THE INDIAN TRIBES
OF NORTH AMERICA

SMITHSONIAN INSTITUTION
BUREAU OF AMERICAN ETHNOLOGY
BULLETIN 145

THE INDIAN TRIBES
OF NORTH AMERICA

By

JOHN R. SWANTON

SMITHSONIAN INSTITUTION PRESS
CITY OF WASHINGTON

Swanton, INDIAN TRIBES OF NORTH AMERICA
(reprint)

ISBN No. 0-87474-179-3   [This is a new number
                            because of changes in
                            cover design, map
                            treatment]

Library of Congress catalog card number 52-61970

ISBN 0-87474-179-3

Originally published 1952.
Fifth Reprint 1979

CONTENTS

ILLUSTRATIONS

MAPS

1. Outline map of North America showing relative position of the four following maps illustrating the locations of the Indian tribes of North America, page 11.

The following maps appear in an envelope inside the back cover.

2. Northwestern North America (section 1 of map 1)
3. Northeastern North America (section 2 of map 1)
4. Southwestern North America (section 3 of map 1)
5. Southeastern North America (section 4 of map 1)

THE INDIAN TRIBES OF NORTH AMERICA

By JOHN R. SWANTON

INTRODUCTION

From the date of its first appearance in 1891 the Powell map of "Linguistic Families of American Indians North of Mexico" has proved of the widest utility. It has been reissued several times and copied into numerous publications. There has, however, been almost equal need of a map giving the location of the tribes under the several families.

To one familiar from his readings in early American history with the names and locations of our prominent eastern "tribes," such as the Delaware, Iroquois, Cherokee, and Choctaw, the preparation of a tribal map would seem to be simple, and it would indeed be so if all Indians had been grouped into bodies as clearly marked as those mentioned. But even in the eastern United States the term "tribe" is quickly found to have no uniform application. The Creeks were a confederation of a few dominant tribes and a number of subordinate bodies, each formerly independent. The name "Delaware" is commonly said to have covered three tribes or subtribes, but while two of these seem never to have been independent of each other, the third, the Munsee, is often treated as if it were entirely separate. The name "Powhatan" was applied to about 30 tribes or subtribes which had been brought together by conquest only a few years before Virginia was settled, and the term "Chippewa," or "Ojibwa," is used for a multitude of small bands with little claim to any sort of governmental unity. In the case of the Iroquois, on the other hand, the tribe was only a part of the governmental unit, the Iroquois Confederation, or Longhouse.

The northern Plains tribes present a certain coherence but farther south and west our difficulties multiply. An early explorer in Texas states that in that region, by "nation" was to be understood only a single town or perhaps a few neighboring villages, and in fact the number of tribal names reported from this section seems almost endless. In the governmental sense, each Pueblo community was a tribe, and if we were to attempt a complete list we should have in the first place a large number of existing, or at least recently existing, tribes, little and big, and a still greater number known only through the early writers or by tradition. In California, Kroeber (1925) states that there were no tribes in the strict sense of the term except among the Yokuts of the San Joaquin Valley and their immediate neighbors. Elsewhere in California, and in western Oregon and Washington as well, tribe and town might be considered convertible terms. As the number of these was continually shifting, it would be impracticable to enter them in that capacity in a work of the present kind.

North of the International Boundary, conditions are, if possible, worse, except in the southernmost section of Canada where lived tribes similar to those in the eastern parts of the United States, such as the Huron, Chippewa, Assiniboin, and Blackfoot, though the Chippewa, as already mentioned, require a somewhat elastic extension of our common concept of a tribe. On the north Pacific coast, however, the conditions noted in western Oregon and Washington are continued. We have numerous local groups associated into several major divisions on linguistic grounds alone. Still farther north and east, among the Algonquians, Athapascans, and Eskimo, we are confronted with a bewildering array of bands and local groups, usually confined to one town and taking their name from it or from a certain territory over which its members hunted, and the numbers and names of these are uncertain even at the present time. Nothing remotely resembling scientific accuracy is possible in placing these bands, if we aim at chronological uniformity, and we must either enter great linguistic groups, embracing sometimes almost an entire stock, or make an arbitrary selection of bands with the idea of including those which we esteem the most important.

Northeastern México and some parts of Central America may also be defined as band areas, but most of North America below the Río Grande was occupied by well-recognized tribal divisions.

From all of the West Indies except Haiti, Cuba, and Puerto Rico nothing like a complete list of tribes has survived, and even for the best documented of these, Haiti, it is impossible to say how many of the caciquedoms mentioned should be given tribal status.

A short study of the conditions above outlined shows that only two alternatives are open in a work like the present. Either one must, in effect, alter it to a town and band map, entering the most minute recorded subdivisions and setting his results forth, not on one map but on dozens, or he must be satisfied with a relatively conventional classification, having in view popular convenience rather than scientific uniformity, and making the best grouping he can of those peoples which did not have real tribal organizations. In the present undertaking the latter plan has been followed, but clues to the more scientific study have been given by including lists of "subdivisions" and "villages." There is no profession that these lists are complete; a perfect presentation of them would demand an investigation for which there is as yet no opportunity. The rest of the accompanying text has been devoted to certain items of information likely to be called for first by the general reader, including: the origin of the tribal name and a brief list of the more important synonyms, the linguistic connections of the tribe—it has not seemed feasible to try to include the physical and cultural connections—its location, a brief sketch of its history, its estimated and actual population at different periods (based mainly on Mooney's (1928) study and the reports of the United States and Canadian Indian Offices), and the "connection in which it has become noted," particularly the extent to which its name has been perpetuated geographically or otherwise. I have also included references to the more important sources of information. Two works have been used as basal authorities. One, the Handbook of American Indians (Hodge, 1907, 1910), is general in scope and may be assumed throughout except for the tribes of México, Central America, and the West Indies. The other, Kroeber's Handbook of the Indians of California (1925), is the basal authority used in treating the Indian groups of that State. In the Gulf area I have utilized the results of my own studies, published and unpublished.

As far as possible each tribe, or group has been treated by itself, but in Washington, Oregon, California, and Alaska, to avoid needless repetition, the history of the tribes is considered as a whole. The section on México, Central America, and the West Indies represents an afterthought. Both map and text material were drawn originally from the "Indian Languages of Mexico and Central America" (Thomas and Swanton, 1911), and Dr. Lehmann's (1920) monumental work on "Zentral Amerikas," but they have been made over thoroughly in the light of the classification and map of Dr. J. Alden Mason (1940) and Frederick Johnson (1940), and no attempt has been made to take up the history of the several tribes or indicate other authorities.

A brief history of the present undertaking will perhaps enable the reader to obtain a better understanding of it, appreciate the difficulties encountered in the compilation, and in consequence view its short-comings, of which as the compiler I am keenly aware, with due charity. It represents an evolution both in method of procedure and in the extent of territory covered. In the beginning I was governed by the older tradition regarding map work of the kind, the idea of entering a tribe in the place where it was first encountered by Whites, but an attempt to carry out this plan soon presented difficulties because neighboring tribes were often encountered a century or more apart and their relative positions may have changed utterly in the interval. There is no certainty, for instance, that the Indians outside of the narrow strip of territory opened to our vision by De Soto's army in 1539–43 were in the same relative position when Carolina was settled about 1670 and Louisiana in 1699. It is particularly to be noted that, while De Soto found eastern Arkansas full of towns, it was almost deserted when Marquette and La Salle visited it in 1673 and 1682. We also know that great alterations took place in the St. Lawrence Valley between the voyages of Cartier in 1534–43 and Champlain's appearance there in 1603.

In view of these difficulties, I gave up this plan and tried the device of putting each tribe in the region with which it was most closely associated historically. But with what region were the Shawnee, Cheyenne, Arapaho, Kiowa, Comanche, and some other tribes most closely associated? The Middle West or the Plains are rather too general terms. Moreover, tribes acquired this close association with certain sections at very different periods and, if this plan were carried out, the map as a whole would be historically inaccurate. Thus the Delaware upon the whole were associated most closely with the valley of the river which bears their name, but when the Foxes had reached Iowa and the Dakota had occupied South Dakota, where they are best known, the Delaware had removed many hundred miles from this region. The Abnaki were most closely associated with western Maine but were uprooted in the middle of the eighteenth century and moved to Canada. The Huron are most closely connected historically with the region of Lake Simcoe, Ontario, but they were driven from there in the middle of the seventeenth century, and a hundred years later under the name Wyandot they, or at least part of them, came to be "closely associated" with Ohio. Thus we have here two associations of the same tribe.

For a time it seemed as if some of these inconsistencies were unavoidable and that any attempt at chronological accuracy was out of the question. Such is indeed the case if we insist upon absolute, documented accuracy, because Alaska, western Canada, and the northwestern part of the United States were almost wholly unknown until the latter half of the eighteenth century and there is no authentic information regarding many tribes until the beginning of the nineteenth when many eastern tribes, and some of those on the Plains, had been displaced or destroyed. But on experimenting along this line I discovered that if we select the year 1650, or rather a few years prior to that date and assume a fairly static condition for 30 or 40 years afterward, we can determine the location of most of the tribes of the eastern and southern United States and eastern Canada in a fairly satisfactory manner, and this arrangement was finally decided upon. Up to 1649 the Hurons were still in Ontario; the Erie, the Neutral Nation, and the Susquehanna had not been destroyed by the

Iroquois; and King Philip's War, which was to scatter the New England Indians, did not break out until 1675. The Virginia Indians had suffered very much as a result of their risings in 1622 and 1644 but continued to occupy the same general territories in which the colonists found them. By 1650 the Gulf region had been traversed by Spanish expeditions and Florida had been settled nearly a hundred years, but there had been little displacement of the aborigines even in Florida, and between the accounts of the Spanish chroniclers and the later narratives of Virginia traders, and the South Carolina colonists after 1670 we are able to get a fair idea of the position of the principal Southeastern peoples at that date. Meantime the French penetrated into the Ohio Valley and as far south on the Mississippi as the mouth of the Arkansas by 1673, and to the ocean by 1682, and they founded Louisiana in 1699. La Salle's Texas colony, established in 1685, however unfortunate for himself and the other participants in the venture, gives a more than fair view of the Indians of that great territory, soon supplemented by the reports of those who accompanied the later Spanish expeditions. Moreover, this data may be checked in some measure by the much earlier reports of Cabeza de Vaca bearing on the years 1528 to 1536 and the chroniclers of Moscoso's invasion of east Texas in 1542. Moving still farther west, we find that New Mexico had been occupied by Spaniards long before the date selected, that Coronado had crossed the southern Plains, and that travelers by sea and land had visited southern California. In the meantime eastern Canada had been penetrated by two European nations from two directions—by the French along St. Lawrence River and the Great Lakes and by the English Hudson's Bay Company through their posts on the body of water which gives them their name. Moose Factory was founded in 1671, Fort Nelson in 1682, and Fort Churchill in 1688. From these as bases explorers and traders soon worked their way far inland, and on the other hand the commandants collected considerable information from the natives themselves regarding the regions from whence they came.

As has been said, there was beyond a great tract of country which remained unvisited by Europeans until well into the eighteenth century, but over much of this area there is no evidence of recent tribal movements, and some movements are known sufficiently well to justify an attempt to reconstruct the earlier conditions. Thus the migration of Haida from the northern end of the Queen Charlotte Islands to Prince of Wales Island evidently occurred in recent times, not earlier than the eighteenth century, and it is clear that they replaced the Tlingit there since the names of their towns in the invaded country are all derived from Tlingit. Whether the movement of the Tsimshian to the coast of British Columbia and the, probably contemporary, removal of a part of the Tlingit northward, happened before or after 1650 we shall never know, but it seems to have taken place long before the Haida emigration just mentioned. It was formerly believed that mass migrations of impressive character took place in the Columbia River Valley about the beginning of the nineteenth century. This idea was perhaps set in motion by George Gibbs (1877) in speaking of the migrations of Klikitat Indians, and was suggested in some particulars by Mooney (1928) but elaborated by James Teit (1928) and adopted and amplified by Berreman (1937). This involved the assumption that before that time both banks of Columbia River from The Dalles to the mouth of Snake River were in possession of Salishan tribes, that south of them lay the Cayuse and Molala, and south of them again the ancestors of all of the Shahaptian peoples except the Nez Percés; and that about the beginning of the nineteenth century the Shoshoneans of the interior moved northward, pushing the Shahaptians ahead of them; and that these in turn, after disrupting the Cayuse and Molala, expelled the Salishans from the valley of the Columbia in the region just indicated. More recent researches by Ray, Murdock, Blyth, and Steward (1938) seem to indicate that this is entirely erroneous and that, except for a displacement of the Molala and a relatively recent expansion of Shahaptians toward the south at the expense of the Shoshoneans, the tribes and stocks seem to have occupied substantially the same areas in the earliest times of which we have any record as they did when the reservations were established. At any rate, supposition of stability in tribal location makes the work of the cartographer much simpler, and we will accept the tribal distribution shown by Ray in his paper published in 1938 as being as near the probable situation in 1650 as can now be determined. From the fact that he indicates the northern boundary of Shoshonean peoples in the eighteenth century, it is assumed that he regards the rest of his map as valid for that century.

For the position of the interior Athapascan tribes before they were attacked by the Cree, I am indebted to Dr. Diamond Jenness, formerly Chief of the Department of Anthropology of the National Museum of Canada, who was also kind enough to go over most of my Canadian section and has made many valuable suggestions and amplifications.

The scope of the work has also been expanded territorially as it progressed. Originally it was intended merely as a convenient guide to the tribes of the several states of the American Union and Alaska, demand for such a work being considerable. But since the original linguistic map of the Bureau had included the Dominion of Canada and Greenland, it was later determined to make this of the same extent. And finally, owing to the representations of a leading anthropologist, it was amplified to take in México, Middle America, and the West Indies.

The method of treatment for Canada and Greenland has been practically identical with that for the United States, but it was thought best to represent on the map not merely the tribes but the band divisions of the larger northern tribes, such as the Chippewa, Cree, Algonkin, Montagnais, and several of the Athapascan groups, including the Kutchin and Khotana of the far Northwest and Alaska. Many of these band names are English and wholly modern, but it is highly probable that some of them correspond to more ancient divisions and, since they have found a place in literature, the identification of their locations will be convenient. For the placing of those in the Northeast I am particularly indebted to the late anthropologists Dr. Frank G. Speck, of the University of Pennsylvania, and Dr. John M. Cooper, of the Catholic University of America.

Objection has been made to entering the names of Eskimo tribes or bands on the map, since almost all refer simply to "people living at such-and-such a place," most of them had little permanence, and there was an enormous number of them, the ones I have mentioned being merely a selection. On the other hand, it may be urged that some groups, notably those in Alaska, had considerable continuity, that most of them probably owed their existence to certain natural food supplies which would tend to reproduce other tribes at the same spots even though these were broken up, and that finally most of the tribes here entered have obtained a place in Eskimo literature and it is convenient to know where they lived even though they may have been no more important than other tribes not mentioned. Besides, if this were not done, the map would have little more value, so far as the Eskimo country is concerned, than the linguistic map. In the text I have indicated the relative lack of importance of the Eskimo tribes by treating all under the one head "Eskimo," and their names, like the band names of the northern Indians just mentioned, are in different type. The West Greenland names are, of course, quite modern but are thought to represent the principal bands of an earlier date.

As already stated, that portion of the map south of the territory of the United States is based on the map of México and Central America published by Dr. Thomas and myself (1911), on the work of Lehmann (1920) mentioned above, but particularly on the papers of Mason (1940) and Johnson (1940). Although European influence in this region goes back to the early part of the sixteenth century, relatively little tribal displacement had taken place by 1650. On the West Indies, however, it was very different, and, if we were to note only the tribes extant there in 1650, little could be inserted. However, it has seemed best to submit to the anachronism here by giving the tribes in occupancy when Spaniards first came among them at the end of the fifteenth century and beginning of the sixteenth. In this part of the map I have followed Lehmann except in Jamaica and Haiti, but I have omitted several of his Jamaica names which seem to be merely those of towns. The tribal distribution in Haiti is the result of my studies of Peter Martyr's "De Orbo Novo," and I have increased the five "provinces" given by Las Casas (1875–76) because it seems to me that Marien in the northwest and Maguana in the center should have independent status. Probably the caciquedoms here and in the other islands were in a constant state of flux.

In treating the linguistic stocks, considerable compromise has been found necessary. Since the publication of Powell's map (1891) the investigations of various students have rendered certain changes necessary, but other proposed changes have not been accepted by all students, and some are violently opposed.

The connection between Shahaptian, Waiilatpuan, and Lutuamian, first suggested by Hewitt (1897) and recently confirmed by Jacobs (1937), has made it necessary to put these three groups of languages into one stock which is here called Shapwailutan, a name made up of the first three syllables of the original stock names and in that form suggested by Hewitt many years ago. The connection of Natchez with the Muskhogean family, originally proposed by Brinton and confirmed by me, has been recognized in the present classification. I have also placed the former Tonikan, Chitimachan, and Attacapan stocks under the stock name Tunican in accordance with the results of my own researches though the inclusion of the first mentioned is not entirely beyond question. Dr. J. P. Harrington's studies (1910) have made the relationship between Kiowan and the Tanoan tongues so evident that they have been placed in one family and given the name Kiowa-Tanoan. There no longer seems to be any excuse for keeping the old Shoshonean, Piman, and Nahuatlan stocks apart, and I have followed Buschmann (1859) and Brinton (1891) in uniting them as Uto-Aztecan. Kiowa-Tanoan is probably related to this but the fact has still to be demonstrated.

In California we are confronted by some puzzling questions as to relationships, which have been made the basis of violent differences of opinion. Some of our ethnologists have been very skeptical regarding the Algonquian connection of Yurok and Wiyot but I let it stand as on Kroeber's Handbook (1925) pending exact determination. On the other hand, the validity of the so-called Penutian stock seems to be recognized by all of those who have had the best opportunities to study the languages composing it and is admitted here. The relationship between some of the languages of the other great stock created by

Dixon and Kroebér (1919), the Hokan, is also allowed by other students. A doubt still remains whether all of the languages classified under this head, even in the original and most conservative usage of the term, should go with it. Or rather, it seems doubtful whether our information is sufficient to justify the erection of this stock over against the Penutian. Mr. J. P. Harrington (personal information) is of the opinion that the distinction betweem Hokan and Penutian is artificial and that the languages of both groups and of various others not as yet brought together are probably related. But since the name Hokan has received literary recognition, it seems best to continue it provisionally for the forms of speech first placed in that category. Kroeber's confirmation of Brinton's suggestion regarding the Serian and Tequistlatecan stocks has served to add them to the Hokan family through Yuman, and Sapir proposed extension to Subtiaba and Coahuilteco. I am favorably disposed toward very considerable extensions of the present family boundaries but feel that more unanimity of opinion is desirable before including the more radical suggestions in a general work of this kind. Personally, I am convinced that a very large part of the vocabulary and structure of the Siouan and Muskhogean languages has had a common origin and believe that it will ultimately be found best to consider them as branches of one stock, but adequate proof has not yet been presented. The Tunican stock also shares certain well-marked structural peculiarities with Muskhogean while having connections also with the ancient Texas stocks, but the meaning of this has yet to be determined. It is plain that the structural parallelism between Athapascan and Tlingit is not accidental, and some striking similarities extend to Haida. Whether the somewhat similar parallelism between Salishan, Chimakuan, and Wakashan means genetic relationship is another problem, but the answers to these are not as yet sufficiently assured to incorporate any changes from the older classification in this work. It is evident that a future map devoted to the distribution of languages in North America must give something more than stocks or supposed stocks. It must show the degree of relationship between languages as well inside as outside of stock boundaries.

No doubt the positions assigned to certain tribes in the present map will surprise many ethnologists. This will be particularly true of the placing of some of those of the Plains like the Arapaho, Kiowa, Kiowa Apache, and Arikara. In fact, some of these locations are extremely speculative but they are governed by the necessity of harmonizing them with the locations of other tribes at the time selected as standard, 1650. In the case of certain tribes removed from their original seats before 1650, or whose locations were learned only at a considerably later time, the date of known occupancy is indicated in parentheses.

The present work was well under way before it was learned that something similar was being undertaken by Professor Kroeber, and Kroeber's work has since appeared (1939) as "Cultural and Natural Areas of Native North America." This magnificent publication will undoubtedly continue to occupy a place all by itself for a long time but it is evidently intended mainly for the university student, though its usefulness will by no means be confined to such students, and in other particulars the purposes of that study were quite distinct from those which the present writer has entertained.

"It aims," says Prof. Kroeber, "first, to review the environmental relations of the native cultures of North America. Its second purpose is to examine the historic relations of the culture areas, or geographical units of cultures." My own compilation has no such ambitious purposes. It is merely intended to inform the general reader what Indian tribes occupied the territory of his State and to add enough data to indicate the place they occupied among the tribal groups of the continent and the part they played in the early period of our history and the history of the States immediately to the north and south of us. It attempts to be rather a gazetteer of present knowledge than a guide to the attainment of more knowledge.

The preparation of this manuscript extended over several years and some new material was added indeed until my retirement from active membership on the staff of the Bureau of American Ethnology in 1944. It is admittedly defective in the use of material published during the years since that date.

In the synonymy only those forms have been given which differ so much from the popular designation of the tribe as to make identification difficult.

Although I have usually leaned very largely on Mooney's population figures (1928) in my over-all estimates, my own for the Southeastern tribes, as shown by those on map 3 of Bulletin 137 (Swanton, 1946), would generally be considerably smaller.

The work has been done from the point of view of the United States, and therefore the Chippewa have been treated under Minnesota, the Huron under Ohio, and the Assiniboin under Montana, although their centers were rather north of the International Boundary.

On the maps the boundary lines between modern political nations and states are indicated by long dashes; those between linguistic stocks or major divisions of that type by short dashes and divisions between smaller tribal or group bodies by dots.[1]

---

[1] NOTE: This has not been consistently carried through on the maps.— J. R. S.

MAP 1.—Outline map of North America showing relative position of the four following maps illustrating the locations of the Indian tribes of North America: Section 1, Northwestern North America (map 2, facing p. 26); section 2, Northeastern North America (map 3, facing p. 106); section 3, Southwestern North America (map 4, facing p. 186); section 4, Southeastern North America (map 5, facing p. 298).

MAINE

Abnaki. Properly Wabanaki, "those living at the sunrise," "those living at the east," "easterners." Also called:

Alnânbaĭ, own name, meaning "Indians," or "men."
Aquannaque, Wabanaki as pronounced by Huron.
Bashabas, name given them from a principal chief.
Cannon-gageh-ronnons, name given by Mohawk.
Moassones, from a name applied to their country; perhaps from Penobscot Maweshenook, "berry place."
Narānkamigdok epitsik arenanbak, "villages of the Narānkamigdog," said to be a collective name for all the Abnaki villages.
Natio Luporum, "Wolf Nation."
Natságana, name given by Caughnawaga Iroquois.
Onagungees, Onnogonges, Anagonges, or Owenagunges, name given by the Iroquois.
Skacewanilom, name given by the Iroquois.
Tarrateens, name given by the tribes of southern New England.

Connections.—The Abnaki belonged to the Algonquian linguistic family, their closest connections being with their neighbors to the east and west. Indeed their name has very commonly been extended to include the Malecite, Penobscot, and Pennacook, and even the Micmac, though on the other hand the Sokoki have sometimes been left out.

Location.—The main body was in western Maine, in the valleys of the Kennebec, Androscoggin, and Saco Rivers and on the neighboring coast, overlapping also into Carroll County, N. H. A single tribe, the Missiassik, was in northwestern Vermont, representing probably a late intrusion. (See also New Hampshire and Vermont.)

Subdivisions

Amaseconti, on Sandy River, Franklin County.
Arosaguntacook, on the lower course of Androscoggin River.
Missiassik, in the valley of Missisquoi River, Franklin County, Vt.
Norridgewock, on Kennebec River.
Ossipee, on Ossipee River and Lake in Maine and New Hampshire.
Pequawket, on Lovell's Pond and the headwaters of Saco River, Maine and New Hampshire.
Rocameca, on the upper course of Androscoggin River.
Sokoki, on Saco River and in the adjacent parts of Cumberland and York Counties.
Wawenoc, on the seacoast of Sagadahoc, Lincoln, and Knox Counties.

Villages

Amaseconti; there were two villages of this tribe, at Farmington Falls and New Sharon, respectively.
Aquadocta, westward of Saco.
Arosaguntacook town, probably near Lewiston.

13

Cobbosseecontee, a town or band on the stream of that name, which empties into the Kennebec River at Gardiner.

Ebenecook, at Ebenecook Harbor, Southport Island.

Kennebec, between Augusta and Winslow.

Ketangheanycke, near the mouth of Kennebec River.

Masherosqueck, near the coast and not certainly Abnaki.

Mecadacut, on the coast between Penobscot and Kennebec Rivers.

Missiassik, belonging to the Missiassik tribe, on Lake Champlain at the mouth of Missisquoi River, Vt.

Moratiggon, probably on the Maine or New Hampshire coast and possibly not Abnaki.

Moshoquen, on or near the coast.

Muscongus, on the coast and probably near Muscongus Island.

Negusset, about the site of Woolwich.

Ossaghrage, Iroquois name of an Abnaki village.

Ossipee, probably on Ossipee Lake.

Ouwerage, probably on Ossipee Lake.

Pasharanack, probably on the coast.

Pauhuntanuc, probably on the coast.

Pemaquid, near Pemaquid, Lincoln County.

Pequawket town, about Fryeburg.

Pocopassum, probably on the coast.

Sabino, at the mouth of the Kennebec River, possibly on the west side.

Sagadahoc, at the mouth of the Kennebec River.

Satquin, on the coast southwest of the Kennebec River.

Segotago, probably identical with Sagadahoc.

Sowocatuck, perhaps the chief village of the Sokoki, Saco River.

Taconnet, at the falls of the Kennebec near Waterville.

Unyjaware, Iroquois name for an Abnaki village.

Wacoogo, probably on or near the coast.

History.—The Abnaki and their neighbors claim to have immigrated into their historic seats from the southwest. Aside from possible Norse visitants in 1000–1010, John Cabot, during his second voyage in 1498, probably brought the first white men within sight of Abnaki territory, but he seems to have had no dealings with the people. From that time on, Breton, Basque, Norman, and English fishermen constantly visited the coast. In 1604 Champlain passed along it from north to south and visited several Abnaki bands, and in 1605 Waymouth penetrated the Wawenoc country. In 1607–08 came an abortive attempt on the part of the Plymouth Company to make a permanent settlement at the mouth of the Kennebec River, but it is probable that English fishermen were on Monhegan Island almost continuously after that date. Pemaquid was also occupied at an early period. The Abnaki were soon afterward missionized from Canada and became attached to the French interest. For a time they were successful in driving the English colonists away but later they suffered several severe defeats—particularly the capture of Norridgewock in 1724 and the defeat of the Pequawket in 1725—were much reduced in numbers, and finally withdrew to Canada where they were settled at Bécancour and Sillery, and later at St. Francis, along with other refugee tribes from the south.

Population.—Mooney (1928) estimates this at 3,000 in 1600, including the Penobscot and Passamaquoddy. The St. Francis Indians, including remnants of other New England tribes, numbered 395 in 1903, and 280 in 1924.

Connection in which they have become noted.—The activities of the missionary Rasles, compilation by him of the Abnaki dictionary, the destruction of Norridgewock, and the defeat of the Pequawket on Lovell Pond, as mentioned above, have made the Abnaki famous.

Malecite. They extended into the northeastern part of the State of Maine from Canada (q. v.).

Passamaquoddy. Signifying "Those who pursue the pollock," but strictly "pollock-plenty-place" (Eckstorm). Also called:

> Machias Tribe, applied to some living on Machias River.
> Quoddy, abbreviation of Passamaquoddy.
> St. Croix Indians, from one of the rivers they inhabited.
> Scotuks, from the name of the Schoodic Lakes.
> Unchechauge or Unquechauge.

Connections.—The Passamaquoddy belong to the Algonquian linguistic family, their closest connections being the Malecite, and their more remote relatives the Abnaki, Penobscot, and Pennacook.

Location.—On Passamaquoddy Bay, St. Croix River, and the Schoodic Lakes. (See also Canada.)

Villages

Gunasquamekook, on the site of St. Andrews, N. B.
Imnarkuan, on the site of Pembroke, Washington County.
Sebaik, at Pleasant Point, Passamaquoddy Bay, near Perry, Washington County.

Other towns were on Lewis Island and at Calais, in Maine, and on the New Brunswick side of St. Croix River.

History.—The early history of the Passamaquoddy was identical with that of the Malecite (q. v.). When the territory of the 13 colonies was separated from English rule, the greater part of this tribe was left on the south side of the boundary. They enjoy, jointly with the Penobscot, the privilege of having a representative in the Maine State legislature, though he speaks only on matters of concern to the two tribes.

Population.—The population of the Passamaquoddy was estimated at about 150 in 1726, 130 in 1804, 379 in 1825, 400–500 in 1859; and was enumerated as 386 in 1910. In 1930, 435 Indians were returned from Washington County, and practically all of these must have belonged to this tribe.

Connection in which they have become noted.—The Passamaquoddy have given their name to Passamaquoddy Bay, which forms part of the eastern boundary of the State of Maine and are the easternmost body of Indians in the United States.

Pennacook. The Accominta and Newichawanoc of the extreme southwestern part of the State belonged to this tribe. (See New Hampshire.)

Penobscot. Meaning "the rocky place," or "the descending ledge place" (Eckstorm), referring to the falls between Oldtown and Bangor. Also called:

Pentagouet, from the name of their principal village near Castine.

Connections.—The Penobscot belonged to the Algonquian linguistic stock, their nearest connections being the Abnaki, Passamaquoddy, Malecite, and Pennacook, with whom they were frequently classed under the name of the first mentioned.

Location.—On both sides of Penobscot Bay and in the entire drainage area of Penobscot River.

Subdivisions

A body of Penobscot on Moosehead Lake were known as "Moosehead Lake Indians," but their separation from the rest was probably temporary.

Villages

Agguncia, said to have been a small settlement near Brewer, Penobscot County, from which the fabulous city of "Norumbega" derived its name.

Asnela, a settlement on an island of the same name in Penobscot Bay.

Catawamtek, at Rockland.

Kenduskeag, at Bangor, near the site of the Penobscot Exchange Hotel.

Mattawamkeag, about Mattawamkeag Point, Penobscot County.

Meecombe, on the lower course of Penobscot River.

Negas, in Penobscot County.

Olamon, on an island in Penobscot River near Greenbush.

Oldtown, the present village on an island of the same name.

Passadumkeag, on an island in Penobscot River near the present Passadumkeag.

Pentagouet, at or near Castine.

Precaute, on the southeast coast of Maine; it may have been a Passamaquoddy town.

Segocket, near the mouth of Penobscot River.

Wabigganus, probably near the mouth of the Penobscot River.

History.—Native tradition brings the Penobscot from the Southwest. They were encountered by French and English fishermen and explorers early in the sixteenth century, and one of their towns came to have a European reputation as a city of fabulous size and importance under the name of Norumbega. In the seventeenth century their chief, known to the Whites as Bashaba, seems to have extended his authority, probably his moral authority only, over the tribes to the westward as far as the Merrimac. The Penobscot were visited by Champlain in 1604 and by numerous later explorers. They assisted the French against the English until 1749, when they made peace and in consequence did not remove to Canada with the Abnaki. They have remained in their old country to the present day, their principal settlement being on Oldtown Island. Conjointly with the Passamaquoddy, they have a representative at the sessions of the Maine State legislature privileged to speak on tribal affairs only.

Population.—The following are early estimates of the Penobscot population: 650 in 1726, 1,000 in 1736, 700 in 1753, 400 in 1759, 700 in 1765, 350 in 1786. According to the United States Census of 1910, there were 266, including 13 scattered outside of the State of Maine. The census of 1930 returned 301 Indians from Penobscot County, practically all belonging to this tribe.

Connection in which they have become noted.—The Penobscot have given their name to a bay, a river, and a county in the State of Maine, to a post village in Hancock County, and a branch post office in Detroit. The title of the chief above mentioned, Bashaba or Bessebes, became the center of a myth among the Whites in which he was elevated to the dignity of a local king or emperor. The widely quoted myth of Norumbega should also be mentioned in this connection. This tribe and the Passamaquoddy constitute the only bodies of Indians of any size remaining in New England.

NEW HAMPSHIRE

Abnaki. Parts of Grafton County were occupied by the Ossipee and Pequawket bands, affiliated with the Sokoki of the Abnaki tribe. (See Maine.)

Pennacook. Gerard (Hodge, 1910) says the name is "cognate with Abnaki *pĕnȧkuk*, or *pena^nkuk*, 'at the botton of the hill or highland,' " but Speck says simply "down hill." Also called:

> Merrimac, from the river of that name.
> Nechegansett, name given by Gookin (1792).
> Owaragees, Iroquois name (fide Colden (1747)).

Connections.—The Pennacook belonged to the Algonquian linguistic stock, their nearest relatives being the Abnaki, with whom they were frequently classed, and the Penobscot, Passamaquoddy, and Malecite.

Location.—In southern and central New Hampshire, northeastern Massachusetts, and the southernmost part of Maine. (See also Maine, Massachusetts, and Vermont.)

Subdivisions and Villages

Accominta, at or near the site of York, Maine.
Agawam, at Ipswich, Mass.
Amoskeag, at Amoskeag Falls on the Merrimack River.
Coosuc, a division along Connecticut River between Upper and Lower Ammo-noosuc Rivers, the principal village apparently near the mouth of the latter.

Nashua, a division along the upper course of Nashua River, the village being near Leominster, Mass.

Naumkeag, at Salem, Mass.

Newichawanoc, a division on upper Piscataqua River and Salmon Falls River in Maine and New Hampshire, the principal village being near Berwick, Maine.

Pennacook, a division on both banks of Merrimack River above and below Concord, the village of the same name being on the site of Concord.

Pentucket, at Haverhill, Mass.

Piscataqua, on Piscataqua River near Dover.

Souhegan, a division on Souhegan River, Hillsborough County, with the village of the same name probably near Amherst, formerly called Souhegan.

Squamscot, on Exeter River near Exeter, Rockingham County.

Wachuset, a division on the upper Nashua River, Mass., the village of the same name being located probably near Princeton.

Wamesit, a division on the south bank of Merrimack River below the mouth of Concord River, Mass., the village of the same name being near Lowell.

Weshacum, at Weshacum Ponds, near Sterling, Mass.

Winnecowet, in Rockingham County.

Winnipesaukee, around the lake of the same name.

History.—The early history of the Pennacook was like that of the Abnaki except that they were earlier affected by the English settlements on Massachusetts Bay. In King Philip's War (1675–76) the Nashua and Wachuset tribes joined the hostiles, but the greater part of the Pennacook, under Wannalancet, remained on friendly terms until the treacherous seizure of about 200 of their number by Waldron in 1676. They then abandoned their country and the greater part removed to Canada, where they ultimately joined the Abnaki and other Indians of St. Francis. The remainder were finally settled at Scaticook, Rensselaer County, N. Y.

Population.—The number of Pennacook is estimated by Mooney (1928) at 2,000 in 1600 and 1,250 in 1676. The remnant is included among the 280 St. Francis Indians returned in 1924.

Connection in which they have become noted.—The town of Penacook and Lake Penacook, Merrimack County, are named after the Pennacook, as well as a branch station of the Concord Post Office, and their name also appears in Whittier's poem "The Bridal of Pennacook."

VERMONT

Abnaki. An Abnaki band known as the Missiassik was at one time settled on Missisquoi River in Franklin County. (See Maine.)

Mahican. Bands of the Mahican hunted in the southwestern and western parts of the State and made temporary settlements from time to time. One Mahican village (Winooskeek) is thought to have been located at the mouth of Winooski River. (See New York.)

Pennacook. The eastern margins of Vermont were occupied by the Pennacook, who must have hunted considerably within its borders. (See New Hampshire.)

Pocomtuc. The northernmost bands of the Pocomtuc extended into the southern parts of the State. (See Massachusetts.)

MASSACHUSETTS

Mahican. The Mahican extended over most of Berkshire County, where they were represented mainly by the Housatonic or Stockbridge Indians. (See New York.)

Massachuset. Meaning "at the range of hills," by which is meant the hills of Milton.

Connections.—The Massachuset belonged to the Algonquian linguistic stock, their tongue being an *n*-dialect, and formed one group with the Narraganset, Niantic (East and West), and Wampanoag, and probably the Nauset.

Location.—In the region of Massachusetts Bay between Salem on the north and Marshfield and Brockton on the south. Later they claimed lands beyond Brockton as far as the Great Cedar Swamp, territories formerly under the control of the Wampanoag.

Subdivisions

Johnson (1881) says that there were "three kingdoms or sagamoreships having under them seven dukedoms or petty sagamores." Some of these undoubtedly correspond to the divisions recently worked out by Speck (1928) by means of provincial documents. He identifies six main divisions, two of them further subdivided, all called by the names of their chiefs, as follows:

(1) Band of Chickataubut (including the later bands of Wampatuck and some other of his heirs and a district and band earlier controlled by Obatinnewat or Obtakiest), all of the Massachuset territory south of Charles River and west of the neighborhood of Ponkapog Pond.

(2) Band of Nanepashemet, all the Massachuset territory north of Charles River. Nanepashemet's domain was afterward divided among his three sons: Winnepurkit, owning about Deer Island and in Boston Harbor; Wonohaquaham, owning about Chelsea and Saugus; and Montowampate, owning about Lynn and Marblehead.

(3) Band of Manatahqua, about Nahant and Swampscott.

(4) Band of Cato, a tract 5 miles square east of Concord River.

(5) Band of Nahaton, around Natick.

(6) Band of Cutshamakin, Cutshamequin, or Kutchamakin, about Dorchester, Sudbury, and Milton.

Villages

Conohasset, about Cohasset.

Cowate, "Praying Indians," at the Falls of Charles River.

Magaehnak, probably "Praying Indians," 6 miles from Sudbury.

Massachuset, location uncertain.

Mishawum, at Charlestown.

Mystic, at Medford.

Nahapassumkeck, in the northern part of Plymouth County, probably on the coast.

Natick, "Praying Indians," near the present Natick.

Neponset, on Neponset River about Stoughton.

Nonantum, on Nonantum hill, in Newton.

Pequimmit, "Praying Indians," near Stoughton.

Pocapawmet, on the south shore of Massachusetts Bay.

Punkapog, "Praying Indians," near Stoughton.

Sagoquas, south of Cohasset.

Saugus, near Lynn.

Seccasaw, in the northern part of Plymouth County.

Titicut, "Praying Indians," possibly Wampanoag, in Middleborough town.

Topeent, on the north coast of Plymouth County.

Totant, at or near Boston.

Totheet, on the north coast of Plymouth County.

Wessagusset, near Weymouth.

Winnisimmet, at Chelsea.

Wonasquam, near Annisquam, Essex County, perhaps a later outvillage.

History.—The Massachuset were visited by several voyagers, beginning at least as far back as the time of John Cabot but were first particularly noted by Captain John Smith, who coasted their territory in 1614. In 1617 they were much reduced by a pestilence and about the same time they were depleted by wars with their northeastern neighbors. The Puritans settled in their country in 1629, and mission work was soon begun among them, and was pursued with particular zeal by John Eliot. The converts were gathered into separate villages, where they gradually declined in numbers and presently disappeared as distinct bodies, though a few descendants of the Punkapog town people are still living in Canton, Mattapan, and Mansfield.

Population.—The number of Massachuset is estimated by Mooney (1928) to have been 3,000 in 1600. In 1631 it was reduced to about 500, and soon considerably below that figure by smallpox.

Connection in which they have become noted.—The Massachuset gave their name to Massachusetts Bay and through that to the present Commonwealth of Massachusetts. The Massachuset are also noted as the tribe in which the famous apostle to the Indians, John Eliot, labored, through whom a large part of them were gathered into villages of "Praying Indians." The "Eliot Bible" and other works by him have preserved a knowledge of the Massachuset language to our own day. Crispus Attucks, who was killed in the Boston massacre and is generally regarded as the first victim of the American Revolution, was of mixed Negro-Massachuset ancestry. The marriage of Winnepurkit, a Massachuset chief whose lands were about Boston Harbor, to the daughter of Passaconaway, chief sachem of the Pennacook, was made by Whittier the subject of a poem, "The Bridal of Pennacook."

Nauset. Meaning unknown. Also called:

Cape Indians, from their situation.

Connections.—(See under discussion of the Massachuset.)

Location.—All of Cape Cod except the extreme western end.

Subdivisions

Speck (1928) has identified the following: Iyanough, Wiananno, or Hyannis (centering about Barnstable); Manomoy, or Monomoy (about Chatham); Nauset (from Eastham to Truro).

Villages

Aquetnet, at Skauton Neck, Sandwich, Barnstable County.

Ashimut or Ashimuit, at a large spring near the junction of Falmouth, Mashpee, and Sandwich Townships, Barnstable County.

Coatuit, near Osterville, Barnstable County.

Codtaumut or Cataumut, in Mashpee Township.

Cummaquid, at Cummaquid Harbor.

Manamoyik, near Chatham.

Mashpee, on the coast of Mashpee Township.

Mattakees or Mattakeset, in Barnstable and Yarmouth Townships.

Meeshawn, in Provincetown or Truro Township.

Nauset, near Eastham.

Nemskaket, on or near Nemskaket Creek.

Nobsqussit or Nobscusset, near Dennis.

Pamet, near Truro.

Pawpoesit, near Barnstable.

Pispogutt or Pispoqutt, in the western part of Barnstable County, near Buzzards Bay.

Poponesset, near Poponesset Bay.

Potanumaquut, on Pleasant Bay near Harwich.

Punonaknit, at Billingsgate near Wellfleet.

Satuit, on Cotuit River near Mashpee.

Sawkatuket or Satucket, in Brewster or Harwich.

Skauton, near Sandwich, probably on Buzzards Bay.

Sokones or Succonesset, near Falmouth.

Wakoquet, or Waquoit, near Waquoit or Weequakit, in Barnstable Township.

Wessquobs or Weesquobs, near Pocasset.

Many of these contained Wampanoag Indians and some Indians of other tribes.

History.—From the exposed position of the Nauset on Cape Cod their territory came under the observation of many of the earliest explorers, but actual contact with the people was not so simple a matter. In 1606 Champlain had an encounter with them. In 1614 Hunt carried off 7 Nauset Indians and 20 Patuxet of the Wampanoag tribe whom he sold into slavery. They seem to have escaped the great New England pestilence of 1617. Although they behaved in a hostile manner toward the Pilgrims at their first landing in 1620, they soon became firm friends and even rendered some assistance against King Philip (1675–76). Most of them had been Christianized before this time and collected into churches.   In 1710 many died of fever, but the number of Indians in Nauset territory was increased by additions from other tribes driven from their proper territories, so that the population of the principal Indian settlement at Mashpee has not fallen below 200 down to the present day, though a great deal of mixture with other races has taken place.

Population.—The number of the Nauset was estimated by Mooney (1928) at 1,200 in 1600.   In 1621 they were believed to number 500; in 1674, 462 were reported in the various inhabited centers on Cape Cod, containing Nauset, Wampanoag, and other Indians.   In 1698, 515 Indians were reported from Mashpee, mainly Nauset and Wampanoag.   In 1767, 292 were reported at the same place and the number has varied between 200 and 300 down to 1930.   The United States Census of 1910 reported 206 Indians of this band, all but 5 in Massachusetts.   Speck (1928) estimates that there were 230 in 1920, all of whom were mixed-bloods.   The census of 1930 returned only 38 Indians from Barnstable County and 54 from Massachusetts, but it may be incomplete.

Connection in which they have become noted.—As already remarked, it was in the Nauset territory and in considerable measure through their blood that the Massachusetts aborigines maintained their existence longest.   Nauset Beach, Nauset Harbor, and Nauset Light perpetuate the name.

Nipmuc.   From *Nipmaug*, "fresh water fishing place."

Connections.—The Nipmuc belonged to the Algonquian linguistic family, their language being an *l*-dialect.   Their nearest relatives were the other tribes of Massachusetts and the tribes of Rhode Island, Connecticut, and the Hudson River Valley.

Location.—The Nipmuc occupied the central plateau of Massachusetts, particularly the southern part of Worcester County, but they extended into northern Rhode Island and Connecticut.   (See also Connecticut and Rhode Island.)

Subdivisions and Villages

Acoomemeck, location uncertain.
Attawaugan, near Attawaugan in the town of Killingly, Conn.
Chabanakongkomun, near Dudley.
Chachaubunkkakowok, location uncertain.
Coweset, in northern Rhode Island west of Blackstone River.
Hassanamesit, at Grafton.
Magunkaquog, at Hopkinton.
Manchaug, near Oxford.
Manexit, near Thompson, Conn.
Mashapaug, at Mashapaug Pond in the town of Union, Conn.
Medfield, at Medfield, native name unknown.

Menemesseg, near New Braintree.
Metewemesick, near Sturbridge.
Missogkonnog, location uncertain.
Muskataquid, location uncertain.
Nashobah, near Magog Pond, in Littleton.
Nichewaug, about Nichewaug, near Petersham.
Okommakamesit, near Marlborough.
Pakachoog, near Worcester, probably in Millbury.
Quabaug, near Brookfield.
Quadick, near the present Quadick Reservoir, Thompson County, Conn.
Quantisset, on Thompson Hill, near Thompson, Conn.
Quinebaug, on Quinebaug River near Quinebaug Station, town of Thompson, Conn.
Quinetusset, near Thompson in northeast corner of Connecticut.
Segunesit, in northeastern Connecticut.
Tatumasket, west of Mendon, in the southern part of Worcester County.
Wabaquasset, about 6 miles from Quinebaug River, south of Woodstock, Conn., sometimes regarded as an independent tribe.
Wacuntug, on the west side of Blackstone River, near Uxbridge.
Wenimesset, at New Braintree.

History.—There was no coherence among the people bearing the name of Nipmuc and some of them were from time to time attached to the more powerful tribes in their neighborhood, such as the Massachuset, Wampanoag, Narraganset, and Mohegan. The Whites first met them after Plymouth and the Massachusetts Bay were settled. In 1674 there were seven villages of Christian Indians among the Nipmuc but in 1675 practically all took part with King Philip against the colonists and at its close fled to Canada or to the tribes on Hudson River.

Population.—Mooney (1928) estimates that there were 500 independent Nipmuc in 1600. If we consider as Nipmuc the Indians returned from Worcester County, Mass., and Windham and Tolland Counties, Conn., in 1910, there were then 81.

Pennacook. The following bands of Pennacook lived in the northeastern part of Massachusetts: Agawam, Nashua, Naumkeag, Pentucket, Wachuset, Wamesit, and Weshacum. (See New Hampshire.)

Pocomtuc. Meaning unknown.

Connections.—The Pocomtuc belonged to the Algonquian linguistic family, and spoke an *r*-dialect, their nearest relatives probably being the Wappinger.

Location.—The Pocomtuc home was in the present counties of Franklin, Hampshire, and Hampden, Mass., and in the neighboring parts of Connecticut and Vermont.

Subdivisions and Villages

Agawam, about Springfield, their principal village of the same name being on
Long Hill.

Mayawaug, near W. Suffield, town of Suffield, Conn.

Nameroke, in the town of Enfield, east of Thompsonville, Conn.

Nonotuc, a division and village about Northampton.

Pocomtuc, a division in Deerfield River Valley and the adjacent parts of the
Connecticut River Valley, the principal town of the same name being near
Deerfield. (See also Vermont.)

Scitico, near the place of that name in the eastern part of the town of Enfield,
Conn.

Squawkeag, on both sides of Connecticut River in the northern part of Franklin
County, their principal village, of the same name, being near Northfield.

History.—The fort of the Pocomtuc proper, on Fort Hill near
Deerfield, was destroyed by the Mohawk in 1666. The Pocomtuc
combined with the Narraganset and Tunxis in attacks on the Mohegan
chief, Uncas, and later joined the hostile Indians under King Philip.
At the close of the war they fled to Scaticook on the Hudson, where
some of them remained until 1754, going then to St. Francis, Canada.

Population.—Mooney (1928) estimates that there were 1,200
Pocomtuc in 1600. If we count as Pocomtuc the Indians returned
from Hampden and Hampshire Counties in 1910, there were then 23
left, but they may have been of quite other origin.

Wampanoag. The name has the same meaning as Abnaki, "eastern
people." Also called:

> Massasoits, from the name of their famous chief.
> Philip's Indians, from King Philip.

Connections.—The Wampanoag belonged to the Algonquian linguistic stock, speaking an *n*-dialect like the neighboring Massachuset,
Narranganset, Niantic (East and West), and the Nauset.

Location.—The Wampanoag occupied Rhode Island east of Narragansett Bay; Bristol County, Mass.; the southern part of Plymouth
County, below Marshfield and Brockton; and the extreme western
part of Barnstable. The Indians of Martha's Vineyard should also be
added to them, and it will be convenient to treat under the same head
those of Nantucket and the Saconnet, or Sakonnet, of Sakonnet Point,
R. I., whose connection was more remote. They controlled Rhode
Island in Narragansett Bay until the Narraganset tribe conquered it
from them. (See also Rhode Island.)

Subdivisions

Speck (1928) gives the following mainland subdivisions:

(1) Band of Massasoit, in a territory called Sowwams on the east side of Narragansett Bay; the western part of Bristol County, Mass.; all of Bristol
County, R. I.; and the eastern part of Providence County, R. I.

(2) Band of Annawon, about Squannaconk swamps in Rehoboth Township.

(3) Band of Weetamoe, a chieftainess, their territory being called Pocasset, in southeastern Rhode Island, about Tiverton and adjacent parts of Bristol County, Mass.

(4) Band of Corbitant or Caunbatant, about Swansea.

(5) Band of Tispaquin or Tuspaquin, lands called Assawampset, about Assawampset Pond.

(6) Band of Tyasks or Tyashk, about Rochester and Acushnet.

(7) Band of Totoson, in a territory centering about Mattapoisett and Rochester.

(8) Band of Coneconam or Cawnacome, in a territory known as Manomet, extending from Manomet to Woods Hole.

(9) Band of Piowant or Piant, between Assonet Bay and Taunton River.

There were several vacant tracts not occupied by any of the above. In 1861 there were bands of Wampanoag at Herring Pond, Dartmouth, Mamatakesett Pond, Tumpum Pond, and Watuppa Pond.

Speck (1928) gives the following bands on Martha's Vineyard, but the classification applies to a time when Indians from various parts of the mainland had begun to settle there:

(1) Band of Nohtooksaet who came from Massachusetts Bay, about Gay Head.

(2) Band of Mankutquet (including the bands of Wannamanhut who came from near Boston (Christian town) and Toohtoowee, on the north shore of Chilmark), in the western part of Martha's Vineyard excluding the preceding.

(3) Band of Tewanticut (including the bands of Cheesehahchamuk, about Homes' Hole; Wampamag, of Sanchakankachet; and Tom Tyler, about Edgartown), in the eastern section of Martha's Vineyard.

(4) Band of Pahkepunnasso, on the island of Chappaquiddick.

There were two bands on Nantucket, the names of which are unknown, and we must also add the Sakonnet, on Sakonnet Point, R. I., and the Indians of the Elizabeth Islands.

Villages

Mainland:

Acushnet, about Acushnet.

Agawam, about Wareham.

Assameekg, probably near Dartmouth.

Assawompset, in Middleborough Township.

Assonet, conjectural village near the present Assonet.

Coaxet, near Little Compton, R. I.

Cohannet, about Fowling Pond near Taunton.

Comassakumkanit or Herring Pond, Herring Pond, Plymouth County.

Cooxissett, probably in Plymouth County.

Cowsumpsit, in Rhode Island.

Jones' River, in Kingston Township.

Kitteaumut, near Monument Pond, Plymouth County.

Loquasquscit, near Pawtucket, R. I.

Mattakeset, near Duxbury.

Mainland—Continued

Mattapoiset, near Mattapoiset, Plymouth County.

Munponset, location unknown.

Namasket, about Middleboro.

Nasnocomacack, on the coast and probably a few miles north of Plymouth.

Nukkehkummees, near Dartmouth.

Pachade, near Middleboro.

Patuxet, at Plymouth.

Pocasset, near Tiverton, R. I.

Pokanoket, on Bristol Peninsula, R. I.

Quittaub, in the southwestern part of Plymouth County.

Saltwater Pond, in Plymouth County.

Shawonet, near Somerset.

Wauchimoqut, probably near Seekonk.

Wawayontat, on Weweantitt River near Wareham.

Martha's Vineyard:

Chaubaqueduck, on the main island or on Chappaquiddick Island.

Gay Head, at Gay Head.

Nashamoiess, in the southeastern part of the island.

Nashanekammuck, at Chilmark.

Nunnepoag, location uncertain.

Ohkonkemme, near Tisbury.

Sanchecantacket, near Edgartown.

Seconchqut, location uncertain.

Nantucket:

Miacomit, location uncertain.

Podpis, a district and probably village.

Nantucket—Continued

Quays, a district and probably village.

Sasacacheh, a district and probably village.

Shaukimmo, a district and probably village, south of Nantucket Harbor.

Siasconsit, a district and probably village, including the site of the present Siasconset.

Squam, a district and probably village.

Talhanio, location uncertain.

Tetaukimmo, a district and probably village.

Toikiming, location uncertain.

History.—With many older writers on the Norse voyages to America, Mount Hope Bay, in the territory of the Wampanoag, was a favorite site for the supposed Icelandic colony (ca. 1000–1010), but the theory is now less popular. In 1602 Gosnold touched at Martha's Vineyard and was kindly treated by the natives. Soon after the Pilgrims had established themselves at Plymouth in 1620 they made a treaty of friendship with the Wampanoag head chief, Massasoit, who played a great part in the early history of the colony. He died in 1662 and was succeeded by two sons in succession, the second of whom, Metacomet or Metacom, is the King Philip of history. Observing the steady influx of White colonists into Indian lands, King Philip organized a native confederacy against them and a bloody war followed (1675–76), in which King Philip was killed and the power of the tribes of southern New England finally destroyed. The Wampanoag survivors settled with the Sakonnet, who had remained neutral, and formed towns with the Nauset in the western part of Barnstable County. In 1763 they suffered severely from an epidemic, but a number of bands have preserved their autonomy, in a much mixed condition, to the present day. The Indians of Martha's Vineyard and Nantucket, like the Sakonnet, had refused to join the confederacy and consequently maintained their numbers relatively intact for a longer period. They continued to decline, however, and in 1764 two-thirds of the Nantucket Indians were destroyed by a fever. Two or three mixed-bloods were left in 1809, and in 1855 Abram Quary, the last of these, died. The Indians of Martha's Vineyard, on the other hand, received considerable accessions from the mainland and have maintained themselves down to our day though, like the mainland Indians, much mixed with other tribes and other races.

Population.—Of Wampanoag proper Mooney (1928) estimated that there were 2,400 in 1600. They probably suffered severely in the epidemic of 1617, but in 1630 they are said to have had about 30 villages. In 1700 the Sakonnet Indians, including most of the Wampanoag remnants, were estimated at 400. In 1861 a partial census gives 258, and we may suppose that the total was about 300. Martha's Vineyard: The estimates of the Indian population of Martha's Vineyard vary greatly. Mooney (1928) estimated the number of Indians at 1,500 in 1600, perhaps taken from an estimate of 1642, which gives the same figure, while a later writer places their number as "not less than 3,000" (Hare, 1932, p. 44). An estimate made in 1698 gave 1,000. In 1764, 313 were returned; in 1807, 360, only about 40 of whom were full-bloods. In 1861, 393 were returned, but in 1910 only 147. Nantucket: Mooney estimates the Indian population of Nantucket to have been 1,500 in 1600 and Mayhew (Speck, 1928) gives the same number in 1642. Hare (1932, p. 44) also estimates the Indian population to have been 1,500. In 1763 there were 358; in 1790, 20; in 1809, 2 or 3. An informant of Dr. Speck gives the total number of Indians in Barnstable, Plymouth, and Bristol Counties in 1928 as 450.

Connection in which they have become noted.—The Wampanoag made their mark in history chiefly through the activities of their chiefs, Massasoit and King Philip. One of the two largest bodies of Indians in southern New England to maintain their identity down to the present day were the Wampanoag of Martha's Vineyard.

RHODE ISLAND

Narraganset.   Their name means "people of the small point."

Connections.—The Narraganset belonged to the Algonquian linguistic family and spoke an *n*-dialect like the neighboring Massachuset, Wampanoag, and probably the Niantic (East and West) and the Nauset.

Location.—The Narraganset occupied the greater part of Rhode Island west of Narragansett Bay, between Providence and Pawcatuck Rivers. At one time they dominated the Coweset (see **Nipmuc**) north of them and the Eastern Niantic, and they drove the Wampanoag from the island which gives its name to the State of Rhode Island and the Pequot from some territory they held in the west. (See also Massachusetts and Connecticut.)

Subdivisions

There are said to have been eight chiefs over as many territorial divisions, all under one head chief.

Villages

Chaubatick, probably within a few miles of Providence.
Maushapogue, in Providence County.

Mittaubscut, on Pawtuxet River, 7 or 8 miles above its mouth.
Narraganset, above the site of Kingston.
Pawchauquet, in western Rhode Island.
Shawomet, near Warwick.

History.—The Narraganset traced their origin to the Southwest. They escaped the great pestilence of 1617 and were in fact increased in numbers by bands of refugees. In 1633 the Narraganset lost 700 in a smallpox epidemic. In 1636 Roger Williams settled among them and through their favor was enabled to lay the foundations of the present State of Rhode Island. They remained on good terms with the Whites until King Philip's war (1675–76), into which they threw their whole strength. In the celebrated swamp fight at Kingston they lost nearly 1,000 killed and captured, and the remnants of the tribe were soon forced to abandon the country. Some probably joined the Mahican and Abnaki or even got as far as Canada and never returned to their own people, but others obtained permission to come back and were settled among the Eastern Niantic who had taken no part in the contest. From that time on the combined tribes were known as Narraganset. In 1788 many of these united with the Brotherton Indians in New York, and a few have gone to live with the Mohegan in Connecticut. The remainder are near Charlestown, R. I.

Population.—The Narraganset are estimated by Mooney (1928) to have numbered 4,000 in 1600, including the Eastern Niantic, and were perhaps as numerous in 1675. Along with the Eastern Niantic, they had a total population of about 140 in 1812, and 80 in 1832, while the census of 1910 returned 16. The same year, however, 284 Indians all told were returned from Rhode Island, and in 1930, 130.

Connection in which they have become noted.—The Narraganset were famed as the most powerful tribe of southern New England and became noted also on account of Roger Williams' dealings with them and his report regarding them. Narragansett Bay, the Town of Narragansett in Washington County, and Narragansett Pier, the well-known summer resort, were named after them.

Niantic, Eastern. The word Niantic signifies, according to Trumbull (1818) "at a point of land on a (tidal) river or estuary."

Connections.—The Eastern and the Western Niantic were parts of one original tribe split in two perhaps by the Pequot; the nearest relatives of both were probably the Narraganset.

Location.—The western coast of Rhode Island and neighboring coast of Connecticut.

Village

Wekapaug, on the great pond near Charlestown.

History.—As has just been stated, the Eastern Niantic were closely connected with the Narraganset, but they refused to join them in King Philip's war and at its close the remnants of the Narraganset were settled among them. Their subsequent history has been given under **Narraganset.**

Population.—(See **Narraganset.**)

Connection in which they have become noted.—Niantic, in the town of Westerly, Washington County, R. I., perpetuates the name. (See **Niantic, Western,** under Connecticut.)

Nipmuc. The Coweset and some other bands of Nipmuc extended into the northwestern part of the State but most of these were under the domination of the Narraganset. (See Massachusetts.)

Pequot. The Pequot originally occupied some lands in the western part of Rhode Island of which the Narraganset dispossessed them. (See Connecticut.)

Wampanoag. The Wampanoag occupied the mainland sections of Rhode Island east of Narragansett Bay and Providence River. At one period they also held the island which gives this State its name but they were driven from it by the Narraganset. (See Massachusetts.)

CONNECTICUT

Mahican. The northwestern corner of Litchfield County was occupied by the Wawyachtonoc, a tribe of the Mahican Confederacy of the upper Hudson, though their main seats were in Columbia and Dutchess Counties, N. Y. (See New York.)

Mohegan. The name means "wolf." They are not to be confused with the Mahican. Also called:

> River Indians.
> Seaside People.
> Unkus [Uncas] Indians, from the name of their chief.
> Upland Indians.

Connections.—The Mohegan belonged to the Algonquian linguistic stock and spoke a *y*-dialect closely related to Pequot.

Location.—The Mohegan originally occupied most of the upper valley of the Thames and its branches. Later they claimed authority over some of the Nipmuc and the Connecticut River tribes, and in the old Pequot territory. (See also New York.)

Villages

Ashowat, between Amston and Federal.
Catantaquck, near the head of Pachaug River.
Checapscaddock, southeast of the mouth of Shetucket River in the town of Preston.
Kitemaug, on the west wide of Thames River between Uncasville and Massapeag.
Mamaquaog, on Natchaug River northeast of Willimantic.

Mashantackack, near Palmertown, town of Montville.

Massapeag, at the place now so-called on the west side of Thames River.

Mohegan, at the present town of Mohegan on the west side of Thames River.

Moosup, at the present Moosup in the town of Plainfield.

Nawhesetuck, on Fenton River north of Willimantic.

Pachaug, at the present Pachaug in the town of Griswold.

Paugwonk, near Gardiner Lake in the town of Salem.

Pautexet, near the present Jewett City in the town of Griswold.

Pigscomsuck, on the right bank of Quinebaug River near the present line between
  New London and Windham Counties.

Poquechanneeg, near Lebanon.

Poquetanock, near Trading Cove, town of Preston.

Shantuck, on the west side of Thames River just north of Mohegan.

Showtucket or Shetucket, near Lisbon in the fork of the Shetucket and Quinebaug
  Rivers.

Wauregan, on the east side of Quinebaug River in the town of Plainfield.

Willimantic, on the site of the present city of Willimantic.

Yantic, at the present Yantic on Yantic River.

History.—The Mohegan were probably a branch of the Mahican.
Originally under Sassacus, chief of the Pequot, they afterward became
independent and upon the destruction of the Pequot in 1637, Uncas,
the Mohegan chief, became ruler also of the remaining Pequot and
set up pretensions to territory north and west beyond his original
borders. At the end of King Philip's War, the Mohegan were the
only important tribe remaining in southern New England, but as
the White settlements advanced they were reduced progressively both
in territory and in numbers. Many joined the Scaticook, and in 1788
a still larger body united with the Brotherton in New York, where they
formed the largest single element in the new settlement. The rest
continued in their old town at Mohegan, where a remnant of mixed-
bloods still survives.

Population.—The number of Mohegan were estimated by Mooney
(1928) at 2,200 in 1600; in 1643, including the remnant of the Pequot
and perhaps other tribes, at between 2,000 and 2,500. In 1705
they numbered 750; in 1774, 206 were reported; in 1804, 84; in 1809,
69; in 1825, 300; in 1832, about 350; in 1910, 22.

Connection in which they have become noted.—The Mohegan became
celebrated on account of the services rendered the Whites by Uncas.
Today their name is perpetuated in Mohegan, on Thames River, and
the name of their chief in Uncasville on the same stream. There is
a post village of this name in McDowell County, W. Va., and a
Mohegan Lake in Westchester County, N. Y., but this is named
after the Mahican.

Niantic, Western. Regarding the name, see **Niantic, Eastern,** under
  Rhode Island.

Connections.—These were the same as for the Eastern Niantic. (See Rhode Island.)

Location.—On the seacoast from Niantic Bay to Connecticut River.

Villages

Niantic or Nehantucket, near the present town of Niantic.   There was another near Old Lyme.

History.—Originally the Western Niantic are thought to have constituted one tribe with the Eastern Niantic and to have been cut apart from them by the Pequot. They were nearly destroyed in the Pequot war and at its close (1637) were placed under the control of the Mohegan. About 1788 many joined the Brotherton Indians. A small village of Niantic was reported as existing near Danbury in 1809, but this perhaps contained remnants of the tribes of western Connecticut, although Speck (1928) found several Indians of mixed Niantic-Mohegan descent living with the Mohegan remnant, descendants of a pure-blood Niantic woman from the mouth of Niantic River.

Population. The Western Niantic population was estimated by Mooney (1928) at 600 in 1600; there were about 100 in 1638; 85 in 1761.

Connection in which they have become noted.—The name of the Western Niantic is perpetuated in Niantic village, Niantic River, and Niantic Bay, in New London County. Post villages in Macon County, Ill., and Montgomery County, Pa., bear the name Niantic.

Nipmuc. Some bands of this tribe extended into the northeastern part of the State. (See Massachusetts.)

Pequot. The name means, according to Trumbull (1818), "destroyers." Also called:

Sickenames, in a Dutch deed quoted by Ruttenber (1872).

Connections.—The Pequot belonged to the Algonquian linguistic stock, and spoke a *y*-dialect closely related to Mohegan.

Location.—The Pequot occupied the coast of New London County from Niantic River nearly to the Rhode Island State line. Until driven out by the Narraganset, they extended into Rhode Island as far as Wecapaug River. (See also Rhode Island.)

Villages

Asupsuck, in the interior of the town of Stonington.
Aukumbumsk or Awcumbuck, in the center of the Pequot country near Gales Ferry.
Aushpook, at Stonington.
Cosattuck, probably near Stonington.
Cuppanaugunnit, probably in New London County.
Mangunckakuck, probably on Thames River below Mohegan.

Maushantuxet, at Ledyard.
Mystic, near West Mystic on the west side of Mystic River.
Monhunganuck, near Beach Pond in the town of Voluntown.
Nameaug, near New London.
Noank, at the present place of that name.
Oneco, at the place of that name in the town of Sterling.
Paupattokshick, on the lower course of Thames River.
Pawcatuck, probably on the river of the same name, Washington County, R. I.
Pequotauk, near New London.
Poquonock, inland from Poquonock Bridge.
Sauquonckackock, on the west side of Thames River below Mohegan.
Shenecosset, near Midway in the town of Groton.
Tatuppequauog, on the Thames River below Mohegan.
Weinshauks, near Groton.
Wequetequock, on the east side of the river of the same name.

History.—The Pequot and the Mohegan are supposed to have been invaders from the direction of Hudson River. At the period of first White contact, the Pequot were warlike and greatly dreaded by their neighbors. They and the Mohegan were jointly ruled by Sassacus until the revolt of Uncas, the Mohegan chief. (See **Mohegan.**) About 1635 the Narraganset drove them from a corner of the present Rhode Island which they had previously held, and 2 years later the murder of a trader who had treated some Indians harshly involved the Pequot in war with the Whites. At that time their chief controlled 26 subordinate chiefs, claimed authority over all Connecticut east of Connecticut River, and on the coast as far west as New Haven or Guilford, as well as all of Long Island except the extreme western end. Through the influence of Roger Williams, the English secured the assistance or neutrality of the surrounding tribes. Next they surprised and destroyed the principal Pequot fort near Mystic River along with 600 Indians of all ages and both sexes, and this disaster crippled the tribe so much that, after a few desperate attempts at further resistance, they determined to separate into small parties and abandon the country (1637). Sassacus and a considerable body of followers were intercepted near Fairfield while trying to escape to the Mohawk and almost all were killed or captured. Those who surrendered were divided among the Mohegan, Narraganset, and Niantic, and their territory passed under the authority of Uncas. Their Indian overlords treated them so harshly, however, that they were taken out of their hands by the colonists in 1655 and settled in two villages near Mystic River, where some of their descendants still live. Numbers removed to other places—Long Island, New Haven, the Nipmuc country, and elsewhere—while many were kept as slaves among the English in New England or sent to the West Indies.

Population.—The Pequot population was estimated by Mooney (1928) at 2,200 in 1600; in 1637, immediately after the Pequot war, there were said to be 1,950, but the figure is probably too high. In 1674 the Pequot in their old territory numbered about 1,500; in 1762, 140. In 1832 there were said to be about 40 mixed-bloods, but the census of 1910 gave 66, of whom 49 were in Connecticut and 17 in Massachusetts.

Connection in which they have become noted.—The Pequot are remembered principally on account of the bitter and, to them, disastrous war related above. The name is borne by a post village in Crow Wing County, Minn.

Wappinger. The valley of Connecticut River was the home of a number of bands which might be called Mattabesec after the name of the most important of them, and this in turn was a part of the Wappinger. (See New York.)

NEW YORK

Delaware. Bands of two of the main divisions of the Delaware Indians, the Munsee and Unami, extended into parts of New York State, including the island of Manhattan. (See New Jersey.)

Erie. The Erie occupied parts of Chautauqua and Cattaraugus Counties. (See Ohio.)

Iroquois. From Algonkin Iri^{n}akhoiw, "real adders," with the French suffix -ois. Also called:

> Oñgwano^{n}sioñni', their own name, meaning "We are of the extended lodge," whence comes the popular designation, "People of the long-house."
>
> Canton Indians.
>
> Confederate Indians.
>
> Five Nations, from the five constituent tribes.
>
> Mat-che-naw-to-waig, Ottawa name, meaning "bad snakes."
>
> Mingwe, Delaware name.
>
> Nadowa, name given by the northwestern Algonquians and meaning "adders."
>
> Six Nations, name given after the Tuscarora had joined them.

Connections.—The Iroquois belonged to the Iroquoian linguistic stock, their nearest relations being the Tuscarora, Neutral Nation, Huron, Erie, and Susquehanna.

Location.—In the upper and central part of the Mohawk Valley and the lake region of central New York. After obtaining guns from the Dutch, the Iroquois acquired a dominating influence among the Indians from Maine to the Mississippi and between the Ottawa and Cumberland Rivers. (See also Indiana, Kansas, Ohio, Oklahoma, Pennsylvania, Wisconsin, and Canada.)

Subdivisions

There were five tribes, as follows: Cayuga, about Cayuga Lake; Mohawk, in the upper valley of Mohawk River; Oneida, about Oneida Lake; Onondaga, in Onondaga County and the neighboring section; Seneca, between Lake Seneca and Genesee River. Later there were added to these, for the most part not on terms of perfect equality, the Tuscarora from North Carolina, some Delaware, Tutelo, Saponi, Nanticoke, Conoy, New England Indians, and other fragments of tribes, besides entire towns from the Huron, Erie, Andaste, and other conquered peoples.

Villages

Cayuga:

Chondote, on the east side of Cayuga Lake a few miles south of Cayuga.

Gandasetaigon, near Port Hope, Ont.

Ganogeh, at Canoga.

Gayagaanhe, near the east shore of Cayuga Lake 3½ miles south of Union Springs.

Gewauga, at Union Springs, town of Springport.

Goiogouen, on the east side of Cayuga Lake on Great Gully Brook, about 4 miles south of the present Union Springs, and 4 leagues from the town of Tiohero.

Kawauka, (?), Kente, on Quinte Bay, Lake Ontario, Ont.

Neodakheat, at Ithaca.

Oneniote, at Oneida on Cayuga Lake.

Onnontare, probably east of Seneca River and at Bluff Point, near Fox Ridge, Cayuga County.

Owego, on the right bank of Owego Creek, about 2 miles from the Susquehanna River, in Tioga County.

Skannayutenate, on the west side of Cayuga Lake, northeast of Canoga, Seneca County.

Tiohero, 4 leagues from Goiogouen.

Mohawk:

Canajoharie, on the east bank of Otsquago Creek nearly opposite Fort Plain.

Canastigaone, on the north side of Mohawk River just above Cohoes Falls.

Canienga, near the bank of Mohawk River.

Caughnawaga, on Mohawk River near the site of Auriesville.

Chuchtononeda, on the south side of Mohawk River—named from a band.

Kanagaro, on the north side of Mohawk River in Montgomery County or Herkimer County.

Kowogoconnughariegugharie, (?).

Nowadaga, at Danube, Herkimer County.

Onoalagona, at Schenectady.

Osquake, at Fort Plain and on Osquake Creek, Montgomery County.

Saratoga, about Saratoga and Stillwater.

Schaunactada, at and south of Albany.

Schoharie, near Schoharie.

Teatontaloga, on the north side of Mohawk River and probably near the mouth of Schoharie Creek in Montgomery County.

Tewanondadon, in the peninsula formed by the outlet of Otsego Lake and Shenivas Creek.

Oneida:

Awegen.

Cahunghage, on the south side of Oneida Lake.

Canowdowsa, near junction of Lackawanna and Susquehanna Rivers.

Chittenango, on Chittenango Creek, Madison County.

Cowassalon, on creek of same name in Madison County.

Ganadoga, near Oneida Castle, Oneida County.

Hostayuntwa, at Camden.

Oneida, name of several of the main towns of the tribe, in the valleys of Oneida
Creek and Upper Oriskany Creek.

Opolopong, on the east branch of Susquehanna, about 30 miles above Shamokin
and 10 miles below Wyoming, Pa.

Oriska, near Oriskany in Oneida County.

Ossewingo, a few miles above Chenango, Broome County.

Ostogeron, probably above Toskokogie on the Chenango River.

Schoherage, probably on the west branch of Chenango River (?) below Tuskokogie.

Sevege, a short distance above Owego on the west side of the east branch of
the Susquehanna River.

Solocka, about 60 miles above Shamokin, on a creek issuing from the Great
Swamp north of the Cashuetunk Mountains, Pa.

Tegasoke, on Fish Creek in Oneida County.

Teseroken, (?).

Teiosweken, (?).

Tkanetota, (?).

Onondaga:

Ahaouet, (?).

Deseroken, traditional.

Gadoquat, at Brewerton, Onondaga County.

Gannentaha, a mission on Onondaga Lake about 5 leagues from Onondaga.

Gistwiahna, at Onondaga Valley.

Onondaga, the principal town of the tribe, which occupied several distinct sites,
the earliest known probably 2 miles west of Cazenovia and east of West
Limestone Creek, Madison County.

Onondaghara, on Onondaga River 3 miles east of Onondaga Hollow.

Onondahgegahgeh, west of Lower Ebenezer, Erie County.

Onontatacet, on Seneca River.

Otiahanague, at the mouth of Salmon River, Oswego County.

Teionontatases, (?).

Tgasunto, (?).

Touenho, south of Brewerton, at the west end of Lake Oneida.

Tueadasso, near Jamesville.

Seneca:

Buckaloon, on the north side of Allegheny River near the present Irvine,
Warren County, Pa.

Canadasaga, near Geneva.

Canandaigua, near Canandaigua.

Caneadea, at Caneadea.

Catherine's Town, near Catherine.

Cattaraugus, on a branch of Cattaraugus Creek.

Chemung, probably near Chemung.

Cheronderoga, (?).

Chinklacamoose, probably mainly Delaware but frequented by Seneca, on the site of Clearfield, Pa.

Chinoshahgeh, near Victor.

Condawhaw, at North Hector.

Connewango, 2 villages, one at Warren, Pa., and one on the left bank of Allegheny River above the site of Tionesta, Pa.

Dayoitgao, on Genesee River near Fort Morris.

Deonundagae, on Livingston River west of Genesee River.

Deyodeshot, about 2 miles southeast of East Avon, on the site of Keinthe.

Deyohnegano, 2 villages: one near Caledonia; one on Allegheny Reservation, Cattaraugus County.

Deyonongdadagana, on the west bank of Genesee River near Cuylerville.

Dyosyowan, on Buffalo Creek, Erie County, Pa.

Gaandowanang, on Genesee River near Cuylerville.

Gadaho, at Castle.

Gahato, probably Seneca, in Chemung County.

Gahayanduk, location unknown.

Ganagweh, near Palmyra.

Ganawagus, on Genesee River near Avon.

Ganeasos, (?).

Ganedontwan, at Moscow.

Ganos, at Cuba, Allegany County.

Ganosgagong, at Dansville.

Gaonsagaon, (?).

Gaousge, probably Seneca, on Niagara River.

Gaskosada, on Cayuga Creek west of Lancaster.

Gathtsegwarohare, (?).

Geneseo, near Geneseo.

Gistaquat, (?).

Goshgoshunk, mainly Munsee and Unami, 3 villages on Allegheny River in the upper part of Venango County, Pa.

Hickorytown, mainly Munsee and Unami, probably about East Hickory or West Hickory, Forest County, Pa.

Honeoye, on Honeoye Creek, near Honeoye Lake.

Joneadih, on Allegheny River nearly opposite Salamanca.

Kanagaro, 2 villages, one on Boughton Hill, directly south of Victor, N. Y.; one with several different locations from 1½ to 4 miles south from the first, and southeast from Victor, on the east side of Mud Creek.

Kanaghsaws, about 1 mile northeast of Conesus Center.

Kannassarago, between Oneida and Onondaga.

Kashong, on Kashong Creek at its entrance into Lake Seneca.

Kaskonchiagon, (?).

Kaygen, on the south bank of Chemung River below Kanestio River.

Keinthe, on the north shore of Lake Ontario, later transferred to Bay of Quinte.

Lawunkhannek, mainly Delaware, on Allegheny River above Franklin, Venango County, Pa.

Mahusquechikoken, with Munsee and other tribes, on Allegheny River about 20 miles above Venango, Pa.

Middle Town, 3 miles above the site of Chemung.

New Chemung, at or near the site of Chemung.

Newtown, on Chemung River near Elmira.

Oatka, at Scottsville, on the west bank of Genesee River.

Old Chemung, about 3 miles below New Chemung.

Onnahee, on the east side of Fall Brook, in the western part of lot 20, town of Hopewell, Ontario County.

Onoghsadago, near Conewango (?).

Onondarka, north of Karaghyadirha on Guy Johnson's map of 1771.

Owaiski, near Wiscoy on the west bank of Genesee River, Allegheny County.

Sheshequin, about 6 miles below Tioga Point, Bradford County, Pa.

Skahasegao, at Lima, Livingston County.

Skoiyase, at Waterloo.

Sonojowauga, at Mount Morris, Livingston County.

Tekisedaneyout, in Erie County.

Tioniongarunte, (?).

Tonawanda, on Tonawanda Creek, Niagara County.

Totiakton, on Honeoye outlet not far from Honeoye Falls in Monroe County.

Venango, at Franklin, at the mouth of French Creek, Venango County, Pa.

Yorkjough, about 12 miles from Honeoye and 6 from New Genesee, probably in Livingston County.

Yoroonwago, on upper Allegheny River near the present Corydon, Warren County, Pa.

Iroquoian villages of unspecified tribe

Adjouquay, (?).

Anpuaqun, (?).

Aratumquat, (?).

Cahunghage, on the south side of Oneida Lake.

Caughnawaga, on Sault St. Louis, Quebec Province, Canada.

Chemegaide, (?).

Churamuk, on the east side of Susquehanna River, 18 miles above Owego.

Codocararen, (?).

Cokanuk, (?).

Conaquanosshan, (?).

Conihunta, 14 miles below Unadilla.

Connosomothdian, (?).

Conoytown, of mixed Conoy and Iroquois, on Susquehanna River between Bainbridge and Sunbury, Pa.

Coreorgonel, of mixed Tutelo and Iroquois, on the west side of Cayuga Lake inlet and on the border of the Great Swamp 3 miles from the south end of Cayuga Lake.

Cowawago, (?).

Cussewago, principally Seneca, on the site of the present Waterford, Erie County, Pa.

Ganadoga, near Toronto, Ontario, Canada.

Ganagarahhare, at Venango, Crawford County, Pa.

Ganeraske, at the mouth of Trent River, Ontario, Canada.

Ganneious, at the site of Napanee, Ontario, Canada.

Glasswanoge, (?).

Indian Point, at Lisbon, N. Y.

Janundat, on Sandusky Bay, Erie County, Ohio.

Jedakne, Iroquois or Delaware, on the west branch of Susquehanna River, probably at Dewart, Northumberland County, Pa.

Johnstown, location not given.

Jonondes, location unknown.

Juaniata, on Duncan Island in Susquehanna River, near the mouth of the Juniata.

Juraken, 2 villages, one on the right bank of the Susquehanna at Sunbury, Pa., the other on the left bank of the east branch of the Susquehanna.

Kahendohon, location unknown.

Kanaghsaws, about 1 mile northwest of Conesus Center, N. Y.

Kannawalohalla, at Elmira, N. Y.

Kanesadageh, a town of the Turtle Clan mentioned in the Iroquois Book of Rites.

Karaken, location unknown.

Karhationni, location unknown.

Karhawenradonh, location unknown.

Kayehkwarageh, location unknown.

Kickenapawling, mixed Delaware (?) and Iroquois, 5 miles north of the present Stoyestown, Pa., at the fork of Quemahoning and Stony Creeks.

Kittanning, mixed Iroquois, Delaware, and Caughnawaga, about the present Kittanning, Armstrong County, Pa.

Kuskuski, mixed Delaware and Iroquois, on Beaver Creek, near Newcastle, Pa.

La Montagne, on a hill on Montreal Island, Quebec Province, Canada.

La Prairie, at La Prairie, Quebec, Canada.

Logstown, Shawnee, Delaware, and Iroquois, on the right bank of the Ohio River, 14 miles below Pittsburgh.

Loyalhannon, on Loyalhanna Creek, Pa.

Manckatawangum, near Barton, Bradford County, Pa.

Matchasaung, on the left bank of the east branch of the Susquehanna River, about 13 miles above Wyoming, Pa.

Mingo Town, near Steubenville, Ohio.

Mohanet, probably Iroquois, on the east branch of the Susquehanna River, Pa.

Nescopeck, mixed Iroquois, Shawnee, and Delaware, formerly at the mouth of Nescopeck River, Luzerne County, Pa.

Newtown, 4 towns: one, probably of the Seneca, on Chemung River near Elmira, N. Y.; one, probably of Iroquois and Delaware, on the north bank of Licking River, near Zanesville, Ohio; one, probably of Iroquois and Delaware, on Muskingum River near Newtown, Ohio; and one, probably of Iroquois and Delaware, on the west side of Wills Creek, near Cambridge, Ohio.

Newtychanning, on the west bank of the Susquehanna River and the north side of Sugar Creek, near North Towanda, Pa.

Ohrekionni, (?).

Oka, mixed Iroquois, Nipissing and Algonkin, on Lake of the Two Mountains, near Montreal, Quebec, Canada.

Onaweron, location unknown.

Onkwe Iyede, location unknown.

Opolopong, on the east branch of the Susquehanna River about 30 miles above Shamokin and 10 miles below Wyoming, Pa.

Oskawaserenhon, location unknown.

Ostonwackin, Delaware and Iroquois, at the mouth of Loyalstock Creek on the west branch of the Susquehanna River, at Montoursville, Pa.

Oswegatchie, at Ogdensburg, N. Y.

Otsiningo, on Chenango River, Broome County, N. Y.

Otskwirakeron, location unknown.

Ousagwentera, "beyond Fort Frontenac."

Pluggy's Town, a band of marauding Indians, chiefly Mingo, at Delaware, Ohio.

Runonvea, near Big Flats, Chemung County, N. Y.

Saint Regis, on the south bank of the St. Lawrence River at the international boundary and on both sides.

Sault au Recollet, near the mouth of the Ottawa River, Two Mountains County, Quebec, Canada.

Sawcunk, mixed Delaware, Shawnee, and Mingo, on the north bank of the Ohio River near the mouth of Beaver Creek and the present town of Beaver, Pa.

Schohorage, on the west bank of the Susquehanna River, a short distance above the Indian town of Oquaga, Pa.

Sconassi, on the west side of the Susquehanna River below the west branch, probably in Union County, Pa.

Scoutash's Town, Mingo or Shawnee, near Lewistown, Logan County, Ohio.

Seneca Town, Mingo, on the east side of Sandusky River in Seneca County, Ohio.

Sevege, a short distance above Owego on the west side of the east branch of Susquehanna River, N. Y.

Sewickley, a Shawnee town occupied in later years by a few Mingo and Delaware, on the north side of Allegheny River about 12 miles above Pittsburgh, near Springdale, Pa.

Shamokin, Delaware, Shawnee, and Iroquois, a short distance from the forks of the Susquehanna and on the northeast branch.

Shenango, 3 towns: one, on the north bank of the Ohio River a short distance below the present Economy, Pa.; one, at the junction of the Conewango and Allegheny Rivers; and one, some distance up the Big Beaver near Kuskuski (see above).

Sheshequin, Iroquois and Delaware, about 8 miles below Tioga Point, Pa.

Sittawingo, in Armstrong County, Pa.

Skenandowa, at Vernon Center, Oneida County, Pa.

Solocka, about 60 miles above Shamokin on a creek issuing from the Great Swamp north of the Cashuetunk Mountains, Pa.

Swahadowri, (?).

Taiaiagon, near Toronto, Ontario, Canada.

Tioga, at Athens, Pa.

Tohoguses Town, at junction of Plum and Crooked Creeks, Armstrong County, Pa.

Tonihata, on an island in the St. Lawrence River supposed to be Grenadier Island, Leeds County, Ontario, Canada.

Tullihas, mixed Delaware, Mahican, and Caughnawaga, on the west branch of the Muskingum River, Ohio, above the forks.

Tuskokogie, just above Schoherage (q. v.) on Chenango River (?).

Unadilla, near Unadilla, Otsego County.

Wakerhon, (?).

Wauteghe, on upper Susquehanna River between Teatontaloga and Oquaga.

Youcham, (?).

History.—In Cartier's time the five Iroquois tribes seem to have been independent and in a state of constant mutual warfare. At a later period, not before 1570 according to Hewitt (1907), they were induced by two remarkable men, Dekanawida and Hiawatha, to form a federal union. While the immediate object of the league was to bring about peace between these and other neighboring tribes, the strength which the federal body acquired and the fact that they were soon equipped with guns by the Dutch at Albany incited them to undertake extensive wars and to build up a rude sort of empire.

The related Tuscarora of North Carolina joined them in successive migrations, the greater part between 1712 and 1722, and the remainder in 1802. In the French-English wars they took the part of the English and were a very considerable factor in their final victory. Later all but the Oneida and part of the Tuscarora sided against the American colonists and as a result their principal towns were laid waste by Sullivan in 1779. The Mohawk and Cayuga, with other Iroquoian tribes in the British interest, were given a reservation on Grand River, Ontario. The remainder received reservations in New York except the Oneida, who were settled near Green Bay, Wis. The so-called Seneca of Oklahoma consist of remnants from all of the Iroquois tribes, the Conestoga, Hurons, and perhaps others, which Hewitt (*in* Hodge, 1910) thinks were gathered around the Erie and perhaps the Conestoga as a nucleus.

Population.—In 1600 the Iroquois are estimated by Mooney (1928) to have numbered 5,500; in 1677 and 1685 their numbers were placed at about 16,000; in 1689 they were estimated at about 12,850; in 1774, 10,000 to 12,500; in 1904 they numbered about 16,100, of whom 10,418 were in Canada; in 1923 there were 8,696 in the United States and 11,355 in Canada; total, 20,051. By the census of 1910 there were reported in the United States 2,907 Seneca, 2,436 Oneida, 365 Onondaga, 368 Mohawk, 81 Cayuga, 1,219 St. Regis, and 61 unspecified, a total of 7,437, besides 400 Tuscarora. In 1930 the figure, including Tuscarora, was 6,866. In 1937, 3,241 Oneida were living in Wisconsin and 732 "Seneca" in Oklahoma.

Connection in which they have become noted.—The group of tribes known as the Iroquois is famous from the fact that it had attained the highest form of governmental organization reached by any people north of the valley of México. It is also noted, largely in consequence of the above fact, for the dominating position to which it attained among the Indian tribes of northeastern North America, and for its long continued alliance with the English in their wars with the French. Hiawatha, the name of one of the founders of the confederation, was adopted by Longfellow as that of his hero in the poem of the name, though the story centers about another people, the Chippewa. Lewis H. Morgan (1851) based his theories regarding the nature of primitive society, which have played a very important part in ethnology and sociology, on studies of Iroquois organization. The name Iroquois has been given to a branch of the Kankakee River, Ill., to an Illinois County and a village in the same, and to villages in South Dakota and Ontario. The names of each of the five constituent tribes have also been widely used.

Mahican. The name means "wolf." This tribe is not to be confused with the **Mohegan** of Connecticut (q. v.), though the names are mere varieties of the same word. Also called:

> Akochakañen, meaning "Those who speak a strange tongue." (Iroquois name.)
> Canoe Indians, so called by Whites.
> Hikanagi or Nhíkana, Shawnee name.
> Loups, so called by the French.
> Orunges, given by Chauvignerie (1736), *in* Schoolcraft (1851–57, vol. 3, p. 554).
> River Indians, Dutch name.
> Uragees, given by Colden, 1747.

Connections.—The Mahican belonged to the Algonquian linguistic family, and spoke an *r*-dialect, their closest connections being with the southern New England Indians to the east.

Location.—On both banks of the upper Hudson from Catskill Creek to Lake Champlain and eastward to include the valley of the Housatonic. (See also Connecticut, Massachusetts, Vermont, and Wisconsin.)

Subdivisions

Mahican proper, in the northern part of the territory.
Mechkentowoon, on the west bank of Hudson River above Catskill Creek.
Wawyachtonoc, in Dutchess and Columbia Counties and eastward to the Housatonic River in Connecticut.
Westenhuck (or Housatonic?), near Great Barrington, Mass.
Wiekagjoc, on the eastern bank of the Hudson River near Hudson.

Villages

Aepjin, at or near Schodac.
Kaunaumeek, in New York about halfway between Albany and Stockbridge, Mass.
Kenunckpacook, on the east side of Housatonic River a little above Scaticook.
Maringoman's Castle, on Murderer's Creek, at Bloominggrove, Ulster County.
Monemius, on Haver Island, in Hudson River near Cohoes Falls, Albany County.
Nepaug, on Nepaug River, town of New Hartford, Litchfield County, Conn.
Peantam, at Bantam Lake, Litchfield County, Conn.
Potic, west of Athens, Greene County.
Scaticook, 3 villages in Dutchess and Rensselaer Counties, and in Litchfield County, Conn., the last on Housatonic River near the junction with Ten Mile River.
Wequadnack, near Sharon, Litchfield County, Conn.
Wiatiac, near Salisbury, Litchfield County, Conn.
Wiltmeet, on Esopus Creek, probably near Kingston.
Winooskeek, on Lake Champlain, probably at the mouth of Winooski River, Vt.
Wyantenuc, in Litchfield County, Conn.

History.—The traditional point of origin of the Mahican was in the West. They were found in occupancy of the territory outlined above by the Dutch, and were then at war with the Mohawk who, in

1664, compelled them to move their capital from Schodac near Albany to the present Stockbridge. They gradually sold their territory and in 1721 a band was on Kankakee River, Ind., while in 1730, a large body settled close to the Delaware and Munsee near Wyoming, Pa., afterward becoming merged with those tribes. In 1736 those in the Housatonic Valley were gathered into a mission at Stockbridge and were ever afterward known as Stockbridge Indians. In 1756 a large body of Mahican and Wappinger, along with Nanticoke and other people, settled in Broome and Tioga Counties under Iroquois protection. In 1788 another body of Indians drawn from New York, Connecticut, and Rhode Island, including Mahican, settled near the Stockbridges at Marshall, N. Y. The Stockbridge and Brotherton Indians later removed to Wisconsin, where they were probably joined by part at least of the band last mentioned. A few Mahican remained about their old home on Hudson River for some years after the Revolution but disappeared unnoticed.

Population.—Mooney (1928) estimates that there were about 3,000 Mahican in 1600; the Stockbridges among the Iroquois numbered 300 in 1796, and 606 in 1923, including some Munsee. The census of 1910 gave 533 Stockbridges and 172 Brotherton. The census of 1930 indicated about 813.

Connection in which they have become noted.—The Mahican tribe has probably attained more fame from its appearance in the title of Cooper's novel. "The Last of the Mohegans," than from any circumstance directly connected with its history. There is a village called Mohegan in the northern part of Westchester County, N. Y., and another, known as Mohican in Ashland County, Ohio, while an affluent of the Muskingum also bears the same name.

Mohegan.   (See Connecticut.)

Montauk.   Meaning "uncertain."

Connections.—The Montauk belonged to the Algonquian linguistic family and spoke an *r*-dialect like that of the Wappinger.

Location.—In the eastern and central parts of Long Island.

Subdivisions

Corchaug, in Riverhead and Southold Townships.
Manhasset, on Shelter Island.
Massapequa, in the southern part of Oyster Bay and Huntington Townships.
Matinecock, in the townships of Flushing, North Hempstead, the northern part of Oyster Bay and Huntington, and the western part of Smithtown.
Merric, in the eastern part of Hempstead Township.
Montauk proper, in Southampton Township.
Nesaquake, in the eastern part of Smithtown and the territory east of it.
Patchogue, on the southern coast from Patchogue to Westhampton.
Rockaway, in Newtown, Jamaica, and Hempstead Townships.

Secatogue, in Islip Township.
Setauket, on the north shore from Stony Brook to Wading River.
Shinnecock, on the coast from Shinnecock Bay to Montauk Point.

Villages

Aquebogue, on a creek entering the north side of Great Peconic Bay.
Ashamomuck, on the site of a White town of the same name in Suffolk County.
Cutchogue, at Cutchogue in Suffolk County.
Massapequa, probably at Fort Neck.
Mattituck, on the site of the present Mattituck, Suffolk County.
Merric, on the site of Merricks, Queens County.
Montauk, above Fort Pond, Suffolk County.
Nesaquake, at the present Nissequague, about Smithtown, Suffolk County.
Patchogue, near the present Patchogue, Suffolk County.
Rechquaakie, near the present Rockaway.

There were also villages at Flushing, Glen Cove, Cold Spring, Huntington, Cow Harbor, Fireplace, Mastic, Moriches, Westhampton, and on Hog Island in Rockaway Bay.

History.—The Montauk were in some sense made tributary to the Pequot, until the latter were destroyed, when they were subjected to a series of attacks by the Narraganset and took refuge, about 1759, with the Whites at Easthampton. They had, meanwhile, lost the greater part of their numbers by pestilence and, about 1788, most of those that were left went to live with the Brotherton Indians in New York. A very few remained on the island, whose mixed-blood descendants are still officially recognized as a tribe by the State of New York, principally under the name Shinnecock.

Population.—Including Canarsee, the Montauk are estimated by Mooney (1928) at 6,000 in 1600. In 1658–59 an estimate gives about 500; in 1788, 162 were enumerated; in 1829, 30 were left on Long Island; in 1910, 167 "Shinnecock," 29 "Montauk," and 1 "Possepatuck." In 1923, 250 were returned, including 30 Montauk, 200 Shinnecock, and 20 Poospatock (Patchoag).

Connection in which they have become noted.—The name of the Montauk is perpetuated in that of the easternmost point of land on Long Island, a post village in the same county, and one in Dent County, Mo. They were among those tribes most active in the manufacture of siwan or wampum.

Neutrals. So called by the French because they remained neutral during the later wars between the Iroquois and Huron. Also called:

> Hatiwanta-runh, by Tuscarora, meaning "Their speech is awry"; in form it is close to the names applied by the other Iroquois tribes and more often quoted as Attiwandaronk.

Connections.—The Neutrals belonged to the Iroquoian linguistic stock; their position within this is uncertain.

Location.—In the southern part of the province of Ontario, the westernmost part of New York, in northeastern Ohio, and in southeastern Michigan. (See also Indiana, Michigan, Ohio, and Canada.)

Subdivisions

It seems impossible to separate these from the names of the villages, except perhaps in the cases of the Aondironon (in Ontario bordering Huron territory), and the Ongniaahra (see below).

Villages

There were 28, but only the names of the following have been preserved:

Kandoucho, in Ontario near the Huron country, i. e., in the northern part of Neutral territory.

Khioetoa, apparently a short distance east of Sandwich, Ontario.

Ongniaahra, probably on the site of Youngstown, N.Y.

Ounontisaston, not far from Niagara River.

Teotongniaton, in Ontario.

History.—Shortly after the destruction of the Huron, the Neutrals became involved in hostilities with the Iroquois and were themselves destroyed in 1650–51, most of them evidently being incorporated with their conquerors, though an independent body is mentioned as wintering near Detroit in 1653.

Population.—The Neutrals were estimated by Mooney (1928) to number 10,000 in 1600; in 1653 the independent remnant included 800. They were probably incorporated finally with the Iroquois and Wyandot.

Connection in which they have become noted.—The chief claim of the Neutrals to permanent fame is the fact that the name of one of their subdivisions, the Ongniaahra, became fixed, in the form Niagara, to the world-famous cataract between New York and Ontario.

Saponi. Some years after leaving Fort Christanna, Va., the Saponi settled among the Iroquois and were formally adopted by the Cayuga tribe in 1753. (See Virginia.)

Tuscarora. After their defeat in the Tuscarora War, 1712–13, bands of this tribe began moving north and in course of time the majority settled in New York so that the Iroquois came to be known afterwards as the "Six Nations" instead of the "Five Nations." (See North Carolina.)

Tutelo. The Tutelo accompanied the Saponi from Virginia and were adopted by the Cayuga at the same time. (See Virginia.)

Wappinger. From the same root as Abnaki and Wampanoag, and meaning "Easterners"

Connections.—The Wappinger belonged to the Algonquian linguistic family and spoke an *r*-dialect, their nearest allies being the Mahican, the Montauk, and next the New England tribes.

Location.—The east bank of the Hudson River from Manhattan Island to Poughkeepsie and the territory eastward to the lower Connecticut Valley. (See also Connecticut.)

Subdivisions or "Sachemships"

Hammonasset, west of the Connecticut River, Conn., at its mouth.

Kitchawank, in the northern part of Westchester County beyond Croton River and between Hudson River and the Connecticut.

Massaco, in the present towns of Simsbury and Canton on Farmington River, Conn.

Menunkatuck, in the present town of Guilford, Conn.

Nochpeem, in the southern part of Dutchess County, N. Y.

Paugusset, in the eastern part of Fairfield County and the western edge of New Haven County, Conn.

Podunk, in the eastern part of Hartford County, Conn., east of Connecticut River.

Poquonock, in the towns of Windsor, Windsor Locks, and Bloomfield, Hartford County, Conn.

Quinnipiac, in the central part of New Haven County, Conn.

Sicaog, in Hartford and West Hartford, Conn.

Sintsink, between Hudson, Croton, and Pocantico Rivers.

Siwanoy, in Westchester County and part of Fairfield County, Conn., between the Bronx and Five Mile River.

Tankiteke, mainly in Fairfield County, Conn., between Five Mile River and Fairfield and extending inland to Danbury and even into Putnam and Dutchess Counties, N. Y.

Tunxis, in the southwestern part of Hartford County, Conn.

Wangunk, on both sides of Connecticut River from the Hartford city line to about the southern line of the town of Haddam.

Wappinger proper, about Poughkeepsie in Dutchess County, N. Y.

Wecquaesgeek, between the Hudson, Bronx, and Pocantico Rivers.

Villages

Alipconk, in the Weckquasgeek sachemdom, on the site of Tarrytown, N. Y.

Appaquag, on the Hockanum River east of Hartford, Conn., in the Podunk sachemdom.

Aspetuck, near the present Aspetuck in Fairfield County, Conn., in the Tankiteke sachemdom.

Canopus, in Canopus Hollow, Putnam County.

Capage, near Beacon Falls on Naugatuck River, Conn., in the Paugusset sachemdom.

Cassacuhque, near Mianus in the town of Greenwich, Conn., Siwanoy sachemdom.

Cockaponset, near Haddam in Middlesex County, Conn., in the Wangunk sachemdom.

Coginchaug, near Durham, Conn., in the Wangunk sachemdom.

Cossonnacock, near the line between the towns of Haddam and Lyme, Conn., in the Wangunk sachemdom.

Cupheag, given as the probable name of a town at Stratford, Conn., but this was perhaps Pisquheege.

Hockanum, at the mouth of Hockanum River, Hartford County, Conn., in the Podunk sachemdom.

Keskistkonk, probably on Hudson River, south of the highlands, in Putnam County, in the Nochpeem sachemdom.

Kitchiwank, about the mouth of Croton River, N. Y., in the Kitchiwank sachemdom.

Machamodus, on Salmon River in Middlesex County, Conn., in the Wangunk sachemdom.

Massaco, near Simsbury on Farmington River, Conn., in the Massaco sachemdom.

Mattabesec, on the site of Middletown, Conn., in the Wangunk sachemdom.

Mattacomacok, near Rainbow in the town of Windsor, Conn., in the Wangunk sachemdom.

Mattianock, at the mouth of Farmington River in the Poquonock sachemdom.

Menunketuck, at Guilford, Conn., in the Menunketuck sachemdom.

Meshapock, near Middlebury, Cònn., in the Paugussett sachemdom.

Mioonktuck, near New Haven, Conn., in the Quinnipiac sachemdom.

Namaroake, on Connecticut River in the town of East Windsor, Conn., in the Podunk sachemdom.

Naubuc, near Glastonbury, Conn., in the Podunk sachemdom.

Naugatuck, near Naugatuck, Conn., in the Paugussett sachemdom.

Newashe, at the mouth of Scantic River, in the Podunk sachemdom.

Nochpeem, in the southern part of Dutchess County.

Noroaton, at the mouth of Noroton River, in the Siwanoy sachemdom.

Norwauke, at Norwalk, Conn., in the Siwanoy sachemdom.

Ossingsing, at the site of Ossining, N. Y.

Pahquioke, near Danbury, Conn., in the Tankiteke sachemdom.

Pashesauke, on Lyndes Neck at the mouth of the Connecticut River in the Hammonassett sachemdom.

Pasquasheck, probably on the bank of Hudson River in Dutchess County.

Pataquasak, near Essex Post Office, Conn., in the Hammonassett sachemdom.

Pattaquonk, near Chester, Conn., in the Hammonassett sachemdom.

Paugusset, on the bank of Housatonic River about 1 mile above Derby, Conn., in the Paugusset sachemdom.

Pauquaunuch, in Stratford Township, Fairfield County, Paugusset sachemdom, apparently the same town as Pisquheege.

Pequabuck, near Bristol, Conn., in the Tunxis sachemdom.

Pisquheege, near Stratford, Fairfield County, in the Paugusset sachemdom.

Pocilaug, on Long Island Sound near Westbrook, Conn., in the Hammonassett sachemdom.

Pocowset, on Connecticut River opposite Middletown, Conn., in the Wangunk sachemdom.

Podunk, at the mouth of Podunk River, Conn., in the Podunk sachemdom.

Pomeraug, near Woodbury, Conn., in the Paugussett sachemdom.

Poningo, near Rye, N. Y., in the Siwanoy sachemdom.

Poquannuc, near Poquonock in Hartford County, Conn., in the Poquonock sachemdom.

Potatuck, the name of one or two towns on or near Potatuck River, in the town of Newtown, Fairfield County, Conn., in the Paugusset sachemdom.

Pyquag, near Wethersfield, Conn., in the Wangunk sachemdom.

Quinnipiac, on Quinnipiac River north of New Haven, Conn., in the Quinnipiac sachemdom.

Ramapo, near Ridgefield, Conn., in the Tankiteke sachemdom.

Sackhoes, on the site of Peekskill, N. Y., in the Kitchawank sachemdom.

Saugatuck, at the mouth of Saugatuck River, Conn., in the Tankiteke sachemdom.

Scanticook, on Scantic River near its junction with Broad Brook, Hartford County, Conn., in the Podunk sachemdom.

Senasqua, at the mouth of Croton River, in the Kitchawank sachemdom.

Shippan, near Stamford, Conn., in the Siwanoy sachemdom.

Sioascauk, near Greenwich, Conn., in the Siwanoy sachemdom.

Squantuck, on the Housatonic River, above Derby, Conn., in the Paugussett sachemdom.

Suckiauk, near W. Hartford, Conn., in the Sicaog sachemdom.

Titicus, near Titicus in the town of Ridgefield, Conn., in the Tankiteke sachemdom.

Totoket, near Totoket in the town of N. Branford, New Haven County, Conn., in the Quinnipiac sachemdom.

Tunxis, in the bend of Farmington River near Farmington, Conn., in the Tunxis sachemdom.

Turkey Hill, near Derby, Conn., in the Paugussett sachemdom, perhaps given under another name.

Unkawa, between Danbury and Bethel, Conn., in the Tankiteke sachemdom.

Weantinock, near Fairfield, Conn., in the Tankiteke sachemdom.

Wecquaesgeek, at Dobbs Ferry, in the Wecquaesgeek sachemdom.

Weataug, near Weatogue in the town of Simsbury, Conn., in the Massaco sachemdom.

Wepowaug, near Milford, Conn., in the Paugusset sachemdom.

Werawaug, near Danbury, Conn., in the Tankiteke sachemdom.

Woodtick, near Woodtick in the town of Wolcott, New Haven County, Conn., in the Tunxis sachemdom.

Woronock, near Milford, Conn., in the Paugusset sachemdom, evidently another name for Wepowaug.

History.—The Wappinger were found by Henry Hudson in 1609 in occupancy of the lands above mentioned. The Connecticut bands gradually sold their territory and joined the Indians at Scaticook and Stockbridge. The western bands suffered heavily in war with the Dutch, 1640–45, but continued to occupy a tract along the coast in Westchester County until 1756, when most of those who were left joined the Nanticoke at Chenango, Broome County, N. Y., and were finally merged, along with them, into the Delaware. Some joined the Moravian and Stockbridge Indians while a few were still living in Dutchess County in 1774, and a few mixed-bloods live now on Housatonic River below Kent. These belong to the old Scaticook settlement founded by a Pequot Indian named Mauwehu or Mahwee, and settled mainly by individuals of the Paugusset, Unkawa, and Potatuck towns of the Paugusset sachemdom.

Population.—Mooney (1928) estimates the population of the New York divisions of Wappinger at about 3,000 in 1600, and places that of the various Connecticut bands at 1,750, a total of 4,750. The war with the Dutch is said to have cost the western bands 1,600, but we have no estimates of their population at a later date, except as parts of the Stockbridge, Brotherton, and Iroquois Indians, and a few mixed-bloods at Scaticook, Conn., a few miles below Kent.

Connection in which they have become noted.—The Wappinger bands were among those particularly engaged in the manufacture of siwan or wampum. They occupied much of the mainland territory of the present Greater New York but not Manhattan Island. Wappingers Falls in Dutchess County, N. Y., preserves the name.

Wenrohronon. Probably meaning "The people or tribe of the place of floating scum," from the famous oil spring of the town of Cuba, Allegany County.

Connections.—The Wenrohronon belonged to the Iroquoian linguistic stock. Their closest affiliations were probably with the Neutral Nation, which part of them finally joined, and with the Erie, who bounded them on the west.

Location.—Probably originally, as indicated in the explanation of their name, about the oil spring at Cuba, N. Y. (See also Pennsylvania.)

History.—The Wenrohronon maintained themselves for a long time in the above territory, thanks to an alliance with the Neutral Nation, but when the protection of the latter was withdrawn, they left their country in 1639 and took refuge among the Hurons and the main body of the Neutrals, whose fate they shared.

Population.—Before their decline Hewitt (*in* Hodge, 1910) estimates the Wenrohronon at between 1,200 and 2,000. Those who sought refuge with the Hurons in 1639 numbered more than 600.

Connection in which they have become noted.—The Wenrohronon are noted merely on account of their association with the oil spring above mentioned.

NEW JERSEY

Delaware. The name is derived from that of Delaware River, which in turn, was named for Lord Delaware, second governor of Virginia. Also called:

Abnaki or Wabanaki, "Easterners," from their position relative to many other Algonquian tribes. (See **Abnaki** under Maine, **Wampanoag** under Massachusetts, and **Wappinger** under New York.)

Ă-ko-tcă-kǎ′nĕⁿ, "One who stammers in his speech," the Mohawk name. The Oneida and Tuscarora names were similar.

Anakwanᵉkĭ, Cherokee name, an attempt at Wabanaki.

Lenni Lenape (their own name), meaning "true men," or "standard men."

Loup, "wolf," so called by the French.

Mochomes, "grandfather," name given by those Algonquian tribes which claimed descent from them.

Nar-wah-ro, Wichita name.

Renni Renape, a form of Lenni Lenape.

Tcă-kǎ′nĕⁿ, shortened form of Mohawk name given above. (The names in the languages of the other four Iroquois tribes are about the same).

Connections.—The Delaware belonged to the Algonquian linguistic stock, their closest relatives being the Nanticoke, Conoy, and Powhatan Indians to the south and the Mahican, Wappinger, and southern New England Indians on the north. The dialect of the northernmost of their major divisions, the Munsee, differed considerably from that of the southern groups.

Location.—The Delaware occupied all of the State of New Jersey, the western end of Long Island, all of Staten and Manhattan Islands and neighboring parts of the mainland, along with other portions of New York west of the Hudson, and parts of eastern Pennsylvania, and northern Delaware. (See also Delaware, Illinois, Indiana, Kansas, Maryland and the District of Columbia, Missouri, New York, Ohio, Pennsylvania, Oklahoma, and the **Munsee** under Kansas, Oklahoma, and Wisconsin.)

Subdivisions

There were three major divisions or subtribes, the Munsee in northern New Jersey and adjacent portions of New York west of the Hudson, the Unalachtigo in northern Delaware, southeastern Pennsylvania, and southern New Jersey, and the Unami in the intermediate territory, extending to the western end of Long Island. Each comprised a great many minor divisions which it is not always easy to classify under the three main heads. As Munsee may probably be reckoned the following:

Catskill, on Catskill Creek, Greene County, N. Y.

Mamekoting, in Mamakating Valley, west of the Shawangunk Mountains, N. Y.

Minisink, on the headwaters of Delaware River in the southwestern part of Ulster and Orange Counties, N. Y., and the adjacent parts of New Jersey and Pennsylvania.

Waranawonkong, in the country watered by the Esopus, Wallkill, and Shawangunk Creeks, mainly in Ulster County, N. Y.

Wawarsink, centered about the junction of Wawarsing and Rondout Creeks, Ulster County, N. Y.

We may class as Unami the following:

Aquackanonk, on Passaic River, N. J., and lands back from it including the tract called Dundee in Passsaic.

Assunpink, on Stony Creek near Trenton.

Axion, on the eastern bank of Delaware River between Rancocas Creek and Trenton.

Calcefar, in the interior of New Jersey between Rancocas Creek and Trenton.

Canarsee, in Kings County, Long Island, on the southern end of Manhattan Island, and the eastern end of Staten Island, N. Y.

Gachwechnagechga, on Lehigh River, Pa.

Hackensack, in the valleys of Hackensack and Passaic Rivers.

Haverstraw, on the western bank of the lower Hudson, in Rockland County, N. Y.

Meletecunk, in Monmouth County.

Mosilian, on the eastern bank of Delaware River about Trenton.

Navasink, on the highlands of Navesink, claiming the land from Barnegat to the Raritan.

Pompton, on Pompton Creek.

Raritan, in the valley of Raritan River and on the left bank of Delaware River as far down as the falls at Trenton.

Reckgawawanc, on the upper part of Manhattan Island and the adjacent mainland of New York west of the Bronx.

Tappan, on the western bank of Hudson River in Rockland County, N. Y., and Bergen County.

Waoranec, near Esopus Creek, Ulster County, N. Y.

The following may be considered as Unalachtigo, though I am in some doubt about the Neshamini:

Amimenipaty, at site of a large pigment plant of the Du Pont Company at Edgemoor, Del.

Asomoche, on the eastern bank of Delaware River between Salem and Camden.

Chikohoki, at site of Crane Brook Church, on west side of Delaware River near its junction with the Christanna River.

Eriwonec, about Old Man's Creek in Salem or Gloucester County.

Hopokohacking, on site now occupied by Wilmington, Del.

Kahansuk, about Low Creek, Cumberland County.

Manta, about Salem Creek.

Memankitonna, on the present site of Claymont, Del., on Naaman's Creek.

Nantuxet, in Pennsylvania and Delaware.

Naraticon, in southern New Jersey, probably on Raccoon Creek.

Neshamini, on Neshaminy Creek, Bucks County, Pa.

Okahoki, on Ridley and Crum Creeks, Delaware County, Pa.

Passayonk, on Schuylkill River, Pa., and along the western bank of Delaware River, perhaps extending into Delaware.

Shackamaxon, on the site of Kensington, Philadelphia, Pa.

Siconesse, on the eastern bank of Delaware River a short distance above Salem.

Tirans, on the northern shore of Delaware Bay about Cape May or in Cumberland County.

Yacomanshaghking, on a small stream about the present Camden.

Villages

It will not be practicable to separate the villages belonging to the three great divisions in all cases. The following are entered in the Handbook of American Indians (Hodge, 1907, 1910):

Achsinnink, Unalachtigo village on Hocking River, Ohio, about 1770.

Ahasimus, probably Unami, in northern New Jersey.

Alamingo, a village, probably Delaware, on Susquehanna River.

Allaquippa, possible name of a settlement at the mouth of the Youghiogheny River, Pa., in 1755.

Anderson's Town, on the south side of White River about Anderson, Ind.

Au Glaize, on a southeastern branch of Maumee River, Ohio.

Bald Eagle's Nest, on the right bank of Bald Eagle Creek near Milesburg, Pa.

Beaversville, near the junction of Buggy Creek and Canadian River, Okla.

Beavertown, on the east side of the extreme eastern head branch of Hocking River near Beavertown, Ohio.

Black Hawk, probably Delaware, about Mount Auburn, Shelby County, Ind.

Black Leg's Village, probably Delaware, on the north bank of Conemaugh River in the southeastern part of Armstrong County, Pa.

Buckstown, probably Delaware, on the southeast side of White River, about 3 miles east of Anderson, Ind.

Bulletts Town, probably Delaware, in Coshocton County, Ohio, on Muskingum River about halfway between Walhonding River and Tomstown.

Cashiehtunk, probably Munsee, on Delaware River near the point where it is met by the New Jersey State line.

Catawaweshink, probably Delaware, on or near Susquehanna River, near Big Island, Pa.

Chikohoki, a Manta village on the site of Burlington, Burlington County, N. J.

Chilohocki, probably Delaware, on Miami River, Ohio.

Chinklacamoose, probably Delaware, on the site of Clearfield, Pa.

Clistowacka, near Bethlehem, Pa.

Communipaw, village of the Hackensack, at Communipaw.

Conemaugh, probably Delaware, about Conemaugh, Pa.

Coshocton, on the site of Coshocton, Ohio.

Crossweeksung, in Burlington County, probably about Crosswicks.

Custaloga's Town, Unalachtigo, two villages, one near French Creek, opposite Franklin, Pa., the other on Walhonding River, near Killbucks Creek in Coshocton County, Ohio.

Edgpiiliik, in western New Jersey.

Eriwonec, about Old Man's Creek in Salem or Gloucester County.

Frankstown, probably Delaware, about Frankstown, Pa.

Friedenshütten, a Moravian mission town on Susquehanna River a few miles below Wyalusing, probably in Wyoming County, Pa.

Friedensstadt, in Beaver County, Pa., probably near Darlington.

Gekelemukpechuenk, in Ohio, and perhaps identical with White Eyes' Town.

Gnadenhütten, three Moravian Mission villages, one on the north side of Mahoning Creek near its junction with the Lehigh about the present Lehighton; a second on the site of Weissport, Carbon County, Pa.; and a third on the Muskingum River near the present Gnadenhutten, Ohio. (Brinton (1885) says there were two more towns of the same name.)

Goshgoshunk, with perhaps some Seneca, on Allegheny River about the upper part of Venango County, Pa.

Grapevine Town, perhaps Delaware, 8 miles up Captina River, Belmont County, Ohio.

Greentown, on the Black Fork of Mohican River near the boundary of Richland and Ashland Counties, Ohio.

Gweghkongh, probably Unami, in northern New Jersey, near Staten Island, or on the neighboring New York mainland.

Hespatingh, probably Unami, apparently in northern New Jersey, and perhaps near Bergen or Union Hill.

Hickorytown, probably about East Hickory or West Hickory, Pa.

Hockhocken, on Hocking River, Ohio.

Hogstown, between Venango and Buffalo Creek, Pa., perhaps identical with Kuskuski.

Jacobs Cabins, probably Delaware, on Youghiogheny River, perhaps near Jacobs Creek, Fayette County, Pa.

Jeromestown, near Jeromesville, Ohio.

Kalbauvane, probably Delaware, on the headwaters of the west branch of Susquehanna River, Pa.

Kanestio, Delaware and other Indians, on the upper Susquehanna River, near Kanestio Creek in Steuben County, N. Y.

Kanhangton, about the mouth of Chemung River in the northern part of Bradford County, Pa.

Katamoonchink, perhaps the name of a Delaware village near West Whiteland, Chester County, Pa.

Kickenapawling, probably Delaware and Iroquois, at the junction of Stony Creek with Conemaugh River, approximately on the site of Johnstown, Pa.

Kiktheswemud, probably Delaware, near Anderson, Ind., perhaps identical with Buckstown or Little Munsee Town.

Killbuck's Town, on the east side of Killbuck Creek, about 10 miles south of Wooster, Ohio.

Kishakoquilla, two towns successively occupied by a chief of the name, one about Kishacoquillas, Mifflin County, Pa., the other on French Creek about 7 miles below Meadville, Crawford County, Pa.

Kiskiminetas, on the south side of lower Kiskiminetas Creek, near its mouth, Westmoreland County, Pa.

Kiskominitoes, on the north bank of Ohio River between the Hocking and Scioto Rivers, Ohio.

Kittanning, divided into several settlements and mixed with Iroquois and Caughnawaga, near Kittanning on Allegheny River, Armstrong County, Pa.

Kohhokking, near "Painted Post" in Steuben County, N. Y., or Elmira, Chemung County, N. Y.

Kuskuski, with Iroquois, on Beaver Creek, near Newcastle, in Lawrence County, Pa.

Languntennenk, Moravian Delaware near Darlington, Beaver County, Pa.

Lawunkhannek, Moravian Delaware on Allegheny River above Franklin, Venango County, Pa.

Lichtenau, Moravian Delaware on the east side of Muskingum River, 3 miles below Coshocton, Ohio.

Little Munsee Town, Munsee, a few miles east of Anderson, Ind.

Macharienkonck, Minisink, in the bend of Delaware River, Pike County, Pa., opposite Port Jervis.

Macocks, some distance north of Chikohoki, which was probably at Wilmington, Del., perhaps the village of the Okahoki in Pennsylvania.

Mahoning, on the west bank of Mahoning River, perhaps between Warren and Youngstown, Ohio.

Mechgachkamic, perhaps Unami, probably near Hackensack, N. J.

Meggeckessou, on Delaware River at Trenton Falls, N. J.

Meniolagomeka, on Aquanshicola Creek, Carbon County, Pa.

Meochkonck, Minisink, on the upper Delaware River in southeastern New York.

Minisink, Minisink, in Sussex County, N. J., near where the State line crosses Delaware River.

Munceytown, Munsee, on Thames River northwest of Brantford, Ontario, Canada.

Muskingum, probably Delaware, on the west bank of Muskingum River, Ohio.

Nain, Moravian Indians, principally Delaware, near Bethlehem, Pa.

Newcomerstown, village of Chief Newcomer, about the site of New Comerstown, Tuscarawas County, Ohio.

Newtown, the name of three towns probably of the Delaware and Iroquois, one on the north bank of Licking River, near the site of the present Zanesville, Ohio; a second about the site of Newtown, Ohio; and a third on the west side of Wills Creek near the site of Cambridge, Ohio.

Nyack, probably Canarsee, about the site of Fort Hamilton, Kings County, Long Island, afterward removed to Staten Island.

Nyack, Unami probably, on the west bank of Hudson River about the present Nyack, N. Y.

Ostonwackin, with Cayuga, Oneida, and other Indians, on the site of the present Montoursville, Pa.

Outaunink, Munsee, on the north bank of White River, opposite Muncie, Ind.

Owl's Town, probably Delaware, on Mohican River, Coshocton County, Ohio.

Pakadasank, probably Munsee, about the site of Crawford, Orange County, N. Y.

Papagonk, probably Munsee, in Ulster County, N. Y., also placed near Pepacton,
Delaware County, N. Y.

Passycotcung, on Chemung River, N. Y.

Peckwes, Munsee or Shawnee, about 10 miles from Hackensack.

Pematuning, probably Delaware, near Shenango, Pa.

Pequottink, Moravian Delaware, on the east bank of Huron River, near Milan,
Ohio.

Playwickey, probably Unalachtigo, in Bucks County, Pa.

Pohkopophunk, in eastern Pennsylvania, probably in Carbon County.

Queenashawakee, on the upper Susquehanna River, Pa.

Ramcock, Rancocas, in Burlington County.

Raystown, (?).

Remahenonc, perhaps Unami, near New York City.

Roymount, near Cape May.

Salem, Moravian Delaware, on the west bank of Tuscarawas River, 1½ miles
miles southwest of Port Washington, Tuscarawas County, Ohio.

Salt Lick, probably Delaware, on Mahoning River near Warren, Ohio.

Sawcunk, with Shawnee and Mingo, near the mouth of Beaver Creek, about the
site of the present Beaver, Pa.

Sawkin, on the east bank of Delaware River in New Jersey.

Schepinaikonck, Minisink, perhaps in Orange County, N. Y.

Schipston, probably Delaware, at the head of Juniata River, Pa.

Schoenbrunn, Moravian Munsee, about 2 miles below the site of New Philadelphia, Ohio.

Seven Houses, near the ford of Beaver Creek just above its mouth, Beaver County,
Pa.

Shackamaxon, on the site of Kensington, Philadelphia, Pa.

Shamokin, with Shawnee, Iroquois, and Tutelo, on north sides of Susquehanna
River including the island at the site of Sunbury, Pa.

Shannopin's Town, on Allegheny River about 2 miles above its junction with the
Monongahela.

Shenango, with other tribes, the name of several towns, one on the north bank of
Ohio River a little below Economy, Pa.; one at the junction of Conewango and
the Allegheny; and one some distance up Big Beaver, near Kuskuski (q. v.).

Sheshequin, with Iroquois, about 6 miles below Tioga Point, Bradford County, Pa.

Soupnapka, on the east bank of Delaware River in New Jersey.

Three Legs Town, named from a chief, on the east bank of Muskingum River
a few miles south of the mouth of the Tuscarawas, Coshocton County, Ohio.

Tioga, with Nanticoke, Mahican, Saponi, Tutelo, etc., on the site of Athens, Pa.

Tom's Town, on Scioto River, a short distance below the present Chillicothe and
near the mouth of Paint Creek, Ohio.

Tullihas, with Mahican and Caughnawaga, on the west branch of Muskingum
River, Ohio, about 20 miles above the forks.

Tuscarawas, with Wyandot, on Tuscarawas River, Ohio, near the mouth of Big
Sandy River.

Venango, with Seneca, Shawnee, Wyandot, Ottawa, etc., at the site of Franklin,
Venango County, Pa.

Wechquetank, Moravian Delaware, about 8 miles beyond the Blue Ridge,
northwest from Bethlehem, Pa., probably near the present Mauch Chunk.

Wekeeponall, on the west bank of the Susquehanna River, about the mouth of
Loyalstock Creek in Lycoming County, Pa., probably identical with Queen
Esther's Town.

Walagamika, on the site of Nazareth, Lehigh County, Pa.

White-eyes Village, named from a chief, on the site of Duncan's Falls, 9 miles below Zanesville, Ohio.

White Woman's Town, near the junction of Walhonding and Killbuck Rivers, about 7 miles northwest of the forks of the Muskingum River, in Coshocton County, Ohio.

Will's Town, on the east bank of Muskingum River at the mouth of Wills Creek, Muskingum County, Ohio.

Woapikamikunk, in the valley of White River, Ind.

Wyalusing, Munsee and Iroquois, on the site of Wyalusing, Bradford County, Pa.

Wyoming, with Iroquois, Shawnee, Mahican, and Nanticoke; later entirely Delaware and Munsee; principal settlement at the site of Wilkes-Barre, Pa.

History.—The traditional history of the Delaware set forth in the famous Walam Olum (see Brinton, 1882–85, vol. 5), gave them an origin somewhere northwest of their later habitat. They were found by the earliest white voyagers in the historic seats above given. The Dutch came into contact with the Unami and Munsee Delaware in 1609 and the Swedes with the Unalachtigo in 1637. Both were succeeded by the English in 1664, but the most notable event in Delaware history took place in 1682 when these Indians held their first council with William Penn at what is now Germantown, Philadelphia. About 1720 the Iroquois assumed dominion over them and they were gradually crowded west by the white colonists, reaching the Allegheny as early as 1724, and settling at Wyoming and other points on the Susquehanna about 1742. In 1751, by invitation of the Huron, they began to form villages in eastern Ohio, and soon the greater part of them were on the Muskingum and other Ohio streams. Backed by the French and by other western tribes, they now freed themselves from Iroquois control and opposed the English settlers steadily until the treaty of Greenville in 1795. Notable missionary work was done among them by the Moravians in the seventeenth and eighteenth centuries. About 1770 they received permission from the Miami and Piankashaw to settle between the Ohio and White Rivers, Ind. In 1789, by permission of the Spanish government, a part moved to Missouri and later to Arkansas, along with a band of Shawnee, and by 1820 they had found their way to Texas. By 1835 most of the bands had been gathered on a reservation in Kansas, but in 1867 the greater part of these removed to the present Oklahoma, where some of them occupied a corner of the Cherokee Nation. Others are with the Caddo and Wichita in southwestern Oklahoma, a few Munsee are with the Stockbridges in Wisconsin, and some are scattered in other parts of the United States. In Ontario, Canada, are three bands—the Delawares of Grand River, near Hagersville; the Moravians of the Thames, near Bothwell; and the Munceys of the Thames, near Muncey— nearly all of whom are of the Munsee division.

Population.—Mooney (1928) estimates that there were 8,000 Delaware in 1600 not including the Canarsee of Long Island; estimates made during the eighteenth century vary between 2,400 and 3,000; nineteenth-century estimates are much lower, and the United States Census of 1910 returned 914 Delawares and 71 Munsee, or a total of 985, to which must be added the bands in Canada, making perhaps 1,600 all together. 140 Delaware were reported on the Wichita Reservation, Okla., in 1937.

Connection in which they have become noted.—The Delaware are noted as one of the very few tribes which have come to be known by an English term, and as one of the chief antagonists of the Whites while the latter were forcing their way westward, but in later years as furnishing the most reliable scouts in White employ. A different sort of fame has been attained by one of their early chiefs, Tamenend, whose name, in the form Tammany, was applied to a philanthropic society, a place of meeting, and a famous political organization. Delaware chiefs signed the famous treaty with Penn under the oak at Shackamaxon, and their tribes occupied Manhattan Island and the shores of New York Harbor at the arrival of the Dutch. The name Delaware has been used for postoffices in Arkansas, Iowa, Kentucky, Missouri, New Jersey, Ohio, and Oklahoma, besides the State of Delaware. Lenape is a post village in Leavenworth County, Kans., and Lenapah in Nowata County, Okla.

PENNSYLVANIA

Delaware. In early times this tribe occupied the eastern parts of Pennsylvania along Delaware River; later they were, for a time, on the Susquehanna and the headwaters of the Ohio. (See New Jersey.)

Erie. The Erie extended over the extreme northwestern corner of the State. (See Ohio.)

Honniasont. An Iroquois term meaning "Wearing something round the neck." Also called:

> Black Minqua, the word "black" said to refer to "a black badge on their breast," while "Minqua" indicated their relationship to the White Minqua, or Susquehanna (q. v.).

Connections.—The Honniasont belonged to the Iroquoian linguistic family.

Location.—On the upper Ohio and its branches in western Pennsylvania and the neighboring parts of West Virginia and Ohio. (See also Ohio.)

History.—The Honniasont appear first as a tribe which assisted the Susquehanna in war and traded with the Dutch, but a little later they are reported to have been destroyed by the Susquehanna and Seneca. The remnant seems to have settled among the Seneca, and a Minqua town, probably occupied by their descendants, is mentioned from time to time among the latter and in the neighborhood of their former country.

Population.—This is unknown, but as late as 1662 the Honniasont must have been fairly numerous if the testimony of five Susquehanna chiefs taken in that year is to be relied upon, which was to the effect that they were then expecting 800 Honniasont warriors to join them.

Iroquois. In very early times these Indians entered Pennsylvania only as hunters and warriors, but at a later period they made numerous settlements in the State. (See New York.)

Saluda. A band of "Saluda" Indians from South Carolina moved to Conestoga in the eighteenth century. They may have been Shawnee. (See South Carolina.)

Saponi. The majority of the Saponi lived at Shamokin for a few years some time after 1740 but then continued on to join the Iroquois. (See Virginia.)

Shawnee. Bands of Shawnee were temporarily located at Conestoga, Sewickley, and other points in Pennsylvania. (See Tennessee.)

Susquehanna. A shortened form of Susquehannock, meaning unknown.

> Akhrakouaehronon, given in Jesuit Relations, from a town name. See Atra'kwae'ronnons' below.
> Andaste or Conestoga, from Kanastóge, "at the place of the immersed pole."
> Atra'kwae'ronnons, from the name of a town, and probably signifying "at the place of the sun," or "at the south."
> Minqua, from an Algonquian word meaning "stealthy," "treacherous."
> White Minqua, to distinguish them from the Black Minqua. (See Honniasont above.)

Connections.—The Susquehanna belonged to the Iroquoian linguistic stock.

Location.—On the Susquehanna River in New York, Pennsylvania, and Maryland.

Subdivisions

Originally Susquehanna may have been the name of a confederacy of tribes rather than a single tribe. Hewitt (*in* Hodge, 1910) suggests that the Wyoming (in the territory about the present Wyoming) may have been such a subtribe. The barely mentioned Wysox, on a small creek flowing into the Susquehanna at the present Wysox, was perhaps another. Mention is made of the Turtle, Fox, and Wolf "families," evidently clans, and of the Ohongeeoquena, Unquehiett, Kaiquariegahaga, Usququhaga, and Seconondihago "nations," also perhaps clans.

Villages

Smith (1884) mentions several, but Hewitt (*in* Hodge, 1910) is of the opinion that the names really belong to independent tribes. Champlain says that there were more than 20 villages, though the only one named is Carantouan, thought to have been on the site of the present Waverly, N. Y.

History.—When encountered by the English, French, and Dutch early in the seventeenth century, the Susquehanna were a numerous people, but even then they were at war with the Iroquois by whom they were conquered in 1676 and forced to settle near the Oneida in New York. Later they were allowed to return to the Susquehanna River and reoccupy their ancient country, but they wasted away steadily and in 1763 the remnant, consisting of 20 persons, was massacred by Whites inflamed with accounts of Indian atrocities on the far frontier.

Population.—Mooney (1928) estimates that the Susquehanna numbered 5,000 in 1600. In 1648 they are said to have had 550 warriors.

Connection in which they have become noted.—The name Susquehanna is perpetuated in that of the Susquehanna River and in the names of a county and a town. Conestoga is the designation of two places in Lancaster County, Pa., and one in Chester County, and was given to a widely used type of wagon.

Tuscarora. These Indians on their way to join the Iroquois bands of New York stopped from time to time in the Susquehanna Valley. (See North Carolina.)

Tutelo. Most of these Indians lived at Shamokin with the Saponi and accompanied them to the Iroquois Nation. (See Virginia.)

Wenrohronon. This tribe occupied some parts of the State along the northwestern border. (See New York.)

DELAWARE

Delaware. The Unalachtigo division of the Delaware occupied all of the northern parts of this State when it was first visited by Europeans. (See New Jersey.)

Nanticoke. Bodies of Indians classed under this general head extended into the southern and western sections. Unalachtigo and Nanticoke are two forms of the same word though, as differentiated, they have been applied to distinct tribes. (See Maryland.)

MARYLAND AND THE DISTRICT OF COLUMBIA

Conoy. Probably a synonym of Kanawha, but the meaning is unknown; also spelled Canawese, and Ganawese. Also called:

> Piscataway, from a village on Piscataway Creek where the Conoy chief resided.

Connections.—The Conoy belonged to the Algonquian linguistic stock and were probably intermediate between the Nanticoke and Powhatan Indians.

Location.—Between the Potomac River and the western shore of the Chesapeake.

Subdivisions

Acquintanacsuak, on the west bank of Patuxent River in St. Marys County.

Conoy proper or Piscataway, in the southern part of Prince Georges County.

Mattapanient, on Patuxent River, probably in St. Marys County.

Moyawance, on the west bank of the Potomac River above the Conoy proper.

Nacotchtank, on the eastern branch of the Potomac, in the District of Columbia.

Pamacocack, about the mouth of Mattawoman Creek and the present Pomonkey, Charles County.

Patuxent, in Calvert County.

Potapaco, in the southern and central parts of Charles County.

Secowocomoco, on Wicomico River in St. Marys and Charles Counties.

Villages

The principal settlement of each of the above subdivisions was generally known by the same name. In addition we have the following:

Catawissa, at Catawissa, Columbia County, Pa.

Conejoholo, on the east bank of the Susquehanna on or near the site of Bainbridge, Lancaster County, Pa.

Conoytown, on Susquehanna River between Conejoholo and Shamokin (Sunbury), Pa.

Kittamaquindi, at the junction of Tinkers Creek with the Piscataway a few miles above the Potomac, Prince Georges County, the principal village of the Conoy proper.

History.—If the name of the Conoy is identical with that of Kanawha River, as appears probable, they must have lived at some period along that stream. They were found by Smith and the Maryland colonists in the location above given and missions were established among them by the Jesuits on the first settlement of Maryland in 1634. They decreased rapidly in numbers and were presently assigned a tract of land on the Potomac, perhaps near the site of Washington. In 1675 they were attacked by the Susquehanna Indians who had been driven from their own territories by the Iroquois, retired up the Potomac River, and then to the Susquehanna, where they were finally assigned lands at Conejoholo near the Nanticoke and Conestoga. Some of them were living with these two tribes at Conestoga in 1742. They gradually made their way northward, stopping successively at Harrisburg, Shamokin, Catawissa, and Wyoming, and in 1765 were in southern New York, at Owego, Chugnut, and Chenango, on the eastern branch of the Susquehanna. They moved west with the Mahican and Delaware and soon became known only as constituting a part of those tribes. They used the Turkey as their signature at a council held in 1793.

Population.—The number of Conoy was estimated by Mooney (1928) at 2,000 in 1600; in 1765 they numbered only about 150.

Connection in which they have become noted.—The name Conoy is perpetuated by Conoy, 2 miles north of Falmouth, Lancaster County, Pa., and probably (see above) by the Great and Little Kanawha Rivers, Kanawha County, Kanawha Ridge, and several places in West Virginia, besides post villages in Hancock County, Iowa, and Red River County, Tex.

Delaware. They probably occupied, or at least hunted over, some territory in the extreme northeastern part of the State. (See New Jersey.)

Nanticoke. From *Nentego*, a variant of Delaware *Unechtgo*, or *Unalachtigo*, "Tidewater people," the neighboring division of Delaware being known by the same name. Also called:

Doegs, Toags, or Taux, by some early writers, probably shortened from Tawachguáns.
Ganniataratich-rone, Mohawk name.
Otayáchgo, Tawachguáns, Mahican and Delaware name, meaning "Bridge people."
Skaniadaradighroonas, "Beyond-the-sea people," Iroquois name.

Connections.—The Nanticoke belonged to the Algonquian linguistic family, their closest connections probably being with the Unalachtigo Delaware—as the name implies—and also with the Conoy.

Location.—Although the Nanticoke are frequently more narrowly delimited, it will be convenient to group under this head all of the Indians of the Eastern Shore of Maryland and southern Delaware.

Subdivisions

Annamessicks, in the southern part of Somerset County.
Choptank, on Choptank River.
Cuscarawaoc, at the head of Nanticoke River in Maryland and Delaware.
Manokin, on Manokin River in the northern part of Somerset County.
Nanticoke proper, on the lower course of Nanticoke River.
Nause, in the southern end of the present Dorchester County.
Ozinies, on the lower course of Chester River; they may have been part of or identical with the Wicomese.
Tocwogh, on Sassafras River, in Cecil and Kent Counties.
Wicocomoco, on Wicocomoco River in Somerset and Wicocomoco Counties.
Wicomese, in Queen Anne's County.

Villages

Ababco, a subtribe or village of the Choptank on the south side of Choptank River in Dorchester County, near Secretary Creek.
Askimimkansen, perhaps Nanticoke, on an upper eastern branch of Pocomoke River, probably in Worcester County.
Byengeahtein, probably in Dauphin or Lancaster County, Pa.
Chenango, a mixed population on Chenango River about Binghamton, N. Y.
Hutsawap, a village or subtribe of the Choptank, in Dorchester County.
Locust Necktown, occupied by a band of Nanticoke proper known as Wiwash, on Choptank River, in Dorchester County.

Matchcouchtin, consisting of Nanticoke proper, probably in Pennsylvania.

Matcheattochousie, Nanticoke proper, probably in Pennsylvania.

Natahquois, Nanticoke proper, probably on the eastern shore of Maryland or on the Susquehanna, Pennsylvania.

Nause, belonging to the tribe of the same name, on the north bank of Nanticoke River near its mouth.

Pekoinoke, Nanticoke proper, still existing in Maryland in 1755.

Pohemkomeati, on lower Susquehanna River, Pennsylvania.

Teahquois, Nanticoke proper, probably on lower Susquehanna River, Pennsylvania.

Tequassimo, a subtribe or village on the Choptank, on the southern shore of Choptank River.

Tocwogh, the principal village of the tribe of that name, said to be on the south side of Chester River in Queen Anne County, but, unless this is a later location, probably on the south side of Sassafras River in Kent County.

Witichquaom, Nanticoke proper, near Susquehanna River in southern Pennsylvania.

History.—Traditionally, the Nanticoke are supposed to have come from the west at about the same time as the Delaware, but they were found in the location above given by the earliest white explorers and settlers. They were at war with the Maryland colonists from 1642 to 1678. In 1698 reservations were set aside for them. Soon after 1722 the greater part of them began to move north, stopping for a time on the Susquehanna at its junction with the Juniata. In 1748 the greater part of the tribe went farther up, and, after camping temporarily at a number of places, settled under Iroquois protection at Chenango, Chugnut, and Oswego. In 1753 part of these joined the Iroquois in western New York, and they were still living with them in 1840, but the majority, in company with the remnants of the Mahican and Wappinger, emigrated west about 1784 and joined the Delaware in Ohio and Indiana, with whom they soon became incorporated, disappearing as a distinct tribe. Yet a part did not leave their old country. Some were living in Maryland in 1792 under the name of Wiwash, and some mixed-bloods still occupy a small territory on Indian River, Delaware. The Choptank, or a part of them, also remained in their old country on the south of Choptank River, Dorchester County, where a few of their descendants, their blood much mixed with that of Negroes, were to be found in 1837. Some Wicocomoco must also have stayed about their ancient seats, since a few mongrels are said to retain the name.

Population.—Mooney (1928) estimated a total Indian population on the eastern shore of Maryland in 1600 of 2,700, including 700 Tocwogh and Ozinies, 400 Wicocomoco, and 1,600 Nanticoke and their more immediate neighbors. In 1722 they are said to have numbered about 500 and in 1765 those who had emigrated to New York were supposed to count about 500 more. In 1792 the Nanticoke proper left in Maryland were said to comprise only 30 persons, but in 1911 Speck (1915) estimated their descendants in southern Maryland at 700.

Connection in which they have become noted.—The name Nanticoke is perpetuated in that of Nanticoke River between Wicomico and Dorchester Counties, and by the town of Nanticoke in the former. There are also places of the name in Broome County, N. Y., and Luzerne County, Pa.

Powhatan. The Accohanoc Indians of the panhandle of Virginia, who extended over into Worcester County, were the only representatives of the Powhatan Indians in Maryland, though the Conoy were closely related to them. (See Virginia.)

Shawnee. Shawnee Indians settled temporarily in western Maryland near the Potomac and in the northeastern part of the State on the Susquehanna. (See Tennessee.)

Susquehanna. They lived along and near the Susquehanna River. (See Pennsylvania.)

VIRGINIA

Cherokee. This tribe claimed territory in the extreme southwestern part of the State. If not actually occupied by them, it at least formed part of their hunting territories. (See Tennessee.)

Manahoac. Meaning "They are very merry," according to Tooker (1895), but this seems improbable. Also called:

Mahocks, apparently a shortened form.

Connections.—The Manahoac belonged to the Siouan linguistic family; their nearest connections were probably the Monacan, Moneton, and Tutelo.

Location.—In northern Virginia between the falls of the rivers and the mountains east and west and the Potomac and North Anna Rivers north and south.

Subdivisions

Subtribes or tribes of the confederacy as far as known were the following:

Hassinunga, on the headwaters of the Rappahannock River.
Manahoac proper, according to Jefferson (1801), in Stafford and Spottsylvania Counties.
Ontponea, in Orange County.
Shackaconia, on the south bank of the Rappahannock River in Spottsylvania County.
Stegaraki, on the Rapidan River in Orange County.
Tanxnitania, on the north side of the upper Rappahannock River in Fauquier County.
Tegninateo, in Culpeper County, at the head of the Rappahannock River.
Whonkentia, in Fauquier County, near the head of the Rappahannock.

Villages

Mahaskahod, on the Rappahannock River, probably near Fredericksburg, is the only town known by name.

History.—Traditional evidence points to an early home of the Manahoac people in the Ohio Valley. In 1608 John Smith discovered them in the location above given and learned that they were allied with the Monacan but at war with the Powhatan Indians and the Iroquois (or perhaps rather the Susquehanna). After this they suddenly vanish from history under a certainly recognizable name, but there is good reason to believe that they were one of those tribes which settled near the falls of the James River in 1654 or 1656 and defeated a combined force of Whites and coast Indians who had been sent against them. They seem to have been forced out of their old country by the Susquehanna. Probably they remained for a time in the neighborhood of the Monacan proper and were in fact the Mahock encountered by Lederer (1912) in 1670 at a point on James River which Bushnell seems to have identified with the site of the old Massinacack town, the fact that a stream entering the James at this point is called the Mohawk rendering his case rather strong. Perhaps the old inhabitants had withdrawn to the lower Monacan town, Mowhemencho. In 1700 the Stegaraki were located by Governor Spotswood of Virginia at Fort Christanna, and the Mepontsky, also placed there, may have been the Ontponea. We hear of the former as late as 1723, and there is good reason to believe that they united with the Tutelo and Saponi and followed their fortunes, and that under these two names were included all remnants of the Manahoac.

Population.—Mooney (1928) estimates that there were 1,500 Manahoac in 1600 but this is probably rather too high, since their numbers and those of the Tutelo together seem to have been 600–700 in 1654. However, it is possible that these figures cover only the Manahoac, while Mooney's include part of the Saponi and Tutelo.

Meherrin. Meaning unknown.

Connections.—The Meherrin belonged to the Iroquoian linguistic family, their closest connections probably being the Nottaway.

Location.—Along the river of the same name on the Virginia-North Carolina border.

History.—The tribal name Meherrin first appears in the form "Maharineck" in the account of an expedition by Edward Blande and others to North Carolina in 1650, and next in an Indian census taken in 1669. Later they seem to have adopted a body of Conestoga or Susquehanna fleeing from Pennsylvania after their dispersal by the Iroquois about 1675. This is the only way to account for the fact that they are all said to have been refugee Conestoga. They were living on Roanoke River in 1761 with the southern bands of Tuscarora and Saponi, and the Machapunga, and probably went north in the last Tuscarora removal in 1802. (For information regarding another possible band of Meherrin see "Nottaway.")

Population.—Mooney (1928) estimates the Meherrin population at 700 in 1600. In 1669 they are said to have had 50 bowmen, or approximately 180 souls. In 1755 they were said to be reduced to 7 or 8 fighting men, but in 1761 they are reported to have had 20.

Connection in which they have become noted.—Meherrin River, an affluent of the Chowan, running through southern Virginia and northeastern North Carolina, and a Virginia town perpetuate the name of the Meherrin.

Monacan. Possibly from an Algonquian word signifying "digging stick," or "spade," but more likely from their own language. Also called:

Rahowacah, by Archer, 1607, *in* Smith (1884).

Connections.—The Monacan belonged to the Siouan linguistic stock. Their nearest connections were the Manahoac, Tutelo, and Saponi.

Location.—On the upper waters of James River above the falls at Richmond.

Villages

(Locations as determined by D. I. Bushnell, Jr.)

Massinacack, on the right bank of James River about the mouth of Mohawk Creek, and a mile or more south of Goochland.

Mohemencho, later called Monacan Town, on the south bank of James River and probably covering some of "the level area bordering the stream in the extreme eastern part of the present Powhatan County, between Bernards Creek on the east and Jones Creek on the west."

Rassawek, at the confluence of the James and Rivanna Rivers and probably "on the right bank of the Rivanna, within the angle formed by the two streams."

Two other towns are sometimes added but as they afterward appeared as wholly independent tribes, the Saponi and the Tutelo, it is probable that their connection with the Monacan was never very intimate. They seem to have been classed as Monacan largely on the evidence furnished by Smith's map, in which they appear in the country of the "Monacans" but Smith's topography, as Bushnell has shown, was very much foreshortened toward the mountains and the Saponi and Tutelo towns were farther away than he supposed. Again, while Massinacack and Mohemencho are specifically referred to as Monacan towns and Smith calls Rassawek "the chiefe habitation" of the Monacan, there is no such characterization of either of the others.

History.—Capt. John Smith learned of the Monacan in the course of an exploratory trip which he made up James River in May 1607. The people themselves were visited by Captain Newport the year following, who discovered the two lower towns. The population gradually declined and in 1699 some Huguenots took possession of the land of Mowhemencho. The greater part of the Monacan had been driven away some years before this by Colonel Bornn (Byrd?). Those who escaped continued to camp in the region until after 1702, as we learn from a Swiss traveler named F. L. Michel (1916). It is probable that the remnant finally united with their relatives the Saponi and Tutelo when they were at Fort Christanna and followed their fortunes, but we have no further information as to their fate.

Population.—The number of the Monacan was estimated by Mooney (1928) at 1,200 in 1600 including part of the Saponi and Tutelo, but they can hardly have comprised over half as many. In 1669 there were still about 100 true Monacan as they were credited with 30 bowmen.

Connection in which they have become noted.—The name Monacan is perpetuated by a small place called Manakin on the north bank of James River, in Goochland County, Va.

Nahyssan. A contraction of Monahassano or Monahassanugh, remembered in later times as Yesa^n.

Connections.—The Nahyssan belonged to the Siouan linguistic stock, their nearest relatives being the Tutelo, Saponi, and probably the Monacan and Manahoac.

Location.—The oldest known location of the Nahyssan has been identified by D. I. Bushnell, Jr. (1930), within very narrow limits as "probably on the left bank of the James, about 1½ miles up the stream from Wingina, in Nelson County."

History.—In 1650 Blande and his companions noted a site, 12 miles south-southwest of the present Petersburg, called "Manks Nessoneicks" which was presumably occupied for a time by the Nahyssan or a part of them, since "Manks" may be intended for "Tanks," the Powhatan adjective signifying "little." In 1654 or 1656 this tribe and the Manahoac appeared at the falls of James River having perhaps been driven from their former homes by the Susquehanna. They defeated a force of colonials and Powhatan Indians sent against them but did not advance further into the settlements. In 1670 Lederer (1912) found two Indian towns on Staunton River, one of which he calls Sapon and the other Pintahae. Sapon was, of course, the town of the Saponi but it is believed that Pintahae was the town of the Nahyssan Indians, though Lederer gives this name to both towns. Pintahae was probably the Hana-thaskie or Hanahaskie town of which Batts and Fallam (1912) speak a year later. About 1675 the Nahyssan settled on an island below the Occaneechi at the junction of the Staunton and Dan Rivers. Before 1701 all of the Siouan tribes who had settled in this neighborhood moved into North Carolina, and it is thought that the Nahyssan followed the Saponi and Tutelo to the headwaters of the Yadkin and that their subsequent fortunes were identical with those of these two. (See Saponi and Tutelo.)

Population.—(See Saponi and Tutelo.)

Nottaway. Meaning "adders," in the language of their Algonquian neighbors, a common designation for alien tribes by peoples of that linguistic stock. Also called:

> Cheroenhaka, their own name, probably signifying "fork of a stream."
> Mangoak, Mengwe, another Algonquian term, signifying "stealthy," "treacherous."

Connections.—The Nottaway belonged to the Iroquoian linguistic family, their closest connections probably being the Meherrin, Tuscarora, and Susquehanna.

Location.—On the river of the same name in southeastern Virginia.

History.—The Nottaway were found by the Virginia colonists in the location given above. Though they were never prominent in colonial history, they kept up their organization long after the other tribes of the region were practically extinct. In 1825 they are mentioned as living on a reservation in Southampton County and ruled over by a "queen." The name of this tribe was also applied to a band of Indians which appeared on the northern frontiers of South Carolina between 1748 and 1754. They may have included those Susquehanna who are sometimes confounded with the Meherrin, and are more likely to have included Meherrin than true Nottaway although they retained the name of the latter (see Swanton, 1946).

Population.—The number of Nottaway, exclusive of those last mentioned, was estimated by Mooney (1928) at 1,500 in the year 1600. In 1709 Lawson reported one town with 30 fighting men, but in 1827 Byrd estimated that there were 300 Nottaway in Virginia. In 1825, 47 were reported. The band that made its appearance on the frontiers of South Carolina was said to number about 300.

Connection in which they have become noted.—The name of the Nottaway is preserved by Nottoway River, Nottoway County, and two towns, one the county seat of the above, the other in Sussex county. There is a Nottawa in St. Joseph County, Mich.

Occaneechi. Meaning unknown.

> The Botshenins, or Patshenins, a band associated with the Saponi and Tutelo in Ontario, were perhaps identical with this tribe.

Connections.—The Occaneechi belonged to the Siouan linguistic stock; their closest connections were probably the Tutelo and Saponi.

Location.—On the middle and largest island in Roanoke River, just below the confluence of the Staunton and the Dan, near the site of Clarksville, Mecklenburg County, Va. (See also North Carolina.)

History.—Edward Blande and his companions heard of them in 1650. When first met by Lederer in 1670 at the spot above mentioned, the Occaneechi were noted throughout the region as traders, and their language is said to have been the common speech

both of trade and religion over a considerable area (Lederer, 1912).
Between 1670 and 1676 the Occaneechi had been joined by the Tutelo
and Saponi, who settled upon two neighboring islands.   In the latter
year the Conestoga sought refuge among them and were hospitably
received, but, attempting to dispossess their benefactors, they were
driven away.   Later, harassed by the Iroquois and English, the
Occaneechi fled south and in 1701 Lawson (1860) found them on the
Eno River, about the present Hillsboro, Orange County, N. C.
Later still they united with the Tutelo and Saponi and followed their
fortunes, having, according to Byrd, taken the name of the Saponi.

   Population.—Mooney (1928) estimates that there were 1,200
Occaneechi in the year 1600.   There is no later estimate, but in 1709
this tribe along with the Shakori, Saponi, Tutelo, and Keyauwee
were about 750.

   Connection in which they have become noted.—The name Occaneechi is
associated particularly with the Occaneechi Trail or Trading Path,
which extended southwest through North and South Carolina from
the neighborhood of Petersburg, Va.

Powhatan.   Said by Gerard to signify "falls in a current of water,"
and applied originally to one tribe but extended by the English to
its chief Wahunsonacock, and through him to the body of tribes
which came under his sway.   Also called:

>   Sachdagugh-roonaw, Iroquois name.

   Connections.—The Powhatan belonged to the Algonquian linguistic
stock, their nearest relatives probably being the Algonquian tribes of
Carolina and the Conoy.

   Location.—In the tidewater section of Virginia from Potomac
River to the divide between James River and Albemarle Sound, and
the territory of the present eastern shore of Virginia.   (See also
Maryland and District of Columbia.)

Subdivisions

Subtribes constituting this group are as follows:

Accohanoc, in Accomac and part of Northampton Counties, Va., and probably
   extending slightly into Maryland.
Accomac, in the southern part of Northampton County, Va.
Appomattoc, in Chesterfield County.
Arrohattoc, in Henrico County.
Chesapeake, in Princess Anne County.
Chickahominy, on Chickahominy River.
Chiskiac, in York County.
Cuttatawomen, in King George County.
Kecoughtan, in Elizabeth City County.
Mattapony on Mattapony River.
Moraughtacund, in Lancaster and Richmond Counties.

Mummapacune, on York River.
Nansemond, in Nansemond County.
Nantaughtacund, in Essex and Caroline Counties.
Onawmanient, in Westmoreland County.
Pamunkey, in King William County.
Paspahegh, in Charles City and James City Counties.
Pataunck, on Pamunkey River.
Piankatank, on Piankatank River.
Pissasec, in King George and Westmoreland Counties.
Potomac, in Stafford and King George Counties.
Powhatan, in Henrico County.
Rappahannock, in Richmond County.
Secacawoni, in Northumberland County.
Tauxenent, in Fairfax County.
Warrasqueoc, in Isle of Wight County.
Weanoc, in Charles City County.
Werowocomoco, in Gloucester County.
Wicocomoco, in Northumberland County.
Youghtanund, on Pamunkey River.

Villages

Accohanoc, on the river of the same name in Accomac or Northampton Counties.
Accomac, according to Jefferson (1801), about Cheriton, on Cherrystone Inlet, Northampton County.
Acconoc, between Chickahominy and Pamunkey Rivers, in New Kent County.
Accoqueck, on Rappahannock River, above Secobec, in Caroline County.
Accossuwinck, on Pamunkey River, King William County.
Acquack, on the north bank of Rappahannock River, in Caroline County.
Appamattoc, on the site of Bermuda Hundred, in Prince George County.
Appocant, on the north bank of Chickahominy River, in New Kent County.
Arrohattoc, in Henrico County on the James River, 12 miles below the falls at Richmond.
Askakep, near Pamunkey River in New Kent County.
Assaomeck, near Alexandria.
Assuweska, on the north bank of the Rappahannock in King George County.
Attamtuck, between the Chickahominy and Pamunkey Rivers in New Kent County.
Aubomesk, on the north bank of the Rappahannock in Richmond County.
Aureuapeugh, on Rappahannock River in Essex County.
Cantaunkack, on York River in Gloucester County.
Capahowasic, about Cappahosic in Gloucester County.
Cattachiptico, on Pamunkey River in King William County.
Cawwontoll, on the north bank of the Rappahannock River in Richmond County.
Chawopo, at the mouth of Chipoak Creek, Surry County.
Checopissowo, on Rappahannock River above Tobacco Creek, in Caroline County.
Chesakawon, above the mouth of Corotoman River, in Lancaster County.
Chesapeake, according to Jefferson on Linnhaven River in Princess Anne County, a small stream flowing north into Chesapeake Bay.
Chiconessex, about Wiseville, in Accomac County.
Chincoteague, about Chincoteague Inlet, in Accomac County.
Chiskiac, on the south side of York River, about 10 miles below the junction of the Mattapony and Pamunkey.

Cinquack, near Smiths Point on the Potomac, in Northumberland County.

Cinquoteck, in the fork of Mattapony and Pamunkey Rivers, in King William County.

Cuttatawomen, (1) on the Rappahannock River at Corotoman River in Lancaster County; (2) about Lamb Creek on the Rappahannock, in King George County.

Gangasco, near Eastville, in Northampton County.

Kapawnich, on the north bank of the Rappahannock, about Corotoman River in Lancaster County.

Kerahocak, on the north bank of the Rappahannock River in King George County.

Kiequotank, on the eastern shore of Accomac County, north of Metomkin.

Kupkipcock, on Pamunkey River in King William County.

Machapunga, (1) in Northampton County; (2) on Potomac River.

Mamanahunt, on Chickahominy River, in Charles City County.

Mamanassy, at the junction of Pamunkey and Mattapony Rivers in King and Queen County.

Mangoraca, on the north bank of the Rappahannock in Richmond County.

Mantoughquemec, on Nansemond River, in Nansemond County.

Martoughquaunk, on Mattapony River in Caroline County.

Massawoteck, on the north bank of Rappahannock River in King George County.

Matchopick, on the north bank of the Rappahannock River in Richmond County.

Matchut, on Pamunkey River, in New Kent County.

Mathomauk, on the west bank of James River, in Isle of Wight County.

Matomkin, about Metomkin Inlet in Accomac County.

Mattacock, on the north bank of York River in Gloucester County.

Mattacunt, on the south side of Potomac River in King George County.

Mattanock, on the west side of Nansemond River, near its mouth, in Nansemond County.

Maysonec, on the north bank of the Chickahominy in New Kent County.

Menacupunt, on Pamunkey River, in King William County.

Menaskunt, on the north bank of Rappahannock River in Richmond County.

Meyascosic, on the north side of James River in Charles City County.

Mohominge, near the falls of James River, in Richmond County.

Mokete, on Warrasqueoc Creek, in Isle of Wight County.

Moraughtacund, near the mouth of Moratico River in Richmond County.

Mouanast, on the north bank of Rappahannock River, in King George County.

Mutchut, on the north bank of the Mattapony River in King and Queen County.

Muttamussinsack, on the north bank of Rappahannock River in Caroline County.

Myghtuckpassu, on the south bank of Mattapony River in King William County.

Namassingakent, on the south bank of Potomac River in Fairfax County.

Nameroughquena, on the south bank of the Potomac River in Alexandria County, opposite Washington, D. C.

Nansemond, probably about Chuckatuck in Nansemond County.

Nantapoyac, on the south bank of James River in Surry County.

Nantaughtacund, on the south side of the Rappahannock River in either Essex County or Caroline County.

Nawacaten, on the north bank of the Rappahannock River in Richmond County.

Nawnautough, on the north bank of the Rappahannock River in Richmond County.

Nechanicok, on the south bank of the Chickahominy in the lower part of Henrico County.

Nepawtacum, on the north bank of the Rappahannock in Lancaster County.

Onancock, near Onancock in Accomac County.

Onawmanient, probably on Nominy Bay, in Westmoreland County.

Opiscopank, on the south bank of the Rappahannock River in Middlesex County.

Oquomock, on the north bank of the Rappahannock River in Richmond County.

Orapaks, in New Kent County, between the Chickahominy and Pamunkey Rivers.

Ottachugh, on the north bank of the Rappahannock River in Lancaster County.

Ozatawomen, on the south bank of the Potomac River in King George County.

Ozenic, on Chickahominy River in New Kent County.

Pamawauk, perhaps identical with Pamunkey.

Pamuncoroy, on the south bank of Pamunkey River in New Kent County.

Pamunkey, probably near West Point in King William County.

Papiscone, on the north bank of the Rappahannock in King George County.

Pasaugtacock, on the north bank of York River in King and Queen County.

Paspahegh, (1) on the south bank of Chickahominy River in Charles City County; (2) on the north bank of James River in Charles City County.

Passaunkack, on the south bank of Mattapony River in the northwestern part of King William County.

Pastanza, on or near Potomac River, possibly on Aquia Creek, in Stafford County.

Pawcocomac, on the north bank of Rappahannock River at the mouth of the Corotoman in Lancaster County.

Peccarecamek, an Indian settlement reported on the southern Virginia border, perhaps mythical.

Pemacocack, on the west bank of Potomac River in Prince William County about 30 miles below Alexandria.

Piankatank, on Piankatank River in Middlesex County.

Pissacoac, on the north bank of Rappahannock River above Leedstown in Westmoreland County.

Poruptanck, on the north bank of York River in Gloucester County.

Potaucac, in New Kent County between the Chickahominy and Pamunkey Rivers.

Potomac, about 55 miles in a straight line from Chesapeake Bay, on a peninsula in what is now Stafford County, formed by Potomac River and Potomac Creek.

Powcomonet, on the north bank of Rappahannock River in Richmond County.

Powhatan, on the north bank of James River at the falls on ground now forming an eastern suburb of Richmond.

Poyektauk, on the north bank of Rappahannock River in Richmond County.

Poykemkack, on the north bank of Rappahannock River in Richmond County.

Pungoteque, in Accomac County, probably near Metomkin Inlet.

Quackcohowaon, on the south bank of the Mattapony in King William County.

Quioucohanock, probably on an eminence now called Wharf Bluff just east of Upper Chipoak Creek in Surry County.

Quiyough, on the south bank of Aquia Creek near its mouth, in Stafford County.

Rappahannock, at the mouth of a creek on Rappahannock River in Richmond County.

Rickahake, probably in Norfolk County.

Righkahauk, on the west bank of Chickahominy River in New Kent County.

Ritanoe, probably Powhatan, in Virginia or North Carolina.

Roscows, in Elizabeth City County.

Secacawoni, at the mouth of Coan Creek on the south bank of the Potomac in Northumberland County.

Secobec, on the south bank of Rappahannock River in Caroline County.

Shamapa, on Pamunkey or York River.

Sockobeck, on the north bank of Rappahannock River in King George County.

Tantucquask, on Rappahannock River in Richmond County.

Tauxenent, about Mount Vernon in Fairfax County.

Teracosick, on the west bank of Nansemond River in Nansemond County.

Utenstank, on the north bank of Mattapony River in Caroline County.

Uttamussac, on the north bank of Pamunkey River in King William County.

Uttamussamacoma, on the south bank of Potomac River in Westmoreland County.

Waconiask, on the north bank of Rappahannock River in King George County.

Warrasqueoc, on the south bank of James River at the mouth of Warrasqueoc Creek in Isle of Wight County.

Weanoc, below the mouth of Appamattox River at the present Weyanoke in Prince George County.

Wecuppom, on the north bank of Rappahannock River in Richmond County.

Werawahon, on the north bank of Chickahominy River in New Kent County.

Werowacomoco, on the north bank of York River in Gloucester County about opposite the mouth of Queen Creek.

Wicocomoco, at the mouth of Wicomico River in Northumberland County.

Winsack, on the north bank of Rappahannock River in Richmond County.

History.—The Powhatan were visited by some very early explorers, including probably the Cabots in 1498. Their territory was well known to the Spaniards in the latter part of the sixteenth century and a Jesuit mission was established among them in 1570 though soon extinguished by the Indians. In 1607 the Virginia colony was planted on James River and from that time on relations between the Whites and Powhatans were of the most intimate character, friendly at first, but later disturbed by the exactions of the newcomers. Peace was restored for a time by the marriage of Powhatan's daughter Pocahontas to John Rolfe, and lasted until Powhatan's death in 1618. In 1622 Powhatan's second successor, Opechancanough, led an uprising against the colonists, as a result of which all of the White settlements except those immediately about Jamestown were destroyed. War continued until 1636 when exhaustion of both sides led to peace, but in 1644 Opechancanough led another uprising as destructive as the first. He was captured and was killed the same year. The tribes made peace separately, and they were placed upon reservations, where they gradually dwindled away. In 1654 or 1656 the Pamunkey assisted the English in resisting an invasion of some inland people, but the allied army was severely defeated (see **Manahoac**). In 1675 these Indians were accused of having committed certain depredations, really caused by the Conestoga, and several unauthorized expeditions were led against them by Nathaniel Bacon. In August 1676, a great body of them gathered in a fort near Richmond which was carried by storm, and men, women, and children indiscriminately massacred. Peace was made with the survivors on condition that an annual tribute be paid by each village. In 1722 in a treaty made at Albany between the English and Iroquois, the latter agreed to cease their attacks upon the Powhatan Indians, but the Powhatans already had been greatly reduced and they continued to decline. Those on the eastern shore of Virginia, who had become very much mixed with Negroes, were driven away in 1831 during the excitement caused by the slave rising under Nat Turner. In 1785 Jefferson reported the Powhatan Indians reduced to two tribes, the Pamunkey and Mattapony, embracing only about 15 men, but he must have overlooked great numbers of these Indians, for at the present time there are several bands, including the Chickahominy, Nansemond, Pamunkey, Mattapony, Upper Mattapony, Rappahannock, Wicocomoco, Potomac, Powhatan, and Werowocomoco (Speck, 1925).

Population.—The Powhatan population was estimated by Mooney (1928) as 9,000 in 1600; Smith (1884) allows them 2,400 warriors; in 1669 a census gave 528 warriors or about 2,000 population, the Wicocomoco being then the largest tribe. In 1705 the Pamunkey by themselves numbered 150 souls. Jefferson in 1785 represented the two tribes which he mentions as having but 15 men; Mooney, however, believed that there must have been a population of something like 1,000 because of the number of mixed-bloods still surviving. The census of 1910 returned 115 Chickahominy and 85 Pamunkey. The United States Office of Indian Affairs Report for 1923 includes still other bands, giving in all a population of 822, and Speck (1925) gives the names of 10 bands aggregating 2,118 in 1923. The census of 1930 returned only 203 Indians from Virginia but evidently missed nearly all except the Pamunkey.

Connection in which they have become noted.—The Powhatan Confederacy is famous as embracing those Indians among whom the first permanent English settlement in North America was made; for the personal character of its chief, Powhatan, who had conquered about 24 tribes, in addition to the 6 under him at his accession, before the appearance of the Europeans; on account of the dealings of the Whites with both Powhatan and his brother Opechancanough, as well as the massacre of the settlers by the latter in 1622 and again in 1644; and not least from the fame attached to Powhatan's daughter, Pocahontas. There are post villages named Powhatan in Jefferson County, Ala.; Lawrence County, Ark.; Natchitoches Parish, La.; McDowell County, W. Va.; a county and county seat of the name in Virginia; Powhatan Point in Belmont County, Ohio; and Powhattan in Brown County, Kans.

Saponi. Evidently a corruption of Monasiccapano or Monasukapanough, which, as shown by Bushnell, is probably derived in part from a native term "moni-seep" signifying "shallow water." Paanese is a corruption and in no way connected with the word "Pawnee."

Connections.—The Saponi belonged to the Siouan linguistic family, their nearest relations being the Tutelo.

Location.—The earliest known location of the Saponi has been identified by Bushnell (1930) with high probability with "an extensive village site on the banks of the Rivanna, in Albemarle County, directly north of the University of Virginia and about one-half mile up the river from the bridge of the Southern Railway." This was their location when, if ever, they formed a part of the Monacan Confederacy. (See also North Carolina, Pennsylvania, and New York.)

Villages

The principal Saponi settlement usually bore the same name as the tribe or, at least, it has survived to us under that name. In 1670 Lederer reports another which he visited called Pintahae, situated not far from the main Saponi town after it had been removed to Otter Creek, southwest of the present Lynchburg (Lederer, 1912), but this was probably the Nahyssan town.

History.—As first pointed out by Mooney (1895), the Saponi tribe is identical with the Monasukapanough which appears on Smith's map as though it were a town of the Monacan and may in fact have been such. Before 1670, and probably between 1650 and 1660, they moved to the southwest and probably settled on Otter Creek, as above indicated. In 1670 they were visited by Lederer in their new home and by Thomas Batts (1912) a year later. Not long afterward they and the Tutelo moved to the junction of the Staunton and Dan Rivers, where each occupied an island in Roanoke River in Mecklenburg County. This movement was to enable them to escape the attacks of the Iroquois, and for the same reason they again moved south before 1701, when Lawson (1860) found them on Yadkin River near the present site of Salisbury, N. C. Soon afterward they left this place and gravitated toward the White settlements in Virginia. They evidently crossed Roanoke River before the Tuscarora War of 1711, establishing themselves a short distance east of it and 15 miles west of the present Windsor, Bertie County, N. C. A little later they, along with the Tutelo and some other tribes, were placed by Governor Spotswood near Fort Christanna, 10 miles north of Roanoke River about the present Gholsonville, Brunswick County. The name of Sappony Creek in Dinwiddie County, dating back to 1733 at least, indicates that they sometimes extended their excursions north of Nottoway River. By the treaty of Albany (1722) the Iroquois agreed to stop incursions on the Virginia Indians and, probably about 1740, the greater part of the Saponi and the Tutelo moved north stopping for a time at Shamokin, Pa., about the site of Sunbury. One band, however, remained in the south, in Granville County, N. C., until at least 1755, when they comprised 14 men and 14 women. In 1753 the Cayuga Iroquois formally adopted this tribe and the Tutelo. Some of them remained on the upper waters of the Susquehanna in Pennsylvania until 1778, but in 1771 the principal section had their village in the territory of the Cayuga, about 2 miles south of Ithaca, N. Y. They are said to have separated from the Tutelo in 1779 at Niagara, when the latter fled to Canada, and to have become lost, but a portion, at least, were living with the Cayuga on Seneca River in Seneca County, N. Y., in 1780. Besides the Person County Indians, a band of Saponi Indians remained behind in North Carolina which seems to have fused with the Tuscarora, Meherrin, and Machapunga and gone north with them in 1802.

Population.—The Saponi and the Tutelo are identified by Mooney (1928) as remnants of the Manahoac and Monacan with an estimated population of 2,700 in 1600. In 1716 the Huguenot Fontaine found 200 Saponi, Manahoac, and Tutelo at Fort Christanna. In 1765, when they were living on the upper Susquehanna, the Saponi are said to have had 30 warriors. The main North Carolina band counted 20 warriors in 1761, and those in Person County, 14 men and 14 women in 1755.

Connection in which they have become noted.—A small place called Sapona, in Davidson County, N. C., east of the Yadkin River, preserves the name of the Saponi.

Shakori. They seem to have lived in the State at one time. (See North Carolina.)

Shawnee. Indians of this tribe were settled for a time in the Shenandoah Valley. (See Tennessee.)

Tutelo. Significance unknown but used by the Iroquois, who seem to have taken it from some southern tongue. Also called:

> Kattera, another form of Tutelo.
> Shateras, a third form of the name.

Connections.—The Tutelo belonged to the Siouan linguistic family, their nearest connections being the Saponi and probably the Monacan.

Location.—The oldest known town site of the Tutelo was near Salem, Va., though the Big Sandy River at one time bore their name and may have been an earlier seat. (See also North Carolina, New York, and Pennsylvania.)

History.—In 1671 Fallam and Batts (1912) visited the town above mentioned. Some years later the Tutelo moved to an island in Roanoke River just above the Occaneechi, but in 1701 Lawson found them still farther southwest, probably about the headwaters of the Yadkin (Lawson, 1860). From that time forward they accompanied the Saponi until the latter tribe separated from them at Niagara as above noted. In 1771 they were settled on the east side of Cayuga Inlet about 3 miles from the south end of the lake. This village was destroyed by Sullivan in 1779, but the Tutelo continued to live among the Cayuga sufficiently apart to retain their own language until 1898, when the last individual who could speak it fluently died.   A certain amount of Tutelo blood flows in the veins of some of the Iroquois. (For further information, see Swanton (1937).)

Population.—(See Saponi.) In 1701–9, according to Lawson (1860), the Tutelo, Saponi, Keyauwee, Occaneechi, and Shakori numbered together about 750.   In 1715 Governor Spotswood reported that the Indians at Fort Christanna, including the Tutelo, Saponi, Occaneechi, and Manahoac, numbered 300.   In 1763 the Tutelo, Saponi, Nanticoke, and Conoy had 200 men, probably less than 1,000 souls.

Connection in which they have become noted.—The Tutelo are noteworthy chiefly as the principal body of Siouan Indians from Virginia to retain their integrity and preserve a knowledge of their language late enough for a permanent record of it to be made.

WEST VIRGINIA

Moneton.   Meaning "Big Water" people.

Connections.—The Moneton belonged to the Siouan linguistic family; their nearest connections were probably the Manahoac and Monacan of Virginia and perhaps the Ofo of Ohio and Mississippi.

Location.—Probably on the lower course of Kanawha River.

History.—The Moneton were first mentioned by Thomas Batts in 1671.   (See Alvord and Bidgood, 1912.) Three years later they were visited by Gabriel Arthur, an indentured servant of the trader Abraham Wood, and this is the last we hear of them as an independent tribe. They probably united with the Siouan people in the Piedmont region of Virginia.

Population.—Unknown. Arthur calls the principal Moneton settlement "a great town."

Cherokee (see Tennessee), **Conoy** (see Maryland), **Delaware** (see New Jersey), **Honniasont** and **Susquehanna** (see Pennsylvania), and **Shawnee** (see Tennessee) settled in various parts of West Virginia from time to time, but none of them was established there at an early date for an appreciable period except perhaps the Conoy, whose name appears to be perpetuated in that of the Kanawha River.   There is no information regarding the Moneton residence there other than the preservation of their name.

NORTH CAROLINA

Bear River Indians.   A body of Indians mentioned by Lawson and associated with Algonquian tribes.   They may have been a part of the Machapunga (q. v.).   Rights (1947) calls them the Bear River or Bay River Indians.   Lawson (1709) gives the name of their town as Raudauqua-quank and estimates the number of their fighting men at 50.   Mooney (1928) places them with the Pamlico in his estimate as of the year 1600 and gives the two a population of 1,000. (See also California for another tribe of the same name.)

Cape Fear Indians. Named from Cape Fear, their native designation being unknown or indeed whether they were an independent tribe or a part of some other.

Connections.—No words of the language of the Cape Fear Indians have been preserved, but early references clearly associate them with the eastern Siouan tribes, and they may have been a part of the Waccamaw, since Waccamaw River heads close to Cape Fear. They would then have been connected with the Siouan linguistic family and probably with the southern Atlantic division of which Catawba is the typical member.

Location.—On Cape Fear River, as above stated. (See also South Carolina.)

Villages

The only village mentioned by name is Necoes, about 20 miles from the mouth of Cape Fear River, probably in Brunswick County. In 1715 five villages were reported.

History.—While the Cape Fear Indians were probably met by several of the early voyagers, our first specific notice of them comes from the narratives of a New England colony planted on Cape Fear River in 1661. These settlers seized some of the Indian children and sent them away under pretense of instructing them in the ways of civilization and were themselves in consequence driven off. In 1663 a colony from Barbadoes settled here but soon left. In 1665 a third colony established itself at the mouth of Oldtown Creek in Brunswick County, on the south side of the river, on land bought from the Indians, but, though the latter were friendly, like the others this attempt at settlement was soon abandoned. They were visited by Capt. William Hilton in 1663. In 1695 they asked to be taken under the protection of Governor Archdale. The protection was granted and shortly afterward they rescued 52 passengers from a wrecked New England vessel who formed the nucleus of Christ Church Parish north of Cooper River. A few Cape Fear Indians accompanied Barnwell on his Tuscarora expedition in 1711–12. They were active in his behalf as scouts and also guarded the region around Port Royal. After the Yamasee War they were removed to South Carolina and settled inland from Charleston, probably in Williamsburg County (Milling, 1940). In the latter part of the eighteenth century, a remnant of this tribe and the Pedee lived in the Parishes of St. Stephens and St. Johns under a chief called King John. By 1808 only a half-breed woman remained of these two tribes, though others may have removed to the Catawba.

Population.—Mooney (1928) estimates a population of 1,000 Cape Fear Indians in 1600. The census of 1715, above mentioned, gives 206. In 1808 White neighbors remembered when as many as 30 Pedee and Cape Fear Indians lived in their old territories.

Catawba. This tribe occupied parts of southwestern North Carolina near Catawba River. (See South Carolina.)

Cheraw. Significance unknown. Also called:

> Ani'-Suwa'lï, Cherokee name.
> Saraw, Suali, synonyms even more common than Cheraw.
> Xuala, Xualla, Spanish and Portuguese forms of the word, the *x* being intended for *sh*.

Connections.—The Cheraw are classed on circumstantial grounds in the Siouan linguistic family though no words of their tongue have been preserved.

Location.—The earliest known location of the Cheraw appears to have been near the head of Saluda River in Pickens and Oconee Counties, S. C., whence they removed at an early date to the present Henderson, Polk, and Rutherford Counties.

Villages

The names given are always those of the tribe, though we have a "Lower Saura Town" and an "Upper Saura Town" on a map dating from 1760.

History.—Mooney (1928) has shown that the Cheraw are identical with the Xuala province which De Soto entered in 1540, remaining about 4 days. They were visited by Pardo at a later date, and almost a hundred years afterward Lederer (1912) heard of them in the same region. Before 1700 they left their old country and moved to the Dan River near the southern line of Virginia, where they seem to have had two distinct settlements about 30 miles apart. About the year 1710, on account of constant Iroquois attacks, they moved southeast and joined the Keyauwee. The colonists of North Carolina, being dissatisfied at the proximity of these and other tribes, Governor Eden declared war against the Cheraw, and applied to Virginia for assistance. This Governor Spotswood refused, as he believed the Carolinians were the aggressors, but the contest was prosecuted by the latter until after the Yamasee War. During this period complaint was made that the Cheraw were responsible for most of the depredations committed north of Santee River and they were accused of trying to draw the coast tribes into an alliance with them. It was asserted also that arms were being supplied them from Virginia. The Cheraw were then living upon the upper course of the Great Pee Dee, near the line between the two colonies and in the later Cheraw district of South Carolina. Being still subject to attack by the Iroquois, they finally—between 1726 and 1739—became incorporated with the Catawba, with whom at an earlier date they had been at enmity. In 1759 a party joined the English in their expedition against Fort Duquesne, but the last notice of them is in 1768 when the remnant was still living with the Catawba.

Population.—During the Spanish period the Cheraw appear to have been of considerable importance but no estimate of their numbers has come down to us. Mooney (1928) gives 1,200 as a probable figure for the year 1600. The census of 1715 gives 140 men and a total of 510, probably including the Keyauwee and perhaps some other tribes. In 1768 the survivors numbered 50 to 60.

Connection in which they have become noted.—The Cheraw are famous as one of the few tribes in the Carolinas mentioned by De Soto's chroniclers which can be identified and located with fair precision. They were noted later for their persistent hostility to the English and have left their name in Suwali Gap in the Blue Ridge Mountains, N. C.; in Saura Town Mountains, Stokes County, N. C.; in the town of Cheraw, Chesterfield County, S. C.; and possibly in the Uwaharrie River and Uwaharrie Mountains of North Carolina. There is a locality named Cheraw in Otero County, Colo.

Cherokee. The Cherokee lived in the mountainous parts of the State in the west. (See Tennessee.)

Chowanoc. Meaning in Algonquian "(people) at the south."

Connections.—The Chowanoc belonged to the Algonquian linguistic family and were evidently most nearly allied to the other North Carolina Algonquians.

Location.—On Chowan River about the junction of Meherrin and Blackwater Rivers.

Villages

Maraton, on the east bank of Chowan River in Chowan County.
Ohanoak, on the west side of Chowan River not far below Nottoway River probably in Hertford County.
Catoking, (probably) near Gatesville, in Gates County.
Metocaum, on Chowan River in the present Bertie County.
Ramushonok, apparently between the Meherrin and Nottoway Rivers in Hertford County.

History.—In 1584–85, when first known to Europeans, the Chowanoc were the leading tribe in northeastern North Carolina. In 1663 they entered into a treaty with the English by which they submitted to the English Crown, but they violated this in 1675 and after a year of warfare were compelled to confine themselves to a reservation on Bennett's Creek which became reduced by 1707 from 12 square miles to 6. They sided with the colonists in the Tuscarora War, and at about the same time were visited by a Church of England missionary, Giles Rainsford. In 1723 a reservation of 53,000 acres was set aside for them conjointly with the Tuscarora and in 1733 they were given permission to incorporate with that tribe. They continued to decline in numbers until in 1755 Governor Dobbs stated that only 2 men and 3 women were left.

Population.—In 1584–85 one of the Chowanoc towns, Ohanoak, was said to contain 700 warriors, and Mooney (1928) estimates their numbers at about 1,500 in 1600. In 1707 they were reduced to one town with about 15 fighting men, but at the end of the Tuscarora War their numbers were placed at 240. In 1731 less than 20 families were reported and by 1755 only 5 individuals, as above noted.

Connection in which they have become noted.—The Chowanoc seem to have been the most powerful Algonquian tribe south of the Powhatan. Their memory is preserved in the names of Chowan River and Chowan County, and in the designation of a small post office in the county of the name, all in North Carolina.

Coree, or Coranine. Meaning unknown.

Connections.—As the final stage of the Coree existence was passed with an Algonquian tribe, some have thought that the affiliations of this people were also Algonquian. On the other hand Lawson (1860) notes that their language and that of a tribe to the north were mutually intelligible and there is reason for thinking that this northern tribe belonged to the Iroquois Confederacy. At least the Coree were closely associated in many ways with the Iroquoian Tuscarora.

Location.—On the peninsula south of Neuse River in Carteret and Craven Counties.

Villages

Coranine, probably on the coast in Carteret County.
Narhantes, among the Tuscarora, 30 miles from Newbern.
Raruta, probably on the coast of Carteret County, south of Neuse River.

History.—When the Coree and the Whites first met is unknown, but they appear in the records of the Raleigh colony under the name Cwarennoc. They were greatly reduced before 1696 in a war with another people. They took part with the Tuscarora in their war against the colonists, and in 1715 the remnant of them and what was left of the Machapunga were assigned a reservation on Mattamuskeet Lake in Hyde County, where they occupied one village, probably until they became extinct. A few of them appear to have remained with the Tuscarora.

Population.—The population of this tribe and the Neusiok was estimated by Mooney (1928) at 1,000 in 1600. In 1707 Lawson says they had 25 fighting men and were living in 2 villages. No later enumeration is known.

Connection in which they have become noted.—Although some distance from the Coree country, Core Creek Station in Craven County, N. C., may perpetuate the name of the Coree.

Eno. Significance unknown, but Speck suggests i'nare, "to dislike," whence, "mean," "contemptible"; ye^{n}i'nare, "People disliked,"

Haynokes, synonym from Yardley (1654).

Connections.—The Eno were probably of the Siouan linguistic stock, though, on account of certain peculiarities attributed to them, Mooney (1895) casts some doubt upon this. Their nearest relatives were the Shakori.

Location.—On Eno River in the present Orange and Durham Counties. (See also South Carolina.)

Villages

The only village name recorded, distinct from that of the tribe, is Adshusheer, a town which they shared with the Shakori. It is located by Mooney (1928) near the present Hillsboro. Lawson (1860) speaks in one place as if it were a tribe but as there is no other mention of it, it is more likely that it was simply the name of the town which the Eno and Shakori occupied.

History.—The Eno are first mentioned by Governor Yeardley of Virginia, who was told that they had valiantly resisted the northward advance of the Spaniards. From this it appears possible that they had formerly lived upon the Enoree River in South Carolina, which lay on the main trail from St. Helena to the Cheraw country at the foot of the Appalachian Mountains. Lederer (1912) mentions them in 1671 and Lawson (1860) in 1701 when they and the Shakori were in the town of Adshusheer. About 1714, together with the Shakori, Tutelo, Saponi, Occaneechi, and Keyauwee, they began to move toward the Virginia settlements. In 1716 Governor Spotswood of Virginia proposed to settle the Eno, Cheraw, and Keyauwee at Eno town "on the very frontiers" of North Carolina but the project was defeated by the latter province on the ground that all three tribes were then at war with South Carolina. From the records it is not clear whether this Eno town was the old settlement or a new one nearer the Albemarle colonists. Owing to the defeat of this plan, the Eno moved into South Carolina. Presumably they finally united with the Catawba, among whom, Adair (1930) states, their dialect was still spoken in 1743.

Population.—Mooney (1928) estimates the combined Eno, Shakori, and Adshusheer at 1,500 in 1600. In 1714 the Eno, Shakori, Tutelo, Saponi, Occaneechi, and Keyauwee totaled 750. There is no other record of their numbers.

Connection in which they have become noted.—In marked distinction from their neighbors, the Eno had taken to a trading life. Their name was given to Eno River in Orange and Durham Counties, N. C., and perhaps to a place called Enno in the southwestern part of Wake County, and to Enoree River in South Carolina (see above), as also to a post village near the last mentioned.

Hatteras. Meaning unknown.

Connections.—The Hatteras belonged to the Algonquian linguistic family.

Location.—Among the sandbanks about Cape Hatteras east of Pamlico Sound and frequenting Roanoke Island.

Village

Sandbanks, on Hatteras Island.

History.—Lawson (1860) thought the Hatteras showed traces of White blood and therefore they may have been the Croatan Indians with whom Raleigh's colonists are supposed to have taken refuge. They disappeared soon after as a distinct tribe and united with the mainland Algonquians. In 1761, the Rev. Alex. Stewart baptized 7 Indians and mixed-blood children of the "Attamuskeet, Hatteras, and Roanoke" tribes and 2 years later he baptized 21 more.

Population.—The Hatteras population has been estimated with the Machapunga and other tribes at 1,200 in 1600; they had 16 warriors in 1701, or a total population of about 80.

Connection in which they have become noted.—The possible connection of the Hatteras with the Croatan has been mentioned and their name has become perpetuated in the dangerous cape at the angle of the outer sand islands of their old country.

Keyauwee. Meaning unknown.

Connections.—From the historical affiliations of Keyauwee, they are presumed to have been of the Siouan linguistic family.

Location.—About the points of meeting of the present Guilford, Davidson, and Randolph Counties. (See also South Carolina.)

Villages

No separately named villages are known.

History.—The Keyauwee do not appear to have been noted by white men before 1701 when Lawson (1860) found them in a palisaded village about 30 miles northeast of Yadkin River near the present Highpoint, Guilford County. At that time they were preparing to join the Saponi and Tutelo for better protection against their enemies, and, shortly afterward, together with the last mentioned tribes, the Occaneechi, and the Shakori, they moved toward the settlements about Albemarle Sound. As mentioned already, Governor Spotswood's project to settle this tribe together with the Eno and Cheraw at Enotown on the frontier of North Carolina was foiled by the opposition of the latter colony. The Keyauwee then moved southward to the Pee Dee along with the Cheraw, and perhaps the Eno and Shakori. In the Jefferys atlas of 1761 their town appears close to the boundary line between the two Carolinas. They do not reappear in any of the historical records but probably united ultimately in part with the Catawba, while some of their descendants are represented among the Robeson County Indians, often miscalled Croatan.

Population.—Mooney (1928) estimates 500 Keyauwee in 1600. In 1701 they are said to have numbered approximately as many as the Saponi, but the population of that tribe also is unknown. Shortly afterward it is stated that the Keyauwee, Tutelo, Saponi, Occaneechi, and Shakori totaled 750 souls. This is all the information that we have.

Machapunga. Said to mean "bad dust," or "much dirt," in the native Algonquian language.

Connections.—The Machapunga belonged to the Algonquian linguistic stock.

Location.—In the present Hyde County and probably also in Washington, Tyrrell, and Dare Counties, and part of Beaufort.

Villages

The only village named is Mattamuskeet (probably on Mattamuskeet Lake in Hyde County). However, we should probably add Secotan on the north bank of Pamlico River in Beaufort County, and perhaps the town of the Bear River Indians (q. v.).

History.—The Machapunga seem to have embraced the larger part of the descendants of the Secotan, who lived between Albemarle and Pamlico Sounds when the Raleigh colony was established on Roanoke Island (1585–86) though the Pamlico may also have been included under the same head. They were reduced to a single village by 1701, took part with other Indian tribes of the region in the Tuscarora War, and at its close were settled on Mattamuskeet Lake with the Coree. In 1761 a small number were still living in North Carolina, evidently at the same place, and the Rev. Alex. Stewart reported that he had baptized seven Indian and mixed-blood children belonging to the "Attamuskeet, Hatteras, and Roanoke." On a second visit 2 years later he baptized 21 more.

Population.—The Machapunga are estimated by Mooney (1928) to have numbered 1,200, including some smaller tribes, in 1600. In 1701 Lawson gives 30 warriors, probably less than 100 souls (Lawson, 1860). In 1775 there were said to be 8 to 10 on the mainland and as many more on the off-shore banks. In 1761 the number of warriors was only 7 or 8. The Bear River Indians (q. v.) may have combined with these.

Connection in which they have become noted.—In the form Machipongo, the name is applied to a post village in Northampton County, Va.

Meherrin. This tribe extended across from Virginia into Northampton and Hertford Counties. (See Virginia.)

Moratok. A place name, but the meaning otherwise unknown.

Connections.—There is little doubt that the Moratok belonged to the Algonquian linguistic stock and were closely related to the other Algonquian tribes of the sound region of North Carolina.

Location.—On Roanoke River and apparently on the north side, and estimated to be 160 miles up the river, though the distance is evidently reckoned from the Raleigh settlement on Roanoke Island.

Villages

The village bearing the name of the tribe is the only one known.

History.—The sole mention of the Moratok is in the narratives of the Raleigh expeditions. They were first recognized as an independent tribe by Mr. Maurice Mook (1943 a).

Population.—Unknown but reported as large.

Natchez. Part of the Natchez Indians sought refuge with the Cherokee after their tribe had been broken up by the French, and most of them appear to have lived along Hiwassee River. They accompanied those Cherokee who moved to Oklahoma and settled on the western margin of the Cherokee Reservation, where a few of them retained their language long enough to have it recorded. (See Mississippi.)

Neusiok. Probably a place name.

Connections.—The form of this name suggests that the Neusiok were of the Algonquian stock, but they may have been Iroquoian like their neighbors the Tuscarora and Coree (?).

Location.—On lower Neuse River particularly on the south side, in Craven and Cartaret Counties.

Village

Chattooka, on the site of Newbern, and Rouconk, exact location unknown.

History.—In 1584 Amadas and Barlowe heard of the Neusiok as a war with the tribes farther north. The later settlers speak of them as Neuse Indians. They dwindled away rapidly after White contact and perhaps united finally with the Tuscarora.

Population.—With the Coree the Neusiok are estimated by Mooney (1928) at 1,000 in the year 1600. In 1709 they numbered but 15 warriors although occupying two towns.

Connection in which they have become noted.—The name Neusiok is connected with that of the River Neuse in North Carolina, and a post village.

Occaneechi. When the Occaneechi lived on Roanoke River, Va., they probably ranged over into Warren, Halifax, and Northampton Counties, N. C. In 1701 they were in Orange County, N. C. (See Virginia.)

Pamlico. Meaning unknown.

Connections.—The Pamlico belonged to the Algonquian linguistic stock.

Location.—On Pamlico River.

History.—The Pamlico are mentioned by the Raleigh colonists in 1585–86 under the name Pomouik. In 1696 they were almost destroyed by smallpox. In 1701 Lawson recorded a vocabulary from them which shows their affiliations to have been as given above (Lawson, 1860). In 1710 they lived in a single small village. They took part in the Tuscarora war, and at its close that part of the Tuscarora under treaty with the English agreed to destroy them. A remnant of the Pamlico was probably incorporated by the Tuscarora as slaves.

Population.—The Pamlico are estimated by Mooney (1928), together with "Bear River" Indians, as 1,000 in 1600. In 1710 they numbered about 75.

Connection in which they have become noted.—The Pamlico have given their name to or shared it with the largest sound in North Carolina and a North Carolina county. They are also noteworthy as having been almost if not quite the most southerly Algonquian tribe on the Atlantic seaboard, and the most southerly one from which a vocabulary has been collected.

Saponi. This tribe lived on Yadkin River and in other parts of the State for a certain period. (See Virginia.)

Shakori. A native name but its significance unknown, though perhaps the same as Sugari, "stingy or spoiled people," or "of the river-whose-water-cannot-be drunk." Also called:

Cacores, a misprint.

Connections.—The Shakori belonged to the Siouan linguistic family, their closest connections being evidently with the southern division of the Siouan tribes of the East. Barnwell (1908) identified them with the Sissipahaw (q. v.).

Location.—The Shakori moved so frequently and there is so much uncertainty regarding their early history, that this is hard to give, but, as they usually kept company with the Eno, tenancy of the courses of Shocco and Big Shocco Creeks in the present Vance, Warren, and Franklin Counties is perhaps the location most closely connected with them in historic times. (See South Carolina and Virginia.)

History.—It is possible that the Shakori gave their name to the province of Chicora visited by Ayllon and his companions in 1521. If so, we must suppose that they moved north later in the sixteenth century or early in the seventeenth, perhaps as a result of the Pardo expeditions. In 1650 Edward Blande and his associates found the "Nottoway and Schockoores old fields" between Meherrin and Nottoway Rivers, but the Indians were not there. In 1654 Governor Yeardley of Virginia was told by a Tuscarora Indian of an inland people called the "Cacores," probably an attempt to indicate this tribe. In 1672 Lederer found them living in a village 14 miles from that of the Eno (Lederer, 1912), and in 1701 Lawson says these two tribes (the Shakori and Eno) were in one village called Adshusheer on Eno River (Lawson, 1860). The later fortunes of the Shakori were bound up with those of the Eno (q. v.).

Population.—Mooney (1928) estimates the Shakori, Eno, and "Adshusheer" at 1,500 in 1600.

Connection in which they have become noted.—The two creeks, Shocco and Big Shocco, and a post office 9 miles south of Warrenton, Warren County, perpetuate the name of the Shakori. If Chicora refers to the same tribe, it appears prominently in Spanish narratives of American exploration, particularly because of the information regarding Indian customs obtained by Peter Martyr from an Indian, Francisco of Chicora.

Sara, see **Cheraw.**

Sissipahaw. Meaning unknown.

Connections.—The Sissipahaw were probably of the Siouan linguistic family though no words of their language are known.

Location.—The principal Sissipahaw settlement appears to have been about the present Saxapahaw on Haw River in the lower part of Alamance County. (See also South Carolina.)

History.—The name of this tribe is possibly preserved in the Sauxpa mentioned by the Spanish officer Vandera in 1569 as a place visited by Juan Pardo. Lawson (1860) spoke of them in connection with his travels through Carolina in 1701, but he did not visit them. Barnwell (1908) identified them with the Shakori with whom they were doubtless nearly allied and of whom they may have been a branch. They united with other tribes of the region against the English in the Yamasee war of 1715, and later with other Siouan remnants probably joined the Catawba.

Population.—Mooney (1928) estimates the Sissipahaw at 800 in 1600. "Haw Old Fields" constituted the largest body of fertile land in the region.

Connections in which they have become noted.—The name Sissipahaw has been brought down to our times by Haw River and the towns of Haw River and Saxapahaw on the same, in Alamance County, N. C.

Sugeree. This tribe occupied parts of Mecklenburg County. (See South Carolina.)

Tuscarora. From their own name Skă-ru'-rĕⁿ, signifying according to Hewitt (*in* Hodge, 1910), "hemp gatherers," and applied on account of the great use they made of *Apocynum cannabinum.* Also called:

Ă-ko-t'ăs'-kă-ro'-rĕⁿ', Mohawk name.
Ani'-Skălâ'lĬ, Cherokee name.
Ă-t'ăs-kă-lo'-lĕⁿ', Oneida name.
Tewohomomy (or Keew-ahomomy), Saponi name.

Connections.—The Tuscarora belonged to the Iroquoian linguistic family.

Location.—On the Roanoke, Tar, Pamlico, and Neuse Rivers. (See also Pennsylvania and New York.)

Subdivisions

The Tuscarora should be considered a confederacy with three tribes or a tribe with three subtribes as follows: Kă'tĕ'nu'ā'kā', "People of the submerged pine tree"; Akawăntca'kā', meaning doubtful; and Skarū'rĕⁿ, "hemp gatherers," i. e., the Tuscarora proper.

Villages

The following were in North Carolina, a more precise location not being possible except in the cases specified:

Annaooka.
Chunaneets.
Cohunche.
Conauhcare.
Contahnah, near the mouth of Neuse River.
Cotechney, on the opposite side of Neuse River from Fort Barnwell, about the mouth of Contentnea Creek.
Coram.
Corutra.
Harooka.
Harutawaqui.
Kenta.
Kentanuska.
Naurheghne.
Neoheroka, in Greene County.
Nonawharitse.
Nursoorooka.
Oonossoora.
Tasqui, a day's journey from Cotechney on the way to Nottaway village.
Tonarooka, on a branch of Neuse River between "Fort Narhantes" and Cotechney.
Torhunte, on a northern affluent of Neuse River.
Tosneoc.

Ucouhnerunt, on Pamlico River, probably in the vicinity of Greenville, in Pitt
County.

Unanauhan.

Later settlements in New York were these:

Canasaraga, on Canaseraga Creek on the site of the present Sullivan.

Ingaren.

Junastriyo.

Jutaneaga.

Kanhats.

Kaunehsuntahkeh.

Nyuchirhaan, near Lewiston, Niagara County.

Ohagi, on the west side of Genesee River a short distance below Cuylersville,
Livingston County.

Oquaga, on the east branch of the Susquehanna on both sides, in the town of
Colesville, Broome County.

Oyonwayea, also called Johnson's Landing, in Niagara County, about 4 miles
east of the outlet of Niagara River at the mouth of Four Mile Creek.

Shawiangto, on the west side of the Susquehanna not far from Windsor, Broome
County.

Tiochrungwe, on the "main road" from Oneida to Onondaga.

Tuscarora, the name of three villages: one a short distance east of "Anatsagane,"
probably the present Stockbridge, in Madison County; the second about 3 miles
below Oquaga, in Broome County, approximately on the site of Windsor; and
the third 12 miles by land and 20 by water below Oquaga, in the vicinity of
Great Bend, in Susquehanna County.

The location of Ganatisgowa is uncertain.

History.—The place or manner of separation of the Tuscarora from
the Iroquois tribes of New York is not known, and they were found
in the tract indicated above when the country was first entered by
white colonists.   John Lawson, Surveyor General of North Carolina,
lived in close contact with these Indians for many years and his
History of Carolina gives us our earliest satisfactory picture of them.
(See Lawson, 1860.)   It was his capture and execution by the tribe
in September 1711, however, which brought on the first Tuscarora
War, though behind it lay a series of encroachments by the Whites
on Tuscarora territory, and the kidnaping and enslavement of numbers of Indians.   Immediately after Lawson's death, part of the
Tuscarora, headed by chief Hencock, and the Coree, Pamlico, Machapunga, and Bear River Indians conspired to cut off the white
settlers and, in consequence, on September 22, 1711, they rose and
massacred about 130 of the colonists on Trent and Pamlico Rivers.
Colonel Barnwell, with 33 white men and about 500 Indians, marched
against the hostiles, by direction of the colony of South Carolina,
drove them from one of their towns with great loss, and invested
Hencock's own town, Cotechney.   But having suffered severely in
two assaults upon the place and fearing lest the white captives in the
hands of the Indians would be killed, he made peace and returned

home. Dissatisfied with the treatment accorded him by the North
Carolina authorities, however, he violated the treaty during his retreat
by seizing some Indians and sending them away as slaves. This brought
on the second Tuscarora War, 1712–13. South Carolina was again
appealed to for assistance, and Colonel James Moore set out for the
north with about 900 Indians and 33 white men, a number which
was considerably swelled before he reached the seat of trouble.
March 20 to 23 he stormed the palisaded town of Neoheroka, inflicting
a loss upon the enemy of about 950. The Tuscarora became so
terrified at this that part of them abandoned Fort Cohunche, situated
at Hencock's town and started north to join their relatives, the
Iroquois. This was only the beginning of the movement, bands of
Tuscarora being noted at intervals as moving north or as having
arrived among the Five Nations. They were adopted by the Oneida
but, contrary to the general impression, were not granted coordinate
rights in the League before September 1722. A part of the Tuscarora
under a chief named Tom Blunt (or Blount), had, however, remained
neutral. They received recognition by the government of North
Carolina, and continued in their former homes under their own chiefs.
In 1766, 155 removed to New York, and the 105 remaining were
brought north in 1802 while a deputation of northern Tuscarora were
in Carolina to obtain payment for the lands they had formerly occupied. When the Tuscarora first moved north they were settled at
various places along the Susquehanna in Pennsylvania and in New
York, some in the Oneida country itself. In 1875, by the treaty of
Fort Herkimer, the Oneida sold to the State of New York, the lands
on which their adopted children, the Tuscarora, had settled, and for a
time the Tuscarora were dispersed in various settlements in New York
State, and even in Pennsylvania. At the outbreak of the American
Revolution, the majority of Tuscarora and Oneida espoused the cause
of the colonists and in consequence they were attacked by Indians
in the British interest, including even some of their Iroquois brethren,
their houses were burned, their crops and other property destroyed,
and they themselves scattered. A large band of them settled, however, at a place called Oyonwayea or Johnson's Landing, on Lake
Ontario. Later a party from this settlement discovered a place in
the northeastern part of the present Tuscarora Reservation which
pleased them so much that they decided to winter there and they
were presently joined by the rest of the inhabitants of Oyonwayea.
At the treaty held at Genesee, September 15, 1797, between Robert
Morris and the Seneca tribe, Morris reserved to the tribe, by grant,
2 square miles, covering their new settlements, and the Seneca there-
upon granted them an additional square mile. As a result of their
appeal to the legislature of North Carolina above mentioned, they

were able to lease lands in the south, and they devoted the proceeds to the purchase of 4,329 acres adjoining their New York reserve. The Tuscarora who had sided with Great Britain were granted lands in severalty on Grand River, Ontario.

Population.—There were 5,000 Tuscarora in 1600 according to an estimate by Mooney (1928). In 1708, Lawson gives 15 towns and 1,200 warriors (Lawson, 1860). Barnwell in 1712 estimates 1,200 to 1,400 fighting men (Barnwell, 1908); Chauvignerie in 1736, 250 warriors, not including those in North Carolina, and on the Susquehanna and Juniata Rivers (Chauvignerie, *in* Schoolcraft, 1851–57, vol. 3, p. 555). In 1752 the southern Tuscarora were said to number 300 men; in 1754 there were said to be 100 men and 200 women and children and these figures are repeated in 1761. In 1766 there were said to be 220 to 230 all told in the south; next year we read that 155 southern Tuscarora had removed and that 105 remained. Other estimates place the total Tuscarora population at 1,000 in 1765, 2,000 in 1778, 1,000 in 1783, and 400 in 1796. In 1885 there were 828 (evenly divided between New York and Canada). In 1909 there were 364 in New York and a year later 416 in Canada, a total of 780. In 1910, 400 were reported in the United States and in 1923, 376 in New York alone. The number in Canada is not separately given.

Connection in which they have become noted.—This tribe is noted historically for its prominence among the peoples of eastern North Carolina, for the two wars which it waged with the colonists, and for the rather spectacular migration of the greater part to the north and its union with the Five Iroquois Nations. The name Tuscarora occurs applied to settlements in Frederick County, Md.; Craven County, North Carolina; Schuylkill County, Pennsylvania; Livingston County, N. Y.; Elko County, Nev.; and Ontario; and to a creek and mountain in Pennsylvania.

Tutelo. This tribe lived for a while on the upper Yadkin and later in Bertie County. (See Virginia.)

Waccamaw. They probably ranged across into North Carolina from the head of Waccamaw River. (See South Carolina.)

Wateree. According to Lederer (1912) they were living in 1670 on the upper Yadkin. (See South Carolina.)

Waxhaw. They extended over into Union County from South Carolina. (See South Carolina.)

Weapemeoc. Meaning unknown, but evidently a place name. Also called:

> Yeopim, a shortened and more usual form.

Connections.—The Weapemeoc were almost certainly of the Algonquian linguistic family and related to the Powhatan Indians to the north and the Chowan, Machapunga, and Pamlico to the south.

Location.—Most of the present Currituck, Camden, Pasquotank, and Perquimans Counties, and part of Chowan County north of Albemarle Sound.

Subdivisions

In the same section in later times are given the following tribes which must be regarded as subdivisions of the Weapemeoc:

Pasquotank, on Pasquotank River.
Perquiman, on Perquimans River.
Poteskeet, location uncertain.
Yeopim, or Weapemeoc proper, on Yeopim River.

Villages

Chepanoc, on Albemarle Sound in Perquimans County.
Mascoming, on the north shore of Albemarle Sound, in Chowan County.
Metachkwem, location unknown.
Pasquenock, perhaps identical with Pasquotank, on the north shore of Albemarle Sound, perhaps in Camden County.
Weapemeoc, probably in Pasquotank County.

History.—The Weapemeoc first appear in history in the narratives of the Raleigh colony of 1585–86. Later they are spoken of under the various subdivisional names. They parted with some of their land in 1662. In 1701, according to Lawson (1860), only 6 of the Yeopim survived though there were 40 warriors of the other subdivisions, including 10 Pasquotank and 30 Potekeet.

Population.—In the time of the Raleigh colony the Weapemeoc are said to have had between 700 and 800 warriors. They were estimated by Mooney (1928) at 800 in 1600. From their number as given by Lawson in 1701 Rights (1947) estimates 200 at that date.

Connection in which they have become noted.—In the form Yeopim the name has been preserved in that of a railroad station in Perquimans County, N. C.

Woccon.   Significance unknown.

Connections.—The Woccon belonged to the Siouan linguistic stock, their closest relations being the Catawba.

Location.—Between Neuse River and one of its affluents, perhaps about the present Goldsboro, Wayne County.

Villages

Tooptatmeer, supposed to have been in Greene County.
Yupwauremau, supposed to have been in Greene County.

History.—The first mention of the Woccon appears to be by Lawson writing about 1701, who recorded 150 words of their language. These show that it was nearer Catawba than any other known variety of speech. Lack of any earlier mention of such a large tribe lends strength to the theory of Dr. Douglas L. Rights that they were originally Waccamaw (q. v., under South Carolina). They took part against the Whites in the Tuscarora Wars and were probably extinguished as a tribe at that time, the remnant fleeing north with the Tuscarora, uniting with the Catawba, or combining with other Siouan remnants in the people later known as Croatan.

Population.—The number of Woccon was estimated by Mooney (1928) at 600 in 1600. Lawson (1860) gives 120 warriors in 1709.

Connection in which they have become noted.—The sole claim of the Woccon to distinction is from the fact that it is the only one of the southern group of eastern Siouan tribes other than the Catawba from which a vocabulary has been preserved.

Yadkin. Meaning unknown.

Connections.—The Yadkin probably belonged to the Siouan linguistic family.

Location.—On Yadkin River.

History.—The Yadkin first appear in history in a letter by the Indian trader, Abraham Wood, narrating the adventures of two men, James Needham and Gabriel Arthur, whom he had sent on an exploring expedition to the west. They passed this tribe and town, which they call "Yattken," in the summer of 1674. Lawson (1860) gives the name as Reatkin but applies it to the river, and there is no later mention of the people.

Connection in which they have become noted.—Their name Yadkin is perpetuated by the Yadkin River, Yadkin County, and the towns and villages of Yadkin College, Yadkin Falls, Yadkin Valley, and Yadkinville, all in the State of North Carolina.

Yeopim, see **Weapemeoc.**

SOUTH CAROLINA

Catawba. Significance unknown though the name was probably native to the tribe. Also called:

> Ani'ta'guä, Cherokee name.
> Iswa or Issa, signifying "river," and specifically the Catawba River; originally probably an independent band which united early with the Catawba proper.
> Oyadagahrœnes, Tadirighrones, Iroquois names.
> Usherys, from iswahere, "river down here"; see Issa.

Connections.—The Catawba belonged to the Siouan linguistic family, but Catawba was the most aberrant of all known Siouan languages, though closer to Woccon than any other of which a vocabulary has been recorded.

Location.—In York and Lancaster Counties mainly but extending into the neighboring parts of the State and also into North Carolina and Tennessee.

Subdivisions

Two distinct tribes are given by Lawson (1860) and placed on early maps, the Catawba and Iswa, the latter deriving their name from the native word meaning "river," which was specifically applied to Catawba River.

Villages

In early days this tribe had many villages but few names have come down to us. In 1728 there were six villages, all on Catawba River, the most northerly of which was known as Nauvasa. In 1781 they had two called in English Newton and Turkey Head, on opposite sides of Catawba River.

History.—The Catawba appear first in history under the name Ysa, Issa (Iswa) in Vandera's narratives of Pardo's expedition into the interior, made in 1566–67. Lederer (1912) visited them in 1670 and calls them Ushery. In 1711–13 they assisted the Whites in their wars with the Tuscarora, and though they participated in the Yamasee uprising in 1715 peace was quickly made and the Catawba remained faithful friends of the colonists ever after. Meanwhile they declined steadily in numbers from diseases introduced by the Whites, the use of liquor, and constant warfare with the Iroquois, Shawnee, Delaware, and other tribes. In 1738 they were decimated by smallpox and in 1759 the same disease destroyed nearly half of them. Through the mediation of the Whites, peace was made at Albany in 1759 between them and the Iroquois, but other tribes continued their attacks, and in 1763 a party of Shawnee killed the noted Catawba King Haigler. The year before they had left their town in North Carolina and moved into South Carolina, where a tract of land 15 miles square had been reserved for them. From that time on they sank into relative insignificance. They sided with the colonists during the revolution and on the approach of the British troops withdrew temporarily into Virginia, returning after the battle of Guilford Court House. In 1826 nearly the whole of their reservation was leased to Whites, and in 1840 they sold all of it to the State of South Carolina, which agreed to obtain new territory for them in North Carolina. The latter State refused to part with any land for that purpose, however, and most of the Catawba who had gone north of the State line were forced to return. Ultimately a reservation of 800 acres was set aside for them in South Carolina and the main body has lived there ever since. A few continued in North Carolina and others went to the Cherokee, but most of these soon came back and the last of those who remained died in 1889. A few Catawba intermarried with the Cherokee in later times, however, and still live there, and a few others went to the

Choctaw Nation, in what is now Oklahoma, and settled near Scully-
ville. These also are reported to be extinct. Some families established themselves in other parts of Oklahoma, in Arkansas, and near
Sanford, Colo., where they have gradually been absorbed by the
Indian and White population. About 1884 several Catawba were
converted by Mormon missionaries and went to Salt Lake City, and
in time most of those in South Carolina became members of the
Mormon Church, although a few are Baptists. Besides the two
divisions of Catawba proper, the present tribe is supposed to include
remnants of about 20 smaller tribes, principally Siouan.

Population.—Mooney (1928) estimates the number of Catawba in
1600, including the Iswa, at 5,000. About 1682 the tribe was supposed to contain 1,500 warriors or about 4,600 souls; in 1728, 400 warriors or about 1,400 souls; and in 1743, after incorporating several
small tribes, as having less than that number of warriors. In 1752
we have an estimate of about 300 warriors, or about 1,000 people;
in 1755, 240 warriors; in 1757, about 300 warriors and 700 souls;
and in 1759, 250 warriors. Although there is an estimate accrediting
them with 300 warriors in 1761, King Haigler declared that they had
been reduced by that year, after the smallpox epidemic of 1760, to
60 fighting men. In 1763 fewer than 50 men were reported, and in
1766 "not more than 60." In 1775 there was estimated a total
population of 400; in 1780, 490; in 1784, 250; in 1822, 450; in 1826,
110. In 1881 Gatschet found 85 on the reservation and 35 on adjoining farms, a total of 120. The census of 1910 returned 124, and
in 1912 there were about 100, of whom 60 were attached to the reservation. The census of 1930 gave 166, all but 7 in South Carolina.

Connection in which they have become noted.—The Catawba, whether
originally or by union with the Iswa, early became recognized as
the most powerful of all the Siouan peoples of Carolina. They are
also the tribe which preserved its identity longest and from which
the greatest amount of linguistic information has been obtained.
The name itself was given to a variety of grape, and has become applied,
either adopted from the tribe directly or taken from that of the grape,
to places in Catawba County, N. C.; Roanoke County, Va.; Marion
County, W. Va.; Bracken County, Ky.; Clark County, Ohio; Caldwell
County, Mo.; Steuben County, N. Y.; Blaine County, Okla.; York
County, S. C.; and Price County, Wis. It is also borne by an island in
Ohio, and by the Catawba River of the Carolinas, a branch of the
Wateree.

Cherokee. The extreme northwestern portion of the State was
    occupied by Cherokee Indians. (See Tennessee.)
Chiaha. A part of this tribe lived in South Carolina at times. (See
    Georgia.)

Chickasaw. The Chickasaw territory proper was in northern Mississippi, at a considerable distance from the State under discussion, but about 1753 a body of Chickasaw Indians settled on the South Carolina side of Savannah River, to be near the English trading posts and to keep in contact with the English, who were their allies. Before 1757 most of them moved over to the immediate neighborhood of Augusta and remained there until the period of the American Revolution. In that war they sided against the colonists and their lands were confiscated in 1783. (See Mississippi.)

Congaree. Meaning unknown.

Connection.—No words of this language have been preserved but the form of the name and general associations of the tribe leave little doubt that it was a Siouan dialect, related most closely to Catawba.

Location.—On Congaree River, centering in the neighborhood of the present State Capital, Columbia.

Village

The only village mentioned bore the same name as the tribe and was sometimes placed on the Congaree opposite Columbia, sometimes on the north side of the river.

History.—The Congaree are mentioned in documents of the seventeenth century as one of the small tribes of the Piedmont region. In 1701 Lawson (1860) found them settled on the northeast bank of Santee River below the mouth of the Wateree. They took part against the Whites in the Yamasee War of 1715, and in 1716 over half of them were captured and sent as slaves to the West Indies. The remnant appear to have retreated to the Catawba, for Adair (1930) mentions their dialect as one of those spoken in the Catawba Nation.

Population.—The Congaree are estimated by Mooney (1928) at 800 in 1600. A census taken in 1715 gives 22 men and a total population of about 40.

Connection in which they have become noted.—Congaree River and a railroad station in Richland County, S. C., preserve the name; Columbia, the State capital, was originally known as the Congarees.

Creeks. In the time of De Soto, Cofitachequi, which seems to have been either Kasihta or Coweta, and a few other Creek towns including perhaps Hilibi and part of the Chiaha Indians were in the territory of the present State of South Carolina near Savannah River. The Coosa of Coosawhatchie, Edisto, and Ashley Rivers may have been Creek in origin, and in later times Creeks constantly resorted to the provincial settlements in this area. (See Alabama.)

Cusabo. Meaning perhaps "Coosawhatchie River (people)."

Connections.—There is little doubt that the Cusabo belonged to the Muskhogean linguistic family. Their closest connections appear to have been with the Indians of the Georgia coast, the Guale.

Location.—In the southernmost part of South Carolina between Charleston Harbor and Savannah River and including most of the valleys of the Ashley, Edisto, Ashepoo, Combahee, Salkehatchie, and Coosawhatchie Rivers.

Subdivisions

These people should be divided first into the Cusabo proper, who occupied all of the coast, and the Coosa, who were inland upon the rivers above mentioned. The Cusabo proper seem to have consisted of a northern group of tribes or subtribes, including the Etiwaw (on Wando River), Wando (on Cooper River), Kiawa (on the lower course of Ashley River), and perhaps the Stono (about Stono Entrance); and a southern group including the Edisto (on Edisto Island), Ashepoo (on lower Ashepoo River), Combahee (on lower Combahee River), Wimbee (between the latter and the lower Coosawhatchie River), Escamacu (between St. Helena Sound and Broad River), and perhaps a few others. Sometimes early writers erroneously include the Siouan Sewee and Santee as Cusabo.

Villages

Ahoya or Hoya, on or near Broad River.
Ahoyabi, near the preceding.
Aluste, near Beaufort, possibly a form of Edisto.
Awendaw, near Awendaw Creek; it may have been Sewee (q. v.).
Bohicket, near Rockville.
Cambe, near Beaufort.
Chatuache, 6–10 leagues north of Beaufort.
Mayon, probably on Broad River.
Talapo, probably near Beaufort.
Touppa, probably on Broad River.
Yanahume, probably on the south side of Broad River.

History.—While their country was most likely skirted by earlier navigators, the first certain appearance of the Cusabo in history is in connection with a slave-hunting expedition sent out by Vasques de Ayllon. This reached the mainland in 1521, probably a little north of the Cusabo territory and introduced the blessings of White civilization to the unsuspecting natives by carrying away about 70 of them. One of these Indians was finally taken to Spain and furnished the historian Peter Martyr with considerable information regarding his country and the names of a number of tribes, some of whom were certainly Cusabo. In 1525 Ayllon sent a second expedition to the region and in 1526 led a colony thither. Dissatisfied with his first landing place, probably near the landfall of the expedition of 1521, he moved the colony "40 or 45 leagues," perhaps to the neighborhood of Savannah River. But it did not prosper, Ayllon died, trouble broke out among the survivors, and finally they returned to Haiti in the middle of the following winter. In 1540 De Soto passed near this country, but apparently he did not enter it, and the next European contact was brought about by the settlement of Ribault's first colony at Port Royal in 1562. The small number of people left by Ribault managed to maintain themselves for some time with the assistance of friendly natives, but, receiving no relief from France, they became discouraged, and built a small vessel in which a few of them eventually reached home. In 1564 a Spanish vessel visited this coast for the purpose of rooting out the French settlement. Later the same year a second Huguenot colony was established on St. Johns River, Florida, and communication was maintained with the Cusabo Indians. In 1565 this colony was destroyed by the Spaniards who visited Port Royal in quest of certain French refugees, and the year following Fort San Felipe was built at the same place. From this time until 1587 a post was maintained here, although with some intermissions due to Indian risings. In 1568–70 a vain attempt was made to missionize the Indians. In 1576 a formidable Indian uprising compelled the abandonment of the fort, but it was soon reoccupied and an Indian town was destroyed in 1579 by way of reprisal. Next year, however, there was a second uprising, making still another abandonment necessary. The fort was reoccupied in 1582 but abandoned permanently 5 years later; and after that time there was no regular post in the country but communication was kept up between the Cusabo and St. Augustine and occasional visits seem to have been made by the Franciscan Friars. Between 1633 and 1655 we have notice of a new mission in Cusabo territory, called Chatuache, but when the English settled South Carolina in 1670 there appears to have been no regular mission there and certainly no Spanish post. Charleston was founded on Cusabo soil, and from the date of its establishment onward relations were close between the English and Cusabo. In 1671 there was a short war between the colonists and the Coosa Indians and in 1674 there was further trouble with this people and with the Stono. In 1675 the Coosa Indians surrendered to the English a large tract of land which constituted Ashley Barony, and in 1682 what appears to have been a still more sweeping land cession was signed by several of the Cusabo chiefs. In 1693 there was another short war, this time between the Whites and the Stono. A body of Cusabo accompanied Colonel Barnwell in his expedition against the Tuscarora in 1711–12, and this fact may have quickened the consciences of the colonists somewhat, because in 1712 the Island of Palawana, "near the Island of St. Helena," was granted to them. It appears that most of their plantations were already upon it but it had inadvertently been granted to a white proprietor. The Cusabo here mentioned were those of the southern group; there is reason to think that the Kiawa and Coosa were not included. Early in 1720 "King Gilbert and ye Coosaboys" took part in Col. John Barnwell's punitive expedition against St. Augustine (Barnwell, 1908). In 1743 the Kiawa were given a grant of land south of the Combahee River, probably to be near the other coast Indians. Part of the Coosa may have retired to the Catawba, since Adair (1930) mentions "Coosah" as one of the dialects spoken in the "Catawba Nation," but others probably went to the Creeks. At least one band of Cusabo may have gone to Florida, because, in "A List of New Indian Missions in the Vicinity of St. Augustine," dated December 1, 1726, there is mention of a mission of San Antonio "of the Cosapuya nation and other Indians" containing 43 recently converted Christians and 12 pagans. Two years later we are informed that "the towns of the Casapullas Indians were depopulated," though whether this has reference to the ones in Florida or to those in their old country is not clear.

Population.—Mooney (1928) estimates the number of southern Cusabo, exclusive of the Edisto, at 1,200 in 1600, the Edisto at 1,000, the Etiwaw at 600, and the Coosa at 600. He classifies the Stono with the Westo, thereby falling into a common error. The colonial census of 1715 gives the number of southern Cusabo as 295, including 95 men, in 5 villages, while the Etiwaw (probably including the other northern Cusabo) had 1 village, 80 men, and a total population of 240. There were thus 535 Cusabo over all. The Coosa are nowhere mentioned by name and were probably included with one or the other of these. The 55 Indians at the Florida mission above mentioned, consisting of individuals of "the Cosapuya nation and other Indians," included 24 men, 13 women, and 18 children.

Connection in which they have become noted.—The first part of the name Coosa is identical in origin with the first part of the name of Coosawhatchie River, S. C., and a post village. The people themselves are noted in history as the first in eastern North America north of Florida among whom European settlements were begun. They had an earlier and longer contact with Europeans than any other Indians on the Atlantic seaboard except those of the Gulf of St. Lawrence.

Eno. This tribe moved into the northern part of the State after 1716 and perhaps united ultimately with the Catawba. At some prehistoric period they may have lived on Enoree River. (See North Carolina.)

Keyauwee. They settled on the Pee Dee after 1716 and probably united with the Catawba. (See North Carolina.)

Natchez. A band of Indians of this tribe lived for several years at a place called Four Hole Springs in South Carolina but left in 1744 fearing the vengeance of the Catawba because of seven of that tribe whom they had killed. (See Mississippi.)

Pedee. Meaning unknown, but Speck (1935) suggests from Catawba pi'ri, "something good," or pi'here, "smart," "expert," "capable."

Connections.—No words of the language have survived but there is every reason to suppose that it was a dialect of the Siouan linguistic family.

Location.—On Great Pee Dee River, particularly its middle course.

Village

No village names are known apart from the tribal name, which was sometimes applied to specific settlements.

History.—The Pedee are first mentioned by the colonists of South Carolina. In 1716 a place in or near their country called Saukey (perhaps Socatee) was suggested as the site for a trading post but the proposition to establish one there was given up owing to the weakness of the Pedee tribe, who were thought to be unable to protect it. In 1744, the Pedee, along with Natchez Indians, killed some Catawba and were in consequence driven from their lands into the White settlements. Soon afterward most of them joined the Catawba, but some remained near the Whites, where they are mentioned as late as 1755. In 1808 the Pedee and Cape Fear tribes were represented by one half-breed woman.

Population.—Mooney, 1928, estimates the number of Pedee as 600 in 1600. The census of 1715 does not give them separate mention, and they were probably included among the 610 Waccamaw or the 106 Winyaw.

Connection in which they have become noted.—The Great and Little Pee Dee Rivers and a station in Marion County, S. C., also a post village in Anson County, N. C., perpetuate the name of the Pedee.

Saluda. Meaning unknown.

Connections.—These are uncertain but circumstantial evidence indicates strongly that the Saluda were a band of Shawnee, and therefore of the Algonquian stock.

Location.—On Saluda River.

History.—Almost all that we know regarding the Saluda is contained in a note on George Hunter's map of the Cherokee country drawn in 1730 indicating "Saluda town where a nation settled 35 years ago, removed 18 years to Conestogo, in Pensilvania." As bands of Shawnee were moving into just that region from time to time during the period indicated, there is reason to think that this was one of them, all the more that a "Savana" creek appears on the same map flowing into Congaree River just below the Saluda settlement.

Population.—Unknown.

Connection in which they have become noted.—The name Saluda is preserved by Saluda River and settlements in Saluda County, S. C.; Polk County, N. C.; and Middlesex County, Va.

Santee.   Named according to Speck (1935), from iswa[n]'ti, "the river," or "the river is there."   Also called:

Seretee, by Lawson (1860).

Connections.—No words of the Santee language have come down to us, but there is little doubt that they belonged to the Siouan linguistic family.

Location.—On the middle course of Santee River.

Villages

The only name preserved is Hickerau, on a branch of Santee River.

History.—The Santee were first encountered by the Spaniards during the seventeenth century, and in the narrative of his second expedition Captain Eçija places them on Santee River.   In 1700 they were visited by John Lawson, who found their plantations extending for many miles along the river, and learned that they were at war with the coast people (Lawson, 1860).   They furnished Barnwell (1908) with a contingent for his Tuscarora campaign in 1711–12, but are said to have taken part against the Whites in the Yamasee War of 1715.   In 1716 they were attacked by the Etiwaw and Cusabo, acting in the interest of the colonists, and the greater part of them were carried away captive and sent to the West Indies.   The remainder were probably incorporated with the Catawba.

Population.—The number of Santee was estimated by Mooney (1928) at 1,000 in 1600.   In 1715 an Indian census gave them 43 warriors and a total population of 80 to 85 in 2 villages.

Connection in which they have become noted.—The name Santee has been given permanency chiefly by its application to the Santee River, S. C., but it has also been applied to a village in Orangeburg County, S. C.

Sewee.   Significance: perhaps, as Gatschet suggested, from sāwe', "island."

Connections.—No words of their language have survived, but the Sewee are regarded as Siouan on strong circumstantial grounds, in spite of the fact that they are sometimes classed with the Cusabo.

Location.—On the lower course of Santee River and the coast westward to the divide of Ashley River about the present Monks Corner, Berkeley County.

Villages

Lawson, writing about 1700, mentions a deserted village in Sewee Bay called Avendaughbough which may have belonged to them (Lawson, 1860). The name seems to be still preserved in the form Awensdaw.

History.—Possibly Xoxi (pronounced Shoshi or Shohi), one of the provinces mentioned by Francisco of Chicora, an Indian carried from this region by the Spaniards in 1521, is a synonym of Sewee. The name is mentioned by Captain Eçija in 1609. They may have been the Indians first met by the English expedition which founded the colony of South Carolina in 1670, when they were in Sewee Bay. They assisted the English against the Spaniards, and supplied them with corn. Lawson (1860) states that they were formerly a large tribe, but in his time, 1700, were wasted by smallpox and indulgence in alcoholic liquors. Moreover, a large proportion of the able-bodied men had been lost at sea in an attempt to open closer trade relations with England. Just before the Yamasee War, they were still living in their old country in a single village, but it is probable that the war put an end to them as a distinct tribe. The remnant may have united with the Catawba.

Population.—Mooney (1928) gives an estimate of 800 Sewee for the year 1600. In 1715 there were but 57.

Connection in which they have become noted.—At an earlier period this name was applied to the body of water now called Bulls Bay. There is a post hamlet with this designation in Meigs County, Tenn., but the name is probably of independent origin.

Shakori. This tribe is thought to have moved south with the Eno after 1716 and to have united ultimately with the Catawba. At some prehistoric period they perhaps lived on or near Enoree River, and there is reason to think that they or a branch gave their name to the Province of Chicora. (See North Carolina.)

Shawnee. In 1680, or shortly before, a band of Shawnee, probably from the Cumberland, settled on Savannah River, and the year following they performed a great service to the new colony of South Carolina by driving off the Westo Indians, whom I consider to have been Yuchi. These Shawnee appear to have been of the band afterward known as Hathawekela. They remained long enough in the neighborhood of Augusta to give their name to Savannah River, but by 1707 some of them had begun to move into Pennsylvania, and this movement continued at intervals until 1731, when all seem to have been out of the State. The Saluda (q. v.) were perhaps one of these bands. In 1715, as a result of the Yamasee War, a body moved from the Savannah to the Chatta-hoochee, and thence to the Tallapoosa. (See Tennessee.)

Sissipahaw. Possibly they were the Sauxpa mentioned by the Spanish officer Vandera in 1569, and if so they may then have been in South Carolina, a proposition considerably strengthened if Chicora is to be identified with the Shakori, since Barnwell (1908) equates these tribes. (See North Carolina.)

Sugeree. Speck (1935) suggests Catawba ye^{n}si'grihere, "people stingy," or "spoiled," or "of the river whose-water-cannot-be-drunk." (Cf. **Shakori.**) Also called:

Suturees, a synonym of 1715.

Connections.—No words of their language have been preserved, but there is every reason to suppose that they belonged to the Siouan linguistic family and were closely related to the Catawba, and perhaps still more closely to the Shakori.

Location.—On and near Sugar Creek in York County, S. C., and Mecklenburg County, N. C.

Villages

There were said to be many but their names have not been preserved.

History.—The Sugeree are hardly mentioned by anyone before Lawson in 1701. They probably suffered in consequence of the Yamasee War and finally united with the Catawba.

Population.—No separate enumeration or estimate of the Sugeree appears ever to have been made, and Mooney (1928) seems to have included them in the population of 5,000 allowed the Catawba.

Connection in which they have become noted.—The name Sugeree has been preserved in Sugar Creek, an affluent of Catawba River in North and South Carolina.

Waccamaw. Meaning unknown.

Connections.—Nothing of their tongue has been preserved but evidence points to a connection of the Waccamaw with the Siouan linguistic family, and presumably with the Catawba dialectic group. The Woccon may have been a late subdivision, as Dr. Rights has suggested. (See North Carolina.)

Location.—On Waccamaw River and the lower course of the Pee Dee. (See North Carolina.)

Villages

The Waccamaw were reported to have had six villages in 1715, but none of the names is preserved.

History.—The name of the Waccamaw may perhaps be recorded in the form Guacaya, given by Francisco of Chicora as that of a "province" in this region early in the sixteenth century. In 1715 the Cheraw attempted to incite them to attack the English, and they joined the hostile party but made peace the same year. In 1716 a trading post was established in their country at a place called Uauenee (Uaunee, Euaunee), or the Great Bluff, the name perhaps a synonym of Winyaw, although we know of no Winyaw there.   There was a short war between them and the colonists in 1720 in which they lost 60 men, women, and children killed or captured.   In 1755 the Cherokee and Natchez are reported to have killed some Pedee and Waccamaw in the White settlements.   Ultimately they may have united with the Catawba, though more probably with the so-called Croatan Indians of North Carolina.   There is, however, a body of mixed bloods in their old country to whom the name is applied.

Population.—The Waccamaw are estimated by Mooney (1928) at 900 in 1600 along with the Winyaw and some smaller tribes.   The census of 1715 gives 210 men and 610 souls, and in 1720 they are said to have had 100 warriors.   (See **Cape Fear Indians** under North Carolina.)

Connection in which they have become noted.—Waccamaw River in North and South Carolina and Waccamaw Lake in North Carolina, which empties into the river, perpetuate their name.

Wateree.   Gatschet suggests a connection with Catawba, *wateran,* "to float on the water."   Also called:

> Chickanee, name for a division of Wateree and meaning "little."
> Guatari, Spanish spelling of their name.

Connections.—The Wateree are placed in the Siouan linguistic stock on circumstantial evidence.

Location.—The location associated most closely with the Wateree historically was on Wateree River, below the present Camden.   (See North Carolina.)

History.—The Wateree are first mentioned in the report of an expedition from Santa Elena (Beaufort) by Juan Pardo in 1566–67. They lived well inland toward the Cherokee frontier.   Pardo made a small fort and left a corporal there and 17 soldiers, but the Indians soon wiped it out.   In 1670 Lederer (1912) places them very much farther north, perhaps on the upper Yadkin, but soon afterward they are found on Wateree River where Lawson met them.   In 1711–12 they furnished a contingent to Barnwell in his expedition against the Tuscarora.   In a map dated 1715 their village is placed on the west bank of Wateree River, possibly in Fairfield County, but on the Moll map of 1730 it is laid down on the east bank.   The Yamasee War reduced their power considerably, and toward the middle of the eighteenth century they went to live with the Catawba, with whom the survivors must ultimately have fused.   They appear as a separate tribe, however, as late as 1744, when they sold the neck of land between Congaree and Wateree Rivers to a white trader.

Population.—The number of Wateree is estimated by Mooney (1928) at 1,000 in 1600. There is no later enumeration.

Connection in which they have become noted.—The Wateree were one of the most powerful tribes of central South Carolina as far back as the time of the Spanish settlements at St. Helena. Their name is preserved in Wateree River, S. C., and in a post village in Richland County in the same State.

Waxhaw. Meaning unknown. Also called:

> Flatheads, a name given to this tribe and others of the Catawba connection owing to their custom of deforming the head.

Connection.—Nothing of their language has been preserved, but circumstantial evidence points to a close relationship between the Waxhaw and the Catawba and hence to membership in the Siouan linguistic stock. Their closest contacts appear to have been with the Sugeree.

Location.—In Lancaster County, S. C., and Union and Mecklenburg Counties, N. C.

Villages

Lawson mentions two villages in 1701 but the names are not given.

History.—The Waxhaw were possibly the Gueza of Vandera, who lived in western South Carolina in 1566–67. Lederer (1912) writing about 1670, speaks of the Waxhaw under the name Wisacky and says that they were subject to and might be considered a part of the Catawba. They were probably identical with the Weesock, whose children were said by Gabriel Arthur (1918) to be brought up in Tamahita (Yuchi) families "as ye Ianesaryes are amongst ye Turkes." Lawson (1860) visited them in 1701. At the end of the Yamasee War, they refused to make peace with the English and were set upon by the Catawba and the greater part of them killed. The rest fled to the Cheraw, but a band numbering 25 accompanied the Yamasee to Florida in 1715 and are noted as still there in 1720.

Population.—The Waxhaw are included by Mooney (1928) in the 5,000 estimated population of the Catawba. No separate estimate of their numbers is given anywhere.

Connection in which they have become noted.—The Waxhaw were distinguished in early times on account of their custom of deforming the heads of their children, Their name is preserved in Waxhaw Creek and in the name of a post town, both in Union County, N. C.; by a hamlet in Lancaster County, S. C.,; and a place in Bolivar County, Miss.

Winyaw. Meaning unknown.

Connections.—The Winyaw are placed in the Siouan linguistic family on circumstantial evidence. Their closest connections were with the Pedee and Waccamaw.

Location.—On Winyaw Bay, Black River, and the lower course of the Pee Dee.

History.—Unless this tribe is represented by the Yenyohol of Francisco of Chicora (1521), the Winyaw were first mentioned by the colonists of South Carolina after 1670. In 1683 it was charged that colonists had raided them for slaves on an insufficiently supported charge of murder by some of their people This unfriendly act did not prevent some of them from joining Barnwell's army in the first Tuscarora War. Along with other Indians they, indeed, withdrew later from the expedition, but they claimed that it was for lack of equipment. In 1715 the Cheraw tried to induce them and the Waccamaw to side against the colonists in the Yamasee War. A year later a trading post was established in the territory of the Waccamaw not far from their own lands. (See **Waccamaw.**) About the same time some of them settled among the Santee, but they appear to have returned to their own country a few years later. Some assisted the Whites in their war with the Waccamaw in 1720. They soon disappear from history and probably united with the Waccamaw.

Population.—Mooney (1928) includes the Winyaw in his estimate of 900 for the "Waccamaw, Winyaw, Hook, &c." as of the year 1600. The census of 1715 gives them one village of 36 men and a total population of 106.

Connection in which they have become noted.—Winyaw Bay, S. C., preserves the name. It was from this tribe or one in the immediate neighborhood that Francisco of Chicora was carried away by the first Ayllon expedition and from which one of the earliest ethnological descriptions of a North American tribe was recorded The name by which the Spaniards knew the province, however, Chicora, was probably derived from the Shakori, Sugeree, or a branch of one of them.

Yamasee. The Yamasee Indians lived originally near the southern margin of the State and perhaps at times within its borders, but they are rather to be connected with the aboriginal history of Georgia. In 1687, having become offended with the Spaniards, they settled on the north side of Savannah River on a tract afterward known as the Indian land and remained there in alliance with the colonists until 1715, when they rebelled and fled to St. Augustine. (See Georgia.)

Yuchi. The Yuchi probably did not enter South Carolina until after the year 1661. The Westo, whom I consider to have been a part of them, were driven away by the Shawnee in 1681, but there was a band of Yuchi higher up the Savannah River which did not move until 1716, and later another body settled between Silver Bluff and Ebenezer Creek. Hawkins says that they had villages at Ponpon and Saltkechers, but that is all the evidence we have of settlements so far east, and these probably belonged to the Yamassee. In 1729 the Yuchi began to move west to join the Creeks and by 1751 completed the evacuation. (See Georgia.)

GEORGIA

Apalachee. After the English and Creeks destroyed the Apalachee towns in Florida in 1704, they established a part of the tribe in a village not far below the present Augusta. In 1715, when the Yamasee War broke out, these Apalachee joined the hostile Indians and went to the Chattahoochee to live near that faction of the Lower Creeks which was favorable to Spain. Soon afterward, however, the English faction gained the ascendency among the Creeks, and the Apalachee returned to Florida. (See Florida.)

Apalachicola. From Hitchiti "Apalachicoli" or Muskogee "Apalachicolo," signifying apparently "People of the other side," with reference probably to the Apalachicola River or some nearby stream. Also called:

> Tálwa láko or Itálwa láko, "big town," name given by the Muskogee Indians·
> Palachicola or Parachukla, contractions of Apalachicola.

Connections.—This was one of those tribes of the Muskhogean linguistic stock which spoke the Atsik-hata or Hitchiti language, and which included in addition the Hitchiti, Okmulgee, Oconee, Sawokli, Tamali, Mikasuki, Chiaha, and possibly the Osochi (but see **Osochi**).

Location.—The earliest known home of the Apalachicola was near the river which bears their name in the center of the Lower Creek country. Later they lived for a considerable period at the point where it comes into existence through the junction of the Chattahoochee and Flint Rivers. (See also Alabama and Florida.)

Subdivisions and Villages

The following names of towns or tribes were given by a Tawasa Indian, Lamhatty, to Robert Beverley (1722) and may well have belonged to the Apalachicola: Aulédley, Ephíppick, Sonepáh, and perhaps Socsoóky (or Socsósky). The census of 1832 returned two distinct bodies of Indians under the synonyms Apalachicola and Tálwa láko.

History.—According to Muskogee legend, the ancestors of the Muskogee encountered the Apalachicola in the region above indicated when they entered the country, and they were at first disposed to fight with them but soon made peace. According to one legend the Creek Confederacy came into existence as a result of this treaty. Spanish documents of the seventeenth century are the earliest in which the name appears. It is there used both as the name of a town (as early as 1675) and, in an extended sense, for all of the Lower Creeks. This fact, Muskogee tradition, and the name Tálwa łáko all show the early importance of the people. They were on more friendly terms with the Spaniards than the Muskogee generally and hence were fallen upon by the Indian allies of the English and carried off, either in 1706 or 1707. They were settled on Savannah River opposite Mount Pleasant, at a place which long bore their name, but in 1716, just after the Yamasee War, they retired into their old country and established themselves at the junction of Chattahoochee and Flint Rivers. Later they moved higher up the Chattahoochee and lived in Russell County, Ala., remaining in the general neighborhood until they removed to new homes in the present Oklahoma in 1836–40. There they established themselves in the northern part of the Creek Reservation but presently gave up their ceremonial ground and were gradually absorbed in the mass of Indians about them.

Population.—In 1715 just before the outbreak of the Yamasee War, there were said to be 2 settlements of this tribe with 64 warriors and a total population of 214. A Spanish census of 1738 also gave 2 settlements with 60 warriors in one and 45 in the other; a French census of 1750, more than 30 warriors; a British enumeration of 1760, 60; one of 1761, 20; an American estimate of 1792, 100 (including the Chiaha); and the United States Census of 1832, a total population of 239 in 2 settlements.

Connection in which they have become noted.—Apalachicola River, Apalachicola Bay, and the name of the county seat of Franklin County, Fla., are derived from this tribe. The Spaniards applied their name to the Lower Creeks generally, and they were also noted as one of the tribes responsible for the formation of the Confederation.

Chatot. Some of these Indians lived at times in the southwest corner of this State. (See Florida.)

Cherokee. From early times the Cherokee occupied the northern and northeastern parts of Georgia, though from certain place names it seems probable that they had been [preceded in that territory by Creeks. (See Tennessee.)

Chiaha. Meaning unknown though it may contain a reference to mountains or highlands. (Cf. Choctaw and Alabama tcaha, Hitchiti tcáihi, "high.") Also called:

> Tolameco or Solameco, which probably signifies "big town," a name reported by the Spaniards.

Connections.—The Chiaha belonged to the Muskhogean linguistic stock and in later times spoke the Muskogee tongue, but there is every reason to class them in the Hitchiti group.   (See **Apalachicola.**)

Location.—In later historic times the Chiaha were on the middle course of Chattahoochee River, but at the earliest period at which we have any knowledge of them they seem to have been divided into two bands, one on Burns Island, in the present State of Tennessee, the other in eastern Georgia near the coast.   (See also South Carolina and Florida.)

Subdivisions

The Mikasuki of northern Florida are said to have separated from these people.

Villages

Hawkins (1848) gives the following:

Aumucculle, on a creek of the same name which enters Flint River "45 miles below Timothy Barnard's."

Chiahutci, Little Chiaha, a mile and a half west of the Hitchiti town, near Auhegee Creek.

Hotalgihuyana, occupied jointly with the Osochi, on the right bank of Flint River 6 miles below Kinchafoonee.

History.—Some confusion regarding this tribe has been occasioned by the fact that in the sixteenth century there appear to have been two divisions. The name first appears in the De Soto narratives applied to a "province" on an island in Tennessee River which J. Y. Brame has identified in a very satisfactory manner with Burns Island close to the Tennessee-Alabama line. They were said to be "subject to a chief of Coça," from which it may perhaps be inferred that the Creek Confederacy was already in existence. Early in 1567 Boyano, Juan Pardo's lieutenant, reached this town with a small body of soldiers and constructed a fort, Pardo joining him in September. When Pardo returned to Santa Elena shortly afterward he left a small garrison here which was later destroyed by the Indians. Possibly Chehawhaw Creek, an eastern affluent of the Coosa indicates a later location of this band. The only remaining reference which might apply to them occurs in the names of two bodies of Creeks called "Chehaw" and "Chearhaw" which appear in the census rolls of 1832–33, but they may have gotten their designations from former residences on or near the creek so called. In 1727 there was a tradition among the Cherokee that the Yamasee Indians were formerly Cherokee driven out by the Tomahitans, i. e., the Yuchi, and in this there may be some reminiscence of the fate of the Chiaha.

In the Pardo narratives the name "Lameco or Solameco" is given as a synonym for the northern Chiaha, and this may have been intended for Tolameco, which would be a Creek term meaning "Chief Town." This was also the name of a large abandoned settlement

near Cofitachequi on the middle course of Savannah River visited by
De Soto in 1540. Since we know that Chiaha were also in this region,
it is a fair supposition that this town had been occupied by people of
this connection. There is a Chehaw River on the South Carolina
coast between the Edisto and Combahee, and as "Chiaha" is used
once as an equivalent for Kiawa, possibly the Cusabo tribe of that
name may have been related. Moreover, we are informed (S. C.
Docs.) that the Chiaha had their homes formerly among the Yamasee.
In 1715 they withdrew to the Chattahoochee with other upper Creek
towns, probably from a temporary abode on Ocmulgee River. After
the Creeks moved to Oklahoma the Chiaha settled in the northeastern
corner of the Creek Reservation and maintained a square ground
there until after the Civil War, but they have now practically lost
their identity. Some of them went to Florida and the Mikasuki are
said by some Indians to have branched off from them. In the country
of the western Seminole there was a square ground as late as 1929
which bore their name.

Population.—There are no figures for the northern band of Chiaha
unless they could have been represented in the two towns of the
1832–33 census given above, which had total populations of 126 and
306 respectively. For the southern division a Spanish census of 1738
gives 120 warriors but this included also the Osochi and Okmulgee.
In 1750 only 20 were reported, but in 1760, 160, though an estimate
the following year reduces this to 120. In 1792 Marbury gives 100
Chiaha and Apalachicola, and the census of 1832–33 returned 381
of the former. In 1799 Hawkins states that there were 20 Indian
families in Hotalgi-huyana, a town occupied jointly by this tribe and
the Osochi, but in 1821 Young raises this to 210. He gives 670 for
the Chiaha proper.

Connection in which they have become noted.—The Chiaha tribe is
of some note on account of the prominence given to one branch of it
in the De Soto narratives. As above mentioned, its name, spelled
Chehawhaw, is applied to a stream in the northern part of Talladega
County, Ala.; it is given in the form Chehaw to a post hamlet of Macon
County, Ala.; to a stream in Colleton County, S. C.; and also to
a small place in Seminole County, Okla.

Chickasaw. A band of Chickasaw lived near Augusta from about
1723 to the opening of the American Revolution, and later they were
for some time among the Lower Creeks. (See Mississippi and
South Carolina.)

Creeks. A part, and perhaps a large part, of the Indians who afterward constituted the Creek Confederacy were living in the sixteenth

century in what the Spaniards called the province of Guale on the present Georgia coast. Some of them moved inland in consequence of difficulties with the Whites, and in the latter half of the seventeenth century most of those afterward known as Lower Creeks were upon Chattahoochee and Ocmulgee Rivers, the latter river being then called Ocheese Creek, from the Hitchiti name given to the Indians living on it. After the Yamasee War (1715) all assembled upon Chattahoochee River and continued there, part on the Georgia side of the river, part on the Alabama side, until they removed to the present Oklahoma early in the nineteenth century. (See **Creek Confederacy** and **Muskogee** under Alabama.)

Guale. Meaning unknown, though it resembles Muskogee wahali, "the south," but it was originally applied to St. Catherines Island, or possibly to a chief living there. Also called:

> Ouade, a French form of Guale.
> Ybaha, Yguaja, Ibaja, Iguaja, Yupaha, Timucua name.

Connections.—The names of villages and the title "mico" applied to chiefs leave little doubt that these Indians belonged to the Muskhogean linguistic family. Part of them were probably true Creeks or Muskogee. (See Alabama.) Their nearest connections otherwise appear to have been with the Cusabo Indians. (See South Carolina.)

Location.—On the Georgia coast between St. Andrews Sound and Savannah River, though the section between St. Catherines Sound and Savannah seems to have been little occupied. (See also Florida.)

Subdivisions

Three rough divisions appear to be indicated by Governor Ibarra of Florida, but this is very uncertain. (See below under Villages.)

Villages

So far as they can be made out, the villages in each of the three groups mentioned above were as follows:

Northern group:

> Asopo, apparently a form of Ossabaw but stated to have been on St. Catherines Island.
> Chatufo.
> Couexis, given in the French narratives as near St. Catherines.
> Culapala.
> Guale, not, it appears, on the island of that name but "on an arm of a river which is a branch of another on the north bank of the aforesaid port in Santa Elena in 32° N. lat.," probably on Ossabaw Island.
> Otapalas.
> Otaxe (Otashe).
> Posache, "in the island of Guale."
> Tolomato, said to have been on the mainland 2 leagues from St. Catherines Island and near the bar of Sapello.

Uchilape, "near Tolomato."

Uculegue.

Unallapa.

Yfusinique, evidently on the mainland.

Yoa, said to have been 2 leagues up a river emptying into an arm of the sea back of Sapello and St. Catherines Sound.

Central group:

Aleguifa, near Tulufina.

Chucalagaite, near Tulufina.

Espogache, near Espogue.

Espogue, not more than 6 leagues from Talaxe.

Fasquiche, near Espogue.

Sapala, evidently on or near Sapello Island.

Sotequa.

Tapala.

Tulufina, probably on the mainland.

Tupiqui, probably the original of the name Tybee, but this town was very much farther south.

Utine.

Southern group:

Aluque.

Asao, probably on St. Simons Island.

Cascangue, which seems to have been reckoned as Timucua at times and hence may have been near the Timucua border.

Falquiche.

Fuloplata, possibly a man's name.

Hinafasque.

Hocaesle.

Talaxe, probably on St. Simons Island or on the Altamaha River, both of which were known by the name Talaxe.

Tufulo.

Tuque.

Yfulo.

To the above must be added the following town names which cannot be allocated in any of the preceding divisions:

Alpatopo.

Aytochuco.

Ayul.

Olatachahane, perhaps a chief's name.

Olatapotoque, given as a town, but perhaps a chief's name.

Olataylitaba, perhaps two names run together, Olata and Litabi.

Olocalpa.

Sulopacaques.

Tamufa.

Yumunapa.

History.—The last settlement of the Ayllon colony in 1526 was on or near the Guale country, as the name Gualdape suggests. When the French Huguenot colony was at Port Royal, S. C., in 1562, they heard of a chief called Ouadé and visited him several times for provisions. After the Spaniards had driven the French from Florida, they continued north to Guale and the Cusabo territory to expel several Frenchmen who had taken refuge there.   In 1569 missionary work was undertaken by the Jesuits simultaneously among the Cusabo and Guale Indians and one of the missionaries, Domingo Augustin, wrote a grammar of the Guale language.   But the spiritual labors of the missionaries proved unavailing, and they soon abandoned the country.   In 1573 missionary work was resumed by the Franciscans and was increasingly successful when in 1597 there was a general insurrection in which all of the missionaries but one were killed.   The governor of Florida shortly afterward burned very many of the Guale towns with their granaries, thereby reducing most of the Indians to submission, and by 1601 the rebellion was over.   Missionary work was resumed soon afterward and continued uninterruptedly, in spite of sporadic insurrections in 1608 and 1645 and attacks of northern Indians in 1661, 1680, and even earlier.   However, as a result of these attacks those of the Guale Indians who did not escape inland moved, or were moved, in 1686, to the islands of San Pedro, Santa Maria, and San Juan north of St. Augustine.   Later another island called Santa Cruz was substituted for San Pedro.   The Quaker, Dickenson, who was shipwrecked on the east coast of Florida in 1699, visited these missions on his way north.   At the time of the removal some Guale Indians appear to have gone to South Carolina, and in 1702 a general insurrection of the remainder took place, and they joined their kinsmen on the outskirts of that colony under the leadership of the Yamasee.   A few may have remained in Florida.   In any event, all except those who had fled to the Creeks were united after the outbreak of the Yamasee in 1715 and continued to live in the neighborhood of St. Augustine until their virtual extinction.   In 1726 there were two missions near St. Augustine occupied by Indians of the "Iguaja nation," i. e., Guale, but that is the last we hear of them under any name but that of the Yamasee (q. v.).

Population.—Mooney (1928), who was not aware of the distinction to be drawn between the Guale Indians and the Yamasee, gives an estimate of 2,000 Guale in the year 1650.   For the two tribes this is probably too low.   The Guale alone, before they had been depleted by White contact and Indian invasions from the north, might well have numbered 4,000, but some of these were later added to the Creeks.   In 1602 the missionaries claimed that there were more than 1,200 Christians in the Guale province, and in 1670 the English estimated that the Spanish missions contained about 700 men.   The first accurate census of the Yamasee and Guale Indians together, made in 1715, perhaps omitting some few of the latter still in Florida, gives 413 men and a total population of 1,215.

Connection in which they have become noted.—Aside from the abortive missionary undertakings of the friars who accompanied Coronado, and a short missionary experience among the Calusa, the provinces of Guale and Orista (Cusabo) were the first north of México in which regular missionary work was undertaken, and the grammar of the Guale language by Domingo Augustin was the first of any language in that region to be compiled.

Hitchiti. Perhaps from Atcik-hata, a term formerly applied to all of the Indians who spoke the Hitchiti language, and is said to refer to the heap of white ashes piled up close to the ceremonial ground. Also called:

> At-pasha-shliha, Koasati name, meaning "mean people."

Connections.—The Hitchiti belonged to the Muskhogean linguistic family and were considered the mother town of the Atcik-hata group. (See **Apalachicola.**)

Location.—The Hitchiti are oftenest associated with a location in the present Chattahoochee County, Ga., but at an earlier period were on the lower course of the Ocmulgee River. (See also Florida and Oklahoma.)

Villages

Hihaje, location unknown.

Hitchitoochee, on Flint River below its junction with Kinchafoonee Creek.

Tuttallosee, on a creek of the same name, 20 miles west from Hitchitoochee.

History.—The Hitchiti are identifiable with the Ocute of De Soto's chroniclers, who were on or near the Ocmulgee River. Early English maps show their town on the site of the present Macon, Ga., but after 1715 they moved to the Chattahoochee, settling first in Henry County, Ala., but later at the site above mentioned in Chattahoochee County, Ga. From this place they moved to Oklahoma, where they gradually merged with the rest of the Indians of the Creek Confederacy.

Population.—The population of the Hitchiti is usually given in conjunction with that of the other confederate tribes. The following separate estimates of the effective male Hitchiti population are recorded: 1738, 60; 1750, 15; 1760, 50; 1761, 40; 1772, 90; in 1832 the entire population was 381.

Connection in which they have become noted.—In early days, as above mentioned, the Hitchiti were prominent as the leaders in that group of tribes or towns among the Lower Creeks speaking a language distinct from Muskogee. Hichita, McIntosh County, Okla., preserves the name.

Kasihta. One of the most important divisions of the Muskogee, possibly identical with the Cofitachequi of the De Soto narratives. (See **Muskogee** under Alabama.)

Oconee.   Significance unknown.

Connections.—The Oconee belonged to the Muskhogean linguistic stock, and the Atcik-hata group.   (See **Apalachicola.**)

Location.—Just below the Rock Landing on Oconee River, Ga. (But see also Florida.)

History.—Early documents reveal at least two bodies of Indians bearing the name Oconee and probably related.   One was on or near the coast of Georgia and seems later to have moved into the Apalachee country and to have become fused with the Apalachee tribe before the end of the seventeenth century.   The other was at the point above indicated, on Oconee River.   About 1685 they were on Chatta-hoochee River, whence they moved to the Rock Landing.   A more northerly location for at least part of the tribe may be indicated in the name of a Cherokee town, though that may have been derived from a Cherokee word as Mooney supposed.   About 1716 they moved to the east bank of the Chattahoochee in Stewart County, Ga., and a few years later part went to the Alachua Plains, in the present Alachua County, Fla., where they became the nucleus of the Seminole Nation and furnished the chief to that people until the end of the Seminole war.   Most of them were then taken to Oklahoma, but they had already lost their identity.

Population.—The following estimates of effective Oconee men in the Creek Nation are preserved: 1738, 50; 1750, 30; 1760, 50; 1761, 50. In 1675 there were about 200 Indians at the Apalachee Mission of San Francisco de Oconi.

Connection in which they have become noted.—The name Oconee is perpetuated in the Oconee River, the town of Oconee, Oconee Mills, and Oconee Siding, all in Georgia, but not necessarily in the name of Oconee County, S. C., which is of Cherokee origin, although there may be some more remote relationship.   There is a place of the name in Shelby County, Ill.

Okmulgee.   Signifying in the Hitchiti language, "where water boils up" and referring probably to the big springs in Butts County, Ga., called Indian Springs.   Also called:

   Waiki lȧko, "Big Spring," Muskogee name.

Connections.—The Okmulgee belonged to the Muskhogean linguistic stock and the Atsik-hȧta group.   (See **Apalachicola** under Georgia.)

Location.—In the great bend of the Chattahoochee River, Russell County, Ala.; earlier, about the present Macon, Ga.   (See also Alabama and Oklahoma.)

History.—The Okmulgee probably separated from the Hitchiti or one of their cognate towns when these towns were on Ocmulgee River and settled at the point above indicated, where they became closely associated with the Chiaha and Osochi. They went west with the other Creeks and reestablished themselves in the most northeastern part of the allotted territory, where they gradually lost their identity. Although small in numbers, they gave the prominent Perryman family to the Creek Nation and its well-known head chief, Pleasant Porter.

Population.—A French census of about 1750 states that there were rather more than 20 effective men among the Okmulgee, and the British census of 1760 gives 30. Young, quoted by Morse, estimates a total population of 220 in 1822. There are few other enumerations separate from the general census of the Creeks.

Connection in which they have become noted.—The name of the city of Okmulgee and that of Ocmulgee River were derived independently from the springs above mentioned. The name Okmulgee given to the later capital of the Creek Nation in what is now Oklahoma was, however, taken from the tribe under consideration. It has now become a flourishing oil city.

Osochi. A division of the Lower Creeks which lived for a time in southwestern Georgia. (See Alabama.)

Sawokli. A division of the Creeks belonging to the group of towns that spoke the Hitchiti language. (See Alabama.)

Shawnee. The Shawnee band which settled near Augusta concerns South Carolina and Georgia almost equally. Their history has already been given in treating the tribes of the former State. (See also Tennessee.)

Tamathli. The name is possibly related to that of a Creek clan with the Hitchiti plural ending, in which case it would refer to "flying creatures," such as birds.

Connections.—Tamathli belonged to the Atsik-hata group in the Creek Confederation.

Location.—The historic seats of the Tamathli were in southwestern Georgia and neighboring parts of Florida.

History.—It is believed that we have our first mention of the Tamathli in the Toa or Toalli of the De Soto narratives. When De Soto passed through Georgia in 1540, it is believed that this tribe was living at Pine Island in Daugherty County. They may have been connected with the Altamaha Yamasee living between Ocmulgee and Oconee Rivers whose name sometimes appears in the form Tama. They afterward drifted into Florida and were established in a mission called La Purificación de la Tama on January 27, 1675, by Bishop Calderón of Cuba, in the Apalachee country 1 league from San Luis. In a mission list dated 1680 appears the name of another mission, Nuestra Señora de la Candelaria de la Tama. The Tamathli suffered the same fate as the Apalachee in general when the latter were attacked by Moore in 1704. At least part of these Indians afterward moved to the neighborhood of St. Augustine, where another mission was established for them, but this was attacked by the Creeks on November 1, 1725, while mass was being celebrated. Many Indians were killed and the remainder moved to other missions. In 1738 we hear of a "Tamaxle nuevo," as the northernmost Lower Creek settlement and a southern division called "Old Tamathle," and are informed that "in the town of Tamasle in Apalachee [i. e., Old Tamathle] there were some Catholic and pagan families." We hear again of these Tamathli Indians from Benjamin Hawkins (1848), writing in 1799, who sets them down as one of the tribes entering into the formation of the Florida Seminole. A town of the same name also appears in the Cherokee country "on Valley River, a few miles above Murphy, about the present Tomatola, in Cherokee County, N. C." The name cannot be interpreted in Cherokee and there may once have been a northern division of the Tamathli.

Population.—The Spanish census dated 1738 enters Old Tamathli, with 12 men, and New Tamathli with 26, but the latter probably was in the main a Sawokli settlement. The French estimate of 1750 entered only the former town with 10 men. In Young's enumeration of Seminole towns (*in* Morse, 1822) this is given a total population of 220.

Timucua. One contact between the Timucua Indians and Georgia is mentioned later in connection with the Osochi. When the Spaniards first came in contact with them, the Timucua occupied not merely northern and central Florida but Cumberland Island and a part of the adjacent mainland. The Timucua evidently withdrew from this territory as a result of pressure exerted by northern Indians in the latter part of the seventeenth century or the very beginning of the eighteenth. (See **Utina** under Florida.)

Yamasee. Meaning unknown, though it has been interpreted by Muskogee yámasi, "gentle." The form given in some early writings, Yamiscaron, may have been derived from a Siouan dialect or from Timucua, as there is no *r* in any of the Muskhogean tongues.

Connections.—The Yamasee town and chief names indicate plainly that they spoke a Muskhogean dialect and tradition affirms that it was connected most closely with Hitchiti, a contention which may be considered probable.

Location.—The earliest references that we have place the Yamasee on Ocmulgee River not far above its junction with the Oconee. They seem to have ranged or extended northeastward of these rivers to or even slightly beyond the Savannah, but always inland. (See also Florida, Alabama, South Carolina.)

Subdivisions and Villages

Immediately before the outbreak of the Yamasee War there were the following:
Upper Towns:

Huspaw, near Huspaw Creek between Combahee River and the Whale Branch.

Pocotaligo, near Pocotaligo River.

Sadkeche, probably near Salkehatchie, a hamlet at the Atlantic Coast Line crossing of the Combahee River.

Tomatly, in the neighborhood of Tomatly, Beaufort County, S. C.

Yoa, near Huspaw.

Lower Towns:

Altamaha, location unknown.

Chasee, location unknown.

Oketee, probaly near one of the places so called on New River, in Jasper and Beaufort Counties, S. C.

Pocasabo.

Tulafina (?), perhaps near Tulafinny Creek, an estuary of the Coosawhatchie River in Jasper County.

Other possible Yamasee settlements were Dawfuskee, Ilcombe, and Peterba.

History.—The first reference to the Yamasee appears to be a mention of their name in the form Yamiscaron as that of a province with which Francisco of Chicora was acquainted in 1521. The "Province of Altamaha" mentioned by De Soto's chronicler Ranjel in 1540 probably included at least a part of the Yamasee people. For a hundred years afterward the tribe remained practically unnoticed except for a brief visit by a Spanish soldier and two missionaries in 1597, but in 1633 they are reported to have asked for missionaries, and in 1639 peace is said to have been made between the allied Chatot, Lower Creeks, and Yamasee and the Apalachee. In 1675 Bishop Calderón of Cuba founded two missions in the Apalachee country which were occupied by Yamasee or their near relatives. The same year there were three Yamasee missions on the Atlantic coast but one of these may have been occupied by Tamathli. Later they moved nearer St Augustine but in the winter of 1684–85 some act of the Spanish governor offended them and they removed to South Carolina, where the English gave them lands on the west side of Savannah River near its mouth. Some of these Indians were probably from the old Guale province, but the Yamasee now took the lead. Eighty-seven warriors of this nation took part in Barnwell's expedition against the Tuscarora (see North Carolina). In 1715 they rose in rebellion against the English and killed two or three hundred settlers but were defeated by Governor Craven and took refuge in Florida, where, until the cession of Florida to Great Britain, the Yamasee continued as allies of the Spaniards. Meanwhile their numbers fell off steadily. Some remained in the neighborhood of the St. Johns River until the outbreak of the Seminole War.

The Oklawaha band of Seminole is said to have been descended from them. Another band accompanied the Apalachee to Pensacola and Mobile, and we find them located near those two places on various charts. They may be identical with those who, shortly afterward, appear among the Upper Creeks on certain maps, though this is the only testimony we have of their presence there. At any rate, these latter are probably the Yamasee found among the Lower Creeks in the nineteenth century and last heard of among the Seminole of west Florida. Of some historical importance is a small band of these Indians who seem to have lived with the Apalachicola for a time, after the Yamasee War, and in 1730 settled on the site of what is now Savannah under the name of Yamacraw. There the Georgia colonists found them three years later, and the relations between the two peoples were most amicable. The name Yamacraw was probably derived from that of a Florida mission, Nombre de Dios de Amacarisse, where some of the Yamasee once lived. Ultimately these Yamacraw are believed to have retired among the Creeks and later may have gone to Florida.

Population.—It is impossible to separate distinctly the true Yamasee from the Guale Indians. Mooney (1928) gives an estimate of 2,000 in 1650, probably too low. A mission list compiled by Gov. Salazar of Florida in 1675 gives 1,190 Yamasee and Tama. In 1708 the two tribes, united under the name Yamasee, were thought to have 500 men capable of bearing arms. In 1715 a rather careful census gives 413 men and a total population of 1,215. Lists dating from 1726 and 1728 give 313 and 144 respectively in the missions about St. Augustine. A fairly satisfactory Spanish census, taken in 1736, indicates that there were then in the neighborhood of St. Augustine more than 360 Yamasee and Indians of Guale. This does not include the Yamasee near Pensacola and Mobile, those in the Creek Nation, or the Yamacraw. In 1761 a body of Yamasee containing 20 men was living near St. Augustine, but by that time the tribe had probably scattered widely. In 1821 the "Emusas" on Chattahoochee River numbered 20 souls.

Connection in which they have become noted.—The Yamasee are famous particularly on account of the Yamasee War, which marked an epoch in Indian and White history in the Southeast. At the end of the seventeenth century a certain stroke was used in paddling canoes along the coast of Georgia, South Carolina, and Florida, which was called the "Yamasee stroke." A small town in Beaufort County, S. C., is called "Yemasee," a variant of this name.

Yuchi. Significance unknown, but perhaps, as suggested by Speck (1909), from a native word meaning "those far away," or "at a distance," though it is also possible that it is a variant of Ochesee

or Ocheese, which was applied by the Hitchiti and their allies to
Indians speaking languages different from their own.   Also called:

Ani'-Yu'tsĭ, Cherokee name.
Chiska, probably a Muskogee translation of the name of one of their bands.
Hughchee, an early synonym.
Round town people, a name given by the early English colonists.
Rickohockans, signifying "cavelanders" (Hewitt, *in* Hodge, 1907), perhaps
     an early name for a part of them.
Tahogaléwi, abbreviated to Hogologe, name given them by the Delaware
     and other Algonquian people.
Tamahita, so called by some Indians, perhaps some of the eastern Siouans.
Tsoyaha, "People of the sun," their own name, or at least the name of
     one band.
Westo, perhaps a name applied to them by the Cusabo Indians of South
     Carolina though the identification is not beyond question.

Connections.—The Yuchi constituted a linguistic stock, the Uchean,
distinct from all others, though structurally their speech bears a
certain resemblance to the languages of the Muskhogean and Siouan
families.

Location.—The earliest known location of the Yuchi was in
eastern Tennessee, perhaps near Manchester, but some of them
extended still farther east, while others were as far west as Muscle
Shoals.   On archeological grounds Prof. T. M. N. Lewis believes that
one main center of the Yuchi was on Hiwassee River.   We find
settlements laid down on the maps as far north as Green River,
Kentucky.   In later times a part settled in West Florida, near the
present Eucheeanna, and another part on Savannah and Ogeechee
Rivers.   (See also Alabama, Florida, Oklahoma, Tennessee, and South
Carolina.)

Subdivisions

There appear to have been three principal bands in historic times: one on
Tennessee River, one in West Florida, and one on Savannah River, but only a
suggestion of native band names has survived.   Recently Wagner has heard of
at least three subdivisional names, including the Tsoyaha, or "Sun People" and
the Root People.

Villages

Most of their settlements are given the name of the tribe, Yuchi, or one of its
synonyms.   In early times they occupied a town in eastern Tennessee called by
the Cherokee Tsistu'yĭ, "Rabbit place," on the north bank of Hiwassee River
at the entrance of Chestua Creek in Polk County, Tenn., and at one time also that
of Hiwassee, or Euphasee, at the Savannah Ford of Hiwassee River.   The
Savannah River band had villages at Mount Pleasant, probably in Screven
County, Ga., near the mouth of Brier Creek, 2 miles below Silver Bluff on Savannah River in Barnwell County; and one on Ogeechee River bearing the name of
that stream, though that was itself perhaps one form of the name Yuchi.
Hawkins (1848) mentions former villages at Ponpon and Saltketchers in South
Carolina, but these probably belonged to the Yamasee.   The following Yuchi
settlements were established after the tribe united with the Lower Creeks:

Arkansaw River, in Oklahoma.

Big Pond Town, Polecat Creek, and Sand Creek, in and near Creek County, Okla.

Blackjack Town.

Deep Fork Creek, Okla.

Duck Creek Town.

Intatchkálgi, on Opilthlako Creek 28 miles above its junction with Flint River, probably in Schley County, Ga.

Padshilaika, at the junction of Patchilaika Creek with Flint River, Macon County, Ga.

Red Fork, location uncertain.

Snake Creek, location uncertain.

Spring Garden Town, above Lake George, Fla.

Tokogalgi, on Kinchafoonee Creek, an affluent of Flint River, Ga.

History.—The chroniclers of the De Soto expedition mention the Yuchi under the name Chisca, at one or more points in what is now Tennessee. In 1567 Boyano, an officer under Juan Pardo, had two desperate encounters with these Indians somewhere in the highlands of Tennessee or North Carolina, and, according to his own story, destroyed great numbers of them. In 1670 Lederer (1912) heard of people called Rickohockans living in the mountains who may have been Yuchi, and two white men sent from Virginia by Abraham Wood visited a Yuchi town on a head stream of the Tennessee in 1674. About this time also, English explorers and settlers in South Carolina were told of a warlike tribe called Westo (probably a division of Yuchi) who had struck terror into all of the coast Indians, and hostilities later broke out between them and the colonists. At this juncture, however, a band of Shawnee made war upon the Westo and drove them from the Savannah. For a time they seem to have given themselves up to a roving life, and some of them went so far inland that they encountered La Salle and settled near Fort St. Louis, near the present Utica, Ill. Later some were located among the Creeks on Ocmulgee River, and they removed with them to the Chattahoochee in 1715. Another band of Yuchi came to live on Savannah River about 20 miles above Augusta, probably after the expulsion of the Westo. They were often called Hogologe. In 1716 they also moved to the Chattahoochee but for a time occupied a town distinct from that of the other Yuchi. It was probably this band which settled near the Shawnee on Tallapoosa River and finally united with them. Still later occurred a third influx of Yuchi who occupied the Savannah between Silver Bluff and Ebenezer Creek. In 1729 a Kasihta chief named Captain Ellick married three Yuchi women and persuaded some of the Yuchi Indians to move over among the Lower Creeks, but Governor Oglethorpe of Georgia guaranteed them their rights to their old land until after 1740, and the final removal did not, in fact, take place until 1751.

A still earlier invasion of southern territories by Yuchi is noted by one of the governors of Florida in a letter dated 1639. These invaders proved a constant source of annoyance to the Spaniards. Finally they established themselves in West Florida not far from the Choctawhatchee River, where they were attacked by an allied Spanish and Apalachee expedition in 1677 and suffered severely. They continued to live in the same region, however, until some time before 1761 when they moved to the Upper Creeks and settled near the Tukabahchee. Eucheeanna in Walton County, Fla. seems to preserve their name.

A certain number of Yuchi remained in the neighborhood of Tennessee River, and at one time they were about Muscle Shoals. They also occupied a town in the Cherokee country, called by the latter tribe Tsistu′yï, and Hiwassee at Savannah Ford. In 1714, the former was cut off by the Cherokee in revenge for the murder of a member of their tribe, instigated by two English traders. Later tradition affirms that the surviving Yuchi fled to Florida, but many of them certainly remained in the Cherokee country for a long time afterward, and probably eventually migrated west with their hosts.

A small band of Yuchi joined the Seminole just before the outbreak of the Seminole War. They appear first in West Florida, near the Mikasuki but later had a town at Spring Garden in Volusia County. Their presence is indicated down to the end of the war in the Peninsula, when they appear to have gone west, probably reuniting with the remainder of the tribe.

The Yuchi who stayed with the Creeks accompanied them west and settled in one body in the northwestern part of the old Creek Nation, in Creek County, Okla.

Population.—For the year 1650 Mooney (1928) makes an estimate of 1,500 for the Yuchi in Georgia, Alabama, and Tennessee, but this does not include the "Westo," for whom, with the Stono, he allows 1,600. The colonial census of 1715 gives 2 Yuchi towns with 130 men and 400 souls, but this probably takes into consideration only 1 band out of 3 or 4. In 1730 the band still on Tennessee River was supposed to contain about 150 men. In 1760, 50 men are reported in the Lower Creek town and 15 in one among the Upper Creeks. In 1777 Bartram (1792) estimated the number of Yuchi warriors in the lower town at 500 and their total population as between 1,000 and 1,500. In 1792 Marbury (1792) reports 300 men, or a population of over 1,000, and Hawkins in 1799 says the Lower Creek Yuchi claimed 250 men. According to the census of 1832–33 there were 1,139 in 2 towns known to have been occupied by Indians of this connection. In 1909 Speck stated that the whole number of Yuchi could "hardly exceed five hundred," but the official report for 1910 gives only 78. That, however, must have been an underestimate as the census of 1930 reported 216. Owing to the number of Yuchi bands, their frequent changes in location, and the various terms applied to them, an exact estimate of their numbers at any period is very difficult. In the first half of the sixteenth century they may well have numbered more than 5,000.

Connection in which they have become noted.—The Yuchi have attained an altogether false reputation as the supposed aborigines of the Gulf region. They were also noted for the uniqueness of their language among the Southeastern tongues. The name is preserved in Euchee, a post hamlet of Meigs County, Tenn.; Eucheeanna, a post village of Walton County, Fla.; Euchee (or Uchee) Creek, Russell County, Ala.; Uchee, a post station of Russell County, Ala.; Uchee Creek, Columbia County, Ga.; and an island in Savannah River near the mouth of the latter.

Yufera. (See Florida.)

FLORIDA

Acuera. Meaning unknown (acu signifies "and" and also "moon").

Connections.—This tribe belonged to the Timucuan or Timuquanan linguistic division of the Muskhogean linguistic family.

Location.—Apparently about the headwaters of the Ocklawaha River.

Towns.—(See **Utina.**)

History.—The Acuera were first noted by De Soto in a letter written at Tampa Bay to the civil cabildo of Santiago de Cuba. According to information transmitted to him by his officer Baltazar de Gallegos, Acuera was "a large town . . . where with much convenience we might winter," but the Spaniards did not in fact pass through it, though, while they were at Ocale, they sent to Acuera for corn. The name appears later in Laudonnière's narrative of the second French expedition to Florida, 1564–65 (1586), as a tribe allied with the Utina. It is noted sparingly in later Spanish documents but we learn that in 1604 there was an encounter between these Indians and Spanish troops and that there were two Acuera missions in 1655, San Luis and Santa Lucía, both of which had disappeared by 1680. The inland position of the Acuera is partly responsible for the few notices of them. The remnant was probably gathered into the "Pueblo de Timucua," which stood near St. Augustine in 1736, and was finally removed to the Mosquito Lagoon and Halifax River in Volusia County, where Tomoka River keeps the name alive.

Population.—This is nowhere given by itself. (See **Utina.**)

Aguacaleyquen, see **Utina.**

Ais.   Meaning unknown; there is no basis for Romans' (1775) derivation from the Choctaw word "isi" (deer).   Also called:

Jece, form of the name given by Dickenson (1699).

Connections.—Circumstantial evidence, particularly resemblance in town names, leads to the conclusion that the Ais language was similar to that of the Calusa and the other south Florida tribes.   (See **Calusa.**)   It is believed that it was connected with the Muskhogean stock.

Location.—Along Indian River on the east coast of the peninsula.

Villages

The only village mentioned by explorers and geographers bears some form of the tribal name.

History.—Fontaneda (1854) speaks of a Biscayan named Pedro who had been held prisoner in Ais, evidently during the sixteenth century, and spoke the Ais language fluently.   Shortly after the Spaniards made their first establishments in the peninsula, a war broke out with the Ais, but peace was concluded in 1570.   In 1597 Governor Mendez de Canço, who traveled along the entire east coast from the head of the Florida Keys to St. Augustine, reported that the Ais chief had more Indians under him than any other.   A little later the Ais killed a Spaniard and two Indians sent to them by Canço for which summary revenge was exacted, and still later a difficulty was created by the escape of two Negro slaves and their marriage with Ais men.   Relations between the Floridian government and these Indians were afterward friendly but efforts to missionize them uniformly failed.   An intimate picture of their condition in 1699 is given by the Quaker Dickenson (1803), who was shipwrecked on the coast farther south and obliged, with his companions, to travel through their territory.   They disappear from history after 1703, but the remnant may have been among those who, according to Romans (1775), passed over to Cuba in 1763, although he speaks of them all as Calusa.

Population.—Mooney (1928) estimates the number of Indians on the southeastern coast of Florida in 1650, including this tribe, the Tekesta, Guacata, and Jeaga, to have been 1,000.   As noted above, the Ais were the most important of these and undoubtedly the largest.   We have no other estimates of population applying to the seventeenth century.   In 1726, 88 "Costa" Indians were reported in a mission farther north and these may have been drawn from the southeast coast.   In 1728, 52 "Costa" Indians were reported.

Connection in which they have become noted.—The Ais were noted as the most important tribe of southeastern Florida, and they were probably responsible for the fact that the watercourse on which they dwelt came to be called Indian River.

Alabama. Early in the eighteenth century the Pawokti, and perhaps some other Alabama bands, lived near Apalachicola River, whence they were driven in 1708. After the Creek-American War a part of the Alabama again entered Florida, but they do not seem to have maintained an independent existence for a very long period. (See Alabama.)

Amacano. A tribe or band perhaps connected with the Yamasee, placed in a mission on the Apalachee coast in 1674 with two others, Chine, and Caparaz (q. v.). The three together had 300 souls.

Amacapiras, see **Macapiras.**

Apalachee. Meaning perhaps "people on the other side" (as in Hitchiti), or it may be cognate with Choctaw apelachi, "a helper."
Connections.—These Indians belonged to the Muskhogean linguistic family, their closest connections having been apparently the Hitchiti and Alabama.
Location.—The Apalachee towns, with few exceptions, were compactly situated in the neighborhood of the present Florida capital, Tallahassee. (See also Georgia, Alabama, Louisiana, and Oklahoma.)

Villages

Aute, 8 or 9 days' journey from the main towns and apparently southwest of them.
Ayubale, 77 leagues from St. Augustine.
Bacica, probably near the present Wacissa River.
Bacuqua, seemingly somewhat removed from the main group of towns.
Calahuchi, north of the main group of towns and not certainly Apalachee.
Cupayca, location uncertain; its name seems to be in Timucua.
Ibitachuco, 75 leagues from St. Augustine.
Iniahica, close to the main group of towns, possibly the Timucua name for one of the others given, since *hica* is the Timucua word for "town."
Ochete, on the coast 8 leagues south of Iniahica.
Ocuia, 84 leagues from St. Augustine.
Ospalaga, 86 leagues from St. Augustine.
Patali, 87 leagues from St. Augustine.
Talimali, 88 leagues from St. Augustine and very likely identical with Iniahica.
Talpatqui, possibly identical with the preceding.
Tomoli, 87 leagues from St. Augustine.
Uzela, on or near Ocilla River.
Yapalaga, near the main group of towns.
Ychutafun, on Apalachicola River.
Yecambi, 90 leagues from St. Augustine.

A few other names are contained in various writings or placed upon sundry charts, but some of these belonged to distinct tribes and were located only temporarily among the Apalachee; others are not mentioned elsewhere but appear to belong in the same category; and still others are simply names of missions and may apply to certain of the towns mentioned above. Thus Chacatos evidently refers to the Chatot tribe, Tama to the Tamaḷi, and Oconi probably to a branch of the Oconee mentioned elsewhere. The Chines were a body of Chatot and derived their name from a chief. Among names which appear only in Spanish we find Santa Fe. Capola and Ilcombe, given on the Popple Map, were probably occupied by Guale and Yamasee refugees. A late Apalachee settlement was called San Marcos.

History.—The Apalachee seem to appear first in history in the chronicles of the Narvaez expedition (Bandelier, 1905). The explorers spent nearly a month in an Apalachee town in the year 1528 but were subjected to constant attacks on the part of the warlike natives, who pursued them during their withdrawal to a coast town named Aute. In October 1539, De Soto arrived in the Apalachee province and remained there the next winter in spite of the unceasing hostility of the natives, who well maintained the reputation for prowess they had acquired 11 years before. Although the province is mentioned from time to time by the first French and Spanish colonists of Florida, it did not receive much attention until the tribes between it and St. Augustine had been pretty well missionized. In a letter written in 1607 we learn that the Apalachee had asked for missionaries and, although one paid a visit to them the next year, the need is reiterated at frequent intervals. It was not until 1633, however, that the work was actually begun. In that year two monks entered the country and the conversion proceeded very rapidly so that by 1647 there were seven churches and convents and eight of the principal chiefs had been baptized. In that year, however, a great rebellion took place. Three missionaries were killed and all of the churches with their sacred objects were destroyed. An expedition sent against the insurgents was repulsed, but shortly afterward the movement collapsed, apparently through a counterrevolution in the tribe itself. After this most of the Apalachee sought baptism and there was no further trouble between them and the Spaniards except for a brief sympathetic movement at the time of the Timucua uprising of 1656. The outstanding complaint on the part of the Indians was that some of them were regularly commandeered to work on the fortifications of St. Augustine. In 1702 a large Apalachee war party was severely defeated by Creek Indians assisted by some English traders, and in 1704 an expedition from South Carolina under Colonel Moore practically destroyed the nation. Moore claims to have carried away the people of three towns and the greater part of the population of four more and to have left but two towns and part of another. Most of these latter appear to have fled to Mobile, where, in 1705, they were granted land on which to settle. The Apalachee who had been carried off by Moore were established near New Windsor, S. C., but when the Yamasee War broke out they joined the hostile Indians and retired for a time to the Lower Creeks. Shortly afterward the English faction among the Lower Creeks became ascendant and the Apalachee returned to Florida, some remaining near their old country and others settling close to Pensacola to be near their relatives about Mobile. By 1718 another Apalachee settlement had been organized by the Spaniards near San Marcos de Apalache and close to their old country. In 1728 we hear of two small Apalachee towns in this neighborhood. Most of them gravitated finally to the neighborhood of Pensacola. In 1764, the year after all French and Spanish possessions east of the Mississippi passed into the hands of Great Britain, the Apalachee, along with several other tribes, migrated into Louisiana, now held by Spain, and settled on Red River, where they and the Taensa conjointly occupied a strip of land between Bayou d'Arro and Bayou Jean de Jean. Most of this land was sold in 1803 and the Apalachee, reduced to a small band, appear to have moved about in the same general region until they disappeared. They are now practically forgotten, though a few mixed-blood Apalachee are still said to be in existence. A few accompanied the Creeks to Oklahoma.

Population.—Mooney (1928) estimates 7,000 Apalachee Indians in 1650, a figure which seems to me to be ample. Governor Salazar's mission-by-mission estimate in 1675 yielded a total of 6,130, and a Spanish memorial dated 1676 gives them a population of 5,000. At the time of Moore's raid there appear to have been about 2,000. The South Carolina Census of 1715 gives 4 Apalachee villages, 275 men, and 638 souls. As the Mobile Apalachee were shortly afterward reduced to 100 men, the number of the entire tribe in 1715 must have been about 1,000. By 1758 they appear to have fallen to not much over 100, and in 1814 Sibley reported but 14 men in the Louisiana band, signifying a total of perhaps 50 (Sibley, 1832). Morse's estimate (1822) of 150 in 1817 is evidently considerably too high.

Connection in which they have become noted.—The Apalachee were mentioned repeatedly as a powerful and warlike people, and this character was attested by their stout resistance to Narvaez and De Soto. The sweeping destruction which overtook them at the hands of the Creeks and Carolinians marks an epoch in Southeastern history. Their name is preserved in Apalachee Bay and River, Fla.; Apalachee River, Ga., Apalachee River, Ala.; and most prominently of all, in the Appalachian Mountains, and other terms derived from them. Tallahassee, the capital of Florida, the name of which signifies

"Old Town," is on the site of San Luis de Talimali, the principal Spanish mission center.   There is a post village named Apalachee in Morgan County, Ga.

Apalachicola.   At times some of the Apalachicola Indians lived south of the present Florida boundary line and they gave their name to the great river which runs through the panhandle of that State.   (See Georgia.)

Calusa.   Said by a Spaniard, Hernando de Escalante Fontaneda, who was a captive among them for many years, to mean "fierce people," but it is perhaps more probable that, since it often appears in the form Carlos, it was, as others assert, adopted by the Calusa chief from the name of the Emperor Charles V, about whose greatness he had learned from Spanish prisoners.

Connections.—From the place names and the few expressions recorded by Fontaneda, I suspect that the Calusa were connected linguistically with the Muskhogean stock and particularly with that branch of it to which the Apalachee and Choctaw belonged, but no definite conclusion on this point is as yet possible.

Location.—On the west coast of the Peninsula of Florida southward of Tampa Bay and including the Florida Keys.   The Indians in the interior, about Lake Okeechobee, while forming a distinct group, seem also to have been Calusa.

Subdivisions

Unknown, except as indicated above.

Villages

In the following list the letters S and I indicate respectively towns belonging to the seacoast division and those of the interior division about Lake Okeechobee. Beyond this allocation the positions of most of the towns may be indicated merely in a general manner, by reference to neighboring towns.

Abir (I), between Ñeguitun and Cutespa.

Alcola (or Chosa), location uncertain.

Apojola Negra, the first word is Timucua; the second seems to be Spanish; location unknown.

Calaobe (S).

Caragara, between Namuguya and Henhenguepa.

Casitoa (S), between Muspa and Cotebo.

Cayovea (S).

Cayucar, between Tonco and Ñeguitun.

Chipi, between Tomçobe and Taguagemae.

Chosa (see Alcola).

Comachica (S).

Cononoguay, between Cutespa and Estegue.

Cotebo, between Casitoa and Coyobia.

Coyobia, between Cotebo and Tequemapo.

Cuchiyaga, said to be southwest from Bahia Honda and 40 leagues northeast of Guarungube, probably on Big Pine Key.

Custavui, south of Jutun.

Cutespa (I), between Abir and Cononoguay.

Elafay, location uncertain.

Enempa (I).

Estame (S), between Metamapo and Sacaspada.

Estantapaca, between Yagua and Queyhicha.

Estegue, between Cononoguay and Tomsobe.

Excuru, between Janar and Metamapo.

Guarungube, "on the point of the Martyrs," and thus probably near Key West.

Guevu (S).

Henhenguepa, between Caragara and Ocapataga.

Janar, between Ocapataga and Escuru.

Judyi, between Satucuava and Soco.

Juestocobaga, between Queyhicha and Sinapa.

Jutun (S), between Tequemapo and Custavui.

Metamapo (S), between Escuru and Estame.

Muspa (S), between Teyo and Casitoa.

Namuguya, between Taguagemae and Caragara.

Ñeguitun, between Cayucar and Abir.

Ño or Non (S).

Ocapataga, between Henhenguepa and Janar.

Queyhicha, between Estantapaca and Juestocobaga.

Quisiyove (S).

Sacaspada (S), between Estame and Satucuava.

Satucuava, between Sacaspada and Judyi.

Sinaesta (S).

Sinapa (S), between Juestocobaga and Tonco.

Soco, between Judyi and Vuebe.

Taguagemae, between Chipi and Namuguya.

Tampa (S), the northernmost town, followed on the south by Yegua, and probably on Charlotte Harbor.

Tatesta (S), between the Tequesta tribe and Cuchiyaga, about 80 leagues north of the latter, perhaps at the innermost end of the Keys.

Tavaguemue (I).

Tequemapo (S), between Coyobia and Jutun.

Teyo, between Vuebe and Muspa.

Tiquijagua (?).

Tomo (S).

Tomsobe (I), between Estegue and Chipi.

Tonco, between Sinapa and Cayucar.

Tuchi (S).

Vuebe, between Soco and Teyo, possibly the same as Guevu.

Yagua (S), between Tampa and Estantapaca.

History.—Most early navigators who touched upon the west coast of Florida must have encountered the Calusa but the first definite appearance of the tribe historically is in connection with shipwrecks of Spanish fleets, particularly the periodical treasure fleet from México, upon the Calusa coast. These catastrophes threw numerous Spanish captives into the hands of the natives and along with them a quantity of gold and silver for which the Calusa shortly became noted. Ponce de Leon visited them in 1513, Miruelo in 1516, Cordova in 1517; and Ponce, during a later expedition in 1521, received from them a mortal wound from which he died after reaching Cuba. Most of our early information regarding the Calusa is obtained from Fontaneda (1854), who was held captive in the tribe from about 1551 to 1569. At the time when St. Augustine was settled attempts were made to establish a post among these Indians and to missionize them, but the post had soon to be withdrawn and the missionary attempt proved abortive. The Calusa do not seem to have been converted to Christianity during the entire period of Spanish control. While their treatment of castaways was restrained, in every other respect they appear to have continued their former manner of existence, except that they resorted more and more to Havana for purposes of trade. Outside of a steady diminution in numbers there is little to report of them until the close of the Seminole War. The Seminole, when hard pressed by the American forces, moved south into the Everglade region and there came into contact with what was left of the Calusa. Romans (1775) states that the last of the Calusa emigrated to Cuba in 1763, but probably the Indians who composed this body were from the east coast and were not true Calusa. The Calusa themselves appear about this time under the name Muspa, which, it will be seen, was the designation of one of their towns. On the movement of the Seminole into their country they became involved in hostilities with the American troops, and a band of Muspa attacked the camp of Colonel Harney in 1839 killing 18 out of 30 men. July 23 of the same year Harney fell upon the Spanish Indians, killed their chief, and hung six of his followers. The same band later killed a botanist named Perrine living on Indian Key and committed other depredations. The Calusa may have been represented by the "Choctaw band" of Indians, which appears among the Seminole shortly after this time. The Seminole now in Oklahoma assert that a body of Choctaw came west with them when they were moved from Florida, but the only thing certain as to the Calusa is that we hear no more about them. Undoubtedly some did not go west and either became incorporated with the Florida Seminole or crossed to Cuba.

Population.—Mooney's (1928) estimate of 3,000 Calusa Indians in 1650 is probably as near the truth as any estimate that could be suggested. No census and very few estimates of the population, even of the most partial character, are recorded. An expedition sent into the Calusa country in 1680 passed through 5 villages said to have had a total population of 960, but this figure can be accepted only with the understanding that these villages were principal centers. In the band that attacked Harney in 1839 there were said to be 250 Indians.

Connection in which they have become noted.—When first discovered the Calusa were famous for the power of their chiefs, the amount of gold which they had obtained from Spanish treasure ships, and for their addiction to human sacrifice. Their name persists in that of Caloosahatchee River and probably also in that of Charlotte Harbor. Another claim to distinction is the adoption by their chief of the name of the great Emperor Charles—if that was indeed the case. The only similar instance would seem to be in the naming of the Delaware Indians, but that was imposed upon the Lenni Lenape, not adopted by them.

Caparaz. A small tribe or band placed in 1674 in connection with a doctrina called San Luis on the Apalachee coast along with two other bands called Amacano and Chine. Possibly they may have been survivors of the Capachequi encountered by De Soto in 1540. The three bands were estimated to contain 300 people.

Chatot. Meaning unknown, but the forms of this word greatly resemble the synonyms of the name Choctaw.

Connections.—The language spoken by this tribe belonged, undoubtedly, to the southern division of the Muskhogean stock.

Location.—West of Apalachicola River, perhaps near the middle course of the Chipola. (See also Georgia, Alabama, and Louisiana).

Villages

From the names of two Spanish missions among them it would appear that there were at least two towns in early times, one called Chacato, after the name of the tribe, and the other Tolentino.

History.—The Chatot are first mentioned in a Spanish document of 1639 in which the governor of Florida congratulates himself on having consummated peace between the Chatot, Apalachicola, and Yamasee on one side and the Apalachee on the other. This, he says, "is an extraordinary thing, because the aforesaid Chacatos never maintained peace with anybody." In 1674 the two missions noted above were established among these people, but the following year the natives rebelled. The disturbance was soon ended by the Spanish officer Florencia, and the Chatot presently settled near the Apalachee town of San Luis, mission work among them being resumed. In 1695, or shortly before, Lower Creek Indians attacked this mission, plundered the church, and carried away 42 Christianized natives. In 1706 or 1707, following on the destruction of the Apalachee towns, the Chatot and several other small tribes living near it were attacked and scattered or carried off captive, and the Chatot fled to Mobile, where they were well received by Bienville and located on the site of the present city of Mobile. When Bienville afterward moved the seat of his government to this place he assigned to them land on Dog River by way of compensation. After Mobile was ceded to the

English in 1763 the Chatot, along with a number of other small tribes near that city, moved to Louisiana. They appear to have settled first on Bayou Boeuf and later on Sabine River. Nothing is heard of them afterward though in 1924 some old Choctaw remembered their former presence on the Sabine. The remnant may have found their way to Oklahoma.

Population.—I would estimate a population of 1,200–1,500 for the Chatot when they were first missionized (1674). When they were settled on the site of Mobile, Bienville (1932, vol. 3, p. 536) says that they could muster 250 men, which would indicate a population of near 900, but in 1725–26 there were but 40 men and perhaps a total population of 140. In 1805 they are said to have had 30 men or about 100 people. In 1817 a total of 240 is returned by Morse (1822), but this figure is probably twice too large.

Connection in which they have become noted.—The Chatot are noted because at one time they occupied the site of Mobile, Ala., and because Bayou Chattique, Choctaw Point, and Choctaw Swamp close by that city probably preserve their name. The Choctawhatchee, which is near their former home, was probably named for them.

Chiaha. A few Creeks of this tribe emigrated from their former towns to Florida before the Creek-American War and after that encounter may have been joined by others. In an early list of Seminole settlements they are credited with one town on "Beech Creek," and this may have been identical with Fulemmy's Town or Pinder Town located on Suwanee River in 1817, which was said to be occupied by Chiaha Indians. The Mikasuki are reported to have branched off from this tribe. (See Georgia.)

Chilucan. A tribe mentioned in an enumeration of the Indians in Florida missions made in 1726. Possibly the name is derived from Muskogee chiloki, "people of a different speech," and since one of the two missions where they are reported was San Buenaventura and elsewhere that mission is said to have been occupied by Mocama Indians, that is, seacoast Timucua, a Timucuan connection is indicated. In the list mentioned, 70 Chilucan were said to be at San Buenaventura and 62 at the mission of Nombre de Dios.

Chine. A small tribe or band associated with two others called Amacano and Caparaz (q. v.) in a doctrina established on the coast of the Apalachee country called San Luis. Other evidence suggests that Chine may be the name of a Chatot chief. Later they may have moved into the Apalachee country, for in a mission list dated 1680 there appears a mission called San Pedro de los Chines. This tribe and the Amacano and Caparaz were said to number 300 individuals in 1674.

Creeks, see **Alabama, Chiaha, Hitchiti, Mikasukee, Muskogee, Oconee, Sawokli, Tawasa,** and **Yuchi.**)

Fresh Water ("Agua Dulce") Indians. A name applied to the people of seven to nine neighboring towns, and for which there is no native equivalent.

Connections.—The same as **Acuera** (q. v.).

Location.—In the coast district of eastern Florida between St. Augustine and Cape Canaveral.

Villages

The following towns are given in this province extending from north to south, but not all of the native names have been preserved:

Anacape, said to have been 20 leagues south of St. Augustine.

Antonico; another possible name is Tunsa.

Equale, location uncertain.

Filache, location uncertain.

Maiaca, a few leagues north of Cape Canaveral and on St. Johns River.

Moloa, south of the mouth of St. Johns River (omitted from later lists).

San Julian, location uncertain.

San Sebastian, on an arm of the sea near St. Augustine, destroyed in 1600 by a flood.

Tocoy, given by one writer as 5 leagues from St. Augustine; by another as 24 leagues.

The names Macaya and Maycoya, which appear in the neighborhood of the last of these are probably synonyms or corruptions of Maiaca, but there seems to have been a sister town of Maiaca at an early date which Fontaneda (1854) calls Mayajuaca or Mayjuaca. In addition to the preceding, a number of town names have been preserved which perhaps belong to places in this province. Some of them may be synonyms of the town names already given, especially of towns like Antonico and St. Julian, the native names of which are otherwise unknown. These include:

Çacoroy, 1½ leagues from Nocoroco.

Caparaca, southwest of Nocoroco.

Chimaucayo, south of St. Augustine.

Çicale, 3 leagues south of Nocoroco.

Colucuchia, several leagues south of Nocoroco.

Disnica, probably south of St. Augustine, though not necessarily in the Fresh Water Province.

Elanogue, near Antonico.

Malaca, south of Nocoroco.

Mogote, in the region of Nocoroco.

Nocoroco, one day's journey south of Matanzas Inlet and on a river called Nocoroco River, perhaps Halifax River.

Perqumaland, south of the last mentioned; possibly two towns, Perqui and Maland.

Pia, south of Nocoroco.

Sabobche, south of Nocoroco.

Tomeo, apparently near or in the Fresh Water province.

Tucura, apparently in the same province as the last mentioned.

Yaocay, near Antonico.

History.—The history of this province differed little from that of the other Timucua provinces, tribes, or confederacies. Ponce de Leon made his landfall upon this coast in 1513. The French had few dealings with the people but undoubtedly met them. Fontaneda (1854) heard of the provinces of Maiaca and Mayajuaca, and later there were two Spanish missions in this territory, San Antonio de Anacape and San Salvador de Maiaca. These appear in the mission list of 1655 and in that of 1680 but from data given with the latter it is evident that Yamasee were then settled at Anacape. All of these Indians were converted rapidly early in the seventeenth century and the population declined with increasing celerity. The last body of Timucua were settled in this district and have left their name in that of Tomoka Creek. (See **Utina.**)

Population.—There are no data on which to give a separate and full statement of the Timucua population in this district. In 1602, however, 200 Indians belonging to it had been Christianized and 100 more were under instruction. (See **Acuera.**)

Guacata. Meaning unknown.

Connections.—On the evidence furnished by place names in this section, the tribe is classified with the south Florida peoples.

Location.—On or near Saint Lucie River in Saint Lucie and Palm Beach Counties.

History.—The Guacata are first mentioned by Fontaneda (1854), who in one place speaks of them as on Lake Mayaimi (Okeechobee), but this probably means only that they ranged across to the lake from the eastern seacoast. Shortly after his conquest of Florida Menendez left 200 men in the Ais country, but the Indians of that tribe soon rose against them and they moved to the neighborhood of the Guacata, where they were so well treated that they called the place Santa Lucia. Next year, however, these Indians rose against them and although they were at first defeated the Spaniards were so hard pressed that they abandoned the place in 1568. They were still an independent body in the time of Dickenson, in 1699, but not long afterward they evidently united with other east coast bands, and they were probably part of those who emigrated to Cuba in 1763.

Population.—No separate estimate has ever been made. (See Ais.)

Guale. In relatively late times many of these Indians were driven from their country into Florida. (See Georgia.)

Hitchiti. The ancient home of the Hitchiti was north of Florida but after the destruction of the earlier tribes of the peninsula, in which they themselves participated, Hitchiti-speaking peoples moved in in great numbers to take their places, so that up to the Creek-American War, the Hitchiti language was spoken by the greater number of

Seminole. The later immigration, as we have indicated above, reduced the Hitchiti element to a minority position, so that what we now call the Seminole language is practically identical with Muskogee. True Hitchiti as distinguished from Hitchiti-speaking peoples who bore other names, do not appear to have been very active in this early movement though Hawkins (1848) mentions them as one of those tribes from which the Seminole were made up. The Hitchiti settlement of Attapulgas or Atap'halgi and perhaps other of the so-called Fowl Towns seem to represent a later immigration into the peninsula. (See Georgia.)

Icafui. Meaning unknown.

Connections.—They were undoubtedly of the Timucuan group though they seem to have been confused at times with a tribe called Cascangue which may have been related to the Muskogee or Hitchiti. On the other hand, Cascangue may have been another name of this tribe, possibly one employed by Creeks or Hitchiti.

Location.—On the mainland and probably in southeastern Georgia near the border between the Timucua and the strictly Muskhogean populations.

Villages

Seven or eight towns are said to have belonged to this tribe but the names of none of them are known with certainty.

History.—Icafui seems to be mentioned first by the Franciscan missionaries who occasionally passed through it on their way to or from interior peoples. It was a "visita" of the missionary at San Pedro (Cumberland Island). Otherwise its history differed in no respect from that of the other Timucuan tribes. (See **Utina.**)

Population.—Separate figures regarding this tribe are wanting. (See Utina.)

Jeaga. Meaning unknown.

Connections.—The Jeaga are classed on the basis of place names and location with the tribes of south Florida, which were perhaps of the Muskhogean division proper.

Location.—On the present Jupiter Inlet, on the east coast of Florida.

Villages

Between this tribe and the Tequesta the names of several settlements are given which may have belonged to one or both of them, viz: Cabista, Custegiyo, Janar, Tavuacio.

History.—The Jeaga tribe is mentioned by Fontaneda (1854) and by many later Spanish writers but it was of minor importance. Near Jupiter Inlet the Quaker Dickenson (1803), one of our best informants regarding the ancient people of the east coast of Florida, was cast ashore in 1699. In the eighteenth century, this tribe was probably merged with the Ais, Tequesta, and other tribes of this coast, and removed with them to Cuba. (See **Ais.**)

Population.—No separate enumeration is known. (See **Ais.**)

Koasati. Appearance of a "Coosada Old Town" on the middle course of Choctawhatchee River on a map of 1823 shows that a band of Koasati Indians joined the Seminole in Florida, but this is all we know of them. (See Alabama.)

Macapiras, or Amacapiras. Meaning unknown. A small tribe which was brought to the St. Augustine missions in 1726 along with some Pohoy, and so apparently from the southwest coast. There were only 24, part of whom died and the rest returned to their old homes before 1728.

Mikasuki. Meaning unknown.

Connections.—These Indians belonged to the Hitchiti-speaking branch of the Muskhogean linguistic family. They are said by some to have branched from the true Hitchiti, but those who claim that they were originally Chiaha (q. v.) are probably correct.

Location.—Their earliest known home was about Miccosukee Lake in Jefferson County. (See also Oklahoma.)

Villages

Alachua Talofa or John Hick's Town, in the Alachua Plains, Alachua County.
New Mikasuki, near Greenville in Madison County.
Old Mikasuki, near Miccosukee Lake.

History.—The name Mikasuki appears about 1778 and therefore we know that their independent status had been established by that date whether they had separated from the Hitchiti or the Chiaha. They lived first at Old Mikasuki and then appear to have divided, part going to New Mikasuki and part to the Alachua Plains. Some writers denounce them as the worst of all Seminole bands, but it is quite likely that, as a tribe differing in speech from themselves, the Muskogee element blamed them for sins they themselves had committed. Old Mikasuki was burned by Andrew Jackson in 1817. Most Mikasuki seem to have remained in Florida where they still constitute a distinct body, the Big Cypress band of Seminole. Those who went to Oklahoma retained a distinct Square Ground as late as 1912.

Population.—Morse (1822) quotes a certain Captain Young to the effect that there were 1,400 Mikasuki in his time, about 1817. This figure is probably somewhat too high though the Mikasuki element is known to have been a large one. They form one entire band among the Florida Seminole.

Connection in which they have become noted.—The Mikasuki attained prominence in the Seminole War. In the form Miccosukee their name has been applied to a lake in Jefferson and Leon Counties, Fla., and a post village in the latter county. In the form Mekusuky it has been given to a village in Seminole County, Okla.

Mocoço, or **Mucoço.** Meaning unknown.

Connections.—They belonged with little doubt to the Timucuan division of the Muskhogean linguistic stock.

Location.—About the head of Hillsboro Bay.

Villages

None are mentioned under any other than the tribal name.

History.—The chief of this tribe gave asylum to a Spaniard named Juan Ortiz who had come to Florida in connection with the expedition of Narvaez. When De Soto landed near the Mocoço town its chief sent Ortiz with an escort of warriors to meet him. Ortiz afterward became De Soto's principal interpreter until his death west of the Mississippi, and the Mocoço chief remained on good terms with the Spaniards as long as they stayed in the neighborhood. There are only one or two later references to the tribe. (See **Utina.**)

Connection in which they have become noted.—The contacts of the Mocoço with De Soto and his followers constitute their only claim to distinction.

Muklasa. A small Creek town whose inhabitants were probably related by speech to the Alabama and Koasati. They are said to have gone to Florida after the Creek War. (See Alabama.)

Muskogee. The first true Creeks or Muskogee to enter Florida seem to have been a body of Eufaula Indians who made a settlement called Chuko tcati, Red House, on the west side of the peninsula some distance north of Tampa Bay.[2] This was in 1761. Other Muskogee drifted into Florida from time to time, but the great immigration took place after the Creek-American War. The newcomers were from many towns, but more particularly those on the Tallapoosa River. They gave the final tone and the characteristic language to the Florida emigrants who had before been dominantly of Hitchiti connection, and therefore the so-called Seminole language is Muskogee, with possibly a few minor changes in the vocabulary. (See Alabama.)

Ocale, or **Etocale.** Meaning unknown, but perhaps connected with Timucua tocala, "it is more than," a comparative verb.

[2] A possible exception to this statement was the temporary entrance of a small body of Coweta Indians under Secoffee, or the Cowkeeper.

Connections.—(See **Acuera.**)

Location.—In Marion County or Levy County north of the bend of the Withlacoochee River.

Villages

Uqueten (first village approaching from the south), and perhaps Itaraholata.

History.—This tribe is first mentioned by the chroniclers of the De Soto expedition. He passed through it in 1539 after crossing Withlacoochee River. Fontaneda also heard of it, and it seems to appear on De Bry's map of 1591. This is the last information that has been preserved.

Population.—Unknown. (See **Acuera** and **Utina.**)

Connection in which they have become noted.—Within comparatively modern times this name was adopted in the form Ocala as that of the county seat of Marion County, Fla. There is a place so called in Pulaski County, Ky.

Oçita, see **Pohoy.**

Oconee. After leaving the Chattahoochee about 1750 the Oconee moved into Florida and established themselves on the Alachua Plains in a town which Bartram calls Cuscowilla. They constituted the first large band of northern Indians to settle in Florida and their chiefs came to be recognized as head chiefs of the Seminole. One of these, Mikonopi, was prominent during the Seminole War, but the identity of the tribe itself is lost after that struggle. Another part of them seem to have settled for a time among the Apalachee (q. v.). (See Georgia.)

Onatheaqua. In the narratives of Laudonnière and Le Moyne this appears as one of the two main Timucua tribes in the northwestern part of Florida, the other being the Hostaqua (or Yustaga). Elsewhere I have suggested that it may have covered the Indians afterward gathered into the missions of Santa Cruz de Tarihica, San Juan de Guacara, Santa Catalina, and Ajoica, where there were 230 Indians in 1675, but that is uncertain. (See **Utina.**)

Osochi. A Creek division thought to have originated in Florida. (See Alabama.)

Pawokti. Meaning unknown.

Connections.—They were probably affiliated either with the Tawasa or the Alabama. In any case there is no reason to doubt that they spoke a Muskhogean dialect, using Muskhogean in the extended sense.

Location.—The earliest known location of the Pawokti seems to have been west of Choctawhatchee River, not far from the shores of the Gulf of México. (See also Alabama.)

History.—Lamhatty (*in* Bushnell, 1908) assigns the Pawokti the above location before they were driven away by northern Indians, evidently Creeks, in 1706-7. Although the name does not appear in any French documents known to me, they probably settled near Mobile along with the Tawasa. At any rate we find them on Alabama River in 1799 a few miles below the present Montgomery and it is assumed they had been there from 1717, when Fort Toulouse was established. Their subsequent history is merged in that of the Alabama (q. v.).

Population.—(See Alabama.)

Pensacola. Meaning "hair people," probably from their own tongue, which in that case was very close to Choctaw.

Connections.—The name itself, and other bits of circumstantial evidence, indicate that the Pensacola belonged to the Muskhogean stock and, as above noted, probably spoke a dialect close to Choctaw.

Location.—In the neighborhood of Pensacola Bay. (See also Mississippi.)

History.—In 1528 the survivors of the Narvaez expedition had an encounter with Indians near Pensacola Bay who probably belonged to this tribe. It is also probable that their territory constituted the province of Achuse or Ochus which Maldonado, the commander of De Soto's fleet, visited in 1539 and whence he brought a remarkably fine "blanket of sable fur." In 1559 a Spanish colony under Tristan de Luna landed in a port called "the Bay of Ichuse," (or "Ychuse") undoubtedly in the same province, but the enterprise was soon given up and the colonists returned to Mexico. The Pensacola tribe seems to be mentioned first by name in Spanish letters dated 1677. In 1686 we learn they were at war with the Mobile Indians. Twelve years afterward, when the Spanish post of Pensacola was established, it is claimed that the tribe had been exterminated by other peoples, but this is an error. It had merely moved farther inland and probably toward the west. They are noted from time to time, and in 1725-6 Bienville (1932, vol. 3, p. 535) particularly describes the location of their village near that of the Biloxi of Pearl River. The last mention of them seems to be in an estimate of Indian population dated December 1, 1764, in which their name appears along with those of six other small tribes. They may have been incorporated finally into the Choctaw or have accompanied one of the smaller Mobile tribes into Louisiana near the date last mentioned.

Population.—In 1725 (or 1726) Bienville (1932, vol. 3, p. 535) says that in the Pensacola village and that of the Biloxi together, there were not more than 40 men. The enumeration mentioned above, made in 1764, gives the total population of this tribe and the Biloxi,

Chatot, Capinans, Washa, Chawasha, and Pascagoula collectively as 251 men.

Connection in which they have become noted.—Through the adoption of their name first for that of Pensacola Bay and secondly for the port which grew up upon it, the Pensacola have attained a fame entirely disproportionate to the aboriginal importance of the tribe. There are places of the name in Yancey County, N. C., and Mayes County, Okla.

Pohoy, Pooy, or **Posoy.** Meaning unknown.

Connections.—They were evidently closely connected with the Timucuan division of the Muskhogean linguistic stock. (See **Utina**).

Location.—On the south shore of Tampa Bay.

Towns.—(See History.)

History.—This tribe, or a part of the same, appears first in history under the names Oçita or Ucita as a "province" in the territory of which Hernando de Soto landed in 1539. He established his headquarters in the town of the head chief on June 1, and when he marched inland on July 15 he left a captain named Calderón with a hundred men to hold this place pending further developments. These were withdrawn at the end of November to join the main army in the Apalachee country. In 1612 these Indians appear for the first time under the name Pohoy or Pooy in the account of an expedition to the southwest coast of Florida under an ensign named Cartaya. In 1675 Bishop Calderón speaks of the "Pojoy River," and in 1680 there is a passing reference to it. Some time before 1726 about 20 Indians of this tribe were placed in a mission called Santa Fe, 9 leagues south of St. Augustine, but they had already suffered from an epidemic and by 1728 the remainder returned to their former homes. (See **Utina**.)

Population.—In 1680 the Pohoy were said to number 300.

Connection in which they have become noted.—The only claim of the Pohoy to distinction is derived from their contacts with the expedition of De Soto.

Potano. Meaning unknown.

Connections.—(See **Utina**.)

Location.—In the territory of the present Alachua County.

Towns

The following places named in the De Soto narratives probably belonged to this tribe: Itaraholata or Ytara, Potano, Utinamocharra or Utinama, Cholupaha, and a town they called Mala-Paz. A letter dated 1602 mentions five towns, and on and after 1606, when missionaries reached the tribe, stations were established called San Francisco, San Miguel, Santa Anna, San Buenaventura, and San Martin(?). There is mention also of a mission station called Apalo.

History.—The name Potano first appears as that of a province through which De Soto passed in 1539. In 1564–65 the French colonists of Florida found this tribe at war with the Utina and assisted the latter to win a victory over them. After the Spaniards had supplanted the French, they also supported the Utina in wars between them and the Potano. In 1584 a Spanish captain sent to invade the Potano country was defeated and slain. A second expedition, however, killed many Indians and drove them from their town. In 1601 they asked to be allowed to return to it and in 1606 missionary work was undertaken among them resulting in their conversion along with most of the other Timucua peoples. Their mission was known as San Francisco de Potano and it appears in the mission lists of 1655 and 1680. In 1656 they took part in a general Timucuan uprising which lasted 8 months. In 1672 a pestilence carried off many and as the chief of Potano does not appear as signatory to a letter written to Charles II by several Timucua chiefs in 1688, it is possible their separate identity had come to an end by that date. Early in the eighteenth century the Timucua along with the rest of the Spanish Indians of Florida were decimated rapidly and the remnant of the Potano must have shared their fate. (See **Utina.**)

Population.—Mooney (1928) estimates the number of Potano Indians at 3,000 in 1650 and this is probably fairly accurate, as the Franciscan missionaries state that they were catechizing 1,100 persons in the 5 towns belonging to the tribe in 1602. In 1675 there were about 160 in the 2 Potano missions. (See **Acuera** and **Utina.**)

Connection in which they have become noted.—The Potano tribe was anciently celebrated as, with one or two possible exceptions, the most powerful of all the Timucua peoples.

Saturiwa. Meaning unknown.

Connections.—(See **Utina.**)

Location.—About the mouth of St. Johns River. Some early writers seem to include Cumberland Island in their jurisdiction.

Villages

Laudonnière (1586) says that the chief of this tribe ruled over 30 subchiefs, but it is uncertain whether these subchiefs represented villages belonging to the tribe, allied tribes, or both. The Spaniards give the following: San Juan del Puerto, the main mission for this province under which were Vera Cruz, Arratobo, Potaya, San Matheo, San Pablo, Hicachirico ("Little Town"), Chinisca, and Carabay. San Diego de Salamototo, near the site of Picolata, on which no villages seem to have depended; and Nuestra Senora de Guadalupe, 3 leagues from St. Augustine, may be classed here somewhat uncertainly.

History.—The Saturiwa were visited by Jean Ribault in 1562 and probably by earlier explorers, but they appear first under their proper name in the chronicles of the Huguenot settlement of Florida of

1564–5. Fort Caroline was built in the territory of the Saturiwa and intimate relations continued between the French and Indians until the former were dispossessed by Spain. The chief, known as Saturiwa at this time, assisted De Gourgues in 1567 to avenge the destruction of his countrymen. It is perhaps for this reason that we find the Spaniards espousing the cause of Utina against Saturiwa 10 years later. The tribe soon submitted to Spain, however, and was one of the first missionized, its principal mission being San Juan del Puerto. There labored Francisco de Pareja to whose grammar and religious works we are chiefly indebted for our knowledge of the Timucua language (Pareja, 1612, 1613, 1886). Like the other Florida Indians, they suffered severely from pestilence in 1617 and 1672. The name of their chief appears among those involved in the Timucua rebellion of 1656, and the names of their missions appear in the list of Bishop Calderón and in that of 1680. We hear nothing more of them, and they evidently suffered the same fate as the other tribes of the group.

Population.—No separate figures for the Saturiwa have been preserved, except that a missionary states in 1602 that there were about 500 Christians among them and in 1675 San Juan del Puerto contained "about thirty persons" and Salamototo "about forty." (See **Utina.**)

Connection in which they have become noted.—The prominence of the Saturiwa was due to the intimate dealings between them and the French colonists. Later the same people, though not under the same name, became a main support of the Spanish missionary movement among the Florida Indians.

Sawokli. A division of Creek Indians belonging to the Hitchiti-speaking group. Anciently it seems to have lived entirely in Florida, but later it moved up into the neighborhood of the Lower Creeks. (See Alabama.)

Seminole. Meaning "one who has camped out from the regular towns," and hence sometimes given as "runaway," but there is too much onus in this rendering. Prof. H. E. Bolton believes it was adopted from Spanish *cimarron* meaning "wild."

> Ikanafáskalgi, "people of the point," a Creek name.
> Ikaniúksalgi, "peninsula people," own name.
> Isti seminole, "Seminole people."
> Lower Creeks, so called by Bartram (1792).
> Ungiayó-rono, "peninsula people," Huron name.

Connections.—As implied above, the Seminole removed from the Creek towns and constituted just before the last Seminole War a fair representation of the population of those towns: perhaps two-thirds Creek proper or Muskogee, and the remaining third Indians of the Hitchiti-speaking towns, Alabama, Yamasee, and besides a band of

Yuchi, latterly a few of the original Indian inhabitants of southern Florida.

Location.—The Seminole towns were first planted about Apalachicola River, in and near the old Apalachee country and in the Alachua country in the central part of the State, although a few were scattered about Tampa Bay and even well down the east coast as far south as Miami. They did not enter the Everglade section of the State until toward the end of the last Seminole War. As a result of that war, the greater part were removed to the territory now constituting Seminole County, Okla. A few remained in their old territory and their descendants are there today.

Villages

Ahapopka, near the head of Ocklawaha River.

Ahosulga, 5 miles south of New Mikasuki, perhaps in Jefferson County.

Alachua, near Ledwiths Lake.

Alafiers, probably a synonym for some other town name, perhaps McQueen's Village, near Alafia River.

Alapaha, probably on the west side of the Suwannee just above its junction with the Allapaha.

Alligator, said to be a settlement in Suwannee County.

Alouko, on the east side of St. Marks River 20 miles north of St. Marks.

Apukasasoche, 20 miles west of the head of St. Johns River.

Attapulgas: first location, west of Apalachicola River in Jackson or Calhoun Counties; second location inland in Gadsden County.

Beech Creek, exact location unknown.

Big Cypress Swamp, in the "Devil's Garden" on the northern edge of Big Cypress Swamp, 15 to 20 miles southwest of Lake Okeechobee.

Big Hammock, north of Tampa Bay.

Bowlegs' Town, chief's name, on Suwannee River and probably known usually under another name.

Bucker Woman's Town, on Long Swamp east of Big Hammock.

Burges' Town, probably on or near Flint or St. Marys River, southwestern Georgia.

Calusahatchee, on the river of the same name and probably occupied by Calusa Indians.

Capola, east of St. Marks River.

Catfish Lake, on a small lake in Polk County nearly midway between Lake Pierce and Lake Rosalie, toward the headwaters of Kissimmee River.

Chefixico's Old Town, on the south side of Old Tallahassee Lake, 5 miles east of Tallahassee.

Chetuckota, on the west bank of Pease Creek, below Pease Lake, west central Florida.

Choconikla, on the west side of Apalachicola River, probably in Jackson County.

Chohalaboohulka, probably identical with Alapaha.

Chukochati, near the hammock of the same name.

Cohowofooche, 23 miles northwest of St. Marks.

Cow Creek, on a stream about 15 miles northeast of the entrance of Kissimmee River.

Cuscowilla (see Alachua).

Etanie, west of St. Johns River and east of Black Creek.

Etotulga, 10 miles east of Old Mikasuki.

Fish-eating Creek, 5 miles from a creek emptying into Lake Okeechobee.

Fulemmy's Town, perhaps identical with Beech Creek, Suwannee River.

Hatchcalamocha, near Drum Swamp, 18 miles west of New Mikasuki.

Hiamonee, on the east bank of Ocklocknee River, probably on Lake Iamonia.

Hitchapuksassi, about 20 miles from the head of Tampa Bay and 20 miles southeast of Chukochati.

Homosassa, probably on Homosassa River.

Iolee, 60 miles above the mouth of Apalachicola River on the west bank at or near Blountstown.

John Hicks' Town, west of Payne's Savannah.

King Heijah's Town, or Koe Hadjo's Town, consisted of Negro slaves, probably in Alachua County.

Lochchiocha, 60 miles east of Apalachicola River and near Ocklocknee River.

Loksachumpa, at the head of St. Johns River.

Lowwalta (probably for Łiwahali), location unknown.

McQueen's Village, on the east side of Tampa Bay, perhaps identical with Alafiers.

Miami River, about 10 miles north of the site of Fort Dallas, not far from Biscayne Bay, on Little Miami River.

Mulatto Girl's Town, south of Tuscawilla Lake.

Negro Town, near Withlacoochee River, probably occupied largely by runaway slaves.

New Mikasuki, 30 miles west of Suwannee River, probably in Madison County.

Notasulgar, location unknown.

Ochisi, at a bluff so called on the east side of Apalachicola River.

Ochupocrassa, near Miami.

Ocilla, at the mouth of Aucilla River on the east side.

Oclackonayahe, above Tampa Bay.

Oclawaha, on Ocklawaha River, probably in Putnam County.

Oithlakutci, on Little River 40 miles east of Apalachicola River.

Okehumpkee, 60 miles southwest from Volusia.

Oktahatki, 7 miles northeast of Sampala.

Old Mikasuki, near Miccosukee in Leon County.

Oponays, "back of Tampa Bay," probably in Hillsboro or Polk Counties.

Owassissas, on an eastern branch of St. Marks River and probably near its head.

Payne's Town, near Koe Hadjo's Town, occupied by Negroes.

Picolata, on the east bank of St. Johns River west of St. Augustine.

Pilaklikaha, about 120 miles south of Alachua.

Pilatka, on or near the site of Palatka, probably the site of a Seminole town and of an earlier town as well.

Red Town, at Tampa Bay.

Sampala, 26 miles above the forks of the Apalachicola on the west bank, in Jackson County, or in Houston County, Ala.

Santa Fe, on the river of the same name, perhaps identical with Washitokha.

Sarasota, at or near Sarasota.

Seleuxa, at the head of Aucilla River.

Sitarky, evidently named after a chief, between Camp Izard and Fort King, West Florida.

Spanawalka, 2 miles below Iolee and on the west bank of Apalachicola River.

Suwannee, on the west bank of Suwannee River in Lafayette County.

Talakhacha, on the west side of Cape Florida on the seacoast.

Tallahassee, on the site of present Tallahassee.

Tallahassee or Spring Gardens, 10 miles from Volusia, occupied by Yuchi.

Talofa Okhase, about 30 miles west southwest from the upper part of Lake George.

Taluachapkoapopka, a short distance west of upper St. Johns River, probably at the present Apopka.

Tocktoethla, 10 miles above the junction of Chattahoochee and Flint Rivers.

Tohopki lagi, probably near Miami.

Topananaulka, 3 miles west of New Mikasuki.

Topkegalga, on the east side of Ocklocknee River near Tallahassee.

Totstalahoeetska, on the west side of Tampa Bay.

Tuckagulga, on the east side of Ocklocknee River between it and Hiamonee.

Tuslalahockaka, 10 miles west of Walalecooche.

Wacahoota, location unknown.

Wachitokha, on the east side of Suwannee River between Suwannee and Santa Fe Rivers.

Wakasassa, on the coast east of the mouth of Suwannee River.

Wasupa, 2 miles from St. Marks River and 18 miles from St. Marks itself.

Wechotookme, location unknown.

Welika, 4 miles east of the Tallahassee town.

Wewoka, at Wewoka, Okla.

Willanoucha, at the head of St. Marks River, perhaps identical with Alouko.

Withlacoochee, on Withlacoochee River, probably in Citrus or Sumter County.

Withlako, 4 miles from Clinch's battle ground.

Yalacasooche, at the mouth of Ocklawaha River.

Yulaka, on the west side of St. Johns River, 35 miles from Volusia or Dexter.

Yumersee, at the head of St. Marks River, 2 miles north of St. Marks, a settlement of Yamasee. (See Georgia.)

History.—The origin of the Seminole has already been given (p. 112). The nucleus of the nation was constituted by a part of the Oconee, who moved into Florida about 1750 and were gradually followed by other tribes, principally of the Hitchiti connection. The first true Muskogee to enter the peninsula were some of the Indians of Lower Eufaula, who came in 1767[3] but these were mixed with Hitchiti and others. There was a second Muskogee immigration in 1778, but after the Creek-American War of 1813–14 a much greater immigration occurred from the Creek Nation, mainly from the Upper Towns, and as the great majority of the newcomers were Muskogee, the Seminole became prevailingly a Muskogee people, what is now called the Seminole language being almost pure Muskogee. Later there were two wars with the Whites; the first from 1817–18, in which Andrew Jackson lead the American forces; and the second, from 1835 to 1842, a long and bitter contest in which the Indians demonstrated to its fullest capacity the possibilities of guerrilla warfare in a semitropical, swampy country. Toward the end of the struggle the Indians were forced from northern and central Florida into the Everglade section of the State. This contest is particularly noteworthy on account of the personality of Osceola, the brains of Seminole resistance, whose capture by treachery is an ineffaceable blot upon all who were connected with it and incidentally upon the record of the American

---

[3] But see footnote p. 134.

Army. Diplomacy finally accomplished what force had failed to effect—the policy put in practice by Worth at the suggestion of General E. A. Hitchcock. The greater part of the hostile Indians surrendered and were sent to Oklahoma, where they were later granted a reservation of their own in the western part of the Creek Nation. Both the emigrants, who have now been allotted, and the small number who stayed behind in Florida have since had an uneventful history, except for their gradual absorption into the mass of the population, an absorption long delayed in the case of the Florida Seminole but nonetheless certain.

Population.—Before the Creek-American war the number of Seminole was probably about 2,000; after that date the best estimates give about 5,000. Exclusive of one census which seems clearly too high, figures taken after the Seminole war indicate a gradual reduction of Seminole in Oklahoma from considerably under 4,000 to 2,500 in 1851. A new census, in 1857, gave 1,907, and after that time little change is indicated though actually the amount of Indian blood was probably declining steadily. In Florida the figures were: 370 in 1847, 348 in 1850, 450 in 1893, 565 in 1895, 358 in 1901, 446 in 1911, 600 in 1913, 562 in 1914, 573 in 1919, 586 in 1937. In 1930 there were 1,789 in Oklahoma, 227 in Florida, and 32 scattered in other States.

Connection in which they have become noted.—The chief claim of this tribal confederation to distinction will always be the remarkable war which they sustained against the American Nation, the losses in men and money which they occasioned having been out of all proportion to the number of Indians concerned. The county in Oklahoma where most of the Seminole were sent at the end of the great war bears their name, as does a county in Florida, and it will always be associated with the Everglade country, where they made their last stand. Towns or post villages of the name are in Baldwin County, Ala.; Seminole County, Okla.; Armstrong County, Pa.; and Gaines County, Tex.

Surruque. Meaning unknown.

Connections.—Somewhat doubtful, but they were probably of the Timucuan linguistic group. (See **Utina.**)

Location.—At or very close to Cape Canaveral.

History.—The Surruque appear first in history as the "Sorrochos" of Le Moyne's map (1875), and his "Lake Sarropé" also probably derived its name from them. About the end of the same century, the sixteenth, trouble arose between them and the Spaniards, in consequence of which the Spanish governor fell upon a Surruque town, killed 60 persons and captured 54. Later they probably united with the Timucua people and shared their fortunes.

Population.—No estimate is possible. (See **Utina.**)

Tacatacuru. The meaning is unknown, though it seems to have something to do with "fire" (taca).

Connections.—(See **Utina.**)

Location.—On Cumberland Island to which the name Tacatacuru was applied.

Villages

It is probable that the same name was used for its chief town, which was missionized by the Spaniards under the name of San Pedro Mocama. Under this mission were those of Santo Domingo and Santa Maria de Sena.

History.—The chief of Tacatacuru (now Cumberland Island), or of the neighboring mainland, met Jean Ribault in 1562 and seems to have remained on good terms with the French during their occupancy of Fort Caroline in 1564–65. He, or a successor, is mentioned among those who joined De Gourgues in his attack upon the Spaniards in 1567, but soon afterward they made peace with Spain and one chief, Don Juan, was of great assistance to the white men in many ways, particularly in driving back the Guale Indians after their rising in 1597. This chief died in 1600, and was succeeded by his niece. The church built by these Indians was said to be as big as that in St. Augustine. The good relations which subsisted between the Tacatacuru Indians and the Spaniards do not appear to have been broken by the Timucua rebellion of 1656. By 1675 the tribe had abandoned Cumberland Island and it was occupied by Yamasee. The mission of San Pedro Mocama consequently does not appear in the mission list of 1680, although it is in that of 1655.[4] The tribe was subsequently amalgamated with the other Timucua peoples and shared their fortunes. (See **Utina.**)

Population.—There is no estimate of the number of Tacatacuru distinct from that of the other Timucua. The missionary stationed among them in 1602 notes that there were then 8 settlements and 792 Christianized Indians in his province, but this province may not have been confined to the tribe. In that year Santo Domingo served 180 Christians and Santa Maria de Sena 112.

Tawasa. Meaning unknown.

Connections.—They spoke a dialect belonging to the Timucuan division of the Muskhogean linguistic family, intermediate between Timucua proper and Choctaw, Hitchiti, Alabama, and Apalachee.

Location.—In 1706–7 in west Florida about the latitude of the junction of the Chattahoochee and Flint Rivers; at an earlier time and again later they were on the Alabama near the present Montgomery. (See also **Louisiana.**)

---

[4] I have stated elsewhere (Swanton, 1946, p. 187) that the name of this mission was wanting in the list drawn up in 1655. I should have given the date as 1680.

Villages

They usually occupied only one town but Autauga on Autauga Creek in the southeastern part of Autauga County, Ala., is said to have belonged to them.

History.—De Soto found the Tawasa near the Montgomery site in 1540. Some time during the next century and a half they moved to the neighborhood of Apalachicola River, but in 1707 they were attacked by the Creeks, who captured some of them, while the greater part fled to the French and were by them given lands near the present Mobile. They occupied several different sites in that neighborhood but in 1717 they moved back to the region where De Soto found them, their main village being in the northwestern suburbs of the present Montgomery. After the Treaty of Fort Jackson in 1814, they were compelled to abandon this place and move into the Creek territories between the Coosa and Talapoosa Rivers, where they remained until the main migration beyond the Mississippi. Previous to this, some of them had gone with other Alabama into Louisiana and they followed their fortunes. The name was remembered by Alabama in Polk County, Tex., until within a few years.

Population.—The French census of 1760 returned 40 Tawasa men and the Georgia census of 1792 "about 60." The census of 1832-33 gives 321 Indians in towns called Tawasa and Autauga, but all of these were quite certainly not Tawasa Indians in the strict application of that term. (See Alabama.)

Connection in which they have become noted.—The Tawasa tribe will be remembered ethnologically on account of the rescue of so much important information regarding the early history of themselves and their neighbors through the captive Indian Lamhatty (*in* Bushnell, 1908), who made his way into Virginia in 1708, and on account of the still more important vocabulary obtained from him.

Tekesta or Tequesta. Meaning unknown.

Connections.—The language of this tribe was probably connected with the languages of the other peoples of the southeast coast of Florida and with that of the Calusa, and may have been Muskhogean.

Location.—In the neighborhood of Miami.

Villages

Besides Tekesta proper, the main town, four villages are mentioned between that and the next tribe to the north, the Jeaga, to whom some of the villages may have belonged. These were, in order from south to north: Tavuacio, Janar, Cabista, and Custegiyo.

History.—The Tekesta do not appear in history much before the time of Fontaneda, who was a captive among the Calusa from 1551 to 1569. In 1566 we learn that they protected certain Spaniards from the Calusa chief, although the latter is sometimes regarded as their overlord. A post was established in their country in 1566 but abandoned 4 years later. Attempts made to convert them to Christianity at that time were without success. In 1573 they are said to have been converted by Pedro Menendez Marques, but later they returned to their primitive beliefs. It was these Indians who, according to Romans (1775), went to Cuba in 1763 along with some others from this coast.

Population.—Mooney (1928) estimates that in 1650 there were 1,000 Indians on the southeast coast of Florida. According to Romans those who went to Cuba in 1763 had 30 men. Adair (1775) says there were 80 families.

Connection in which they have become noted.—Although the name has found ńo topographical lodgement, the Tekesta may be remembered as the earliest known body of people to occupy the site of Miami.

Tocobaga. Meaning unknown, though toco means in Timucua "to come out," "to proceed from."

Connections.—(See **Utina.**)

Location.—About Old Tampa Bay.

Villages

The main town was at or near Safety Harbor at the head of Old Tampa Bay.

History.—Narvaez probably landed in the territory of this tribe in 1528, but his chroniclers speak of meeting very few Indians. Eleven years later De Soto's expedition disembarked just south in Tampa Bay but came into little contact with this tribe. Two years after driving the French from St. Johns River in 1565, Menendez visited Tocobaga, and left a captain and 30 soldiers among them, all of whom were wiped out the year following. In 1612 a Spanish expedition was sent to punish the chiefs of Pohoy and Tocobaga because they had attacked Christian Indians, but spent little time in the latter province. There is no assured reference to a mission nearer than Acuera, nor do the Tocobaga appear among the tribes which participated in the great Timucua revolt of 1656. Ultimately it is probable that they joined the other Timucua and disappeared with them, though they may have united with the Calusa. It is also possible that they are the "Tompacuas" who appear later in the Apalachee country, and if so they may have been the Indians placed in 1726 in a mission near St. Augustine called San Buenaventura under the name "Macapiras" or "Amacapiras." (See **Utina.**)

Population.—Unknown. (See **Utina.**)

Connection in which they have become noted.—The principal claim to notoriety on the part of the Tocobaga is the fact that Narvaez landed in their country in 1528.

Ucita, see **Pohoy.**

Utina or Timucua. The first name, which probably refers to the chief and means "powerful," is perhaps originally from uti, "earth," while the second name, Timucua, is that from which the linguistic stock, or rather this Muskhogean subdivision of it, has received its name.

Connections.—As given above.

Location.—The territory of the Utina seems to have extended from the Suwannee to the St. Johns and even eastward of the latter, though some of the subdivisions given should be rated as independent tribes. (See **Timucua** under Georgia.)

Towns

Laudonnière (1586) states that there were more than 40 under the Utina chief, but among them he includes "Acquera" (Acuera) and Moquoso far to the south and entirely independent, so that we are uncertain regarding the status of the others he gives, which are as follows: Cadecha, Calanay, Chilili, Eclauou, Molona, Omittaqua, and Onachaquara.

As the Utina, with the possible exception of the Potano, was the leading Timucua division and gave its name to the whole, and as the particular tribe to which each town mentioned in the documents belonged cannot be given, it will be well to enter all here, although those that can be placed more accurately will be inserted in their proper places.

In De Soto's time Aguacaleyquen or Caliquen seems to have been the principal town. In the mission period we are told that the chief lived at Ayaocuto.

Acassa, a town inland from Tampa Bay.

Aguacaleyquen, a town in the province of Utina between Suwannee and Santa Fe Rivers.

Ahoica, probably near the Santa Fe River.

Alachepoyo, inland from Tampa Bay.

Alatico, probably on Cumberland Island.

Albino, 40 leagues or 4 days inland from St. Augustine and within 1½ to 2 leagues of two others called Tucuro and Utiaca.

Alimacani, on an island of the same name not far north of the mouth of St. Johns River.

Amaca, inland from Tampa Bay.

Anacapa, in the Fresh Water Province 20 leagues south of St. Augustine.

Anacharaqua, location unknown.

Antonico, in the Fresh Water Province.

Apalu, in the province of Yustaga.

Arapaja, 70 leagues from St. Augustine, Probably on Alapaha River.

Araya, south of the Withlacoochee River.

Archaha, location unknown.

Assile, on or near Aucilla River.

Astina, location unknown.

Atuluteca, probably near San Pedro or Cumberland Island.

Ayacamale, location unknown.

Ayaocute, in the Utina country 34 leagues from St. Augustine.

Ayotore, inland from Cumberland Island and probably southwest.

Beca, location unknown.

Becao, location unknown.

Bejesi, location unknown, perhaps the Apalachee town of Wacissa.

Cachipile, 70 leagues west of St. Augustine.

Çacoroy, south of St. Augustine and 1½ leagues from Nocoroco, probably in the Fresh Water Province.

Cadecha, allied with Utina.

Calany, allied with Utina.

Caparaca, south of St. Augustine, southwest of Nocoroco and probably in the Fresh Water Province.

Casti, location unknown.

Cayuco, near Tampa Bay.

Chamini, 70 leagues west of St. Augustine.

Chimaucayo, south of St. Augustine.

Chinica, 1½ leagues from St. Augustine.

Cholupaha, south of Aguacaleyquen in the Potano Province.

Chuaquin, 60 leagues west of St. Augustine.

Çicale, south of St. Augustine and 3 leagues south of Nocoroco, perhaps in the Fresh Water Province.

Cilili, said to be a Utina town.

Colucuchia, several leagues south of Nocoroco.

Coya, location unknown.

Disnica, south of St. Augustine, perhaps should be Tisnica.

Eçalamototo, on the site of Picolata.

Eçita, near Tampa Bay, possibly a variant of Oçita.

Eclauou, location unknown.

Edelano, on an island of the same name in St. Johns River.

Elajay, location unknown, perhaps Calusa.

Elanogue, in the Fresh Water Province near Antonico.

Emola, location unknown.

Enecaque, location unknown.

Equale, in the Fresh Water Province.

Ereze, inland from Tampa Bay.

Esquega, a town or tribe on the west coast.

Exangue, near Cumberland Island.

Filache, in the Fresh Water Province.

Guacara, on Suwannee River in northwestern Florida.

Guaçoco, probably a town on a plain so called in the Urriparacoxi country.

Heliocopile, location unknown.

Helmacape, location unknown.

Hicachirico ("Little town"), one league from the mission of San Juan del Puerto, which was probably at the mouth of St. Johns River in the Saturiwa Province.

Hiocaia, the probable name of a town giving its name to a chief, location unknown.

Huara, inland from Cumberland Island.

Itaraholata, south of Potano, Potano Province.

Juraya, a rancheria, apparently in the Timucua territory.

Laca, another name for Eçalamototo.

Lamale, inland from Cumberland Island.

Luca, between Tampa Bay and the Withlacoochee River in the Urriparacoxi country.

Machaba, 64 leagues from St. Augustine, near the northern border of the Timucua country inland.

Maiaca, the town of the Fresh Water Province most distant from St. Augustine, a few leagues north of Cape Canaveral and on St. Johns River.

Malaca, south of Nocoroco.

Marracou, location unknown.

Mathiaqua, location unknown.

Mayajuaca, near Maiaca.

Mayara, on lower St. Johns River.

Mocama, possibly a town on Cumberland Island, province of Tacatacuru, but probably a province.

Mogote, south of St. Augustine in the region of Nocoroco.

Moloa, on the south side of St. Johns River near its mouth, province of Saturiwa.

Napa, on an island one league from Cumberland Island.

Napituca, north of Aguacaleyquen, province of Utina.

Natobo, a mission station and probably native town 2½ leagues from San Juan del Puerto at the mouth of St. Johns River, province of Saturiwa.

Nocoroco, at the mouth of a river, perhaps Halifax River, one day's journey south of Matanzas Inlet, Fresh Water Province.

Ocale, in a province of the same name in the neighborhood of the present Ocala.

Oçita, probably on Terra Ceia Island, on Hillsborough Bay.

Onathaqua, a town or tribe near Cape Canaveral.

Osigubede, a chief and probably town on the west coast.

Panara, inland from Cumberland Island.

Parca, location unknown.

Patica, on the seacoast 8 leagues south of the mouth of St. Johns River.

Patica, on the west bank of St. Johns River in the Utina territory.

Pebe, a chief and probably a town on the west coast.

Pentoaya, at the head of Indian River.

Perquymaland, south of Nocoroco; possibly the names of two towns, Perqui and Maland, run together.

Pia, on the east coast south of Nocoroco.

Pitano, a mission station and probably a native town a league and a half from Puturiba.

Pohoy, a town or province, or both, at Tampa Bay, and perhaps a synonym of Oçita.

Potano, the principal town of the Potano tribe, on the Alachua plains.

Potaya, 4 leagues from San Juan del Puerto at the mouth of St. Johns River.

Puala, near Cumberland Island.

Punhuri, inland from Cumberland Island.

Puturiba, probably near the northern end of Cumberland Island, province of Tacatacuru. There was another town of the same name west of the Suwannee River.

Sabobche, near the coast south of Nocoroco.

Saint Julian, in the Fresh Water Province.

San Mateo, about 2 leagues from San Juan del Puerto at the mouth of St. Johns River, province of Saturiwa.

San Pablo, about 1½ leagues from San Juan del Puerto, province of Saturiwa.

San Sebastian, on an arm of the sea near St. Augustine.

Sarauahi, a quarter of a league from San Juan del Puerto.

Sena, on an "inlet" north of the mouth of St. Johns River, perhaps Amelia River.

Siyagueche, near Cape Canaveral.

Socochuno, location unknown.

Soloy, not far from St. Augustine and probably on the river called Seloy by the French.

Surruque, a town or tribe near Cape Canaveral.

Tacatacuru, the name of Cumberland Island and Province, and perhaps of the chief town, on the mainland side of the island near the southern end, 2 leagues from the Barra de San Pedro.

Tafocole, inland from Tampa Bay.

Tahupa, inland from Cumberland Island.

Tanpacaste, a chief and perhaps town north of Pohoy, i. e., north of Tampa Bay.

Tarihica, 54 leagues from St. Augustine, and perhaps in the Onatheaqua Province.

Tocaste, on a large lake south of the Withlacoochee River, province of Urriparacoxi.

Tocoaya, very near Cumberland Island.

Tocobaga, the chief town of the province so called, in Safety Harbor, Tampa Bay.

Tocoy, in the Fresh Water Province 5 leagues south of St. Augustine.

Tolapatafi, probably toward the west coast of the peninsula of Florida near Aucilla River.

Toloco, location unknown.

Tomeo, near the Fresh Water Province.

Tucura, near the Fresh Water Province.

Tucuro, see Abino.

Tunsa, possibly a synonym of Antonico.

Uçachile, a town or tribe in the Yustaga Province, perhaps the mother town of the Osochi.

Uqueten, the southernmost village of the province of Ocale on Withlacoochee River entered by De Soto.

Urica, 60 leagues from St. Augustine.

Uriutina, just north of the river of Aguacaleyquen, perhaps at Lake City.

Urubia, near Cape Canaveral and 1½ leagues from the town of Surruque.

Utayne, inland from Cumberland Island.

Utiaca, see Abino.

Utichini, inland from Cumberland Island and within a league and a half of Puturiba.

Utinamocharra, 1 day's journey north of Potano, Potano Province.

Vera Cruz, half a league from San Juan del Puerto, province of Saturiwa.

Vicela, a short distance south of Withlacoochee River, province of Urriparacoxi.

Xapuica, near the Guale country, perhaps a synonym of Caparaca.

Xatalalano, inland from Cumberland Island.

Yaocay, near Antonico in the Fresh Water Province.

Ycapalano, inland from Cumberland Island and probably within half a league or a league of Puturiba.

Yufera, inland and probably northwest from Cumberland Island.

History.—The Utina were evidently those Indians occupying the province called Aguacaleyquen which De Soto passed through in 1539. In 1564 the French came in contact with them after the establishment of Fort Caroline. On one occasion they sent a contingent to help them defeat the neighboring Potano. After the Spaniards had supplanted the French, the Timucua allied themselves with the former and in 1576 or 1577 a body of soldiers was sent to support them against several neighboring tribes. They were missionized at a comparatively early date, and afterward followed the fortunes of the rest of the Timucua.

Following is a brief over-all sketch of the history of the tribes constituting the Timucuan group. They first came into contact with Europeans during Ponce de Leon's initial expedition in 1513 when the peninsula and subsequently the State received its name. Narvaez in 1528 and De Soto in 1539 passed through the country of the western tribes. Ribault visited those on and near St. Johns River in 1562, and the French settlers of Fort Caroline on that river in 1564–65 were in close contact with them. A considerable part of our knowledge regarding these Indians is contained in the records of that colony. The Spaniards supplanted the French in 1565 and gradually conquered the Timucua tribes while the Franciscans missionized them. Our knowledge of the Timucua language is derived mainly from religious works by the missionaries Pareja and Mouilla and a grammar compiled by the former. During the early half of the seventeenth century the missions were in a flourishing condition but a general rebellion in 1656 occasioned some losses by death and exile. They also suffered severely from pestilences which raged in the missions in 1613–17, 1649–50, and 1672. It is probable that some decline in population took place even before the great rebellion but that and the epidemics occasioned considerable losses. Toward the end of the seventeenth century, however, all the Florida Indians began to suffer from the invasion of Creek and Yuchi Indians to the northward, and this was accentuated after the break-up of the Apalachee in 1704 by the expedition under Moore. Most of the remaining Timucua were then concentrated into missions near St. Augustine, but this did not secure immunity against further attacks by the English and their Indian allies. Sometime after 1736 the remnants of these people seem to have removed to a stream in the present Volusia County which in the form Tomoka bears their name. Here they disappear from history, and it is probable that they were swallowed up by the invading Seminole.

Population.—The Timucua, in the wide extent of the term, are estimated by Mooney (1928) to have numbered 13,000 in 1650, including 3,000 Potano, 1,000 Hostaqua, 8,000 Timucua proper and their allies, and 1,000 Tocobaga. In a letter dated February 2, 1635, it is asserted that 30,000 Christian Indians were connected with the 44 missions then maintained in the Guale and Timucua provinces. While this figure is probably too high, it tends to confirm Mooney's (1928) estimate. In 1675 Bishop Calderón of Cuba states that he confirmed 13,152 in the four provinces of Timucua, Guale, Apalache, and Apalachicoli, but Governor Salazar estimates only 1,400 in the Timucua missions that year. Later, pestilences decimated the Timucua very rapidly, and their ruin was completed by attacks of the English and the northern Indians, so that by 1728 the single town which seems to have contained most of the survivors had but 15 men and 20 women. Eight years later 17 men were reported there. Not long after this time the tribe disappears entirely, though it is highly probable that numbers of individuals who had belonged to it had made their homes with other Indians.

As to the Utina tribe by itself, we have a missionary letter dated 1602 which estimates its population as 1,500, in this case probably an understatement.

Connection in which they have become noted.—This tribe, known as the Utina or Timucua, is noteworthy (1) for having given its name to the peoples of the Timucuan or Timuquanan stock now regarded as part of the Muskogean family, and (2) as having been, next perhaps to the Potano, the most powerful tribe constituting that stock.

The Timucuan group has left its name in that of the river above mentioned.

Yamasee. Some tribes affiliated with the Yamasee settled in the Apalachee country in the latter part of the seventeenth century. The great body came to Florida from South Carolina after their war with the English colonists in 1715, and most of them remained in the northeastern part of the peninsula. Their final appearance is as the Ocklawaha band of Seminole. Part of them moved west, however, and settled near Mobile, and either this or a third party lived among the Creeks for a time, after which they seem to have returned to west Florida, where they were represented by the "Yumersee" town of the Seminole. A considerable number of them were captured by the Creek Indians and incorporated with them. (See Georgia.)

Yuchi. In the seventeenth century a body of Yuchi established themselves west of Apalachicola River, but moved north to join the Upper Creeks before 1761. At a much later date a body of eastern Yuchi joined the Seminole and in 1823 had a settlement called Tallahassee or Spring Gardens 10 miles from Volusia. They probably moved to Oklahoma at the end of the last Seminole war. (See Georgia.)

Yufera. This is the name of a town or group of towns reported as located somewhere inland from Cumberland Island, and perhaps in the present territory of Georgia. The name is derived through Timucua informants but it may have referred to a part of the Muskogee tribe called Eufaula.

Yui. Meaning unknown.

Connections.—(See **Utina.**)

Location.—On the mainland 14 leagues inland from Cumberland Island and probably in the southeastern part of the present state of Georgia.

Villages

They had five villages but the names of these are either unknown or unidentifiable.

History.—The name of the Yui appears first in Spanish documents. They were visited by the missionary at San Pedro (Cumberland Island) and appear to have been Christianized early in the seventeenth century. No individual mission bore their name and they. are soon lost sight of, their history becoming that of the other Timucua tribes.

Population.—The missionaries estimated more than 1,000 Indians in this province in 1602. (See **Utina.**)

Yustaga. Meaning unknown.

Connections.—No words of the Yustaga language have been preserved but circumstantial evidence indicates they belonged to the Timucuan branch of the Muskhogean linguistic stock, although occasionally the provinces of Timucua and Yustaga are spoken of as if distinct.

Location.—Approximately between Aucilla and Suwannee Rivers, somewhat toward the coast.

Villages

The Yustaga villages cannot be satisfactorily identified though the missions of Asile, San Marcos, Machaba, and San Pedro seem to have belonged to it.

History.—The Yustaga are first mentioned by Biedma (*in* Bourne, 1904), one of the chroniclers of De Soto, who gives the title to a "province" through which the Spaniards marched just before coming to Apalachee. While the French Huguenots were on St. Johns River, some of them visited this tribe, and later it is again mentioned by the Spaniards but no mission bears the name. Its history is soon merged in that of the Timucuan peoples generally. The last mention of the name appears to be in 1659. It is of particular interest as the province from which the Osochi Indians who settled among the Lower Creeks probably emigrated in 1656 or shortly afterward.

Population.—In 1675, 40 Indians were reported in the mission of Asile and 300 in each of the others, giving a total very close to Mooney's (1928) estimate of 1,000 as of the year 1600.

ALABAMA

Abihka, see **Creek Confederacy** and **Muskogee.**

Alabama. Perhaps connected with the native word "albina," meaning "to camp," or alba amo, "weed gatherer," referring to the black drink. Also called:

Ma'-mo aⁿ-ya -di, or Ma'-mo haⁿ-ya, by the Biloxi.
Oke-choy-atte, given by Schoolcraft (1851–57), the name of an Alabama town, Oktcaiutci.

Connections.—The Alabama language belonged to the southern division of the Muskhogean stock, and was perhaps connected with the tongues of the Muklasa and Tuskegee, which have not been preserved. It was closely related to Koasati and more remotely to Hitchiti and Choctaw.

Location.—The principal historic seat of this tribe was on the upper course of Alabama River. (See also Florida, Louisiana, Oklahoma, and Texas.)

Subdivisions

The Tawasa and Pawokti, which later formed two Alabama towns, were originally independent tribes (see under Florida), though the former, at least, was not properly Alabama. The same may have been true of some other Alabama towns, though we have no proof of the fact.

Villages

Besides the above:

Autauga, on the north bank of Alabama River about the mouth of Autauga Creek in Autauga County.

Kantcati, on Alabama River about 3 miles above Montgomery and on the same side.

Nitahauritz, on the north side of Alabama River west of the confluence of the Alabama and Cahawba Rivers in Dallas County.

Okchayutci, in Benjamin Hawkins' time (about 1800) on the east bank of Coosa River between Tuskegee and the Muskogee town of Otciapofa. (See Hawkins, 1848, 1916.)

Wetumpka, a branch village reported in 1761.

History.—Native tradition assigns the origin of the Alabama to a point at the confluence of Alabama and Tombigbee Rivers, but we seem to hear of the tribe first historically in what is now northern Mississippi west of the Chickasaw country. This is in the narratives of De Soto's chroniclers, which, however, do not altogether agree, since one writer speaks of a province of the name, two others bestow the designation upon a small village, and only Garcilaso (1723), the least reliable, gives the title Fort Alibamo to a stockade—west of the village above mentioned—where the Spaniards had a severe combat. While this stockade was probably held by Alabama Indians, there is no certainty that it was. The next we hear of the tribe it is in its historic seats above given. After the French had established themselves at Mobile they became embroiled in some small affrays between the Alabama and Mobile Indians, but peace was presently established and thereafter the French and Alabama remained good friends as long as French rule continued. This friendship was cemented in 1717 by the establishment of Fort Toulouse in the Alabama country and the admission among them of one, or probably two, refugee tribes, the Tawasa and Pawokti. (See Florida.) About 1763 a movement toward the west began on the part of those Indians who had become accustomed to French rule. Some Alabama joined the Seminole in Florida. Others accompanied the Koasati to Tombigbee River but soon returned to their own country. Still another body went to Louisiana and settled on the banks of the Mississippi River, where they were probably joined from time to time by more. Later they advanced further toward the west and some are still scattered in St. Landry and Calcasieu Parishes, but the greatest single body finally reached Polk County, Tex., where they occupy a piece of land set aside for them by the State. Those who remained behind took a very prominent part in the Creek-American War and lost all their land by the treaty of Fort Jackson, 1814, being obliged to make new settlements between the Coosa and Tallapoosa. They accompanied the rest of the Creeks to Oklahoma, and their descendants are to be found there today, principally about a little station bearing the name just south of Weleetka.

Population.—In 1702 Iberville (*in* Margry, 1875–86, vol. 4, p. 514) estimated that there were 400 families of Alabama in two villages, and the English census of 1715 gives 214 men and a total population of 770 in four villages. These figures must have been exclusive of the Tawasa and Pawokti, which subsequent estimates include. About 1730–40 there is an estimate of 400 men in six towns. In 1792 the number of Alabama men is given as 60, exclusive of 60 Tawasa, but as this last included Kantcati the actual proportion of true Alabama was considerably greater. Hawkins, in 1799, estimated 80 gunmen in four Alabama towns, including Tawasa and Pawokti, but he does not include the population of Okchaiyutci. (See Hawkins, 1848.) In 1832 only two towns are entered which may be safely set down as Alabama, Tawasa and Autauga, and these had a population of 321 besides 21 slaves. The later figures given above do not include those Alabama who had moved to Louisiana. In 1805 Sibley (1832) states there were two villages in Louisiana with 70 men; in 1817 Morse (1822) gives 160 Alabama all told in Texas, but this is probably short of the truth. In 1882 the United States Indian Office reported 290 Alabama, Koasati, and Muskogee in Texas, the larger number of whom were probably Alabama. In 1900 the figure is raised to 470. In 1910 a special agent from the Indian Office reported 192 Alabama alone. The census of 1910 gave 187 in Texas and 111 in Louisiana, a total of 298. The 176 "Creek" Indians returned from Polk County, Tex., in 1930, were mainly Alabama. The number of Alabama in Oklahoma has never been separately reported.

Connection in which they have become noted.—The Alabama attained early literary fame from Garcilaso de la Vega's (1723) description of the storming of "Fort Alibamo." Their later notoriety has rested upon the fact that their name became attached to Alabama River, and still more from its subsequent adoption by the State of Alabama.   A railroad station in Oklahoma is named after them, and the term has been applied to places in Genesee County, N. Y., and in Polk County, Wis.   There is an Alabama City in Etowah County, Ala., and Alabam in Madison County, Ark.

Apalachee.   A part of this tribe lived for a time among the Lower Creeks and perhaps in this State.   Another section settled near Mobile and remained there until West Florida was ceded to Great Britain when they crossed the Mississippi.   A few seem to have joined the Creeks and migrated with them to Oklahoma.   (See Florida.)

Apalachicola.   Very early this tribe lived on the Apalachicola and Chattahoochee Rivers, partly in Alabama.   Sometime after 1715 they settled in Russell County, on the Chattahoochee River where they occupied at least two different sites before removing with the rest of the Creeks to the other side of the Mississippi.   (See Georgia.)

Atasi.   A division or subtribe of the Muskogee (q. v.).

Chatot.   This tribe settled near Mobile after having been driven from Florida and moved to Louisiana about the same time as the Apalachee.   (See Florida.)

Cherokee.   In the latter part of the eighteenth century some Cherokee worked their way down the Tennessee River as far as Muscle Shoals, constituting the Chickamauga band.   They had settlements at Turkeytown on the Coosa, Willstown on Wills Creek, and Coldwater near Tuscumbia, occupied jointly with the Creeks and destroyed by the Whites in 1787.   All of their Alabama territory was surrendered in treaties made between 1807 and 1835.   (See Tennessee.)

Chickasaw.   The Chickasaw had a few settlements in northwestern Alabama, part of which State was within their hunting territories. At one time they also had a town called Ooe-asa (Wĭ-aca) among the Upper Creeks.   (See Mississippi.)

Choctaw.   This tribe hunted over and occupied, at least temporarily, parts of southwestern Alabama beyond the Tombigbee.   (See Mississippi.)

Creek Confederacy.   This name is given to a loose organization which constituted the principal political element in the territory of the present States of Georgia and Alabama from very early times, probably as far back as the period of De Soto.   It was built around a dominant tribe, or rather a group of dominant tribes, called Muskogee. The name Creek early became attached to these people because when they were first known to the Carolina colonists and for a considerable period afterward the body of them which the latter knew best was living upon a river, the present Ocmulgee, called by Europeans "Ocheese Creek." The Creeks were early divided geographically into two parts, one called Upper Creeks, on the Coosa and Tallapoosa Rivers; the other, the Lower Creeks, on the lower Chattahoochee and Ocmulgee. The former were also divided at times into the Coosa branch or Abihka and the Talla-poosa branch and the two were called Upper and Middle Creeks respectively. Bartram (1792) tends to confuse the student by denominating all of the true Creeks "Upper Creeks" and the Seminole "Lower Creeks." The dominant Muskogee gradually gathered about them—and to a certain extent under them—the Apalachicola, Hitchiti, Okmulgee, Sawokli, Chiaha, Osochi, Yuchi, Alabama, Tawasa, Pawokti, Muklasa, Koasati, Tuskegee, a part of the Shawnee, and for a time some Yamasee, not counting broken bands and families from various quarters. The first seven of the above were for the most part among the Lower Creeks, the remainder with the Upper Creeks. (For further information, see the separate tribal names under Alabama, Georgia, and Florida.)

Eufaula. A division or subtribe of the **Muskogee** (q. v.).

Fus-hatchee. A division of the **Muskogee** (q. v.).

Hilibi. A division or subtribe of the **Muskogee** (q. v.).

Hitchiti. This tribe lived for considerable period close to, and at times within, the present territory of Alabama along its south-eastern margin. (See Georgia.)

Kan-hatki. A division of the **Muskogee** (q. v.).

Kealedji. A division of the **Muskogee** (q. v.).

Koasati. Meaning unknown; often given as Coosawda and Cou-shatta, and sometimes abbreviated to Shati.

Connections.—They belonged to the southern section of the Musk-hogean linguistic group, and were particularly close to the Alabama.

Location.—The historic location of the Koasati was just below the junction of the Coosa and Tallapoosa Rivers to form the Alabama and on the east side of the latter, where Coosada Creek and Station still bear the name. (See also Florida, Mississippi, Louisiana, Texas, and Oklahoma.)

Villages

Two Koasati towns are mentioned as having existed in very early times, one of which may have been the Kaskinampo. (See Tennessee.) At a later period a town known as Wetumpka on the east bank of Coosa River, in Elmore County, near the falls seems to have been occupied by Koasati Indians. During part of its existence Wetumpka was divided into two settlements, Big Wetumpka on the site of the modern town of the same name, and Little Wetumpka above the falls of Coosa.

History.—It is probable that from about 1500 until well along in the seventeenth century, perhaps to its very close, the Koasati lived upon Tennessee River. There is good reason to think that they are the Coste, Acoste, or Costehe of De Soto's chroniclers whose principal village was upon an island in the river, and in all probability this was what is now known as Pine Island. There is also a bare mention of them in the narrative of Pardo's expedition of 1567 inland from Santa Elena, and judging by the entries made upon maps published early in the eighteenth century this tribe seems to have occupied the same position when the French and English made their settlements in the Southeast. About that time they were probably joined by the related Kaskinampo. Not long after they had become known to the Whites, a large part of the Koasati migrated south and established themselves at the point mentioned above. A portion seems to have remained behind for we find a village called Coosada at Larkin's Landing in Jackson County at a much later date. The main body continued with the Upper Creeks until shortly after France ceded all of her territories east of the Mississippi to England in 1763, when a large part moved to Tombigbee River. These soon returned to their former position, but about 1795 another part crossed the Mississippi and settled on Red River. Soon afterward they seem to have split up, some continuing on the Red while others went to the Sabine and beyond to the Neches and Trinity Rivers, Tex. At a later date a few Texas bands united with the Alabama in Polk County, where their descendants still live, but most returned to Louisiana and gathered into one neighborhood northeast of Kinder, La. The greater part of the Koasati who remained in Alabama accompanied the Creeks to Oklahoma, where a few are still to be found. Previous to this removal, some appear to have gone to Florida to cast in their lot with the Seminole.

Population.—The earliest estimates of the Alabama Indians probably included the Koasati. In 1750 they are given 50 men; in 1760, 150 men. Marbury (1792) credits them with 130 men. In 1832, after the Louisiana branch had split off, those who remained numbered 82 and this is the last separate enumeration we have. Sibley (1806) on native authority gives 200 hunters in the Louisiana bands; in 1814 Schermerhorn estimates that there were 600 on the Sabine; in 1817 Morse places the total Koasati population in Louisiana and Texas at 640; in 1829 Porter puts it at 180; in 1850 Bollaert gives the number of men in the two Koasati towns on Trinity River as 500.

In 1882 the United States Indian Office reported 290 Alabama, Koasati, and Muskogee in Texas, but the Census of 1900 raised this to 470. The Census of 1910 returned 11 Koasati from Texas, 85 from Louisiana, and 2 from Nebraska; those in Oklahoma were not enumerated separately from the other Creeks. The 134 "Creeks" returned from Louisiana in 1930 were mainly Koasati.

Connection in which they have become noted.—Coosada, a post village in Elmore County, Ala., near the old Koasati town, and Coushatta, the capital of Red River Parish, La., preserve the name of the Koasati.

Kolomi. A division of the Muskogee (q. v.).

Mobile. Meaning unknown, but Halbert (1901) suggests that it may be from Choctaw moëli, "to paddle," since Mobile is pronounced moila by the Indians. It is the Mabila, Mauilla, Mavila, or Mauvila of the De Soto chroniclers.

Connections.—The language of the tribe was closely connected with that of the Choctaw and gave its name to a trade jargon based upon Choctaw or Chickasaw.

Location.—When the French settled the seacoast of Alabama the Mobile were living on the west side of Mobile River a few miles below the junction of the Alabama and Tombigbee.

History.—When they make their first appearance in history in 1540 the Mobile were between the Alabama and Tombigbee Rivers, and on the east side of the former. Their chief, Tuscaloosa, was a very tall and commanding Indian with great influence throughout the surrounding country. He inspired his people to attack the invading Spaniards and a terrific battle was fought October 18, 1540, for the possession of one of his fortified towns (Mabila), which the Spaniards carried with heavy losses to themselves in killed and wounded, while of the Indians 2,500 or more fell. It is probable that the village of Nanipacna, through which a force of Spaniards of the De Luna colony passed in 1559, was occupied by some of the survivors of this tribe. At a later date they may have settled near Gees Bend of the Alabama River, in Wilcox County, because early French maps give a village site there which they call "Vieux Mobiliens." A Spanish letter of 1686 speaks of them as at war with the Pensacola tribe. When the French came into the country, the Mobile were, as stated above, settled not far below the junction of the Tombigbee and Alabama. After a post had been established on the spot where Mobile stands today, the Mobile Indians moved down nearer to it and remained there until about the time when the English obtained possession of the country. They do not appear to have gone to Louisiana like so many of the smaller tribes about them and were probably absorbed in the Choctaw Nation.

Population.—After allowing for all exaggerations, the number of Mobile Indians when De Soto fought with them must have been very considerable, perhaps 6,000 to 7,000. Mooney (1928) estimates 2,000 Mobile and Tohome in 1650, over a hundred years after the great battle. In 1702 Iberville states that this tribe and the Tohome together embraced about 350 warriors; in 1725–26 Bienville (1932, vol. 3, p. 536), gives 60 for the Mobile alone, but in 1730 Régis de Rouillet (1732) cuts this in half. In 1758 De Kerlérec (1907) estimates the number of warriors among the Mobile, Tohome, and Naniaba at about 100.

Connection in which they have become noted.—The Mobile have attained a fame altogether beyond anything which their later numerical importance would warrant: (1) on account of the desperate resistance which they offered to De Soto's forces, and (2) from the important Alabama city to which they gave their name. There is a place called Mobile in Maricopa County, Ariz.

Muklasa. Meaning in Alabama and Choctaw, "friends," or "people of one nation."

Connections.—Since the Muklasa did not speak Muskogee and their name is from the Koasati, Alabama, or Choctaw language, and since they were near neighbors of the two former, it is evident that they were connected with one or the other of them.

Location.—On the south bank of Tallapoosa River in Montgomery County. (See Florida and Oklahoma.)

History.—When we first hear of the Muklasa in 1675 they were in the position above given and remained there until the end of the Creek-American War, when they are said to have emigrated to Florida in a body. Nothing is heard of them afterward, however, and although Gatschet (1884) states that there was a town of the name in the Creek Nation in the west in his time, I could learn nothing about it when I visited the Creeks in 1911–12.

Population.—In 1760 the Muklasa are said to have had 50 men, in 1761, 30, and in 1792, 30. These are the only figures available regarding their numbers.

Muskogee. Meaning unknown, but perhaps originally from Shawnee and having reference to swampy ground. To this tribe the name Creeks was ordinarily applied. Also called:

> Ani'-Gu'sa, by the Cherokee, meaning "Coosa people," after an ancient and famous town on Coosa River.
> Ku-û'sha, by the Wyandot.
> Ochesee, by the Hitchiti.
> Sko'-ki haⁿ-ya, by the Biloxi.

Connections.—The Muskogee language constitutes one division of the Muskhogean tongues proper, that which I call Northern.

Location.—From the earliest times of which we have any record these people seem to have had towns all the way from the Atlantic coast of Georgia and the neighborhood of Savannah River to central Alabama.   (See also Florida, Louisiana, Oklahoma, Tennessee, and Texas.)

Subdivisions and Villages

It is difficult to separate major divisions of the Muskogee from towns and towns from villages, but there were certainly several distinct Muskogee tribes at a very early period.   The following subdivisional classification is perhaps as good as any:

Abihka (in St. Clair, Calhoun, and Talladega Counties):
   Abihka-in-the-west, a late branch of Abihka in the western part of the Creek Nation, Okla.
   Abihkutci, on Tallassee Hatchee Creek, Talladega County, on the right bank 5 miles from Coosa River.
   Kan-tcati, on or near Chocolocko, or Choccolocco, Creek and probably not far from the present "Conchardee."
   Kayomalgi, possibly settled by Shawnee or Chickasaw, probably near Sylacauga, Talladega County.
   Lun-ham-ga, location unknown.
   Talladega, on Talladega Creek, Talladega County.
   Tcahki lako, on Choccolocco Creek in Talladega or Calhoun County.
Atasi: Location (1) on the upper Ocmulgee River, (2) on the Chattahoochee, (3) on the Tallapoosa in Tallapoosa County, (4) on the south side of the Talla-poosa in Macon County, and (5) on the north side near Calebee Creek in Elmore County.
Coosa:
   Abihkutci, a division of Okfuskee, which apparently came into existence after the Creeks had removed to Oklahoma.
   Atcinaulga, on the west bank of Tallapoosa River in Randolph County.
   Big Tulsa, on the east bank of Tallapoosa River at the mouth of Ufaubee Creek in Tallapoosa County.
   Chatukchufaula, possibly identical with the last, on Nafape Creek or Tallapoosa River.
   Chuleocwhooatlee, on the left bank of Tallapoosa River, 11 miles below Nuyaka, in Tallapoosa County.
   Holitaiga, on Chattahoochee River in Troup County, Ga.
   Imukfa, on Emaufaw Creek in Tallapoosa County.
   Ipisagi, on Sandy Creek in Tallapoosa County.
   Kohamutkikatsa, location unknown.
   Little Tulsa, on the east side of Coosa River, 3 miles above the falls, Elmore County.
   Lutcapoga, perhaps near Loachapoka in Lee County, or on the upper Tallapoosa.
   Nafape, on a creek of the same name flowing into Ufaubee Creek.
   Okfuskee, location (1) at the mouth of Hillabee Creek, (2) at the mouth of Sand Creek, both in Tallapoosa County.
   Okfuskutci, (1) on Chattahoochee River in Troup County, Ga.; (2) on the upper Tallapoosa in Tallapoosa County, Ala.; (3) another town of the name or an earlier location of the first somewhere near the lower Tallapoosa.
   Old Coosa, near the junction of the Coosa and Tallapoosa Rivers.

Otciapofa, on the east side of the Coosa River in Elmore County, just below the falls.

Saoga-hatchee, on Saogahatchee Creek, in Tallapoosa or Lee County.

Suka-ispoga, on the west bank of Tallapoosa River below the mouth of Hillibee Creek, in Tallapoosa County.

Tallassehasee, on Tallassee Hatchee Creek in Talladega County.

Tcahkiłako, on Chattahoochee River near Franklin, Heard County, Ga.

Tcatoksofka, seemingly a later name of the main Okfuskee town.

Tcawokela, 25 miles east northeast of the mouth of Upatoie Creek, probably near Chewacla Station, Lee County.

Tcułakonini, on Chattahoochee River in Troup County, Ga.

Tohtogagi, on the west bank of Tallapoosa River, probably in Randolph County.

Tukabahchee Tallahassee, later called Talmutcasi, on the west side of Tallapoosa River in Tallapoosa County.

Tukpafka, on Chattahoochee River in Heard County, Ga., later moved to Tallapoosa, settled on the left bank 11 miles above Okfuskee, Tallapoosa County, and renamed Nuyaka.

Tulsa Canadian, a branch of Tulsa on the Canadian River, Okla.

Tulsa Little River, a branch of Tulsa near Holdenville, Okla.

Coweta (early location on the upper Ocmulgee, later on the west bank of Chattahoochee River in Russell County, Ala., opposite Columbus, Ga.):

Coweta Tallahassee, later Łikatcka or Broken Arrow, probably a former location of the bulk of the tribe, on the west bank of Chattahoochee River in Russell County, Ala.

Katca tàstånågi's Town "at Cho-lose-parp-kari."

Settlements on "Hallewokke Yoaxarhatchee."

Settlements on "Toosilkstorkee Hatchee."

Settlements on "Warkeeche Hatchee."

Wetumpka, a branch of the last on the main fork of Big Uchee Creek 12 miles northwest from the mother town, Coweta Tallahassee.

Eufaula:

A branch among the Seminole called Kan-tcati.   (See Florida, **Seminole**.)

A branch village of Eufaula hopai on a creek called "Chowokolohatchee."

Eufaulahatchee or Eufaula Old Town, on Talladega Creek, also called Eufaula Creek, 15 miles from its mouth.

Lower Eufaula or Eufaula hopai, above the mouth of Pataula Creek, in Clay County, Ga.

Upper Eufaula, on the right bank of Tallapoosa River 5 miles below Okfuskee, in Tallapoosa County—at one time separated into Big Eufaula and Little Eufaula.

Hilibi (at the junction of Hillabee and Bear Creeks, Tallapoosa County):

Anetechapko, 10 miles above Hilibi on a branch of Hillabee Creek.

Etcuseislaiga, on the left bank of Hillabee Creek, 4 miles below Hilibi.

Kitcopataki, location unknown.

Łanutciabala, on the northwest branch of Hillabee Creek, probably in Tallapoosa County.

Little Hilibi, location unknown.

Oktahasasi, on a creek of the name 2 miles below Hilibi.

Hołiwahali (on the north bank of Tallapoosa River in Elmore County):

Łapłako, on the south side of Tallapoosa in Montgomery County nearly opposite Hołiwahali.

Kasihta (best-known location on the east bank of Chattahoochee River, at the
    junction of Upatoie Creek in Chattahoochee County, Ga.):
Apatai, in the forks of Upatoie and Pine Knob Creeks in Muskogee County, Ga.
Salenojuh, on Flint River 8 miles below Aupiogee Creek (?).
Settlements bearing the same name (Kasihta).
Settlements on Chowockeleehatchee Creek, Ala.
Settlements on Little Uchee Creek, Ala.
Settlements on "Tolarnulkar Hatchee."
Sicharlitcha, location unknown.
Tallassee Town, on Opillikee Hatchee, perhaps in Schley or Macon Counties,
    Ga.
Tuckabatchee Harjo's Town, on Osenubba Hatchee, a west branch of the
    Chattahoochee, Ala.
Tuskehenehaw Chooley's Town, near West Point, Troup County, Ga.
Okchai:
Asilanabi, on Yellow Leaf Creek in Shelby County.
Łałogálga, or Fish Pond, on a branch of Elkhatchee Creek, 14 miles up, in
    Tallapoosa or Coosa County.
Okchai, location (1) on the east side of the lower Coosa in Elmore County; (2)
    in the southeastern part of Coosa County, on a creek bearing their name,
    which flowed into Kialaga Creek.
Potcas hatchee, probably a branch of this on the upper course of Hatchet
    Creek in Clay or Coosa County.
Tcahki łako, on Chattahoochee River.
Tulsa hatchee, location uncertain.
Pakana:
Pakan Tallahassee, on Hatchet Creek, Coosa County.
The Pakana who settled near Fort Toulouse at the junction of Coosa and
    Tallapoosa Rivers and afterward moved to Louisiana, living on Calcasieu
    River for a while.
Tukabahchee (in the sharp angle made where Tallapoosa River turns west in
    Elmore County):
Only one small out village is mentioned, Wihili, location unknown.
Wakokai (on the middle course of Hatchet Creek in Coosa County):
Sakapadai, probably on Sacapartoy, a branch of Hatchet Creek, Coosa County.
Tukpafka, on Hatchet Creek, Coosa County.
Wiogufki, on Weogufka Creek in Coosa County.
Besides the Muskogee tribes noted above, there were the following:
Fus-hatchee. Not a major division; on the north bank of Tallapoosa River in
    Elmore County, 2 miles below Hołiwahali. They may have been related to
    the Hołiwahali.
Kan-hatki. Not a major division; just below Kolomi on the north bank of
    Tallapoosa River in Elmore County. Possibly related to the Hołiwahali.
Kealedji. Not a primary division; perhaps a branch of Tukabahchee; location
    (1) on the Ocmulgee, (2) on Kialaga Creek in Elmore County or Tallapoosa
    County, having one branch Hatcheetcaba, west of Kealedji, probably in Elmore
    County.
Kolomi. Probably not a major division; location (1) on the Ocmulgee, (2) on the
    middle Chattahoochee in Russell County, Ala., (3) on the north side of the
    lower Tallapoosa in Elmore County. They may have been related to the
    Hołiwahali.

Wiwohka. Not a primary division but a late town; location (1) near the mouth of Hatchet Creek in Coosa County, (2) on Weoka Creek in Elmore County.

In addition to the above there were a number of towns and villages which cannot be classified, or only with extreme doubt. They are as follows:

Acpactaniche, on the headwaters of Coosa River, perhaps meant for Pakana.

Alkehatchee, an Upper Creek town.

Atchasapa, on Tallapoosa River not far below Tulsa, possibly for ᐧtcheechubba.

Aucheucaula, in the northwestern part of Coosa County.

Auhoba, below Autauga. (See Alabama.)

Breed Camp, an Upper Creek town, probably meant for the Chickasaw settlement of Ooe-asa.

Cauwaoulau, a Lower Creek village in Russell County west of Uchee Post Office and south of the old Federal road.

Chachane, the Lower Creek town farthest downstream.

Chanahunrege, between the Coosa and Tallapoosa Rivers in or near Coosa County.

Chananagi, placed by Brannon (1909) "in Bullock County, just south of the Central of Georgia Railroad near Suspension."

Chichoufkee, an Upper Creek town in Elmore County, east of Coosa River and near Wiwoka Creek.

Chinnaby's Fort, at Ten Islands in the Coosa River.

Chiscalage, in or near Coosa County, perhaps a body of Yuchi.

Cholocco Litabixee, in the Horseshoe Bend of Tallapoosa River.

Chuahla, just below White Oak Creek, south of Alabama River.

Cohatchie, in the southwestern part of Talladega County on the bank of Coosa River.

Conaliga, in the western part of Russell County or the eastern part of Macon, somewhere near the present Warrior Stand.

Cooccohapofe, on Chattahoochee River.

Cotohautustenuggee, on the right bank of Upatoie Creek, Muscogee County, Ga.

Cow Towns, location uncertain.

Donnally's Town, on the Flint or the Chattahoochee River.

Ekun-duts-ke, probably on the south bank of Line Creek in Montgomery County.

Emarhe, location uncertain.

Eto-husse-wakkes, on Chattahoochee River, 3 miles above Fort Gaines.

Fife's Village, an Upper Creek village a few miles east of Talladega, Ala.

Fin'halui, a Lower Creek settlement, perhaps the Yuchi settlement of High Log.

Habiquache, given by the Popple Map as on the west side of Coosa River.

Ikan atchaka, "Holy Ground," in Lowndes County, 2½ miles due north of White Hall, just below the mouth of Holy Ground Creek on the Old Sprott Plantation.

Istapoga, in Talladega County near the influx of Estaboga Creek into Choccolocco Creek, about 10 miles from Coosa River.

Kehatches, somewhere above the bend of Tallapoosa River and between it and the Coosa.

Keroff, apparently on the upper Coosa.

Litafatchi, at the head of Canoe Creek in St. Clair County.

Lustuhatchee, above the second cataract of Tallapoosa River.

Melton's Village, in Marshall County, Ala., on Town Creek, at the site of the present "Old Village Ford."

Ninnipaskulgee, near Tukabahchee.

Nipky, probably a Lower Creek town.

Oakchinawa Village, in Talladega County, on both sides of Salt Creek, near the point where it flows into Big Shoal Creek.

Old Osonee Town, on Cahawba River in Shelby County.

Opillako, on Pinthlocco Creek in Coosa County.

Oti palin, on the west bank of Coosa River, just below the junction of Canoe Creek. (See Chinnaby's Fort.)

Oti tutcina, probably between Coosa and Opillako or Pakan Tallahassee and on Coosa River.

Pea Creek, perhaps an out settlement of Tukabahchee, location unknown.

Pin Huti, somewhere near Dadeville in Tallapoosa County.

Rabbit Town, possibly a nickname, location unknown.

St. Taffery's, location unknown.

Satapo, on Tennessee River.

Talipsehogy, an Upper Creek settlement.

Talishatchie Town, in Calhoun County east of a branch of Tallasehatchee Creek, 3 miles southwest of Jacksonville.

Tallapoosa, said to be within a day's journey of Fort Toulouse at the junction of the Coosa and Tallapoosa Rivers and probably on the river of that name.

Talwa Hadjo, on Cahawba River.

Tohowogly, perhaps intended for Sawokli, 8 to 10 miles below the falls of the Chattahoochee.

Turkey Creek, in Jefferson County, on Turkey Creek north of Trussville, probably Creek.

Uncuaula, in the western part of Coosa County on Coosa River.

Wallhal, an Upper Creek town given on the Purcell map, perhaps intended for Eufaula, or an independent town on Wallahatchee Creek, Elmore County.

Weyolla, a town so entered on the Popple Map, between the Coosa and Tallapoosa but near the former; probably a distorted form of the name of some well-known place.

History.—Muskogee tradition points to the northwest for the origin of the nation. In the spring of 1540, De Soto passed through some settlements and a "province" called Chisi, Ichisi, and Achese, in southern Georgia, which may have been occupied by Muskogee because they are known to Hitchiti-speaking people as Ochesee. Somewhat later he entered Cofitachequi, probably either the later Kasihta, or Coweta, and the same summer he entered Coosa and passed through the country of the Upper Creeks. Companions of De Luna visited Coosa again in 1559 and assisted it in its wars with a neighboring tribe to the West, the Napochi. Cofitachequi was visited later by Juan Pardo and other Spanish explorers and some of Pardo's companions penetrated as far as Coosa. It is probable that part if not all of the province of Guale on the Georgia coast was at that time occupied by Muskogee, and relations between the Guale Indians and the Spaniards continued intimate from 1565 onward. Soon afterward the Spaniards also encountered the Creeks of Chattahoochee River. At what time the confederacy of which the Muskogee were the most important part was established is unknown but the nucleus probably existed in De Soto's time. At any rate it was in a flourishing condition in 1670 when South Carolina was colonized and probably continued to grow more rapidly than before owing to the accession of

Creek tribes displaced by the Whites or other tribes whom the Whites had displaced. Before 1715 a large body were living on Ocmulgee River but following on the Yamasee outbreak of that year they withdrew to the Chattahoochee from which they had moved previously to be near the English trading posts. Occupying as they did a central position between the English, Spanish, and French colonies, the favor of the Creeks was a matter of concern to these nations, and they played a more important part than any other American Indians in the colonial history of the Gulf region. For a considerable period they were allied with the English, and they were largely instrumental in destroying the former Indian inhabitants of Florida and breaking up the missions which had been established there. Finding the territory thus vacated very agreeable and one abounding in game, they presently began to settle in it permanently, particularly after it was ceded to Great Britain in 1763. The first of the true Muskogee to emigrate to Florida, except for a small band of Coweta, were some Eufaula Indians, and the Muskogee do not seem to have constituted the dominant element until after the Creek-American war, 1813–14. In the last decades of the eighteenth century, the internal organization of the Confederacy was almost revolutionized by Alexander McGillivray, the son of a Scotch trader, who set up a virtual dictatorship and raised the Confederacy to a high position of influence by his skill in playing off one European nation against another. After his death friction developed between the factions favorable to and those opposed to the Whites. Inspired by the Shawnee chief, Tecumseh, a large part of the Upper Creeks broke out into open hostilities in 1813, but nearly all of the Lower Creeks and some of the most prominent Upper Creek towns refused to join with them and a large force from the Lower Creeks under William MacIntosh and Timpoochee Barnard, the Yuchi chief, actively aided the American army. This war was ended by Andrew Jackson's victory at Horsehoe Bend on the Tallapoosa River, March 27, 1814. One immediate result of this war was to double or triple the number of Seminole in Florida, owing to the multitude of Creeks who wished to escape from their old country. From this time on friction between the pro-White and anti-White Creek factions increased. When the United States Government attempted to end these troubles by inducing the Indians to emigrate, the friction increased still more and culminated in 1825 when the Georgia commissioners had induced William MacIntosh, leader of the pro-American faction, and some other chiefs to affix their signatures to a treaty ceding all that was then left of the Creek lands. For this act formal sentence of death was passed upon MacIntosh, and he was shot by a band of Indians sent to his house for that purpose May 1, 1825. However, the leaders of the Confederacy finally agreed to the removal, which took place between 1836 and 1840, the Lower Creeks settling in the upper part of their new lands and the Upper Creeks in the lower part.   The former factional troubles kept the relations between these two sections strained for some years, but they were finally adjusted and in course of time an elective government with a chief, second chief, and a representative assembly of two houses was established, which continued until the nation was incorporated into the State of Oklahoma.

Population.—Except where an attempt is made to give the population by towns, it is usually impossible to separate the Muskogee from other peoples of the Confederacy.   Correct estimates of all Creeks are also rendered difficult because they were taking in smaller tribes from time to time and giving off colonists to Florida and Louisiana.   In 1702 Iberville placed the whole number of Creek and Alabama families at 2,000.   In 1708 South Carolina officials estimated about 2,000 warriors.   In 1715 something approaching a census was taken of the tribes in their vicinity by the government of South Carolina and a total of 1,869 men and a population of 6,522 was returned for the Creeks, exclusive of the Alabama, Yuchi, Shawnee, Apalachicola, and Yamasee.   A town by town enumeration made by the Spaniards in 1738 shows 1,660 warriors; a French estimate of 1750, 905; another of 1760, 2,620; a North Carolina estimate of 1760, 2,000 warriors; an English estimate of 1761, 1,385; one of about 3,000 the same year; an American estimate of 1792, 2,850; and finally the census taken in 1832–33 just before the emigration of the Creeks to their new lands across the Mississippi, showed a total of 17,939 in the true Muskogee towns.   Besides these more careful statements, we have a number of general estimates of warriors in the eighteenth century ranging from 1,250 up to between 5,000 and 6,000.   This last was by Alexander McGillivray and is nearest that shown by the census of 1832–33.   It would seem either that the earlier estimates were uniformly too low or that the Confederacy increased rapidly during the latter part of the eighteenth century and the first part of the nineteenth.   After the removal estimates returned by the Indian Office and from other sources ranged between 20,000 and 25,000.   When a new census was taken in 1857, however, less than 15,000 were returned, and there was a slow falling off until 1919 when there were about 12,000.   It must be noted that the census of 1910 returned only 6,945, a figure which can be reconciled with that of the United States Indian Office only on the supposition that it is supposed to cover only Indians of full or nearly full blood.   The report of the United States Indian Office for 1923 gives 11,952 Creeks by blood. Regarding the later population it must be remembered that it has become more and more diluted.   The United States Census of 1930 gave 9,083 but included the Alabama and Koasati Indians of Texas and Louisiana and individuals scattered through more than 13 other States outside of Oklahoma, where 8,760 lived. These "general estimates" include the incorporated tribes.

Connection in which they have become noted.—In the form Muskhogean, the name of this tribe was adopted by Powell (1891) for that group of languages to which the speech of the Muskogee belongs. In the form Muscogee it has been given to a county in western Georgia, and to a railroad junction in it, and to a post-village in Escambia County, Fla. In the form Muskogee it is the name of the capital of Muskogee County, Okla., the third largest city in that state. The political organization of which they constituted the nucleus and the dominant element represents the most successful attempt north of México at the formation of a superstate except that made by the Iroquois, and the part they played in the early history of our Gulf region was greater than that of any other, not even excepting the Cherokee. They were one of the principal mound-building tribes to survive into modern times and were unsurpassed in the elaborate character of their ceremonials (except possibly by the Natchez), while their prowess in war was proven by the great contest which they waged with the United States Government in 1813–14, and the still more remarkable struggle which their Seminole relatives and descendants maintained in Florida in 1835–1842. Their great war speaker, Hopohithli-yahola, was probably surpassed in native greatness by no chief in this area except the Choctaw Pushmataha. (See Foreman, 1930.)

Napochi. If connected with Choctaw Napissa, as seems not unlikely, the name means "those who see," or "those who look out," probably equivalent to "frontiersmen."

Connection.—They belonged to the southern division of the Muskhogeans proper, and were seemingly nearest to the Choctaw.

Location.—Along Black Warrior River.

History.—The tribe appears first in the account of an attempt to colonize the Gulf States in 1559 under Don Tristan de Luna. A part of his forces being sent inland from Pensacola Bay came to Coosa in 1560 and assisted its people against the Napochi, whom they claimed to have reduced to "allegiance" to the former. After this the Napochi seem to have left the Black Warrior, and we know nothing certain of their fate, but the name was preserved down to very recent times among the Creeks as a war name, and it is probable that they are the Napissa spoken of by Iberville in 1699, as having recently united with the Chickasaw. Possibly the Acolapissa of Pearl River and the Quinipissa of Louisiana were parts of the same tribe.

Population.—Unknown.

Connection in which they have become noted.—The only claim the Napochi have to distinction is their possible connection with the remarkable group of mounds at Moundville, Hale County, Ala.

Natchez. One section of the Natchez Indians settled among the the Abihka Creeks near Coosa River after 1731 and went to Oklahoma a century later with the rest of the Creeks. (See Mississippi.)

Okchai. A division of the **Muskogee** (q. v.).

Okmulgee. A Creek tribe and town of the Hitchiti connection. (See Georgia.)

Osochi. Meaning unknown.

Connections.—Within recent times the closest connections of this tribe have been with the Chiaha, though their language is said to have been Muskogee, but there is some.reason to think that they may have been originally a part of the Timucua. (See below.)

Location.—Their best known historic seat was in the great bend of Chattahoochee River, Russell County, Ala., near the Chiaha. (See also Georgia and Florida.)

Villages

The town of Hotalgi-huyana was populated in part from this tribe and in part from the Chiaha. The census of 1832 gives two settlements, one on the Chattahoochee River and one on a stream called Opillike Hatchee.

History.—The suggestion that the Osochi may have been Timucua is founded (1) on the resemblance of their name to that of a Timucua division in northwest Florida called by the Spaniards Ossachile or Uçachile, (2) on the fact that after the Timucua uprising of 1656 some of the rebels "fled to the woods," and (3) the later mention of a detached body of Timucua in the neighborhood of the Apalachicola. Early in the eighteenth century they seem to have been living with or near the Apalachicola at the junction of the Chattahoochee and Flint. From what Hawkins (1848) tells us regarding them, we must suppose that they moved up Flint River somewhat later and from there to the Chattahoochee, in the location near the Chiaha above given. They migrated to Oklahoma with the rest of the Lower Creeks, and maintained their separateness in that country for a while but were later absorbed in the general mass of the Creek population.

Population.—The following estimates of the effective male population of the Osochi occur: 1750, 30; 1760, 50; 1792, 50. The census of 1832–33 returned a total of 539, but one of the two towns inhabited by these Indians may have belonged to the Okmulgee.

Pakana. A division of the **Muskogee** (q. v.).

Pawokti. This tribe moved from Florida to the neighborhood of Mobile along with the Alabama Indians and afterward established a town on the upper course of Alabama River. Still later they were absorbed into the Alabama division of the Creek Confederacy. (See Florida.)

Pilthlako. A division of the Creeks, probably related to the Muskogee (q. v.), and possibly a division of the Okchai.

Sawokli. Possibly meaning "raccoon people," in the Hitchiti language, and, while this is not absolutely certain, the okli undoubtedly means "people."

Connections.—The Sawokli belonged to the Muskhogean linguistic stock and to the subdivision called Atcik-hata. (See **Apalachicola.**)

Location.—The best known historic location was on Chattahoochee River in the northeastern part of the present Barbour County, Ala. (See Florida and Georgia.)

Villages

Hatchee tcaba, probably on or near Hatchechubbee Creek, in Russell County, Ala.

Okawaigi, on Cowikee Creek, in Barbour County, Ala.

Okiti-yagani, in Clay County, Ga., not far from Fort Gaines.

Sawokli, several different locations, the best known of which is given above.

Sawoklutci, on the east bank of the Chattahoochee River, in Stewart County, Ga.

Tcawokli, probably on Chattahoochee River in the northeastern part of Russell County, Ala.

History.—When first known to the Spaniards the Sawokli were living on Chattahoochee River below the falls. A Spanish mission, Santa Cruz de Sabacola, was established in one section of the tribe by Bishop Calderón of Cuba in 1675, and missionaries were sent to a larger body among the Creeks in 1679 and again in 1681. Most of the Indians surrounding these latter, however, soon became hostile and those who were Christianized withdrew to the junction of the Chattahoochee and Flint Rivers, where they were settled not far from the newly established Chatot missions. The Sawokli appear to have remained in the same general region until 1706 or 1707, when they were displaced by hostile Indians, probably Creeks. At least part lived for a while on Ocmulgee River and returned to the Chattahoochee, as did the residents of many other Indian towns, about 1715, after which they gradually split up into several settlements but followed the fortunes of the Lower Creeks. In the seventeenth century there may have been a detached body as far west as Yazoo River, since a map of that period gives a "Sabougla" town there and the name is preserved to the present day in a creek and post village.

Population.—In 1738 a Spanish report gives the Sawokli 20 men, evidently an underestimate. In 1750 four settlements are given with more than 50 men, and in 1760 the same number of settlements and 190 men, including perhaps the Tamałi, but to these must be added 30 men of Okiti-yakani. In 1761, including the neighboring and probably related villages, they are reported to have had 50 hunters. Hawkins in 1799 gives 20 hunters in Sawoklutci but no figures for the other towns. (See Hawkins, 1848.) In 1821 Young (*in* Morse, 1822) estimates 150 inhabitants in a town probably identical with this, and, according to the census of 1832–33, there were 187 Indians in Sawokli besides 42 slaves, 157 Indians in Okawaigi, and 106 in Hatcheetcaba; altogether, exclusive of the slaves, 450.

Connection in which they have become noted.—Sawokla is the name of a small place in Oklahoma, and a branch of this town has had its name incorporated in that of a stream, the Chewokeleehatchee, in Macon County., Ala., and in a post office called Chewacla in Lee County, Ala.

Shawnee. In 1716 a band of Shawnee from Savannah River moved to the Chattahoochee and later to the Tallapoosa, where they remained until early in the nineteenth century. A second band settled near Sylacauga in 1747 and remained there until some time before 1761 when they returned north. (See Tennessee.)

Taensa. This tribe was moved from Louisiana in 1715 and given a location about 2 leagues from the French fort at Mobile, one which had been recently abandoned by the Tawasa, along a watercourse which was named from them Tensaw River. Soon after the cession of Mobile to Great Britain, the Taensa returned to Louisiana. (See Louisiana.)

Tohome. Said by Iberville to mean "little chief," but this is evidently an error.

Connections.—They belonged to the southern branch of the Muskhogean linguistic group, their closest relatives being the Mobile.

Location.—About McIntosh's Bluff on the west bank of Tombigbee River, some miles above its junction with the Alabama.

Subdivisions

Anciently there were two main branches of this tribe, sometimes called the Big Tohome and Little Tohome, but the Little Tohome are known more often as Naniaba, "people dwelling on a hill," or "people of the Forks;" the latter would be because they were where the Alabama and Tombigbee Rivers unite.

Villages

No others are known than those which received their names from the tribe and its subdivisions.

History.—Cartographical evidence suggests that the Tohome may once have lived on a creek formerly known as Oke Thome, now contracted into Catoma, which flows into Alabama River a short distance below Montgomery. When first discovered by the Whites, however, they were living at the point above indicated. In the De Luna narratives (1559–60) the Tombigbee River is called "River of the Tome." Iberville learned of this tribe in April 1700, and sent messengers who reached the Tohome village and returned in May. In 1702 he went to see them himself but seems not to have gone beyond the Naniaba. From this time on Tohome history is identical with that of the Mobile and the two tribes appear usually to have been in alliance although a rupture between them was threatened upon one occasion on account of the murder of a Mobile woman by one of the Tohome. In 1715 a Tohome Indian killed an English trader named Hughes who had come overland from South Carolina, had been apprehended and taken to Mobile by the French and afterward liberated. A bare mention of the tribe occurs in 1763 and again in 1771–72. They and the Mobile probably united ultimately with the Choctaw.

Population.—In 1700 Iberville estimated that the Tohome and Mobile each counted 300 warriors, but 2 years later he revised his figures so far that he gave 350 for the two together. In 1730 Regis de Rouillet estimated that there were 60 among the Tohome and 50 among the Naniaba. In 1758 Governor De Kerlerec estimated that the Mobile, Tohome, and Naniaba together had 100 warriors. (See **Mobile.**)

Tukabahchee.   One of the four head tribes of the Muskogee (q. v.).

Tuskegee.   Meaning unknown, but apparently containing the Alabama term táska, "warrior."

Connections.—The original Tuskegee language is unknown but it was probably affiliated with the Alabama, and hence with the southern branch of Muskhogeans.

Location.—The later and best known location of this tribe was on the point of land between Coosa and Tallapoosa Rivers, but in 1685 part of them were on the Chattahoochee River near modern Columbus and the rest were on the upper Tennessee near Long Island. (See also Oklahoma and Tennessee.)

Villages

None are known under any except the tribal name.

History.—In 1540 De Soto passed through a town called Tasqui 2 days before he entered Coosa. In 1567 Vandera was informed that there were two places in this neighborhood near together called Tasqui and Tasquiqui, both of which probably belonged to the Tuskegee.

By the close of the seventeenth century the Tuskegee appear to have divided into two bands one of which Coxe (1705) places on an island in Tennessee River. This band continued to live on or near the Tennessee for a considerable period but in course of time settled among the Cherokee on the south side of Little Tennessee River, just above the mouth of Tellico, in the present Monroe County, Tenn. Sequoya lived there in his boyhood. Another place which retained this name, and was probably the site of an earlier settlement was on the north bank of Tennessee River, in a bend just below Chattanooga, while there was a Tuskegee Creek on the south bank of Little Tennessee River, north of Robbinsville, in Graham County, N. C. This band, or the greater part of it, was probably absorbed by the Cherokee. A second body of Tuskegee moved to the location mentioned above where the Coosa and Tallapoosa Rivers come together. It is possible that they first established themselves among the Creek towns on the Ocmulgee, moved with them to the Chattahoochee in 1715 and finally to the point just indicated, for we have at least two documentary notices of Tuskegee at those points and they appear so situated on a number of maps. It is more likely that these were the Tuskegee who finally settled at the Coosa-Tallapoosa confluence than a third division of the tribe but the fact is not yet established. In 1717 the French fort called Fort Toulouse or the Alabama Fort was built close to this town and therefore it continued in the French interest as long as French rule lasted. After the Creek removal, the Tuskegee formed a town in the southeastern part of the Creek territories in Oklahoma, but at a later date part moved farther to the northwest and established themselves near Beggs.

Population.—There are no figures for the Tuskegee division which remained on Tennessee River. The southern band had 10 men according to the estimate of 1750, but this is evidently too low. Later enumerations are 50 men in 1760, 40 in 1761, including those of Coosa Old Town, 25 in 1772 and 1792, 35 in 1799. The census of 1832-33 returned a population of 216 Indians and 25 Negro slaves.

Connection in which they have become noted.—The name Tuskegee became applied locally to several places in eastern Tennessee and western North Carolina, and one in Creek County, Okla., but the most important place to receive it was Tuskeegee or Tuskegee, the county seat of Macon County, Ala. The Tuskegee Normal and Industrial Institute for colored people, located at this place, has, under the guidance of the late Booker T. Washington, made the name better known than any other association.

Wakokai. A division or subtribe of the **Muskogee** (q. v.).

Wiwohka. A division of the Muskogee made up from several different sources. (See **Muskogee.**)

Yamasee. There was a band of Yamasee on Mobile Bay shortly after 1715, at the mouth of Deer River, and such a band is entered on maps as late as 1744. It was possibly this same band which appears among the Upper Creeks during the same century and in particular is entered upon the Mitchell map of 1755. Later they seem to have moved across to Chattahoochee River and later to west Florida, where in 1823 they constituted a Seminole town. (See Florida.)

Yuchi. A band of Yuchi seems to have lived at a very early date near Muscle Shoals on Tennessee River, whence they probably moved into east Tennessee. A second body of the same tribe moved from Choctawhatchee River, Fla., to the Tallapoosa before 1760 and established themselves near the Tukabahchee, but they soon disappeared from the historical record. In 1715 the Westo Indians, who I believe to have been Yuchi, settled on the Alabama side of Chattahoochee River, probably on Little Uchee Creek. The year afterward another band, accompanied by Shawnee and Apalachicola Indians, established themselves farther down, perhaps at the mouth of Cowikee Creek in Barbour County, and not long afterward accompanied the Shawnee to Tallapoosa River. They settled beside the latter and some finally united with them. They seem to have occupied several towns in the neighborhood in succession and there is evidence that a part of them reached the lower Tombigbee. The main body of Yuchi shifted from the Savannah to Uchee Creek in Russell County between 1729 and 1740 and continued there until the westward migration of the Creek Nation. (See Georgia.)

MISSISSIPPI

Acolapissa. When first known to Europeans, this tribe lived on Pearl River, partly in what is now Mississippi, partly in Louisiana, but they were more closely associated with Louisiana in later times and will be treated among the tribes of that State. (See Louisiana.)

Biloxi. Apparently a corruption of their own name Taneks aⁿya, "first people," filtered over the tongues of other Indians. Also called:

>Ananis, Anaxis, Annocchy, early French spellings intended for Taneks.
>Polu'ksalgi, Creek name.

Connections.—They belonged to the Siouan linguistic family.

Location.—Their earliest historical location was on the lower course of Pascagoula River. (See also Louisiana, Oklahoma, and Texas.)

Villages

None are known except those bearing the name of the tribe, unless we assume the "Moctobi" or "Capinans" to be a part of them. These, however, may have been merely synonyms of the tribal name.

History.—It is possible that the Biloxi are the Capitanesses who appear west of Susquehanna River on early Dutch charts. On the De Crenay map of 1733, a Biloxi town site appears on the right bank of the Alabama River, a little above the present Clifton in Wilcox County, Ala. This was probably occupied by the Biloxi during their immigration from the north. Individuals belonging to the tribe were met by Iberville on his first expedition to Louisiana in 1699, and in June of the same year his brother Bienville visited them. In 1700 Iberville found their town abandoned and does not mention encountering the people themselves, though they may have been sharing the Pascagoula village at which he made a short stop. A few years later, Pénicaut says (1702–23), St. Denis persuaded the Biloxi to abandon their village and settle on a small bayou near New Orleans but by 1722 they had returned a considerable distance toward their old home and were established on the former terrain of the Acolapissa Indians on Pearl River. They continued in this neighborhood and close to the Pascagoula until 1763, when French government east of the Mississippi came to an end. Soon afterward, although we do not know the exact date, they moved to Louisiana and settled not far from Marksville. They soon moved farther up Red River and still later to Bayou Boeuf. Early in the nineteenth century they sold their lands, and, while part of them remained on the river, a large body migrated to Texas and settled on Biloxi Bayou, in Angelina County. All of these afterward left, either to return to Louisiana or to settle in Oklahoma. A few Biloxi are still living in Rapides Parish, La., and there are said to be some in the Choctaw Nation, but the tribe is now practically extinct. In 1886 the Siouan relationship of their language was established by Dr. Gatschet of the Bureau of American Ethnology, and a considerable record of it was obtained by Mr. James O. Dorsey of the same institution in 1892–93. (See Dorsey and Swanton, 1912.)

Population.—On the basis of the imperfect records available, I have made the following estimates of Biloxi population at different periods: 420 in 1698, 175 in 1720, 105 in 1805, 65 in 1829, 6–8 in 1908. Mooney (1928) estimated that this tribe, the Pascagoula, and the "Moctobi" might number 1,000 in 1650.

Connection in which they have become noted.—The Biloxi are remarkable (1) as having spoken a Siouan dialect unlike all of their neighbors with one possible exception; (2) as the tribe first met by Iberville when he reached the coast of Louisiana and established the French colony of that name; (3) as having furnished the names of the first two capitals of Louisiana, Old and New Biloxi; that of the present Biloxi, Miss.; and the name of Biloxi Bay.

Capinans. The name of a body of Indians connected in French references with the Biloxi and Pascagoula and probably a branch of one of them.

Chakchiuma. Proper spelling Shâktci homma, meaning "Red Crawfish [People]."

Connections.—They spoke a dialect closely related to Choctaw and Chickasaw. Their nearest relatives were the **Houma** (q. v.), who evidently separated from them in very recent times.

Location.—In the eighteenth century on Yalobusha River where it empties into the Yazoo but at an early period extending to the head of the Yalobusha and eastward between the territories of the Choctaw and Chickasaw tribes as far as West Point.

Subdivisions

A French map dated about 1697 seems to call that section of the tribe on Yazoo River, Sabougla, though these may have been a branch of the Sawokli. (See Georgia.)

History.—According to tradition, this tribe came from the west at the same time as the Chickasaw and Choctaw and settled between them. When De Soto was among the Chickasaw, an expedition was directed against the Chakchiuma "who the [Chickasaw] Cacique said had rebelled," but their town was abandoned and on fire. It was claimed that they had planned treachery against the Spaniards. The chief of the tribe at this time was Miko Lusa (Black Chief). After the French settlement of Louisiana a missionary was killed by these people and in revenge the French stirred up the neighboring tribes to attack them. They are said to have been reduced very considerably in consequence. Afterward, they remained closely allied with the French, assisted them after the Natchez outbreak, and their chief was appointed leader of the Indian auxiliaries in the contemplated attack upon the Chickasaw in 1739. The animosity thus excited probably resulted in their destruction by the Chickasaw and absorption into the Chickasaw and Choctaw tribes. From De Crenay's map it appears that a part had gone to live with the Chickasaw by 1733. The rest may have gone to the Choctaw, for a band bearing their name constituted an important division of that nation. Tradition states that they were destroyed by the united efforts of the Chickasaw and Choctaw, but the latter were uniformly allied with the French and hostile to the Chickasaw when this alliance is supposed to have been in existence.

Population.—Mooney (1928) estimates 1,200 souls among the Chakchiuma, Ibitoupa, Taposa, and Tiou in 1650; exclusive of the Tiou, my own would be 750. In 1699 they are said to have occupied 70 cabins. In 1702 it is claimed that there were 400 families, which in 1704 had been reduced to 80, but probably the first figure is an exaggeration. About 1718–30 there were 50 Chakchiuma cabins and in 1722 the total population is placed at 150.

Chickasaw. Meaning unknown, though the ending suggests that it might have been a place name. Also called:

> Ani'-Tsĭ'ksû, Cherokee name.
> Kasahá únûⁿ, Yuchi name.
> Tchaktchán, Arapaho name.
> Tchíkasa, Creek name.
> Tci'-ka-sa', Kansa name.
> Ti-ka'-jă, Quapaw name.
> Tsi'-ka-cĕ, Osage name.

Connections.—Linguistically the Chickasaw were closely connected with the Choctaw and one of the principal tribes of the Muskhogean group.

Location.—In northern Mississippi, principally in Pontotoc and Union Counties. (See South Carolina, Georgia, Alabama, Arkansas, Kentucky, Oklahoma, and Tennessee.)

Subdivisions

Aside from some incorporated tribes such as the Napochi and Chakchiuma, no major subdivisions other than towns are mentioned until late in Chickasaw history when we hear of three such subdivisions: those of Tishomingo, Sealy, and McGilvery, named after their chiefs. These, however, were probably superficial and temporary.

Villages

Ackia.
Alaoute, mentioned only by Iberville.
Amalahta.
Apeonné.
Apile faplimengo (Iberville).
Ashukhuma.
Ayebisto (Iberville).
Chatelaw.
Chinica (Iberville).
Chucalissa.
Chukafalaa.
Coüi loussa, (French Memoir of 1755).
Latcha Hoa, on Latcha Hoa Run, an affluent of Ahoola Ihalchubba, a western tributary of Tombigbee River, northeastern Mississippi.
Etoukouma (De Batz).
Falatchao.
Gouytola (Iberville).

Ogoula-Tchetoka (De Batz).
Onthaba atchosa (Iberville).
Ooe-asa, in Creek Nation near Sylacauga.
Oucahata (Iberville).
Oucthambolo (Iberville).
Outanquatle (French Memoir of 1755).
Tanyachilca (Iberville).
Thanbolo (Iberville).
Tuckahaw.
Tuskawillao.
Yaneka.

All of the above, with one or two exceptions noted, were close to one another in the general location given above.

History.—Like most of the other Muskhogean peoples, the Chickasaw believed they had come from the west. They thought that they had settled for a time at a spot in northern Alabama on the north side of the Tennessee River long known as Chickasaw Old Fields. There is little doubt that Chickasaw had once lived at that place whether or not the whole tribe was so located. The first Europeans to become acquainted with the tribe were the Spaniards under De Soto, who spent the months of January, February, and March 1541, in the Chickasaw country, and in the latter month were attacked by the tribe with such fury that they were nearly destroyed. Little is heard of the Chickasaw from this time until French explorers and colonists arrived, at the end of the seventeenth century. They found the tribe in approximately the position in which De Soto had encountered them, and they found them as warlike as before. Although the French tried to make peace with them, English traders had effected establishments in their country even before the settlement of Louisiana, and they remained consistent allies of England while England and France were fighting for the possession of North America. In the south their alliance meant much the same to the English as Iroquois friendship meant to them in the north. As practically all of the surrounding peoples were devoted to the French, and the Chickasaw were not numerous, they were obliged to maintain a very unequal struggle until the final victory of England in 1763, and they suffered severely in consequence. They supported the Natchez when they revolted in 1729, and when French expeditions from the north and south were hurled upon them simultaneously in 1736, they beat both off with heavy losses. In 1740 a gigantic attempt was made to conquer them, but the greater part of the force assembled dissolved without accomplishing anything. A small French expedition under Céloron succeeded in obtaining a treaty of peace advantageous to the French but this soon became a dead letter, and French communications up and down the Mississippi River were constantly threatened and French voyageurs constantly attacked in the period following. In

1752 and 1753 the French commanders Benoist and Reggio were defeated by the Chickasaw. At an earlier period, shortly before 1715, they and the Cherokee together drove the Shawnee from their settlements on the Cumberland, and in 1745 they expelled another Shawnee band from the same region. In 1769 they utterly routed the Cherokee on the site of the Chickasaw Old Fields. In 1793–95 war broke out with the Creeks, who invaded their territories with 1,000 men, but while they were attacking a small stockade, a band of about 200 Chickasaw fell upon them, whereupon an unaccountable terror took possession of the invaders, and they fled precipitately. There was at one time a detached body of Chickasaw on the lower Tennessee not far from its mouth. They also had a town among the Upper Creeks for a brief period (Ooe-asa), and a settlement near Augusta, Ga., from about 1723 to the opening of the American Revolution. The Chickasaw maintained friendship with the American Government after its establishment, but, being pressed upon by white settlers, parted with their lands by treaties made in 1805, 1816, 1818, and 1832. The actual migration to new homes in what is now Oklahoma began in 1837 and extended to 1847. The Chickasaw and Choctaw mingled rather indiscriminately at first but their lands were separated in 1855 and the Chickasaw set up an independent government modeled on that of the United States which lasted until merged in the new State of Oklahoma.

Population.—Mooney (1928) estimates that there were about 8,000 in 1600. In 1702 Iberville estimated that there were 2,000 families of Chickasaw, but in 1715 a rather careful enumeration made by the colony of South Carolina, gave 6 villages, 700 men, and a population of 1,900. In 1761, a North Carolina estimate gives about 400 men; in 1766, about 350. Most of the subsequent estimates of the number of warriors made during the eighteenth century vary between 250 and 800. In 1817 Morse (1822) places the total population at 3,625; in 1829 General Peter B. Porter estimates 3,600 (*in* Schoolcraft, 1851–57, vol. 3); and a more accurate report in Schoolcraft gives 4,715 in 1833. The figures of the United States Indian Office between 1836 and the present time vary from 4,500 for 1865 to 1870 to nearly 11,000 in 1923, but this latter figure includes more than 5,000 freedmen and persons intermarried in the tribe, and, when we allow for mixed bloods, we shall find that the Chickasaw population proper has usually stood at between 4,500 and 5,500 during the entire period. There has probably been a slow decline in the absolute amount of Chickasaw blood owing to constant intermixture with other peoples. The 1910 census returned 4,204 Chickasaw and that of 1930, 4,745.

Connection in which they have become noted.—The Chickasaw were noted (1) as one of the most warlike tribes of the Gulf area, (2) as the tribe of all those encountered by the Spaniards who came nearest putting an end to De Soto's army, (3) as the constant allies of the English without whom the control of the Gulf region by the latter would many times have been jeopardized. There are post villages of the name in Mobile County, Ala., and Mercer County, Ohio, and Chickasha, a variant form, is the name of the county seat of Grady County, Okla.

Choctaw. Meaning unknown, though Halbert (1901) has suggested that they received their name from Pearl River, "Hachha". Also called:

> Ani'-Tsa'ta, Cherokee name.
> Flat Heads, from their custom of flattening the heads of infants.
> Hennē'sh, Arapaho name.
> Nabuggindebaig, probably the Chippewa name for this tribe, signifying "flat heads."
> Paⁿs falaya, "Long Hairs," given by Adair.
> Sanakíwa, Cheyenne name, meaning "feathers sticking up above the ears."
> Tá-qta, Quapaw name.
> Tca-qtá aⁿ-ya-dí, or Tca-qtá haⁿ-ya, Biloxi name.
> Tca-tá, Kansa name.
> Têtes Plates, French equivalent of "Flat Heads."
> Tsah-tû, Creek name.

Connections.—This was the largest tribe belonging to the southern Muskhogean branch. Linguistically, but not physically, it was most closely allied with the Chickasaw and after them with the Alabama.

Location.—Nearly all of the Choctaw towns were in the southeastern part of Mississippi though they controlled the adjoining territory in the present State of Alabama. The small tribes of Mobile were sometimes called Choctaw. (See also Louisiana, Texas, Oklahoma, Alabama, and Arkansas.)

Subdivisions and Villages

From the earliest times of which we have any knowledge the Choctaw villages were distributed into three divisions: a southern, a northeastern, and a western, though a central group may also be distinguished. The southern division is fairly well defined by our several informants, but there is considerable disagreement with reference to the others. One authority gives but two divisions, an eastern and a western, and even cuts up the southern group between them. The following locations were established largely by Mr. H. S. Halbert (1901):

Southern or Sixtown Division:

> Bishkun, in the northern part of Jasper County.
> Bissasha, on the west side of Little Rock Creek, in Newton County, sect. 23, tp. 8, range 12, east.
> Boktoloksi, on Boguetuluksi Creek, a southwest affluent of Chickasawhay River.
> Chickasawhay, on Chickasawhay River about 3 miles south of Enterprise, Clarke County.

Chinakbi, on the site of Garlandville, in Jasper County.

Chiskilikbacha, probably in Jasper County.

Coatraw, 4 miles southwest of the town of Newton in sect. 17, tp. 5, range 11, east, Newton County.

Inkillis tamaha, in the northeastern part of Jasper County.

Nashobawenya, in the southwestern part of Jasper County.

Okatalaia, in the eastern part of Smith County or the western part of Jasper County.

Oktak chito tamaha, location unknown.

Oskelagna, probably in Jasper County.

Puskustakali, in the southwest corner of Kemper County or the proximate part of Neshoba County.

Siniasha, location uncertain.

Tala, in the southern part of Newton County, between Tarlow and Bogue Felamma Creeks.

Talahoka, in Jasper County.

Yowani, on the east side of Chickasawhay River, in the southern part of Clarke County.

Western Division:

Abissa, location uncertain.

Atlantchitou, location unknown.

Ayoutakale, location unknown.

Bok chito, probably on Bogue Chitto, in Neshoba and Kemper Counties.

Bokfalaia, location uncertain.

Bokfoka, location unknown.

Boktokolo, location unknown.

Cabea Hoola, location unknown.

Chunky, on the site of Union, Newton County.

Chunky chito, on the west bank of Chunky Creek, about half a mile below the confluence of that creek with Talasha Creek—later this belonged to the southern district.

East Kunshak chito, near Moscow, in Kemper County.

Filitamon, location unknown.

Halunlawi asha, on the site of Philadelphia, in Neshoba County.

Hashuk chuka, location unknown.

Hashuk homa, location unknown.

Imoklasha, on the headwaters of Talasha Creek, in Neshoba County, in sections 4, 9, and 16, tp. 9, range 13, east.

Iyanabi, on Yannubbee Creek, about 8 miles southwest of De Kalb, in Kemper County.

Itichipota, between the headwaters of Chickasawhay and Tombigbee Rivers.

Kafitalaia, on Owl Creek, in section 21, tp. 11, range 13, east, in Neshoba County.

Kashtasha, on the south side of Custusha Creek, about 3 miles a little south of West Yazoo Town.

Konshak osapa, somewhere west of West Imoklasha.

Koweh chito, northwest of De Kalb, in Kemper County.

Kushak, on Lost Horse Creek, 4 miles southeast of Lazelia, Lauderdale County.

Kunshak bolukta, in the southwestern part of Kemper County some 2 miles from Neshoba County line and 1½ miles from the Lauderdale County line.

Kunshak chito, on or near the upper course of Oktibbeha River.

Lushapa, perhaps on Lussalaka Creek, a tributary of Kentarcky Creek, in Neshoba County.

Oka Chippo, location unknown.

Oka Coopoly, on Ocobly Creek, in Neshoba County.

Oka hullo, probably on or near the mouth of Sanoote Creek, which empties into Petickfa Creek in Kemper County.

Oka Kapassa, about Pinckney Mill, in sect. 23, tp. 8, range 11, east, in Newton County—possibly in the southern section.

Okalusa, in Romans' time on White's Branch, Kemper County.

Okapoola, location unknown.

Okehanea tamaha, location unknown.

Oklabalbaha, location unknown.

Oklatanap, location unknown.

Oony, south of Pinckney Mill, in Newton County—possibly in the southern division.

Osak talaia, near the line between Neshoba and Kemper Counties.

Osapa chito, on the site of Dixon Post Office, in Neshoba County.

Otuk falaia, location unknown.

Pante, at the head of Ponta Creek, in Lauderdale County.

Shinuk Kaha, about 7 miles a little north or east of Philadelphia, in Neshoba County.

Shumotakali, in Kemper County, between the two head prongs of Black Water Creek.

Tiwaele, location unknown.

Tonicahaw, location unknown.

Utapacha, location unknown.

Watonlula, location uncertain.

West Abeka, location unknown.

West Kunshak chito, in Neshoba County, near the headwaters of Oktibbeha Creek.

Wiatakali, about 1 mile south of the De Kalb and Jackson road, in Neshoba County.

Yazoo, or West Yazoo, in Neshoba County, near the headwaters of Oktibbeha Creek, in sections 13 and 24, tp. 10, range 13, east.

Northeastern Divison:

Alamucha, 10 miles from Sukenatcha Creek, in Kemper County.

Athlepele, location unknown.

Boktokolo chito, at the confluence of Running Tiger and Sukenatcha Creeks, about 4 miles northwest of De Kalb.

Chichatalys, location unknown.

Chuka hullo, on the north side of Sukenatcha Creek, somewhere between the mouths of Running Tiger and Straight Creeks, in Kemper County.

Chuka lusa, location unknown.

Cutha Aimethaw, location unknown.

Cuthi Uckehaca, probably on or near the mouth of Parker's Creek, which empties into Petickfa, in sect. 30, tp. 10, range 17, east.

East Abeka, at the junction of Straight Creek with the Sukenatcha, in Kemper County.

Escooba, perhaps on or near Petickfa Creek, in Kemper County.

Hankha Ula, on a flat-topped ridge between the Petickfa and Black Water Creeks, in Kemper County.

Holihta asha, on the site of De Kalb, in Kemper County.

Ibetap okla chito, perhaps on Straight Creek, in Kemper County.

Ibetap okla iskitini, at the head of the main prong of Yazoo Creek, in Kemper County.

Imoklasha iskitini, on Flat Creek, the eastern prong of Yazoo Creek, in Kemper County.

Itokchako, near East Abeka, in Kemper County.

Kunshaktikpi, on Coonshark Creek, a tributary of Kentarky Creek, in Neshoba County.

Lukfata, on the headwaters of one of the prongs of Sukenatcha River.

Oka Altakala, probably at the confluence of Petickfa and Yannubbee Creeks, in Kemper County.

Osapa issa, on the north side of Blackwater Creek, in Kemper County.

Pachanucha, location unknown.

Skanapa, probably on Running Tiger Creek, in Kemper County.

Yagna Shoogawa, perhaps on Indian branch of Running Tiger Creek.

Yanatoe, probably in southwest Kemper County.

Yazoo iskitini, on both sides of Yazoo Creek.

The following were outside the original town cluster:

Bayou Chicot, south of Cheneyville, St. Landry Parish, La.

Boutté Station, in St. Charles Parish, La.

Cahawba Old Towns, in Perry County, Ala., and probably on Cahawba River.

Cheponta's Village, on the west bank of the Tombigbee River in the extreme southeastern part of Choctaw County, Ala.

Chisha Foka, on the site of Jackson.

Coila, in Carroll County, probably occupied by Choctaw.

Heitotowa, at the site of the later Sculleyville, Choctaw Nation, Okla.

Shukhata, on the site of Columbus, Ala.

Teeakhaily Ekutapa, on the lower Tombigbee River.

Tombigbee, on or near Tombigbee River.

A few other names of towns placed in the old Choctaw country appear on various maps, but most of these are probably intended for some of the villages given above.

History.—After leaving the ruins of Mabila, De Soto and his followers, according to the Gentleman of Elvas (see Robertson, 1933), reached a province called Pafallaya, but, according to Ranjel, to a chief river called Apafalaya. Halbert is undoubtedly right in believing that in these words we have the old name of the Choctaw, Paⁿsfalaya, "Long Hairs," and this is the first appearance of the Choctaw tribe in history. We hear of them again, in Spanish Florida documents of the latter part of the seventeenth century, and from this time on they occupied the geographical position always associated with them until their removal beyond the Mississippi. The French of necessity had intimate dealings with them from the time when Louisiana was first colonized, and the relations between the two peoples were almost invariably friendly. At one time an English party was formed among the Choctaw, partly because the prices charged by the Carolina traders were lower than those placed upon French goods. This was led by a noted chief named Red Shoes and lasted for a considerable time, one of the principal Choctaw towns being burned before it came to an end with the defeat of the British party in 1750. In 1763, after French Government had given way to that of the English east of the Mississippi, relations between the latter and the Choctaw were peaceful though many small bands of Indians of this tribe crossed the Mississippi into Louisiana. The American Revolution did not alter conditions essentially, and, though Tecumseh and his emissaries endeavored to enlist the Choctaw in his favor, only about 30 individuals joined the hostile Creeks. The abstinence of the tribe as a whole was due very largely to the personal influence of the native statesman, Pushmataha, whose remains lie in the Congressional Cemetery in Washington, surmounted by an impressive monument. Meanwhile bands of Choctaw continued moving across the Mississippi, but the great migration occurred after the Treaty of Dancing Rabbit, September 30, 1830, by which the tribe ceded their old lands. However, a considerable body of Choctaw did not leave at this time. Many followed, it is true, at the time of the allotment in Oklahoma, but upward of a thousand still remain, principally in the neighborhood of Philadelphia, Miss. The western Choctaw established a government on the model of those of the other civilized tribes and that of the United States, and it was not given up until merged in the State of Oklahoma early in the present century.

Population.—Estimates of the number of Choctaw warriors between 1702 and 1814 vary between 700 and 16,000. A North Carolina estimate made in 1761 says they numbered at least 5,000 men. Common estimates are between 4,000 and 5,000, but even these figures may be a trifle low since the first reliable census, that of Armstrong, in 1831, gave 19,554. However, there may have been a slight increase in population after the beginning of the nineteenth century, when an end was put to intertribal wars. Figures returned by the Indian Office since that time show a rather unusual constancy. They go as low as 12,500, and at the other extreme reach 22,707, but the average is from 18,000 to 20,000. The census of 1910 gave 15,917, including 1,162 in Mississippi, 14,551 in Oklahoma, 115 in Louisiana, 57 in Alabama, and 32 in other States, but the United States Indian Office Report for 1923 has 17,488 Choctaw by blood in Oklahoma, 1,600 "Mississippi Choctaw" in Oklahoma, and 1,439 in the State of Mississippi, not counting about 200 in Louisiana, Alabama, and elsewhere. A few small tribes were gathered into this nation, but only a few. The census of 1930 returned 17,757, of whom 16,641 were in Oklahoma, 624 in Mississippi, 190 in Louisiana, and the rest in more than 14 other States. In 1937 the Mississippi Choctaw numbered 1,908, from which it seems that many of the Mississippi Choctaw were missed in 1930 unless the "Mississippi Choctaw" already in Oklahoma are included.

Connection in which they have become noted.—The Choctaw were noted (1) as the most numerous tribe in the Southeast next to the

Cherokee, (2) as depending more than most other tribes in the region on agriculture, (3) for certain peculiar customs such as head deformation, extensive use of ossuaries for the dead, and the male custom of wearing the hair long, (4) as faithful allies of the French against the English but always at peace with the United States Government, (5) as having furnished the names to counties in Alabama, Mississippi, and Oklahoma, and settlements in the same States, and in Van Buren County, Ark.

Choula. Bernard de La Harpe gives this as the name of a small tribe of 40 individuals on the Yazoo River. There is some reason to think it was applied to a part of the Ibitoupa tribe (q. v.). The name means "fox" in Chickasaw and Choctaw.

Grigra. Said to have been given them from the frequent occurrence of these two syllables in their speech. They sometimes appear as the "Gray Village" of the Natchez.

Connections.—The fact that the language of this tribe contained an *r* suggests a probable relationship with the tribes of the Tunican group.

Location.—When first known to us, it formed one of the Natchez villages on St. Catherines Creek, Miss.

Villages

Only one village is mentioned called by a shorter form of the name given to the tribe, Gris or Gras.

History.—The Grigra had been adopted by the Natchez at an earlier period than the Tiou (q. v.) and, like them, may once have resided on Yazoo River, but there is no absolute proof of this. They are mentioned as one of three Natchez tribes belonging to the anti-French faction. Otherwise their history is identical with that of the Natchez.

Population.—One estimate made about 1720–25 gives about 60 warriors.

Houma. Literally "red," but evidently an abbreviation of săktci homma, "red crawfish."

Connections.—They spoke a Muskhogean language very close to Choctaw, and it is practically certain from the fact that their emblem was the red crawfish that they had separated from the Chakchiuma (q. v.).

Location.—The earliest known location of the Houma was on the east side of the Mississippi River some miles inland and close to the Mississippi-Louisiana boundary line, perhaps near the present Pinckney, Miss. (See also Louisiana.)

Villages

At one time the people of this tribe were distributed between a Little Houma village 2 leagues below the head of Bayou La Fourche and a Great Houma village half a league inland from it. This was after they had moved from their earlier home.

History.—La Salle heard of the Houma in 1682, but he did not visit them. Tonti made an alliance with them 4 years later, and in 1699 their village was the highest on the Mississippi reached by Iberville before returning to his ships. In 1700 Iberville visited them again and left a missionary among them to build a church, which was an accomplished fact when Gravier reached the tribe in November of the same year. A few years later the Tunica, who had been impelled to leave their old town, were hospitably received by this tribe, but in 1706 they rose upon their hosts, destroyed part of them, and drove the rest down the Mississippi. These reestablished themselves on Bayou St. John near New Orleans, but not long afterward they reascended the river to the present Ascension Parish and remained there for a considerable period. In 1776 they sold a part at least of their lands to two French Creoles but seem to have remained in the neighborhood until some years after the purchase of Louisiana by the United States. By 1805 some had gone to live with the Atakapa near Lake Charles. Most of the remainder appear to have drifted slowly across to the coast districts of Terrebonne and La Fourche Parishes, where their descendants, with Creole and some Negro admixture, still live.

Population.—Mooney (1928) estimates a Houma population in 1650 of 1,000. In 1699 Iberville gives 140 cabins and about 350 warriors, while the Journal of the second vessel in this expedition gives a population of 600–700. In 1718, after the tribe had suffered from both pestilence and massacre, La Harpe estimates 60 cabins and 200 warriors. In 1739 a French officer who passed their town rates the number of their warriors at 90–100 and the whole population at 270–300. In 1758 there is an estimate of 60 warriors and in 1784 one of 25 while, in 1803, the total Houma population is placed at 60. In 1907 the native estimate of mixed-blood population calling itself Houma was 800–900, but the census of 1910 returned only 125 Indians from Terrebonne. To these there should probably be added some from La Fourche but not a number sufficient to account for the discrepancy. In 1920, 639 were returned and in 1930, 936 from Terrebonne besides 11 from La Fourche. Speck estimates double the number.

Connection in which they have become noted.—Houma, the capital of Terrebonne Parish, preserves the name.

Ibitoupa. Meaning probably, people "at the source of" a stream or river.

Connections.—No words of this language are known unless the tribal name itself is native, but from this and Le Page du Pratz's (1758) statement that their language, unlike that of the Tunica group, was without an *r*, there is every reason to class it as Muskhogean and closely related to Chackchiuma, Chickasaw, and Choctaw.

Location.—On Yazoo River in the present Holmes County, perhaps between Abyatche and Chicopa Creeks.

Villages

Only one village is known, and that called by the tribal name, though it is possible that the **Choula,** (q. v.) mentioned by La Harpe were an offshoot.

History.—The Ibitoupa are mentioned in 1699 by Iberville, and in Coxe's Carolana (1705). Before 1722 they had moved higher up and were 3 leagues above the Chakchiuma (q. v.), who were then probably at the mouth of the Yalobusha. They probably united with the Chickasaw soon after the Natchez War, though they may first have combined with the Chakchiuma and Taposa. They were perhaps related to the people of the Choctaw towns called Ibetap okla.

Population.—All that we know of the population of the Ibitoupa is that in 1722 it occupied 6 cabins; in the same year there are said to have been 40 Choula, a possible offshoot.

Connection in which their name has become noted.—It seems to have been the original of the name of Tippo Bayou, Miss.

Koasati. A band of Koasati moved from Alabama to Tombigbee River in 1763 but returned to their old country a few years later impelled by the hostilities of their new neighbors. (See Alabama.)

Koroa. Meaning unknown. Also called:

Kúlua, Choctaw name, the Muskhogean people being unable to pronounce *r* readily.

Connections.—The name and associations, together with Le Page du Pratz's (1758) statement that their language possessed an *r* sound, are practically conclusive proof that this tribe belonged to the Tunican linguistic group.

Location.—The Koroa appear oftenest in association with the Yazoo on the lower course of Yazoo River, but at the very earliest period they were on the banks of the Mississippi or in the interior of what is now Louisiana on the other side of that river. (See also Louisiana.)

Villages

None are known under any other name.

History.—In the De Soto narratives a people is mentioned called Coligua and Colima which may be the one under discussion. If not, the first appearance of the Koroa in history is on Marquette's map applying to 1673, though they are there misplaced. The La Salle narratives introduce us, apparently, to two tribes of the name, one on Yazoo River, the other below Natchez, but there are reasons for thinking that the latter was the tribe elsewhere called Tiou. In Tonti's account of his expedition overland to the Red River in 1690 we learn of a Koroa town west of the Mississippi, and also of a Koroa River. In 1700 Bienville also learned of a trans-Mississippi Koroa settlement. From the time of Tonti's expedition to the mouth of the Mississippi in 1686 there seems to have been a Koroa town on or near the lower Yazoo, as mentioned above. When the Natchez outbreak occurred, this tribe and the Yazoo joined them and destroyed the French post on Yazoo River, but they suffered severely from Indians allied with the French and probably retired soon afterward to the Chickasaw, though part, and perhaps all of them, ultimately settled among the Choctaw. The Choctaw chief Allen Wright claimed to be of Koroa descent.

Population.—Mooney (1928) estimates that there were 2,000 Koroa, Yazoo, Tunica, and Ofo in 1650. Le Page du Pratz places the number of Koroa cabins in his time at 40. In 1722 the total population of the Koroa, Yazoo, and Ofo is given as 250, and in 1730 the last estimate of the Koroa and Yazoo together gives 40 warriors, or perhaps 100 souls.

Moctobi. This name appears in the narratives of the first settlement of Louisiana, in 1699, applied to a tribe living with or near the Biloxi and Pascagoula. It is perhaps the name of the latter in the Biloxi language, or a subdivision of the Biloxi themselves, and is best treated in connection with the latter.

Natchez. Meaning unknown (the *z* should not be pronounced). Also called:

Ani'-Na'tsɪ, Cherokee name.
Sunset Indians, given by Swan (*in* Schoolcraft (1851–57)).
Theloël or Thécoël, name used by the Natchez but seemingly derived from that of a town.

Connections.—The Natchez were the largest of three tribes speaking closely related dialects, the other two being Taensa and Avoyel, and this group was remotely related to the great Muskhogean family.

Location.—The historic seat of the Natchez Indians was along St. Catherines Creek, and a little east of the present city of Natchez. (See also Alabama, Louisiana, North Carolina, Oklahoma, South Carolina, and Tennessee.)

Villages

Iberville gives the following list of Natchez villages: "Natchés, Pochougoula, Ousagoucoulas, Cogoucoulas, Yatanocas, Ymacachas, Thoucoue, Tougoulas, and

Achougoulas." This list was obtained through the medium of the Mobilian trade language and part of the names are undoubtedly translated into it. Thus we find the Mobilian and Choctaw word for people, okla, "ougoula," or "oucoula," in five of these. The term Tougoulas probably designates the town of the Tiou (q. v.), an adopted tribe, and one of the others is perhaps a designation for the adopted tribe of Grigra (q. v.). Later writers usually speak of but five settlements, including that of the Grigra. One of these, the town of the "walnuts," is evidently the Ousagoucoulas of Iberville's informants, meaning, in reality, the town of the Hickories. The Great Village was probably the town called Naches or Natchez, and Pochougoula, the Flour Village, but the others mentioned, Jenzenaque or Jensenac and the White Apple or Apple Village cannot be identified. A White-earth village is mentioned by one writer, probably intended for the White Apple village. The Natchez among the Cherokee lived for a time at a town called Guhlaniyi.

History.—Undoubtedly tribes of the Natchez group were encountered by De Soto and his companions in 1541–43, and it is highly probable that the chief Quigaltanqui, who figures so prominently in the pursuit of the Spaniards when they took to the Mississippi, was leader of the tribe in question or of one of its divisions. The name Natchez appears first, however, in the narratives of La Salle's descent of the Mississippi in 1682. Relations between the French and Natchez were at first hostile, but peace was soon made and in 1699 a missionary visited the latter with a view to permanent residence. The next year Iberville, who had stopped short of the Natchez in his earlier ascent of the Mississippi, opened negotiations with the Natchez chief. A missionary was left among them at this time and the mission was maintained until 1706. In 1713 a trading post was established. The next year four Canadians, on their way north, were killed by some Natchez Indians and this resulted in a war which Bienville promptly ended. Immediately afterward a stockaded fort was built on a lofty bluff by the Mississippi and named Fort Rosalie. Several concessions were granted in the neighborhood and settlers flowed in until this was one of the most flourishing parts of the new colony. Between 1722 and 1724 there were slight disturbances in the good relations which had prevailed between the settlers and Indians, but they were soon smoothed over and harmony prevailed until a new commandant named Chépart, who seems to have been utterly unfit for his position, was sent to take command of Fort Rosalie. In consequence of his mismanagement a conspiracy was formed against the French and on November 28, 1729, the Indians rose and destroyed both post and settlement, about 200 Whites being slain. Next year the French and their Choctaw allies attacked the forts into which the Natchez had retired and liberated most of their captives but accomplished little else, and one night their enemies escaped across the Mississippi, where they established themselves in other forts in the marshy regions of northeastern Louisiana. There they were again attacked and about 400 were induced to surrender, but the greater part escaped during a stormy night and withdrew to the Chickasaw, who had been secretly aiding them. Later they divided into two bands, one of which settled among the Upper Creeks while the other went to live with the Cherokee. Afterward each followed the fate of their hosts and moved west of the Mississippi with them. Those who had lived with the Creeks established themselves not far from Eufaula, Okla., where the last who was able to speak the old tongue died about 1890. The Cherokee Natchez preserved their language longer, and a few are able to converse in it at the present day (1925).

Population.—Mooney's (1928) estimate of Natchez population in 1650 is 4,500; my own, as of 1698, 3,500. In 1731, after the losses suffered by them during their war with the French, Perrier estimated that they had 300 warriors. In 1735, 180 warriors were reported among the Chickasaw alone. During the latter half of the eighteenth century estimates of the warriors in the Creek band of Natchez vary from 20 to 150, and in 1836 Gallatin conjectures that its numbers over all were 300, which is probably above the fact. There are no figures whatever for the Cherokee band of Natchez.

Connection in which they have become noted.—The Natchez have become famous in a number of ways: (1) because they were the largest and strongest tribe on the lower Mississippi when Louisiana was settled by the French, (2) on account of their monarchical government and the peculiar institution of the Sun caste, (3) on account of the custom of destroying relatives and companions of a dead member of the Sun caste to accompany him or her into the world of spirits, (4) for the massacre of the French post at Natchez and the bitter war which succeeded it, (5) from the name of the city of Natchez, Miss., adopted from them. The name is also borne by post villages in Monroe County, Ala.; and Natchitoches Parish, La.; and a post hamlet in Martin County, Ind.

Ofo, or **Ofogoula,** see **Mosopelea** under Ohio.

Okelousa. A tribe living at one time in northern Mississippi. (See Louisiana.)

Pascagoula. "Bread people." Also called:

> Mískigúla, Biloxi name.

Connections.—They were probably Muskhogeans although closely associated with the Siouan Biloxi.

Location.—Their earliest known location was on the river which still bears their name, about 16 French leagues from its mouth. (See also Louisiana and Texas.)

Villages

Unknown, but see **Biloxi.**

History.—Iberville heard of the Pascagoula in 1699 when he made the first permanent settlement in Louisiana. That summer his brother Bienville visited them, and the following winter another brother, Sauvolle, who had been left in charge of the post, received several Pascagoula visitors. Some Frenchmen visited the Pascagoula town the next spring and Pénicaut (*in* Margry, 1875–86, vol. 5) has left an interesting account of them. In Le Page du Pratz's time (early eighteenth century) they were on the coast, but they did not move far from this region as long as France retained possession of the country. When French rule ended the Pascagoula passed over to Louisiana and settled first on the Mississippi River and later on Red River at its junction with the Rigolet du Bon Dieu. In 1795 they moved to Bayou Boeuf and established themselves between a band of Choctaw and the Biloxi. Early in the nineteenth century all three tribes sold these lands. A part of the Pascagoula remained in Louisiana for a considerable period, Morse mentioning two distinct bands, but a third group accompanied some Biloxi to Texas and lived for a time on what came to be called Biloxi Bayou, 15 miles above its junction with the Neches. I have been able to find no Indians in Louisiana claiming Pascagoula descent, but in 1914 there were two among the Alabama who stated that their mother was of this tribe, their father having been a Biloxi.

Population.—Mooney (1928) estimates that in 1650 there were 1,000 all told of the Biloxi, Pascagoula, and Moctobi. My own estimate for about the year 1698 is 875 of whom I should allow 455 to the Pascagoula. In 1700 Iberville states that there were 20 families, which would mean that they occupied the same number of cabins, but Le Page du Pratz raises this to 30. In 1758 the Pascagoula, Biloxi, and Chatot are estimated to have had about 100 warriors. In 1805 Sibley (1832) gives 25 among the Pascagoula alone. Morse (1822) estimates a total Pascagoula population of 240, and Schoolcraft (1851–57) cites authority for 111 Pascagoula in 1829. This is the last statement we have bearing upon the point.

Connection in which they have become noted.—The Pascagoula tribe is of some note as a constant companion of the Siouan Biloxi, and from the fact that it has bequeathed its name to Pascagoula River, Pascagoula Bay, and Pascagoula Port, Miss.

Pensacola. This tribe moved inland from Pensacola Bay near the end of the seventeenth century and in 1725–26 had established themselves near the Biloxi on Pearl River. (See Florida.)

Quapaw. When the French discovered this tribe in 1673 one town was on the east side of the Mississippi, but before 1700 it moved to the western bank. (See Arkansas.)

Taposa. Meaning unknown.

Connections.—As this tribe is said to have been allied with the Chickasaw and, unlike the Tunica and Tiou, did not have an *r* sound in their language, there is every reason to suppose that they belonged to the Muskhogean stock. Probably they were most closely affiliated with their neighbors, the Chakchiuma and Chickasaw.

Location.—Their earliest known location was on Yazoo River a few miles above the Chakchiuma.

History.—The Taposa are first mentioned by Iberville and the missionary De Montigny, in 1699. On the De Crenay map of 1733 (1910) their village is placed very close to that of the Chakchiuma, whose fortunes they probably followed.

Population.—The only hint as to the size of this tribe is given by Le Page du Pratz who says that the Taposa had about 25 cabins, half the number he assigns to the Chakchiuma. Other writers usually include them with the Chakchiuma (q. v.).

Tiou. Meaning unknown. The name has occasionally been misprinted "Sioux," thus causing confusion with the famous Sioux or Dakota of Minnesota and the Dakotas.

Connections.—The Tiou are proved by a statement of Diron d'Artaguiette (1916) to have belonged to the Tunica linguistic group of the Tunican family.

Location.—Their earliest location was near the upper course of Yazoo River; later they lived a little south of the Natchez and then among them.

History.—Shortly before 1697 the Tiou appear to have been in the locality first mentioned, and a map of that date seems to give two towns of Tiou, one above the Tunica and one below them. By 1699 part had settled among the Natchez, having been driven from their former homes, according to Le Page du Pratz (1758), by the Chickasaw. Before establishing themselves finally with the Natchez, they seem to have lived for a time a short distance below them on the Mississippi River, where La Salle and his companions speak of them as Koroa. Part of the tribe appears to have remained on the Yazoo for some years after the rest had left. At a later period the Bayogoula called in Tiou and Acolapissa to take the places of the Mugulasha with whom they had formerly lived and whom they had destroyed. Soon after Fort Rosalie had been built, the Tiou sold the lands upon which they had settled to the Sieur Roussin and moved elsewhere. After the Natchez massacre the hostile Indians sent them to the Tunica in a vain endeavor to induce the latter to declare against the French. In 1731, if we may trust a statement by Charlevoix, they were utterly cut off by the Quapaw, and while the completeness of this destruction may well be doubted, we hear nothing of them afterward.

Population.—No estimate of Tiou population separate from that of the Natchez is known.

Tunica. Meaning "the people," or "those who are the people." Also called:

Yoron, their own name.

Connections.—They were the leading tribe of the Tunica group of the Tunican stock, the latter including also the Chitimacha and Atakapa.

Location.—On the lower course of Yazoo River, on the south side about 4 French leagues from its mouth. (See also Arkansas.)

History.—There is evidence that tribes belonging to the Tunica group were encountered by De Soto west of the Mississippi and very probably the name of the tribe is preserved in that of the town of Tanico mentioned by Elvas (*in* Robertson, 1933), where people made salt, for in later years we find the Tunica engaged in the making and selling of this commodity. An early location for them on the eastern side of the Mississippi is indicated by the "Tunica Oldfields" near Friar Point, not many miles below Helena, Ark. The name appears on Marquette's map (1673) but there they are wrongly placed. In 1682 La Salle and his companions learned of this tribe, then located as given above, but neither he nor his lieutenant Tonti visited them on this or any subsequent expedition, though they learned of Tunica villages in the salt-making region of northeastern Louisiana. The Yazoo town of the tribe was first seen, apparently, by three missionary priests from Canada, one of whom, Father Davion, established himself among them in 1699. In 1702 he fled from his charges, but two or three years later was induced by them to return, and he remained among them for about 15 years more. In 1706 this tribe left the Yazoo and were received into the Houma town nearly opposite the mouth of Red River, but later, according to La Harpe (1831), they rose upon their hosts and killed more than half of them, and for a long period they continued to live in the region they had thus appropriated. They were firm friends of the French and rendered them invaluable service in all difficulties with the tribes higher up, and particularly against the Natchez, but in 1719 or 1720 Davion was so much discouraged at the meager results of his efforts that he left them. The anger excited against them by their support of the French resulted in an attack by a large party of Natchez and their allies in 1731 in which both sides suffered severely and the head chief of the Tunica was killed. The

Tunica remained in the same region until some time between 1784 and 1803, when they moved up Red River and settled close to the present Marksville, La., on the land of the Avoyel Indian village which they claimed to have bought from the Avoyel tribe.   Before this event took place, in company with the Ofo, Avoyel, and some Choctaw, they attacked the pirogues of a British expedition ascending the Mississippi, killed six men, wounded seven, and compelled the rest to turn back. A few families descended from the Tunica are still settled on the site just mentioned, which forms a small reservation.   Sibley (1832) says that in his time Tunica had settled among the Atakapa, and it was perhaps some of their descendants of whom Dr. Gatschet heard as living near Beaumont, Tex., about 1886.   Mooney (1928) learned of some Tunica families in the southern part of the Choctaw Nation, Okla., but they had lost their old language.

Population.—Mooney (1928) estimated that in 1650 the total population of the Tunica, Yazoo, Koroa, and Ofo was 2,000, and this very figure, except that it does not include the Koroa, is given by the missionary De Montigny in 1699.   My own figure for the same date is somewhat higher, 2,450, out of which I estimate about 1,575 were Tunica.   In 1719 the number of Tunica was conjectured to be 460 and in 1803, 50 to 60, though a second statement of about the same period gives 25 warriors.   Morse (1822) reports 30 Tunica in Louisiana. The census of 1910 gives 43 Tunica in all, but among these are included some Indians of other tribes and there were many mixed-bloods. The census of 1930 gives only 1, he being the only one who could speak the old language.

Connection in which they have become noted.—The Tunica were prominent in history (1) from the fact that their language was the principal dialect of a stock on the lower Mississippi which received its name from them, (2) for their sedentary character, (3) for their devotion to the French interest and their part in the Natchez wars, (4) from the perpetuation of their name in Tunica County, and Tunica Oldfields, Miss., and a post village of the name in West Feliciana Parish, La.

Yazoo.   Meaning unknown.

Connections.—The associations of this tribe with the Koroa and the fact that their language contained an *r* sound make it reasonably certain that they belonged to the Tunican group and stock.

Location.—On the south side of Yazoo River about 4 French leagues above its mouth.   (See also Arkansas.)

History.—The Yazoo appear to have been the first of the tribes living on the lower part of the Yazoo River to have established themselves there, and hence it was from them that the stream received its name. They are mentioned by La Salle and his companions in connection with their voyage to the mouth of the Mississippi in 1682. A French post was established near them in 1718, and in 1727 a Jesuit missionary, Father Seuel, settled nearby. In 1729, however, the Yazoo joined the Natchez in their uprising, murdered the missionary, and massacred the French garrison. Their subsequent fortunes were identical with those of the Koroa, and they were probably absorbed into the Chickasaw or Choctaw. It is not improbable that there is some connection between the name of this tribe and that of two of the Yazoo towns among the Choctaw, but if so it goes back beyond recorded history.

Population.—I have estimated that in 1698 there were somewhat more than 600 Yazoo and Koroa together. In 1700 Gravier reported 30 Yazoo cabins, but a quarter of a century later Le Page du Pratz (1758) estimated 100. In 1722 the Yazoo, Koroa, and Ofo together are said to have numbered 250. In 1730, however, the number of Yazoo and Koroa warriors is placed at 40.

Connection in which they have become noted.—The Yazoo are noted principally from the fact that they have transmitted their name to Yazoo River, Miss., and secondarily to Yazoo County and its capital city, in the same State.

LOUISIANA

Acolapissa. Meaning "those who listen and see," indicating possibly "borderers" or "scouts." Also called:

> Aquelou pissas, by Le Page du Pratz (1758, 2: 219).
> Cenepisa, by La Salle (*in* Margry, 1875–86, 1: 564).
> Colapissas, in 1699 by Pénicaut (*in* French, 1869, p. 38).
> Coulapissas, in 1700 by Sauvole (*in* Margry 1875–86, 4: 462).
> Equinipichas, by Sauvole (*in* French, 1851, 3: 225).
> Kinipissa, by Tonti (*in* Margry, 1875–86; 1: 604).
> Kolapissas, in 1700 by Gravier (*in* French, 1875, p. 88).

Connections.—The Acolapissa belonged to the Muskhogean linguistic family and evidently spoke a language closely related to Choctaw and Chickasaw. They may have been more intimately connected with the Napissa who united with the Chickasaw and who were perhaps identical with the Napochi (q. v.) of De Luna, but their closest relatives were the Tangipahoa (q. v.).

Location.—Their earliest known location was on Pearl River about 11 miles above its mouth. (See also Mississippi.)

Villages

Iberville was told that they consisted of six villages and that the Tangipahoa constituted a seventh, but we treat the latter separately, and the names of the six are not given.

History.—The Acolapissa are not mentioned among the tribes that came to Iberville in 1699 to form an alliance with him, but after his departure for France, Bienville visited them and was well received, although at first they were terrified because of a slave raid made upon them 2 days before by the English and Chickasaw. In 1702 (or 1705) they moved from Pearl River and settled on a bayou on the north side of Lake Pontchartrain called "Castembayouque" (now Castine Bayou). Six months later the Natchitoches Indians (q. v.) descended to the French fort on the Mississippi from their town on Red River to ask assistance from St. Denis, the commandant there, because of the ruin of their crops. St. Denis sent them under the charge of Pénicaut to the Acolapissa, who welcomed them and assigned a place for them to settle close to their own village. Late in 1713 or early in 1714 St. Denis, who had received a commission to proceed to Texas to examine the Spanish settlements, sent for the Natchitoches intending to reestablish them in their former seats, but upon hearing of this project the Acolapissa fell upon them and killed and captured a considerable number. In 1718, according to Pénicaut, but in any case before 1722, they moved over to the Mississippi River and settled on the east side 13 leagues from New Orleans. In 1739 they constituted practically one settlement with the Bayogoula and Houma, with whom they finally merged. Their later history is one with that of the **Houma** (q. v.).

Population.—Mooney (1928) estimated that in 1650 the population of the Acolapissa and the Tangipahoa together was 1,500. My own calculation as of 1698 is 1,050, based on La Harpe's (1831) estimate of 300 Acolapissa warriors in 1699 and Iberville's estimate of 250 families 3 years later. In 1722 Charlevoix states that there were 200 warriors and in 1739 there are said to have been of the Acolapissa, Houma, and Bayogoula together 90 to 100 warriors and 270 to 300 people exclusive of children.

Adai. Meaning unknown.

Connections.—This tribe was at first thought to have constituted an independent linguistic stock and the name Adaizan was given to it, but later Dr. Gatschet determined that the Adai language was a somewhat aberrant Caddo dialect, and it was therefore placed in the Caddoan stock.

Location.—Near the present Robeline in Natchitoches Parish.

History.—In 1699 Iberville mentions the Adai under the name Natao. In 1717 the mission of San Miguel de Linares was established among them by Spanish Franciscan missionaries. The buildings were destroyed in 1719 by a force of French and Indians, but they were rebuilt 2 years later as San Miguel de los Adaes, and the mission was not finally abandoned until 1773.   In October 1721 a military post called Nuestra Señora del Pilar de los Adaes was located close to the mission and continued until the latter was given up.   For 50 years this post was the capital of Texas in spite of, or because of, the fact that it was on its extreme eastern frontier.   In 1778 De Mézières states (*in* Bolton, 1914) that the tribe was almost extinct, but in 1805 Sibley reported a small Adai settlement on Lake Macdon near an affluent of Red River.   The survivors probably combined with the other Caddoan tribes of the region and followed their fortunes.

Population.—Bienville reported 50 warriors among them in 1700 but twice as many in 1718.   When the mission of San Miguel was rebuilt it is said to have served 400 Indians.   In 1805 the Adai village contained only 20 men but the number of women was much greater. The total Adai population in 1825 was 27.   My own estimate for 1698 is about 400.

Connection in which they have become noted.—The Adai were peculiar in having spoken a dialect so diverse from the other Caddo forms of speech that, as already stated, Powell (1891) at first gave them an independent status as constituting the Adaizan linguistic family. Historically, the Adai Indian and White settlement was noted as the easternmost outpost of the Spaniards and of the Franciscan Spanish missions, and it was the capital of the Province of Texas for 50 years.

Alabama.   Some of this tribe moved to Louisiana shortly after the territory east of the Mississippi was abandoned by the French. Most of them finally passed on into Texas, but a few are still settled in the southwestern part of the State.   (See Alabama.)

Apalachee.   A band of Apalachee Indians moved from the neighborhood of Mobile to Louisiana in 1764, remained for a short time on the Mississippi River and then moved up to Red River, where they obtained a grant of land along with the Taensa.   Later they sold this land and part of them probably removed to Oklahoma, but others remained in Louisiana and amalgamated with other tribes. (See Florida.)

Atakapa.   Meaning in Choctaw and Mobilian, "man eater," because they and some of the Indians west of them at times ate the flesh of their enemies.

> Skunnemoke, the name of a chief, extended to the whole people.
> Tûk-pa'-haⁿ-ya-di, Biloxi name.
> Yuk'hiti ishak, own name.

Connections.—The Atakapa were originally placed in an independent linguistic stock, including also the Bidai, Deadose, and probably the Opelousa, but it has now been determined that they belonged to one family with the Chitimacha, their eastern neighbors, and probably

the Tunican group on the Mississippi, the whole being called the
Tunican stock.

Location.—Atakapa bands extended along the coast of Louisiana
and Texas from Vermillion Bayou to and including Trinity Bay.
(See **Akokisa** under Texas.)

Subdivisions and Villages

The Atakapa about Trinity Bay and the lower course of Trinity River were
called Akokisa by the Spaniards, but they differed in no respect from the Atakapa
of Lake Charles. There was, however, an eastern Atakapa dialect which was
distinctly different from the one current in the Lake Charles and Trinity Bay
sections and was spoken by two different bands, one about Vermillion Bay and
one on the Mermentou River. There were a number of small villages but their
names are unknown.

History.—In 1528 Cabeza de Vaca learned of the existence of some
of these Indians, calling them Han. The portion of the Atakapa
living in Louisiana came to the attention of the French after the latter
had established themselves on the Mississippi River, but it so happened that they had more dealings with the people of Trinity Bay,
the Akokisa. This was owing in the first place to the romantic adventures of a French officer, Simars de Belle-Isle, left upon this coast in
1719. In 1721 Bernard de la Harpe and Captain Beranger accompanied by Belle-Isle visited the bay and carried some Indians off
with them to New Orleans. Fortunately for us, Beranger recorded
a number of words in their language which prove it to have been
almost identical with the Atakapa of Lake Charles. The Indians
subsequently escaped and are reported to have reached their own
country. In 1779 the band of Atakapa on Vermillion Bayou furnished 60 men and the Mermentou band 120 men to Galvez for his
expedition against the British forts on the Mississippi. In the latter
part of the eighteenth century numerous plots of land were sold to
French Creoles by the Atakapa Indians, but the last village of the
easternmost band was not abandoned until early in the nineteenth
century. The last village of the Atakapa who spoke the eastern
dialect was on the Mermentou and Indians are said to have lived
there down to 1836. The Calcasieu band held together for a longer
period, so that in 1908 a few persons were living who once made their
homes in the last native village on Indian Lake or Lake Prien. It
was from two of these that Dr. Gatchet, in January 1885, obtained
his Atakapa linguistic material. (See Gatschet and Swanton, 1932.)
Although in 1907 and 1908 I found a few Indians who knew something of the old tongue, it is today practically extinct. (See also
J. O. Dyer, 1917.) As early as 1747 a Spanish mission was proposed
for the Akokisa Indians, and in 1756, or about that time, it was established on the left bank of Trinity River, a short distance below the

present Liberty. It was named Nuestra Señora de la Luz, and near it was the presidio of San Agustín de Ahumada erected the same year. Before 1772 both of these had been abandoned. In 1805 the principal Akokisa village was on the west side of Colorado River about 200 miles southwest of Nacogdoches, but there was another between the Neches and the Sabine. The ultimate fate of the tribe is unknown.

Population.—Exclusive of the Akokisa, Mooney (1928) estimates a population of 1,500 Atakapa in 1650, which the Akokisa would perhaps swell to 2,000. In 1747 a Spanish report gives 300 Akokisa families, a figure which is probably too high. In 1779 the Bayou Vermillion and Mermentou bands had 180 warriors. Sibley (1832) states that in 1805 there were 80 warriors in the only Atakapa town remaining but that 30 of these were Houma and Tunica. The same writer adds that in 1760–70 the Akokisa numbered 80 men.

Connection in which they have become noted.—The traditional fame of the Atakapa rests upon the sinister reputation it had acquired as a body of cannibals. After the French began to settle southwestern Louisiana, they distinguished as the Atakapas district a section of southern Louisiana including the parishes of St. Mary, Iberia, Vermillion, St. Martin, and Lafayette, a usage which continues in commercial reports to the present day. The capital of this district, the modern St. Martinville, was known as the Atakapas Post. In Spartanburg County, S. C., is a place called Tucapau, the name of which may have been taken from this tribe.

Avoyel. The name signifies probably "people of the rocks," referring to flint and very likely applied because they were middlemen in supplying the Gulf coast tribes with flint. Also called:

> Little Taensa, so-called from their relationship to the Taensa (q. v.).
> Tassenocogoula, name in the Mobilian trade language, meaning "flint people."

Connections.—The testimony of early writers and circumstantial evidence render it almost certain that the Avoyel spoke a dialect of the Natchez group of the Muskhogean linguistic family.

Location.—In the neighborhood of the present Marksville, La.

History.—The Avoyel are mentioned first by Iberville in the account of his first expedition to Louisiana in 1699, where they appear under the Mobilian form of their name, Tassenocogoula. He did not meet any of the people, however, until the year following when he calls them "Little Taensas." They were encountered by La Harpe in 1714, and Le Page du Pratz (1758) gives a short notice of them from which it appears that they acted as middlemen in disposing to the French of horses and cattle plundered from Spanish settlements. In 1764 they took part in an attack upon a British regiment ascending the Mississippi (see **Ofo**), and they are mentioned by some later writers, but Sibley (1832) says they were extinct in 1805 except for two or three women "who did live among the French inhabitants of Washita." In 1930 one of the Tunica Indians still claimed descent from this tribe.

Population.—I have estimated an Avoyel population of about 280 in 1698. Iberville and Bienville state that they had about 40 warriors shortly after this period. (See **Taensa.**)

Connection in which they have become noted.—The name of the Avoyel is perpetuated in that of Avoyelles Parish, La.

Bayogoula. Meaning "bayou people," either from their location or from the fact that their tribal emblem was the alligator.

Connections.—Their language was of the southern Mushkogean division, not far removed from Houma and Choctaw.

Location.—Near the present Bayou Goula, in Iberville Parish.

History.—Unless this tribe was the Pishenoa encountered by Tonti in 1686 and not mentioned subsequently, it was first visited by Iberville in 1699. It then occupied one town with the **Mugulasha** (q. v.). In the winter of 1699–1700 the Bayogoula suffered severely from a surprise attack of the Houma. In the spring of 1700, for what cause we know not, the Bayogoula attacked their fellow townsmen, the Mugulasha, and destroyed them, but in 1706 they suffered a similar fate at the hands of the Taensa who had sought refuge with them. The remnant of the Bayogoula was given a place near New Orleans, but some time later they moved up the river to the present Ascension Parish, where they were found in 1739 between the Houma and Acolapissa. Yet our informant states that the three tribes were virtually one and the same, the distinction being kept up merely because the chief of each band was descended from the tribe mentioned. The subsequent history of the Bayogoula is identical with that of the Houma. (See **Houma** under Mississippi.)

Population.—Mooney (1928) estimates that in 1650 there were 1,500 of the Bayogoula, Quinipissa, and Mugulasha together. My own estimate for the same tribes, as of 1698, is 875. In 1699 Iberville gave about 100 cabins and 200–250 warriors, and the Journal of his companion ship, *Le Marin*, has 400–500 people. In 1700, after the destruction of the Mugulasha, Gravier gives a population of 200, and about 1715 they are said to have had 40 warriors. For their numbers in 1739, see **Houma** under Mississippi.

Connection in which they have become noted.—This tribe shared with the Washa the distinction of having been the first Indians within the limits of the present State of Louisiana to meet Iberville in the year in which the French colony of Louisiana was founded. The name is preserved in the post village of Bayou Goula, Iberville Parish, La., which seems to be close to the location of the original Indian town.

Biloxi. The Biloxi settled in Louisiana about 1764, and a very few are still living there. (See Mississippi.)

Caddo. The Caddo Indians are given under five different heads: the **Adai** and the **Natchitoches Confederacy** in Louisiana; the **Eyeish**, the **Hasinai Confederacy**, and the **Kadohadacho Confederacy** in Texas.

Chatot. The Chatot entered Louisiana about 1764, lived for a while on Bayou Boeuf, and later moved to Sabine River, after which nothing more is heard of them. (See Florida.)

Chawasha. Meaning unknown, though possibly "raccoon place (people)."

Connections.—A reference to this tribe and the Washa by Bienville places them in the Chitimacha division of the Tunican linguistic stock. I had erroneously concluded at an earlier period, on slender circumstantial evidence, that they were Muskhogeans.

Location.—On Bayou La Fourche and eastward to the Gulf of Mexico and across the Mississippi.

History.—After the relics of De Soto's army had escaped to the mouth of the Mississippi River and while their brigantines were riding at anchor there, they were attacked by Indians, some of whom had "staves, having very sharp heads of fish-bone." (See Bourne 1904, vol. 2, p. 202.) These may have belonged to the Chawasha and Washa tribes. The same two tribes are said, on doubtful authority, to have attempted to attack an English sea captain who ascended the Mississippi in 1699, but they were usually friendly to the French. In 1712 [5] they were moved to the Mississippi by Bienville and established themselves on the west side, just below the English Turn. In 1713 (or more probably 1715) they were attacked by a party of Chickasaw, Yazoo, and Natchez, who killed the head chief and many of his family, and carried off 11 persons as prisoners. Before 1722 they had crossed to the east side of the river, half a league lower down. In 1730, in order to allay the panic in New Orleans following on the Natchez uprising of 1729 which resulted in the massacre of the Whites at Natchez, Governor Perrier allowed a band of Negro slaves to attack the Chawasha, and it is commonly reported that they were then destroyed. The French writer Dumont (1753) is probably right, however, when he states that only seven or eight adult males were killed. At any rate they are mentioned as living with the Washa at Les Allemands on the west side of the Mississippi above

---

[5] So given by Bienville in an unpublished ms. (See page 294.)

New Orleans in 1739, and in 1758 they appear as constituting one village with the Washa. Except for one uncertain reference, this is the last we hear of them, but they may have continued for a considerable period longer before disappearing as a distinct body.

Population.—Mooney (1928) gives an estimate of 1,400 for the Washa, Chawasha, and Opelousa together in the year 1650. My own estimate for the first two and the Okelousa, as of 1698, is 700. This is based on Beaurain's (La Harpe's) estimate (1831) of 200 warriors for the 3 tribes. About 1715 there are said to have been 40 Chawasha warriors; in 1739, 30 warriors of the Washa and Chawasha together; and in 1758, 10 to 12.

Connection in which they have become noted.—The Chawasha attained temporary notoriety on account of the massacre perpetrated upon them in the manner above mentioned.

Chitimacha. Perhaps derived from the name of Grand River in the native tongue, which was Sheti, though Gatschet (1883) interprets it through the Choctaw language as meaning "those who have pots."

Connections.—The Chitimacha have given their name to a group of languages under the Tunican linguistic stock, including also the Chawasha and Washa.

Location.—On Grand River, Grand Lake, and the lower course of Bayou La Teche.

Subdivisions and Villages

The earliest French writers couple with this tribe the name of a tribe or supposed tribe called Yakna-Chitto, "Big Earth," but it is not known whether they were a part of the Chitimacha or an entirely independent people. In later times the Chitimacha were drawn into two unnamed subdivisions, one near the upper end of Bayou La Fourche and the other on Grand Lake. Following are the known villages:

Ama'tpan na'mu, two villages: (1) 3 miles east of Charenton on Bayou Teche; (2) on the east side of Grand Lake opposite Charenton.

Grosse Tête na'mu, 2 miles from the village at Plaquemine.

Hi'pinimsh na'mu, at the Fausse Pointe in the western part of Grand Lake, near Bayou Gosselin.

Ka'me naksh tcat na'mu, at Bayou du Plomb, near Bayou Chêne, 18 miles north of Charenton.

Ku'shuh na'mu, on Lake Mingaluak, near Bayou Chêne.

Na'mu ka'tsi, the Bayou Chêne village, St. Martin's Parish.

Ne'kun tsi'snis, opposite Ile aux Oiseaux, in the Lac de la Fausse Pointe.

Ne Pinu'nsh, on Bayou Teche, 2 miles west of Charenton.

Oku'nkiskin, probably at some sharp bend on Bayou La Teche judging from their name.

Shatshnish, at Jeanerette.

She'ti na'mu, on Grand River west of Plaquemine.

Sho'ktangi ha'ne hetci'nsh, on the south side of Graine à Volée Inlet, Grand Lake.

Tca'ti kuti'ngi na'mu, at the junction of Bayou Teche with the Atchafalaya Bayou.

Tcat kasi'tunshki, on the site of Charenton.

Tsa'htsinshup na'mu, the Plaquemine village, on Bayou des Plaquemines near Grand River.

Waitinimsh, at Irish Bend near Franklin.

There are said to have been others at the shell bank on the shore of Grand Lake, close to Charenton, and at a place called "Bitlarouges."

History.—Iberville made an alliance with the Chitimacha in 1699, shortly after his arrival in the present Louisiana. In August 1706, the Taensa captured some Chitimacha by treachery and enslaved them, and later the same year a Chitimacha war partly killed St. Cosme, missionary to the Natchez, and three other Frenchmen encamped with him. War followed between the Chitimacha on one hand and the French and their Indian allies on the other, which dragged along until 1718. The Chitimacha suffered severely during these 12 years and this war was responsible for the fact that in the early days of the Louisiana colony the greater part of the Indian slaves were Chitimacha. By the terms of the peace concluded in 1718, the Chitimacha agreed to settle at a designated spot upon the Mississippi, not far from the present Plaquemine. This, they or rather the eastern portion of them, did in 1719. In 1739 they seem to have been farther down, near the head of Bayou La Fourche. In 1784 one village is reported on Bayou La Fourche and two on the Teche. By 1881 the only survivors were near Charenton, where they occupied a small part of what had once been a considerable reservation. In that year and the year following Dr. A. S. Gatschet of the Bureau of American Ethnology collected from them a considerable body of linguistic material and some ethnological information. (See Gatschet, 1883.) Descendants of the tribe, mostly mixed-bloods, occupy the same section at the present time, but the Plaquemine band has disappeared.

Population.—Mooney (1928) estimated that in 1650 the Chitimacha numbered 3,000 souls. The present writer allowed 750 warriors to the tribe in 1698, based on Beaurain's estimate of 700–800 in 1699, which would mean about 2,625 souls. In 1758 the Mississippi band counted only about 80 warriors and in 1784 Hutchins gives 27. The size of the western band is nowhere indicated separately but the census of 1910 gives 69 for the entire tribe, 19 of whom were then at school in Pennsylvania. In 1930, 51 were returned.

Connection in which they have become noted.—The Chitimacha were the most powerful tribe of the northern Gulf coast west of Florida in United States territory. They also attained prominence in early Louisiana history on account of their long war with the French and the number of Chitimacha slaves in colonial families arising from that fact. The survivors are noteworthy as the best basket makers in the whole Gulf region.

Choctaw. Choctaw began moving into Louisiana not long after the settlement of New Orleans, at first temporarily, but later for permanent occupancy, especially after the territory east of the Mississippi had been ceded to Great Britain. Some settled on the northern shores of Lake Pontchartrain, where a few still remain, while other bands established themselves on the Nezpique, Red River, Bayou Boeuf, and elsewhere. Most of these drifted in time to the Choctaw Nation of Oklahoma, but a few families are still scattered about the State of Louisiana. (See Mississippi.)

Doustioni. A small tribe of the Natchitoches Confederacy (q. v.).

Houma. When first encountered by Europeans, the Houma lived near the present boundary line between Mississippi and Louisiana, if not actually on the Louisiana side. In 1706 or shortly afterward they moved altogether within the limits of Louisiana, where their descendants have remained to the present day. (See Mississippi.)

Koasati. Part of this tribe entered Louisiana near the end of the eighteenth century and lived on Red River and in the western part of the State. At the present day, the largest single band of Koasati in existence is northeast of Kinder, La. (See Alabama.)

Koroa. The Koroa camped, hunted, and had at times more permanent settlements in northeastern Louisiana. (See Mississippi.)

Mugulasha. This was a tribe which formerly lived in the same town as the Bayogoula on the lower course of the Mississippi. Some early writers state that they were identical with the Quinipissa and they will be treated in connection with that tribe.

Muskogee. The true Muskogee were represented by one band, a part of the Pakana tribe, which moved into the colony about 1764. They were settled upon Calcasieu River in 1805. Later they seem to have united with the Alabama now living in Polk County, Tex., but there are no known survivors at the present day. (See Alabama.)

Natchez. When this tribe was attacked by the French after they had destroyed the Natchez post, they escaped into Louisiana and fortified themselves at Sicily Island, from which most of them again escaped. A part under the chief of the Flour Village attacked the French post at Natchitoches in the fall of 1731, drove the Natchitoches from their town, and intrenched themselves in it. St. Denis, commander of that post, attacked them, however, having been previously reinforced by some Caddo and Atakapa, and inflicted upon them a severe defeat. After this no considerable number of Natchez seem to have remained in Louisiana. (See Mississippi.)

Natchitoches Confederacy. The word "Natchitoches" is generally supposed to be derived from "nạshitosh", the native word for pawpaw but an early Spanish writer, José Antonio Pichardo, was told that it was from a native word "nacicit" signifying "a place where the soil is the color of red ochre," and that it was applied originally to a small creek in their neighborhood running through red soil. The following are synonyms:

Nachittoos, Yoakum, 1855–56, vol. 1, p. 392.
Nachtichoukas, Jefferys, 1761, pt. 1, p. 164.
Nacitos, Linares (1716) *in* Margry, 1875–86, vol. 6, p. 217.
Nactythos, Iberville (1699) *in* Margry, 1880, 1875–86, vol. 4, p. 178.
Nadchito, Bienville (1700), *in* Margry, 1875–86, vol. 4, p. 434.
Naketosh, Gatschet, Caddo and Yatassi MS., p. 77, B. A. E.
Napgitache, McKenney and Hall, 1854, vol. 3, p. 82.
Naquitoches, Belle-Isle (1721), *in* Margry, 1875–86, vol. 6, p. 341.
Nashi'tosh, Mooney, 1896, p. 1092.
Nasitti, Joutel (1687) *in* Margry, 1875–86, vol. 3, p. 409.
Natsytos, Iberville (1699) *in* Margry, 1875–86, vol. 4, p. 178.
Notchitoches, Carver, 1778, map.
Yatchitcohes, Lewis and Clark, 1840, p. 142.
As part of the Caddo, the same terms were applied to them as appear under Kadohadacho (q. v.).

Connections.—They belonged to the Caddo division of the Caddoan linguistic stock, their nearest relatives being the Indians of the Kadohadacho and Hasinai Confederacies.

Location.—In northwestern Louisiana.

Subdivisions

Doustioni, appearing sometimes as Souchitioni, a small tribe near the present Natchitoches.
Natchitoches, close to the present site of Natchitoches.
Ouachita, on Ouachita River not far from the present Columbia.
Yatasi, on Red River near Shreveport.
A tribe called Capiché is mentioned by Tonti, but it is otherwise never referred to. Another called Nakasa, Nakasé, Natchés or Nataché was probably a part of the Yatasi, and Tonti mentions a tribe called Choye, probably the Chaye of Joutel (1713), as a people associated with the Yatasi. At a relatively late date part of the Yatasi went to live with the Indians of the Kadohadacho Confederation while the rest settled close to the Natchitoches.

History.—Moscoso, De Soto's successor, perhaps encountered some of the tribes of this group though his route lay farther north and west. On February 17, 1690, Tonti reached the villages of these Indians coming from the Taensa on Lake St. Joseph, and went on up the river to the Kadohadacho, visiting the Yatasi on the way.

In March 1700 Bienville followed the same route from the Taensa and reached the Natchitoches Indians in April, stopping at the Ouachita town en route. He went up Red River as far as the Yatasi and then returned to Biloxi. In 1702 the Natchitoches tribe, having lost their crops, descended the Red River and the Mississippi to the French fort near the mouth of the latter, then commanded by Louis Juchereau de St. Denis, who received them kindly and sent them to live with the Acolapissa Indians on Lake Pontchartrain. A few years later St. Denis visited the Natchitoches country himself. In 1707 four Indians of this tribe took part in an expedition against the Chitimacha to avenge the death of the missionary St. Cosme. In 1713–14 St. Denis sent for the Natchitoches Indians in order to take them back to their old country, where he had planned to establish a post. On learning of the intentions of their neighbors, the Acolapissa Indians fell upon them, killed 17 and captured 50 women and girls, but the latter were apparently recovered soon afterward and all were returned to their old town, where the post was established according to plan in 1714. From this time until his death St. Denis' career was intimately bound up with this post and the Indians about it, though he was frequently engaged in expeditions into and across Texas. He was formally appointed commandant of the post July 1, 1720, and retained it until his death in June 1744. In 1731, with the assistance of his Indians and a detachment of soldiers from the Spanish post of Adai, he won a signal victory over a large body of Natchez Indians, the only clear-cut advantage which the French gained in the Natchez War. In the meantime Natchitoches had become the center of a flourishing trade with the Indians extending far to the north and west, and when St. Denis died his son, Louis de St. Denis continued to enjoy the advantages of it and to share the prestige of his father. During all of this time, however, the Natchitoches Indians seem to have been decreasing, and toward the end of the eighteenth century they parted with most of their lands to French Creoles, though their relations with the latter seem to have been uniformly cordial. Part of them remained in their old country permanently and either died out or mixed with the newcomers, while the rest joined their relatives of the Kadohadacho and Hasinai Confederations and followed their fortunes.

Population.—In 1700 Bienville estimated that there were 400–450 warriors in the Natchitoches Confederacy, but in 1718 he reported that the number had fallen to 80, while La Harpe (1831) reported a total population of 150–200. In 1805 Sibley (1832) reported 52 warriors and for the Natchitoches tribe by itself, 32, and 20 years later a total population of 61 was returned. An estimate of 1,000 for all of these tribes before White contact would probably be ample.

Connection in which they have become noted.—The city of Natchi-toches, La., is named after this group of tribes and is noteworthy as the oldest permanent settlement in the State. The victory which they enabled St. Denis to win over the Natchez Indians occupies a noteworthy place in the history of the section.

Ofo. This tribe entered Louisiana some time in the latter half of the eighteenth century and finally united with the Tunica, settling with them at Marksville. (See the article **Mosopelea** under Ohio and **Tunica** under Mississippi.)

Okelousa. Meaning "black water."

Connections.—The associations of this tribe were mainly with Muskhogean peoples and this fact, coupled with the Muskhogean name, indicates their linguistic affiliations with a fair degree of certainty.

Location.—The Okelousa moved about considerably. The best-determined location is the one mentioned by Le Page du Pratz (1758), on the west side of the Mississippi back of and above Pointe Coupée. (See History below.) (See also Mississippi.)

History.—After De Soto reached the principal Chickasaw town, the head chief came to him, January 3, 1541, "and promptly gave the Christians guides and interpreters to go to Caluça, a place of much repute among the Indians. Caluça is a province of more than 90 villages not subject to anyone, with a savage population, very warlike and much dreaded, and the soil is fertile in that section." (See Bourne, 1904, 1922, vol. 2, p. 132.) There is every reason to think that Caluça is a shortened form of Okalousa and it is rather likely that the later Okelousa were descended from these people, but if so either De Soto's informants had very much exaggerated their numbers or they suffered immense losses before we hear of them again. The name in De Soto's time may, however, have been applied to a geo-graphical region. Nicolas de la Salle, writing in 1682, quotes native informants to the effect that this tribe, in alliance with the Houma, had destroyed a third. La Harpe (1831) mentions them as allied with the Washa and Chawasha and wandering near the seacoast, a state-ment which led me to the erroneous conclusion that the three tribes thus associated were related. The notice of them by Le Page du Pratz has been mentioned above. They finally united with the Houma, the Acolapissa, or some other Muskhogean band on the lower Mississippi.

Population.—Unknown, but for an estimate, see **Chawasha** (p. 202).

Opelousa. Probably from Mobilian and Choctaw Aba lusa, "black above," and meaning "black headed" or "black haired."

Connections.—No words of the Opelousa language have survived, but the greater number of the earlier references to them speak as if they were allied with the Atakapa, and it is probable that they belonged to the Atakapan group of tribes.

Location.—In the neighborhood of the present Opelousas.

History.—The Opelousa seem to have been mentioned first by Bienville in an unpublished report on the Indians of the Mississippi and Gulf regions. They were few in numbers and led a wandering life. They maintained some sort of distinct tribal existence into the nineteenth century but disappeared by the end of the first quarter of it.

Population.—About 1715 this tribe was estimated to have 130 warriors; in 1805 they are said to have had 40, and in 1814 the total population of the tribe is placed at 20.

Connection in which they have become noted.—The Opelousa gave their name to an important post and the district depending upon it.

Ouachita. A tribe of the Natchitoches Confederacy (q. v.).

Pascagoula. This tribe entered Louisiana about 1764 and lived on Red River and Bayou Boeuf. Their subsequent history is wrapped in uncertainty. (See Mississippi.)

Quapaw. From 1823 to 1833 the Quapaw lived with the Kadohadacho on a southern affluent of Red River. (See Arkansas.)

Quinipissa. Signifying "those who see," perhaps meaning "scouts," or "outpost."

Connections.—The Quinipissa belonged to the southern division of the Muskhogean stock, and probably were very closely related to the Choctaw.

Location.—On the west bank of the Mississippi River and some distance above New Orleans.

History.—There may have been a connection between this tribe, the **Acolapissa** (q. v.) and the Napissa or Napochi. (See Mississippi.) They were met first by La Salle and his companions when the latter were on their way to the Gulf of Mexico in 1682. They treated the explorers in a hostile manner but made peace with Tonti in 1686. When Iberville ascended the river in 1699, no tribe of the name was to be found, but later it was learned that the chief of the Mugulasha tribe, then forming one village with the Bayogoula, was the same Quinipissa chief who had had dealings with La Salle and Tonti. According to some writers, the Mugulasha were identical with the Quinipissa; according to others, the Mugulasha had absorbed the remains of the Quinipissa. In May 1700, the Bayogoula rose against the Mugulasha and destroyed them as a tribe, though they probably adopted many of them as individuals. We hear nothing further regarding them.

Population.—There is no separate estimate of the number of the Quinipissa. (See **Bayogoula**.)

Connection in which they have become noted.—The Quinipissa are noted only for the encounter, ultimately hostile, which La Salle had with them in 1682 when he descended to the mouth of the Mississippi.

Souchitioni, see Natchitoches Confederacy.

Taensa. Meaning unknown, but the name is evidently derived from that of one of the tribe's constituent towns.

Connections.—They were one of the three known tribes of the Natchez division of the Muskhogean stock.

Location.—At the western end of Lake St. Joseph, in Tensas Parish. (See also Alabama.)

Villages

The only list of Taensa villages preserved was obtained by Iberville through the medium of the Mobilian trade language and it is uncertain how much of each name is a Mobilian translation. In four of them we recognize the Mobilian word for people, okla. These villages are: Taënsas, Ohytoucoulas, Nyhougoulas, Couthaougoula, Conchayon, Talaspa, and Chaoucoula. Gatschet has endeavored to interpret all but one of them; Taënsas by reference to taⁿ'tci, "corn"; Ohytoucoulas from u'ti, "chestnut"; Couthaougoula from uk'ha'tax, "lake"; Conchayon from ko'nshak, "reed"; Talaspa from ta'lapi, "five" or ta'lepa, "hundred"; Chaoucoula from issi, "deer" or ha'tche, "river." Most of these seem in the highest degree doubtful. All of the towns were situated close together in the place above indicated.

History.—It is altogether probable that the Spaniards under De Soto encountered the Taensa or bands afterward affiliated with them, and the probability is strengthened by the fact that La Salle in 1682 was shown some objects of Spanish origin by the chief of the Taensa. However, La Salle and his companions are the first Europeans known to have met them. The French were treated with great kindness and no war ever took place between the two peoples. The Taensa were subsequently visited by Tonti and by Iberville. When the latter was in their town in 1700 the temple was destroyed by fire, whereupon five infants were thrown into the flames to appease the supposedly offended deity. De Montigny undertook missionary work among them for a brief period but soon went to the Natchez as presenting a larger field and his place was never filled. In 1706 the Taensa abandoned their villages on account of the threatening attitude of the Yazoo and Chickasaw and settled in the town of the Bayogoula whom they afterward destroyed or drove away in the tragic manner above described. (See Bayogoula.) The Taensa appear to have moved shortly to a spot in the vicinity of Edgard, St. John Baptist Parish, and later to the Manchac. In 1715 they left this latter place and moved to Mobile, where they were assigned a townsite 2 leagues from the French post, at a place formerly occupied by the Tawasa. Before 1744 they had crossed the Tensaw River, to which they gave their name, and made a new settlement which they retained until Mobile was surrendered to the British in 1763. Soon after that event, they moved to Red River. In April 1764, they asked permission to establish themselves on the Mississippi River at the upper end of Bayou La Fourche, but they seem never to have gone there. For more than 40 years they occupied a tract of land on Red River adjoining that of the Apalachee. Early in the nineteenth century both tribes sold their lands and moved to Bayou Boeuf. Still later the Taensa seem to have moved farther south to a small bayou at the head of Grand Lake which still bears their name, where they intermarried with the Chitimacha, Alabama, and Atakapa. Some Taensa blood is known to run in the veins of certain Chitimacha, but as a tribe they are entirely extinct.

Population.—Mooney's estimate (1928) for the Taensa and Avoyel in 1650 is 800, and my own for 1698 slightly greater or nearly the same, although De Montigny (*in* Shea, 1861), writing in 1699, gives only 700. In 1700 Iberville estimated 120 cabins and 300 warriors, but in 1702 allows them 150 families. Somewhat later Le Page du Pratz (1758) says they had about 100 cabins. In 1764 this tribe, with the Apalachee and Pakana Creeks, counted about 200 all told. Sibley (1832) places the number of Taensa warriors in 1805 at 25.

Connection in which they have become noted.—The Taensa were noted for (1) the peculiarity of their customs, which were like those of the Natchez, (2) the tragic destruction of their temple in 1700 and the human sacrifices which followed, (3) the perpetuation of their name in Tensas Parish, Tensas River, and Tensas Bayou, La., and the Tensaw River and Tensaw Village in Baldwin County, Ala.

Tangipahoa. Meaning probably "corncob gatherers," or "corncob people."

Connections.—The name of this tribe and its affiliations with the Acolapissa indicate that it belonged to the southern division of the Muskhogean stock.

Location.—Probably on the present Tangipahoa River, Tangipahoa Parish.

History.—The original home of the Tangipahoa seems to have been as given above, and their relations with the Acolapissa must have been very close, for Iberville was informed by some Indians that they constituted a seventh Acolapissa town. In 1682 La Salle's party discovered a town on the eastern side of the Mississippi, 2 leagues below the settlement of the Quinipissa, which had recently been destroyed, and one of his companions calls this "Tangibao," while others speak of it as Maheouala or Mahehoualaima. The last two terms may refer to the name of the town and the first to that of the tribe which occupied it. Probably a part of the Tangipahoa only settled here, but, as we hear little of them after this period, we must assume that they had been absorbed by some other people, most likely the Acolapissa.

Population.—(See **Acolapissa.**)

Connection in which they have become noted.—Tangipahoa Parish, Tangipahoa River, in Amite and Pike Counties, Miss., and Tangipahoa Parish, La., and the post town of Tangipahoa preserve the name of the Tangipahoa.

Tawasa. Some Tawasa accompanied the Alabama to Louisiana but not until after the separate existence of the tribe had been ended. (See Alabama.)

Washa. Appearing oftenest in literature in the French form Ouacha, meaning unknown.

Connections.—The nearest relations of the Washa were the Chawasha (q. v.) and both belonged to the Chitimachan branch of the Tunican linguistic family.

Location.—Their earliest known location was on Bayou La Fourche, perhaps in the neighborhood of the present Labadieville, Assumption Parish.

Villages

None are known under any but the tribal name.

History.—As stated in treating the Chawasha, this tribe and the one just mentioned may have been those which attacked Moscoso's flotilla at the mouth of the Mississippi. Shortly after Iberville reached America in 1699, the Washa and three other tribes west of the Mississippi came to make an alliance with him and a little later, on his way up the great river, he fell in with some of them. He calls Bayou La Fourche "the River of the Washas." In July 1699, Bienville made a vain attempt to establish friendly relations with them, but we hear little more of them until 1715 [6] when Bienville moved them to the Mississippi and settled them 2 leagues above New Orleans on the south side of the Mississippi. In 1739 the Washa and Chawasha were found living together at Les Allemands, and they probably continued in the same neighborhood until a considerably later period. Sibley (1832) says the tribe in 1805 was reduced to 5 persons (2 men and 3 women) scattered in French families.

---

[6] So stated in a ms. by Bienville. In Swanton (1911) this date was given erroneously as 1718 on other authority.

Population.—A memoir attributed to Bienville states that in 1715 the Washa numbered 50 warriors, having been reduced from 200. This is the only separate estimate of them. (See **Chawasha** for the combined population of the two tribes at other periods.)

Connection in which they have become noted.—The name Washa is preserved in Washa Lake, near the seacoast of Terrebonne Parish, La., and it was formerly given to Lake Salvador, southeast of New Orleans.

Yatasi. A tribe of the **Natchitoches Confederacy** (q. v.).

ARKANSAS

Caddo. These Indians are treated under the five following heads: Adai and the Natchitoches Confederacy in Louisiana, Eyeish and the Hasinai Confederacy in Arkansas, and Kadohadacho Confederacy in Texas. Tribes of the Kadohadacho Confederacy are the only ones known to have lived in Arkansas.

Cahinnio. One of the tribes connected with the Kadohadacho Confederacy (q. v. under Texas).

Cherokee. Some Cherokee lived in this State while they were on their way from their old territories to Oklahoma, and a tract of land in northwestern Arkansas was granted them by treaty in 1817, which in 1828 they re-ceded to the United States Government. (See Tennessee.)

Chickasaw. Chickasaw passed through Arkansas on their way to Oklahoma but owned no land there. (See Mississippi.)

Choctaw. The Choctaw had a village on the lower course of Arkansas River in 1805 and they owned a large strip of territory in the western part of the State, granted to them by the treaty of Doak's Stand, October 18, 1820. They surrendered the latter in a treaty concluded at Washington, January 20, 1825. (See Mississippi.)

Illinois. When Europeans first descended the Mississippi an Illinois division known as Michigamea, "Big Water", was settled in northeastern Arkansas about a lake known by their name, probably the present Big Lake in Mississippi County. They had probably come from the region now embraced in the State of Illinois only a short time before, perhaps from a village entered on some maps as "the old village of the Michigamea." Toward the end of the seventeenth century they were driven north again by the Quapaw or Chickasaw and united with the cognate Kaskaskia. (See Illinois.)

Kaskinampo. This tribe appears to have been encountered by De Soto in what is now the State of Arkansas in 1541. (See Tennessee.)

Michigamea.   (See **Illinois** above.)

Mosopelea, see **Ofo.**

Ofo.   If these are the Mosopelea, as seems assured, they appear to
have lived for a short time near the end of the seventeenth century
in the neighborhood of the Quapaw on the lower course of Arkansas
River before moving farther south.   (See Mississippi.)

Osage.   The Osage hunted over much of the northern, and particularly northwestern, part of Arkansas and claimed all lands now
included in the State as far south as Arkansas River.   They ceded
most of their claims to these to the United States Government in a
treaty signed at Fort Clark, Louisiana Territory, in 1808, and the
remainder by treaties at St. Louis, September 25, 1818, and June 2,
1825.   (See Missouri.)

Quapaw.   Meaning "downstream people."   They were known by
some form of this word to the Omaha, Ponca, Kansa, Osage, and
Creeks.   Also called:

> Akansa, or Arkansas, by the Illinois and other Algonquian Indians, a
> name probably derived from one of the Quapaw social subdivisions.
> Beaux Hommes, a name given them by the French.
> Bow Indians, so-called probably because the bow wood from the Osage
> orange came from or through their country.
> Ima, by the Caddo, probably from one of their towns.
> Papikaha, on Marquette's map (1673).
> Utsúshuat, Wyandot name, meaning "wild apple," and referring to the
> fruit of the Carica papaya.

Connections.—The Quapaw were one of the five tribes belonging to
what J. O. Dorsey (1897) called the Ȼegiha division of the Siouan
linguistic stock.

Location.—At or near the mouth of Arkansas River.   (See also
Louisiana, Kansas, Mississippi, Oklahoma, and Texas.)

Villages

Tongigua, on the Mississippi side of Mississippi River above the mouth of the
Arkansas, probably in Bolivar County, Miss.
Tourima, at the junction of White River with the Mississippi, Desha County,
probably the town elsewhere called Imaha.
Ukakhpakhti, on the Mississippi, probably in Phillips County.
Uzutiuhi, on the south side of the lower course of Arkansas River not far from
Arkansas Post.

History.—Before the French became acquainted with this tribe (in
1673) the Quapaw had lived on Ohio River above its junction with the
Wabash, and that portion of the Ohio was known as Arkansas River
by the Illinois from this circumstance.   It was formerly thought that
the Pacaha or Capaha met by De Soto in this part of Arkansas were

the tribe in question, but it is not probable that they had left the Ohio then, and the name Capaha, the form on which the relationship is supposed to be established, is probably incorrect. In 1673 Marquette visited them and turned back at their towns without descending the Mississippi any farther. La Salle in 1682, Tonti in 1686, and all subsequent voyagers down and up the Mississippi mention them, and they soon became firm allies of the French. Shortly after Marquette's visit they were ravaged by pestilence and the Ukakhpakhti village was moved farther downstream. A few years later and before 1700 the people of Tongigua moved across and settled with those of Tourima, and still later all of the towns moved from the Mississippi to the Arkansas. Le Page du Pratz (1758) encountered them about 12 miles above the entrance of White River. Sibley (1832) found them in 1805 on the south side of Arkansas River about 12 miles above Arkansas Post. By a treaty signed at St. Louis, August 24, 1818, the Quapaw ceded all their claims south of Arkansas River except a small territory between Arkansas Post and Little Rock, extending inland to Saline River. The latter was also given up in a treaty signed November 15, 1824, at Harrington's, Arkansas Territory, and the tribe agreed to live in the country of the Caddo Indians. They were assigned by the Caddo a tract on Bayou Treache on the south side of Red River, but it was frequently overflowed, their crops were often destroyed, and there was much sickness, and in consequence they soon returned to their old country. There they annoyed the white settlers so much that by a treaty signed May 13, 1833, the United States Government conveyed to them 150 sections of land in the extreme southeastern part of Kansas and the northeastern part of Indian Territory, to which they in turn agreed to move. February 23, 1867, they ceded their lands in Kansas and the northern part of their lands in Indian Territory. In 1877 the Ponca were brought to the Quapaw Reservation for a short time, and when they removed to their own reservation west of the Osage most of the Quapaw went with them. Still later the lands of the Quapaw were allotted in severalty and they are now citizens of Oklahoma.

Population.—Mooney (1928) estimated that in 1650 the Quapaw numbered 2,500. In 1750 Father Vivier stated that they had about 400 warriers or about 1,400 souls. In 1766, however, the British Indian Agent, John Stuart, reported that they had but 220 gunmen. Porter estimated that the total Quapaw population in 1829 was 500. In 1843 it was 476. In 1885 there were 120 on the Osage Reservation and 54 on the Quapaw Reservation, and in 1890, 198 on both. The census of 1910 gave 231, but the Indian Office Report of 1916, 333, and that of 1923, 347. The census of 1930 returned 222.

Connection in which they have become noted.—The native form of the name of this tribe, Quapaw, is but seldom used topographically, although there is a village of the name in Ottawa County, Okla., but Arkansas; the term applied to them by the Illinois Indians, has become affixed to one of the largest branches of the Mississippi and to one of the States of the American Union. It has also been given to a county and mountain in Arkansas and to cities in that State and in Kansas.

Tunica. From some names given by the chroniclers of De Soto it is probable that the Tunica or some tribes speaking their language were living in Arkansas in his time. In fact it is not unlikely that the Pacaha or Capaha, who have often been identified with the Quapaw, were one of these. In later historic times they camped in the northeastern part of Louisiana and probably in neighboring sections of Arkansas. (See Mississippi.)

Yazoo. Like the Tunica this tribe probably camped at times in northeastern Louisiana and southeastern Arkansas, but there is no direct evidence of the fact. (See Mississippi.)

TENNESSEE

Catawba. For a brief period in their later history the Catawba lived among the Cherokee and they may have occupied lands in Tennessee at that time. There are indications that they may have been in eastern Tennessee at a more remote epoch. (See South Carolina.)

Cherokee. Meaning unknown, but possibly from Creek tciloki, "people of a different speech." The middle and upper dialects substitute *l* for *r*. Also called:

> Alligewi or Alleghanys, a people appearing in Delaware tradition who were perhaps identical with this tribe.
> Ani'-Kĭtu'hwagĭ, own name, from one of their most important ancient settlements, and extended by Algonquian tribes to the whole.
> Ani'-Yûn'-wiyâ', own name, meaning "real people."
> Bäniatho, Arapaho name (Gatschet, MS., B. A. E.).
> Entari ronnon, Wyandot name, meaning "mountain people."
> Mâⁿtĕrâⁿ', Catawba name, meaning "coming out of the ground."
> Ochie'tari-ronnon, a Wyandot name.
> Oyata' ge'ronóñ, Iroquois name, meaning "inhabitants of the cave country."
> Shánaki, Caddo name.
> Shánnakiak, Fox name (Gatschet, Fox MS., B. A. E.).
> Talligewi, Delaware name (in Walam Olum), see Alligewi.
> Tcálke, Tonkawa name.
> Tcerokiéco, Wichita name.
> Uwatáyo-róno, Wyandot name, meaning "cave people."

Connections.—The Cherokee language is the most aberrant form of speech of the Iroquoian linguistic family.

Location.—From the earliest times of which we have any certain knowledge the Cherokee have occupied the highest districts at the southern end of the Appalachian chain, mainly in the States of Tennessee and North Carolina, but including also parts of South Carolina, Georgia, Alabama, and Virginia. (See also Arkansas, Kansas, Kentucky, Oklahoma, and Texas.)

Subdivisions and Villages

There were anciently three Cherokee dialects which probably corresponded in some measure to the three groups of towns into which early traders and explorers divided the tribe. These groups, with the towns belonging to each according to the Purcell map, but following as far as possible the Handbook (Hodge, 1907, 1910) orthography, are as follows:

Lower Settlements:

Estatoee, 2 towns: Old Estatoee on Tugaloo River below the junction of Chattooga and Tullalah Rivers, in Oconee County, S. C.; and Estatoee in the northwestern part of Pickens County.

Keowee, 2 towns: Old Keowee on Keowee River near Fort George, Oconee County, S. C.; and New Keowee on the headwaters of Twelve-mile Creek in Pickens County, S. C., the latter also called probably Little Keowee.

Kulsetsiyi, 3 towns: (1) on Keowee River, near Fall Creek, Oconee County, S. C.; (2) on Sugartown or Cullasagee Creek near Franklin, Macon County, N. C.; (3) on Sugartown Creek, near Morganton, Fannin County, Ga.

Oconee, on Seneca Creek near Walhalla, Oconee County, S. C.

Qualatchee, 2 towns: (1) on Keowee River, S. C.; (2) on the headwaters of Chattahoochee River, Ga.

Tomassee, 2 towns: (1) on Tomassee Creek of Keowee River, Oconee County, S. C.; (2) on Little Tennessee River near the entrance of Burningtown Creek, Macon County, S. C.

Toxaway, on Toxaway Creek, a branch of Keowee River, S. C.

Tugaloo, on Tugaloo River at the junction of Toccoa Creek, Habersham County, Ga.

Ustanali, several towns so called: (1) on Keowee River below the present Fort George, Oconee County, S. C.; (2) probably on the waters of Tuckasegee River in western North Carolina; (3) just above the junction of Coosawatee and Conasauga Rivers to form the Oostanaula River in Gordon County, Ga.; (4) perhaps on Eastanollee Creek of Tugaloo River, Franklin County, Ga.; (5) perhaps on Eastaunaula Creek flowing into Hiwassee River in Mc-Minn County, Tenn.; and (6) possibly another.

Middle Settlements:

Cowee, about the mouth of Cowee Creek of Little Tennessee River, about 10 miles below Franklin, N. C.

Coweeshee, probably between the preceding and Yunsawi.

Ellijay, 4 towns: (1) on the headwaters of Keowee River, S. C.; (2) on Ellijay Creek of Little Tennessee River near Franklin, N. C.; (3) about Ellijay in Gilmer County, Ga.; and (4) on Ellejoy Creek of Little River near Marysville in Blount County, Tenn.

Itseyi, 3 towns: (1) on Brasstown Creek of Tugaloo River, Oconee County, S. C.; (2) on Little Tennessee River near Franklin, N. C.; and (3) on upper Brasstown Creek of Hiwassee River, Towns County, Ga.

Jore, on Iola Creek, an upper branch of Little Tennessee River, N. C.

Kituhwa, on Tuckasegee River and extending from above the junction of the Oconaluftee nearly to the present Bryson City, Swain County, N. C.

Nucassee, at the present Franklin, N. C.

Stikayi, 3 towns: (1) on Sticoa Creek, near Clayton, Rabun County, Ga.; (2) on Tuckasegee River at the old Thomas homestead just above Whittier, Swain County, N. C.; and (3) on Stekoa Creek of Little Tennessee River, a few miles below the junction of Nantahala, Graham County, N. C.

Tawsee, on Tugaloo River, Habersham County, Ga.

Tekanitli, in upper Georgia.

Tessuntee, on Cowee River, south of Franklin, N. C.

Tikaleyasuni, on Burningtown Creek, an upper branch of Little Tennessee River, western North Carolina.

Watauga, 2 towns: (1) on Watauga Creek, a branch of Little Tennessee River, a few miles below Franklin, N. C.; (2) traditionally located at Watauga Old Fields, about Elizabethtown, on Watauga River, in Carter County, Tenn.

Yunsawi, on West Buffalo Creek of Cheowa River, Graham County, N. C.

Over-the-Hills and Valley Settlements, or Overhill Settlements:

Chatuga, 3 towns: (1) on Chattooga River, on the boundary between South Carolina and Georgia; (2) probably on upper Tellico River, Monroe County, Tenn.; (3) perhaps on Chattooga River, a tributary of the Coosa, in northwest Georgia.

Chilhowee, on Tellico River in Monroe County, Tenn., near the North Carolina border.

Cotocanahut, between Natuhli and Niowe.

Echota, 5 towns: (1) Great Echota, on the south side of Little Tennessee River, a short distance below Citico Creek, Monroe County, Tenn.; (2) Little Echota on Sautee Creek, a head stream of the Chattahoochee west of Clarksville, Ga.; (3) New Echota, at the junction of Oostanaula and Conasauga Rivers, Gordon County, Ga.; (4) the old Macedonian Mission on Soco Creek, of the North Carolina Reservation; and (5) at the great Nacoochee mound. (See Naguchee below.)

Hiwassee, 2 towns: (1) Great Hiwassee on the north bank of Hiwassee River at the present Savannah Ford, above Columbus, Polk County, Tenn.; (2) at the junction of Peachtree Creek with Hiwassee River, above Murphy, N. C., probably the Guasuli of the De Soto Chroniclers.

Natuhli, on Nottely River, a branch of Hiwassee River at or near the site of the present Ranger, Cherokee County, N. C.

Nayuhi, seems to have been the name of four towns: (1) probably of the Lower Settlements, on the east bank of Tugaloo River, S. C.; (2) on the upper waters of Tennessee River, apparently in North Carolina, and (3 and 4) in the same general region, the last three being mentioned by Bartram (1792).

Sitiku, on Little Tennessee River at the entrance of Citico Creek, Monroe County, Tenn.

Tahlasi, on Little Tennessee River about Talassee Ford in Blount County, Tenn.

Tallulah, 2 towns: (1) on the upper Tallulah River, Rabun County, Ga.; (2) on Tallulah Creek of Cheowa River in Graham County, N. C.

Tamahli, 2 towns: (1) on Valley River a few miles above Murphy, about the present Tomatola, Cherokee County, N. C.; (2) on Little Tennessee River about Tomotley Ford, a few miles above Tellico River in Monroe County, Tenn.

Tellico, 4 towns: (1) Great Tellico, at Tellico Plains on Tellico River, Monroe County, Tenn.; (2) Little Tellico, on Tellico Creek of Little Tennessee River about 10 miles below Franklin, N. C.; (3) (also called Little Tellico at times) on Valley River about 5 miles above Murphy, N. C.; (4) Tahlequah, capital of the Cherokee Nation in what is now Oklahoma.

Tennessee, 2 towns: (1) on Little Tennessee River a short distance above its junction with the main stream in east Tennessee; (2) on an extreme head branch of Tuckasegee River, above the present Webster, N. C.

Toquo, on Little Tennessee River about the mouth of Toco Creek, Monroe County, Tenn.

Tsiyahi, 3 towns: (1) on a branch of Keowee River, near the present Cheochee, Oconee County, S. C.; (2) a modern settlement on Cheowa River about Robbinsville, N. C.; (3) a former settlement in Cades Cove, on Cover Creek, Blount County, Tenn.

Ustanali; according to Purcell's map, there was a town of this name different from those already given, on the upper waters of Cheowa River, Graham County, N. C.

Besides the above, the following settlements are given by Mooney and other writers:

Amahyaski, location unknown.
Amkalali, location unknown.
Amohi, location unknown.
Anisgayayi, a traditional town on Valley River, Cherokee County, N. C.
Anuyi, location unknown.
Aquohee, perhaps at the site of Fort Scott, on Nantahala River, Macon County, N. C.
Atsiniyi, location unknown.
Aumuchee, location unknown.
Ayahliyi, location unknown.
Big Island, on Big Island, in Little Tennessee River a short distance below the mouth of Tellico River.
Briertown, on Nantahala River about the mouth of Briertown Creek, Macon County, N. C.
Broomtown, location unknown.
Brown's Village, location unknown.
Buffalo Fish, location unknown.
Canuga, 2 towns: (1)apparently on Keowee River, S. C.; (2) a traditional town on Pigeon River probably near Waynesville, Haywood County, N. C.
Catatoga, on Cartoogaja Creek of Little Tennessee River above Franklin, N. C.
Chagee, near the mouth of Chatooga Creek of Tugaloo River at or near Fort Madison, southwest Oconee County, S. C.
Cheesoheha, on a branch of Savannah River in upper South Carolina.
Chewase, on a branch of Tennessee River in East Tennessee.
Chicherohe, on War Woman Creek in the northwestern part of Rabun County, Ga.
Chickamauga, a temporary settlement on Chickamauga Creek near Chattanooga.
Conisca, on a branch of Tennessee River.
Conontoroy, an "out town."
Conoross, on Conoross Creek which enters Keowee or Seneca River from the west in Anderson County, S. C.
Coyatee, on Little Tennessee River about 10 miles below the Tellico, about the present Coytee, Loudon County, Tenn.
Crayfish Town, in upper Georgia.
Creek Path, with Creeks and Shawnee at Gunter's Landing, Ala.

Crowmocker, on Battle Creek which falls into Tennessee River below Chattanooga, Tenn.

Crow Town, on the left bank of Tennessee River near the mouth of Raccoon
Creek, Cherokee County, Ala.

Cuclon, an unidentified town.

Cusawatee, on lower Coosawatee River in Gordon County, Ga.

Dulastunyi, on Nottely River, Cherokee County, N. C., near the Georgia line.

Dustayalunyi, about the mouth of Shooting Creek, an affluent of Hiwassee River,
near Hayesville, Clay County, N. C.

Ecochee, on a head stream of Savannah River in northwest South Carolina or
northeast Georgia.

Elakulsi, in northern Georgia.

Etowah, 2 towns: (1) on Etowah River about the present Hightower, Forsyth
County, Ga.; (2) a possible settlement on Hightower Creek of Hiwassee River,
Towns County, Ga.

Euforsee, location unknown.

Fightingtown, on Fightingtown Creek, near Morgantown, Fannin County, Ga.

Frogtown, on a creek of the same name, north of Dahlonega, Lumpkin County,
Ga.

Guhlaniyi, occupied by Cherokee and Natchez, at the junction of Brasstown
Creek with Hiwassee River a short distance above Murphy, N. C.

Gusti, traditional, on Tennessee River near Kingston, Roane County, Tenn.

Halfway Town, about halfway between Sitiku and Chilhowee on Little Tennessee
River about the boundary of Monroe and Loudon Counties, Tenn.

Hemptown, on Hemptown Creek near Morgantown, Fannin County, Ga.

Hickory Log, on Etowah River a short distance above Canton, Cherokee County,
Ga.

High Tower Forks, probably one of the places called Etowah.

Ikatikunahita, on Long Swamp Creek about the boundary of Forsyth and Cherokee Counties, Ga.

Ivy Log, on Ivy Log Creek, Union County, Ga.

Johnstown, on the upper waters of Chattahoochee River and probably in the
northern part of Hall County, Ga.

Kalanunyi, a district or town laid off on the Eastern Cherokee Reserve in Swain
and Jackson Counties, N. C.

Kanastunyi, on the headwaters of French Broad River near Brevard in Transyl-
vania County, N. C., also possibly a second on Hiwassee River.

Kansaki, 4 towns: (1) on Tuckasegee River a short distance above the present
Webster in Jackson County, N. C.; (2) on the lower course of Canasauga Creek
in Polk County, Tenn.; (3) at the junction of Conasauga and Coosawatee
Rivers, the later site of New Echota, Gordon County, Ga.; (4) mentioned in
the De Soto narratives but perhaps identical with No. 2.

Kanutaluhi, in northern Georgia.

Kawanunyi, about the present Ducktown, Polk County, Tenn.

Kuhlahi, in upper Georgia.

Kulahiyi, in northeastern Georgia near Currahee Mountain.

Leatherwood, at or near Leatherwood in the northern part of Franklin County,
Ga.

Long Island, at the Long Island in Tennessee River on the Tennessee-Georgia
line.

Lookout Mountain Town, at or near the present Trenton, Dade County, Ga.

Naguchee, about the junction of Soquee and Sautee Rivers in Nacoochee Valley at the head of Chattahoochee River, Habersham County, Ga.

Nanatlugunyi, traditional, on the site of Jonesboro, Washington County, Tenn.

Nantahala (see Briertown).

Nickajack, on the south bank of Tennessee River in Marion County, Tenn.

Nununyi, on Oconaluftee River near Cherokee, Swain County, N. C.

Ocoee, on Ocoee River near its junction with the Hiwassee, about Benton, Polk County, Tenn.

Oconaluftee, probably at the present Birdtown, on the Eastern Cherokee Reservation.

Ooltewah, about the present Ooltewah, on Ooltewah Creek, James County, Tenn.

Oothcaloga, on Oothcaloga (Ougillogy) Creek of Oostanaula River near Calhoun, Gordon County, Ga.

Paint Town, on lower Soco Creek, within the reservation in Jackson and Swain Counties, N. C.

Pine Log, on Pine Log Creek in Bartow County, Ga.

Quacoshatchee, in northwest Pickens County, S. C.

Qualla, agency of the Eastern Cherokee on a branch of Soco River, Jackson County, N. C.

Quanusee, location unknown.

Rabbit Trap, in upper Georgia.

Red Bank, on Etowah River, at or near Canton, Cherokee County, Ga.

Red Clay, on Oconaluftee River in Swain County, N. C., Eastern Cherokee Reservation.

Running Water, on the southeast bank of Tennessee River below Chattanooga, near the northwestern Georgia line and 4 miles above Nickajack.

Sanderstown, in northeastern Alabama.

Selikwayi, on Sallacoa Creek probably at or near the present Sallacoa, Cherokee County, Ga.

Seneca, on Keowee River about the mouth of Conneross Creek in Oconee County, S. C.

Setsi, traditional, on the south side of Valley River, about 3 miles below Valleytown, Cherokee County, N. C.

Skeinah, on Toccoa River, Fannin County, Ga.

Soquee, on Soquee River, near Clarksville, Habersham County, Ga.

Spikebuck Town, on Hiwassee River at or near Hayesville, Clay County, N. C.

Spring Place, a mission station in Murray County, Ga.

Standing Peach Tree, on Chattahoochee River, at the mouth of Peachtree Creek, northwest of Atlanta, Ga.

Sutali, on Etowah River, probably in southwestern Cherokee County, Ga.

Suwanee, on Chattahoochee River about the present Suwanee, Gwinnett County, Ga.

Tagwahi, 3 towns: (1) on Toccoa Creek east of Clarkesville, Habersham County, Ga.; (2) on Toccoa or Ocoee River about the present Toccoa in Fannin County, Ga.; (3) perhaps on Persimmon Creek which enters Hiwassee River some distance below Murphy, Cherokee County. N. C.

Takwashnaw, a Lower Cherokee town.

Talahi, location unknown.

Talaniyi, in upper Georgia.

Talking Rock, on Talking Rock Creek, an affluent of Coosawattee River, Ga.

Tasetsi, on the extreme head of Hiwassee River in Towns County, Ga.

Taskigi, 3 towns occupied originally by Tuskegee Indians (see Alabama): (1) on Little Tennessee River above the junction of the Tellico, Monroe County,

Tenn.; (2) on the north bank of Tennessee River just below Chattanooga, Tenn.; (3) perhaps on Tuskegee Creek of Little Tennessee River near Robbinsville, Graham County, N. C.

Tikwalitsi, on Tuckasegee River at Bryson City, Swain County, N. C.

Tlanusiyi, at the junction of Hiwassee and Valley Rivers on the site of Murphy, N. C.

Tocax, location unknown, perhaps connected with Toxaway or Toccoa.

Torsalla, one of the Keowee towns.

Tricentee, one of the Keowee towns.

Tsilaluhi, on a small branch of Brasstown Creek of Hiwassee River, just within the lines of Towns County, Ga.

Tsiskwahi, a district or town in the Eastern Cherokee Reservation, Swain County, N. C.

Tsistetsiyi, on South Mouse Creek, a branch of Hiwassee River in Bradley County, Tenn.

Tsistuyi, on the north bank of Hiwassee River at the entrance of Chestua Creek, in Polk County, Tenn., at one time occupied by Yuchi.

Tsudinuntiyi, on lower Nantahala River, in Macon County, N. C.

Tucharechee, location unknown.

Tuckasegee, 2 towns: (1) about the junction of the two forks of Tuckasegee River, above Webster, Jackson County, N. C.; (2) on a branch of Brasstown Creek of Hiwassee River, in Towns County, Ga.

Turkeytown, on the west bank of Coosa River opposite the present Center, Cherokee County, Ala.

Turniptown, on Turniptown Creek above Ellijay, Gilmer County, Ga.

Turtletown, in upper Georgia.

Tusquittah, on Tusquittee Creek near Hayesville, Clay County, N. C.

Two Runs, on Etowah River at the crossing of the old Indian trail between Coosa and Tugaloo Rivers, Bartow County, Ga.

Ustisti, one of the Lower Towns.

Valleytown, at Valleytown on Valley River, Cherokee County, N. C.

Wahyahi, on upper Soco Creek on the Eastern Cherokee Reservation, Jackson County, N. C.

Wasasa's Village, on Brown's Creek, a southern affluent of Tennessee River in northern Alabama.

Willstown, on Wills Creek, below Fort Payne, De Kalb County, Ala.

History.—There seems to have been a Cherokee migration legend something like that of the Creeks according to which the tribe entered their historic seats from some region toward the northeast.

In 1540 De Soto seems to have passed through only one town that has a Cherokee name, but Pardo in 1566 learned of another, Tanasqui, which has a Cherokee appearance and may have given its name to Tennessee River. Continuous contact between the Cherokee and the Whites began after Virginia was settled, when traders from that colony commenced to work their way into the Appalachian Mountains. Contact became more intimate with the founding of the Carolina colonies, and a contingent of 310 Cherokee joined Moore in his attack on the Tuscarora in 1713. In 1730 Sir Alexander Cuming staged a personal embassy to the Cherokee and afterward took seven of the Indians to England with him. In 1738 an enemy more serious even than White men made its first appearance in this tribe, namely smallpox, which cut down their numbers by nearly 50 percent. In 1755 the Cherokee won a great victory over the Abihka Creeks, who forthwith withdrew from the Tennessee River. Relations with the Whites were upon the whole friendly until 1759 when the Indians refused to accede to the demand of the Governor of South Carolina that a number of Indians including two leading chiefs be turned over to him for execution under the charge that they had killed a White man. He had asked also to have 24 other chiefs sent to him merely on suspicion that they entertained hostile intentions. War followed, and the Indians captured Fort Loudon, a post in the heart of their country, August 8, 1760, after having defeated an army which came to relieve it. The year following, however, the Indians were defeated on June 10, by a larger force under Col. James Grant, who laid the, greater number of the Middle Cherokee settlements in ashes, and compelled the tribe to make peace. In 1769 they are said to have suffered a severe defeat at the hands of the Chickasaw at the Chickasaw Oldfields. On the outbreak of the American Revolution they sided with the British and continued hostilities after its close down to 1794. Meanwhile parties of Cherokee had pushed down Tennessee River and formed new settlements near the present Tennessee-Alabama boundary. Shortly after 1800 missionary work was begun among them, and in 1820 they adopted a regular form of government modeled on that of the United States. In the meantime large numbers of them, wearied of the encroachments of the Whites, had crossed the Mississippi and settled in the territory now included in the State of Arkansas. In 1821 Sequoya, son of a mixed-blood Cherokee woman by a White man, submitted a syllabary of his own devising to the chief men of the nation, and, on their approval, the Cherokee of all ages set about learning it with such zeal that in a few months numbers of them were able to read and write by means of it. In 1822 Sequoya went west to teach his alphabet to the Indians of the western· division, and he remained among them permanently. The pressure of the Whites upon the frontiers of the Eastern Cherokee was soon increased by the discovery of gold near the present Dahlonega, Ga., and after a few years of fruitless struggle the nation bowed to the inevitable and by the treaty of New Echota, December 29, 1835, sold all of their territories not previously given up and agreed to remove to the other side of the Mississippi to lands to be set apart for them. These lands were in the northeastern part of the present Oklahoma, and thither the greater part of the tribe removed in the winter of 1838–39, suffering great hardships and losing nearly one-fourth of their number on the way. Before the main migration took place one band of Cherokee had established themselves in Texas where they obtained a grant of land from the Mexican government, but the Texas revolutionists refused to recognize this claim although it was supported by Gen. Sam Houston. In consequence, the Cherokee chief Bowl was killed in 1839, along with many of his men, and the rest were expelled from the State. At the time of the great migration, several hundred Cherokee escaped to the mountains where they lived as refugees until in 1842, through the efforts of William H. Thomas, an influential trader, they received permission to remain on lands set apart for their use in western North Carolina, the Qualla Reservation, where their descendants still reside. The early years of the reestablished Cherokee Nation west of the Mississippi were troubled by differences between the faction that had approved removal and that which had opposed it. Afterward the tribal life was entirely disrupted for a few years by the Civil War. In 1867 and 1870 the Delaware and Shawnee were admitted from Kansas and incorporated into the nation. March 3, 1906, the Cherokee government came to an end, and in time the lands were allotted in severalty, and the Cherokee people soon became citizens of the new State of Oklahoma.

Population.—Mooney (1928) estimates that in 1650 there was a total Cherokee population of 22,000. In 1715 a rather careful estimate, yet in all probability too low, gave a total of 11,210 (Lower Cherokee 2,100; Middle 6,350; Upper 2,760), including 4,000 warriors and distributed among 60 villages. In 1720 two estimates were made, of 10,000 and 11,500 respectively, but in 1729 the estimate jumps to 20,000, with 6,000 warriors, distributed in 64 towns. In 1755 a North Carolina estimate gives 5 divisions of the tribe and a total of 2,590 men. In 1760 we find a flat figure of 2,000; in 1761, about 3,000. Even before this time the Cherokee are supposed to have lost heavily from smallpox, intoxicants, and wars with the colonists, but at the time of their forced removal to the west in 1838 those in their old country had increased to 16,542. Those already in the west were estimated at about 6,000. The Civil War interfered with their growth but in 1885 they numbered 19,000, about 17,000 being in the west. In 1902 there were officially reported in the west 28,016 persons of Cherokee blood, including all degrees of admixture, but this includes several thousand persons repudiated by the tribal courts. The Census of 1910 returned 31,489 Cherokee, 29,610 of whom were in Oklahoma, 1,406 in North Carolina, and the rest scattered in 23 other States. In 1923 the report of the United States Indian Office gave 36,432 Cherokee "by blood" in Oklahoma, and 2,515 in North Carolina: total 38,947. In 1930, 45,238 were returned: 40,904 in Oklahoma, 1,963 in North Carolina, and the rest in more than 36 other States. In 1937 the number of eastern Cherokee was given as 3,327.

Connection in which they have become noted.—The Cherokee tribe is one of the most famous in all North America, (1) on account of its size and strength and the prominent part it played in the history of our country, (2) from the fact that the invention of the Cherokee alphabet by Sequoya was the only case of the adoption of a system of writing without immediate White prompting in the annals of our Indians, (3) from the perpetuation of numerous place names from Cherokee sources and of the name itself in counties in Alabama, Georgia, Iowa, Kansas, Oklahoma, North Carolina, South Carolina, and Texas, and places in some of these States and California, Kentucky, and Arkansas; in Colbért County, Ala.; Cherokee County, Iowa; Crawford County, Kans.; Lawrence County, Ky.; and the name of stations in Louisville, Ky.; Swain County, N. C.; Alfalfa County, Okla.; and San Saba County, Tex. There is a Cherokee City in Benton County, Ark.; Cherokee Dam at Jefferson City, Tenn.; and Cherokee Falls in Cherokee County, S. C. Several prominent Americans were descended from this tribe, including Senator Robert Owen and Will Rogers.

Chiaha. A part of this tribe was encountered by De Soto in 1540, in the territory now forming this State, probably, as shown by Mr. J. Y. Brame, on what is now Burns Island. They are also mentioned in connection with the explorations of Juan Pardo in 1567. (See Georgia.)

Chickasaw. In historic times the Chickasaw claimed the greater part of western Tennessee, and twice drove Shawnee Indians from the Cumberland Valley, the first time with the assistance of the Cherokee, according to the claim of the latter. At an early date they had a settlement on the lower Tennessee River but it is doubtful whether this was in Tennessee or Kentucky. (See Mississippi.)

Kaskinampo. Meaning unknown, though -nampo may be the Koasati word for "many."

Connections.—The Kaskinampo were probably closely related to the Koasati, and through them to the Alabama, Choctaw, and other Muskhogean people.

Location.—Their best-known historic location was on the lower end of an island in the Tennessee River, probably the one now called Pine Island. (See also Arkansas.)

History.—There is every reason to believe that this tribe constituted the Casqui, Icasqui, or Casquin "province" which De Soto entered immediately after crossing the Mississippi River, and it was probably in what is now Phillips County, Ark. We hear of the Kaskinampo next in connection with the expeditions of Marquette and Joliet but do not learn of their exact location until 1701, when they seem to have been on the lower end of the present Pine Island. We are informed, however, by one of the French explorers that they had previously lived upon Cumberland River, and there is evidence that, when they first moved to the Tennessee, they may have settled for a short time near its mouth. Both the Cumberland and the Tennessee were known by their name, and it stuck persistently to the latter stream until well along in the eighteenth century. After the early years of the eighteenth century we hear little more of them, but there is reason to believe that they united with the Koasati.

Population.—Our only clue to the population of the Kaskinampo is in an unpublished report of Bienville, who estimates 150 men, or a total population of about 500.

Connection in which they have become noted.—The Kaskinampo are distinguished only for the prominent part they played in the De Soto narratives and for the application of their name for a time to Tennessee River.

Mosopelia. This tribe probably established themselves on Cumberland River and at one or two points on the Tennessee shore of the Mississippi on their way from Ohio to Mississippi. (See **Ofo** under Mississippi and Ohio.)

Muskogee. Although we do not have records of any settlement in Tennessee by the true Muskogee, it is probable that some of them occupied part of its territory in prehistoric times, and at a later date their war parties constantly visited it. (See Alabama.)

Natchez. After being driven from Mississippi and Louisiana, one band of Natchez lived among the Cherokee. (See Mississippi.)

Ofo, see **Mosopelia.**

Shawnee. Meaning "southerners," the best-known variants of the name being the French form Chaouanons, and that which appears in the name of Savannah River. Also called:

> Ani'-Sawănu'gĭ, by the Cherokee.
> Ontwagana, "one who stutters," "one whose speech is unintelligible," applied by the Iroquois to this tribe and many others.
> Oshawanoag, by the Ottawa.
> Shawala, by the Teton Dakota.

Connections.—The Shawnee belonged to the Algonquian linguistic stock, their closest relatives being the Fox, Sauk, and Kickapoo.

Location.—There was scarcely a tribe that divided so often or moved so much as the Shawnee, but one of the earliest historic seats of the people as a whole was on Cumberland River. (See also Alabama, Georgia, Illinois, Indiana, Kansas, Kentucky, Maryland and the District of Columbia, Missouri, Ohio, Oklahoma, Pennsylvania, South Carolina, Texas, Virginia.)

Subdivisions and Villages

There were five subdivisions of long standing, Chillicothe, Hathawekela, Kispokotha, Mequachake, and Piqua. The Hathawekela, Kispokotha, and Piqua later formed one body known as Absentee Shawnee. The following names of villages have been preserved:

Bulltown, or Mingo, on Little Kanawha River, W. Va.

Chillicothe, 3 or 4 towns: (1) on Paint Creek on the site of Oldtown, near Chillicothe in Ross County, Ohio; (2) on the Little Miami about the site of Oldtown in Greene County, Ohio; (3) on the Great Miami River at the present Piqua in Miami County; (4) probably the native name of Lowertown (see below).

Conedogwinit, location unknown.

Cornstalk's Town, on Scippo Creek opposite Squaw Town, Pickaway County, Ohio.

Girty's.Town, on St. Mary's River, east of Celina Reservoir, Auglaize County, Ohio.

Grenadier Squaw's Town, on Scippo Creek, Pickaway County, Ohio.

Hog Creek, on a branch of Ottawa River in Allen County, Ohio.

Kagoughsage, apparently in Ohio or western Pennsylvania.

Lewistown (and Seneca), near the site of the present Lewistown, Logan County, Ohio.

Lick Town, probably Shawnee, on upper Scioto River, probably near Circleville, Ohio.

Logstown, with Delaware, and later Iroquois, on the right bank of Ohio River about 14 miles below Pittsburgh, in Allegheny County, Pa.

Long Tail's Settlement, in Johnson County, Kans.

Lowertown, 2 towns; (1) on Ohio River just below the mouth of the Scioto and later built on the opposite side of the river about the site of Portsmouth, Ohio; (2) in Ross County, also called Chillicothe.

Mequachake: There were several towns of the name occupied by people of this division; they also had villages on the headwaters of Mad River, Logan County, Ohio.

Old Shawnee Town, on Ohio River in Gallia County, Ohio, 3 miles above the mouth of the Great Kanawha.

Peixtan (or Nanticoke), on or near the lower Susquehanna River in Dauphin County, Pa., possibly on the site of Paxtonville.

Pigeon Town, Mequachake division, on Mad River, 3 miles northwest of West Liberty, Logan County, Ohio.

Piqua, 4 towns: (1) Pequea on Susquehanna River at the mouth of Pequea Creek, in Lancaster County, Pa.; (2) on the north side of Mad River, about 5 miles west of Springfield, Clark County, Ohio; (3) Upper Piqua on Miami River 3 miles north of the present Piqua in Miami County, Ohio, and (4) Lower Piqua, a smaller village on the site of the modern town of that name, Ohio.

Sawanogi, on the south side of Tallapoosa River in Macon County, Ala.; but see Muskogee in Alabama.

Scoutash's Town (or Mingo), near Lewistown, Logan County, Ohio.

Shawneetown, on the west bank of Ohio River about the present Shawneetown, Gallatin County, Ill.

Sonnioto, at the mouth of Scioto River, Ohio, perhaps the same as Lowertown.

Tippecanoe, on the west bank of the Wabash River, just below the mouth of Tippecanoe River in Tippecanoe County, Ind.

Wapakoneta, on the site of the present Wapakoneta, Auglaize County, Ohio.

Will's Town, at the site of Cumberland, Md.

History.—Tradition and the known linguistic connections of the Shawnee indicate that they had migrated to the Cumberland River Valley from the north not long previous to the historic period. They were on and near the Cumberland when French explorers first heard of them, although there are indications that they had been in part on the Ohio not long before. Shortly after 1674 the Hathawekela or that part of the Shawnee afterward so called, settled upon Savannah River, and in 1681 they proved of great assistance to the new colony of South Carolina by driving a tribe known as Westo, probably part of the Yuchi, from the middle Savannah. Early in the following century, or possibly very late in the same century, some of these Hathawekela began to move to Pennsylvania and continued to do so at intervals until 1731. Meanwhile, however, immediately after the Yamasee War, a part had retired among the Creeks, settling first on Chattahoochee River and later on the Tallapoosa, where they remained until some years before the removal of the Creeks to the west. Of the remaining bands of Shawnee—those which had stayed upon the Cumberland—part of the Piqua moved eastward into Pennsylvania about 1678, and more in 1694, so that they were able to welcome their kinsmen from the south a few years later. A French trader named Charleville established himself at Nashville among the rest of the tribe, but soon afterward they were forced out of that region by the Cherokee and Chickasaw. They stopped for a time at several points in Kentucky, and perhaps at Shawneetown, Ill., but about 1730, by permission of the Wyandot, collected along the north bank of the Ohio between the Allegheny and Scioto Rivers. Shortly after the middle of the eighteenth century they were joined by their kinsmen who had been living in Pennsylvania. One Pennsylvania band continued on south to the Upper Creeks with whom they lived for several years before returning north. Their return must have occurred soon after 1760, and they are said to have settled for a time in the old Shawnee country on the Cumberland but were soon ejected by the Chickasaw, this time unassisted by the Cherokee. From the beginning of the French and Indian War to the treaty of Greenville in 1795 the main body of Shawnee were almost constantly fighting with the English or the Americans. They were the most active and pertinacious foes of the Whites in that section. Driven from the Scioto, they settled upon the headwaters of the Miami, and later many of them assisted the Cherokee and Creeks in their wars with the Americans. In 1793, however, one considerable body, on invitation of the Spanish Government, occupied a tract of land near Cape Girardeau, Mo., along with some Delaware. After the treaty of Greenville, the Shawnee were obliged to give up their lands on the Miami, and part retired to the headwaters of the Auglaize, while the more hostile element swelled the numbers of those who had gone to Missouri. In 1798 a part of the Shawnee in Ohio settled on White River, Ind., by invitation of the Delaware. Shortly afterward a Shawnee medicine man named Tenskwátawa, known to the Whites as "the Shawnee prophet," began to preach a new doctrine which exhorted the Indians to return to the communal life of their ancestors, abandoning all customs derived from the Whites. His followers increased rapidly in numbers and established themselves in a village at the mouth of Tippecanoe River, Ind. Their hostile attitude toward the Whites soon becoming evident, they were attacked here in 1811 by Gen. W. H. Harrison and totally defeated. While this war was going on Tecumseh, Tenskwátawa's famous brother, was in the south endeavoring to bring about an uprising among the tribes in that section. In the war between the Americans and British which broke out in 1812 Tecumseh acted as leader of the hostiles and was killed at the battle of the Thames in 1814. In 1825 the Shawnee in Missouri, who are said to have taken no part in these wars, sold their lands, and most of them moved to a reservation in Kansas, but a large part had previously gone to Texas, where they remained until expelled by the American colonists in 1839. About 1831 the Shawnee still in Ohio joined those in Kansas, and about 1845 the Hathawekela, Kispokotha, and Piqua moved from Kansas to Oklahoma and established themselves on Canadian River, becoming known later as the Absentee Shawnee. In 1867, a band which had been living with the Seneca also moved to what is now Oklahoma and came to be known as Eastern Shawnee; and still later the main body became incorporated with the Cherokee. One band, known as Black Bob's band, at first refused to remove from Kansas, but later joined the rest. All have now become citizens of Oklahoma.

Population.—Owing to the number of separate bodies into which this tribe became divided, and their complex history, estimates of Shawnee population in early times are difficult. Mooney (1928) places their entire number at 3,000 in 1650. Estimates made by various writers during the eighteenth and early nineteenth centuries vary between 1,000 and 2,000, 1,500 being the favorite figure. In 1760 the Abihka and Tallapoosa bands numbered 100 warriors. In 1909 the Eastern Shawnee numbered 107; the Absentee Shawnee, 481; and those incorporated with the Cherokee Nation, about 1,400. The census of 1910 returned only 1,338. In 1923, 166 Eastern Shawnee were enumerated and 551 Absentee, but no figures were given for that part of the tribe in the Cherokee Nation. The census of 1930 gave 1,161, most of whom were in Oklahoma. There were 916 in Oklahoma in 1937.

Connection in which they have become noted.—Although prominent by virtue of its size, the Shawnee tribe is noteworthy rather on account of numerous migrations undertaken by its various branches and the number of contacts established by them, involving the history of three-quarters of our southern and eastern States. They constituted the most formidable opposition to the advance of settlements through the Ohio Valley, and under Tecumseh and Tenskwátawa attempted an extensive alliance of native tribes to oppose the Whites. The name Shawnee is preserved in various forms in Pennsylvania, Tennessee, Wisconsin, Kansas, New York, Ohio, Oklahoma, Missouri, and Illinois, and most conspicuously of all, perhaps, in the name of the river Savannah and the city of Savannah, Ga. There are places called Shawnee in Park County, Colo.; Johnson County, Kans.; Perry County, Ohio; Pottawatomie County, Okla.; and Converse County, Wyo.; Shawnee-on-Delaware in Monroe County, Pa.; Shawanee in Claiborne County, Tenn.; Shawanese in Luzerne County, Pa.; Shawano in Shawano County, Wis.; Shawneetown in Gallatin County, Ill., and Cape Girardeau County, Mo.

Tali. A tribe met by De Soto near the great bend of the Tennessee and found in the same region by the earliest English and French explorers, living in what is now northern Alabama and perhaps also in Tennessee. It is probable that they were a part of the **Creeks** (q. v.).

Tuskegee. One band of Tuskegee formed a settlement or settlements in the Cherokee Nation. (See **Cherokee,** and **Tuskegee** under Alabama.)

Yuchi. The greater part of the Yuchi probably lived at one period in and near the mountains of eastern Tennessee though one band of them was on the Tennessee River just above Muscle Shoals and there is evidence for an early occupation of the Hiwassee Valley. Some remained with the Cherokee until a very late date. (See Georgia.)

KENTUCKY

Cherokee. The Cherokee claimed some land in southeastern Kentucky and traces of culture of Cherokee type are said to be found in archeological remains along the upper course of the Cumberland, but no permanent Cherokee settlement is known to have existed in historic times within this State. (See Tennessee.)

Chickasaw. The westernmost end of Kentucky was claimed by the Chickasaw, and at a very early period they had a settlement on the lower course of Tennessee River, either in Kentucky or Tennessee. (See Mississippi.)

Mosopelea. This tribe may have lived within the boundaries of Kentucky for a brief time, perhaps at the mouth of the Cumberland River, when they were on their way from Ohio to the lower Mississippi. (See Ohio, and see also **Ofo** under Mississippi.)

Shawnee. The Shawnee had more to do with Kentucky in early times than any other tribe, but maintained few villages in the State for a long period. Their more permanent settlements were farther south about Nashville. At one Shawnee town, located for a short time near Lexington, Ky., the noted Shawnee chief, Blackhoof, was born. The tribe crossed and recrossed the State several times in its history and used it still more frequently as a hunting ground. (See Tennessee.)

Yuchi. According to some early maps, the Yuchi had a town in this State on a river which appears to be identical with Green River. (See Georgia.)

Hunting bands of Illinois, Miami, Iroquois, and Delaware at times visited Kentucky, but these tribes can hardly be said to have played much of a part in Kentucky history. (See New York, New Jersey, Indiana, and Illinois.)

OHIO

Chippewa. Representatives of this tribe appear as parties to the Treaty of Greenville, 1795, and to treaties concluded in 1807 and 1817 by which lands in this State were relinquished to the Whites. (See Minnesota.)

Delaware. The Delaware lived in Ohio for a considerable period in the course of their migration west under White pressure   (See New Jersey.)

Erie. Meaning in Iroquois, "long tail," and referring to the panther, from which circumstance they are often referred to as the Cat Nation. Also called:

Gä-quä'-ga-o-no, by L. H. Morgan (1851).

Connection.—The Erie belonged to the Iroquoian linguistic family.

Location.—All of northern Ohio, except possibly the northwestern corner, and in portions of northwestern Pennsylvania and western New York. In the southeastern part of the State they perhaps reached the Ohio River. (See also Indiana, New York, and Pennsylvania.)

Subdivisions and Villages

The names of but two villages are known, Gentaienton and Riqué. There are supposed to have been several subdivisions, but their names have not been preserved.

History.—Little is known of this tribe until the final struggle which resulted in its destruction as a nation at the hands of the Iroquois and the incorporation of most of the remnants among the conquerors. The war lasted from 1653 to 1656 and seems to have been unusually bloody, the victory of the Iroquois having been determined probably by the fact that they possessed firearms. Some of the so-called Seneca of Oklahoma may be descended from Erie refugees.

Population.—Hewitt (1907) considers 14,500 a conservative estimate of Erie population at the time of the last war, but Mooney (1928) allows only 4,000.

Connection in which they have become noted.—The historical prominence of the Erie tribe itself is confined to the war in which it was destroyed. Its claim to present remembrance arises from the adoption of the name for one of the Great Lakes; for an important city in Pennsylvania upon its shores; counties in New York, Ohio, and Pennsylvania; places in Weld County, Colo.; Whiteside County, Ill.; Neosho County, Kans.; Monroe County, Mich.; Cass County, N. Dak.; Loudon County, Tenn.; Erieside in Lake County, Ohio; and Erieville in Madison County, N. Y., and some smaller settlements; also an important railroad.

Honniasont. This tribe occupied parts of the eastern fringe of Ohio after it had been incorporated into the Iroquois and perhaps before. (See Pennsylvania.)

Illinois. Representatives of the Illinois were parties to the Treaty of Greenville by which lands of the State of Ohio were relinquished to the Whites. (See Illinois.)

Iroquois. After the destruction or dispersal of the Erie and other native tribes of Ohio, many Iroquois settlements were made in the State, particularly by the westernmost tribe, the Seneca. Some of these so-called Iroquois villages were no doubt occupied by people of formerly independent nations. (See New York.)

Kickapoo. Representatives of this tribe were parties to the Treaty of Greenville by which Ohio lands were relinquished to the Whites. (See Wisconsin.)

Miami. After the original tribes of Ohio had been cleared away, some Miami worked their way into the State, particularly into the western and northern parts, and they gave their name to three Ohio rivers, the Miami, Little Miami, and Maumee. (See Indiana.)

Mosopelea. Significance uncertain, though probably from an Algonquian language. Also called:

Chonque, by Tonti in 1690, probably the Quapaw name.
Ofo, own name, perhaps an abbreviation of the Mobilian term, Ofogoula, though this last may mean simply "Ofo people." Ofogoula may also be

interpreted Ofi okla, "Dog People." They were, in fact, known to some of the other tribes as "Dog People."

Ouesperie, Ossipe, Ushpee, names by which they were known to other tribes and evidently shortened forms of Mosopelea, which has a variant in *r*.

Connections.—The Mosopelea spoke a Siouan dialect most closely related to Biloxi and Tutelo and secondarily to Dakota.

Location.—When the French first heard of them, they were in southwestern Ohio, but their best-known historical location was on the lower Yazoo, close to the Yazoo and Koroa Indians. (See also Arkansas, Indiana, Kentucky, and Tennessee.)

Villages

Anciently they had eight villages, but none of the names of these have been preserved.

History.—After abandoning southwestern Ohio some time before 1673, the Mosopelea appear to have settled on the Cumberland, driven thither probably by the Iroquois, and to have given it the name it bears in Coxe's map (1741), Ouesperie, a corruption of Mosopelea. By 1673 they had descended to the Mississippi and established themselves on its western side below the mouth of the Ohio. Later they appear to have stopped for a time among the Quapaw, but before 1686 at least part of them had sought refuge among the Taensa. Their reason for leaving the latter tribe is unknown, but Iberville found them in the historic location above given in 1699. He inserts their name twice, once in the form Ofogoula and once as "Ouispe," probably a corruption of Mosopelea. When their neighbors, the Yazoo and Koroa, joined in the Natchez uprising, the Ofo refused to side with them and went to live with the Tunica, who were French allies. Shortly before 1739 they had settled close to Fort Rosalie, where they remained until after 1758. In 1784 their village was on the western bank of the Mississippi 8 miles above Point Coupée, but nothing more was heard of them until 1908, when I found a single survivor living among the Tunica just out of Marksville, La., and was able to establish their linguistic connections.

Population.—In 1700 the Mosopelea are said to have occupied 10–12 cabins, but some years later Le Page du Pratz (1758) gives 60. In 1758 they are reported to have had 15 warriors and in 1784, 12.

Connection in which they have become noted.—The most noteworthy circumstance connected with this tribe is its romantic history and the recovery of the knowledge of the same.

Neutrals. The Neutral Nation may have occupied a little territory in the extreme northwest of Ohio. (See New York.)

Ofo, see **Mosopelea.**

Ottawa. In the eighteenth century, Ottawa worked into the northern part of Ohio and established settlements along the shore of Lake Erie. (See Michigan.)

Potawatomi. Representatives of this tribe were parties to the Treaty of Greenville in 1795 and to treaties made in 1805, 1807, and 1817 by which lands in this State were relinquished to the Whites. (See Michigan.)

Seneca, see **Iroquois**, under New York.

Shawnee. It is probable that some Shawnee were in Ohio at very early periods. After they had been driven from the Cumberland Valley by the Chickasaw and Cherokee shortly after 1714, they worked their way north into this State and, as they were joined by the former eastern and southern bands, Ohio became the Shawnee center for a considerable period, until after the Treaty of Greenville. (See Tennessee.)

Wyandot. Meaning perhaps "islanders," or "dwellers on a peninsula." Occasionally spelled Guyandot. At an earlier date usually known as Huron, a name given by the French from huré, "rough," and the depreciating suffix -on. Also called:

> Hatindia8ointen, Huron name of Huron of Lorette.
> Nadowa, a name given to them and many other Iroquoian tribes by Algonquians.
> Telamateno, Delaware name, meaning "coming out of a mountain or cave."
> Thastchetci', Onondaga name.

Connection.—The Wyandot belonged to the Iroquoian linguistic family.

Location.—The earliest known location of the Huron proper was the St. Lawrence Valley and the territory of the present province of Ontario from Lake Ontario across to Georgian Bay. The Tionontati were just west of them on Lake Huron. (See also Illinois, Indiana, Kansas, Michigan, Minnesota, and Wisconsin.)

Subdivisions and Villages

There are said to have been four confederated Huron tribes in the time of Champlain.

Cartier, who first met these people, gives the following town names:

Araste, on or near St. Lawrence River below the site of Quebec.

Hagonchenda, on St. Lawrence River not far from the point where it is joined by Jacques Cartier River.

Hochelaga, on Montreal Island.

Hochelay, probably near Point Platon, Quebec.

Satadin, location uncertain.

Stadacona, on the site of the present Quebec.

Starnatan, just below the site of Quebec.

Tailla, near Quebec.

Teguenondahi, location uncertain.

Tutonaguay, 25 leagues above the site of Quebec.

The following towns, some under their native names and others under the names of the missions established by the French Jesuits, existed in Ontario between Lake Simcoe and Georgian Bay in the first half of the seventeenth century:

Andiata.

Angoutenc, between the refugee Wenrohronon town and Ossossané and about 2 miles from the latter.

Anonatea, 1 league from Ihonatiria.

Arendaonatia.

Arente.

Arontaen, near Point Cockburn, on the north shore of Nattawasaga Bay.

Cahiague, where was the mission of St. John the Baptist.

Carhagouha, in Tiny Township about 2 miles northwest of Lafontaine.

Carmaron.

Ekiodatsaan.

Endarahy.

Iahenhouton.

Ihonatiria, where was the mission of the Immaculate Conception.

Karenhassa.

Khinonascarant, the name of three small villages.

Onentisati, in Tiny Township.

Ossossané, where was the mission of the Immaculate Conception after it was moved from Ihonatiria.

Ste. Agnes.

Ste. Anne.

St. Antoine.

Ste. Barbe.

Ste. Catherine.

Ste. Cècile.

St. Charles, 2 villages.

St. Denys.

St. Etienne.

St. François Xavier.

Ste. Geneviève.

St. Joachim.

St. Louis.

Ste. Madeleine.

St. Martin.

Ste. Marie, 2 villages.

Ste. Térèse.

Scanonaerat, where was the mission of St. Michel.

Taenhatentaron, where was the mission of St. Ignace.

Teanaustayaé, whither the mission of St. Joseph was moved from Ihonatiria (?).

Teandewiata.

Tondakhra, on the west side of the northern peninsula of Tiny Township, 4 miles northwest of Lafontaine and about 1 mile southeast of Clover Point.

Touaguainchain, perhaps where the mission of Ste. Madeleine was established.

After the Huron had been broken up by the Iroquois there was for a time a Huron mission on Mackinac Island, called St. Ignace, which was soon moved to

Point Ignace on the shore to the northward. A part of the tribe settled successively in villages called Ancienne Lorette and Jeune Lorette, 8 miles northwest of Quebec.

The following names of Huron or Wyandot towns are recorded in Ohio after the part of the tribe which moved west and south had collected there:

Cranetown, 2 towns: (1) on the site of the present Royalton, Fairfield County; (2) in Crawford County, 8 or 10 miles northeast of the present Upper Sandusky.

Junqueindundeh, on Sandusky River 24 miles above its mouth.

Junundat, on a small creek that empties into a little lake below the mouth of Sandusky River, Seneca County.

Sandusky, 2 towns: (1) Lower Sandusky on the site of Sandusky, Erie County; (2) Upper Sandusky near the present town of that name in Wyandot County.

There was a Wyandot village in Wayne County, Mich., called Brownstown, occupied by people of this tribe from 1809 to 1818.

History.—The St. Lawrence territories seem to have been occupied by two of the four Huron tribes when Cartier explored the St. Lawrence River in 1534–43; at any rate Hurons were in occupancy. When Champlain came into the country in 1603, they were all living south of Georgian Bay. The French soon entered into amicable relations with them and, beginning in 1615, missionaries undertook to convert them to Christianity. These efforts were crowned with considerable success, but were brought to an end when the tribe was attacked and disrupted by the Iroquois in 1648–49. Part of the Huron were then adopted by their conquerors, while part placed themselves under the protection of the French at Quebec, their descendants being known today as the Hurons of Lorette, and others fled to the Neutrals, the Erie, the Tionontati, and other tribes. In 1649, however, the Tionontati were attacked in their turn and forced along with their Huron guests to take refuge on Christian Island in Lake Huron. Then followed a long course of wandering; to Michilimackinac; Manitoulin Island; Green Bay; the Potawatomi; the Illinois; the neighborhood of the Ottawa on Chequamigon Bay, on the south shore of Lake Superior; and again to Michilimackinac. In the latter part of the seventeenth century some moved to Sandusky, Ohio, and Detroit, Mich. In 1745 a considerable party of Huron under the leadership of the war chief Orontony or Nicholas went from Detroit to the marshlands of Sandusky Bay, but in 1748, on the failure of a conspiracy Orontony had attempted against the French, he abandoned his villages and removed to White River, Ind. After his death the Hurons seem to have returned to Detroit and Sandusky and gradually extended their claims over Ohio, so that it was by their permission that the Shawnee from the south and the Delaware from the east settled north of Ohio River. The Wyandot allied themselves with the British in the War of 1812. At its close a large tract of land in

Ohio and Michigan was confirmed to them, but they sold much of it in 1819, under treaty provisions, reserving a small portion near Upper Sandusky, Ohio, and a smaller area on Huron River, near Detroit, until 1842, when these tracts also were sold, and the tribe removed to Wyandotte County, Kans. In 1867 they were placed upon a small reservation in the northeastern part of the Indian Territory and are now citizens of the State of Oklahoma.

Population.—Mooney (1928) estimates that in 1600 there were 10,000 Huron and 8,000 Tionontati. French estimates of the first half of the seventeenth century range from 20,000 to 30,000, the former figure being one that Hewitt (*in* Hodge, 1907) is inclined to accept. After the dispersal, the Hurons of Lorette were estimated at 300 in 1736 but placed officially at 455 in 1904. The following figures are given for the other Huron: 1,000 in 1736; 500 and 850 in 1748; 1,250 in 1765; 1,500 in 1794–95; 1,000 and 1,250 in 1812. In 1885 the Huron in Oklahoma numbered 251; in 1905, 378; and by the census of 1910, 353. In 1923 there were 502 in Oklahoma and in 1924, 399 at Lorette, Canada: total 901. The census of 1930 returned exactly the same number in the United States as had the census of 1910. In 1937, 783 were reported in Oklahoma.

Connection in which they have become noted.—The Wyandot tribe is famous, (1) from the fact that it was the chief tribe or group of tribes encountered by Cartier when he explored the St. Lawrence, (2) for the flourishing missions maintained among them by the French Jesuits, (3) for the tragic destruction of their confederacy by the Iroquois, (4) from the various applications of the names Huron and Wyandot, the former including one of the Great Lakes and also rivers and counties in Michigan, Ohio, and Ontario; places in Fresno County, Calif.; Lawrence County, Ind.; Atchison County, Kans.; Erie County, Ohio; Beadle County, S. Dak.; Henderson County, Tenn.; and the Huron Mountains in Marquette County, Mich. Wyandot was applied in the forms Wyandot or Wyandotte to counties in Ohio and Kansas; to places in Wyandot County, Ohio; Crawford County, Ind.; Butte County, California; Ottawa County, Okla.; and Wayne County, Mich.; and a famous cave, Wyandotte Cave, 4 miles northeast of Leavenworth, Ind. In the form Guyandotte, the name of the Wyandot has been given to a river, mountains, and a town in West Virginia.

INDIANA

Chippewa. Representatives of this tribe appear as parties to the Treaty of Greenville in 1795 and treaties made in 1817 and 1821 by which lands in Indiana were relinquished to the Whites. (See Minnesota.)

Delaware. About 1770 the Delaware, most of whom were then living in Ohio, received permission from the Miami and Piankashaw to occupy that part of Indiana between the Ohio and White Rivers, where at one period they had six villages. In course of time, all moved west of the Mississippi to Missouri, Kansas, and Oklahoma. (See New Jersey.)

Erie. Erie tribal territory may once have extended into the northeastern part of the State, but this tribe played but little part in the known history of the region covered by it. (See Ohio.)

Illinois. Representatives of this tribe appear as parties to the Treaty of Greenville in 1795, relinquishing land in Indiana to the Whites. (See Illinois.)

Iroquois. The earlier Indian occupants of Indiana were largely driven out by the Iroquois, particularly by the westernmost of the Iroquois tribes, the Seneca, yet they seem to have had few settlements in the State. (See New York.)

Kickapoo. When the Kickapoo were on Vermilion River, Ill., they undoubtedly occupied some of western Indiana for brief periods. (See Wisconsin.)

Miami. The name is thought to be derived from the Chippewa word Omaumeg, signifying "people on the peninsula," but according to their own traditions, it came from the word for pigeon. The name used by themselves, as recorded and often used by early writers, is Twightwees, derived from the cry of a crane. Also called:

> Naked Indians, a common appellation used by the colonists, from a confusion of twa^{n}h, twa^{n}h, the cry of a crane, with tawa, "naked."
> Pkíwi-léni, by the Shawnee, meaning "dust or ashes people."
> Sä^{n}shkiá-a-rúnû, by the Wyandot, meaning "people dressing finely, or fantastically."
> Tawatawas, meaning "naked." (See Naked Indians above.)
> Wa-yä-tä-no'-ke, cited by Morgan (1851).

Connections.—The Miami belonged to the Algonquian linguistic stock, their nearest immediate connections being with the Illinois.

Location.—For territory occupied in Indiana, see History. (See also Illinois, Kansas, Michigan, Ohio, Oklahoma, and Wisconsin.)

Subdivisions and Villages

French writers divided the Miami into the following five bands: Piankashaw, Wea, Atchatchakangouen, Kilatika, Mengakonkia, and Pepicokia. The first two later became recognized as independent tribes, the last may have been absorbed by the Piankashaw but this and the other three divisions are no longer recognized. The following villages are mentioned:

Chicago, on the site of the present city, probably occupied by Wea.

Chippekawkay (Piankashaw), perhaps containing originally the Pepicokia band, on the site of Vincennes, Knox County, Ind.

Choppatee's Village, on the west bank of St. Joseph River, a few miles from Fort Wayne, Allen County, Ind.

Flat Belly's Village (see Papakeecha).

Kekionga, on the east bank of St. Joseph River, in Allen County, Ind., opposite Fort Wayne.

Kenapacomaqua, a Wea village on the west bank of Eel River, near its mouth, 6 miles above Logansport, Cass County, Ind.

Kokomo, on the site of the present Kokomo, Ind.

Kowasikka or Thorntown, on Sugar Creek near the present Thornton, Boone County, Ind.

Little Turtle's Village, on Eel River, Ind., about 20 miles northwest of Fort Wayne.

Meshingomesia, on a reservation on the northeastern side of Mississinewa River, in Liberty Township, Wabash County, Ind.

Missinquimeschan, probably Piankashaw, near the site of Washington, Daviess County, Ind.

Mississinewa, on the east side of Mississinewa River at its junction with the Wabash in Miami County, Ind.

Osaga, location uncertain.

Papakeecha, named from its chief, east of Turkey Lake at the present Indian village, Noble County, Ind.

Piankashaw, occupied by Piankashaw, on Wabash River at the junction of the Vermilion.

Pickawillanee, on Miami River at the site of the present Piqua, Miami County, Ohio.

Saint Francis Xavier, mission for Miami and Mascouten on Fox River, Wis., near De Pere, Brown County.

Seek's Village, on Eel River about 3 miles from Columbia City, in Whitley County, Ind.

Thornton (see Kowasikka).

White Raccoon's Village, near the present Aboite, Allen County, Ind.

History.—Miami were living in the neighborhood of Green Bay, Wis., when knowledge of the tribe first came to Europeans shortly after the middle of the seventeenth century. In 1670 they were at the headwaters of Fox River, but soon afterward they formed new settlements at the southern end of Lake Michigan and on Kalamazoo River, Mich. It is quite possible that bands of this tribe had moved from Wisconsin at a still earlier period and were in northern Indiana. Their first settlements at the lower end of Lake Michigan were at Chicago and on St. Joseph River. In 1703 there was a Miami village at Detroit, but the greater part of the tribe continued to live on St. Joseph River for a considerable period. By 1711 they had reached the Wabash, and presently they were forced from St. Joseph River by the Potawatomi, Kickapoo, and other northern tribes. In consequence they moved farther south and also eastward to Miami River, and perhaps as far as the Scioto. After the peace of 1763, they abandoned these eastern territories to the Shawnee and retired to Indiana. They took a prominent part in all subsequent wars in this section, but soon after the War of 1812 began to dispose of their lands and by 1838 had parted with most of them, the United States Government agreeing to provide them with new lands west of the Mississippi. In 1840 all of their remaining territories were ceded except one tract reserved for a part of the tribe called Meshingomesia's band, which had chosen to remain in their old country. In 1867 the rest accompanied the Illinois to Oklahoma, where they were given a reservation in the northeastern corner of the State. Their lands now have been allotted in severalty, and they are citizens of the State of Oklahoma. The lands of Meshingomesia's band in Indiana were divided among the survivors in 1872 and their descendants are citizens of Indiana.

Population.—Mooney (1928) estimated 4,500 Miami, including the Wea and Piankashaw, in the year 1650. An estimate of 1764 gives them 1,750, but a year later another substracts 500 from this figure. In 1825 the Miami, Wea, and Piankashaw, entered as tribes, were supposed to total about 1,400, of whom 327 were Wea. In 1885 only 57 Miami proper were officially recognized in Indian Territory, while the Wea and Piankashaw were enumerated with the Illinois, the whole numbering 149. These last had increased to 191 in 1903. In 1905 the total number of Miami in Indian Territory was 124. In 1900 the Miami in Indiana, including many White-Indian mixed-bloods, numbered 243. The census of 1910 returned 226 Miami, of whom 123 were in Oklahoma and 90 in Indiana. The United States Indian Office Report of 1923 gave 125 Indians in Indiana, most of whom certainly belonged to this tribe. The census of 1930 returned 284 Miami and Illinois; the 47 reported from Indiana were, of course, all Miami. In 1937, 287 were reported from Oklahoma.

Connection in which they have become noted.—Historically the Miami were noted as one of those tribes which offered steady resistance to the westward movement of White population in the eighteenth century. Their name has been given to three Ohio rivers of some importance, the Great Miami, Little Miami, and Maumee; counties in Ohio, Indiana, and Kansas; and to places in California, Indiana, Oklahoma, Missouri, Ohio, Texas, and Manitoba, Canada; also to a creek in Missouri. There are places of the name in Gila County, Ariz.; Miami County, Ind.; Saline County, Mo.; Colfax County, N. Mex.; Ottawa County, Okla.; Roberts County, Tex.; Kanawha County, W. Va. Miamisburg is in Montgomery County, Miamitown in Hamilton County, and Miamiville in Clermont County, all in Ohio; and Miami Station is in Carroll County, Mo. The name of Miami, Fla., and the derived Miami Beach and Miami Springs, Fla., have a different origin. The

Miami tribe had a famous chief, Little Turtle, whose name often appears in historical narratives.

Mosopelea. Before this tribe left its former territory north of the Ohio, it probably extended into the extreme southeastern part of Indiana. (See Ohio.)

Neutrals. The Neutral Nation may have extended slightly into the northeastern portion of this State, though this is uncertain. (See New York.)

Ottawa. Representatives of the Ottawa appear as parties to the Treaty of Greenville in 1795, relinquishing Indiana land to the Whites, and as parties to similar treaties in 1817 and 1821. (See Michigan.)

Potawatomi. The Potawatomi pushed into the northern part of Indiana during the eighteenth century and were in occupancy until they ceded their lands to the United States Government in the first half of the nineteenth century. (See Michigan.)

Seneca, see Iroquois.

Shawnee. There was an ancient Shawnee town in Posey County, Ind., at the junction of the Wabash and Ohio. At a later period the tribe had settlements along the southern and eastern borders, and the soil of Indiana was the scene of the activities of the Shawnee prophet and his brother Tecumseh until after Gen. Harrison's victory at Tippecanoe. (See Tennessee.)

Wyandot. Representatives of this tribe appear as parties to the Treaty of Greenville in 1795, relinquishing land in Indiana to the Whites. (See Wisconsin and Ohio.)

ILLINOIS

Chippewa. Representatives of this tribe appear in treaties made in 1795, 1816, 1829, and 1833 relinquishing Illinois land to the Whites. (See Minnesota.)

Delaware. While they were being slowly crowded west by the Whites, the Delaware passed across Illinois, and their connection with the State was transitory in both senses of the term. (See New Jersey.)

Foxes. This tribe, together with the Sauk, drove the Illinois Indians from the northwestern part of the State of Illinois in the latter part of the eighteenth century and took their places, but ceded the territory to the United States Government by a treaty signed November 3, 1804. (See Wisconsin.)

Illinois. A native word signifying "men," "people." Also called:

> Chicktaghicks, Geghdageghroano, or Kighetawkigh Roanu, by the Iroquois.
> Oudataouatouat, applied by the Wyandot to the Ottawa and later to the Illinois.
> Witishaχtánu, the Huron name for the Illinois and Miami, from Ushaχtáno, "Illinois River."

Connections.—The Illinois belonged to the Algonquian linguistic family, and were more closely connected with the Chippewa than with any other Algonquian tribe, except the Miami.

Location.—In historic times they lived principally along the Illinois and Mississippi Rivers, one division, the Michigamea, being as far south as northeastern Arkansas (q. v.). (See also Indiana, Iowa, Kansas, Missouri, Ohio, Oklahoma, and Wisconsin.)

Subdivisions and Villages

The Illinois were in reality a group of related tribes, of which the best known are the following:

Cahokia, later home about Cahokia, Ill.

Kaskaskia, before 1700 near the present Utica, La Salle County, later at or near Kaskaskia, Ill.

Michigamea, probably on Big Lake, between the St. Francis and Mississippi Rivers, Ark.

Moingwena, in Iowa near the mouth of Des Moines River.

Peoria, their early location probably in northeastern Iowa, later near the present Peoria.

Tamaroa, on both sides of Mississippi River about the mouths of the Illinois and Missouri.

The following were perhaps minor Illinois tribes:

Albivi, given by only one writer and it is doubtful whether this was a true Illinois band.

Amonokoa, mentioned by Hennepin, 1680.

Chepoussa, probably a band from Kaskaskia River connected with the Michigamea.

Chinko, mentioned by Allouez and La Salle.

Coiracoentanon, mentioned by La Salle.

Espeminkia, mentioned by La Salle.

Tapouaro, mentioned by La Salle.

The villages noted in history are:

Cahokia, near the present Cahokia.

Immaculate Conception, a mission among the Kaskaskia, near Rockford.

Kaskaskia, as given above.

Matchinkoa, 30 leagues from Fort Crevecoeur, near the present Peoria.

Moingwena, as given above.

Peoria, as given above.

Pimitoui, on Illinois River near the mouth of Fox River in La Salle County.

History.—In 1667 the French priest Allouez met a party of Illinois Indians who had come to La Pointe on Lake Superior to trade. In 1673 Marquette, while descending the Mississippi, found the Peoria and Moingwena west of the river near the mouth of the Des Moines, but before his return they had moved to the neighborhood of the present Peoria, and most of the other Illinois tribes, except the Mitchigamea, were then on Illinois River. In 1700 the Kaskaskia moved to southern Illinois and settled on Kaskaskia River. About the time of La Salle's visit in 1682 the Illinois were at war with a number of neighboring peoples, and the Iroquois, who were then just beginning raids against them, caused them heavy losses in the succeeding years. The murder of Pontiac by a Kaskaskia Indian set the northern tribes in motion against the Illinois and in the ensuing wars the latter were reduced to a fraction of their former strength and the Sauk, Foxes, Kickapoo, and Potawatomi dispossessed them of the greater part of their territories. The remnant settled near the French at Kaskaskia, where they continued to decline in numbers until, in 1800, only about 150 were left. In 1832 the survivors sold their lands and removed west of the Mississippi, to the present Kansas, whence they removed again in 1867 and became consolidated with the Wea and Piankashaw in the northeastern corner of the present State of Oklahoma.

Population.—Mooney (1928) estimated that in 1650 the Illinois numbered about 8,000. About 1680 Hennepin gives 400 houses and 1,800 warriors. Rasles estimated 300 cabins of 4 fires each, indicating a population of 9,000, which is probably excessive. About the year 1750 there were supposed to be from 1,500 to 2,000 souls. In 1778 the Kaskaskia numbered 210 and the Peoria and Michigamea together 170. In 1800 all these were reduced to 150. In 1885 the mixed-blood remnant in Indian territory, including the Wea and Piankashaw, numbered 149, and in 1905, 195. The census of 1910 gave 128, of whom 114 were in Oklahoma, and the census of 1930, 284 Illinois and Miami. In 1937 there were 370 "Peoria" in Oklahoma.

Connection in which they have become noted.—The chief claim of the Illinois to distinction is the adoption of its name for an important branch of the Mississippi and more particularly its later adoption as the name of the State of Illinois. The name is also given geographical application in Arkansas, Texas, Oregon, and Oklahoma. The name appears in Illinois Bend, Montague County, Tex.; Illinois City, Rock Island County, Ill.; and Illiopolis, Sangamon County, Ill.

Kickapoo. This tribe, after helping destroy the Illinois, settled on Vermilion River and extended its territories to Illinois River. It ceded this land to the United States Government July 30, 1819. (See Wisconsin.)

Miami. In very early times the Miami had a town where now stands Chicago, and later their territorial claims covered parts of the eastern sections of the State.   (See Indiana.)

Ottawa. Some Ottawa worked down to the northernmost part of the State in the eighteenth century.   (See Michigan.)

Potawatomi. This tribe succeeded the Miami in the region of Chicago, and, after the destruction of the Illinois, occupied still more territory in the northeastern part of the State.   (See Michigan.)

Sauk. The Sauk assisted their relatives the Foxes in expelling the Illinois tribes from the Rock River region, and they occupied it with them until the lands were ceded to the Whites and they moved farther west.   (See Wisconsin.)

Shawnee. There were Shawnee for a while in the southern part of Illinois.   (See Tennessee.)

Winnebago. Representatives of this tribe were parties to an Illinois land cession in 1829.   (See Wisconsin.)

Wyandot. Some Wyandot were parties to the Greenville Treaty in 1795 relinquishing land in Illinois to the Whites.   (See Ohio.)

MICHIGAN

Chippewa. At a very early period, Chippewa lived about the Sault St. Marie and on the northern shore of Lake Michigan.   (See Minnesota.)

Foxes. Since the Sauk are known to have lived in Michigan at an early period, it is probable that the Foxes did also, but this is still uncertain.   (See Wisconsin.)

Hurons, see **Wyandot.**

Kickapoo. The same probability of an early residence in Michigan applies to the Kickapoo as to the Foxes and for a similar reason.   (See Wisconsin.)

Menominee. This tribe ceded its claim to a portion of the upper peninsula of Michigan in 1836.   (See Wisconsin.)

Miami. The Miami, or a portion of them, at one time occupied the valley of St. Joseph River and other parts of the southern Michigan border.   (See Indiana.)

Neutrals. Bands of the Neutral Nation extended, in the seventeenth century, into what is now southeastern Michigan.   (See New York.)

Noquet. Meaning probably "bear foot," another name for the Bear gens in Chippewa. The Bear gens may have been prominent in this tribe.

Connections.—The Noquet are thought to have been related to the Menominee of the Algonquian linguistic family.

Location.—About Big Bay de Noquet and Little Bay de Noquet and extending across the northern peninsula of Michigan to Lake Superior. (See also Wisconsin.)

History.—In 1659 the Noquet was one of the tribes attached to the mission of St. Michel. They were never prominent and were probably absorbed at a very early date by the Menominee or Chippewa.

Population.—Unknown.

Connection in which they have become noted.—The name Noquet is perpetuated in the two bays above mentioned.

Ottawa. From a native word signifying "to trade," because they were noted as middlemen. It occurs shortened to Tawa. Also called:

> Andatahouats, Ondatawawat, Huron name.
> Udawak, Penobscot name.
> Ukua'-yata, Huron name, according to Gatschet (1877).
> Waganha's, Iroquois name, meaning "stammerers".
> Watawawininiwok, Chippewa name, meaning "men of the bulrushes", from the many bulrushes in Ottawa River.
> Wdǫwǫ, Abnaki name.

Connections.—The Ottawa belonged to the Algonquian linguistic stock and were related most closely with the Chippewa and Potawatomi.

Location.—The earliest known home of this tribe was Manitoulin Island and neighboring parts of the north shore of Georgian Bay. Their connection with Michigan came later. (See also Illinois, Indiana, Iowa, Kansas, Minnesota, Ohio, Oklahoma, Wisconsin, and Canada.)

Subdivisions and Villages

The following four main divisions are given by early writers: The Kishkakon or Bear Gens, the Nassauaketon, or Fork People, the Sable Gens and the Sinago or Gray Squirrel Gens, to which a fifth, the Keinouche or Pickerel Gens, is sometimes added. The Kishkakon, Sinago, and Keinouche were closely associated.

Villages:

Aegakotcheising, in Michigan.
Anamiewatigong, in Emmet County, lower Michigan.
Apontigoumy, probably in Ontario.
Machonee, near the mouth of Au Vaseau River which flows into Lake St. Clair, in lower Michigan.
Manistee, in Michigan, perhaps near the village of Weganakisi on Little Traverse Bay.
Menawzhetaunaung, on an island in the Lake of the Woods.
Meshkemau, on Maumee Bay, Lucas County, Ohio.
Michilimackinac, on Mackinac Island.
Middle Village, location unknown.

Obidgewong, with Chippewa, on the western shore of Lake Wolseley, Manitoulin Island, Ontario.

Oquanoxa, on the west bank of the Little Auglaize, at its mouth, in Paulding County, Ohio.

Roche de Boeuf, on the northwestern bank of Maumee River, near Waterville, Lucas County, Ohio.

Saint Simon, a mission on Manitoulin Island.

Shabawywyagun, apparently on the eastern shore of Lake Michigan.

Tushquegan, on the south bank of Maumee River opposite Toledo, Ohio.

Waganakisi, on the site of Harbor Springs, Emmet County, Mich.

Walpole Island, on the island of that name, Ontario.

Waugau, near the mouth of Maumee River, in Lucas County, Ohio.

Wolf Rapids, on Maumee River, Ohio, about the boundary of Wood and Henry Counties.

Additional bands:

Maskasinik, position uncertain, mentioned in Jesuit Relation of 1657–58 with Nikikouek and Missisauga.

Nikikouek, position uncertain, associated with Missisauga and dwelling east of them on the north shore of Lake Huron.

Outaouakamigouk, on the northeast coast of Lake Huron in 1648, probably Ottawa.

Sagnitaouigama, in 1640 southeast of Ottawa River, perhaps same as Sinago.

History.—It is uncertain whether the Ottawa River in Ontario received its name because the Ottawa once lived upon it or because the Ottawa had obtained a monopoly of the trade passing up and down it. When the French actually came among them they were in the region above indicated. After the destruction of their allies, the Hurons, in 1648–49, the Iroquois attacked the Ottawa in turn, who fled to the islands at the entrance of Green Bay, part of them later passing to Keweenaw Bay, while the rest accompanied the Hurons to an island near the entrance of Lake Pepin on the Mississippi. Harassed by the Dakota, the Ottawa settled on Chequamegon Bay but in 1670–71 were induced by the French to return to Manitoulin Island. By 1680 most of them had left Manitoulin Island and joined the Hurons about the mission station at Mackinaw. About 1700 the Hurons removed to Detroit, and a portion of the Ottawa seem to have obtained a foothold on the west shore of Lake Huron between Saginaw Bay and Detroit, but they returned to Mackinaw about 1706. Soon afterward the chief seat of a portion of the tribe was fixed at L'Arbre Croche in Emmett County, whence they spread down the east side of Lake Michigan to St. Joseph River, a few finding their way into Wisconsin and northeastern Illinois. At the same time some of them were living in their old country on Manitoulin Island and about Georgian Bay, and others were scattered along the southern shore of Lake Erie from Detroit to the vicinity of Beaver Creek, Pa. They took part successively against the English and the American colonists in all wars during the latter half of the eighteenth century and the beginning of the nineteenth until the end of the War of 1812. The famous chief Pontiac was an Ottawa. The Canadian Ottawa are on Manitoulin and Cockburn Islands and the adjacent shores of Lake Huron. In 1831 two bands of Ottawa known as the Ottawa of Blanchard's Fork of Great Auglaize River and the Ottawa of Roche de Boeuf on Maumee River were granted lands on Marais des Cygnes River, Kans., but they re-ceded the greater part of these lands in 1846, and in 1862 they agreed to allotment in severalty and to the relinquishment of their remaining territory. Further treaties regarding the disposal of their lands were made in 1867 and 1872. In 1867 they received a plot of land in Oklahoma which had been ceded by the Shawnee. A few Ottawa went west with the Prairie Potawatomi but were soon fused with them or scattered to other places. A few others have continued to occupy parts of Kansas down to the present day but after 1868 most of them removed to Oklahoma. A still larger body of Ottawa remained in Michigan, scattered among a number of small villages.

Population.—Mooney (1928) estimated that in 1600 there were of the combined Algonkin and Ottawa about 6,000. The scattered condition of the tribe during their earlier history prevented their contemporary chroniclers from obtaining satisfactory figures. In 1906 the Chippewa and Ottawa on Manitoulin and Cockburn Islands numbered 1,497, of whom about half were Ottawa; there were 197 under the Seneca School, Okla.; and in Michigan there were 5,587 in 1900 of whom about two-thirds were Ottawa. According to the census of 1910, there were 2,717 Ottawa in the United States, 2,454 being in Michigan, 170 in Oklahoma, and the rest in Wisconsin, Nebraska, Kansas, and Pennsylvania. In 1923 there were 274 in Oklahoma and a much larger number in Michigan and Canada. The United States Census of 1930 gives 1,745, of whom 1,469 were in Michigan, 167 in Oklahoma, and 84 in Wisconsin. In 1937 there were 422 in Oklahoma.

Connection in which they have become noted.—Although a prominent tribe in early times, the Ottawa will now be especially remembered from the fact that they have given their name to the most important branch of the St. Lawrence River and the city on its banks which became the capital of the Dominion of Canada. Their name is also borne by counties in Kansas, Michigan, and Ohio, and the province of Quebec; by important cities in La Salle County, Ill., and Franklin County, Kans.; and by smaller places and streams in Rockcastle County, Ky.; Waukesha County, Wis.; Le Sueur County, Minn.; Putnam County, Ohio; Boone County, Wis.; Boone County, Va.; and Ottawa Beach in Ottawa County, Mich., and Ottawa Lake in Monroe County in the same State. The tribe will be noted furthermore as that to which belonged the famous Indian patriot, Pontiac.

Potawatomi. Meaning "people of the place of the fire," and hence sometimes known as the Fire Nation. Also called:

> Atsistarhonon, Huron name.
> Kúnu-háyanu, Caddo name, meaning "watermelon people."
> Ndaton8atendi, Undatomátendi, Huron name.
> Peki'neni, Fox name, meaning "grouse people."
> Tcáshtálálgi, Creek name, meaning "watermelon people."
> Wah-hō'-na-hah, Miami name, meaning "fire makers."
> Wáhiúȼaxá, Omaha name.
> Wáhiúyaha, Kansa name.
> Woraxa, Iowa, Oto, and Missouri name.
> Woráxĕ, Winnebago name.

Connections.—The Potawatomi belonged to the Algonquian linguistic family, being most closely affiliated with the Chippewa and Ottawa.

Location.—The ancient home of this tribe was evidently in the lower peninsula of Michigan. (See also Illinois, Indiana, Iowa, Kansas, Ohio, Oklahoma, and Wisconsin.)

Subdivisions and Villages

In the course of their later history, the Potawatomi became separated into several distinct bands but these do not seem to have corresponded to any old, well-determined classification.

Villages:

> Abercronk, not certainly Potawatomi, in northeastern Porter County, Ind.
> Ashkum's Village, on the north side of Eel River, about Denver, Miami County, Ind.
> Assiminehkon, probably Potawatomi, in Lee County, Ill.
> Aubbeenaubbee's Village, in Aubbeenaubbee Township in Fulton County, Ind.
> Checkawkose's Village, on the south side of Tippecanoe River, about Harrison Township, Kosciusko County, Ind.
> Chekase's Village, on the west side of Tippecanoe River between Warsaw and Monoquet, Kosciusko, Ind.
> Chichipé Outipé, near South Bend, St. Joseph County, Ind.
> Chippoy, on Big Shawnee Creek, in Fountain County, Ind.
> Comoza's Village, on Tippecanoe River in Fulton County, Ind.
> Kinkash's Village, on Tippecanoe River, Kosciusko County, Ind.
> Little Rock Village, on the north bank of Kankakee River about the boundary of Kankakee and Will Counties, Ill.
> Macon, location unknown.
> Macousin, on the west bank of St. Joseph River, Berrien County, Mich.
> Mangachqua, on Peble River in southern Michigan.
> Maquanago, probably Potawatomi, near Waukesha, in southeastern Wisconsin.
> Masac's Village, on the west bank of Tippecanoe River in the northeastern part of Fulton County, Ind.
> Matchebenashshewish's Village, on Kalamazoo River probably in Jackson County, Mich.
> Maukekose's Village, near the head of Wolf Creek in Marshall County, Ind.
> Menominee's Village, on the north side of Twin Lakes near the site of Plymouth, Marshall County, Ind.

Menoquet's Village, on Cass River, lower Michigan.

Mesheketeno's Village, on Kankakee River, a short distance above the present Kankakee in northeastern Illinois.

Mesquawbuck's Village, near Oswego, Kosciusko County, Ind.

Mickkesawbee, at the site of the present Coldwater, Mich.

Milwaukee, with Foxes and Mascouten, at or near the present Milwaukee, Wis.

Minemaung's Village, near Grantpark, Kankakee County, Ill.

Mota's Village, just north of Tippecanoe River near Atwood, Kosciusko County, Ind.

Muskwawasepeotan, near Cedarville, Allen County, Ind.

Natowasepe, on St. Joseph River about the present Mendon, St. Joseph County, Mich.

Nayonsay's Village, probably Potawatomi, in the northeastern part of Kendall County, Ill.

Pierrish's Village, on the north bank of Eel River, just above Laketon, Wabash County, Ind.

Pokagon, in Berrien County, near the west bank of St. Joseph River just north of the Indiana line.

Prairie Ronde, about the boundary of Cass and Van Buren Counties, Mich.

Rock Village in northeastern Illinois.

Rum's Village, about 4 miles south of South Bend, St. Joseph County, Ind.

Saint Joseph, a mission on St. Joseph River near the south end of Lake Michigan.

Saint Michael, a mission in southern Wisconsin.

Sawmehnaug, on Fox River, Ill.

Seginsavin's Village, on Rouge River near Detroit, Mich.

Shaytee's Village, probably Potawatomi on Fox River, Ill.

Shobonier's Village, near the present Shabbona, De Kalb County, Ill.

Soldier's Village, in northern Illinois.

Tassinong, probably Potawatomi, in Porter County, Ind.

Toisa's Village, on the west bank of Tippecanoe River, nearly opposite Bloomingsburg, Fulton County, Ind.

Tonguish's Village, near Rouge River in the southern part of Oakland County, or the northern part of Wayne County, Mich.

Topenebee's Village, on St. Joseph River opposite Niles, Berrien County, Mich.

Waisuskuck's Village, in northeastern, Illinois.

Wanatah, in La Porte County, Ind., a short distance east of the present Wanatah.

Wimego's Village, on the north bank of Indian Creek, in the northern part of Cass County, Ind.

Winamac's Village, near the present Winamac, Pulaski County, Ind.

Wonongoseak, probably Potawatomi, between the northern and southern branches of Elkhart River, apparently in Noble County, Ind.

History.—Shortly before the Potawatomi were encountered by the French they seem to have been living in the lower peninsula of Michigan. According to native traditions, the Ottawa, Chippewa, and Potawatomi reached the upper end of Lake Huron in company from some region farther east, and the Potawatomi crossed from that point into the peninsula. By 1670 they had been driven to the neighborhood of Green Bay west of Lake Michigan, whence they slowly moved south until by the end of the century they had established themselves on Milwaukee River, at Chicago, and on St. Joseph River. After the conquest of the Illinois Indians about 1765, they took possession of still more of what is now the northern part of the State of Illinois and extended their settlements eastward over southern Michigan as far as Lake Erie.   After 1795, against the protests of the Miami, they moved down the Wabash and advanced their occupancy as far as Pine Creek. They sided actively first with the French against the English and then with the English against the Americans until a general peace was brought about in 1815.   As White settlers increased in numbers in their neighborhood, the Potawatomi gradually parted with their lands, the greatest cessions being made between 1836 and 1841, and most of them retired beyond the Mississippi.   Part of the Prairie band of Potawatomi returned to Wisconsin, while another band, the Potawatomi of Huron, are in lower Michigan.   A few escaped into Canada and are now on Walpole Island in St. Clair County.   Part of the Potawatomi living in Wisconsin sold their lands and received in exchange a reservation in southwestern Iowa.   These received the name of Prairie Potawatomi.   In 1846 they also disposed of their Iowa territory and in 1847-48 passed over into Kansas and established themselves just east of the Potawatomi of the Woods, who had come from Indiana in 1840 to occupy a reserve on Osage River, in Kansas.   In 1846, however, the latter re-ceded this and settled the following year between the Shawnee and Delaware Indians in the present Shawnee County, Kans.   The Potawatomi of the Prairie remained in Kansas and received allotments there, but the Potawatomi of the Woods went to a new reservation in Oklahoma in 1869-71 near the Kickapoo.   A few have accompaied the Kickapoo to Mexico.

Population.—Mooney's (1928) estimate for the Potawatomi, as of the year 1650, is 4,000.   Estimates made between 1765 and 1843 vary from 1,200 to 3,400, but it would seem that they must have averaged 2,000 to 2,500.   In 1908, 2,522 Potawatomi were reported in the United States, distributed as follows: Citizen Potawatomi in Oklahoma, 1,768; Prairie band in Kansas, 676; and Potawatomi of Huron, in Calhoun County, Mich., 78.   A few besides these were scattered through their ancient territory and at various other points. Those in Canada are all in the Province of Ontario and number about 220, of whom 176 are living with Chippewa and Ottawa on Walpole Island and the remainder, no longer officially reported, are divided between Caradoc and Riviére aux Sables, where they reside by permission of the Chippewa and Munsee.   The United States Census of 1910 returned 2,440, of whom 866 were living in Oklahoma, 619 in Kansas, 461 in Michigan, and 245 in Wisconsin, while the remainder were scattered in 11 other States.   The United States and Canadian Indian Office Reports of 1923-24 give 2,227 in Oklahoma, 803 in Kansas, and 170 on Walpole Island, Ontario, but those in Michigan are not separately entered. The United States Census of 1930 returned 1,854, of whom 654 were in Kansas, 636 in Oklahoma, 425 in Wisconsin, and 89 in Michigan. In 1937 there were 142 in Michigan, 311 in Wisconsin, 1,013 in Kansas, and 2,667 in Oklahoma: total 4,133.

Connection in which they have become noted.—In the form Pottawatomie the name of this tribe is used as a designation of counties in Kansas and Oklahoma and a post township of Coffey County, Kans., and in the form Pottawattamie as the designation of a county in Iowa.

Sauk. At some time shortly before European contact the Sauk lived about Saginaw Bay and the present name of the bay is derived from them. They were probably driven beyond Lake Michigan by the Ottawa allied with the Neutral Nation. (See Wisconsin.)

Wyandot. After the disruption of their nation by the Iroquois these people lived for limited periods at several different points in the territory now included in the State of Michigan. They were temporarily at Michilimackinac, Detroit, and other places. (See Ohio.)

WISCONSIN

Chippewa. This tribe pushed its way west in the latter part of the seventeenth century as far as the territory lying within the present State of Wisconsin, and the trading post established by the French at La Pointe became an important Chippewa base. Early in the eighteenth century they are said to have driven the Foxes out of northern Wisconsin, and they have continued to occupy that part of the State until the present time, having two reservations there. (See Minnesota.)

Dakota. In very early times the Dakota occupied a little of the northwestern margin of Wisconsin. (See South Dakota.)

Foxes. A name thought to have been derived from that of the Fox clan and to have been applied to the tribe through a misunderstanding. Also called:

Beshde'ke, Dakota name.
Mĕshkwa kihŭgⁱ, own name signifying "red earth people," from the kind of earth from which they are supposed to have been created.
O-dug-am-eeg, Chippewa name, meaning "those who live on the opposite side."
Skaxshurunu, Wyandot name, meaning "fox people."
Skuakîsagi, Shawnee name.
To-che-wah-coo, probably the Arikara name.
Wăkushég, Potawatomi name, meaning "foxes."

Connections.—The Foxes belonged to the Algonquian linguistic family and in one group with the Sauk and Kickapoo.

Location.—In the vicinity of Lake Winnebago or along Fox River. (See also Illinois, Iowa, Kansas, Michigan, Minnesota, Missouri, Nebraska, and Oklahoma.)

History.—Since the closely related Sauk Indians came to Wisconsin from Saginaw Bay, Mich., it is probable that the Foxes once lived in that region as well, but it is uncertain. There is also a tradition that they were in northern Wisconsin and were driven south by the Chippewa. The French missionaries heard of them as early as 1640, and in 1670 found them in the location above given, where they remained for a long period. They were constantly at war with the Chippewa, and though they received aid from the Dakota, obtained little advantage in these contests. It was on account of assistance rendered the Chippewa by the French that the Foxes came to assume a hostile attitude toward the latter and finally went to war with them. In 1712 they planned an attack on the French fort at Detroit which nearly succeeded. Between 1729 and 1733 occurred a bitter war with the French in which the Foxes, though assisted by some Sauk, lost heavily. Before 1746 they were in the habit of exacting a toll from all white traders passing up Fox River, and for this reason they were attacked by a band of French, defeated, and driven down Wisconsin River, settling on the north bank of that stream about 20 miles from its mouth. In 1780, in alliance with the Dakota, they attacked the Chippewa at St. Croix Falls and were defeated. Shortly before this they had assisted the Sauk in driving the Illinois tribes from the northwestern part of the Rock River country, and they occupied these territories, but early in the nineteenth century they drew away from the Sauk and settled in Iowa. In 1842 the Foxes and the Sauk, who had taken refuge with them after the Black Hawk War, sold their lands in Iowa and were given in exchange a tract across the Missouri in Kansas. About 1857–59 the Foxes became angered at the Sauk for entering into an agreement for the disposition of the lands of the two tribes during the absence of the former, and they returned to Iowa where a few of their people had always remained. There they bought land near Tama City on Iowa River, which they increased by purchase until they had more than 3,000 acres. They have remained on this reservation down to the present day.

Population.—Mooney (1928) estimated that in 1650 there must have been about 3,000 Foxes, but this figure seems to be somewhat too high. In 1728 Guignes stated that they had 200 warriors, probably an underestimate, but most of the figures before 1850 fall between 1,500 and 2,500. Michelson (1919) says that the most reliable early estimate is that of Lewis and Clark in 1805, which gives 1,200. Since that date they have usually been enumerated with the Sauk. In

1885 the Indians at Tama, most of whom were Foxes, numbered 380. In 1909 the United States Indian Office gives 352 (nearly all Foxes) in Iowa, besides the bands in Oklahoma and Kansas, most of whom were Sauk. The United States Census of 1910 gives only 257 in Iowa, but the Indian Office Report of 1923 raises this again to 354. In 1930 there were 887 Sauk and Fox, and it is assumed that the 344 returned from Iowa were nearly all Fox. In 1937, 441 were returned from Iowa. (See **Sauk.**)

Connection in which they have become noted.—Historically this tribe is remarkable (1) as having been almost the only Algonquian tribe of consequence to undertake a serious war with the French, and (2) from its connection with the Sauk at the time of the uprising of the latter under Black Hawk. It has given its name to Fox River, Wis., and to a second Fox River, also called Pishtaka, which rises in Wisconsin and flows through Illinois, into the Illinois River. Some small places have also been named from it.

Housatonic, see Stockbridges.

Illinois. At one time Illinois Indians probably occupied some of the southern and southwestern sections of Wisconsin. (See Illinois.)

Iowa. A rather pronounced tradition points to the Winnebago as the mother tribe of the Iowa, Oto, and Missouri, and the latter are supposed to have stopped at certain places within the State of Wisconsin during their migration to the southwest. (See Iowa.)

Iroquois. The Iroquois anciently played an important part in the aboriginal history of the Indian tribes of Wisconsin, usually as enemies. In very late times the Oneida were given a reservation here where their descendants still live. (See New York.)

Kickapoo. From Kiwĕgapaw[a], "he stands about," "he moves about, standing now here, now there." Also called:

A'-uya$_x$, Tonkawa name, meaning "deer eaters."
Hígabu, Omaha and Ponca name.
I'-ka-dŭ', Osage name.
Shake-kah-quah, Wichita name.
Shígapo, Shikapu, Apache name.
Sik'-a-pu, Comanche name.
Tékapu, Huron name.
Yu[n]tara'ye-ru'nu, a second Huron name, meaning "tribe living around the lakes."

Connections.—The Kickapoo belonged to the Algonquian linguistic stock, and in a special group with the Foxes and Sauk.

Subdivisions and Villages

The villages were: Etnataek (shared with the Foxes), rather a fortification than a village, near the Kickapoo village on Sangamon River, Ill., and Kickapougowi, on the Wabash River in Crawford County, Ill., about opposite the mouth of Turman Creek.

Location.—For territory occupied in Wisconsin, see History. (See also Illinois, Indiana, Kansas, Michigan, Missouri, Ohio, and Oklahoma.)

History.—As suggested in the case of the Foxes, the Kickapoo may once have lived near the Sauk in the lower peninsula of Michigan but such a residence cannot be proven. If the name Outitchakouk used by the Jesuit missionary Druillettes refers to this tribe, as seems probable, knowledge of them was brought to Europeans in 1658. At any rate they were visited by Allouez about 1667–70 and were then near the portage between Fox and Wisconsin Rivers, perhaps about Alloa, Columbia County, Wis. Early in the eighteenth century a part of them settled somewhere near Milwaukee River, and after the destruction of the Illinois about 1765, they moved still farther south and lived about Peoria. One portion then pushed down to the Sangamon, while another worked east to the Wabash, and made their headquarters on Vermilion River. The former became known as the Prairie band and the latter as the Vermilion band. They took part against the colonists in the War of 1812 and the Black Hawk War, but in 1837 a hundred of them were engaged to assist the United States Government against the Seminole. In 1809 and 1819 they ceded their lands in Illinois and soon removed to Missouri and thence to Kansas. About 1852 a large party of Kickapoo, along with some Potawatomi, went to Texas and thence to México, where they became known as "Mexican Kickapoo." In 1863 another dissatisfied band joined them, and though in 1873 part were induced to return to Indian Territory, and others afterward followed, nearly half the tribe remained and were granted a reservation in the Santa Rosa Mountains of eastern Chihuahua. The remainder are divided between Oklahoma and Kansas.

Population.—Mooney (1928) estimates that in 1650 there were 2,000 Kickapoo. In 1759 they were estimated at 3,000; in 1817, at 2,000; and in 1825, at 2,200. In 1875 those in the United States were officially estimated at 706 and there were supposed to be about 100 more in México. In 1885 those in the United States were estimated at 500 and those in México at 200. In 1905, 247 were reported in Oklahoma and 185 in Kansas, a total of 432, and almost as many more were thought to be in México. The census of 1910 returned 348 in the United States, of whom 211 were in Kansas and 135 in Oklahoma. In 1923 the United States Indian Office gave 277 in Kansas and 200 in Oklahoma, total 477. In 1930 there were 523, half in Kansas and half in Oklahoma. In 1937, 332 were returned from Kansas and 260 from Oklahoma.

Connection in which they have become noted.—The Kickapoo have given their name to a river in Wisconsin, creeks in Illinois and Texas, and some small places in these States and Kansas.

Mahican, see Stockbridges.

Mascouten. A name applied at times to the Prairie band of the Potawatomi, but more often to the Peoria band of Illinois who, in early days, lived with or near the Kickapoo.

Menominee. Meaning "Wild Rice Men," because they lived largely upon the wild rice of the lakes in and near their country. Hence the French "Nation de la Folle Avoine," and English "Wild Rice Men." Also called:

> Addle-Heads, a misinterpretation of Folles Avoines.
> Omanomini, Chippewa name.
> White Indians, so given by Long (*in* Keating, 1824).

Connections.—The Menominee belonged to the Algonquian linquistic family and to the same section as the Cree and Foxes.

Location.—On and near the Menominee River, Wis. (See also Michigan.)

Subdivisions

(As given by Skinner, 1921)

Kaka′pa′kato′ Wini′niwûk, "Barricade Falls people," at Keshena Falls of Wolf River.
Kakä′nikone Tusi′-niniwûg, "Portage people," at Portage, Wis.
Kipisa′′kia Wini′wiwûk, "River Mouth people," at Prairie du Chien.
Mani′towûk Tusi′niniwûg, "Manitou Place people," at Manitowoc, Wis.
Mätc Sua′mäko Tusi′nini^u, "Great Sand Bar people," on the sand dunes at what is now called Big Suamico, on Green Bay.
Minika′ni Wini′niwuk, "Village people," at the mouth of Menominee River.
Misi′nimäk Kimiko Wini′niwûk, "Michilimackinac People," near the old fort at Mackinac, Mich.
Muhwä′o Se′peo Wini′niwûk, "Wolf River people," on the upper stretches of Wolf River.
Nämä′o Wikito′ Tusi′ni^u, "Sturgeon Bay people," at Sturgeon Bay.
Nomä′kokon Se′peo Tusi′niniwûg, "Beaver River people," near Winneconne, Fond du Lac, and Oshkosh.
Oka′to Wini′niwûk, "Pike Place people," at the mouth of the Oconto River.
Pä′sä′tiko Wini′niwûk, "Peshtigo River people," at the mouth of Peshtigo River.
Powahe′kune Tusi′niniwûg, "Rice-gathering-place people," on Lake Poygan.
Sua′makosa Tusi′nini^u, "Little Sand Dune people," on the sandhills of Little Suamico.
Wi′skos Se′peo Wini′niwûk, "Wisconsin River people"—the name Wisconsin being derived from wi′skos or wi′sko^{n}s, "muskrat"—on the Mississippi near Wisconsin River.

There were other settlements of Menominee at Milwaukee and at Fort Howard in the present city of Green Bay.

About the time of the arrival of the Whites the old bands were broken up or renamed after their chiefs, and the following bands of this kind are recorded by Hoffman:

Aia'miqta.

Äqkâ'mot.

Kĕshok, or Kē'so.

Le Motte.

Mä'nabŭ'shō

O'hopē'sha.

Osh'kosh.

Pĕsh'tiko, evidently one of the old local groups.

Piwä'qtinet.

Sha'kitŏk.

Shu'nu' ni'ŭ or Shu'nien.

History.—Tradition says that the Menominee were driven into the region later identified with them, from the neighborhood of Michilimackinac, but when they were first known to white men they were already there, and they remained there until 1854, though their villages sometimes extended to Fox River and their later claims reached to the mouth of Milwaukee River on Lake Michigan and on the west side of Green Bay to the headwaters of Menominee and Fox Rivers. Westward they claimed the height of land between Green Bay and Lake Superior. In 1854 they ceded all their lands except a reserve on Wolf River, where they have continued to the present day.

Population.—Mooney (1928) estimates that there were 3,000 Menominee in 1650. The most conservative estimates made during the nineteenth century range from 1,600 to 1,900. In the first decade of the twentieth century their numbers were placed at 1,600, of whom 1,370 were under the Green Bay School superintendency, Wisconsin. The census of 1910 returned 1,422; 1,350 in Wisconsin and the rest scattered over 8 States. The United States Indian Office Report for 1923 gave 1,838. The census of 1930 returned 1,969, and the United States Indian Office Report of 1937, 2,221.

Connection in which they have become noted.—The name Menominee has become applied to a county in Michigan and a city of some size in the same State, also to a small place in Illinois. In the form Menomonee, it is given to a considerable river of Wisconsin which flows into Green Bay, and to various other places in Wisconsin. A city in the same State, capital of Dunn County, bears the name Menomonie. Menomonee Falls are in Waukesha County, Wis. There is a place called Menominee in Menominee County, Mich.

Miami. This tribe, or at least portions of it, lived in southern Wisconsin when it was first known to French explorers and missionaries but later it moved south entirely out of the State. (See Indiana.)

Missouri. (See Iowa.)

Munsee. Some Munsee moved into Wisconsin with the Stockbridges (q. v.).

Noquet. This tribe may have been related to the Menominee or the Chippewa. At times it probably overlapped the northeastern border of Wisconsin. (See Michigan.)

Oneida, see **Iroquois.**

Oto. (See Iowa.)

Ottawa. Some Ottawa lived in Wisconsin temporarily after they had been driven from their old homes by the Iroquois. They settled first on the islands at the mouth of Green Bay, and a part of them lived later upon Black River and at Chequamegon Bay before returning to their old country. (See Michigan.)

Potawatomi. When first encountered by the French the Potawatomi were on the islands at the mouth of Green Bay. Later they pushed down the coast of Lake Michigan to Milwaukee River and thence to Chicago after which they drew further south into Illinois, Indiana, and southern Michigan. (See Michigan.)

Sauk. From Osā'kiwŭg, meaning "people of the outlet," or "people of the yellow earth." Also called:

> Hotĭ'nestakoⁿ', Onondaga name.
> Satoeronnon, Huron name.
> Quatokeronon, Huron name.
> Za'-ke, Santee and Yankton Dakota name.

Connections.—The Sauk belonged to the Algonquian linguistic stock and the same subdivision as that embracing the Foxes and Kickapoo.

Location.—On the upper part of Green Bay and lower course of Fox River. (See also Illinois, Iowa, Kansas, Michigan, Minnesota, Missouri, and Oklahoma.)

History.—The earliest known home of the Sauk was about Saginaw Bay, Mich., which still bears their name. Shortly before the appearance of the Whites they were expelled from this country by the Ottawa and the Neutral Nation, and settled in the region above indicated where they remained for a considerable period. In 1766 Carver (1796) found their chief villages on Wisconsin River. After the destruction of the Illinois they extended their territories over the Rock River district of northwestern Illinois. In 1804 a band of Sauk wintering near St. Louis were induced to enter into a treaty ceding to the United States Government the Sauk territories in Illinois and Wisconsin, but this transaction created so much indignation among the rest of the tribe when it became known that the band who made the treaty never returned to the rest and they have received independent recognition as the Missouri River Sauk. As the rest of the Sauk refused to move, other negotiations were entered into which were broken off in 1832 by the Indian outbreak known as the Black Hawk

War. As a result of this struggle, the Sauk abandoned their country east of the Mississippi and sought refuge with the Foxes, already established in Iowa. In 1842 the Sauk, with the Foxes, ceded their lands in Iowa also in exchange for a tract in Kansas. About 1857–59, in the absence of the Foxes, the Sauk agreed to take up land in severalty and cede the remainder of this Kansas territory, and the Foxes, when they learned of this, returned to Iowa. In 1867 the Sauk ceded their lands in Kansas and removed to the Indian territory, and in 1889 they took up land in severalty and sold their surplus territories to the government.

Population.—Mooney (1928) estimates that there were 3,500 Sauk in 1650. The principal early estimates of the Sauk are: in 1736, 750 persons; in 1759, 1,000; in 1766, 2,000; in 1783, 2,250; in 1810, 2,850; in 1825, 4,800; in 1834, 2,500. Michelson (1919) states, however, that the best was that of Lewis and Clark, which would make them about 2,000 in 1805. In 1885 there were 457 in Indian Territory, including a few Foxes, and 87 in southeastern Nebraska. The Indian Office Report for 1909 gives 536 (chiefly Sauk) in Oklahoma, and 87 (chiefly Sauk) in Kansas. The census of 1910 gives 347 in Oklahoma and 69 in Kansas, Sauk and Fox not being discriminated. It also records a number of individuals of both tribes scattered over nine other States. In 1923 the United States Report on Indian Affairs gave 673 in Oklahoma, and 93 in Kansas; total 766. The census of 1930 returned 887 Sauk and Fox, rather more than two-thirds being Sauk. In 1937 the United States Indian Office reported 126 "Sac and Fox" in Kansas and 861 in Oklahoma, principally Sauk.

Connection in which they have become noted.—Whatever prominence the Sauk have attained they owed almost entirely to the war which, under Black Hawk, they sustained against the Whites. Their name is perpetuated in Sauk River, Minn.; Sauk County, Wis.; and places in these two States. In the form Sac, it has been applied to a county and its capital in Iowa, a river in Missouri, and a small place in Tennessee. There is a post village called Sauk in Skagit County, Wash.; a Sauk City in Sauk County, Wis.; a Saukville in Ozaukee County in the same State; Sauk Rapids in Benton County, Minn.; and in the same State but in Stearns County, Sauk Centre which has a reputation all its own.

Stockbridges. This name was given to a body of Indians most of whom belonged to the Housatonic and other tribes of the Mahican group, who in 1833 were placed upon a reserve in the neighborhood of Green Bay, along with the Oneida Indians and some Munsee. In 1856 all but a few who desired to become citizens removed to a reservation west of Shawano, Shawano County, Wis., where they still live. (See New York.)

Tionontati. Remnants of this tribe were in Wisconsin as part of the **Wyandot** (q. v.).

Winnebago. Signifying in the Fox and the Sauk languages "people of the filthy water," for which reason they were sometimes known to the French as Puants and to the English as Stinkards. Also called:

> Aweatsiwaenhronon, a form of the Huron name (see below).
> Banabeouiks, a shortened form of Winnebago.
> Bay Indians, so called by Lapham, Blossom, and Dousman (1870).
> Hati'hshi'rû'nû, Huron name, meaning "afraid of sticking in the mire."
> Hotanka, Dakota name.
> Hotcangara, own name, signifying "(people of the) big or real speech," but, through a confusion of words, often misinterpreted "fish eaters."
> Nipegon, so called by Long (in James (1823)).

Connections.—The Winnebago belong to the Siouan linguistic family, and to a subdivision comprising also the group called by J. O. Dorsey (1897) Chiwere, which includes also the Iowa, Oto, and Missouri.

Location.—The most ancient known habitat of this tribe was on the south side of Green Bay extending inland as far as Lake Winnebago. (See also Illinois, Iowa, Minnesota, and South Dakota.)

Villages

Those that are known by name are:
Prairie la Crosse, in southeastern Wisconsin.
Sarrochau, on the site of Taycheeday, Fond du Lac County, Wis.
Spotted Arm's Village, near Exeter, Green County, Wis.
Village du Puant, on Wildcat Creek about a mile above its junction with the Wabash, above Lafayette, in Tippecanoe County, Ind.
Wuckan, on Lake Poygan, Winnebago County, Wis.
Yellow Thunder, at Yellow Banks, Green Lake County, Wis.

History.—The Winnebago were occupants of the territory above mentioned from the earliest times of which we have any record. During the eighteenth century they spread up Fox River and still later extended their villages to Wisconsin and Rock Rivers. It is reported that they were nearly destroyed by the Illinois some time before 1671 but, if so, they soon recovered entirely from this shock. They managed to remain on better terms with the surrounding tribes than most of their neighbors. By treaties made in 1825 and 1832 they ceded all of their lands south of Wisconsin and Fox Rivers to the United States Government in return for a reservation on the west side of the Mississippi above upper Iowa River. In 1836 they suffered severely from the smallpox. In 1837 they relinquished the title to their old country east of the Mississippi, and in 1840 they removed to the Neutral Ground in the territory of Iowa. Many, however, remained in their old lands. In 1846 the rest surrendered their reservation for one in Minnesota north of Minnesota River, and in 1848 removed to Long Prairie Reservation, bounded by Crow Wing, Watab, Mississippi, and Long Prairie Reservations, Minn. In 1853 they removed to Crow River and in 1856 to Blue Earth, Minn., where they remained until the Dakota outbreak of 1862, when the Whites in the section demanded their removal. In consequence they were taken to Crow Creek Reservation, S. Dak., but suffered so much from sickness, and in other ways, that they escaped to the Omaha for protection. There a new reservation was assigned to them on the Omaha lands, where they have since been allotted land in severalty. Some however, remained in Minnesota when the tribe was removed from that State and a larger number did not leave Wisconsin.

Population.—Mooney (1928) estimates that there were 3,800 individuals belonging to the Winnebago tribe in 1650. The following figures have been given from time to time: In 1806, 1,750; in 1820, 5,800; in 1837 and 1843, 4,500; in 1867, 1,750 in Nebraska and 700 in Wisconsin. In 1876 there were 1,463 on the Nebraska Reservation and 860 in Wisconsin, but 204 of the latter removed to Nebraska in 1877. In 1886 there were 1,222 in Nebraska and 930 in Wisconsin. In 1910 the United States Indian Office gave 1,063 in Nebraska and 1,270 in Wisconsin, but the United States Census of the same date gave a total Winnebago population of 1,820, of whom 1,007 were in Nebraska, 735 in Wisconsin, and the remainder scattered among 10 other States. In 1923 the Report of the United States Commissioner of Indian Affairs gave 1,096 in Nebraska. In 1930 the figure was 1,446, of whom 937 were in Wisconsin and 423 in Nebraska. In 1937 the United States Indian Office reported 1,456 in Wisconsin, and 1,212 in Nebraska: total, 2,668.

Connection in which they have become noted.—The Winnebago tribe is noted for the unique position it occupied, as a Siouan tribe surrounded by Algonquian peoples, probably having been left behind in the general Siouan movement west, and its reputation as one of the mother tribes of the Siouan stock. Its name is perpetuated in that of Winnebago Lake, Wis.; the names of counties in Iowa, Illinois, and Wisconsin; and places in Winnebago County, Ill.; Faribault County, Minn.; Winnebago County, Wis.; and Thurston County, Nebr.

Wyandot. After being driven out of Ontario by the Iroquois, part of the Wyandot, along with some Ottawa, went to Michilimackinac and from there to Green Bay, after which they lived successively at several different points within the boundaries of the present State of Wisconsin until they finally removed to Detroit. (See Ohio.)

MINNESOTA

Arapaho. There are traditions that they once lived along Red River, in the present North Dakota and Minnesota, (See Wyoming.)

Cheyenne. The earliest known home of this tribe was in that part of Minnesota bounded roughly by the Mississippi, Minnesota, and upper Red Rivers. From here they moved to the Sheyenne branch of Red River, North Dakota. (See South Dakota.)

Chippewa or Ojibwa. Traditional significance of name in their own language, "to roast until puckered up," referring to the puckered seam in their moccasins. Also called:

>An-ish-in-aub-ag, another native term meaning "spontaneous men."
>Axshissayé-rúnu, Wyandot name.
>Bawichtigouek, name in Jesuit Relations.
>Bedzaqetcha, Tsattine name, meaning "long hairs."
>Bedzietcho, Kawchodinne name.
>Bungees, so called by Hudson Bay traders.
>Cabellos realzados, the Spanish translation of French Cheveux-relevés.
>De-wǎ-kǎ-nhǎ', Mohawk name.
>Dshipowē-hága, Caughnawaga name.
>Dwǎ-kǎ-nĕⁿ, Onondaga name.
>Eskiaeronnon, Huron name, meaning "people of the falls."
>Haḣatonwan, Dakota name.
>Haḣatonway, Hidatsa name, meaning "leapers."
>Jumpers, incorrect rendering of Saulteurs.
>Kútaki, Fox name.
>Leapers, same as Jumpers.
>Né-a-ya-og, Cree name, meaning "those speaking the same language."
>Ne-gá-tcĕ, Winnebago name.
>Nwǎ'-kǎ, Tuscarora name.
>Ostiagahoroones, Iroquois name.
>Paouichtigouin, name in Jesuit Relations.
>Saulteurs, or Saulteaux, given to part of the tribe from the falls at Sault Sainte Marie.
>Sotoes, Anglicization of above.
>Wah-kah-towah, Assiniboin name, according to Tanner.

Connections.—The Chippewa are the type tribe of one of the two largest divisions of the Algonquian linguistic stock.

Location.—The earliest accounts of the Chippewa associate them particularly with the region of Sault Sainte Marie, but they came in time to extend over the entire northern shore of Lake Huron and both shores of Lake Superior, besides well into the northern interior and as far west as the Turtle Mountains of North Dakota. (See also Illinois, Indiana, Iowa, Kansas, Michigan, Montana, North Dakota, Ohio, Wisconsin, and Canada.)

Subdivisions

There were a number of major and numerous minor divisions of this tribe. According to Warren, there were 10 major divisions, as follows:

Betonukeengainubejig, in northern Wisconsin.

Kechegummewininewug, on the south shore of Lake Superior.

Kechesebewininewug, on the upper Mississippi in Minnesota.

Kojejewininewug, on Rainy Lake and River, about the northern boundary of Minnesota.

Mukmeduawininewug, or Pillagers, on Leech Lake, Minn.

Munominikasheenhug, at the headwaters of St. Croix River in Wisconsin and Minnesota.

Ottawa Lake Men, on Lac Courte Oreilles, Wis.

Sugwaundugahwininewug, north of Lake Superior.

Wahsuahgunewininewug, at the head of Wisconsin River.

Wazhush, on the northwest side of Lake Superior at the Canadian border.

Villages and Small Bands

Amikwa, on the north shore of Lake Huron, opposite Manitoulin Island.

Angwassag, near St. Charles, Saginaw County, Mich.

Anibiminanisibiwininiwak, a band, on Pembina River in the extreme northern part of Minnesota and the adjacent part of Manitoba.

Bagoache, a band, about the northern shore of Lake Superior.

Bay du Noc, perhaps Chippewa, probably on Noquet Bay in upper Michigan.

Beaver Island Indians, on the Beaver Islands of Lake Michigan, at the outlet.

Big Rock, the location of a reservation in lower Michigan.

Blackbird, on Tittibawassee River, Saginaw County, Mich.

Burnt Woods, Chippewa, on Bois Brulé River near the west end of Lake Superior, northern Wisconsin.

Chetac Lake, on the lake of the same name in Sawyer County, Wis.

Crow Wing River, at the mouth of Crow Wing River in north central Minnesota.

Doki's Band, at the head of French River where it leaves Lake Nipissing, Ont.

Epinette, on the north shore of Lake Superior, east of Michipicoton River, Ont.

Flying Post, about the post of that name in Ontario.

Fond du Lac, on St. Louis River near Fond du Lac, Minn.

Gamiskwakokawininiwak, about Cass Lake, near the head of the Mississippi, in Minn.

Gasakaskuatchimmekak, location uncertain.

Gatagetegauning, on Lac (Vieux) Desert or Gatagetegauning on the Michigan-Wisconsin State line.

Gawababiganikak, about White Earth Lake, Minn.

Grand Portage, at Grand Portage on the northern shore of Lake Superior in Minn.

Gull Lake Band, on Gull Lake on the upper Mississippi, in Cass County, Minn.

Kahmetahwungaguma, on Sandy Lake, Cass County, Minn.

Kawkawling, location uncertain.

Kechepukwaiwah, on the lake of the same name near Chippewa River, Wis.

Ketchewaundaugenink, on Shiawassee River on the trail between Detroit and Saginaw Bay, Mich.

Kishkawbawee, on Flint River in lower Michigan.

Knife Lake, location uncertain.

Lac Courte Oreilles, on the lake of the same name at the headwaters of Chippewa River, in Sawyer County, Wis.

Little Forks, a reservation on Tittibawassee River, in lower Michigan.

Long Lake, on Long Lake north of Lake Superior, between Nipigon and Pic River, Ont.

Matawachkirini, Matachewan, about Fort Matachewan, Ont.

Mattagami, about Mattagami Lake.

Mekadewagamitigweyawininiwak, on Black River, Mich.

Menitegow, on the east bank of Saginaw River in lower Michigan.

Menoquet's Village, on Cass River, lower Michigan.

Michilimackinac, on Mackinac Island, Mich.

Michipicoten, a band on Michipicoten River, Ont.

Midinakwadshiwininiwak, a band in the Turtle Mountain region, N. Dak.

Misisagaikaniwininiwak, a band on Mille Lacs, Minn.

Miskwagamiwisagaigan, a band about Red Lake River, Minn.

Nabobish, at the mouth of Saginaw River, Mich.

Nagonabe, in lower Michigan.

Nameuilni, a band northwest of Lake Superior, between Rainy Lake and Lake Nipigon in Algoma, Ont.

Nibowisibiwininiwak, in Saskatchewan north of Lake Winnipeg.

Nipissing, about Lake Nipissing.

Obidgewong, with Ottawa, on the west shore of Lake Wolseley, Manitoulin Island, Ont.

Ommunise, or Ottawa, on Carp River, Mich.

Onepowesepewenenewak, in Minnesota.

Ontonagon, a band on Ontonagon River in upper Michigan.

Oschekkamegawenenewak, 2 bands: (1) near Rainy Lake (1753); (2) east of Mille Lacs.

Ouasouarini, on Georgian Bay, Ont.

Oueschekgagamiouilimy, the Caribou gens of Rainy River, Minn.

Outchougai, on the east side of Georgian Bay and probably south of French River, connected with the Amikwa.

Otusson, on upper Huron River in Sanilac County, Mich.

Pawating, at Sault Ste. Marie, on the south bank of St. Mary's River, Chippewa County, Mich.

Pic River, at the mouth of Pic River on the north shore of Lake Superior, Ont.

Pokegama, on Pokegama Lake, Pine County, Minn.

Portage du Prairie, in Manitoba.

Rabbit Lake Chippewa, a band on Rabbit Lake, Minn.

Reaum's Village, in Flint River, Mich., about the boundary of Genesee and Saginaw Counties.

Red Cedar Lake, on Red Cedar Lake, Barron County, Wis.

Red Cliff, near the west end of Lake Superior, in Wisconsin or Minnesota.

Rice Lake Band, on Rice Lake, Barron County, Wis.

Saginaw, with Ottawa, near Saginaw, Mich.

Saint Francis Xavier, a mission, on Mille Lacs, Aitkin County, Minn.

Shabwasing, a band, probably in lower Michigan.

Shaugawaumikong, on Long Island, on the west coast of Lake Superior, in Ashland County, Wis.

Sukaauguning, on Pelican Lake, Oneida County, Wis.

Thunder Bay, Chippewa or Ottawa, a band on Thunder Bay, Alpena County, Mich.

Timagimi, about Lake Timagimi.

Trout Lake, location uncertain.

Turtle Portage, in Wisconsin.

Wabasemowenenewak, near a white rock perhaps in Minnesota.
Walpole Island, with other tribes, Ontario.
Wanamakewajejenik, near the Lake of the Woods.
Wapisiwisibiwininiwak, a band, on Swan Creek, near Lake St. Clair, Mich.
Wauswagiming, on Lac du Flambeau, Lac du Flambeau Reservation, Wisconsin.
Wequadong, near L'Anse at the head of Keweenaw Bay, Baraga County, Mich.
Whitefish, on Sturgeon River.
Wiaquahhechegumeeng, at the head of Lake Superior in Douglass County, Wis.
Winnebegoshishiwininewak, a band on Lake Winnibigashish, Minn.
Yellow Lake, on Yellow Lake, Burnett County, Wis.

History.—According to tradition, the Chippewa were part of a large body of Indians which came from the east—how much east of their later homes is uncertain—and after reaching Mackinaw separated into the Chippewa, Ottawa, and Potawatomi. The Chippewa afterward pushed their way west along both shores of Lake Superior, and in the eighteenth century, assisted by the adoption of firearms, drove the Dakota from Mille Lacs, and spread over the northern part of Minnesota and southern Manitoba as far as the Turtle Mountains. They also flowed back around Lake Huron. During the nineteenth century they were gradually gathered into reservations on both sides of the International Boundary, but none were ever removed from their original country except two small bands and some scattered families which went to Kansas early in 1839, and in 1866 agreed to settle among the Cherokee in Oklahoma.

Population.—Mooney (1928) considered that there were 35,000 Chippewa in 1650. The tribe was so large and has so many ramifications that few early estimates are very close to the truth. The principal are: In 1764, about 25,000; in 1783 and 1794, about 15,000; in 1843, about 30,000; in 1851, about 28,000. In 1884 there were in Dakota 914; in Minnesota, 5,885; in Wisconsin, 3,656; in Michigan, 3,500 returned separately and 6,000 combined Chippewa and Ottawa, of whom perhaps one-third were Chippewa; in Kansas, 76 Chippewa and Munsee. In Canada the Chippewa of Ontario, including the Nipissing, numbered at the same time about 9,000, while in Manitoba and the Northwest Territories there were 17,129 Chippewa and Cree on reservations under the same agencies. The census of 1910 gave 20,214 in the United States, of whom 8,234 were in Minnesota, 4,299 in Wisconsin, 3,725 in Michigan, 2,966 in North Dakota, and the balance scattered among 18 States. The United States Indian Office Report for 1923 gave 22,599. In Canada there were probably somewhat less than 25,000, giving a total for the tribe of about 45,000. It must, however, be remembered that the present population of Chippewa includes thousands of mixed-bloods, partly representing mixtures with other tribes and partly mixtures with Whites. The United States Census of 1930 gives 21,549, including 9,495 in Minnesota, 4,437 in

Wisconsin, 3,827 in North Dakota, 1,865 in Michigan, and 1,549 in Montana. In 1937, 15,160 were returned from Minnesota, 4,303 from Wisconsin, 6,513 from North Dakota, and 481 from Montana; a total in the United States of 26,457.

Connection in which they have become noted.—From early times the Chippewa were one of those tribes most prominent in the minds of writers on American Indians. This fact they owed in the first place to their numbers and the extent of country covered by their bands; secondly, to their central position and the many White men who became acquainted with them; and, thirdly, to the popularization given them by Henry M. Schoolcraft (1851–57), and the still wider popularity which they and their myths attained through the use of Schoolcraft's material by Longfellow in his famous poem of Hiawatha, for while the name Hiawatha is drawn from Iroquois sources, the stories are nearly all Chippewa. The name is preserved by streams in Wisconsin, Ohio, Michigan, Minnesota, and Ontario; by counties in Michigan, Wisconsin, and Minnesota; by various places in Pennsylvania, New York, Wisconsin, Michigan, Ohio, and Ontario; and by Chippewa Bay, St. Lawrence County, N. Y.; Chippewa Falls, Chippewa County, Wis.; Chippewa Lake, Mecosta County, Mich.; Chippewa Lake, Medina County, Ohio; and Ojibwa in Sawyer County, Wis.

Dakota. When first known to Europeans the Dakota were mainly in southern Minnesota. They gradually moved westward but did not cede all of their lands in Minnesota until 1863, and even then retained rights to the famous Red Pipestone Quarry. (See South Dakota.)

Foxes. In 1830 representatives of this tribe were a party to a treaty ceding Minnesota lands to the Whites. (See Wisconsin.)

Iowa. According to tradition, this tribe lived for a time near the famous Red Pipestone Quarry in southwestern Minnesota, and were at the mouth of Minnesota River when the Dakota reached that country. They appear to have been near the mouth of Blue Earth River just before Le Sueur arrived there in 1701. Dakota informed him that Blue Earth River belonged to the Dakota of the West, the Iowa, and the Oto. (See Iowa.)

Missouri. Representatives of this tribe were a party to the treaty of 1830, ceding Minnesota lands to the Whites. (See Missouri.)

Omaha. At one time the Omaha lived about the Red Pipestone Quarry in Minnesota. (See Nebraska.)

Oto. As noted above (under Iowa), the Oto are reported to have shared at one time the ownership of Blue Earth River with the Iowa and the Western Dakota. (See Nebraska.)

Ottawa. A band of Ottawa, in company with some Wyandot, once wintered on Lake Pepin. (See Michigan.)

Ponca. This tribe was probably in southwestern Minnesota at the same time as the Omaha. (See Nebraska.)

Sauk. In 1830 Sauk representatives were a party to a treaty ceding Minnesota lands to the Whites. (See Wisconsin.)

Winnebago. A part of the Winnebago lived in Minnesota from 1848 to 1862 after surrendering their reservation in Iowa Territory. (See Wisconsin.)

Wyandot. This tribe visited the borders of Minnesota for a short period in company with the Ottawa. (See **Ottawa,** above, and Ohio.)

IOWA

Chippewa. Part of the Chippewa, together with the Potawatomi and Ottawa, ceded lands in this State in 1846. (See Minnesota.)

Dakota. After the Iowa Indians moved from the northern part of the present State of Iowa, the Dakota occupied much of the territory they had abandoned until the Sauk and Fox settled in their neighborhood shortly before and immediately after the Black Hawk War of 1832 and harassed them so constantly that they withdrew. (See South Dakota.)

Foxes. This tribe began moving into Iowa sometime after 1804 and by the end of the Black Hawk War all were gathered there. In 1842 they parted with their Iowa lands and most of them removed to Kansas with the Sauk, but shortly after the middle of the nineteenth century some began to return to the State and by 1859 nearly all had come back. They bought a tract of land near Tama City to which they added from time to time and where they have lived ever since. (See Wisconsin.)

Illinois. Franquelin (1688) seems to locate the Peoria on the upper Iowa River, but Marquette, on his descent of the Mississippi in 1673, found that tribe and the Moingwena near the mouth of the Des Moines. When he returned he found that they had moved to the neighborhood of Peoria, Ill. The name Des Moines is derived from that of the Moingwena. (See Illinois.)

Iowa. Apparently borrowed by the French from Ayuhwa, the Dakota term applied to them, which, according to Riggs, signifies "sleepy ones." Skinner (1926) states that Iowa is their own name, but I feel sure that it has been borrowed in later years. Also called:

Nadouessioux Maskoutens, Algonkin name meaning "Dakota of the Prairies."
Nez Percés, a traders' nickname.

Pahodja, own name, meaning "dusty noses." Skinner (1926) gives a different
    translation, but I am inclined to accept that furnished by J. O. Dorsey.
Pashóhan, Pawnee name.
Pierced Noses, traders' name.
Wa-ōtc', Winnebago name.

Connections.—The Iowa were a tribe of the Siouan linguistic stock
and of the Chiwere subdivision, which included also the Oto, and
Missouri.

Location.—The Iowa moved about a great deal but mainly within
the boundaries of the State which bears their name. (See also Kansas,
Minnesota, Missouri, Nebraska, Oklahoma, and Wisconsin.)

Subdivisions and Villages

The only subdivisions mentioned are those of the moieties and gentes. But
one village, the Wolf village, appears in the historical narratives.

History.—In the earliest historical period the Iowa were living on
a western affluent of the Mississippi conjectured by Mott (1938) to
have been the Upper Iowa. Later they moved into the northwestern
part of the present State of Iowa about the Okoboji Lakes and probably extended into southwestern Minnesota to the neighborhood of
the Red Pipestone Quarry and to the Big Sioux River. In the latter
part of the eighteenth century they passed over to the Missouri and
settled south of the spot where Council Bluffs now stands and on the
east side of the river. About 1760 they moved east and came to live
along the Mississippi between the Iowa and Des Moines Rivers.
Their principal town was on the Des Moines River and for a long
time at a spot in the northwestern part of Van Buren County. Early
in the nineteenth century part of them seem to have moved farther
up the Des Moines while others established themselves on Grand and
Platte Rivers, Mo. At this time they seem to have come into contact
with the Dakota and to have suffered considerably in consequence.
There is a tradition that they were defeated by Black Hawk in 1821.
In 1814 they were allotted lands in what was known as "the Platte
Purchase" extending from the Platte River of Missouri through
western Iowa even to the Dakota country. By treaties signed
August 4, 1824, July 15, 1830, September 17, 1836, and November
23, 1837, they ceded all of their claims to lands in Missouri and Iowa,
and by that of Prairie du Chien, signed August 19, 1825, they surrendered all claims to land in Minnesota. The treaty of 1836 assigned
part of them a reservation along Great Nemaha River, in the present
Richardson County, Nebr., and Brown County, Kans., but it was
considerably reduced by treaties of May 17, 1854, and March 6, 1861.
Later part removed to Oklahoma to find homes in the present Lincoln
and Noble Counties.

Tradition assigns to this tribe a single origin with the Winnebago, Oto, and Missouri, and it is borne out by the close linguistic relationship between them. Rather specific migration legends have been preserved giving an account of the movements of this tribal complex and the time and circumstances of the separation. If we are to believe these traditions, after separation from the Winnebago, the Iowa-Oto-Missouri mother tribe moved first to Rock River, Ill., near its junction with the Mississippi, and thence to the Des Moines River some distance above its mouth, after separating at the Iowa River into two bands, the one which became the Iowa moving to the northwest while the Oto-Missouri went on to the mouth of Grand River, where part remained becoming the Missouri while the rest, the Oto, went on westward up the Missouri. The historical documents do not bring the Iowa so far south and they also seem to link the Oto and Iowa closely together. We should, therefore, be inclined to dismiss the native traditions altogether were it not that we have to account for the Missouri who are not mentioned in early times in close conjunction with the other two but had reached the mouth of Grand River as early as 1687. It is, of course, possible that the Missouri separated from the Iowa-Oto or Iowa at Upper Iowa River instead of Iowa River, but it is also possible that the entire tribal complex moved somewhat farther south before their separation. The later stages of Iowa history given in the tradition already noted conform sufficiently well with the known historical facts to give us some confidence regarding the rest of the story though it varies in details. According to this, the Iowa went from the neighborhood of the Red Pipestone Quarry to the mouth of the Platte, and then in succession to the headwaters of the Little Platte River, Mo., to the west bank of the Mississippi slightly above the mouth of the Des Moines, to a point a little higher up on the same side of the Mississippi, southwestwardly to Salt River and up it to its extreme headwaters, to the upper part of Chariton River, to Grand River, and thence to Missouri River opposite Fort Leavenworth, where they lived in 1848 at the time when this narrative was related and the map accompanying it drawn.

By agreement, the Oklahoma tract held by the Iowa was granted to its occupants in severalty.

Population.—In 1702 Iberville estimated that the war power of the Iowa was about 300 "good men." In 1736 Chauvignerie placed it as low as 80. An estimate made in 1760 gives the total population as 1,100 souls. In 1777 Cruzat reported that there were 250 warriors, and Lewis and Clark, in 1804, 200 warriors and a total population of 800. In 1829 we find an estimate of 1,000, and in 1832 Catlin gives one of the highest, 1,400. In 1836, however, an attempted census returned 992 but only 7 years later the United States Indian Office reported only 470. In 1885 there were 138 in Kansas, and 88 in Oklahoma. In 1905 the figures were 225 and 89 respectively. The census of 1910 returned 244 of whom 124 were in Kansas, 79 in Oklahoma, and 38 in Nebraska. The United States Indian Office Report of 1923 gave 338 in Kansas and 82 in Oklahoma, a total of 420. The census of 1930 returned 10 in Brown County, Kans.; 83 in Richardson County, Nebr.; 32 in Lincoln County, Okla.; 24 in Noble County, Okla.; and 5 in other States, or a total of 154. In 1937 there were 112 in Oklahoma. Although we have estimates of Iowa population higher than any above given, in one case as high as 8,000, it is evident that the figure suggested by Mooney (1928) as giving the probable population in 1780, i. e., 1,200, is nearer the truth—too high if anything.

Connection in which they have become noted.—The Iowa were relatively inconspicuous in the early days, but their name will always be prominent because it was adopted as that of one of the great agricultural States of the Middle West. Iowa City, two rivers, a county, and several smaller places in the same State bear the name. There is also a county so designated in Wisconsin and villages in Kansas and California.

There is a place of the name in Calcasieu Parish, La.; Iowa Falls in Hardin County, Iowa; Iowa Colony in Brazoria County, Tex.; Iowa Park in Wichita County in the same State, and Iowa Hill in Placer County, Calif.

Missouri. This tribe is said to have had the same origin as the Iowa and to have moved with them and the Oto to Iowa River, where the Iowa remained while the others continued on to the Missouri. (See Missouri.)

Moingwena. (See Illinois above.)

Omaha. While the Omaha usually lived west of the Missouri, they wandered for a time in western Iowa before moving over into Nebraska. (See Nebraska.)

Oto, see **Missouri** above, and **Missouri,** page 269.)

Ottawa. Representatives of this tribe were a party to a treaty made in 1846, ceding Iowa lands to the Whites. (See Michigan.)

Peoria. (See Illinois above.)

Ponca. The Ponca accompanied the Omaha while they were in western Iowa. (See Nebraska.)

Potawatomi. The Prairie Potawatomi settled in western Iowa before removing to Kansas. They ceded their lands in 1846. (See Michigan.)

Sauk. The Sauk moved into Iowa after the Black Hawk War and from there to Kansas in 1842. (See Wisconsin.)

Winnebago. In 1840 this tribe went to the Neutral Ground in Iowa assigned to them by treaty of September 15, 1832, whence they removed in 1848 to Minnesota. (See Wisconsin.)

MISSOURI

Caddo. Within historic times no Caddoan tribe is known to have lived within the limits of the present State of Missouri, but occupancy by Caddo is indicated by certain archeological remains in the extreme southwestern section. (See Texas.)

Dakota. Representatives of this tribe were a party to a treaty made in 1830, relinquishing lands in Missouri to the Whites. (See South Dakota.)

Delaware. In 1818 a grant of land in southern Missouri was made to some of the Delaware Indians but it was re-ceded by them in 1829. (See New Jersey.)

Foxes. Representatives of this tribe were a party to treaties with the United States Government concerning Missouri lands made in 1804 and 1830. (See Wisconsin.)

Illinois. Some of the tribes of the Illinois group at one time lived close to, and probably for a short time within, the eastern boundaries of Missouri. (See Illinois.)

Iowa. The Iowa perhaps lived for a time in that part of Missouri north of Missouri River. (See Iowa.)

Kickapoo. The Kickapoo lived in Missouri for awhile after they had sold their lands in Illinois but soon passed on to Kansas. (See Wisconsin.)

Missouri. Meaning either "(people having) dugout canoes," or "(people having) wooden canoes," which amounts to the same thing. Through a misunderstanding, the name has been supposed to apply to the river which now bears the name, and it has been interpreted as meaning "big muddy." They were also called:

> Niútachi, their own name.
> Waçux¢a, by the Osage.
> Wa-ju'-xd¢ă, by the Quapaw.

Location.—The best-known historical location of the Missouri was on the river which bears their name on the south bank near the mouth of Grand River. Berry and Chapman (1938) have recently sought to identify this site, and probably correctly, with what they call the Utz site at a place called The Pinnacles in Saline County, Mo., a few miles above the mouth of the Grand. (See also Iowa, Kansas, Minnesota, Nebraska, Oklahoma, and Wisconsin.)

Connection.—The Missouri belonged to the Chiwere division of the Siouan linguistic family, the other tribes under this head being the Iowa and Oto.

According to tradition, the Missouri, Iowa, and Oto separated from the Winnebago at some indefinite period in the past and moved southwest to Iowa River where the Iowa remained, the others continuing to the Missouri, which they reached at the mouth of Grand River. Here, in consequence of a dispute between two chiefs, the tribe split again, the Missouri remaining where they were, while the Oto continued on up the Missouri River. From what we know of the relationship between the tribes in question, such successive fissions are not inherently improbable, though they may not have occurred at the places indicated. No doubt, events that happened gradually have been represented as occurring abruptly within limited periods. (For a further discussion of the Chiwere migration legends, see **Iowa** under Iowa and **Oto** under Nebraska.) Whatever their earlier history Marquette (1698) reported their presence on the Missouri River in 1673, and they were probably at the point above indicated, though his map is too inaccurate to place this beyond question. Here, or in the immediate neighborhood, they remained until 1798, when they suffered a terrible defeat at the hands of the Sauk and Fox Indians and scattered to live for a time among the Osage, Kansa, and Oto. By 1805 they had recovered to some extent, and Lewis and Clark found them in villages south of the River Platte. As a result of another unfortunate war, however, this time with the Osage, part joined the Iowa but the greater part went to the Oto to live, and followed their fortunes, participating with them in all treaties from 1830 onward.

Population.—Mooney (1928) estimates that there were 1,000 Missouri in 1780. In 1702 there were supposed to be 200 families. In 1805 Lewis and Clark placed the entire population of the tribe at 300 souls, but in 1829, when they were with the Oto, they counted but 80. Only 13 Indians of the Missouri tribe were returned by the census of 1910, and in 1930 they were not separated from the Oto (q. v.).

Connection in which they have become noted.—Historically the Missouri tribe itself is remembered particularly for the tragic manner in which it was almost destroyed, but, as in many other cases, its name has attained a distinction out of all proportion to the aboriginal standing of the people. It is associated with that of the largest branch of the largest river of North America and to one of the great States of the American Union. There is a post town in Clay County, Mo., called Missouri City; another Missouri City in Fort Bend

County, Tex.; and a city in Harrison County, Iowa, known as Missouri Valley, besides a Missouri Branch in Wayne County, W. Va.

Omaha. Representatives of this tribe were party to a treaty made in 1830 relinquishing lands in Missouri to the United States Government. (See Nebraska.)

Osage. A corruption of their own name Wazhazhe, which in turn is probably an extension of the name of one of the three bands of which the tribe is composed. Also called:

> Anahou, a name used by the French, perhaps the Caddo name.
> Bone Indians, given by Schoolcraft.

Connections.—The Osage were the most important tribe of the division of the Siouan linguistic stock called by J. O. Dorsey (1897) Dhegiha, which included also the Omaha, Ponka, Kansa, and Quapaw.

Location.—The greater part of this tribe was anciently on Osage River, Mo., but from a very early period a smaller division known as Little Osage was on the Missouri River near the village of the Missouri Indians (q. v.). (See also Arkansas, Kansas, and Oklahoma.)

Subdivisions and Villages

The two principal local divisions were the Great and Little Osages, mentioned above. About 1802 a third division, the "Arkansas Band," was created by the migration of nearly half of the Big Osage to Arkansas River under a chief known as Big-Track. The names of the following Osage villages, some of them having the names of their chiefs, have been recorded:

Big Chief, 4 miles from the Mission in Indian Territory in 1850.
Black Dog, 60 miles from the Mission in Indian Territory in 1850.
Heakdhetanwan, on Spring Creek, a branch of Neosho River, Indian Territory.
Intapupshe, on upper Osage River about the mouth of Sac River, Mo.
Khdhasiukdhin, on Neosho River, Kans.
Little Osage Village, on Osage Reservation, Okla., on the west bank of Neosho River.
Manhukdhintanwan, on a branch of Neosho River, Kans.
Nanzewaspe, in Neosho valley, southeastern Kansas.
Nikhdhitanwan, at the junction of the Sac and Osage Rivers, Mo.
Paghuukdhinpe, on the east side of Verdigris River, Okla.
Pasukdhin, an ancient village name and also name of a late village on Verdigris River, Okla.
Santsepasu, location uncertain.
Santsukhdhin, native name of the Arkansas band, the village being located on Verdigris River, Okla., 60 miles above its mouth.
Takdheskautsiupshe, unidentified.
Tanwakanwakaghe, at the junction of Grand and Osage rivers, Mo.
Tanwanshinka, on Neosho River, Okla.
Wakhakukdhin, on Neosho River, Okla.
White Hair's Village, on the east side of Little Osage River in the northern part of the present Vernon County, Mo.

History.—Tradition indicates a prehistoric seat of the Osage on the Ohio River, but the first historical notice of them appears to be on Marquette's autograph map of 1673, where they are located in the region with which they are usually associated. They continued there until the separation of the Arkansas band already mentioned. By that time the Little Osage had moved from the Missouri to a position within 6 miles of the Great Osage. During the eighteenth century and the first part of the nineteenth, the Osage were at war with practically all the other tribes of the Plains and a large number of those of the woodlands, to many of which their name was a synonym for enemy. On November 10, 1808, the Osage signed a treaty ceding all their territorial claims in the present States of Missouri and Arkansas to the United States. The remainder was further curtailed by treaties signed in 1825, 1839, and 1865, and the limits of their later reservation were established by act of Congress of July 15, 1870. They have since been allotted land in severalty and are now citizens of Oklahoma.

Population.—Mooney's (1928) estimate of Osage population as of the year 1780 is 6,200. In 1804 Lewis and Clark estimated 500 warriors in the Great Osage band, nearly half as many Little Osages, and 600 in the Arkansas band. Sibley (1832), about the same time, gave 1,250 warriors. Morse (1822) estimated that there was an Osage population of 5,200; in 1829 Porter gave 5,000; in 1843 the United States Indian Office enumerated 4,102; Schoolcraft (1851–57) records 3,758 exclusive of an important division known as Black Dog's band; in 1877 the United States Indian Office had 3,001; in 1884, 1,547; in 1886, 1,582; and in 1906, 1,994. The census of 1910 gives 1,373, all but 28 in Oklahoma, but the United States Indian Office Report for 1923 has 2,099. In 1930, 2,344 were reported, and in 1937, 3,649.

Connection in which they have become noted.—As above stated, the Osage attained a high reputation as fighters among all the tribes of the southern Plains and many of those of the Gulf region. They are also remarkable for their social organization as set forth in the reports of Dr. Francis La Flesche (1921, 1925, 1928). The name became affixed to the Osage River, a considerable branch of the Missouri, which rises in Kansas but flows principally through the State of Missouri; also to counties in Kansas and Missouri; a fork of the Gasconade River, Mo.; a creek in Arkansas; and to places in Carroll County, Ark.; Franklin County, Ill.; Mitchell County, Iowa; Becker County, Minn.; Osage County, Okla.; Coryell County, Tex.; Monongalia County, W. Va.; Weston County, Wyo.; Osage Beach in Camden County, Mo.; Osage City in Cole County, Mo.; and Osage

City in Kansas.   Indirectly they have also furnished one of the popular names of the bois d'arc, Osage orange, the favorite wood for making bows among the tribes of the southern Plains between the lower Mississippi and the Pueblo country.

Oto.   As stated in treating of the Missouri (q. v.), the Oto accompanied that tribe into this State, left them when they were both on the Missouri River near Grand River, and moved northeast into Kansas. (See Nebraska.)

Sauk.   Representatives of this tribe were parties to the treaties involving Missouri land cessions made in 1804 and 1830. (See Wisconsin.)

Shawnee.   A part of the Shawnee Indians settled about Cape Girardeau in southeastern Missouri early in the nineteenth century. They ceded their lands to the U. S. Government in 1825. (See Tennessee.)

NORTH DAKOTA

Arapaho.   Certain traditions indicate that the Arapaho at one time lived in the Red River Valley in what is now Minnesota and North Dakota, but they had left before the historic period. (See Wyoming.)

Arikara.   Signifying "horns," or "elk," and having reference to their ancient manner of wearing the hair with two pieces of bone standing up, one on each side of the crest; -ra is the plural suffix. Also called:

>   Ă da ka' da ho, Hidatsa name.
>   Ah-pen-ope-say, or A-pan-to'-pse, Crow name.
>   Corn eaters, given as their own name.
>   Ka'-nan-in, Arapaho name, meaning "people whose jaws break in pieces."
>   O-no'-ni-o, Cheyenne name.
>   Padani, Pani, applied to them by various tribes.
>   Ree, abbreviation of Arikara.
>   Sanish, "person," their own name, according to Gilmore (1927).
>   S'qŭĭes'tshi, Salish name.
>   Stâr-râh-he' [tstarahi], their own name, according to Lewis and Clark (1904–05).
>   Tanish, their own name, meaning "the people," according to Hayden (1862). Perhaps a misprint of Sanish.
>   Wa-zi'-ya-ta Pa-da'-nin, Yankton name, meaning "northern Pawnee."

Connections.—The Arikara belonged to the Caddoan linguistic stock and were a comparatively recent offshoot of the Skidi Pawnee.

Location.—In historic times they have occupied various points on the Missouri River between Cheyenne River, South Dakota, and Fort Berthold, North Dakota. (See also Montana and Nebraska.)

Subdivisions and Villages

The Arikara are sometimes spoken of as a confederacy of smaller tribes each occupying its own village, and one account mentions 10 of these, while Gilmore (1927) furnishes the names of 12, including 4 of major importance under which the others were grouped. These were as follows:

Awahu, associated with which were Hokat and Scirihauk.
Hukawirat, with which were associated Warihka and Nakarik.
Tukatuk, with which were associated Tsininatak and Witauk.
Tukstanu, with which were associated Nakanusts and Nisapst.

Earlier sources give other names which do not agree with these:

Hachepiriinu.
Hia.
Hosukhaunu, properly the name of a dance society.
Hosukhaunukarerihu, properly the name of a dance society.
Kaka.
Lohoocat, the name of a town in the time of Lewis and Clark.
Okos.
Paushuk.
Sukhutit.

History.—After parting from the Skidi in what is now Nebraska, the Arikara gradually pushed north to the Missouri River and on up that stream.

In 1770 when French traders opened relations with them they were a little below Cheyenne River. Lesser and Weltfish (1932) suggest that they may have been the Harahey or Arahey of whom Coronado was told rather than the Pawnee (q. v.). Lewis and Clark found them, reduced considerably in numbers, between Grand and Cannonball Rivers. In 1823 they attacked the boats of an American trader, killing 13 men and wounding others, and in consequence of this trouble they abandoned their country and went to live with the Skidi on Loup River. Two years later they returned to the Missouri, and by 1851 they had pushed as far north as Heart River. Meantime wars with the Dakota and the smallpox had reduced them so much that they were glad to open friendly relations with two other tribes, similarly reduced, the Hidatsa and Mandan. In 1862 they moved to Fort Berthold. In 1880 the Fort Berthold Reservation was created for the three tribes, and the Arikara have ever since lived upon it, though they are now allotted land in severalty, and on the approval of the allotments, July 10, 1900, they became citizens of the United States.

Population.—Mooney (1928) estimates that in 1780 there were about 3,000 Arikara. In 1804 Lewis and Clark gave 2,600. In 1871 they numbered 1,650; in 1888 only 500; and in 1904, 380. The census of 1910 returned 444 of whom 425 were in North Dakota. In 1923 the United States Indian Office gave 426. The census of 1930 returned 420, and the United States Indian Office in 1937, 616.

Connection in which they have become noted.—The Arikara are noted merely as the most northerly of the Caddoan tribes and from their probable influence in introducing a knowledge of agriculture to the people of the upper Missouri. Arickaree in Washington County, Colo., perpetuates the name.

Assiniboin. In early days the Assiniboin were constantly coming across from Canada to fight and trade with the tribes of the upper Missouri, but they did not settle within the limits of North Dakota for any considerable period. (See Montana, and also **Dakota** under South Dakota.)

Cheyenne. When they left Minnesota the Cheyenne settled for a while on the Sheyenne fork of Red River after which they moved beyond the limits of the State of North Dakota. (See South Dakota.)

Chippewa. After they had obtained guns the Chippewa pushed westward as far as the Turtle Mountains which gave their name to a Chippewa band. There were 2,966 Chippewa in North Dakota in 1910. (See Minnesota.)

Dakota. While working their way west from Minnesota, bands of Dakota occupied at various times parts of the eastern, southern, and southwestern margins of North Dakota and a part of the Standing Rock Agency is within the limits of the State. In 1910 1,190 Dakota were making their homes on its soil. (See South Dakota.)

Hidatsa. Derived from the name of a former village and said, on somewhat doubtful authority, to signify "willows." Also called:

> A-gutch-a-ninne-wug, Chippewa name, meaning "the settled people."
> A-me-she′, Crow name, meaning "people who live in earth houses."
> Gi-aucth-in-in-e-wug, Chippewa name, meaning "men of the olden time."
> Gros Ventres of the Missouri, traders' name, probably derived from the sign for them in the sign language.
> Hewaktokto, Dakota name.
> Minitari, meaning "they crossed the water," said to have been given to them by the Mandan, from the tradition of their first encounter with the tribe on the Missouri.
> Wa-nuk′-e-ye′-na, Arapaho name, meaning "lodges planted together."
> Wetitsaán, Arikara name.

Connections.—The Hidatsa belonged to the Siouan linguistic stock, their closest relations within it being the Crow.

Location.—They lived at various points on the Missouri between the Heart and Little Missouri Rivers. (See also Montana and Canada.)

Villages

Lewis and Clark (1804–5) give the following three names:

Amahami or Mahaha, on the south bank of Knife River, formerly an independent but closely related tribe.
Amatiha, on the south bank of Knife River.
Hidatsa, on the north bank of Knife River.

The band names given by Morgan are rather those of social divisions.

History.—According to tradition, the Hidatsa formerly lived by a lake northeast of their later country, one sometimes identified with Devil's Lake. They moved from there to the mouth of Heart River, where they met and allied themselves with the Mandan, and from them they learned agriculture. As we have seen, Lewis and Clark found them on Knife River. In 1837 a terrible smallpox epidemic wasted them so completely that the survivors consolidated into one village which was moved in 1845 to the neighborhood of Fort Berthold, where the tribe has ever since continued to reside. They have now been allotted lands in severalty and are citizens of the United States.

Population.—Mooney (1928) estimates the Hidatsa and Amahami together as numbering 2,500 in 1780. Lewis and Clark give 600 warriors, or about 2,100 people. In 1905 they totaled 471, and the census of 1910 gives 547, a figure repeated by the United States Indian Office in 1923. In 1930, 528 were returned and in 1937, 731.

Connection in which they have become noted.—The Hidatsa appear most prominently, along with the Mandan, in connection with the ascent of the Missouri by Lewis and Clark and later expeditions into the same region. The name of Minatare, Scotts Bluff County, Nebr., probably refers to this tribe.

Mandan. Probably a corruption of the Dakota word applied to them, Mawatani. Also called:

>A-rach-bo-cu, Hidatsa name (Long, 1791).
>As-a-ka-shi, Us-suc-car-shay, Crow name.
>How-mox-tox-sow-es, Hidatsa name (?).
>Kanit', Arikara name.
>Kwowahtewug, Ottawa name.
>Métutahanke, own name since 1837, after their old village.
>Mo-no'-ni-o, Cheyenne name.
>Numakaki, own name prior to 1837, meaning "men," "people."
>U-ka'-she, Crow name, meaning "earth houses."

Connections.—The Mandan belonged to the Siouan linguistic stock. Their connections are with the Tutelo and Winnebago rather than the nearer Siouan tribes.

Location.—When known to the Whites, the Mandan were on the same part of the Missouri River as the Hidatsa, between Heart and Little Missouri Rivers. (See also South Dakota.)

Subdivisions and Villages

The division names given by Morgan (1851) appear to have been those of their former villages and are as follows: Horatamumake, Matonumake, Seepoosha, Tanatsuka, Kitanemake, Estapa, and Neteahke. In 1804 Lewis and Clark found two villages in existence, Metutahanke and Ruptari, about 4 miles below the mouth of Knife River.

They were divided socially into two moieties named like those of the Hidatsa, the Four-Clan Moiety and Three-Clan Moiety, and many of the clans constituting these bear village names. One of Dr. Lowie's (1917) informants gave the Prairie-chicken people, Young white-headed Eagle, People all in a bunch, and Crow people, as clans of the first Moiety; and the Maxi''kina, Tamĭ'sik, and Nū'pta as clans of the second. Another informant gave the following clans altogether: Si'pucka, Xtaxta'nū'mᵃkᵉ, Village above, Maxáhe, Tamĭ'sik, Seven-different-kinds, Hilltop village, Scattered village, White-bellied mouse people, and Nūptarɛ. Curtis (1907–9) and Maximilian (1843) give a Badger clan; Curtis, Red Butte and Charcoal clans; Maximilian, Bear and Cactus villages, perhaps intended for clans; and Morgan, Wolf, Good Knife, Eagle, and Flathead clans. Some of Lowie's informants substituted other names for Nū'pta, which latter is also the name of a village.

History.—When first visited by the Whites, the Mandan had distinct traditions of an eastern origin, and they may have come from the neighborhood of the Winnebago or from the Ohio country. Tradition also affirms that they first reached the Missouri at the mouth of White River, South Dakota, whence they moved to Moreau River and thence to Heart River, where the Whites found them. The first recorded visit to them was by Varendrye in 1738. The nine villages which they had in 1750 were merged into two by 1776 which were about 4 miles below the mouth of Knife River when Lewis and Clark visited them in 1804. In 1837 they were almost destroyed by smallpox, only 31 souls being left out of 1,600, according to one account. In 1845 some Mandan accompanied the Hidatsa to Fort Berthold, others followed at intervals, and the tribe has continued to reside there down to the present time, though lands are now allotted to them in severalty and they are citizens of the United States.

Population.—Mooney's (1928) estimate of Mandan population for 1780 is 3,600. In 1804 Lewis and Clark estimated there were 1,250, and in 1837, just before the great smallpox epidemic, there were supposed to be 1,600. In 1850 the total number was said to be 150, but in 1852 it had apparently increased to 385. In 1871 there were 450; in 1877, 420; in 1885, 410; and 1905, 249; while the census of 1910 returned 209, and the United States Indian Office Report of 1923, 273. The census of 1930 gives 271, and the Indian Office Report for 1937, 345.

Connection in which they have become noted.—The Mandan attained wide notoriety among the Whites (1) from their intimate dealings with the early White explorers and traders in the upper Missouri region; (2) from the fact that their customs and ceremonies were made particular matters of record by Maximilian (1843), Catlin (1844), and other White visitors; (3) from the reputation these Indians acquired of an unusually light skin color and theories of Welsh or, at least European, origin based upon these characters; and (4) from the tragic decimation of the tribe by smallpox as above mentioned. The name has been adopted as that of a city in North Dakota, the capital of Morton County.

SOUTH DAKOTA

Arapaho. According to tradition, the Arapaho at one time lived in the neighborhood of the Black Hills and warriors of the tribe often traversed the western parts of this State. (See Wyoming.)

Arikara. The Arikara lived at various points on the Missouri River in South Dakota during their migration northward after separating from the Skidi Pawnee. (See North Dakota.)

Cheyenne. From a Dakota term applied to them meaning "people of alien speech," literally, "red talkers." Also called:

> A-was-she-tan-qua, Hidatsa name (Long, 1791).
> Báhakosin, Caddo name, meaning "striped arrows."
> Dog Indians, so called sometimes owing to a confusion of the name with the French word *chien*.
> Dzĭtsi'stäs, own name.
> Gatsalghi, Kiowa Apache name.
> Hĭtäsi'na or Ĭtäsi'nă. Arapaho name, meaning "scarred people."
> I-sōnsh'-pu-she, Crow name.
> Itah-Ischipahji, Hidatsa name (Maximilian, 1843).
> I-ta-su-pu-zi, Hidatsa name, meaning "spotted arrow quills."
> Ka'neaheăwastsĭk, Cree name, meaning "people with a language somewhat like Cree."
> Nanonĭks-karĕ'nĭki, Kichai name.
> Niere'rikwats-kûni'ki, Wichita name.
> Păgănävo, Shoshoni and Comanche name, meaning "striped arrows."
> Săk'o'ta, Kiowa name.
> Scarred Arms, from a misinterpretation of the tribal sign.
> Sha-hō, Pawnee name.

Connections.—Cheyenne was one of the three most aberrant languages of the Algonquian linguistic family, and was shared by no other tribe except the Sutaio, whose speech differed only in minor points.

Location.—This tribe moved frequently; in South Dakota they were associated with the Cheyenne River and the Black Hills. (See also Colorado, Kansas, Minnesota, Montana, Nebraska, North Dakota, Oklahoma, and Wyoming.)

Subdivisions

Following are the bands which had a well-recognized place in the camp circle, as given by Mooney (1928); Hevĭqs'-nĭ''pahĭs, Mŏĭséyu, Wŭ'tapíu, Hévhaitä'nio, Oĭ'vimána, Hĭsíometä'nio, Sŭtáio (formerly a distinct tribe; see below), Oqtógŭnä, Hó'nowä, Măsĭ''kotä, O'mĭ'sĭs. Other band names not commonly recognized as divisional names, are these: Moqtávhaitä'niu, Ná'kuimána, Anskówĭnĭs, Pĭ'nûtgû', Máhoyum, Wóopotsĭ't, Totoimana (on Tongue River), Black Lodges (near Lame Deer), Ree Band, Yellow Wolf Band, Half-breed Band.

History.—Before 1700 the Cheyenne lived in what is now the State of Minnesota. There are very definite traditions of a time when they were on Minnesota River, from which region the Cheyenne who visited La Salle's fort in Illinois in 1680 probably came. A little later they seem to have moved to the neighborhood of Lake Traverse and still later part of them occupied a stockaded town on the Sheyenne River of North Dakota near the present Lisbon, N. Dak. Some years before 1799, perhaps in the decade 1780 to 1790, this town was surprised by Chippewa Indians and destroyed while most of the men were off hunting. The Cheyenne who escaped first settled along the Missouri where other bands of Cheyenne seem to have preceded them. There were a number of villages belonging to the tribe along the Missouri near the point where the boundary line between North and South Dakota crosses it until just before the time of Lewis and Clark, or, as Grinnell (1923) believes, for a number of years after the date of their expedition (1804–1806). However, they accustomed themselves more and more to a nomadic life and moved on toward the Black Hills whither they had been preceded by a cognate tribe known as the Sutaio. It is very probable that the Cheyenne had met the Sutaio east of the Missouri. At first the attitude of the two people toward each other is said to have been hostile, but presently they became friendly and finally united. On leaving the Missouri, the Cheyenne seem to have given up raising corn and making pottery. During the early part of the nineteenth century they moved to the headwaters of the Platte. When Bent's Fort was built on the upper Arkansas in 1832 a large part decided to establish themselves near it but the rest continued to rove about the headwaters of the North Platte and the Yellowstone. This separation in the tribe was made permanent by the Treaty of Fort Laramie in 1851, the two sections being known respectively as Southern Cheyenne and Northern Cheyenne. In the meantime they had met and formed an alliance with the Arapaho, though there is no memory of the date or the circumstances.

They were at war with the Kiowa from the time of their settlement on the upper Arkansas until 1840, but afterward acted with them against other tribes and the Whites. In 1849 they suffered severely in the cholera epidemic, and later between 1860 and 1878, in wars with the Whites. The southern division took a leading part in the general outbreak of 1874–75, and the Northern Cheyenne joined the hostile Dakota in 1876 and shared in the Custer massacre. Finally, the Northern Cheyenne were assigned a reservation in Montana. The Southern Cheyenne were similarly assigned to a reservation in the present Oklahoma in 1867 but could not be induced to remain upon it until after the general surrender of 1875. In 1901–02 the lands of the Southern Cheyenne were allotted in severalty.

Population.—Mooney (1928) places the number of Cheyenne and Sutaio at 3,500 in 1780. In 1904 the number of Southern Cheyenne was given as 1,903, and the Northern Cheyenne as 1,409, a total of 3,312. The census of 1910 returned 3,055, of whom 1,522 were in Oklahoma and 1,346 in Montana, but the United States Indian Office Report of 1923 gives 3,248, composed of 1,831 Southern Cheyenne, and 1,417 Northern Cheyenne. The census of 1930 returned 2,695, the Northern Cheyenne being slightly more numerous then the Southern division. In 1937 there were 1,561 Northern Cheyenne and 2,836 Southern Cheyenne and Arapaho together.

Connection in which they have become noted.—This Cheyenne tribe was one of the most famous of the Plains, and was conspicuous on account of the frequent wars which it waged against other tribes, as well as against the Whites. It is also noted on account of its romantic history, having originally been a corn-raising tribe in southern Minnesota and later having become thoroughly adjusted to Plains life. The name is preserved by the State Capital of Wyoming; by a river in South Dakota; by counties in Colorado, Nebraska, and Kansas; by the Cheyenne Mountains and Cañons in Colorado; by a river of North Dakota (spelled Sheyenne); and by Cheyenne Wells in Colorado, and Sheyenne in Eddy County, N. Dak. There is also a place of the name in Roger Mills County, Okla.; and another in Winkler County, Tex.

Dakota. Signifying "allies" in the Santee or eastern dialect; in Yankton and in Assiniboin it is Nakota; in Teton, Lakota. They are more often known as Sioux, an abbreviation of Nadouessioux, the name applied to them by the Chippewa, as transmitted through French; it signifies "adders," and by derivation "enemies." Also called:

> Ab-boin-ug, Boinug or Obwahnug, Wanak, Chippewa name, meaning "roasters" from their custom of torturing foes.
> Ba-akush′, Caddo name.
> Ba-ra-shŭp′-gi-o, Crow name.

Chah'-ra-rat, Pawnee name.

Coupe-gorges, French rendering of a name given them in the sign language.

Cut-throats, English equivalent of same.

Hand Cutters, translation of Ute name.

Ita ha'tski, Hidatsa name, meaning "long arrows."

Kaispa, Sarsi name.

K'odalpa-Kiñago, Kiowa name, meaning "necklace people."

Mar-an-sho-bish-ko, Crow name, meaning "cutthroats."

Minishúpsko, Crow name of opprobrious meaning.

Nadouessioux, general Algonquian name received through the French.

Natni or Natnihina, Arapaho, meaning "cutthroats."

Na'-to-wo-na, Cheyenne name for easternmost bands of Sioux.

Nuktusem or Nktusem, Salish name.

Ocheti shakowin, own name, meaning "the seven council fires."

O-o'-ho-mo-i'-o, Cheyenne name, meaning "those on the outside."

Oshahak, Fox name.

Pambizimina, Shoshoni name, meaning "beheaders."

Pámpe Chyimina, Ute name, meaning "Hand Cutters."

Papitsinima, Comanche name, meaning "beheaders."

Píshakulk, Yakima name, meaning "beheaders."

Poualak or Pouanak, name given in early French records, for Ab-boin-ug.

Sáhagi, Shawnee name.

Shahañ, Osage, Kansa, and Oto name.

Shánana, Kiowa Apache name.

Tsaba'kosh, or Ba-akush', Caddo name, meaning "cutthroats."

Túyĕtchískĕ, Comanche name, meaning "cutthroats."

Wä-sä-sa-o-no, Iroquois name.

Yuⁿssáha, Wyandot name, meaning "birds."

Connections.—The Dakota belonged to the Siouan linguistic family, their closest relations being the Hidatsa.

Location.—The earliest known home of this tribe was on and near the Mississippi in southern Minnesota, northwestern Wisconsin, and neighboring parts of Iowa. In 1825, after they had spread somewhat farther west, Long (1791) gives their boundaries thus: They were bounded by a curved line extending east of north from Prairie du Chien on the Mississippi, so as to include all the eastern tributaries of the Mississippi, to the first branch of Chippewa River; thence by a line running west of north to Spirit Lake; thence westwardly to Crow Wing River, Minn., and up that stream to its head; thence westwardly to Red River and down that stream to Pembina; thence southwest-wardly to the eastern bank of the Missouri near the Mandan villages; thence down the Missouri to a point probably not far from Soldiers River; thence east of north to Prairie du Chien. At a later time they occupied less territory toward the east but extended much farther westward between the Yellowstone and Platte Rivers. (See also Iowa, Minnesota, Missouri, Montana, Nebraska, North Dakota, Wisconsin, Wyoming, and Canada.)

Subdivisions

Early explorers usually distinguished an Eastern or Forest and a Western or Prairie division, but the following is a more accurate classification: (1) Mdewkanton, (2) Wahpeton, (3) Wahpekute, (4) Sisseton, (5) Yankton, (6) Yanktonai, including (a) Upper Yanktonai, and (b) Lower Yantonai or Hunkpatina, from whom also the Assiniboin are said to have separated, and (7) Teton, including (a) the Brulé (Upper and Lower), (b) Hunkpapa, (c) Miniconjou, (d) Oglala, (e) Oohenonpa or Two Kettle, (f) San Arcs, (g) Sihasapa or Blackfoot.   Numbers 1 to 4 constituted the Santee or Eastern division.

Minor Bands, Villages, Etc.

Black Tiger, near Fort Peck Agency.

Broken Arrows, possibly the Cazazhita.

Casarba, 35 leagues up St. Peters River in 1804.

Cazazhita, probably Tetons and perhaps the same as the Wannawega.

Chansuushka, unidentified.

Chasmuna, unidentified.

Cheokhba, a band of the Hunkpapa Teton.

Congewichacha, a Dakota division, perhaps Teton.

Farmers Band, probably a band of the Mdewakanton, below Lake Traverse, Minn.

Fire Lodge, below Lake Traverse.

Flandreau Indians, a part of the Santee who settled at Flandreau, S. Dak.

Grey Eagle Band, below Lake Traverse, Minn.

Lake Comedu, unidentified.

Lean Bear, below Lake Traverse, Minn.

Long Sioux, near Fort Peck.

Magayuteshni, a Mdewakanton division.

Menostamenton, unidentified.

Micacoupsiba, on the upper St. Peters, Minn.

Minisha, an Oglala band.

Neecoweegee, unidentified, possibly Minneconjou.

Nehogatawonahs, near St. Croix River in Minnesota or Wisconsin.

Newastarton, an unidentified band on the Mississippi above the St. Peters (Minnesota) River; probably the Mdewakanton.

Ocatameneton, an eastern Dakota band.

Ohanhanska, a band of the Magayuteshni division of the Mdewakanton on Minnesota River.

Oughetgeodatons, a village or subdivision of one of the western bands.

Oujatespouitons, west of the Mississippi.

Peshlaptechela, an Oglala Teton band.

Pineshow, a band of Wahpeton, on Minnesota River, 15 miles from its mouth.

Psinchaton, belonging to the Western Dakota in Minnesota.

Psinoumanitons, a division of the Eastern Dakota, probably in Wisconsin.

Psinoutanhinhintons, a band of Western Dakota in Minnesota.

Rattling Moccasin Band, a band of Mdewakanton Dakota on Minnesota River below Lake Traverse, Minn.

Red Leg's Band, a Wahpekute band in Minnesota.

Redwood, location uncertain.

Star Band, a band of Mdewakanton.

Takini, an Upper Yanktonai band.

Talonapin, a Hunkpapa band.

Tashunkeota, a Sihasapa band.
Tateibombu's Band, location uncertain.
Touchouasintons, a band of the Western Dakota, perhaps the Wazikute.
Traverse de Sioux, a part of the Sisseton formerly on Minnesota River, Minn.
Waktonila, unidentified.
Wazikute, a band of Upper Yanktonai.
White Cap Indians, on the south Saskatchewan River, in Assiniboia, Canada.
White Eagle Band, location unknown.
Wiattachechah, an unidentified village.

History.—The first historical mention of the Dakota is in the Jesuit Relation for 1640 when they were probably in the eastern part of the territory indicated above. Rev. A. L. Riggs, for many years a missionary among them, claims that their traditions pointed to the northeast as the place of their origin and that they once lived about the Lake of the Woods. There are, however, strong grounds for believing that they pushed their way up into the present Minnesota from the southeast, though there is no doubt that the Chippewa forced them back in later times from some of the most easternmost lands they occupied and their expulsion from Mille Lacs is an historical event. It is thought that few Dakota crossed the Missouri before 1750, yet it is claimed that some of them reached the Black Hills by 1765. In 1862 the Eastern Dakota under Little Crow rose upon the Whites and in the war which followed 700 settlers and 100 soldiers were killed, while the hostile bands lost all of the rest of their lands in Minnesota and were forced to move to Dakota and Nebraska. On the discovery of gold in the Black Hills the rush of miners to that region became the occasion for a war with the Western Dakota rendered famous by the cutting off of General Custer and five companies of cavalry on the Little Bighorn, June 25, 1876. An incipient rising at Wounded Knee Creek, resulting from the spread of the Ghost Dance religion, was the last scene of the struggles between the Dakota and the Whites, and the tribe is now allotted lands in severalty, principally in South Dakota, but in part in North Dakota and Nebraska.

Population.—Mooney (1928) estimated that in 1780 there were 25,000 Dakota of all divisions, exclusive of the Assiniboin (q. v. under Montana). In 1904 their distribution on agencies and their numbers were as follows: Cheyenne River (Minniconjou, Sans Arcs, and Oohenonpa), 2,477; Crow Creek (Lower Yanktonai), 1,025; Fort Totten School (Sisseton, Wahpeton, and Yanktonai), 1,013; Riggs Institute (Santee), 279; Fort Peck (Yankton), 1,116; Lower Brulé (Lower Brulé), 470; Pine Ridge (Oglala), 6,690; Rosebud (Brulé, Waglukhe, Lower Brulé, Northern, Oohenonpa, and Wazhazha), 4,977; Santee (Santee), 1,075; Sisseton (Sisseton and Wahpeton), 1,908; Standing Rock (Sihasapa, Hunkpapa, and Yanktonai), 3,514; Yankton (Yankton), 1,702; under no agency (Mdewakanton in Minnesota) 929; total, 27,175. The census of 1930 returned 25,934, of whom 20,918 were in South Dakota, 2,307 in North Dakota, 1,251 in Montana, 690 in Nebraska, and the remainder in more than 22 other States. The Report of the United States Office of Indian Affairs for 1937 gave 33,625, including 27,733 in South Dakota, 2,797 in North Dakota, 1,292 in Nebraska, 1,242 in Minnesota, and 561 in Montana.

Connections in which they have become noted.—The Dakota are one of the most famous tribes of North America, thanks to their numbers and prowess, their various wars with the Whites and the spectacular character of one of the last encounters with them, the celebrated "Custer massacre," not to mention the conspicuous nature of their connection with the Ghost Dance cult and the tragic affray at Wounded Knee Creek which grew out of it. The name is preserved in two of the States of our Union, North and South Dakota; by a river which flows through them; by counties in Minnesota and Nebraska; and by places in Stephenson County, Ill.; Winona County, Minn.; in Wisconsin and Nebraska; and as Dakota City in Humboldt County, Iowa, and Dakota County, Nebr. The other popular name for this tribe, Sioux, has been given to Sioux City, Iowa, and Sioux Falls, S. Dak.; to counties in Iowa and Nebraska; and small places in Nebraska, Iowa, and Minnesota; as Sioux in Yancey County, N. C.; Sioux Center in Sioux County, Iowa; Sioux Rapids in Buena Vista County, Iowa; and Sioux Pass in Richland County, Mont. It appears as Lacota (the Teton form of the name) in Marion County, Fla., and Van Buren County, Mich., and with the spelling Lakota in Kossuth County, Iowa; Nelson County, N. Dak.; and Culpeper County, Va.

Kiowa. The Kiowa lived in and about the Black Hills for a time before they were succeeded by the Sutaio and Cheyenne. (See Oklahoma.)

Mandan. According to tradition, this tribe reached the Missouri River near the mouth of White River, and settled at several places along the former within the borders of this State before passing out of it into North Dakota. (See North Dakota.)

Omaha. After having been driven from the region of the Pipestone Quarry in Minnesota, the Omaha settled on the Missouri in the territory of South Dakota and later moved downstream under pressure from the Dakota to their later seats in Nebraska. (See Nebraska.)

Ponca. This tribe was with the Omaha when it left the region of the Pipestone Quarry, but separated from it on the Missouri and went into the Black Hills for a time, after which it retired to the Missouri and settled in the present Nebraska. (See Nebraska.)

Sutaio. Significance uncertain. A Cheyenne informant of Grinnell (1923) believed it was derived from *issŭht'*, "ridge."

Connection.—The Sutaio belonged to the Algonquian linguistic stock, their nearest relatives being the Cheyenne.

Location.—When first brought distinctly to the knowledge of Whites, this tribe was west of Missouri River, between it and the Black Hills.

History.—The Sutaio may have been the "Chousa" band of Cheyenne of whom Perrin du Lac (1805) heard. At any rate they were probably not far distant from the Cheyenne during their migrations from Minnesota to the Missouri River and beyond, though whether in front of them, or to one side, it is impossible to tell. According to Cheyenne tradition as reported by Grinnell (1923), the two tribes met three different times. At any rate we know that they lived side by side in the region eastward of the Black Hills for some time and that they finally united there into one body, the Sutaio taking their place as one band in the Cheyenne tribal camping circle.

Population.—Unknown. (See **Cheyenne.**)

Winnebago. After leaving Minnesota in 1862 and before they took refuge with the Omaha, part of this tribe lived for a while on the Crow Creek Reservation. (See Wisconsin.)

NEBRASKA

Arapaho. The Arapaho ranged for a considerable period over the western part of this State. (See Wyoming.)

Arikara. This tribe lived in the territory now included in Nebraska with the Skidi Pawnee at some prehistoric period, and after 1823 they returned to the same tribe for 2 years. (See North Dakota.)

Cheyenne. Like the Arapaho, the Cheyenne ranged to some extent over the western territories of the State. (See South Dakota.)

Comanche. At an early day the Comanche must have lived in or near the western part of Nebraska, before moving south. (See Texas.)

Dakota. The Dakota had few settlements of any permanency in the territory of Nebraska but they were constantly raiding into and across it from the north. (See South Dakota.)

Foxes. The Foxes were parties to a land cession made in 1830. (See Wisconsin.)

Iowa. When the Omaha lived about the Pipestone Quarry in Minnesota, they were accompanied by the Iowa, who afterward went with them to South Dakota and thence to Nebraska. They, however, continued southeast into the territory of the present State of Iowa (q. v.).

Kansas. They were parties to a cession of Nebraska land made in 1825. (See Kansas.)

Kiowa. The Kiowa were at one time on the western margin of Nebraska and later followed the Comanche south. (See Oklahoma.)

Missouri. After they had been driven from Missouri by the Sauk and Fox, the remnant of this tribe lived for a while in villages south of Platte River. (See Missouri.)

Omaha. Meaning "those going against the wind or current"; sometimes shortened to Maha. Also called:

> Ho'-măⁿ-hăⁿ, Winnebago name.
> Hu-úmûi, Cheyenne name.
> Onĭ'hă°, Cheyenne name, meaning "drum beaters" (?).
> Pŭk-tĭs, Pawnee name.
> U'-aha, Pawnee name.

Connections.—The Omaha belonged to that section of the Siouan linguistic stock which included also the Ponca, Kansa, Osage, and Quapaw, and which was called by J. O. Dorsey (1897) Dhegiha.

Location.—Their principal home in historic times was in northeastern Nebraska, on the Missouri River. (See also Iowa, Minnesota, Missouri, and South Dakota.)

History.—According to strong and circumstantial traditions, the Omaha and others belonging to the same group formerly lived on the Ohio and Wabash Rivers. It is usually said that the Quapaw separated from the general body first, going down the Mississippi, but it is more likely that they were left behind by the others and later moved out upon the great river. The Osage remained on Osage River, and the Kansa continued on up the Missouri, but the Omaha, still including the Ponca, passed north inland as far as the Pipestone Quarry in Minnesota, and were afterward forced west by the Dakota, into what is now the State of South Dakota. There the Ponca separated from them and the Omaha settled on Bow Creek, in the present Nebraska. They continued from that time forward in the same general region, the west side of the Missouri River between the Platte and the Niobrara, but in 1855 made their last movement of consequence to the present Dakota County. In 1854 they sold all of their lands except a portion kept for a reserve, and they gave up the northern part of this in 1865 to the Winnebago. (See Wisconsin.) In 1882, through the efforts of Miss Alice C. Fletcher, they were granted lands in severalty with prospects of citizenship, and Miss Fletcher was given charge of the ensuing allotment. Citizenship has now been granted them.

Population.—Mooney (1928) estimates that there were about 2,800 Omaha in 1780. In 1802 they were reduced by smallpox to about 300. In 1804 the estimated number was 600; in 1829, 1,900;

in 1843, 1,600. Schoolcraft (1851–57) gives 1,349 in 1851; Burrows, 1,200 in 1857; and the same number appears in the census returns for 1880. In 1906 the United States Indian Office returned 1,228, and the census of 1910 gave 1,105. The Report of the United States Indian Office for 1923 showed an increase to 1,440. The census of 1930 gave 1,103, principally in Nebraska. The United States Indian Office reported 1,684 in 1932.

Connection in which they have become noted.—The Omaha will be remembered particularly from the fact that its name has been adopted by the City of Omaha, Nebr. It has also been given to small places in Boone County, Ark.; Stewart County, Ga.; Gallatin County, Ill.; Morris County, Tex.; Knott County, Ky.; and Dickenson County, Va.

It will be remembered furthermore as the scene of the humanitarian labors of Miss Alice C. Fletcher and the ethnological studies of Miss Fletcher and Dr. Francis La Flesche.

Oto. From Wat'ota, meaning "lechers." It often appears in a lengthened form such as Hoctatas or Octoctatas. Also called:

> Che-wae-rae, own name.
> Matokatági, Shawnee name.
> Motútatak, Fox name.
> Wacútada, Omaha and Ponca name.
> Wadótata, Kansa name.
> Watohtata, Dakota name.
> Watútata, Osage name.

Connections.—The Oto formed, with the Iowa and Missouri, the Chiwere group of the Siouan linguistic family and were closely connected with the Winnebago.

Location.—The Oto moved many times, but their usual location in the historic period was on the lower course of the Platte or the neighboring banks of the Missouri. (See also Iowa, Kansas, Minnesota, Missouri, Oklahoma, and Wisconsin.)

History.—From the maps of the Marquette expedition it would seem that at the time when they were drawn, 1673, the Oto were some distance up Des Moines River. Their name was often coupled with that of the related Iowa who lived north of them, but they always seem to have occupied a distinct area. Shortly after this time they moved over to the Missouri and by 1804 had established their town on the south side of the Platte River not far from its mouth. According to native traditions, this tribe, the Iowa, and the Missouri were anciently one people with the Winnebago, but moved southwest from them, and then separated from the Iowa at the mouth of Iowa River and from the Missouri at the mouth of Grand River. Their language proves that they were closely related to these tribes whether or not the separations occurred in the manner and at the places indicated. Their split with the Missouri is said to have been brought about by a quarrel between two chiefs arising from the seduction of the daughter of one by the son of the other, and from this circumstance the Oto are supposed to have derived their name. In 1700 they were, according to Le Sueur, on Blue Earth River near the Iowa, and it is probable that they moved into the neighborhood of the Iowa or Missouri at several different times, but their usual position was clearly intermediate along a north-south line. In 1680 two Oto chiefs came to visit La Salle in Illinois and reported that they had traveled far enough west to fight with people using horses, who were evidently the Spaniards, a fact which proves their early westward range.

By treaties signed July 15, 1830, and October 15, 1836, they and the Missouri ceded all claims to land in Missouri and Iowa, and by another signed September 21, 1833, the two ceded all claims to land south of the Little Nemaha River. By a treaty signed March 15, 1854, they gave up all their lands except a strip 10 miles wide and 25 miles long on the waters of Big Blue River, but when it was found that there was no timber on this tract it was exchanged on December 9 for another tract taken from the Kansas Indians. In a treaty signed August 15, 1876, and amended March 3, 1879, they agreed to sell 120,000 acres off the western end of their reserve. And finally, a treaty signed on March 3, 1881, provided, the consent of the tribe being obtained, for the sale of all of the remainder of their land in Kansas and Nebraska, and the selection of a new reservation. Consent to the treaty was recorded May 4 following, and the tribe removed the following year to the new reservation which was in the present Oklahoma southwest of Arkansas River on Red Rock and Black Bear Creeks, west of the present Pawnee. The first removal to Oklahoma is said to have been due to a fission in the tribe resulting in the formation of two bands, a conservative band called Coyotes and the Quakers, who were progressives. The Coyotes moved in 1880 and the Quakers joined them 2 years later.

Population.—Mooney (1928) estimated that in 1780 the Oto numbered about 900. In 1805 Lewis and Clark estimated 500 then living, but Catlin in 1833 raised this to 1,300, a figure which includes the Missouri. Burrows in 1849 gives 900, and the United States Indian Office in 1843, 931. This and all later enumerations include both the Oto and the Missouri. In 1862 they numbered 708; in 1867, 511; in 1877, 457; in 1886, 334; in 1906, 390; and by the census of 1910, 332. The census of 1930, however, showed a marked increase to a total of 627, all but 13 of whom were in Oklahoma, 376 in Noble County, 170 in Pawnee, 34 in Kay, and 17 in Osage. There were 7 in California, 1 in Kansas, and 1 in Nebraska. In 1937, 756 were reported in Oklahoma.

Connection in which they have become noted.—The name Oto has been applied to some small settlements in Woodbury County, Iowa, and in Missouri, and in the form Otoe to a county and post village in Nebraska.

Pawnee. The name is derived by some from the native word paríki, "a horn," a term said to be used to designate their peculiar manner of dressing the scalp lock; but Lesser and Weltfish (1932) consider it more likely that it is from parisu, "hunter," as claimed by themselves. They were also called Padani and Panana by various tribes. Also known as:

> Ahihinin, Arapaho name, meaning "wolf people."
> Awahi, Caddo and Wichita name.
> Awahu, Arikara name.
> Awó, Tonkawa name, originally used by the Wichita.
> Chahiksichahiks, meaning "men of men," applied to themselves but also to all other tribes whom they considered civilized.
> Dárāzhazh, Kiowa Apache name.
> Harahey, Coronado documents (somewhat uncertain).
> Ho-ni'-i-tañi-o, Cheyenne name, meaning "little wolf people."
> Kuitare-i, Comanche name, meaning "wolf people."
> Paoneneheo, early Cheyenne name, meaning "the ones with projecting front teeth."
> Páyiⁿ, Kansa form of the name.
> Pi-ta'-da, name given to southern tribes (Grinnell, 1923).
> Tśe-sa do hpa ka, Hidatsa name meaning "wolf people."
> Wóhesh, Wichita name.
> Xaratenumanke, Mandan name.

Connections.—The Pawnee were one of the principal tribes of the Caddoan linguistic stock. The Arikara (q. v.) were an offshoot, and the Wichita were more closely related to them than were the Caddo.

Location.—On the middle course of Platte River and the Republican fork of Kansas River. (See also Kansas, Oklahoma, and Wyoming.)

Subdivisions

The Pawnee consisted in reality of four tribes, or four known in historic times, viz: The Chaui or Grand Pawnee, the Kitkehahki or Republican Pawnee, the Pitahauerat or Tapage Pawnee, and the Skidi or Skiri Pawnee, the first three speaking the same dialect and being otherwise more closely connected with one another than with the last. The Kitkehahki embraced two divisions, the Kitkehahki proper and the Little Kitkehahki. Murie gives two others, the Black Heads and Karikisu, but Lesser and Weltfish (1932) state that the first was a society and the second the name of the women's dance or ceremony before corn planting. The Pitahauerat consisted of the Pitahauerat proper and the Kawarakis, sometimes said to be villages.

History.—Some of the Pawnee trace their origin to the southwest, some to the east, and some claim always to have lived in the country with which later history associates them. The first White men to meet any members of these tribes were the Spaniards under Coronado in 1541. French explorers heard of them again early in the eighteenth century and French traders were established among them before the middle of it. The Spaniards of New Mexico became acquainted with them at about the same time on account of the raids which they conducted in search of horses. They lay somewhat out of the track of the first explorers from the east, and in consequence suffered less diminution in numbers through White influences than did many of their neighbors, but they were considerably reduced through wars with the surrounding tribes, particularly with the Dakota. Although some of the early traders and trappers were treated harshly by them, their relations with the United States Government were friendly from the first, and they uniformly furnished scouts for the frontier armies. By treaties negotiated in 1833, 1848, and 1857, they ceded all of their lands in Nebraska except one reservation and in 1876 this tract was also surrendered and the entire tribe given new lands in Oklahoma, where they still live. The land has been allotted to them in severalty and they are now citizens of the United States.

Population.—Mooney (1928) estimates 10,000 Pawnee in 1780. In 1702 Iberville estimated 2,000 families. In 1838 they numbered about 10,000 according to an estimate of Dunbar and Allis (1880–82), and one authority places the figure as high as 12,500. In 1849, after the cholera epidemic, they were reported at 4,500; in 1856, 4,686 were returned, but in 1861, only 3,416. In 1879, after suffering severely in consequence of the removal to Indian Territory, they had dropped to 1,440, and by 1906 they had fallen to 649. The census of 1910 returned 633, but according to the Report of the United States Indian Office for 1923, they had then increased to 773. The census of 1930 gave 730. In 1937, 959 were reported.

Connection in which they have become noted.—The Pawnee tribe is distinguished (1) for its peculiar language and culture; (2) because of its numbers and warlike prowess, its constant hostility to the Dakota, and consistent assistance to the American forces operating upon the Plains; and (3) as having given its name to a city in Oklahoma; to counties in Oklahoma, Kansas, and Nebraska; to streams in Colorado and Kansas; and to places in Morgan County, Colo.; Sangamon County, Ill.; Montgomery County, Ind.; Pawnee City in Pawnee County, Nebr.; Pawnee Rock in Barton County, Kans.; Pawnee Station in Bourbon County, Kans.; and a creek and buttes in northeastern Colorado.

Ponca. Own name, meaning unknown. Also called:

> Díhit, Li-hit' or Ríhit, Pawnee name.
> Kan'kaⁿ, Winnebago name.
> Tchiáxsokush, Caddo name.

Connections.—The Ponca spoke practically the same language as the Omaha and formed with them, the Osage, Kansa, and Quapaw, the Dhegiha group of the Siouan linguistic family.

Location.—On the right bank of the Missouri at the mouth of the Niobrara. (See also Iowa, Minnesota, Oklahoma, and South Dakota.)

History.—The early life of the Ponca seems to have run parallel with that of the Omaha (q. v.). They are said to have separated from the latter at the mouth of White River, S. Dak., and to have moved west into the Black Hills but to have rejoined the Omaha a little later. These two tribes and the Iowa then descended the Missouri together as far as the mouth of the Niobrara, where the Ponca remained while the Omaha established themselves below on Bow Creek. They remained in approximately the same situation until 1877 when the larger part of them were forcibly removed to Indian Territory. This action was the occasion for a special investigation, as a result of which about three-quarters continued in the Territory while the remainder preferred to remain in their old country. Their lands have now been allotted to them in severalty.

Population.—Mooney (1928) gives 800, as the probable size of the Ponca tribe in 1780. In 1804 Lewis and Clark estimate only 200 but they had been greatly reduced just before by smallpox. In 1829 they had increased to 600 and in 1842 to about 800. In 1871 they numbered 747. In 1906 the Ponca in Oklahoma numbered 570 and those in Nebraska 263; total, 833. The census of 1910 gave 875 in all, including 619 in Oklahoma and 193 in Kansas. The Report of the United States Indian Office for 1923 was 1,381, evidently including other tribes. The census of 1930 returned 939. In 1937 the United States Indian Office gave 825 in Oklahoma and 397 in Nebraska.

Connection in which they have become noted.—The name Ponca is preserved by a river in South Dakota, Ponca City in Kay County, Okla., and places in Newton County, Ark., and Dixon County, Nebr.

Sauk. Like the Foxes, they were parties to the land cession of 1830 involving territories in this State. (See Wisconsin.)

Winnebago. Part of the Winnebago settled close to the Omaha after they had been driven from Minnesota following the Dakota outbreak of 1862. A reservation was later assigned them there and in course of time they were allotted land in severalty upon it. (See Wisconsin.)

KANSAS

Apache, see **Jicarilla.**

Arapaho. The Arapaho ranged at one time over much of the western part of this State. (See Wyoming.)

Cherokee. By the terms of the Treaty of New Echota, the Cherokee obtained title to lands in southeastern Kansas, part in one block known as the "Neutral land," and the rest in a strip along the southern boundary of the State. These were re-ceded to the United States Government in 1866. (See Tennessee.)

Cheyenne. Like the Arapaho they at one time ranged over the western part of the State. (See South Dakota.)

Chippewa. In 1836 two bands of Chippewa living in Michigan and known as the Swan Creek and Black River bands were given a tract of territory on Osage River, Kans. They arrived in 1839. In 1866 they agreed to remove to the Cherokee country in what is now Oklahoma and to unite with that tribe. A small number of families of Chippewa living west of Lake Michigan accompanied the Prairie Potawatomi to southwestern Iowa, but they were either absorbed by the Potawatomi or subsequently separated from them. (See Minnesota.)

Comanche. They ranged over the western part of the State. (See Texas.)

Delaware. A strip of land in northeastern Kansas was granted to the Delaware in 1829 and was again surrendered by treaties made in 1854, 1860, and 1886. In 1867 they agreed to take up their residence with the Cherokee in Oklahoma. Four sections of land were, however, confirmed to a body of Munsee ("Christian Indians"), who in turn sold it in 1857. This sale was confirmed by the United States Government in 1858, and a new home was found for these Indians among the Swan Creek and Black River Chippewa whom they accompanied to the Cherokee Nation in Oklahoma in 1866. Nevertheless, a few Munsee have remained in the State. (See New Jersey.)

Foxes. The Foxes lived for a time on a reservation in eastern Kansas but about 1859 returned to Iowa. (See Wisconsin.)

Illinois. The remnants of these people were assigned a reservation about the present Paola in 1832. In 1867 they removed to the northeastern corner of the present Oklahoma, where they received lands which had formerly belonged to the Quapaw. (See Illinois.)

Iowa. This tribe was placed on a reservation in northeastern Kansas in 1836, and part of them continued in this State and were allotted land here in severalty, while the rest went to Oklahoma. (See Iowa.)

Iroquois. Lands were set aside in Kansas in 1838 for some Iroquois, part of the Munsee, and remnants of Mahican and southern New England Indians but only a few of the Indians involved moved to them. They were later declared forfeited, and the rights of 32 bona fide Indian settlers were purchased in 1873. (See **Seneca** and also New York, Massachusetts, Rhode Island, and Connecticut.)

Jicarilla. This was one of the so-called Apache tribes. They lived in Colorado and New Mexico and ranged over parts of Texas, Oklahoma, and Kansas. (See Colorado.)

Kansa. Name derived from that of one of the major subdivisions; a shortened form Kaw is about equally current. Also called:

> Alähó, Kiowa name.
> Guaes, in Coronado narratives, thought to be this tribe.
> Hútañga, own name.
> Móhtawas, Comanche name, meaning "without a lock of hair on the forehead."
> Úkase, Fox name.

Connections.—The Kansa belonged to the Siouan linguistic stock and constituted, with the Osage, Quapaw, Omaha, and Ponca a distinct subgroup called by Dr. J. O. Dorsey (1897) Dhegiha.

Location.—They were usually on some part of the Kansas River, which derives its name from them. (See also Nebraska and Oklahoma.)

Villages

Bahekhube, near a mountain south of Kansas River, Kans.
Cheghulin, 2 villages; (1) on the south side of Kansas River, and (2) on a tributary of Kansas River, on the north side east of Blue River.
Djestyedje, on Kansas River near Lawrence.
Gakhulin, location uncertain.
Gakhulinulinbe, near the head of a southern tributary of Kansas River.
Igamansabe, on Big Blue River.
Inchi, on Kansas River.
Ishtakhechiduba, on Kansas River.
Manhazitanman, on Kansas River near Lawrence.
Manhazulin, on Kansas River.
Manhazulintanman, on Kansas River.
Manyinkatuhuudje, at the mouth of Big Blue River.
Neblazhetama, on the west bank of the Mississippi River a few miles above the mouth of Missouri River, in the present Missouri.
Niudje, on Kansas River, about 4 miles above the site of Kansas City, Mo.
Padjegadjin, on Kansas River.
Pasulin, on Kansas River.
Tanmangile, on Big Blue River.
Waheheyingetseyabe, location uncertain.
Wazhazhepa, location uncertain.

Yuzhemakancheubukhpaye, location uncertain.
Zandjezhinga, location uncertain.
Zandzhulin, at Kaw Agency, Indian Territory, in 1882.
Zhanichi, on Kansas River.

History.—According to tradition, the Kansa and the others of the same group originated on Ohio River, the Kansa separating from the main body at the mouth of Kansas River. If the Guaes of Coronado were the Kansa, the tribe was first heard of by white men in 1541. During at least a part of the eighteenth century, they were on Missouri River above the mouth of the Kansas, but Lewis and Clark met them on the latter stream. They occupied several villages in succession along Kansas River until they settled at Council Grove, on Neosho River, in the present Morris County, where a reservation was set aside for them by the United States Government in 1846, when they ceded the rest of their lands. They remained on this reservation until 1873 when it was sold and another reserve purchased for them in Oklahoma next to the Osages. Their lands have now been allotted to them in severalty.

Population.—Mooney (1928) estimates a Kansa population of 3,000 in 1780. In 1702 Iberville estimated 1,500 families. Lewis and Clark (1804) give 300 men. In 1815 there were supposed to be about 1,500 in all, and in 1822, 1,850. In 1829 Porter estimated 1,200, but the population as given by the United States Indian Office for 1843 was 1,588. After this time, however, the tribe lost heavily through epidemics and in 1905 was returned at only 209. The census of 1910 gave 238, but the United States Indian Office Report of 1923 gave 420. The census of 1930 returned 318. In 1937 the number was given as 515.

Connection in which they have become noted.—The Kansa will be remembered particularly from the fact that they have given their name to Kansas River and the State of Kansas, and secondarily to Kansas City, Mo., and Kansas City, Kans. It is also applied to places in Walker County, Ala.; Edgar County, Ill.; Seneca County Ohio; Seneca and Delaware Counties, Okla.; and in the form Kaw, to a village in Kay County, Okla., and a station out of the Kansas City, Mo., P. O. Kansasville is in Racine County, Wis.

Kickapoo. A reservation was granted this tribe in southeastern Kansas in 1832, and though it was progressively reduced in area, part of them have continued to live there down to the present time. (See Wisconsin.)

Kiowa. Signifying (in their own language) "principal people." Also called:

Be'shĭltchă, Kiowa Apache name.
Datŭmpa'ta, Hidatsa name, perhaps a form of Wi'tapähä'tu below.

Gahe'wa, Wichita and Kichai name.

Ko'mpabi'änta, Kiowa name, meaning "large tipi flaps."

Kwü'da, old name for themselves, meaning "going out."

Manrhoat, mentioned by La Salle, perhaps this tribe.

Na'la'ni, Navaho name, including southern plains tribes generally, but particularly the Comanche and Kiowa.

NI'chihinĕ'na, Arapaho name, meaning "river man."

Quichuan, given by La Harpe (1831) and probably this tribe.

Te'pdă', ancient name for themselves, meaning "coming out."

Tepki'nägo, own name, meaning "people coming out."

Tideing Indians, Lewis and Clark (1904–5).

Vi'täpätúi, name used by the Sutaio.

Wi'tapahatu, Dakota name, meaning "island butte people." (The Cheyenne name was similar.)

Connections.—Though long considered a separate linguistic stock, the researches of J. P. Harrington make it evident that the Kiowa were connected with the Tanoan stock as the Kiowa-Tanoan stock and probably with the Shoshonean stock also.

Location.—The best-known historic location of these people was a plot of territory including contiguous parts of Oklahoma, Kansas, Colorado, New Mexico, and Texas. (See also Montana, Nebraska, South Dakota, and Wyoming.)

Subdivisions

The bands constituting their camp circle, beginning on the east and passing round by the south were: Kata, Kogui, Kaigwu, Kingep, Semat (i. e., Apache), and Kongtalyui.

History.—According to tradition, the Kiowa at one time lived at the head of Missouri River near the present Virginia City. Later they moved down from the mountains and formed an alliance with the Crows but were gradualy forced south by the Arapaho and Cheyenne, while the Dakota claim to have driven them from the Black Hills. They made peace with the Arapaho and Cheyenne in 1840 and afterward acted with them. When they reached the Arkansas, they found the land south of it claimed by the Comanche. These people were at first hostile, but after a time peace was made between the two tribes, the Kiowa passed on toward the south, and the two ever after acted as allies. Together they constantly raided Mexican territory, advancing as far south as Durango. The Kiowa were among the most bitter enemies of the Americans. They were placed on a reservation in southwestern Oklahoma in 1868 along with the Commanche and Kiowa Apache and have now been allotted lands in severalty.

Population.—Mooney (1928) estimates that there were 2,000 in 1780. In 1905 their population was 1,165; the census of 1910 gave it as 1,126, and the United States Indian Office Report for 1923, 1,679, including the Kiowa Apache. The census of 1930 returned 1,050, but in 1937 the United States Office of Indian Affairs reported 2,263.

Connection in which they have become noted.—The Kiowa were one of the leading tribes on the southern Plains and were surpassed only by the Comanche and Apache in the raids which they undertook into México. The name has become affixed to counties in Colorado and Kansas, a creek in Colorado; and small places in Barber County, Kans.; Pittsburg County, Okla.; and Elbert County, Colo.

Kiowa Apache. The name is derived from that of the Kiowa and from the circumstance that they spoke a dialect related to those of the better-known Apache tribes, though they had no other connection with them. Also called:

> Bad-hearts, by Long (1823). (See Kaskaias.)
> Cancey or Kantsi, meaning "liars," applied by the Caddo to all Apache of the Plains, but oftenest to the Lipan.
> Essequeta, a name given by the Kiowa and Comanche to the Mescalero Apache, sometimes, but improperly, applied to this tribe.
> Gáta'ka, Pawnee name.
> Gĭnä's, Wichita name.
> Gû'ta'k, Omaha and Ponca name.
> K'á-pätop, Kiowa name, meaning "knife whetters."
> Kaskaias, possibly intended for this tribe, translated "bad hearts."
> Kĭsínahĭs, Kichai name.
> Mûtsĭănă-täníu, Cheyenne name, meaning "whetstone people."
> Nadíisha-déna, own name, meaning "our people."
> Pacer band of Apache, H. R. Doc.
> Prairie Apaches, common name.
> Sádalsómte-k'íägo, Kiowa name, meaning "weasel people."
> Tâ'gugála, Jemez name for Apache tribes including Kiowa Apache.
> Tagúi, an old Kiowa name.
> Tágukerish, Pecos name for all Apache.
> Tashĭn, Comanche name for all Apache.
> Tha'ká-hinĕ'na, Arapaho name, meaning "saw-fiddle man."
> Yabipais Natagé, Garcés Diary (1776).

Connections.—The Kiowa Apache belonged to the Athapascan linguistic family, their nearest relatives being the Jicarilla and Lipan (Hoijer).

Location.—They have been associated with the Kiowa from the earliest traditional period. (See also Colorado, New Mexico, Oklahoma, and Wyoming.)

History.—The first historical mention of the Kiowa Apache is by La Salle in 1681 or 1682, who calls them Gattacka, the term by which they are known to the Pawnee. As intimated above, their history was in later times the same as that of the Kiowa, and they occupied a definite place in the Kiowa camp circle. For 2 years only, 1865–67, they were at their own request detached from the Kiowa and adjoined to the Cheyenne and Arapaho, on account of the unfriendly attitude of the Kiowa toward the Whites.

Population.—Mooney (1928) gives an estimate of 300 Kiowa Apache as of 1780, adopting the estimate made by Lewis and Clark in 1805.   In 1891 their population was 325, but like the associated tribes they suffered heavily from measles in 1892 and in 1905 there were only 155 left.   The census of 1910 returned 139, that of 1930, 184, and in 1937 they appear to have increased to 340 but other Apache may be included.

Connection in which they have become noted.—The Kiowa Apache are remarkable merely as an example of a tribe incorporated into the social organism of another tribe of entirely alien speech and origin.

Miami.   In 1832 the Miami subdivisions known as Piankashaw and Wea were assigned lands along with the Illinois in Eastern Kansas. In 1840 the rest of the Miami were granted lands in the immediate neighborhood but just south, and all but one band removed there from Indiana.   In 1854 they ceded part of this territory and in 1867 accompanied the Illinois to the present Oklahoma.   (See Indiana.)

Missouri.   The remnant of this tribe accompanied the Oto when they lived in this State.   (See Missouri.)

Munsee.   A band of Munsee or "Christian Indians" owned land in Kansas between 1854 and 1859.   (See **Delaware** in New Jersey, etc.)

Osage.   The southeastern part of Kansas was claimed by the Osage and was ceded by them to the United States Government in treaties made in 1825, 1865, and 1870.   (See Missouri.)

Oto.   The Oto were on the eastern border of Kansas several times during their later history.   (See Nebraska.)

Ottawa.   In 1831 two bands of Ottawa were granted lands on Marais des Cygnes or Osage River.   They relinquished these in 1846 and in 1862 agreed to allotment of land in severalty, giving up their remaining lands.   Further treaties regarding these were made in 1867 and 1872.   A few families of Ottawa accompanied the Prairie Potawatomi when they removed from Wisconsin to Iowa, but they were soon absorbed or else scattered.   Ottawa bands called Ottawa of Blanchard's Fork and Ottawa of Roche de Boeuf occupied lands in Kansas between 1832 and 1865 when they moved to Oklahoma. (See Michigan.)

Pawnee.   A part of the Pawnee occupied the valley of the Republican Fork of Kansas River.   (See Nebraska.)

Potawatomi.   In 1837 the United States Government entered into a treaty with five bands of Potawatomi living in the State of Indiana

by which it was agreed to convey to them by patent a tract of country on Osage River, southwest of the Missouri, in the present State
of Kansas. This was set apart the same year and the Indians, the
Potawatomi of the Woods, moved into it in 1840, but they ceded
it back in 1846 and were given a reserve between the Shawnee and
the Delaware, in the present Shawnee County, which they occupied
in 1847. By a series of treaties, culminating in the Treaty of
Chicago, 1833, the Potawatomi west of Lake Michigan surrendered
their lands and received a large tract in southwestern Iowa. They
were accompanied by a few Chippewa and Ottawa. In 1846 this
reserve was re-ceded to the United States Government and in
1847–48 the Indians, now known as the Prairie Potawatomi,
moved to lands in Kansas just east of the lands of the Potawatomi
of the Woods. Michigan Potawatomi did not come to this place
until 1850. About the end of the Civil War some of the Prairie
band moved back to Wisconsin but the greater part of them remained and accepted lands in severalty. In 1869 the Potawatomi
of the Woods began a movement to secure lands in Oklahoma, and
by 1871 most of them had gone thither. (See Michigan.)

Quapaw. Between 1833 and 1867 lands in the southeastern tip of
Kansas belonged to their reserve in Indian Territory (Oklahoma),
but in the latter year they ceded this back to the Government.
(See Arkansas.)

Sauk. After leaving Iowa, the Sauk and Fox Indians occupied a
reserve in the eastern part of Kansas, but about 1859 the Foxes
returned to Iowa, and in 1867 the Sauk ceded their Kansas territories and moved to Oklahoma. (See Wisconsin.)

Seneca. Seneca Indians were joint owners with other tribes of land
in the extreme southwestern part of Kansas. They ceded this to
the United States Government in 1867. (See New York.)

Shawnee. In 1825 the Shawnee residing in Missouri received a grant
of land along the south side of Kansas River, west of the boundary
of Missouri. In 1831 they were joined by another body of Shawnee
who had formerly lived at Wapaghkonnetta and on Hog Creek,
Ohio. In 1854 nearly all of this land was re-ceded to the United
States Government and the tribe moved to Indian Territory, the
present Oklahoma. (See Tennessee.)

Wyandot. The Wyandot purchased land in eastern Kansas on Missouri River from the Delaware in 1843 and parted with it again in
1850. A few Wyandot also held title to land along with other
tribes on the border of Oklahoma and re-ceded it along with them
in 1867. (See Ohio.)

OKLAHOMA

Alabama. This was one of the tribes of the Creek Confederacy, part of which accompanied the Creeks to Oklahoma early in the nineteenth century and settled near Weleetka, where a small station on the Frisco Railway bears their name. (See Alabama.)

Apache. The name was given to a tribe or rather a group of tribes. (See **Jicarilla** under Colorado; **Kiowa Apache,** under Kansas; **Lipan** under Texas; also **Apache** under New Mexico.)

Apalachee. A few individuals of this tribe removed to Oklahoma from Alabama or Louisiana. Dr. Gatschet learned the names of two or three individuals about 1884. (See Florida.)

Arapaho. In early times the Arapaho ranged to some extent over the western sections of Oklahoma, and part of them (the Southern Arapaho) were finally given a reservation and later allotted land in severalty in the west central part along with the Southern Cheyenne. (See Wyoming.)

Biloxi. A few Biloxi reached Oklahoma and settled with the Choctaw and Creeks. (See Mississippi.)

Caddo. The Caddo moved to Oklahoma in 1859 and were given a reservation in the southwestern part about Anadarko, where they were allotted land in severalty. (See Texas.)

Cherokee. The Cherokee were moved to a large reservation in the northeastern part of Oklahoma in the winter of 1838–39. After nearly 70 years of existence under their own tribal government they were allotted land in severalty and became citizens of the United States. (See Tennessee.)

Cheyenne. The history of the Southern Cheyenne parallels that of the Southern Arapaho as given above. (See South Dakota.)

Chickasaw. The Chickasaw moved to the present Oklahoma between 1822 and 1840. They had their own government for many years but are now citizens. (See Mississippi.)

Choctaw. This tribe moved to Oklahoma about the same time as the Chickasaw though several thousand remained in their old country. Like the Chickasaw they had their own national government for a long time but are now citizens at large of Oklahoma. (See Mississippi.)

Comanche. The western part of Oklahoma was occupied by the Comanche during their later history, and they were finally given a reservation in the southwestern part of it, where they were allotted land in severalty and given the privileges of citizenship. (See Texas.)

Creeks. The tribes constituting the Creek Confederacy came to Oklahoma between 1836 and 1841 and were given a reservation in the northeastern part, where they maintained a national government until early in the present century when their lands were allotted in severalty, and they became citizens. (See Alabama, Florida, and Georgia.)

Delaware. In 1867 a part of the Delaware were removed from Kansas to the northeastern part of what is now Oklahoma and incorporated with the Cherokee Nation. Another band of Delaware is with the Caddo and Wichita in southwestern Oklahoma. (See New Jersey.)

Foxes. A few Fox Indians accompanied the Sauk (q. v.) to Oklahoma in 1867. (See Wisconsin.)

Hitchiti. This is a subtribe of the Creek Confederacy. (See Georgia; also **Creeks** and **Creek Confederacy** above and under Alabama, Florida, and Georgia.)

Illinois. In 1868 the surviving Illinois Indians, principally Peoria and Kaskaskia, previously united with the Miami bands, Wea and Piankashaw, moved to Oklahoma and occupied a reserve in the northeastern part of the State under the name Peoria. (See Illinois.)

Iowa. Part of the Iowa were moved from Kansas to a reserve in central Oklahoma set apart in 1883; they were allotted land in severalty in 1890. (See Iowa.)

Iroquois. Some Iroquois Indians, together with the Tuscarora, some Wyandot, and probably Indians of the former Erie Nation, all under the name of Seneca Indians, were given a reservation in northeastern Oklahoma, where their descendants still live, now as citizens of the United States. (See New York and Ohio.)

Jicarilla. This was one of those Athapascan tribes known as Apache. In early times they ranged over parts of western Oklahoma. (See Colorado.)

Kansa. In 1873 the Kansa were moved to Oklahoma and given a reservation in the northeastern part of the State. (See Kansas.)

Kichai. In very early times this tribe lived on, or perhaps north of, Red River, but later they worked their way south to the headwaters of the Trinity. In 1859 they returned to the north side of the river in haste in fear of attack by the Texans and have since lived with the Wichita in the neighborhood of Anadarko. (See Texas.)

Kickapoo. In 1873 some Kickapoo were brought back from México and settled in the central part of Oklahoma, where all but a certain portion of the Mexican band were afterward gathered. (See Wisconsin.)

Kiowa and Kiowa Apache. These tribes formerly ranged over much of the western part of this State. (See Kansas.)

Koasati. The Koasati were one of the tribes of the Creek Confederacy. They removed to northeastern Oklahoma with the rest of the Creeks and settled in the western part of the Creek territory. (See Alabama and Louisiana.)

Lipan. The Lipan were the easternmost band of Apache; some of them are with the Tonkawa. (See Texas.)

Miami. Part of the Miami were brought from Indiana and given a reservation in the extreme northeastern part of Oklahoma along with the Illinois (q. v.). (See Indiana.)

Mikasuki. Some of these Indians accompanied the Seminole to Oklahoma and as late as 1914 had a Square Ground of their own. (See Florida.)

Missouri. The remnant of the Missouri came to Oklahoma with the Oto in 1882 and shared their reservation. (See Missouri.)

Modoc. In 1873, at the end of the Modoc War, a part of the defeated tribe was sent to Oklahoma and placed on the Quapaw Reservation where a few yet remain. (See Oregon.)

Muklasa. A small Creek division said to have kept its identity in Oklahoma. (See Alabama.)

Munsee. A few Munsee accompanied the Delaware proper to Oklahoma and 21 were reported there in 1910. (See New Jersey.)

Muskogee. This was the name of the principal tribe or group of tribes of the Creeks (q. v.).

Natchez. A small band of Natchez accompanied the Creeks to Oklahoma and settled near Eufaula, where they later became merged in the rest of the Creek population. Another band of Natchez settled in the Cherokee Nation, near Illinois River, and a very few still preserve something of their identity. (See Mississippi.)

Nez Percé. Chief Joseph's band of Nez Percé were sent to Oklahoma in 1878, but they suffered so much from the change of climate that they were transferred to Colville Reservation in 1885. (See Idaho.)

Okmulgee. A Creek tribe and town belonging to the Hitchiti division of the Nation. Its name is perpetuated in the city of Okmulgee, former capital of the Creek Nation in Oklahoma. (See Georgia.)

Osage. The Osage formerly owned most of northern Oklahoma and after they had sold the greater part of it still retained a large reservation in the northeast, which they continue to occupy, though they have now been allotted land in severalty. (See Missouri.)

Oto. In 1880 a part of the Oto moved to the lands of the Sauk and Fox Indians in Oklahoma and in 1882 the rest followed. (See Nebraska.)

Ottawa. When they surrendered their lands in Michigan and Ohio, some Ottawa bands including those of Blanchard's Fork and Roche de Boeuf migrated to Kansas, and about 1868, to Oklahoma, settling in the northeastern part of the State. (See Michigan.)

Pawnee. The Pawnee moved to Oklahoma in 1876 and were given a reservation in the north central part of the State, where they have now been allotted land in severalty. (See Nebraska.)

Peoria. (See Illinois.)

Piankashaw, see Miami.

Ponca. In 1877 the Ponca were moved by force to Oklahoma and, though some individuals were finally allotted land in severalty in their old country, the greater part settled permanently near the Osage in northeastern Oklahoma.

Potawatomi. The Potawatomi of the Woods were moved from Kansas to Oklahoma in 1867–81 and given a reservation in the central part of the State. (See Michigan.)

Quapaw. Lands were granted to the Quapaw in the extreme southeastern part of Kansas and the extreme northeastern part of Oklahoma in 1833. In 1867, they ceded all their lands in Kansas and have since confined themselves within the limits of Oklahoma, though a large part have removed to the reservation of the Osage. (See Arkansas.)

Sauk. In 1867 the Sauk ceded their lands in Kansas in exchange for a tract in the central part of Oklahoma, where they have continued to live down to the present time. (See Wisconsin.)

Seminole. The greater part of the Seminole were removed to Oklahoma after the Seminole War in Florida. (See Florida.)

Seneca, see Iroquois.

Shawnee. The Absentee Shawnee moved from Kansas to what is now central Oklahoma about 1845; in 1867 a second band, which had been living with the Seneca in Kansas, also moved to Oklahoma but settled in the extreme northeastern part of the State; and in 1869

the third and largest section removed to the lands of the Cherokee
by agreement with that tribe. (See Tennessee.)

Tawakoni. Said to refer to "a river bend among red hills," or "neck
of land in the water." The synonyms should not be confounded
with those of the Tonkawa. Also called:

> Three Canes, an English form resulting from a mistaken attempt to trans-
> late the French spelling of their name, Troiscannes.

Connections.—The Tawakoni belonged to the Caddoan linguistic
stock and were most closely connected with the Wichita, the two
languages differing but slightly.

Location.—They were on the Canadian River about north of the
upper Washita. (See also Texas.)

Villages

Flechazos, on the west side of Brazos River near the present Waco.

History.—The Tawakoni were first met in the above location in
company with the Wichita and other related tribes. Within the next
50 years, probably as a result of pressure on the part of more northerly
peoples, they moved south and in 1772 they were settled in two groups
on Brazos and Trinity Rivers, about Waco and above Palestine. By
1779 the group on the Trinity had rejoined those on the Brazos. In
1824 part of the Tawakoni were again back on Trinity River. In
1855 they were established on a reservation near Fort Belknap on the
Brazos, but in 1859 were forced, by the hostility of the Texans, to move
north into southwestern Oklahoma, where they were officially incorporated with the Wichita.

Population.—Mooney (1928) includes the Tawakoni among the
Wichita (q. v.). In 1772 Mézières reported 36 houses and 120
warriors in the Trinity village and 30 families in the Brazos village,
perhaps 220 warriors in all. In 1778–79 he reported that these two
towns, then on the Brazos, contained more than 300 warriors. Sibley
(1832) reported that in 1805 the Tawakoni, probably including the
Waco, numbered 200 men. In 1859 they were said to number 204
exclusive of the Waco. The census of 1910 records only a single
survivor of this tribe.

Tawehash. Meaning unknown. Lesser and Weltfish (1932) suggest
that this group was identical with a Wichita band reported to them
as Tiwa. They have been given some of the same synonyms as
the Wichita (q. v.).

Connections.—The Tawehash belonged to the Caddoan linguistic
stock and were related closely to the Wichita, Tawakoni, Waco, and
Yscani.

Location.—Their earliest known home was on Canadian River north of the headwaters of the Washita.

Villages

In 1778 Mézières found two native villages to which he gave the names San Teodoro and San Bernardo.

History.—The Tawehash were encountered in the above situation by La Harpe in 1719. They moved south about the same time as the Tawakoni and other tribes of the group and were found on Red River in 1759, when they defeated a strong Spanish force sent against them. They remained in this same region until in course of time they united with the Wichita and disappeared from history. Their descendants are among the Wichita in Oklahoma.

Population.—Most writers give estimates of the Tawehash along with the Wichita and other related tribes. In 1778 they occupied two villages aggregating 160 lodges and numbered 800 fighting men and youths.

Tonkawa. In 1884 the remnant of the Tonkawa were removed to Oklahoma and the next year settled on a reservation near Ponca, where they were finally allotted land in severalty. (See Texas.)

Tuskegee. A Creek division believed to be connected linguistically with the Alabama Indians. It removed to Oklahoma with the other Creeks and established itself in the northwestern part of the allotted territory. (See Alabama.)

Waco. According to Lesser and Weltfish (1932), from Wehiko, a corruption of México, and given the name because they were always fighting with the Mexicans. The same authorities report that the Waco are thought to have been a part of the Tawakoni without an independent village but separated later. Also called:

Gentlemen Indians, by Bollaert (1850).
Houechas, Huanchané, by French writers, possibly intended for this tribe.

Connections.—The Waco were most closely related to the Tawakoni of the Wichita group of tribes belonging to the Caddoan Stock.

Location.—They appear first in connection with their village on the site of the present Waco, Tex., though their original home was in Oklahoma with the Wichita.

Villages

Quiscat, named from its chief, on the west side of the Brazos on a bluff or plateau above some springs and not far from the present Waco.

History.—According to native informants as reported by Lesser and Weltfish (1932), the Waco are formerly supposed to have constituted a part of the Tawakoni without an independent village. It has also been suggested that they may have been identical with the Yscani, but Lesser and Weltfish identify the Yscani with another band. Another possibility is that the Waco are descendants of the Shuman tribe. (See Texas.) In later times the Waco merged with the Tawakoni and Wichita.

Population.—In 1824 the Waco had a village of 33 grass houses and about 100 men, and a second village of 15 houses and an unnamed number of men. In 1859, just before their removal from Texas, they numbered 171. They are usually enumerated with the Wichita (q. v.), but the census of 1910 returned 5 survivors.

Connection in which they have become noted.—Almost the sole claim to special remembrance enjoyed by the Waco is the fact that its name was adopted by the important city of Waco, Tex. It also appears as the name of places in Sedgwick County, Kans.; Madison County, Ky.; Jasper County, Mo.; Smith County, Miss.; Haralson County, Ga.; York County, Nebr.; Cleveland County, N. C.; Stark County, Ohio; and in Tennessee; but it is uncertain whether the designations of all these came originally from the Waco tribe.

Wea, see **Miami.**

Wichita. From wits, "man." Also known as:

> Black Pawnee, common early name.
> Do'gu'at, Kiowa name, meaning "tattooed people."
> Do'kănă, Comanche name, meaning "tattooed people."
> Freckled Panis, from above.
> Guichita, Spanish form of the name.
> Hinásso, Arapaho name.
> Höxsúwitan, Cheyenne name.
> Ki'-ǥi-ku'-ǥuc, Omaha name.
> Kirikiris, Kirikurus, or Kitikitish, reported as own name but properly the name of one of their bands.
> Mítsitá, Kansa name.
> Páǥiⁿ wasábĕ, Ponca and Omaha name, meaning "Black bear Pawnee."
> Paneassa, various early writers.
> Panis noirs, early French name.
> Panis piqués, early French name.
> Pányi Wacéwe, Iowa, Oto, and Missouri name.
> Picks, from Panis piqués.
> Pitchinávo, Comanche name, meaning "painted breasts."
> Prickled Panis, referring to their tattooing.
> Quirasquiris, French form of native name.
> Quivira, from chronicles of Coronado expedition.
> Sónik'ni, Comanche name, meaning "grass lodges."
> Speckled Pawnee, referring to their tattooing.
> Túxquĕt, see Do'gu'at.

Connections.—The Wichita were one of the principal tribes of the Caddoan linguistic family.

Location.—Their earliest certain location was on Canadian River north of the headwaters of the Washita.   (See also Texas.)

Subdivisions

Most of the so-called subdivisions of the Wichita were independent tribes, some of which, including the Tawakoni, Waco, Tawehash, and Yscani, have been treated separately.   The others—Akwits or Akwesh, Kirikiris, Isis (see Yscani), Tokane (see Yscani), and Itaz—were probably only temporary bands.   Mooney (1928) also mentions the Kirishkitsu (perhaps a Wichita name for the Kichai) and the Asidahetsh and Kishkat, which cannot be identified.

History.—The Wichita rose to fame at an early period owing to the fact that they were visited by Coronado in 1541, the Spaniards calling the Wichita country the province of Quivira.   They were then farther north than the location given above, probably near the great bend of the Arkansas and in the center of Kansas.   A Franciscan missionary, Juan de Padilla, remained 3 years among them in the endeavor to convert them to Christianity, but he was finally killed by them through jealousy on account of his work for another tribe.   In 1719 La Harpe found the Wichita and several allied tribes on the south Canadian River in the territory later embraced in the Chickasaw Nation. Within the next 50 years they were forced south by hostile northern and eastern tribes and by 1772 were on the upper courses of the Red and Brazos Rivers.   In 1835 they made their first treaty with the United States Government.   They continued to live in southwestern Oklahoma until the Civil War, when they fled to Kansas until it was over.   In 1867 they returned and were placed on a reservation in Caddo County, Okla., where they have since remained.

Population.—In 1772 the Wichita and the Tawehash seem to have had about 600 warriors.   Mooney (1928) estimates that in 1780 the confederated Wichita tribes had a population of about 3,200.   Bolton (1914), on information derived from Mézières, estimated about 3,200 for the Wichita proper in 1778.   In 1805 Sibley estimated the Wichita at 400 men.   In 1868, 572 were reported in the confederated tribes. The census of 1910 gives 318, including the remnant of the Kichai. In 1937 there were 385.

Connection in which they have become noted.—Although a tribe of considerable power in early days, the Wichita will be remembered in future principally from the prominence of the city of Wichita, Kans., which bears their name.   It is also the name of counties in Kansas and Texas, a ridge of hills in southwestern Oklahoma called the Wichita Mountains, a river in Texas, and places in Oklahoma, besides Wichita Falls in Wichita County, Tex.   The identification of this tribe with the Province of Quivira gives it additional interest.

Wyandot. In 1867 a part of the Wyandot who had been living in Kansas was removed to the northeastern corner of Oklahoma where they have since remained. It is probable that this body includes more of the old Tionontati than of the true Wyandot. (See Ohio.)

Yscani. Meaning unknown. Also spelled Ascani, Hyscani, Ixcani.

Connections.—This was one of the confederated Wichita tribes and therefore without doubt related to them in speech, and thus of the Caddoan linguistic family.

Location.—The Yscani are first mentioned in connection with the Wichita and allied tribes on the South Canadian in the territory later assigned to the Chickasaw Nation. Part, however, were reported to be living 60 leagues farther toward the northwest.

History.—The Yscani evidently moved south from the above-mentioned location at the same time as the other tribes. They kept particularly close to the Tawakoni, with whose history their own is almost identical. As the name Yscani disappears from the early annals shortly before the name Waco appears in them, it has been thought that the Waco were the Yscani under a new name, but Lesser and Weltfish (1932) identify the Waco with the Isis or Tokane, perhaps both. (See **Waco** above.)

Population.—In 1772 their village was reported to contain 60 warriors, and about 1782 the entire tribe was said to have about 90 families.

Yuchi. Although originally an independent tribe, the Yuchi united with the Creeks before coming west, and they settled in the Creek Nation, in the northwestern part of that territory, where their descendants still live. (See Georgia.)

TEXAS

Akokisa. The name Akokisa, spelled in various ways, was given by the Spaniards to those Atakapa living in southeastern Texas, between Trinity Bay and Trinity River and Sabine River. (See **Atakapa** under Louisiana.)

Alabama. Alabama Indians came to Texas early in the nineteenth century, and the largest single body of Alabama still lives there on a State reservation in Polk County. (See Alabama.)

Anadarko. The name of a tribe or band belonging to the Hasinai Confederacy (q. v.).

Apache. The Jicarilla and other Apache tribes raided across the boundaries of this State on the northwest and west in early times, but the only one of them which may be said to have had its headquarters inside for any considerable period was the **Lipan** (q. v.).

Aranama. The Aranama were associated sometimes with the Karankawa in the Franciscan missions but were said to be distinct from them. Although a small tribe during all of their known history, they held together until comparatively recent times, and Morse (1822) gives them a population of 125. They were remembered by the Tonkawa, when Dr. A. S. Gatschet visited the latter, and he obtained two words of their language, but they are said to have been extinct as a tribe by 1843. While their affiliations are not certainly known, they were undoubtedly with one of the three stocks, Karankawan, Tonkawan, or Coahuiltecan, probably the last mentioned, and will be enumerated provisionally with them. (See **Coahuiltecan Tribes**.)

Atakapa, see **Akokisa** above and under Louisiana.

Bidai. Perhaps from a Caddo word signifying "brushwood," and having reference to the Big Thicket near the lower Trinity River about which they lived. Also called:

> Quasmigdo, given as their own name by Ker (1816).
> Spring Creeks, the name given by Foote (1841).

Connections.—From the mission records it appears that the Bidai were of the Atakapan linguistic stock.

Location.—On the middle course of Trinity River about Bidai Creek and to the westward and southwestward.

History.—The Bidai were living in the region above given when first known to the Europeans and claimed to be aborigines of that territory. The Franciscan mission of San Ildefonso was founded for them and the Akokisa, Deadose, and Patiri. In the latter part of the eighteenth century they are said to have been chief intermediaries between the Spaniards and Apache in the sale of firearms. The attempt to missionize them was soon abandoned. In 1776–77 an epidemic carried away nearly half their number, but they maintained separate existence down to the middle of the nineteenth century, when they were in a village 12 miles from Montgomery. They have now entirely disappeared.

Population.—Mooney (1928) estimates for them a population of 500 in 1690. In 1805 there were reported to be about 100.

Connection in which they have become noted.—The name is perpetuated in that of a small creek flowing into Trinity River from the west and in a village known as Bedias or Bedais in Grimes County, Tex.

Biloxi. Some Biloxi entered Texas before 1828. In 1846 a band was camped on Little River, a tributary of the Brazos. Afterward they occupied a village on Biloxi Bayou in the present Angelina County, but later either returned to Louisiana or passed north to the present Oklahoma. (See Mississippi.)

Caddo Tribes.   Under this head are included the Adai and the Natchitoches Confederacy (see Louisiana); and the Eyeish, the Hasinai
Confederacy, and the Kadohadacho Confederacy in Texas.

Cherokee.   A band of Cherokee under a chief named Bowl settled in
Texas early in the nineteenth century, but they were driven out by
the Texans in 1839 and their chief killed.   (See Tennessee.)

Choctaw.   Morse (1822) reported 1,200 Choctaw on the Sabine and
Neches Rivers, and some bands continued to live for a while in
eastern Texas.   One band in particular, the Yowani Choctaw, was
admitted among the Caddo there.   All the Choctaw finally removed to Oklahoma.   (See Mississippi.)

Coahuiltecan Tribes.   The name was derived from that of the Mexican
State of Coahuila, the tribes of this group having extended over
the eastern part of that province as well as a portion of Texas.
Also called:

>   Tejano, an alternative name for the group.

Connections.—As Coahuiltecan are included all of the tribes known
to have belonged to the Coahuiltecan linguistic family and some
supposed on circumstantial evidence to be a part of it.   It is probable
that most of the so-called Tamaulipecan family of México were really
related to this, and that the Karankawan and Tonkawan groups were
connected as well, though more remotely.

Location.—The Coahuiltecan tribes were spread over the eastern
part of Coahuila, México, and almost all of Texas west of San Antonio
River and Cibolo Creek.   The tribes of the lower Rio Grande may
have belonged to a distinct family, that called by Orozco y Berra
(1864) Tamaulipecan, but the Coahuiltecans reached the Gulf coast
at the mouth of the Nueces.   Northeast of that point they were
succeeded by Karankawan tribes.   Toward the north it is probable
that the Coahuiltecans originally extended for a long distance before
they were displaced by the Apache and Comanche.   (See also México.)

Subdivisions

In considering the Coahuiltecan stock it has been found necessary to change
the original plan of giving separate consideration to each tribe because we are
here confronted by an enormous number of small tribal or band names, of many
of which we do not know even the location.   In lieu of subdivisions, therefore,
we shall give as complete a list as possible of these small tribes or bands, as far as
they are known.   They are as follows:

Aguastayas.	Asan.
Alasapas.	Atajal.
Andacaminos.	Atastagonies.
Annas.	Borrados.
Apayxam.	Cabia.
Aranama (see above).	Cacafes.

Cachopostales.
Camai.
Cantunas.
Casas Chiquitas.
Casastles.
Chaguantapam.
Chagustapa.
Chapamaco.
Ghemoco.
Choyapin (perhaps Tonkawan).
Chuapas.
Cimataguo.
Cluetau.
Cocomeioje.
Comecrudo.
Cotonam.
Cupdan.
Escaba.
Espopolames.
Gabilan.
Geies.
Guanipas.
Gueiquesales.
Guerjuatida.
Guisoles.
Haeser.
Hapes.
Harames.
Heniocane.
Hiabu.
Hihames.
Huacacasa.
Huanes.
Hume.
Juamaca.
Jueinzum.
Juncatas.
Junced.
Macapao.
Macocoma.
Mallopeme.
Mamuqui.
Manam.
Manico.
Manos Colorados.
Manos de Perro.
Manos Prietas.
Maquems.
Maraquites.
Matucar.
Matuime.
Maubedan.
Mauyga.

Mazapes.
Menenquen.
Mescales.
Mesquites.
Milijaes.
Morbanas.
Mulatos.
Muruam (perhaps Tonkawan).
Narices.
Natao.
Nazas.
Necpacha.
Nigco (probably meant for Sinicu).
Nonapho (perhaps Tonkawan).
Obozi (?).
Ocana.
Odoesmades.
Ohaguames.
Orejones.
Oydican.
Paac.
Paachiqui.
Pabor.
Pacaruja (given by Uhde, 1861).
Pachal.
Pachalaque.
Pachaloco.
Pachaquen.
Pachaug.
Pacpul.
Pacuaches.
Pacuachiam.
Paguan.
Paguanan.
Pajalat.
Pajarito.
Pakawa.
Pamaque.
Pamaya.
Pamoranos.
Pampopas.
Papanac.
Paquache.
Parantones.
Parchaque.
Parchinas.
Pasalves.
Pasnacanes.
Pasqual.
Pastaloca.
Pastancoyas.
Pasteal.
Patague.

Patan.

Patanium.

Pataquilla (perhaps Karankawan).

Patou.

Patzau.

Pausanes.

Pausaqui.

Pausay.

Payaya.

Payuguan.

Peana.

Pelones.

Pescado (?).

Piedras Blancas.

Piquique.

Pinanaca.

Piniquu.

Pintos.

Pita.

Pitahay.

Pomuluma.

Prietos.

Psaupsau.

Pulacuam (perhaps Tonkawan).

Putaay.

Quanataguo.

Quems.

Quepanos.

Quesal.

Quide (?).

Quioborique (?).

Quisabas (?).

Quitacas.

Quivi (?).

Salapaque (?).

Salinas (?).

Samampac.

Sampanal.

Sanipao.

Saracuam (?).

Secmoco.

Semonan (?).

Senisos.

Siaguan.

Siansi.

Sijame (perhaps Tonkawan).

Sillanguayas.

Simaomo (perhaps Tonkawan).

Sinicu.

Siupam.

Sonaque.

Sonayan.

Suahuaches (?).

Suanas.

Sulujame.

Tacame.

Taimamares.

Tamcan (?).

Tamique (?).

Tanpacuazes.

Tarequano.

Teana.

Tecahuistes.

Tejones.

Teneinamar.

Tenicapeme.

Tepachuaches.

Tepemaca.

Terocodame.

Tet.

Tetanauoica.

Tetecores.

Tetzino (perhaps Tonkawan).

Tilijaes.

Tinapihuayas.

Tiopane (perhaps Karankawan).

Tiopines.

Tishim.(perhaps Tonkawan).

Tocas.

Tonzaumacagua.

Tripas Blancas.

Tuancas.

Tumamar.

Tumpzi.

Tusanes.

Tusonid.

Tuteneiboica.

Unojita (?).

Uracha.

Utaca (?).

Venados.

Vende Flechas.

Viayam.

Viddaquimamar.

Xarame.

Xiabu.

Yacdossa.

Ybdacax.

Yemé.

Yman.

Ymic.

Yoricas.

Ysbupue.

Yué.

Yurguimes.

Zorquan.

As indicated, some of these were perhaps Tonkawan, Karankawan, or of other affiliations. Some were represented by single individuals and no doubt many of the names are synonyms or have become distorted in the process of recording. The exact nature of these groups can now never be known. The above list does not include a great many names given only by Cabeza de Vaca or La Salle and his companions in the same region. The multiplicity of tribes and confusion in names is not so serious in any other region north of México.

History.—The Coahuiltecan tribes were first encountered by Cabeza de Vaca and his companions who passed through the heart of their country, and by the Spaniards when they invaded Coahuila and founded Parral. From the early part of the seventeenth century onward, their country was traversed repeatedly. In 1675 the Coahuiltecan country on both sides of the Rio Grande was invaded by Fernando del Bosque, and in 1689 and 1690 the Texas portion was again traversed by De Leon and Manzanet. In 1677 a Franciscan mission for Coahuiltecan tribes was established at Nadadores and before the end of the century others were started along the Rio Grande and near San Antonio. Great numbers of Indians were gathered into these missions during the first part of the eighteenth century but the change of life entailed upon roving people, disease, and the attacks of hostile tribes from the north reduced their numbers rapidly. Today none of these Indians are known to survive in Texas. In 1886 Dr. A. S. Gatschet found remnants of two or three tribes on the south side of the Rio Grande and some of their descendants, survive, but they are no longer able to speak their ancient language.

Population.—Mooney (1928) estimated that in 1690 the Coahuiltecan peoples totaled 15,000; no figures embracing all of them occur in the various narratives.

Comanche. Significance unknown. Also called:

Allebome, given by Lewis and Clark as the French·name.
Bald Heads, so called by Long (1823).
Bo'dălk' iñago, Kiowa name, meaning "reptile people," "snake men."
Ca'-tha, Arapaho name, meaning "having many horses."
Cintu-aluka, Teton Dakota name.
Dătsĕ-aⁿ, Kiowa Apache name (Gatschet, MS, BAE).
Gyai'-ko, Kiowa name, meaning "enemies."
Idahi, Kiowa Apache name (Mooney, 1896).
Indá, Jicarilla name.
La Plais, French traders' name, perhaps corrupted from Tête Pelée.
La'-ri'hta, Pawnee name.
Los Mecos, Mexican name.
Mahán, Isleta name.
Máhana, Taos name.
Na'ⁿlani, Navaho name, meaning "many aliens," or "many enemies" (collective for Plains tribes).
Na'nita, Kichai name.
Nar-a-tah, Waco name.

Na'tăa, Wichita name, meaning "snakes," i. e., "enemies."

Ne'me nē, or Nimĕnim, own name, or Nüma, meaning "people."

Padouca, common early name, evidently from the name of the Penateka band.

Sänko, obsolete Kiowa name.

Sau'hto, Caddo name.

Selakampóm, Comecrudo name for all warlike tribes but especially for the Comanche.

Shĭshĭnówŭtz-hitä'neo, Cheyenne name meaning "snake people."

Snake Indians, common name.

Tête Pelée, French traders' name, identification somewhat doubtful.

Yampah or Yä'mpaini, Shoshoni name, meaning "Yampa people," or "Yampa eaters."

Connections.—The Comanche belonged to the Shoshonean linguistic family, a branch of Uto-Aztecan, its tongue being almost identical with that of the Shoshoni.

Location.—In northwestern Texas and the region beyond as far as Arkansas River. (See also Colorado, Kansas, Nebraska, New Mexico, Oklahoma, and Wyoming.)

Subdivisions

The following are the names of Comanche bands so far as these are known:

Detsanayuka or Nokoni.	Pagatsu.
Ditsakana, Widyu, Yapa or Yamparika.	Penateka or Penande.
Kewatsana.	Pohoi (adopted Shoshoni).
Kotsai.	Tanima, Tenawa or Tenahwit.
Kotsoteka, Kwahari or Kwahadi.	Waaih.
Motsai.	

Various writers also mention the following:

Guage-johe.	Muvinabore.
Ketahto.	Nauniem.
Kwashi.	Parkeenaum.

History.—Although differing today in physical type, on account of their close linguistic relationship it is supposed that the original Comanche must have separated from the Shoshoni in the neighborhood of eastern Wyoming. The North Platte was known as Padouca Fork as late as 1805. In 1719, however, the Comanche are placed by early writers in southwestern Kansas. For a long time the Arkansas River was their southern boundary, but finally they moved below it attracted by opportunities to obtain horses from the Mexicans and pushed on by other peoples. The Apache, who were in the country invaded, attacked them but were defeated. In this movement the Penateka Comanche were in advance and from the name of this band comes Padouca, one of the old terms applied to the entire people. For a long time the Comanche were at war with the Spaniards and the Apache, and later with the Americans. Texas suffered so much from their depredations that the famous Texas Rangers were organized as a protection against them and proved extremely effective. In 1854, by permission of the State of Texas, the Federal Government established two reservations upon Brazos River and some of the Comanche and Kiowa were placed upon the upper reserve. Friction with the settlers, however, continued and compelled the abandonment of these reserves in 1859 and the removal of the Indians to the territory embraced in the present State of Oklahoma. By a treaty concluded October 18, 1865, a reservation was set apart for the Comanche and Kiowa consisting of the Panhandle of Texas and all of Oklahoma west of Cimarron River and the 98th meridian of west longitude. By a treaty concluded October 21, 1867, they surrendered all of this except a tract of land in southwestern Oklahoma between the 98th meridian, Red River, the North Fork of Red River, and Washita River. They did not settle finally upon this land, however, until after the last outbreak of the southern prairie tribes in 1874–75. Their descendants continue to live in the same territory.

Population.—Mooney (1928) estimated that there must have been 7,000 Comanche about 1690. The census of 1904 gives 1,400; the census of 1910, 1,171; and the United States Indian Office Report for 1923 shows a total of 1,697. The census of 1930 returned 1,423. In 1937 the figure given is 2,213.

Connection in which they have become noted.—The Comanche were one of the most famous tribes of the Plains, particularly the southern Plains. They were remarkable (1) for their numbers, horsemanship, and warlike character; (2) for the frequent clashes between them and the White expeditions or bodies of emigrants; (3) as largely instrumental in introducing horses to the Indians of the northern Plains. They gave place names to counties in Kansas and Texas; a mountain in Texas; and places in Yellowstone County, Mont.; Comanche County, Tex.; and Stephens County, Okla. There is a Comanche River in Colorado.

Creeks, see **Muskogee,** under Alabama.

Deadose. An Atakapa tribe or subtribe in south central Texas. (See Louisiana.)

Eyeish, or Háish. Meaning unknown. Also called Aays, Aix, Aliche, Yayecha, etc.

Connections.—The Eyeish belonged to the Caddoan linguistic stock, their closest relatives probably being the Adai, and next to them the peoples of the Kadohadacho and Hasinai Confederacies, with which, in fact, Lesser and Weltfish (1932) classify them.

Location.—On Ayish Creek, northeastern Texas, between the Sabine and Neches Rivers.

History.—In 1542 the Eyeish were visited by the Spaniards under Moscoso, De Soto's successor. They are next noted in 1686–87 by the companions of La Salle. In 1716 the mission of Nuestra Señora de los Dolores was established among them by the Franciscans, abandoned in 1719, reestablished in 1721, and finally given up in 1773, the success of the mission having been very small. Their proximity to the road between the French post at Natchitoches and the Spanish post at Nacogdoches seems to have contributed to their general demoralization. Sibley (1832) reported only 20 individuals in the tribe in 1805 but in 1828 there were said to be 160 families. Soon afterward they joined the other Caddo tribes and followed their fortunes, and they must have declined very rapidly for only a bare memory of them is preserved.

Population.—In 1779, 20 families were reported; in 1785, a total population of 300; in 1805, 20 individuals; in 1828, 160 families. (See **Caddo Confederacy,** under Louisiana.)

Connection in which they have become noted.—Ayish Bayou, a tributary of the Angelina River on which they formerly lived, perpetuates the name of the Eyeish.

Guasco. A tribe or band which attained some prominence from the importance attached to it in the narratives of the De Soto expedition. (See **Hasinai Confederacy.**)

Hainai. An important band of the Hasinai Confederacy (q. v.).

Hasinai Confederacy. Hasinai signifies "our own folk." The name often occurs in the forms Assinay or Cenis.

Connections.—The Hasinai Confederacy constituted one of the major divisions of the Caddo, the others being the Kadohadacho Confederacy, the Natchitoches Confederacy, and the Adai and Eyeish, the two last probably connected but not confederated. All belonged to the Caddoan linguistic stock.

Location.—In northeastern Texas between the headwaters of the Neches and Trinity Rivers.

Subdivisions

The following tribes or bands were included:

Anadarko, northwest of Nacogdoches in the present Rusk County.

Guasco, position unknown.

Hainai, 3 leagues west of Nacogdoches.

Nabedache, 3 to 4 leagues west of Neches River and near Arroyo San Pedro, at a site close to the old San Antonio road, which became known as San Pedro.

Nacachau, just north of the Neches tribe and on the east side of Neches River.

Nacanish, north of the Hainai.

Nacao, probably part of the Nacanish.

Nacogdoche, at the present Nacogdoches.

Nacono, southeast of the Neches and Nabedache and 5 leagues from the former.

Namidish or Nabiti, on Angelina River north of the Hainai.

Nasoni, two towns: (1) about 27 miles north of Nacogdoches near the Anadarko; (2) in the Kadohadacho Confederacy.

Nechaui, southeast of the Nabedache, half a league from the Nacono, and 5 leagues from the crossing of the Neches at the Neches village.

Neches, the main village 1 league or more east of Neches River, nearly west of the present Nacogdoches and near the mounds southwest of Alto, Cherokee County.

The following names may belong to other allied tribes but next to nothing is known of them:

Naansi.	Nadamin.	Neihahat.
Nabeyeyxa.	Natsshostanno.	Tadiva.

Lesser and Weltfish (1932) speak of a tribe called Kayamaici, but this was probably a local group on Kiamichi River.

Villages

As recorded by our authorities, these almost always bore the names of the tribes occupying them.

History.—On their way west in 1542 after the death of De Soto, in an endeavor to reach México overland, the Spaniards who had followed him passed through the Caddo country, and the names of the Nabedache, Nasoni, Anadarko, and Nacanish seem to be recognizable. In 1686–87 La Salle and his companions spent some time in their villages, and it was near one of them that La Salle was murdered by his own people. In 1690 the Spaniards entered their country and opened the first mission among them at the Nabedache village in May of that year. A number of missions were established in the other villages. All were abandoned in 1719 in expectation of a French attack, but they were reestablished in 1721. They did not prove successful, however, and were gradually removed to the neighborhood of San Antonio. Early in the nineteenth century the Hasinai were joined by the Louisiana Caddo, and all were placed upon a reservation on the Brazos River in 1855. Threatened with massacre by some of their White neighbors, they fled to Oklahoma 4 years later, were granted new lands near the present Anadarko, and finally allotted land in severalty.

Population.—Mooney (1928) estimates that in 1690 the entire Caddo population, including the Hasinai, the Kadohadacho and Natchitoches Confederacies, and the Adai and Eyeish tribes, amounted to 8,500, 700 more than the number I arrived at. He does not give figures for the Hasinai by themselves, but it is probable that he would have allowed between 4,000 and 5,000. The former figure is the one I suggested (see Swanton, 1942).

Referring to earlier estimates, we are told that a Canadian who had lived for several years among the Hasinai stated in 1699 that they had between 600 and 700 warriors, which would indicate a population of 2,500–3,000.   In 1716 Don Diego Ramon, under whom the missions were established, gave it as his opinion that they were serving a population of 4,000–5,000.   When Aguayo reestablished them in 1721 he distributed presents to the inhabitants of the principal towns.   His figures are evidently incomplete, but even so they suggest some falling off in the 5 years that had elapsed.   At any rate it is evident that these Indians lost very heavily during the eighteenth century and that their numbers did not exceed 1,000 at the opening of the nineteenth century.   A rather careful estimate by Jesse Stem in 1851 would indicate a population of about 350.   In 1864 the United States Indian Office reported 150, and in 1876 and subsequent years still smaller figures appear which are evidently incomplete.   The first seemingly accurate census taken by the Indian Office was in 1880, when the figure for the united Caddo people was given as 538.   It varied little from this until after 1910 when it showed steady gains.   In 1937, 967 Caddo were reported.

Connection in which they have become noted.—The Hasinai are noted as the Indians among whom La Salle came to his untimely end, and along with the Kadohadacho and Natchitoches as makers of the beautiful Caddo pottery.   (See **Kadohadacho Confederacy.**)   Texas, a common name applied to them, was adopted as the designation of a Republic and later State of the American Union.   It has been given to places in Washington County, Ky., and Baltimore County, Md.; to Texas City, Galveston County, Tex.; Texas Creek, Fremont County, Colo.; and in the combined form Texarkana to a city on the boundary line between Texas and Arkansas, entering also into Texhoma, Texas County, Okla., and Sherman County, Tex.

Isleta del Sur, see **Pueblos** under New Mexico.

Jicarilla.   The Jicarilla ranged into this State (Texas) at times. (See Colorado.)

Kadohadacho Confederacy.   The word Kadohadacho signifies in the native language "real chiefs," kadi being the word for "chief," and it is from an abbreviation of this term that we get the word Caddo. They were also called:

At'-ta-wits, by the Comanche, according to Ten Kate (1907).
Dä'sha-i, or Táshash, by the Wichita.
Érawika, by the Pawnee.
'H'-doum-dei-kiн, by the Kiowa.
Ka-lŏX-la'-tce, by the Choctaw.
Kalu-χnádshu or Kasseye'i, by the Tonkawa.
Kul-hŭl-atsĬ, by the Creeks.
Ma'-seip'-kiн, by the Kiowa, signifying "pierced noses."
Ni'rĬs-hări's-kĬ'riki, another Wichita name.

Otä's-itä'niuw', Cheyenne name, signifying "pierced nose people" (or Utásĕta).

Su'-dẹ̆ĕ, by the Quapaw.

Tani'bänĕn, by the Arapaho, signifying "pierced nose people."

Witúne, by the Comanche, according to Gatschet (MS., B. A. E.).

Connections.—The Kadohadacho belonged to the Caddo division of the Caddoan linguistic stock, the other members being the closely related Hasinai (q. v.) and Natchitoches (see under Louisiana), and the more remotely connected Adai of Louisiana and Eyeish of Texas.

Location.—The Kadohadacho lived in northeastern Texas and southwestern Arkansas at the Great Bend of Red River, though they are usually associated with the region around Caddo Lake which they occupied at a later period. (See also Arkansas and Louisiana.)

Subdivisions

Cahinnio, near Ouachita River, Ark.

Kadohadacho, on the north side of Red River near the point where the present Arkansas-Texas boundary line reaches it.

Nanatsoho, on the south side of Red River not far from the point reached by the present Arkansas-Oklahoma State line.

Upper Nasoni, on the south side of Red River nearly opposite the present Ogden.

Upper Natchitoches, on the south side of Red River between the Nanatsoho and Nasoni.

Upper Yatasi, a part of the Yatasi which joined them in very late times.

History.—In October 1541, De Soto and his army entered a province called Tula believed to be the country of the Indians later known as Cahinnio, a tribe for whose bravery the Spaniards came to have a wholesome respect. The next encounter between these people and white men was in the summer of 1687 when, after the murder of the Sieur de la Salle, six survivors of his expedition, including Joutel and Father Anastasius Donay, passed through the Kadohadacho towns on their way to the Mississippi, visiting the Nasoni, Kadohadacho, and Cahinnio. Tonti visited them also 4 years later. In November and December 1691, Domingo Teran (Castaneda, 1936) spent a miserable week in this country exploring it and taking soundings of Red River, and we owe to him the first map of the region. In 1700 Bienville undertook to reach them but got no farther than the Yatasi village halfway between the Natchitoches and Kadohadacho. In 1719 the French officer Bernard de la Harpe (1831) spent some time among them and established a trading post which endured for a considerable period. French traders quickly monopolized the Kadohadacho trade, the principal trading point being Natchitoches, but no missions were established. This group of tribes proved to be a strong bulwark against the warlike northern Indians, particularly the Osage, but they suffered much in consequence, and late in the eighteenth century the Kadohadacho or a part of them moved to another location some miles below their ancient village. The town established in the new location, however, was also attacked by the Osages, who inflicted such losses upon its inhabitants that they removed again about 1800 and established themselves on Sodo Creek northwest of the present Shreveport. In 1824 a treaty was signed between the United States Government and the Quapaw Indians by which the latter agreed to give up their lands on the Arkansas and remove to the country of the Caddo Indians. The Quapaw removed the year following but suffered such losses on account of floods in Red River that in 1833 they surrendered these lands and removed to Oklahoma. Two years later the Kadohadacho and their allies also subscribed to a treaty by which they surrendered all of their lands within the territory of the United States. In consequence, they removed to Texas and settled near their Hasinai kindred, whose fortunes they afterward followed although the two parties remained distinct for a considerable period. Some united themselves for a time with the Cherokee under Chief Bowl. Some also took up their residence with the Chickasaw in the Indian Territory. Those who remained in Texas were fellow victims with the Hasinai of the increasing friction with their white neighbors embittered by Comanche and Apache depredations for which they were in no way responsible. We may now call these united peoples by the simple term "Caddo." In an endeavor to end these difficulties a reservation was set apart for the Caddo on Brazos River in 1852 but trouble arose again of such a violent character that in 1859 the Caddo abandoned Texas and were assigned a new reservation in the southwestern part of the present State of Oklahoma, where their descendants still live, most of the scattered bands having been gathered into one section. Most of the Caddo sided with the Federal Government during the Civil War and went to Kansas, where they remained until it was over, though experiencing many hardships in consequence and losing many of their people in epidemics. They took considerable interest in the Ghost Dance Religion and still more in the Peyote Cult, John Wilson, a mixed-blood Caddo and Delaware, being one of the prominent leaders. The fact that they had always cultivated the ground has made their adjustment to the new economic system fairly easy. In 1902 they were allotted land in severalty.

Population.—My estimate for the Kadohadacho division of the Caddo before White contact is 2,000. Bienville and La Harpe place it in 1700–1709 between 2,000 and 2,500. In 1718, however, Bienville asserts that it had fallen to 200 warriors, which would mean about 800 people, and Sibley (1832) indicates the same figures as late as 1805. In 1829 Porter (*in* Schoolcraft, vol. 3) gives an estimate of 450, and in 1851 Stem (1851) who is likely to be reliable, places it at 476. In 1857 Neighbors returns a partial enumeration of 235, and in 1876, the last time they were returned separately from the Hasinai, the Indian Office reported 467. It is evident, however, that this also includes part of the Hasinai and all of the Adai and Eyeish besides the remnants of the Natchitoches group. After this date the population of the united Caddo group remained around 500, but during the present century it has been steadily increasing and in 1937, 967 were reported.

Connection in which they have become noted.—The Kadohadacho group is noted as containing the tribe which ultimately gave the name Caddo to the linguistic family of which it is a part. The name Caddo has been applied to a parish and lake in Louisiana; a county in Oklahoma; a creek and gap in Arkansas; to the village of Caddo Gap, Montgomery County, Ark.; and to villages in Bryan County, Okla., and Stephens County, Tex.; and in Hunt County, Tex., is Caddo Mills.

Karankawan Tribes. The name Karankawa is derived from one of the constituent tribes, but the significance is unknown.

> Nda kun-dadéhe, Lipan name, meaning "people walking in the water."
> Quĕlancouchis, Clamcoets, names given by the French.
> Yákokon kápai, Tonkawa, meaning "without moccasins," but this name includes the coast Coahuiltecan tribes.

Connections.—The Karankawan tribes are placed in an independent linguistic stock, which was connected most closely, it would seem, with the Coahuiltecan group.

Location.—On the coast of the Gulf of México between Trinity and Aransas Bays.

Subdivisions

Five principal tribes constituted the Karankawan stock. They were as follows:
Coapite.
Coaque or Coco, on Galveston Island and at the mouth of Brazos River.
Karankawa, on Matagorda Bay.
Kohani, near the mouth of Colorado River.
Kopano, on Copano Bay.

To these should perhaps be added the Tiopane and Tups, and perhaps also the Pataquilla, and the Quilotes mentioned by Cabeza de Vaca (1851).

History.—The Karankawan coast was skirted by a number of early voyagers but the first contact with its inhabitants worth noting was by Cabeza de Vaca and other shipwrecked members of Pamphilo de Narvaez's expedition. There is little doubt that the people among whom Cabeza de Vaca was cast away in 1528 were the Coaque or Coco. In 1685 La Salle landed in their country supposing that he was near the mouth of the Mississippi, and he built a fort (Fort St. Louis) in which the French maintained themselves for 2 years. In 1689 the region was visited by a Spanish expedition under De Leon intent upon driving the Frenchmen out of the country. Shortly afterward the Spaniards began to colonize Texas and, though few settlements were made near the coast, missions were established from time to time to gather in the Karankawan Indians. The neophytes could never be induced to remain long at these missions, however, and continued during the Spanish period in about the same condition of savagery in which they had been found, though they decreased steadily in numbers. After the American settlements had begun, the coast tribes annoyed them by constant pilfering, and the reprisals which the Karankawans suffered finally destroyed them entirely. The last are said to have perished shortly before the Civil War. The only Karankawan vocabulary of undoubted purity was recorded in 1720 by the French Captain Beranger. In 1891 Dr. A. S. Gatschet published two others, one obtained from Tonkawa Indians and the other, much longer, from a white woman named Oliver who had lived near the last band of Karankawa in her girlhood and had learned a considerable number of words. But this band is said to have been much mixed with Coahuiltecan, a contention which an examination of the material seems to confirm.

Population.—Mooney's (1928) estimate of 2,800 for the Karankawan tribes in 1690 appears to me decidedly too high, but there are practically no data upon which to make a satisfactory determination.

Connection in which they have become noted.—The Karankawan tribes will be longest remembered as those among which Cabeza de Vaca and his companions were cast away in 1528, and where La Salle's colony was established in 1685. The name of one Karankawan tribe (Kopano) is preserved by Copano Bay.

Kichai or (more phonetically) **Kitsei.** Their own name and said to mean "going in wet sand," but the Pawnee translate their rendering of it as "water turtle." Also called:

> Gíts'ajĭ, Kansa name.
> Ki-ȼi'-tcac, Omaha name.
> Kiétsash, Wichita name.
> Ki'-tchēsh, Caddo name.
> Quichais, Spanish variant.
> Quidehais, from French sources (La Harpe, 1831).

Connections.—The Kichai were a tribe of the Caddoan stock whose language lay midway between Wichita and Pawnee.

Location.—On the upper waters of Trinity River, and between that stream and Red River. (See also Oklahoma.)

History.—It is probable that in the prehistoric period the Kichai lived north of Red River but they had gotten south of it by 1701 when the French penetrated that country and they continued in the same general region until 1855. They were then assigned to a small reservation on Brazos River, along with several other small tribes.

In 1858, however, alarmed at threats of extermination on the part of the neighboring Whites, they fled to the present Oklahoma, where they joined the Wichita. They have remained with them ever since.

Population.—Mooney (1928) estimates a total Kichai population of 500 in 1690. In 1772 the main Kichai village contained 30 houses and there were estimated in it 80 warriors, most of whom were young. In 1778 the number of Kichai fighting men was estimated at 100. The census of 1910 returned a total population of only 10, and that of 1930 included them with the Wichita, the figure for the two tribes, nearly all Wichita however, being 300.

Connection in which they have become noted.—Their name Kichai is perpetuated in the Keeche Hills, Okla.; Keechi Creek, Tex.; a branch of the Trinity, Keechi; a post hamlet of Leon County, Tex.; and perhaps Kechi, a post township of Sedgwick County, Kans.

Kiowa. This tribe hunted in and raided across northern Texas. (See Kansas.)

Koasati. Early in the nineteenth century bands of Koasati had worked over from Louisiana into Texas, settling first on the Sabine and later on the Neches and the Trinity. In 1850 the bulk of the entire tribe was in Texas but later, partly it is said on account of a pestilence, they suffered heavy losses and most of the survivors returned to Louisiana, where the largest single body of Koasati is living. Among the Alabama in Polk County, Tex., there were in 1912 about 10 of this tribe. (See Alabama and Louisiana.)

Lipan. Adapted from Ipa-n'de, apparently a personal name; n'de meaning "people." Also called:

> Ä-tagúi, Kiowa name, meaning "timber Apache"; used also for Mescalero.
> Cances, Caddo name, meaning "deceivers."
> Hu-ta'-ci, Comanche name, meaning "forest Apache" (Ten Kate, 1884, *in* Hodge, 1907).
> Húχul, Tonkawa name. (See Uχul.)
> Na-izhă'ñ, own name, meaning "ours," "our kind."
> Navóne, Comanche name (Gatschet, MS., B. A. E.).
> Shi'îni, former Mescalero name, meaning "summer people"(?).
> Tu-tsän-nde, Mescalero name, meaning "great water people."
> Uχul, Tonkawa name, meaning a spiral shell and applied to this tribe because of their coiled hair.
> Yabipai Lipan, so called by Garcés in 1776.

Connections.—This is one of the tribes of the Athapascan linguistic stock to which the general name Apache was applied. Their closest relations politically were with the Jicarilla, with whom they formed one linguistic group.

Location.—The Lipan formerly ranged from the Rio Grande in New Mexico over the eastern part of the latter State and western

Texas southeastward as far as the Gulf of México. (See also New
Mexico and Oklahoma.)

Subdivisions

The Lipan were reported during the early part of the nineteenth century to
consist of three bands, probably the same which Orozco y Berra (1864) calls
Lipanjenne, Lipanes de Arriba, and Lipanes Abajo.

History.—The position of the Lipan prior to the eighteenth century
is somewhat obscure, but during that century and the early part of
the nineteenth they ranged over the region just indicated. In 1757
the San Saba mission was established for them, but it was broken up
by their enemies, the Comanche and Wichita. In 1761–62 the missions of San Lorenzo and Candelaria were organized for the same
purpose but met a similar fate in 1767. In 1839 the Lipan sided
with the Texans against the Comanche but suffered severely from the
Whites between 1845 and 1856, when most of them were driven into
Coahuila, México. They remained in Coahuila until October 1903,
when the 19 survivors were taken to northwest Chihauhua, and remained there until 1905. In that year they were brought to the
United States and placed on the Mescalero Reservation, N. Mex.,
where they now live. A few Lipan were also incorporated with the
Tonkawa and the Kiowa Apache.

Population.—Mooney (1928) estimates that the Lipan numbered
500 in 1690. In 1805 the three bands were reported to number 300,
350, and 100 men respectively, which would seem to be a too liberal
allowance. The census of 1910 returned 28.

Connection in which they have become noted.—The Lipan were noted
as persistent raiders into Texas, New Mexico, and México. Their
name has been given to a post village in Hood County, Tex.

Muskogee. A few Muskogee came to Texas in the nineteenth century,
most belonging to the Pakana division. Two or three individuals
lived until recently near Livingston, Tex. (See Alabama.)

**Nabedache, Nacachau, Nacanish, Nacogdoche, Nadaco, Namidish,
Nechaui, Neches,** and one section of the **Nasoni.** Small tribes
or bands belonging to the Hasinai Confederacy (q. v.).

Nanatsoho, Nasoni (Upper). Small tribes or bands connected with
the Kadohadacho Confederacy (q. v.).

Pakana. A Muskogee division. (See **Muskogee** above and also under
Alabama.)

Pascagoula. Bands belonging to the Pascagoula, entered Texas from
Louisiana early in the nineteenth century, and one band lived on
Biloxi Bayou, a branch of the Neches, for a considerable period,
together with some Biloxi Indians. All had disappeared in 1912

except two Indians, only half Pascagoula, living with the Alabama in Polk County. (See Mississippi).

Patiri. A tribe associated with the Akokisa, Bidai, and Deadose in the mission of San Ildefonso west of Trinity River. Since related tribes are said to have been put in the same mission in that period (1748–49), it is believed that the Patiri spoke an Atakapan language. Their former home is thought to have been along Caney Creek.

Pueblos. There were two late settlements of Pueblo Indians, Isleta del Sur and Senecú del Sur, near El Paso, Tex., composed principally of Indians brought back by Governor Otermin in 1681 after an unsuccessful attempt to subdue the Pueblo Indians of the Rio Grande. Senecú del Sur was, however, actually in Chihuahua, México. The people of these pueblos are now almost completely Mexicanized. (See New Mexico.)

Quapaw. Between 1823 and 1833 the Quapaw lived with the Caddo Indians in northwestern Louisiana and northeastern Texas, and one band of them known as Imaha were reckoned as a constituent element of the Caddo Confederacy. (See Arkansas.)

Senecú del Sur. (See **Pueblos** above.)

Shawnee. A band of Shawnee entered eastern Texas for a brief period during the middle of the nineteenth century. They were afterward moved to Oklahoma. (See Tennessee.)

Shuman. More often known as Jumano or Humano, significance unknown. Also called:

> Borrados, from Spanish sources, "striped"(?).
> Chouman, French form of name.
> Humanas, Jumanas, Xumanas, Spanish forms of name.
> Ipataragüites, from Mota-Padilla, probably intended for this tribe.
> Patarabueyes, given by Espejo in 1582.
> Suma, sometimes regarded as a separate tribe but considered by Sauer merely as a synonym.

Connections.—The eastern division of the Shuman, that to which the name Jumano is oftenest applied, was once thought to have belonged to the Caddoan stock, but Sauer (1934) appears to have shown that in all probability it was Uto-Aztecan. The western section, oftener called Suma, has been classed, erroneously of course, as Tanoan.

Location.—In early times most of the Shuman lived along the Rio Grande between the mouth of the Concho and the present El Paso but extending westward as far as the Casas Grandes in Chihuahua. Later a part of them entered the Plains in western Texas and eastern New Mexico. (See also New Mexico.)

Subdivisions and Villages

Besides the two main divisions to which the names Shuman or Jumano and Suma have been applied respectively, the Suma later became separated into two groups, one about El Paso and the other in the region of the Casas Grandes. The only villages named are: Atripuy, Genobey, Quelotetrey, and Pataotrey.

History.—The Shuman were first met by Cabeza de Vaca and his companions about the beginning of the year 1536 although De Vaca does not mention them by name. In 1582 they were visited by Antonio de Espejo and in 1598 by Juan de Oñate. At the latter date a part of them at least were near the Salinas, east of the Rio Grande in what is now New Mexico. About 1622 they were visited by the Franciscan missionary of the Pueblo of Isleta, and in 1629 an independent mission was established for them. By this time, the eastern section of the tribe had gotten as far east as the Conchos, a headstream of the Nueces. About 1670 there were Shuman not far from Pecos River, and from that time through the eighteenth century they seem to have resided principally in the region indicated. As late as the middle of the nineteenth century they are mentioned in connection with the Kiowa, and again as living near Lampazas, Nuevo Leon, México. Possibly they were the tribe later known as Waco. The name of the western Shuman appears in the form Suma as early as 1630 when it was used by Benavides, and in 1659 some of the northern Suma were at San Lorenzo. During the Pueblo revolt of 1680 they became hostile and united with the Manso and Jano in an outbreak in 1684, but they were reduced 2 years later and formed into several settlements about El Paso, San Lorenzo being the only one to endure. They declined steadily in numbers until in 1897 only one was known to be living, at Senecú. The mission of Casas Grandes was established among the southern branch of the Suma in 1664. Then and for some years afterward they were allied with the Apache and Jocome in raids against the Piman tribes west of them, particularly the Opata, but are supposed to have been destroyed ultimately by the Apache.

Population.—In 1582 Espejo believed that the Shuman numbered 10,000, probably an overestimate. Mooney (1928) does not give them separate entry in his estimates] of population. In 1744 the northern branch of that part of the tribe called Suma had become reduced to 50 families; in 1765 there were only 21 families; and in 1897 only one individual was supposed to be left.

Soacatino, or **Xacatin.** A tribe met by the companions of De Soto in northwestern Louisiana or northeastern Texas. It was undoubtedly Caddo but has not been identified satisfactorily with any known Caddo tribe.

Tawakoni. The Tawakoni were a subdivision of the Wichita, or at least a tribe closely affiliated with them. (See Oklahoma.)

Tonkawan Tribes. The name derived from the most important and only surviving tribe of the family. Gatschet (1891 a) says that Tonkawa is a Waco word, Tonkaweya, meaning "they all stay together." The synonyms are not to be confounded with those of the Tawakoni. Also called:

Kádiko, Kiowa name, probably a corruption of Kúikogo, "man-eating men" (Gatschet, MS., B. A. E.).
Kariko, Comanche name, from above.
K'inähi-píäko, Kiowa name, meaning "maneaters" (Mooney, 1898).
Konkoné or Komkomé, early French name.
Maneaters, common translation of some of above synonyms.
Miúxsĕn, Cheyenne name.
Némeréxka, Comanche name (Gatschet, MS., B. A. E.).
Títskan wátitch, own name.

Connections.—The Tonkawan tribes constitute a distinct linguistic family but with affinities for the Coahuiltecan and probably Karankawan and Tunican groups.

Location.—In central Texas from Cibolo Creek on the southwest to within a few miles of Trinity River on the northeast. (See also Oklahoma.)

Subdivisions

The tribes or bands certainly included under this head were the Tonkawa, Yojuane, Mayeye, and Ervipiame, but there should probably be added the Sana, Emet, Cava, Toho, Tohaha, Quiutcanuaha, Tenu, Tetzino, Tishin, Tusolivi, and Ujuiap, and perhaps also the Nonapho, Sijame, Simaomo, Muruam, Pulacuam, and Choyapin, though the last three at least were probably Coahuiltecan.

History.—Tribes of Tonkawan stock were undoubtedly encountered by Cabeza de Vaca early in the sixteenth century; certainly so if the Muruam were Tonkawan for they are evidently his Mariames. In 1691 the Tonkawa and Yojuane are mentioned by Francisco Casañas de Jesus Maria as enemies of the Hasinai (Swanton, 1942, p. 251), and in 1714 the Yojuane destroyed the main fire temple of the Hasinai. Between 1746 and 1749 the Tonkawa were gathered into missions on San Xavier (San Gabriel) River but these were given up in 1756, and 2 years later the Tonkawa assisted in the destruction of the San Sabá Mission established for the Apache. From that time until well into the nineteenth century the tribe continued to reside in the same section, rarely settling down for any considerable period. In 1855 they and several other Texas tribes were gathered by the United States Government on two small reservations on Brazos River. In 1859 however, the threatening attitude of their white neighbors resulted in their removal to Washita River in what is now Oklahoma. On the night of October 25, 1862, the Tonkawa camp there was fallen upon by a body of Delaware, Shawnee, and Caddo Indians desiring to pay off old scores but pretending that the Tonkawa and their agent were in sympathy with the Southern Confederacy. Out of about 300

Tonkawa 137 were massacred, and the survivors, after some years of miserable wandering, were gathered into Fort Griffin, Tex., where they might be protected from their enemies. In 1884 all that were left were given a small reservation in northern Oklahoma, near the Ponca, where their descendants still live.

Population.—Mooney (1928) estimated that in 1690 there were about 1,600 Tonkawa. A Spanish estimate of 1778 gives 300 warriors but the following year, after an epidemic of smallpox, this is cut in half. In 1782, 600 were said to have attended a certain meeting and this was only a portion of the tribe. Sibley (1832) estimated that in 1805 they had 200 men. In 1809 there were said to be 250 families and in 1828, 80. In 1847 the official estimate was 150 men. Before the massacre of 1862 there were supposed to be about 300 all told, but when they were placed on their reservation in 1884 there were only 92. In 1908 there were 48 including a few intermarried Lipan; the census of 1910 gave 42, but that of 1930 restores the figure to 48, and in 1937 there were said to be 51.

Connection in which they have become noted.—The Tonkawan tribes have the following claims to remembrance: (1) On account of the uniqueness of their language, (2) for their reputed addiction to cannibalism, (3) on account of the massacre perpetrated upon them partly in consequence of this reputation, as above described. The city of Tonkawa in Kay County, Okla., perpetuates the name.

Waco. The Waco were a subtribe or tribe of the Wichita group which lived near the present Waco for a limited period before removal to Oklahoma (q. v.).

Wichita. The Wichita lived for a time along both sides of Red River in northern Texas. (See Oklahoma.)

NEW MEXICO

Apache. Probably from ápachu, "enemy," the Zuñi name for the Navaho who were designated "Apaches de Nabaju" by the early Spaniards in New Mexico. The name has also been applied to some Yuman tribes, the Apache Mohave (Yavapai) and the Apache Yuma. Also called:

> Ahuádjĕ, Havasupai name for at least Tonto and White Mountain Apache.
> Ai-a'-ta, Panamint name.
> Atokúwe, Kiowa name.
> Awátch or Awátche, Ute name.
> Chah'-shm, Santo Domingo Keres name.
> Chĭshyë, Laguna name.
> Ha-ma-kaba-mitc kwa-dig, Mohave name, meaning "far-away Mohave."
> H'iwana, Taos name.
> Igihua'-a, Havasupai name.

Inde or Nde, own name.

Jarosoma, Pima name (from Kino).

Mountain Comanche, by Yoakum (1855–56).

Muχtsuhintan, Cheyenne name.

Oop, Papago name.

Op, or Awp, Pima name.

Póanĭn, Sandia and Isleta name (Hodge, 1895).

P'ónin, Isleta name (Gatschet, MS., B. A. E.).

Shis-Inday, own name meaning "men of the woods," because their winter quarters were always in the forest.

Tá-ashi, Comanche name, meaning "turned up," and having reference to their moccasins.

Tagúi, Old Kiowa name.

Tágukerésh, Pecos name.

Tashĭn, Comanche name (Mooney, 1898).

Taχkáhe, Arapaho name.

Thah-a-i-nin', Arapaho name, meaning "people who play on bone instruments," meaning two bison ribs, one notched, over which the other is rubbed.

Tinnä'-ash, Wichita name.

Tshishé, Laguna name.

Utce-cí-nyu-mûh or Utsaamu, or Yotché-eme, Hopi name.

Xa-hë'-ta-ño', Cheyenne name meaning "those who tie their hair back."

Connections.—Together with the Navaho, the Apache constituted the western group of the southern division of the Athapascan linguistic stock (Hoijer, 1938).

Location.—In southern New Mexico and Arizona, western Texas, and southeastern Colorado, also ranging over much of northern Mexico. (See also Kansas, Oklahoma, and México.)

Subdivisions

On linguistic grounds Hoijer (1938) divides the southern Athapascans into two main groups, a western and an eastern. The latter includes the Jicarilla, Lipan, and Kiowa Apache, the two former being more closely related to each other than either is to the Kiowa Apache. In the western group Hoijer again distinguishes two major subdivisions, the Navaho, and the San Carlos-Chiricahua-Mescalero. The Navaho are always regarded as a distinct tribe and will be so treated here. Separate treatment is also being given to the Jicarilla, Lipan, and Kiowa Apache. The rest of the southern Athapascans will be placed under the present head, it being freely admitted at the same time that such treatment is mainly a matter of convenience and that it is impossible to say how many and what southern Athapascan divisions should be given tribal status. What is here called the Apache Tribe may be classified as follows with the locations of the divisions, basing the scheme on the classifications of Hoijer and Goodwin (1935):

1. San Carlos Group:
   San Carlos proper:
   > Apache Peaks Band, in the Apache Mountains, northeast of Globe.
   > Arivaipa Band, on Arivaipa Creek.
   > Pinal Band, between Salt and Gila Rivers in Gila and Pinal Counties.
   > San Carlos Band, in the region of San Carlos River between Gila and Salt Rivers.

1. San Carlos Group—Continued.
    White Mountain Group:
        Eastern White Mountain Band, in the region of the upper Gila and Salt
        Rivers in southeastern Arizona.
        Western White Mountain Band, in the same region between the Eastern
        Band and the San Carlos Band.
    Cibecue Group:
        Canyon Creek Band, centering on Canyon Creek in Gila and Navajo
        Counties.
        Carrizo Band, on Carrizo Creek in Gila County.
        Cibicue Band, on Cibecue Creek between the two last.
    Southern Tonto Group:
        Mazatzal Band, about the Mazatzal Mountains.
        Six semibands: north of Roosevelt Lake; on the upper Tonto Creek;
        between the upper Tonto and the East Verde; west of the preceding
        between the East Verde, Tonto, and Verde; north of the East Verde;
        and from Cherry Creek to Clear Creek.
    Northern Tonto Group:
        Bald Mountain Band, about Bald Mountain, south of Camp Verde.
        Fossil Creek Band, on Fossil Creek between Gila and Yavapai Counties.
        Mormon Lake Band, centering on Mormon Lake south of Flagstaff.
        Oak Creek Band, about Oak Creek south of Flagstaff.
2. Chiricahua-Mescalero Group:
    Gileños Group:
        Chiricahua Band, about the Chiricahua Mountains in southeastern
        Arizona.
        Mimbreño Band, centered in the Mimbres Mountains in southwestern
        New Mexico.
        Mogollon Band, about the Mogollon Mountains in Catron and Grant
        Counties, N. Mex.
        Warm Spring Band, at the head of Gila River.
    Mescalero Group:
        Faraon or Apache Band of Pharaoh, a southern division of the Mescalero.
        Mescalero Band, mainly between the Rio Grande and Pecos Rivers,
        N. Mex.

The term Querecho, as well as Vaquero, was applied rather generally to Apache
by the Spaniards but probably more particularly to the Mescalero and their
allies. Under Llanero were included Mescalero, Jicarilla, and even some Comanche. The term Coyotero has been applied to some of the San Carlos divisions
and recently by Murdock (1941) to all.

History.—The Apache tribes had evidently drifted from the north
during the prehistoric period, probably along the eastern flanks of
the Rocky Mountains. When Coronado encountered them in 1540
under the name Querechos, they were in eastern New Mexico and
western Texas, and they apparently did not reach Arizona until after
the middle of the sixteenth century. They were first called Apache
by Oñate in 1598. After that time their history was one succession
of raids upon the Spanish territories, and after the United States
Government had supplanted that of México in the Southwest, the
wars with the Apache constituted some of the most sensational

chapters in our military annals.   Except for some Apache in México
and a few Lipans with the Tonkawa and Kiowa in Oklahoma, these
people were finally gathered into reservations in New Mexico and
Arizona.

Population.—Mooney (1928) estimated that all of the Apache
proper numbered 5,000 in 1680.   The census of 1910 gives 6,119
Apache of all kinds, excluding only the Kiowa Apache, and the
Report of the United States Indian Office for 1923 enumerates 6,630.
If an increase has actually occurred, it is to be attributed to the
captives taken by these people from all the surrounding tribes and
from the Mexicans.   The census of 1930 returned 6,537 but this
includes the Jicarilla and Lipan.   The Apache proper would number
about 6,000.   However, the Indian Office Report for 1937 gives
6,916 exclusive of the Jicarilla.

Connection in which they have become noted.—Apache is one of the
best-known Indian tribal names.   This is due (1) to the warlike
character of the people bearing it, (2) to their constant depredations
along the Spanish and American frontiers, and (3) to the severe and
difficult fighting made necessary before they were forced to give up
their ancient raiding proclivities.   The word has, therefore, been
taken over to some extent into literature when it is desired to describe
fierce and ruthless individuals, and in this sense it has been given
local application to some of the criminal elements of Paris.   The
name Apache is given to villages in Cochise County, Ariz., and Caddo
County, Okla., and Apache Creek is a place in Catron County, N. Mex.

Comanche.   In the Spanish period, the Comanche raided into and
across the territory of New Mexico repeatedly.   (See Texas.)

Jemez.   Corrupted from Ha'-mish or Hae'-mish, the Keresan name
of the pueblo.   Also spelled Amayes, Ameias, Amejes, Emeges,
Gemes, etc.   Also called:

> Maí-děc-kǐž-ne, Navaho name, meaning "wolf neck."
> Tu'-wa, own name of pueblo.
> Uala-to-hua or Walatoa, own name of pueblo, meaning "village of the
> bear."
> Wŏng'-ge, Santa Clara and Ildefonso name, meaning "Navaho place."

Connections.—With the now extinct Pecos, the Jemez constituted
a distinct group of the Tanoan linguistic family now a part of the
Kiowa-Tanoan stock.

Location.—On the north bank of Jemez River, about 20 miles northwest of Bernalillo.

Villages

The following names of villages have been recorded as formerly occupied by
the Jemez but the list may contain some duplication:

Amushungkwa, on a mesa west of the Hot Springs, about 12 miles north of Jemez
pueblo.

Anyukwinu, north of Jemez pueblo.
Astialakwa, on the summit of a mesa that separates San Diego and Guadalupe Canyons at their mouths.
Bulitzequa, exact site unknown.
Catróo, site not identified.
Ceca, not identified.
Guatitruti, not identified.
Guayoguia, not identified.
Gyusiwa, one-half mile north of Jemez Hot Springs, on a slope descending to the river from the east in Sandoval County.
Hanakwa, not identified.
Kiashita, in Guadalupe Canyon, north of Jemez pueblo.
Kiatsukwa, not identified.
Mecastria, not identified.
Nokyuntseleta, not identified.
Nonyishagi, not identified.
Ostyalakwa, not identified.
Patoqua, on a ledge of the mesa which separates Guadalupe and San Diego Canyons, 6 miles north of Jemez pueblo.
Pebulikwa, not identified.
Pekwiligii, not identified.
Potre, not identified.
Seshukwa, not identified.
Setokwa, about 2 miles south of Jemez pueblo.
Towakwa, not identified.
Trea, not identified.
Tyajuindena, not identified.
Uahatzae, not identified.
Wabakwa, on a mesa north of Jemez pueblo.
Yjar, not identified.
Zolatungzezhii, not identified.

History.—The Jemez came from the north, according to tradition, settling in the valleys of the upper tributaries of the Jemez River and at last in the sandy valley of the Jemez proper. Castañeda, the chronicler of Coronado's expedition, mentions seven towns belonging to the Jemez tribe besides three in the region of Jemez Hot Springs. After they had been missionized they were induced to abandon their towns by degrees until about 1622 they became concentrated into the pueblos of Gyusiwa and probably Astialakwa. Both pueblos contained chapels, probably dating from 1618, but before the Pueblo revolt of 1680 Astialakwa was abandoned and another pueblo, probably Patoqua, established. About the middle of the seventeenth century, in conjunction with the Navaho, the Jemez twice plotted insurrection against the Spaniards. After the insurrection of 1680 the Jemez were attacked by Spanish forces led successively by Otermin, Cruzate, and Vargas, the last of whom stormed the mesa in July 1694, killed 84 Indians, and after destroying Patoqua and two other pueblos, returned to Santa Fé with 361 prisoners and a large quantity of stores. Gyusiwa was the only Jemez pueblo reoccupied, but in 1696 there was a second revolt and the Jemez finally fled to the Navaho country, where they remained for a considerable time before returning to their former home. Then they built their present village, called by them Walatoa, "Village of the Bear." In 1728, 108 of the inhabitants died of pestilence. In 1782 Jemez was made a visita of the mission of Sia. In 1838 they were joined by the remnant of their relatives, the Pecos Indians from the upper Rio Pecos. Their subsequent history has been uneventful.

Population.—Mooney (1928) estimates the Jemez population at 2,500 in 1680. In 1890 it was 428; in 1904, 498, including the remnant of Pecos Indians; in 1910, 499. In 1930 the entire Tanoan stock numbered 3,412. In 1937 the Jemez Indians numbered 648.

Jicarilla. An Apache tribe which ranged over the northeastern corner of New Mexico. (See Colorado.)

Keresan Pueblos. Keresan is adapted from K'eres, their own designation. Also called:

> BiernI'n, Sandia name.
> Cherechos, Oñate in 1598.
> Drinkers of the Dew, Zuñi traditional name.
> Ing-wĕ-pi'-raⁿ-di-vi-he-maⁿ, San Ildefonso Tewa name.
> PabiernI'n, Isleta name.

Connections.—These Indians constituted an independent stock having no affiliations with any other.

Location.—On the Rio Grande, in north central New Mexico, between the Rio de los Frijoles and the Rio Jemez, and on the latter stream from the pueblo of Sia to its mouth.

Subdivisions and Villages

The Keresan Indians are divided dialectically into an Eastern (Queres) Group and a Western (Sitsime or Kawaiko) Group, comprising the following pueblos:

Eastern (Queres) Group:

> Cochiti, on the west bank of the Rio Grande, 27 miles southwest of Santa Fé.
> San Felipe, on the west bank of the Rio Grande about 12 miles above Bernalillo.
> Santa Ana, on the north bank of the Rio Jemez.
> Santo Domingo, on the east bank of the Rio Grande about 18 miles above Bernalillo.
> Sia, on the north bank of Jemez River about 16 miles northwest of Bernalillo.

Western (Sitsime or Kawaiko) Group:

> Acoma, on a rock mesa or peñol, 357 feet in height, about 60 miles west of the Rio Grande, in Valencia County.
> Laguna, on the south bank of San José River, in Valencia County.

In addition to the above principal towns, we have the following ancient towns and later out-villages recorded:

Former towns of Cochiti and San Felipe:
  At the Potrero de las Vacas.
  At Tyuonyi or Rito de los Frijoles.
  Haatze, near the foot of the Sierra San Miguel, about Cochiti Pueblo.
  Hanut Cochiti, about 12 miles northwest of Cochiti Pueblo.
  Kuapa, in the Cañada de Cochiti, 12 miles northwest of Cochiti Pueblo.
Former towns of Santo Domingo:
  At the Potrero de la Cañada Quemada.
  Gipuy, two towns: (1) on the banks of the Arroyo de Galisteo, more than a
    mile east of the present station of Thornton; (2) west of No. 1.
  Huashpatzena, on the Rio Grande.
Former towns of Sia:
  Opposite Sia are the ruins of a town called Kakanatzia and south of it another
    called Kohasaya which may have been former Sia settlements.
Former towns of Acoma:
  Kashkachuti, location unknown.
  Katzimo or the Enchanted Mesa, about 3 miles northeast of the present Acoma
    Pueblo.
  Kowina, on a low mesa opposite the spring at the head of Cebollita Valley,
    about 15 miles west of Acoma.
  Kuchtya, location unknown.
  Tapitsiama, on a mesa 4 or 5 miles northeast of their present pueblo.
  Tsiama, the ruins are situated at the mouth of Cañada de la Cruz, at or near
    the present Laguna village of Tsima.
Later villages:
  Acomita, about 15 miles north of Acoma.
  Heashkowa, about 2 miles southeast of Acoma.
  Pueblito, about 15 miles north of Acoma.

History.—Like the other Pueblo peoples of New Mexico, the Keresans traced their origin to the underworld, whence they had emerged at an opening called Shipapu. According to the tradition, they afterward drifted south slowly to the Rio Grande, where they took up their residence in the Rito de los Frijoles, or Tyuonyi, and constructed the cliff dwellings found there today excavated in the friable volcanic tufa. Long before the coming of Europeans, they had abandoned the Rito and moved farther south, separating into a number of autonomous village communities. Coronado, who visited them in 1540, reported seven of these. In 1583 Espejo encountered them and in 1598 Oñate. Missions were established in most of the principal towns early in the seventeenth century, but they were annihilated and Spanish dominion temporarily brought to an end by the great Pueblo rebellion of 1680, which was not finally quelled until about the end of the eighteenth century. Afterward, missionary work was resumed but without pronounced success, while the native population itself gradually declined in numbers. Although some of the most conservative pueblos belong to this group, they will not be able indefinitely to resist the dissolving force of American civilization in which they are immersed.

Population.—In 1760 there were 3,956 Keresans; in 1790–93, 4,021; in 1805, 3,653; in 1850, 3,342; in 1860, 2,676; in 1871, 3,317; in 1901–5, 4,249; in 1910, 4,027; in 1930, 4,134; in 1937, 5,781.

Kiowa. The Kiowa raided into and across New Mexico in the Spanish and early American period. (See Oklahoma.)

Kiowa Apache. The Kiowa Apache were an Athapascan tribe incorporated into and accompanying the Kiowa. (See Oklahoma.)

Lipan. The Lipan were the easternmost of the Apache tribes. (See **Apache** and also **Texas**.)

Manso. A Spanish word meaning "mild." Also called:

> Gorretas, by Zarate-Salmeron.
> Lanos, by Perea (1632–33).

Connections.—The Manso belonged to the Tanoan division of the Kiowa-Tanoan linguistic stock.

Location.—About Mesilla Valley, in the vicinity of the present Las Cruces, N. Mex.

Villages

The mission of Nuestra Señora de Guadalupe de los Mansos was founded among them but none of the native names of their villages are known.

History.—Shortly before the appearance of the Spaniards in their country, the Manso lived in substantial houses like the Pueblo Indians generally but changed these to dwellings of reeds and wood. They were relocated at a spot near El Paso in 1659 by Fray Garcia de San Francisco, who established the above-mentioned mission among them. The remnant of the Manso are now associated in one town with the Tiwa and Piro.

Population.—In 1668, when the mission of Nuestra Señora de Guadalupe de los Mansos was dedicated, Vetancourt states that it contained upward of 1,000 parishioners. Very few of Manso blood remain.

Navaho, Navajo. From Tewa Navahú, referring to a large area of cultivated land and applied to a former Tewa pueblo, and by extension to the Navaho, known to the Spaniards as "Apaches de Navajó," who intruded on the Tewa domain or who lived in the vicinity, to distinguish them from other so-called Apache bands. Also called:

> Bágowits, Southern Ute name.
> Dacábimo, Hopi name.
> Dávaχo, Kiowa Apache name.
> Díné', own name.
> Djëné, Laguna name.
> Hua'ámú'u, Havasupai name.
> I'hl-dëné, Jicarilla name.
> Moshome, Keresan name.
> Oop, Oohp, Pima name.

Págowitch, southern Ute name, meaning "reed knives."

Ta-cáb-cí-nyu-mûh, Hopi name.

Ta'hlï'mnïn, Sandia name.

Tasámewé, Hopi name (Ten Kate, 1885) meaning "bastards."

Te'liémnim, Isleta name.

Tenyé, Laguna name.

Wild Coyotes, Zuñi nickname translated.

Yabipais Nabajay, Garcés (1776).

Yátilatlávi, Tonto name.

Yoetahá or Yutahá, Apache name, meaning "those who live on the border of the Ute."

Yu-i'-ta, Panamint name.

Yutílapá, Yavapai name.

Yutilatláwi, Tonto name.

Connections.—With the Apache tribes, the Navaho formed the southern division of the Athapascan linguistic family.

Location.—In northern New Mexico and Arizona with some extension into Colorado and Utah.

History.—Under the loosely applied name Apache there may be a record of this tribe as early as 1598 but the first mention of them by the name of Navaho is by Zarate-Salmeron about 1629. Missionaries were among them about the middle of the eighteenth century, but their labors seem to have borne no fruits. For many years previous to the occupation of their country by the United States, the Navaho kept up an almost constant predatory war with the Pueblo Indians and the White settlers. A revolution in their economy was brought about by the introduction of sheep. Treaties of peace made by them with the United States Government in 1846 and 1849 were not observed, and in 1863, in order to put a stop to their depredations, Col. "Kit" Carson invaded their country, killed so many of their sheep as to leave them without means of support, and carried the greater part of the tribe as prisoners to Fort Sumner and the Bosque Redondo on the Rio Pecos. They were restored to their country in 1867 and given a new supply of sheep and goats, and since then they have remained at peace and prospered greatly, thanks to their flocks and the sale of their famous blankets.

Population.—Mooney (1928) estimates that there were 8,000 Navaho in 1680. In 1867 an incomplete enumeration gave 7,300. In 1869 there were fewer than 9,000. The census of 1890, taken on a faulty system, gave 17,204. The census of 1900 returned more than 20,000 and that of 1910, 22,455. The report of the United States Indian Office for 1923 gives more than 30,000 on the various Navaho reservations, and the 1930 census 39,064, while the Indian Office Report for 1937 entered 44,304.

Connection in which they have become noted.—This tribe has acquired considerable fame from its early adoption of a shepherd life after the introduction of sheep and goats, and from the blankets woven by Navaho women and widely known to collectors and connoisseurs. The name has become affixed, in the Spanish form Navajo, to a county, creek, and spring in Arizona; a post village in Apache County, Ariz.; a mountain in New Mexico; and a place in Daniels County, Mont. In southwestern Oklahoma is a post village known as Navajoe. The tribe has attracted an unusual amount of attention from ethnologists and from writers whose interests are purely literary.

Pecos. From P'e'-a-ku', the Keresan name of the pueblo. Also called:

> Acuyé, Cicuyé, probably the name of a former pueblo, Tshiquité or Tziquité.
> Aqiu, Pecos and Jemez name.
> Hiokŭŏ'k, Isleta Tiwa name.
> K'ok'-o-ro-t'ŭ'-yu, Pecos name of pueblo.
> Los Angeles, mission name.
> Nuestra Señora de los Angeles de Porciúncula, full church name.
> Paego, Keresan name of Pueblo.
> Paequiu or Paequiuala, Keresan name of tribe.
> P'a-qu-láh, Jemez name.
> Péahko, Santa Ana name.
> Peakŭní, Laguna name of Pueblo.
> Tamos, from Espejo.

Connections.—The Pecos belonged to the Jemez division of the Tanoan linguistic family, itself a part of the Kiowa-Tanoan stock.

Location.—On an upper branch of Pecos River, about 30 miles southeast of Santa Fé.

Villages

The following are names of ruined Pecos villages:

Kuuanguala, a few miles southeast of Pecos, near Arroyo Amarillo, at the present site of Rowe.

Pomojoua, near San Antonio del Pueblo, 3 miles southeast of San Miguel, San Miguel County.

San Jose, modern Spanish name of locality.

Seyupa, a few miles southeast of Pecos, at the site of the village of Fulton, San Miguel County.

Tonchuun, 5 miles southeast of Pecos Pueblo.

History.—According to tradition, the Pecos came originally from some place to the north of their historic seats, but their last migration was from the southeast where they occupied successively the now ruined pueblos at San José and Kingman before locating at their final settlement. Pecos was first visited by Coronado in 1540 and afterward by Espejo in 1583, Castaño de Sosa in 1590–91, and Oñate in 1598. During the governorship of Oñate, missionaries were assigned to Pecos, and the great church, so long a landmark of the Santa Fé Trail, was erected about 1617. The town suffered severely

from attacks of the Apache of the Plains and afterward from the
Comanche. In the Pueblo revolts of 1680–96 it took an active part
and suffered proportionately. In 1782 the Pecos mission was abandoned, the place becoming a visita of Santa Fé. A few years later
nearly every man in the Pecos tribe is said to have been killed in a
raid by the Comanche, epidemics decreased the numbers of the
remainder, and in 1838 the old town of Pecos was abandoned. The
17 surviving Pecos Indians moved to Jemez, where their descendants
still live.

Population.—At the time of Coronado's visit in 1540 the population
was estimated as 2,000–2,500. In 1630 and 1680 there were 2,000
Pecos; in 1760, 599 (including Galisteo); in 1790–93, 152; in 1805,
104; in 1838, 17; in 1910, 10.

Connection in which they have become noted.—The name Pecos seems
assured of permanent preservation as applied to Pecos River, Tex.,
the largest branch of the Rio Grande, as well as to Pecos County,
Tex., and its principal town, and also to a place in San Miguel County,
New Mex., adjacent to the ruins of the aboriginal village. The
latter are well known as a result of the archeological work done there
by Dr. A. V. Kidder for the Department of Archeology, Phillips
Academy, Andover, Mass.

Piro Pueblos.   Significance of Piro unknown.   Also called:

> Norteños, "northerners" in Spanish, because inhabiting the region of
> El Paso del Norte (may also refer to Tiwa).
> Tükahun, Isleta Tiwa name for all pueblos below their village, meaning
> "southern pueblos."

Connections.—They were a division of the Tanoan linguistic family,
which in turn is a part of the Kiowa-Tanoan stock.

Location and major subdivisions.—In the early part of the seventeenth century the Piro comprised two divisions, one inhabiting the
Rio Grande Valley from the present town of San Marcial, Socorro
County, northward to within about 50 miles of Albuquerque, where
the Tiwa settlements began; and the other, sometimes called Tompiros
and Salineros, occupying an area east of the Rio Grande in the
vicinity of the salt lagoons, or salinas, where they adjoined the eastern
group of Tiwa settlements on the south.

Towns

Abo, on the Arroyo del Empedradillo, about 25 miles east of the Rio Grande and
    20 miles south of Manzano, in Valencia County.
Agua Nueva, on the Rio Grande between Socorro and Servilleta.
Alamillo, on the Rio Grande about 12 miles north of Socorro.
Barrancas, on the Rio Grande near Socorro.
Qualacu, on the east bank of the Rio Grande near the foot of the Black Mesa,
    on or near the site of San Marcial.

San Felipe, on the Rio Grande, probably near the present San Marcial, Socorro County.

San Pascual, on the east bank of the Rio Grande, opposite the present San Antonio village, Socorro County.

Senecu, on the west bank of the Rio Grande, at the site of the present village of San Antonio, 13 miles below Socorro.

Senecu del Sur (also Tiwa), on the southeast bank of the Rio Grande, a few miles below El Paso, in Chihuahua, México.

Sevilleta, on the east bank of the Rio Grande about 20 miles above Socorro.

Socorro or Pilabo, on the site of the present Socorro.

Socorro del Sur, on both sides of the Rio Grande a few miles below El Paso, Tex.

Tabira, at the southern apex of the Mesa de los Jumanos, northeast of the present Socorro.

Tenabo, probably at the Siete Arroyos, northeast of Socorro and east of the Rio Grande.

Teypana, nearly opposite the present town of Socorro, on the east bank of the Rio Grande, in Socorro Couuty.

Tenaquel (?).

Following are names of deserted pueblos near the lower Rio Grande which were also in all probability occupied by the Piro:

Amo.

Aponitre.

Aquicabo.

Atepua.

Ayqui.

Calciati.

Canocan.

Cantensapué.

Cunquilipinoy.

Encaquiagualcaca.

Huertas, 4 miles below Socorro.

Peixolóe.

Pencoana.

Penjeacú.

Pesquis.

Peytre.

Polooca.

Preguey.

Pueblo Blanco, on the west rim of the Médano, or great sand-flow, east of the Rio Grande.

Pueblo Colorado, same location as Pueblo Blanco.

Pueblo de la Parida, same location as Pueblos Blanco and Colorado.

Pueblo del Alto, on the east side of the Rio Grande, 6 miles south of Belen.

Queelquelu.

Quialpo.

Quiapo.

Quiomaquí.

Quiubaco.

Tecahanqualahámo.

Teeytraan.

Tercáo.

Texa.

Teyaxa.

Tobol.

Trelagú.

Trelaquepú.

Treyéy.

Treypual.

Trula.

Tuzahe.

Vumahein.

Yancomo.

Zumaque.

The following deserted pueblos were inhabited either by the Piro or the Tiwa:

Acoli.

Aggey.

Alle.

Amaxa.

Apena.

Atuyama.

Axauti.

Chein.

Cizentetpi.

Couna.

Dhiu.

Hohota.

Mejia, 5 leagues below Isleta.

Quanquiz.

Salineta, 4 leagues from Guadelupe Mission at El Paso, Tex.

San Bautista, on the Rio Grande, 16 miles below Sevilleta.

San Francisco, on the lower Rio Grande between El Paso, Tex., and San Lorenzo.

Xatoe.

Xiamela (?).

Yonalus.

All the above pueblos not definitely located were probably situated in the Salinas in the vicinity of Abo.

History.—The western or Rio Grande branch of the Piro was visited by members of Coronado's Expedition in 1540, by Chamuscado in 1580, by Espejo in 1583, by Oñate in 1598, and by Benavides in 1621–30. The establishment of missionaries among them began in 1626, and the efforts of the monks combined with the threats of Apache raids to induce the Indians to concentrate into a smaller number of towns. The first actual mission work among the Piros of the Salinas began in 1629 and was prosecuted rapidly, but before the Pueblo rebellion of 1680 Apache raids had become so numerous that all of the villages of the Salinas region and Senecu on the Rio Grande were abandoned. The Piro were not invited to take part in the great rebellion and when Governor Otermin retreated to El Paso nearly all of them joined him, while the few who remained subsequently scattered. Those who accompanied the governor were settled at Senecu del Sur and Socorro del Sur, where their descendants became largely Mexicanized.

Population.—The Piro population was estimated at 9,000 early in the sixteenth century, but is now about 60. (See **Tewa.**)

Pueblo Indians. A general name for those Indians in the Southwest who dwelt in stone buildings as opposed to the tribes living in more fragile shelters, pueblo being the word for "town" or "village" in Spanish. It is not a tribal or even a stock name, since the Pueblos belonged to four distinct stocks. Following is the classification of Pueblos made by F. W. Hodge (1910) except that the Kiowa have since been connected with the Tanoans and a few minor changes have been introduced:

Kiowa-Tanoan linguistic stock:
> Tewa Group:
>> Northern Division: Nambe, Tesuque, San Ildefonso, San Juan, Santa Clara, Pojoaque (recently extinct), Hano.
>> Southern Division: Tano (practically extinct).
> Tiwa Group: Isleta, Isleta del Sur (Mexicanized), Sandia, Taos, Picuris.
> Jemez Group: Jemez, Pecos (extinct).
> Piro Group: Senecu, Senecu del Sur (Mexicanized).

Keresan linguistic stock:
> Eastern Group: San Felipe, Santa Ana, Sia, Cochiti, Santo Domingo.
> Western Group: Acoma, Laguna, and outlying villages.

Zuñian linguistic stock:
   Zuñi Group: Zuñi and its outlying villages.
Shoshonean linguistic stock, part of the Uto-Aztecan stock:
   Hopi Group: Walpi, Sichomovi, Mishongnovi, Shipaulovi, Shongopovi, Oraibi.

The Pueblo Indians in New Mexico are being considered at length under the following heads: Jemez, Keresan Pueblos, Piro Pueblos, Tewa Pueblos, Tiwa Pueblos, and Zuñi; the Hopi are considered under Arizona. (See also Colorado, Nevada, and Texas.)

Connection in which they have become noted.—The Pueblo Indians have become famous from the fact that, unlike all of their neighbors, they lived in communal stone houses and in stone dwellings perched along the canyon walls; from their peculiar customs and ceremonies, such as the Snake Dance; and from their real and supposed connection with the builders of the stone ruins with which their country and neighboring parts of the Southwest abound. In recent years they have been subjects of interest to artists and writers and an attempt has been made to base a style of architecture upon the type of their dwellings. They are of historic interest as occupants of one of the two sections of the United States first colonized by Europeans.

Shuman. The Shuman lived at various times in or near the southern and eastern borders of New Mexico. (See Texas.)

Tewa Pueblos. The name Tewa is from a Keres word meaning "moccasins." Also called:

   Tŭ'-ba-na, Taos name.
   Tu'-vĕn, Isleta and Sandia name.

Connections.—They constituted a major division of the Tanoan linguistic family, itself a part of the Kiowa-Tanoan stock.

Location.—Along the valley of the Rio Grande in the northern part of New Mexico, except for one pueblo, Hano, in the Hopi country, Arizona.

Subdivisions

They consisted of two main branches, the Northern Tewa, from near Santa Fé to the mouth of the Rio Chama, including also Hano; and the Southern Tewa or Tano, from Santa Fé to the neighborhood of Golden, back from the Rio Grande.

Towns

Northern Tewa towns and villages still occupied:

Hano, the easternmost pueblo of Tusayan, Ariz.
Nambe, about 16 miles north of Santa Fé, on Nambe River, a small tributary of the Rio Grande.
San Ildefonso, near the eastern bank of the Rio Grande, about 18 miles northwest of Santa Fé.
San Juan, near the eastern bank of the Rio Grande 25 miles northwest of Sante Fé.

Santa Clara, on the western bank of the Rio Grande, about 30 miles above Santa Fé.

Tesuque, 8 miles north of Santa Fé.

Towns and villages formerly occupied by the Northern Tewa:

Abechiu, at a place called Le Puente, on a bluff close to the southern bank of Rio Chama, 3 miles southeast of the present town of Abiquiu, Rio Arriba County.

Agawano, in the mountains about 7 miles east of the Rio Grande, on Rio Santa Cruz.

Analco, at the place where there is now the so-called "oldest house," adjacent to San Miguel Chapel, in Santa Fé.

Axol, location uncertain.

Camitria, in Rio Arriba County.

Chipiinuinge, on a small but high detached mesa between the Cañones and Polvadera Creek, 4 miles south of Chama and about 14 miles southwest of Abiquiu, Rio Arriba County.

Chipiwi, location uncertain.

Chupadero, location uncertain.

Cuyamunque, on Tesuque Creek, between Tesuque and Pojoaque, about 15 miles northwest of Santa Fé.

Fejiu, at the site of the present Abiquiu on the Rio Chama, Rio Arriba County.

Fesere, on a mesa west or south of the Rio Chama, near Abiquiu, Rio Arriba County.

Homayo, on the west bank of Rio Ojo Caliente, a small western tributary of the Rio Grande, in Rio Arriba County.

Howiri, at the Rito Colorado, about 10 miles west of the Hot Springs, near Abiquiu, Rio Arriba County.

Ihamba, on the south side of Pojoaque River, between Pojoaque and San Ildefonso Pueblos.

Jacona, a short distance west of Nambe, on the south side of Pojoaque River, Santa Fé County.

Junetre, in Rio Arriba County.

Kaayu, in the vicinity of the "Santuario" in the mountains about 7 miles east of the Rio Grande, on Rio Santa Cruz, Santa Fé County.

Keguayo, in the vicinity of the Chupaderos, a cluster of springs in a mountain gorge, about 4 miles east of Nambe Pueblo.

Kuapooge, with Analco occupying the site of Santa Fé.

Kwengyauinge, on a conical hill about 15 feet high, overlooking Chama River, at a point known as La Puenta, about 3 miles below Abiquiu, Rio Arriba County.

Luceros, partially Tewa.

Navahu, in the second valley south of the great pueblo and cliff village of Puye, west of Santa Clara Pueblo, in the Pajarito Park.

Navawi, between the Rito de los Frijoles and Santa Clara Canyon, southwest of San Ildefonso.

Otowi, on a mesa about 5 miles west of the point where the Rio Grande enters White Rock Canyon, between the Rito de los Frijoles and Santa Clara Canyon, in the northeastern corner of Sandoval County.

Perage, a few rods from the west bank of the Rio Grande, about 1 mile west of San Ildefonso Pueblo.

Pininicangui, on a knoll in a valley about 2 miles south of Puye and 3 miles south of Santa Clara Creek, on the Pajarito Plateau, Sandoval County.

Pojiuuingge, at La Joya, about 10 miles north of San Juan Pueblo.

Pojoaque, on a small eastern tributary of the Rio Grande, about 18 miles north-west of Santa Fé.

Ponyinumbu, near the Mexican settlement of Santa Cruz, in the northern part of Santa Fé County.

Ponyipakuen, near Ojo Caliente and El Rito, about the boundary of Taos and Rio Arriba Counties.

Poseuingge, at the Rito Colorado, about 10 miles west of the hot springs near Abiquiu.

Potzuye, on a mesa west of the Rio Grande in northern New Mexico, between San Ildefonso Pueblo on the north and the Rito de los Frijoles on the south.

Pueblito, opposite San Juan Pueblo, on the west bank of the Rio Grande in Rio Arriba County.

Pueblo Quemado (or Tano), 6 miles southwest of Santa Fé.

Puye, on a mesa about 10 miles west of the Rio Grande and a mile south of Santa Clara Canyon, near the intersection of the boundaries of Rio Arriba, Sandoval, and Santa Fé Counties.

Sajiuwingge, at La Joya, about 10 miles north of San Juan Pueblo, Rio Arriba County.

Sakeyu on a mesa west of the Rio Grande in northern New Mexico, between San Ildefonso Pueblo and Rito de los Frijoles.

Sandia, not the Tiwa pueblo of that name.

Santa Cruz, east of the Rio Grande, 30 miles northwest of Santa Fé, at the site of the present town of that name.

Sepawi, in the valley of El Rito Creek, on the heights above the Ojo Caliente of Joseph, and 5 miles from the Mexican settlement of El Rito.

Shufina, on a castlelike mesa of tufa northwest of Puye and separated from it by Santa Clara Canyon.

Teeuinge, on top of the mesa on the south side of Rio Chama, about ¼ mile from the river and an equal distance below the mouth of Rio Oso, in Rio Arriba County.

Tejeuingge Ouiping, on the southern slope of the hills on which stands the present pueblo of San Juan, on the Rio Grande.

Tobhipangge, 8 miles northeast of the present Nambe Pueblo.

Triapí, location uncertain.

Triaque, location uncertain.

Troomaxiaquino, in Rio Arriba County.

Tsankawi, on a lofty mesa between the Rito de los Frijoles on the south and Los Alamos Canyon on the north, about 5 miles west of the Rio Grande.

Tsawarii, at or near the present hamlet of La Puebla, or Pueblito, a few miles above the town of Santa Cruz, in southeastern Rio Arriba County.

Tseweige, location uncertain.

Tshirege, on the northern edge of the Mesa del Pajarito about 6 miles west of the Rio Grande and 7 miles south of San Ildefonso Pueblo.

Yugeuingge, on the west bank of the Rio Grande, opposite the present pueblo of San Juan, near the site of the village of Chamita.

The following extinct villages are either Tewa or Tano:

Chiuma, location uncertain.

Guia, on the Rio Grande in the vicinity of Albuquerque.

Guika, on the Rio Grande near Albuquerque.

Peñas Negras, on an eminence west of Pecos Road, near the edge of a forest, 8 miles south-southeast of Santa Fé.

The following were inhabited by either the Tiwa or the Tewa:

Axoytre, perhaps the same as Axol above?

Camitre, perhaps the same as Camitria above?

Paniete, location uncertain.

Piamato, location uncertain.

Quiotráco, probably in Rio Arriba County.

So far as known the following pueblos belonged to the Southern Tewa:

Ciénega (also contained Keresan Indians), in the valley of Rio Santa Fé, 12 miles southwest of Santa Fé.

Dyapige, southeast of Lamy, "some distance in the mountains."

Galisteo, 1½ miles southeast of the present hamlet of the name and about 22 miles south of Santa Fé.

Guika (or Tewa), on the Rio Grande near Albuquerque.

Kayepu, about 5 miles south of Galisteo, Santa Fé County.

Kipana, south of the hamlet of Tejon, in Sandoval County.

Kuakaa, on the south bank of Arroyo Hondo, 5 miles south of Santa Fé.

Ojana, south of the hamlet of Tejon, Sandoval County.

Paako, south of the mining camp of San Pedro, Santa Fé County.

Pueblo Blanco, on the west rim of the Médano, or great sand-flow, east of the Rio Grande.

Pueblo Colorado, on the south border of the Galisteo plain.

Pueblo de los Silos, in the Galisteo Basin, between the Keresan pueblos of the Rio Grande and Pecos.

Pueblo Largo, about 5 miles south of Galisteo.

Pueblo Quemado (or Tewa), 6 miles southwest of Santa Fé.

Puerto (or Keresan).

San Cristóbal, between Galisteo and Pecos.

San Lázaro, 12 miles southwest of the present Lamy, on the south bank of the Arroyo del Chorro, Santa Fé County.

San Marcos, 18 miles south-southwest of Santa Fé.

Sempoai, near Golden, Santa Fé County.

She, about 5 miles south of Galisteo in Santa Fé County.

Tuerto, near the present Golden City, Santa Fé County.

Tungge, on a bare slope near the banks of a stream called in the mountains farther south Rio de San Pedro; lower down, Uña de Gato; and in the vicinity of the ruins Arroyo del Tunque, at the northeastern extremity of the Sandia Mountains, in Sandoval County.

Tzemantuo, about 5 miles south of Galisteo, Santa Fé County.

Tzenatay, opposite the little settlement of La Bajada, on the declivity sloping from the west toward the bed of Santa Fé Creek, 6 miles east of the Rio Grande and 20 miles southwest of Santa Fé.

Uapige, east of Lamy Station on the Atchison, Topeka, and Santa Fé Railway, some distance in the mountains.

History.—When Coronado passed through the southern end of Tewa territory in 1540, he found it had been nearly depopulated by the Teya, a warlike Plains tribe, perhaps Apache, about 16 years before. The Tewa were next visited by Espejo. In 1630 there were but five Southern Tewa towns remaining and those were entirely broken up during the Pueblo revolts of 1680–96, most of the Indians removing to the Hopi in Arizona, after 1694. The greater part of the remainder were destroyed by smallpox early in the nineteenth century, though there are still a few descendants of this group living in the other pueblos along the Rio Grande, particularly Santo Domingo. The history of the Northern Tewa was similar to that of the Southern but they suffered much less and remain a considerable body at the present day though with a stationary population. The Pueblo of Hano was established among the Hopi as a result of the rebellion of 1680–92.

Populations.—The population of the Northern Tewa is given as follows: In 1680, 2,200; in 1760, 1,908; in 1790–93, 980; in 1805, 929; in 1850, 2,025; in 1860, 1,161; in 1871, 979, in 1901–05, 1,200; in 1910, 968. In 1930 the entire Tanoan stock numbered 3,412. In 1937, 1,708 were returned from the Tewa excluding the Hano, which were enumerated with the Hopi.

In 1630 Benavides estimated the Southern Tewa population at 4,000; in 1680 Galisteo, probably including San Cristóbal, had an estimated population of 800 and San Marcos of 600. No later separate figures are available.

Connection in which they have become noted.—Tano, the alternative name of the Southern Tewa, has been used as a designation of the stock to which the entire group—Tewa, Tiwa, Piro, Pecos, and Jemez— belong, a stock now merged with the Kiowa-Tanoan.

Tiwa Pueblos. The name Tiwa is from Ti'wan, pl. Tiwesh', their own name. Also spelled Tebas, Tigua, Tiguex, Tihuas, Chiguas. Also called:

> E-nagh-magh, a name given by Lane (*in* Schoolcraft, 1851–57) to the language of "Taos, Picuris, Tesuqua, Sandia," etc.

Connections.—The Tiwa Pueblos are a division of the Tanoan linguistic family, itself a part of the Kiowa-Tanoan stock.

Location and Subdivisions.—The Tiwa Pueblos formed three geographic divisions, one occupying Taos and Picuris (the most northerly of the New Mexican Pueblos), on the upper waters of the Rio Grande; another inhabiting Sandia and Isleta, north and south of Albuquerque respectively; and the third living in the pueblos of Isleta del Sur and Senecu del Sur, near El Paso, Tex., in Texas and Chihuahua, México, respectively.

Towns and Villages
(As far as known)

Alameda, on the east side of the Rio Grande about 10 miles above Albuquerque.
Bejuituuy, near the southern limit of the Tiwa habitat on the Rio Grande, at the present Los Lunas.
Carfaray, supposed to have been east of the Rio Grande beyond the saline lakes.
Chilili, on the west side of the Arroyo de Chilili, about 30 miles southeast of Albuquerque.

Isleta, on the west bank of the Rio Grande about 12 miles south of Albuquerque.

Isleta del Sur, on the northeast side of the Rio Grande, a short distance below El Paso, Tex.

Kuaua, north of the present bridge across the Rio Grande above Bernalillo.

Lentes, on the west bank of the Rio Grande near Los Lunas.

Manzano, near the present village so called, 6 miles northwest of Quarai and about 25 miles east of the Rio Grande.

Mojualuna, in the mountains above the present Taos Pueblo.

Nabatutuei, location unknown.

Nachurituei, location unknown.

Pahquetooai, location unknown.

Picuris, inhabited, about 40 miles north of Santa Fé.

Puaray, on a gravelly bluff overlooking the Rio Grande in front of the southern portion of the town of Bernalillo.

Puretuay, on the summit of the round mesa of Shiemtuai, or Mesa de las Padillas, 3 miles north of Isleta.

Quarai, about 30 miles straight east of the Rio Grande, in the eastern part of Valencia County.

San Antonio, east of the present settlement of the same name, about the center of the Sierra de Gallego, or Sierra de Carnué, between San Pedro and Chilili, east of the Rio Grande.

Sandia, inhabited, on the east bank of the Rio Grande, 12 miles north of Albuquerque.

Santiago, probably about 12½ miles above Bernalillo, on the Mesa del Cangelon.

Senecu del Sur, including Piro Indians, on the southeastern bank of the Rio Grande, a few miles below El Paso, in Chihuahua, México.

Shumnac, east of the Rio Grande in the vicinity of the present Mexican settlements of Chilili, Tajique, and Manzano.

Tajique, about 30 miles northeast of Belen, close to the present settlement of the same name, on the southern bank of the Arroyo de Tajique.

Taos, inhabited, on both sides of Taos River, an eastern tributary of the Rio Grande, in Taos County.

The following pueblos now extinct were probably also Tiwa:

Locations entirely unknown:
Acacafui.
Guayotrí.
Henicohio.
Leyvia.
Paniete.
Poxen.
Trimati.
Tuchiamas.
Vareato.

Locations known:
Ranchos, about 3 miles from Taos Pueblo.
Shinana, on the Rio Grande near Albuquerque.
Tanques, also on the Rio Grande near Albuquerque.
Torreon, at the modern town of the same name, about 28 miles east of Belen.

History.—The first two Tiwa divisions above mentioned occupied the same positions when Coronado encountered the Tiwa in 1540–42. Relations between his followers and the Indians soon became hostile and resulted in the capture of two pueblos by his army. In 1581 three missionaries were sent to the Tiwa under an escort but all were killed as soon as the escort was withdrawn. In 1583 Espejo approached Puaray, which Coronado had attacked, but the Indians fled. Castaño de Sosa visited the Tiwa in 1591 and Oñate in 1598. Missionary work was begun among them early in the seventeenth century, and the Indians were withdrawn progressively until only four pueblos were occupied by them at the time of the great rebellion of 1680, in which they took part. In 1681 Governor Otermin stormed Isleta and captured 500 Indians most of whom he settled near El Paso. Part of the Isleta fled to the Hopi country and remained there until 1709 or 1718, when the people of Isleta returned and reestablished their town. The Sandia Indians, however, remained away until 1742, when they were brought back by some missionaries and settled in a new pueblo near their former one. Since then there have been few disturbances of importance, but the population until very lately slowly declined.

Population.—In 1680 there were said to be 12,200 Tiwa; in 1760, 1,428 were reported; in 1790–93, 1,486; in 1805, 1,491; in 1850, 1,575; in 1860, 1,163; in 1871, 1,478; in 1901–5, 1,613; in 1910, 1,650; in 1937, 2,122. (See **Tewa Pueblos.**)

Ute. The Ute were close to the northern border of New Mexico, extending across it at times and frequently raiding the tribes of the region and the later white settlements. (See Utah.)

Zuñi. A Spanish adaptation of the Keresan Sünyyitsi, or Sŭ'nyitsa of unknown meaning. Also spelled Juñi. Synonyms are:

A'shiwi, own name, signifying "the flesh."
Cibola, early Spanish rendering of A'swiwi.
La Purísima de Zuñi, mission name.
Nai-tĕ'-zi, Navaho name.
Narsh-tiz-a, Apache name.
Nashtezhĕ, Navaho name.
Nuestra Señora de Guadalupe de Zuñi, mission name.
Saraí, Isleta and Sandia name of the pueblo; Sarán, Isleta name of the people.
Saray, Tiwa name of the pueblo.
Sà'u'ú, Havasupai name.
Siete Ciudades de Cibola, or Seven Cities of Cibola.
Sŭ'nyitsa, Santa Ana name of the pueblo.
Sünyítsi, Laguna name.
Tâa Ashiwani, sacred name of tribe, signifying "corn peoples."
Xaray, the Tiwa name.
Ze-gar-kin-a, given as Apache name.

Connections.—The Zuñi constitute the Zuñian linguistic stock.

Location.—On the north bank of upper Zuñi River, Valencia County.

Villages

Halona (extinct), on both sides of Zuñi River, on and opposite the site of Zuñi Pueblo.
Hampasawan (extinct), 6 miles west of Zuñi Pueblo.

Hawikuh (extinct), about 15 miles southwest of Zuñi Pueblo, near the summer village of Ojo Caliente.

Heshokta (extinct), on a mesa about 5 miles northwest of Zuñi Pueblo.

Heshota Ayathltona (extinct), on the summit of Taaiyalana, or Seed Mountain, commonly called Thunder Mountain, about 4 miles southeast of Zuñi Pueblo.

Heshota Hluptsina (extinct), between the "gateway" and the summer village of Pescado, 7 miles east of Zuñi Pueblo.

Heshota Imkoskwin (extinct), near Tawyakwin, or Nutria.

Heshotapathltaie, or Kintyel, on Leroux Wash, about 23 miles north of Navaho Station, on the Atchison, Topeka, and Santa Fé Railway, Ariz.

Heshota Uhla (extinct), at the base of a mesa on Zuñi River, about 5 miles west of the summer village of Ojo Pescado, or Heshotatsina.

Kechipauan (extinct), on a mesa east of Ojo Caliente, or Kyapkwainakwin, 15 miles southwest of Zuñi Pueblo.

Kiakima (extinct), at the southwestern base of Thunder Mountain, 4 miles southeast of Zuñi Pueblo.

Kwakina (extinct), 7 miles southwest of Zuñi Pueblo.

Kwakinawan (extinct), south-southeast of Thunder Mountain, which lies 4 miles east of Zuñi Pueblo.

Matsaki (extinct), near the northwestern base of Thunder Mountain and 3 miles east of Zuñi Pueblo.

Nutria, at the headwaters of an upper branch of Zuñi River, about 23 miles northeast of Zuñi Pueblo.

Ojo Caliente, about 14 miles southwest of Zuñi Pueblo.

Pescado, about 15 miles east of Zuñi Pueblo.

Pinawan (extinct), about 1½ miles southwest of Zuñi Pueblo, on the road to Ojo Caliente.

Shopakia (extinct), 5 miles north of Zuñi Pueblo.

Wimian (extinct), 11 miles north of Zuñi Pueblo.

History.—According to Cushing (1896), the Zuñi are descended from two peoples, one of whom came originally from the north and was later joined by the second, from the west or southwest (from the country of the lower Colorado), who resembled the Yuman and Piman peoples in culture. Although indefinite rumors of an Indian province in the far north, containing seven cities, were afloat in Mexico soon after its conquest, the first definite information regarding the Zuñi was supplied by Fray Marcos de Niza, who set out in 1539, with a Barbary Negro named Estevanico as guide, to explore the regions of the northwest. In the present Arizona he learned that Estevanico who, together with some of his Indian companions, had been sent on ahead, had been killed by the natives of "Cibola," or Zuñi. After approaching within sight of one of the Zuñi pueblos, Fray Marcos returned to México with such glowing accounts of the "Kingdom of Cibola" that the expedition of Francisco Vasquez de Coronado was fitted out the next year. The first Zuñi Indians were encountered near the mouth of Zuñi River, and the Spaniards later carried the Zuñi pueblo of Hawikuh by storm, but it was discovered that the Indians had already moved their women and children, together with the greater part of their property, to their stronghold on Taaiyalone Mesa. Thither the men also escaped. The invaders were bitterly disappointed in respect to the riches of the country, and, after the arrival of the main part of the army, they removed to the Rio Grande to go into winter quarters. Later, Coronado returned and subjugated the Zuñi.

In 1580 the Zuñi were visited by Francisco Sanchez Chamuscado, and in 1583 by Antonio de Espejo, the first to call them by the name they commonly bear. By this time one of the seven original pueblos had been abandoned. In 1598, the Zuñi were visited by Juan de Oñate, the colonizer of New Mexico. The first Zuñi mission was established by the Franciscans at Hawikuh in 1629. In 1632 the Zuñi murdered the missionaries and agáin fled to Taaiyalone Mesa, where they remained until 1635. On August 7, 1670, the Apache or Navaho raided Hawikuh, killed the missionary, and burned the church. The mission was not reestablished, and it is possible that the village itself was not rebuilt. In 1680 the Zuñi occupied but three villages, excluding Hawikuh, the central mission being at Halona, on the site of the present Zuñi pueblo. They took part in the great rebellion of 1680 and fled to Taaiyalone Mesa, where they remained until their reconquest by Vargas in 1692. From this time on the people were concentrated in the single village now known as Zuñi, and a church was erected there in 1699. In 1703 they killed the missionary and again fled to their stronghold, returning in 1705. A garrison was maintained at Zuñi for some years after this, and there were troubles with the Hopi, which were finally composed in 1713. The mission continued well into the nineteenth century, but the church was visited only occasionally by priests and gradually fell into ruins. In recent years the United States Government has built extensive irrigation works and established a large school, where the younger generation are being educated in the ways of civilization.

Population.—In 1630 the Zuñi population was estimated at 10,000, probably much too high a figure; and in 1680, at 2,500. In 1760 it was given as 664; in 1788, 1,617; in 1797–98, 2,716; in 1805, 1,470; in 1871, 1,530; in 1889, 1,547; in 1910, 1,667; in 1923, 1,911; in 1930, 1,749; in 1937, 2,080.

Connections in which they have become noted.—The Zuñi have become widely known (1) from their association with the "Kingdom of Cibola"; (2) from the size of the pueblo and the unique character of the language spoken there; and (3) from the close study made of them by Cushing, Mrs. Stevenson, Kroeber, and others. The name Zuñi is borne by a detached range of mountains in the northwestern part of New Mexico. Besides Zuñi post village in McKinley County, N. Mex., there is a place named Zuñi in Isle of Wight County, Va.

ARIZONA

Apache.   Bands of Apache occupied the Gila River region in Arizona
within historic times and periodically overran much of the territory
of the State.   (See New Mexico.)

Cocopa.   Significance of name unknown.

Connections.—The Cocopa belong to the Yuman linguistic family,
a branch of the Hokan stock.

Location.—About the mouth of Colorado River.   (See also México.)

Subdivisions

River Cocopa and Mountain Cocopa.   Cuculato and Llagas are also mentioned, the latter a name applied by the Spaniards to a group of villages.

Villages

Gifford (1923) reports as follows: "Settlement sites on W. bank of Colorado
from Hardy confluence N. (when river flowed near Colonia Lerdo): 1, A'u'ewawa;
2, Kwinyakwa'a; 3, Yishiyul, settlement of Halyikwamai in 1848; 4, Heyauwah,
5 miles N. of Yishiyul and opposite Colonia Lerdo (8 hours' slow walk from
Colorado-Hardy confluence); 5, Amanyochilibuh; 6, Esinyamapawhai (Noche Buena
of the Mexicans)."   There was also a town called Hauwala below or above No. 5.

"Settlement sites on W. bank of Hardy from confluence N.: 1, Karukhap; 2,
Awiahamoka; 3, Nümischapsakal; 4, EweshespiL; 5, Tamanikwawa, (meaning
'mullet (tamanik) place') on lagoon 4 or 5 miles SE of Cocopah mts; 6, ᵃwikukapa
(Cocopa mt.); 10, WeLsuL; 11, Awisinyai, northernmost Cocopa village, about 5
miles S. of Mexicali.

"Lumholtz (p. 251) lists following Cocopa settlements in the first decade of
20th century; Noche Buena (20 families), Mexical (40–50 families), Pescador (15
families), Pozo Vicente (more than 100 families)."

History.—Without question this tribe was first met by Hernando de
Alarcón in 1540.   They are mentioned by Oñate in 1604–5, by Kino
in 1701–2 under the name "Hogiopas," and by Francisco Garcés in
1776.   Most of their territory was outside of the limits of the United
States, but a small part of it passed under United States Government
control with the Gadsden Purchase.   Those Cocopa who remained on
the northern side of the International Boundary were placed on the
Colorado River Reservation.

Population.—Garcés estimated 3,000 in 1776.   In 1857 Heintzelman
placed the former strength of the tribe at about 300 warriors.   There
are now said to be 800 in northern Baja California.   There were 99
in the United States in 1930, and 41 in 1937.

Halchidhoma.   Significance unknown.

Connections.—The Halchidhoma belonged to the Yuman branch of
the Hokan linguistic stock and are said to have spoken the same
language as the Yuma tribe and to have been closely connected also
with the Maricopa.

Location.—At various points on the Colorado River near the mouth
of the Gila.   (See also California.)

Villages

Asumpción, a group of villages on or near the Colorado River, in California, more than 50 miles below the mouth of Bill Williams Fork.

Lagrimas de San Pedro, a group of villages in the neighborhood of Asumpción.

San Antonio, in the same general location as Lagrimas but only 35 or 40 miles below the mouth of Bill Williams Fork.

Santa Coleta, a group of villages in the same region as Asumpción and Lagrimas de San Pedro.

History.—The Halchidhoma were probably encountered by Alarcón in 1540, though he does not mention them. In 1604–5 Oñate found them occupying eight villages on the Colorado below the mouth of the Gila; Father Eusebio Kino in 1701–2 came upon them above the Gila, and by Garcés' time (1776) their villages were scattered on both sides of the Colorado, beginning about 38 miles below Bill Williams' Fork and extending the same distance downstream. Later they moved farther north, along with the Kohuana, but were soon forced downstream again by the Mohave and ultimately took refuge with the Maricopa on Gila River, by whom they were ultimately absorbed.

Population.—Mooney (1928) estimates 3,000 in 1680, but this is evidently based on Garcés' figure of 2,500 in 1776, which Kroeber (1920) believes much too high. Kroeber suggests about 1,000 as of the year 1770.

Halyikwamai. Significance unknown. Also spelled Jallicumay, Quigyuma, Tlalliguamayas, Kikima (by Mason, 1940), and in various other ways.

Connections.—The Halyikwamai belonged to the Yuman linguistic stock, their dialect being reported as close to Cocopa and Kohuana.

Location.—(See History.)

Villages

Presentacion, probably Quigyuma, on the west side of the Colorado River, in Baja California.

San Casimiro, probably on the east bank of the Colorado River, above tidewater, in northwest Sonora, México.

San Felix de Valois, apparently on the east bank of the Rio Colorado, between its mouth and the junction of the Gila, probably about the present Arizona-Sonora boundary line.

San Rudesindo, probably on the east bank of the Colorado River, just above its mouth, in northwestern Sonora, México.

Santa Rosa, a group of villages on the eastern side of the lower Rio Colorado, about latitude 32°18' N., in northwestern Sonora, México.

History.—The Halyikwamai were discovered in 1540 by Alarcón, who calls them Quicama. In 1604–5 Oñate found them in villages on the Colorado River below the mouth of the Gila River and above the Cocopa Indians. In 1762 they dwelt in a fertile plain, 10 or 12 leagues in length, on the eastern bank of the Colorado, and here they were found by Father Garcés in 1771 in a group of villages which he named Santa Rosa. By 1775, when he revisited the tribe, they had moved to the west side of the river, their first villages on the north being in the vicinity of Ogden's Landing, about latitude 32°18′ N., adjacent to the Kohuana. It is probable that they were finally absorbed by the Cocopa or some other Yuman people.

Population.—Mooney (1928) estimates a population for the Halyik-wamai in 1680 of 2,000, which is Garcés' estimate in 1775. Oñate estimated 4,000–5,000 in 1605, but all of these figures are probably much too high.

Havasupai. Signifying "blue (or green) water people," abbreviated into Supai. Also called:

> Ăk′-ba-sū′-pai, Walapai form of name.
> Ká'nína, Coconino, Cosnino, Kokonino, Zuñi name said to have been borrowed from the Hopi and to signify "piñon nut people."
> Nation of the Willows, so called by Cushing.
> Yabipai Jabesua, so called by Garcés in 1776.

Connections.—The Havasupai belong to the Yuman branch of the Hokan linguistic stock, being most closely connected with the Walapai, and next with the Yavapai.

Location.—They occupy Cataract Canyon of the Colorado River, northwestern Arizona.

History.—The nucleus of the Havasupai Tribe is believed to have come from the Walapai. The Cosnino caves on the upper Rio Verde, near the northern edge of Tonto Basin, central Arizona, were named for them, from a traditional former occupancy. Garcés may have met some of these Indians in 1776, but definite notices of them seem to be lacking until about the middle of the last century. Leroux (1888) appears to have met one of this tribe in 1851, and since then they have come increasingly to the knowledge of the Whites.

Population.—Mooney (1928) estimates about 300 Havasupai in 1680, but Spier (1928) believes this figure somewhat too high. In 1869, 300 were reported; in 1902, 233; in 1905, 174; in 1910, 174; and in 1923, 184. In 1930, with the Walapai and Yavapai, they numbered 646. In 1937 the number estimated was 208.

Hopi. Contracted from their own name Hópitu, "peaceful ones," or Hópitu-shínumu, "peaceful all people." Also called:

> A-ar-ke, or E-ar′-ke, Apache name, signifying "live high up on top of the mesas."
> Ah-mo-kái, Zuñi name.
> Ai-yah-kín-nee, Navaho name.
> A′-mu-kwi-kwe, Zuñi name, signifying "smallpox people."
> Asay or Osay, by Bustamante and Gallegos (1582).
> Bokeaí, Sandia Tiwa name.

Buhk'hérk, Isleta Tiwa name for Tusayan.

Bukín, Isleta name for the people.

Eyaníni diné, Navaho name (Gatschet).

Hapeka, a Zuñi name, referring to excrement.

Joso, Tewa name.

Khoso, Santa Clara name.

Kosho, Hano Tewa name.

K'o-so-o, San Ildefonso Tewa name.

Maastoetsjkwe, given by Ten Kate, signifying "the land of Másawé," god of the earth, given as the name of their country.

Mastutc'kwe, same as preceding.

Moki, signifying "dead" in their own language, but probably from some other, perhaps a Keresan dialect.

Topin-keua, said to be a Zuñi name of which Tontonteac is a corruption.

Tusayan, name of the province in which the Hopi lived, from Zuñi Usaya-kue, "people of Usaya," Usaya referring to two of the largest Hopi villages.

Whiwunai, Sandia Tiwa name.

Connections.—The Hopi constitute a peculiar dialectic division of the Shoshonean branch of the Uto-Aztecan linguistic family, and they are the only Shoshonean people, so far as known, who ever took on a Pueblo culture, though the Tanoans are suspected of a remote Shoshonean relationship.

Location.—On Three Mesas in northeastern Arizona.

Towns

Awatobi (destroyed), on a mesa about 9 miles southeast of Walpi.

Hano, occupied by Tewa (see **Tewa Pueblos** under New Mexico).

Homolobi, near Winslow, was formerly occupied by the ancestors of various Hopi clans.

Kisakobi, at the northwest base of the East Mesa.

Kuchaptuvela, on the terrace of the First or East Mesa below the present Walpi village.

Mishongnovi, on the Second or Middle Mesa.

Moenkapi, about 40 miles northwest of Oraibi, a farming village of Oraibi.

Oraibi, on the Third or West Mesa.

Shipaulovi, on the Second or Middle Mesa.

Shongopovi, on the Second or Middle Mesa.

Sichomovi, on the First or East Mesa.

Walpi, on the First or East Mesa.

Kisatobi and Kuchaptuvela were successively occupied by the ancestors of the Walpi before the later Walpi was built.

History.—According to tradition, the Hopi are made up of peoples who came from the north, east, and south. Their first contact with Europeans was in 1540, when Coronado, then at Zuñi, sent Pedro de Tobar and Fray Juan de Padilla to visit them. They were visited by Antonio de Espejo in 1583, and in 1598 Juan de Oñate, governor and colonizer of New Mexico, made them swear fealty and vassalage to the King of Spain. In 1629 a Franciscan mission was established at Awatobi, followed by others at Walpi, Shongopovi, Mishongnovi, and Oraibi. These were destroyed in the general Pueblo outbreak of 1680, and an attempt to reestablish a mission at Awatobi in 1700 led to its destruction by the other pueblos. The pueblos of Walpi, Mishongnovi, and Shongopovi, then situated in the foothills, were probably abandoned about the time of the rebellion, and new villages were built on the adjacent mesas for defense against a possible Spanish attack which did not materialize. After the reconquest of the Rio Grande pueblos by Vargas, some of the people who formerly occupied them fled to the Hopi and built a pueblo called Payupki on the Middle Mesa. About the middle of the eighteenth century, however, they were taken back and settled in Sandia. About 1700 Hano was established on the East Mesa, near Walpi, by Tewa from near Abiquiu, N. Mex., on the invitation of the Walpians. About the time when the Payupki people returned to their old homes, Sichomovi was built on the First Mesa by clans from the Rio Grande, and Shipaulovi was founded by a colony from Shongopovi. The present Hopi Reservation was set aside by Executive order on December 16, 1882.

Population.—Mooney (1928) estimates a Hopi population of 2,800 in 1680. In 1890 the population of Oraibi was 905, and in 1900 the other pueblos (exclusive of Hano) had 919. In 1904 the total Hopi population was officially given as 1,878. The Census of 1910 returned 2,009, apparently including Hano, and the Report of the United States Indian Office for 1923 gave 2,336. The United States Census of 1930 returned 2,752. In 1937 there were 3,248, including the Tewan Hano.

Connections in which they have become noted.—The Hopi are noted as a tribe Shoshonean in language but Puebloan in culture, and also deserve consideration as one of the Pueblo divisions to which particular attention has been paid by ethnologists, including Fewkes, the Stevensons, Hough, Voth, Forde, Lowie, etc. Great popular attention has been drawn to them on account of the spectacular character of the Snake Dance held every 2 years.

Kohuana. Significance unknown. Also given as Cajuenché, Cawina, and Quokim.

Connections.—The Kohuana belonged to the Yuman branch of the Hokan linguistic stock, spoke the Cocopa dialect, and were also closely connected with the Halyikwamai.

Location.—In 1775–76 the Kohuana lived on the east bank of the Colorado River below the mouth of the Gila, next to the Halyikwamai, their villages extending south to about latitude 32°33′ N., and into southern California, at about latitude 33°08′ N., next to the eastern Diegueno. (See also México.)

Villages

Merced, a group of rancherias in northeastern Baja California, west of the Colorado and 4 leagues southwest of Santa Olalla, a Yuma village.

San Jacome, probably Cajuenche, near the mountains, about latitude 33°8′ N., in southern California.

San Sebastian, Cajuenche or Diegueño, in southern California, latitude 33°8′ N., evidently at Salton Lake.

History.—The Kohuana are the Coana mentioned by Hernando de Alarcón, who ascended the Colorado River in 1540. Juan de Oñate visited them in 1604–5, and they are probably the Cutganas of Kino (1701–2), while Francisco Garcés in 1776 reported that they were numerous and at enmity with the Cocopa. From Mohave tradition, it appears that at a somewhat later period they lived along the river near Parker together with the Halchidhoma, whom they followed to the fertile bottom lands higher up. Later the Mohave crowded them southward but still later compelled them to return to the Mohave country where they remained for 5 years. At the end of that period they determined to go downstream again to live with the Yuma; but, one of their number having been killed by the Yuma, they joined the Maricopa, with whom they ultimately became merged.

Population.—Mooney (1928) estimates that there were 3,000 Kohuana in 1680, the figure given by Garcés in 1775–76. Kroeber (1920) believes these estimates are too high. In 1851 Bartlett reported 10 of this tribe living with the Maricopa, and, according to a Mohave informant of Kroeber's, there were 36 about 1883.

Maricopa. Significance of the name unknown. Also called:

Atchihwa′, Yavapai name (Gatschet 1877–92).
Cocomaricopa, an old form.
Cohpáp, or Awo-pa-pa, Pima name.
Pipatsje, own name, signifying "people."
Si-ke-na, Apache name for Pima, Papago, and Maricopa, signifying "living in sand houses."
Tá'hba, Yavapai name (Gatschet, 1877–92).
Tchihogásat, Havasupai name.
Widshi itíkapa, Tonto name, also applied to Pima and Papago.

Connections.—The Maricopa belong to the Yuman linguistic stock, a part of the Hokan family, and are said to be related most closely to the Yuma tribe proper and the Halchidhoma.

Location.—On Gila River, with and below the Pima, to the mouth of the river. Anciently they are said to have had some rancherias in a valley west of the Colorado.

Villages

The following villages were all on the Gila River unless otherwise specified:

Aicatum.

Amoque.

Aopomue.

Aqui.

Aquimundurech.

Aritutoc, on the north side at or near the present Oatman flat and the Great Bend of the river.

Atiahigui.

Aycate.

Baguiburisac, probably Maricopa, near the Gila River.

Caborh.

Caborica.

Cant, probably Maricopa, not far below the mouth of Salt River.

Choutikwuchik.

Coat, probably Maricopa, location uncertain.

Cocoigui.

Cohate.

Comarchdut.

Cuaburidurch.

Cudurimuitac.

Dueztumac, about 120 miles above the mouth of the Gila.

Gohate.

Guias.

Hinama, its people now on the south bank of Salt River east of the Mormon settlement of Lehi, Maricopa County.

Hiyayulge.

Hueso Parado, with Pima, on the Pima and Maricopa Reservation.

Khauweshetawes.

Kwatchampedau.

Norchean.

Noscario.

Oitac.

Ojiataibues.

Pipiaca.

Pitaya.

Sacaton, mainly Pima, on the Gila River about 22 miles east of Maricopa Station.

San Bernadino, at Agua Caliente, near the Gila River; another place on the river was called by the same name.

San Geronimo, 20 leagues from Merced and 27 leagues from the Gila River.

San Martin, on the Gila River west of the Great Bend.

San Rafael, probably Maricopa, in southern Arizona.

Sasabac.

Shobotarcham.

Sibagoida, probably Maricopa, location uncertain.

Sibrepue.

Sicoroidag, on the Gila River below Tucsani.

Soenadut.

Stucabitic.

Sudac.

Sudacsasaba.

Tadeovaqui.

Tahapit.

Toa.

Toaedut.

Tota, probably Maricopa.

Tuburch.

Tuburh, location uncertain.

Tubutavia.

Tucavi, perhaps identical with Tucsani.

Tucsani.

Tucsasic.

Tuesapit.

Tumac, said to have been the westernmost Maricopa village on the Gila River.

Tuquisan.

Tutomagoidag.

Uitorrum, a group of rancherias on the south bank of the Gila River not far west of the Great Bend.

Uparch.

Upasoitac, near the Great Bend of the Gila River.

Urchaoztac.

Yayahaye.

History.—The Maricopa are thought to have separated from the Yuma and to have moved slowly up the Colorado River to the lower Gila River; or, as later history would indicate, they may have been forced into this region by hostile tribes. They were encountered by Juan de Oñate in 1604–5, and by Kino in 1701–2. From 1775 until recent times they were at war with the Yuma, and in 1857, in alliance with the Pima, they inflicted a severe defeat upon the Yuma near Maricopa Wells. A reservation was set apart for the Maricopa and Pima by Act of Congress February 28, 1859; it was enlarged by Executive order of August 31, 1876, but was revoked and other lands were set apart by Executive order of June 14, 1879. This was again enlarged by Executive orders May 5, 1882, and November 15, 1883. No treaty was ever made with them.

Population.—Mooney (1928) estimates that there were 2,000 Maricopa in 1680. Venegas (1758) says that in 1742 there were about 6,000 Pima and "Cocomaricopa" on Gila River, and in 1775 Garcés estimates a population of 3,000 Maricopa. In 1905 there were 350 under the Pima School Superintendent. The census of 1910 gives 386, and the Report of the United States Indian Office for 1923, 394. The census of 1930 returned 310, and the Report of the United States Indian Office of 1937, 339.

Connection in which they have become noted.—The name of the Maricopa is preserved in that of Maricopa County, Ariz., and in the name of a post village in Pinal County and another in Kern County, Calif.

Mohave. From a native word "hamakhava," referring to the Needles and signifying "three mountains." Also given as Amojave, Jamajabs. Synonyms are:

Nāks'-ăt, Pima and Papago name.
Soyopas, given by Font (1775).
Tzi-na-ma-a, given as their own name "before they came to the Colorado River."
Wamákava, Havasupai name.
Wili idahapá, Tulkepaya name.

Connections.—The Mohave belonged to the Yuman linguistic family.

Location.—On both sides of the Colorado River—though chiefly on the east side—between the Needles and the entrance to Black Canyon.

Villages

Pasion, a group of rancherias on the east bank of the Colorado, below the present Fort Mohave.
San Pedro, on or near the west bank of the Colorado, about 8 miles northwest of Needles, Calif.

Santa Isabel, a group of rancherias situated at or in the vicinity of the present Needles.

History.—Possibly Alarcón may have reached the Mohave territory in 1540. At any rate, Oñate met them in 1604, and in 1775–76 Garcés found them in the above-named villages. No treaty was made with them by the United States Government, but by Act of March 3, 1865, supplemented by Executive orders in 1873, 1874, and 1876, the Colorado River Reservation was established and it was occupied by the Mohave, Chemehuevi, and Kawia.

Population.—Mooney (1928) gives 3,000 Mohave in 1680, and Kroeber (1925) the same as of 1770, the estimate made by Garcés in 1775–76. About 1834 Leroux estimated 4,000. In 1905 their number was officially given as 1,589, of whom 508 were under the Colorado River School Superintendent, 856 under the Fort Mohave School Superintendent, 50 under the San Carlos Agency, and about 175 at Camp McDowell, on the Verde River. The Indians at Fort Mohave and Camp McDowell, however, were apparently Yavapai, commonly known as Apache Mohave. The census of 1910 gives 1,058 true Mohave. The United States Indian Office Report for 1923 seems to give 1,840, including Mohave, Mohave Apache, and Chemehuevi. The census of 1930 returned 854, and the Report of the United States Office of Indian Affairs for 1937, 856.

Connection in which they have become noted.—The name Mohave has been preserved in the designation of the Mohave Desert and Mohave River in California, and Mohave County, Ariz., and also in the name of a post-village in Arizona. There is also a post village named Mojave in Kern County, Calif.

Navaho. The Navaho occupied part of the northeastern section of Arizona. (See New Mexico.)

Paiute. The southern or true Paiute occupied or hunted over some of the northernmost sections of Arizona. (See Nevada.)

Papago. Signifying "bean people," from the native words papáh, "beans," and óotam, "people." Also called:

> Saikinné, Si'-ke-na, Apache name for Pima, Papago, and Maricopa.
> Táh'ba, Yavapai name.
> Texpamais, Maricopa name.
> Tóno-oöhtam, own name, signifying "people of the desert."
> Vidshi itikapa, Tonto name.

Connections.—The Papago belong to the Piman branch of the Uto-Aztecan linguistic stock and stand very close to the Pima.

Location.—In the territory south and southeast of the Gila River, especially south of Tucson; in the main and tributary valleys of the

Santa Cruz River; and extending west and southwest across the desert waste known as the Papaguería, into Sonora, México.

Subdivisions and Villages

Acachin, location uncertain.

Alcalde, probably in Pima County.

Ana, probably in Pima County.

Anicam, probably in Pima County.

Areitorae, south of Sonorita, Sonora, México.

Ati, on the west bank of Rio Altar, between Uquitoa and Tubutama, just south of the Arizona boundary.

Babasaqui, probably Papago, 3 miles above Imuris, between Cocospera and Magdalena, Sonora, México.

Bacapa, in northwestern Sonora, México, slightly southeast of Carrizal.

Baipia, slightly northwest of Caborca, probably on the Rio Altar, northwestern Sonora, México.

Bajío, location uncertain.

Batequi, east of the Rio Altar in northwestern Sonora, México.

Boca del Arroyo, probably in Pima County.

Caborica, on the Gila River.

Caca Chimir, probably in Pima County.

Cahuabi, in Arizona near the Sonora border.

Canoa, between Tubac and San Xavier del Bac, on Rio Santa Cruz.

Casca, probably in Pima County.

Charco, probably identical with Chioro.

Chiora, probably in Pima County.

Chuba, location uncertain.

Coca, location uncertain.

Comohuabi, in Arizona on the border of Sonora, México.

Cops, west of the Rio San Pedro, probably in the vicinity of the present Arivaca, southwest of Tubac.

Cubac, in the neighborhood of San Francisco Atí, west from the present Tucson.

Cuitoat, between San Xavier del Bac and the Gila River.

Cujant, in northwest Sonora, between the mouth of the Rio Gila and Sonorita.

Cumaro, southern Arizona near the Sonora border.

Elogio, probably in Pima County.

Fresnal, probably in Pima County.

Guadalupe, about 10 leagues south of Areitorae.

Gubo, probably Papago, 13 leagues east of Sonorita, just below the Arizona boundary.

Guitciabaqui, on the west bank of the Santa Cruz River, near the present Tucson.

Juajona, near San Xavier del Bac, southern Arizona.

Junostaca, near San Xavier del Bac.

Macombo, probably in Pima County.

Mata, probably Papago, north of Caborica.

Mesquite, probably in Pima County.

Milpais, location uncertain.

Nariz, probably in Pima County.

Oapars, in Arizona between San Xavier del Bac and the Gila River.

Ocaboa, location uncertain.

Oísur, on the Santa Cruz River, 5 or 6 leagues north of San Xavier del Bac, southern Arizona.

Onia, probably in Pima County.

Ooltan, in northwest Sonora, México, 3 leagues northwest of Busanic.

Oteàn, location uncertain.

Perigua, Arizona, south of the Gila River.

Perinimo, probably in Pima County.

Piato, probably the same as Soba, in the region of Tubutama and Caborica, Sonora, México.

Pitic, on the Rio Altar, northwest Sonora.

Poso Blanco, in Arizona south of the Gila River.

Poso Verde, south of the Arizona-Sonora boundary, opposite Oro Blanco, Ariz.

Purificación, probably Papago, near the Arizona-Sonora boundary, 12 leagues from Agua Escondida, probably in a southeasterly direction.

Quitovaquita, on the headwaters of Rio Salado of Sonora, near the Arizona-Sonora boundary line.

Raton, location uncertain.

San Bonifacio, probably Papago, south of the Gila River between San Angelo and San Francisco, in the present Arizona.

San Cosme, probably Papago, directly north of San Xavier del Bac, on the Santa Cruz River, Ariz.

San Ignacio, with Pima, on the north bank of Rio San Ignacio, latitude 30°45′ N., longitude 111° W., Sonora, México.

San Ildefonso, 4 leagues northwest of Caborica, Sonora, México.

San Lazaro, probably Papago, on the Rio Santa Cruz in longitude 110°30′ W., just below the Arizona-Sonora boundary.

San Luis Babi, in northwest Sonora, México, between Busanic and Cocospera.

San Martin, probably Papago, on the Gila River, west of the Great Bend of the Colorado.

San Rafael, in southern Arizona near the headwaters of the Rio Salado of Sonora.

Santa Barbara, probably Papago, 4 miles southwest of Busanic, near the headwaters of the north branch of the Rio Altar, in Sonora, México.

Santa Rosa, south of the Gila River and west of Tucson.

Saric, probably Papago, on the west bank of Rio Altar, in northern Sonora, México.

Saucita, in southern Arizona.

Shuuk, or Pima, on the Gila River Reservation, southern Arizona.

Sierra Blanca, probably in Pima County.

Soba, a large body of Papago, including the villages of Carborica, Batequi, Mata, Pitic, and San Ildefonso.

Sonoita, on the headwaters of the Rio Salado of Sonora, just below the Arizona-Sonora boundary.

Tachilta, in southern Arizona or northern Sonora.

Tacquison, on the Arizona-Sonora boundary.

Tecolote, in southwestern Pima County, Ariz., near the Mexican border.

Tubasa, probably on the Rio Santa Cruz River between San Xavier del Bac and the Gila River, southern Arizona.

Tubutama, on the eastern bank of the northern branch of the Rio Altar, in northwest Sonora, México.

Valle, probably in Pima County.

Zuñiga, probably Papago, in northwest Sonora, México.

History.—Father Eusebio Kino was probably the first white man to visit the Papago, presumably on his first expedition in 1694. Their subsequent history has been nearly the same as that of the Pima, except that they were not brought quite as much in contact with the Whites.

Population.—Mooney (1928) places the number of Papago at 6,000 in 1680. In 1906 they were reported as follows: Under the Pima School Superintendent, 2,233; under the farmer at San Xavier, 523 allottees on the reservation and 2,225 in Pima County. In addition, 859 Papago were officially reported in Sonora, México, in 1900, probably an underestimate. In 1910, 3,798 were reported in the United States, but the Report of the United States Indian Office for 1923 gives 5,672; the 1930 census, 5,205; and the Indian Office Report for 1937, 6,305.

Pima. Signifying "no" in the Nevome dialect and incorrectly applied through misunderstanding by the early missionaries. Also called:

> Â'-â'tam, own name, signifying "people," or, to distinguish them from the Papago, Â'-â'tam â'kimûlt, "river people."
> Nashteîse, Apache name, signifying "live in mud houses."
> Paînyá, probably name given by Havasupai.
> Saikiné, Apache name, signifying "living in sand (adobe) houses," also applied to Papago and Maricopa.
> Teχ-păs, Maricopa name.
> Tihokahana, Yavapai name.
> Widshi Iti'kapa, Tonto-Yuma name.

Connections.—The Pima gave their name to the Piman linguistic stock of Powell, which is now recognized to be a subdivision of the great Uto-Aztecan stock, also including the Nahuatlan and Shoshonean families. The tribes connected most intimately with the Pima were the Papago (see above) and the Quahatika (q. v.), and after them the so-called Pima Bajo or Nevome of México.

Location.—In the valleys of the Gila and Salt Rivers. (See also México.)

Subdivisions

Formerly the name Pima was applied to two tribes called respectively tne Pima Bajo and Pima Alto, but the former, living chiefly in Sonora, México, are now known as Nevome, the term Pima being restricted to the Pima Alto.

Villages

Agua Escondida, probably Pima or Papago, southwest of Tubac, southwestern Arizona.
Agua Fria, probably Pima, on Gila River Reservation.
Aquitun, 5 miles west of Picacho, on the border of the sink of the Santa Cruz River.
Aranca, two villages, location unknown.
Arenal, probably Pima, on the Pima and Maricopa Reservation, Gila River.
Arivaca, west of Tubac.
Arroyo Grande, southern Arizona.

Bacuancos, 7 leagues south of the mission of Guevavi, northwestern Sonora, México.

Bisani, 8 leagues southwest of Caborica, Sonora, México.

Blackwater.

Bonostac, on the upper Santa Cruz River, below Tucson.

Busanic, southwest of Guevavi, near the Arizona-Sonora boundary, latitude 31°10′ N. longitude 111°10′ W.

Cachanila, probably Pima, on the Pima and Maricopa Reservation, Ariz.

Casa Blanca, on the Gila.

Cerrito, probably Pima, on the Pima and Maricopa Reservation, Ariz.

Cerro Chiquito, probably Pima, on the Pima and Maricopa Reservation, Ariz.

Chemisez, on the Gila.

Chupatak, in southern Arizona.

Chutikwuchik.

Chuwutukawutuk, in southern Arizona.

Cocospera, on the headwaters of the Río San Ignacio, latitude 31° N., Sonora, México.

Comac, on the Gila River, 3 leagues (miles?) below the mouth of Salt River, Ariz.

Estancia, 4 leagues south of the mission of Saric, which was just south of the Arizona boundary.

Gaibanipitea, probably Pima, on a hill on the west bank of the San Pedro River, probably identical with the ruins known as Santa Cruz, west of Tombstone, Ariz.

Gutubur, locality unknown.

Harsanykuk, at Sacaton Flats, southern Arizona.

Hermho, on the north side of Salt River, 3 miles from Mesa, Maricopa County, Ariz.

Hiatam, north of Maricopa Station on the Southern Pacific R. R., southern Arizona.

Hormiguero, probably Pima, on the Pima and Maricopa Reservation, Ariz.

Huchiltchik, below Santa Ana, on the north bank of the Gila.

Hueso Parado, with Maricopa, on the Pima and Maricopa Reservation, Ariz.

Imuris, near the eastern bank of Río San Ignacio, or Magdalena, latitude 30°50′ N. longitude 110°50′ W., in the present Sonora, México.

Judac, on the Gila.

Kamatukwucha, at the Gila crossing.

Kamit, in southern Arizona.

Kawoltukwucha, west of the Maricopa and Phoenix R. R., in Maricopa County, Ariz.

Kikimi, on the Gila River Reservation.

Kookupvansik, in southern Arizona.

Mange, on the Gila.

Merced, northeast of San Rafael, in what is now southern Arizona.

Nacameri, on the east bank of Río Horcasitas, Sonora, México.

Napeut, on the north bank of the Gila.

Ocuca, in Sonora, México, near the Rio San Ignacio, northwest of Santa Ana.

Oquitoa, on the Rio del Altar, northwestern Sonora, México.

Ormejea, in southern Arizona.

Oskakumukchochikam, in southern Arizona.

Oskuk, on the Gila.

Peepchiltk, northeast of Casa Blanca, southern Arizona.

Pescadero, in northern Sonora, México.

Petaikuk, in southern Arizona.

Pitac, on the Gila.

Potlapigua, about Babispe, Baserac, and the frontier in Sonora, México, but this was Opata territory.

Remedios, a mission on the San Ignacio branch of the Río Asunción, in Sonora, Mexico.

Rsanuk, about 1 mile east of Sacaton Station, on the Maricopa and Phoenix R. R., southern Arizona.

Rsotuk, northwest of Casa Blanca, southern Arizona.

Sacaton, on the Gila, about 22 miles east of Maricopa Station and 16 miles north of Casa Grande Station on the Southern Pacific R. R., Ariz.

San Andrés Coata, near the junction of the Gila and Salado Rivers, Ariz.

San Fernando, 9 leagues east of the ruins of Casa Grande, near the Gila.

San Francisco Ati, west of the Santa Cruz River, Ariz.,

San Francisco de Pima, 10 or 12 leagues above the Río Asunción from Pitic, about latitude 31° N., Sonora, México.

San Serafin, northwest of San Xavier del Bac, southern Arizona.

Santan, on the north bank of the Gila, opposite the Pima Agency.

Santos Angeles, in Sonora, México.

Saopuk, at The Cottonwoods, on the Gila River.

Sepori, south of the Gila River, Ariz.

Shakaik, on the north side of the Gila, northwest of Casa Blanca.

Statannyik, on the south bank of the Gila, between Vaaki (Casa Blanca) and Huchiltchik.

Stukamasoosatick, on the Gila River Reservation.

Sudacson, on the Gila River, Pinal County, Ariz., between Casa Grande and a point 10 leagues below.

Tatsituk, about Cruz's store in southern Arizona.

Taumaturgo.

Tubuscabors, on or near the Gila River, southern Arizona.

Tucson, probably with Papago and Sobaipuri, on the site of modern Tucson.

Tucubavia, on the headwaters of Río Altar, northern Sonora, Mexico.

Tutuetac, about 16 miles northwest of Tucson and west of the Santa Cruz River, in southern Arizona.

Uturituc, on the Gila and probably on the site of the present Sacaton.

Wechurt, at North Blackwater, southern Arizona.

History.—According to native tradition, the Pima originated in the Salt River Valley and spread later to the Gila River. They attribute the large adobe ruins in their country, including the Casa Grande, to their ancestors, and tell stories of their occupancy of them, but the connection is still in doubt. The Nevome and Opata of the Altar, Magdalena, and Sonora Rivers are said to have sprung from Pima colonies. They claim that their old manner of life was ended by three bands of foreigners from the east, who destroyed their pueblos, devastated their fields, and killed or enslaved many of their people. The rest fled to the mountains, and when they returned they did not rebuild the substantial adobe structures which they had formerly occupied, but lived in dome-shaped lodges of pliable poles covered with thatch and mud. Russell (1908) considers it unlikely that Coronado encountered the Pima, but in 1694 Father Eusebio Francisco Kino reached the Casa Grande and undoubtedly met them. Under his inspiration, an expedition was sent to the Gila in 1697 to ascertain the disposition of the tribe. In 1698 he again visited them and between that date and 1702 entered their country four times more. In 1731 Fathers Felipe Segresser and Juan Bautista Grashoffer took charge of the missions of San Xavier del Bac and San Miguel de Guevavi and became the first permanent Spanish residents of Arizona. Padre Ignacio Javier Keller visited the Pima villages in 1736–37 and in 1743, and Sedelmayr reached the Gila in 1750. The first military force to be stationed among the Pima was a garrison of 50 men at Tubac on the Santa Cruz. The presidio was moved to Tucson about 1776 and in 1780 it was increased to hold 75 men. Between 1768 and 1776 Father Francisco Garcés made five trips from Xavier del Bac to the Pimas and beyond. In 1851 parties of the Boundary Survey Commission passed down the Gila River, and J. R. Bartlett, the American Commissioner, has left an excellent description of the Pima Indians (Bartlett, 1854). After the California gold rush began, the Pima frequently assisted parties of explorers and travelers who were making the southern route, and they often protected them from the Apache. In 1853 the Gadsden Purchase transferred the Pima to the jurisdiction of the United States. Surveys for a railroad through Pima territory were made in 1854 and 1855, but it was not constructed until 1879. In the meantime the Pima were subjected to contact with White outlaws and border ruffians of the worst description, and White settlers threatened to absorb their supplies of water. In 1857 the first United States Indian Agent for the territory acquired by the Gadsden Purchase was appointed. In 1871 the first school among them was opened.

Population.—Mooney (1928) estimates that there were 4,000 Pima in 1680. In 1775 Garcés placed the number of those on the Gila River at 2,500. In 1906 there were 3,936 in all; in 1910, according to the United States Census, 4,236; and in 1923, according to the Report of the United States Indian Office, 5,592. The 1930 census returned 4,382. The Indian Office reported 5,170 in 1937.

Connections in which they have become noted.—Pima County, Ariz., and a post town in Graham County, Ariz., preserve the name of the Pima, which has also been made familiar to ethnographers and geographers by the use to which it has been put in the Powell classification to cover a supposed linguistic stock. There is little doubt, however, that this supposed stock is merely a part of a much larger stock, the Uto-Aztecan.

Quahatika. Significance unknown. Also spelled Kohátk.

Connections.—The Quahatika belonged to the Piman division of the Uto-Aztecan stock, and were most closely related to the Pima, of which tribe they are said to have been a branch.

Location.—In the desert of southern Arizona, 50 miles south of the Gila River.

Villages

The chief Quahatika settlement is Quijotoa, in the western part of Pima County, southern Arizona. Early in the eighteenth century they are said to have shared the village of Aquitun with the Pima. (See Pima.)

History.—The history of the Quahatika has, in the main, been parallel with that of the Pima and Papago (q. v.). They are said to have left Aquitun about 1800, and to have introduced cattle among the Pima from the Mexicans about 1820.

Population.—The Quahatika seem to have been enumerated with the Pima.

Sobaipuri. Significance unknown. Also called:

Rsársavinâ, Pima name, signifying "spotted."

Connections.—The Sobaipuri were intimately connected with, if not a part of, the Papago, of the Piman division of the Uto-Aztecan linguistic stock.

Location.—In the main and tributary valleys of the San Pedro and Santa Cruz Rivers, between the mouth of the San Pedro River and the ruins of Casa Grande, and possibly eastward of this area in southern Arizona.

Villages

Alamos, on Rio Santa Cruz, southern Arizona.

Aribaiba, on the San Pedro River, not far from its junction with the Gila.

Babisi, probably Sobaipuri, at the southern boundary near Suamca.

Baicadeat, on the San Pedro River, Ariz.

Busac, probably Sobaipuri, apparently on Arivaipa Creek, a tributary of the San Pedro, east of old Camp Grant, Ariz.

Camani, probably Sobaipuri, on the Gila River, not far from Casa Grande, Ariz.

Causac, on the San Pedro.

Comarsuta, on the San Pedro, between its mouth and its junction with Arivaipa Creek.

Esqugbaag, probably Sobaipuri, on or near the San Pedro, near the Arizona-Sonora boundary.

Guevavi, on the west bank of the Santa Cruz, below Tubac, at or near the present Nogales.

Jiaspi, on the western bank of San Pedro, probably near the present Prospect, Ariz.

Juamalturgo, or Pima, in Arizona south of the ruins of Casa Grande.

Muiva, on the San Pedro, probably near the mouth of Arivaipa Creek.

Ojio, on the eastern bank of the San Pedro River, near its junction with the Gila River and not far from the present Dudleyville, Ariz.

Optuabo, probably Sobaipuri, near the present Arizona-Sonora boundary and probably in Arizona.

Quiburi, on the western bank of the San Pedro, perhaps not far from the present Benson, Ariz.

Quiquiborica, on the Santa Cruz, 6 leagues south of Guevavi, near the Arizona-Sonora boundary.

Reyes, probably Sobaipuri, on the Santa Cruz, in the present southern Arizona.

San Angelo, near the western bank of the Santa Cruz, below its mouth, in southern Arizona.

San Clemente, probably Sobaipuri, on the western bank of the Santa Cruz, north of the present Tucson, Ariz.

San Felipe, at the junction of the Santa Cruz and Gila Rivers.

San Salvador, on the San Pedro River, above Quiburi, southern Arizona.

San Xavier del Bac, on Santa Cruz, 9 miles south of Tucson in the northeast corner of what is now the Papago Reservation.

Santa Eulalia, probably Sobaipuri, slightly northwest of Busanic, just south of the Arizona-Sonora boundary line.

Sonoita, on the Santa Cruz, north of the present Nogales and 7 leagues east northeast of Guevavi.

Suamca, on the headwaters of the Santa Cruz, in the vicinity of Terrenate, Sonora, México, just below the Arizona-Sonora boundary line.

Tubo, probably Sobaipuri, apparently on Arivaipa Creek, a tributary of the San Pedro River, east of old Camp Grant, Ariz.

Tumacacori, probably Sobaipuri, on the Santa Cruz, south of Tubac and 8 leagues north northwest of Guevavi.

Turisai, probably Sobaipuri, probably on or near the Santa Cruz River, southern Arizona.

Tusonimon, about 4 leagues west of Casa Grande, near the Gila River.

Tutoida, on the San Pedro, probably between Arivaipa Creek and the Gila.

History.—The Sobaipuri were visited by Kino, 1694–1702, and missions were established among them, but at a later period the tribe was broken up by the Apache and seems to have sought refuge among the Papago, with whom it became merged.

Population.—Mooney (1928) estimates that there were 600 Sobaipuri in 1680. They are now extinct as an independent tribe.

Tonto. This name has been applied to a number of distinct groups of Apache and Yuman peoples. It is said to have been given to a mixture of Yavapai, Yuma, and Maricopa, with some Pinaleño Apache, placed on the Verde River Reservation, Ariz., in 1873, and transferred to the San Carlos Reservation in 1875; also to a body of Indians, descended mostly from Yavapai men and Pinaleño women. (See New Mexico.)

Walapai. From the native word Xawálapáiyᵃ, "pine-tree folk" (fide J. P. Harrington). Also called:

E-pa, by A. Hrdlička (information, 1906), given as their own name.
Gualiba, by Garcés in 1776 (Diary, p. 404, 1900); Yavapai name.
Hawálapai, by Curtis (1907–9, vol. 2, p. 116).
Jaguallapai, by Garcés in 1776 (Diary, p. 308, 1900).
Matávĕkĕ-Paya, by Corbusier MS. p. 27. Meaning "people to the north"(?); Yavapai name.
Oohp, by Ten Kate (1885, p. 160), Pima name.

Páxuádo ámĕti, by Gatschet (1886, p. 86), meaning "people far down the river," Yavapai name.
Setá Kóχninăme, by Ten Kate (1884, p. 9), Hopi name.
Tăbkĕpáya—Gatschet (1883, p. 124), Yavapai name; abbreviated from Matávĕkĕ-Paya.
Tiqui-Llapais, by Domenech (1860, vol. 1, p. 444).

Connections.—The Walapai belonged to the Yuman branch of the Hokan linguistic stock and were connected especially closely with the Havasupai, the Yavapai apparently standing next.

Location.—On the middle course of the Colorado River, above the Mohave Indians, between Sacramento Wash and National Canyon and inland, extending south almost to Bill Williams Fork.

Subdivisions and Villages

Kroeber and his collaborators give the following:

A. *Mata'va-kopai* (*north people*) (the northwestern division). Villages: Hadū'-ba, Hai'ya, Hathekáva-kió, Huwuskót, Kahwága, Kwa'thekithe'i'ta, Mati'bika, Tanyika";

B. *Soto'lve-kopai* (*west people*) (the Cerbat Mountains and the country west to the Colorado). Villages: Chimethi'ap, Ha-kamuê", Háka-tovahádja, Hamté", Ha'thewelī'-kio', Ivthī'ya-tanákwe, Kenyuā'tci, Kwatehá, Nyi'ī'ta, Quwī'-nye-há, Thawinúya, Waika'ī'la, Wa-nye-ha', Wi'ka-tavata'va, Wi-kawea'ta, Winya'-ke-tawasa, Wiyakana'mo;

C. *Ko'o'u-kopai* (*mesa people*) (north central section).—Villages: Crozier (American name), Djiwa'ldja, Hak-tala'kava, Haktutu'deva, Hê'l, Katha't-nye-ha', Muketega'de, Qwa'ga-we', Sewi", Taki'otha'wa, Wi-kanyo";

D. *Nyav-kopai* (*east people*) (east of the point where Truxton Canyon begins to cut its way down to Hualpai Valley).—Villages: Agwa'da, Ha'ke-takwī'va, Haksa", Hā'nya-djiluwa'ya, Tha've-nalnalwi'dje, Wiwakwa'ga, Yiga't;

E. *Hakia' tce-pai* (?) or *Talta'l-kuwa* (*cane?*) (about the Mohon Mountains).—Villages: Hakeskia'l, Hakia'ch, Ka'nyu'tekwa', Tha'va-ka-lavala'va, Wi-ka-tāva, Witevikivol, Witkitana'kwa;

F. *Kwe'va-kopai* (*south people*).—Villages: Chivekaha', Djimwā'nsevio", Ha-djiluwa'ya, Hapu'k, Kwakwa', Kwal-hwa'ta, Kwathā'wa, Tak-mi'nva;

G. *Hua'la-pai, Howā'laᵃ-pai* (*pine people*) (at the northern end of the Hualpai Mountains, extending in a rough half-circle from east to west.)—Villages: Hake-djeka'dja, Ilwi'-nya-ha', Kahwa't, Tak-tada'pa.

History.—It is possible that some of the Walapai were encountered by Hernando de Alarcón in 1540, and at any rate Marcos Farfan de los Godos met them in 1598, and Francisco Garcés in 1776. Their history since that time has been little different from that of the other Yuman tribes of the region.

Population.—Mooney (1928) estimates that there were 700 Walapai in 1680, but estimates of native informants regarded by Kroeber and his associates as reliable would give a population of more than 1,000 previous to 1880. There were 728 in 1889; 631 in 1897; 501 in 1910, according to the census of that year; 440 in 1923; and 449 in 1932; 454 in 1937. (See **Havasupai**.)

Yavapai. According to the Handbook of American Indians (Hodge, 1907, 1910), from enyaéva, "sun," and pai, "people," and thus signifying "people of the sun," but the southeastern Yavapai interpreted it to mean "crooked-mouth people," that is, a "sulky" people who do not agree with other peoples (fidé Gifford, 1936). Also called:

Apache Mohaves, in Rep. Office Ind. Aff., 1869, p. 92; 1870.

Apáches, by Garcés in 1775–76 (Diary, p. 446, 1900); also by Spaniards.

Cruzados, by Oñate in 1598 (Col. Doc. Inéd., vol. 16, p. 276, 1864–84).

Dil-zha, by White (MS.); Apache name meaning "Indians living where there are red ants."

E-nyaé-va Pai, by Ewing (1892, p. 203), meaning "sun people" because they were sun worshipers.

Gohún, by Ten Kate, (1884, p. 5), Apache name.

Har-dil-zhays, by White (1875 MS.), Apache name.

Inʸa'vapé, by Harrington (1908, p. 324), Walapai name.

Jum-pys, by Heintzelman, (1857, p. 44)

Kohenins, by Corbusier (1886, p. 276), Apache name.

Ku-we-vĕ-ka pai-ya, by Corbusier (MS., p. 27); said to be own name, because they live in the south.

Nyavapai, by Corbusier (1886, p. 276).

Taros, by Garcés in 1775–76 (Diary, p. 446, 1900), Pima name.

Yampaos, by Whipple (1856, p. 103).

Connections.—The Yavapai belonged to the Yuman branch of the Hokan linguistic family, their closest cultural affiliations being with the Havasupai and Walapai.

Location.—In western Arizona from the Pinal and Mazatzal Mountains to the country of the Halchidhoma and Chemehuevi in the neighborhood of Colorado River and from Williams and Santa Maria Rivers, including the valleys of the smaller branches, to the neighborhood of the Gila River.

Subdivisions

Gifford gives the following:

A. Kewevikopaya or Southeastern Yavapai, which included the Walkamepa Band (along the southerly highway from Miami to Phoenix via Superior), and the Wikedjasapa Band (along the present Apache trail highway from Phoenix to Miami via Roosevelt Dam). These included the following exogamous bands: Limited to the Walkamepa Band: Ilihasitumapa (original home in the Pinal Mountains); limited to the Wikedjasapa Band: Amahiyukpa (claiming as their homeland the high mountains on the west side of the Verde River, just north of Lime Creek and directly opposite the territory of the Yelyuchopa Clan), Atachiopa (who originated in the mountains west of Cherry), Hakayopa (whose inland homeland was Sunflower Valley, south of Mazatzal Peak, high in the Mazatzal Mountains, and west of Fort Reno in the Tonto Basin), Hichapulvapa (whose country was the Mazatzal Mountains southward from the East Verde River and westward from North Peak and Mazatzal Peak); represented in both bands: Iiwilkamepa (who considered the mountainous country between the Superstition and Pinal Mountains as their homeland), Matkawatapa (said to have originated from intermarriage between people of the Walkamepa Band and Apache from the Sierra Ancha), Onalkeopa (whose original homeland was in the Mazatzal Mountains between the lands of the Hichapulvapa and Yelyuchopa clans but who moved later south into the territory of the Walkamepa Band), Yelyuchopa (who claimed as their homeland the Mazatzal Mountains between the territories of the Hakayopa and Hichapulvapa clans). Cuercomache (on one of the heads of Diamond Creek, near the Grand Canyon of the Colorado) is given as a village. Amanyiká was the principal camp site of the Wikedjasapa south of the Salt River.

B. Yavepe or Northeastern Yavapai, including:

a. Yavepe proper (claiming upper Verde Valley and the mountains on either side, including the Montezuma National Monument), whose bands were: Wipukupa (occupying caves in Redrock country, probably in the region designated as Red Buttes on maps, and descending Oak Creek to plant maize in certain moist flats and to gather mesquite in Verde Valley), Matkitwawipa (people of upper Verde Valley, East Verde River, Fossil Creek, Clear Creek, ranging south to Cave Creek, and Walkey-anyanyepa (people of the massif to which Jerome clings).

b. Mat-haupapaya (inhabiting the massif from Prescott to Crown King and Bumble Bee), and including: Wikutepa (the Granite Peak Band) and Wikenichapa (the Black Mountains or Crown King Band).

C. Tolkepaya or Western Yavapai, including: Hakupakapa or Inyokapa (inhabitants of mountains north of Congress); Hakehelapa Wiltaikapaya (people of Harquahala and Harcuvar Mountains on either side of Wiltaika (Salome); People's Valley, Kirkland Valley (upper drainage of Hassayampa Creek near Wickenburg and region around Hillside); Haka-whatapa or Matakwarapa (who formerly lived at La Paz and Castle Dome).

History.—Gifford (1936) states that "the earliest probable mention" of the Yavapai "is by Luxan of the Espejo expedition, who in 1582–1583 apparently visited only the country of the Northeastern Yavapai." In 1598 Marcos Farfan de los Godos met them and called them Cruzados because they wore small crosses on their heads, and in 1604 Juan de Oñate also visited them, as did Father Francisco Garcés in 1776, after which time contact with Europeans was pretty regular. They were removed to the Verde River Agency in May 1873. In 1875 they were placed on the San Carlos Apache Agency, but by 1900 most of the tribe had settled in part of their old home on the Verde River, including the abandoned Camp McDowell Military Reservation, which was assigned to their use, November 27, 1901, by the Secretary of the Interior, until Congress should take final action. By Executive Order of September 15, 1903, the old reservation was set aside for their use, and the claims of the white settlers purchased under Act of April 21, 1904.

Population.—Mooney (1928) estimates 600 Yavapai in 1680. Gifford's (1936) estimate would about double that, though he does not believe they ever exceeded 1500. In 1873 they were said to number about 1,000 and in 1903 between 500 and 600. In 1906, 520 were reported, 465 at Camp McDowell and Upper Verde Valley, and 55 at San Carlos. In 1910, 289 were reported by the Census, but the same year the Indian Office reported 178 under the Camp McDowell School

Superintendent, 282 under the Camp Verde School, and 89 under the San Carlos School; total, 549. In 1823 the Indian Office reported 708 under the Camp Verde School and Salt River Superintendencies. In 1932 the Indian Office reported only 193, but the "Yuma Apache" would add 24. In 1937 there were 194.

Connection in which they have become noted.—(See **Havasupai.**) The name has been perpetuated in that of Yavapai County, Ariz.

Yuma. Said to be an old Pima and Papago term for this tribe and in some cases the Kamia and Maricopa also (Forde, 1931). Also called:

Cetguanes, by Venegas (1759).
Chirumas, an alternative name given by Orozco y Berra (1864).
Club Indians, by Emory (1848).
Cuchan, or, strictly, Kwitcʸánª, own name.
Dil-zhay's, Apache name for this tribe and the Tonto and Mohave, signi-
    fying "red soil with red ants" (White, MS.).
Garroteros, by Emory (1848).
Guichyana, Chemehuevi name.
Hatilshe', same as Dil-zhay's.
Húkwats, Paiute name, signifying "weavers."
Kún, said to be Apache name for this tribe and the Tulkepaia.
Wamákava, applied by Havasupai to Mohave and perhaps to this tribe
    also.

Connections.—The Yuma were one of the chief tribes of the old Yuman linguistic stock, to which they have given their name, but their closest immediate relatives were the Maricopa and Halchidhoma. The Yuman stock is now considered a part of the larger Hokan family.

Location.—On both sides of the Colorado River next above the Cocopa, or about 50 or 60 miles from the mouth of the river, at and below the junction of the Gila River, Fort Yuma being in about the center of their territory. (See also California.)

Villages

Forde (1931) gives the following:
Ahakwedehor (axakweδexor), about 2 miles northeast of Fort Yuma.
Avikwotapai, some distance south of Parker on the California side of the Colorado.
Huksil (xuksī'l), along the Colorado River near Pilot Knob, a few miles south of
    Algodones and across the International Boundary.
Kwerav (ava'io), about 2 miles south of the present Laguna Dam and on the
    California side of the Colorado.
Unnamed town, a little east of the present site of Picacho, at the foot of the
    Chocolate Mountains.

History.—Neither Alarcón, who ascended the Colorado River in 1540, nor Oñate, who visited it in 1604, mentions the Yuma, but in the case of Oñate this may be accounted for by the fact that these Indians were then living exclusively on the west side of the river, which he did not reach. The first explorer to mention them by name seems to have been Father Kino, 1701–2; and Garcés, 1771, and Anza, 1774 and 1775, have a great deal to say about them. Garcés and Eixarch remained among them in 1775. (See Kino (1726), and Garcés (1900).) Most of their territory passed under the control of the United States by the treaty of Guadalupe Hidalgo in 1848, and the remainder in consequence of the Gadsden Purchase of 1853. After the founding of Fort Yuma, contacts between the Whites and this tribe became intimate. Most of them were ultimately concentrated on the Colorado River and Yuma Reservations.

Population.—Garcés (1776) estimated that there were 3,000 Yuma, but Anza (see Coues, 1900) raises this to 3,500. An estimate attributed to M. Leroux dating from "early in the 19th century," again gives 3,000. According to the Report of the United States Indian Office for 1910, there were then 655 individuals belonging to the tribe, but the census of that year gives 834. The Indian Office figure for 1923 is 826 and that for 1929, 826, but the United States Census for 1920 increases it very materially, to 2,306. However, the Report of the Indian Office for 1937 gives only 848.

Connections in which they have become noted.—Besides giving its name to the Yuman stock, the name Yuma is preserved by counties in Arizona and Colorado; localities in Yuma County, Ariz.; Yuma County, Colo.; Cloud County, Kans.; Taylor County, Ky; Wexford County, Mich.; and Carroll County, Tenn.

COLORADO

Apache. A number of the Apache bands extended their raids from time to time over the territory of what is now Colorado, but only one of them, the Jicarilla, may be said to have been permanent occupants of any part of the State within the historic period. This tribe is considered under the name Jicarilla below; for an account of the other Apache tribes except the Lipan, see New Mexico. The Lipan are treated under Texas.

Arapaho. The Arapaho hunted and warred over parts of eastern Colorado. (See Wyoming.)

Bannock. This tribe and the Shoshoni roamed over the extreme northwestern corner of the State. (See Idaho.)

Cheyenne. The same may be said of the Cheyenne as of the Arapaho. (See South Dakota.)

Comanche. Like the Arapaho and Cheyenne, this tribe hunted and warred in the eastern parts of the State. (See Texas.)

Jicarilla. A Mexican Spanish word, meaning "little basket," given to the tribe on account of the expertness of Jicarilla women in making baskets. Also called:

Bĕ'-χai, or Peχ'-gĕ, Navaho name.
Kinya-inde, Mescalero name.
Kᵉop-tagúi, Kiowa name, signifying "mountain Apache."
Pi'-ke-e-wai-i-ne, Picuris name.
Tan-nah-shis-en, by Yarrow (1879) and signifying "men of the woodland."
Tashi'ne, Mescalero name.
Tinde, own name.
Tu-sa-be', Tesuque name.

Connections.—The Jicarilla were one of the so-called Apache tribes, all of which belonged to the great Athapascan linguistic stock, but with the Lipan (see Texas) constituted a group distinct from the Apache proper. (See New Mexico.)

Location.—Within historic times the homes of the Jicarilla have been in southeastern Colorado and northern New Mexico, though they have ranged into the adjacent parts of Kansas, Oklahoma, and Texas.

Subdivisions

Mooney (1928) gives the following:
Apatsiltlizhihi, who claim the district of Mora, N. Mex.
Dachizhozhin, original home around the present Jicarilla Reservation, N. Mex.
Golkahin, claiming a former home south of Taos Pueblo, N. Mex.
Ketsilind, claiming a former home south of Taos Pueblo, N. Mex.
Saitinde, claiming the vicinity of present Espanola, N. Mex., as their original home.

History.—There is little doubt that the Jicarilla traveled southward at no very remote period from among the Athapascan tribes in northwestern Canada, very likely by way of the eastern flanks of the Rocky Mountains. They were probably among the Querechos met by Coronado in 1540–42, the same people known to the later Spanish explorers as Vaqueros. They first received mention under their own name early in the eighteenth century. In 1733 a Spanish mission was established for them near Taos, N. Mex., but it did not last long, and their relations with the Spaniards were generally hostile. In 1853 the governor of New Mexico induced 250 of the tribe to settle on the Puerco River, but failure to ratify the treaty he had made with them caused them to go on the warpath, and they continued hostile until their defeat by United States troops in 1854. In 1870 they resided on the Maxwell grant in northeastern New Mexico, but the sale of it necessitated their removal. In 1872 and again in 1873 attempts were made to move them to Fort Stanton, but most of them were permitted to go to the Tierra Amarilla, on the northern confines of the territory, on a reservation of 900 square miles set aside in 1874. Their annuities having been suspended in 1878 on account of their refusal to move southward in accordance with an Act of Congress of that year, they resorted to thieving. In 1880 the Act of 1878 was repealed, and a new reservation was set aside on the Navajo River, to which they were removed. Here they remained until 1883, when they were transferred to Fort Stanton. On February 11, 1887, however, a reservation was set aside for them in the Tierra Amarilla region by Executive Order. They removed to this territory and there they have now been allotted land in severalty.

Population.—Mooney (1928) estimated that there were about 800 Jicarilla in 1845. In 1905 they numbered 795; according to the Census of 1910, there were 694; the Report of the United States Indian Office for 1923 gave 608, and that for 1937, 714.

Connection in which they have become noted.—The name Jicarilla is given to mountains and a post village in Lincoln County, N. Mex.

Kiowa. Like the Arapaho, Cheyenne, and Comanche, the Kiowa formerly hunted and warred across parts of eastern Colorado. (See Oklahoma.)

Kiowa Apache. This tribe always accompanied the Kiowa. (See Oklahoma.)

Navaho. The Navaho lived just south of the Colorado boundary, entering that State only occasionally. (See New Mexico.)

Pueblos. Most of the Pueblo tribes trace their origin to some place in the north and there is no doubt that the ancestors of many of them lived in what are now the pueblo and cliff ruins of Colorado. In historic times the principal dealings of Colorado Indians with the Pueblos have been with the Pueblo of Taos, which was once a trading point of importance. Many of its people intermarried with the Ute. (See New Mexico.)

Shoshoni. Together with the Bannock, the Shoshoni roamed over the extreme northwestern part of Colorado. (See Idaho.)

Ute. The Ute formerly occupied the entire central and western portions of Colorado. (See Utah.)

UTAH

Bannock. This tribe and the Shoshoni roamed over the northern part of Utah as far as the Uintah Mountains, and beyond Great Salt Lake. (See Idaho.)

Gosiute. The Gosiute were a small body of Indians inhabiting the region about Great Salt Lake in northern Utah. They were long supposed to be a mixture of Ute and Shoshoni but are now known to have been connected only with the Shoshoni. They attracted particular attention because of their wretched manner of life, which reports frequently exaggerated unduly. (See **Shoshoni, Western,** under Idaho.)

Navaho. This tribe occupied, at least at times, a small part of the southeastern section of Utah as far as the San Juan River. (See New Mexico.)

Paiute, Southern. The Southern Paiute occupied the southwestern part of Utah. (See Nevada.)

Shoshoni, Western. The Western Shoshoni extended into northern Utah; they included the Gosiute, as above stated. (See Idaho.)

Ute. Significance unknown. Also called:

> Grasshopper Indians, Pattie (1833).
> Iätä-go, Kiowa name.
> Ietan, a form of their name used widely for Indians of the Shoshonean stock.
> Mactciñgeha waiⁿ, Omaha and Ponca name, signifying "rabbit skin robes.'
> Moh-tau-hai'-ta-ni-o, Cheyenne name, signifying "the black men."
> Násuia kwe, Zuñi name, signifying "deer-hunting men."
> No-ochi or Notch, own name.
> Nota-á, Navaho name.
> Quazula, seems to be the Jemez name for them.
> Sápa wichasha, Dakota name, signifying "black people."
> Tâ'hana, Taos name.
> Tcingawúptuh, former Hopi name.
> Wáatenĭhts, Atsina name, signifying "black."

Connections.—The Ute belonged to the Shoshonean division of the Uto-Aztecan linguistic stock and were related more closely to the true Paiute, Kawaiisu, and Chemehuevi.

Location.—In central and western Colorado and all of eastern Utah, including the eastern part of Salt Lake Valley and Utah Valley and extending into the upper drainage area of the San Juan River in New Mexico. (See also Nevada and Wyoming.)

Subdivisions

Capote, in the Tierra Amarilla and Chama River country, northwestern New México.

Elk Mountain Ute (perhaps the Sabuaguanos of Escalante (1882) and Tah-bah-was-chi of Beckwith (1882), especially if the initial letter in one or the other case has been misread, in the Elk Mountains of Colorado.

Kosunats, on Uintah Reservation in 1873.

Moache, in southwest Colorado and northwest New Mexico.

Pahvant, around the lower portion of Sevier Lake and River, Utah.

Pavógowunsin, on the upper course of the Sevier River, south of the Salina River.

Pikakwanarats, on the Uinta Reservation in 1873.

Sampits or Sanpet, around Manti on San Pitch Creek but wintering on Sevier River, Utah.

Seuvarits or Sheberetch, in the Castle Valley country and on headwaters of San Rafael River, in east central Utah.

Tabeguache, in southwest Colorado, chiefly about Los Pinos.

Tumpanogots or Timpaiavats, about Utah Lake, Utah.

Uinta, in northeastern Utah.

Wiminuche, in southwest Colorado, chiefly in the valley of the San Juan and its northern tributaries.

Yampa, on and about Green and Colorado Rivers in eastern Utah.

The Sogup, in or near New Mexico, and Yubuincariri, west of Green River, Utah, are also given as former bands, and a few others of uncertain status also appear, such as the Kwiumpus, Nauwanatats, and Unkapanukints. In later years the recognized divisions were reduced to three: Tabeguache or Uncompahgre, Kaviawach or White River, and Yoovte or Uinta.

History.—The Ute occupied the region above indicated when they came to the knowledge of the Spaniards, who were the first Europeans to encounter them. Their warlike disposition was early accentuated by the introduction of horses among them. Our first intimate knowledge of them is derived from the diary of Fray Silvestre Velez de Escalante, who penetrated their country in 1776. For a brief period they were organized into a confederacy under a chief named Tabby (Taíwi). The first treaty between the United States Government and the Ute was concluded December 30, 1849. By Executive order of October 3, 1861, Uintah Valley was set apart for the Uinta Band, while the remainder of the land claimed by them was taken without formal purchase. By a treaty of October 7, 1863, a reservation was assigned to the Tabeguache, and the remainder of their land was taken without formal purchase. On May 5, 1864, various reserves, established in 1856 and 1859 by Indian agents, were ordered vacated and sold. By a treaty of March 2, 1868, a reservation was created in Colorado for the Tabeguache, Moache, Capote, Wiminuche, Yampa, Grand River, Uinta, and other bands, who relinquished the remainder of their lands, but by an agreement of September 13, 1873, a part of the reservation was ceded to the United States. When it was found that a portion of this last cession was included in the Uncompahgre Valley, the part so included was retroceded to the Ute by Executive order of August 17, 1876. By Executive order of November 22, 1875, the Ute Reservation was enlarged, but this additional tract was restored to the public domain by an order of August 4, 1882. By Act of June 18, 1878, a portion of the Act of May 5, 1864, was repealed, and several tracts included in the reservations thereunder established were restored to the public domain. Under an agreement of November 9, 1878, the Moache, Capote, and Wiminuche ceded their right to the confederated Ute Reservation established by the 1868 treaty, the United States agreeing to establish a reservation for them on San Juan River, a promise which was finally fulfilled by Executive order of February 7, 1879. On March 6, 1880, the Southern Ute and the Uncompahgre acknowledged an agreement to settle respectively on La Plata River and on the Grand River near the mouth of the Gunnison, while the White River Ute agreed to move to the Uinta Reservation in Utah. Sufficient agricultural land not being found at the point designated as the future home of the Uncompahgre, the President, by Executive order of January 5, 1882, established a reserve for them in Utah, the boundaries of which were defined by Executive order of the same date. By Act of May 24, 1888, a part of the Uinta Reservation was restored to the public domain. The tribe has since been allotted land in severalty.

Population.—Mooney (1928) estimates that there were 4,500 Ute in 1845, including the Gosiute. In 1870 there were supposed to be 4,000. The official reports give 3,391 in 1885 and 2,014 in 1909. The census of 1910 returned 2,244; the United States Indian Office in 1923, 1,922, including some Paiute; and the Indian Office in 1937, 2,163.

Connections in which they have become noted.—The Ute shared with the Shoshoni the reputation of being the strongest and most warlike of the Plateau people. The State of Utah derives its name from the Ute. Utah is also the name of a county and a lake in this State. There is a place called Utahville in Clearfield County, Pa., and localities called Ute in Montrose County, Colo., and Monona County, Iowa, and Ute Park in Colfax County, N. Mex.

NEVADA

Koso. This is properly a California tribe, though it sometimes ranged into Nevada. (See California.)

Paiute, Northern. The significance of the word "Paiute" is uncertain, though it has been interpreted to mean "water Ute" or "true Ute." Also called:

> Monachi, Yokuts name.
> Monozi, Maidu name.
> Mono-Paviotso, name adopted in the Handbook of American Indians (Hodge, 1907, 1910), from an abbreviated form of the above and Paviotso.
> Nutaa, Chukchansi Yokuts name, signifying that they were east or upstream.
> Paviotso, a native term applied by Powell (1891) to a part of the Nevada Indians of this group.
> Snake, name commonly given to the Northern Paiute of Oregon.

Connections.—With the Bannock, the Northern Paiute constituted one dialectic group of the Shoshonean Branch of the Uto-Aztecan stock.

Location.—The Northern Paiute were not properly a tribe, the name being used for a dialectic division as indicated above. They covered western Nevada, southeastern Oregon, and a strip of California east of the Sierra Nevada as far south as Owens Lake except for territory occupied by the Washo. According to the students of the area, they were pushed out of Powder River Valley and the upper course of John Day River in the nineteenth century by Shahaptian tribes and the Cayuse. (See also Idaho.)

Subdivisions and Villages

There were no true tribes or bands except in the extreme western and northeastern parts of the area covered, but topography enforced concentration into certain valleys. Aside from the detached Bannock, the Northern Paiute were divided by the Sierra Nevada Mountains into a widely spread eastern division and a small division confined to California, the Eastern and Western Mono of Kroeber. Kroeber (1925) distinguishes six divisions of the latter as follows:

Balwisha, on the Kaweah River, especially on its south side.
Holkoma, on a series of confluent streams—of which Big Burr and Sycamore Creeks are the most important—entering Kings River above Mill Creek.
Northfork Mono, for whom no native name has survived, on the North Fork of San Joaquin River.
Posgisa or Poshgisha, of the San Joaquin, on Big Sandy Creek, and toward, if not on, the heads of Little and Big Dry Creeks.
Waksachi, on Limekiln and Eshom Creeks and the North Fork of Kaweah River.
Wobonuch, at the head of Mill Creek, a southern affluent of Kings River, and in the pine ridges to the north.

Away from Owens Valley and the immediate neighborhood the Paiute have been divided into a large number of bands with names which usually signify that they were "eaters" of some particular kind of food. Although the entire area has been filled in with such names, they have been given largely by Indians from areas outside those of the supposed bands; different names are given by different informants, the same name occurs in a number of places, at times widely separated, and there is lack of agreement among informants, including Steward (1933), Kelly (1937), Park (1938), and Blyth (1938), as to the numbers, names, and locations of the groups under consideration. Instead of attempting any sort of classification, therefore, I will simply insert a miscellaneous list of villages and local settlements though these were almost as fluctuating and impermanent as the larger groups. In most cases, however, it may be assumed that the location was determined by economic factors and mention of such a site has, therefore, some permanent value however often the name may have changed or the composition of the village fluctuated.

Gifford (1932) gives the following hamlets belonging to Kroeber's Northfork Mono besides 83 fishing places and campsites, the exact locations of which are entered in his report and accompanying map:

Apasoraropa.	Homohomineu.
Apayiwe.	Howaka.
Asiahanyu.	Kodiva.
Bakononohoi.	Konahinau.
Dipichugu.	Kotuunu.
Dipichyu.	Kunugipü.
Ebehiwe.	Monolu.
Homenadobema.	Moyopaso.

Muchupiwe.
Musawati.
Nakamayuwe.
Napasiat.
Noboihawe.
Nosidop.
Ohinobi.
O'oneu.
Oyonagatü.
Pahabitima.
Pakasanina.
Papavagohira.
Pasawapü.
Pasiaputka.
Pausoleu.
Payauta.
Pekeneu.
Pimishineu.
Poniaminau.
Poniwinyu.
Ponowee.
Saganiu.
Saiipü.
Saksakadiu.
Sanita.
Sigineu.

Sihuguwe.
Sikinobi.
Sipineu.
Siügatü.
Soyakanim.
Sukuunu.
Supanaminau.
Takapiwe.
Takatiu.
Tasineu.
Tiwokiiwe.
Topochinatü.
Tübipakwina.
Tükweninewe.
Tumuyuyu.
Tüpipasagüwe.
Waapüwee.
Wadakhanau.
Wegigoyo.
Wiakwü.
Wokoiinaha.
Wokosolna.
Yatsayau.
Yauwatinyu.
Yauyau.

Steward enumerates the following "districts" of Owens Valley and neighboring valleys, each with communistic hunting and seed rights, political unity, and a number of villages:

Kwina patü, Round Valley.

Panatü, the Black Rock territory, south to Taboose Creek.

Pitana patü, extending from the volcanic tableland and Norton Creek in the Sierra to a line running out into Owens Valley from Waucodayavi, the largest creek south of Rawson Creek.

Tovowahamatü, centering at Big Pine, south to Big Pine Creek in the mountains, but with fishing and seed rights along Owens River nearly to Fish Springs.

Tunuhu witü, of uncertain limits.

Utü'ütü witü, from the warm springs, now Keough's, south to Shannon Creek.

The people of Deep Springs Valley called their valley Patosabaya and themselves Patosabaya nünemua; the Fish Lake Valley people to the north of these did not constitute a unified band but were distributed into the following villages:

Ozanwin, on the east or south slope of the Sylvania Mountains and near Tü'nava.

Pau'uva, in the vicinity of McNett ranch.

Sohodühatü, at the present Oasis ranch.

Suhuyoi, at the Patterson ranch.

Tuna'va, the present Geroux ranch, marked McFee on the United States Geological Survey.

Tü'nava, at Pigeon Spring at the east end of Fish Lake Valley.

Watühad, Moline ranch on Moline Creek.

Yogamatü, several miles from the mountains at the present Chiatovich ranch.

Steward (1933) gives the following village names in and near Owens Valley:

An unnamed site west of Deep Springs Lake.

Ahagwa, on Division Creek.

Antelope Springs, native name not recorded.

Hudu matu, on Cottonwood Creek.

Hunadudugo, camp near Wyman Creek.

Ka'nasi, camp at Dead Horse Meadow on Wyman Creek.

Mogahu' pina, scattered along Hogback, Lone Pine, Tuttle, and Diez Creeks.

Mogohopinan watu, on Richter Creek.

Muhu witu, on Tinnemaha Creek.

Nataka' matu, at Independence.

Nuvahu' matu, near Thibaut Creek.

Oza'n witu, southeast of Deep Springs Lake.

Padohahu matu, on Goodale Creek.

Pahago watu, on Tuttle Creek.

Pakwazi' natu, at Olancha.

Pa'natu, on Owens River, near mouth of Birch Creek.

Pau'wahapu, at Hines Spring.

Pawona witu, on Bishop Creek below Bishop.

Pa'yapo'o'ha, south of Bishop.

Pazi'wapi'nwuna, at Independence.

Posi'da witu, on Baker Creek.

Suhubadopa, at Fish Springs Creek, at least in prehistoric times.

Suhu'budu mutu, on Carroll Creek.

Suhuvakwazi natu, on Wyman Creek.

Tanova witu, south of Independence.

Ti'numaha witu, on Tinnemaha Creek.

To'owiawatu, at Symmes Creek.

Totsitupi, on Thibaut Creek.

To'vowaha'matu, at Big Pine on Big Pine Creek.

Tsagapu witu, at Shepherd Creek.

Tsaki'shaduka, near Old Fort Independence.

Tsaksha witu, at Fort Independence.

Tsa'wawua'a, on Bishop Creek.

Tsigoki, beyond Owens ranch, east of Bishop.

Tuhunitogo, near upper course of Birch Creek.

Tuinu'hu, on Sawmill Creek.

Tunwa'pu, at the mouth of Taboose Creek.

Tupico, on Birch Creek, west of Hunadudugo.

Tupuzi witu, at George's Creek.

Waushova witu, on Lone Pine Creek.

Steward gives the following villages in Fish Lake Valley:

Oza'nwin, on the east or south slope of the Sylvania Mountains and near Tu'nava.

Pau'uva, in the vicinity of McNett ranch.

Sohoduhatu, at the present Oasis ranch.

Suhuyoi, at the Patterson ranch.

Tuna' va, at the present Geroux ranch.

Tu' nava, at Pigeon Springs at east end of Fish Lake Valley.

Watuhad, at Moline ranch.

Yogamatu, several miles from the mountains at the present Chiatovich ranch.

The following are miscellaneous local groups of Northern Paiute, the names drawn from various sources:

Agaivanuna, at Summit Lake, western Nevada.

Duhutcyatikadu, on Silver and Summer Lakes, Oreg.

Genega's Band, at the mouth of Truckee River

Gidutikadu, in Surprise, Calif.; Coleman; Warner, Oreg.; and probably also Long Valleys, in California, Nevada, and Oregon.

Goyatikendu, at Yainax and Beatty, Oreg., brought from Silver Lake.

Hadsapoke's Band, at Gold Canyon, Carson River.

Hoonebooey, east of the Cascades and south of the Blue Mountains of Oregon.

Itsaatiaga, about Unionville, Nev.

Kaivaningavidukw, in Surprise Valley, northeastern California.

Koeats, in north central Nevada.

Kosipatuwiwagaiyu, about Carson Sink.

Koyuhow, about McDermitt, Nev.

Kuhpattikutteh, on Quinn River, Nev.

Kuyuidika, near the site of Wadsworth on Truckee River.

Kuyuitikadu, at Pyramid Lake, Nixon, Nev.

Kwinaduvaa, at McDermitt, Nev.

Laidukatuwiwait, about the sink of the Humboldt.

Lohim, an isolated Shoshonean band, probably of this connection, on Willow Creek, a southern affluent of the Columbia, Oreg.

Loko, on or near Carson River, Nev.

Nogaie (with 4 subbands), in the vicinity of Robinson District, Spring Valley, Duckwater, and White River Valley.

Odukeo's Band, around Carson and Walker Lakes.

Oualuck's Band, in Eureka Valley, Oreg.

Pamitoy, in Mason Valley.

Paxai-dika, in Bridgeport Valley, Calif.

Petodseka, about Carson and Walker Lakes.

Piattuiabbe (with 5 bands), near Belmont, Nev.

Pitanakwat or Petenegowat, in Owens Valley, but formerly in Esmeralda County, Nev.

Poatsituhtikuteh, on the north fork of Walker River.

San Joaquin's Band, at the forks in Carson Valley.

Sawagativa, about Winnemucca.

Shobarboobeer, probably of this connection, in the interior of Oregon.

Shuzavi-dika, in Mono Valley, Calif.

Togwingani, about Malheur Lake, Oreg.

Tohaktivi, about the White Mountains, near the head of Owens River, Calif.

Toitikadu, at Fallon and Yerington, Nev.

Toiwait, about the lower Sink of the Carson.

Tonawitsowa (with 6 bands), in the vicinity of Battle Mountain and Unionville.

Tonoyiet's Band, below Big Meadows, Truckee River.

Torepe's Band, near the lower crossing of Truckee River.

Tosarke's Band, near Carson and Walker Lakes.

Tsapakah, in Smith Valley.

Tubianwapu, about Virginia City.

Tubuwitikadu, east of Steens Mountain, Oreg.

Tupustikutteh, on Carson River.

Tuziyammos, about Warner Lake, Oreg.

Wahi's Band, at the big bend of Carson River.

Wadatikadu, at Burns, Malheur District, Oregon, and Susanville, Calif.

Wahtatkin, east of the Cascade Mountains and south of the Blue Mountains, Oreg.

Walpapi, on the shores of Goose, Silver, Warner, and Harney Lakes, Oreg.

Warartika, about Honey Lake, northeastern California.

Watsequeorda's Band, on Pyramid Lake.

Winemucca's Band, said to have had a specific location on Smoke Creek near Honey Lake, northeastern California, but to have been extended to other northern Paiute living west of the Hot Springs Mountains in Nevada, who do not seem to have been united into one body until brought together to defend themselves against the Whites.

Wobonuch, at the head of Mill Creek, California, and in the pine ridges to the north.

Yahuskin, about the shores of Goose, Silver, and Harney Lakes, Oreg.

Yammostuwiwagaiya, in Paradise Valley, Nev.

History.—Although the territory of the Northern Paiute has been occupied for a long period by human beings and has been modified from time to time along its margins by neighboring cultures, there seem to have been few fundamental changes in the culture of the region taken as a whole, the economic life having been based on hunting and gathering. Contacts with Europeans began at a comparatively late period, probably with the entrance of trappers about 1825. Jedediah Smith made journeys across Nevada in 1825 and Old Greenwood may have visited it still earlier. Peter Skene Ogden visited the Paiute of eastern Oregon between 1826 and 1828 and probably reached Humboldt River in Nevada. These men were followed by Walker (1833), Russell (1834–43), and many others. During this period relations with the Indians seem to have been uniformly friendly, but clashes became more numerous with the great stream of immigration which began about 1840 and swelled to tidal proportions with the discovery of gold in California. The Paiute in the remote valleys, however, remained for a long time little affected. Descriptions of Indian life in the numerous reports of travelers are disappointing. A great crisis in the affairs of the Indians was brought about by the discovery of the Comstock lode at Virginia City, Nev., since in the next 10 years prospectors penetrated every part of the territory, says Steward, "and boom towns sprang up in the midst of sheer desert." A greater menace to the lives of the Indians was the introduction of livestock and consequent destruction of native food plants. Pinyon trees were also cut down for fuel. By this time the natives had both guns and horses and were in consequence much more capable of inflicting damage in the clashes which began about 1860 and in consequence of which several military posts were established. With the completion of the first transcontinental railroad in 1869, the native period came practically to an end. On October 1, 1863, the United States Government extended its authority without formal purchase over the territory of the "Western Shoshoni" and included within it the northern part of the lands occupied by the Northern Paiute under discussion. The Government assumed "the right of satisfying their claim by assigning them such reservations as might seem essential for their occupancy, and supplying them in such degree as might seem proper with necessaries of life" (Royce, 1899). By virtue of the authority thus granted, a mill and timber reserve was created on Truckee River by Executive order, April 24, 1864, for the Pyramid Lake Indians. In December 1864 Eugene Monroe surveyed a reservation for the Paiute at Walker River, and in January 1865 he surveyed another at Pyramid Lake. The former was set aside by Executive order March 19, 1874, and the latter 4 days later. "The remainder of the Pai Ute country," says Royce, "[was] taken possession of by the United States without formal relinquishment by the Indians." On the other hand, the Indians by no means confined themselves to these reservations.

Population.—Mooney (1928) estimated that this division, i. e., the tribes embraced under the name of Northern Paiute, and the true or Southern Paiute numbered 7,500 in 1845. The figures given in the Report of the Indian Office for 1903 indicate a population of about 5,400 for the group. The Census of 1910 reports 1,448 "Mono" and 3,038 Paviotso, a total of 4,486, but the United States Indian Office Report of 1923 seems to give a total of more than 13,000. This is evidently erroneous since the United States Census of 1930 reported 4,420. The figures of the United States Indian Office in 1937 seem to yield 4,108, after substracting 270, which plainly belonged to the Southern Paiute.

Paiute, Southern.   Also called:

> Auölasús, Pima name.
> Chemegué Cuajála, by Garcés in 1776, the first name on account of their association with the Chemehuevi (see under California; for Cuajála, see Kohoaldje below).
> Da-da'-ze ni'-ka-ci^n'-ga, Kansa name, signifying "grasshopper people."
> Diggers, a popular name sometimes used for them.
> Hogăpä'goni, Shoshoni name, signifying "rush-arrow people."
> Kohoaldje, originally Mohave name of Virgin River Paiute.
> Nüma, own name, signifying "people," "Indians."
> Pa'gonotch, Southern Ute name.
> Pah-rú-sá-páh, Chemehuevi name.
> Snake Diggers, or Ute Diggers, by Simpson (1859).
> Yabipai Cajuala, by Garcés in 1776.

Connections.—The Southern Paiute belonged to the Ute-Chemehuevi group of the Shoshonean branch of the Uto-Aztecan stock.

Location.—In western Utah, northwestern Arizona, southeastern Nevada, and parts of southeastern California.

Subdivisions

Powell and Ingalls give the following "tribes" which, as Steward (1933) suggests, were more likely villages or restricted local groups:

Ho-kwaits, in the vicinity of Ivanspaw ("Ivanpah Mountain").

I'-chu-ar'-rum-pats, in Moapa Valley, "probably in Overton-St. Thomas vicinity" (Kelly, 1932).

Kai'vav-wits, in the vicinity of Kanab ("Kaibab Plateau"—Kelly).

Kau-yai'-chits, at Ash Meadows but actually in Shoshoni territory.

Kwai-an'-tikwok-ets, east of Colorado, which is perhaps what the name means (Palmer, 1928).

Kwi-en'-go-mats, at Indian Springs.

Kwi-um'-pus, in the vicinity of Beaver.

Mo-a-pa-ri'-ats, in Moapa Valley (on Moapa Creek).

Mo-quats, in Kingston Mountains.

Mo-vwi'-ats, at Cottonwood Island.

Nau-wan'-a-tats, in Moapa Valley.

No-gwats, in the vicinity of Potosi ("in Spring Mountains"—Kelly).

Nu-a'gun-tits, in Las Vegas Valley.

Pa-ga'-its, in the vicinity of Colville.

Pa-gu'-its, at Pagu Lake.

Pa-ran-i-guts, in Pa-ran-i-gut Valley.

Pa-room'-pai-ats, in Moapa Valley "head of Moapa Creek, at Home ranch."

Pa-room'-pats, at Pa-room Spring.

Pa-ru'-guns, in the vicinity of Parawau "Paragonah Lakes" (Kelly, 1932).

Pa-spi'-kai-vats, in the vicinity of Toquerville, "a district on lower Ash Creek" (Kelly).

Pin'-ti-ats, in Moapa Valley.

Sau-won'-ti-ats, in Moapa Valley.

Shi'-vwits, on Shi'-vwits Plateau.

Tim-pa-shau'-wa-got-sits, at Providence Mountains.

Tsou-wa'-ra-its, in Meadow Valley.

U'-ai-Nu-ints, in the vicinity of St. George.

U-in-ka'-rets, in Mountains ("Mount Trumbull"—Kelly).

Un-ka-ka'-ni-guts, in Long Valley.

Un-ka'-pa-Nu-kuints', in the vicinity of Cedar (perhaps "second creek south of Kanarra . . . slightly southeast of New Harmony"—Kelly).

U-tum'-pai-ats, in Moapa Valley ("site of Wiser Ranch, near Glendale, Nevada"—Kelly).

Ya'-gats, at Armagoza ("spring just north of Tecopa, in Armagosa Valley"—Kelly).

Kelly (1932) reduces the number of "tribes" or "bands" to 14, some of which agree with those given by Powell, while others seem to contain the remnants of a number of his "tribes." She also gives two not appearing in his list, viz: the Kaiparowits and a band at Gunlock.

History.—The Southern Paiute came in contact with the Spaniards in the sixteenth and seventeenth centuries but were little disturbed by them. The first attempt to describe them systematically seems to have been made by Father Escalante, who traversed their territory in 1776. After the annexation of California and New Mexico to the

United States, their country was slowly but steadily encroached upon, and they were in part removed to reservations though by far the greater number remained scattered through the country. There has been comparatively little friction between these Indians and the Whites.

Population.—Mooney (1928) gives the population of the Southern Paiute and Northern Paiute together as 7,500 in 1845. In 1906 there were reported to be 129 Indians at Moapa Reservation, 267 at Duck Valley, and those not under an agent in Nevada were estimated 6 years before to number 3,700, but this includes the Northern Paiute; in Utah there were 76 Kaibab, 154 Shivwits, and 370 not under an agency; and in Arizona there were 350 Paiute under the Western Nevada School Superintendent, altogether slightly more than 5,000. Even allowing for the Northern Paiute, this figure must be too high or the enumerators of 1910 missed a great many Indians, for the census of that date reports only 780 Paiute altogether. The Indian Office Report for 1923 gives 226 in Nevada and southwestern Utah, but others in Utah are enumerated with the Ute. The census of 1930 enumerates 294 exclusive of the Chemehuevi. According to the Report of the United States Indian Office for 1937, there seem to have been 439 in that year.

Connections in which they have become noted.—The name Paiute has become identified with the name "Diggers." Both have been used in a contemptuous sense. A county of south-central Utah is named Paiute.

Panamint, see **Paiute, Northern.**

Pueblo. In historic times none of the Pueblo Indians have occupied any part of Nevada, but remains in the southern section of the State testify to former occupancy by these Indians. (See New Mexico and Arizona.)

Shoshoni. The Western Shoshoni occupied northeastern Nevada as far as, and including, Reese River Valley. (See Idaho.)

Ute. The Ute claimed a small part of eastern Nevada. (See Utah.)

Washo. From the native term Washiu, signifying "person." Also called:

Tsaisuma, name given them by the northeastern Maidu.

Connections.—Until recently the Washo were regarded as constituting a distinct linguistic stock, but it is now believed that they were related to some of the tribes of California. J. P. Harrington has announced a linguistic connection between them and the Chumash, but other students place them in the Hokan linguistic family.

Subdivisions

Lowie gives the following:

Ha'nale'lti, about Woodfords and in Antelope Valley.
Pa'walu, near Minden and Gardnerville.
We'lmelti, about Reno.

Location.—On Truckee River as far down as the Meadows, though their right to the latter was disputed by the Northern Paiute tribes; Carson River down to the first large canyon below Carson City; the borders of Lake Tahoe; and Sierra and other valleys as far as the first range south of Honey Lake, Calif.

History.—There is some evidence that the Washo were once established in valleys farther east than the location above given and were driven thence by Northern Paiute tribes. In 1860–62, according to Mooney (1928), the Northern Paiute conquered them in a contest over the site of Carson and forbade them thenceforth to own horses. They had little contact with Whites until very recent years. In later times they lived between Reno and a point a short distance south of Carson City, where they adopted a parasitic mode of life, depending almost entirely on the towns and ranches. In 1865 it was proposed to set aside two reservations for these Indians in Carson and Washoe Valleys, but white settlers had already occupied the territory and the plan was abandoned.

Population.—Mooney (1928) made an estimate of 1,000 as of 1845. In 1859 they numbered about 900. In 1907, 300 were reported. The census of 1910 reported 819; that of 1930, 668. In 1937, 629 were reported.

Connections in which they have become noted.—The name Washo is preserved in the names of Washoe County, Washoe Lake, Washoe Valley, and Washoe, a post hamlet, all in Nevada. Another locality called Washoe is in Carbon County, Mont.

WYOMING

Arapaho, possibly from the Pawnee tirapihu or larapihu, signifiying "trader." Also called:

Ähyä'to, Kiowa name.
Ano's-anyotskano, Kichai name.
Bĕtidĕĕ, Kiowa Apache name.
Detseka'yaa, Caddo name, signifying "dog eaters."
Dog Eaters.
E-tah-leh, Hidatsa name, signifying "bison path Indians."
Hitänwo'Iv, Cheyenne name, signifying "cloud men" or "sky men."
Inûna-ina, own name, signifying "our people."
Ita-Iddi, Hidatsa name (Maximilian).
Kaninahoish, Chippewa name.
Komséka-Ki'ñahyup, former Kiowa name, signifying "men of the worn-out leggings."

Kun na-nar-wesh or Gens des Vach[es], by Lewis and Clark (1804).

Maḣpíyato, Dakota name, signifying "blue cloud."

Niă'rharĭ's-kûrikiwa'ahûski, Wichita name.

Särĕtĭka, Comanche and Shoshoni name, signifying "dog eaters"; the Pawnee, Wichita, and Ute names were forms of this.

Connections.—Together with their near relatives, the Atsina, the Arapaho constitute the most aberrant group of the Algonquian linguistic stock.

Location.—The Arapaho have occupied a number of different regions in the historic period, but after they crossed the Missouri they became most closely identified with northeastern Wyoming, where the main or northern part of the tribe resided for a long period and where they were finally given a reservation. (See also Colorado, Kansas, Montana, Nebraska, North Dakota, Oklahoma, South Dakota, and Canada.)

Subdivisions

The Arapaho recognized five main divisions, which were evidently originally distinct tribes. Mooney (1928) calls these: (1) Nákasinĕ'na, Báachinĕna, or Northern Arapaho; (2) Náwunĕna, or Southern Arapaho; (3) Aä'ninĕna, Hitúnĕna, Atsina, or Gros Ventres of the Prairie, today usually reckoned as a distinct tribe (see Montana); (4) Bäsawunĕna, principally with the Northern Arapaho; and (5) Hánahawunĕna, or Aanû'nhawă, later incorporated with the Northern Arapaho. The corresponding names given by Kroeber (1902 b) are: Hinanaē'inaⁿ (Arapaho proper), Nāⁿwaçinähä'änaⁿ (evidently Southern Arapaho), Hitōune'naⁿ (Gros Ventres), Bääsaⁿwūune'naⁿ, and Hāⁿanaxawūune'naⁿ. Kroeber also states that four more divisions recognized in the tribe were evidently in reality divisions of the Hinanaē'inaⁿ. These are: Wāⁿxuē'içi ("ugly people"), about Cantonment, Okla.; Haxāaⁿçine'naⁿ ("ridiculous men"), on the South Canadian, Okla.; Bāⁿtcline'naⁿ ("red-willow men"), in Wyoming; and a fourth whose name has been forgotten. The following are relatively modern local bands of the Arapaho: Forks-of-the-River Men, Bad Pipes, Greasy Faces, Wáquithi, Aqáthinĕ'na, Gawunĕna, Háqihana, Säsábäithi, of which the first three were among the Northern Arapaho.

History.—According to tradition, the Arapaho were once sedentary and seem to have lived in the Red River Valley, whence they moved southwest across the Missouri at some time prior to the passage of that stream by the Cheyenne. Sometime afterward the Atsina separated from the rest, possibly cut off from the main body by the Crow, and moved off to the north; and within the last century the rest of the tribe have slowly divided into a northern and a southern branch, the Northern Arapaho living along the edges of the mountains at the headwaters of the Platte, while the Southern Arapaho continued on toward the Arkansas. About 1840 they made peace with the Dakota, Kiowa, and Comanche but were at war with the Shoshoni, Ute, and Pawnee until they were confined to reservations. By the treaty of Medicine Lodge in 1867 the Southern Arapaho were placed upon a reservation in Oklahoma along with the Southern Cheyenne; this was thrown open to white settlement and the Indian lands were allotted in severalty in 1892. The Northern Arapaho were assigned to a reservation on Wind River, Wyo., after having made peace with the Shoshoni who occupied the same reserve. The Atsina were associated with the Assiniboin on Fort Belknap Reservation, Mont.

Population.—Mooney (1928) estimated that there were 3,000 Arapaho in 1780 and the same number of Atsina. In 1894 there were 2,638 of the two tribes together; in 1904 there were 889 Northern Arapaho and 859 Southern Arapaho, a total of 1,748. The census of 1910 reported 1,419 Arapaho, while the United States Indian Office Report for 1923 gives 921 Arapaho in Wyoming and 833 in Oklahoma, a total of 1,754. The 1930 census reported 1,241, of whom 867 belonged to the northern division. In 1937 there were 1,164 Northern Arapaho and 2,836 Southern Arapaho and Cheyenne together.

Connections in which they have become noted.—The Arapaho were one of the famous raiding tribes of the Plains; their name appears frequently coupled with that of the Cheyenne. The name Arapahoe has been given to a county and a mountain in Colorado and to localities in Furnas County, Nebr.; Pamlico County, N. C.; Cheyenne County, Colo.; and Fremont County, Wyo.; and the name Arapaho to the county seat of Custer County, Okla.

Bannock. Some Bannock ranged into western Wyoming. (See Idaho.)

Cheyenne. The Cheyenne hunted and warred to some extent in the eastern part of Wyoming; were long allied with the Arapaho. (See South Dakota.)

Comanche. Before separating from the Shoshoni the Comanche probably occupied territory in Wyoming, afterward moving southward. (See Texas.)

Crows. The Crows occupied in Wyoming the valleys of Powder, Wind, and Big Horn Rivers and ranged as far south as Laramie. (See Montana.)

Dakota. Dakota hunting and war parties frequently reached the territory of Wyoming, but the tribe had no permanent settlements there. In 1876 they participated with the Northern Arapaho and Northern Cheyenne in the cession of the northeastern territory of Wyoming. (See South Dakota.)

Kiowa. According to tradition, a tradition reinforced by other evidence, the Kiowa lived for a time in or near the Black Hills before moving south. (See Oklahoma.)

Kiowa Apache. This tribe lived in close conjunction with the Kiowa. (See Oklahoma.)

Pawnee. The Pawnee were known to Wyoming only as hunters and warriors. (See Nebraska.)

Shoshoni. The Northern Shoshoni formerly occupied the western part of Wyoming. (See Idaho.)

Ute. The Ute were just south of the present Wyoming and entered its territory at times to hunt or fight. (See Utah.)

MONTANA

Arapaho. The Arapaho proper occupied, or camped in, parts of southeastern Montana at various periods of their history. (See Wyoming.)

Arikara. Some Arikara hunted in eastern Montana. In 1869 and 1880, together with the Hidatsa and Mandan, they relinquished rights to land in the southeastern part of the State. (See North Dakota.)

Assiniboin. From a Chippewa term signifying "one who cooks by the use of stones."

> E-tans-ke-pa-se-qua, Hidatsa name, from a word signifying "long arrows" (Long, 1823).
> Guerriers de pierre, French name.
> Hohe, Dakota name, signifying "rebels."
> Sioux of the Rocks, English name.
> Stonies, or Stone Indians, English name translated from the Indian.
> Tlū'tlämä'ekä, Kutenai name, signifying "cutthroats," the usual term for Dakota derived from the sign language.
> Weepers, given by Henry (1809).

Connections.—The Assiniboin belonged to the Siouan linguistic family, and were a branch of the Dakota (see South Dakota), having sprung traditionally from the Yanktonai whose dialect they spoke.

Location.—The Assiniboin were most prominently associated historically with the valleys of the Saskatchewan and Assiniboin Rivers, Canada. In the United States they occupied the territory north of the Milk and Missouri Rivers as far east as the White Earth. (See also North Dakota.)

Subdivisions

The latest list is that given by Professor Lowie (1939). He states that, anciently, there were three principal tribal divisions, viz: Hō'ke (Like-Big-Fish), Tu-wan'hudan (Looking-like-Ghosts), and Sitcon'-ski (Tricksters, lit. "Wrinkled-Ankles"). Lowie obtained the names of the following smaller bands: Tcanxta'daa, Unska'ha (Roamers), Wazī'a wintca'cta, (Northern People), Watō'paxna-on wan or Wato'paxnatun, Tcan'xe wintca'cta (People of the Woods), Tanin'tä`bin (Buffalo-Hip), Hu'decä`bine (Red-Butt), Wacī'azī hyābin (Fat-Smokers), Witcī'-

abin, Iⁿ'yaⁿtoⁿ'waⁿbin (Rock People), Watŏ'pabin (Paddlers), Cuñtcĕ'bi (Canum Mentulae), Cahĭ'a iye'skābin (Speakers of Cree (Half-Crees)), Xe'natoⁿwan (Mountain People), Xĕ'bina (Mountain People), Icna'umbisᵃ, (Those-who-stay-alone), and Ini'na u'mbi. Hayden (1862) mentions a band called Min'-i-shi-nak'-a-to, or Lake People, which does not seem to be identifiable with any of the above. This last may be the band called by Henry (1809) Those-who-have-water-for-themselves-only. The following bands cited by Henry are wholly unidentifiable: Red River, Rabbit, Eagle Hills, Saskatchewan, Foot, and Swampy Ground Assiniboin.

History.—According to tradition, this tribe separated from the Wazikute band of Yanktonai. The separation evidently took place before contact with the Whites, but there is evidence that when Europeans first heard of the tribe they were south of their later habitat, probably in the vicinity of the Lake of the Woods and Lake Nipigon. Thence they moved northwest toward Lake Winnipeg and later to the banks of the Assiniboin and Saskatchewan Rivers. In the meantime they had allied themselves with the Cree and had become enemies of their own southern relatives with whom they were afterward almost constantly at war. This northward movement and alliance with the Cree was due in large measure to the establishment of British posts on Hudson Bay and the desire of the Assiniboin Indians to have access to them and thus supply themselves with firearms and other European articles. The Assiniboin in the United States were gathered under the Fort Belknap and Fort Peck agencies; those in Canada under the Battleford, Edmonton, and Assiniboin agencies, at Moose Mountain, and on Stoney Reservation.

Population.—Mooney (1928) estimated that there were 10,000 Assiniboin in 1780. In 1829 Porter gave 8,000, and Drake (*in* Church, 1825) thought that there were 10,000 before the smallpox epidemic of 1836, when 4,000 died. The United States Indian Office Report of 1843 gave 7,000; in 1890 they numbered 3,008; and in 1904, 1,234 in the United States, and 1,371 in Canada, a total of 2,605. The census of 1910 gave 1,235 in the United States, and the United States Indian Office Report for 1923 gave 1,400, while there was an approximately equal number in Canada. The United States Census of 1930 gave 1,581. In 1937, 2,232 were returned in the United States.

Connections in which they have become noted.—The Assiniboin attained prominence during the dealings of explorers and traders with the Indians along the upper Missouri. As Assiniboin or Assiniboine, the name has been adopted for an important affluent of the Red River of the North in Manitoba and Saskatchewan Provinces. Mount Assiniboin is in the Rocky Mountains near the boundary between British Columbia and Alberta, about 20 miles south of Banff.

Atsina. Probably from Blackfoot ăt-se'-na, supposed to mean "gut people." Also called:

Acapatos, by Duflot de Mofras (1844).
A-re-tear-o-pan-ga, Hidatsa name.
Bahwetego-weninnewug, Chippewa name, signifying "fall people."
Bot-k'in'ago, signifying "belly men."
Fall Indians, common early name.
Gros Ventres des Plaines, derived from an incorrect interpretation of the tribal sign and the qualifying phrase "des Plaines" to distinguish them from the Hidatsa, the Gros Ventres de la Rivière.
Haáninin or Aä'ninĕna, own name, said to signify "white-clay people," "lime-men," or "chalk-men."
His-tu-i'-ta-ni-o, Cheyenne name.
Hitúnĕna, Arapaho name, signifying "beggars" or "spongers."
Minnetarees of the Plains, Minnetarees of the Prairies, so called to avoid confusion with the Hidatsa (q. v. under North Dakota).
Rapid Indians, from Harmon (1820).
Sä'pani, Shoshoni name, signifying "bellies."
Sku'tani, Dakota name.

Connections.—The Atsina were a part of the Arapaho, of which tribe they are sometimes reckoned a division, and both belong to the Algonquian linguistic family.

Location.—On Milk River and adjacent parts of the Missouri, in what is now Montana, ranging northward to the Saskatchewan. (See also Canada.)

Subdivisions

Kroeber (1908 b) has recorded the following names of bands or clans, some of which may, however, be duplications:

Names of clans whose position in the camp circle is known, beginning at the south side of the opening at the east: Frozen or Plumes, "Those-who-water-their-horses-once-a-day"; Tendons, "Those-who-do-not-give-away," or "Buffalo-humps"; Opposite (or Middle) Assiniboin, "Ugly-ones or Tent-poles worn smooth [from travel]"; Bloods, "Fighting-alone."

Other clan names: Berry-eaters, Breech-cloths, Coffee, Dusty-ones, Gray-ones or Ash-colored, Kaⁿhutyi (the name of a chief), Night-hawks, Poor-ones, Torn-trousers, Weasel-skin headdress.

History.—If the Arapaho once lived in the Red River country, the Atsina were probably with them. At least, the languages of both point to the region of the Algonquian tribes northeast of the Plains for their origin. At the same time Kroeber (1900 b) thinks that they must have been separated for at least 200 years. According to Hayden (1860), they were south of the Saskatchewan about 1800. In 1818 they joined the Arapaho and remained with them until 1823 when they returned to the location given above in the neighborhood of Milk River. For a long time they maintained an alliance with the Blackfeet but later joined the Crow against them and in the course of the ensuing war, in 1867, suffered a severe defeat. Later they were placed on Fort Belknap Reservation, Mont., with the Assiniboin.

Population.—Mooney (1928) estimates that the Atsina numbered 3,000 in 1780. In 1904 there were 535. The census of 1910 reported 510, and the United States Office of Indian Affairs in 1923 reported 586; 631 were reported by the census of 1930, and 809 in 1937.

Bannock. The Bannock ranged into the western part of the State. (See Idaho.)

Cheyenne. The Cheyenne frequently entered the eastern part of Montana and the Northern Cheyenne were ultimately assigned a reservation within the State. (See South Dakota.)

Chippewa. The Chippewa had little contact with the region now included in Montana until very recent times when a considerable number came to live there, 486 according to the census of 1910. (See Minnesota.)

Cree. The original homes of the Cree were north of the present United States, though their war parties frequently came into the territory now occupied by this country to fight the Dakota, Blackfoot, and other tribes. In comparatively late times a number, given by the census of 1910 as 309, settled in Montana, and others were reported from Washington (91), Michigan, Oregon, North Dakota, Idaho, Kansas, and Minnesota. (See also Canada.)

Crow. A translation, through the French gens des corbeaux, of their own name Absároke, "crow-, sparrowhawk-, or bird-people." Also called:

Hahderuka, Mandan name.
Haideroka, Hidatsa name.
Hounena, Arapaho name, signifying "crow men."
Issắppo', Siksika name.
Kanġitoka, Yankton Dakota name.
Ka'-xi, Winnebago name.
Kihnatsa, Hidatsa name, signifying "they who refused the paunch," and referring to the tradition regarding the separation of these two tribes.
Kokokiwak, Fox name.
Long-haired Indians, by Sanford (1819).
O-e'-tun'-i-o, Cheyenne name, signifying "crow people."
Par-is-ca-oh-pan-ga, Hidatsa name, signifying "crow people" (Long, 1823).
Stémchi, Kalispel name.
Stémtchi, Salish name.
Stimk, Okinagan name.
Yaχka'-a, Wyandot name, signifying "crow."

Connections.—The Crow belonged to the Siouan linguistic stock and were most closely related to the Hidatsa, from whom they claim to have separated.

Location.—On the Yellowstone River and its branches, extending as far north as the Musselshell and as far south as Laramie Fork on the Platte, but centering particularly on three southern tributaries of Yellowstone River, the Powder, Wind, and Big Horn Rivers. (See also Wyoming and Canada.)

Subdivisions

There were formerly three local divisions, known to the people themselves as Minĕ'sepĕre, Dung-on-the-river-banks?, or Black Lodges; the A˅c'arahō', Many-Lodges; and the Erarapī'o, Kicked-in-their-bellies. The first of these is called River Crow by some writers and the last two collectively Mountain Crow. They were also divided into 12 clans arranged in pairs.

History.—As stated above, the Crow tribe claims to have separated from the Hidatsa, a tradition shared by the Hidatsa. It is at least certain that the two are more closely related linguistically than is either to any other Siouan group. Their separation into bands must have occurred in the first quarter of the nineteenth century at latest. In 1804 they were found in their historic seats and have been in approximately the same region ever since, the reservation to which they were finally assigned being on the Big Horn River.

Population.—Mooney's (1928) estimate for the year 1780 is 4,000 Crow. In 1804 Lewis and Clark estimated 350 lodges and 3,500 souls. In 1833 there were said to be 1,200 warriors and a population of from 3,250 to 3,560. In 1890 a total population of 2,287 was reported, and in 1904, 1,826. The census of 1910 gave 1,799, and the United States Indian Office Report for 1923, 1,777. The census of 1930, reported 1,674, and the Indian Office Report for 1937, 2,173.

Connections in which they have become noted.—The Crow tribe was prominent in the early history of the Northwest, though not to the extent of the Dakota and Blackfeet. The Indian form of the name, Absarokee, is borne by a post village of Stillwater County, Mont.; in the form Absaraka it appears as the name of a place in Cass County, N. Dak.; and as Absaroka, more prominently, as the name of a range of mountains and a National Forest in the Yellowstone National Park.

Dakota. The Dakota entered Montana at times to hunt and fight the Crow but were not permanent residents of the State. (See South Dakota.)

Hidatsa. Together with the Arikara and Mandan, in 1869 and 1880 the Hidatsa took part in treaties ceding territory in southeastern Montana to the United States Government. (See North Dakota.)

Kalispel. This tribe probably visited the westernmost parts of Montana at times and most of them finally settled upon the Flathead Reservation in that State. Some of them, together with the Salish and Kutenai, ceded Montana lands in 1855. (See Idaho.)

Kiowa. According to tradition, the Kiowa at one time lived in the southeastern part of this State. (See Oklahoma.)

Kutenai. Said to be from a term applied to this tribe by the Blackfoot Indians and believed by Turney-High (1937) to have come originally from the name of a Kutenai tribe or division called Tunaha. Also called:

> Flatbows, the name given often to the Lower Kutenai, the origin of which is unknown.
>
> Kúspĕlu, their Nez Percé name, signifying "water people."
>
> Sán'ka or asán'ka, own name, significance unknown.
>
> Shalsä'ulk°, by the Sinkiuse and said to be from a place name, but see below.
>
> Skelsá-ulk, Salish name, signifying "Water People."
>
> Slender Bows, name sometimes given as an interpretation of their own name, but erroneously.

Connections.—The Kutenai were placed by Powell in a distinct stock called Kitunahan, but some linguists regard them as remote relatives of the Algonquians and Salishans.

Location.—On Kootenay River, Kootenay Lake, Arrow Lake, and the upper course of the Columbia River, except for the bend between Donald and Revelstoke; in southeastern British Columbia; northwestern Montana; northeastern Washington; and the northern tip of Idaho. In modern times they have settled as far southeast as Flathead Lake. (See also Canada.)

Subdivisions

The Kutenai were separated into two general divisions, the line between extending roughly from north to south through Libby, Mont. The Upper Kutenai lay to the east on upper Kootenay River and depended more upon hunting, especially of the bison, while the Lower Kutenai were largely fishermen. Turney-High (1937) gives the following bands: (1) Tunáxa, whose original home was on the Plains and who have now been destroyed and their descendants incorporated with the other bands; (2) Tobacco Plains or People-of-the-Place-of-the-Flying-Head, esteemed to be the mother band of the tribe (on Kootenay River at the International Boundary Line—the Fernie Band was a subdivision); (3) Jennings Band (about Jennings, Mont.); (4) Libby Band (at Libby, Mont.); (5) Bonner's Ferry Band (at Bonner's Ferry, Idaho); (6) Fort Steele Band (at Steele, B. C.); (7) Creston Band (at Creston, B. C.); (8) Windermere Band (a very modern band at Windermere, B. C.). To these may be added the very modern Dayton-Elmo Band on Flathead Lake drawn from the Jennings and Libby bands.

History.—From information collected by Turney-High (1937), it would seem that the Kutenai formerly lived east of the Rocky Mountains, extending at least as far as MacLeod, Alberta. Their oldest settlement in their present territories would seem to have been at Tobacco Plains whence they gradually spread to the north, west, and south, and in recent times to the southeast. Their country was traversed early in the nineteenth century by David Thompson (1916) in the interest of the Northwest Company, and Kootenai House was established in 1807.   With the running of the International Boundary, their country was divided between the Dominion of Canada and the United States to the considerable inconvenience of the tribe.   Missionary work among them, particularly work among the Upper Kutenai, has been very successful.

Population.—Mooney (1928) estimated the Kutenai population to be 1,200 in 1780.   In 1890 those in the United States were estimated at 400 to 500.   In 1905 they numbered 554, and those in British territory the year preceding were enumerated at 553.   The census of 1910 gave 538 in the United States.   The Report of the Canadian Department of Indian Affairs for 1924 returned about 450, and that of the United States Indian Office only 129 under that name.   The latter figure is evidently defective, as the Census of 1930 returned 287 of whom 185 were in Montana and 101 in Idaho.   In 1937 there were 118 in Idaho.

Connections in which they have become noted.—The Kutenai are noted for their peculiar language, which differs from the speech of all their neighbors and has been given an independent position as the Kitunahan stock.   They have given their name to Kootenay or Kootenai River, also called the Flat Bow or MacGillivray, which flows through British Columbia, Montana, and Idaho; to Kootenay Lake in British Columbia; to Kootenai Mountains, and Kootenai Falls, Mont.; Kootenai County, Idaho; and to a post village, Kootenai, in Bonner County, Idaho.

Mandan.   The Mandan were parties to treaties made in 1869 and 1880 ceding their claims to land in southeastern Montana.   (See North Dakota.)

Nez Percé.   Individuals belonging to this tribe sometimes entered the southwestern part of Montana.   (See Idaho.)

Piegan.   The Piegan were the southernmost subtribe of the Siksika (q. v.).

Salish,   Probably a place name, the last syllable, -ish, "people."   Also called:

> A-shu'-e-ka-pe, Crow name, signifying, "flatheads."
> A-too-ha-pe, Hidatsa name.
> Flatheads, widely so called because, in contradistinction to the tribes west of them, they left their heads in the natural condition, flat on top, instead of sloping backward to the crown.
> Ka-ka-i-thi, Arapaho name, signifying, "flathead people."
> Ka-ko'-is-tsi'-a-ta'-ni-o, Cheyenne name, signifying, "people who flatten their heads."
> Ko-tōh'-spi-tup'-i-o, Siksika name.
> Nebagindibe, Chippewa name, signifying, "flat head."

Pa O-bde'-ca, Yankton Dakota name, signifying, "heads cornered or edged."

Têtes-Plates, common French term.

Connections.—The Salish belonged to the interior division of the Salishan linguistic family, to which they have given their name.

Location.—In western Montana originally, extending from the Rocky Mountains on the west; south to the Gallatin; east to Crazy Mountain and Little Belt Ranges, north to some hilly country north of Helena. Later they were centered farther west around Flathead Lake. (See also Idaho.)

Subdivisions

It is said that there was a distinct band of Salish Indians on a river near Helena, another band near Butte, another somewhere east of Butte, and another somewhere in the Big Hole Valley; and there are traditions of still others.

History.—According to Teit (1930) the Salish once extended farther to the east, and there were related tribes in that region which he calls Sematuse and Tunahe. As Turney-High (1937) has pointed out, however, the Tunahe were evidently a Kutenai division; and the Sematuse, if not mythical, seem to have been an alien people in possession of this country before the Salish entered it. Teit states that these Salish were driven westward out of the Plains by the Blackfoot, particularly after that tribe obtained guns. Turney-High, on the other hand, regards the Salish as rather late intruders into the Plains from the west. However, the pressure of tribes westward by their neighbors to the east as soon as the latter obtained guns is such a common story that it hardly seems probable that the Salish could have escaped its effects. Just how far the Salish retired westward may be a matter of argument, nor does it affect the theory of an earlier eastward migration if such a movement can be substantiated on other grounds. Salish relations with the Whites were always friendly and they were successfully missionized by Roman Catholics under the lead of the famous Father De Smet. By the treaty of July 16, 1855, they ceded all of their lands in Montana and Idaho except a reserve south of Flathead Lake and a second tract in Bitter Root Valley which was to be made into a reserve for them if it were considered advisable. It was, however, not so considered, and acting upon an Act of Congress of June 5, 1872, the Salish were removed to the former reservation, where they still live.

Population.—Mooney (1928) estimated that there were 600 Salish in 1780, evidently accepting the figure given by Lewis and Clark for 1806. Teit (1930) considers this much too low, the data collected by him indicating a Salish population of perhaps 3,000, but this would seem to err in the opposite direction. The Indian Office figure for 1905 is 557 and that for 1909, 598. The census of 1910 reported 486, of whom 400 were in Montana, 46 in Washington, 27 in Oregon, 6 in Idaho, 6 in Nebraska, and 1 in Kansas. The census of 1830 reported 2,036 Interior Salish from Montana, but did not give separate figures for the tribe under discussion. The United States Office of Indian Affairs reported 3,085 in 1937.

Connections in which they have become noted.—It was among the Salish Indians that the noted Father De Smet worked as a missionary. The large group of languages to which this tribe belongs is known to ethnologists as the Salishan linguistic family. Flathead or Selish Lake, Flathead Pass, and Flathead County, all in Montana, also derive their names from the Salish or "Flathead" Indians.

Sematuse (phonetically SEmtē'use). Signifying "foolish" according to some, derived from an old place name according to others. Teit (1930) identified the Sematuse as a former tribe of the Salishan stock, closely related to the Salish tribe. According to his informants, one band of these people was on Big Blackfoot River, another at a place later known as "Big Camas," or "Camas Prairie," and some thought that a smaller band had headquarters near Deer Lodge, and there may have been one at Phillipsburg. Others were said to have been on the Little Blackfoot and Salmon-Trout Rivers but may not have constituted a band. Turney-High (1937), however, thinks that this tribe was mythical or else that it was the name of a non-Salishan people who preceded the Salish in western Montana.

Shoshoni. Before European weapons reached the eastern tribes, bands of Shoshoni ranged over a considerable part of eastern Montana as far north as Milk River. (See Idaho.)

Siksika. A native word signifying "black feet," by which term the tribe is best known. By some they are said to be called Blackfeet from the discoloration of their moccasins by the ashes of prairie fires, but more probably their moccasins were dyed black. Also called:

Ah-hi'-tä-pe, former name for themselves, signifying "blood people."
Ayatchinini, Chippewa name.
Ayatchiyiniw, Cree name, signifying "stranger," or "enemy."
Beaux Hommes, so given by Dobbs (1744).
Carmeneh, Crow name.
Choch-Katit, Arikara name.
Ish-te-pit'-e, Crow name.
Í tsi sí pi ša, Hidatsa name, signifying "black feet."
Katce, Sarsi name.
Ka-wi-'na-han, Arapaho name, signifying "black people."
Makadewana-ssidok, Chippewa name.
Mämakatä'wana-si'tä'-ak, Fox name.

Mkatewetitéta, Shawnee name.

Mukkudda Ozitunnug, Ottawa name (Tanner, 1830).

Netsepoyè, sometimes used by the Confederacy and signifying "people who speak our language."

Pah-kee, Shoshoni name.

Po'-o-mas, Cheyenne name, signifying "blankets whitened with earth."

Sāhā'ntlā, Kutenai name, signifying "bad people."

Sawketakix, name sometimes used by themselves, signifying "men of the plains."

S'chkoé, or S'chkoeishin, Kalispel name, from koài, "black."

Sicä'bê, Kansa name.

Si-ha'-sa-pa, Yankton Dakota name, signifying "black feet."

Skuäíshĕni, Salish name, signifying "black feet."

Stχuaíχn, Okinagan name, signifying "black."

Toñkoñko, Kiowa name, signifying "black legs."

Tuhu'vti-ómokat, Comanche name.

Wateni'hte, Arapaho name.

Connections.—The Siksika belong to the Algonquian linguistic stock, forming the most aberrant of all the well-recognized tongues of that family except Arapaho and Atsina.

Location.—In the territory stretching from North Saskatchewan River, Canada, to the southern headstreams of the Missouri in Montana, and from about longitude 105° W. to the base of the Rocky Mountains.

Subdivisions

The Siksika are divided into the following subtribes: The Siksika or Blackfeet proper, occupying the northern part of the above territory; the Kainah or Bloods south of the preceding; and the Piegan, south of the Kainah, the one best represented in the United States.

Each of the above divisions was subdivided into bands as follows:

Siksika bands:
  Aisikstukiks.
  Apikaiyiks.
  Emitahpahksaiyiks.
  Motahtosiks.
  Puhksinahmahyiks.
  Saiyiks.
  Siksinokaks.
  Tsiniktsistsoyiks.
Kainah or Blood bands:
  Ahkaiksumiks.
  Ahkaipokaks.
  Ahkotashiks.
  Ahkwonistsists.
  Anepo.
  Apikaiyiks.
  Aputosikainah.
  Inuhksoyistamiks.
  Isisokasimiks.
  Istsikainah.
  Mameoya.
  Nitikskiks.
  Saksinahmahyiks.
  Siksahpuniks.
  Siksinokaks.
Piegan bands:
  Ahahpitape.
  Ahkaiyikokakiniks.
  Apikaiyiks.
  Esksinaitupiks.
  Inuksikahkopwaiks.
  Inuksiks.
  Ipoksimaiks.
  Kahmitaiks.
  Kiyis.
  Kutaiimiks.
  Kutaisotsiman.
  Miahwahpitsiks.

Miawkinaiyiks.
Mokumiks.
Motahtosiks.
Motwainaiks.
Nitakoskitsipupiks.
Nitawyiks.
Nitikskiks.

Nitotsiksisstaniks.
Sikokitsimiks.
Sikopoksimaiks.
Sikutsipumaiks.
Susksoyiks (Hayden, 1862).
Tsiniksistsoyiks.

History.—According to certain traditions, the Siksika moved into their present territory from the northeast, and it is at least evident that they had gravitated westward, their movement probably accelerated by the acquisition of horses. They were at war with nearly all of their neighbors except the Athapascan Sarsi and the Atsina; both of these tribes usually acted with them. They were on relatively friendly terms with the English of the Hudson's Bay posts in Canada, upon whom they depended for guns and ammunition, but were hostile to the Whites on the American side, in large measure because through them their enemies received the same kind of supplies. They were several times decimated by smallpox but suffered less than many tribes not so far removed from White influences, and have never been forced to undergo removal from their home country. They are now gathered under agencies on both sides of the International Boundary and are slowly adapting themselves to White modes of life.

Population.—Mooney (1928) estimates that in 1780 there were 15,000 Blackfeet. Mackenzie (1801) gave 2,250 to 2,500 warriors for 1790, which would reduce Mooney's (1928) figures by about one-half, but in the meantime the smallpox epidemic of 1780–81 had occurred. The official Indian Report for 1858 gave 7,300 and another estimate of about the same period, said by Hayden (1862) to have been made "under the most favorable circumstances," reported 6,720. In 1909 the official enumeration of those in the United States was 2,195, and of those in Canada 2,440, a total of 4,635. The census of 1910 gave 2,367 in the United States, all but 99 of whom were Piegan. The United States Indian Office Report for 1923 gives 3,124 Blackfeet and the Report of the Canadian Department of Indian Affairs for 1924, 2,236; total, 5,360. The United States census of 1930 reported 3,145. In 1937 the Office of Indian Affairs reported 4,242.

Connections in which they have become noted.—The Siksika were peculiar (1) as one of the largest and most warlike tribes of the northern Plains, next to the Dakota alone in prominence; (2) as speaking one of three highly specialized languages of the Algonquian stock; (3) as among the bitterest opponents of explorers and traders on the American side of the International Boundary; and (4) as having given the name Blackfoot to a considerable town in Idaho, capital of Bingham County, to a creek in the same county, to mountains in Idaho and Alberta, to a river in Montana, and to a village in Glacier County, in the same State.

Spokan. Some Spokan probably entered western Montana at times and, in 1910, 134 were reported as residents of the State. (See Washington.)

Tunahe (Tunā'xe). Given by Teit (1930) as the name of an extinct Salishan tribe living in west central Montana, but identified by Turney-High (1937) as a former eastern or plains band of the Kutenai Indians, that band, in fact, from which the name Kutenai is derived.

IDAHO

Bannock. From their own name Bana'kwŭt. Also called:

Diggers, by many writers.
Ogoize, by the Kalispel.
Panai'ti, form of name given by Hoffman (1886).
Pun-nush, by the Shoshoni.
Robber Indians, by Ross (1855).
Ush-ke-we-ah, by the Crow Indians.

Connections.—The Bannock belonged to the Shoshonean branch of the Uto-Aztecan linguistic stock, being a detached branch of the Northern Paiute.

Location.—In historic times their main center was in southeastern Idaho, ranging into western Wyoming, between latitude 42° and 45° North and from longitude 113° West eastward to the main chain of the Rocky Mountains. At times they spread well down Snake River, and some were scattered as far north as Salmon River and even into southern Montana. (See also Colorado, Oregon, and Utah.)

Subdivisions

A few local group names have been preserved, such as the Kutsshundika or Buffalo-eaters, Penointikara or Honey-eaters, and Shohopanaiti or Cottonwood Bannock, but these are not well defined.

History.—Bridger met the Bannock Indians in the country above indicated as early as 1829, but contacts between them and the Whites became much more intimate with the establishment of Fort Hall in 1834. In 1869 Fort Hall Reservation was set aside for them and the Shoshoni, but they were in the habit of wandering widely and it was a long time before they were gathered into it. They claimed the territory in southwestern Montana in which are situated Virginia City and Bozeman, and it is probable that they were driven across the mountains into the Salmon River Valley at a comparatively recent period. Before 1853 they were decimated by the smallpox and were finally gathered under the Lemhi and Fort Hall agencies. Loss of their lands, failure of the herds of buffalo, and lack of prompt relief on the part of the Government occasioned an uprising of the tribe in 1878, which was suppressed by General O. O. Howard.

Population.—Bridger, in 1829, stated that the Bannock had 1,200 lodges, or a population of about 8,000, but he evidently included the neighboring Shoshoni. Mooney (1928) estimated that in 1845 there were about 1,000, but Forney, in 1858 (p. 213) gave only 400 to 500. In 1870 Jones estimated 600 and Mann 800 "Northern Bannocks." In 1901 they numbered 513 but were so intermixed with Shoshoni that the figure is uncertain. The census of 1910 reported 413, all but 50 of whom were in Idaho, and the census of 1930 gave 415, including 313 in Idaho. In 1937, 342 were reported.

Connections in which they have become noted.—The only prominence attained by the Bannock was for a brief period during the Bannock War. The name is perpetuated by a river, a range of mountains, and a county. There is also a place named Bannock in Belmont County, Ohio, and another in Butler County, Ky., but these are probably not connected with the tribe.

Kalispel. From a native term said to mean "Camas"; they were given the name Pend d'Oreilles, because when they were first met by Europeans nearly all of them wore large shell earrings. Also called:

> Ak-min'-e-shu'-me, by the Crow and meaning "the tribe that uses canoes".
> Camas People, a translation of Kalispel.
> Earring People, an English translation of Pend d'Oreilles.
> Hanging Ears, English translation of Pend d'Oreilles.
> Ni-he-ta-te-tup'i-o, Siksika name.
> Papshpûn'lĕma, Yakima name, signifying "people of the great fir trees."

Connections.—The Kalispel belonged to the interior division of the great Salishan family.

Location.—On Pend Oreille River and Lake, Priest Lake, and the lower course of Clark's Fork. They were said to have extended eastward to Thompson Lake and Horse Plains and to have hunted over some of the Salmon River country, Canada, and were formerly said to have extended to Flathead Lake and Missoula. (See also Montana and Washington.)

Subdivisions

(1) Upper Kalispel or Upper Pend d'Oreilles (in Montana from Flathead Lake and Flathead River to about Thompson Falls on Clark Fork of the Pend Oreille River, including the Little Bitterroot, southward about to Missoula and northward to the International Boundary), with bands at Flathead Lake, near Kalispel, at or near Dayton, near Polson at the foot of the lake, and possibly one at Columbia Falls; some wintered on the Bitterroot and a large band at St. Ignatius.

(2) Lower Kalispel or Lower Pend d'Oreilles or Kalispel proper (from Thompson Falls down Clark Fork, Pend Oreille Lake, Priest Lake, and Pend Oreille River nearly to the International Boundary and hunting territories along Salmon River, British Columbia).

(3) The Chewelah (in the country west of the Calispell or Chewelah Mountains in the upper part of the Colville Valley).

The Lower Kalispel also included several minor bands, the Chewelah apparently two. The Chewelah subdivision spoke a slightly different dialect and was sometimes regarded as an independent tribe.

History.—The Kalispel were visited by Lewis and Clark in 1805, and in 1809 a post was established on Pend Oreille Lake by the Northwest Company and another on Clark Fork the same year called Salish House. Emissaries of the American Fur Company reached them later, and in 1844 they were missionized by the Roman Catholic Church. July 16, 1855, the Upper Kalispel, Kutenai, and Salish surrendered all of their lands except an area about Flathead Lake which became the Jocko Reservation. The greater part of the Kalispel settled here, but part of the Lower Kalispel were gathered on Colville Reservation with the Okanagon, Colville, and a number of other tribes.

Population.—Mooney (1928) estimated that the Kalispel numbered 1,200 in 1780, but Teit (1930) considered that the prehistoric population must have been between 5,000 and 6,500, an estimate which would seem to be excessive. In 1805 Lewis and Clark estimated that there were 30 lodges of these people and a population of 1,600. In 1905 there were 640 Upper and 197 Lower Pend d'Oreilles under the Flathead Agency (Jocko Reservation) and 98 under the Colville Agency. The census of 1910 reported 386 from Montana, 157 from Washington, 15 from Idaho, and 6 from three other States. They were not separately enumerated in 1930, but the United States Office of Indian Affairs reported 97 in 1937.

Connections in which they have become noted.—The name Kalispel is preserved in that of the banking city of Kalispell, county seat of Flathead County, Mont., by Calispell Lake, and by the Calispell Mountains. The name Pend d'Oreilles is preserved in Pend Oreille Lake in northern Idaho and in Pend Oreille River in Montana, Idaho, and Washington.

Kutenai. This tribe occupied the extreme northern part of Idaho. (See Montana.)

Nez Percé. A French appellation signifying "pierced noses." Also called:

> Â'dal-k'ato'igo, Kiowa name, signifying "people with hair cut across the forehead."
> Aníporspi, Calapooya name.
> A-pa-o-pa, Atsina name (Long, 1823).

A-pū-pe', Crow name, signifying "to paddle," "paddles."
Blue Muds, name applied by traders.
Chopunnish, Lewis and Clark.
Green Wood Indians, Henry-Thompson Journal.
I'-na-cpĕ, Quapaw name.
Kamŭ'inu, own name.
Ko-mun'-i-tup'-i-o, Siksika name.
Mikadeshitchísi, Kiowa Apache name.
Nimipu, own name, signifying "the people."
Pa ka'-san-tse, Osage name, signifying "plaited hair over the forehead."
Pe ga'-zan-de, Kansa name.
Pierced Noses, English translation of name.
Po'-ge-hdo-ke, Dakota name.
Sa-áptin, Okanagon name.
Shi'wanĭsh, Tenino name for this tribe and the Cayuse, signifying "strangers
    from up the river."
Tchaxsúkush, Caddo name.
Thoig'a-rik-kah, Shoshoni name, signifying "louse eaters(?)."
Tsuhárukats, Pawnee name.
Tsútpĕli, own name.

Connections.—The Nez Percé Indians were the best known tribe of the Shahaptian division of the Shapwailutan linguistic stock, to which they gave the name commonly applied to them by Salish tribes.

Location.—The Nez Percé occupied a large part of central Idaho, and sections of southeastern Washington and northeastern Oregon. (See also Montana and Oklahoma.)

Subdivisions

The following bands are given by Spinden (1908):

Alpowĕ'ma, on Alpaha (Alpowa) Creek.
Atskaaiwawixpu, at the mouth of the northern fork of Clearwater River.
Esnime, Slate Creek Band, the Upper Salmon River Indians.
Hasotino, at Hasutin, opposite Asotin City, Wash.
Hatwĕme, on Hatweh Creek.
Heswéiwewipu, at the month of Asotin Creek.
Hĭnsepu, at Hansens Ferry on the Grande Ronde.
Imnáma, on Imnaha River.
Inantoĭnu, at the mouth of Joseph Creek.
Isäwisnemepu, near Zindels, on the Grande Ronde.
Iwatōĭnu, at Kendrick on Potlatch Creek.
Kamiaxpu, at Kamiah, at the mouth of Lawyer's Creek; this band also called
    Uyame.
Lamtáma, on Salmon River.
Lapwĕme, on Lapwai and Sweetwater Creeks.
Makapu, on Cottonwood or Maka Creek.
Painĭma, near Peck, on Clearwater River.
Pipū'ĭnĭmu, on Big Cañon Creek.
Saiksaikinpu, on the upper portion of the Southern Fork of Clearwater River.
Sakánma, between the mouth of Salmon River and the mouth of Grande Ronde.
Sálwĕpu, on the Middle Fork of Clearwater River, about 5 miles above Kooskia,
    Idaho.

Saxsano, about 4 miles above Asotin City, Wash., on the east side of Snake River.

Simīnekempu, at Lewiston, Idaho.

Taksehepu, at Agatha on Clearwater River.

Tamanmu, at the mouth of Salmon River.

Tewepu, at the mouth of Oro Fino Creek.

Toiknimapu, above Joseph Creek on the north side of the Grande Ronde.

Tsokolaikiinma, between Lewiston and Alpowa Creek.

Tukē′līklīkespu, at Big Eddy.

Tukpäme, on the lower portion of the South Fork of Clearwater River.

Tunèhepu, at Juliaetta on Potlatch Creek.

Walwáma, in Willowa Valley.

Wewi′me, at the mouth of the Grande Ronde.

Witkispu, about 3 miles below Alpowa Creek, on the east side of Snake River.

Yaktō′īnu, at the mouth of Potlatch Creek.

Yatóīnu, on Pine Creek.

The Nuksiwepu, Sahatpu, Wawawipu, Almotipu, Pinewewewixpu, Tokalatoinu, and other bands extended about 80 miles down Snake River from Lewiston.

History.—In 1805 Lewis and Clark passed through the territory of the Nez Percé Indians. The first friction between this tribe and the Whites followed upon the discovery of gold in the West and the consequent influx of miners and settlers. By treaties concluded in 1855 and 1863 they ceded all of their lands to the United States Government with the exception of one large reservation. The occupants of Wallowa Valley refused to agree to the final cessions, and the Nez Percé war of 1877 resulted, distinguished by the masterly retreat of Chief Joseph toward the Canadian line, which was almost attained by him before he was overtaken. Joseph and his followers to the number of 450 were sent to Oklahoma, but they lost so heavily from disease that in 1885 they were removed to the Colville Reservation, Wash., where a few still live.

Population.—Mooney (1928) estimates a population of 4,000 Nez Percé in 1780. In 1805 Lewis and Clark computed the total number at 6,000, if we deduct the estimated population of the two tribes later reckoned as distinct. Wilkes (1849) gives 3,000 and Gibbs (1877) estimates more than 1,700 in 1853. In 1885 the official figure was 1,437. In 1906 there were 1,534 on Lapwai Reservation and 83 on Colville Reservation, Wash. The census of 1910 reported 1,259, of whom 1,035 were in Idaho. The Report of The United States Indian Office for 1923 gave 1,415 and the report for 1937, 1,426. In 1930 the Shahaptian division of the Shapwailutan stock numbered 4,119.

Connections in which they have become noted.—The Nez Percé have claims to remembrance, (1) as the largest and most powerful tribe of the Shapwailutan stock, (2) as having given a name applied to them to the principal division of the formerly independent Shahaptian family. From this tribe Nez Perce County, Idaho, and the post village of Nezperce in Lewis County derive their names.

Paiute, Northern. Indians of this group entered the southwestern part of Idaho at times. (See Nevada.)

Palouse. This tribe extended up the Palouse River into Idaho. (See Washington.)

Salish, or Flathead. The present State of Idaho was visited to some extent by Indians of this tribe. (See Montana.)

Shoshoni, Northern. Significance of the word Shoshoni is unknown. Also called:

> Aliatan, a name taken originally from that of the Ute and subsequently applied to many Shoshoni tribes, including the Shoshoni proper.
> Bik-ta'-she, Crow name, signifying "grass lodges."
> E-wu-h·a'-wu-si, Arapaho name, signifying "people that use grass or bark for their houses or huts."
> Gens du Serpent, by the French.
> Ginebigônini, Chippewa name, signifying "snake men."
> Kinebikowininiwak, Algonkin name, signifying "serpents."
> Ma-buc-sho-roch-pan-ga, Hidatsa name.
> Miká-atí, Hidatsa name, signifying "grass lodges."
> Mi'kyashĕ, Crow name, signifying "grass lodges."
> Pezhi'-wokeyotila, Teton Dakota name, signifying "grass-thatch dwellers."
> Pi-ci'-kse-ni-tup'i-o, Siksika name.
> Sin-te'-hda wi-ca-sa, Yankton Dakota name, signifying "rattlesnake Indians."
> Sisízhanĭn, Atsina name signifying "rattlesnake men."
> Snake Indians, common English name.
> Snóă, Okanagon name.
> Wákidoħka-numak, Mandan name, signifying "snake man."
> Wĕs'ănikaciⁿga, Omaha and Ponca name, signifying "snake people."
> Zuzéca wićása, Teton Dakota name, signifying "snake people."

Connections.—The Northern Shoshoni belonged to the Shoshoni-Comanche dialectic group of the Shoshonean division of the Uto-Aztecan linguistic family.

Location.—The Northern Shoshoni occupied eastern Idaho, except the territory held by the Bannock; western Wyoming; and northeastern Utah.

Subdivisions

Their only subdivisions were a number of bands headed by popular chiefs, the make up of which was constantly shifting.

Villages

Lemhi and Central Idaho:
> Bohodai, near the junction of Middle Fork with the Salmon, and an unnamed site on upper Salmon River where a few families from Sohodai sometimes wintered.
> Guembeduka, about 7 miles north of the town of Salmon.
> Padai, scattered along Lemhi River about Salmon.

Pagadut, on Red Rock Creek, about Lima, Mont.; possibly a few families lived near Dillon, Mont.

Pasasigwana, at a warm spring in the mountains north of Clayton.

Pasimadai, on Upper Salmon River.

Sohodai, on the upper Middle Fork of Salmon River, near Three Rivers.

Fort Hall Shoshoni:

No band names given.

Bannock Creek (Kamdüka) Shoshoni (Pocatello's Band):

Biagamugep, the principal village, near Kelton.

Cache Valley (Pangwiduka) Kwagunogwai:

Along the Logan River above its junction with the Little Bear River.

Salt Lake Valley:

There are said to have been bands in the Ogden, Weber, and Salt Lake Valleys, but their names have not been preserved; they are sometimes called Ute, but Steward is certain that they were affiliated with the Shoshoni.

History.—At one time the Northern Shoshoni extended farther eastward into the Plains but there is no reason to suppose that they did not at the same time retain the mountain territories later held by them. They were affected only indirectly by the Spanish settlements to the south and southwest. In 1805 they were met by Lewis and Clark who were guided by a famous woman of their nation, Sacagawea, and from that time on contact with the Americans became fairly common. The Northern Shoshoni, particularly those under the famous chief Washakie, were unusually friendly to the Whites. They were finally gathered upon the Lemhi and Fort Fall Reservations in Idaho and the Wind River Reservation in Wyoming. By the Treaty of Fort Bridger, July 3, 1868, the eastern bands of the Shoshoni and Bannock ceded all rights to their territories in Wyoming and Idaho except the Wind River Reservation in the former state for the Shoshoni and a reservation to be set apart for the Bannock whenever they desired it. On July 30, 1869, Fort Hall Reservation was set aside for the Bannock but subsequently occupied in part by the Shoshoni. February 12, 1875, the Lemhi Reservation was established for these two tribes and the Sheepeater band of Western Shoshoni.

Population.—Mooney (1928) estimated 4,500 in the year 1845, including the Western Shoshoni. The United States Census of 1910 gave 3,840 "Shoshoni," of which number about 2,000 appear to have belonged to this division. The Report of the Office for Indian Affairs of 1917 indicated about 2,200. The census of 1930 reported 3,994 for the Northern and Western Shoshoni combined, but in 1937 the United States Office of Indian Affairs reported 3,650 Northern Shoshoni alone.

Connections in which they have become noted.—The Northern Shoshoni are the most prominent and strongest tribe of the upper plateau. They were also distinguished by the fact that their name was employed by Gallatin (1936) and later adopted by Powell (1891) for application to a linguistic stock, a stock now considered a branch of a much larger group, the Uto-Aztecan.   The Shoshoni came into prominence in the last century (1) because Sacagawea or Bird Woman, the famous guide and interpreter of Lewis and Clark in their expedition to the Pacific, was a member of this tribe; and (2) because of the ability of chief Washakie and his constant friendship for the Whites.   The name Shoshone has been applied to rivers and mountains in Wyoming and Nevada; to a lake in Yellowstone National Park; to the Shoshone Falls of Snake River; to a county in Idaho; and to places in Inyo County, Calif.; Lincoln County, Idaho; White Pine County, Nev.; and Fremont County, Wyo.

Shoshoni, Western.   Significance of the word Shoshoni is unknown.

Connections.—The same as for the Northern Shoshoni.

Location.—Central and western Idaho, northwestern Utah, central and northeastern Nevada, and a small territory in California north of and about Death and Panamint Valleys.

Subdivisions

The names of a great many local groups have been recorded, usually signifying that they were "eaters" of certain kinds of food, but most of these seem to have belonged to territories rather than people, the "eaters" in each being subject to change.   A few of these have, however, acquired special interest and some measure of permanence as, for instance, the Tukuarika, Tukuadüka, or Sheep Eaters, extending from the Yellowstone National Park to the middle course of Salmon River; the Gosiute of northern Utah and eastern Nevada and the Panamint or Koso, the Californian representatives of the division.

Villages

Steward (1938) gives the following villages under the several natural areas occupied by these Indians:

Lida and vicinity:
  Clayton Valley.
  Kamuva, or Wipa, several miles east of Goldfield.
  Montezuma.
  Old Camp, on the north side of Gold Mountain.
  Pauwaha' (Lida).
  Tumbasai'uwi, at Stonewall Mountain.
Eastern California:
  Saline Valley:
    Isha'mba (Waucoba Spring).
    Ko (Saline Valley).
    Navadu, at the Springs in Cottonwood Canyon which runs west from Death Valley.
    Tuhu, at Goldbelt Spring.
  Little Lake and Koso Mountains:
    Mua'ta (Coso Hot Springs).
    Pagunda (Little Lake).
    Pakwa'si (at Alancha).
    Uyuwu'mba, about 5 miles south of Darwin.

Panamint Valley:
    No villages given.
Northern Death Valley:
    Mahunu (springs in Grapevine Canyon and probably Grapevine Springs).
    Ohyu, at Surveyor's Well.
    Panuga (Mesquite Springs).
Central and Southern Death Valley:
    Tumbica, at the several springs at Furnace Creek.
    Village (perhaps) some 15 miles south of Furnace Creek.
Beatty and Belted Mountains (camps):[7]
    Howell Ranch, near Springdale.
    Hunusu, at Burn's Ranch.
    Indian Camp, at the head of Oasis Valley.
    Mutsi, in the vicinity of the water holes marked merely "Tanks" on the U. S. Geol. Surv. map.
    Sivahwa, a few miles north of the last.
    Tunava, at Whiterock Springs.
    Takanawa, at Hick's Hot Springs.
    Sakaiñaga, at the mouth of Beatty Wash on the Amagrosa River.
    Panavadu, somewhere near the last.
    Wuniakuda, 2 or 3 miles east of the Ammonia Tanks.
    Wiva, at Oaksprings.
    Kuikun (Captain Jack Spring).
    Tupipa, at Tippipah Springs.
    Pokopa, at Topopah Spring.
    Pagambuhan (Cane Spring).
Ione Valley, Reese River, and Smith Creek Valley:
    Reese River Valley (camps):[7]
        Wiyunutuahunupi, at the first creek south of Austin.
        Angasikigada, 1 mile from the last.
        Tutumbihunupi, 1½ miles from the last.
        Ohaogwaihunupi, 1 mile from the last.
        Bambishpahunupi, about 2 miles from last.
        Songwatumbihun, about 1½ miles from the last.
        Gunuvijep, about 1½ miles from the last.
        Biahunupi, at Big Creek, west of Kingston.
        Mezaguahunupi, 2 miles from the last.
        Oapihunupi, 2 miles from the last.
        Tudupihunupi, 1½ miles from the last.
        Yudigivoihunupi, 2 miles from the last.
        Aihyuhunupi, about 2 miles from the last.
        Navahodava, 3 miles from the last.
        Guvadakuahunupi, 2 miles from the last or about halfway between Austin and Bell's Ranch.
        Baiambasahunupi, about 1 mile from the last.
        Kwinahunupi, 2 miles from the last.
        Tosakuahunupi, 3 miles from the last.
        Asunguahunupi, 1 mile from the last.
        Wakaihunupi, 1 mile from the last.
        Boyuwihunupi, 3 miles from the last.
        Yumbahunupi, 3 miles from the last.
        Onihunupi, about 2½ miles from the last.

---

[7] Camps given in order of location; names not alphabetized.

Adumbihunupi, about 2½ miles from the last.

Bukwiyohunupi, about 4 miles from the last and a little south of Bell's Ranch

Reese River Valley (winter sites): [8]

Sunungoi, about 10 miles northwest of Austin and slightly north of Mount Airy.

Sova, a spring near the summit of Mount Airy.

Tuosava, 2 or 3 miles south of the last.

Yutomba, 1 mile from the last.

Evimba, 3 or 4 miles from the last.

Dumboi, 2 or 3 miles from the last.

Hukumba, about 2 miles from the last.

Kosiva, 3 miles from the last.

Wupayagahunupi, 3 miles from the last.

Dawishiwuhunupi, 2 miles from the last.

Kunuvidumbihunupi, about 1½ miles from the last.

Pazuyohoi, 4 miles from the last.

Wangodusikihunupi, 2 miles from the last.

Ava, 2 miles from the last.

Bohoba, a spring 3 miles from the last.

Dongwishava, slightly south of Ione, west of the Bell Ranch.

There is also a camp southwest of Berlin Peak at a spring called Wanzi awa.

Great Smoky Valley and Monitor Valley:

No villages given.

Kawich Mountains (winter camps):

Breen Creek.

Hot Creek, about 10 miles north of Tybo.

Hot Springs, to the south, had several winter encampments.

Hugwapagwa (Longstreet Canyon or Horse Canyon).

Kunugiba (Tybo Creek).

Reveille Mill.

Tuava (Rose Spring).

Little Smoky Valley and vicinity:

Little Smoky Valley:

Dzishava (Moore Station).

Indian Creek (Bagumbush?), 6–7 miles north of Kwadumba.

Kwadumba (Snowball), 8 miles north of Sapava.

Kwatsugu (Fish Creek).

Sapava (Hick's Station), 12 miles north of Morey.

Tutoya, at a spring 4 or 5 miles south of Morey, on the west side of the valley.

Fish Springs Valley:

Butler's Place, about 20 miles north of Wongodoya.

Udulfa (Hot Creek).

Wongodoya, at a spring in the hills west of Fish Springs.

Railroad Valley (camps in north end of valley):

Akamba, or probably also Watoya, at a spring west of Mount Hamilton.

Bambasa, on the west side of Mount Hamilton.

Bauduin (Warm Spring).

Bawazivi (Currant Creek).

Biadoyava, at Blue Eagle Springs.

Nyala, native name unknown.

Suhuva (Duckwater).

Wongodupijugo, southeast of Green Spring.

---

[8] Winter sites given in order of location; names not alphabetized.

Steptoe Valley:
"There were . . . villages at Ely, on Duck Creek, about 8 miles northwest of McGill, and at Warm Spring, Schellbourne, Egan Canyon, and Cherry Creek."
Spring, Snake, and Antelope Valleys:
Spring Valley:
Aidumba, at a spring west of Aurun.
Basamba, slightly up the hill west of Sogowosugu.
Basiamba, in vicinity of Oceola.
Basawinuba, either 3 or 4 miles northwest of Aurun.
Basawinuba (Mud Springs), about 7 miles south of Aurun.
Basonip, about 7 miles (?) south of Cleveland Ranch.
Bauumba, near Shoshone.
Biabauwundu, at Cleveland Ranch.
Haiva, about 6 miles north of Cleveland or two canyons south of Wongovitwuninogwap.
Sogowosugu, at Aurun.
Supuva, at Anderson's Ranch.
Taiwudu, on west slope of Snake Mountains.
Toziup, on west slope of Mount Moriah.
Tuhuva, between Yellen's and Cleveland Ranches.
Tupa, about 7 miles north of Anderson's Ranch.
Wongovitwuninogwap, on Valley Creek, about 10 miles north of Cleveland
Antelope Valley:
Bohoba, at Mike Springs south of the villages in Antelope Valley.
Hugapa, at Chinn Creek.
Kwadumba, at a spring about 3 miles south of Tippetts.
Suhuva, at a spring near Kwadumba.
Toiva, at a spring at north end of valley.
Wadoya, at a spring 15 miles north of Toiva.
Snake Valley:
Bauwunoida, at the present Baker.
Biaba, at Big Spring.
Tosakowaip, at Silver Creek.
Tunkahniva, near a cave near Lehman Cave in the canyon west of Baker.
Cave Valley, south of Steptoe Valley:
Daint.
Gosiute Shoshoni:
A cave on the north end of the Skull Valley Mountains a short distance from the present highway.
Haiyashawiyep, near present town called Iosepa.
Iowiba, in mountains just east of Skull Valley Reservation.
Ongwove, a few miles south of Orr's Ranch.
Suhudaosa, at the present Orr's Ranch (?).
Tiava, on present reservation.
Tozava, at a spring on west side of Lakeside Range.
Tutiwunupa, on west slope of the Cedar Mountains, just east of Clive.
Utcipa, south of Tutiwunupa on west slope of Cedar Mountains.
Wanapo'ogwaipi, at Indian Springs, south of Ongwove.
Pine Creek and Diamond Valley:
Bauwiyoi, a group of at least 6 encampments at the foot of the Roberts Mountains.

Todzagadu, on the west side of the Sulphur Spring Mountains.

Tupagadu, west of the Alkali flat in Diamond Valley.

Ruby Valley and Vicinity:

A settlement on south side of Spruce Mountains.

A village on the east slope of the Pequop Mountains.

Baguwa, in the flats near Overland.

Butte Valley, at north end on a canyon called Natsumbagwic.

Medicine Spring, on the west slope of the Cedar Mountains, east of Franklin Lake.

Suhuwia, on the headwaters of Franklin River.

Toyagadzu (Clover Valley).

Waihamuta, on the creek against the hills, west of the Neff Ranch.

Wongogadu, on north side of Spruce Mountains.

Yuogumba or Sihuba (Long Valley).

Humboldt River (districts):

A village in a valley a little south of Elko.

A village somewhere on upper Huntington Creek.

Banadia, scattered along both sides of Lamoille Creek.

Badukoi, village about 3 miles below Carlin.

Elko, preferred site for village being at the mouth of the South Fork.

Independence Valley, in the valley of what is called Magpie or Maggie Creek.

Kinome, 5 miles north of Huntington.

Palisade, people lived near here along Humboldt River.

Sahoogep, at Lee.

The valley of North Fork.

Toyagadzu, at Wells.

Tukwampandai, at Deeth.

Battle Mountain and Vicinity:

There was a concentration of population between Battle Mountain and Iron Point.

Snake River (three villages between Hagerman and Bruneau):

Ototumb, near Bliss.

Pazintumb, about 8 miles below Hagerman.

Saihunupi, about 4 miles below Hagerman.

Boise River and Vicinity:

No village names recorded.

Grouse Creek:

Kuiva, on Raft River, probably near Lynn and Yost.

O'o or Podongoe, a little southwest of Lucin.

Paduyavavadizop (Dove (?) Creek).

Tusaid or Angapuni (Grouse Creek).

Promontory Point (Hukundu''ka):

Nagwituwep, on Blue Creek, north of the old railroad.

Nanavadzi, near Little Mountain, east of Promontory Point.

Sudotsa, scattered along valley of Bear River from near Bear River City to Deweyville.

Tongishavo, on the west side of Promontory Point near Mount Tarpey.

The following names, derived from various sources, may be appended:

Kaidatoiabie (with 6 subbands), in northeastern Nevada.

Nahaego, in Reese River Valley, and about Austin, Nev.

Pagantso (with 3 subbands), in Ruby Valley, Nev.

Sunananahogwa, on Reese River, Nev.
Temoksee, in Reese River Valley, Nev.
Toquimas, in lower Reese River Valley, Nev.

History.—The history of the Western Shoshoni was practically identical with that of the Northern Shoshoni and Northern Paiute, except that their territory was somewhat more remote from the paths followed by American explorers in the north and Spaniards in the south. In 1825 Jedidiah Smith made several journeys across Nevada and may have been preceded by Old Greenwood. In 1847 the Mormons settled Nevada and came in contact with some of the eastern representatives of this Shoshonean division. Narratives of explorers generally waste few words on these Indians or the neighboring Paiute, classing them indiscriminately as "diggers" and dismissing them all with a few contemptuous words. They were affected materially by the discovery of the Comstock Lode. Although it was not in their territory, prospectors penetrated everywhere, stock was introduced which sorely affected the food supplies of the natives, and the resulting friction affected first the Northern Paiute and somewhat later the Shoshoni. Steward says:

By 1865, Shoshoni of Battle Mountain and Austin were involved. Meanwhile south of the Great Salt Lake in Utah and in eastern California, Shoshoni, especially those known as Gosiute, were committing depredations against immigrants, raiding the pony express and attacking the stage line which ran through this territory. . . . For protection, Fort Ruby in Ruby Valley was built in 1862. . . . An army unit massacred a large number of Shoshoni in Steptoe Valley in 1862, but by 1865 the strife was ended. In 1869 the railroad across the continent was completed and the native period was at an end. Shoshoni of central Nevada and of the more remote valleys seem to have kept pretty well out of the conflict. The treaty of 1863 included all the Shoshoni of northern Nevada. They were given the Western Shoshone or Duck Valley Reservation in 1877 (by Executive Order of April 16), but by no means all Shoshoni went to it. A few of the more westerly Shoshoni joined Paiute on reservations in western Nevada, but most Shoshoni remained near their native haunts, gradually abandoning their native economy and attaching themselves to ranches or mining towns. (Steward, 1938, p. 7.)

The Carlin Farms Reservation northwest of Elko was set aside by Executive Order of May 10, 1877, but restored to the public domain by Executive Order of January 16, 1879.

Population.—Mooney (1938) estimated that there were 4,500 Northern and Western Shoshoni together in 1845. The United States Census of 1910 gave 3,840, a figure which included about 1,800 Western Shoshoni. The United States Indian Office Report for 1917 indicated perhaps 1,500. The census of 1930 raised this figure into the neighborhood of 2,000, but in 1937 the Indian Office returned only 1,201.

Skitswish. From their own name; significance unknown. Also called:

> Coeur d'Alêne, a French appellation meaning "awl heart," said to have been used originally by a chief to indicate the size of a trader's heart.
> Q'ma'shpăl, Yakima name, meaning "camas people."
> Pointed Hearts, derived from the word Coeur d'Alêne.

Connections.—The Skitswish belonged to the inland division of the Salishan stock, their closest relatives being the Kalispel or Pend d'Oreilles, and other eastern tribes.

Location.—On the headwaters of Spokane River from a little above Spokane Falls to the sources, including Coeur d'Alêne Lake and all its tributaries, and the head of the Clearwater.

Subdivisions and Villages

Teit (1930) reports the following divisions and villages, noting that the last in reality may have included two sections, the Coeur d'Alêne Lake Division and the Spokane River Division:

St. Joe River Division:

Ntcaamtsen (.ntcäa'mtsɛn), at the confluence of the St. Joe and St. Maries Rivers.

Stiktakeshen (.sti'qᵘtakɛcɛn?), near the mouth of St. Joe River, on the river, or nearby on the lake.

Stotseawes (stotsɛäwɛs), on St. Joe River, at the place now called Fish Trap by the Whites.

Takolks (ta'x.olks) (?), on upper Hangman's River, at a spring near the foot of the hill just south of De Smet.

Tcatowashalgs (tcat'owacalgs), on St. Joe River a little above Stotseawes.

Tcetishtasheshen (tcêti'ctacɛcɛn), probably on the lake, near the Stiktakeshen, on the north or east side, not far from the mouth of the river.

Coeur d'Alêne River Division:

Athlkwarit (ałqwarit), at Harrison.

Gwalit (gwa'lît), near the lake and close to Harrison.

Hinsalut (hînsä'lut), on Coeur d'Alêne River a little above Smakegen.

Kokolshtelps (qoqolc'têlps), a little above Nestagwast.

Nalstkathlkwen (nalstqa'łxwɛn), a little above Senshalemants.

Neatskstem (ne'atsxstɛm), on Coeur d'Alêne River a little above Athlkwarit.

Nêstagwast (nest'a'gwast), at Black Lake, at a tributary river and lake here.

Senshalemants (sɛncä'lɛmänts), a little above Hinsalut.

Smakegen (sma'qɛgen), at Medimont.

Skwato (sk'wat'o'), at old mission.

Tclatcalk (tcła'tcalxw), on Coeur d'Alêne Lake, close to the mouth of Coeur d'Alêne River.

Coeur d'Alêne Lake and Spokane River Division.

Ntaken (nt'a'q'ɛn) Hayden Lake), north of Coeur d'Alêne Lake.

Tcelatcelitcemen (tcêlätcelîtcɛmɛn), halfway down Coeur d'Alêne Lake, on the east side.

Ntcemkainkwa (ntc'ɛmqa'inqwa), at Coeur d'Alêne City.

Smethlethlena (smɛłɛłe'na), near the last on the same side.

Tpoenethlpem, very near the preceding, on the same side.

Nsharept (ncã'rɛpt), a little below the next to the last.
Stcatkwei (stcatkwe'i), a little below the last.
Kamilen (q'ämi'len), at Post Falls.
Hinsaketpens (hinsaq'a'tpɛns), about one mile above the Spokane bridge.
Newashalks (ne'ɛwa'calqs), a little below the preceding.
Ntsetsawolsako (ntsetsakwolsa'ko?), on Tamarack Creek, toward the moun-
tains.
Neshwahwe (nesxwa'xxwe), on the river a little below the last two.
Nesthlihum (nesłi'xum), a little below the last.
Tcanokwaken (tcanokwã'kɛn?), a little below the last.
Mulsh (mu'lc), at Green Acres.
Tcatenwahetpem (tcatenwa'xetpɛm), a short distance below Green Acres,
and about 20 miles above Spokane City.

History.—There is no tradition of any Skitswish migrations. Like
so many other tribes in the region, the Skitswish were first brought
clearly to the attention of Whites by Lewis and Clark. Although
suffering the usual heavy losses following contact with Europeans,
they continued to live in the same country and were finally allotted
a reservation there bearing their name.

Population.—Mooney (1928) estimated that the Skitswish may have
numbered 1,000 in 1780, but Teit (1930) raises this to from 3,000 to
4,000. In 1905 the United States Indian Office returned 494, all on the
one reservation. The census of 1910 gave 293, probably below the
true figure, as the United States Indian Office reported 601 on the
reservation, including probably some Spokane, and in 1937 it returned
608.

Connections in which they have become noted.—Coeur d'Alêne Lake in
northern Idaho and a town on its shores preserve the memory of the
Skitswish, as they bear the name given this tribe by the French.

Snakes, see **Paiute, Northern.**

Spokan. The Spokan extended a few miles into this State along its
western boundary. (See Washington.)

WASHINGTON

The State of Washington was occupied by a great number of Indian
tribes formerly very populous, particularly those along the coast.
There are few traditions regarding migrations and those which we
have apply almost entirely to the interior people. After the Whites
came it was unlikely that the Indians would move eastward in the
face of the invasion and impossible for them to move westward;
hence we do not have to trace various stages of long migrations due to
displacement by the Whites and the overland retreat which followed,
so marked in the history of the eastern Indians. Contrary to an older
view, which held that Salishan tribes formerly extended to the lower
Columbia and were driven north by Shahaptians, pushed forward in

turn by Shoshonean peoples, it seems that the relative positions of
Salishans and Shahaptians has been unchanged for an uncertain
period of time and that, as a matter of fact, the Shoshoneans have
been pushed southward although this movement was very recent.
The Athapascan Kwalhioqua must represent a comparatively late
invasion although that may not have been so recent as their anoma-
lous position would lead one to suppose. There is also evidence of a
much earlier movement when the Salishans came down upon the
coast. The earliest European to meet any of the peoples of Washington was probably Juan de Fuca, a Greek navigator sailing under
the Spanish flag, who, in 1592, visited the straits which now bear
his name. Other Spanish explorers followed, and were later succeeded
by English and Americans. The continual resort of trading vessels
to Nootka on the west coast of Vancouver Island served to distribute
European commodities and had a considerable influence among the
tribes of Washington. In the latter part of the eighteenth century
traders of the Hudson Bay and Northwest Companies made their
appearance, but the Washington peoples first come squarely out
upon the stage of history with the descent of the Columbia by Lewis
and Clark in 1805–6. These pioneers gave the first general description of the region, enumerated the aboriginal peoples found in occupancy, and attempted estimates of their numbers. For some time
afterward the territory was dominated by representatives of British
companies and the land was claimed by England, while the only
attempt to exploit it on the part of Americans, the settlement of
Astoria, was soon abandoned. Following upon the acceptance of
the 49th parallel of latitude as the International Boundary, however,
and still more the discovery of gold in California and the opening
up of the "Oregon trail," settlers from the Eastern States began to
pour in in numbers. It was thereafter inevitable that friction should
develop between the newcomers and the aborigines. There were
wars with the Nez Percé, Yakima, and other tribes, but the Indians
suffered less in this way than from European diseases, particularly the
smallpox, which began their ravages before Lewis and Clark appeared,
from spirituous liquors, and from a general dislocation of their aboriginal adjustments. The destruction was greatest in the Columbia
Valley, which as the main artery of travel and trade was peculiarly
exposed to epidemics, and within a few years the greater part of the
once teeming populations of the lower valley were practically wiped
out of existence. Roman Catholic missions sprang up at an early
date in the eastern part of the territory, and were soon followed by
those of Protestant denominations, notable among which was that
conducted among the Cayuse by Marcus Whitman (1838–47). As
in other parts of the United States, the Indians gradually parted

with their lands and were placed upon reservations, though in most cases they were not removed so far from their original homes as in the eastern parts of the Union.

The above sketch will show enough of the history of most of the tribes in this area, though some details have been added in certain cases (i. e., in connection with the Cayuse, Chilluckittequaw, Chimakum, Chinook, Klickitat, and Yakima. (See Ray, 1932, and Spier and Sapir, 1930.)

Cathlamet. Significance unknown. Also called:

> Guasámas, or Guithlamethl, by the Clackamas.
> Kathlamet, own name.
> Kwillu'chini, by the Chinook.

Connections.—The Cathlamet belonged to the Chinookan stock. The dialect to which they have given their name was spoken as far up the Columbia River as Ranier.

Location.—On the south bank of Columbia River near its mouth, claiming the territory between Tongue Point and the neighborhood of Puget Island, and on the north bank from the mouth of Grays Bay to a little east of Oak Point.

Villages

Ika'naiak, on the north side of the Columbia River at the mouth of Coal Creek Slough just east of Oak Point.

Ilo'humin, on the north side of Columbia River opposite Puget Island and near the mouth of Alockman Creek.

Kathla'amat, on the south side of Columbia River about 4 miles below Puget Island.

Ta'nas ilu', on Tanas Ilahee Island on the south side of the Columbia River.

Wa'kaiyakam, across Alockman Creek opposite Ilo'humin.

Population.—Mooney (1928) estimated 450 Cathlamet in 1780. In 1805–6 Lewis and Clark gave 300. In 1849 Lane reported 58. They are now extinct as a separate group.

Connection in which they have become noted.—The capital of Wahkiakum County, Washington, perpetuates the name of the Cathlamet.

Cathlapotle. Meaning "people of Lewis (Na'p!ōɪx.) River."

Connections.—The Cathlapotle belonged to the Chinookan linguistic stock and were placed by Spier (1936) in the Clackamas division of Upper Chinook but by Berreman (1937) apparently with the Multnomah.

Location.—On the lower part of Lewis River and the southeast side of the Columbia River, in Clarke County.

Villages

The main village of the Cathlapotle was Nahpooitle, at the mouth of Lewis River, but to this should perhaps be added Wakanasisi, opposite the mouth of Willamette River.

Population.—Mooney (1928) estimated 1,300 Cathlapotle in 1780; Lewis and Clark, 900 in 1806.

Connection in which they have become noted.—Lewis River was once known by the name of Cathlapotle.

Cayuse.   The Cayuse were located about the heads of Wallawalla, Umatilla, and Grande Ronde Rivers, extending from the Blue Mountains to Deschutes River, Washington and Oregon.   (See Oregon.)

Chehalis.   Meaning "sand," the name derived originally, according to Gibbs (1877), from a village at the entrance of Grays Harbor. Also called:

> Atchiχe′lish, Calapooya name.
> Ilga′t, Nestucca name.
> Lower Chehalis, name used by Spier (1927).
> Staq-tûbc, Puyallup name.

Connections.—The Chehalis belonged to the coastal division of the Salishan linguistic family, being most intimately related to the Humptulips, Wynoochee, and Quinault.

Location.—On the lower course of Chehalis River, especially on the south side, and on the south side of Grays Bay.   In later times the Chehalis occupied territory to and about Willapa Bay that had formerly been held by the Chinook.

Villages

Chehalis (Gibbs, 1877), on the south side of Grays Harbor near Westport, in country earlier occupied by the Chinook.

Chiklisilkh (Gibbs), at Point Leadbetter, Willapa Bay, in territory earlier occupied by Chinook.

Hlakwun (Curtis, 1907–9), near Willapa on Willapa River in territory earlier occupied by the Chinook.

Kaulhlak (Curtis), at the head of Palux River, earlier in Chinook country.

Klumaitumsh (Gibbs and Boas personal information), given doubtfully as the name of a former band or village on the south side of Grays Harbor at its entrance.

Nai′yasap (Curtis), on Willapa River in territory earlier occupied by Chinook.

Nickomin (Swan 1857 and Boas, personal information), on North River which flows into Willapa Bay, in territory earlier occupied by the Chinook.

Noohooultch (Gibbs), on the south side of Grays Harbor.

Noosiatsks (Gibbs), on the south side of Grays Harbor.

Nooskoh (Gibbs), on a creek opposite Whishkah River.

Qyan (Gairdner, 1841), on the north point of Grays Harbor.

Talal (Gibbs), at Ford's Prairie on the Chehalis River near Centralia, and therefore far outside of the Chehalis territory proper.
Willapa, on Willapa River and in earlier Chinook country.

The following villages were originally occupied by Chinook but seem to have shifted in population or language or both so as to become Chehalis: Hwa'hots, Nutskwethlso'k, Quela'ptonlilt, Quer'quelin, Tske'lsos.

Population.—Mooney (1928) estimated a population of 1,000 in the year 1780 for the Lower and Upper Chehalis, the Cowlitz, the Humptulips, and related tribes, but the number had sunk to 170 by 1907. However, the census of 1910 gives 282 for the same group exclusive of the Cowlitz. In 1923 the United States Indian Office returned 89, and in 1937, 131.

Connections in which they have become noted.—A river, county, and city in Washington preserve the name of the Chehalis. There is a Chehalis in Minnesota but its name probably has no connection with that of the Washington tribe.

Chelan. The name is derived from Chelan Lake.

Connections.—An interior Salish tribe speaking the Wenachee dialect and separated tentatively from that tribe by Spier (1927).

Location.—At the outlet of Lake Chelan.

Population.—No data.

Connections in which they have become noted.—The name Chelan is shared not only by the lake above mentioned but by Chelan Falls, a range of mountains, a county, and two post villages, Chelan and Chelan Falls.

Chilluckittequaw. Significance unknown.

Connections.—The Chilluckittequaw belonged to the Chinookan linguistic stock.

Location.—As reported by Lewis and Clark, the Chilluckittequaw lay along the north side of Columbia River, in the present Klickitat and Skamania Counties, from about 10 miles below the Dalles to the neighborhood of the Cascades. Spier (1936) thinks they may have been identical with the White Salmon or Hood River group of Indians and perhaps both. In the latter case we must suppose that they extended to the south side of the Columbia.

Subdivisions and Villages

Itkilak or Ithlkilak (occupied jointly with Klickitat), at White Salmon Landing.
Nanshuit (occupied jointly with Klickitat), at the present Underwood.
Smackshop, a band of Chilluckittequaw extending from the River Labiche (Hood River ?) to the Cascades.
Tgasgutcu (occupied jointly with Klickitat), said to be about ½ mile west of a long, high mountain opposite Mosier, Oreg., and at the same time about a mile above White Salmon Landing, an apparent inconsistency.

Thlmieksok or Thlmuyaksok, ½ mile from the last; in 1905 the site of the Burket Ranch.

Historical Note.—According to Mooney (1928), a remnant of the Chilluckittequaw lived near the mouth of the White Salmon River until 1880 when they removed to the Cascades, where a few still resided in 1895.

Population.—Mooney (1928) estimated 3,000 for this tribe in 1780. In 1806 Lewis and Clark placed the figure at 1,400, besides 800 Smackshop, or a total of 2,200.

Chimakum.   Significance of the name is unknown.   Also called:

> Aqokúlo, own name.
> Port Townsend Indians, popular name.

Connections.—The Chimakum, the Quileute, and the Hoh (q. v.) together constituted the Chimakuan linguistic stock, which in turn was probably connected with the Salishan stock.

Location.—On the peninsula between Hood's Canal and Port Townsend.

History.—The Chimakum were constantly at war with the Clallam and other Salish tribes and, being inferior in numbers, suffered very much at their hands.   They were included in the Point-no-Point Treaty of 1855 and placed on the Skokomish Reservation, where they gradually diminished in numbers until, in 1890, Boas was able to find only three individuals who could speak their language, and then but imperfectly.

Population.—Mooney (1928) estimates 400 Chimakum in 1780, and Gibbs (1877), 90 in 1855.   The census of 1910 enumerated 3.

Connection in which they have become noted.—Attention was called to the Chimakum in early days by their warlike character and the uniqueness of their language.

Chinook.   From Tsinúk, their Chehalis name.   Also called:

> Ala'dshūsh, Nestucca name.
> Flatheads, a name shared with a number of other tribes in the region from their custom of deforming the head.
> Thlála'h, Clackama name.

Connections.—The Chinook belonged to the Lower Chinook division of the Chinookan family.

Location.—On the north side of the Columbia River from its mouth to Grays Bay (not Grays Harbor), a distance of about 15 miles, and north along the seacoast to include Willapa or Shoalwater Bay.   Ray (1938) makes a separate division to include the Shoalwater Chinook but it will be more convenient to treat them under one head.   It is understood that they differed not at all in dialect.

Towns

(As given by Ray (1938), except as otherwise indicated)

Clamoitomish (Sapir, 1930), in Grays Bay.

Hakelsh, at the mouth of Smith Creek on the northeast shore of Willapa Bay.

Hwa'hots, at a former settlement called Bruceport about 3 miles north of the mouth of Palix River.

Ini'sal, on Naselle River where it enters the arm of Willapa Bay.

Iwa'lhat, at the mouth of Wallicut River, which bears its name in a corrupted form.

Kalawa'uus, on the peninsula at Oysterville Point.

Killaxthokle (Lewis and Clark, 1905–6), probably on Willapa Bay.

Kwatsa'mts, on Baker Bay at the mouth of Chinook River, north side of the Columbia.

Lapi'lso, on an island in an arm of Willapa Bay below the mouth of Naselle River.

Ma'hu, at the mouth of Nemah River below the present town of Nemah.

Mo'kwal, at the mouth of Deep River on Grays Bay.

Nahume'nsh, on the west side of North River at its mouth on the north shore of Willapa Bay.

Namla'iks, at Goose Point.

Na'mstcats, at a site now called Georgetown between Tokeland and North Cove.

Nokska'itmithls, at Fort Canby on Cape Disappointment.

No'skwalakuthl, at Ilwaco, named after its last chief.

Nu'kaunthl, at Tokeland, named after its chief.

Nu'patstcthl, at the site of Nahcotta, on the peninsula opposite the mouth of Nemah River.

Nutskwethlso'k, on Willapa Bay west of Bay Center.

Nuwi'lus, on the site of Grayland on the coast.

Quela'ptonlilt (Swan, 1857), at the mouth of Willapa River.

Querquelin (Swan), at the mouth of Querquelin River, which flows into Palix River from the south near the mouth of the latter.

Se'akwal, on the north bank of the Columbia a short distance below Mo'kwal.

Tokpi'luks, at the mouth of Palix River.

Tse'yuk, at Oysterville on the peninsula north of Nahcotta.

Tske'lsos, on Willapa River between South Bend and Raymond.

Ya'kamnok, at Sandy Point 3 miles south of Goose Point, the extreme north point at Bay Center.

History.—Though the Chinook had been known to traders for an indefinite period previously, they were first described by Lewis and Clark, who visited them in 1805. From their proximity to Astoria and their intimate relations with the early traders, they soon became well known, and their language formed the chief Indian basis for the Chinook jargon, first employed as a trade language, which ultimately extended from California to Alaska. In the middle of the nineteenth century they became mixed with the Chehalis with whom they ultimately fused entirely, dropping their own language. The Chinook of later census returns are composed of a number of other tribes of the same stock.

Population.—Mooney (1928) estimates that there were 800 of these Indians in 1780, "including the Chinook and Killaxthokl." In 1805 Lewis and Clark gave 400 on Columbia River alone. In 1885 Swan states that there were 112. They are now nearly extinct though Ray (1938) discovered three old people still living as late as 1931–36.

Connection in which they have become noted.—The name of the Chinook tribe became famous (1) because of intimate dealings between the Chinook and British and American traders, (2) on account of the extension of their name to the related tribes now classed in the Chinookan stock, (3) because the name was also extended to the Chinook jargon or Oregon Trade Language known throughout the entire Northwest, (4) because of its application to the Chinook or Pacific wind, and (5) from its application to towns in Pacific County, Wash., and Blaine County, Mont.

Clackamas. Placed on both sides of the Columbia, but I prefer to follow Berreman (1937) in limiting the term to groups living on the Oregon side. (See Oregon.)

Clallam. Meaning "strong people." Also spelled Nu-sklaim, S'Klallam, Tla'lem.

Connections.—The Clallam were a tribe of the coastal division of the Salishan linguistic stock most closely connected with the Songish.

Location.—On the south side of the Strait of Juan de Fuca, between Port Discovery and Hoko River. Later the Clallam occupied the Chimakum territory also and a small number lived on the lower end of Vancouver Island.

Villages

Elwah, at the mouth of Elwah River.

Hoko, at the mouth of Hoko Creek.

Huiauulch, on the site of modern Jamestown, 5 miles east of Dungeness.

Hunnint or Hŭnglʹnglt, on the east side of Clallam Bay; this town and Klatlawas together were called Xainañt by Erna Gunther (1927).

Kahtai, at Port Townsend, occupied after the destruction of the Chimakum.

Kaquaith (or Skakwiyel), at Port Discovery.

Klatlawas, the Tlătlăwaiʹis of Curtis (1907–9), on the west side of Clallam Bay; see Hunnint.

Kwahamish, a fishing village on the Lyre River.

Mekoös, on Beecher Bay, Vancouver Island, B. C.

Pistchin, on Pysht Bay.

Sequim or Suktcikwiiñ, on Sequim Bay or Washington Harbor.

Sestietl, Upper Elwah.

Stehtlum, at new Dungeness.

Tclanuk, on Beecher Bay, Vancouver Island, B. C.

Tsako, at the former mouth of Dungeness River.

Tsewhitzen, on Port Angeles Spit, 2 or 3 miles west of the old town of Stehtlum.

Yennis, at Port Angeles or False Dungeness.

Population.—Mooney (1928) estimated 2,000 Clallam in 1780. In 1854 Gibbs estimated 800. In 1855, 926 were reported. In 1862 Eells estimated 1,300 but gave 597 in 1878. In 1881 he reduced this to 485. In 1904, 336 were returned. By the census of 1910, 398 were reported; by the United States Indian Office in 1923, 535, and in 1937, 764.

Connections in which they have become noted.—The name Clallam is perpetuated by its application to a bay, a county, a river, and a precinct in the State of Washington.

Clalskanie. (See Oregon.)

Columbia or **Sinkiuse-Columbia.** So called because of their former prominent association with Columbia River, where some of the most important bands had their homes. Also called:

Bō'tcaced, by the Nez Percé, probably, meaning "arrows" or "arrow people."
Isle-de-Pierre, a traders' name, perhaps from a place in their country or for a band of the tribe.
Middle Columbia Salish, so called by Teit (1928) and Spier (1930 b).
Papspê'lu, Nez Percé name, meaning "firs," or "fir-tree people."
.sa'ładebc, probably the Snohomish name.
Sinkiuse, the name applied to themselves and most other neighboring Salish tribes, and said to have belonged originally and properly to a band which once inhabited Umatilla Valley.
Suwa'dabc, Snohomish name for all interior Indians, meaning "inland people," or "interior people."
.swā'dab.c, Twana name for all interior Indians, meaning "inland people."
.swa'namc, Nootsak name for all interior Indians, meaning "inland people."
Ti'attłuxa, Wasco Chinook name.
.tskowā'xtsɛnux or .skowa'xtsɛnɛx, applied by themselves, meaning has something to do with "main valley."

Connections.—The Sinkiuse-Columbia belonged to the inland division of the Salishan linguistic stock, their nearest relatives being the Wenatchee and Methow.

Subdivisions or Bands
(According to Teit, 1930)

.nkeē'us or .s.nkeiē'usox (Umatilla Valley).
Stata'ketux, around White Bluffs on the Columbia.
.tskowā'xtsɛnux or .skowa'xtsɛnɛx, also called Moses-Columbia or Moses Band after a famous chief (Priest's Rapids and neighboring country).

Curtis (1907–9) gives the following: "Near the mouth of the sink of Crab Creek were the Sĭnkŭmkŭnătkuh, and above them the Sĭnkolkolumínuh. Then came in succession the Stapĭ'sknuh, the Skukulăt'kuh, the Skoáhchnuh, the Skĭhlkĭntnuh, and, finally, the Skultaqchĭ'mh, a little above the mouth of Wenatchee River." Spier (1927) adds that the Sinkowarsin met by Thompson in 1811 might have been a band of this tribe.

Location and History.—The Sinkiuse-Columbia lived on the east side of Columbia River from Fort Okanogan to the neighborhood of Point Eaton. Later a reservation was created for them known as Columbia Reservation. In 1870 Winans placed them "on the east and south sides of the Columbia River from the Grand Coulée down to Priest's Rapids." They are now under the jurisdiction of Colville Agency and one band, the Moses-Columbia Band, is in the southern part of Colville Reservation.

Population.—The Sinkiuse-Columbia are estimated by Mooney (1928) to have numbered 800 in 1780, but were probably considerably more numerous as Teit (1927) considers that this tribe and the Pisquow together must have totaled something like 10,000 before the smallpox reached them. In 1905, 355 were reported; in 1908, 299; and in 1909, perhaps including some others, 540 were returned. The census of 1910 gave 52.

Colville. The name is derived from Fort Colville, a post of the Hudson's Bay Company at Kettle Falls, which was in turn named for the London governor of the company at the time when the post was founded, i. e., in 1825. Also called:

Basket People, by Hale (1846).
Chaudière, French name derived from the popular term applied to them, Kettle Falls Indians.
Kettle Falls Indians, as above.
Sälsχuyilp, Okanagon name.
Skuyélpi, by other Salish tribes.
Whe-el-po, by Lewis and Clark, shortened from above.

Connections.—The Colville belonged to the inland division of the Salishan linguistic stock and to that branch of the latter which included the Okanagon, Sanpoil, and Senijextee.

Location.—On Colville River and that part of the Columbia between Kettle Falls and Hunters.

Villages and Subdivisions

(From Ray, 1932)

Kakalapia, home of the Skakalapiak (across from the present town of Harvey, at the point where the ferry now crosses).
Kilumaak, home of the Skilumaak (opposite the present town of Kettle Falls, about 1½ miles above Nchumutastum).
Nchaliam, home of the Snchalik (about 1½ miles above the present town of Inchelium).
Nchumutastum, home of the Snchumutast (about 6 miles above Nilamin).
Nilamin, home of the Snilaminak (about 15 miles above Kakalapia).
Nkuasiam, home of the Snkuasik (slightly above the present town of Daisy, on the opposite side of the river).
Smichunulau, home of the Smichunulauk (at the site of the present State bridge at Kettle Falls).

History.—The history of the Colville was similar to that of the neighboring tribes except that Kettle Falls was early fixed upon as the site of an important post by the Hudson Bay Company and brought with it the usual advantages and disadvantages of White contact.

Population.—Mooney (1928) estimated the number of the Colville at 1,000 as of 1780, but Lewis and Clark placed it at 2,500, a figure also fixed upon by Teit (1930). In 1904 there were 321; in 1907, 334; and in 1937, 322.

Connections in which they have become noted.—The name Colville was applied to an important Indian Reservation and later to a town, the county seat of Stevens County, Wash., but the original, of course, was not Indian.

Copalis. Significance unknown.

Connections.—The Copalis belonged to the coastal division of the Salishan linguistic family.

Location.—Copalis River and the Pacific Coast between the mouth of Joe Creek and Grays Harbor.

Population.—Lewis and Clark in 1805 estimated a population of 200 Copalis in 10 houses. The 5 individuals assigned to a "Chepalis" tribe in an enumeration given by Olson of the year 1888 probably refers to them.

Connections in which they have become noted.—The name Copalis is perpetuated in that of Copalis River, and in the post villages of Copalis Beach and Copalis Crossing, Grays Harbor County, Wash.

Cowlitz. Significance unknown. Also called:

Nū-sō-lupsh, name given by Indians not on the Sound to Upper Cowlitz and Upper Chehalis.

Connections.—The Cowlitz belonged to the coastal division of the Salishan linguistic family, yet shared some peculiarities with the inland tribes.

Location.—Most of the lower and all the middle course of Cowlitz River. Later they were divided between Chehalis and Puyallup Reservations.

Towns

Ray (1932) gives: Awi'mani, at the mouth of Coweman River, south of Kelso, and Manse'la, on site of Longiew. (See Curtis, 1907–9.)

Population.—Mooney (1928) estimated the number of the Cowlitz, along with the Chehalis, Humptulips, and some other tribes, at 1,000 in 1780. In 1853 Gibbs stated that they and the Upper Chehalis counted not more than 165. About 1887 there were 127 on Puyallup Reservation. The census of 1910 returned 105. The United States Indian Office Report of 1923 gives 490, probably including other tribes.

Connections in which they have become noted.—The name Cowlitz is perpetuated by Cowlitz River and Cowlitz Pass; by Cowlitz Glacier, which radiates from Mount Ranier; and by Cowlitz County, Cowlitz

Park, Cowlitz Chimney, Cowlitz Cleaver, and some small towns in the same region.

Duwamish. A place name.

Connections.—The Duwamish belonged to the Nisqually dialectic group of the coast division of the Salishan linguistic stock.

Subdivisions and Villages

(According to Smith, 1940)

A. The Duwamish River from its mouth up to and including the Black and Cedar Rivers, with the following villages:

Dsidsila'letc, at Yesler Way and Jackson St., Seattle.

Duwe'kwulsh, at Maple Valley.

Kati'lbabsh, at the present town of Renton.

Sakwe'kwewad, on Cedar River about 2 miles from Renton.

Skwa'lko, where the Black and White Rivers join to form the Duwamish.

Tkwabko', at south end of Lake Washington.

Tola'ltu, below Duwamish Head, Seattle.

Tupa'thlteb, at the mouth of the easternmost estuary of the Duwamish.

Tuduwa'bsh, at the mouth of the Duwamish River.

B. From where the Black River flows into the Duwamish to the junction of the White and Green Rivers, including these villages:

Stak and Tcutupa'lhu, on the east bank of the White River between its junction with the Black River and the mouth of the Green River.

C. The Green River villages:

Ila'lkoabsh, at the junction of the Green and White Rivers.

Su'sabsh, on Suise Creek.

Perhaps several groups of houses: (1) on the upper Green River, including Tskoka'bid (at the bend now spanned by the highway bridge about 4 miles east of Auburn); (2) on the north bank of the Robert Wooding Place; (3) on the Du Bois Place, and (4) at the mouth of Newaukum Creek.

D. The White River village, Sbalko'absh (on White River near a small stream at the southeast corner of the present Muckleshoot Reservation and to the east on Boise Creek).

E. The Lake Washington people, including the Thluwi'thalbsh (at Union Bay), the Sammamish (at the mouth of Sammamish River), and the peoples of Salmon Bay. In 1856 they were removed to the eastern shore of Bainbridge Island but as the place lacked a fishing ground they were shortly afterward taken to Holderness Point, on the west side of Eliot Bay, which was already a favorite place for fishing. They are now under the Tulalip School Superintendency.

Population.—The Duwamish were estimated by Mooney (1928), with the Suquamish and other tribes, at 1,200 in 1780. About 1856 they are variously given at from 64 to 312. The census of 1910 returned 20.

Connections in which they have become noted.—The Duwamish will be remembered mainly as one of the tribes formerly located on the site of Seattle, and one of the two of which the Indian who gave his name to that city was chief. The name Duwamish itself is preserved in Duwamish River and in the name of a small town.

Hoh. Significance unknown.

Connections.—The Hoh spoke the Quileute language and were often considered part of the same tribe, constituting one division of the Chimakuan linguistic stock and more remotely connected with the Salishan family.

Location.—On Hoh River on the west coast of Washington.

Population.—Mooney (1928) estimates 500 in the Hoh and the Quileute together in 1780. In 1905 the Hoh numbered 62.

Connection in which they have become noted.—The name Hoh is preserved in that of the Hoh River.

Humptulips. Said to signify "chilly region."

Connections.—The Humptulips belonged to the coastal division of the Salishan linguistic stock, being connected most closely with the Chehalis.

Location.—On the Humptulips River, and part of Grays Harbor, including also Hoquiam Creek and Whiskam River.

Villages

Hli'mŭmi (Curtis, 1907–9), near North Cove.
Hoquiam, on Hoquiam Creek.
Hooshkal (Gibbs), on the north shore of Grays Harbor.
Kishkallen (Gibbs), on the north shore of Grays Harbor.
Klimmim (Gibbs), 1877).
Kplelch (Curtis), at the mouth of North River.
Kwapks (Curtis, 1907–9), at the mouth of North River.
Mo'nilŭmsh (Curtis), at Georgetown.
Nooachhummik (Gibbs), on the coast north of Grays Harbor.
Nookalthu (Gibbs), north of Grays Harbor.
Nu'moihanhl (Curtis), at Tokeland.
Whishkah, on Whishkah River.

These are placed under the Humptulips only on account of their locations as described.

Population.—See **Chehalis.** In 1888 according to Olsen 18 Humptulips were reported. In 1904 there were 21.

Connection in which they have become noted.—Humptulips River and a village in Grays Harbor County preserve the name of the Humptulips Indians.

Kalispel. The Kalispel extended over into the eastern edge of the State from Idaho (q. v.).

Klickitat. From a Chinook term meaning "beyond" and having reference to the Cascade Mountains. Also called:

Awi-adshi, Molala name.
Lûk'-a-tatt, Puyallup name.
Máhane, Umpqua name.
MI-Çlauq'-tcu-wûn'-ti, Alsea name, meaning "scalpers."

Mûn-an'-nĕ-qu' tûnnĕ, Naltunnetunne name, meaning "inland people."
Qwû'lh-hwai-pûm, own name, meaning "prairie people."
Tlakäï'tat, Okanagon name.
Tsĕ la'kayät amím, Kalapuya name.
Tluwänxa-ikc, Clatsop name.
Wahnookt, Cowlitz name.

Connections.—The Klickitat belonged to the Shahaptian division of the Shapwailutan linguistic family.

Subdivisions and Villages

Possibly the Atanum or Atanumlema should be added to the Klickitat. Mooney (1928) reports that their language was distinct from, though related to, both Klickitat and Yakima.

The following villages are mentioned:

Itkilak or Ithlkilak, at White Salmon Landing, which they occupied jointly with the Chilluckquittequaw.
Nanshuit (occupied jointly with the Chilluckquittequaw), at Underwood.
Shgwaliksh, not far below Memaloose Island.
Tgasgutcu (occupied jointly with the Chilluckquittequaw), said to be about ½ mile west of a long high mountain opposite Mosier, Oreg., and about 1 mile above White Salmon Landing but the exact location seems to be in doubt.
Wiltkun (exact location unknown).

History.—The original home of the Klickitat was somewhere south of the Columbia, and they invaded their later territory after the Yakima crossed the river. In 1805 Lewis and Clark found them wintering on Yakima and Klickitat Rivers. Taking advantage of the weakness of the Willamette tribes following upon an epidemic of fever between 1820 and 1830, the Klickitat crossed the Columbia and forced their way as far south as the valley of the Umpqua but were soon compelled to retire to their old seats. They were active and enterprising traders, profiting by their favorable location to become middlemen between the coast tribes and those living east of the Cascades. They joined in the Yakima treaty at Camp Stevens, June 9, 1855, by which they ceded their lands to the United States, and most of them settled upon the Yakima Reservation.

Population.—Mooney (1928) estimated that the Klickitat, including the Taitinapam, numbered 600 in 1780. In 1805 Lewis and Clark placed their total population at about 700. The census of 1910 returned 405

Connections in which they have become noted.—The Klickitat were early distinguished from other tribes of central Washington owing to their propensity for trading. The name is perpetuated in that of a small affluent of the Columbia and in the name of the county, and a post village in the county.

Kwaiailk. Meaning unknown. Also called:

> Kwū-teh-ni, Kwalhioqua name.
> Nū-sō-lupsh, by Sound Indians, referring to the rapids of their stream.
> Stak-ta-mish, a name for this and other inland tribes, meaning "forest people."
> Upper Chehalis, common name.

Connections.—The Kwaiailk belonged to the coastal division of the Salishan linguistic family but a part of them were associated with the inland tribes by certain peculiarities of speech. Their nearest relatives seem to have been the Cowlitz and Chehalis.

Location.—On the upper course of Chehalis River.

Subdivisions and Villages

Cloquallum, on Cloquallum River.

Population.—In 1855, according to Gibbs (1877), the Kwaiailk numbered 216 but were becoming amalgamated with the Cowlitz. (See **Chehalis.**)

Kwalhioqua. From their Chinook designation, meaning "a lonely place in the woods." Also called:

> Axwē'lāpc, "people of the Willapa," by the Chinook and Quinault Indians.
> Gilā'q!ulawas, from the name of the place where they usually lived.
> Owhillapsh or Willapa, applied to this tribe erroneously.
> Tkulhiyogoā'ikc, Chinook name.

Connections.—The Kwalhioqua belonged to the Athapascan linguistic stock.

Location.—On the upper course of Willopah River, and the southern and western headwaters of the Chehalis. Gibbs (1877) extends their territory eastward of the Cascades, but Boas (1892) doubts the correctness of this.

Subdivisions

Suwal, on headwaters of the Chehalis.
Wela'pakote'li, on Willapa River.

Population.—Mooney (1928) estimated 200 in 1780; Hale (1846) gives about 100, but in 1850 it is said that only 2 males and several females survived, which indicates that an error had been made by one or the other.

Connection in which they have become noted.—The Kwalhioqua were distinguished almost solely by the fact that they belonged to the great Athapascan group yet were the only tribe of that stock in the State of Washington in historic times, having become entirely isolated from their relatives.

Lummi. Significance unknown. Also spelled Há-lum-mi, Nuh-lum-mi, and Qtlumi. Also called:

Nūkhlésh, by the Skagit, who also included the Clallam in the designation.

Connections.—The Lummi belonged to the coastal division of the Salishan linguistic family and spoke, according to Boas (1911), the same dialect as the Songish of Vancouver Island.

Location.—On the upper part of Bellingham Bay and about the mouth of Nooksack River. Formerly the Lummi are said to have resorted at times to a group of islands east of Vancouver Island. They were finally placed on Lummi Reservation.

Villages
(According to Stern, 1934)

Elek, near the upper end of Bellingham Bay.
Hwetlkiem, near the upper end of Bellingham Bay west of Nooksack River.
Kwakas, on the north side of Nooksack River.
Momli, near the mouth of Nooksack River.
Skalisan, north of Point Francis and opposite Lummi Island.

The following fishing stations are also cited:

Hoholos, a point on Orcas Island south of Freeman Island.
Hwitcosang, in Upright Channel south of Shaw Island.
Hwtcihom or Bee Station, north of Sandy Point.
Skalekushan or Village Point, on Lummi Island.
Skoletc, on Lopez Island opposite Lopez.
Tceltenem, Point Roberts.
Tlkwoloks, on Orcas Island.

Population.—Mooney (1928) estimates the number of Lummi at 1,000 in 1780, including the Samish and Nooksack. In 1905 there were 412; according to the census of 1910, 353; according to the United States Indian Office Report for 1923, 505; and according to that for 1937, 661.

Connection in which they have become noted.—Lummi River, Washington, preserves the name.

Makah. Meaning "cape people." Also called:

Ba-qa-ŏ, Puyallup name.
Cape Flattery Indians, from their location.
Classet, Nootka name, meaning "outsiders."
Kwe-nēt-che-chat, own name, meaning "cape people."
Tlā'asath, Nootka name, meaning "outside people."

Connections.—The Makah belonged to the Nootka branch of the Wakashan linguistic family.

Location.—About Cape Flattery, claiming the coast east as far as Hoko River and south to Flattery Rocks, besides Tatoosh Island. Later they were confined to the Makah Reservation.

Villages

Winter towns:

Baada, on Neah Bay.

Neah, on the site of the old Spanish fort, Port Nuñez Gaona, Neah Bay.

Waatch, at the mouth of Waatch Creek, 4 miles from Neah Bay.

Summer villages:

Ahchawat, at Cape Flattery.

Kehsidatsoos, location unknown.

Kiddekubbut, 3 miles from Neah Bay.

Tatooche, on Tatoosh Island, off Cape Flattery.

Population.—Together with the Ozette, the Makah were estimated by Mooney (1928) to number 2,000 in 1780, a figure evidently based on that given by Lewis and Clark in 1805. In 1905 there were 435; the census of 1910 gave 360, and the United States Indian Office Report for 1923 gave 425, including the people of Ozette. In 1937, 407 were returned besides the Ozette Indians.

Connection in which they have become noted.—The Makah and the Ozette are peculiar as the only tribes of the Nootka group and the Wakashan stock in the United States.

Methow. Meaning unknown. The Battle-le-mule-emauch of Ross (1847, p. 290).

Connections.—The Methow spoke a dialect belonging to the interior division of the Salishan linguistic stock.

Location.—On Methow River. A detached band called Chilowhist wintered on the Okanogan River between Sand Point and Malott.

Population.—Mooney (1928) estimated that this band and the Columbia Indians, or rather Moses' band of Columbia Indians, numbered 800 in 1780. In 1907 there were 324.

Connection in which they have become noted.—Methow River and Valley and a post village perpetuate the name of the Methow Indians.

Mical. Significance unreported.

Connections.—The Mical were a branch of the Shahaptian tribe called Pshwanwapam.

Location.—On the upper course of Nisqually River.

Population.—No separate data.

Muckleshoot. From the native word o'kelcuł, significance unknown.

Connections.—The Muckleshoot belonged to the Nisqually dialectic group of the coastal division of the Salishan linguistic family.

Location.—On White River, their territory extending from Kent eastward to the mountains, but it seems also to have included Green River.

Subdivisions

The following names appear applied to bands in their territory:

Sekamish, on White River.

Skopamish, on upper Green River.

Smulkamish, on upper White River

Smith (1940) adds Dothliuk, at South Prairie below where Cole Creek enters South Prairie Creek, an affluent of Carbon River.

Population.—The Muckleshoot are probably included in the 1,200 "Nisqually, Puyallup, etc." estimated by Mooney (1928) as in existence in 1780. The Skopamish numbered 222 in 1863 and the Smulkamish about 183 in 1870. Mooney estimated a total of 780 in 1907 for the group above given. In 1937 the United States Office of Indian Affairs reported 194 Indians of this tribe.

Connection in which they have become noted.—The name of the Muckleshoot is preserved in that of Muckleshoot Indian Reservation.

Neketemeuk. A supposed Salishan tribe placed by Teit's informants at an early period near and above the Dalles. Ray (1932), however, discredits the existence of an independent tribe of this name.

Nespelem, a division of the Sanpoil (q. v.).

Nez Percé. The Nez Percé occupied territory in the extreme southeastern part of the state. (See Idaho.)

Nisqually. From Skwale′absh, the native name of Nisqually River. Also spelled Quallyamish, and Skwalliahmish. Also called:

>Askwalli, Calapooya name.
>Ltsxe′als, Nestucca name.
>Suketĭ′kenuk, Sukotĭ′kenuk, by Columbia Indians along with all other coast people, meaning "people of the other side," with reference to the Cascades.
>Tsĕ Skua′lli ami′m, Luckamiut Kalapooian name.

Connections.—They gave their name to one dialectic division of the coastal division of the Salishan linguistic stock.

Location.—On Nisqually River above its mouth and on the middle and upper courses of Puyallup River.

Subdivisions and Villages

Basha′labsh, on Mashell Creek and neighboring Nisqually River, the town on a highland below Eatonville on Mashell Creek.

Sakwi′absh, Clear Creek and neighboring Nisqually River, the main settlement on a hill near the junction of Clear Creek and the Nisqually River.

Sigwa′letcabsh, on Segualitcu River, the main settlement where Dupont Creek enters the Sqwualitcu River.

Tsakwe′kwabsh, on Clarks Creek and neighboring Puyallup River, the main settlement where Clarks Creek empties into Puyallup River, but seems to have included also Skwa′dabsh, at the mouth of a creek entering Wappato Creek above the Wappato Creek village.

Sta′habsh, where the Stuck River enters the Puyallup.

Tsuwa′diabsh, on what is now the Puyallup River above its junction with the Carbon, and just below the site of the Soldiers′ Home.

Tuwha′khabsh, above Ortig where Vogt Creek enters the Carbon River.

Yisha′ktcabsh, on Nisqually Lake, the principal settlement being at the mouth of a sizable creek.

Yokwa'lsshabsh, on Muck Creek and the neighboring parts of Nisqually River, the main settlement located where Muck Creek enters Nisqually River, and a division on Clover Creek.

Population.—Mooney (1928) estimated that in 1780 there were about 3,600 Nisqually of whom, in 1907, between 1,100 and 1,200 survived. About 1,100 were returned in the census of 1910, but the Indian Office Report for 1937 gives only 62, evidently a minor tribe which gave its name to the larger body.

Connection in which they have become noted.—The memory of the Nisqually tribe, or cluster of bands, has been preserved in the name of Nesqually or Nisqually River, and in the post village of Nisqually in Thurston County.

Nooksack. Meaning "mountain men." Also spelled Nooksak and Nootsak.

Connections.—The Nooksack belonged to the coastal division of the Salishan linguistic family. Hill-Tout (1902) says they separated from the Squawmish of British Columbia and speak the same dialect.

Location.—On Nooksack River, Whatcom County. (See also Canada.)

Population.—In 1906, 200 Nooksack were officially returned, but Hill-Tout (1902) states that in 1902 there were only about 6 true male members of the tribe. The census of 1910 gives 85 under this name, and the Report of the United States Office of Indian Affairs for 1937 returned 239. (See **Lummi.**)

Connection in which they have become noted.—Nooksack River and Nooksack town in Whatcom County, Washington, preserve the name.

Ntlakyapamuk. The southern bands of this tribe hunted over in the territory now embraced in Washington. (See Canada.)

Okanagon. From the native term Okanā'qēn, Okanāqē'nix, or Okinā'qēn. The name is derived from some place on the Okanogan River, near Okanogan Falls at the mouth of the Similkameen, where is said to have been the headquarters of a large band of the tribe and is even given as the place of origin of the entire tribe. Also called:

>Akênuq'lã'lãm or Kōkenu'k'kē, by Kutenai (Chamberlain, 1892).
>Isonkuafli, own name, meaning "our people."
>Kãnk.'utlã'atlam, Kutenai name, meaning "flatheads" (Boas, 1911).
>KEnãke'n, by Tobacco Plains Band of Klickitat.
>OtcEnãke', OtcEnã.qai'n, or UtcEnã'.qai'n, by the Salish and their allies.
>Soo-wãn'-a-mooh, Shuswap name.
>.SoqEnãqai'mEx, Columbia name.
>Tcutzwã'ut, Tcitxûã'ut, Tsawa'nEmux, or OkEnã.qai'n, Ntlakyapamuk names.
>WEtc.nãqei'n, Skitswish name.

Connections.—The Okanagon belonged to the interior division of the Salishan stock, but their closest relatives were the Sanpoil, Colville, and Senijextee.

Location.—On Okanagan River above the mouth of the Similkameen to the Canadian border and in British Columbia along the shores of Okanagan Lake and in the surrounding country; in later times they have displaced an Athapascan tribe and part of the Ntlakyapamuk from the Similkameen Valley. (See also Canada.)

Subdivisions and Villages

The Similkameen Okanagon were divided into three bands, the Okanagon proper into four; with the villages belonging to each, they are as follows:

Upper Similkameen Band:

> Ntkaihelok (Ntkai'xelôx), about 11 miles below Princeton, north side of Similkameen River.
>
> Snazaist (Snäzäi'st), on the north shore of Similkameen River, a little east of Twenty-mile Creek and the town of Hedley.
>
> Tcutcuwiha (Tcutcuwî'xa) or Tcutcawiha (Tcutcawî'xa), on the north side of Similkameen River, a little below the preceding.

Ashnola Band:

> Ashnola (Acnū'lôx), on the south side of Similkameen River, near the mouth of Ashnola Creek.
>
> Nsrepus (Nsre'pus) or Skanek, .sa'nEx, a little below the Ashnola, but on the north side of Similkameen River.

Lower Similkameen Band:

> KekerEmyeaus (KekerEmyē'aus), across Similkameen River from Keremyeus.
>
> Keremyeus (KerEmye'us), on the north side of Similkameen River, near Keremeos.
>
> Nkura-elok (Nkuraē'lôx), on the south side of Similkameen River and about 4 miles below KerEmyeaus.
>
> Ntleuktan (Ntleuxta'n), on the south side of Similkameen River, opposite Skemkain.
>
> Skemkain (Skemquai'n), a short distance below Nkuraelok.
>
> Smelalok (Smela'lox), on the south side of Similkameen River, about 10 miles below Nsrepus.

To the villages listed above must be added the following old Similkameen village sites in Washington:

> Hepulok (Xe'pulôx).
>
> Konkonetp (Ko'nkonetp), near the mouth of Similkameen River.
>
> Kwahalos (Kwaxalo's), a little back from Similkameen River, below Hepulok.
>
> Naslitok (Nä.sli'tok), just across the International Boundary in Washington.
>
> Skwa'nnt, below Kwahalos.
>
> Tsakeiskenemuk (Tsakei'sxEnEmux), on a creek along the trail between Keremeous and Penticton.
>
> Tseltsalō's, below Kwahalos.

Douglas Lake Band:

> Kathlemik (Kā.'ĺEmix), near Guichons, at the mouth of the Upper Nicola River, where it falls into Nicola Lake.
>
> Komkonatko (Komkona'tko) or Komkenatk (KomkEna'tkk), at Fish Lake on the headwaters of the Upper Nicola River.
>
> Kwiltcana (Kwiltca'na) at the mouth of Quilchene Creek.
>
> Spahamen (Spä'xamEn) or Spahamen (Spä'xEmEn), at Douglas Lake.

Komaplix or Head of the Lake Band:

Nkamapeleks (Nkama'pElɛks) or Nkomapeleks (Nkoma'pElɛks), near the head of Okanagan Lake, about 8 miles north of Vernon.

Nkekemapeleks (Nkekema'pElɛks), at the head of Long Lake, a little over a mile from Vernon.

Nkokosten (Nxok.o'stɛn), a place near Kelowna, and also a general name for the district around there and Mission.

Skelaunna (SkElā'un.na), at Kelowna, near the present town.

Sntlemukten (SntlEmuxte'n), (Black Town), a little north of the head of Okanagan Lake.

Stekatelkeneut (Stekatelxenē'ut), a little above Mission(?) on Long Lake opposite Tselotsus.

Tseketku (Tse'kEtku), at a small lake a little north of Black Town.

Tselotsus (TsElo'tsus), at the narrows of Long Lake.

Tskelhokem (TsxElho'qEm), near the lower end of Long Lake about 19 miles south of Vernon.

Penticton Band:

Penticton (Pentī'ktEn), Penticton, near the foot of Okanagan Lake.

Stekatkothlkneut (StEkatkoɫxne'ut) or Stekatethlkeneut (StEkatEɫxenē'ut), on the opposite side of Long Lake from Mission.

Nkamip Band:

Nkamip (Nkamī'p), on the east side of the upper end of Osoyoos Lake.

Sci'yus, near Haynes or the old customhouse just north of the American line.

Skohenetk (Sxoxenē'tkuᵘ), at the lower end of Dog Lake.

To the villages listed above must be added the following names of old village sites on Okanagan River south of the Canadian line:

Milkemahituk (MilkEmaxi-tuk) or Milkemihituk (MilkEmixī'tuk), a general name for the district around the mouth of Similkameen River and of the river itself.

Okinaken (Ōkinā'qēn), an old name for Sathlilk.

Sathlilk (Saɫi'lxᵘ), near the mouth of Similkameen River.

SmElkammin (Smelkammī'n), thought to be the old name of a place at the mouth of Similkameen River.

History.—The history of the Okanagon differed little from that of the Ntlakyapamuk and other neighboring tribes except that they were affected by the fact that a part of them were on the south side of the International Boundary. During the last two centuries, however, there has been a steady movement of the tribe northward, where they have displaced the Shuswap, who once hunted down to the head of Okanagan Lake and in the hinterland on the east side of it down to the latitude of Penticton. They have also displaced the Stuwik(?) and the Ntlakyapamuk in the Similkameen Valley.

Population.—Mooney (1928) estimated that there were about 2,200 Okanagon in 1780. Teit (1900) gives the population as between 2,500 and 3,000. In 1905, according to the Canadian and United States Departments of Indian Affairs, there were 1,516 Indians belonging to this tribe, including 824 in Canada and 692 in the United States. In 1906 the numbers were given as 824 and 527, respectively.

Connections in which they have become noted.—The name of the Okanagon in the form Okanogan has been given to a county, a town in that county, a precinct, and a river in the State of Washington, and in the form Okanagan to a lake and a town in British Columbia.

Ozette. Significance unknown.

Connections.—The Ozette were a southern branch of the Makah and belonged to the Nootka branch of the Wakashan linguistic family.

Location.—On the Ozette Lake and Ozette River in Clallam County.

Villages

Ozette, at Flattery Rocks.
Sooes, 4 miles south of the Makah village of Waatch.

Population.—(See **Makah.**)   A single Ozette Indian was reported in 1937.

Connections in which they have become noted.—An island, a lake, a river, and a village are named Ozette after them.

Palouse. Significance unknown.   Also called:

> Pallotepellows, by Lewis and Clark in 1806.
> .spalu'.soχ, so called by Sinkiuse, said to be from a place name.

Connections.—The Palouse belonged to the Shahaptian division of the Shapwailutan linguistic stock, and were most closely connected with the Nez Percé.

Location.—In the valley of Palouse River in Washington and Idaho and on a small section of Snake River, extending eastward to the camas grounds near Moscow, Idaho.   The Palouse were included in the Yakima treaty of 1855 but have never recognized the treaty obligations and have declined to lead a reservation life.

Subdivisions and Villages

Almotu, on the north bank of Snake River about 30 miles above the mouth of Palouse River.
Chimnapum, on the northwest side of Columbia River near the mouth of Snake River and on lower Yakima River.
Kasispa, at Ainsworth, at the junction of Snake and Columbia Rivers, Wash.
Palus, on the north bank of Snake River just below its junction with the Palouse.
Sokulk or Wanapum, on Columbia River above the mouth of Snake River.
Tasawiks, on the north bank of Snake River, about 15 miles above its mouth.

History.—The Palouse are said to have separated from the Yakima.

Population.—Estimated by Mooney (1928) at 5,400 in 1780.   In 1805 Lewis and Clark gave 1,600.   In 1854 they were said to number 500.   The census of 1910 returned 82.

Connection in which they have become noted.—Palouse or Pelouse River, in Idaho and Washington, and the city of Palouse in Whitman County, Washington, preserve the name of the Palouse Indians.

Pshwanwapam. Meaning "the stony ground." Also called Upper Yakima.

Connections.—The Pshwanwapam belonged to the Shahaptian division of the Shapwailutan linguistic family, and probably were most closely connected with the Yakima.

Location.—On the upper course of Yakima River.

Puyallup. From Pwiya'lap, the native name of Puyallup River.

Connections.—The Puyallup belonged to the Nisqually dialectic group of the Coastal division of the Salishan linguistic family.

Location.—At the mouth of Puyallup River and the neighboring coast, including Carr Inlet and the southern part of Vashon Island.

Subdivisions and Villages

Esha'ktlabsh, on Hylebos Waterway.

Kalka'lak, at the mouth of Wappato Creek.

Klbalt, at Glencove.

Puyallup or Spwiya'laphabsh, on Commencement Bay and Puyallup River as far up as the mouth of Clarks Creek, including the main settlement of the same name at the mouth of Puyallup River.

Sha'tckad, where Clay Creek empties into the Puyallup River.

Sko'tlbabsh, on Carr Inlet, including a Sko'tlbabsh settlement on Carr Inlet above the town of Minter.

Skwapa'bsh, on the south part of Vashon Island and the land west of the Narrows, including a town of the same name at the mouth of a stream at Gig Harbor.

Skwlo'tsid, at the head of Wollochet Bay.

Steilacoom, on Steilacoom Creek and the neighboring beach, the main village on the present site of Steilacoom.

Tsugwa'lethl, at Quartermaster Harbor.

Tule'lakle, at the head of Burley Lagoon, Carr Inlet.

Twa'debshab, at the mouth of a creek formerly entering Commencement Bay and now covered by Tacoma.

Population.—(See **Nisqually.**) The report of the United States Office of Indian Affairs for 1937 gave 322 Puyallup.

Connections in which they have become noted.—The name Puyallup is preserved by a river, an Indian reservation, a glacier, an important town in Pierce County, and in the ridge called Puyallup Cleaver.

Queets or Quaitso. Significance unknown.

Connections.—The Queets belonged to the Coastal division of the Salishan linguistic family and were most intimately related to their neighbors to the south, the Quinault.

Location.—On Queets River and its branches.

Population.—Lewis and Clark in 1805 estimated that the Queets numbered 250. They then occupied 18 houses. Mooney (1928) estimated that in 1780 they and the Quinault together numbered 1,500, but Olson (1936) regards this figure as too high. Olson prints an estimate of 82 as their present population, including 23 males over 18, 32 females over 14, and 16 children between 6 and 16. In 1909 there were 62.

Connection in which they have become noted.—The name of the Queets is perpetuated in that of Queets River.

Quileute. Meaning unknown.

Connections.—Together with the Hoh and Chimakum, the Quileute constituted the Chimakuan linguistic family which is possibly more remotely related to Wakashan and Salishan.

Location.—On Quilayute River, on the west coast of Washington. They are now on the Quileute and Makah Reservations.

Population (including the Hoh).—Mooney (1928) estimates that in 1780 there were of the Quileute and the Hoh 500 Indians. Olson (1936) quotes a figure of 64 in 1888. The census of 1910 returned 303 and the United States Office of Indian Affairs in 1937 gave 284.

Connections in which they have become noted.—The town of Quillayute in Clallam County, preserves the name of the Quileute and it was formerly that of Soleduck River. Otherwise the tribe is particularly noted on account of the uniqueness of its language, which was spoken by no other known tribes except the Hoh and Chimakum (q. v.).

Quinault. "A corruption of kwi'naił, the name of the largest settlement situated at the present site of the village (Taholah)" at the mouth of the Quinault River.

Connections.—The Quinault belonged to the coastal division of the Salishan linguistic family.

Location.—The valley of Quinault River and the Pacific coast between Raft River and Joe Creek.

Subdivisions

Lewis and Clark mention a division or associated band called Calasthocle.

Towns

(Olson's (1936) list modified phonetically)

A'alatsis, 3 miles below Lake Quinault.

Djagaka'lmik, ½ mile above Nosklako's.

Djekwe'ls, on the north bank of Quinault River about 400 yards above Thlathle'-lap).

Gutse'lps, 6 miles below Lake Quinault.

Hagwi'shtap, about 1½ miles above Cook Creek.

He'shnithl or Kuku'mnithl, on the south bank of Quinault River about 500 yards above Pini'lks.

Kwakwa'h, not far from Hagwi'shtap.

Kwakwa'nikatctan, 4 miles below Lake Quinault.

Kwatai'tamik, 3 miles above Kwakwa'h.

Kwatai'tumik, on the south bank about 500 yards above Kwi'naithl.

Kwikwa'la, perhaps ½ mile above Sunuksunu'ham.

Kwi'naithl, at present site of Taholah.

Lae'lsnithl, on north bank a mile or less above Heshnithl.

La'lshithl, perhaps a mile above Djagaka'lmik on Quinault River.

Ma'atnithl, 1 mile below the fork of upper Quinault River.

Magwa'ksnithl, 300 yards above Kwikwa'la.

Me'tsugutsathlan, on south bank of Quinault River at its mouth.

Nago'olatcan, not far from Nossho'k.

Negwe'thlan, at the mouth of Cook Creek.

Nokedja'kt or Thla'a'lgwap, on south bank a few hundred yards above Tonans.

Nomi'lthlostan, just above Kwakwa'h.

No'omo'thlapsh, at mouth of Moclips River, which bears its name in a corrupted form.

No'omo'thlapshtcu, not far above Magwa'ksnithl.

No'skathlan, a few miles above Kwi'naithl, on the north bank of Quinault River.

Noskthlako's, on south bank of Quinault River perhaps 1 mile above No'skathlan.

Nossho'k, not far above Nokedja'kt.

No'sthluk, not far from Djekwe'ls.

Pina'alathl, located where the upper Quinault River enters Lake Quinault.

Pini'lks, close to La'lshithl.

Pino'otcan tci'ta, on the upper Quinault below Ma'anithl.

Po'iks, on the upper Quinault above Finley Creek.

Pote'lks, 1 mile above Tsimi'sh.

Sunuksunu'ham, not far from Nomi'lthlostan.

Tamo'ulgutan, just below No'omo'thlapshtcu.

Tci'tano'sklakalathl, at the outlet of Lake Quinault.

Thlathle'lap, at the mouth of Quinault River and on the north bank.

To'nans, less than ½ mile above He'shnithl.

Tsi'i'sh, 2 miles above Magwaksnithl.

Population.—Lewis and Clark in 1805 estimated 800 Quinault proper and 200 Calasthocle. Mooney (1928) estimated 1,500 in 1780 including the Quaitso, but Olson (1936) suggests 800 and regards that as too high if anything. This would reduce Mooney's figure considerably since the Quaitso were a much smaller tribe. A tabulation recovered by Olson but believed to be from some Indian agent gave 95 Quinault in 1888. The Indian Office figure for the two tribes in 1907 was 196. The census of 1910, however, returned 288, presumably including the Quaitso. In 1923 the Indian Office returned 719 on the Quinault Reservation, perhaps representing several tribes, but that for 1937 gave 1,228 of the Quinault alone.

Connection in which they have become noted.—Quinault Lake and River and a small town, all in Grays Harbor County, preserve the name of the Quinault.

Sahehwamish. Meaning unknown but evidently that of a locality.

Connections.—The Sahehwamish belonged to the Nisqually dialectic group of the coastal division of the Salishan linguistic stock.

Location.—On the innermost inlets of Puget Sound as indicated by the positions of the subdivisions given below.

Subdivisions

Elo'sedabsh, on Medicine Creek and the lower reaches of Nisqually River, including a main settlement at the mouth of Nisqually River and Tuda'dab, at the mouth of McAllister or Medicine Creek.

Sahehwamish or Sahe'wabsh, on Shelton Inlet, including the main settlement of Sahe'wabsh, at Arcadia, and a village opposite the town of Shelton.

Skwayaithlhabsh, on Mud Bay or Eld Inlet.

Statca'sabsh, on Budd Inlet, with its principal settlement at Tumwater.

Tapi'ksdabsh, with its main settlement on Oyster Bay or Totten Inlet below the town of Oyster Bay.

Tutse'tcakl, on South Bay or Henderson Inlet, between the creek at the head and that on the south.

Population.—The group to which this tribe belonged is estimated by Mooney (1928) to have numbered 1,200 in 1780, and he gives 780 for the year 1907.

Samish. Signification unknown.

Connections.—The Samish belonged to the coastal division of the Salishan linguistic family.

Location.—On Samish Bay and Samish Island, Guemes Island, and the northwest portion of Fidalgo Island. The Samish were later placed on Lummi Reservation.

Villages

Atse'ked, on the south side of the slough at Edison on Samish Bay.
Dikwi'bthl.
Gunguna'la, on Guemes Island facing west toward Cypress Island.
Hwaibathl, at Anacortes.
Kwalo'l, at Summit Park on Fidalgo Bay.
Nukhwhaiimikhl, on the southwest side of Guemes Island.

The name of the last village listed above is from Gibbs (1877) and may be another name for Gunguna'la, and Gibbs' Aseakum is perhaps Atse'ked.

Population.—Mooney (1928) estimates the Samish tribe, together with the Lummi and Nooksack, at 1,000 in 1780. No later estimate is given.

Connection in which they have become noted.—Samish River, Samish Bay, Samish Island, and a post hamlet on Bellingham Bay perpetuate the name of the Samish Indians.

Sanpoil. A native word in spite of its French aspect; meaning unknown. Also called:

> Hai-ai'-nĭma, by the Yakima.
> Ipoilq, another Yakima name.
> Nesilextcī'n, .n.selixtcī'n, by Sanpoil, and probably meaning "Salish-speaking."
> N'poch-le, a shortened form of the name.

Connections.—The Sanpoil belonged to the inland division of the Salishan linguistic stock, and were related most closely to its eastern section.

Location.—On Sanpoil River and Nespelem Creek and on the Columbia below Big Bend. They were later placed on Sanpoil and Colville Reservations.

Subdivisions and Villages

The Nespelim of Nespelem Creek were often given independent status. Ray gives the following villages and camps:

Nespelim villages:

Haimisahun, a summer settlement of the Suspiluk, on the north bank of Columbia River about a half mile above the mouth of Nespelem River.

Masmasalimk, home of the Smasmasalimkuwa, approximately a mile and a half above Skik.

Nekuktshiptin, home of the Snekuktshiptimuk, at the site of the present Condon's Ferry, on the north side of the river.

Nspilem, home of the Snspiluk, on the lower Nespelem from the falls to the mouth of the river.

Salkuahuwithl, home of the Salkuahuwithlau, across the river from the present town of Barry.

Skik, home of the Skik, about a mile above Salkuahuwithl on the same side of the river.

Skthlamchin, fishing grounds of the Salkuahuwithlau, across the river from the mouth of the Grand Coulee.

Sanpoil villages:

Enthlukaluk, about a mile and a half north of the mouth of the river.

Hahsulauk, home of the Shahsulauhuwa, near Plum.

Hulalst, home of the S-hulalstu, at Whitestone, about 8 miles above Npuiluk.

Hwatsam, a winter camp, about 3 miles above Snukeilt.

Kakamkam, on the islands in the Sanpoil River a short distance above the mouth.

Kathlpuspusten, home of the Kathlpuspustenak, about a mile above Plum, on the opposite side of the river.

Ketapkunulak, on the banks of the Columbia just east of the Sanpoil River.

Naak, home of the Snaakau, about a mile below Plum but on the north side of the river.

Nhohogus, fishing grounds of the S-hulalstu.

Npokstian, a winter camp, about 2 miles above Hwatsam.

Npuiluk, home of the Snpuiluk, at the mouth of Sanpoil River, made up of the following camps: Snkethlkukwiliskanan, near the present landing of the Keller ferry; a branch of the last called by the same name, several hundred yards north of the first between the cliff and the Sanpoil River, on the west side; Kethltselchin, on the first bench above the Columbia, west of the Sanpoil River.

Nthlahoitk, a winter camp of the Snpuiluk, about halfway between Skthlamchin and Naak.

Saamthlk, home of the Saamthlk, on the opposite side of the river from Kathlpuspusten.

Skekwilk, on the west side of Sanpoil River about a mile above the mouth.

Snputlem, on the east bank of Sanpoil River, about an eighth of a mile above the mouth.

Snukeilt, home of the Snukeiltk, on the west side of Columbia River about ½ mile above the mouth of Spokane River.

Tkukualkuhun, home of the Stkukualkuhunak, at Rodger's Bar just across the river from Hunters.

Tsaktsikskin, a winter camp of the Snpuiluk, about a half mile below Naak.

Wathlwathlaskin, home of the Swathlwathlaskink, ½ mile up the river from Nthlahoitk.

Temporary camp sites of the Sanpoil on Sanpoil River; beginning with the first temporary camp beyond Npuiluk:

Enluhulak, about 3 miles above the mouth of the river.

Ksikest, on the west side of the river about halfway between the Columbia River and Keller.

Aklaiyuk, ½ mile above Ksikest.

Snkloapeten, a short distance below Keller.

Pupesten, at the present site of Keller.

Nmhoyam, about a quarter of a mile north of Keller.

Nhwiipam, a mile above Alice Creek on the east side of the river.

Seaachast, at Alice Creek.

Achhulikipastem, about half a mile north of Alice Creek.

Nloklokekuelikten, about 2 miles south of Cash Creek.

Nhatlchinitk, on the west side of the river at Cash Creek.

Snthulusten, on the east side of the river at the foot of a cliff, about ¼ mile above Cash Creek.

Nlupiam, 1½ miles above Snthulusten, on the same side of the river.

Slakumulemk, directly across the river from Nlupiam.

Nklakachin, on the east side of the river, at Thirty-mile Creek.

Malt, ½ mile above Thirty-mile Creek.

Lulukhum, at Devil's Elbow.

The following possible camp sites are higher up:

Akthlkapukwithlp, 8 miles below West Fork.

Kthliipus, at the present site of Republic.

Tkwiip, near the creek at West Fork.

Population.—Mooney (1928) estimates 800 Sanpoil in 1780 but Ray (1932) raises this to 1,600–1,700, and considers that there were about 1,300 immediately following the middle of the nineteenth century. In 1905 the United States Indian Office returned 324 Sanpoil and 41 Nespelim; in 1910 the census gave 240 and 46; in 1913, as the result of a survey, the Office of Indian Affairs returned 202 and 43.

Connection in which they have become noted.—Sanpoil River, a northern tributary of the Columbia, perpetuates the name of the Sanpoil. Nespelem River is named for the subgroup, and a town.

Satsop. Significance unknown.

Connections.—The Satsop belonged to the coastal division of the Salishan linguistic family, and have usually been classed with the Lower Chehalis.

Location.—On Satsop River, a branch of the Chehalis.

Population.—The population of the Satsop is usually given with that of the Chehalis (q. v.), but in 1888 a census of the Satsop alone, obtained by Olson (1936), gave 12.

Connections in which they have become noted.—Satsop River and a village called Satsop in Grays Harbor County preserve the name of the Satsop.

Semiahmoo. Significance unknown. Also called:

> Birch Bay Indians, from a place occupied by them.

Connections.—The Semiahmoo belonged to the coastal division of the Salishan linguistic stock.

Location.—About Semiahmoo Bay in northwest Washington and southwest British Columbia.

Population.—In 1843 the Semiahmoo numbered 300; in 1909 there were 38 in British Columbia; none were enumerated on the American side of the line.

Connections in which they have become noted.—The name of the Semiahmoo is preserved in Semiahmoo Bay and a township in Whatcom County, Wash.

Senijextee. Significance unknown. Also called:

> Lake Indians, a popular name for them because they lived on the Arrow Lakes.

Connections.—The Senijextee belonged to the inland division of the Salishan linguistic stock, and were most closely connected with the Sanpoil.

Location.—On both sides of the Columbia River from Kettle Falls to the Canadian boundary, the valley of Kettle River, Kootenay River from its mouth to the first falls, and the region of the Arrow Lakes, B. C. The Lake Indians on the American side were placed on Colville Reservation.

Population.—Mooney (1928) estimates their numbers at 500 in 1780. In 1909 the United States Office of Indian Affairs reported 342 on Colville Reservation. The census of 1910 identifies them with the Colville and returns 785.

Sinkaietk. Significance unknown; an Anglicized form of their own name.

Connections.—The Sinkaietk are sometimes classed with the Okanagon, and called Lower Okanagon, both constituting a dialectic group of interior Salishan Indians.

Location.—Okanagan River from its mouth nearly to the mouth of the Similkameen.

Subdivisions

Kartar, from the foot of Lake Omak to the Columbia River.

Konkonelp, winter sites, from about 3 miles above Malott to the turn of the Okanagan River at Omak.

Tonasket, from Riverside upstream to Tonasket.

Tukoratum, winter sites, from Condon's Ferry on the Columbia to the mouth of the Okanagan River and up the latter to about 4 miles above Monse, Wash. Ray (1932) mentions four villages belonging to the Kartar and Tukoratum Bands.

Population.—Included with the Okanagon (q. v.).

Sinkakaius. Meaning "between people."

Connections.—The Sinkakaius belonged to the interior division of the Salishan linguistic stock and were composed largely of people from the Tukoratum Band of Sinkaietk and the Moses Columbia people.

Location.—Between Columbia River and the Grand Coulee in the latitude of Waterville.

Skagit. Significance unknown. Also called:

Hum-a-luh, own name, meaning "the people."

Connections.—The Skagit belonged to the coastal division of the Salishan linguistic stock.

Location.—On Skagit and Stillaguamish Rivers except about their mouths.

Subdivisions and Villages
(Smith, 1941)

Base'lelotsed, on Skagit River from Van Horn to roughly 3 miles above Rockport and Sauk River almost to the mouth of Suiattle, including the village of Tca'gwalk, at the mouth of Sauk River.

Baska'dsadsiuk, on the south bank of Skagit River from Hamilton to Birdsview, including a village opposite Hamilton.

Baske'kwiuk, on Skagit River above Rockport, including a village at Marble Mount at the mouth of the Cascade River.

Baslo'halok, on the north bank of the Skagit from Hamilton to Birdsview, including a settlement at Hamilton.

Duwa'ha, on the mainland drainages from South Bellingham to Bayview including part of Lake Whatcom, Lake Samish and Samish River, including the village of Batsla'thllaos, at Bayview on Padilla Bay.

Nookachamps, on Skagit River from Mount Vernon to Sedro Woolley and Nookachamps River drainage including Big Lake, including a village back of Mount Vernon just below the concrete bridge, and Tsla'tlabsh on Big Lake.

Sauk, on Sauk River above the confluence of the Suiattle River, including a settlement on Sauk prairie above Darrington.

Sba'leuk, on Skagit River from above Birdsview to above Concrete, including a village at Concrete.

Sikwigwi'lts, on Skagit River from Sedro Woolley to below Lyman, including a village on the flats near Sedro Woolley.

Stillaguamish, on Stillaguamish River from Arlington up, including villages at Arlington and Trafton.

Suiattle, on Suiattle River, including a village not far about the mouth of Suiattle River.

Tcubaa'bish, on Skagit River from Lyman to below Hamilton, including Day Creek drainage, and including a village at the mouth of Dry Creek.

Population.—The Skagit population is given by Mooney (1928), with the Swinomish and some other tribes, as 1,200 in 1780. Gibbs (1877) estimated there were 300 Skagit proper in 1853. The census of 1910 returned 56 under this name. In 1923 the United States Indian Office entered 221 "Swinomish" in their returns, including evidently the Skagit and some other tribes; in 1937 it gave an estimate of 200 Skagit.

Connection in which they have become noted.—Skagit River, which flows into Puget Sound, Skagit County, and a post hamlet preserve the name of the Skagit Indians.

Skilloot. Significance unknown.

Connections.—The Skilloot belonged to the Clackamas dialectic division of the Chinookan linguistic family.

Location.—On both sides of Columbia River above and below the mouth of Cowlitz River. (See also Oregon.)

Subdivisions and Villages

Cooniac (at Oak Point on the south side of Columbia River, below the mouth of the Cowlitz, in the present Columbia County, Oregon) was their principal village in later times. The Hullooetell, reported to Lewis and Clark as a numerous nation north of Columbia River on Cowlitz and Lewis Rivers, may have been a subdivision, although perhaps Salishan. The Seamysty, at the mouth of Cowlitz River before 1835, were undoubtedly a Skilloot band, and the Thlakalama and Tlakatlala of Boas (1901, and personal information 1905), at the mouth of Kalama River, about 3 miles above Oak Point, had best be added.

Population.—Mooney (1928) estimates the number of Skilloot at 3,250 in 1780 including 250 Tlakalama. In 1806 Lewis and Clark give 2,500 and in 1850 Lane places the Skilloot population at 200. They have now entirely disappeared as an independent group.

Skin. Taken from a town name.

Connections.—The Skin belonged to the Shahaptian division of the Shapwailutan linguistic stock.

Location.—On Columbia River from The Dalles to a point about 75 miles above.

Villages

Ka'sawi, on the Columbia opposite the mouth of Umatilla River.

Skin, opposite the mouth of Deschutes River.

Uchi'chol, on the north bank of the Columbia in Klickitat County.

Waiya'mpam, about Celilo.

Eneeshur is used by Lewis and Clark for part of the above people, perhaps all of them.

Population.—Mooney (1928) includes the Skin in a group under the general name Tapanash, which he estimates to have numbered 2,200 in 1780.

Snohomish. Meaning unknown but evidently the name of a place. Also called:

>   Ashnuhumsh, Kalapuya name.

Connections.—The Snohomish belonged to the Nisqually dialectic group of the coastal division of the Salishan linguistic stock.

Location.—On the lower course of Snohomish River and on the southern end of Whidbey Island.

Subdivisions and Villages

Sdugwadskabsh, the south portion of Whidbey Island, including villages opposite Mukilteo on Whidbey (Neg^{u}ā'sx) Island and at Newell on Useless Bay.

Skwilsi'diabsh, from Preston Point, above Everett, to the southern tip of Camano Island, including a village at Marysville and Tcatcthlks opposite Tulalip on Tulalip Bay.

Snohomish, Port Gardner Bay and Snohomish River as far up as Snohomish, including Tctlaks at Everett on the south side of the mouth of Snohomish River and Hibolb on the north side of its mouth.

Tukwetlbabsh, on Snohomish River from Snohomish to Monroe, including villages at Snohomish at the mouth of Pilchuck Creek and below Monroe 2 miles from the confluence of the Skykomish and the Snoqualmie.

Population.—Mooney (1928) estimated the population of the Snohomish, the Snoqualmie, the Tulalip, and some others at 1,200 in 1780. In 1850 there were 350 Snohomish. The census of 1910 gives 664, evidently including other bands, and the United States Office of Indian Affairs, 667 in 1937.

Connections in which they have become noted.—The name of the Snohomish is perpetuated in Snohomish River, Snohomish County, and a city in that county.

Snoqualmie. From the native word sdo'kwalbiuq^u.

Connections.—The Snoqualmie belonged to the Nisqually branch of the coastal division of the Salishan linguistic family.

Location.—On Snoqualmie and Skykomish Rivers.

Subdivisions and Villages

Skykomish, on Skykomish River above Sultan, and on the same below Goldbar.

Snoqualmie, on Snoqualmie River, including villages at Cherry Valley, on Snoqualmie River opposite the mouth of Tolt River; at Fall City; and below Snoqualmie Falls.

Stakta'ledjabsh, on Skykomish River as far up as Sultan, including Sultan Creek, including villages above Monroe at the mouth of Sultan Creek and on Sultan Creek 4 miles above its mouth.

Population.—(See **Snohomish.**) The population of the Snoqualmie alone was reported as 225 in 1857.

Connections in which they have become noted.—The name of the Snoqualmie is perpetuated by Snoqualmie River and a town upon it in King County.

Spokan. Phonetically Spōkē'.n or Spō.qē'in); said by some to signify "Sun (people)," though this origin is doubtful. Also called:

> Lêcĺē'cuks, Wasco name probably intended for this tribe.
> Lar-ti-e-lo, by Lewis and Clerk in 1806.
> Sɛnoxamī'naɛx, by the Okanagon, from their principal division.
> Sɛntutū' or Sɛnoxma'n, by the Upper Kutenai from the Salish names for the Middle and Little Spokan respectively.

Connections.—The Spokan belonged to the inland division of the Salishan linguistic stock, and were most closely connected with the Kalispel, Pend d'Oreilles, Sematuse, and Salish.

Location.—On the Spokane and Little Spokane Rivers, southward to, and perhaps including, Cow Creek, and northward to include all of the northern feeders of the Spokane. (See also Idaho and Montana.)

Subdivisions

The Lower Spokan (about the mouth and on the lower part of Spokane River, including the present Spokane Indian reserve), the Upper Spokan or Little Spokan (occupying the valley of the Little Spokane River and all the country east of the lower Spokane to within the borders of Idaho), the South or Middle Spokan (occupying at least the lower part of Hangmans Creek, extending south along the borders of the Skitswish).

History.—Like so many other tribes of the Columbia region, the Spokan enter the arena of history with the appearance of Lewis and Clark in their territory in 1805. Teit (1930) thinks it possible that the several bands were once so many distinct tribes which have become fused in course of time, but of this there is no certainty. The Lower and most of the Middle Spokan, and part of the Upper Spokan, were finally placed under the Colville Agency; the rest are on the Flathead Reservation in Montana.

Population.—Mooney (1928) estimated that about 1780 there might have been 1,400 Spokan, but Teit's figures would raise this to something like 2,500. In 1806 Lewis and Clark thought there were 600 but they may have included only one of the three divisions. In 1905 the United States Indian Office gave 277 Lower Spokan and 177 Middle and Upper Spokan under the Colville Agency and 135 on the Flathead Reservation; in 1909 it gave 509 all together under the Colville Agency and 138 on the Flathead Reservation. The United States Census of 1910 returned 643 all told; the Indian Office Report for 1923, 669; and the Indian Office Report for 1937, 847.

Connections in which they have become noted.—The fame of the Spokan will rest in the future mainly upon the importance of the Washington city of Spokane. Their name is also attached to a river in Idaho and Washington, and to the county of which Spokane is the metropolis. It has also been applied to post hamlets in Custer County, S. Dak.; in Christian County, Mo.; and in Trumbull County, Ohio; also to Spokane Bridge, Spokane County, Wash.

Squaxon or **Squakson.**   Their own name.

Connections.—The Squaxon belonged to the Nisqually branch of the coast division of the Salishan linguistic family.

Location.—On North Bay, Puget Sound.

Villages

On North Bay at the mouth of Coulter Creek and at Allyn at the mouth of Mason Creek.

Population.—With the Skokomish and Toanho (Twana), Mooney (1928) estimated that there were 1,000 Squaxon in 1780. In 1909 there were 98 under this name, and in 1937, 32.

Suquamish.   From a native place name.

Connections.—They belonged to the Nisqually branch of the coastal division of the Salishan linguistic stock, their closest connections being with the Duwamish. The famous Seattle was chief of both tribes.

Location.—On the west side of Puget Sound, according to Paige (1857) claiming the territory from Applegate Cove to Gig Harbor.

Subdivisions and Villages

Saktabsh, on Sinclair Inlet, Dyes Inlet, and southern Blakely, Blakely Island, with villages at Bremerton and on Eagle Harbor.

Suquamish, on Liberty Bay, at Port Madison, and on the northern part of Blakely Island, with villages at Suquamish, above Poulsbo, and at Point Monroe.

Population.—(See **Duwamish.**) The Suquamish numbered 441 in 1857, 180 in 1909, and 307 in 1910, according to the census of that year. The United States Indian Office returned 204 "Susquamish" Indians in 1910, probably meaning this tribe. In 1937 it returned 168 "Suquamish."

Connection in which they have become noted.—The name Suquamish is applied to a town in Kitsap County, Wash.

Swallah.   A name applied by Eells (1889). Also called:

Swalash, by Mallet (*in* Ind. Aff. Rep., 1877, p. 198).

Connections.—The Swallah belonged to the coastal division of the Salishan linguistic family.

Location.—On Orcas Island and San Juan Island and the group to which they belong.

Villages

Hutta'tchl, on the southeast end of Orcas Island.
Klala'kamish, on the east side of San Juan Island.
Lemaltcha, on Waldron Island.
Stashum, on Waldron Island.

Swinomish.   A place name.

Connections.—The Swinomish belonged to the coastal division of the Salishan linguistic family, and are sometimes called a subdivision of the Skagit.

Location.—On the northern part of Whidbey Island and about the mouth of Skagit River.

Subdivisions and Villages

Ho'baks, on the upper end of Penn's Cove, not far from San de Fuca, Batsa'dsali at Coupeville, Ba'asats between Coupeville and Snaklem Point west of Long Point, and Tcubaa'ltced on the north side of Snaklem Point about 4 miles from Coupeville.

Kikia'los, on Skagit Bay from the South Fork of Skagit River to the north tip of Camano Island, with a village at the mouth of Carpenter Creek between Conway and Fir, and another called Atsala'di at Utsalady on Camano Island.

Kwa'dsakbiuk, on the lower reaches of Stillaguamish River and Port Susan, with a village at the mouth of the Stillaguamish.

Skagit, on Whidbey Island, from Oak Harbor south to Snaklem Point, with a village at Oak Harbor.

Skwada'bsh, on the North Fork of the Skagit River and the eastern part of Whidbey Island lying north of Oak Harbor, with Skwi'kwikwab at the mouth of the North Fork of the Skagit, and Tcotab on a point across Skagit Bay.

Swinomish (on southern Padilla Bay, Swinomish Slough which joins Padilla Bay and Skagit Bay, Skagit Bay from Sullivan Slough north, and the southeast portion of Fidalgo Island), with the following villages: Kale'kut (not far from Whitney at the highway bridge), Sde'os (near Lone Tree Point, Shuptada'tci (on Swinomish Slough 3 miles from La Conner), and another village (on Sullivan Slough just east of La Conner).

Population.—The Swinomish are usually enumerated with the Skagit (q. v.). The Skagit and Swinomish together numbered 268 in 1909. In 1937 there were 285 Swinomish reported.

Taidnapam.   Also called Upper Cowlitz.

Connections.—The Taidnapam belonged to the Shahaptian division of the Shapwailutan linguistic family.

Location.—On the headwaters of Cowlitz River and perhaps extending over into the headwaters of the Lewis River.

Population.—Mooney estimates the population of the Taidnapam and the Klickitat together at 600 in 1780, but extinct as independent tribes by 1907.

Twana. Said to signify "a portage," referring to that between the upper end of Hoods Canal and the headwaters of Puget Sound. Also called:

> Tu-a'd-hu, own name.
> Skokomish, from the name of a principal division.
> Wi'lfa Ampa'fa ami'm, Luckiamute-Kalapuya name.

Connections.—The Twana constituted one dialectic group of the coastal division of the Salishan stock.

Location.—On both sides of Hoods Canal. Later they were placed on Skokomish Reservation.

Subdivisions and Villages

Eels (1877) gave the following:

Kolsid, on Quilcene and Dabop Bays.

Skokomish, around Annas Bay and the drainage area of Skokomish River.

Soatlkobsh, on both sides of the canal from Seabeck and Oak Head to Port Gamble and Squamish Harbor opposite.

Smith (1941) lists the following villages:

Habha'b, at Eldon on the Canal at the mouth of the Hammerhammer River.

Li'liwap, at Lilliwap on the Canal.

Skoko'bsh, at the mouth of the Skokomish River.

Tule'lalap, at the east branch of the Canal at the mouth of Mission Creek.

Two towns at Duckabush and Brinnon.

Population.—Mooney (1928) gives the Twana, Skokomish, and Squaxon together a population of 1,000 in 1780. In 1853 they were estimated to total about 265. The census of 1910 gave 61 Twana and 195 Skokomish, and the United States Office of Indian Affairs returned 206 Skokomish in 1937.

Wallawalla. Meaning "little river"; called Walula by Spier (1936).

Connections.—The Wallawalla language belongs to the Shahaptian division of the Shapwailutan linguistic stock and is very closely related to the Nez Percé.

Location.—On the lower Wallawalla River, except perhaps for an area around Whitman occupied by Cayuse, and a short span along the Columbia and Snake Rivers near their junction, in Washington and Oregon. They are now on Umatilla Reservation, Oregon.

Population.—Mooney (1928) gives 1,500 for the Wallawalla and the Umatilla together in 1780. In 1805 Lewis and Clark estimated 1,600 but they included other bands now known to be independent. The census of 1910 gave 397, the Report of the United States Office of Indian Affairs for 1923, 628, and that for 1937, 631, the two last evidently including some other peoples.

Connections in which they have become noted.—The name Walla-walla is perpetuated in that of the city of Walla Walla, Wash.; Walla Walla County; Walla Walla River, which flows through Oregon and Washington; and appears in the name of a small place in Illinois.

Wanapam. Significance unknown.

Connections.—The Wanapam belonged to the Shahaptian division of the Shapwailutan linguistic stock and were connected closely with the Palouse.

Location.—In the bend of Columbia River between Priest Rapids and a point some distance below the mouth of Umatilla River, and extending east of the Columbia north of Pasco.

Subdivisions

They seem to have included two branches, the Chamnapum and Wanapam proper.

Population.—Mooney (1928) estimates their population as 1,800 in 1780.

Watlala. The Watlala occupied the north side of Columbia River from the Cascades to Skamania and perhaps to Cape Horn, but a larger territory on the south side. (See under Oregon.)

Wauyukma. Significance unknown.

Connections.—They belonged to the Shahaptian division of the Shapwailutan linguistic family and were very closely related to the Palouse.

Location.—On Snake River below the mouth of the Palouse.

Population.—Unknown but probably included with the Palouse, which Mooney (1928) estimates to have numbered 1,800 in 1780.

Wenatchee (Wīna′t.ca). So called by the Wasco, and it has become a popular name for them. Also called:

> Awena′tchela, by the Klickitat, meaning "people at the coming-out or source," said to refer to the fact that they occupied the country at the heads of the rivers or above the Yakima.
>
> Pisquow, from .s.npeskwau′zux, their own name, variants of which appear in the appelations given them by other Salish tribes in the neighborhood.
>
> Tsō′kwob.c, by the Snohomish.

Connections.—The Wenatchee belonged to the inland division of the Salishan linguistic family, their nearest relations being the Sinkiuse-Columbia Indians.

Subdivisions

(From Curtis (1907–9) and Ray (1932))

Sinia′lkumuk, on the Columbia between Entiat Creek and Wenatchee River.
Sinkumchi′muk, at the mouth of the Wenatchee.
Sinpusko′isok, at the forks of the Wenatchee, where the town of Leavenworth now stands.

Sintia'tkumuk, along Entiat Creek.

Stske'tamihu, 6 miles down river from the present town of Wenatchee.

Minor divisions mentioned are the following:

Camiltpaw, on the east side of Columbia River.

Shanwappom, on the headwaters of Cataract (Klickitat) and Tapteel Rivers.

Siapkat, at a place of this name on the east bank of Columbia River, about Bishop Rock and Milk Creek, below Wenatchee River.

Skaddal, originally on Cataract (Klickitat) River, on the west bank of Yakima River and later opposite the entrance to Selah Creek.

Location.—On Methow and Wenatchee Rivers and Chelan Lake. The Wenatchee are now under the Colville Agency.

Population.—Mooney (1928) estimated there were 1,400 Wenatchee in 1780, but Teit (1928) considers this considerably too low. The four bands of this tribe mentioned by Lewis and Clark in 1805 totaled 820. The census of 1910 gave 52.

Connection in which they have become noted.—Wenatchee River, Lake Wenatchee, and Wenatchee Mountain preserve the name, as also the town of Wenatchee, county seat of Chelan County.

Wishram. From Wu'cxam, the name given them by the Yakima and Klickitat Indians. Also called:

> E-che-loot, by Lewis and Clark in 1806, from their own name.
> Ila'xluit, their own name and from this called Tlakluit.

Connections.—They belonged to the Chinookan stock, and spoke the same dialect as the Wasco.

Location.—On the north side of Columbia River in Klickitat County.

Villages

Atatathlia itcagitkok, on a small island near Celilo Falls, or more likely Ten-Mile Rapids.

Chalaitgelit, a short distance east of The Dalles.

Gawilapchk, a winter village below The Dalles.

Gawishila, a fishing station above The Dalles.

Hladakhat, about 10 miles below The Dalles.

Hliluseltshlikh, below Big Eddy.

Kwalasints, opposite The Dalles.

Nayakkhachikh, a winter village below Gawilapchk.

Niukhtash, at Big Eddy.

Shabanahksh, 1 mile below Wishram (?).

Shgwaliksh, perhaps Klickitat, about 12 miles (?) below The Dalles.

Shikeldaptikh, about a half mile below The Dalles.

Shkagech, below Crate's Point.

Shkonana, opposite Crate's Point.

Shkukskhat, below The Dalles.

Tsapkhadidlit, a wintering place below Nayakkhachikh.

Waginkhak, below The Dalles and the lowest Tlakluit town on the river.

Wakemap, above Wishram.

Wasnaniks, below Skukskhat.

Wayagwa, above The Dalles, the easternmost town.

Wishram (properly called Nixlúidix'), about 5 miles above The Dalles.

Population.—Mooney (1928) estimated that in 1780 there were about 1,500 Wishram, but Spier and Sapir (1930) suggest 1,000 about 1800. The latter figure is the one given by Lewis and Clark in 1806. The census of 1910 returned 274, and in 1937, under the designation "Upper Chinook," the United States Office of Indian Affairs gave 124.

Connection in which they have become noted.—A town in Klickitat County preserves the name of the Wishram.

Wynoochee. Significance of word is unreported.

Connections.—The Wynoochee were closely connected with the Chehalis Indians and belonged to the coastal division of the Salishan linguistic stock.

Location.—On the Wynoochee, an affluent of Chehalis River.

Yakima. Meaning "runaway." Also called:

> Cuts-sáh-nem, by Clark in 1805 in Lewis and Clark Journals (1904–5).
> Pa' kiut'lĕma, own name, "people of the gap."
> Shanwappoms, from Lewis and Clark in 1805.
> Stobshaddat, by the Puget Sound tribes, meaning "robbers."
> Waptai'lmĭn, own name, "people of the narrow river." Both of their names for themselves refer to the narrows in Yakima River at Union Gap where their chief village was formerly situated.

Connections.—The Yakima belonged to the Shahaptian division of the Shapwailutan linguistic family.

Location.—On the lower course of Yakima River.

Subdivisions

(As given by Spier (1936), quoting Mooney and Curtis)

Átanum-lema, on Atanum Creek.
Nakchi'sh-hlama, on Naches River, and hence possibly Pshwa'nwapam.
Pisko, about the mouth of Toppenish Creek.
Se'tas-lema, on Satus Creek.
Si'-hlama, on Yakima River above the mouth of Toppenish Creek.
Si'la-hlama, on Yakima River between Wenas and Umtanum Creeks.
Si'mkoe-hlama, on Simcoe Creek.
Tkai'waichash-hlama, on Cowiche Creek.
Topinish, on Toppenish Creek.
Waptailmin, at or below Union Gap.

It is quite possible that under the term Yakima several distinct tribes were included.

History and location.—The Yakima are mentioned by Lewis and Clark under the name of Cutsahnim, but it is not known how many and what bands were included under that term. In 1855 the United States made a treaty with the Yakima and 13 other tribes of Shapwailutan, Salishan, and Chinookan stocks, by which these Indians ceded the territory from the Cascade Mountains to Palouse and Snake Rivers and from Lake Chelan to the Columbia. The Yakima

Reservation was established at the same time and upon it all the participating tribes and bands were to be confederated as the Yakima Nation under the leadership of Kamaiakan, a distinguished Yakima chief. Before this treaty could be ratified, however, the Yakima War broke out, and it was not until 1859 that its provisions were carried into effect. The Palouse and certain other tribes have never recognized the treaty or come on the reservation. Since the establishment of the reservation, the term Yakima has been generally used in a comprehensive sense to include all the tribes within its limits, so that it is now impossible to estimate the number of true Yakima.

Population.—Mooney (1928) estimated the Yakima proper at 3,000 in 1780. In 1806 Lewis and Clark give an estimated population of 1,200 to their Cutsahnim (see above). The census of 1910 gives 1,362 "Yakima," and the Report of the United States Indian Office for 1923, 2,939, but as already stated, this name now covers many people beside the true Yakima tribe. In 1937 the population of the same body of Indians was given as 2,933.

Connections in which they have become noted.—The Yakima first attained prominence on account of the extension of their name over a number of related, and some unrelated, peoples as above mentioned, and its use to designate the Yakima Reservation. It has attained greater permanence as the designation of a branch of Columbia River, a county in Washington, and a town in the same County and State.

OREGON

The history of the Oregon Indians was similar to that of the Indians of Washington. The coast tribes seem to have been affected little or not at all by the settlements of the Spaniards in California, and those of the interior were influenced only in slightly greater measure by them through the introduction of the horse. Nor were these tribes reached so extensively by the employees of the great fur companies. Contact with such advance agents of civilization was principally along the valley of the Columbia River, and Astoria will always be remembered as bearing witness to the transient attempts of the American Fur Company to establish a permanent trading organization in this region under the American flag. As in the case of Washington, Oregon and its tribes were first brought to the acquaintance of our Eastern States in an intimate way by the expedition of Lewis and Clark in 1805–6. Here also settlement was delayed until the fixation of the International Boundary line and the rush westward following upon the discovery of gold in California. From the middle of the nineteenth century onward, however, the native tribes were rapidly dispossessed, placed upon reservations, and reduced in

numbers. At a later period the decrease became less marked, but
it has continued nevertheless, partly as an actual extinction of the
aboriginal population and partly as an absorption in the dominant
race. Most of the Chinookan tribes were finally placed upon Warm
Springs and Grande Ronde Reservations and on Yakima Reservation
in Washington; all of the Athapascan tribes upon the Siletz Reservation, except the Umpqua, who went to Grande Ronde; the Kusan and
Yakonan tribes upon the Siletz Reservation; the Salishan peoples
of Oregon upon the Grande Ronde and Siletz Reserves; most of the
Kalapooian peoples upon the Grande Ronde, though a few on the
Siletz; most of the Molala upon the Grande Ronde; the Klamath
upon Klamath Reserve; the Modoc mostly on Klamath Reserve but
a few upon the Quapaw Reservation in Oklahoma; the Shahaptian
tribes of Oregon upon the Umatilla Reservation; and the Northern
Paiutes upon the Klamath Reservation.

Ahantchuyuk. Own name, significance unknown. Also called:

> French Prairie Indians, by early settlers.
> Pudding River Indians, by various authors, and adopted by Berreman
> (1937).

Connections.—The Ahantchuyuk belonged to the Kalapooian linguistic stock.

Location.—On and about Pudding River, which empties into the
Willamette from the east about 10 miles south of Oregon City.

Population.—(See **Calapooya.**) Not given separately.

Alsea. A corruption of Älsé, their own name, meaning unknown.
Also called:

> Kûnis'tûnnĕ, Chastacosta name.
> Päifan amím, Luckiamute Kalapuya name.
> Si ni'-tĕ-lĭ tunnĕ, Naltunne name, meaning "flatheads."
> Tcha yáχo amim, Luckiamute Kalapuya name.
> Tĕhayesátlu, Nestucca name.

Connections.—The Alsea belonged to the Yakonan linguistic stock.
Location.—On Alsea River and Bay.

Villages

Chiink, on the south side of Alsea River.
Kakhtshanwaish, on the north side of Alsea River.
Kalbusht, on the lower course of Alsea River.
Kauhuk, on the south side of Alsea River.
Kaukhwan, on the north side of Alsea River at Beaver Creek.
Khlimkwaish, on the south side of Alsea River.
Khlokhwaiyutslu, on the north side of Alsea River.
Kutauwa, on the north side of Alsea River at its mouth.
Kwamk, on the south side of Alsea River.
Kwulisit, on the south side of Alsea River.

Kyamaisu, on the north side of Alsea River at its mouth.

Panit, on the south side of Alsea River.

Shiuwauk, on the north side of Alsea River.

Skhakhwaiyutslu, on the south side of Alsea River.

Tachuwit, on the north side of Alsea River.

Thlekuhweyuk, on the south side of Alsea River.

Thlekushauk, on the south side of Alsea River.

Population.—Mooney (1928) estimates the number of Indians belonging to the Yakonan stock at 6,000 in 1780. The census of 1910 returned 29 Indians under this name, and that of 1930 only 9 under the entire Yakonan stock.

Connection in which they have become noted.—Alsea or Alseya River, Alsea Bay and the village of Alsea, Benton County, Oreg., preserve the name of the Alsea Indians.

Atfalati. Meaning unknown. Often shortened to Fallatahs. Sometimes spelled Tuálati, or Tualatin (Berreman, 1937). Also known as:

Tualatin, Palmer *in* Ind. Aff. Rep., p. 260, 1859.

Wapato Lake Indians, a common name used by travelers.

Connections.—The Atfalati belonged to the northern dialectic branch of the Kalapooian linguistic family.

Location.—On the Atfalati plains, the hills about Forest Grove and the shores and vicinity of Wapato; they are also said to have extended as far as the site of Portland.

Villages and Bands

Chachambitmanchal, 3½ miles north of Forest Grove.

Chachamewa, at Forest Grove, 6 miles from Wapato Lake.

Chachanim, on Wapato Lake prairie.

Chachif, on Wapato Lake.

Chachimahiyuk, between Wapato Lake and Willamette River, Washington County.

Chachimewa, on or near Wapato Lake, Yamhill County.

Chachokwith, at a place of the same name north of Forest Grove, Washington County.

Chagindueftei, between Hillsboro and Sauvies Island, Washington County.

Chahelim, in Chehelim Valley, 5 miles south of Wapato Lake, Yamhill County.

Chakeipi, about 10 miles west of Oregon City.

Chakutpaliu, northeast of Hillsboro, Washington County.

Chalal, near the outlet of Wapato Lake.

Chalawai, southeast of Wapato Lake.

Chamampit, on Wapato Creek at the east end of Wapato Lake.

Chapanaghtin, north of Hillsboro, Washington County.

Chapokele, 4 miles west of Wapato Lake.

Chapungathpi, at Forest Grove, Washington County.

Chatagihl, at the upper end of Wapato Lake.

Chatagithl, at the upper end of Wapato Lake.

Chatagshish, in Washington County.

Chatakuin, 7 miles north of Hillsboro, Washington County.

Chatamnei, 10 miles north of Wapato Lake, in Washington County.
Chatilkuei, 5 miles west of Wapato Lake, in Yamhill County.
Chawayed, west of Forest Grove, in Washington County.

Population.—(See **Calapooya.**) The census of 1910 returned 44 Atfalati.

Connection in which they have become noted.—The name Atfalati is preserved in the form Tualatin by a town in Washington County.

Bannock. The Bannock came over into the eastern borders of the state between Powder and Owyhee Rivers in more recent times. (See Idaho.)

Calapooya. Meaning unknown. Also called:

> Kait-ka, by the Umpqua.
> Tsänh-alokual amím, by the Luckiamute Kalapuya.

Connections.—The Calapooya belonged to the Calapooya dialectic division of the Kalapooian linguistic stock.

Location.—On the headwaters of Willamette River including McKinzie, Middle, and West Forks.

Subdivisions or Bands

Ampishtna, east of upper Willamette River.
Tsanchifin, on the site of Eugene City.
Tsanklightemifa, at Eugene City.
Tsankupi, at Brownsville, Lynn County.
Tsawokot, north of Eugene City.

Population.—Mooney (1928) estimates the population of the entire Kalapooian stock at 3,000 in 1780. The Kalapooian bands on Grande Ronde Reservation numbered 351 in 1880; 164 in 1890; 130 in 1905. The census of 1910 returned 5 of the Calapooya tribe by itself, and 106 in the entire stock; and that of 1930, 45 individuals in the stock.

Connections in which they have become noted.—The Calapooya tribe is of note (1) because its name has been used for all the tribes of the stock; and (2) from its later application to Calapooya River, a branch of the Willamette; Calapooya Creek, an affluent of the Umpqua; and the Calapooya Mountains.

Cayuse. Significance unknown.

> Haí'luntchi, Molalla name.
> Wailĕtpu, own name.

Connections.—The Cayuse were placed by Powell (1891) in the Waiilatpuan linguistic stock along with the Molala (q. v.), but this is now recognized as a branch of the Shapwailutan family.

Location.—About the heads of Wallawalla, Umatilla, and Grande Ronde Rivers and extending from the Blue Mountains to Deschutes River, Washington and Oregon.

History.—Anciently the Cayuse are said to have had their headquarters on the Upper Grande Ronde but to have extended west later to the region of Deschutes River, where they may have met the Molala. They entered the historical arena with the expedition of Lewis and Clark and were afterward well known to explorers, hunters, and settlers. In 1838 a mission was established among them by the noted Marcus Whitman at the site of the present town of Whitman, but in 1847 smallpox carried off a large number of the tribe, and the Indians, believing the missionaries to be the cause, murdered Whitman and a number of other Whites and destroyed the mission. By 1851 they were much reduced in numbers and had become partially merged in the Nez Percé. In 1853 they joined in the treaty by which Umatilla Reservation was formed and made their homes upon it from that time forward. Their language is now nearly extinct.

Population.—Mooney (1928) estimates 500 Cayuse in 1780. In 1904, 404 were officially reported; the census of 1910 gave 298, while the United States Indian Office in 1923 returned 337. The census of 1930 reported 199 Cayuse and Molala, and the United States Indian Office of Cayuse alone in 1937, 370.

Connection in which they have become noted.—The Cayuse were reputed one of the most warlike tribes of Washington and Oregon. Horses were early bred among them and an Indian pony came to be known to the white settlers as a "cayuse." There is a place called Cayuse in Umatilla County, Oreg.

Chastacosta. From Shista-kwŭsta, their own name, significance unknown. Also called:

> Atcháshti amē'nmei, by the Atfalati Kalapuya.
> Atchashti ámim, another form of the Kalapuya name.
> Katuku, by the Shasta.
> Wálamskni, by the Klamath.
> Wálamswash, by the Modoc.

Connections.—The Chastacosta belonged to the Athapascan stock.

Location.—On the lower course of Illinois River, both sides of Rogue River for some distance above its confluence with the Illinois, and on the north bank somewhat farther.

Villages

Dorsey recorded the following:

Chetuttunne.

Chunarghuttunne, east of the junction of Rogue River and Applegate River.

Chunsetunneta.

Chunsetunnetun.

Chushtarghasuttun.

Chusterghutmunnetun, the highest on Rogue River.

Chuttushshunche.

Khloshlekhwuche.

Khotltacheche.

Khtalutlitunne.

Kthelutlitunne, at the junction of Rogue River and a southern affluent.

Kushlatata.

Mekichuntun.

Musme.

Natkhwunche.

Nishtuwekulsushtun.

Sechukhtun.

Senestun.

Setaaye.

Setsurgheake.

Silkhkemechetatun.

Sinarghutlitun.

Skurgnut.

Sukechunetunne.

Surghustesthitun.

Tachikhwutme, above the mouth of
    Illinois River.

Takasichekhwut.

Talsunme.

Tatsunye.

Thethlkhuttunne.

Tisattunne.

Tsetaame, east of the junction of Rogue
    River with Applegate River.

Tsetutkhlalenitun.

Tukulittatun.

Tukwilisitunne.

Tuslatunne.

Twenty of these at least were on the north side of Rogue River. The following may be synonymous with some in the above list: Klothchetunne, on or in the vicinity of Rogue River; Sekhatsatunne, on the north bank of Rogue River; Tasunmatunne, in the Rogue River country.

Drucker (1937) merely gives the "Chasta Costa (cista kwusta)" as one town near the Rogue-Illinois confluence divided into three parts called Tleattli'ntun, Tcetci'-wut, and Setla'tun.

Population.—Mooney (1928) estimates the population of the Chastacosta and 10 other Athapascan tribes in the vicinity at 5,600. In 1856 the remnant which was removed to Siletz Reservation numbered but 153, and the census of 1910 returned only 7. The 1930 census returned a total Athapascan population in Oregon of 504. The United States Office of Indian Affairs reported 30 Chastacosta in 1937.

Chelamela. Significance unknown. Also called:

Long Tom Creek Indians.

Connections.—The Chelamela belonged to the Calapooya dialectic division of the Kalapooian linguistic stock.

Location.—On Long Tom Creek, a western tributary of the Willamette River.

Population.—(See **Calapooya.**)

Chepenafa. Significance unknown. Also called:

Api'nefu, or Pineifu, by the other Kalapuya.

Marys River Indians, the official and popular name.

Connections.—The Chepenafa belonged to the Calapooya dialectic division of the Kalapooian linguistic stock, and were sometimes regarded as a subdivision of the Luckamiut (q. v.).

Location.—At the forks of St. Marys Creek, near Corvallis.

Population.—(See **Calapooya.**) The census of 1910 returned 24.

Chetco. Own name, meaning "close to the mouth of the stream."

Connections.—The Chetco belonged to the Athapascan linguistic stock and differed little in culture from the other Athapascan groups immediately north of them and the Tolowa to the south.

Location.—On each side of the mouth of Chetco River and about 14 miles up it as well as on Winchuck River. (See also California.)

Villages

As recorded by Dorsey (*in* Hodge, 1907):

Chettanne, Khuniliikhwut, Nukhsuchutun, Setthatun, Siskhaslitun, and Tachukhaslitun, on the south side of Chetco River.

Chettannene, on the north side of Chetco River.

Nakwutthume, on Chetco River above all the other villages.

Thlcharghiliitun, on the upper course of a south branch of Chetco River.

As recorded by Drucker (1937):

Hosa'tun, at the mouth of Winchuck River.

Natltene'tun, about where the modern town of Brookings stands.

Shrī'choslintun, on Chetco River a little above the following.

Tcagitlī'tun, on Chetco River at the mouth of the north Fork.

Tcet or Tcetko, at the mouth of Chetco River, really a town on each side.

Tūme'stun, near Shrī'choslintun.

Drucker adds that "the coast town which Parrish calls Wishtenatan (Water man, xustene'ten) may have been affiliated more closely with Chetco River than with the Lower Rogue River group."

Population.—See Chastacosta. In 1854, a year after the Chetco had been removed to the Siletz Reservation, they numbered 241. In 1861 they numbered 262. In 1877 there were only 63 on the reservation. The census of 1910 returned 9.

Connection in which they have become noted.—A river and a post hamlet in Curry County, Oregon, perpetuate the name of the Chetco.

Clackamas. From their own name, Guithla'kimas, significance unknown.

Also spelled Tlăkĭmĭsh, and called:

A'kimmash, by the Atfalati Kalapuya.

Gitā'q!ēmas, by the Clatsop.

Nsekau's or Ns tiwat, by the Nestucca.

Tu'hu tane, by the Umpqua.

Connections.—The Clackamas belonged to the Chinookan linguistic stock and to a dialectical division to which they have given their name.

Location.—On Clackamas River, claiming the country on the east side of Willamette River from a few miles above its mouth nearly to Oregon City and east as far as the Cascade Mountains. (See also Washington.)

Population.—Mooney (1928) estimates that the Clackamas numbered 2,500 in 1780. In 1806 Lewis and Clark set down their probable number as 1,800. In 1851 there were 88; the 1910 census returned 40; and United States Office of Indian Affairs in 1937, 81. The census of 1930 reported a total of 561 Indians in the Chinookan stock.

Connection in which they have become noted.—The name Clackamas is perpetuated by a river, a county, and a town in Oregon.

Clatskanie. Significance unknown. Also spelled A'látskné-i, Clack-star, Klatskanai, Tlatskanai, etc.

Connection.—The Clatskanie belonged to the Athapascan linguistic stock.

Location.—According to Gibbs (1877) the Clatskanie at one time owned the prairies bordering Chehalis River, Washington, at the mouth of Skookumchuck River, but on the failure of game, crossed the Columbia and occupied the mountains about Clatskanie River, their best-known historic seat. For a long time they exacted toll of all who passed going up or down the Columbia.

Population.—Mooney (1928) estimates 1,600 Clatskanie in 1780. In 1851 they were reduced to three men and five women. The census of 1910 returned three. (See **Chastacosta.**)

Connection in which they have become noted.—Like the Kwahlioqua, the Clatskanie are noted for their isolation from other branches of the Athapascan stock. Their name is preserved by Clatskanie Creek and Clatskanie town in Columbia County, Oreg.

Clatsop. From a native word meaning "dried salmon."

Connection.—The Clatsop belonged to the Lower Chinook dialectic division of the Chinookan linguistic stock.

Location.—The Clatsop centered about Cape Adams, on the south side of Columbia River, extending up the latter as far as Tongue Point, and southward on the Pacific coast to Tillamook Head.

Villages

As far as known these were:

Konope, near the mouth of Columbia River.

Neacoxy, the principal winter village, at the site of Seaside, at the mouth of Neacoxie Creek.

Neahkeluk, at Point Adams.

Niakewankih, south of Point Adams at the mouth of Ohanna Creek.

Neahkstowt, near the present Hammond.

Necotat, at the site of Seaside.

Population.—Mooney (1928) estimates 300 Clatsop in 1780. In 1806 Lewis and Clark gave 300. In 1875 the few survivors were moved to Grande Ronde Reservation, where the census of 1910 returned 26. (See **Clackamas.**)

Connection in which they have become noted.—Clatsop County and the town of Clatsop, Oreg., preserve the name.

Clowwewalla. Significance unknown. Phonetically GiLā'wēwalamt. Also called:

Fall Indians, Tumwater Indians, popular names.

Willamette Indians, Willamette Falls Indians, popular names.

Connections.—The Clowwewalla belonged to the Clackamas division of the Chinookan linguistic stock.

Location.—At the falls of Willamette River.

Subdivisions

The Clowwewalla may have included the Cushooks, Chahcowahs, and Nemalquinner of Lewis and Clark.

Population.—The Clowwewalla, or a part of them, were called Cushook by Lewis and Clark, who estimated that they numbered 650 in 1805–6. On this basis Mooney (1928) estimated there might have been 900 in 1780. They were greatly reduced by the epidemic of 1829 and in 1851 numbered 13. They are now apparently extinct.

Dakubetede. Own name, significance unknown. Also called:

> Applegate River Indians, from their habitat.
> Nĭ'ckitc hĭtclûm, Alsea name, meaning "people far up the stream."
> Ts'û-qûs-li'–qwŭt-me' tunne, Naltûnnetûnne name.

Connections.—The Dakubetede belonged to the Athapascan linguistic stock, using a dialect identical with that of the Taltushtuntude.

Location.—On Applegate River.

Population.—Mooney (1928) estimates the Dakubetede, the Nahankhotane (part of the Umpqua), the Taltushtuntude, and the Umpqua to have numbered 3,200 in 1780. They are nowhere separately enumerated. (See **Chastacosta.**)

Hanis. Own name, significance unknown.

Connections.—The Hanis formed one dialectic group of the Kusan linguistic family, the other being Miluk. It is probable that this stock was connected with the Yakonan.

Location.—On Coos River and Bay.

Villages

Anasitoh, on the south side of Coos Bay.
Melukitz, on the north side of Coos Bay.

Population.—Mooney (1928) estimates that the Hanis and the Miluk together numbered 2,000 in 1780. In 1805 Lewis and Clark estimated 1,500 Hanis. The census of 1910 returned 93 for the entire stock and that of 1930, 107, while, again for the stock, the United States Office of Indian Affairs reported 55 in 1937.

Klamath. A word of uncertain origin but probably used first by Columbia River or other outside tribes. Their own name is máklaks, meaning "people," "community." They are also called:

> Aĭgspaluma, abbreviated to Aĭgspalo, Aĭspalu; Nez Percé name for all Indians on Klamath Reservation and in the vicinity, meaning "people of the chipmunks."

Alámmimakt ísh (from ala'mmig, "Upper Klamath Lake"), said to be the
Achomawi name.

Athlámeth, C̓alapooya name.

Aúksiwash, in Yreka dialect of Shasta.

Dak'-ts!a^am-al-a^ɛ or Dak'-ts!a^ɛw-an-a'ɛ, "those above the lakes," by the
Takelma.

Ê-ukshik-ni máklaks, meaning "people of the lakes," also their own name.

Makaítserk, by the western Shasta.

Plaíkni, collective name for Klamath, Modoc, and Snakes on Sprague River.

Sáyi, Northern Paiute name.

Tapáadji, Ilmawi name.

Wols, name given by the Latgawa.

Connections.—Together with the Modoc (q. v.), the Klamath constituted the Lutuamian division of the Shapwailutan linguistic family.

Location.—On Upper Klamath Lake, Klamath Marsh, and Williamson and Sprague Rivers.

Subdivisions and Villages

These are given as follows by Spier (1930), maintaining his order:

I. ă'ukckni (the Klamath marsh—Williamson River group), with the following
villages: mŭ'tcuia'ksi (near the bridge toward the eastern end of Klamath marsh),
k'ɛtaiwa's (along the eastern side of the marsh), gŭpgŭa'ḵsi, (east side of Klamath
marsh south of last), i'wal (along a southeastern tongue of the marsh), kla'djŏḵsi
(ibid.), du''îlkŭt (on the south shore of Klamath marsh), awa'lwaskăn (west of
preceding), wa'ktale's (on the higher ground where Williamson River leaves the
marsh), la'laks (ibid.), lobŏ'kstsŏksi (on the bluff on the left bank of the Sprague
River at the railroad bridge) called by Gatschet (1891 b) ktaí-tú-pakshi), an unnamed site (on the south side of Sprague River below the dam), ḵ!ŏtcwă'ĕts (about
2 miles above the dam on the south bank of Sprague River), komă'ĕksi (on both
sides of Sprague River south of Braymill, 4 miles from Chiloquin), ḵa'umkăn
(about 6 miles above last), [Yainax] (settlements of some sort near here), hícdĭc-
luĕ'lukc (west of Gearhart Mountain), bɛzŭkse'was (on the right bank of Williamson River below the mouth of Sprague River), tăkalma'kcda (on the right bank of
Williamson River below preceding), djĭgiă's (below last two on both sides of river),
ḵ!o'ltawas (on both banks below
preceding but principally on left bank), at'awĭkc (below last, principally on right
bank), ya'ak (right bank below preceding), tsa'k'wi (below last, principally on
right), wĭtă'mŭmpsi (on a high bluff on the right bank above an eddy in the sharp
bend in the river), goyɛmske'ɛgĭs or k̇iɛk̇e'tsŭs (on right bank below last), wɛla'lksi
(on the eastern shore of Agency Lake), loḵ'o'gŭt (on the higher land near Agency
Lake by a little warm spring), tcŏ'klalŭmps (overlooks the lake where the Chiloquin road meets the Agency Lake highway), "other towns may have been at
ya'mzi, on the western side of Yamsay Mountain, and kokenă'oke, Spring Creek,
a large northern affluent of Klamath marsh."

II. kowa'cdikni, perhaps part of the first division, occupying: kowa'cdi (on
Agency Lake).

III. du'kwakni (on the delta of Williamson River), affiliated most closely with
the next division, and including: mo'aḵsda (on the left bank of Williamson River
nearly a mile above the mouth), wĭckămdi (below the preceding on the right bank),
la'wa'lstŏt (on the point forming the right side of the mouth of Williamson River),

mo'giŋkŭnks (on the left bank of Williamson River a quarter of a mile above the mouth), djĭŋgŭs (at a spring on the lake front to the east of the mouth of Williamson River).

IV. gu'mbŏtkni (on Pelican Bay and the marsh to the north) including: sle'tsksi (on the west side of Seven Mile Creek near its mouth), wudŏ'kăn (in the marsh a mile from the last and east of Seven Mile Creek), iwŭnau'ts (on the western side of a little creek emptying into Klamath Lake 2 miles east of Recreation P. O., and extending along the marsh shore to the northern side of Pelican Bay), dŭnŏ'ksi (an open space overlooking the northern end of Pelican Bay), e'o'ķai (a few hundred yards up Four Mile Creek on the left bank), wa'lŏ'kdi (above the last mentioned on the opposite side of the creek), waķ'a'k (south of the high ridge south of Odessa), gai'lŏks or gaila'lķs (on the point south of Odessa, or more probably between Howard and Shoalwater Bays), stŏ'kmatc (at Eagle Point); to which should perhaps be added: e'o'ķaķ (on Wood River, toward the mountains), and e'uķwa'lksi (on the east side of Wood River, and possibly the same site as the other).

V. iu'la'loŋkni (the people of Klamath Falls (Link River) and the eastern shore of Klamath Lake), including the following villages: kɛt!ai'ksi (extending southward from a promontory 2 miles or so northwest of Modoc Point), suwiaka̋'ĕks (at Modoc Point), iulă'u (on the east side of Klamath Lake), diu'wiaks (at the railroad point Ouxy), ķau'ŏmŏt (a half mile south of the preceding on the lake shore), dĭ'tk!aķs (at a hot spring known as Barclay Spring near the last mentioned), kŏlwa'l (at Rattlesnake Point at Algoma), wuķlo'twas (on Buck Island in Klamath Lake), lama'tcksi (on the point east of Buck Island), k!su'nk!si (three-fourths of a mile south of the preceding on the shore of Klamath Lake), iwau'wŏne (on both sides of Link River at the highway bridge), iu''laloŋe (at the mouth of Klamath River), wĕķa̋'ĕls (on the shore of Klamath Lake a mile west of the mouth of Klamath River), wut!ana'kŏķs (at one end of a little marsh (now drained) on the west side of Klamath Lake), iup!a'tŏna (at the other end of the same marsh), woksa'lks (on the north shore of Wokas marsh near Klamath Lake), dŏ'ktcŏŋks (on the west shore of Klamath Lake opposite Buck Island), sa'stĭtķa'-wals (at Squaw Point).

Population.—Mooney (1928) estimated the Klamath at 800 in 1780 but Spier (1930) raises this to 1,200. In 1905, including former slaves and members of other tribes more or less assimilated with them, they numbered 755. The census of 1910 returned 696. In 1923 there were 1,201 Indians under the Klamath Superintendency including Klamath, Modoc, and other Indians. In 1930, 2,034 were returned as Klamath and Modoc. In 1937 the United States Office of Indian Affairs reported 1,912 Klamath.

Connection in which they have become noted.—The name Klamath is perpetuated by Klamath Lake, Klamath County, and the town of Klamath Falls, Klamath County, Oreg.; by Klamath River, Oreg. and Calif.; and by a village in Humboldt County, Calif.

Kuitsh. Significance unknown. Also called:

> Ci-sta'-qwût-mê' tunnĕ', Mishikwutmetunne name, meaning "people dwelling on the stream called Shista."
> Lower Umpqua, or Umpwua, popular name.
> Tu'kwil-mă̋'-k'i, Alsea name.

Connections.—The Kuitsh belonged to the Yakonan linguistic stock, though so remotely connected that Frachtenberg (1911, p. 441) thought of placing them in an independent family, the Siuslawan.

Location.—On Lower Umpqua River.

Villages

According to Dorsey these were:

Chitlatamus.	Paiuiyunitthai.
Chukhuiyathl.	Skakhaus.
Chukukh.	Takhaiya.
Chupichnushkuch.	Thukhita.
Kaiyuwuntsunitthai.	Tkimeye.
Khuwaihus.	Tsalila.
Kthae.	Tsetthim.
Kuiltsh.	Tsiakhaus.
Mikulitsh.	Tsunakthiamittha.
Misun.	Wuituthlaa.
Ntsiyamis.	

Population.—The Kuitsh are usually classed with the Siuslaw. Mooney (1928) estimates the entire Yakonan stock at 6,000 in 1780, and by 1930 this had been reduced to 9. The Kuitsh are nowhere separately enumerated.

Latgawa. Signifying "those living in the uplands." Also called:

Walumskni, by the Klamath.

Connections.—With the Takelma proper, the Latgawa constituted the Takilman linguistic family which, in turn, was probably affiliated with the Shastan stock.

Location.—On Upper Rogue River eastward about Table Rock and Bear Creek and in the neighborhood of the present town of Jacksonville.

Village

Sapir (1915) records one village belonging to this tribe known by the tribal name and also called Latgauk.

Population.—See **Takelma.**

Lohim. Significance unknown. (See **Paiute, Northern.**)

Connections.—Reported as a band of Shoshoneans which entered Oregon at a late period.

Location.—On Willow Creek, a southern affluent of the Columbia.

Population.—In 1870 the number of Lohim was reported as 114, but the name has not appeared in recent official reports. They have generally been regarded as renegades belonging to the Umatilla Reservation, and Ray's (1938) informants denied the presence of Shoshoneans here, asserting that the name was applied to Yakima.

Luckiamute, Lakmiut. Significance unknown.

> Alakĕma'yuk, Atfalati name.
> Suck-a-mier, Chelukimaukes, forms appearing in Reports of the Office of Indian Affairs.

Connections.—The Luckiamute belonged to the Calapooya dialectic division of the Kalapooian linguistic stock.

Location.—The Luckiamute River.

Subdivisions or Bands

Ampalamuyu, on Luckiamute River.
Mohawk, on Mohawk River.
Tsalakmiut, on Luckiamute River.
Tsamiak, near Luckiamute River.
Tsantatawa, south of Luckiamute River.
Tsantuisha, on Luckiamute River.

Population.—(See **Calapooya.**) The number of Luckiamute was given as 28 in 1905. The census of 1910 returned only 8.

Connection in which they have become noted.—This tribe has given its name to Luckiamute River, Oreg.

Miluk. Significance unknown; also called Lower Coquille.

Connections.—The Miluk spoke the southern of the two dialects of the Kusan linguistic family, and were related more remotely to the Yakonan stock.

Location.—At the mouth of Coquille River.

Villages

Miluk or Mulluk, on the north side of the Coquille River at the site of the present town of Randolph.
Nasumi, on the south side of Coquille River on the coast of Oregon, near the site of the present Bandon.

Population.—Mooney (1928) estimated 2,000 in 1780 for the Miluk and Hanis together. In 1910 they numbered 93. (See **Hanis.**) In 1937 the population of the "Kus" Indians was given as 55.

Mishikhwutmetunne. Signifying "people who live on the stream called Mishi." Also called:

> Coquille, or Upper Coquille, from their habitat.
> De-d'á tené, Tutuni name, meaning "people by the northern water."
> Ithalé tĕni, Umpqua name.
> Kukwil', Alsea name (from Coquille).

Connections.—The Mishikhwutmetunne belonged to the Athapascan linguistic stock, their relations being particularly close with the Tututni.

Location.—On upper Coquille River.

Villages

The following were recorded by J. O. Dorsey (1884):

Chockreletan, near the forks of Coquille River.
Chuntshataatunne.
Duldulthawaiame.
Enitunne.
Ilsethlthawaiame.
Katomemetunne.
Khinukhtunne.
Khweshtunne, next above Coquille City.
Kimestunne.
Kthukhwestunne.
Kthunataachuntunne.
Meshtshe.
Nakhituntunne
Nakhochatunne.
Natarghiliitunne.
Natsushltatunne.
Nilestunne.
Rghoyinestunne.
Sathlrekhtun.
Sekhushtuntunne.

Sunsunnestunne.
Sushltakhotthatunne.
Thlkwantiyatunne.
Thltsharghiliitunne.
Thltsusmetunne.
Thlulchikhwutmetunne.
Timethltunne.
Tkhlunkhastunne, next to the Kusan people and below Coquille City.
Tsatarghekhetunne
Tthinatlitunne, at the site of Coquille.
Tulwutmetunne.
Tuskhlustunne.
Tustatunkhuushi.

Drucker (1937) recorded besides:
Hweshtun (perhaps partly Kusan).
Natgrilitun.
Stonerutltutl, a suburb of Natgrilitun.
Tlunhoshtun, said to have come from Umpqua.

Population.—(See **Chastacosta.**) The census of 1910 returned 15 Mishikhwutmetunne under the name Upper Coquille.

Modoc. From Móatokni, meaning "southerners." Also called:

Aígspaluma, Nez Percé name for all Indians on Klamath Reservation and in the vicinity.
La-la-cas, said to be the original name.
Lutmáwi, by a part of the Pit River Indians.
Lutuami, Ilmawi name.
Pχánai, Yreka Shasta name.
Saidoka, Shoshoni name.

Connections.—With the Klamath (q. v.), the Modoc constituted the Lutuamian division of the Shapwailutan linguistic stock.

Location.—On Little Klamath Lake, Modoc Lake, Tule Lake, Lost River Valley, and Clear Lake, extending at times as far east as Goose Lake. (See also California and Oklahoma.)

Subdivisions

The most important bands of the Modoc are said to have been at Little Klamath Lake, Tule Lake, and in the valley of Lost River.

Villages

Agawesh, on lower Klamath Lake, Calif., and on Hot Creek.
Chakawech, near Yaneks, on Sprague River, Klamath Reservation.
Kalelk, on the north shore of Tule or Rhett Lake.

Kawa, at Yaneks on Sprague River.

Keshlakchuis, on the southeast side of Tule (Rhett) Lake, Calif.

Keuchishkeni, on Hot Creek near Little Klamath Lake, Calif.

Kumbatuash (with Klamath), southwest of Tule (Rhett) Lake, Calif., extending from the lake shore to the lava beds.

Leush, on the north side of Tule (Rhett) Lake, Oreg.

Nakoshkeni, at the junction of Lost River with Tule Lake.

Nushaltkagakni, at the headwaters of Lost River near Bonanna.

Pashka, on the northwest shore of Tule (Rhett) Lake.

Shapashkeni, on the southeast side of Little Klamath Lake, Calif.

Sputuishkeni, on Lower Klamath Lake, Calif.

Stuikishkeni, on the north side of Little Klamath Lake.

Waisha, on Lost River, 3 or 4 miles northwest of Tule Lake, and near the hills that culminate in Laki Peak.

Wachamshwash, on Lost River near Tule (Rhett) Lake, in Klamath County.

Welwashkeni, on the southeast side of Tule Lake, at Miller's Farm, Calif.

Wukakeni, on the east side of Tule Lake, Calif.

Yaneks (with Klamath and Shoshoni), along middle Sprague River, Lake County.

Yulalona (with Klamath), at the site of the present Linkville.

History.—The Modoc came into contact with the Whites in comparatively late times, and acquired an unfortunate reputation from frequent conflicts with white immigrants in which atrocities were committed on both sides. In 1864 the Modoc and the Klamath together ceded their territory to the United States and retired to Klamath Reservation, but they were never contented there and made persistent efforts to return to their old country. Finally, in 1870, a chief named Kintpuash, better known to the Whites as Captain Jack, led the more turbulent element of the tribe back to the California border and refused to return. The first attempt to bring the runaways back precipitated the Modoc War of 1872–73. The Modoc retreated to the lava beds of northern California and for several months resisted all attempts to dislodge them, but they were finally overcome and Kintpuash and five other leaders hanged in October of that year. Part of the tribe was then sent to Indian Territory and placed on the Quapaw Reservation and the remainder on the Klamath Reservation.

Population.—Mooney (1928) estimates that there were 400 Modoc in 1780, but Kroeber (1925), with whom Spier (1930) seems to concur, allows twice as many. In 1905 there were 56 on the Quapaw Reservation and 223 on the Klamath Reservation. The census of 1910 returned 282, of whom 212 were in Oregon, 33 in Oklahoma, 20 in California, and the remainder scattered among 5 other States. In 1930 31 were in Oklahoma. (See **Klamath.**) In 1937, 329 were reported.

Connections in which they have become noted.—The chief claim of the Modoc to remembrance is on account of the remarkable defensive war they maintained in the lava beds of California, as above stated. A California county is named for them and places called Modoc are to be found in Phillips County, Ark.; in Emanuel County, Ga.; in Louisiana; in Ohio; and in McCormick County, S. C.; Randolph County, Ill.; and Randolph County, Ind.; also in the name of Modoc Point, Oreg.; in Scott County, Kans.; and in the name of the Modoc Lava Beds, Calif.

Molala. Derived from the name of a creek in the Willamette Valley from which one of their bands drove the original inhabitants. Also called:

> Amolélish, by the Kalapuya.
> Kúikni, by the Klamath.
> Láti-u or La'tiwĕ, their own name.
> Ya'-ide'sta, by the Umpqua.

Connections.—Together with the Cayuse, the Molala constituted the Waiilatpuan division of the Shapwailutan linguistic stock. According to Cayuse tradition, the Molala formerly lived with them and were separated and driven westward in consequence of wars with hostile tribes.

Location.—At an early date the Molala are believed to have been in the valley of the Deschutes River and to have been driven west, as above intimated, into the valleys of the Molala and Santiam Rivers. Either part of them subsequently went south to the headwaters of Umpqua and Rogue Rivers or they were separated from the rest in the movement above mentioned, as Berreman (1937) thinks.

Subdivisions

The following are said to have been Molala bands or settlements:

Chakankni, on the headwaters of Rogue River, northwest of Klamath Lake, absorbed later by the neighboring tribes, particularly the Klamath.
Chimbuiha, on the headwaters of Santiam River.
Mukanti, on the western slope of the Cascade Mountains.

Population.—Mooney (1928) believes the Molala were still with the Cayuse in 1780, whose numbers he fixes at about 500. In 1849 the Molala were estimated at 100. In 1877 Gatschet found several families living on the Grande Ronde Reservation, and in 1881 there were said to be 20 individuals in the mountains west of Klamath Lake. The census of 1910 returned 31, all but 6 of whom were in Oregon. (See **Cayuse.**)

Connection in which they have become noted.—The Molala are noteworthy in the first place for the uniqueness of their language, which is closely related only to Cayuse. Molalla River or Creek and a post village, both in Clackamas County, Oreg., bear the name.

Multnomah. Significance unknown. Also called:

> Wappato, originally the Cree or Chippewa name of a bulbous root (*Sagittaria variabilis*) used as food by the Indians of the west and northwest It means literally "white fungus." It passed into the Chinook jargon

with the meaning "potato" and became applied to Sauvies Island in Columbia River, at the mouth of the Willamette, and the Indian tribes living on or near it. It was so used by Lewis and Clark, though there was little or no political connection between the numerous bands so designated.

Connections.—The Multnomah belonged to the Clackamas division of the Chinookan linguistic stock.

Location.—As above indicated, on and near Sauvies Island.

Subdivisions or Bands

Cathlacomatup, on the south side of Sauvies Island on a slough of Willamette River.

Cathlacumup on the west bank of the lower mouth of the Willamette River and claiming as their territory the bank of the Columbia from there to Deer Island.

Cathlanaquiah, on the southwest side of Sauvies Island.

Clahnaquah, on Sauvies Island.

Claninnata, on the southwest side of Sauvies Island.

Kathlaminimin, at the south end of Sauvies Island, later said to have become associated with the Cathlacumup and Nemoit.

Multnomah, on the upper end of Sauvies Island.

Nechacokee, on the south bank of Columbia River a few miles below Quicksand (Sandy) River.

Nemalquinner, at the falls of the Willamette but with a temporary house on the north end of Sauvies Island.

Shoto, on the north side of Columbia River, a short distance from it and nearly opposite the mouth of the Willamette.

Population.—Mooney (1928) gives the population of all of these bands of the Multnomah as 3,600 in 1780. Their descendants are probably included among the 315 Indians returned as Chinook by the census of 1910. (See **Clackamas.**)

Connection in which they have become noted.—There is a county, town, and river channel of the name in Oregon. The name "Wappato" secondarily applied to the Multnomah besides its former use as a name of Sauvies Island, is given, with the spelling Sapato, to a lake and place near Portland in Oregon—the latter in Multnomah County, the former between Yamhill and Washington Counties—and to a place in the State of Washington.

Naltunnetunne, a small Athapascan tribe between the Tututni and Chetco, apparently included by later writers under the former.

Nez Percé. They extended into northeastern Oregon. (See Idaho.)

Paiute, Northern. These people occupied the southeastern part of Oregon and formerly extended far enough north to include the valley of Powder River and the upper course of John Day River of which they were dispossessed by Shahaptians. (See Nevada.)

Santiam. Significance unknown. Also called:

Aha'lpam, by the Atfalati Kalapuya.

Connections.—The Santiam belonged to the Calapooya dialectic division of the Kalapooian linguistic stock.

Location.—Santiam River.

Subdivisions or Bands

Chamifu, on Yamhill Creek.
Chanchampenau, east of Willamette River.
Chanchantu, location not specified.
Chantkaip, below the junction of the Santiam forks.

Population.—(See **Calapooya**.)   In 1906 there were 23 Santiam on Grande Ronde Reservation.   The census of 1910 returned 9.

Connection in which they have become noted.—The name Santiam is perpetuated in Santiam River, a branch of the Willamette.

Shasta.   The Shasta extended at least into the territory watered by Jenny Creek from their main seats in California (q. v.).

Siletz.   Significance unknown.   Also called:

> Tsä Shnádsh amím, Luckiamute Kalapuya name.

Connections.—The Siletz belonged to the Salishan linguistic stock.

Location.—On Siletz River.

Population.—Mooney (1928) estimates the population of all of the Salishan tribes of Oregon as 1,500 in 1780.   They are not now separately recorded, but in the census of 1930, 72 Salishan Indians were returned from Oregon besides the Tillamook.

Connections in which they have become noted.—The Siletz are of note as having been the southernmost of the Salishan linguistic family. Siletz River and a post village, both in Lincoln County, Oreg., preserve the name.

Siuslaw.   Significance unknown.   Also called:

> K'çu-qwĭc'tŭnnĕ, Naltunne name.
> K'qlo-qwec tŭnnĕ, Chastacosta name.
> Tsaná-uta amím, Luckiamute Kalapuya name.

Connections.—The Siuslaw belonged to the Siuslawan division of the Yakonan linguistic stock.

Location.—On and near Siuslaw River.

Villages

Dorsey (1884) gives the following:

Chimuksaich.	Khalakw.
Hauwiyat.	Kumiyus.
Hilakwitiyus.	Kumkwu.
Khachtais.	Kupimithlta.
Khaikuchum.	Kuskussu.
Khaiyumitu.	Kwsichichu (south of Eugene City).
Khakhaich.	Kwulhauunnich.

Kwultsaiya.
Kwunnumis.
Kwuskwemus.
Matsnikth.
Mithlausmintthai.
Paauwis.
Pia.
Pilumas.
Pithlkwutsiaus.
Skhutch.

Stthukhwich.
Thlachaus.
Thlekuaus.
Tiekwachi.
Tsahais.
Tsatauwis.
Tsiekhaweyathl.
Waitus.
Wetsiaus.
Yukhwustitu.

Population.—(See **Alsea**.)   The census of 1910 reported 7 Siuslaw.

Connection in which they have become noted.—The name Siuslaw is preserved by Siuslaw River, in Lane County, Oreg.

Skilloot.   The Skilloot occupied part of Oregon opposite the mouth of Cowlitz River.   (See Washington.)

Snake.   (See **Northern Paiute** under Nevada.)

Takelma.   Own name, meaning "those dwelling along the river."

> Kyu'-kŭtc hítclûm, Alsea name meaning "people far down the stream (or country)."
> Lowland Takelma, of Berreman (1937).
> Na-tcté tûnně, Naltunne name.
> Rogue River Indians, from their habitat.

Connections.—Together with the Latgawa (q. v.), the Takelma constituted the Takilman linguistic stock.   It is possible that this is distantly connected with the Shastan stock of northern California.

Location.—On the middle course of Rogue River from above Illinois River to about Grant's Pass and on the northern tributaries of Rogue River between these limits and the upper course of Cow Creek; also south nearly to the California boundary.

Villages

The following names were recorded by J. O. Dorsey mainly in one of the Athapascan dialects of the region:

Hashkushtun, on the south side of Rogue River.
Hudedut, at the forks of Rogue River and Applegate River.
Kashtata, on the south side of Rogue River above Leaf Creek and Galice Creek.
Kthotaime, on the south side of Rogue River.
Nakila, on the south side of Rogue River about 10 miles above Yaasitun.
Salwahka, near the mouth of Illinois River or one of its tributaries.
Seethltun, on the south side of Rogue River, the village nearest the Chastacosta.
Sestikustun, on the south side of Rogue River.
Sewaathlchutun, ibid.
Shkashtun, ibid.
Skanowethltunne, ibid.
Talmamiche, ibid.
Talotunne, ibid.

Tthowache, on the south side of Rogue River near "Deep Rock".
Yaasitun, on the south side of Rogue River.
Yushlali, ibid.

The following names, probably covering in part the same towns, were recorded by Dr. Edward Sapir in 1906, and are enumerated from the Latgawa country downstream:

Hatil, east of Table Rock.
Gelyalk, below Table Rock.
Dilomi, near the falls of Rogue River.
Gwenpunk.
Hayaal balsda.
Daktgamik.
Didalam, on the present site of Grant's Pass, the county seat of Josephine County.
Daktsasin or Daldanik, on Rogue River near Jump Off Joe Creek.
Hagwal, on Cow Creek.
Somouluk.
Hatonk.

Population.—Mooney (1928) estimates the entire Takilman stock at 500 in 1780. Only 1 was returned under that name by the census of 1910, but under the general head of "Rogue River" the Indian Office Report for 1937 gives two bodies of Indians numbering 58 and 46 individuals, respectively.

Connection in which they have become noted.—Together with the Latgawa, the Takelma are remarkable for the peculiarity of their language, accentuated by the fact that they are almost entirely surrounded by Athapascan peoples. A post village called Takilma in Josephine County, Oreg., perpetuates the name.

Taltushtuntude. Own name, meaning unknown. Also called:

> Galice Creek Indians, from their habitat.
> Kû-lïs'-kitc hïtc'lûm, Alsea name.

Connections.—The Taltushtuntude belonged to the Athapascan linguistic stock, and spoke the same dialect as the Dakubetede but culturally had become assimilated with the Takelma.

Location.—On Galice Creek.

Population.—In 1856, 18 Taltushtuntude were reported living on the Siletz Reservation. Under the name "Galice Creek" 42 Indians were reported in 1937.

Tenino. Significance unknown. Also called:

> Mĕli'-lĕma, own name.
> Warm Springs Indians, the common official designation.

Connections.—The Tenino constituted a division of the Shahaptian branch of the Shapwailutan linguistic stock.

Subdivisions and Villages

Kowasayee, on the north bank of Columbia River nearly opposite the mouth of the Umatilla.

Ochechote or Uchichol, on the north bank of Columbia River, the exact region being uncertain though they derive their name from a rock near the mouth of the Deschutes River.

Skinpah, on the north bank of Columbia River above the mouth of the Deschutes.

Tapanash, on the north bank of Columbia River, near the mouth of the Deschutes and a little above Celilo, the name being later extended over most of the above bands.

Tilkuni, between White and Warm Springs Reservations.

Tukspush on John Day River, and hence called often John Day Indians.

Wahopum, on the north bank of Columbia River near the mouth of Olive Creek.

Waiam, near the mouth of the Deschutes River.

History.—The Tenino were mentioned by Lewis and Clark in 1805. By the treaty of 1855 they gave up their lands and settled, along with other Shahaptian tribes and some Salishan tribes, on Yakima Reservation, Washington. Since then they have not had separate official recognition.

Population.—Mooney (1928) estimated that in 1780 there were 3,600 including the Atanum of the Yakima and the Tyigh. The United States Office of Indian Affairs reported 460 in 1937 of the Yakima and associated bands.

Connection in which they have become noted.—A town in Thurston County, Wash., perpetuates the name.

Tillamook.   A Chinook term meaning "people of Nekelim (or Nehalem). Also spelled Calamox, Gillamooks, Killamook, etc.

Higgahaldahu, Nestucca name.

Kyaukw, Alsea name.

Nsietshawas, so called by Hale (1846).

Si ni'-tĕ-lĭ, Mishikwutmetunne name for this tribe and the Alsea, meaning "flatheads."

Connections.—The Tillamook were the principal tribe in Oregon belonging to the Salishan linguistic family, coastal division.

Location.—The coast from the Nehalem to Salmon River.

Subdivisions and Villages

Nehalem, on Nehalem River.

Nestucca, on Nestucca Bay and the streams flowing into it.

Salmon River, on the river of that name.

Tillamook, on Tillamook Bay and the streams flowing into it, including the following villages enumerated by Lewis and Clark: Chishucks (at the mouth of Tillamook River), Chucktin (the southernmost Tillamook village, on a creek emptying into Tillamook Bay), Kilherhursh (at the entrance of Tillamook Bay), Kilherner (on Tillamook Bay, at the mouth of a creek 2 miles from Kilherhursh), Towerquotten (on a creek emptying into Tillamook Bay).

Population.—See **Siletz**. Lewis and Clark estimated 2,200 Tillamook in 1805. In the reports of the Wilkes Exploring Expedition (1845) their number is given as 400, and by Lane in 1849 as 200. The census of 1910 returned 25, and that of 1930, 12.

Connection in which they have become noted.—The Tillamook seem to have been the most powerful tribe on the coast of Oregon. A bay, and also a county and its capital in the former country of the tribe preserve the name; also a cape, Tillamook Head.

Tututni. Meaning unknown. Also called:

> H'lilush, Nestucca name.
> Lower Rogue River Indians, or Rogue River Indians, from their habitat.
> Tálĕmaya, Umpqua name.
> Ta-qu'-qûc-cĕ, Chetco name, meaning "northern language."

Connections.—The Tututni belonged to the Athapascan linguistic stock, and were related closely with the Mishikhwutmetunne.

Location.—On lower Rogue River and the Pacific coast north and south of its mouth.

Villages

J. O. Dorsey (1884) gave the following villages or bands:

On the north coast of Rogue River:
> Chemetunne, popularly called Joshuas, just north of Rogue River.
> Kaltsergheatunne, at Port Orford.
> Kosotshe, between Port Orford and Sixes Creek, perhaps earlier on Flores Creek.
> Kwatami, on or near Sixes River.
> Kthukwuttunne.
> Kthutetmeseetuttun, just north of Rogue River.
> Kwusathlkhuntunne, said to have been at the mouth of Mussel Creek, 5 miles south of Mount Humbug.
> Natutshltunne, between Coquille River and Flores Creek.
> Niletunne, the first village south of the Miluk village of Nasumi, south of Coquille River.
> Yukichetunne, on Euchre Creek.

On Rogue River:
> Chetlesiyetunne, on the north side.
> Enitunne, near the mouth of a southern affluent of Rogue River.
> Etaatthetunne.
> Kunechuta.
> Kushetunne, on the north side.
> Mikonotunne, on the north side 14 miles from its mouth.
> Nakatkhaitunne, on the north side of Rogue River.
> Targheliichetunne, on the north side.
> Targhutthotunne, near the coast.
> Testthitun, on the north side.
> Thechuntunne, on the north side.
> Thethlkhttunne, or Chastacosta, on the north side.

On or near the coast south of Rogue River:
> Aanetun.

Chetleschantunne, on Pistol River and the headlands from the coast 6 miles south of Rogue River.

Khainanaitetunne.

Kheerghia, about 25 miles south of Pistol River.

Khwaishtunnetunne, near the mouth of a small stream locally called Wishtenatin, after the name of the settlement, that enters the Pacific about 10 miles south of Pistol River, at a place later known as Hustenate.

Natthutunne, on the south side of Rogue River.

Nuchumatuntunne, on the north side of Rogue River near the mouth.

Sentethltun, on the south side of Rogue River and perhaps at its mouth.

Skumeme, on the south side of Rogue River near its mouth.

Tsetintunne, the highest of 4 villages on a stream emptying into Rogue River near its mouth.

Tsetuttunne.

Drucker (1937) gives the following village names:

On Rogue River:

Gwī'sat huntun, on Mussel Creek near Sixes River and sometimes separated as the Sixes tribe.

Kusū'me, on what is now called Flores Creek.

Kwataime, a short distance north of last.

Kwuse'tun, near and possibly a suburb of Megwinō'tun, on the coast.

Megwinō'tun, a few miles up river.

Skame'me, between Pistol River and mouth of Rogue River; Waterman places it at Hunter's Creek.

Sukwe'me or Sukwe'tce, at mouth of Sixes River.

Tagrilī'tun, a suburb of Tū'tutun.

Tce'metun or Tce'me, really two towns, one on each side of the river's mouth.

Tce'tlersh tcuntun, on Pistol River, perhaps belonging to the Chetco.

Tū'tutun, 5 to 6 miles from the river's mouth, divided into two parts called Tatre'tun, "downriver," and Na'gutretun "upriver."

Yukwī'tce or Yu'gwitce, on what is now called Euchre Creek.

Berreman (1937) makes seven major divisions as follows: Kwatami or Sixes River; Euchre Creek (Yukichetunne); Mikono tunne; Pistol River (Chetleschantunne); Joshua; Tututunne (Tututni); Kwaishtunne or Khustenete.

Population.—(See **Chastacosta.**) In 1854 the Tututni population was 1,311. The census of 1910 returned 383, but in 1930 the United States Indian Office gave only 41 under this name, 55 under that of "Meguenodon" (see above), and 45 under that of "Joshua" (Tce'metun).

Tyigh. Significance unknown. Also spelled Attayes, Iyich, Ta-ih, Thy, Tyh, etc.

Teáxtkni, or Télknikni, Klamath name.

Tsĕ Amínĕma, Luckiamute Kalapuya name.

Connections.—The Tyigh belonged to the Tenino branch of the Shahaptian division of the Shapwailutan linguistic stock.

Location.—The country about Tygh and White Rivers.

Subdivisions and Villages

No names are recorded.

History.—The history of the Tyigh was identical with that of the Tenino (q. v.).

Population.—With the other Oregon tribes of the Tenino group, the Tyigh numbered 1,400 in 1780 according to Mooney's (1928) estimate. In 1854 they were said to number 500 and in 1859, 450; but both of these figures must be overestimates. They are not now enumerated separately from the Warm Spring Indians, placed at 550 by the census of 1910.

Connection in which they have become noted.—Tygh Creek and a place called Tygh Valley in Wasco County, Oreg., bears the name of the Tyigh.

Umatilla. Significance unknown.

Connections.—The Umatilla belonged to the Shahaptian division of the Shapwailutan linguistic stock.

Location.—On Umatilla River and the banks of Columbia River adjacent to the mouth of the Umatilla.

Population.—Mooney (1928) estimates this tribe and the Wallawalla together at 1,500 in 1780. The census of 1910 returned 272, the United States Indian Office Report for 1923, 145, and the Indian Office Report for 1937, 124.

Connections in which they have become noted.—An Indian reservation has received the name Umatilla, and it has also been applied to a river, a county, and a post village, all in Oregon; also to a place in Lake County, Fla.

Umpqua. Significance unknown.

Amgútsuish, Shasta name.
Cactaⁿ'-qwût-me'tûnně, Naltunne name.
Ci-cta'-qwût-me'tûnně, Tututni name, meaning "Umpqua River people."
Ci-sta'-qwût, Chastacosta name.
Etnémitane, own name (Gatschet, 1877).
Tsan Ámpkua amím, Luckiamute Kalapuya name, meaning "people on the Umpqua."
Upper Umpqua, Berreman (1937).
Yaᵃgalá', Takelma name.

Connections.—The Umpqua belonged to the Athapascan linguistic stock.

Location.—On upper Umpqua River, east of the Kuitsh.

Subdivisions

The Umpqua on Cow Creek are often spoken of separately under the name Nahankhuotana. Parker (1840) mentions a people called Palakahu which was probably an Athapascan or Yakonan tribe but cannot now be identified, and also the Skoton and Chasta, probably parts of the Chastacosta or Tututni. This is all the more likely as he includes the Kwatami band of the Tututni and the entirely independent Chilula of California. Their chief village was Hewut.

Population.—(See **Dakubetede.**)   Hale (1846) says that in his time the Umpqua were supposed to number not more than 400.   In 1902 there were 84 on Grande Ronde Reservation.   The census of 1910 returned 109.   In 1937, 43 Indians are given under this name.   (See **Chastacosta** and **Dakubetede.**)

Connection in which they have become noted.—Umpqua River, and the settlement of Umpqua or Umpqua Ferry in Douglas County, preserve the name.

Wallawalla.   The Wallawalla extended somewhat into northeastern Oregon.   (See Washington.)

Walpapi.   Significance unknown.   Commonly called Snakes.   A part of the Northern Paiute.   (See under Nevada.)

Wasco.   From a native word wacq!ó, "cup or small bowl of horn," the reference being to a cup-shaped rock a short distance from the main village of the tribe; from this the tribal name Gałasq'ó, "those that have the cup," is derived and variations of it frequently appear in the literature.   Also called:

> Afúlakin, by the Kalapuya.
> Ámpχänkni, meaning "where the water is," by the Klamath.
> Awásko ammim, by the Kalapuya.
> Sáχlatks, by the Molala.

Connections.—They belonged to the upstream branch of the Chinookan linguistic stock, their closest relatives being the Wishram on the opposite side of the river.

Location.—In the neighborhood of The Dalles, in the present Wasco County.

Villages and Fishing Stations

The following are given by Sapir (1930) in order from east to west: Hlgahacha, Igiskhis, Wasco (a few miles above the present town of The Dalles), Wogupan, Natlalalaik, Gawobumat, Hliekala-imadik, Wikatk, Watsokus, Winkwot (at The Dalles), Hlilwaihldik, Hliapkenum, Kabala, Gayahisitik, Itkumahlemkt, Hlgaktahlk, Tgahu, Hliluktik, Gahlentlich, Gechgechak, Skhlalis.

Population.—Morse (1822) estimated the number of Wasco at 900. The census of 1910 returned 242, and the United States Office of Indian Affairs, 227 in 1937.   (See **Clackamas** and **Watlala.**)

Connections in which they have become noted.—The Wasco were the strongest Upper Chinook tribe and that which ultimately absorbed the rest.   The name is preserved by Wasco County, Oreg., and a town in Sherman County in the same State; also places in Kern County, Calif., and Kane County, Ill.

Watlala. Significance of word is unknown. Also called:

>   Cascade Indians, the popular English name.
>   Gila'xicatck, by the Chinook.
>   Katlagakya, own name.
>   Shahala, from Chinook saxala, meaning "above," by Chinook.

Connections.—The Watlala belonged to the Chinookan linguistic stock and the Clackamas dialectic group.

Location.—At the Cascades of Columbia River and extending down to the mouth of the Willamette River.

Subdivisions

The following names have been applied by various writers to the Indians in this neighborhood and may be subdivisions of this tribe, or perhaps refer to the entire tribe itself:

Cathlakaheckit, at the Cascades.
Cathlathlala, just below the Cascades.
Clahclellah, near the foot of the Cascades.
Neerchokioon, on the south side of Columbia River a few miles above Sauvies Island.
Washougal, near Quicksand River.
Yehuh, just above the Cascades.

Population.—Mooney (1928) estimates that the Watlala and the Wasco together numbered 3,200 in 1780. In 1805–6 Lewis and Clark estimated that there were 2,800. In 1812 the two first-mentioned bands were estimated to number 1,400. They are no longer enumerated separately and are probably incorporated at the present time with the Wishram and the Wasco.

Yahuskin. One of the two chief peoples in Oregon belonging to the Northern Paiute division of the Shoshonean and therefore Uto-Aztecan linguistic stock. (See Nevada.)

Yamel. Significance unknown, often spelled Yam Hill. Also called:

>   Ychă-yamel-amim, by the Atfalati Kalapuya.

Connections.—The Yamel belonged, along with the Atfalati, to the northern dialectic division of the Kalapooian linguistic stock.

Location.—Yamhill River.

Subdivisions

Gatschet (1877) records these as follows:

Andshankualth, on a western tributary of the Willamette.
Andshimmampak, on Yamhill River.
Chamifu, in the forks of Yamhill River.
Chamiwi, on Yamhill River.
Champikle, on Dallas (La Creole) Creek.
Chinchal, on Dallas Creek.

Population.—(See **Calapooya.**) The census of 1910 returned 5 Yamel.

Connection in which they have become noted.—The name of the Yamel, in the form Yamhill, is perpetuated by an affluent of the Willamette and by the county through which it flows.

Yaquina. Significance unknown.

Să-ákl, Nestucca name.
Sĭs'-qûn-me'tûnnĕ, Chetco name.
Tcha yákon amim, Luckiamute Kalapuya name.

Connections.—The Yaquina were one of the tribes of the Yakonan linguistic stock to which they gave their name.
Location.—About Yaquina River and Bay.

Villages

The following list is from J. O. Dorsey (1884):

On the north side of Yaquina River:

Holukhik.	Mittsulstik.
Hunkkhwitik.	Shash.
Iwai.	Thlalkhaiuntik.
Khaishuk.	Thlekakhaik.
Khilukh.	Tkhakiyu.
Kunnupiyu.	Tshkitshiauk.
Kwulaishauik.	Tthilkitik.
Kyaukuhu.	Ukhwaiksh.
Kyuwatkal.	Yahal.
Mipshuntik.	Yikkhaich.

On the south side of the river:

Atshuk.	Kwullakhtauik.
Chulithltiyu.	Kwutichuntthe.
Hakkyaiwal.	Mulshintik.
Hathletukhish.	Naaish.
Hitshinsuwit.	Paiinkhwutthu.
Hiwaitthe.	Pikiiltthe.
Kaku.	Pkhulluwaaitthe.
Khaiyukkhai.	Pkuuniukhtauk.
Khitalaitthe.	Puuntthiwaun.
Kholkh.	Shilkhotshi.
Khulhanshtauk.	Shupauk.
Kilauutuksh.	Thlekwiyauik.
Kumsukwum.	Thlelkhus.
Kutshuwitthe.	Thlinaitshtik.
Kwaitshi.	Thlukwiutshthu.
Kwilaishauk.	Tkulmashaauk.
Kwulchichicheshk.	Tuhaushuwitthe.
Kwullaish.	Tulshk.

Population.—(See **Alsea.**) The census of 1910 returned 19 Yaquina.
Connecton in which they have become noted.—The name of this tribe Yaquina, was given some scientific prominence by its use, in the form

Yakonan, for a small linguistic stock in the Powellian classification. It is preserved in Yaquina River, Yaquina Bay and a town called Yaquina in Lincoln County.

Yoncalla. From Ayankĕld, or Tch'Ayankē'ld, "those living at Ayankeld," own name.

Connections.—The Yoncalla were the southernmost tribe of the Kalapooian linguistic stock, forming one of the three dialectic divisions.

Location.—On Elk and Calapooya Creeks, tributaries of Umpqua River.

Subdivisions

According to Gatschet (1887), there were two bands, called Chayankeld and Tsantokayu by the Luckiamute, but it seems likely that the former name (Tch' Ayankē'ld) is merely the native tribal name.

Population.—(See **Calapooya.**)   The census of 1910 returned 11 Yoncalla.

Connection in which they have become noted.—Yoncalla, a post village of Douglas County, Oreg., preserves the name.

CALIFORNIA

The territory of the present State of California was discovered in 1542 by a Portuguese navigator in the Spanish service, J. R. Cabrillo. In 1578 Sir Francis Drake landed at Drake's Bay, opened communication with the natives, and took possession of the country in the name of England, calling it New Albion. It was explored by the Spaniard S. Viscayno in 1602, but no attempt was made at colonization until the Franciscan Fathers established a mission at San Diego in 1769. Within the next 50 years they founded 21 missions and gathered 20,000 Indians about them, but the number of neophytes continually fell off and the power of the missions declined with them, especially after Mexican government had succeeded to Spanish. Transfer of the country to the United States and the rush of immigrants following upon the discovery of gold in 1848 was still more disastrous to the Indians and this disaster extended to parts of the State which the Spaniards had not reached. From this time on the history of the Indians of this area is one long story of debauchery and extermination. Reservations were set aside for most of the tribes, but the greater part of the survivors live scattered through the country as squatters or on land purchased by themselves.

In dealing with the tribes of California, I have adopted the names given by Dr. Kroeber in his Handbook of the Indians of California (1925). An inspection of these shows us at once, however, that the tribal concept in most parts of the State is one imposed upon the

Indians as a result of ethnological investigation rather than something recognized by themselves. It has a dialectic rather than a governmental or ceremonial base, but it is the best that can be done unless we adopt the impracticable alternative of treating each village group as a tribe. It is to be understood that, from the ordinary point of view as to what constitutes a tribe, this expedient is largely artificial. Under these circumstances it has seemed best not to follow a strictly alphabetic system throughout, or rather, to enter those tribes defined by their names as parts of larger groups under the more common group names, the qualifying word following, as: Paiute, Northern, and Yuki, Coast, instead of Northern Paiute and Coast Yuki.

Connections in which they have become noted.—That few names of California tribes have found permanent lodgment in the geography of the region is not surprising when we consider the small number of names of this kind at all prominent. This is in keeping with the fact that tribal organizations as they were known in eastern North America were wanting over much of the State, and that where they existed they were generally small and insignificant. It also happens that a few real tribal names, or names that have been used to cover tribal groups, include peoples which extended into neighboring States and have been treated elsewhere. Under this head come the names of Modoc County, Klamath River, Mohave River, Mono County and Lake, and Piute Peak. Still other names are derived from villages and small tribes, mere subdivisions of the main bodies. Among these may be mentioned Tuolumne County, Mokelumne Peak and River, Cosumnes River, Kaweah River. While the designation of the Shasta is a conspicuous one it is rather the mountain which has given name to the tribe than the tribe to the mountain, though in fact both are derived from a chief of the Shasta people. Following from the use of the term for Mount Shasta we have Shasta River, Shasta, Shasta Retreat, Shasta Springs. The history of the name Hupa has been somewhat similar. It has remained attached to the valley to which it was originally applied and to the tribe secondarily. Nevertheless, the valley name now serves to preserve in memory that of the people who occupied it.

Achomawi.   From adzúma or achóma, "river."

>Kō'm-maidüm, Maidu name, meaning "snow people."
>Shawash, Yuki name for the Achomawi taken to Round Valley Reservation.

Connections.—The Achomawi were originally classed with the Atsugewi as one stock under the name Palaihnihan, the Achomawan stock of Merriam (1926), and this in turn constitutes the eastern branch

of the Shastan stock, which in turn is now placed under the widely
spread Hokan family.

Location.—In the drainage area of Pit River from near Montgomery
Creek in Shasta County to Goose Lake on the Oregon line, with the
exception of the territory watered by Burney, Hat, and Horse or Dixie
Valley Creeks.

Subdivisions

Kroeber (1925) gives the following:

Achomawi, on Fall River.
Astakiwi, in upper Hot Springs Valley.
Atuami, in Big Valley.
Hamawi, on the South Fork of Pit River.
Hantiwi, in lower Hot Springs Valley.
Ilmawi, on the south side of Pit River opposite Fort Crook.
Madehsi, the lowest on Pit River along the big bend.

C. H. Merriam (1926) says that Achomawi is the Madehsi name for the Astakiwi
which occupied all of Hot Springs Valley, and he adds the names of two other
tribes between the last mentioned and Goose Lake, the Ko-se-al-lak'-te, and,
higher up, at the lower end of the lake, the Hā'-we-si'-doc.

Population.—Together with the Atsugewi, the Achomawi are estimated by Kroeber (1925) to have numbered 3,000 in 1770; in 1910
there were 985. According to the census of 1930, the entire Shastan
stock numbered 844, and in 1937, 418 "Pit River" Indians were enumerated, only a portion of the stock apparently.

Alliklik. Designation bestowed by the Ventureño Chumash; meaning unknown.

Connections.—The Alliklik belonged to the Californian group of the
Shoshonean division of the Uto-Aztecan linguistic stock, their closest
relatives probably being the Serrano.

Location.—On the upper Santa Clara River.

Villages

Akavavi Kashtu, Etseng, Huyang, Küvung, and Pi'idhuku (on Piru Creek, the
last mentioned at Piru); Kamulus (on Castac Creek); Kashtük Tsawayung (on
a branch of Castac Creek).

Population.—The Alliklik together with the Serrano, Vanyume, and
Kitanemuk, numbered 3,500 in 1770 and 150 in 1910. The census of
1930 returned 361 southern California Shoshoneans.

Atsugewi. Their own name or that which the Achomawi applied to
them; significance unknown.

Adwanuqdji, Ilmawi name.
Hat Creek Indians, popular English name.
Tcunoíyana, Yana name.

Connections.—With the Achomawi, the Atsugewi constituted the Palaihnihan or eastern group of the Shastan- stock, more recently placed by Dixon and Kroeber (1919) in the Hokan family.

Location.—On Burney, Hat, and Dixie Valley or Horse Creeks.

Subdivisions

Kroeber (1925) gives: Apwarukei (Dixie Valley people), Hat Creek people (native name unknown), and Wamari'i (Burney Valley people). C. G. Merriam (1926) calls the Hat Creek people collectively At-soo-kā'-e (Atsugewi) and treats most of the Burney Valley Indians as part of the Atsugewi proper.

Population.—Kroeber estimates that in 1770 there were 3,000 of the Atsugewi and the Achomawi together. The Shastan Indians numbered 844 in 1930.

Bear River Indians. A body of Indians living along Bear River in the present Humboldt County for whom no suitable native name has been preserved. Also called:

Ni'ekeni', name they applied to themselves and to the Mattole.

Connections.—The Bear River Indians belonged to the Athapascan linguistic family, and were most closely connected with the Mattole, Sinkyone, and Nongatl tribes to the south and east.

Location.—As given above. (See North Carolina for a tribe similarly named.)

Villages

From the mouth of Bear River inland as given by Nomland (1938):

Tcalko', at the mouth of Bear River.
Chilshĕck, on the site of the present Capetown.
Chilenchĕ, near the present Morrison Ranch.
Selsche'ech, on a site marked by a large red rock 3–4 miles above the last.
Tlanko, above the preceding.
Estakana, at Gear's place, on the largest flat in the upper valley above Tlanko.
Sehtla, about 7 miles above Capetown.
Me'sseah, name for a natural amphitheater, the training place for shamans, about which lived a few families.

Population.—Included with the Nongatl (q. v.). 1,129 were returned in the census of 1930. The United States Office of Indian Affairs reported 23 "Bear River" Indians in 1937.

Cahuilla. A name perhaps of Spanish origin, but its significance is unknown. Also spelled Kawia.

Connections.—The Cahuilla belonged to the southern California group of the Shoshonean division of the Uto-Aztecan stock.

Location.—Mainly in the inland basin between the San Bernardino Range and the range extending southward from Mount San Jacinto.

Subdivisions

Desert Cahuilla, at northern end of the Colorado Desert.
Mountain Cahuilla, in the mountains south of San Jacinto Peak.
Western or Pass Cahuilla, centering in Palms Springs Canyon.

Villages

Duasno, on or near the Cahuilla Reservation.
Juan Bautista, in San Bernardino County.
Ekwawinet, at La Mesa, 2 miles south of Coachella.
Kavinish, at Indian Wells.
Cahuilla, on the Cahuilla Reservation.
Kwaleki, in the San Jacinto Mountains.
Lawilvan or Sivel, at Alamo.
Malki, on the Potrero Reservation in Cahuilla Valley east of Banning.
Pachawal, at San Ygnacio.
Palseta, at Cabezon.
Paltewat, at Indio in Cahuilla Valley.
Panachsa, in the San Jacinto Mountains.
Sechi, in Cahuilla Valley.
Sokut Menyil, at Martinez.
Sapela, at San Ygnacio.
Temalwahish, at La Mesa.
Torres, on Torres Reservation.
Tova, at Agua Dulce.
Wewutnowhu, at Santa Rosa.

Population.—Kroeber (1925) estimates 2,500 Cahuilla in 1770; in
1910 there were about 800. (See **Alliklik**.)

Connection in which their name has become noted.—The name Cahuilla is preserved in that of a village called Kaweah in Tulare County.

Chemehuevi. The Yuman name for this tribe and for the Paiute;
significance unknown. Also called:

> Ah'alakàt, Pima name, meaning "small bows."
> Mat-hat-e-vátch, Yuma name, meaning "northerners."
> Tä'n-ta'wats, own name, meaning "southern men."

Connections.—The Chemehuevi were a part of the true Paiute and
were associated with them and the Ute in one linguistic subdivision
of the Shoshonean division of the Uto-Aztecan linguistic stock.

Location.—Anciently in the eastern half of the Mohave Desert.
At a later date the Chemehuevi settled on Cottonwood Island, in
Chemehuevi Valley, and at other points on Colorado River.

Subdivisions
(So far as known)

Hokwaits, in Ivanpah Valley.
Kauyaichits, location unknown.
Mokwats, at the Kingston Mountains.
Moviats, on Cottonwood Island.

Shivawach or Shivawats, in the Chemehuevi Valley, perhaps only the name of a
locality.
Tümpisagavatsits or Timpashauwagotsits, in the Providence Mountains.
Yagats, at Amargosa.

Population.—Kroeber (1925) estimates between 500 and 800
Chemehuevi in ancient times.   In 1910, 355 were returned of whom
260 were in California.

Chetco.   The Chetco extended slightly across into northern California
from its home in Oregon (q. v.).

Chilula.   An American rendering of Yurok Tsulu-la, "people of
Tsulu," the Bald Hills.

Connections.—With the Hupa and Whilkut, the Chilula formed one
group of the Athapascan linguistic stock.

Location.—On or near lower Redwood Creek from near the inland
edge of the heavy redwood belt to a few miles above Minor Creek.

Villages

The following are known and are given in order beginning with the one farthest
down Redwood Creek: Howunakut, Noleding, Tlochime, Kingkyolai, Kingyu-
kyomunga, Yisining'aikut, Tsinsilading, Tondinunding, Yinukanomitseding,
Hontetlme, Tlocheke, Hlichuhwinauhwding, Kailuhwtahding, Kailuhwchengetld-
ing, Sikingchwungmitahding, Kinahontahding, Misme, Kahustahding.

Population.—Kroeber (1925) estimates 500 to 600 Chilula before
White contact.   Now reduced to two or three families and a few
persons incorporated with the Hupa.   (See **Bear River Indians.**)

Chimariko.   From the native word chimar, "person."   Also called:

Kwoshonipu, name probably given them by the Shasta of Salmon River.
Meyemma, given by Gibbs (1853).

Connections.—Originally considered a distinct stock, the Chimariko
are now classed in the Hokan linguistic family.

Location.—On the canyon of Trinity River from about the mouth
of New River to Canyon Creek.

Villages

Chalitasum, at the junction of New and Trinity Rivers.
Chichanma, at Taylor Flat.
Himeakudji, at Big Creek.
Hodinakchohoda, at Cedar Flat.
Maidjasore, at Thomas.
Paktunadji, at Patterson.
Tsudamdadji, at Burnt Ranch.

Population.—The Chimariko were estimated by Kroeber (1925) at
250 in 1849; only a few mixed-bloods are now living.

Chumash. A term originally applied to the Santa Rosa islanders. Also called:

> Santa Barbara Indians, a popular name.

Connections.—At first considered a distinct linguistic stock, the Chumash are now included in the larger Hokan family.

Location.—The Chumash occupied the three northern islands of the Santa Barbara group, the coast from Malibu Canyon to Estero Bay, and extended inland to the range that divides the drainage of the great valley from the coast, except on the west where their frontier was the watershed between the Salinas and the Santa Maria and short coast streams, and on the east where some small fragments had spilled over into part of the most southerly drainage of the San Joaquin-Kern system.

Subdivisions

Barbareño Chumash, on the coast from Point Conception nearly to Ventura River.

Cuyama Chumash, in the valley of Cuyama River and the upper valley of the Santa Maria River.

Emigdiano Chumash, beyond the coast range in the southernmost extremity of the great valley of California.

Island Chumash, on San Miguel, Santa Rosa, and Santa Cruz Islands.

Obispeño Chumash, on the coast from a point a little north of Santa Maria River to Salinan territory.

Purisimeño Chumash, on the coast between the lands of the Obispeño and Barbareño divisions.

Santa Ynez Chumash, inland along Santa Ynez River between the Barbareño and Cuyama divisions.

Ventureño, on the coast from the Ventura River to the end of Chumash territory on the southeast and the drainage areas of Ventura River, Calleguas Creek, and most of that of Santa Clara River inland.

Villages

A'hwai (at Ojai).
Ala-hulapun, at Santa Ynez Mission.
Alka'ash, on the coast west of Santa Barbara.
Alpincha, at Santa Barbara.
Alwatalam, in the Goleta marsh.
Amolomol, on the coast close to Santa Barbara.
Amuwu, at Mission Purisima near Santa Ynez River.
Anawupu, on a small stream emptying into the Pacific at Gaviota.
Antap, near Ventura.
Awawilashmu, near the Cañada del Refugio.
Chikachkach, at the mouth of Ventura River.
Ch'oloshush, at the west end of Santa Cruz Island.
Ch'üshü, on the north shore of Santa Cruz Island.
Chwayük, on the coast west of Ventura River.
Elhelel, on the coast east of Santa Barbara.
Elhiman, in the Goleta marsh.

Hahas, on the north shore of Santa Cruz Island toward the east end.
Hanawani, on the south shore of Santa Cruz Island.
Halam, on Jalama Creek near the coast.
Hanaya, northeast of Santa Barbara Mission.
Heliok, on the coast southwest of Goleta.
Helo, on the coast south of Goleta.
Hipuk, inland on Maliba Creek.
Honmoyanshu, near Ventura.
Ho'ya or Huya, said to have been the name of a village on Santa Cruz Island.
Humkaka, at Point Conception.
Ishwa, at the mouth of Santa Clara River.
Kachyoyukuch, near Ventura.
K'ahü, on the coast between Cañada del Refugio and Dos Pueblos Canyon.
Kamupau, inland on San Emigdio Creek.
Kashiwe, inland northeast of Santa Susana.
Kashwa, northeast of Santa Barbara Mission.
Kasil, at the mouth of Cañada del Refugio.
Katstayüt, on the coast west of Gaviota.
Kayewüsh, inland on Calleguas Creek.
Kichüwün, on the northeast coast of Santa Rosa Island.
Kinapuich', near Ventura.
Kohso, a short distance inland from the mouth of Ventura River.
Kolok, at Carpinteria.
K'shiuk'shiu, on the northeast coast of Santa Rosa Island.
Kulalama, near Santa Barbara Mission.
Kuyamu, near the mouth of Dos Pueblos Canyon.
L'aka'amu, on the north coast of Santa Cruz Island near its west end.
L'alalü, on the north coast of Santa Cruz Island.
Lapau, on the Cañada de los Uvas north of Old Fort Tejon.
Liyam, on the south shore of Santa Cruz Island.
Lu'upsh, near the east end of Santa Cruz Island.
Mahalal, at San Cayetano.
Mah'auh, inland near the middle course of Calleguas Creek.
Maliwu, at the mouth of Maliba Creek.
Mashch'al, on the east coast of Santa Cruz Island.
Masuwük, near Los Alamos.
Ma'tilha, inland on Matilija Creek.
Mich'iyu, on the coast east of Gaviota.
Mikiw, at the mouth of Dos Pueblos Canyon.
Mishopshno (near Carpinteria), near Santa Ynez River above Cachuma Creek.
Mishtapalwa, near Ventura.
Mismatuk, in Arroyo Burro near Santa Barbara Mission.
Mispu, on the coast southwest of Santa Barbara.
Mitskanakan, at Ventura Misslon.
Nupu, at Santa Paula.
Nushüm, on the coast between Ventura Mission and Carpinteria.
Muwu, on the coast near the mouth of Calleguas Creek.
Nahayalewa, on the headwaters of Santa Ynez River northwest of Chismahoo
    Mountain.
Nawani, on the west coast of Santa Rosa Island.
Niakla, on the north coast of Santa Rosa Island.
Nila'lhuyu, on the south coast of Santa Rosa Island.
Nimalala, on the north coast of Santa Cruz Island.

Nümkülkül, on the north coast and near the west end of Santa Rosa Island.
Onohwi, on Nojoqui Creek, a branch of Santa Ynez River.
Onomyo, at Gaviota.
Sahpilil, on the coast southwest of Goleta.
Salnobalkaisikw, a short distance west of Ojai.
Sati'k'oi, at Saticoy on Santa Clara River.
Sek'spe, at Sespe.
Shalawa, on the coast north of Santa Barbara.
Shawa, on the west coast of Santa Cruz Island.
Shimiyi, at Simi on Calleguas Creek.
Shisholop, on the coast near Point Conception.
Shisholop, a second town of the name at Ventura Mission.
Shishwashkui, on the coast south of Rincon Creek.
Shtekolo, at the Cienega near Santa Barbara Mission.
Shuku, at the mouth of Rincon Creek.
Shushuchi, on the coast west of the Cañada del Refugio.
Shuwalashu, on the coast at the lower end of Sycamore Canyon.
Siliwihi, on the north coast of Santa Rosa Island.
Simo'mo, at the mouth of Calleguas Creek.
Sis'a, on Sisar Canyon northwest of Santa Paula.
Sitoptopo, inland northeast of Ojai.
Siuhtun, at Santa Barbara Mission.
Skonon, in Arroyo Burro near Santa Barbara Mission.
S'ohmüs, inland on the middle course of Calleguas Creek.
Swahül, at the eastern point of Santa Cruz Island.
Swetete, on the coast east of Santa Barbara.
Ta'apu, inland north of Santa Susana.
Takuyo, inland on Tecuya Creek, northwest of old Fort Tejon.
Tashlipunau, inland on San Emigdio Creek north of San Emigdio Mountains.
Teneknes, at Carpinteria.
Tenenam, near Santa Barbara Mission.
Tokin, near Santa Barbara Mission.
Tuhmu'l, on the coast east of Gaviota.
Upop, near Point Conception.
Ushtahash, inland northwest of Santa Barbara Mission.
Wene'me, at Hueneme.
Wichachet, on the coast east of the mouth of Calleguas Creek.

Cabrillo's sixteenth century relation gives the names of a number of villages, part of which Kroeber (1925) has been able to identify, at least with a fair degree of probability, while some are evidently duplications. Eliminating the duplications, we have the following additional village names:

Aguin.
Anacot.
Asimu.
Bis.
Caacat (or Caacac), though this last may be a synonym for Ciucut (Siuhtun).
Gua (or Quannegua).
Maquinanoa.
Misinagua.
Nacbuc (or Anacbuc).
Nocos.
Olesino.
Opia (or Opistopia).
Potoltuc (Paltate, Partocac, or Paltocac).
Quiman.
Sopono (Misesopono, or Garomisopona).
Xotococ.
Yutum.

Population.—The number of Chumash has been estimated by Kroeber (1925) at 10,000 in 1770; at the present time a mere remnant is left, given as 38 in the census of 1910 and 14 in that of 1930.

Costanoan.   From Spanish Costaños, "coast people."   Also called:

Mutsun, Gatschet extended this term over these and other peoples.

Connections.—The Costanoan formed one division of the Penutian linguistic stock.

Location.—On the coast between San Francisco Bay and Point Sur, and inland probably to the Mount Diablo Range.

Subdivisions

Monterey Costanoan, from Pajaro River to Point Sur and the lower courses of the latter stream and Salinas and Carmel Rivers.
Saclan Costanoan, between San Francisco and San Pablo Bays.
San Francisco Costanoan, between San Francisco Bay and the Pacific Ocean.
San Juan Bautista Costanoan, along San Benito River and San Felipe Creek.
Santa Clara Costanoan, on Coyote and Calaveras Creeks.
Santa Cruz Costanoan, on the coast between Pescadero and Pajaro River.
Soledad Costanoan, on the middle course of Salinas River.

Villages

As far as Kroeber has been able to locate them, they are as follows:
Ahala-n, south of Martinez.
Altah-mo, on the west shore of San Francisco Bay.
Aulin-tak, on the coast close to Santa Cruz Mission.
Ausai-ma, on San Felipe Creek.
Awas-te, near San Francisco.
Chatu-mu, near Santa Cruz Mission.
Hotochtak, just west of the preceding.
Huchiu-n, northeast of Oakland.
Huime-n, near San Pablo.
Huris-tak, at the junction of San Felipe and San Benito Creeks.
Imuna-kan, northeast of Salinas.
Kakon-ta-ruk, near Point Sur.
Kalinta-ruk, at the mouth of Salinas River.
Kino-te, inland south of San Francisco Bay.
Matala-n, inland south of San Francisco Bay.
Mus-tuk, inland east of the mouth of Salinas River.
Mutsu-n, at San Juan Bautista Mission.
Olho-n, south of San Francisco.
Orbiso-n, at San Jose Mission.
Paisi-n, on San Benito River.
Posol-mi, near the south end of San Francisco Bay.
Romano-n, south of San Francisco.
Rumse-n, on Carmel River.
Saho-n, on Salinas River south of Salinas.
Sakla-n, south of Martinez.
Salso-n, at San Mateo.
Sirhin-ta-ruk, on the coast north of Point Sur.

Sokel, at Aptos, east of Santa Cruz.
Tamie-n, on Coyote River near Santa Clara Mission.
Tamo-tk, near Monterey.
Tulo-mo, south of San Francisco.
Ulis-tak, on Coyote River north of Santa Clara Mission.
Urebure, near the west shore of San Francisco Bay.
Wacharo-n, near Soledad Mission on Salinas River.
Werwerse-n, inland east of San José.
Wolwo-n, inland northwest of Mt. Diablo.

Population.—Kroeber (1925) estimates that there were about 7,000 Costanoan in 1770. Today there are only a few mixed-blood descendants remaining. The census of 1910 returned 10; that of 1930, none.

Cupeño. From Kupa, the name of one of their towns.

Connections.—The Cupeño spoke a dialect belonging to the Luiseño-Cahuilla branch of the Shoshonean division of the Uto-Aztecan linguistic stock.

Location.—A mountainous district on the headwaters of San Luis Rey River, not over 10 by 5 miles in extent.

Villages

Kupa, near the famous hot springs of Warner's Ranch.
Wilakal, at San Ysidro.

Population.—Kroeber (1925) estimates not over 500 in 1770, and in 1910, 150. (See **Alliklik**.)

Dakubetede. An Athapascan tribe of Oregon which extended slightly beyond the northern border of California. (See Oregon.)

Diegueño. Derived from the name of the Mission of San Diego.

Connections.—The Diegueño belonged to the Central division of the Yuman linguistic group, being most closely connected with the Kamia and Kiliwa, but that is reckoned a branch of the Hokan stock.

Subdivisions

Northern Diegueño, in the eastern part of San Diego County and extending an indefinite distance southward into the Mexican State of Baja California.
Southern Diegueño, in the modern districts of Campo, La Posta, Manzanita, Guyapipe, and La Laguna, and some territory in Baja California.

Villages

Aha-hakaik, at La Laguna.
Akmukatikatl, inland on San Dieguito River.
Ahta ("cane") or Hapawu, at Carrizo.
Ahwat, in Baja California.
Amai'-tu, at La Posta.
Amat-kwa'-ahwat, on the stream above Campo.
Amotaretuwe, inland between San Diego and Sweetwater Rivers.
Anyaha, at the headwaters of San Diego River.

Atlkwanen, on the head of San Dieguito River.
Awaskal, location unknown.
Ekwiamak, on the head of Sweetwater River.
Emitl-kwatai, at Campo.
Ewiapaip, at Guyapipe.
Hakum, in or near Jacumba Pass.
Hakutl, south of San Marcos Creek.
Hamacha, on the middle course of Sweetwater River.
Hamul, at the head of Otay River.
Hanwi, location uncertain.
Hapai, south of San Dieguito River.
Hasasei, location uncertain.
Hasumel, location uncertain.
Hata'am, location uncertain.
Hawai, location uncertain.
Hawi, at Vallecitos.
Inomasi, location uncertain.
Inyahkai, at La Laguna.
Kamachal, location uncertian.
Kohwat, location uncertain.
Kokwitl, location uncertain.
Kosmit, at the head of San Diego River.
Kosoi, at San Diego.
Kwalhwut, location uncertain.
Kulaumai, on the coast near the mouth of San Dieguito River.
Kwatai, at the head of Cottonwood Creek.
Maktati, location uncertain.
Maramoido, location uncertain.
Mat-ahwat-is, location uncertain.
Matamo, location uncertain.
Met-hwai, southwest of San Ysidro Mountain.
Meti, location uncertain.
Mitltekwanak, on San Felipe Creek and the head of San Dieguito River.
Netlmol, location uncertain.
Nipawai, on lower San Diego River.
Otai, about Otai Mountain.
Pamo, between the heads of San Dieguito and San Diego Rivers.
Paulpa, at the north end of San Diego Bay.
Pauwai, inland between San Dieguito and San Diego Rivers.
Pokol, location uncertain.
Pu-shuyi, inland east of San Diego.
Sekwan, on the middle course of Sweetwater River.
Setmunumin, southeast of Mesa Grande.
Shana, location uncertain.
Sinyau-pichkara, on the middle course of San Dieguito River.
Sinyau-tehwir, at the head of San Diego River.
Sinyeweche, northeast of San Diego.
Suapai, location uncertain.
Tapanke, location uncertain.
Tawi, west of San Ysidro Mountain.
Tlokwih, near North Peak.
Totakamalam, at Point Loma.
Tukumak, at Mesa Grande.

Wemura, location uncertain.
Witlimak, on a head branch of San Diego River.

Population.—Kroeber (1925) estimates 3,000 Diegueño and Kamia together in 1770; in 1925, between 700 and 800. The census of 1930 gave 322.

Esselen. Probably the name of a village; significance unknown.

Connections.—Originally given the status of a distinct stock, the Esselen are now placed in the Hokan linguistic family, their affinities being rather with the Yuman division, to the south, and with the Pomo, Yana, and other groups to the north than with their closer neighbors of this stock, the Salinan and Chumash tribes.

Location.—On the upper course of Carmel River, Sur River, and the coast from Point Lopez almost to Point Sur.

Villages

Echilat, 12 miles southeast of Mission Carmelo.
Ekheya, in the mountains.
Ensen, at Buena Esperanza.
Ichenta, at San José.
Pachhepes, near the next.
Xaseum, in the sierra.

Population.—Kroeber (1925) estimates 500 Esselen in 1770; they are now extinct.

Fernandeño. So-called from San Fernando, the name of one of the two Franciscan missions in Los Angeles County.

Connections.—The nearest relatives of the Fernandeño were the Gabrielino and both belonged to the California section of the Shoshonean Division of the Uto-Aztecan linguistic stock.

Location.—In that part of the valley of Los Angeles River above Los Angeles.

Villages

Hahamo, north of Los Angeles.
Kawe, northwest of Los Angeles.
Mau, north of Los Angeles.
Pasek, at San Francisco Mission.

Population.—Kroeber (1925) estimates that, with the Gabrielino and Nicoleño, the Fernandeño numbered 5,000 in 1770; they are now practically extinct.

Gabrielino. Derived from San Gabriel, one of the two missions in Los Angeles County. Also called:

Kizh, reported by Gatschet (1876); Hale (1846) has Kij.

Playsanos, a name which seems to be applied to the California Shoshoneans living in the lowlands, especially near the coast in the region of Los Angeles.

Tobikhars, said to mean "settlers," but probably from Tobohar, the mythical first man.

Tumangamalum, Luiseño name.

Connections.—The nearest connections of the Gabrielino were the Fernandeño; both belonged to the California branch of the Shoshonean Division of the Uto-Aztecan stock.

Location.—In the drainage area of the San Gabriel River, the territory about Los Angeles, and all the country southward to include half of Orange County, also Santa Catalina Island and probably San Clemente.

Villages

Ahau, near Los Angeles River north of Long Beach.
Akura, near San Gabriel Mission.
Akura-nga, at La Presa.
Aleupki-nga, at Santa Anita.
Apachia, just east of Los Angeles.
Asuksa, west of Azusa.
Awi, between Pomona and the San Gabriel River.
Chokish-nga, at Jaboneria.
Chowi, near San Pedro.
Engva, near Redondo.
Hout, south of San Gabriel Mission.
Hutuk, inland on Santa Ana River.
Isantka-nga, at Mission Vieja.
Kinki or Kinkipar, on San Clemente Island.
Kukamo, southwest of Cucamonga Peak.
Lukup, near the mouth of Santa Ana River.
Masau, on the coast near San Pedro.
Moyo, on the coast south of the mouth of Santa Ana River.
Nakau-nga, at Carpenter's.
Pahav, southeast of Corona.
Pasino, southeast of Pomona.
Pimoka-nga, at Rancho de los Ybarras.
Pimu or Pipimar, on Santa Catalina Island.
Pubu, inland on San Gabriel River, east of Long Beach.
Saan, on the coast south of Santa Monica.
Sehat, inland near the middle course of San Gabriel River.
Shua, near Long Beach.
Siba, at San Gabriel Mission.
Sisitkan-nga, at Pear Orchard.
Sona-nga, at White's.
Sua-nga, near Long Beach.
Tibaha, north of Long Beach between Los Angeles and San Gabriel Rivers.
Toibi, at Pomona.
Wenot, at Los Angeles.

Population.—Kroeber (1925) estimates 5,000 Gabrielino, Fernandeño, and Nicoleño in 1770; they are now practically extinct.

Halchidhoma. On the middle Colorado. (See Arizona.)

Huchnom. The name applied to this tribe by the Yuki and apparently by themselves; said to signify "mountain people." Also called:

> Redwoods, a popular name.
> Ta'-tu, by the Pomo of Potter Valley.

Connection.—The Huchnom belonged to the Yukian linguistic stock, though resembling the Pomo somewhat more closely in culture.

Location.—In the valley of South Eel River from Hullville nearly to its mouth, together with the valley of its affluent, Tomki Creek, and the lower course of the stream known as Deep or Outlet Creek.

Villages

Ba'awel, name in Pomo; on South Eel River a couple of miles from Ukumna (q. v.).
Hatupoka, on Tomki Creek below the village of Pukemul.
Komohmemut-kuyuk, on South Eel River between Lilko'ol and Mumemel.
Lilko'ol, on South Eel River between Ba'awel and the preceding.
Mot, on South Eel River between Yek and Mupan.
Mot-kuyuk, on South Eel River at the mouth of Tomki Creek.
Mumemel, on South Eel River just below the forks at Hullville.
Mupan, on South Eel River between Mot and Mot-kuyuk.
Nonhohou, on South Eel River between Shipomul and Yek.
Pukemul, on Tomki Creek above the village of Hatupoka.
Shipomul, on South Eel River at the mouth of Outlet Creek.
Ukumna, near the head of the eastern source of Russian River.
Yek, on South Eel River between Nonhohou and Mot.

There is one village of uncertain name and possibly Yuki on the headwaters of the South Fork of Eel River.

Population.—The Huchnom were estimated at 500 in 1770 by Kroeber (1925); the census of 1910 returned 7 full-bloods and 8 half-breeds. (See **Yuki**.)

Hupa. Derived from the Yurok name of the valley, Hupo. Also called:

> Cha'parahihu, Shasta name.
> Hích'hu, Chimariko name.
> Kishakevira, Karok name.
> Nabiltse, given by Gibbs (1877) and translated "man."
> Natinnoh-hoi, own name, after Natinnoh, "Trinity River."
> Num-ee-muss, Yurok name.
> Trinity Indians, translation of their own name.

Connections.—The Hupa belonged to the Athapascan linguistic stock, forming one closely knit linguistic group with the Chilula and Whilkut.

Location.—On the middle course of the Trinity River and its branches, particularly a beautiful stretch of 8 miles known as Hupa (or Hoopa) Valley, and on New River. C. H. Merriam (1926) treats these latter as a distinct tribe of Shastan affinities, but J. P. Harrington (personal information) states that they were Hupa.

Villages

Aheltah, name perhaps Yurok; said to be in the upper part of Hupa territory.

Cheindekotding, on the west bank of Trinity River between Kinchuhwikut and Miskut.

Dakis-hankut, on the west bank of Trinity River between Honsading and Kinchuhwikut.

Djishtangading, on the east bank of Trinity River between Howunkut and Haslinding.

Haslinding, in the "Sugar Bowl" above Hupa Valley.

Honsading, the village farthest down Trinity River and on the east bank.

Howunkut, on the west side of Trinity River between Medilding and Djishtangading.

Kachwunding, on Trinity River near the mouth of Willow Creek.

'Kek-kah'-nä-tung, at Martha Ziegler's place on the lower part of New River.

Kinchuhwikut, on the east bank of Trinity River between Dakishankut and Cheindekotding.

Ki-ooᶜʰ-wet-tung, at Sally Noble's place on New River, about a quarter of a mile below the mouth of Panther Creek.

Klo-neś-tung, at the present site of Quinby on New River.

Medilding, on the east bank of Trinity River between Totltsasding and Howunkut.

Me-yemma, possibly belonging to this tribe, but more likely Chimariko, on Trinity River just below the mouth of New River.

Mingkutme, on Trinity River near the mouth of Willow Creek.

Miskut, on the east bank of Trinity River between Cheindekotding and Takimitlding.

Sehachpaya, the name perhaps Yurok; said to have been in the upper part of the Hupa territory.

Sokeakeit, ibid.

Takimitlding, on the east bank of Trinity River between Miskut and Tsewenalding.

Tashuanta, the name perhaps Yurok; said to have been in the upper part of the Hupa territory.

Tlelding, at the forks of the Trinity River.

Tl'okame, a subsidiary settlement of the preceding, 5 miles up the South Fork of Trinity River.

Totltsasding, on the west bank of Trinity River between the preceding and Medilding.

Tsa-nah'-ning-ah'-tung, on the bar or flat at New River Forks, at the junction of East Fork with main New River.

Tsewenalding, on the east bank of Trinity River between Takimitlding and Totltsasding.

Waugullewatl, the name perhaps Yurok; said to have been in the upper part of the Hupa territory.

Population.—Kroeber (1925) places the number of Hupa at 1,000 in 1770; the census of 1910 returned 500. In 1937 the United States Office of Indian Affairs returned 575. (See **Bear River Indians.**)

Connection in which they have become noted.—A village in Humboldt County, preserves the name of the Hupa.

Juaneño. Derived from the mission of San Juan Capistrano. Also called:

> Gaitchim, given by Gatschet (1876).
> Netela, given by Hale (1846), meaning "my language."

Connections.—The Juaneño belonged to the Shoshonean branch of the Uto-Aztecan linguistic stock, their speech being a variant of Luiseño.

Location.—From the Pacific Ocean to the crest of the southern continuation of the Sierra Santa Ana. Southward, toward the Luiseño, the boundary ran between the San Onofre and Las Pulgas; on the north, toward the Gabrielino, it is said to have followed Alisos Creek.

Villages

Ahachmai, on the lower course of San Juan Creek below the mission of San Juan Capistrano.

Alona, north of the Mission of San Juan Capistrano.

Hechmai, near the coast south of Arroyo San Onofre.

Humai, on the middle course of San Juan Creek.

Palasakeuna, at the head of Arroyo San Mateo.

Panhe, near the mouth of Arroyo San Mateo.

Piwiva, on San Juan Creek above San Juan Capistrano.

Pu-tuid-em, near the coast between San Juan and Aliso Creeks.

Population.—The Juaneño were estimated by Kroeber (1925) at 1,000 in 1770; the census of 1910 returned 16. (See **Alliklik.**)

Kamia. From their own term Kamiyai or Kamiyahi, which they applied also to the Diegueño. Also called:

> Comeya, common synonym used by Bartlett in 1854 and adopted in Handbook of American Indians (Hodge, 1907, 1910).
> I'-um O'-otam, Pima name for Kamia and Diegueño.
> New River Indians, from their location.
> Quemayá, so called by Garcés in 1775–76.
> Tipai, own name, also meaning "person."
> Yum, same as I'-um.

Connections.—They belonged to the Yuman stock of Powell now considered a subdivision of the Hokan family, their closest affinities being with the eastern Diegueño who were sometimes considered one tribe with themselves.

Location.—In Imperial Valley, and on the banks of the sloughs connecting it with Colorado River. (See also México.)

Villages

There were no true villages.

Population.—Gifford (1931) says there could not have been more than a few hundred Kamia in aboriginal times. Heintzelman (1857) gives 254 under the chief Fernando in 1849. (See **Diegueño.**)

Connection in which they have become noted.—Whatever notoriety the Kamia, an inconspicuous tribe, has attained is due entirely to the fame of their valley home.

Karok. Properly Karuk, signifying in their own language "upstream," but not used as a tribal designation.

> Ara, given by Gatschet (1890), signifying "man."
> Ivap'i, Shasta name.
> Orleans Indians, a name sometimes locally used, especially downstream from the Karok territory.
> Petsikla, Yurok name, meaning "upstream."

Connections.—Originally considered an independent stock, the Karok are now classsed in a much larger linguistic connection known as the Hokan family. Their closest relatives are the Chimariko and Shasta.

Location.—On the middle course of Klamath River between the Yurok and Shasta and all of the branches of the Klamath except the upper course of Salmon River.

Subdivisions

The Karok were divided into the Upper Karok above Independence Creek and the Lower Klamath below that stream.

Villages

Aftaram, on Klamath River, probably above the mouth of Salmon River.
Ahoeptimi, 10 to 12 miles above Ashipak (q. v.).
Akoteli, a village or portion of a village near the mouth of Salmon River.
Amaikiara, on the west side of Klamath River below a fall about a mile below the mouth of Salmon River.
Aranimokw, Yurok name of a Lower Karok town on Klamath River.
Ashanamkarak, at the fall just mentioned, and on the east side of Klamath River.
Ashipak, on Klamath River a few miles above the mouth of Salmon River.
Asisufunuk, at Happy Camp, at the mouth of Indian Creek.
Aukni, Shasta name for a village above Happy Camp.
Ayis, some distance above the mouth of Salmon River.
Chamikininich, on the south or east bank of Klamath River in the Orleans district.
Chiniki, on Klamath River below Camp Creek.
Chinits, at Sims Ferry on Klamath River.
Inam, at the mouth of Clear Creek.
Inoftak, a village or section of a village near the mouth of Salmon River.
Ishipishi, opposite Katimin, the Karok center of the world just above the mouth of Salmon River.
Iwatak, a village or section of a village near the mouth of Salmon River.
Katipiara, on the east bank of Klamath River above the flat at Orleans.
Kaus, a village or section of a village near the mouth of Salmon River.
Kumawer, Yurok name of a village above the mouth of Salmon River.
Nupatsu, Shasta name of a village below Happy Camp.
Oler, Yurok name of a village below Camp Creek.

Panamenik, on the flat at Orleans.

Sanipa, on Klamath River below Camp Creek.

Segoashkwu, Yurok name of a village below Camp Creek.

Shavuram or Sahwuram, on Klamath River above Tu'i.

Tachanak, on the west bank of Klamath River at the mouth of Camp Creek.

Ti, 10 to 12 miles above Ashipak.

Tishrawa, a village or section of a village near the mouth of Salmon River.

Tsofkaram or Tasofkaram, at Pearch on Klamath River.

Tu'i, Yurok name of a village on Klamath River below Camp Creek.

Unharik, a village or section of a village near the mouth of Salmon River.

Ussini, Shasta name of a village at the mouth of China Creek.

Wetsitsiko or Witsigo, Yurok name of a village in the Orleans district.

Wopum, the Karok village farthest down Klamath River opposite Red Cap
Creek.

Yutuirup, a neighbor or suburb of Ishipishi (q. v.).

Population.—The number of Karok were estimated by Kroeber (1925) at about 1,500 in 1770. In 1905, 576 were returned, and in 1910, 775, but the latter figure is probably too high, though the census of 1930 returned 755.

Kato. A Pomo place name meaning "lake." Also called:

> Batem-da-kai-ee, given by Gibbs (1853).
> Kai Po-mo, given by Powers (1877).
> Laleshiknom, Yuki name.
> Tlokeang, own name.

Connections.—The Kato belonged to the Athapascan linguistic stock, and spoke a dialect peculiar to themselves.

Location.—On the uppermost course of the South Fork of Eel River.

Villages

There are said to have been nearly 50 of these, probably an overestimate, but none of their names are known.

Population.—Kroeber (1925) estimates 500 Kato in 1770; about 50 persons, mostly full-bloods are still reckoned as Kato. (See **Bear River Indians**.)

Kawaiisu. So-called by the Yokuts; the signification of the word is unknown.

Connections.—The Kawaiisu belonged to the Shoshonean branch of the Uto-Aztecan linguistic family, and were a more immediate off-shoot, apparently, of the Chemehuevi.

Location.—In the Tehachapi Mountains.

Population.—Kroeber (1925) estimates an aboriginal Kawaiisu population of perhaps 500 and a present (1925) population of nearly 150. (See **Alliklik**.)

Kitanemuk. Perhaps from the stem ki, "house,"; other synonyms are Kikitanum, and Kikitamkar.

Connections.—The Kitanemuk belonged to the Shoshonean division of the Uto-Aztecan linguistic stock and to a subgroup which included also the Alliklik, Vanyume and Serrano.

Location.—On upper Tejon and Paso Creeks, the streams on the rear side of the Tehachapi Mountains in the same vicinity and the small creeks draining the northern slope of the Liebre and Sawmill Range, with Antelope Valley and the westernmost end of the Mohave Desert.

Villages

The present principal Kitanemuk village is called Nakwalki-ve, and is situated where Tejon Creek breaks out of the hills. (Other names given do not seem unquestionably those of villages).

Population.—Kroeber (1925) estimates that in 1770 there were 3,500 Serrano, Vanyume, Kitanemuk, and Alliklik, and that these were represented by about 150 in 1910. (See **Alliklik**.)

Konomihu. Their own name, significance unknown.

Connections.—The Konomihu was the most divergent of the Shastan group of tribes of the Hokan linguistic family.

Location.—Territory centering about the forks of Salmon River.

Villages

The principal Konomihu village, called, apparently by the Karok, Shamnam, was between the forks of Salmon River in Siskiyou County, on the right side of the south branch just above the junction.

Population.—Together with the Chimariko, New River Shasta, and Okwanuchu, the Konomihu are estimated by Kroeber (1925) to have numbered about 1,000 in 1770; they are not now enumerated separately from the Shasta, of whom 844 were returned in 1930.

Koso. Significance unknown.

Ke-at, given by Gatschet (Wheeler Survey, p. 411, 1879).
Panamint, name more often used.

Connections.—The Koso formed the westernmost extension of the Shoshoni-Comanche branch of the Shoshonean division of the Uto-Aztecan linguistic stock.

Location.—On a barren tract of land in the southeastern part of the State between the Sierra and the State of Nevada, and including Owens Lake, the Coso, Argus, Panamint, and Funeral Mountains and the intervening valleys.

Population.—Kroeber (1925) estimates an aboriginal Koso population of not over 500; since 1880 they have been placed at about 100 to 150.

Lassik. The name derived from that of a chief.

Connections.—The Lassik belonged to the Athapascan linguistic family and were connected very closely with the Nongatl, who lay just to the north.

Location.—On a stretch of Eel River, from a few miles above the mouth of the South Fork not quite to Kekawaka Creek; also Dobbins Creek, an eastern affluent of the main stream, and Soldier Basin at the head of the North Fork; to the east they extended to the head of Mad River.

Population.—Kroeber (1925) estimates that in 1770, along with the Nongatl and Sinkyone, the Lassik numbered 2,000, and in 1910, 100. (See **Alliklik**.)

Luiseño. From the name of the Mission of San Luis Rey de Francia. Also called:

Ghecham or Khecham, from the native name of San Luis Rey Mission.

Connections.—The Luiseño belonged to the Shoshonean division of the Uto-Aztecan linguistic family.

Location.—In the southwest part of the state from the coast toward but wholly west of the divide that extends south from Mount San Jacinto; bounded northward by the cognate Juaneño, Gabrielino, and Serrano and south by the Diegueño.

Villages

Ahuya, near the upper course of San Luis Rey River.
Akipa, near Kahpa.
Alapi, south of the middle course of the San Luis Rey River.
Awa', on a head branch of Santa Margarita River.
Hurumpa, west of Riverside.
Huyulkum, on the upper course of San Luis Rey River.
Ikaimai, near San Luis Rey Mission.
Kahpa, on the middle course of San Luis Rey River.
Katukto, between Santa Margarita and San Luis Rey Rivers, north of San Luis Rey.
Keish, south of San Luis Rey Mission.
Keweyu, on the upper course of San Luis Rey River.
Kolo, near the upper course of San Luis Rey River.
Kuka, on the upper course of San Luis Rey River.
Kwalam, on the lower course of San Luis Rey River.
Malamai, northeast of Pala.
Meha, on Santa Margarita River northwest of Temecula.
Mehel-om-pom-pauvo, near Escondido.
Ngorivo, near the headwaters of San Luis Rey River.
Pa'auw, near Ta'i.
Paiahche, on Elsinore Lake.
Pala, at Pala.
Palamai, on the coast between Buena Vista and Agua Hedionda Creeks.
Panakare, north of Escondido.

Pashkwo, near the headwaters of San Luis Rey River.
Paumo, east of Pala.
Pu-chorivo, on the upper course of San Luis Rey River.
Saumai, south of the middle course of San Luis Rey River.
Shakishmai (Luiseño or Diegueño), on the boundary line between the two peoples.
Shikapa, west of Escondido.
Sovovo, east of San Jacinto.
Taghanashpa, east of Pala.
Takwi, at the head of Santa Margarita River.
Takwishpo-shapila, near Palomar Mountain.
Ta'i, close to Palomar Mountain.
Tapomai, north of Katukto.
Temeku, east of Temecula.
Tomkav, west of Pala.
Ushmai, near the mouth of Santa Margarita River.
Wahaumai, on San Luis Rey River above San Luis Rey.
Wiawio, at the mouth of San Luis Rey River.
Wissamai, east of San Luis Rey.
Woshha, near the upper course of San Luis Rey River.
Yami, near Huyulkum.

Population.—Kroeber (1925) estimates 4,000 to be a liberally allowed maximum for the Luiseño in 1770. The United States Indian Office returned over 2,500 in 1856; 1,300 in 1870; 1,150 in 1885; and in recent returns, less than 500. (See **Alliklik.**)

Maidu.   A native term meaning "person." Also called:

Wawáh, Paiute name for all Sacramento River tribes.

Connections.—Formerly considered an independent stock, the Maidu have now been placed in the Penutian linguistic family.

Location.—In the drainage areas of the Feather and American Rivers.

Subdivisions

The Maidu are divided, mainly on dialectic grounds, into the Nishinam or Southern Maidu (holding the whole of the American drainage plus that of the Bear and Yuba Rivers), the Northeastern Maidu (on the upper reaches of the North and Middle Forks of Feather River), and the Northwestern Maidu (below the high Sierra, part in the foothills where the South, Middle, North, and West Branches of Feather River converge, and on upper Butte and Chico Creeks and part in the open Sacramento Valley along the lower courses of the same streams).

Villages

Southern Division:
Bamo, southwest of Placerville.
Bushamul, on Bear River below the foothills.
Chapa, between the South and Middle Forks of American River.
Chikimisi, on a branch of the North Fork of Cosumnes River.
Chuemdu, on Bear River below the foothills.
Ekele-pakan, west of Placerville.
Helto, on an east branch of Feather River.
Hembem, on the North Fork of American River.

Homiting, on Bear River below the foothills.
Honkut, on Feather River north of Marysville.
Hoko, on Feather River below Marysville.
Indak, at Placerville.
Intanto, on Bear River below the foothills.
Kaluplo, on Bear River below the foothills.
Kapaka, on Bear River below the foothills.
Kolo-ma, on the South Fork of American River.
Kulkumish, at Colfax.
Kushna, on the South Fork of Yuba River.
Lelikian, on Bear River below the foothills.
Lidlipa, on Bear River below the foothills.
Mimal, on Feather River just south of Marysville.
Molma, at Auburn.
Mulamchapa, on Bear River below the foothills.
Okpa, on Feather River below Marysville.
Ola, on the east bank of Sacramento River above the mouth of Feather River.
Oncho-ma, south of Placerville.
Opelto, on Bear River below the foothills.
Opok, on the North Fork of Cosumnes River.
Pakanchi, on Bear River below the foothills.
Pan-pakan, on a south branch of Yuba River.
Pitsokut, northwest of American River midway between Auburn and Sacra-
    mento.
Pulakatu, on Bear River below the foothills.
Pushuni, northeast of Sacramento.
Seku-mni, on the lower course of American River.
Shokumimlepi, on Bear River below the foothills.
Shutamul, on Bear River below the foothills.
Sisum, on Feather River below Marysville.
Siwim-pakan, inland between the Middle and South Forks of American River.
Solakiyu, on Bear River below the foothills.
Taisida, southeast of Marysville.
Talak, on Bear River below the foothills.
Tomcha, on the east side of Feather River above Marysville.
Tonimbutuk, on Bear River below the foothills.
Toto, on an east branch of Feather River.
Tsekankan, at Grass Valley.
Tumeli, on the South Fork of American River northeast of Placerville.
Usto-ma, east of Grass Valley.
Wapumni, near the middle course of Cosumnes River.
Wokodot, on a south branch of Yuba River northeast of Grass Valley.
Woliyu, on Bear River below the foothills.
Yalisu-mni, on the lower course of the South Fork of American River.
Yamakü, near the junction of the South Fork of American River with the main
    stream.
Yikulme, on Feather River above the junction of Bear River.
Yodok, at the junction of the South Fork of American River with the main
    stream.
Yokolimdu, on Bear River below the foothills.
Yükülü, on the lower course of the South Fork of American River.
Yupu, close to Marysville.

Northeastern Division:
  Hopnom-koyo, on a north branch of Indian Creek.
  Ko-tasi, north of the middle course of Indian Creek.
  Nakangkoyo, on the headwaters of the North Fork of Feather River.
  Oidoing-koyo, on the headwaters of the North Fork of Indian Creek.
  Silong-koyo, at Quincy.
  Tasi-koyo, on the middle course of Indian Creek.
  Yota-moto, on the middle course of Indian Creek.
Northwestern Division:
  Bahyu, on a west branch of the North Fork of Feather River.
  Bauka, on the west side of Feather River below Oroville.
  Bayu, on the west side of Feather River below Oroville.
  Benkümkümi, inland between the Middle and North Forks of Feather River.
  Botoko, on the west bank of Feather River below Oroville.
  Eskini, on a branch of Sacramento River southeast of Chico.
  Hoholto, near the lower course of the Middle Fork of Feather River.
  Hokomo, near the lower course of the Middle Fork of Feather River.
  Kalkalya, near the lower course of the Middle Fork of Feather River.
  Konkau, near the lower course of the North Fork of Feather River.
  Kulayapto, near the lower course of the Middle Fork of Feather River.
  Michopdo, southeast of Chico.
  Nim-sewi, northeast of Chico.
  Ololopa, west of Oroville.
  Otaki, northeast of Chico.
  Paki, north of Chico.
  Tadoiko, south of Chico.
  Taichida, on the west bank of Feather River below Oroville.
  Taikus, on a west branch of the North Fork of Feather River, near its lower
    course.
  Toto-ma, on the lower course of the North Fork of Feather River.
  Tsaktomo, at the junction of the Middle and South Forks of Feather River.
  Tsam-bahenom, near the lower course of the Middle Fork of Feather River.
  Tsuka, near the South Fork of Feather River.
  Tsulum-sewi, a considerable distance northeast of Chico.
  Yauku, northeast of Chico.
  Yuma, at Oroville.
  Yunu, east of Chico.

Helto, Toto, Honkut, and Tomcha should perhaps be included in the last division instead of among the Nishinam.

Inhabited sites not included among the above were Hoktem, Kiski, Kphes, Natoma, Tankum, Tsamak, Wesnak, and Wili.

The following list of Northwestern Maidu "districts" or "tribelets" was given to Dr. Kroeber by a Wintun half-breed, who had spent most of his life associated with the Chico Maidü:

Shǐ'dä-wi, between Sacramento River and lower Pine Creek.
Mu'lǐ, on the Sacramento between Pine and Chico Creeks.
Ts'êno or Ch'ê'no, on the west side of the river about opposite the mouth of Chico
  Creek.
Su''nūsi, on the Sacramento from Chico Creek to the Llano Seco or Parrott grant
  about opposite Jacinto or a couple of miles above.
Batsi', near Jacinto, on the west side, opposite and perhaps including the Llano
  Seco grant.

Pi'nhuk, the principal settlement, at Butte City, of a tribelet covering a considerable extent of country.

Micho'pdo, from Dayton to Chico east of Little Chico Creek.

O'da-wi, from Chico City water tank to the foothills and from Edgar slough to Sandy Gulch.

E'sken, from Durham to the foothills and Butte Creek to Clear Creek.

Shi'udu, from Clear Creek to Feather River and from near Oroville to past Liveoak.

Kū'lu, east of Shi'udu from Feather River toward the foothills about as far as the Oroville branch of the Southern Pacific Railroad and from Oroville inclusive south not quite to Marysville.

Yū'pu, from the Southern Pacific bridge over the Feather River north of Marysville to about 2 miles south of the city and from a short distance west of the Feather to the foothills (this was a Nishinam village).

Dr. Kroeber (1925) attempts to reconstruct the names of the Nishinam or Southern Maidu tribelets as follows: Following downstream: Yupu (at mouth of Yuba into Feather River), Kochuk or (and) Yokol-Liman-Hokok, Wolok or Ola (at efflux of Feather into Sacramento), Leuchi, Wijuna, Totola or Nawean, Pujune (on American River just above its mouth), Sek or Sekumne, Kadema and perhaps others up American River, Sama (below Sacramento city). This is incomplete.

Population.—Kroeber (1925) estimates that 9,000 Maidu about the year 1770 would be a liberal estimate; the census of 1910 returned 1,100, and that of 1930 only 93.

Mattole. Perhaps from the name of a village. Also called:

Tul'bush, Wailaki name, meaning "foreigners."

Connections.—The Mattole constitute one of the primary divisions of those Indians of the Athapascan stock living in California.

Location.—On Bear River and Mattole River drainages; also on a few miles of Eel River and its Van Dusen Fork immediately above the Wiyot.

Population.—Kroeber (1925) estimates that there were 500 Mattole in 1770; the census of 1910 returned 34, including 10 full-bloods. (See **Bear River Indians.**)

Miwok. The native word signifying "people."

Connections.—Originally a distinct stock in the classificatory system of Powell, Miwok has now been made a subdivision of the Penutian linguistic family.

Location.—The Miwok lived in three detached groups as follows: (1) The main body on the long western slope of the Sierra Nevada between Fresno and Cosumnes Rivers and in that part of the valley which is intersected by the winding arms of the deltas of the San Joaquin and the Sacramento; (2) the Coast Miwok from the Golden Gate north to Duncan's Point and eastward to Sonoma Creek; and (3) the Lake Miwok in the basin of Clear Lake, including the drainage of two small streams flowing into the lowest mile or two of Clear Lake, and the southern bank of Cache Creek, the lake outlet, for a short distance beyond.

Subdivisions

Apart from the natural groups indicated above, the following dialectic subdivisions may be made out:

The Lake Miwok, identical with the geographical group just described.
The Bodega Miwok, about Bodega Bay in the coastal area.
The Coast Miwok, occupying the rest of the coastal area.
The Plains Miwok, in the deltas of the San Joaquin and Cosumnes Rivers.
The Northern Miwok, in the upper valleys of Mokelumne and Calaveras Rivers.
Central Miwok, in the upper valleys of the Stanislaus and Tuolumne.
The Southern Miwok, along the headwaters of the Merced and Chowchilla and on Mariposa Creek.

The Lake Miwok were furthermore subdivided into two, or possibly three, district or tribal groups: (1) about the present Lower Lake, (2) on the headwaters of Putah Creek, and perhaps (3) in Pope Valley.

Villages

Lake Miwok:
Kado' i'-yomi-pukut, Cookman Ranch, toward Lower Lake.
Kai-yomi-pukut, in Pope Valley at the limit of Miwok territory.
Kala'u-yomi, in Coyote Valley.
Kawi-yomi, a town reported by Barrett (1908 b) on north frontier of Miwok, perhaps originally Pomo.
Kilinyo-ke, at Eaton Ranch in Coyote Valley.
Ki'tsin-pukut, Gamble, in Coyote Valley.
Laka'h-yomi, on Weldon's ranch a mile and a half from Middletown and on Putah Creek.
Lă'lmak-pukut, at north end of Middletown.
Ole'-yomi, on the Berry place in Coyote Valley on Putah Creek.
Sha'lshal-pukut and Shanák-yomi-pukut, at Asbill in Coyote Valley.
Tsitsa-pukut, according to Barrett (1908 b), a site at the north end of Miwok territory but believed by Kroeber's informants to have been occupied by Miwok only in late times.
Tsôk-yomi-pukut or Shôkomi, 3 miles below the store or town of Pope Valley.
Tsu'keliwa-pukut, "at the new Siegler swimming resort."
Tu'bud or Tu'bul, on Asbill property toward Lower Lake.
Tule'-yomi, 2–3 miles south of the American town of Lower Lake.
Tumi'stumis-pukut, given by Barrett (1908 b).
Wi'lok-yomi, near the present rancheria or reservation but may have been Wappo.
Wodi'daitepi, in Jerusalem Valley.
Yawi'-yomi-pukut, above Tsu'keliwa-pukut in a canyon.
Coast Miwok:
Amayelle, on San Antonio Creek.
Awachi, at the mouth of Estero Americano.
Awani-wi, at San Rafael.
Bauli-n, on Bolinas Bay.
Chokeche, near Novato.
Echa-kolum, on Tomales Bay south of Marshall.

Echa-tamai, at Nicasio.
Etem, at Petaluma.
Ewapalt, near Valley Ford.
Ewu, north of San Rafael.
Helapattai, on Bodega Bay.
Hime-takala, on Bodega Bay.
Ho-takala, on Bodega Bay.
Huchi, at Sonoma.
Kennekono, at Bodega Corners.
Kotati, at Cotati.
Likatiut, on Petaluma River north of Petaluma.
Liwanelowa, at Sausalito.
Lumen-takala, northeast of Cotati.
Meleya, on San Antonio Creek southwest of Petaluma.
Olema-loke, at Olema.
Olompolli, northwest of Novato.
Oye-yomi, near Freestone.
Pakahuwe, near Freestone.
Patawa-yomi, near Freestone.
Payinecha, west of Cotati.
Petaluma, east of Petaluma River and the present Petaluma.
Pulya-lakum, on the ocean near the mouth of Salmon Creek.
Puyuku, south of Ignacio.
Sakloki, opposite Tomales Point.
Shotokmo-cha, southeast of Ignacio.
Shotomko-wi, on Tomales Bay near the mouth of San Antonio Creek.
Susuli, northwest of Petaluma.
Suwutenne, north of Bodega Corners.
Temblek, west of Sonoma.
Tiwut-huya, on the coast outside of Bodega Bay.
Tokau, on Bodega Bay.
Tuchayelin, northwest of Petaluma.
Tuli, northwest of Sonoma.
Tulme, northwest of Petaluma.
Uli-yomi, at the head of Estero Americano.
Utumia, near Tomales.
Wotoki, on the south side of Petaluma River.
Wugilwa, on Sonoma Creek.
Valley Miwok:
Plains Division:
Chuyumkatat, on Cosumnes River.
Hulpu-mni, on the east bank of Sacramento River below Sacramento.
Lel-amni, on Mokelumne River.
Lulimal, near Cosumnes River.
Mayeman, on Cosumnes River.
Mokel(-umni), on Mokelumne River.
Mokos-umni, on Cosumnes River.
Ochech-ak, on Jackson Creek.
Sakayak-umni, on Mokelumne River.
Sukididi, on Cosumnes River.
Supu, on Cosumnes River.
Tukui, on Cosumnes River.
Umucha, near Cosumnes River.

Yomit, on Cosumnes River.

Yumhui, near Cosumnes River.

Northern Division:

Apautawilü, between Mokelumne and Calaveras Rivers.

Chakane-sü, on Jackson Creek?

Kechenü, at the head of Calaveras River.

Heina, between Mokelumne River and the head of Calaveras River.

Huta-sü, at San Andreas.

Kaitimü, at the head of Calaveras River.

Ketina, between Mokelumne and Calaveras Rivers.

Künüsü, near Mokelumne River.

Mona-sü, on the headwaters of Calaveras River.

Noma, near the South Fork of Cosumnes River.

Omo, near the South Fork of Cosumnes River.

Penken-sü, inland south of Mokelumne River.

Pola-sü, near Jackson.

Seweu-sü, on Jackson Creek?

Sopochi, between Mokelumne River and Jackson Creek.

Tukupe-su, at Jackson.

Tumuti, on the headwaters of Jackson Creek.

Upüsüni, on Mokelumne River.

Yule, south of Cosumne River.

Yuloni, on Jackson Creek.

Central Division:

Akankau-nchi, two towns of the name, (1) near Sonora, (2) a considerable distance to the southwest.

Akawila, between a branch of Tuolumne River and Stanislaus River.

Akutanuka, northwest of Stanislaus River.

Alakani, east of San Andreas.

Chakachi-no, southwest of Sonora.

Hangwite, on the South Fork of Stanislaus River.

Hechhechi, on the headwaters of Tuolumne River.

Hochhochmeti, on Tuolumne River.

Humata, on a branch of Calaveras River.

Hunga, northeast of Sonora.

Kapanina, southwest of Sonora.

Katuka, on a branch of Calaveras River.

Kawinucha, near the North fork of Stanislaus River.

Kesa, a short distance east of Sonora.

Kewe-no, on Stanislaus River.

Kosoimuno-nu, between Stanislaus River and San Andreas.

Kotoplana, a short distance west of Sonora.

Kulamu, on a branch of Tuolumne River.

Kuluti, at Sonora.

Loyowisa, near the junction of the Middle and South Forks of Stanislaus River.

Newichu, between Stanislaus River and a head branch of Calaveras River.

Olawiye, east of Sonora.

Oloikoto, on Stanislaus River.

Pangasema-nu, on a northern branch of Tuolumne River.

Pasi-nu, on Tuolumne River southeast of Sonora.

Pigliku (Miwok pronunciation of "Big Creek"), south of Tuolumne River.

Pokto-no, a short distance west of Sonora.

Pota, a short distance northwest of Sonora.
Sala, just south of Pigliku.
Sasamu, almost due east of San Andreas.
Shulaputi, just southeast of the preceding.
Siksike-no, south of Sonora near Tuolumne River.
Singawü-nu, at the head of a branch of Tuolumne River.
Sopka-su, southwest of Sonora between Stanislaus and Tuolumne Rivers.
Suchumumu, southwest of Sonora.
Sukanola, southeast of Sonora.
Sukwela, east of Sonora.
Sutamasina, on the South Fork of Stanislaus River.
Takema, on the Middle Fork of Stanislaus River.
Telese-no, northeast of Sonora.
Tel'ula, northeast of Sonora.
Tipotoya, on Stanislaus River.
Tulana-chi, on Stanislaus River.
Tulsuna, between the South and Middle Forks of Stanislaus River.
Tunuk-chi, northeast of Sonora.
Tuyiwü-nu, on Stanislaus River.
Waka-che, southwest of and near Sonora.
Wokachet, on the South Fork of Stanislaus River.
Wolanga-su, south of the junction between the South and Middle Forks of
    Stanislaus River.
Wüyü, on Stanislaus River.
Yungakatok, near the junction of the North and Middle Forks of Stanislaus
    River.
Southern Division:
Alaula-chi, on Merced River.
Angisawepa, on Merced River.
Awal, on Merced River.
Awani, close to Yosemite.
Hikena, on Merced River.
Kakahula-chi, on Merced River.
Kasumati, near Mariposa.
Kitiwana, on Merced River.
Kuyuka-chi, on Merced River.
Nochu-chi, near Mariposa.
Nowach, on the headwaters of Chowchilla River.
Olwia, on the headwaters of Chowchilla River.
Owelinhatihü, on Merced River.
Palachan, on a southern branch of Merced River.
Sayangasi, between the middle courses of Merced and Tuolumne Rivers.
Siso-chi, on Merced River.
Sope-nchi, on a northern branch of Merced River.
Sotpok, on a southern branch of Merced River.
Wasema, near the head of Fresno River.
Wehilto, on the upper waters of Fresno River.
Wilito, on Merced River.
Yawoka-chi, on Merced River.

Many other village names have been recorded, but the above list contains all
those which are well authenticated independent settlements.

Population.—Kroeber (1925) estimates that in 1770 there were about 500 Lake Miwok, 1,500 Coast Miwok, and 9,000 Plains and Sierra Miwok, bringing the total to 11,000. The census of 1910 returned 670, but Kroeber estimates about 700 of the Plains and Sierra Miwok alone. The census of 1930 returned 491.

Modoc. This tribe extended into the northern part of the State. (See Oregon.)

Mohave. The Mohave occupied some territory in the neighborhood of the Colorado River. (See Arizona.)

Nicoleño. From San Nicolas, the most eastward of the Santa Barbara Islands.

Connections.—They belonged to the Shoshonean Division of the Uto-Aztecan linguistic stock, but their more immediate affiliations are uncertain.

Location.—On the island above mentioned.

Population.—Kroeber (1925) gives an estimate of their population in conjunction with the Gabrielino and Fernandeño (q. v.). (See also **Alliklik.**)

Nongatl. Significance unknown. Also called:

Saia, by the Hupa, along with other Athapascans to the south; meaning "far off."

Connections.—The Nongatl belonged to the Athapascan linguistic family and were closely connected with the Lassik (q. v.).

Location.—In the territory drained by three right-hand affluents of Eel River—Yager Creek, Van Dusen Fork, and Larrabee Creek—and on the upper waters of Mad River.

Population.—The Nongatl were estimated by Kroeber (1925) to number in 1770, along with the Sinkyone and Lassik, 2,000, and 100 in 1910. (See **Bear River Indians.**)

Okwanuchu. Significance unknown.

Connections.—The Okwanuchu belonged to the Shastan Division of the Hokan linguistic stock.

Location.—On the upper Sacramento from about the vicinity of Salt and Boulder Creeks to its headwaters; also on the McCloud River and Squaw Creek from about their junction up.

Population.—See **Chimariko** and **Shasta.**

Paiute, Northern. The Northern Paiute occupied part of the Sierra in the southeastern part of the State and the desert country east of it and also a strip of land in the extreme northeast. (See Nevada.)

Patwin. Signifying "person" in their own language.

Connections.—The Patwin formed the southernmost and most

diverse dialetic division of the former Wintun (or Copehan) linguistic family, now considered part of the Penutian stock.

Location.—On the western side of Sacramento Valley, and extending from San Francisco Bay to a point a little south of Willows, occupying both sides of Sacramento River from a few miles above its junction with Feather River to the northern boundaries of their territory.

Subdivisions, or "Tribelets," and Villages
(As given by Kroeber, 1932)

River Patwin:
  Colusa Dialect:
    Katsi'l, less than a mile below the present Katsi'l Reservation.
    Ke'ti', on the site of the present Princeton.
    Koru', in Colusa city, named from it.
    Kukui, one and a half miles below Koru'.
    Sôma, 2 miles below modern Katsi'l, somewhat off the river, and not certainly an independent unit.
    Tatno, perhaps 2 miles above Colusa.
    Ts'a', 3 miles below Princeton.
    Wa'itere, 2 or 3 miles above the present Katsi'l, or "Colusa rancheria."
  Grimes Dialect:
    Ko'doi(–dihi), a mile below Sāka, on the J. Brown place.
    Kusêmpu, on the east side of Sacramento River, perhaps a mile below No'matsapin.
    Lo'klokma-ti'nbe, in the southern outskirts of Grimes.
    No'matsapin, about 5 miles downstream from Sāka.
    Nōwi(–dihi), 1 mile below Lo'klokma-ti'nbe.
    P'ālo, 1 or 2 miles downstream from Tsaki, some 3 miles above Kirkville.
    Sāka, little more than 100 yards from last, at Eddy's Ferry.
    Tsaki, 7 or 8 miles below Sāka.
    T'inik(–dihi), on the east side about opposite Ko'doi, status uncertain.
    Yali, opposite Sāka, on east bank.
  Knight's Landing Dialect (only ones remembered):
    Hololum (?), between Kirkville and Knight's Landing.
    Yo'doi, at Knight's Landing giving name to Yolo.
Hill Patwin (from south to north):
  South of Cache no names of tribelets are known but villages called Suskol, Tuluka, Ula-to, Topai-dihi, and Liwai-to.
  On Lower Cache Creek Barrett places Pulupulu, Churup, Kachituli, also Moso (at Capay).
  C. H. Merriam (1929) gives Kopā' (Kope) (in the broad flat part of Capay Valley near Brooks), and Kroeber (1932) Hacha (3 miles below Capay).
  Kisi, a village upstream on Cache Creek, may have been a tribal center.
  Imil, a village apparently in a tribal territory (near Guinda), and Sūya, a village (half a mile north of Guinda), besides 16 inhabited sites mentioned by one informant.
  Lopa and Tebti (on or near Cache Creek), villages probably belonging to a tribelet.
  Sukui-sel, whose principal village was Sukui (2–3 miles above Sulphur Creek).
  Kuikui, a village was Sukui (2–3 miles above Sulphur Creek).

Kuikui, a village (on Cache Creek 2 miles below the mouth of Bartlett), and Opi, a village (on Cache Creek at the mouth of Bartlett), probably in a tribelet.

Tebti-sel, including the villages of Tebti (on Bartlett Creek at the mouth of Long Valley Creek), and Helu'supet or Helu'sapet (downstream within 2 or 3 miles of Cache Creek).

Lol-sel, located at village of A'li-ma-ti'nbe (some 5 miles up Long Valley Creek).

Loli (either on Bartlett Creek 3 miles from Tebti or in Indian Valley) was a village in an unnamed tribelet.

Wor-pa'ntibe, one of whose villages was Wa'i-taluk (in Morgan Valley south of Cache Creek).

Tsuhel-mem or Chuhel-mem, a village on Indian Creek above Ladoga and Kabal-mem or Kabel-mem, a later village.

A tribelet called Edī' or Edī'la.

A tribelet with villages at Bahka(labe) (not far from the mouth of Indian Creek).

Kula'(-la) (some miles up), and Dikikala'i (downstream from Bahka).

Yakut (on Sand Creek), perhaps a tribelet by itself.

Wa'ikau-sel, with villages at Let(-labe) (near Cortina Creek).

Wa'ikau (on main Cortina Creek), and perhaps Kotu (1½ or 2 miles upstream from Wa'ikau).

A tribelet at Pone (on Grapevine Canyon or Road, three or more miles north of Sites).

Potba-sel, or a village called Potba(-labe), (at a spring in a gulley half a dozen miles north of the last.

Population.—(See **Wintun.**)

Pomo. From the native ending -pomo or -poma, placed after the names of village or local groups, the exact meaning of which is unknown. Also called:

Nokonmi, Yuki name.

Connections.—The Pomo were originally placed in a distinct linguistic stock (Kulanapan) but are now attached to the widely scattered Hokan family.

Location.—The Pacific Coast between Cleone and Duncan's Point, and inland, with some interruptions, as far as Clear Lake; there was a detached group on Stony Creek.

Subdivisions

The Pomo were divided dialectically into the following groups:

Salt Pomo or Northeastern Pomo, on the headwaters of Stony Creek.

Eastern Pomo, on the northern and southern affluents of Clear Lake.

Southeastern Pomo, about Lower Lake.

Northern Pomo, from the northern boundary of Pomo territory to Navarro River and some distance above Ukiah on Russian River.

Central Pomo, from the above boundaries to Gualala on the coast and a point north of Cloverdale on Russian River.

Southern Pomo or Gallinomero, in the inland portion of the remaining Pomo territory.

Southwestern or Gualala Pomo, on the coast section of the remaining territory.

Certain divisions larger than villages were recognized in an indefinite way by the people themselves.

Village Communities

Northeastern Pomo:

Bakamtati, at Stony Ford.

Cheetido, at the salt deposit.

Turururaibida, above the forks of Stony Creek.

The status of the last two of these is somewhat uncertain.

Eastern Pomo:

Bidamiwina, Nonapotl, and Shabegok were names of three places which were at different times centers of a community called Habe-napo or "rock people," around Kelseyville.

Danoha, some miles up an eastern affiluent of lower Scott Creek, connected with which was Badonnapoti on Bloody Island in Upper Lake off the mouth of Scott Creek and Behepel or Gabehe between the two.

Howalek, on Middle Creek near Upper Lake town.

Kashibadon, at Lakeport on the west side of the lake.

Shigom, on the east side of main Clear Lake.

Yobutui, on the opposite side of lower Scott Creek from the northern Pomo village of Mayi.

Southeastern Pomo:

Elem, on Rattlesnake or Sulphur Bank Island in the Bay known as East Lake.

Kamdot or Lemakma, on Buckingham Island near the entrance to Lower Lake.

Koi, Hoyi, Shutauyomanok, or Kaubokolai, on an island near the outlet of the lake.

Northern Pomo:

Bakau, at Little Lake north of Willits.

Buldam, at the mouth of Big River.

Chomchadila, on the West Fork near Calpella.

Chauishak, near Willits.

Dapishu or Kachabida, in Redwood Canyon.

Kachake, on Mill Creek, separate position uncertain.

Kadiu, at the mouth of Noyo River.

Kalaili, at the mouth of Little River.

Katuli, above Navarro River at Christine.

Komli, at Ukiah.

Kulakai, at a lake south of Sherwood.

Lemkolil, on Anderson Creek near Boonville.

Masut or Shiyol, on the West Fork of Russian River near the mouth of Seward Creek.

Mato, northwest of Sherwood.

Mayi, on Scott Creek near Tule Lake, not far from the town of Upper Lake.

Nabo or Nato, near Willits.

Naboral, on Scott Creek northwest of Lakeport.

Pomo, in Potter Valley downstream from Sedam.

Shabakana, Bitadanek, and Kobida, three sites successively inhabited by one group, whose home was on Forsythe Creek.

Sedam, in Potter Valley downstream from Shanel.

Shachamkau, Chamkawi or Bomaa, downstream?, in Coyote Valley.

Shanekai, in a small elevated valley between the heads of an affluent of southern Eel River and a tributary of Middle Creek which drains into the head of Clear Lake.

Shanel or Seel or Botel, at the north end of Potter Valley on the East Fork of Russian River.

Shotsiu, east of Willits.

Tabate, below Philo on Navarro River.

Tsakamo, on Russian River at the mouth of Cold Creek.

Tsamomda, west of Willits.

Tsiyakabeyo, on a tributary of Middle Creek which drains into the head of Clear Lake, probably only a part of Shanekai.

On the North Fork of Navarro River were three sites, Chaida, Chulgo, and Huda, which may have constituted a community.

Central Pomo:

Danokeya, name uncertain, on Rancheria Creek.

Kahwalau, Russian River at the mouth of Pieta Creek.

Kodalau, on Brush Creek.

Koloko, Russian River at the mouth of Squaw Creek.

Lachupda, on the upper waters of the North Fork of Gualala River.

Lema, on McNab Creek a mile or two up from Russian River.

Pdahau or Icheche, on Lower Garcia River.

Shanel, near the mouth of McDowell and Feliz Creeks, in Hopland Valley.

Shepda, on Russian River at the entry of Wise Creek.

Shiego, on Russian River at the mouth of McNab Creek.

Shokadjal, on Russian River in Ukiah Valley.

Tatem, downstream from the last and in the same valley.

Southern Pomo or Gallinomero:

Batiklechawi, at Sebastopol at the head of the slough known as Laguna de Santa Rosa, an important village and probably the head of a district.

Hiwalhmu, a village and probably the head of a community on the Gualala River drainage.

Hukabetawi, near Santa Rosa City and perhaps the head of a community.

Kalme, a community in the Russian River drainage.

Kubahmoi, a village and probably the head of a community on the Gualala River drainage.

Makahmo, on the Russian drainage at the mouth of Sulphur Creek.

Ossokowi, a village and probably the center of a community on Russian River extending from the mouth of Elk Creek halfway up to Geyserville.

Shamli, a village on Gualala River drainage, perhaps the head of a community.

Shawako, on Dry Creek at the mouth of Piña Creek.

Wilok, at the head of Santa Rosa Creek.

Wotokkaton, head of a community in the vicinity of Healdsburg.

Southwestern or Gualala Pomo:

Ashachatiu, a village at the mouth of Russian River connected probably with Chalanchawi.

Chalanchawi (see Ashachatiu).

Chiti-bida-kali, north of Timber Cove.

Danaga, at Stewart's Point.

Hibuwi, on the Middle Fork of the Gualala.

Kowishal, at Black Point.

Meteni, perhaps the name of a group at the site of Fort Ross, though another name, Madshuinui is also mentioned.

Potol, on Haupt and Hopper Creeks, perhaps the center of a group.

Population.—Kroeber (1925) estimates 8,000 Pomo in 1770; the census of 1910 returned 777, but this figure perhaps does not include all, as Kroeber gives 1,200 for the same year. According to the census of 1930, there were then 1,143.

Salinan. From Salinas River which drains most of their territory.

Connections.—Formerly considered a distinct linguistic stock, they are now connected with the Hokan linguistic family.

Location.—From the headwaters of the Salinas—or perhaps only from the vicinity of the Santa Margarita Divide—north to Santa Lucia Peak and an unknown point in the valley somewhere south of Soledad; and from the sea presumably to the main crest of the Coast Range.

Subdivisions

On linguistic grounds the Salinan have been divided into the San Miguel Salinas on the upper course of Salinas River, the San Antonio Salinas below the preceding to Costanoan territory, and the Playano along the coast.

Villages

San Antonio Division:
   Chahomesh, at the head of San Antonio River.
   Chohwahl, near the mouth of San Antonio River.
   Chukilin, at the head of Nacimiento Creek.
   Holamna Jolon, southeast of San Antonio Mission.
   Nasihl Pleyto, on lower San Antonio River.
   Sapewis, below the preceding.
   Skotitoki, north of San Antonio Mission.
   Tesospek, on San Antonio River above San Antonio Mission.
   Tetachoya Ojitos, on lower San Antonio River.
San Miguel Division:
   Cholame, probably on Cholame Creek or at the mouth of Estrella Creek.
   Teshaumis, on the upper course of Cholame Creek.
   Teshaya, at San Miguel Mission.
   Trolole, near Cholame or near Santa Margarita.
Playano:
   Ehmahl, located conjecturally near Lucia.
   Lema, perhaps lower down the coast than the preceding.
   Ma'tihl'she, located conjecturally still farther south.
   Tsilakaka, placed conjecturally near San Simeon.

Population.—Kroeber (1925) estimates that there may have been 3,000 Salinan in 1770 but that 2,000 is a safer estimate; about 40 remain. The census of 1910 returned 16; that of 1930, none.

Serrano. A Spanish word, meaning "mountaineers." Also called:
   Banumints, Chemehuevi name.
   Ców-ang-a-chem, own name (Barrows 1900).
   Cuabajái, applied by Mohave to those about Tejon Creek.
   Genigueches, by Garcés in 1776.
   Gikidanum, or Gitanemuk, Serrano of upper Tejon and Paso Creeks in the San Joaquin Valley drainage.

Hanakwiche, by some Yuman tribes.

Hanyuveche, Mohave name.

Kaiviat-am, given by a native as their own name, from kai-ch, "mountain."

Kuvahaivima, Mohave name for those about Tejon Creek.

Marangakh, by their southern and other neighbors.

Marayam, Luiseño name.

Mayintalap, southern Yokuts name for Serrano of upper Tejon, Paso, and possibly Pastoria Creeks, meaning "large bows."

Möhineyam, name for themselves, given by Mohave River Serrano.

Panumits, Chemehuevi name for Serrano north of the San Bernardino Range, toward Tehachapi Mountains.

Pitanta, Chemehuevi name for those Serrano north of San Bernardino Range in Mohave Desert and on Tejon Creek.

Takhtam, by Gatschet (*in* Wheeler Surv., vol. 7, p. 413, 1879), meaning "men."

Tamankamyam, by the related Aguas Calientes.

Witanghatal, Tubatulabal name for the Tejon Creek Serrano.

Connections.—The Serrano belonged to the Shoshonean Division of the Uto-Aztecan linguistic stock.

Location.—In the San Bernardino Range; a tract of unknown extent northward; the San Gabriel Mountains or Sierra Madre west to Mount San Antonio; and probably a tract of fertile lowland south of the Sierra Madre, from about Cucamonga east to above Mentone and as far as San Gorgonio Pass.

Villages

The following place names have been recorded and many of these probably were names of villages:

Acha-va-t, east of Bear Lake.

Aka-va-t, west of Banning.

Arhangk, near Colton.

Atan-pa-t, northeast of Acha-va-t.

Hikavanü-t, west of Colton.

Hisaku-pa, on the outlet of Bear Lake.

Hunga-va-t, in San Timotec Canyon.

Kayah-pia-t, at Bear Lake.

Kotaina-t, on Santa Ana River east of San Bernardino.

Malki, northeast of Banning.

Maronga, on Morongo Creek.

Musku-pia-bit, northwest of San Bernardino.

Nilengli, near San Bernardino Peak.

Nanamü-vya-t, at the head of Mohave River.

Padjüdjü-t, at the head of Mohave River.

Puwipuwi, near San Gorgonio Mountain.

Toloka-bi, in San Timoteo Canyon.

Wacha-vak, where San Timoteo Canyon comes out on Santa Ana River.

Wahinu-t, in Cajon Canyon.

Yamiwu, perhaps Cahuilla, north of San Jacinto Peak.

Population.—Kroeber gives 1,500 Serrano as an ample allowance in aboriginal times; the census of 1910 returned 118. (See **Alliklik.**)

Shasta. Probably from a chief called Sasti. Also called:

Ekpimi, Ilmawi name.
Mashukhara, Karok name.
Wúlx, Takelma name, meaning "enemies."

Connections.—The Shasta constituted part of the Shastan division of the Hokan linguistic stock.

Location.—On Klamath River from a point between Indian and Thompson Creeks to a spot a few miles above the mouth of Fall Creek; also the drainage areas of two tributaries of the Klamath— Scott River and Shasta River—and a tract on the north side of the Siskiyous in Oregon on the affluents of Rogue River known as Stewart River and Little Butte Creek.

Subdivisions

Ahotireitsu, in Shasta Valley.
Cecilville Indians, about Cecilville; they spoke a distinct dialect; the Indians called by Merriam (1926) Haldokehewuk.
Iruaitsu, in Scott Valley.
Kahosadi, on the affluents of Rogue River.
Kammatwa or Wiruhikwairuk'a, on Klamath River.

The term New River Shasta is incorrectly used since there were no Shasta on New River.

Villages

Ahotiretsu Division:
Ahawaiwig, Asta, Ihiweah, Ikahig, Kusta.
Iruaitsu Division:
Itayah and Crowichaira the only ones known.
Kammatwa Division (in order up stream):
Chitatowoki (north side), Ututsu (N.), Asouru (N.), Sumai (N.), Arahi (S.), Harokwi (N.), Kwasuk (S.), Aika (N.), Umtahawa (N.), Itiwukha (N.), Ishui (N.), Awa (N.), Waukaiwa (N.), Opshiruk (N.), Ishumpi (N.), Okwayig (N.), Eras (S.), Asurahawa (S.), Kutsastsus (N.).

Population.—Kroeber (1925) estimates that there were about 2,000 Shasta in 1770; in 1910 there were only about 100. The entire Shastan stock numbered 844 according to the returns of the 1930 census, and in 1937, 418 "Pit River" Indians were enumerated, a portion of this stock.

Connections in which they have become noted.—Mount Shasta, Shasta County, and a place in the county preserve the name of the Shasta Indians.

Sinkyone. From Sinkyo, the name of the South Fork of Eel River.

Connections.—The Sinkyone were one of the tribes of the southern California group of the Athapascan family.

Location.—On the South Fork of Eel River and its branches and the adjacent coast from near Four Mile Creek to Usal Lagoon.

Land Areas

(Given by native informants to Nomland (1935) instead of villages)

Anse'ntakūk, the land south of Briceland.
Chashīngūk, the ridge north of Briceland.
Senkē'kūk, to the South Fork from Garberville.
Shusashīsh'ha, the region north of Garberville.
Totro'bē, the land around Briceland.
Yenekūk, an area southeast of Briceland.
Yese', coast area to the Mattole boundary at Four Mile Creek.
Yēsē'kūk, the Mattole River area.

Population.—(See **Lassik** and **Bear River Indians**).

Tolowa. So-called by the Yurok. Also called:

> Ăqŭstă, by Dorsey (MS.); meaning "southern language," Naltunnetunne name.
> Lagoons, by Heintzleman (*in* Ind. Aff. Rep., 1857, p. 392; 1858).
> Lopas, by Heintzleman (op. cit.).

Connections.—The Tolowa constituted one of the divisions into which the California peoples of the Athapascan linguistic stock are divided, but they were closely connected with the Athapascan tribes of Oregon immediately to the north.

Location.—On Crescent Bay, Lake Earl, and Smith River.

Villages

(According to Drucker, 1937)

Etcūlet, at end of point in Lake Earl.
Ha'tsahothwut, long abandoned site.
Kehoslī'hwut, on east bank, lower course of Smith River.
Mestlte'tltun, on Crescent Bay.
Mī'litcuntun, on middle course of Smith River.
Mu'nsontun, on east bank, on lower course of Smith River.
Munshrī'na taso', long abandoned site.
Muslye', on North Fork of Smith River.
Na'kutat, a suburb of Tatítun,
Numore'tun, long abandoned site.
Sitragī'tum, on the west bank of Smith River below Mill Creek.
Ta'gestlsatun, on coast at mouth of Wilson Creek, mixed with Yurok.
Ta'tatun, on Crescent Bay.
Tati'tun, on shore of Crescent Bay near north end.
Tcestu'mtun, on South Fork of Smith River.
Tcunsu'tltun, on east bank of Smith River at mouth of Mill Creek.
Te'nītcuntun, between North and South Forks of Smith River at junction.
Tltru'ome, on Crescent Bay toward south end.
Tro'let, a small suburb of Yotokut near mouth of Smith River.
Tunme'tun, on a small branch of the North Fork of Smith River.
Tushroshku'shtun, on peninsula between two arms of Lake Earl.
Yoto'kut, on coast south of mouth of Smith River.

Population.—Kroeber estimates "well under" 1,000 Tolowa in 1770 and indicates a possible modification to 450; the census of 1910 returned 121.   In 1930 the "Oregon Athapascans," including the Tolowa, were reported to number 504.

Tübatulabal. A Shoshonean word meaning "pine-nut eaters." Also called:

>Bahkanapül or Pahkanapïl, own name, said to refer to all those who speak their language.
>
>Kern River Indians, popular name.
>
>Pitanisha, the usual Yokuts name, from Pitani-u, the place-name of the forks of Kern River.
>
>Wateknasi, by Yokuts, meaning "pine-nut eaters."

Connections.—Under the name of Kern River Shoshoneans, the Tübatulabal are given a position as one of the major divisions of the Shoshonean branch of the Uto-Aztecan linguistic family.

Location.—In the upper part of the valley of Kern River.

Subdivisions

Bankalachi, on west slopes of Greenhorn Mountains.
Palagewan, on Kern River above mouth of South Fork.
Tübatulabal, on lower reaches of South Fork of Kern River.

Villages

E. W. Voegelin (1938) gives the following:
Palagewan sites:

>Holit, near mouth of Bull Run Creek, SW. quar., sec. 4, T. 25 S., R. 33 E.
>Pashgeshtap, at hot spring on east edge of Hot Springs Valley, SE. quar., sec. 31, T. 26 S., R. 33 E.
>Tcuhkayl, at hot springs in foothills, SE. quar. sec. 26, T. 25 S., R. 33 E.

Tübatulabal sites:

>Hahalam, South Fork Kern River, NW. quar., sec. 16, T. 26 S., R. 34 E.
>Kolokum, near springs on Fay Creek, NE. quar., sec. 22, T. 25 S., R. 34 E.
>Omomíp, (1) on north bank of South Fork Kern River, NW. quar., sec. 3, T. 26 S., R. 35 E. (2), north bank of South Fork of Kern River, SW., quar., sec. 4, T. 26 S., R. 35 E.
>Padazhap, below and above spring, in foothills south of South Fork Valley, SW. quar., sec. 31, T. 26 S., R. 34 E.
>Tcebunun, south bank of South Fork of Kern River, SW. quar., sec. 35, T. 25 S., R. 35 E.
>Tushpan, on floor of South Fork Valley, SW. quar., sec. 14, T. 26 S., R. 34 E.
>Umubílap, below spring on flat, near west end of South Fork Valley, SE. quar., sec. 12, T. 26 S., R. 33 E.
>Uupulap, on flat west side of South Fork of Kern River, NW. quar., sec. 24, T. 25 S., R. 35 E.
>Yítiyamup, at springs in foothills, north edge of South Fork Valley, SE. quar., sec. 35, T. 25 S., R. 34 E.
>Yowolup, at spring on floor of South Fork Valley.
>Name unknown, on South Fork of Kern River, NE. quar., sec. 18, T. 26 S., R. 34 E.

History.—From the specialization of their language, Kroeber (1925) inferred that these people had occupied their country for a long time

but later researches by Whorf (1935) make this less certain.   The first
white person to visit them was Father Garcés in 1776 and during the
next 50 years they were brought in contact with the San Buenaventura
Mission, founded in 1782 near Ventura.   By 1846 white settlers had
established ranches in South Fork Valley, and in 1857 the Kern River
gold rush began in Palagewan territory.   During 1862 a few Tübatulabal joined the Owens Valley Paiute in hostilities against the
Whites, and about this time a group of Koso Indians settled in the
Tübatulabal area, intermarrying chiefly with the Kawaiisu, however.
In 1863, 35–40 Tübatulabal and Palagewan men were massacred near
Kernville by American soldiers.   Between 1865 and 1875 the Tübatulabal began to practice agriculture and in 1893 the majority of them
and a few Palagewan survivors were allotted land in South Fork
and Kern Valleys.

Population.—Kroeber (1925) makes an estimate of 1,000 Tübatulabal for the year 1770 but Voegelin (1938) regards this as "probably
too high."   Henley in 1854 gives a figure of 100 which seems to
apply to the Tübatulabal and Palagewan Bands, but Voegelin points
out that it may be necessary to double this on account of a band
temporarily absent from the country, and the same writer estimates
that Henley indicates a band of perhaps 50 which may have been the
Bankalachi.   A village site estimate obtained by Voegelin (1938)
from native informants suggested a total about 1855–60 of 228
Tübatulabal, and 65 Palagewan, or 293 combined.   An estimate for
1863 based on the total of adult males indicates a population of 220.
The United States Census of 1910 returned 105 and a field census
taken by Voegelin in 1832 including all mixtures, 145.

Vanyume.   Name applied by the Mohave; significance unknown,
   though it is probably related to the term Panamint given to the
   Koso.

Connections.—The Vanyume belonged to the Shoshonean Division
of the Uto-Aztecan linguistic stock, their closest connections being
probably with the Kitanemuk, and secondly with the Serrano.

Location.—On Mohave River.

Population.—(See **Alliklik**.)   They are now extinct as a tribe.

Wailaki.   A Wintun word meaning "north language," applied to
   other Wintun groups and to some foreign groups.   Also called:

   Kak'-wits, Yuki name, meaning "northern people."

Connections.—The Wailaki belonged to the Athapascan linguistic
stock and to the southern California group.

Location.—On Eel River from the Lassik territory to the Big
Bend, several affluents on the west side, Kekawaka Creek on the
east side, and the whole of the North Fork except the head.

Subdivisions and Village Communities [9]

On main Eel River:

Sehlchikyo-kaiya, on the east side, Big Bend Creek to McDonald Creek.
Ninkannich-kaiya, opposite Sehlchikyo-kaiya.
Nehlchikyo-kaiya, on the east side downstream to the mouth of North Fork.
Sehlchikyo-kaiya, on the east side downstream.
Tatisho-kaiya, on the west side opposite the mouth of North Fork.
Bas-kaiya, on the east side below Sehlchikyo-kaiya.
Sla-kaiya, on the east side below Bas-kaiya.
Chisko-kaiya, on the east side below Sla-kaiya.
Seta-kaiya, on the west side below Tatisho-kaiya.
Kaikiche-kaiya, on the west side below Seta-kaiya.
Dahlso-kaiya, Set'ahlchicho-kaiya, K'andang-kaiya—in order downstream on the west side.
Ihikodang-kaiya, on the west side below Chisko-kaiya.
Kasnaikot-kaiya, on the east side at the mouth of Kakawaka Creek.

On the lower part of North Fork:

Setandong-kiyahang, Secho-kiyahang, Kaiye-kiyahang—in order upstream.

Higher up North Fork:

T'odannang-kiyahang, on the North Fork below Hull Creek.
T'okyah-kiyahang, upstream on North Fork.
Chokot-kiyahang, on and above Red Mountain Creek.
Ch'i'ankot-kiyahang, on Jesus Creek.

Population.—The Wailaki were estimated by Kroeber (1925) as 1,000 about 1770; they were given as 227 in the census of 1910. (See **Bear River Indians.**)

Wappo. An Americanization of Spanish Guapo. "brave," given them on account of their stubborn resistence to Spanish military aggression. Also called:

Ash-o-chĭ-mi, a name given by Powers (1877).
Soteomellos or Sotomieyos, names given by Taylor (1860–63).

Connections.—The Wappo language constituted a very divergent form of speech of the Yukian linguistic family.

Location.—On the headwaters of Napa River and Pope and Putah Creeks, and a stretch of Russian River.

Subdivisions and Villages

Following are their dialectic divisions and the villages in each, the names in italic being principal towns in as many village communities:

Southern Wappo:

Anakota-noma, at St. Helena.
Kaimus, at Yountville.
Tsemanoma, northeast of St. Helena.
Wilikos, near the head of Sonoma Creek.

Central Wappo:

Maiyakama, south of Calistoga.
Mêlka'wa-hotsa-noma, at site of Middletown—Driver.
Mutistul, between the Napa River and Russian River drainage.
Nihlektsonoma, north of Calistoga.
Tselmenan, north of Calistoga.

[9] Arranged in order of location; not alphabetized.

Northern Wappo:
  Lok-noma, northeast of Middletown.
  Petinoma, north of Middletown.
  Uyuhanoma, east of Middletown.
Western Wappo:
  Ashaben, near Lytton.
  Gayechin, near Lytton.
  Hol-tcu'kolo, location unknown.
  Koloko, on Russian River below Geyserville.
  Malalachahl, at Lytton.
  Nêts-tul, northeast of Tsimitu-tsonoma.
  Oso'yûk-eju, west of Russian River and southeast of Geyserville.
  Owotêl-pêti, east of Tsimitutsonoma.
  Pipoholma, on Russian River below Geyserville.
  Shêi-kana, location unknown.
  Shimela, on Russian River below Geyserville.
  Tsi'mitu-tso-noma, on the east bank of Russian River some miles below Geyserville.
  Tekenan-tso-noma, near Geysers in Sulphur Creek drainage.
  Unutsa'wa-holma-noma, north of Tsi'mitu-tso-noma.
Lile'ek Wappo:
  Daladan, on Cole Creek.
  Kabetsawam, on Cole Creek.

Driver (1939) adds the following names of camp sites, presumably in the country of the Western Wappo: Halîsh-wahûk-holma, Ho'lko-mota, Hut-mitul, Nuya-hotsa, Tcano-nayuk, Ts'awo-tul, Tikomota, Walma-pêsite.

Population.—Kroeber (1925) estimates 1,000 Wappo in 1770 as a maximum; the census of 1910 returned 73.   (See **Yuki.**)

Washo.   The range of this tribe extended over considerable Californian territory about the angle in the eastern boundary line of the State.   (See Nevada.)

Whilkut.   From Hupa Hoilkut-hoi.   Also called:

  Redwood Indians, the popular name for them.

Connections.—The Whilkut belonged to the Hupa dialectic group of the Athapascan linguistic family.

Location.—On the upper part of Redwood Creek above the Chilula Indians and Mad River, except in its lowest course, up to the vicinity of Iaqua Butte.

Population.—Kroeber (1932) estimates about 500 Whilkut in aboriginal times; the census of 1910 returned 50 full-bloods and some mixed-bloods.

Wintu.   The native word meaning "people."

  For synonyms see Wintun.

Connections.—The Wintu were the northernmost division of the Copehan stock of Powell, later called Wintun by Kroeber (1932) and now regarded as part of the Penutian family.

Location.—In the valleys of the upper Sacramento and upper Trinity Rivers north of Cottonwood Creek and extending from Cow Creek on the east to the South Fork of the Trinity on the west.

Subdivisions
(As given by Du Bois (1935) but placing the native name first)

Dau-nom, "in-front-of-west" (Bald Hills), a flat valley area at the foot of the hills south of Reading and east of the coastal range.

Dau-pom, "in-front-of-place" (Stillwater), comprising the plateau to the north of Reading.

Elpom, "shore place" (Keswick), extending from a point somewhat south of Kennett on the Sacramento chiefly along the west bank southward almost to Reading, and including the former Indian settlements around the mining town of Old Shasta.

Hayfork Wintu, on the Hayfork branch of Trinity River and on Trinity River about Junction City, extending also from about Middletown westward to the South Fork of the Trinity.

Klabalpom (French Gulch), on the upper reaches of Clear Creek.

Nomsus, "west-dwelling" (Upper Trinity), on the East Fork of Trinity River and Trinity River proper as far south as Lewiston.

Nomtipom, "west-hillside-place" (Upper Sacramento), along the precipitous reaches of the upper Sacramento above Kennett.

Waimuk, "north inhabitant(?)," in the narrow valley of the upper McCloud River.

Winimen, "middle-water" (McCloud), in the McCloud and lower Pit Valleys.

Du Bois (1935) mentions Nomkentcau and Nomkali as two villages in Watson Gulch.

Population.—(See **Wintun.**)

Wintun. The word for "people" in the northern Wintun dialects. Also called:

> Wawáh, Mono name for all Sacramento River tribes, meaning "strangers."
> Xátūkwiwa, Shasta name for a Wintun Indian.

Connections.—The Wintun were formerly considered a part of Powell's Copehan stock and the Wintun of Kroeber (1932) but are now placed in the Penutian family.

Location.—On the west side of the Sacramento Valley from the river up to the coast range, but falling short of this in spots and extending beyond it in others, and from Cottonwood Creek on the north to about the latitude of Afton and Stonyford on the south.

Wintun Tribelets
(Generally south to north)

Dahchi'mchini-sel, in a village called Dahchi'mchini (upstream of Brisco Creek and 4 miles above Elk Creek).

Toba, reported by Barrett (1919) as a town at the mouth of Brisco Creek.

A tribelet probably located at Tolokai or Doloke (at the mouth of Elk Creek).

Pomtididi-sel, at the village of Pomtididi (where Grindstone Creek enters Stony Creek).

A tribelet at a village called Kalaiel (on the North Fork of Stony Creek).

Soninmak (at a "butte" named Son-pom down Stony Creek).

Pelti-kewel (reported north of preceding by one informant).

A tribelet at the villages of Sohu's-labe (3 or 4 miles south of Fruto) and Nomê'l-mim-labe (2 or 3 miles farther south still).

Nom-kewel or Nom-laka, with their village, Lo-pom (south of Thomas Creek).

Walti-kewel, with villages called Noitikel, Kenkopol, and Saipanti (close together on the north side of Thomas Creek below Nom-kewel).

Olwenem-wintun, at O'lwenem (near the mouth of Thomas Creek on the Sacramento).

A tribelet at Mĭ'tenek (at Squaw Hill Ferry).

Pelmem-we, at Pelmem (near Vina and the mouth of Deer Creek).

Tehêmet, (at Tehama).

Dă-mak (where Redbank Creek comes in below Red Bluff).

Wai-kewel (on Elder Creek).

A tribelet at Chuidau (on the South Fork of Cottonwood Creek).

Population.—Kroeber (1932) estimates 12,000 Wintun in 1770 and about 1,000 in 1910. The census of 1930 returned 512 Wintun, Wintu, and Wappo.

Wiyot. Properly the name of one of the three Wiyot districts but extended by most of their neighbors over the whole people. Also called:

>Dilwishne, Sinkyone name.
>Humboldt Bay Indians, popular term.
>Sulatelik, used by the Wiyot to designate their language, and approaching a tribal designation in its usage.
>Wishosk, probably a misapplication of the Wiyot name for their Athapascan neighbors.

Connections.—In the Powellian classification the Wiyot were given an independent position as the Wishoskan stock. Later California investigators combined them with the Yurok under the name Ritwan but still later believed that they had established a relationship between them and the great Algonquian family of the east. This allocation is, however, questioned by other ethnologists.

Location.—On lower Mad River, Humboldt Bay, and lower Eel River.

Subdivisions

Batawat, on lower Mad River.

Wiki, on Humboldt Bay.

Wiyot, on lower Eel River.

Villages

Bimire, on the lower part of Humboldt Bay.

Dakduwaka, or Hiluwitl(?), on the southern point at the entrance to Humboldt Bay.

Dakwagerawakw, on Eel River.

Dulawat, on an island in Humboldt Bay.

Hakitege (?), at the junction of Eel and Van Duzen Rivers.

Ho'ket (?), near the mouth of Eel River.

Kachewinach (?), on Mad River.
Kotsir (?), at the northern end of Humboldt Bay.
Kumaidada, on Freshwater Creek.
Legetku (?), at the southern end of Humboldt Bay.
Ma'awor, Yurok name; at the mouth of Mad River.
Osok, Yurok name; on Mad River,
Potitlik, Cherokigechk, of Pletswak (?), opposite the entrance of Humboldt Bay.
Tabagaukwa (?), at the mouth of Mad River.
Tabayat or Witki (?), on Humboldt Bay.
Tokelomigimitl (?), north of Humboldt Bay.
Watsayeriditl (?), on Eel River.
We'tso (?), on the south side of Mad River.
Wuktlakw (?), on the north side of Eel River.
Yachwanawach, at the end of Humboldt Bay.

Population.—Kroeber (1932) estimates 1,000 Wiyot in 1770 and 100 in 1910. The census of 1930 gives 236 but probably includes Indians of other connections.

Yahi. Meaning "person" in their own language.

Connections.—The Yahi constituted the southernmost group of the Yanan division of the Hokan linguistic stock.

Location.—On Mill and Deer Creeks.

Villages

Bushkuina, Tolochuaweyu, and Tuliyani were on or near Mill Creek; Bopmay-huwi, Gahma, K'andjauha, Puhiya, and Yisch'inna on or near Deer Creek.

Population.—Included in the Yana (q. v.).

Yana. Meaning "person" in their own language. Also called:

Kom'-bo, Maidu name.
Nó-si or Nó-zi, a name given by Powers (1877).
Tisaiqdji, Ilmawi name.

Connections.—The Yana were originally considered an independent linguistic stock but are now placed in the larger Hokan family.

Location.—Including the Yahi, the Yana extended from Pit River to Rock Creek, and from the edge of the upper Sacramento Valley to the headwaters of the eastern tributaries of Sacramento River.

Subdivisions

Aside from the Yahi (q. v.), they embraced three dialectic subdivisions, a northern (on the drainage of Montgomery Creek into Pit River and that of Cedar Creek, an affluent of Little Crow Creek), a central (the entire Cow Creek drainage and Bear Creek), and a southern (on Battle, Payne, and Antelope Creeks and one or two smaller streams).

Villages

Northern Division:
Djewintaurik'u, south of Montgomery.
Djitpamauwid'u, on Cedar Creek.
K'asip'u, south of Round Mountain.

Central Division:
  Badjiyu, on Clover Creek.
  Ban'ha, inland between the two forks of Cow Creek.
  Djichitpemauna, on Bear Creek.
  Hamedamen, at Millville.
  Haudulimauna, near the South Fork of Cow Creek.
  Hodjinimauna, on the North Fork of Bear Creek.
  Luwaiha, on Old Cow Creek.
  Pawi, on Clover Creek.
  Pulsu'aina, near the North Fork of Cow Creek.
  Ship'a, between Little Cow Creek and Oak Run.
  Unchunaha, between the North Fork of Cow Creek and Clover Creek.
  Wamarawi, west of Shingletown.
  Wichuman'na, on the South Fork of Cow Creek.
Southern Division:
  K'uwiha, on Battle Creek.

Population.—Kroeber (1932) estimates 1,500 Yana in 1770 including the Yahi, and states that there are less than 40 full- and mixed-bloods today, all of the Northern and Central Divisions. Only 9 appear under the head of Yanan in the census of 1930.

Yokuts. The name for "person," or "people," in many of the dialects of the group. Also called:

> Mariposan, a name derived from Mariposa County, and applied to the stock to which these people were originally assigned by Powell.
> Noche, a name used by Garcés in 1775–76 (1900).

Connections.—The Yokuts were originally considered a distinct linguistic family but have now been made a part of the large Penutian stock.

Location.—On the entire floor of San Joaquin Valley from the mouth of San Joaquin River to the foot of Tehachapi, and the adjacent lower slopes or foothills of the Sierra Nevada, up to an altitude of a few thousand feet, from Fresno River south.

Subdivisions and Villages

These were as follows:

Buena Vista Group:
  Tulamni (on Buena Vista Lake), including the villages of Tulamniu (on the west or northwest shore of the lake), and Wogitiu (at McKittrick).
  Hometwoli or Humetwadi (on Kern Lake), including the villages of Halau (near the entrance of Kern River into the channel connecting Kern and Buena Vista lakes).
  Loasau (somewhere on the north side of Kern Lake), and Sihetal Daal or Pohalin Tinliu (on the south shore).
  Tuhohi, Tohohai, or Tuohayi (among the channels and tule-lined sloughs of lower Kern River, perhaps ranging as far as Grass Lake), including the village of Tahayu (location unknown).
Poso Creek Group:
  Paleuyami, Padeuyami, Peleuyi, or Paluyam (on Poso Creek and neighboring parts of Kern River), including the villages of Altau (just south of Poso

Creek), Bekiu (in Poso Flat), Shikidapau (in Poso Flat), Holmiu (in Linn's Valley) and Kumachisi, Komechesi, Kometsicsi, or Kumachesi (centered about Hoschiu on White River), including the villages of Hoschiu (on White River), and Kelsiu (just south of White River).

Tule-Kaweah Group:

Yaudanchi, Yaulanchi, or Nutaa (Tule River in the foothills especially the North and Middle Forks), including the villages of Shawahtau (above Springville), and Ukun'ui (above Daunt), and perhaps Uchiyingetau (at the painted rocks).

Bokninuwad, or Bokninwal (on Deer Creek in the foothills), including K'eyau (near the valley), and perhaps Hoin Tinliu (not far from Deer Creek Hot Springs, though this may have been Bankalachi), and Uchiyingetau (see above).

Wüchamni, Wikchamni, or Wikchomni (on Kaweah River and the adjacent hills).

Yokod or Yokol (west of the latter and south of Kaweah River), their principal village being on a flat near Kaweah Railroad Station, and on the south side of Kaweah River, north of Exeter.

Gawia or Kawia (on the north side of Kaweah River), including a settlement on the north side of Kaweah River and Chidepuish (at Calvin Hill on Big Dry or Rattlesnake Creek).

Kings River Group:

Choinimni (on Kings River), including the village of Tishechu (on the south side of Kings River at the mouth of Mill Creek).

Michahai (on Mill Creek), including the village of Hehshinau (on the north side of the stream on a flat at the foot of the pine covered ridge).

Chukaimina (in Squaw Valley on a small southern affluent of Mill Creek), including the villages of Dochiu (at the north side of the valley), and Mashtinau (on the east side of the valley).

Toihicha (below the Choinimni on the north side of Kings River), including the villages of Tanaiu (at Hughes Creek), and Bochiptau (location uncertain).

Aiticha (farther down Kings River on the south side), including the village of K'ipayu (somewhat nearer Centerville than to Tishechu).

Kocheyali (location and even existence uncertain as the name is given as a synonym for the last).

Gashowu (on Big Dry Creek and Little Dry Creek), including the villages of Pohoniu (below Letcher on Big Dry Creek), Yokau (on Auberry Valley on Little Dry Creek), and Ochopou (possibly belonging to the Kechayi).

Northern Group of the Foothill Division:

Toltichi (the Yokuts tribe farthest up the San Joaquin, possibly Mono), including the village of Tsopotipau (at the electric power site on the large bend of the river below the entrance of the North Fork).

Kechayi (holding the south bank of the San Joaquin for some miles above Millerton), including Kochoyu and Kowichkowicho (farther up).

Dumna (on the north side of the San Joaquin about opposite the Kechayi), including the village of Dinishneu (at Belleville).

Dalinchi (on Fine Gold Creek), including the villages of Moloneu (on this creek), and Dalinau (over the divide in the Coarse Gold Creek drainage).

Chukchansi, Shukshansi, or Shukshanchi (on Coarse Gold Creek and the head of Cottonwood Creek), including the villages of Hapasau (near Fresno Flats), Chukchanau or Suksanau (well up on Fresno River), Tsuloniu (near the headwaters of Coarse Gold Creek), Kowoniu or Kohoniu (on Picayune

Creek), Kataniu (the present Picayune rancheria), and Ch'eyau (on Cottonwood Creek near Bates).

Southern Group of the Valley Division:

Yauelmani (a strip of territory between Tejon Ranch on Paso Creek and Poso Creek), including the villages of Tinliu (below the Tejon Ranch House), Woilo (at Bakersfield), K'ono-ilkin (on Kern River), Shoko (on Kern River), but Shoko and K'ono-ilkin were shared, however, with the Paleuyami, so that it is not known which claimed ownership.

Tsineuhiu (a short distance above Bakersfield on Kern River), and Kuyo (on a channel draining toward Kern Lake), and the people of this subdivision also lived at times at Hoschiu on White River and at Chididiknawasi (in the Deer Creek country).

Koyeti (on lower Tule River from Porterville down), including the village of Chokowisho (Porterville).

Choinok (probably on Deep and Outside Channels of Kaweah River), including the village of Ch'iuta (somewhere south of Tulare).

Wo'lasi or Wo'ladji (at and below Farmersville, perhaps on Cameron channel).

Telamni (at Visalia and Goshen), including the village of Waitatshulul (about 7 miles north of Tulare City).

Wechihit (about Sanger on lower Kings River), including the village of Musahau (in the low bottoms opposite Sanger), and perhaps Wewayo (on Wahtoke Creek) although this latter was rather a kind of no-man's-land.

Nutunutu (south of lower Kings River), including the villages of Chiau (a little south of Kingston), and Hibek'ia (location uncertain).

Wimilchi (on the north side of lower Kings River), including the town of Ugona (southwest of Kingston).

Wowol (on the southeastern shores of Tulare Lake), including the village of Sukuwutnu or Dulau (on an island off the eastern shore of the lake).

Chunut (the Tulare Lake shore in the Kaweah Delta region), including the villages of Miketsiu and Chuntau which cannot be definitely located.

Tachi (the tract from northern Tulare Lake and its inlet or outlet Fish Slough west to the Mount Diablo chain of the Coast Range), including the villages of Udjiu (downstream from Coalinga), Walna (where the western hills approach the lake), Colon (Huron), Chi (west of Heinlen), and Waiu (on Mussel Slough).

Apiachi (north of Kings River and east of its outlet slough), including the village of Wohui (beyond Telweyit or Summit Lake, in the direction of Elkhorn).

Northern Group of the Valley Division:

Pitkachi or Pitkati (on the south side of the San Joaquin), including the villages of Kohuou (near Herndon or Sycamore), Weshiu (on a slough), and Gawachiu (still farther downstream).

Wakichi (on the south side of San Joaquin River above the last), including the village of Holowichniu (near Millerton).

Hoyima (on the north side of the San Joaquin opposite the Pitkachi), including the villages of K'eliutanau (on a creek entering the San Joaquin from the north), and Moyoliu (above the mouth of Little Dry Creek).

Heuchi (on Fresno River at least on its north side), including the village of Ch'ekayu (on Fresno River 4 miles below Madera).

Chauchila or Chaushila, or Toholo (on the several channels of Chauchilla River), including a village at Shehamniu (on Chowchilla River apparently at the edge of the plains some miles below Buchanan), and perhaps Halau (near Berenda), although this may have been Heuchi.

Nupchinche or Noptinte (not located).
Tawalimnu (probably on Tuolumne River).
Lakisamni (perhaps about Takin rancheria at Dents of Knights Ferry on the
    Stanislaus River).
Siakumne (location uncertain).
Hannesuk (location uncertain).
Coconoon (on Merced River).
Chulamni (about Stockton, their territory extending at least some miles down
    the San Joaquin and up the Calaveras, and possibly as far west as Mount
    Diablo), including the villages of Yachik and Wana (both near Stockton).

Population.—Kroeber (1932) estimates 18,000 Yokuts in 1770 and
600 in 1910, based on the census report of 533. The census of 1930
returned 1,145.

Yuki. Derived from the Wintun language and meaning "stranger,"
or "foe." Also called:

    Chu-mai-a, Pomo name.
    Noam-kekhl, Wintun name, meaning "west dwelling," or "western tribe."

Connections.—The Yuki constituted an independent stock called
Yukian.

Location.—All the land lying in the drainage of Eel River above
the North Fork, except for a stretch on South Eel River where the
allied Huchnom were situated.

Subdivisions

Huititno'm, on the South Fork of Middle Eel River.
Onkolukomno'm, from the forks of the South Eel River to their sources.
Sukshaltatano'm, on the North Fork of Middle Eel River.
Ta'no'm, on main Eel River.
Ukomno'm, about Round Valley on the north side of Middle Fork.
Utitno'm, about the forks made by the Middle and South Eel Rivers.
Witukomno'm, on the south side of Middle Eel River, especially on its branches.

Villages

The following villages constituted a group in the northern portion of Round
Valley west of the agency: Chochhanuk, Mameshishmo U'wit, Hake, Son, and
there were still others whose names have been forgotten.

There was another group in the northern part of Round Valley east of the
agency and northeast over the hills to include Williams Valley: Pomo, in Round
Valley, and, in successive order upstream in Williams Valley, Mo't-huyup,
Kilikot, Lelhaksi, Nonakak, Yukuwaskal, Moyi.

A third group was in the northeastern corner of Round Valley and eastward to
Middle Eel River, as follows: Titwa or Ona[n]s, Sonkash, Molkus, (all in Round
Valley), and other villages east of the valley toward the river, whose names and
sites are not known.

The names of six subdivisions of the Ta'no'm are known: Kichilpitno'm,
Kasha[n]sichno'm, Pomaha[n]no'm, Ma[n]tno'm, Ha[n]chhotno'm, and Ulamolno'm.
Probably these corresponded to the Ukonno'm groups. Names of places are:
Kasha[n]sich, Pomaha[n], and Hanchhot.

The following names belong to settlements or communities in various parts of the Yuki territory:

Alniukino'm, in the northwest part of Round Valley.

K'ilikuno'm, in the north or lower end of Eden Valley.

Witukomno'm, a village near the head of Eden Valley.

Sukano'm, Sonlaⁿlno'm, Chakomno'm, and Chahelilno'm—names of parts of a group of unknown designation, between the Ukomno'm and the Witukomno'm.

Liltamno'm and Nonlachno'm (perhaps synonymous), at Bluenose north or northeast of Round Valley.

Ukachimno'm, in Poorman's Valley, northeast of Round Valley.

Shipimaⁿino'm and Kichilukomno'm, in Williams Valley; one of these may be the name of the second group given above, in Round Valley.

Maⁿlchalno'm, at one of the heads of Middle Eel River.

Onkolukomno'm, in Gravelly Valley near Hullville.

Hunkalich, a village near Hullville.

Matamno'm, a group perhaps belonging to the Witukomno'm division.

Population.—Kroeber (1932) estimates 2,000 Yuki in 1770; the census of 1910 returned 95, and that of 1930, 177, including the Yuki, Coast Yuki, and Huchnom.

Yuki, Coast; or Ukhotno'm. (See **Yuki.**) The second name is applied to them by the interior Yuki, signifying "ocean people."

Connections.—The Coast Yuki believe themselves to be an offshoot from the Huchnom but linguistic examination seems to place them near the Yuki.

Location.—The Pacific coast from Cleone to a point halfway between Rockport and Usal and inland to the divide between the coast streams and Eel River.

Villages

These have not been recorded but the following places were probably inhabited: On the coast from north to south:

On-chil-ka or On-chil-em, beyond Rockport.

Es'im, at Rockport or Hardy Creek.

Melhom-i'iken (Warren Creek).

Hisimel-auhkem (the next creek).

Lil-p'in-kem (De Haven).

Shipep or Shipoi (Westport).

K'etim, Chetman Gulch.

Lilim, Mussel Rock.

Ok'omet or Shipoi, Kabesilah.

Methuyak-olselem (the creek north of Ten Mile River).

Metkuyaki or Metkuyakem (the mouth of Ten Mile River and also the river).

Mil-hot-em (Cleone).

Sus-mel-im, at the mouth of Pudding Creek.

Ol-hepech-kem (Noyo River).

Nehkinmelem (Casper).

Onp'otilkei (in Sherwood Valley).

Ukemim (near Willits).

Population.—Kroeber (1932) estimates that in 1770 and 1850 there were 500 Coast Yuki; the census of 1910 reported 15.   (See **Yuki.**)

Yuma.   This tribe extended into the extreme southeastern corner of the State along the Colorado River.   (See Arizona.)

Yurok.   Signifying "downstream" in the language of the neighboring Karok.   Also called:

> Kiruhikwak, by the Shasta of Salmon River.
> Weitchpec, a name sometimes locally used, especially in Hupa and Karok territory, to which Weichpec is at present the nearest Yurok village.

Connections.—The Yurok were originally regarded as an independent stock, later combined with the Wiyot into the Ritwan family, and still later identified by Kroeber and Sapir as a part of the great Algonquian family of the east.   This last identification has not, however, met with entire acceptance.

Location.—On the lower Klamath River and along the coast to the north and south of it.

Subdivisions

Two dialects differing but little from each other may be distinguished; one spoken in the southernmost coast section, the districts of the Big Lagoon and Trinidad; the other, in the remainder of Yurok territory.

Villages

Ayotl, above the mouth of Blue Creek.
Erner, at the mouth of Blue Creek.
Ertlerger, at the mouth of Trinity River on the west side.
Espau, on the coast north of Redwood Creek.
Hergwer, on Stone Lagoon.
Himetl, on the north side of Klamath River.
Ho'pau, on Klamath River a few miles from the coast.
Keihkem, 2 towns: (1) on Big Lagoon;   (2) on the north side of Klamath River.
Kenek, on the south side of Klamath River.
Kenekpul, on the south side of Klamath River, a short distance below Kenek.
Kepel, on the north side of Klamath River.
Ko'otep, on the north side of Klamath River.
Lo'olego on the north side of Klamath River above the mouth of the Trinity.
Ma'ats, on Big Lagoon.
Merip, on the north bank of Klamath River.
Meta, on the south or west bank of Klamath River.
Metskwo, at the mouth of Little River.
Murekw, on the north bank of Klamath River.
Nagetl, on the south or west side of Klamath River opposite the mouth of Blue Creek.
Nohtskum, on the south bank of Klamath River.
Omen, on the coast north of Klamath River.
Omenhipur, on the coast north of Klamath River.
Opyuweg, between Big Lagoon and the coast.
Orau, on Redwood Creek.

Orekw, on the south side of Redwood Creek at its mouth.
Osegen, on the coast south of Klamath River.
Oslokw, on the east side of Big Lagoon.
Otmekwor, on the north side of the mouth of Redwood Creek.
Otsepor, on the south side of Klamath River below the mouth of Bluff Creek.
Otwego, on the south side of Klamath River near its mouth.
Pa'ar, near the north end of Big Lagoon.
Pekwan, on the north side of Klamath River.
Pekwututl, on the south side of Klamath River at the mouth of the Trinity.
Rekwoi, on the north side of the mouth of Klamath River.
Sa'a, on the south side of Klamath River.
Sa'aitl, on the north side of Klamath River some miles above its mouth.
Serper, on the north side of Klamath River.
Sregon, on the north or east side of Klamath River.
Tlemekwetl, on the north side of Klamath River below Blue Creek.
Tmeri, just below Requa.
Tsahpekw, on the west side of Stone Lagoon.
Tsetskwi, on the north or east side of Klamath River.
Tsotskwi, near the south end of Stone Lagoon.
Tsurau, near Trinidad.
Turip, on the south side of Klamath River a few miles from the coast.
Wa'asel, on the north side of Klamath River.
Wahsekw, on the north or east side of Klamath River below Weitchpeg.
Weitspus, opposite the mouth of Trinity River.
Wetlkwau, on the south side of the mouth of Klamath River.
Wohkel, on the south side of Klamath River a short distance above its mouth.
Wohkero, on the north side of Klamath River.
Wohtek, close to the preceding.
Yohter, on the south or west side of Klamath River.

Population.—Kroeber (1932) estimates 2,500 Yurok in 1770; the census of 1910 returned 668, and that of 1930, 471.

ALASKA

Ahtena.   Signifying "Ice People."   Also called:

> Copper River Indians, popular name.
> Intsi Dindjich, Kutchin name, meaning "men of iron."
> Ketschetnäer or Kolshina, Russian name meaning "ice people."
> Mednofski, Russian name meaning "copper river people."
> Yellowknife Indians, by Ross (quoted by Dall, 1877).
> Yullit, Ugalakmiut name.

Connections.—The Ahtena belonged to the Athapascan linguistic stock. Physically they are said to bear a close resemblance to the Koyukukhotana. (See **Koyukan.**)

Location.—In the basin of Copper River.

Subdivisions

According to Allen (1887):
> Miduusky, on Copper River from its mouth to Tazlina River, and its branches.
> Tatlazan, above the Tazlina.

According to Hoffman (ms.):

Ikherkhamut, near the mouth of Copper River.

Kangikhlukhmut, at the head of Copper River.

Kulchana, about headwaters of the Kuskokwim and extending probably into the valley of Copper River, but Osgood (1936) calls this "an erroneous generalized extension of the Ahtena people."

Kulushut, on Copper River next above the Ikherkhamut.

Shukhtutakhlit, on Copper River next above the Kangikhlukhmut.

Vikhit, next below the Kulchana (?).

Villages

Alaganik, with Ugalakmiut near the mouth of Copper River.

Batzulnetas, near upper Copper River where the trail for Tanana River begins.

Liebigstag, on the left bank of Copper River, latitude 61°57′ N., longitude 145°45′ W.

Miduuski, on the east bank of Copper River below the mouth of Tonsina Creek.

Skatalis, near the mouth of Copper River, probably the original Alaganik.

Skolai, on Nizina River near the mouth of Chitistone River, latitutde 61°21′ N., longitude 143°17′ W.

Slana, at the confluence of Slana and Copper Rivers.

Titlogat, probably of the Kulchana division. (But cf. Osgood above.)

Toral, on Copper River at the mouth of Chitina River.

History.—The mouth of Copper River was discovered by Nagaieff in 1781, but expeditions into the interior met with such consistent hostility on the part of the natives that for a long time they were a simple record of failure. The attempts of Samoylof in 1796, Lastóchkin in 1798, KJimoffsky in 1819, and Gregorief in 1844 all ended in the same way. Serebrannikof ventured up the river in 1848, but his disregard for the natives cost him his life and the lives of three of his companions. In 1882 after the cession of Alaska to the United States, a trader named Holt ascended as far as Taral but on a subsequent visit he was killed by the natives. In 1884 Lt. Abercrombie explored a part of the river, and in 1885 a thorough exploration of the whole region was made by Lt. Allen, who visited the Ahtena villages on Copper River and on its principal tributaries. From that time on intercourse between the river people and Whites has been increasingly intimate.

Population.—Mooney (1928) estimated 500 Ahtena for the year 1740. Petroff (1884) placed their numbers in 1880 at not more than 300. Allen (1887) gave 366 on the river and its branches. The census of 1890 returned 142, and that of 1910, 297. In 1920 the total native population of Alaska speaking Athapascan dialects was 4,657; in 1930, 4,935.

Aleut. A name of unknown origin but traced with some plausibility to the Chukchi word aliat, meaning "island," which is supposed to have been bestowed upon the inhabitants of the Aleutian Islands through a misunderstanding.   Also called:

Takhayuna, Knaiakhotana, name according to Petroff (1884).
U-nung'ŭn, own name, according to Dall (1886).

Connections.—The Aleut constituted the only widely divergent branch of the Eskimauan linguistic stock, the remainder of the tongues of that family being closely related.

Location.—On the Aleutian Islands, the Shumagin Islands, and the western part of Alaska Peninsula.

Subdivisions

There were two main subdivisions distinguished by difference in dialect: (1) the Atka, on Andreanof, Rat, and Near Islands; and (2) the Unalaska on the Fox and Shumagin Islands and Alaska Peninsula.

Villages

I. Atka Division·
Attu, on Holt Bay (Chichagof Harbor ?), Attu Island.
Korovinski, at Korovin Bay, on Atka Island.
Nazan, on Atka Island.
Unalga, on Unalga Island, Andreanof group;
The following ruined places on the single island of Agattu: Agonakagna, Atku-
    lik, Atkigyin, Hachimuk, Hamnulik, Hanilik, Hapkug, Higtiguk, Hilksuk,
    Ibin, Imik, Iptugik, Isituchi, Kakuguk, Kamuksusik, Kaslukug, Kigsitatok,
    Kikchik, Kikun, Kimituk, Kitak, Kuptagok, Magtok, Mukugnuk, Navisok,
    Siksatok, Sunik, Ugiatok, Ugtikun, Ugtumuk, Ukashik.
II. Unalaska Division:
Akutan, on Akutan Island, close to Unalaska Island.
Avatanak, on Avatanak Island, between Unalaska and Unimak Islands.
Belkofski, near the end of Alaska Peninsula.
Biorka, on Biorka Island near Unalaska.
Chernofski, on Unalaska Island.
Eider, on Captain Bay, Unalaska Island.
Iliuliuk, on Unalaska Island.
Kashiga, on Unalaska Island.
Korovinski, on Korovin Island.
Makushin, on Makushin Bay, Unalaska Island.
Mashik, at Port Moller, Alaska Peninsula.
Morzhovoi, at the end of Alaska Peninsula, formerly at the head of Morzhovoi
    and later on Traders Cove which opens into Isanotski Bay.
Nateekin, on Nateekin Bay, Unalaska Island.
Nikolaief, on Alaska Peninsula north of Belkofski.
Nikolski, on Umnak Island.
Pavlof, at Selenie Point, Pavlof Bay, Alaska Pensinsula.
Pogromni, near Pogromni volcano, on the north shore of Unimak Island.
Popof, at Pirate Cove, Popof Island, one of the Shumagins.
Saint George, on St. George Island, Pribilof group.
Saint Paul, on Saint Paul Island, Pribilof group.
Sannak, on Sannak Island.
Unga, on Unga Island, Shumagin group.
Vossnessenski, on Vossnessenski Island, in the Shumagin group.

Villages reported by later writers:

Agulok, on Unalaska Island.
Akun, on Akun Island, between Unalaska and Unimak.
Artelnof, on Akun Island.
Beaver, on Unalaska Island.
Chaliuknak, on Beaver Bay, Unalaska Island.
Ikolga, on Unalaska Island.
Imagnee, on Summer Bay, Unalaska Island.
Itchadak, on one of the east Aleutian Islands.
Kalekhta, on Unalaska Island.
Kutchlok on Unalaska Island.
Riechesni, on Little Bay, Akun Island in the Krenitzin group.
Seredka, on Seredka Bay in Akun Island.
Sisaguk, on Unimak Island.
Takamitka, on Unalaska Island.
Tigalda, on Tigalda Island, one of the east Aleutians.
Totchikala, on Unalaska Island..
Tulik, on Umnak Island, near a volcano of the same name.
Ugamitzi, on Unalaska Island.
Uknodok, on Hog Island, Captains Bay, Unalaska.
Veselofski, at Cape Cheerful, Unalaska.

History.—The Aleut became known to the Russians immediately after the voyages of Chirikoff and Bering in 1741, the discovery of the islands themselves being attributed to Mikhaíl Nerodchikof, September 1745. Though the natives at first resisted the exactions of the foreign traders with courage, their darts were no match for firearms, and they were not only cruelly treated themselves but were forced into the service of their masters as allies in attacks upon more distant peoples. It is said they were soon reduced to one-tenth of their former numbers. In 1794–1818 the Russian Government interfered to protect them from exploitation, and their condition was somewhat improved, but most of the improvement they experienced at Russian hands was due to the noted missionary Veniamínoff, who began his labors in 1824. Through his efforts and those of his fellow missionaries of the Greek Church, all of the Aleut were soon converted, and they were to some extent educated. In 1867 they, with the rest of the population of Alaska, passed under the control of the United States.

Population.—Mooney (1928) estimated that in 1740 there were 16,000 Aleut. Veniamínoff (1840) gave the Atka population as 750 in 1834 and the Unalaska population as 1,497. In 1848 Father Shaiesnekov enumerated 1,400 all told, a figure which was reduced to 900 as a result of the smallpox epidemic of that year. Dall (1877) estimated that there were about 2,000, and according to the census of 1890 there were 1,702, including 734 mixed-bloods. The census of 1910 returned 1,451. The native Alaskan population speaking Eskimauan dialects was 13,698 in 1920 and 19,028 in 1930.

Connection in which they have become noted.—The name of the Aleut is perpetuated in that of the Aleutian Islands, and from their language is derived the word Alaska, applied to Alaska Territory, and to Alaska Peninsula, which such a large number of the Aleut inhabit.

Dihai-kutchin.   Signifying "Kutchin farthest downstream."

Connections.—The Dihai-kutchin were a band or tribe of the Kutchin division of the Athapascan linguistic stock.   They are added to Osgood's (1936) list of true Kutchin tribes on the authority of Robert McKennan (1935).

Location.—The Dihai-kutchin lived about the north fork of Chandalar River, and the Middle and South Forks of the Koyokuk River, Alaska.

Population.—The Dihai-kutchin were never numerous and are now extinct as a separate body of Indians.

Eskimo.   All of the coast lands of Alaska from Kayak Island near the mouth of Copper River to the Canadian boundary on the Arctic coast were fringed with Eskimo settlements except the upper end of Cook Inlet and that part of Alaska Peninsula which, with the Aleutian Islands, was occupied by the cognate Aleut. (See **Aleut** and Canada.)

Haida.   A part of this tribe settled on Prince of Wales and Dall Islands early in the eighteenth century and are locally known as Kaigani. (See **Haida** under Canada.)   The Kaigani population in 1910 numbered 530; in 1920, 524; and in 1930, 588.

Han.   Signifying "those who dwell along the river."

Connections.—Athapascan linguistic stock.

Location.—The Yukon River drainage between latitude 64° and 66° N., in east central Alaska and Yukon Territory, Canada.

Subdivisions

Katshikotin or Eagle group (about the village of Eagle on Yukon River), including Johnny's Village and probably also Charlie's Village or Tadush (near the mouth of Kandik River), Takon of Nuklako (centering at the confluence of the Klondike and Yukon Rivers), and perhaps a third, Fetutlin (near the mouth of Forty Mile Creek.).

Population.—Mooney (1928) estimates that there were 200 Han in 1740.

Ingalik.   Name given by the Eskimo but widely used as applied to these Indians.

Connections.—The Ingalik were one of the westernmost divisions of the Athapascan linguistic stock.

Location.—Between Anvik and Holy Cross on the lower Yukon River, including the drainage of the Anvik River and the region southeast to the Kuskokwim River, including its drainage above Georgetown.

Subdivisions

Osgood (1934) makes the following subdivisions:
(1) Anvik-Shageluk group, centering around the villages bearing these names.
(2) Bonasila group, centering around the village of the same name.
(3) Holy Cross-Georgetown group, centering around the villages bearing those names.
(4) McGrath group, the people of the drainage of the upper Kuskokwim River; this group somewhat arbitrarily constructed.

Villages Reported in this Area

Akmiut, a litte above Kolmakof on Kuskokwim River.
Anvik, at the junction of Anvik and Yukon Rivers.
Chagvagchat, near the headwaters of Anvik River.
Inselnostlinde, on Shageluk River.
Intenleiden, on the east bank of Shageluk River.
Khugiligichakat, on Shageluk River.
Khunanilinde, near the headwaters of Kuskokwim River.
Koserefski, on the left bank of the Yukon near the mouth of Shageluk Slough, later an Ikogmiut Eskimo village.
Kuingshtetakten, on Shageluk River.
Kvigimpainag, on the east bank of Yukon River, 20 miles from Kvikak.
Napai, on the north bank of Kuskokwim River.
Palshikatno, on Innoko River.
Tigshelde, on Innoko River.
Tlegoshitno, on Shageluk River.
Vagitchitchate, near the mouth of Innoko River.

Population.—(See **Ahtena.**)

Koyukon. A contraction of Koyukukhotana, "people of Koyukuk River."

Connections.—The Koyukon belonged to the Athapascan linguistic stock.

Location.—On the drainage of the Yukon River south of the mouth of the Tanana to about latitude 63° N., including the drainage of the Innoko River north of the latitude named, and of the Koyukuk River in west central Alaska.

Subdivisions

Kaiyuhkhotana, on Yukon River between the Anvik and Koyukuk, including the drainage of Innoko River north of latitude 63° N.
Koyukukhotana, the drainage of the Koyukuk River.
Yukonikhotana, the drainage of Yukon River south of the mouth of the Tanana to the mouth of the Koyukuk.

Villages

(1) Kaiyuhkhotana villages:
Anilukhtakpak, on Innoko River.
Chinik, on the east bank of Yukon River at the junction with the Talbiksok.
Iktigalik, on Unalaklik River.

Innoka, on Tlegon River.

Ivan, on the divide between Unalaklik and Yukon Rivers.

Kagogagat, on the north bank of Yukon River at the mouth of Medicine Creek.

Kaiakak, on the west bank of Yukon River.

Kaltag, on the left bank of Yukon River.

Khogoltlinde, on Yukon River.

Khulikakat, on Yukon River.

Klamaskwaltin, on the north bank of Yukon River near the mouth of Kaiyuh River.

Kunkhogliak, on Yukon River.

Kutul, on Yukon River 50 miles above Anvik.

Lofka, on the west bank of Yukon River.

Nulato, on the north bank of Yukon River about 100 miles from Norton Sound.

Taguta, on the north bank of Yukon River 15 miles below the mouth of the Kaiyuh.

Takaiak, east of Yukon River near Nulato.

Talitui, on Tlegon River.

Tanakot, on the right bank of Yukon River near the mouth of Melozi River.

Terentief, on the Yukon below Koyukuk River.

Tutago, on Yukon River at the mouth of Auto River.

Wolasatux, on the east bank of Yukon River on a small stream north of Kaiyuh River.

(2) Koyukukhotana villages:

Batza, on Batza River.

Bolshoigor, on Yukon River 25 miles above the mouth of Koyukuk River.

Dotle, on Koyukuk River.

Hussliakatna, on the right bank of Koyukuk River, 2 miles above the south end of Dall Island.

Kakliaklia, on Koyukuk River at the mouth of Ssukloseanti River.

Kaltat, on an island in Yukon River not far from its junction with Koyukuk River.

Kanuti, on Koyukuk River in latitude 66°18' N.

Kautas, on Koyukuk River.

Kotil, at the junction of Kateel River with Koyukuk River.

Koyukuk, near the junction of Koyukuk and Yukon Rivers.

Mentokakat, on the left bank of Yukon River 20 miles above the mouth of Melozi River.

Nohulchinta, on the South Fork of Koyukuk River 3 miles above the junction.

Nok, on the west bank of Koyukuk River near its mouth.

Notaloten, on Yukon River 20 miles above the mouth of Koyukuk River.

Oonigachtkhokh, on Koyukuk River.

Soonkakat, on the left bank of the Yukon River below Nulato.

Tashoshgon, on Koyukuk River.

Tlialil, on Koyukuk River.

Tok, on an island at the junction of Koyukuk River with the Yukon.

Zakatlatan, on the north bank of Yukon River, in longitude 156°30' W.

Zogliakten, on the east bank of Koyukuk River.

Zonagogliakten, on the east bank of Koyukuk River.

(3) Yukonikhotana villages:

Chentansitzan, on the north bank of Yukon River 30 miles below the mouth of Melozi River.

Medvednaia, on the south side of Yukon River.

Melozikakat, on Melozikakat River.

Noggai, on Yukon River.

Nowi, on the south side of Yukon River at the mouth of Nowikakat River.

Tohnokalong, on the north bank of Yukon River in longitude 154°25′ W.

Tuklukyet, on the north bank of Yukon River 15 miles below the mouth of Tozi River.

History.—Russian influences began to penetrate the country of the Koyukon after the establishment of the Russian settlement of Kodiak before any settlements had been made on the Kuskokwim or Yukon. In 1838 the most important Russian settlement on the lower Yukon was made at Nulato, and this was the center of one of the very few native uprisings. The post was attacked by neighboring Indians in 1851 and most of the inmates butchered. With American ownership in 1867 the influences of civilization began to increase, and the current was swollen still further by the discovery of gold, though this last was hardly to the advantage of the aborigines. (See **Ahtena.**)

Population.—Mooney (1928) estimated that there were 1,500 Koyukon in the year 1740. In 1890, 940 were returned.

Kutcha-kutchin. Signifying "those who dwell on the flats," called Yukon Flats Kutchin by Osgood (1936). They have also been called as follows, but the Eskimo terms are applicable to any Kutchin:

Fort Indians, Ross (MS).

Ik-kil-lin, Gilder quoted by Murdoch (1892).

Itchali, 11th Census, Alaska, p. 154.

It-ka-lya-rūin, Dall (1877, p. 30); Nuwukmiut Eskimo name.

Itkpe′lit, Petitot (1876, Vocab., p. 42).

Itku′dliñ, Murdoch (1892).

Lowland people, Whymper (1868, p. 247).

Na-Kotchρô-tschig-Kouttchin, Petitot (1891, p. 361).

O-til′-tin, Dawson (1888, p. 202B).

Youkon Louchioux Indians, Ross (MS.).

Connections.—The Kutcha-kutchin were a tribe belonging to the Kutchin division of the northern section of the Athapascan linguistic family.

Location.—Along the valley of the Yukon from the widening of the river a few miles above Circle to about Birch Creek below Fort Yukon.

Villages

One at Fort Yukon and one at Senati, on the middle Yukon.

History.—The history of all the Kutchin tribes had best be treated in one place. They were first brought into contact with Europeans when Alexander Mackenzie met some of them in 1789 during his descent of the river which bears his name. This became more intimate with the establishment of the first Fort Good Hope in 1847. Until Alaska passed into the hands of the United States practically all of the relations which the Kutchin tribes had with Europeans were through the Hudson's Bay Company. Since then influences from the west have been more potent. The discovery of gold in the Klondike region and the rush which followed marked the opening of a new era for these people, but one in which the bad for a long time outweighed the good.

Population.—Mooney (1928) estimated that there were about 500 of these Indians in 1740. The Kutcha-kutchin and the Tranjik-kutchin may be put together as Kutchin in the census of 1910, which enters 359. The Hudson's Bay Co.'s census of 1858 gave 842 Kutchin belonging to six tribes as resorting to Fort Yukon. Osgood (1936), who quotes this, believes that the entire Kutchin population at that date might be set down at 1,200. (See **Ahtena**.)

Connection in which they have become noted.—The Kutchin tribes were noted for their greater energy and more warlike character, as compared with neighboring Athapascans, and for a peculiar three-caste system in their social organization.

Nabesna. From the name of Nabesna River, the meaning of which is unknown.

Connections.—The Nabesna belonged to the Athapascan linguistic family.

Location.—In the entire drainage area of the Nabesna and Chisana Rivers, including the tributaries of the Tanana River, which they form at their confluence, as far down as the Tok River; the upper White River, including its tributaries the Beaver and the Snag, and the headwaters of the Ladue; together an area roughly enclosed between latitude 61°31′ and 63°30′ N., and longitude 141°30′ and 143°30′ W. (Dr. Robert C. McKennan through Osgood, 1936).

Subdivisions

According to McKennan (1935), including the following "extremely fluid bands:"
(1) Ranged about Last Tetling Lake and the Tetling River.
(2) Ranged about the mouth of the Nabesna River.
(3) Ranged from the head of the Nabesna through the upper Chisana River to the White.
(4) Ranged from Scottie Creek to the Snag.

The first of these evidently includes the Nutzotin of earlier writers with their villages of Nandell near Wagner Lake and Tetling, and the third the Santotin. Khiltats, at the mouth of Nabesna River, must have belonged to the second division.

Villages

Allen (1887) mentions the village of Khiltats at the mouth of the Nabesna River.

History.—White contact with these people was made in 1885 and a settlement established at Chisana in 1913.

Niska. This is a tribe of the Chimmesyan linguistic family which lived just beyond the boundaries of Alaska to the southeast and at times hunted over some of its territory. It belonged properly to British Columbia. (See Canada.)

Natsit-kutchin. Signifying "those who dwell off the flats [i. e., Yukon River]." Also called:

> Gens du Large, by Ross (MS), from which came the name of Chandelar River.
> Natche'-Kutchin, by Dall (1877, p. 430).
> Neyetse-kutchi, by Richardson (1851, vol. 1, p. 399).
> Tρe-ttchié-dhidié-Kouttchin, by Petitot (1891).

Connections.—The Natsit-kutchin were one of the tribes of the Kutchin group of the northern division of the Athapascan linguistic stock.

Location.—On Chandelar River.

Population.—Mooney (1928) estimated 200 Natsit-kutchin as of the year 1740. The census of 1910 returned 177. (See **Kutcha-kutchin.**)

Tanaina. Own name, meaning "people" exclusive of Eskimo and Europeans. Also called Knaiakhotana.

Connections.—The Tanaina belonged to the Athapascan linguistic stock.

Location.—According to Osgood (1934): "The drainage of Cook Inlet north of Seldovia (59°20′ N. lat.), the north half of Iliamna Lake and its drainage, including Clark Lake. Since contact, possibly slight incursions have been made into territory formerly occupied by the Eskimo, notably Seldovia Bay and portions of Iliamna Lake."

Subdivisions

Osgood (1936) gives the following:

(1) Lower Inlet (Seldovia and Kachemak Bay).
(2) Middle Inlet (Tustamena, Skilak, and Kenai Lakes and the adjacent coast).
(3) Upper Inlet (Knik arm of Cook Inlet and its drainage).
(4) Susitna (Susitna River and drainage).
(5) Tyonek (west coastal region of Cook Inlet).
(6) Iliamna (region of the north part of Iliamna Lake and its drainage).
(7) Clark Lake (the region about Clark Lake).

Villages

Chinila, on the east side of Cook Inlet near the mouth of Kaknu River.
Chuitna (not given by Osgood), on Cook Inlet at the mouth of Chuit River.
Eklutna, at the head of Knik Arm.
Iliamna, near the mouth of the Iliamna River.
Kasilof, on the east coast of Cook Inlet at the mouth of Kasilof River.
Kasnatchin, at Anchor Point, Kenai Peninsula.
Kenai, on the east side of Cook Inlet at the mouth of Kaknu River.

Kilchik (not noted by Osgood), on Lake Clark.

Knakatnuk, opposite Nitak on the west side of Knik Arm, at the head of Cook Inlet.

Knik, near the mouth of Knik River.

Kultuk, on the east side of Cook Inlet near Nikishka.

Kustatan, on the west side of Cook Inlet below Tyonek.

Nikhkak, on Lake Clark.

Nikishka, near East Foreland at the head of Cook Inlet.

Ninilchik, on the east coast of Cook Inlet south of the mouth of Kasilof River.

Nitak, on the east side of Knik Bay at the head of Cook Inlet and near Eklutna.

Skilak, on the south side of Skilak Lake, Kenai Peninsula.

Skittok, on Kaknu River and forming part of the Kenai settlement.

Susitna, on Susitna River, Cook Inlet.

Titukilsk, on the east shore of Cook Inlet and near Nikishka.

Tyonek, on the west side of Cook Inlet.

Zdluiat, on the east side of Knik Bay south of Nitak.

History.—Cook Inlet received its name from Captain Cook who entered it in May 1778, but all of the natives met by him seem to have been Eskimo. The Russian settlement of Kodiak in 1784 marked an important event for the history of the region because the Russians, assisted by Aleut hunters, at once began to exploit the animal wealth of the neighboring region, and Cook Inlet was a principal scene of their activities. In July 1786, Portlock and Dixon went to the very head of Cook Inlet and must have had dealings with the Tanaina because they met with considerable success in their trading operations. Captain Douglas visited the inlet in 1788. Russian ownership gave place to ownership by the United States in 1867, but Cook Inlet was exploited relatively little until the railroad line was built from Seward to Fairbanks and skirted the head of the inlet for many miles. The Tanaina Indians were one of the last groups in Alaska to receive attention from ethnologists.

Population.—Mooney (1928) estimated that there were about 1,200 Tanaina in 1740. In 1818, 1,471 natives were enumerated in Cook Inlet. In 1825 Baron Wrangell returned 1,299. Veniamínoff (1840) gave 1,628 and in 1860 the Holy Synod returned 937. In 1869 Halleck and Colyer returned the grossly exaggerated estimate of 25,000. The census of 1880 returned 614 and that of 1890, 724. Mooney estimated 890 in 1900. (See **Ahtena.**)

Tanana. Named from the Tanana River.

Connections.—The Tanana belonged to the northern division of the Athapascan linguistic family. They were formerly erroneously classed among the Kutchin tribes.

Location.—"The drainage of the lower Tanana River below the Tok River, the region about the confluence of the Tanana and Yukon, and the region along the latter river above the confluence." [Osgood, 1936.]

Subdivisions and Villages

Clatchotin, on Tanana River.
Huntlatin, on Tanana River.
Minchumina Lake people, around the lake of that name.
Nuklukayet, a rendezvous for various tribes, on the north bank of the Yukon just below the mouth of the Tanana.
Nukluktana, on Tanana River just below Tutlut River.
Tatsa, on Yukon River.
Tolwatin, on Tanana River.
Tozikakat, north bank of the Yukon at the mouth of Tozi River.
Tutlut, at the junction of Tutlut and Tanana Rivers.
Weare, at the mouth of Tanana River.

Population.—Mooney (1928) estimates a possible population of 500 in 1740 including the Nabesna. Richardson (1851) cut this estimate to 100. Dall (1870) made it 500, Petroff (1884), 300–700, Allen (1887) 600, the census of 1890, 373. In 1900, 370 were given and by the census of 1910, 415. (See **Ahtena.**)

Tennuth-kutchin. Meaning "middle people." Also called:

> Birch Creek Kutchin, Osgood (1934, p. 172).
> Birch River Indians, Whymper (1868, p. 255).
> Gens de Bouleaux, Dall (1870 p. 431).

Connections.—The Tennuth-Kutchin were a tribe of the Kutchin group of the northern division of the Athapascan stock.

Location.—In the region of Birch Creek.

Population.—Mooney (1928) estimated that there were about 100 Tennuth-Kutchin in 1740. They have long been extinct having been swept away in 1863, according to Dall (1870), by an epidemic of scarlet fever. (See **Kutcha-kutchin.**)

Tlingit (literally Łĭngi′t). Signifying "people," in their own language. Also called:

> Koluschan, a name given to them as a linguistic family by Powell (1891), originally a Russian or Aleut term referring to the labrets worn by their women.

Connections.—The Tlingit were originally constituted into one linguistic stock by Powell, but show resemblances to the Athapascan dialects and to Haida which have induced Sapir (1915) to class the three together as the Na-déné. The exact nature of the relationship is still disputed.

Location.—All of the coast and islands of Alaska from Yakutat Bay inclusive southward with the exception of the southern ends of Prince of Wales and Dall Islands and Annette Island, though these latter have been alienated from them only in comparatively recent times.

Subdivisions and Villages

Auk, on Stephens Passage and Douglas and Admiralty Islands, including the following villages:

Anchguhlsu, opposite the north end of Douglas Island.

Tsantikihin, on the site of the present Juneau.

Chilkat, about the head of Lynn Canal, including these villages:

Chilkoot, on the northeast arm of Lynn Canal.

Deshu, at the head of Lynn Canal.

Dyea, at the modern place of the same name.

Katkwaahltu, on Chilkat River about 6 miles from its mouth.

Klukwan, on Chilkat River 20 miles from its mouth.

Skagway, at the site of the modern town of that name at the head of Lynn Canal.

Yendestake, at the mouth of Chilkat River.

Gonaho, at the mouth of Alsek River.

Hehl, on Behm Canal.

Henya or Hanega, on the west coast of Prince of Wales Island between Tlevak Narrows and Sumner Strait, including the following villages:

Klawak, on the west coast of Prince of Wales Island.

Shakan, a summer village on the northwest coast of Prince of Wales Island.

Tuxican, on a narrow strait on the northwest coast of Prince of Wales Island.

Huna, on Cross Sound, encamping in summer northward beyond Lituya Bay, with these villages:

Akvetskoe, a summer village on Lituya Bay.

Gaudekan, the chief town, now usually called Huna, in Port Frederick on the north shore of Chichagof Island.

Hukanuwu, on the north side of Cross Sound between the mainland and Chichagof Island.

Klughuggue, given by Petroff (1884) as a town on Chichagof Island but probably identical with one given by Krause (1885) on the opposite mainland, and perhaps the same as Tlushashakian.

Kukanuwu, on the north side of Cross Sound.

Tlushashakian, on the north side of the west entrance to Cross Sound.

Hutsnuwu, on the west and south coasts of Admiralty Island, with these villages:

Angun, north of Hood Bay, Admiralty Island.

Killisnoo, on Killisnoo Island near Admiralty Island.

Nahltushkan, on Whitewater Bay, on the west coast of Admiralty Island.

Kake, on Kupreanof Island, the designation being sometimes extended to cover Kuiu and Sumdum, and including a village of the same name.

Kuiu, on Kuiu Island, with a village of the same name in Port Beauclerc.

Sanya, about Cape Fox, their village being called Gash, at Cape Fox.

Sitka, on the west coasts of Baranof and Chichagof islands, with these villages:

Dahet.

Keshkunuwu.

Kona.

Kushtahekdaan.

Old Sitka, a summer camp on Baranof Island.

Sitka, site of the modern town.

Tlanak.

Tluhashaiyikan, as indicated by the native word straight opposite Mount Edgecombe.

Silver Bay, a summer camp.

Stikine, on Stikine River and the neighboring coasts, with these villages:

Kahltcatlan, a place called also Old Wrangell.

Katchanaak, on the site of modern Wrangell.

Shakes' Village, on Etolin Island.

Sumdum, at Port Houghton, the village and location being the same.

Taku, on Taku River and Inlet, Stevens Channel, and Gastineau Channel, with the following villages:

Sikanasankian, on Taku Inlet.

Takokakaan, at the mouth of Taku River, as the name itself implies.

Tongass, at the mouth of Portland Canal, on the north side, with a village of the same name on Tongass Island, Alexander Archipelago.

Yakutat, principally about Yakutat Bay but extending westward in later times to the mouth of Copper River, including these villages:

Chilkat, a village or group of villages on Controller Bay.

Gutheni, north of Dry Bay.

Hlahayik, on Yakutat Bay behind an island called Hlaha which gave it the name.

Yakutat, on Yakutat Bay.

History.—According to native tradition, some Tlingit families came into their present territories from the coast farther south while others entered from the interior. In 1741 Chirikoff and Bering discovered the Tlingit country, and they were soon followed by other Russian explorers as well as by explorers and traders from México, England, France, and New England. Among the noteworthy events of this period was the visit of La Pérouse to Lituya Bay in 1786 and the tragic loss of two of his boats loaded with men in the tide rips at its entrance. In 1799 the Russians built a fort near the present Sitka. In 1802 the Sitka Indians rose upon this post, killed part of its inmates, and drove the rest away, but 2 years later Baranoff drove them from their fort in turn and established on its site a post which grew into the present Sitka, the capital successively of Russian America and Alaska Territory until 1906. Russian rule was so harsh that there were frequent outbreaks among the natives so long as the territory remained under their control. In 1836 to 1840 occurred a terrible epidemic of smallpox, brought up from the Columbia River, which swept away hundreds of Indians. In 1840 the Hudson's Bay Company took a lease from the Russian American Company of all their lands between Cape Spencer and latitude 54° 40′ N. In 1867 the Tlingit were transferred with the rest of the Alaskan people to the jurisdiction of the United States and since then they have been suffering ever more rapid transformation under the influences of western civilization.

Population.—Mooney (1928) estimated that there were 10,000 Tlingit in 1740. Veniamínoff (1840) gave 5,850 for the year 1835, and an enumeration made by Sir James Douglas 4 years later showed

5,455 exclusive of the Yakutat. In 1861 Lt. Wehrman of the Russian Navy reported 8,597 as the result of a census. Petroff (1884) in the census of 1880 gave 6,763, but the census of 1890 showed only 4,583, not counting the Tlingitized Ugalakmiut. The census of 1910 returned 4,426; that of 1920, 3,895; and that of 1930, 4,462.

Connection in which they have become noted.—The Russian capital and the first American territorial capital Sitka was on Tlingit land, as is the later and present territorial capital Juneau. The ports of this tribe, especially those in the Chilkat country, figured prominently in the great Klondike rush.

Tranjik-kutchin. Signifying "one who dwells along the river [i. e., the Black River]." Also called:

> Black River Kutchin, by Osgood (1936).
> Cache River People, by Cadzow (1925).

Connections.—The Tranjik-kutchin belonged to the Kutchin group of tribes of the northern division of the Athapascan linguistic stock.
Location.—In the country around Black River.
History.—(See **Kutcha-kutchin.**)
Population.—(See **Kutcha-kutchin.**)

Tsimshian. The home of the Tsimshian is on Skeena River, British Columbia, and the coast to the southward. In 1887, however, Rev. William Duncan, missionary of the Church of England at Metlakatla, 15 miles south of Port Simpson, having become involved in difficulties with his superiors, moved to Annette Island, Alaska, with the greater part of the Indians who had been under his charge. A grant of land was subsequently obtained from the United States Government, and the Tsimshian have continued in occupancy. The census of 1910 reported 729; that of 1920, 842; and that of 1930, 845. (See Canada.)

Vunta-kutchin. Signifying "those who dwell among the lakes." Also called:

> Crow River Kutchin, by Osgood (1934, p. 173), from a stream in their country.
> Gens des Rats, by Dall (1877, p. 31).
> Rat People, by Dall (1869, p. 261).
> Zjén-ta-Kouttchin, by Petitot (1891, p. 361), meaning "muskrat people," a name probably based on a legend, though a tributary of the Porcupine is called Rat River.

Connections.—The Vunta-kutchin are one of the group of Kutchin tribes belonging to the northern division of the Athapascan linguistic family.
Location.—On the middle course of Porcupine River and the country to the northward, including Old Crow Creek.

Population.—Mooney (1928) estimated that the Vunta-Kutchin together with the Tukkuth-kutchin, and "Tutcone-kutchin" comprised a population of 2,200 in 1670, but they had been reduced to 1,700 in 1906 and the census of 1910 returned only 5 under this name by itself. (See **Kutcha-kutchin.**)

CANADA

Algonkin. Significance uncertain, but Hewitt (Hodge, 1907) suggests Micmac algoomeaking or algoomaking, "at the place of spearing fish or eels [from the bow of a canoe]." It was applied originally to one band, the Weskarini.

Connections.—The Algonkin were the easternmost division of the Chippewa group of the Algonquian linguistic stock.

Location.—On Ottawa River but particularly its northern tributaries.

Subdivisions

Abitibi, about Lake Abitibi.

Barrière, about Barrière and Kakabong Lakes.

Dumoine, on Dumoine River and Lake, Ontario.

Kichesipirini, on Allumette Island in Ottawa River and hence often called Algonkins of the Island.

Kipawa, on Kipawa River, Maganasibi River, and the north bank of Ottawa River opposite Mattawa.

Lac des Quinze, Lac des Quinze and to the north and east.

Maniwaki or River Desert, from the upper course of the Rivière Lièvre to Black River.

Ononchataronon, between St. Lawrence and Ottawa Rivers and near Montreal.

Sagaiguninini, southwest of Ottawa River in 1640, perhaps not of this group, as nearly all the other bands are on or northeast of the Ottawa River.

Timiskaming, on and near Lake Timiskaming.

Weskarini, on the north side of Ottawa River below Allumette Island and on Gatineau River.

Villages

Egan, Maniwaki township, Ottawa County, Quebec.

Hartwell, in Ottawa County, Quebec.

Isle aux Tourtes, mission, for Algonkin and Nipissing, probably on Ottawa River but soon removed to Oka.

History.—The Algonkin were encountered by the French when that nation first settled Canada and became firmly attached to them. In the war between the French and Iroquois many bands were driven out of their country, some uniting with the Ottawa, while others fled to the north and east and drifted back into their old territories on the cessation of hostilities. They have since continued in the same region though suffering steady modification in culture and manner of life from contact with Europeans.

Population.—Mooney (1928) estimated that in 1600 there were 6,000 in the Algonkin and Ottawa bands combined. In 1884, 3,874 were returned from Quebec Province and eastern Ontario. The total population of the bands recognized as Algonkin in 1900, but including a few Iroquois, was 1,536.

Connection in which they have become noted.—The principal claim of these people to notoriety rests on the fact that they, or rather one of their bands, first bore the name Algonkin from which the name of the great Algonquian linguistic stock was derived, as well as a multitude of names of places and terms of various sorts.

Arapaho. This tribe probably occupied Canadian territory in prehistoric times in southern Saskatchewan and perhaps in southern Manitoba. (See Wyoming.)

Assiniboin. A tribe of the Siouan linguistic family which separated from the Dakota in the late prehistoric period, living first, it is thought, about Rainy Lake and Lake of the Woods but, from about 1675, on Assiniboin and Saskatchewan Rivers west of Lake Winnipeg. Their lands extended southward to the Missouri and a part of the tribe were finally placed on reservations in Montana. (See Montana.)

Atsina. These were a branch of the Arapaho and were popularly known as Gros Ventres, or, in order to distinguish them from another tribe so called, Gros Ventres of the Plains. They were sometimes known as Fall Indians from the circumstance that they were supposed formerly to have lived at the falls of the Saskatchewan River, near the junction of its north and south branches. (See Montana.)

Bellabella. An Indian corruption of the word Milbank taken back into English. Also called:

Elk·ba′sumн, Bellacoola name.
Hē′iltsuq, own name.
Milbank Sound Indians, popular name.

Connections.—Dialectically the Bellabella were closely related to the Kwakiutl south of them and more remotely to the Nootka of the west coast of Vancouver Island and Cape Flattery, Washington, the whole constituting the Wakashan linguistic family.

Location.—The coast of British Columbia from Rivers Inlet to Douglas Channel inclusive.

Subdivisions

Haisla Dialect:
Kitamat, on Douglas Channel.
Kitlope, on Gardiner Canal.

Heiltsuk Dialect:

Bellabella proper, embracing the Kokaitk on the north shore of Milbank Sound, Oealitk on the south shore of Milbank Sound, and the Oetlitk on the middle section of Milbank Sound.

China Hat, on Tolmie Channel and Mussel Inlet.

Nohuntsitk, at the lower end of Wikeno Lake.

Somehulitk, at the north end of Wikeno Lake.

Wikeno, on Rivers Inlet.

Villages

The Wilkeno had the following, all with one possible exception, on Rivers nlet: Niltala, Nuhitsomk, Somhotnechau, Tlaik, Tsiomhau, Wikeno.

History.—Bodega and Maurelle passed along the coast occupied by the Bellabella in 1775, and they were immediately afterward visited by English and American explorers and traders. The Hudson's Bay post of Fort McLoughlin was established in their territory in 1833, but the foundation of Victoria in 1843 probably had greater influence on the lives of these people. The traders were soon followed by missionaries and permanent white settlers.

Population.—Mooney (1928) estimated that in 1780 there were 2,700 Indians of the Bellabella group. In 1906 there were 852.

Connection in which they have become noted.—These people are interesting as exhibiting an apparent replacement of a patrilineal system of descent by a matrilineal system.

Bellacoola. A name applied by the Kwakiutl; significance unknown. Phonetic form of name Bī′lxula. Also called:

Tallion Nation, from the name of a town, in early reports of the Canadian Indian Office.

Connections.—They are an isolated body of Indians belonging to the Salishan linguistic family.

Location.—On North Bentinck Arm, South Bentinck Arm, Dean Channel and River, and Bella Coola River, B. C.

Subdivisions

At the present time there are but two bodies of Bellacoola: The Kimsquit, on Dean Inlet; and the Bella Coola, at the mouth of Bella Coola River. Older writers speak of the Nuhalk, which was the name of Bella Coola Valley; Taliomk, at the head of South Bentinck Arm, abandoned about 20 years ago; and the Noothlakamish, reported by Tolmie and Dawson (1884) on North Bentinck Arm.

Villages

(as given by McIlwraith)

Aimats, north of Anutskwakstl near the Peisela River.

Aketi, on the south side of Dean River about 1 mile from the sea.

Anutlitlk, near the mouth of Dean River, still occupied.

Anutskwakstl, an eastern extension of Tlokotl.

Aseik, on a stream flowing into a bay at the southwest end of South Bentinck Arm.

Asenane, on the shore of a bay on the south side of Bella Coola River.

Asktlta, at Salmon House on Upper Dean River.

Atlklaktl, near the south bank of Peisela River about ¼-mile from the sea.

Ikwink, on Dean River 28 miles from the sea.

Kadis, on the east side of South Bentinck Arm, about ¼-mile from Nuik River.

Kameik, on the west bank of Necleetsconnay about ¾-mile from the sea.

Kankilst, on the east side of South Bentinck Arm "slightly north of the island opposite the hot springs on the west side of the fiord."

Koapk, on the east side of the mouth of a creek entering the head of South Bentinck Arm from the south.

Komkutis, the upper (eastern) continuation of Stskeitl.

Kwiliutl, on the north side of the Atnarko a few hundred yards above the forks.

Nuekmak, near some stagnant pools on the north side of Bella Coola River a short distance above Snoönikwilk.

Nuhwilst, on the shore of Dean Channel six miles from Satsk.

Nuiku, on a raised mound on South Bentinck Arm south of the mouth of Nuik River.

Nukaakmats, on the north shore of Bella Coola River about a mile above Tsilkt.

Nukits, on the south side of Bella Coola River 11¼ miles from the sea.

Nuskapts, on the south bank of Dean River about 25 miles from the sea.

Nuskek, on the shore of North Bentinck east of the creek that flows into it at Green Bay.

Nuskelst, on the north side of Bella Coola River opposite the mountain of the same name.

Nutal, on the bank of Dean River at the bottom of the canyon.

Nutltleik, 200 yards from Bella Coola River on a creek flowing in from the north and about 31 miles from the sea.

Nutskwatlt, on the south side of Dean River about 1¼-miles from the sea.

Okmikimik, at the present village of Hagensburg 11 miles from the sea.

Ososkpimk, on the north shore of Bella Coola River about ½-mile above Aimats.

Satsk, at the mouth of the Kimsquit River.

Senktl, on the south side of Bella Coola River opposite Tciktciktelpats.

Setlia, on the east side of South Bentinck Arm about ¼-mile from its junction with North Bentinck.

Siwalos, on the north side of Dean River about 35 miles from the sea, where the trail to the interior left the river valley.

Skomeltl, on the south side of Bella Coola River about 3 miles from the sea.

Snoönikwilk, on a curving promontory on the south bank of Bella Coola River about 4 miles from the sea.

Snutele, on the south bank of Bella Coola River above Nukaakmats.

Snutlelelatl, on the north side of the Atnarko about 10 miles from the forks.

Stskeitl, on the south bank of Bella Coola River about ¼-mile from the sea.

Stuik, on the point between the Atnarko and Whitewater Rivers, which join to form the Bella Coola.

Talio, on the west side of the mouth of the river, last location, which was frequently changed.

Tasaltlimk, on the shore of North Bentinck Arm west and north of the mouth of the Necleetsconnay.

Tciktciktelpats, some distance from the north bank of the Bella Coola River, the river course having changed.

Tlokotl, above Atlklaktl on Peisela River.

Tsaotltmem, on the east side of South Bentinck Arm about 4 miles from Kankilst.
Tsilkt, on the north shore of Bella Coola River above Tsomootl.
Tsomootl, the upper continuation of Skomeltl.

Boas (1898) gives also the following names, most of which are probably synonyms for some of the above: Koatlna, Nusatsem, Osmakmiketlp, Peisela, Sakta, Selkuta, Slaaktl, Sotstl, Tkeiktskune, Tskoakkane.

History.—Alexander Mackenzie entered the country of the Bellacoola after crossing the Rocky Mountains in 1793 at about the same time that they began to have dealings with vessels of European explorers and traders. The rest of their history has been the usual one of modification in customs, missionization, supervision by Indian Office officials, and at least temporary decline.

Population.—Mooney (1928) estimates that there were 1,400 Bellacoola in 1780; in 1902 only 311 were returned.

Connection in which they have become noted.—The Bellacoola are noted particularly for their isolated position, a Salishan island among Kwakiutl Indians, for their peculiar cosmologic system recorded by Boas (1897), and as having given their name to Bella Coola River.

Beothuk. Probably from a native word signifying "man," or "human being." Also called:

Macquaejeet or Ulnŏ mequäegit, Micmac name, signifying "red man," and evidently a translation of the popular English name.
Ulnŏbah, Abnaki name.

Connections.—While certain Algonquian elements are to be found in the remnants of the Beothuk language which have been preserved, the greater part of it is so different that these Indians have been placed in an independent linguistic stock, the Beothukan.

Location.—When first brought to the knowledge of Europeans, the Beothuk seem to have occupied all of the island of Newfoundland except possibly the northernmost extremity.

History.—The Beothuk were probably first met by Europeans under John Cabot in 1497, and from that time forward were frequently visited by explorers and fishermen. Differences having arisen between them and the French, they were gradually reduced in numbers, and the Micmac, who had settled meanwhile in the southern part of the island, drove them north until they were confined to some territory near Exploits River. In 1810 Sir Thomas Duckworth issued a proclamation for their protection, but in 1827 when Carmack's expedition, conducted on behalf of the Beothuk Institution for the civilization of the native savages, made a careful search for them, not one was encountered. The last of them may have crossed the Strait of Belle Isle to unite with the Algonquian Indians of Labrador. (See Hodge, 1907, article on Beothukan family.)

Population.—Mooney (1928) estimates the total Beothuk population in 1600 to have been 500.

Connections in which they have become noted.—The Beothuk were noted for their great use of red ocher, from which came the name usually bestowed upon them by Europeans; for their linguistic distinctiveness; and for the mystery surrounding their connections with other tribes and their ultimate fate.

Carriers. The name was derived from a native custom whereby a widow was obliged to carry about with her in a basket for 3 years the ashes of her deceased husband.   Also called:

> Atlăshimih, Bellacoola name.
> Takulli, by several Athapascan tribes, and said to mean "people who go upon the water."

Connections.—The Carriers spoke an Athapascan dialect.

Location.—Around Eutsuk, Francis, Babine, and Stuart Lakes and the headwaters of the Fraser River as far south as the neighborhood of Quesnel.

Subdivisions

The lists collected by different investigators vary to some extent.   The following names are adapted from Morice (1906):

Southern Carriers:

> Tautin, on Fraser River about old Fort Alexander.
> Naskotin, in Chentsithala and Nesietsha villages, on Fraser River near the mouth of Blackwater.
> Tanotenne, at the junction of Stuart and Nechako Rivers.
> Ntshaautin, on Blackwater River and upper Nechaco River.
> Natliatin, inhabiting Natleh and Stella, at either end of Fraser Lake.

Northern Carriers:

> Nikozliautin, on the southern half of Stuart Lake and on Pintce River, in two villages, Nakraztli at the outlet of Stuart Lake, and Pintce on Stuart Lake at the mouth of Pintce River.
> Tatshiautin, at the head of Stuart Lake and on Tachi River and Thatlah, Tremblay, and Connolly Lakes, in the following villages: Kezche on Taché River, Sasthut on Connolly Lake, Tachy at the mouth of Taché River, Tsisli at the mouth of Tatlah River, Tsisthainli on Lac Trembleur, Yucuche at the head of Stuart Lake and on the portage between it and Sabine Lake, and probably Saikez south of Nechaco River.

Babines:

> Nataotin, on middle Babine River and Babine lake, in two towns: Lathakrezla (on the north side of Babine Lake) and Neskollek (on Babine Lake).
> Hwotsotenne, on Bulkley River, hunting as far as Francis Lake, and occupying the following villages:
>> Hagwilget, on Bulkley River 3 miles southeast of Hazleton.
>> Hwotat, on the east side of Babine Lake near its outlet.
>> Keyerhwotket, on Bulkley River.
>> Lachalsap, on Bulkley River.
>> Tsechah, on Bulkley River.
>> Tselkazkwo, on Bulkley River.

Dawson (1880 b) makes the people of Kezche distinct from the Tatshiautin under the name of Kustsheotin, the people of Tachy distinct from the rest of the Tatshiautin under the name Tatshikotin, and the people of Stella distinct from the other Natliatin under the name Stelatin.

History.—The Carriers were visited in 1793 by Alexander Mackenzie when on his way from Athabaska Lake to the Pacific Ocean. When Fort McLeod was built in the Sekani country by Simon Fraser in 1805, it served for a time as a trading point for the Carriers, but in 1806 Fort St. James was established in their own country, near the outlet of Stuart Lake. Missionary work was begun among them in 1843 by the Roman Catholic priest, Father Demers, and proved very successful. After that time white traders, miners, and settlers came in increasing numbers, and finally the country was penetrated by the Canadian transcontinental railroad to Prince Rupert.

Population.—Mooney (1928) estimates that the Carrier tribe numbered 5,000 in 1780. It was given as 2,625 in 1839. Morice (1889) gave an estimate of 1,600, while the Canadian Office of Indian Affairs reported 1,551 in 1902 and 1,614 in 1909.

Connection in which they have become noted.—The Carriers attracted attention at an early period on account of the peculiar custom to which they owe their name. Later they were particularly commended to the attention of ethnologists as furnishing an excellent illustration of the manner in which cultures spread on account of the mixture of coastal and interior features, and for the very thorough studies of them made by Rev. A. G. Morice.

Chilcotin. More phonetically rendered Tsilkotin, meaning "people of young man's [Chilcotin] river."

Connections.—The Chilcotin belong to the Athapascan linguistic stock.

Location.—Chiefly in the valley of Chilcotin River.

Subdivisions

In later years a distinction has grown up between the reservation Chilcotin and those who have continued their aboriginal customs at a distance from the reservations, the latter being called the "Stone Chilcotin" or "Stonies." The former Morice (1889) divides into the Tlathenkotin (in Ilothenka village on Chilcotin River), Tleskotin (in the village of Tlesko on Chilcotin River near its junction with Fraser River), and Toosey (near Williams Lake Agency).

History.—Alexander Mackenzie (1801) passed through their territory in 1793, and Fort Chilcotin was established among them in 1829. To employees of the Hudson's Bay Company soon succeeded miners and more permanent settlers.

Population.—Mooney (1928) estimates that in 1780 there were 2,500 Chilcotin. In 1906 they were placed at 450.

Connection in which they have become noted.—The name of the Chilcotin is perpetuated by Chilcotin River, Chilko River, and Chilko Lake.

Chippewa or Ojibwa. Bands of this immense tribe extended from Lake Nipissing westward along the north shore of Lake Superior, and in later times they settled in southern Manitoba, in the northern part of the present States of Minnesota and North Dakota and along the southern shore of Lake Superior. The Saulte Ste. Marie was considered by them their ancient center of dispersion. Northward they reached the upper course of Albany River. (See Minnesota.)

Chipewyan. From a Cree word meaning "pointed skins," referring to the pointed parkas or shirts which they wore. Also called:

> Montagnais, French name.
> Mountaineers, English name.
> Yatcheé-thinyoowuc, Cree name, meaning "strangers."

Connections.—The Chipewyan formed a dialectic division of the Athapascan linguistic stock.

Location.—The boundaries of this group of Indians have changed considerably but in general their territory lay north of Churchill River, between Great Slave Lake and Slave and Áthabaska Rivers on the west and Hudson Bay on the east.

Subdivisions

The principal subdivisions seem to have been as follows:

Athabaska, between Lake Athabaska and Great Slave Lake and in the territory eastward.

Desnedekenade, along Slave River, near Fort Resolution.

Etheneldeli or Caribou-Eaters, mainly about Lakes Caribou, Axe, and Brochet.

Thilanottine, in later times on the shores of Lacrosse Lake and between Cold Lake and Fort Locha.

The Tatsanottine or Yellow Knives, sometimes considered a subdivision, Jenness (1932) believes to have been independent. It is doubtful whether the distinction represented by these divisions was more than temporary. (See the section on History.)

History.—Petitot (1876 a) states that the Chipewyan tribe was living on Peace River in 1718, that after the Cree had obtained guns they drove the Etchaottine or Slaves from their hunting grounds along Slave River, but that they were attacked in turn by the Chipewyan and expelled from the country, the Chipewyan taking their places. Jenness wholly discredits this tradition, however, and gives the following summary of events bearing on the relative position of Chipewyan and Cree tribes during this period: He thinks that when the fur-trading posts were established on Hudson Bay the

Chipewyan already occupied the country from the Great Slave Lake and Lake Athabaska eastward—

. . . but that the intense fusion resulting from the fur trade obliterated the old subdivisions into tribes or bands and broke down also dialectic differences.   Then the Cree pushed northward and seized the country between Lake Athabaska and Great Slave Lake [the Slave River], driving the Beaver up the Peace River [the Beaver and Cree together driving the Sekani into the Rockies] and confining the Chipewyan or Northern Indians to the territory designated by Hearne.   Then came the smallpox epidemic that decimated both Cree and Chipewyan, but particularly the Cree, who were forced to withdraw a little from Chipewyan territory, allowing the latter to reoccupy Lake Athabaska, the Slave River, and the southern and eastern shores of Great Slave Lake, though a few Cree still lingered on Lake Athabaska and on the Slave River.   This was the condition in Mackenzie's day, who defines the territory of the Chipewyans as extending from 100°–110° W. by 60°–65° N., although his unpublished MS. and that of Roderic Mackenzie make them the principal inhabitants of Lake Athabaska, especially its eastern end.   The establishment of posts on Lake Athabaska broke the Chipewyans up into two groups, an eastern that still traded at the posts on Hudson Bay, and a western that traded at Lake Athabaska.   Subsequently the Cree recovered a little and penetrated this western country in greater numbers, so that today there are practically no Chipewyans near the Mackenzie River except at Fond du Lac, at the east end of Lake Athabaska, and at Fort Resolution and around the south shores of Great Silver Lake.   Slave River is occupied by Cree, as is also Fort Chipewyan; and the Cree dwell all along the Peace River up to Peace River Landing, and have a large colony at Hudson Hope. [Jenness.]

The Athabaska division consisted simply of those Chipewyan who chose to trade at Lake Athabaska.   The Athabaska or "Athapuskow" Indians of Hearne (1795) were Cree.

Population.—Alexander Mackenzie (1801) estimated that there were about 400 Athabaska Chipewyan, and Mooney (1928) that there were 3,500 Chipewyan in all, including 1,250 Caribou-eaters, in 1670. In 1906 there were 2,420, of whom 900 were Caribou-eaters.

Connection in which they have become noted.—From one of their Chipewyan bands, the Athabaska, has come the term Athapascan selected by Powell (1891) for the designation of the linguistic stock to which the Chipewyan belong, although, curiously enough. the name does not appear to be Athapascan at all.

Comox.   Significance unknown; so called by the Lekwiltok.   Also called:

Catlō'ltx, own name.

Connections.—The Comox constituted a dialetic group of the coastal division of the Salishan linguistic family.

Location.—On the east coast of Vancouver Island including both sides of Discovery Passage, between the Puntlatch and Kwakiutl.

Subdivisions

Clahoose, on Toba Inlet.
Comox, on both sides of Discovery Passage between Chancellor Channel and Cape Mudge.
Eëksen, about Oyster Bay.
Homalko, on the east side of Bute Inlet.
Kaäke, on the southeast coast of Valdes Island.
Kakekt, at Cape Lazo.
Sliammon, on Malaspina Inlet.
Tatpoös, on the eastern part of Valdes Island.

History.—The Comox were visited by Europeans somewhat later than the Cowichan (q. v.), otherwise their history has been the same.

Population.—Mooney (1928) estimated that in 1780 there were 400 Comox on Vancouver Island and 1,400 on the mainland. In 1906 he gives 59 and 265 respectively.

Connection in which they have become noted.—An important port on Vancouver Island is named after the Comox.

Cowichan. Significance unknown.

Connections.—The Cowichan were one of the principal dialectic groups of the coastal division of the Salishan linguistic stock. They were closely connected with the Salishan Indians, who occupied the valley of Fraser River from its mouth nearly to Spuzzum. (See **Stalo.**)

Location.—On the southeast coast of Vancouver Island between Nanoos Bay and Saanich Inlet.

Subdivisions

Clemclemalats, in Cowichan Valley.
Comiakin, in Cowichan Valley.
Hellelt, on Chimenes River.
Kenipsim, in Cowichan Valley.
Kilpanlus, in Cowichan Valley.
Koksilah, in Cowichan Valley.
Kulleets, on Chimenes Bay.
Lilmalche, on Thetis Island.
Malakut, on Saanich Inlet.
Penelakut, on Kuper and Galiano Islands.
Quamichan, in Cowichan Valley.
Siccameen, on Oyster Bay.
Somenos, in Cowichan Valley.
Tateke, on Valdes Island, southeast of Vancouver Island and north of Galiano Island.
Yekolaos, on Thetis Island.

History.—These people (the Cowichan) may have been visited by Juan de Fuca in 1592 and were certainly met by several later expeditions to the northwest coast by Spaniards, English, and Americans. Early in the nineteenth century Hudson's Bay Company traders began to come into the country, and, most important for the history of the native people, was the founding of Victoria in 1843. The rush of miners came a few years later and the subsequent history of the Cowichan has been that of most tribes subjected to continuous contact with Europeans, though they have never been driven entirely out of their ancient territories.

Population.—Mooney's (1928) estimate of the Vancouver Island Cowichan for the year 1780 is 5,500 as against a population of 1,298 in 1907.

Connection in which they have become noted.—The name of the Cowichan has been given to a lake, river and valley on Vancouver Island.

Cree. Contracted from Kristinaux, the French form of Kenistenoag, given as a name they applied to themselves. Also called:

> Ana, Annah, Ennas, Eta, various forms of an Athapascan word, meaning "foes."
>
> Iyiniwok, or Nehiyawok, own name, meaning "those of the first race."
> Nathehwy-within-yoowuc, meaning "southern men" (Franklin, 1823).
> Nehiyaw, Chippewa name.
> O'pimmitish Ininiwuc, meaning "men of the woods."
> Shahĕ', Hidatsa name.
> Saie'kuŭn, Siksika name.
> Sha-i-yé, or Shi-é-ya, Assiniboin name, meaning "enemies."
> Shi-e-á-la, Dakota name.
> Southern Indians, by the Hudson Bay traders.

Connections.—The Cree are one of the type people of one of the two greatest divisions of the Algonquian linguistic family.

Location.—When the Cree first came to the knowledge of Europeans they extended from James Bay to the Saskatchewan, the Tête de Boule of the upper Ottawa forming a detached branch. For their later extensions see History below.

Subdivisions

A major distinction is usually drawn between the Paskwawininiwug (Plains Cree) and Sakawininiwug (Woodland Cree). The former are subdivided into the Sipiwininiwug (River Cree) and Mamikininiwug (Lowland Cree). Hayden (1862) gives the following band names, nearly all said to have been derived from the name of a chief: Apistekaihe, Cokah, Kiaskusis, Mataitaikeok, Muskwoikakenut, Muskwoikauepawit, Peisiekan, Piskakauakis, Shemaukau, Wikyuwamkamu-senaikata. These are probably identical in part with the following bands of Plains Cree given by Skinner (1914): Katepoisipi-wiinuŭk (Calling River (Qu'Appelle) Band) also called Kagiciwuinuwuk (Loud Voices Band, from their famous chief), Wabuswaianŭk (Rabbit Skins), Mämäkitce-wiinuŭk (Big Gizzard People), Paskokopa-wiinuŭk (Willow People), Nutimi-iniuŭk (Poplar People), Cipi-winiuŭk (River People), Saka-winouŭk (Bush People), Masnipiwiniuŭk (Painted or Pictured People), "Little Dogs," (Piapot's Band), Asinskau-winiuŭk (Stone People), Tcipoaian-winiuŭk (Chipewyan People), Niopwätŭk (Cree-Assiniboine), Sakbwatsŭk (Bush Assiniboine). Skinner (1914) expresses uncertainty as to whether the names of the last three were nicknames due to intimacy between the bands so designated and the foreign tribes mentioned, or whether the tribes themselves were of mixed ancestry. For the following names of bands of the

Woodland Cree I am indebted to Dr. John M. Cooper (personal information): Barren Ground Cree (on the west side of James Bay at its entrance), Fort Albany Band (on the lower course of Albany River), Kesagami Lake Band (at the southern end of James Bay), Moose Factory Band (the Monsoni proper), on the lower course of Moose River, Northern Tête de Boule (at the head of St. Maurice River), Southern Tête de Boule (on the middle course of St. Maurice River). This list is incomplete, leaving out of consideration particularly the bands later formed toward the west, though two of these latter were the Sakittawawininiwug (Cree of Cross Lake) and the Ayabaskawininiwug (Athabaska Lake Cree). It must not be supposed that any of these have had a connected history from early times. They represent, for the most part, the later rearrangement following on the establishment of trading posts. However, the location of some of them was no doubt determined in the first instance by that of the old bands or by the same geographic advantages originally responsible for them. (See section on History.)

History.—The Cree were known to French traders and missionaries as early as the first half of the seventeenth century, and about the end of that century they rose to a position of importance owing to the use made of them as guides and hunters in the prosecution of the fur trade. The English first came in contact with them through the posts of the Hudson's Bay Company established in their territory on Hudson Bay beginning in 1667 and for a time there was great rivalry between the French and English for their favor and patronage. At an early period the Cree formed an alliance with the Assiniboin, who wished to be on good terms with them so that they could have access to the Hudson Bay posts where they could obtain guns and powder to assist them in their wars with their kindred, the Dakota. This alliance also enabled the Cree to push southward as far as Red River and territories of the present United States. Acquisition of rifles and the impetus given by the fur trade also induced them to undertake adventurous journeys to the west and north. A party of Cree reached the delta of the Mackenzie River just before Sir Alexander Mackenzie, and other Cree bands were raiding the Sekani up the Peace River into the Rocky Mountains at the same time. Today there are many of the Cree descendants in the north and west, around Little Slave Lake, at Hudson Hope on Peace River, along the Lower Peace, and on Lake Athabaska and Slave River down to Great Slave Lake. The trails they blazed in their raids were followed by Mackenzie and other fur-traders. There is a little band among the Sarsi, and they have mingled their blood with every Plains tribe, even including the Blackfeet.[1]

Their later history has been closely bound up with the activities of the Hudson's Bay and Northwest Fur Companies, and though Europeans and European influence have steadily filtered into their country,

---

[1] For much of this information I am indebted to Mr. D. Jenness, formerly Chief of the Anthropological Division of the National Museum of Canada, Ottawa, Canada.

the utility of the Cree in the promotion and preservation of the fur trade has prevented that displacement and depletion so common among the tribes of the United States.

Population.—Mooney (1928) estimated 20,000 Cree at the period of first white contact, including 5,000 Monsoni and related peoples in 1600 and 15,000 Cree proper and Maskegon in 1670. This agrees very closely with another estimate for the year 1776. At the present day they are supposed to number all told about 10,000.

Connection in which they have become noted.—The principal claim of the Cree to notoriety has been in connection with the activities of the Hudson's Bay Company and the fur trade.

Crow. A tribe of the Siouan linguistic family which may have lived on the north side of the International Boundary in late prehistoric times in the region indicated on the map, though this is uncertain. (See Montana.)

Dakota. A well-known tribe of the same family as the Crow. As already noted, the Assiniboin branched from them in prehistoric times, but some bands of Dakota, notably that of Sitting Bull, resorted to Canadian territory at a later period. (See South Dakota.)

Eskimo. Said to be from Abnaki Algonquian Esquimantsic, or possibly from its Chippewa equivalent Ashkimeq, signifying "eaters of raw flesh." This may be described as the traditional interpretation, but Dr. Thalbitzer, an eminent authority on the Eskimo, believes it to have been derived from a term applied to them by the French missionaries, signifying "the excommunicated ones" (Thalbitzer, 1950), from which he also derives the place name Escoumains. Also called:

> A'lvayê'lɪlɪt, Chukchi name, meaning "those of alien language."
> Anda-kρoen, Kutchin name.
> Ara-k'e, Bastard Loucheux (Kutchin) name.
> En-na-k'e, Kawchodinne name, meaning "enemies."
> En-na-k'ié, Slave name, meaning "enemies."
> Eshkibod, Chippewa form given by Baraga.
> Hŭsky, by Hudson's Bay Company employees.
> Innuit, Innuin, etc., own name, meaning "people."
> Kaladlit, name adopted for themselves by Greenland Eskimo, said to be a corruption of Skandinavian Skraeling.
> Nottaway, term used by most Algonquian people for all enemies, meaning "snakes."
> Ot'el'nna, Montagnais name.
> Seymôs, term used by sailors of the Hudson's Bay Company's ships, and derived from a native term of greeting, said to be Seymo or Teymo.
> Skraellingar, Scandinavian name, meaning "small people."
> Ta-kutchi, Kutchin name, meaning "ocean people."
> Tciĕᶜk-rúnĕⁿ, Seneca name, meaning "seal people."
> Ultsēhaga, Kenai name, meaning "slaves."

Connections.—The Eskimo constituted one linguistic stock, the dialects of which were in general very close together, but the Aleut (q. v.) of Alaska formed a somewhat divergent group. Chiefly on physical grounds they are usually set apart from all other aborigines of America.

Location.—The Eskimo are known to have extended anciently from Mingan opposite Anticosti Island, in the Gulf of St. Lawrence, around the entire northeastern and northern coasts of Canada to the Alaskan boundary except for the southwest coast of Hudson Bay, and to have occupied Baffin Land and many of the other Islands of the Arctic Archipelago, both sides of Smith Sound, and the entire west coast and most of the east coast of Greenland. In later times they retired from northeastern Greenland, from the north coast of the Gulf of St. Lawrence, and from part of the west coast of Hudson Bay. Their occupancy of the Mingan section of Labrador appears to have been brief. They fringed the coast of Alaska almost completely to Copper River and in part a little beyond, and had settled along the north coast of Siberia. (See also Alaska.)

Subdivisions

The Eskimo were subdivided into a very large number of local groups always changing, and any list of these is highly conventional. The following is believed to include the most important names and is based upon the best authorities available. The enumeration is from east to west, except for Greenland, omitting of course those territories occupied in early historic times and now abandoned.

I. Labrador Eskimo:
   Aivitumiut, about Rigolet.
   Avitumiut, about Hopedale.
   Chuckbuckmiut, in Saglek Bay.
   Itivimiut, on the east coast of Hudson Bay.
   Ḱanithlualukshuamiut, on George River.
   Kigiktagmiut, on the Belcher Islands and other islands off the east shore of
       Hudson Bay.
   Killinunmiut, at Cape Chidley.
   Koksoakmiut, between Whale and Payne Rivers, especially on Koksoak River.
   Konithlushuamiut, Okkak.
   Netcetumiut, about Cartwright, in Sandwich Bay.
   Nunenumiut, about Nain.
   Nuvugmiut, at Cape Wolstenholme.
   Puthlavamiut, in Battle Harbor, Labrador.
   Unavamiut, at Hopes Advance.
II. Central Eskimo:
   Aivillirmiut, in Wager Inlet and along the coast from Cape Fullerton to Cape
       Penrhyn.
   Akudnirmiut, from Home Bay to Scott Inlet.
   Akuliarmiut, from Icy Cape to beyond Amadjuak Bay.
   Akulliakatagmiut, on the south shore of Dolphin and Union Straits.
   Arveqtormiut, in Bellot Strait.
   Arviligyuarmiut, from Committee Bay nearly to Rae Strait.

Asiagmiut, opposite Melbourne Island.
Ekaluktogmiut, from Dease Strait to Denmark Bay.
Haneragmiut, on the north shore of Dolphin and Union Straits west of the last.
Haningayormiut, on the upper course of Backs River.
Harvaqtormiut, on Mistake Bay.
Hauheqtormiut, from Pistol Bay to Rankin Inlet.
Iglulirmiut, on Fury and Hecla Straits.
Iluilermiut, on Adelaide Peninsula and King William Island.
Kanghiryuachiakmiut, in Minto Inlet.
Kanghiryuarmiut, on the south coast of Banks Island and Prince Albert Sound.
Kiglinirmiut, on the eastern end of Victoria Island.
Kilusiktomiut, on Bathurst Inlet, on the mainland.
Kingnaitmiut, over most of the northern shore of Cumberland Sound.
Kogloktogmiut, on the lower course of Coppermine River.
Nagyuktogmiut, on the north shore of Coronation Gulf.
Nedlungmiut, between Jones' Sound and Norwegian Bay, Ellesmere Land.
Nenitagmiut, on Arctic Sound.
Netsilingmiut, on Boothia Peninsula.
Noahonirmiut, at Cape Krusenstern.
Nugumiut, in Frobisher Bay.
Padlimiut, two groups: (1) from Cape Dier to Home Bay; (2) from Cape
    Esquimaux to Ferguson River on the west coast of Hudson Bay.
Pilingmiut, at the end of Fox Channel(?).
Pingangnaktogmiut, on the south shore of Coronation Gulf.
Puivlirmiut, on the north shore of Dolphin and Union Strait west of Lady
    Franklin Point.
Qaernermiut, Chesterfield Inlet.
Qaumauangmiut, from Resolution Island to Icy Cove, Baffin Island.
Qinguamiut, at the head of Cumberland Sound.
Sagdlirmiut,. on the south coast of Southampton Island.
Saumingmiut, between Cape Mercy and Exeter Sound.
Sikosuilarmiut, about King Charles Cape.
Sinimiut, on Pelly Bay.
Talirpingmiut, on the south shore of Cumberland Sound and Netilling Lake.
Tununerusirmiut, in Admiralty Inlet.
Tununirmiut, in Ponds Inlet and Eclipse Sound and on both sides of Lancaster
    Sound at its east end.
Ukkusiksaligmiut, on the lower part of Backs River.
Wallirmiut, from Rae River to Dease Bay on Great Bear Lake.
III. Mackenzie Eskimo:
Avvagmiut, between Franklin Bay and Liverpool Bay.
Kigirktarugmiut, from the mouth of the Mackenzie River into Alaska.
Kittegaryumiut, on the west side of Mackenzie Delta.
Kurugmiut, on Hutchison Bay.
Nuvorugmiut, from Anderson River to Cape Brown.
IV. The Greenland tribes are as follows, these divisions being named for the most
    part for modern places:

Agto.	Disko.
Ameralik.	Egedesminde.
Anarkat.	Fiskernaes.
Angmagsalingmiut.	Frederikshaab.
Arsuk.	Godhavn.

Godthaab.

Holstensborg.

Igdlorssuit.

Ita Eskimo.

Ivigtut

Jakobshavn.

Julianehaab.

Kangamiut.

Kangatsiak.

Kangerdlugsiatsiak.

Karajak.

Nanortalik.

Nugsuak (two groups (1) on the south side of Nugsuak Peninsula; (2) from Melville Bay to Cape Shackleton).

Pamiagdluk.

Pisigsarfik.

Pröven.

Puisortok.

Sukkertoppen.

Tasiusak, about the place so-called.

Tingamirmiut.

Umanak.

Upernivik, about Upernivik.

V. Alaskan Eskimo tribes and towns:

Aglemiut, from the mouth of Nushagak River to Heiden Bay, including these villages:

Igagik, at the mouth of Ugaguk River.

Ikak, near Naknek Lake.

Kingiak, on the north side of the mouth of Naknek River, Bristol Bay.

Paugwik, with Aleut, at the mouth of Naknek River, on the south side.

Ugashik, at the mouth of Ugashik River.

Unangashik, at Heiden Bay, Alaska Peninsula.

Chingigmiut, in the region of Cape Newenham and Cape Peirce; villages:

Aziavik, near Cape Peirce.

Kinegnak, on Cape Newenham.

Tzahavak, near Cape Newenham.

Chnagmiut, on the shore of Pastol Bay, in the Yukon Delta, and on both banks of Yukon River as far as Razboinski; villages:

Aiachagiuk, on the right bank of the Yukon near the head of the delta.

Aimgua, near the mouth of Yukon River.

Alexeief, in the Yukon Delta.

Andreafski, on the north bank of Yukon River 5 miles above a former Russian redoubt of that name.

Ankachak, on the right bank of the lower Yukon, perhaps identical with Kenunimik.

Apoon, on Apoon Pass, the northern mouth of the Yukon River.

Ariswaniski, on the right bank of the lower Yukon.

Avnulik, the exact location not given.

Chatinak, near the mouth of Yukon River.

Chefoklak, near the head of Yukon Delta.

Chukchuk, in the Yukon Delta.

Claikehak, on the north bank of Yukon River above Tlatek.

Fetkina, on the north arm of Yukon Delta.

Ingichuk, in the Yukon Delta.

Kanig, on the north bank of Yukon River near its mouth.

Kashutuk, on an island in the Yukon Delta.

Kenuninuk, given as 15 miles above Andreafski on the right bank but perhaps identical with Ankachak.

Komarof, on the north bank of Yukon River.

Kotlik, on Kotlik River.

Kusilvak, on Kusilvak Island at the mouth of Yukon River.

Kwiahok, at the southern mouth of the Kwikluak Pass of the Yukon River.

Nigiklik, at the head of the Yukon Delta.

Ninvok, near the Yukon Delta.

Nokrot, near Cape Romanzof on the coast of Norton Sound.

Nunapithlugak, in the Yukon Delta, on the right bank of Apoon Pass.

Onuganuk, at the Kwikluak mouth of the Yukon.

Pastoliak, on the right bank of Pastoliak River near the southern shore of Norton Sound.

Razboinski, on the right bank of the Yukon near the head of the delta.

Starik, on the south bank of Yukon River above the head of the delta.

Takshak, on the north bank of the Yukon near Razboinski.

Tiatiuk, in the Yukon Delta.

Tlatek, on the north bank of Yukon River 35 miles above Andreafski.

Chugachigmiut, from the western extremity of, Kenai Peninsula to the delta of Copper River; villages:

Ingamatsha, on Chenega Island, Prince William Sound.

Kanikluk, on the north shore of Prince William Sound.

Kiniklik, on the north shore of Prince William Sound.

Nuchek, where the Russians established a stockade and trading post known as Fort Konstantine, at Port Etches, Hinchinbrook Island, Prince William Sound.

Tatitlek, on the northeastern shore of Prince William Sound.

Ikogmiut, on both banks of Yukon River from the territory of the Chnagmiut as far inland as Makak; villages:

Asko, on the right bank of the lower Yukon below Anvik.

Bazhi, on the Yukon at the upper mouth of Innoko River.

Ignok, on the right bank of the Yukon near Koserefski.

Ikatlek, on the Yukon 30 miles below Anvik.

Ikogmiut, also called "Mission," on the Yukon near its southernmost bend.

Ikuak, on the Yukon at its southernmost bend.

Ingrakak, on the right bank of the Yukon near longitude 161°30' W.

Katagkak, on Innoko River above its junction with the Yukon.

Khaik, on the northern bank of Yukon River nearly opposite Koserefski; given once apparently as Claikehak.

Kikhkat, on the north bank of Yukon River near Ikogmiut.

Kochkok, on the right bank of Yukon River near the Kuskokwim portage.

Koko, on the north bank of the Yukon below Ikogmiut.

Koserefski, formerly Kaiyuhkhotana, on the left bank of the Yukon near the mouth of Shageluk slough.

Kuyikanuikpul, on the right bank of Yukon River below Koserefski.

Kvikak, formerly Kaiyuhkhotana, on Yukon River 30 miles above Anvik.

Makak, on the right bank of the Yukon below Anvik.

Nukluak, on the left bank of the Yukon opposite Ikogmiut Mission.

Nunaikak, on the Yukon opposite Koserefski, perhaps the same as Ukak.

Nunaktak, on Yukon River above Anvik.

Paimiut, on the southern bank of the Yukon 38 miles above Ikogmiut, latitude 62°10' N., longtitude 160°10' W.

Pogoreshapka, on the right bank of the Yukon about 20 miles from Koserefski.

Ribnaia, on the right bank of the Yukon above Ikogmiut.

Staria Selenie, on the Yukon River below Ikogmiut.

Uglovaia, on the right bank of the lower Yukon between Ikogmiut and Razboinski.

Ukak, on the Yukon nearly opposite Koserefski, perhaps the same as Nunaikak.

Imaklimiut, on Big Diomede Island in Bering Strait in U. S. S. R. territory.

Inguklimiut, on Little Diomede Island in Bering Strait; their village called Inalik.

Kagmalirmiut, on the lower course of Colville River but not extending to its mouth.

Kaialigmiut, north of the Kuskwogmiut, between Kuguktik River and Cape Romanzof and on Nelson Island; villages:

Agiukchuk, opposite the southern shore of Nelson Island.

Anogok, on the coast just west of Kuskokwim Bay; given by Porter (1893) as Magemiut but actually Kaialigmiut.

Asiknuk, on Hooper Bay near Cape Romanzof.

Chichinak, on a small river flowing into Etolin Strait.

Kaialik, in the Yukon Delta near Azun River.

Chalit, on the left bank of Kuguklik River, northwest of Kuskokwim Bay.

Igiak, inland from Scammon Bay and near Magemiut territory.

Kashigalak, in the center of Nelson Island.

Kashunuk, near the Kaskunuk outlet of the Yukon River.

Kenachananak, on the coast opposite Nunivak Island.

Kuskunuk, on Hooper Bay.

Kvigatluk, in the lake district northwest of Kuskokwim River.

Nuloktolok, on the south side of Nelson Island.

Nunvogulukhluguk, in the Big Lake region.

Nushanamut, south of Hooper Bay.

Sfaganuk, between Dall Lake and Etolin Strait.

Ukak, on Hazen Bay.

Ukuk, on Nelson Island.

Unakagak, at the head of Hazen Bay.

Kaniagmiut, on Kodiak Island and the mainland coast from Iliamna Lake to Ugashik River, and the southern coast to longitude 159° W.; villages:

Afognak, comprising 3 settlements on Afognak Island.

Aiaktalik, on one of the Goose Islands near Kodiak.

Akhiok, on Alitak Bay, Kodiak Island.

Aleksashkina, on Wood Island in St. Paul Harbor, Kodiak Island.

Alexandrovsk, on Graham Harbor.

Ashivak, near Cape Douglas.

Chiniak, at the east end of Kodiak Island.

Fugitive, at Hobson Harbor, Sitkalidak Island near Kodiak.

Igak, on Afognak Island east of Afognak.

Kaguyak, on the southwestern coast of Kodiak Island.

Kaluiak, on Chignik Bay.

Kanatak, on Shelikof Strait.

Karluk, on the northern coast of Kodiak Island.

Katmai, on the southeastern coast of Alaska Peninsula.

Kattak, on Afognak Island east of Afognak.

Kiliuda, on the eastern coast of Kodiak Island.

Kodiak, established by the Russians, on the eastern end of Kodiak Island.

Kuiukuk, on the southeastern coast of Alaska Peninsula.

Kukak, on Kukak Bay on the coast of Alaska Peninsula.

Liesnoi, on Wood Island near Kodiak.

Mitrofania, on Mitrofania Island, south of Chignik Bay.

Nauklak, 15 miles east of Naknek Lake, Alaska Peninsula.

Nunamiut, on Three Saints Harbor, Kodiak Island.

Nunikiak, on the southwestern shore of Afognak Island.

Orlova, at Eagle Harbor, Ugak Bay, Kodiak Island.

Ostrovki, on Kachemak Bay, on the coast of Kenai Peninsula.

Seldovia, on the south side of Kachemak Bay, on the west coast of Kenai Peninsula.

Sutkum, on Sutwik Island off the southern coast of Alaska Peninsula.

Three Saints, on the site of the oldest Russian settlement in Alaska, Kodiak Island.

Uganik, on the northern coast of Kodiak Island.

Uhaskek, on the southeastern coast of Kodiak Island.

Ukshivikak, on the southwestern coast of Kodiak Island.

Uyak, near the salmon canneries on Uyak Bay, Kodiak Island.

Uzinki, on Spruce Island, Kodiak group.

Yalik, on Nuka Bay, eastern coast of Kenai Peninsula.

Yelovoi, on Spruce Island, Kodiak group.

Kañianermiut, on the headwaters of Colville River.

Kaviagmiut, on the southern part of Seward Peninsula westward from Norton Bay, many wintering on the eastern shore of Norton Sound; villages:

Aiacheruk, near Cape Nome.

Akpaliut, on Norton Sound west of Golofnin Bay.

Anelo, at Port Clarence.

Anlik, on Golofnin Bay.

Atnuk, near Darby Cape.

Aziak, on Sledge Island.

Chaik, on the shore of Norton Sound.

Chainruk, at Port Clarence.

Chinik, on Golofnin Bay.

Chiukak, on the peninsula enclosing Golofnin Bay.

Iknetuk, on Golofnin Bay.

Imoktegokshuk, at Cape Nome.

Kachegaret, at Port Clarence.

Kalulek, at Port Clarence.

Kaveazruk, at Port Clarence.

Kaviak, southeast of Port Clarence.

Kogluk, at Cape Nome.

Kovogzruk, at Port Clarence.

Metukatoak, at Port Clarence.

Netsekawik, on Golofnin Bay.

Okinoyoktokawik, on the coast opposite Sledge Island.

Opiktulik, on the north shore of Norton Sound.

Perebluk, at Port Clarence.

Senikave, on the mainland opposite Sledge Island.

Shinnapago, at Port Clarence.

Siningmon, on Golofnin Bay.

Sitnazuak, west of Cape Nome.

Sunvalluk, on the coast opposite Sledge Island.

Takchuk, east of Port Clarence.

Tubuktolik, on the north shore of Norton Sound.

Uinuk, at the mouth of Nome River.

Ukivok, on King Island.

Ukodlint, on Golofnin Bay.

Kevalingamiut, on the coast of the Arctic Ocean from Cape Seppings and
Cape Krusenstern inland to Nunatak River. Later they moved farther
north, expelling the Tikeramiut from Port Hope and the district beyond;
villages:
Ipnot, at Point Thomson.
Kechemudluk, at Cape Seppings.
Kivualinak, near Port Hope.
Ulezara, near Cape Kruzenstern.
Kiatagmiut, on Kvichivak River and Iliamna Lake; villages:
Chikak, on Iliamna Lake.
Kakonak, on the south shore of Iliamna Lake.
Kaskanak, on Kvichak River where it flows from Lake Iliamna.
Kichik, on Kichik Lake east of Iliamna Lake.
Kogiung, on Bristol Bay at the mouth of Kvichak River.
Kvichak, on Kvichak River.
Nogeling, on the outlet of Lake Clark.
Kigirktarugmiut, between Manning Point and the mouth of the Mackenzie
River.
Killinermiut, on the middle course of Colville River.
Kinugumiut, on Seward Peninsula in the region about Cape Prince of Wales;
villages:
Eidenu, at Cape Prince of Wales.
Kigegen, inland from Cape Prince of Wales.
Mitletukeruk, location unknown.
Nuk, at Port Clarence.
Pikta, near Cape Prince of Wales.
Shishmaref, at Shishmaref Cape.
Sinauk, on the north shore of Port Clarence.
Niktak, on Cape Prince of Wales.
Kowagmiut, on Kowak River east of Kotzebue Sound; villages:
Kikiktak, at the mouth of Hotham Inlet, Kotzebue Sound.
Kowak, at the mouth of Kowak River.
Umnokalukta, on Black River, a branch of Kowak River.
Unatak, on Kowak River.
Sheshalek, on the north shore of Kotzebue Sound, near the mouth of Noatak
River, a trading settlement for several towns.
Kukparungmiut, on the Arctic Ocean between Point Belcher and Cape Beaufort;
village:
Kokolik, at Point Lay.
Kunmiut, on Kuk River above Wainright Inlet; village:
Kilimantavie, on the Arctic coast west of Wainright Inlet.
Kuskwogmiut, on the shores of Kuskokwim Bay and the banks of Kuskokwim
River as far inland as Kolmakof; villages:
Agomekelenanak, in the Kuskokwim district.
Agulakpak, near Kuskokwim River.
Aguliak, on the eastern shore of Kuskokwim Bay.
Agumak, location not given.
Akiachak, on Kuskokwim River.
Akiak, on Kuskokwim River.
Aklut, on Kuskokwim River at the mouth of the Eek.
Akmiut, on Kuskokwim River 10 miles above Kolmakof, also given as a
Taiyanyanokhotana (Koyukon) village, perhaps Eskimoized in later time :.
Anagok, on the coast near Cape Avinof.

Apahiachak, location uncertain.

Apokak, near the mouth of Kuskokwim River.

Atchaluk, location uncertain.

Bethel, a Moravian Mission, close to Mumtrelek.

Chimiak, on Kuskokwim River.

Chuarlitilik, on Kanektok River.

Ekaluktaluk, location uncertain.

Etoluk, location uncertain.

Igiakchak, location uncertain.

Iliutak, on Kuskokwim Bay.

Kahmiut, location uncertain.

Kakuiak, on Kuskokwim River.

Kaltshak, on the right bank of Kuskokwim River about longitude 161°
    (159° ?) W.

Kaluktuk, location uncertain.

Kamegli, on the right bank of Kuskokwim River above Bethel.

Kanagak, location uncertain.

Kanak, location uncertain.

Kenachananak, on the coast opposite Nunivok Island.

Kiktak, on an island in Kuskokwim River 25 miles above Bethel.

Kinak, on the north bank of the Kuskokwim River.

Kinegnagak, location uncertain.

Klchakuk, on the east side of the entrance to Kuskokwim Bay.

Kleguchek, on the right bank of Kuskokwim River at its mouth.

Klutak, location uncertain.

Kolmakof, a Moravian mission consisting of Eskimo mixed with Athapascans,
    200 miles from the mouth of the Kuskokwim River.

Kongiganak, near the entrance to Kuskokwim Bay.

Kuilkluk, on the left bank of Kuskokwim River, perhaps identical with a
    town given as Quieclohchamiut or Quiechochlogamiut.

Kukluktuk, on the left bank of Kuskokwim River 30 miles below Kolmakof.

Kulvagavik, on the west shore of Kuskokwim Bay.

Kuskok, on Kuskokwim River near its mouth.

Kuskovak, on the west bank of Kuskokwim River near its mouth.

Kweleluk, on a small river in the tundra north of Kuskokwim Bay.

Kwik, on the right bank of Kuskokwim River 10 miles above Bethel.

Kwikak, on upper Kuskokwim River.

Kwilokuk, location uncertain.

Kwinak, on the east side of Kuskokwim River near its mouth.

Lomavik, on the left bank of Kuskokwim River.

Mumtrak, on Good News Bay.

Mumtrelek, on the west bank of lower Kuskokwim River.

Nak, on the north bank of Kuskokwim River.

Nakolvakik, on the left bank of Kuskokwim River near the mouth.

Napai, mixed with Athapascans, on the bank of Kuskokwim River a little
    above Kolmakof.

Napaiskak, on the left bank of Kuskokwim River about 4 miles below
    Bethel.

Napakiak, on the right bank of Kuskokwim River about 10 miles below
    Bethel.

Nochak, on Chilitna River.

Novotoklak, location uncertain.

Okaganak, on the south bank of Kuskokwim River.

Oknagak, on the north bank of Kuskokwim River.

Oyak, on the east shore of Kuskokwim Bay, just north of the mouth of Kanektok River.

Papka, on the north shore of Kuskokwim Bay.

Shevenak, on the left bank of Kuskokwim River.

Shiniak, on the east shore of Kuskokwim Bay at the end of deep-water navigation.

Shokfak, on a lake in the tundra north of Kuskokwim Bay.

Takiketak, on the east shore of Kuskokwim Bay.

Togiaratsorik, on the left bank of Kuskokwim River.

Tuklak, on Kuskokwim River below the Yukon portage.

Tuluka, on the right bank of Kuskokwim River.

Tuluksak, on the left bank of Kuskokwim River 40 miles above Bethel.

Tunagak, location uncertain.

Ugovik, on the right bank of Kuskokwim River.

Uknavik, on Kuskokwim River 10 miles below the Yukon portage.

Ulokak, location uncertain.

Vinasale, a trading post on the upper Kuskokwim.

Yakchilak, near the mouth of Kuskokwim River.

Magemiut, in the lake country of Alaska from Cape Romanzof almost to the Yukon River, villages:

Anogok, see Kaialigmiut.

Chefoklak, on the left bank of Yukon River at the head of the delta.

Gilak, near Cape Romanzof.

Kipniak, at the mouth of the southern arm of Yukon River.

Kweakpak, in the tundra south of the Yukon Delta.

Kwikak, on the coast of the Yukon Delta, south of Black River.

Nanvogaloklak, on one of the lakes connected with Kvichivak River.

Nunochok, in the Big Lake region.

Tefaknak, south of the Yukon Delta.

Tiengak, on Kvichavak River.

Malemiut, on the coast of Norton Sound north of Shaktolik, and on the neck of Seward peninsula; villages:

Akchadak-kochkond, location uncertain.

Atten, near the source of Buckland River.

Chamisso, on Chamisso Island in Eschscholtz Bay.

Inglutaligemiut, on Inglutalik River.

Kongik, on Buckland or Konguk River.

Koyuktolik, on Koyuk River.

Kugaluk, on Spafarief Bay on the shore of Kotzebue Sound.

Kungugemiut, on Buckland River.

Kviguk, at the mouth of Kviguk River, on the shore of Norton Sound.

Kvinkak, on Kvinkak River at the upper end of Norton Sound.

Kwik, two villages: (1) on a stream near the head of Norton Sound; (2) on the west side of Bald Head, Norton Bay.

Nubviakchugaluk, on the north coast of Norton Sound.

Nuklit, near Cape Denbigh, Norton Sound.

Shaktolik, on the east coast of Norton Sound.

Taapkuk, at Cape Espenberg, Kotzebue Sound.

Ulukuk, on Ulukuk River east of Norton Sound.

Ungalik, at the mouth of Ungalik River at the eastern end of Norton Sound.

Noatagmiut, on the lower course of Noatak River; villages:
    Aniyak, on the Arctic coast just north of Kotzebue Sound (?).
    Noatak, on the lower course of Noatak River.
Nunatagmiut, on the upper course of Noatak River.
Nunivagmiut, occupying the greater part of Nunivak Island and a small district about Cape Vancouver on Nelson Island; villages:
    Chulik, on Nunivak Island, in 1880 comprising two villages called Chuligmiut and Upper Chuligmiut.
    Inger, on Nunivak Island.
    Kaliukluk, south of Cape Vancouver on Nelson Island.
    Koot, near Cape Etolin, Nunivak Island.
    Kwik, on the southern shore of Nunivak Island.
    Tanunak, near Cape Vancouver, Nelson Island.
Nushagagmiut, on the banks of Igushik, Wood, and Nushagak Rivers and the shores of Nushagak Bay; villages:
    Agivavik, on Nushagak River.
    Akak, location uncertain.
    Akuliukpak, on Pamiek Lake.
    Akulivikchuk, on Nushagak River.
    Anagnak, on Wood River.
    Angnovchak, location uncertain.
    Annugamok, on an eastern tributary of Nushagak River.
    Ekuk, near the mouth of Nushagak River.
    Golok, location uncertain, perhaps the same as Kalignak.
    Igivachok, location uncertain.
    Igushik, on Igushik River.
    Imiak, at the outlet of Aleknagik Lake.
    Insiachak, location uncertain.
    Kakuak, 60 miles up Nushagak River.
    Kalignak, on a tributary of Nushagak River.
    Kanakanak, on Nushagak Bay.
    Kanulik, on the left bank of Nushagak River near its mouth.
    Mulchatna, on Mulchatna River, a branch of Nushagak River.
    Stugarok, on Nushagak Bay.
    Tikchik, on Lake Tikchik, on the Kuskokwim portage.
    Trinachak, location uncertain.
    Vuikhtulik, on the northern shore of Lake Alaknakik.
    Yaoherk, location uncertain, perhaps identical with Ekuk.
Nuwukmiut, at Point Barrow; villages:
    Isutkwa, on the site of the United States Signal Station at Point Barrow.
    Nuwuk, at Point Barrow.
    Pernyu, on the western shore of Elson Bay, close to Point Barrow.
    Ongovehenok, on Kugrua River near Point Barrow.
Selawigmiut, on Selawik Lake east of Kotzebue Sound:
Sidarumiut, west of Point Barrow; villages:
    Atnik, near Point Belcher.
    Attenok, on Seahorse Islands.
    Charnroruit, on Seahorse Islands.
    Nunaria, near Point Belcher.
    Perignak, on Seahorse Islands.
    Pinguishuk, on Seahorse Islands.
    Sidaru, between Wainwright Inlet and Point Belcher.

Tikeramiut, at Point Hope; village:

Tikera or Nuna, at Point Hope.

Togiagmiut, about Togiak Bay and River; villages:

Aguliukpak, on lake of same name at head of Wood River.

Eklik, on Togiak River near its mouth.

Kashaiak, on Togiak River near its junction with the Kashaiak River.

Kassiank, on Togiak River.

Kulukak, on Kukulak Bay.

Togiak, at the mouth of Togiak River.

Tuniakpuk, on lower Togiak River.

Ualik, on Kulukak Bay.

Ugalakmiut, at the mouth of Copper River and on Kayak Island; in later
years they became thoroughly altered by contact with the Tlingit so that
they were often classed with the latter people.   Village:

Eyak, at the entrance of Prince William Sound.

Unaligmiut, extending from the eastern shore of Norton Sound inland to the
coast range; villages:

Anemuk, on Anvik River.

Iguik, on Norton Sound.

Kiktaguk, on the southern coast of Norton Sound.

Pikmiktalik, near the mouth of Pikmiktalik River, just north of Cape
Romanzof.

Tachik, on St. Michael Island, near the Russian redoubt, and now included
in the town of St. Michael.

Topanika, on the eastern coast of Norton Sound.

Unalaklik, at the mouth of Unalalik River.

Utkiavinmiut, on the Arctic coast west of Point Barrow; villages and summer
camps:

Ernivwin, inland from Point Barrow.

Imekpung, near Point Barrow.

Ipersua, not accurately located.

Kuosugru, on a dry place inland from Point Barrow.

Nakeduxo, not accurately located.

Nunaktuau, close to Refuge Inlet.

Pengnok, near Cape Smythe.

Sakamna, inland from Point Barrow.

Sinyu, inland from Point Barrow.

Utkiavi, at Cape Smythe.

Walakpa, not located definitely.

Utukamiut, originating at Icy Cape; they later ranged along the Arctic coast
from Point Hope to Wainright Inlet, and inland to Colville River; villages:

Kaiaksekawik, on the north side of Icy Cape.

Kelemanturuk, near Icy Cape.

Utuka, at Icy Cape.

Yuit, around East Cape, Indian Point, and Cape Chukotsky, Siberia, and on
St. Lawrence Island, Alaska; and divided into:

(1) The Noökalit, at East Cape; villages:

Enmitahin, north of East Cape.

Nabukak, on East Cape.

Ulak, inhabited in part by Chukchi, just north of East Cape.

(2) The Aiwanat, about Indian Point; villages:

Avak, near Cape Chukotsky.

Imtuk, near Indian Point.

Napakutak, on an island near Indian Point (?).
Nasskatulok, at the head of Plover Bay.
Rirak, in Plover Bay.
Tesik, occupied partly by Chukchi, on the west shore of Chechin Bay.
Unisak, on Indian Point.
(3) The Wuteëlit, at Cape Ulakhpen; villages:
Chenlin, including Chukchi, west of the next.
Cherinak, near Cape Ulakhpen.
(4) The Eiwhuelit, on St. Lawrence Island; villages:
Chibukak, at Northwest Cape.
Chitnak, on the south coast.
Kialegak, near Southeast Cape.
Kukuliak, on the north coast.
Puguviliak, at Southwest Cape.
Punuk, on Punuk Island, east of St. Lawrence Island.

History.—The Norse settlers of Greenland were the first white men
to come in contact with Eskimo, though it is probable that the latter
had relatively little to do with the extermination of the European
colonists as was once thought. They were rediscovered by Frobisher
or perhaps even earlier explorers and contact between White and Eskimo was continuous from that time forward. In the eighteenth century the Danes began to resettle Greenland, and about the same time
relations were opened between the western Eskimo and the Russians.
The Eskimo of Labrador were missionized by Moravians, whose efforts
among them are famous in the annals of missionary work. The central
Eskimo were not reached until much later than those of the east and
west, the first Europeans to come in contact with them being usually
whalers, though some of the eighteenth-century explorers, such as
Hearne (1795), reached them overland from the south. Many of
their tribes were scarcely known at all until the recent explorations of
Stefánsson (1914) and Jenness (1922, 1923).

Population.—Mooney (1928) gives an estimate of 3,600 Eskimo in
Labrador in 1600 and 22,300 in the rest of Canada in 1670; 10,000 in
Greenland in 1721; and 40,000 in Alaska in 1740. As Mooney in preparing the data for each of his areas selects a date just before contact
with the Whites made itself felt appreciably, we may assume that the
figures given had remained relatively stationary for a considerable
period and add them together for our total, which is 75,900. For the
entire Eskimo population we must add 1,200 living in Asia, which gives
us 77,100. To obtain the population of the linguistic stock we must
increase this by the number of the Aleut, 16,000, making 93,100.
Jenness thinks Mooney's estimates are much too high. He has kindly
supplied me with the following figures for the present population:
Canada, 6,184 (Ann. Rep. Dept. Ind. Aff. for 1927); Greenland, 14,066
(Statistisk Aarbog for 1922, Copenhagen, 1922), including, however,

about 300 Europeans; Alaska, 13,698 (census of 1920); Labrador (from an estimate before it was entirely united to Canada), probably not over 1,200 since a large part of the Peninsula was included in Canada. This gives a total of approximately 35,000.

Connection in which they have become noted.—From the time when they were first known to Europeans, the Eskimo were marked off from all other peoples in the minds of the former by their peculiar physical type, and the unique character of their customs and manner of life. They are distinguished as having been the first of all people of America to encounter Europeans, and they have earned an honorable name for themselves through the assistance they have rendered to Arctic explorers at all periods. They may be called the one people who did not have to discover America, since they lived on both sides of Bering Strait and hence in both the New and the Old Worlds.

Etchaottine. Significance unknown. Also called:

> Awokànak, Cree name, meaning "slaves."
> Brushwood Indians, by Franklin (1823).
> Slaves, Slavey, by traders by translation of the Cree term.

Connections.—The Etchaottine belonged to the Athapascan linguistic stock, their closest relatives having been, apparently, the Kawchottine.

Location.—In the valley of Mackenzie River between Great Slave Lake and Fort Norman.

Subdivision

The following names are mainly from Petitot (1891):

Desnedeyarelottine, on the banks of upper Mackenzie River.

Eleidlinottine, at the confluence of Liard and Mackenzie Rivers, their territory extending to La Martre, Grandin, and Taché Lakes.

Etchaottine, between Liard River and the Divide, along Black, Beaver, and Willow Rivers.

Etcheridiegottine, on the middle course of Liard River.

Etechesottine, between Great Slave and La Martre Lakes.

Klodesseottine, on Hay River.

Petitot speaks of another band at Fort Norman, but applies no special name to it.

History.—Petitot (1891) states that the Etchaottine anciently extended as far south as Lake Athabaska but that the Cree, on obtaining guns, drove them out of that region and, when they had taken refuge in the islands in Great Slave Lake, pursued them thither and slaughtered many. Although it is by no means certain that the Etchaottine ever extended as far as Lake Athabaska (see history of the Chipewyan), they no doubt suffered, like other Athapascan tribes of the region, from the invasion of the Cree. In 1789 Mackenzie passed through the entire length of the country and trading posts soon followed. They have since continued to occupy the territory above indicated while it has gradually been metamorphosed by the activities of the Hudson's Bay Company and the missionaries.

Population.—Mooney (1928) estimated that in 1670 there were 1,250 Etchaottine.

Connection in which they have become noted.—The Etchaottine have appeared in history principally under the name of "Slaves" owing to the dominating position which the Cree obtained over them and the contemptuous attitude of that tribe toward them in consequence.

Haida. Their own name, meaning "people."

Connections.—The Haida constitute the Skittagetan linguistic family, the speech of which has certain structural resemblances with that of the Tlingit and Athapascans, with which Sapir (1915) combined it under the term Na-déné.

Location.—Originally on the Queen Charlotte Islands, but early in the eighteenth century a part of the Haida settled on the southern part of Prince of Wales Island, Alaska, where they came to be known as Kaigani, from a summer camp where they were in the habit of gathering to meet trading vessels.

Subdivisions and Villages

The following are large local groups perhaps entitled to the appellation of tribes:

Chaahl, on the northwest coast of Moresby Island.
Cumshewa, at the north entrance of Cumshewa Inlet, Moresby Island.
Dadens, on the south coast of North Island, fronting Parry Passage.
Gahlinskun, on the east coast of Graham Island, north of Cape Ball.
Haena, on the east end of Maude Island, Skidegate Inlet.
Hlielung, on the right bank of Hi-ellen River, at its mouth, Graham Island.
Howkan, on Long Island, Alaska, facing Dall Island.
Kaisun, on the northwest coast of Moresby Island.
Kasaan, on Skowl Arm of Kasaan Bay, east coast of Prince of Wales Island.
Kayung, on the east side of Masset Inlet just above Masset.
Kiusta, on the northwest coast of Graham Island, opposite North Island.
Klinkwan, on Cordova Bay, Prince of Wales Island, Alaska.
Kloo, at the east end of Tanoo Island.
Kung, at the mouth of Naden Harbor, Graham Island.
Kweundlas, on the west coast of Long Island, Alaska.
Masset, on the east coast of Masset Inlet near its entrance.
Naikun, Rose Spit or Nekoon, at the northeast angle of Graham Island.
Ninstints, on Anthony Island at the south end of Moresby Island.
Skedans, on a point of land which extends into Hecate Strait from the east end of Louise Island.
Skidegate, on the north shore of Skidegate Inlet near its entrance.
Sukkwan, on Cordova Bay, Alaska.
Tiun or Tigun, on the west coast of Graham Island south of Point Lewis.
Yaku, on the northwest coast of Graham Island opposite North Island.
Yan, on the west side of Masset Inlet near its mouth.

Small towns and camps so far as known are as follows:

Aiodjus, on the west side of Masset Inlet at its mouth.
Atana, on House or Atana Island off the east coast of Moresby Island.
Atanus, on the northeast coast of Hippa Island.

Chaahl, on the east coast of North Island.

Chatchini, near Kasaan, Prince of Wales Island.

Chets, on an island at the mouth of Tsooskahli, Masset Inlet.

Chuga, near Houston Stewart Channel and the town of Ninstints.

Chukeu, on the southwest coast of Moresby Island.

Dadjingits, on the north shore of Bearskin Bay, Skidegate Inlet.

Dahua, north of Lawn Hill at the mouth of Skidegate Inlet.

Daiyu, on Shingle Bay, east of Welcome Point, Moresby Island.

Djigogiga, legendary town on Copper Bay, Moresby Island.

Djigua, legendary town on the north shore of Cumshewa Inlet.

Djihuagits, on a creek just south of Rose Spit, Graham Island.

Edjao, around Edjao Hill at the east end of Masset Village.

Gachigundae, on the northeast shore of Alliford Bay, Moresby Island.

Gado, two towns: (1) traditional, on the south side of De la Beche Inlet, Moresby Island; (2), on the east side of Lyell Island.

Gaedi, on the northeast shore of a small inlet just northeast of Houston Inlet.

Gaesigusket, on Murchison Island at a point opposite Hot Springs Island.

Gaiagunkun, legendary, near Hot Springs Island.

Gaodjaos, on the south shore of Lina Island, Bearskin Bay.

Gasins, on the northwest shore of Lina Island, Bearskin Bay.

Gatgainans, on Hippa Island.

Gitinkalana, on the north shore of Masset Inlet where it expands into the inner bay.

Guhlga, legendary, on the north shore of Skidegate Inlet one mile above Skidgate Village.

Gulhlgildjing, on the south shore of Alliford Bay, Moresby Island.

Gwaeskun, at Gwaeskun, the northernmost point on the Queen Charlotte Islands.

Hagi, on or near the largest of the Bolkus Islands.

Heudao, on the east side of Gull Point, Prevost Island.

Hlagi, on an island near the east end of Houston Stewart Channel.

Hlakeguns, on Yagun River at the Head of Masset Inlet.

Hlgadun, on Moresby Island facing Anthony Island.

Hlgaedlin, on the south side of Tanoo Island.

Hlgahet, near Skidegate.

Hlgai, at the head of Skedans Bay.

Hlgaiha, north of Dead Tree Point at the entrance of Skidegate Inlet.

Hlgaiu, south of Dead Tree Point at the entrance of Skidegate Inlet.

Hlgihla-ala, north of Cape Ball, on the east shore of Graham Island.

Hlkia, on the outer side of Lyell Island.

Hluln, in Naden Harbor.

Hotao, legendary, on the southwest coast of Maude Island.

Hotdjohoas, on Lyell Island near the north end of Darwin Sound.

Hoyagundla, on a stream of the same name a short distance south of Cape Fife.

Huados, near Hlgihla-ala, north of Cape Ball.

Kadadjans, on the northwest end of Anthony Island.

Kadusgo, at the mouth of a creek of the same name on Louise Island, flowing into Cumshewa Inlet from the south.

Kae, on Skotsgai Bay above Skidegate.

Kaidju, on Hewlett Bay, east coast of Moresby Island.

Kaidjudal, on Moresby Island opposite Hot Springs Island.

Kaigani, at the southeast end of Dall Island, Alaska.

Kasta, legendary, on Copper Bay, Moresby Island.

Katana, on Louise Island.

Kesa, on the west coast of Graham Island.

Ket, on Burnaby Strait, Moresby Island.

Kil, on Shingle Bay, Skidegate Inlet.

Koagoagit, on the north shore of Bearskin Bay.

Koga, on McKay Harbor, Cumshewa Inlet.

Kogalskun, on Masset Inlet.

Kostunhana, a short distance east of Skidegate.

Kundji, 2 towns: (1) legendary, on the south shore of Copper Bay, Moresby Island; (2), on the west side of Prevost Island.

Kungga, on the south shore of Dog Island.

Kungielung, on the west side of the entrance to Masset Inlet.

Kunhalas, just inside of Cumshewa Inlet.

Kunkia, on the north coast of North Island.

Kuulana, in Naden Harbor.

Lanadagunga, south of Tangle Cove, Moresby Island.

Lanagahlkehoda, on a small island opposite, Kaisun, Moresby Island.

Lanahawa, 2 towns: (1) on the west coast of Graham Island opposite Hippa Island; (2) on the west coast of Burnaby Island south of Ket.

Lanahilduns, on the southwest side of Rennell Sound, Graham Island.

Lanaslnagai, 3 towns: (1) on the east coast of Graham Island south of Cape Ball, (2) on the west side of Masset Inlet where the inner expansion begins; (3) on Yagun River.

Lanaungsuls, on Masset Inlet.

Nagus, in an inlet on the southwest coast of Moresby Island.

Sahldungkun, on the west side of Yagun River at its mouth.

Sakaedigialas, traditional, on or near Kuper Island.

Sgilgi, in an inlet on the southwest coast of Moresby Island.

Sindaskun, near the south end of the islands.

Sindatahls, near Tsoo-skahli, an inner expansion of Masset Inlet.

Singa, on the north side of Tasoo Harbor, west coast of Moresby Island.

Skae, close to Cape St. James at the south end of the Queen Charlotte Islands.

Skaito, on the west coast of Moresby Island near Gold Harbor.

Skaos, at the entrance of Naden Harbor.

Skena, legendary, just south of Sand Spit Point, Moresby Island.

Skudus, on the north side of Lyell Island.

Stlindagwai, in an inlet on the west coast of Moresby Island.

Stunhlai, on the northwest coast of Moresby Island.

Sulustins, on the east coast of Hippa Island.

Ta, on the east coast of North Island.

Te, on the west coast of Graham Island opposite Frederick Island.

Tlgunghung, on the north side of Lyell Island.

Tlhingus, on Louise Island.

Tohlka, on the north coast of Graham Island just west of the entrance to Masset Inlet.

Widja, on the north coast of Graham Island just west of the entrance of Masset Inlet.

Yagun, on the north coast of Graham Island.

Yaogus, on the southwest side of Louise Island.

Yastling, in Naden Harbor, Graham Island.

Yatza, on the north coast of Graham Island between North Island and Virago Sound.

Youahnoe, given as a Kaigani town, perhaps identical with the town of Kaigani.

History.—According to native traditions, the oldest Haida settlements were on the mainland side of the islands. The Haida towns in Alaska date back to the early part of the eighteenth century, i. e., their establishment was almost within the historic period. So far as is known, the Spanish Ensign Juan Perez in the corvette *Santiago* was the first white man to visit the islands. This was in the year 1774. In 1775 Bodega and Maurelle touched there. La Perouse coasted the shores of the group in 1786 and Dixon spent a month about them in 1787. He was followed by Douglas, Ingraham, Marchand, Vancouver, and numerous explorers and traders whose names have not been preserved. The Hudson's Bay Company located a post at Masset and mission stations were established at Masset and Skidegate by the Church of England and the Methodists respectively. Smallpox, consumption, liquor, and immorality depleted the native population rapidly even before any Whites settled upon the islands, but the remnant of the people now seems to have reached an adjustment to the new conditions.

Population.—Mooney (1928), estimated that in 1780 there were 8,000 Haida on the Queen Charlotte Islands and 1,800 in Alaska. A detailed enumeration made between 1836 and 1841 gave 6,593 and 1,735 respectively, a total of 8,328. Dawson (1880) thought that there were between 1,700 and 2,000 on the Queen Charlotte Islands and in 1888 the Canadian Office of Indian Affairs estimated 2,500, but the next year, when an actual census was taken of all but one settlement, the total was 637, and in 1894, when all were included, it was only 639. In 1895 there were reported 593; in 1902, 734; and in 1904, 587. In 1880 Petroff (1884) gave 788 Kaigani but Dall (1886) estimated 300. In 1890, 391 were returned and in 1905 the number was estimated as 300. The United States Census of 1910 gave 530; that of 1920, 524; and that of 1930, 588.

Connection in which they have become noted.—The Haida have been noted for much the same things as the Tsimshian; beautiful carvings, peculiar social and ceremonial customs, and large and well-made dugouts. The slate from which so many artistic objects have been made is all obtained at one spot in their country. They are usually regarded as the typical totem-pole people.

Hidatsa. Like their relatives, the Crow, the Hidatsa may have lived on the north side of the International Boundary in late prehistoric times, but this is as yet uncertain. (See North Dakota.)

Huron. When Canada was first settled, the Huron lived in the region of Lake Simcoe, Ontario, but a hundred years earlier part of them occupied the lower St. Lawrence Valley. (See **Wyandot** under Ohio.)

Iroquois. Bands belonging to the tribes of the Iroquois Confederacy lived in Canada at various times and some are there at the present day. (See New York.)

Kawchottine. Signifying "people of the great hares." Also called:

Hare Indians, English appellation derived from their own name.
Kkρayttchare ottiné, Chipewyan name.
Nouga, Eskimo name, meaning "spittle."
Peaux-de-Lièvres, French appellation from their own name.
Rabbitskins, English appellation derived from their own name.

Connections.—The Kawchottine belonged to the Athapascan linguistic family, being most intimately connected with the tribes higher up Mackenzie River.

Location.—West and northwest of Great Bear Lake.

Subdivisions

Petitot (1893) gives the following:

Chintagottine, also called Katagottine, on Mackenzie River north of Fort Good Hope and between the river and Great Bear Lake.
Etatchogottine, north and east of Great Bear Lake and on Great Cape.
Kawchogottine, on the border of the wooded region northeast of Fort Good Hope.
Kfwetragottine, south of Fort Good Hope along Mackenzie River.
Nellagottine, on Lake Simpson and along Anderson River.
Nigottine, also given as a part of the Kawchogottine, along the outlet of Great Bear Lake.
Satchotugottine, immediately north of Great Bear Lake, omitted from a later list.

History.—The country of the Kawchottine was reached by Alexander Mackenzie in 1789. The establishment of Fort Good Hope in 1804 and Fort Norman in 1810 brought them in closer touch with Europeans, and the intimacy has increased steadily from that day to the present.

Population.—Mooney (1928) estimated that there were 750 Kawchottine in 1670. In 1858 Ross (1858) gave their number as 467.

Kitksan. Their own name, meaning "people of Skeena River." Phonetically rendered Gyitkshan.

Connections.—The Kitksan constituted one of the three great tribes or tribal groups of the Chimmesyan linguistic family.

Location.—On the upper waters of Skeena River.

Subdivisions and Villages

(The second name, where there are two, is the one given by Barbeau, 1929)

Kispiox or Kispayaks, at the junction of Kispiox and Skeena Rivers.
Kitanmaiksh or Gitenmaks, at Hazelton.
Kitgargas or Kisgagas, on the north bank of Babine River, 3 or 4 miles above its junction with the Skeena.

Kitsegukla or Gitsegyukla, on Skeena River between Hazelton and Kitwanga.

Kitwancool or Gitwinlkul, 14 miles above Kitwanga on the Grease trail to the Nass.

Kitwanga, on the north bank of Skeena River about 150 miles from the coast.

Kuldo or Qaldo, near the headwaters of Skeena River.

Meamskinisht, a modern mission village founded in 1889.

History.—According to Barbeau (1929), many of the leading families of the Kitksan came from the north, from among the interior Athapascans and from the Tlingit, within the last two centuries. Contact with the Whites became intimate after the establishment of Fort Kilmaurs (Babine) in 1822, Fort Connolly in 1826, and Fort Stager, and European influences began to come up the river with greater strength after the foundation of Fort Simpson in 1831 and Fort Essington in 1835.

Population.—(See **Tsimshian.**)   In 1904 there were 1,120 Kitksan.

Connection in which they have become noted.—(See **Tsimshian.**)

Kutchin.   The Kutchin occupied the entire central portion of Yukon territory and extended to the lower course of the Mackenzie, which they occupied on both sides from New Fort Good Hope to the delta.   (See **Nakotcho-kutchin, Takkuth-kutchin, Tatlit-kutchin,** and Alaska.)

Kutenai.   The Kutenai were located on Kootenay River and Lake and extended into the United States, occupying the northern parts of Montana and Idaho.   In later prehistoric times they extended some distance into the Plains.   (See Montana.)

Kwakiutl.   Own name, signifying according to themselves, "smoke of the world," but probably meaning "beach at the north side of the river."

Connections.—With the Bellabella (q. v.), the Kwakiutl constituted one grand division of the Wakashan linguistic family, the Nootka forming the other.

Location.—On both shores of Queen Charlotte Sound, and the northern end of Vancouver Island.

Subdivisions

The bands or septs, with the relations which they bear to one another, are indicated in the following list, based upon information obtained by Boas (1897):

Koskimo Subdialect:

Klaskino, on Klaskino Inlet, Vancouver Island.

Koprino, at the entrance of Quatsino Sound.

Quatsino, at the entrance of Quatsino Sound, Vancouver Island.

Nawiti Subdialect:

Nakomgilisala, originally at Cape Scott, Vancouver Island.

Tlatlasikoala, formerly at the northeast end of Vancouver Island.

Kwakiutl Subdialect:
Awaitlala, on Knight Inlet.
Goasila, on Smith Inlet.
Guauaenok, on Drury Inlet.
Hahuamis, on Wakeman Sound.
Koeksotenok, on Gilford Island.
Kwakiutl, including Guetela, Komkutis, Komoyue, Matilpe, and Walas Ḳwakiutl most of whom lived at Fort Rupert.
Lekwiltok, between Knight and Bute Inlets.
Mamalelekala, on Village Island.
Nakoaktok, on Seymour Inlet.
Nimkish, on and near Nimkish River.
Tenaktak, on Knight Inlet.
Tlauitsis, on Cracroft Island.
Tsawatenok, on Kingcombe Inlet.
An extinct band was called Hoyalas.

Villages

Awaitlala and Tenaktak: Kwatsi, at Point Macdonald, Knight Inlet. (See Tsawatenok.)
Goasila: Waitlas, at the mouth of Samo River, Smith Inlet.
Guauaenok: Hohopa, on the west coast of Baker Island; Kunstamish, on the east side of Clayton Bay, Wells Passage. (See Tsawatenok.)
Hahuamis. (See Tsawatenok.)
Koeksotenok: Kwakwakas, on the west coast of Gilford Island.
Koeksotenok and Mamalelekala: Memkumlis, on Village Islands, at the mouth of Knight Inlet.
Lekwiltok: Husam, at the mouth of Salmon River; Tatapowis, on Hoskyn Inlet; Tsaiiyeuk, at the entrance of Bute Inlet; Tsakwalooin, near Cape Mudge.
Mamalelekala. (See Koeksotenok).
Matilpe: Etsekin, on Havannah Channel.
Nakoaktok: Awuts, on the lagoon above Shelter Bay; Kikwistok, on the lower part of Seymour Inlet; Mapakum, on Deserter's Island of the Walker Group.
Quatsino: Owiyekumi, on Forward Inlet, Quatsino Sound; Tenate, on the north shore of Forward Inlet.
Tenaktak: (See Awaitlala.)
Tlauitsis: Kalakowis, on the west end of Turnour Island.
Tsawatenok: Hata, at the head of Bond Sound; Kwae, at the head of Kingcombe Inlet.
Tsawatenok, Hahuamis, and Guauaenok together: Kwaustums, on Gilford Island.

History.—If the voyage of Fuentes in 1640 is authentic, he was probably the first European to encounter any of the Kwakiutl Indians. Bodega and Maurelle passed along their coast in 1775, and from this time on they were visited by English and American explorers and traders at frequent intervals. The establishment of a Hudson's Bay post at Victoria in 1843 marked an epoch in their dealings with the Whites which since then have been more and more intimate. Mission work among the Bellabella was very successful but the southern branches of the family held on to their ancient customs with more tenacity.

Population.—Mooney (1928) estimated that in 1780 there were 4,500 southern Kwakiutl Indians. In 1906 there were 1,257. The Report of the Canadian Department of Indian Affairs for 1909 gives 2,090 Kwakiutl.

Connection in which they have become noted.—These tribes are noteworthy for the very complete studies of their social organization and potlatch customs made by Boas (1897), assisted by George Hunt, and the important part these studies have played in the development of general theories of exogamy and totemism.

Lillooet. Signifying "wild onion." The name seems to have been given originally to a part of the Lower Lillooet. Also called:

Stla'tliumH, own name, applied properly to the Upper Lillooet.

Connections.—The Lillooet belong to the interior division of the Salishan linguistic family, their nearest relatives being the Shuswap and Ntlakyapamuk.

Location.—On the upper part of Harrison Lake, Lillooet River, Bridge River, and part of Fraser River above and below the mouth of the latter stream and between the Shuswap and Ntlakyapamuk, and on the heads of some of the streams flowing into the Gulf of Georgia.

Subdivisions

The Lillooet are divided primarily into the Lower Lillooet and the Upper Lillooet, each consisting of two principal bands as follows:

Lower Lillooet: Lillooet River or Douglas (on Little Harrison Lake and the lower Lillooet River up to Lower or Little Lillooet Lake), Pemberton (on Lillooet Lake, Pemberton Meadows, Pole River, Upper Lillooet River, Green Lake, etc.).

Upper Lillooet: Lake (on Anderson and Seaton Lakes, Cayuse River to Duffey Lake and westerly to the headwaters of the streams flowing into Jervis Inlet and the northwest sources of Bridge River), Fraser River (from about 5 miles below the mouth of Cayuse Creek to a few miles below the mouth of Pavilion Creek, a few miles up Cayuse Creek, in Three Lake Valley and on the neighboring hills between the Fraser River and Hat Creek, lower Bridge River and northwest to near the head of Big Creek).

Villages

Lillooet River:

Hahtsa or (by Whites) Douglas, on Little Harrison Lake, about 4 miles from Tipella on Great Harrison Lake.

Kwehalaten, on Little Lillooet Lake.

Lalakhen, on Lower Lillooet River, 10 miles above Douglas.

Samakum, on Lower Lillooet River about 25 miles above Douglas.

Sektcin or (by Whites) Warm Springs, near Lower Lillooet River about 23 miles from Douglas.

Shomeliks, near Lower Lillooet River, 10 miles above Douglas.

Skatin or (by Whites) Skookum Chuck, on Lower Lillooet River about 17 or 18 miles above Douglas.

Smemits, a short distance above Lalakhen.

Pemberton:

Hazilkwa, at head of slough, 1 mile above Nkimsh.

Lakemitc, less than 1 mile above Hazilkwa.

Nkimsh, on Upper Lillooet River, a little above the head of Lillooet Lake.

Stlalek or Stlaluk or (by Whites) Pemberton, near the big bridge across Upper Lillooet River, about 1 mile above Lakemitc.

Sulpauthltin, on Upper Lillooet River, about 2 miles above Stlalek.

Lake:

Heselten, about one-third up Seaton Lake on the north side.

Nkaiot, at the foot of Anderson Lake.

Nkuatkwa, at the head of Anderson Lake.

Skemkain, at the foot of Seaton Lake, about 4 miles from Lillooet.

Slaus, at the head of Seaton Lake.

Tcalethl, about two-thirds up Seaton Lake on the north side.

Fraser River:

Hahalep or Fountain, on the east side of Fraser River near Fountain Creek and about 9 miles above Setl.

Nhoisten, on the upper side of the mouth of Bridge River, about 4 miles above Setl.

Setl or Lillooet village, just west of Lillooet town, on the west side of Fraser River.

Skakethl, on the west side of Fraser River about 3½ miles above Setl.

Skulewas or Skulewes, on the south side of the mouth of Cayuse River.

Tseut, on the east side of Fraser River about 2 miles above Setl.

History.—The first white man to penetrate the country of the Lillooet was probably Simon Fraser in 1809. Contact with traders was practically continuous from that time forward and with the miners from 1858. The Lillooet suffered more than any other tribe from the great smallpox epidemic of 1863.

Population.—Mooney's (1928) estimate of Lillooet population as of the year 1780 is 4,000, perhaps copied from that of Teit (1900). The report of the Canadian Office of Indian Affairs of 1904 seems to give 978 Lillooet, but there are probably omissions, as Teit's estimate of about the same time is 900 Lower Lillooet and 700 Upper Lillooet, a total of 1,600.

Connection in which they have become noted.—The Lillooet have given their name to Lillooet Lakes and Lillooet River.

Malecite. Many explanations of the name have been offered but the most probable is that of Chamberlain (MS.), who says it is from Malisit, the Micmac term for them, which means "broken talkers." Also called:

Etchemin, perhaps from tchinem, "men."

"Muskrats," by some of their neighbors.

Wula'stegwi·ak, meaning "Good River People," name used by themselves, referring to the St. John.

Connections.—The Malecite belonged to the Algonquian linguistic family, their nearest relatives being the Passamaquoddy, and after them the Penobscot, Abnaki, and Pennacook.   They were frequently classed with these under the general name Abnaki.

Location.—In the valley of St. John River, New Brunswick, but extending slightly into the northeastern corner of Maine.

Subdivisions

Maurault (1866) makes a distinction between Malecite and Etchemin, but there seems to have been no valid foundation for this.

Villages

Medoctec, about 10 miles below Woodstock, N. B.
Okpaak, on the middle course of St. John River, N. B.
Saint Anne, on an island near Frederickton, N. B.
Viger, in Viger township, Temiscòuata County, Quebec Province.

History.—Like the Abnaki, the Malecite trace their origin to some region in the southwest.   Early in the sixteenth century some of them were probably encountered by French and English explorers and fishermen, but they were first referred to specifically by Champlain in 1604, though his "Etechemins" were on the St. Croix River and were perhaps Passamaquoddy.   Some years later Fort La Tour was built on St. John River, and it became a noted resort for members of this tribe.   After the English gained possession of Malecite territory, certain lands were assigned to the Indians.   In 1856, according to Schoolcraft (1851–57), these had become reduced to the valley of "the Tobique river, and the small tract at Madawaska, Meductic Point, and Kingsclear, with their small rocky islands near St. John, containing 15 acres."   The descendants of the Malecite live partly in New Brunswick and partly in the province of Quebec, while a few appear in the population statistics of the State of Maine.

Population.—The Malecite population is estimated by Mooney to have been 800 in 1600.   In 1884 there were 767 (584 in New Brunswick; 183 in Quebec); in 1904, 805 (702 in New Brunswick; 103 in Quebec).   The United States Census of 1910 returned 142 living on the south side of the International Boundary, of whom 138 were in Maine.

Connection in which they have become noted.—The name of the Malecite is preserved in that of a small town called Maliseet in New Brunswick, and one of its synonyms in Etchemin River, Province of Quebec.

Micmac.   From the native term Migmac, meaning "allies."   Also called:

Matu-ĕs'-wi skitchi-nú-ûk, Malecite name, meaning "porcupine Indians," on account of their use of porcupine quills in ornamentation.
Shŏnăck, Beothuk name, meaning "bad Indians."
Souriquois, name by which they were known to the French.

Connections.—The Micmac belonged to the Algonquian linguistic stock and to that part of the Central Algonquian group represented typically by the Cree, though their speech differed in some striking particulars. Their closest relatives, however, were the Malecite, Passamaquoddy, Penobscot, and Abnaki.

Location.—Nova Scotia, Cape Breton Island, Prince Edward Island, the eastern shore of New Brunswick as far north as Restigouche, the head of the Bay of Fundy, and, in later times, Newfoundland.

Subdivisions

Rand (1894) states that the Micmac distinguished seven districts, Prince Edward Island where the head chief lived, constituting one of these. The other six consisted of two groups of three each: one, called Sigunikt, including the districts of Memramcook, Pictou (at the north end of Nova Scotia), and Restigouche (in northern New Brunswick and neighboring parts of Quebec); the other, called Kespoogwit (south and east Nova Scotia), including Annapolis (in southwest Nova Scotia), Eskegawage (in east Nova Scotia from Canso to Halifax), and Shubenacadie (in north central Nova Scotia).

Villages

Antigonishe (?), probably on or near the site of the present Antigonishe, Nova Scotia.
Beaubassin, a mission, probably Micmac, site unknown.
Boat Harbor, near Pictou, Nova Scotia.
Chignecto, Nova Scotia.
Eskusone, on Cape Breton Island.
Indian Village, near Lake Badger, Fogo County, Newfoundland.
Isle of St. Johns, probably in Nova Scotia.
Kespoogwit, given by one authority as a village, see under subdivisions.
Kigicapigiak, on Cascapediac River, Bonaventure County, Quebec.
Le Have, near the mouth of Mercy River, about Lunenberg, Nova Scotia.
Maria, in Maria township, Bonaventure County, Quebec.
Minas, in Nova Scotia.
Miramichi, on the right bank of Miramichi River at its mouth.
Nalkithoniash, perhaps in Nova Scotia.
Nipigiguit, Bathurst, at the mouth of Nipisiguit River, New Brunswick.
Pictou, at the north end of Nova Scotia.
Pohomoosh, probably in Nova Scotia.
Restigouche, on the north bank of Restigouche River near its mouth, Bonaventure County, Quebec.
Richibucto, at the mouth of Richibucto River, Kent County, New Brunswick.
Rocky Point, on Prince Edward Island.
Shediac, at Shediac on the east coast of New Brunswick.
Shubenacadie, at the head of Shubenacadie River, Nova Scotia.
Tabogimkik, probably in Nova Scotia.

History.—Some Micmac may have been encountered by Norse voyagers about A. D. 1000. They were probably seen next by John Cabot in 1497, and from that time on they were constantly visited by explorers and even more by fishing vessels from France and England. During this period they acted as middlemen between the Europeans and the Indians farther west and south and found this profitable. Early in the seventeenth century they were missionized by the French and became so devoted to French interests that after the cession of Acadia to England in 1713 disputes and difficulties between them and the English continued until 1779.   Since then they have been peaceful occupants of the territory with which they have always been associated and have gradually adopted the ways and customs of European civilization.

Population.—Mooney's (1928) estimate for the Micmac applying to the year 1600 is 3,500.   This seems to be based on Biard's 1611 estimate of 3,000 to 3,500.   (See Jesuit Relations, 1858.)   In 1760 they were reported to number sonewhat under 3,000 but after that date they increased and in 1884 were officially reported as 4,037.   The Canadian Report of Indian Affairs for 1904 gives 3,861, but it does not include the Micmac of Newfoundland.

Connections in which they have become noted.—The Micmac are remarkable (1) as having been one of the earliest Indian tribes of the North American continent, if not the very earliest, to be encountered by Europeans, and (2) that, in spite of that fact and contrary to the general impression, they suffered no permanent decline in numbers and continued to occupy the territories, or at least a part of the territories, in which they had been found.

Montagnais-Naskapi.   The first component, a French word meaning "mountaineers," and so called from the character of their country; and the second, a term of reproach applied by the Montagnais themselves to their more northern kindred.   Also called:

> Chauhaguéronon, Huron name.
> Kebiks, said to have been so named on account of their warning cry of "Kebik!" when approaching in canoes the rapids of the St. Lawrence near Quebec.
> Ne-e-no-il-no, a name used by themselves, meaning "perfect people."
> Shŏudămŭnk, Beothuk name, meaning "good Indians."
> Tshe-tsi-uetin-euerno, a name used by themselves and said to signify "people of the north-northeast."
> Ussagĕne'wi, Penobscot name, meaning "people of the outlet."
> Ussaghenick, Malecite name.

Connections.—The Montagnais-Naskapi belong to the Algonquian linguistic stock, their nearest relatives being the Cree from whom they are set off by certain phonetic peculiarities.

Location.—Between St. Maurice River and the hinterland of Labrador, and from the River and Gulf of St. Lawrence to James Bay, including also the entire interior of the Labrador Peninsula.   The Labrador division has sometimes been made independent under the name "Nascapee" (Naskapi) but without sufficient justification.

Bands

The southern bands of this group were encountered by Europeans early in the seventeenth century while the northern ones, except for some on James Bay, were but little known until the nineteenth century. To this circumstance, more than anything else, we owe the two names Montagnais and Naskapi. Bands which probably existed in some form or other in 1650, although not necessarily under the names given, were the following:

Bersimis, on Bersimis River.

Chicoutimi, at Chicoutimi and northward.

Chisedec, on Seven Islands and Moisie River.

Escoumains, on and near Escoumains River.

Godbout, on Godbout River.

Mistassini, about Lake Mistassini.

Nichikun, about Nichikun Lake.

Ouchestigouetch, at the heads of Manikuagan and Kaniapiskau Rivers.

Oumamiwek or Ste. Marguerite, on Ste. Marguerite River and to the westward.

Papinachois, at the head of Bersimis River and eastward.

Tadousac, on the west side of the lower Saguenay River.

By 1850 (following Speck, 1942) we find that some of these, including the Chisedec, Oumamiwek, and Papinachois, have disappeared or been renamed, and the following added:

Barren Ground, on the middle course of George River.

Big River, on Great Whale and Fort George Rivers.

Davis Inlet, south of the Barren Ground band.

Eastmain, on and to the northward of Eastmain River.

Kaniapiskau, at the head of Kaniapiskau River.

Michikamau, around Mishikamau Lake.

Mingan, on Mingan River.

Musquaro or Romaine, on Olomanoshibo River.

Natashkwan, on Natashkwan River.

Northwest River, north of Hamilton Inlet and on Northwest River.

Petisikapau, on Petisikapau Lake and in the surrounding country.

Rupert House, on Rupert Bay and River.

St. Augustin, on St. Augustin River.

Shelter Bay, on Shelter Bay River, a modern subdivision.

Ungava, southwest of Ungava Bay.

Waswanipi, on Waswanipi River.

White Whale River, between Lake Minto and Little Whale River and eastward to Kaniapiskau River or even to Whale River.

The territory of the Kaniapiskau and Petisikapau seems to be within that of the earlier Ouchestigouetch. The Shelter Bay band is of very recent origin and seems to have been in the land of the Oumamiwek. The Mingan, Musquaro or Romaine, Natashkwan, Northwest River, and St. Augustine bands are in a region formerly occupied by Eskimo.

Villages

Appeelatat, on the south coast of Labrador.

Assuapmushan, a mission, probably at the entrance of Ashuapmouchouan River into Lake St. John.

Bonne Espérance, at the mouth of Eskimo River on the north coast of the Gulf of St. Lawrence.

Chicoutimi, a mission, on the right bank of the Saguenay at the present place of the same name, Quebec Province.

Esquimaux Point, on the north shore of the Gulf of St. Lawrence, about 20 miles east of Mingan.

Godbout, on the north shore of St. Lawrence River at the mouth of Godbout River.

Itamameou, a mission, on the north bank of St. Lawrence River east of Natash-quan.

Islets de Jeremie, probably Montagnais, on lower St. Lawrence River.

Mingan, on the north shore of the Gulf of St. Lawrence, near the mouth of Mingan River.

Moisie, a summer village of Montagnais and Naskapi, at the mouth of Moisie River.

Mushkoniatawee, on the south coast of Labrador.

Musquarro, on the north shore of the Gulf of St. Lawrence, opposite Anticosti Island.

Nabisipi, on the north shore of the Gulf of St. Lawrence, opposite Anticosti Island.

Natashkwan, on the north shore of the Gulf of St. Lawrence, at the mouth of Natashkwan River.

Pashasheebo, on the north shore of the Gulf of St. Lawrence.

Romaine, at the mouth of Olomanoshibo River on the north shore of the Gulf of St. Lawrence.

St. Augustine, with Naskapi, on the north shore of the Gulf of St. Lawrence.

History.—Montagnais were met by Champlain in 1603 at the mouth of the Saguenay. Missionary work was begun among them in 1615 and they remained firm friends of the French. During the wars between the French and Iroquois, the latter drove some Montagnais bands out of their old seats, but they reoccupied them again on the restoration of peace. The first explorers of the Gulf of St. Lawrence found its northern shore as far west as Mingan in possession of the Eskimo, but the latter people soon retired from this region and the Montagnais took their places. They have gradually adjusted themselves to the new conditions brought about by European colonization, the fur trade serving to protect them from the expropriation suffered so much by the Indians farther south.

Population.—Mooney (1928) estimates the Montagnais and Naskapi together as numbering 5,500 in 1600. In 1812 they were supposed to total 1,500; in 1857 they were estimated at 1,100; and in 1884 they were officially reported at 1,395, but this figure includes only seven bands. In 1906 the Montagnais in the same territory, together with the Naskapi, numbered 2,183.

Nahane. Signifying "people of the west." Also called:

Gōnana, Tlingit name (applied to all interior Indians).

Connections.—The Nahane form a major division of the Athapascan linguistic stock.

Location.—In northern British Columbia and the Yukon Territory between the coast range and the Rocky Mountains and latitude 57° and 60° N., some bands extending to the Mackenzie River in Mackenzie Territory.

Subdivisions

There is no consistency in the lists given by various writers, and Jenness reports a great deal of displacement since the early nineteenth century. The following bands or tribes may, however, be enumerated:

Esbataottine, in the valleys of Beaver, Nahanni, and North Nahanni Rivers.
Etagottine, in the valleys of Gravel and Dahachuni Rivers.
Kaska, on the upper Liard River.
Pelly River Indians, the country in the vicinity of Ross and Perry Rivers.
Tagish, about Tagish and Marsh Lakes.
Takutine, on Teslin River and Lake and upper Taku River.
Titshotina, between the Cassiar Mountains and Liard and Dease Rivers, British Columbia.

The Tahltan (q. v.) are sometimes regarded as a Nahane band.

History.—Some of the easternmost bands of Nahane may have been met by Mackenzie in 1789. Fort Simpson, at the junction of the Liard and Mackenzie Rivers became the base of operations for exploitation of the Nahane country. This was established at the very beginning of the nineteenth century and shortly afterward Fort Liard at the junction of the Liard and Black Rivers and Fort Nelson on the south branch of the Liard, now Fort Nelson River, brought the Hudson Bay factors still farther into Nahane territory. The last-mentioned fort was destroyed by the Indians but reestablished in 1865. Fort Halkett, on the upper Liard, and in the very heart of Nahane territory, was established soon after the union of the Northwest and Hudson's Bay Companies, which took place in 1821. Forty or fifty years later it was abandoned but a smaller post called Toad River was built some time afterward, halfway between the site of Halkett and Fort Liard. In 1834 Chief Trader John M. McLeod pushed up through the mountains and discovered Dease River and Dease Lake. In 1838, a trading post was established on the latter by Robert Campbell, a Scotch officer, and in the summer of that year he pushed across the Pacific slope to the headwaters of the Stikine. His post excited the hostility of the coast Indians, however, who had enjoyed a monopoly of trade with the Athapascans, and Campbell was forced to abandon it, and it was burned by the coast Indians. In 1840 he went north from Fort Halkett as far as Pelly River. In 1842 he built a fort at Lake Francis and Pelly Banks and in 1848 Fort Selkirk at the junction of the Pelly and Lewis Rivers. Two years afterward this latter was destroyed by the Chilkat, whose trade monopoly it threatened. In the meantime European influences had been working inland through the medium of the same coast tribes, from the Russian and from British and American trading vessels, and later on through the Hudson's Bay Company along the passageway marked by the Stikine River. The Nahane were powerfully affected by the Klondike rush, and since then European influences have been growing ever stronger.

Population.—Mooney (1928) estimates that there were about 2,000 Nahane in the present British Columbia in 1780 and 800 in the Yukon Territory in 1670, besides 400 "Mountain Indians" (Tsethaottine). A few hundred must be added for the Nahane in Mackenzie District. In 1906 there were 374 Nahane in British Columbia, 600 in Yukon Territory, and 250 in Mackenzie District. This total, 1,224, agrees fairly well with the 1,000 estimate of Morice (1904).

Nakotcho-kutchin. Signifying "those who dwell on the flats." Also called:

> Gens de la Grande Riviere, by Ross (MS.).
> Loucheux, by Franklin (1823, p. 261).
> Mackenzie Flats Kutchin, by Osgood (1934, p. 174).
> Mackenzie's River Louchioux, by Ross (MS.).

Connections.—The Nakotcho-kutchin were one of the tribes of the Kutchin group of the northern division of the Athapascan linguistic stock.

Location.—On the lower course of Mackenzie River north of the Kawchodinneh and extending to the head of the Mackenzie Delta.

Population.—With two neighboring tribes, Mooney (1928) estimates a population of 800 Nakotcho-kutchin in 1670. In 1906 he estimates there were 600. (See **Kutcha-kutchin** under Alaska.)

Nanaimo. A contraction of Snanaimux, meaning "people of Snonowas (Nanoose)."

Connections.—The Nanaimo belonged to the Cowichan branch of the coastal division of the Salishan linguistic family.

Location.—On the east coast of Vancouver Island about Nanaimo Harbor and Nanoose Bay.

Subdivisions

Nanaimo, about Nanaimo Harbor.
Snonowas, about Nanoose Bay.

History.—The history of the Nanaimo was practically identical with that of the Cowichan.

Population.—(See **Cowichan.**) In 1906 there were 161 Nanaimo and in 1909, 14 Snonowas.

Connection in which they have become noted.—The Nanaimo have given their name to an important port, owing its existence largely to the lignite coal deposits in the vicinity.

Neutral. This name was applied to a confederacy of Iroquoian tribes found by the Whites in occupancy of the southern part of Ontario, the western extremity of New York, and portions of Michigan and Ohio. (See New York.)

Niska. Significance unknown. Phonetically spelled Nisk`a'. Also called:

Nass River Indians, from their habitat.

Connections.—The Niska were one of the three tribes or tribal groups constituting the Chimmesyan linguistic family.

Location.—On Nass River and the neighboring coast. (See also Alaska.)

Subdivisions and Villages

There were four divisions or tribes which, including the village or villages of each, are as follows:

Kithateh or Gitrhatin, including the villages of Kincolith, on Nass Inlet, and Lakkulzap or Greenville.

Kitgigenik or Gitwinksilk, including the village of Lahanla or Lakungida, near the mouth of Nass River.

Kitwinshilk, including the village of Lahulyans or Underleaf.

Kitanwilksh, including the village of Kitlakdamik or Gitlarhdamks, above the canyon of Nass River, and Aiyansh, on the lower course of Nass River.

The following names of villages are also given by various writers:

Kitaix, near the mouth of Nass River.

Gwinwah, on Nass River.

Kisthemuwelgit or Willshilhunhtumwillwillgit, on the north side of Nass River near its mouth.

Qunahhair, on the south bank of Nass River just below the canyon.

Sheaksh, on the south bank of Nass River, 5 miles above the canyon.

Kitahon, Kitangata, Kitlakaous, and Andeguale may be additional towns or synonymous names for some of the above.

Emmons (*in* Hodge, 1910) divides the Niska into the Kitkahteen (Kithatch), including those below the canyon, and the Kitanweliks (Kitanwilksh), those above the canyon.

History.—The history of the Niska was almost the same as that of the Tsimshian (q. v.), though the resort of so many tribes to Nass River during the eulachon run may have given them a more cosmopolitan character than the other Chimmesyans.

Population.—(See **Tsimshian.**) In 1902 the population of the Niska towns was given as 842, in 1906 as 814.

Connection in which they have become noted.—Besides the connections mentioned in treating of the Tsimshian, the Niska were noteworthy from the fact that the territory they occupied included Nass Inlet, which was a place of resort for tribes from all sections during the eulachon season, and that the myths of many of these tribes center around it. Perhaps it was owing to this circumstance that the

Nass River seems to have been the center of the northwest cultural area.

Nooksak. A tribe, living mainly in the State of Washington, which is said to have branched off from the Squawmish of British Columbia. (See Washington.)

Nootka. Significance unknown. The name was originally applied to a tribe also known as Mooachaht living at Nootka Sound but was afterward extended to all of the tribes of the same group even including the Makah of the State of Washington, though the latter are more often treated independently. (See **Makah** under Washington.) Also called:

> Aht, from the endings of their divisional names.
> Tc'ecā'atq, Skokomish name.

Connections.—The Nootka constituted one of the two great branches of the Wakashan linguistic family, the other being the Kwakiutl.

Location.—All the Nootka are located on the west coast of Vancouver Island from Cape Cook on the north to beyond Port San Juan, except the Makah and Ozette, who live about Cape Flattery, in the State of Washington.

Subdivisions or Tribes

Ahousaht, about Clayoquot Sound.
Chaicclesaht, on Ououkinsh and Nasparte Inlets.
Clayoquot, on Meares Island and Torfino Inlet.
Ehatisaht, on Esperanza Inlet.
Ekoolthaht, on Barclay Sound.
Hachaaht, on or north of Barclay Sound.
Hesquiat, on Hesquiat Harbor.
Kelsemaht, on Clayoquot Sound.
Klahosaht, north of Nootka Sound.
Kwoneatshatka, toward the north end of Vancouver Island.
Kyuquot, on Kyuquot Sound.
Makah, about Cape Flattery.
Manosaht, at Hesquiat Point.
Mooachaht, on the north side of Nootka Sound.
Muchalat, on Muchalat Arm of Nootka Sound.
Nitinat, on the tidal lake of Nitinat near the southwest coast of Vancouver Island.
Nuchatlitz, on Nuchalitz and Esperanza Inlets.
Oiaht, on Barclay Sound.
Opitchesaht, on Alberni Canal, Somass River, and neighboring lakes.
Pacheenaht, on San Juan Harbor.
Seshart, on Barclay Sound and Alberni Canal.
Toquart, on the north shore of Barclay Sound.
Uchucklesit, on Uchucklesit Harbor, Barclay Sound.
Ucluelet, at the north entrance of Barclay Sound.

Villages

Exclusive of the Makah and Ozette towns (see Washington), the names of the following Nootka villages have been recorded:

Acous (Chaicclesaht).
Ahadzooas (Oiaht).
Ahahsuinnis (Opitchesaht).
Aktese (Kyuquot).
Carmanah (Nitinat).
Cheshish (Muchalat).
Clo-oose (Nitinat).
Elhlateese (Uchucklesit).
Heshque (Hesquiat).
Ittatso (Ucluelet).
Kukamukamees (Kyuquot).

Mahcoah (Toquart).
Mahktosis (Ahousaht).
Nuchatl (Nuchatlitz).
Oke (Ehatisaht).
Pacheena (Pacheenaht).
Tsahahch (Seshart).
Tsooquahna (Nitinat).
Wyah (Nitinat).
Yahksis (Kelsemaht).
Yucuatl (Mooachaht).

History.—Juan de Fuca (1592) is the first white man known to have visited the Nootka country. Fuentes, if he and his voyage be not myths, was among these people, or at least near them, in 1640. Ensign Juan Perez is believed to have anchored in Nootka Sound in 1774, and the next year Bodega and Maurelle passed along the Nootka coasts on their way south. From March to April 1778, Captain Cook was at Nootka Sound, and we owe one of our oldest accounts of the Indians there to him. In 1786 English vessels under Captains Hanna, Portlock, and Dixon visited them and from that time on British and American trading vessels constantly resorted to them, usually calling at Nootka Sound. Between 1792 and 1794 Capt. George Vancouver visited the country. In 1803 the *Boston*, from the New England port of that name, was destroyed by Nootka Indians and all on board killed except two persons, one of whom, John Jewett (1815), has left us an important account of his captivity and his captors. A new era was opened with the settlement of Victoria in 1843 and since then absorption in European culture has gone on apace. The Nootka have been missionized principally by the Roman Catholic Church.

Population.—Mooney (1928) estimated that, in 1780, there were 6,000 Nootka proper and 2,000 Makah. In 1906 there were 2,159 and 435 respectively.

Connections in which they have become noted.—The claim of the Nootka to special recognition rests, (1) on the fact that, with the exception of a few of their neighbors, they were the only Indians on the Pacific coast who hunted whales; and, (2) from the part played by Nootka Sound in the early history of the northwest coast.

Ntlakyapamuk. From their own name Nʟakˑaʹpamux. Also called:

Cêʹqtamux (c=sh), Lillooet name, from their name for Thompson River.
Knife Indians, by the employees of the Hudson's Bay Company.
Lükatimüʹx, Okanagon name.
Nkoʹatamux, Shuswap name.

Salic, Okanagon name.

Semā'mila, by the Cowichan of Fraser River.

Thompson River Indians, popular name given by the Whites.

Connections.—The Ntlakyapamuk were a tribe of the interior division of the Salishan linguistic stock.

Location.—On Fraser and Thompson Rivers, B. C. (See also Washington.)

Subdivisions and Villages

Lower Thompson, on Fraser River from a short distance below Spuzzum nearly to Cisco:

Chetawe, on the east side of Fraser River about 16½ miles above Yale.

Kalulaadlek, on the east side of Fraser River about 24 miles above Yale.

Kapachichin, on the west side of Fraser River about 28 miles above Yale.

Kapaslok, on Fraser River above Suk.

Kimus, on the east side of the Fraser between Yale and Siska.

Kleaukt, on Fraser River below North Bend.

Koiaum, on the east side of Fraser River 25 miles above Yale.

Nkakim, near Spuzzum, on Fraser River.

Nkattsim, on the east side of Fraser River about 38 miles above Yale and near Keefer's Station.

Nkoiam, on Fraser River below Cisco.

Noieltsi, on the west side of Fraser River about 23 miles above Yale.

Npiktim, on the east side of Fraser River about 30 miles above Yale.

Ntsuwiek, on the west side of Fraser River 27 miles above Yale.

Sintaktl, on the west side of Fraser River 30 to 40 miles above Yale.

Skohwak, on the west side of Fraser River about 15 miles above Yale.

Skuzis, on Fraser River above Spuzzum.

Skwauyik, on the west side of Fraser River.

Spaim, on the east side of Fraser River.

Spuzzum, on the west side of Fraser River below Spuzzum Station.

Stahehani, on the east side of Fraser River between Keefer's Station and Cisco.

Suk, on the east side of Fraser River below Keefer's Station.

Takwayaum, on Fraser River below North Bend.

Tikwalus, on the east side of Fraser River 13 miles above Yale.

Tliktlaketin, on the east side of Fraser River 3 miles below Cisco.

Tzauamuk, on Fraser River 6 or 7 miles above Boston Bar.

Upper Thompson; Lytton band (Lytton and vicinity):

Anektettim, on the east side of Fraser River, 3 miles above Lytton.

Cisco, on Fraser River 8 miles below Lytton.

Kittsawat, near Lytton.

Natkelptetenk, on the west side of Fraser River about 1 mile above Lytton.

Nchekchekokenk, on the west side of Fraser River, 15 miles above Lytton.

Nehowmean, on the west side of Fraser River, 1½ miles above Lytton.

Nikaomin, on the south side of Thompson River, 10 miles above Lytton.

Nkoikin, on the east side of Fraser River, 8 miles above Lytton.

Nkya, on the west side of Fraser River, 2 miles below Lytton.

Noöt, on the west side of Fraser River, 12 miles above Lytton.

Npuichin, on the west side of Fraser River, 8 miles above Lytton.

Ntlaktlakitin, at Kanaka Bar, Fraser River, about 11 miles below Lytton.

Staiya, on the east bank of Fraser River just below Lytton.

Stryne, on the west side of Fraser River, 5 miles above Lytton.

Tlkamcheen on the south side of Thompson River at its junction with the Fraser.

Tuhezep, on the east side of Fraser River about 1 mile above Lytton.

Upper Fraser Band, from the territory of the Lytton band up Fraser River for a distance of 40 miles:

Ahulka, on Fraser River just below Siska.

Nesikeep, on the west side of Fraser River, 38 miles above Lytton.

Nkaktko, on the west side of Fraser River 28 miles above Lytton.

Ntlippaem, on the west side of Fraser River 22 miles above Lytton.

Skekaitin, on the west side of Fraser River 43 miles above Lytton.

Tiaks, at Fosters Bar on the east side of Fraser River, 28 miles above Lytton.

Spences Bridge band, from the territory of the Lytton band up Thompson River nearly to Ashcroft:

Atchitchiken, on the north side of Thompson River 3 miles back in the mountains from Spences Bridge.

Klukluuk, on Nicola River 8 miles from Spences Bridge.

Nkamchin, on the south side of Thompson River at its junction with the Nicola, about 24½ miles above Lytton.

Nkoeitko, on the south side of Thompson River 30 miles above Lytton.

Nokem, at Drynoch, on the south side of Thompson River 16 miles above Lytton.

Nskakaulten, on the south side of Thompson River, ½ mile below Spences Bridge.

Ntekem, on the north side of Thompson River about 1 mile back from the stream and 39 miles above Lytton.

Nukaatko, on the north side of Thompson River 43 miles above Lytton.

Pekaist, on the south side of Thompson River, 32 miles above Lytton.

Pemainus, on the south side of Thompson River 28 miles above Lytton.

Semehau, on the north side of Thompson River 32 miles above Lytton.

Snapa, on the south side of Thompson River, 1½ miles back from the stream and 42 miles above Lytton.

Spatsum, on the south side of Thompson River, 35 miles above Lytton.

Stlaz, at Cornwalls near Ashcroft, 1 mile back from Thompson River.

Tlotlowuk, on Nicola River about 8 miles from Spences Bridge.

Zakhauzsiken, on the south side of Thompson River, half a mile back from the stream and 31 miles above Lytton.

Nicola band, in the valley of Nicola River:

Hanehewedl, near Nicola River, 27 miles above Spences Bridge.

Huthutkawedl, near Nicola River, 23 miles above Spences Bridge.

Koiskana, near Nicola River, 29 miles above Spences Bridge.

Kwilchana, on Nicola Lake.

Naaik, near Nicola River, 39 miles above Spences Bridge.

Nchekus, about 1 mile back in the mountains from Kwilchana.

Nsisket, near Nicola River a few miles from the west end of Nicola Lake.

Nrstlatko, near Nicola River a few miles from the west end of Nicola Lake.

Petutek, on Nicola river about 41 miles above Spences Bridge.

Shahanik, near Nicola River, 16 miles above Spences Bridge.

Tsulus, near Nicola River about 40 miles above Spences Bridge.

Zoht, near the west end of Nicola Lake, 50 miles above Spences Bridge.

History.—Simon Fraser passed through the territory of the Ntlakyapamuk in 1809 and was followed by numerous employees of the

Northwest and Hudson's Bay Companies. More injurious to the welfare of the Indians by far was the invasion of the miners in 1858. In 1863 the tribe was decimated by smallpox, and this and other epidemics have cut down numbers of them at various periods. They have continued to live in their ancestral territories though crowded into narrower quarters by the invasion and settlements of the Whites.

Population.—Mooney (1928) estimates that in 1780 there were 5,000 Ntlakyapamuk. The report of the Canadian Department of Indian Affairs for 1902 gives 1,826 and that for 1906, 1,776.

Okanagon. A tribe living on Okanagan Lake and later in the Similkameen Valley, and extending southward on the west side of Okanogan River to old Fort Okanogan in the State of Washington. (See Washington.)

Ottawa. This tribe occupied Manitoulin Island and bands belonging to it extended eastward toward Ottawa River. At a very early period they made settlements in the southern peninsula of Michigan. (See Michigan.)

Passamaquoddy. A tribe affiliated with the Malecite, living on Passamaquoddy Bay and St. Croix River, in New Brunswick and Maine. (See Maine.)

Puntlatsh. Phonetically rendered Pentlatc, significance unknown.

Connections.—The Puntlatsh constituted a dialectic group of the coastal division of the Salishan linguistic family.

Location.—On the east coast of Vancouver Island between the Cowichan and Comox tribes.

Subdivisions

Hwahwatl, on Englishman River.
Puntlatsh, on Baynes Sound and Puntlatsh River.
Saämen, on Kwalekum River.

History.—The history of the Puntlatsh is practically the same as that of the Cowichan (q. v.).

Population.—Mooney (1928) estimates 300 Puntlatsh in 1780; reduced to 13 in 1906.

Connection in which they have become noted.—The Puntlatsh have given their name to Puntlatsh River, B. C.

Sarcee or Sarsi. From the Siksika (Blackfoot) words *sa arsi*, "not good." Also called:

Castors des Prairies, by Petitot, (1891, p. 362).
Circee, by Franklin, (1824, vol. 1, p. 170).
Ciriés, by Gairdner in 1835 (1841. p. 257).
Isashbahátsĕ, by Curtis (1907–9, p. 180), meaning "bad robes": Crow name.

Mauvais Monde des Pieds-Noirs, by Petitot (1891).

Sussee, by Umfreville in 1790 (1859, p. 270).

Sussekoon, by Henry, Blackfoot MS. vocab., 1808: Siksika name.

Tcŏ′kŏ, or Tsū′qŏs, by Chamberlain (1892, p. 8): Kutenai name.

Tsŏ-Ottinè, by Petitot (1891, p. 362), meaning "people among the beavers".

Ussinnewudj Eninnewug, by Tanner (1830, p. 316), meaning "stone mountain men": Ottawa name.

Connections.—The Sarcee were connected with the Sekani and Tsattine divisions of the Athapascan linguistic family and probably separated from the latter.

Location.—When first known to Europeans, the Sarcee were usually found on the upper courses of the Saskatchewan and Athabaska Rivers toward the Rocky Mountains.

Subdivisions

Jenness (1938) states that the tribe is constituted of the following five bands at the present time :

(1) Bloods, Klowanga or Big Plume's band, of mixed Sarcee and Blood (Blackfoot) descent.

(2) Broad Grass, Tents Cut Down, or Crow-Child's band, mixed Cree and Sarcee, hence their name, signifying that they came from the north where the grass is thick and long.

(3) People who hold aloof or Crow-Chief's band, nearly all pure Sarcee.

(4) Uterus or Old Sarcee's band, part Blackfoot, part Sarcee.

(5) Young Buffalo Robe or Many Horses' band, occasionally called also "Those who keep together."

History.—The Sarcee evidently drifted to the Saskatchewan River from the north and, as Jenness (1938) thinks, "possibly towards the end of the seventeenth century." They are first mentioned by Matthew Cocking in 1772–73, but the erection of a trading fort at Cumberland House, followed by others farther up North Saskatchewan River, soon made them well-known to the traders. Early in the nineteenth century the Indians of the section acquired horses and guns, intertribal warfare was increased to such an extent that several tribes united for mutual protection, and the Sarcee allied themselves for this purpose with the Blackfoot. Nevertheless, they continued to suffer from attacks of the Cree and other tribes, and their numbers were still farther reduced by epidemics, particularly the smallpox epidemics of 1836 and 1870 and one of scarlet fever in 1856. In 1877, along with the Blackfoot and Alberta Assiniboine, they signed a treaty ceding their hunting grounds to the Dominion Government, and in 1880 submitted to be placed upon a reservation, where they declined steadily in numbers until 1920.

Population.—Mooney (1928) estimated that there was a Sarcee population of 700 in 1670. Mackenzie (1801) estimated that there were 120 Sarcee warriors in 1801 and that their tents numbered 35.

Thompson (1916 ed.) and Henry (1801 ed.) allowed 90 tents, 150 warriors and about 650 souls. Sir John Franklin (1824) estimated that they had 100 tents. When their reservation life began Jenness (1938) believes that they numbered between 400 and 450, but they seem to have declined steadily and in 1924 there were 160 on the reserve, "all commonly considered Sarcee though an uncertain proportion were originally Cree and Blackfoot."

Connection in which they have become noted.—The Sarcee are noted as the only northern Athapascan band which is known to have become accustomed to life on the Plains, though it is probable that they merely represent a recent case of Plains adaptation such as took place at an earlier period with the Apache and Kiowa Apache successively.

Seechelt. From their own name Sīciatl (c=sh). Also called:

Nīciatl, Comox name.

Connections.—The Seechelt constituted a distinct dialectic group of the coastal division of the Salishan linguistic family.

Location.—On Jervis and Seechelt Inlets, Nelson Island, and the southern part of Texada Island, B. C.

Subdivisions

Anciently there were four divisions or septs of the Seechelt, as follows:

Kunechin, at the head of Queen's Reach, Jervis Inlet.

Skaiakos, with no fixed abode.

Tsonai, at Deserted Bay at the junction of Queen's Reach and Princess Royal Reach, Jervis Inlet.

Tuwanek, at the head of Narrow's Arm, Seechelt Inlet.

The Kunechin and Tsonai are said to be descended from Kwakiutl from Fort Rupert. Later all Seechelt came to live in one town called Chatelech, on Trail Bay, at the neck of Seechelt Peninsula.

History.—As above noted, two of the original four septs of the Seechelt trace their origin to Kwakiutl Indians from Fort Rupert. On physical grounds Hill-Tout (1902) thought them to be related to the Lillooet. Their history after the coming of Europeans has been similar to that of their neighbors. They were converted to Roman Catholicism by Bishop Durieu.

Population.—Mooney (1928) estimates that there were 1,000 Seechelt in 1780. In 1902 Hill-Tout gave a population of 325 but the Canadian Department of Indian Affairs only 236. The latter authority has 244 in 1909.

Connection in which they have become noted.—The Seechelt have given their name to Seechelt Inlet.

Sekani. Signifying "dwellers on the rocks." Also called:

Al-ta-tin, by Dawson (1888, p. 192 B).

Lhtaten, by Morice (1889, p. 118), meaning "inhabitants of beaver dams": applied also to Nahane.

Rocky Mountain Indians, by Bancroft (1886–90, vol. 1, p. 35, map).

Sastotene, by Teit quoted by Jenness (1937, p. 5): Kaska name for certain bands, meaning "black bear people".

Thé-ké-né, by Petitot (MS.), meaning "dwellers on the mountains."

Tsekenné, by Morice (1889, p. 112), meaning "inhabitants of the rocks." ["people of the contorted rocks," according to James Teit (1900)].

Tseloni, by Teit quoted by Jenness (1937, p. 5): Kaska name for certain bands, meaning "mountain top people".

T'set'sa'ut, by Jenness (1937, p. 5): so called by the Indians on Skeena and Nass Rivers.

Connections.—The Sekani formed a group of bands or tribes of the Athapascan linguistic stock, and were dialectically affiliated with the Tsattine and Sarcee.

Location.—On the headwaters of Peace and Liard Rivers and some of the neighboring western slopes of the Rocky Mountains.

Subdivisions

Jenness (1937) gives the following:

(1) Sasuchan or Sasuten, occupying all of the basin of Finlay River from the mouth of the Omineca north and west, including Thutade and Bear Lakes.

(2) Tsekani, occupying the country from McLeod Lake south to the divide, and east to the edge of the prairies.

(3) Tseloni, occupying the plateau country between the headwaters of Finlay and Liard Rivers, the Fox in its upper reaches, and the Kechika or Muddy River flowing through the center of their domain.

(4) Yutuwichan, in the country from the north end of McLeod Lake down the Parsnip and Peace Rivers to Rocky Mountain canyon and westward to the headwaters of the Manson and Nation Rivers, including Carp Lake and the upper reaches of Salmon River.

Morice (1889) counted nine bands, but he extended the name Sekani over the Tsattine and Sarcee and included three minor groups whose independent position is uncertain, and which have probably resulted from later mixtures.

History.—Jenness (1937) believes that the Sekani were driven into the Rocky Mountains as a result of the westward thrust of the Cree. Morice (1889) tells us that the first Sekani encountered by Europeans were evidently the band met by Alexander Mackenzie on June 9, 1793, when on his way to the Pacific Ocean. One of these guided him to the head of Parsnip River but deserted shortly before they came to the Fraser. In 1797 James Finlay ascended the river which now bears his name. A few years later James McDougall penetrated the Sekani country, and in 1805 Simon Fraser established Fort McLeod on McLeod Lake for the Sekani trade. Since then the contact of the tribe with the Whites has been continuous and cumulative. Traders were followed by miners and missionaries and all the influences of a more complicated civilization.

Population.—Mooney (1928) estimated that there were 3,200 Sekani in 1780, not counting the Esbataottine, of whom he thought there might have been 300 in 1670. Drake (1848), estimated 1,000 in 1820, and Morice 500 in 1887 and 1893. Mooney (1928) estimated there were 750 in 1906, including 250 Esbataottine, but a census taken by the Canadian Department of Indian Affairs in 1923 returned only 160.

Senijextee or **Lake Indians.** These were a Salish people living on the Arrow Lakes and across the International Boundary in the State of Washington as far down the Columbia as Kettle Falls. (See Washington.)

Shuswap. From Suxwa'pmux, their own name, meaning unknown. Also called:

> Atena or Atna, from a Carrier word, meaning "stranger."
> Tlik'atewū'mtlat, Kutenai name, meaning "without shirts or trousers."

Connections.—The Shuswap belong to the interior division of the Salishan linguistic stock.

Location.—The Shuswap occupied a territory on the middle course of the Fraser River, a second section of the Fraser near its head, the drainage of Thompson River above Kamloops Lake, and a large part of the valley of the upper Columbia above the Arrow Lakes.

Subdivisions

Stlemhulehamuk (SLemxu'lExamux), in the valley of Fraser River from High Bar to Soda Creek, including the people of Clinton.
Setlemuk (Se'tLmux), or Setlomuk (Set'Lomux) west of the Fraser, from about Churn Creek to beyond Riskie Creek.
Stietamuk (Stie'tamux), the interior of the plateau between Fraser and North Thompson Rivers.
Tekkakalt (Texqa'kallt) or Tekkekaltemuk (TExqê'kalltemux), people of the North Thompson region.
Skstellnemuk (Sxstê'llnEmux), on the Upper South Thompson, Shuswap Lake, and Spallumcheen River.
Stkamlulepsemuk (Stkamlu'lEpsEmux) or, sometimes, Sekwapmukoe (Sexwap-mux'ō'ē), the people of Kamloops and Savona.
Zaktcinemuk (Zaxtci'nEmux), in the valley of the Bonaparte River to near Ash-croft on the main Thompson, Cache Creek, Loon Lake, the lower part of Hat Creek, through Marble Canyon to Pavilion, and on both sides of Fraser River near that point.

Bands and the Principal Village of Each

Fraser River Division: Soda Creek (Hatsu'thl or Ha'tsu'thl), Buckskin Creek (Tcukkehwank), Williams Lake or Sugar Cane (Pethltcoktcitcen), Alkali Lake (Skat), Dog Creek (Ratltem or Ratlt), Canoe Creek (Teawak), Empire Valley (Tcekweptem or Tcekiuptem), Big Bar (Stekauz), High Bar (Thlenthlenaiten), Clinton (Pethlteket).
Cañon Division: Riskie Creek (Pek), North Cañon (Snhahalaus), South Cañon (Snhahelaus), Chilcotin Mouth (Tekhoilups).

Lake Division: Lake la Hache (Hatlinten or Hallinten), Canim Lake (Tskasken), Green Timber (Pelstsokomus).

North Thompson Division: Upper Thompson (Pesskalalten), Lower North Thompson (Tcoktcekwallk), Kinbaskets.

Bonaparte Division: Pavilion (Skwailak), Bonaparte River (Nhohieilten), Main Thompson.

Kamloops Division: Savona or Deadman's Creek (Sketskitcesten or Stskitcesten), Kamloops (Stkamluleps).

Shuswap Lake Division: South Thompson (Halaut), Adams Lake, Shuswap Lake (Kwaut), Spallumcheen (Spelemtcin), Arrow Lake.

History.—This tribe was encountered by Alexander Mackenzie in 1793 and Simon Fraser in 1808. Mackenzie is thought to have been the first white man to meet any of them and Fraser was the first to explore the northern and western parts of their country. They were followed by fur traders of the Hudson's Bay Company, among them a band of Iroquois who came about the year 1816. The appearance of miners in 1858 introduced much greater changes into their lives which have since undergone rapid alterations though they have not, as in the case of so many Indian tribes of the United States, been driven out of their ancient territories.

Population.—Mooney (1928) estimated that in 1780 the population of the Shuswap was 5,300. Teit (1909) obtained an estimate from an intelligent old Indian which would give a population in 1850 of 7,200. The returns of the Canadian Indian Office for 1903 were 2,185; for 1906, 2,236.

Connection in which they have become noted.—The Shuswap have given their name to a lake and hamlet in British Columbia.

Siksika (Blackfoot). In historic times this tribe was on the upper course of the Saskatchewan River and extended southward into the present State of Montana. Their eastern boundary was in the neighborhood of the 150th meridian, and they stretched westward to the Rocky Mountains. At an earlier period all seem to have been some distance north of the International Boundary. (See Montana.)

Songish. Name given to the principal band of the group by the Whites, who adopted it, in a corrupt form, from the name of a sept, the Stsâ'ñges. Also called:

Etzāmish, by the tribes of the south part of Puget Sound.
Lku'ngEn, own name.

Connections.—The Songish constituted one of the dialectic groups of the coastal division of the Salishan linguistic family.

Location.—At the southern end of Vancouver Island and on the west coast of San Juan Island, State of Washington.

Subdivisions

There were three principal bands or tribes: the Sanetch, Songish, and Sooke.

The Sanetch consisted of the following septs or bands: Mayne Island, Panquechin, Tsartilp, Tsawout, Tsehump, to which the Saturna Island Indians should be added.

The following are Songish bands or septs: Chikauach (at McNeill Bay, Vancouver Island), Chkungen (at McNeill Bay, Vancouver Island), Kekayeken (between Esquimalt and Beecher Bay, Vancouver Island), Kltlasen (at McNeill Bay), Ksapsem (at Esquimalt), Kukoak (at McNeill Bay), Kukulek (at Cadboro Bay, Vancouver Island), Lelek (at Cadboro Bay, Vancouver Bay), Sichanetl (at Oak Bay, Vancouver Island), Skingenes (on Discovery Island off Vancouver Island), Skuingkung (at Victoria), Stsanges (between Esquimalt and Beecher Bay).

History.—The Songish were probably first encountered by the Greek pilot Juan de Fuca in 1592, when he discovered the straits bearing his name. Spanish, English, and American exploring and trading vessels visited their country in ever-increasing numbers but the greatest change in their lives followed upon the settlement of Victoria, first as a Hudson's Bay Company post, in 1843. As this rose to be the capital of the province of British Columbia, it became a rendezvous of Indian tribes from all quarters and for all classes of Whites. It was at the same time a potent cause of the civilizing of the Songish and of their decline.

Population.—Mooney (1928) estimates that there were 2,700 people of the Songish group in 1780; they had become reduced to 488 in 1906.

Connection in which they have become noted.—The only claim of the Songish to special recognition is the fact that Victoria, the provincial capital of British Columbia, was founded in their country. The name of the Sanetch, a Songish band, is perpetuated in Saanich Peninsula and that of another Songish band, the Sooke, in Sooke Inlet.

Squawmish. Significance unknown. Phonetically spelled Sk'qo'mic.

Connections.—Together with the Nooksak of Washington, the Squawmish constituted a subdialect of the coastal division of the Salishan linguistic stock.

Location.—On Howe Sound and Burrard Inlet, north of the mouth of Fraser River.

Villages

Chakkai, on the east side of Howe Sound.

Chalkunts, on Gambier Island.

Chants, on Burrard Inlet.

Chechelmen, on Burrard Inlet.

Chechilkok, at Seymour Creek, Burrard Inlet.

Chekoalch, on Burrard Inlet.

Chewas, on the west side of Howe Sound.

Chiakamish, on Chiakamish Creek, a tributary of Squawmisht River.

Chichilek, on Burrard Inlet.

Chimai, on the left bank of Squawmisht River.

Chukchukts, on the left bank of Squawmisht River.

Ekuks, on the right bank of Squawmisht River.
Etleuk, on the right bank of Squawmisht River.
Hastings Saw Mill Indians.
Helshen, on Burrard Inlet.
Homulschison, at Capilano Creek, Burrard Inlet.
Huikuayaken, on Howe Sound.
Humelsom, on Burrard Inlet.
Ialmuk, at Jericho, Burrard Inlet.
Ikwopsum, on the left bank of Squawmisht River.
Itliok, on the left bank of Squawmisht River.
Kaayahunik, on the west bank of Squawmisht River.
Kaksine, on Mamukum Creek, left bank of Squawmisht River.
Kapkapetlp, at Point Grey, Burrard Inlet.
Kauten, on the right bank of Squawmisht River
Kekelun, on the west side of Howe Sound.
Kekios, on the right bank of Squawmisht River.
Kekwaiakin, on the left bank of Squawmisht River.
Kelketos, on the east coast of Howe Sound.
Ketlalsm, on the east side of Howe Sound.
Kiaken, on the left bank of Squawmisht River.
Kiaken, on Burrard Inlet.
Kicham, on Burrard Inlet.
Koalcha, at Linn Creek, Burrard Inlet.
Koekoi, on the west side of Howe Sound.
Koikoi, on Burrard Inlet.
Kolelakom, on Bowen Island, Howe Sound.
Komps, on the right bank of Squawmisht River.
Kotlskaim, on Burrard Inlet.
Kuakumchen, on Howe Sound.
Kukutwom, on the east side of Howe Sound.
Kulatsen, on the east side of Howe Sound.
Kulaten, on Burrard Inlet.
Kwanaken, on Squawmisht River.
Kwichtenem, on the west side of Howe Sound.
Kwolan, on the right bank of Squawmisht River.
Male, shared with the Musqueam, north of Sea Island in the delta of Fraser River.
Mitlmetlelch, on Passage Island, Howe Sound.
Nkukapenach, on the right bank of Squawmisht River.
Nkuoosai, on Howe Sound.
Nkuoukten, on Howe Sound.
Npapuk, on the east side of Howe Sound.
Npokwis, on the right bank of Squawmisht River.
Nthaich, on the right bank of Squawmisht River.
Papiak, on Burrard Inlet.
Poiam, on the right bank of Squawmisht River.
Pokaiosum, on the left bank of Squawmisht River.
Sauktich, Hat Island, Howe Sound.
Schilks, on the east side of Howe Sound.
Schink, at Gibson's Lodge, on the west side of Howe Sound.
Selelot, on Burrard Inlet.
Shemps, on the left bank of Squawmisht River.
Shishaiokoi, on the east coast of Howe Sound.

Siechem, on the right bank of Squawmisht River.

Skakaiek, on the right bank of Squawmisht River.

Skauishan, on the right bank of Squawmisht River.

Skeakunts, on Burrard Inlet.

Skeawatsut, at Port Atkinson on the east side of Howe Sound.

Skelsh, on Burrard Inlet.

Sklau, on the left bank of Squawmisht River.

Skoachais, on Burrard Inlet.

Skumin, on the left bank of Squawmisht River.

Skutuksen, on the east side of Howe Sound.

Skwaius, on Burrard Inlet.

Slokoi, on the right bank of Squawmisht River.

Smelakoa, on Burrard Inlet.

Smok, on the left bank of Squawmisht River.

Snauk, at False Creek, Burrard Inlet.

Spapak, on the right bank of Squawmisht River.

Stamis, on the left bank of Squawmisht River.

Stetuk, on Burrard Inlet.

Stlaun, on Burrard Inlet.

Stoktoks, on Howe Sound.

Stotoii, on the right bank of Squawmisht River.

Suntz, on Burrard Inlet.

Sutkel, on Burrard Inlet.

Swaiwi, on Burrard Inlet.

Swiat, on the west side of Howe Sound.

Thetsaken, on the east side of Howe Sound.

Thetuksem, on the west side of Howe Sound.

Thetusum, on the west side of Howe Sound.

Thotais, on the right bank of Squawmisht River.

Tktakai, on the right bank of Squawmisht River.

Tlakom, on Anvil Island in Howe Sound.

Tlastlemauk, in Burrard Inlet.

Tleatlum, on Burrard Inlet.

Toktakamai, on the right bank of Squawmisht River.

Tseklten, on Howe Sound.

Tumtls, on the east side of Howe Sound.

Ulksin, on Burrard Inlet.

Yukuts, on the right bank of Squawmisht River.

There were a few more villages at the upper end of Burrard Inlet. Modern villages are: Burrard Inlet, No. 3. Reserve; False Creek (same as Snauk, q. v.), Kapilano (see Homulchison), Seymour Creek (see Checkilkok), and Squamish (on Howe Sound).

History.—The history of the Squawmish has been practically identical with that of the other coast Salish tribes in their neighborhood.

Population.—Mooney (1928) estimates 1,800 Squawmish in 1780. In 1909, 174 were returned.

Connection in which they have become noted.—The Squawmish have given their name to Squawmisht River, B. C.

Stalo. Significance of name unknown. Also called:

Cowichan of Fraser River, on account of their close linguistic connection with the Cowichan proper of Vancouver Island.

Halkōme'lēm, said to be a name which they applied to themselves.

Hue-la-muh or Hum-a-luh, said to be the name by which at least a part of them called themselves.

Sa-chinco, Shuswap name for the upper Stalo, meaning "strangers."

Tē'it, name for those above Nicomen and Chilliwack Rivers, so-called by the lower bands.

Connections.—The Stalo belonged to the coastal division of the Salishan linguistic stock, their nearest relatives being the Cowichan of Vancouver Island with whom they are often classed.

Location.—On the lower Fraser River from a point below Spuzzum to the mouth of the river.

Subdivisions and Villages

Chehalis, along the middle course of Harrison River.

Chilliwack, on Chilliwack River; they formerly spoke Nooksak.

Coquitlam, in Fraser River Valley just above the delta, but owning no land because practically slaves of the Kwantlen.

Ewawoos, in a town called Skeltem, 2 miles above Hope, on Fraser River.

Katsey, in villages called Seltsas and Shuwalethet, on Pitt Lake and River.

Kelatl, in a town called Asilao, on Fraser River above Yale.

Kwantlen, in villages called Kikait, Kwantlen, Skaiametl, Skaiets, and Wharnock, between Stave River and the mouth of the southern arm of Fraser River and Sumass Lake.

Musqueam, in the northern part of Fraser Delta.

Nicomen, in villages called Skweahm and Lahuai, on Nicomen slough and at the mouth of Wilson Creek.

Ohamil, on the south side of Fraser River just below Hope.

Pilalt, in villages called Chutil, Kwalewia, Skelautuk, Skwala, Schachuhil, and perhaps Cheam, on lower Chilliwack River and part of Fraser River.

Popkum, in a town of the same name on lower Fraser River.

Scowlits, in a town of the same name at the mouth of Harrison River.

Sewathen, on the coast south of the mouth of Fraser River.

Siyita, in a village called Skuhamen, at Agassiz on Fraser River.

Skwawalooks, on Fraser River below Hope.

Snonkweametl, in a village called Snakwametl, on Fraser River.

Squawtits, on Fraser River between Agassiz and Hope.

Sumass, on Sumass Lake and River.

Tsakuam, in a town called Shilekuatl, at Yale.

Tsenes, location uncertain.

History.—The first visitors to the Stalo were probably Spaniards, possibly the companions of Juan de Fuca in 1592. In 1809 Simon Fraser passed through their country, and his name is perpetuated in that of the river upon which most of them lived. Afterward traders connected with the Northwest and Hudson's Bay Companies entered their territory more and more frequently and posts were established. They were followed about the middle of the nineteenth century by miners and the latter by more permanent settlers. Complete opening up of the country followed upon its penetration by the Canadian Pacific Railway and the consequent establishment of the port of Vancouver for trans-Pacific trade.

Population.—Mooney (1928) estimated that in 1780 there were 7,100 Stalo and in 1907, 1,451.

Stuwihamuk, So called by the Ntlakyapamuk Salish, significance unknown. Also called:

> Sɛi'lɛqamuǫ, another Ntlakyapamuk name, meaning "people of the high country."
>
> Smîlê'kamuǫ, a third Ntlakyapamuk name.

Connections.—The Stuwihamuk belonged to the Athapascan stock but to what particular branch of it is unknown.

Location.—In Nicola Valley.

History.—At some prehistoric period the Stuwihamuk forced their way into the midst of the territory occupied by Salishan tribes and were finally absorbed by the Ntlakyapamuk of Thompson River.

Population.—Mooney (1928) estimated that in 1780 there were 150 Stuwihamuk, basing his conclusions on Boas' (1895) estimate of 120 to 150 at a later period (1895).

Tahltan. Properly, according to Morice (1904 b), "Thalhthan, a contraction of Tha-sælhthan," from tha or thu, "water," and saelhthan, a verb that refers to some heavy object lying thereon, which seems to be confirmed by a myth reported to Emmons (1911), though some of the older people told the latter it was from a foreign tongue; some, however, derived it from "thalla-a, point, the first living place on the rocky tongue of land between Stikine and Tahltan Rivers; and still others claim that it originated from the exhibition or giving away of a piece of steel, thal, by a chief at a great feast given at this point in early days, in celebration of the bringing out of his daughter."

Connections.—The Tahltan belong to the Athapascan linguistic family, and have usually been classed with the Nahane, but we follow Jenness (1932) in treating them separately.

Location.—In the drainage basin of Stikine River down to the mouth of Iskut River, Dease Lake, and Dease River halfway to McDane Creek (though anciently the head of Dease Lake was not in their territory), the northern sources of the Nass and some of the southern branches of the Taku in Alaska and British Columbia.

Villages

Gikahnegah, a fishing village on the south bank of the Stikine opposite Nine Mile flat.

Lakneip, a subdivision or village on the upper course of Nass River.

Tahltan, called by themselves Goontdarshage, the modern village, 1½ miles northwest of the mouth of Tahltan River.

Teetch-aranee, on the south bank of the Tahltan near its mouth.

Thludlin, on Tahltan River some 12 miles above its mouth.

Tratuckka, a fishing village at Nine Mile flat on the Stikine River.

Tsaqudartsee, several miles beyond Teetch-aranee on the rock ledge separating the Stikine and Tahltan Rivers.

There were some others of which the names have not survived.

History.—The Tahltan claim descent from people from several different directions—the head of the Nass, Tagish Lake, the headwaters of the Taku, the Liard (or Peace) River, and also from the coast. Intimate contact with the Whites was delayed until placer gold was discovered in the river bottom below Glenora in 1861 when some desultory prospecting began, but constant contact only followed on the Cassiar gold excitement of 1874. They suffered in many ways from White contact, particularly during the smallpox epidemics of 1864 and 1868.

Population.—Mooney (1928) placed the entire Nahane population including this tribe at 2,000 in 1780. In 1909 there were 229 Tahltan.

Connection in which they have become noted.—The Tahltan are noted as a tribe whose organization has been made over by contact with coastal people.

Takkuth-kutchin. Significance uncertain but possibly "squinters." Also called:

Dakaz, by Morice (1906, p. 261).

Dakkadhè, by Petitot (1876, p. 20).

Deguthee Dennee, by Franklin (1828, p. 40).

Gens de rats, by Whymper (1868, 255).

Klovén-Kuttchin, by Petitot (1876).

Kukuth-kutchin,' by Bancroft (1886–90, vol. 1, p. 147).

Lapiene's House Indians, by Kirkby in Hind (1863, vol. 2, p. 254).

Louchieux Proper, by Ross (MS., p. 474).

Nattsae-Kouttchin, by Petitot (1891, p. 361), meaning "marmot people."

Porcupine River Indians, by Whymper (1868, p. 255).

Quarrelers, by Mackenzie (1801, p. 51).

Rat Indians, by Hardisty (1867, p. 311).

Rat River Indians, by Whymper (1868, p. 255).

Squint-Eyes, by Franklin (1824, p. 261).

Takadhé, by Petitot (MS.).

Tä-Kuth-Kutchin, by Hind (1863, p. 254).

Tykothee-dinneh, by Franklin (1824, p. 261).

Upper Porcupine River Kutchin, by Osgood (1934, p. 176).

Yukuth Kutchin, by Bancroft (1886–90, vol. 1, p. 115).

Connections.—The Takkuth-kutchin were the central and most characteristic tribe of the Kutchin group of the northern division of the Athapascan linguistic stock.

Location.—On the upper course of Porcupine River.

Population.—With the Vunta-kutchin and Tutcone, Mooney (1928) estimated that there were about 2,200 Takkuth-kutchin in 1670. In 1866 they had been reduced to 15 hunters or 40 men in all. Dawson (1888) gave 337 of this tribe and the Tatlit-kutchin; Morice (1906) estimated 150 in 1906. In 1910, 6 were living in Alaska. (See **Nakotcho-kutchin, Tatlit-kutchin**, and also **Kutcha-kutchin** under Alaska.)

Tatlit-kutchin. Signifying "those who dwell at the source of the river [i. e., the Peel River]." Also called:

> Fon du Lac Loucheux, by Hooper (1853, p. 270).
> Gens du fond du lac, by Ross (MS)..
> Peel River Kutchin, by Osgood (1934, p. 174).
> Sa-to-tin, by Dawson (1888).
> Tρe-tliet-Kouttchin, by Petitot (1891, p. 361).

Connections.—The Tatlit-kutchin belonged to the Kutchin group of tribes of the northern division of the Athapascan linguistic family, being particularly closely connected with the Takkuth-kutchin.

Location.—On Peel River and neighboring parts of the Mackenzie.

Population.—Mooney (1928) gives 800 to the Tatlit-kutchin and the Nakotcho-kutchin, together. In 1866, 30 hunters and 60 men in all were reported. (See **Nakotcho-kutchin, Takkuth-kutchin**, and also **Katcha-kutchin** under Alaska.)

Tatsanottine. Signifying "people of the scum of water," "scum" being a figurative expression for copper. Also called:

> Copper Indians, from the fact that copper was obtained in their country.
> Couteaux Jaunes, French-Canadian name.
> Red-knife Indians, referring to copper.
> Yellow-knife Indians, referring to copper.

Connections.—The Tatsanottine belonged to the Athapascan linguistic stock and were later classified with the Chipewyan, but their original position within the stock is unknown.

Location.—On the northern shores and eastern bays of Great Slave Lake.

History.—The Tatsanottine derived their name from the ore in a low mountain near Coppermine River which they formerly made into knives, axes, and other cutting tools and traded at fabulous prices, until the introduction of articles of European manufacture broke the market and they moved away from the mine toward trading posts in the south.

Population.—Mooney (1928) estimates that there were 430 in 1670. In 1859 a census, which may, however, have been only partial, returned 219. A later estimate by Morice (1906) gave 500.

Connection in which they have become noted.—The Tatsanottine have become noteworthy merely on account of their association with the copper deposit above mentioned.

Thlingchadinne, signifying "dog-flank people." Also called:

> Atticmospicayes or Attimospiquaies, by La Potherie, and said to mean "dog-ribs."
>
> Dog Ribs, popular English name from their own designation.
>
> Flancs-de-Chien or Plats-Côtes-de-Chien, French name derived from their own designation.
>
> Lintcanre, nickname applied by their congeners.

Connections.—The Thlingchadinne belonged to the Athapascan linguistic stock.

Location.—Between Great Bear Lake and Great Slave Lake but not extending to the Mackenzie River.

Subdivisions

Petitot (1891) gives the following divisions:

Lintchanre, north and east of the northern arm of Great Slave Lake.

Takfwelottine, southeast of Great Bear Lake and at the source of Coppermine River.

Tsantieottine, on La Martre Lake and River.

Tseottine, along the south shore of Great Bear Lake.

History.—The name of the Thlingchadinne appears as early as 1744. It is said that they were gradually forced northwest by the Cree but it is probable that this was true of only a part of them, the greater portion having occupied approximately the same territories. Their later history is bound up with that of the Hudson's Bay Company, the purveyors of European civilization to most of the Indians of northwestern Canada.

Population.—Mooney (1928) estimated that in 1670 there were 1,250 Indians of this tribe. In 1858 Ross (1858) gave their total population as 926. Morice (1906) estimated 1,150.

Tionontati, Signifying according to Hewitt (*in* Hodge, 1910), "there the mountain stands". Also called:

> Gens du Petun, French name, meaning "tobacco nation," first used by Champlain (1616), on account of their agricultural activities.
>
> Quieunontati, a slightly different form of Tionontati, meaning "where the mountain stands," used by some early writers.
>
> Tobacco Indians, Tobacco Nation, popular English name.

Connections.—The Tionontati belonged to the Iroquoian linguistic stock, being most closely connected probably with the Huron whose designation was sometimes extended over them.

Location.—In the highland south of Nottawasaga Bay, in Grey and Simcoe Counties, Ontario. (See also Wisconsin.)

Villages

Ehouae (mission of St. Pierre and St. Paul), Ekarenniondi (St. Matthieu), Etarita (St. Jean), St. Andre, St. Barthelemy, St. Jacques, St. Jacques et St. Philippe, St. Simon et St. Jude, St. Thomas.

History.—The Tionontati were first visited by Europeans, the French, in 1616, and in 1640 the Jesuits established a mission among them. When the Huron villages were destroyed by the Iroquois in 1648–49, many Hurons took refuge with this tribe, in consequence of which the Iroquois turned against them, and attacked Etarita in December 1649, during the absence of the warriors, destroying the mission and many of the inhabitants. In consequence the Tionontati abandoned their country and followed the fortunes of the Huron, with whom they subsequently became amalgamated. Hewitt believed that they are represented to a greater extent in the Wyandot of Ohio than were the Huron proper. (See **Wyandot** under Ohio.)

Population.—Mooney (1928) estimates that in 1600 the Tionontati had a population of 8,000. They are no longer separable from the Huron.

Connection in which they have become noted.—The Tionontati were noted solely for the extent to which they cultivated tobacco.

Tsattine. Signifying "dwellers among the beavers." Also called:

Beaver Indians, English term derived from their own name.

Connections.—The Tsattine belonged to the same branch of the Athapascan family as the Sekani and Sarcee.

Location.—On the prairies south of Peace River and east of the Rocky Mountains and on the upper part of Peace River.

History.—The Tsattine and the Sekani were originally one people, the separation having come about by the gradual penetration of the Sekani westward into the mountains. The Sarcee evidently branched off from the Beaver. The invasion of the Cree probably had something to do with all this. Some of the Indians of this tribe resorted to the Hudson's Bay Company's posts before there was a post in their own country. Mackenzie (1801) says that they first secured firearms in 1782. This was perhaps a result of the establishment of a post on Athabaska River by Peter Pond for the Northwest Company in 1778. It was abandoned a few years later and never rebuilt but other forts took its place, such as Athabaska Landing, Peace River Landing, Fort St. John, Fort Dunvegan, and a post on Little Slave Lake. Mackenzie spent the winter of 1792–93 with one band of Beaver near Peace River Crossing before setting out for the Pacific. Goddard (1916) states that they are now divided into three groups, one trading at Fort St. John, a second living about Dunvegan, and a third near Vermilion. There is also a large band at Hudson Hope.

Tsetsaut. Name given them by the Niska and signifying "people of the interior."

Connections.—The Tsetsaut belonged to the Athapascan stock and were usually considered as a Nahane tribe. Their dialect is said to be similar to Tahltan, yet they are reported to have branched off from the Kaska.

Location.—According to Teit, "their [the Tsetsaut's] country lay in a strip from near Bradfield canal and the Iskut across the streams flowing into Behm Canal perhaps to about the head of Boca de Quadra. They occupied all of the upper part of Portland Canal around Stewart, and Salmon and Bear Rivers. They may have come down the canal as far as Maple Bay. They occupied all the White River and Meziadin Lake basins and one of their original headquarters, especially for salmon fishing, was at Meziadin Lake. They stretched across the head of the Skeena River above Kuldo River over to Bear and Sustut lakes" (Teit's Note *in* D. Jenness, 1932).

History.—Once a large tribe they were almost exterminated by the Lakweip and Tlingit about 1830. They once lived further down Behm Canal and were friendly with the Sanya Tlingit until they discovered that the latter had determined to kill them and enslave their women and children, when they emigrated to Portland Canal and, becoming reduced in numbers, fell under the control of the Niska, among whom the last of them found homes.

Population.—About 1830 the Tsetsaut numbered 500; in 1895 they were reduced to 12.

Tsimshian. A native term meaning "people of Skeena River." Also called:

> Kilat, by the Masset Haida.
> Kilgat, by the Skidegate Haida.
> Kwē'tela, Heiltsuk Kwakiutl name.
> Skeena Indians, an English translation of their own name.
> Ts'ōtsqE'n, Tlingit name.

Connections.—The Tsimshian are the largest of the three divisions of the Chimmesyan linguistic stock, to which they have given their name.

Location.—On the lower course of Skeena River and the neighboring parts of the Pacific Coast. (See also Alaska.)

Subdivisions and Villages

The following are at the same time tribal or band, and town groups:
Kilutsai, near Metlakatla.
Kinagingeeg, near Metlakatla.
Kinuhtoiah, near Metlakatla.
Kishpachlaots, at Metlakatla.
Kitlani, near Metlakatla.
Kitsalthlal, between Nass and Skeena Rivers.

Kitunto, near the mouth of Skeena River.

Kitwilgioks, near the mouth of Skeena River.

Kitwilksheba, near Metlakatla and the mouth of Skeena River.

Kitzeesh, near Metlakatla.

These were the Tsimshian proper, but in a more extended sense the name applies to the Kitzilas, who occupied two towns in succession—Old Kitzilas just above the canyon of Skeena River, and New Kitzilas just below, and Kitzimgaylum, on the north side of Skeena River below the canyon. In a still more extended sense it covered the Kitkahta, on Douglas Channel; Kitkatla, on Porcher Island; and the Kittizoo, on the south side of Swindle Island, northwest of Milbank Sound. Modern towns are:

New Metlakatla, at Port Chester on Annette Island, Alaska.

Old Metlakatla, 15 miles south of Port Simpson.

Port Essington, at the mouth of Skeena River.

Port Simpson, between Old Metlakatla and the mouth of Nass River.

History.—Traditional and other evidence indicates that the Tsimshian formerly lived inland and have pushed down to the Pacific in relatively late times, probably displacing the Tlingit. Spanish navigators reached the latitude of their coast in very early times but it is questionable whether any actually touched there. In the latter part of the eighteenth century English and American explorers and traders met them and this contact became more intimate as time went on. Later the Hudson's Bay Company's posts were established at Fort Simpson in 1831 and at Fort Essington in 1835, and still later their country was overrun by miners and prospectors, particularly during the great Klondike rush. In 1857 Rev. William Duncan established a mission of the Church of England at Metlakatla, but, on account of differences with his superiors over the conduct of this work, he removed to Annette Island, Alaska, in 1887 with the greater part of the Indians under his charge and obtained the grant of this island for his colony. A still closer contact between them and the outside world resulted from the establishment of the terminus of the Grand Trunk (now the Canadian National Railway) among them at Prince Rupert.

Population.—Mooney (1928) estimated that in 1780 there were 5,500 Indians belonging to the Chimmesyan linguistic stock of which the Tsimshian were a part. In 1908 there were 1,840 Tsimshian, including 465 in Alaska.

Connection in which they have become noted.—The Indians of this stock, including the Tsimshian, are noted for their beautiful carvings, equaled if at all only by those of the neighboring Haida. They and the Haida together occupy the very center of the remarkable cultural area of the north Pacific coast, and their social and ceremonial institutions have attracted particular attention. Their language occupies a unique position among the tongues of the northwest.

608   BUREAU OF AMERICAN ETHNOLOGY   [BULL. 145]

Tutchone. Usually called Tutchone-kutchin, but their connection with the true Kutchin seems to be denied by later investigators; meaning of name "Crow People." Also called:

> Caribou Indians, by Dall (1877, p. 32).
> Gens de bois, by Whymper (1869, p. 255).
> Gens des Foux, by Dall (1870, p. 429).
> Klo-a-tsul-tshik', by Dawson (1889, p. 202).
> Mountain Indians, by Hardisty (1867, p. 311).
> Nehaunee, by Dall (1877, p. 32). (So called by Hudson's Bay Co. men.)
> Tatanchaks, by Colyer (1870, p. 593).
> Wood Indians, by Dawson (1889, p. 202). (So called by fur traders.)

Connections.—The Tutchone belonged to the Athapascan stock and were probably most closely related to the Han Indians on the Yukon River to the north and the Nabesna Indians to the west.

Location.—Between the Han Indians and the Nahane country.

Population.—Hodge (1910), gives 1,100, on what authority is not stated, and it is uncertain how many other tribes may be included in whole or in part.

THE WEST INDIES

INDIAN TRIBES OF HAITI

Bainoa.

Connections.—So far as known, the Bainoa belonged to the Arawakan linguistic family.

Location.—The Bainoa tribe or "province" included all of the present Republic of Haiti south of the San Nicolas Mountains, except that portion west of the River Savane, and also southwestern Santo Domingo to the River Maguana or San Juan.

Subdivisions

(As given by Peter Martyr (1912))

Amaquei.	Diaguo.
Anninici.	Guahabba.
Atiec.	Guarricco.
Attibuni, on the River Artibonite.	Honorucco.
Azzuei.	Iacchi.
Bauruco.	Iagohaiucho.
Buiaz.	Maccazina.
Camaie.	Maiaguarite.
Caunoa.	Neibaimao.
Dabaigua.	Yaguana.
Dahibonici.	Xaragua.

However, I have omitted from his list Marien and Maguana, which I believe should be considered distinct.

Cahibo or Cibao.

Connections.—The Cahibo belonged, so far as known, to the Arawakan linguistic family, except that a different language is said to have been spoken in the provinces of Cubana and Baiohaigua, but the difference may have been dialectic. Peter Martyr's words render it impossible to suppose the language of this entire tribe was distinct from the speech of the remaining Haitians.

Location.—The northwestern mountain section of Santo Domingo, about the Desert Mountains or Cordilleras del Cibao.

Subdivisions

Baiohaigua, Cotoy, Cubana, Cybaho, Dahaboon, Manabaho, and mountainous districts called Hazue, Mahaitin and Neibaymao.

Caizcimu.

Connections.—So far as known, all the Indians in this province belonged to the Arawakan linguistic family.

Location.—The eastern part of the present Dominican Republic, extending on the south side of the Bay of Samana to a point near the mouth of the Juna River and on the south coast of the whole island to the neighborhood of the mouth of the San Juan or Maguana. Peter Martyr (1912) defines it as reaching only to the coast just west of the present Ciudad Trujillo (formerly Santo Domingo City), but the subdivisions he names indicate the greater extension given above.

Subdivisions

Peter Martyr (1912), gives the following "districts or cantons": Arabo, Aramana, Baguanimabo, Caicoa, Guanama, Guiagua, Hazoa, Higuey, Macorix, Reyre, Xagua, and the rugged district of Haiti to the north.

Guaccaiarima.

Connections.—Cave dwellers were reputed to live here, from which circumstance at least the western part of the territory indicated is sometimes supposed to have been occupied by a people who preceded the Arawak, the Guanacahibes, who were also represented in western Cuba. No language of this province is known, however, distinct from Arawak.

Location.—All of the southwestern peninsula of the Republic of Haiti west of the River Savane.

Subdivisions

Peter Martyr gives the following "cantons": Ayqueroa, Cahaymi, Guabaqua, Habacoa, Ianaizi, Little Bainoa, Manabaxao, Navicarao, Nimaca, Taquenazabo, Zavana.

Hubabo (or Ciguayo)

Connections.—Peter Martyr (1912) seems to say that the inhabitants of this province spoke a language distinct from other Haitians, but the wording is obscure and may refer to the province or tribe of Cahibo.

Location.—In the northern part of Santo Domingo between the Yaqui del Norte and Juna Rivers and the Atlantic and from the Peninsula of Samana to about Point Blanco.

Subdivisions

Peter Martyr knew only the following: Canabaco, Cubao, and Xamana. If my interpretation of his words is correct, the people of this province were called Macoryzes. Elsewhere they seem to be called Ciguana.

Maguana

Connections.—The Maguana probably spoke an Arawakan dialect but their position is uncertain. Peter Martyr gives this as a district or canton of the Bainoa province, but his description of it extends it so far, and the importance of its chief was so great that I have thought it best to give it an independent status. It seems possible that this is identical with the district of Magua assigned to the province of Cahibo.

Location.—In the upper Artabonite Valley, and the valleys of San Tome and San Juan, and Constanza Valley, apparently as far as the Bay of Samana.

Subdivisions

None are given.

Marien

Connections.—The Marien probably spoke an Arawak language and are attached to the province of Bainoa by Peter Martyr (1912), but their chief seems to have acted independently of all others, and Marien is sometimes called a "province."

Location.—The northwestern coast districts of the present Dominican Republic and the northern coast of Haiti from the site of Isabella to the Windward Passage.

Subdivisions

None are known.

INDIAN TRIBES OF CUBA

(After Lehmann, 1920)

Bani.	Cubanacan.
Baracoa.	Cuciba.
Barajagua.	Guaimaro.
Barbacoa.	Guamahaya.
Bayamo.	Guanacahibe.
Bayaquitiri.	Guaniguanico.
Boyaca.	Havana.
Camagüey.	Hanamana.
Cayaguayo.	Iagua.

INDIAN TRIBES OF CUBA—continued

Macaca.

Macorixe.

Maguano.

Maisi.

Maiyé.

Mangon.

Maniabon.

Marien.

Ornofay.

Sabaneque.

Sagua.

Lucayans in Bahamas.

Caribs in Lesser Antilles.

INDIAN TRIBES OF PUERTO RICO

(After Lehmann, 1920)

Agueynaba.

Arecibo.

Aymamon.

Bayamo.

Coamo.

Guanica.

Guarionex.

Humacao.

Loaiza.

Mabodamaca.

Mayaguex.

Urayoan.

Utuado.

Yagueca.

Yauco.

INDIAN TRIBES OF JAMAICA

Aguacadiba.

Ameyao.

Anaya.

Guaygata.

Huereo.

Maynoa.

Oristan.

Vaquabo.

MEXICO AND CENTRAL AMERICA

The latest and most detailed attempt to classify the languages of México and Central America is that of Dr. J. Alden Mason assisted by Mr. Frederick Johnson (1940). Aside from some unaffiliated families and some languages of uncertain affiliations, these writers classify the known languages of this area into 4 great phyla embracing 15 stocks and under these in turn 23 families. In his table Dr. Mason also makes use of such divisions as subphyla, substock, subfamily, and groups, and he continues his classification down to languages, varieties, dialects, and variations. For our purposes, the minor distinctions are unnecessary, many of them being uncertain and subject to constant revision, but the phyla, stocks, and families it is useful to keep in mind, and they may be indicated in small compass by reproducing the essential parts of the legend on Mr. Johnson's map, as follows, merely changing Mosumalpan to Misumalpan, as in Mason's text:

Phylum	Stock	Family
Hokan-Siouan	Hokan	Yuman. Serian. (Tequistlatecan). Waicurian.
	Supanecan. Coahuiltecan	Tamaulipecan. Janambrian (?).
Macro-Otomangue	Otomanguean	Otomian. Popolocan. Triquean. Chorotegan.
	Mixtecan	Mixtecan. Cuicatecan. Amusgan.
	Chinantecan. Zapotecan.	
Macro-Penutian	Uto-Aztecan (or Utaztecan)	Taracahitian. Aztecoidan. Piman.
	Mayan	Mayoid (Lowland Mayan). Quichoid (Highland Mayan).
	Mizocuavean	Mixe-Zoquean. Huavean.
	Totonacan. Xincan. Lencan.	
Macro-Chibchan	Misumalpan	Mosquitoan. Suman. Matagalpan.
	Chibchan.	
Unaffiliated stocks	Jicaquean. Payan. Tarascan.	

Such a classification does not represent, and is not supposed by its authors to represent, the last word on the subject, and some of the classifications, particularly the reduction of almost all languages under four phyla, are certain to receive vigorous opposition. Some of the stock groupings also will not meet with unqualified approval. The family divisions, however, and most of the stocks have already obtained general acceptance. In referring to each tribe, therefore, I shall not ordinarily attempt to go beyond mention of the family and stock affiliations.

Three of the four phyla, it will be noticed, are represented outside of the area under discussion, the Hokan-Siouan, and Macro-Penutian to the northward, and the Macro-Chibchan in South America. This applies also to the Hokan, Coahuiltecan, Uto-Aztecan, and Chibchan stocks, and to the Yuman, Taracahitian, and Piman families.

This classification also omits one phylum, stock, and family mentioned in the text, the Athapascan, disregarded evidently because it intruded into México only at a late period and in fact had no permanent settlements there.

The words "tribe," "band," and "division" will be employed rather indiscriminately in what follows.   One of the lessons resulting from any attempt to classify or "give the number of" Indian tribes— a remark which might be made still more general—is the fact noted already in the Introduction, that there is no specific definition of such names that will apply in all cases.   Sometimes a tribe is a tribe because of its political unity, sometimes because of its dialectic unity, sometimes from a mere "consciousness of kind" on the part of the individuals composing it.   A "band" is supposedly a subdivision of a "tribe" but, the definition of a tribe being such as it is, it is frequently impossible to say whether we have a tribe or a band.   The word "division" assumes, of course, a larger unit but there are divisions which would be tribes from one point of view and divisions or bands from others.   Still the application of a name to any group of Indians whether by themselves or by outsiders means that they share something in common whether that something be a common territory, a common language, a common or similar culture, or a common government.   The common territory, language, culture, or government may, however, extend beyond the tribe.   A common territory may be shared by two or more tribes, as for instance in the case of the Hidatsa, Mandan, and Arikara Indians of North Dakota.   A common language is shared by tribes bitterly hostile to each other, such as the Dakota and Assiniboin and the Choctaw and Chickasaw.   A common culture is shared by numbers of Indians in California who differ in language, and a common government is shared by the five tribes of the Iroquois Confederacy and the several tribes of the Creek Confederation.   For all that, each tribal name means something and a knowledge of them, or at least directory to them, with some intimation as to their geographical and linguistic position, as basal ordinarily to their cultural position, is of distinct service to ethnologists and ethnographers.

Only the names of the most important divisions have been placed upon the map.

Abasopalme, a band of Concho Indians.

Abra, a division ("province") of Guetare mentioned by Peralta (1895).

Acasaquastlan, location of a division of Nahuatl in the Republic of Honduras.

Acaxee, a tribe belonging to the Taracahitian branch of the Uto-Aztecan linguistic stock, located on the headwaters of the

Culiacán River and centering about the valleys of San Andres and Topia. Subdivisions: Acaxee, Sabaibo, and Tebaca; the Papudo and Tecaya are also mentioned.

Accerri, a division ("province") of Guetare mentioned by Peralta.

Achire, a division of Guasave at the southern end of their territory, near the mouth of the Río Lorenzo.

Acolhua, one of the three Nahuatl tribes which formed the Aztec Confederacy.

Aguacatec I, a tribe belonging to the Quichoid division of the Mayan family, in the region of Aguacatán in the northeastern part of the Mam territory.

Aguacatec II, in the Zoque subfamily of the Mizocuavean stock, located in the Quiche territory in southwestern Guatemala, in the region of Aguacatán.

Ahomama, a Lagunero band.

Ahome, a division of the Guasave about the mouth of the Río Fuerte.

Ahuachapan, the location of a detached body of Pokomam in the eastern part of El Salvador.

Aibine, a division of Xixime.

Akwa'ala, or **Paipai,** a Yuman (Hokan) tribe which occupied an inland territory at the northern end of the peninsula of Baja California.

Alaguilac, a tribe whose language resembled Pipil and therefore belonged to the Uto-Aztecan stock, located on the Río Motagua in the eastern part of Guatemala.

Alamama, a Lagunero band.

Amusgo, or **Amishgo,** a tribe of the Miztecan family occupying a wedge-shaped area between the states of Oaxaca and Guerrero, and extending to the Pacific Ocean.

Anachiquaies (the Anacasiguais of Orozco y Berra, 1864), a Tamaulipec tribe about Escandón.

Apache, name given to several Athapascan tribes which invaded México in post-Columbian times. (See New Mexico.)

Apostata, a Tamaulipec tribe about Burgos.

Ara, an unclassified tribe but supposed to be Chibchan.

Aracanaes, the Anacana of Orozco y Berra (1864), a Tamaulipec tribe about Altamira.

Aretino, a Tamaulipec tribe mentioned by Orozco y Berra (1864).

Aripa, a Waicuri division in the northwestern part of the Waicuri territory.

Atzinca, a division of the Matlatzinca at San Juan Acingo, México.

Aycalme, a band of the Concho.

Aztec, the most prominent of all the Nahuatl tribes, located on the site of the present City of México.

Bachilmi, a Concho band.

Baciroa, a tribe probably cognate with the Conicari and Tepahue and therefore in the Taracahitian family, located south of the Conicari and between the Mayo and Tehueco.

Bagaces, an Aztecoidan (Uto-Aztecan) tribe in the interior of Costa Rica northward from the head of the Gulf of Nicoya.

Baimena, a division of the Zoe, in the southern part of the Zoe territory.

Baldam, a division of the Mosquito Indians near the Tuapi Lagoon.

Bambana, a mixed Mosquito-Sumo tribe on the Río Bambana in eastern Nicaragua.

Bamoa, a tribe of Cahita south of the Río Sinaloa.

Baopapa, a Concho band.

Bawihka, a Sumo tribe in the northern interior of Nicaragua, east of Wanks River near its mouth.

Bayano, a Cuna tribe (Chibchan stock).

Baymunana, a tribe of possibly Sumo affiliations (Misumalpan stock) south of Cape Gracias á Dios.

Boa, a Sumo tribe on the headwaters of the Río Grande near the Matagalpa Indians, central Nicaragua.

Borrado, a Tamaulipec tribe near Dolores.

Boruca, a Chibchan tribe on the Pacific coast in southeastern Costa Rica about Coronado Bay.

Bribri, a Chibchan tribe speaking the Talamanca language, and located on the upper course of the Río Tarire in the territory of the present Republic of Panamá and adjacent parts of Costa Rica.

Burica, a Chibchan tribe of the Dorasque division located in the southwestern corner of the Republic of Panamá and neighboring parts of Costa Rica.

Burucaca, a Chibchan tribe related to the Boruca and living in the eastern part of Costa Rica in the interior.

Cabecar, a Chibchan tribe of the Talamanca division located in eastern Costa Rica inland. A synonym for Chiripo.

Cabezas, a tribe or band mentioned by Orozco y Berra (1864) and possibly connected with the Toboso, who were sometimes regarded as belonging to the Athapascan family.

Cacalote, a Tamaulipec tribe about Mier.

Cacalotito, a Concho band (Uto-Aztecan stock).

Cacaopera, a tribe speaking a Matagalpa dialect and living in the extreme northeastern part of El Salvador in the villages of Cacaopera and Lislique.

Cadimas (Orozco y Berra (1864) has Cadinias), a Tamaulipec tribe living about Guemes.

Cahita, a Uto-Aztecan tribe of the Taracahitian family living in south-western Sonora and northwestern Sinaloa, principally in the middle and lower portions of the valleys of the Río Yaqui, Río Mayo, Río Fuerte, and Río Sinaloa, and extending from the Gulf of California to the Sierra Madre except for the coastal tract south of the Esto de Agiabampo. They included the Bamoa (south of Río Sinaloa), Sinaloa or Cinaloa (on upper Río Fuerte), Mayo (on Río Mayo), Tehueco (on Río Oteros), Yaqui (on Río Yaqui), and Zuaque (on the lower course of the Río Fuerte).

Caimanes, a Cuna tribe.

Cakchiquel, a tribe belonging to the Quichoid division of the Mayan linguistic stock located in central Guatemala between Lake Atitlán and the site of Guatemala City and southward to the Pacific Ocean.

Camaleones, a Tamaulipec tribe about Santillana.

Canaynes, given by Orozco y Berra (1864) as the name of a Tamaulipec tribe.

Caramariguanes, given by Orozco y Berra as the name of a Tamauli-pec tribe.

Caramiguaies, given by Orozco y Berra as the name of a Tamauli-pec tribe.

Carib, a tribe not entered upon the map because they were post-Columbian arrivals from the Lesser Antilles upon the northern coast of Honduras whence they spread to the west coast of the Gulf of Honduras and as far north as Stann Creek, British Honduras.

Caribayes, given by Orozco y Berra (1864) as the name of a Tamaulipec tribe.

Carrizos, a Tamaulipec tribe about Camargo.

Catapa, a Chibchan tribe of the Rama-Corobici subfamily.

Caviseras, a Lagunero tribe.

Cazcan, a tribe of the Nahuatlan (Aztecoidan) division of the Uto-Aztecan linguistic stock, located in the southernmost part of the State of Zacatecas, northern Jalisco, and perhaps a small part of Aguas Calientes, extending south to Lake Chapala and beyond the Río Grande de Santiago. The Cazcan proper were in the northern part of this territory, the Tecuexe in the southern part, and the Coca west of Lake Chapala.

Chacahuaztli, a division of the Totonacan family.

Chalchuapa, site occupied by a detached body of Pokomam Indians (Mayan stock) in the Pipil territory.

Chaliva, a Chibchan tribe the minor affiliations of which are unknown.

Chamelcón, a valley near Naco, Honduras, where a band of Nahuatl Indians lived.

Chañabal, a tribe forming one group with the Tzeltal, Tzotzil, Quelene, and Chuj in the Mayoid division of the Mayan linguistic stock. They were located in the southeastern part of Chiapas near the Mexican-Guatemalan boundary.

Changuena, a Chibchan tribe of the Dorasque division, located in the westernmost part of the Republic of Panamá, inland and southwest of Río Tilorio.

Chapagua, the site of a Nahuatl colony, northern Honduras.

Chatino, a tribe belonging to the Zapotecan family living in the southern part of the State of Oaxaca between Oaxaca City and the Pacific Ocean, and on the Río Verde.

Chato, a Matagalpa (or possibly Lenca) tribe, perhaps identical with the Dule and occupying part of the Tegucigalpa area, Honduras.

Chiapanec, a tribe belonging to a family called Chiapanecan or Chorotegan and centering about Tuxtla Gutierrez in western Chiapas but formerly occupying a much larger territory.

Chicomuceltec, a tribe belonging to the Mayoid division of the Mayan linguistic stock, located in the extreme southeastern part of Chiapas close to the Guatemalan frontier.

Chilanga, a division of Lenca Indians in the northeastern part of the Republic of El Salvador.

Chinantec, a tribe constituting an independent stock, the Chinantecan, located in the district of Tuxtepec in the northern part of the State of Oaxaca, México. Mason and Johnson (1940) give the following dialectic varieties: Hume, Ojitlan, Wahmi, and Yolox.

Chinarra, an important subdivision of the Concho living between the Río Santa Maria and the Río Conchos, State of Chihuahua, México, in the northern section.

Chinipa, a tribe placed by Mason and Johnson in the Varohío group of the Taracahitian linguistic family and located on a river of the same name, a branch of the Río Fuerte, State of Chihuahua.

Chiripo, a synonym for Cabecar (q. v.).

Chiru, an "unassigned" tribe on the Gulf of Panamá west of Panamá City.

Chizo, an important subdivision of the Concho living about the big bend of the Río Grande.

Chocho (of Oaxaca), a tribe placed by Mechling (1912) in his Mazatec stock but by Mason and Johnson in the Popolocan family and Otomanguean stock; located in the northern part of the State of Oaxaca.

Chocho (of Puebla), see **Popoloca.**

Chol, a Mayan tribe including two divisions, the Chol Lacandon of eastern Chiapas along the Río Usumacinta and a second about the head of the same.

Cholo, a tribe placed by Mason and Johnson in the "unassigned" group but by Lehmann (1920) connected with the Choco Indians of Colombia, in the extreme southeastern part of the Republic of Panamá on the Pacific coast.

Cholutec, a tribe which has been called Mangue to the exclusion of the Diriá and Orotina but are properly independent of but related to the Mangue. They have been united into one stock with the Chiapanec called by Thomas (1911) Chiapanecan but by Mason and Johnson Chorotegan; Lehmann (1920) connected them with the Otomi. They lived in southern Honduras along the Gulf of Fonseca.

Chontal, signifying in Nahuatl "stranger," (1) a Mayan tribe connected closely with the Tzeltal, Chol, and Tzotzil and occupying the entire eastern part of the State of Tabasco.

Chontal (2), see **Tequistlatec.**

Chorti, a tribe of the Choloid branch of the Mayan stock living in the easternmost part of Guatemala and the neighboring Copan district of Honduras.

Chuchures, a tribe living in the neighborhood of Point Manzanillo on the north coast of the Republic of Panamá, by some placed in the Nahuatlan (Aztecoidan) division of the Uto-Aztecan linguistic family and by others connected with the Suma of the Chibchan family.

Chucunaque, a Cuna tribe belonging to the Chibchan stock.

Chuj, or **Chuje,** a Mayan tribe closely connected with the Jacaltec and belonging to the same group as Chol, located in northwestern Guatemala between Nenton and San Sebastian.

Chumulu, a Chibchan tribe.

Cinaloa, a Cahita tribe on the upper course of the Río Fuerte, State of Sinaloa.

Coahuiltecan tribes, the name given a great number of small tribes or bands in the State of Coahuila, México, and also in Neuvo León, Tamaulipas, and southern Texas as far as the River San Antonio. (See Texas.)

Coano, a division of Cora Indians on the Río Santiago, Nayarit, México.

Coca, a division of Cazcan Indians west of the Lago de Chapala, State of Jalisco, México.

Cochimi, a Yuman tribe in Baja California between latitude 26° N. and latitude 31° N.; Laymon is a northern division.

Coco, a Sumo division.

Cocomacaque, a division of Pima Bajo north of the Río de Sonora, State of Sonora, México.

Cocopa, an Arizona tribe which occasionally crossed into Sonora. (See Arizona.)

Cocora, a tribe belonging to the Rama-Corobici subfamily of the Chibchan stock, on the Río Cocora in southeastern Nicaragua.

Coiba, signifying "distant"(?), the western division of the Cunan branch of the Chibchan linguistic stock located in the neighborhood of the present Panama Canal and westward.

Colotlan, a tribe on the river of the same name, closely connected with the Teul and Tepecano Indians and therefore in the Piman division of the Uto-Aztecan linguistic stock.

Comanito, a tribe placed by Mason and Johnson in the Tahue group of their Cahitan linguistic subfamily and Taracahitian family of the Uto-Aztecan stock.

Comecamotes, a Tamaulipec tribe about Soto la Marina.

Comecrudo, a Coahuiltec or Tamaulipec tribe about San Fernando, Tamaulipas.

Comopori, a division of the Guasave north of the Esto. de Agiabampo.

Concho, a tribal division in the valley of the Río Concho above its mouth and extending westward to the neighborhood of the Casas Grandes. They are placed by Mason and Johnson in the Taracahitian division of the Uto-Aztecan linguistic stock. There were two major subdivisions, the Chinarra around the salt lakes and sand dunes of northern Chihuahua, and the Chizo east of the Concho and near the big bend of the Río Grande; and the following minor bands: Abasopalme, Aycalme, Bachilmi, Baopapa, Cacalotito, Concho, Conejo, Coyamit, Guamichicorama, Guelasiguicme, Guiaquita, Julime, Mamite, Mesquite, Mosnala, Obone (or Oposine), Olobayaguame, Olojasme, Polacme, Posalme, Sucayi, Tatamaste, Tocone, Topacolme, Xiximole, Yacchicaua, Yaculsari, Yaochane (Ahuchan or Ochan), Yeguacat.

Conguaco, or **Popoluca,** a tribe classed by Thomas (1911), following Juarros (1824), with the Lenca but by Lehmann (1920), followed doubtfully by Mason and Johnson, in the Xincan family. They were in the extreme southeastern part of Guatemala near the Pacific coast.

Conicari, a tribe connected by Sauer (1934) with the Cahita and therefore assigned by Mason and Johnson to their Taracahitian family of the Uto-Aztecan stock; they were located about the junction of the Mayo and Cedros Rivers.

Cooc, given by Peralta (1895) as a "province" of the Guetare Indians.

Cora, (1) calling themselves Nayarit or Nayariti, a tribe belonging to the Taracahitian division of the Uto-Aztecan linguistic family, located in the Sierra de Nayarit, on the middle course of the Río Grande de Santiago, State of Jalisco, and a section of the San Pedro, and including the coast of the present Nayarit. Subdivisions: Coano (in the barrancas of Mochitiltic in the extreme south), Huaynamota (on an east branch of the Río Grande de Santiago), Zayahueco (south and southwest margins of Cora country).

Cora, (2) a subdivision of the Waicuri on the east coast of Baja California from about Dolores to the southeastern point of the peninsula.

Corobici, a Chibchan tribe closely related to the Guatuso and living to the east of Lake Nicaragua in Costa Rica.

Coto, or **Cocto,** a Chibchan tribe related to the Boruca and located in the interior of Costa Rica north of the Gulf of Dulce.

Coyamit, a band of Concho Indians.

Cuahcomeca, a tribe of unknown affinities located in western Guerrero.

Cuercos quemados, a Tamaulipec tribe about Revilla.

Cuicatec, a major division of the Mixtecan linguistic family living in the district of Cuicatlán on the northeastern border of the Mixtec, State of Oaxaca, México.

Cuitlatec, a people of unknown affiliations living in the present States of Guerrero and Michoacán between the country of the Tarasco and the Pacific Ocean.

Cuna, the eastern branch of the Cunan family of the Chibchan stock, occupying all of the eastern part of the Republic of Panamá except some territory on the Pacific coast and a small enclave in the interior.

Cuyuteca, a tribe of unknown affiliations living in the State of Jalisco.

Daparabopos, a band of Lagunero Indians.

Desaguedero, a body of Indians believed to have belonged to the Aztecoidan division of the Uto-Aztecan stock, located at the mouth of the Río San Juan between the present republics of Nicaragua and Costa Rice.

Didú, a tribe in Baja California of uncertain location believed to have belonged to the Waicurian family.

Diegueño, a Yuman tribe occupying territory in southwestern California and the northwestern part of Baja California. (See California.)

Diriá, a division of the Mangue, belonging to the Chiapanecan or Chorotegan linguistic stock, connected by Lehmann (1920) with the Otomi. They were located between Lake Nicaragua and the Pacific Ocean.

Doleguas, a Guaymi tribe on Río Chiriqui, Republic of Panamá.

Dorasque, a tribe of the Chibchan linguistic stock living in the northwestern part of the Republic of Panamá on the Atlantic coast about the Bahia del Almirante and extending across to the Pacific.

Dudu, a Sumo tribe placed by Mason and Johnson in the Misumalpan linguistic stock.

Dule, a tribe, possibly identical with the Chato, placed somewhat doubtfully in the Matagalpan family, and located in the area of Tegucigalpa, Honduras.

Duy, a Chibchan tribe related to the Dorasque.

Edú, a Baja California tribe of uncertain location but probably belonging to the Waicurian family.

Escoria, an "unassigned" tribe inland from the Gulf of Parita in the western part of the Republic of Panamá.

Estrella, a Chibchan tribe of otherwise uncertain position.

Eudeve, a division of the Opata of the Uto-Aztecan linguistic stock, in the southern part of the Opata territory near the Jova.

Garabito, given by Peralta (1895) as a Guetare "province," and hence falling in the Chibchan linguistic stock.

Gocoyome, a band of Toboso Indians and perhaps belonging to the Athapascan stock.

Gotane, a tribe of the Chibchan stock and Rama-Corobici subfamily.

Guachichile, a tribe or group of tribes regarded as connected with the Huichol and classed with the Aztecoidan division of the Uto-Aztecan linguistic family. They occupied a long strip of territory extending from the borders of Michoacán northward to Saltillo and lying between longitude 100° and 103° W.

Gualaca, a Chibchan tribe otherwise "unclassified" living near the mouth of Río Chiriquí in the Gulf of Chiriquí.

Guamichicorama, a band of the Concho.

Guanexico, a tribe believed to belong to the Ulva group of the Suman family and Misumalpan stock.

Guarco, a Guetare band or "province" mentioned by Peralta.

Guasapar, a tribe belonging to the Varohio division of the Taracahitian family and Uto-Azetcan stock, in the present state of Chihuahua midway between the Río Oteros or Chínipa and the Río Urique.

Guasave, a tribe of the Cahita group, Taracahitian family and Uto-Aztecan stock located on the Pacific coast of the State of Sinaloa between the Esto. de Agiabampo and the Río San Lorenzo. Sauer (1934) gives the following subdivisions: Achire (at the southern end of the Guasave territory), Ahome (about the mouth of Río Fuerte), Comopori (north of the Esto. de Agiabampo),

and Vacoregue (between the Ahome and the Esto. de Agiabampo).
The following names of settlements are also given: Pohui,
Sisinicari, Tamazula, and Ure.

Guatijigua, a settlement of Lenca Indians in the northeastern part
of El Salvador.

Guatinicamame, a Mazatec tribe belonging to the Popolocan family
and Otomanguean stock.

Guatuso, a tribe which formed one group of the Chibchan stock with
the Corobici Indians, and lived in the interior of the Republic
of Costa Rica south of Lake Nicaragua.

Guaxiquero, a body of Lenca Indians living in Honduras.

Guayma, a band of Seri Indians living on the Gulf of California near
Guaymas.

Guaymi, signifying "man," a Chibchan tribe or group of tribes
(Guaymi-Dorasque subfamily), in the Republic of Panamá from
David Bay on the Pacific coast and the Río Guaymi on the Atlan-
tic side eastward to about the present Chame and Salud. The
following are given as subdivisions or tribes: Doleguas (on Río
Chiriquí), Move (east of Río Chiriquí), Muoi (south of Chiriquí
Lagoon), Murire (about the Gulf of Chiriquí), Muite, Pariza (?),
Penomeño (on the Gulf of Parita).

Guelasiguicme, a Concho band.

Guetare, a tribe belonging to the Talamanca division of the Chibchan
linguistic stock. Subdivisions: Besides Voto, the name of an
independent tribe, Peralta (1895) gives the following as "provinces": Abra, Accerri, Catapa, Cooc, Garabito, Guarco, Pacaca,
Tayopan, Tice, Turriarba.

Guiaquita, a Concho band.

Guixolotes, a Tamaulipec tribe according to Orozco y Berra (1864).

Halyikwamai, or **Kikima,** a Yuman tribe on the frontier between
Sonora and Arizona. (See Arizona.)

Himeri, a division of Pima Indians of the Piman family and Uto-
Aztecan stock living on and near the upper Río Altar, Sonora.

Hine, a Xixime division on the headwaters of the Río Piaxtla.

Hoeras, a Lagunero band.

Huastec, the northernmost representatives of the Mayan linguistic
stock in the northern part of the present State of Veracruz,
southern Tamaulipas, and part of San Luis Potosí; Mason and
Johnson mention Potosino and Veracruzano as dialects.

Huave, a tribe belonging to the Mizocuavean stock, formerly considered independent, living in the coastal parts of the districts of
Juchitlan and Tehuantepec, State of Oaxaca, México.

Huaynamota, a division of the Cora of Nayarit living on an east
branch of the Río Grande de Santiago.

Huichol, a tribe supposed to be closely related to the Guachichil and with them forming a branch of the Aztecoidan (Nahuatlan) family and Uto-Aztecan stock, located in the mountains between the State of Zacatecas and the territory of Nayarit. They are divided into three principal districts with the villages of Santa Catarina, San Sebastian, and San Andrés Coamiata as their respective seats of government.

Huite, signifying "bowmen," a tribe placed by Mason and Johnson in one group with the Ocoroni and Nio and in the Taracahitian linguistic family and Uto-Aztecan stock. They lived about the junction of the Otero and Urique Rivers.

Hume (1), a division of the Chinantec Indians, Chorotegan family.

Hume (2), a division of the Xixime on the Presidio and Baluarte Rivers.

Icaiche, a Maya subdivision.

Ika, a body of Indians in Baja California probably belonging to the Waicurian family.

Inocoples, a Tamaulipec tribe about Hoyos.

Intibucat, a body of Lenca Indians in the Republic of Honduras.

Ipapana, given by Zembrano as a Totonac dialect spoken in the missions of the Augustines.

Irritila, a Lagunero band; Orozco y Berra (1864) applied their name to all of the Lagunero.

Itza, a Maya tribe about Lake Petén, Guatemala.

Itzuco, a tribe of unknown affiliations located in northern Guerrero.

Ixcatec, a tribe of the Popolocan family and Otomanguean stock living in the northern part of the Mixtec territory, State of Oaxaca, México.

Ixil, a Quichoid tribe of the Mayan linguistic stock living in an area slightly west of the center of Guatemala, and including the pueblos of Nebaj, Cotzal, and Chajul as the chief towns.

Izalco, a tribe belonging to the Aztecoidan branch of the Uto-Aztecan linguistic stock, with a dialect regarded by Lehmann (1920) as the oldest type of Pipil. They lived about Izalco, south of San Salvador City, El Salvador.

Iztepeque, a body of Pokomam Indians, Mayan linguistic family, living east of San Salvador City.

Jacaltec, a Mayan tribe speaking a dialect allied to Motozintlec, and located around the pueblo of Jacaltenango, near the northwestern boundary of Guatemala.

Janambre, on slight evidence Orozco y Berra (1864) was induced to separate this tribe and the Pisone from the other tribes in Tamaulipas, and he has been followed by others without more reason. It is probable that these two tribes were Tamaulipecan or connected with the Pame and Otomi. They lived in the south-western part of the State of Tamaulipas.

Jano, a predatory tribe on the northern frontier of México constantly complained of in late seventeenth-century documents. Sauer (1934) believes that they were Apache and specifically possibly the Mimbreño Apache. (See **Apache** under New Mexico.)

Jicaque, signifying in Nahuatl "ancient person," a tribe or group of tribes in northwestern Honduras retained for the present as an independent linguistic stock though they have resemblances to the languages of the Paya, Lenca, and Xinca. Mason and Johnson express uncertainty as to whether their language should be classed with those to the south or those to the north. The Jicaque of Yoro and Jicaque of Palmar (or Sula) are mentioned as dialects by Lehmann (1920). Mason adds that of Leany Mulia.

Jocome, a predatory tribe mentioned constantly in seventeenth-century documents in conjunction with the Jano and said to have the same speech. Sauer (1934) believes they were Apache and seems to suggest that they might have been the Chiricahua Apache.

Jova, a tribe connected with the Opata and classed in the Taracahitian family and Uto-Aztecan stock. They occupied the upper part of the valley of the Río Yaqui, and the following Jova villages are mentioned: Bacaniyagua, Baipoa or Baypon, Natora, Oparrapa, Orasaqui, Sereba, and Setasura.

Julime, a Concho band.

Jumano, a tribe on the Río Grande above the big bend, probably part of the Suma. (See **Shuman** under Texas.)

Kabo, a division of the Mosquito Indians on the east coast of Nicaragua, north of the mouth of the Río Grande.

Kamia, a Yuman tribe whose main seat was in the Imperial Valley, California, but which ranged across the international boundary. (See California.)

Karawaka, a division of the Panameka.

Kekchi, a tribe constituting with the Pokomam and Pokonchi one division of the Quichoid family of the Mayan stock, and living on both sides of the upper Río Cahabón, extending westward to the Río Chixoy.

Kikima. (See **Halyikwamai.**)

Kiliwa, or **Kiliwi,** a Yuman tribe connected somewhat closely with the Kamia and Diegueño and living in the Peninsula of Baja California on the west side of the Gulf of California near its head.

Kiwahka, a mixed Mosquito-Sumo tribe.

Kohuana, a tribe on the Río Colorado. (See Arizona.)

Ku, a Sumo tribe of the Misumalpan stock located on the middle course of Wanks River, Nicaragua.

Kukalaya, a mixed Mosquito-Sumo tribe.

Lacandon, a Mayan tribe in the south central part of the Peninsula of Yucatan.

Lagunero, from the Spanish signifying "lake people," a tribe or group of tribes assigned somewhat doubtfully to the Aztecoidan branch of the Uto-Aztecan stock and living about the lakes of the tablelands of Mapimi. The following bands or subtribes are named by Alegre: Ahomamas, Alamamas, Caviseras, Daparabopos, Hoeras, Irritila, Maiconeras, Meviras, Miopacoas, Ochoes, Paogas, Vassapalles, Yanabopos.

Lakus, a Sumo tribe (Suman family) living, with the Pispis Indians on the Río Uani, in Usabane, on the upper course of the Río Pispis and on the Río Bambana.

Lari, an unclassified tribe but probably Chibchan.

Laymon, a northern section of the Cochimi of the Yuman family, sometimes treated as independent.

Lenca, a tribe or group of tribes usually placed in a family (the Lencan) independent of all others though the language contains resemblances to Xincan. It occupied the Valley of Olancho and extended westward into the departments of Tegucigalpa, Comayagua, Intibuca, and Gracias and into the eastern part of El Salvador east of the Lempa River. The following dialects are mentioned: Guaxiquero, Intibucat, Opatoro, and Similaton in Honduras, and Chilanga and Guatijigua in El Salvador. Conguaco is sometimes placed in this stock but Lehmann (1920) classes it with Xinca.

Loreto, a site in Baja California occupied by Indians who constituted a division of the Cochimi of the Yuman family.

Macoyahui, a tribe regarded by Sauer (1934) as "pretty certainly" related to the Cahita and therefore classed by Mason and Johnson in their Taracahitian family of the Uto-Aztecan stock. They lived on the Río Mayo above the Conicari and in the hills southeastward from the Mayo.

Maiconeras, a Lagunero band.

Malinchenos, given by Orozco y Berra (1864) as a Tamaulipec band or tribe.

Mam, (1) a Quichoid tribe said to have spoken one of the most archaic of the Mayan dialects. They lived in southeastern Guatemala and part of the district of Soconusco, México.

Mam, (2) a Mosquito tribe living about the Caratasca Lagoon, Honduras.

Mamite, a Concho band.

Manche, a Mayan tribe thought to belong to the Choloid group under the Mayoid division of the stock, and located at the head of the Bay of Honduras.

Mandinga, a Cuna tribe, Chibchan stock.

Mangue, a tribe of the Chorotegan family or substock located in Nicaragua between Lake Managua and the Pacific Ocean. Divisions: Diriá and Nagrandan.

Maribichicoa-Guatajigiala, a small branch of the Maribio or Subtiaba of Nicaragua which in turn is believed to belong to the Hokan linguistic stock. They lived in the northeastern part of El Salvador.

Mariguanes, a Tamaulipec tribe living about Horcasitas.

Matagalpa, a tribe or group of tribes originally placed in an independent stock of the same name, by Lehmann (1920) connected with the Suma and Tawahka, Ulua, and Mosquito Indians, but put in their Misumalpan stock by Mason and Johnson. They occupied the central part of Nicaragua, extending almost to the northern end of Lake Nicaragua and north through southern Honduras to the northeastern corner of El Salvador. According to Conzemius (1932), they formerly inhabited the western portion of the Mosquito coast. The Cacaopera constituted a separate dialect.

Matlame, a subdivision of the Matlatzinca which belonged to the Otomian linguistic family and Otomanguean stock.

Matlatzinca, or **Pirinda,** a tribe belonging to the Otomian linguistic family and Otomanguean stock, occupying a narrow strip of territory south of the Mazahua, extending southwest from Toluca. The recorded subdivisions are: Atzinca (at San Juan Acingo), Ocuiltec (at Ocuila), and Quata.

Maya, the type division of the Mayan linguistic family occupying all of the Peninsula of Yucatán including the present British Honduras, northern Guatemala, and neighboring parts of Tabasco. Subdivisions or tribes were the following: Icaiche (east of the Río Hondo in the east central part of the peninsula), Itza (about Lake Petén in northern Guatemala and in adjoining parts of Yucatán and British Honduras), Lacandon (in the south central part of the peninsula), Maya proper (in the greater part of the peninsula and part of Tabasco), Mopan or Moapan (in the southern part of British Honduras and adjoining sections of Guatemala), Santa Cruz (in the northeastern part of Yucatán).

Mayo, a Cahita tribe belonging to the Taracahitian family of the Uto-Aztecan stock, living on the Río Mayo, Sonora.

Mazahua, a tribe of the Otomian linguistic family living in the western portion of the State of México and probably occupying some adjoining territory in Michoacán.

Mazatec, a tribe in the northern part of the States of Oaxaca and Guerrero and extending into the State of Veracruz. Mechling (1912) made it the type tribe of a distinct stock but Lehmann (1920) afterward united it with Chinantec and Otomian while Mason and Johnson connect it primarily with Cuicatec and place it in their Otomanguean stock, and they give the following subdivisions: Mazatec of Oaxaca, Guerrero, and Tabasco, and Guatinicamame.

Melchora, a tribe of the Chibchan stock closely connected with the Rama and located in the Republic of Nicaragua northeast of Lake Nicaragua.

Mesquite, a band of Concho Indians.

Meviras, a Lagunero band.

Meztitlanec, a tribe of the Aztecoidan division of the Uto-Aztecan linguistic stock located in the region north of Tezcuco between the Sierra Madre and Huastec territory.

Miopacoas, a Lagunero band.

Mixe, one of the two main divisions of the former Zoquean linguistic family, now the Mizocuavean stock of Mason and Johnson, in the sierra northeast of the Zapotec in the States of Oaxaca, Veracruz, and Chiapas.

Mixtec, a tribe or tribal group in the western part of the State of Oaxaca and neighboring parts of Guerrero and Puebla. They were formerly, but seemingly erroneously, placed in one stock with the Zapotec. Mason and Johnson, who give them an independent stock position, do, however, place them in one "philum" with the Zapotec, Chinantec and Otomi. They distinguish the Mixteca Alta and Mixteca Baja as two main subdivisions.

Mocorito, a tribe on the Río Mocorito in the State of Sinaloa placed by Mason and Johnson in the Tahue group of the Taracahitian family.

Monqui, a Waicurian division on the east coast of the Peninsula of Baja California between Dolores and Loreto.

Mopan, or **Moapan,** a Mayan tribe in the southern part of British Honduras and in adjoining sections of Guatemala.

Mosnala, a Concho band.

Mosquito, or **Miskito,** a group of tribes regarded by Thomas (1911) as forming an independent stock, connected by Lehmann (1920) with the Matagalpa, Ulua, and Sumo Indians, and through them with the Chibchan stock. Mason and Johnson, however, assign them to their Misumalpan stock. They lived on the Atlantic coast of Nicaragua north of Bluefields and on the Honduran coast as far west as Río Patuca. Mason and Johnson give the following as dialects: Baldam, Kabo, Mam, Tawira, Wanki.

Motozintlec, a Mayan tribe belonging to the same dialectic group as the Jacaltec and located about Motozintla in the southeastern corner of Chiapas close to the Tapachula and Mam.

Move, a Chibchan tribe of the Guaymi division, living on the Golfo de los Mosquitos on the northwest coast of Panamá.

Muite, a tribe belonging to the Guaymi division of the Chibchan linguistic stock.

Muoi, a tribe of the Guaymi division of the Chibchan stock located in the western part of the Republic of Panamá.

Murire, a tribe of the Guaymi division of the Chibchan stock located in the southwestern part of the Republic of Panamá.

Musutepes, a Suman tribe of the Misumalpan linguistic stock.

Naco, see **Chamelcón.**

Nagrandan, a division of Mangue of the Chorotegan family.

Nahuatl or **Mexicano,** popularly known as Aztec from the dominant tribe at the period of the Spanish conquest, a group of tribes belonging to the Aztecoidan family of the Uto-Aztecan linguistic stock. They were located from México City eastward to the coast of the Gulf of México near Veracruz and southeast along that coast to the eastern part of Tabasco, southward from México City nearly, if not quite, to the Pacific Ocean and in the coast districts of Michoacán. There was a detached area on the seacoast of Chiapas and another at the mouth of Usumacinta River; also a number of others as indicated below. There were many tribes including the three allied tribes of Aztec, Acolhua, and Tlacopan, and the Tlascaltec, Meztitlanec, Tepanec, the Sigua in Panamá, the Desaguadero at the mouth of the Río San Juan, Nicaragua, and Costa Rica, and the following detached groups in Honduras: Acasaguastlan, in the highlands of Olancho, in the Chamelcón Valley, Chapagua and Papayeca near Trujillo, and others near Comayagua and Naco.

Nahuatlato, an Aztecoidan tribe connected with the Pipil belonging to the Uto-Aztecan linguistic stock, and living on the east side of the entrance to the Bay of Fonseca in the Republic of Nicaragua. (See **Olomeca** on map.)

Nata, a tribe of unknown affiliations located on the Gulf of Parita, in the western part of the Republic of Panamá.

Nebome, a division of Pima Bajo Indians living on both sides of the Río Yaqui in the State of Sonora.

Nicarao, an Aztecoidan tribe of the Uto-Aztecan linguistic stock affiliated with the Pipil. They lived between Lake Nicaragua and the Pacific Ocean in the present Republic of Nicaragua. (See **Niquisan** on map.)

Nicoya, an Orotiña tribe of the Chorotegan stock living on Nicoya Peninsula, Costa Rica.

Nio, a tribe placed by Mason and Johnson in one linguistic group with the Ocoroni and Huite in the Taracahitian family of the Uto-Aztecan stock. They lived on the Río Sinaloa about the mouth of the Ocoroni.

Niquisan, see **Nicarao.**

Obone, or **Oposine,** a Concho tribe.

Ochoes, a Lagunero band.

Ocoroni, placed by Mason and Johnson in one group with the Nio and Huite tribes and hence in the Taracahitian family of the Uto-Aztecan linguistic stock. They lived on a river of the same name, a branch of the Río Sinaloa.

Ocuiltec, a division of the Matlatzinca Indians of the Otomian linguistic family, occupying the eastern part of their territory.

Ojitlan, a division of the Chinantec of the Chorotegan linguistic family.

Olancho, location of a Nahuatl division in Honduras.

Olive, a tribe said to have been brought from the country beyond the Río Grande by a returning Spanish expedition early in the sixteenth century, but to which of the Texas linguistic stocks they belonged is unknown, though it was probably either the Coahuiltecan or the Karankawan. They were settled by the Spaniards in southern Tamaulipas.

Olmec, an extinct people of uncertain affiliations but formerly of great importance.

Olobayaguame, a Concho band.

Olojasme, a Concho band.

Olomega, see **Nahuatlato.**

Oluta, a division of the Popoloca of Veracruz belonging to the Mixe branch of the Mizocuavean linguistic stock.

Opata, from Pima signifying "hostile people," "enemies," a tribe or tribal group belonging to the Taracahitian division of the Uto-Aztecan linguistic stock extending east and west from longitude 109° to 111° W. and north and south from the International Boundary of México and the United States to the main fork of the Río Yaqui, about latitude 28°30′ N. The Eudeve, in the southern part of Opata territory near the Jova were a subdivision. Villages were: Acônche, Aibin, Alamos, Aribêtzi, Arispe, Babiácora, Babispes, Bacadévatzi, Bacanôra, Bacóbitzi,

Banámitzi, Bátsines, Batuco, Bátziner, Chinapa, Cuchuricác, Cucúripe, Cúmupas, Cuquíaratzì, Debatzi, Matape, Nacori, Oppósura, Oppotu, Saracãtzi, Sauaripa, Setásura, Teúricatzi, Toâpa, Tonitzí, Uasserác, Uépaca, Vásdabas, Zenoquippe.

Opatoro, a division of the Lenca living in the Republic of Honduras.

Orosi, an Orotiña division living south of Lake Nicaragua and belonging to the Chorotegan family.

Orotiña, a tribe living in the extreme western part of the present Republic of Costa Rica between Lake Nicaragua and the Pacific Coast and connected with the Chorotegan family. Subdivisions: Nicoya (on Nicoya Peninsula) and Orosi (south of Lake Nicaragua).

Osa, a subdivision of Boruca Indians about the Gulf of Dulce on the Pacific coast of Costa Rica.

Otomi, the principal tribe of the Otomian linguistic family occupying the greater part of the States of Queretero and Guanajuato, the northwestern portion of Hidalgo and parts of the State of México. A northern division of this tribe was known as Serrano, and a detached body is reported to have lived near the Pacific coast west of Colima. The Mazahua (q. v.) are sometimes regarded as a subdivision.

Pacaca, given by Peralta (1895) as a Guetare "province."

Pachera, a subdivision of the Tarahumare at the extreme headwaters of the northern branch of the Río Nonoava, under the municipality of Guerrero. They belonged to the Taracahitian family, Uto-Aztecan stock.

Pame, a tribe constituting a very divergent branch of the Otomian linguistic family. They were located mainly in the southeastern part of San Luis Potosí but also in adjoining areas of Tamaulipas and Queretero and are said to have extended into Guanajuato and to have included a mission (Cerro Prieto) in the State of México. Pimentel gives three dialects, one spoken in San Luis de la Paz, one in the city of Maiz, and one in Purísima Concepción de Arnedo.

Panamaka, a tribe of the Suman family, Misumalpan stock, located in the northern interior of Nicaragua. The following subdivisions are mentioned: Karawala, Panamaka, Tunki.

Panguayes, mentioned by Orozco y Berra (1864) as a Tamaulipec tribe.

Pantasma, a tribe given a doubtful status in the Matagalpan family.

Paogas, a Lagunero band.

Papabuco, a division of the Chatino of the Zapotecan stock.

Papago, a tribe in Sonora and Arizona. (See Arizona.)

Papantla, a dialectic division of the Totonac, Totonacan stock.

Paparos, a detached body of Indians classified by Lehmann (1920) in the Chocoan linguistic stock the main body of which lay along the Pacific coast of the Republic of Colombia. The territory of this tribe lay on the eastern borders of the Republic of Panamá inland but nearer to the Atlantic than to the Pacific coast.

Papayeca, a Nahuatl colony near Trujillo, Republic of Honduras.

Papudo, a division of the Acaxee of the Taracahitian linguistic family and Uto-Aztecan stock, not mentioned by Sauer (1934).

Pasitas, according to Orozco y Berra (1864) a tribe of Tamaulipec.

Patica, a Chibchan tribe belonging to the Rama-Corobici division.

Paya, a tribe constituting an independent family and living between the Río Aguán and the upper reaches of the Patuca, as also probably on the Bay Islands. A modern division is called Seco.

Penomeño, A Chibchan tribe of the Guaymi division located on the west coast of the Gulf of Panamá.

Pericu, a tribe connected on circumstantial evidence with the Waicurian family though only some proper names in their language are known. They lived about Cape San Lucas and extended northward on the west coast of the Peninsula of Baja California to about latitude 23°30′ N. No subdivisions are known, though the Waicurian Cora have sometimes been connected with them.

Piato, an Upper Pima (Pima Alto) tribe, Piman family and Uto-Aztecan stock, on the middle and lower Altar in Sonora. (See **Pima** under Arizona.)

Pima Alto, see **Pima** under Arizona.

Pima Bajo or **Lower Pima,** a tribe belonging to a linguistic family bearing their name, itself in turn a section of the Uto-Aztecan linguistic stock and located in the Río Yaqui region, Sonora, but extending eastward into Chihuahua and northward to about latitude 30°. Sauer (1934) gives three main divisions: the Yécora, neighbors of the Varohío on the borders of Chihuahua and Sonora; the Nebome, on both sides of the Río Yaqui; and the Ures, inhabiting the flood plain of the Río Sonora below the gorge of Ures and downstream as far as water was available. He also enters on his map the Cocomacaque in the northern part of Pima territory.

Pipil, a tribe or group of tribes belonging to the Nahuatl branch of the Nahuatlan family, Uto-Aztecan stock. They occupied several separate areas, the largest chiefly along the Pacific coast in western Salvador and some adjacent parts of Guatemala; a second a little farther west, east of Escuintla in Guatemala; a third along the upper Río Motagua in eastern Guatemala between the Chol and Pokomam, a small area in Honduras north of Comayagua, another on the Río Chamelecón, and a doubtful enclave between the Jicaque and Paya.

Pirinda, see **Matlatzinca.**

Pisone, a tribe associated by Orozco y Berra (1864) with the Janambre. (See **Janambre.**)

Pispis, a division of Sumo Indians.

Pitas, a Tamaulipec tribe about Santander, perhaps identical with Orozco y Barra's Pintos.

Pochutla, a tribe speaking one of the most aberrant dialects of the Aztecoidan family, Uto-Aztecan stock, and located about Porto Angel on the Pacific coast of Oaxaca.

Pocora, a tribe belonging to the Rama-Corobici branch of the Chibchan linguistic stock.

Pocosi, a tribe connected with the Cabecar of the Talamanca division of the Chibchan stock, living in the neighborhood of the present Limón, Costa Rica.

Pokomam, a Mayan tribe closely connected with the Pokonchi and belonging to the Quichoid division. They occupied a considerable region in southeastern Guatemala, including the capital, extending northward to the Río Grande or Upper Motagua, and eastward to the boundary line between Guatemala and El Salvador. There were detached bodies in Pipil territory at Ahuachapán, Chalchuapa, Iztepeque, and San Salvador.

Pokonchi, a tribe forming with the Pokomam one linguistic group of the Quichoid division of the Mayan family. They extended over a fairly wide territory in the center of Guatemala about the headwaters of the Río Cahabón.

Polacme, a Concho band.

Popoloca (of Conguaco), a body of Indians at the pueblo of Conguaco near the southeastern corner of the Republic of Guatemala. Juarros (1884), followed by Thomas (1911), places them in the Lencan stock but Mason and Johnson incline to agree with Lehmann (1920) that they should be classed as Xincan.

Popoloca (of Oaxaca), see **Chocho.**

Popoloca (of Puebla), a tribe which gives its name to the Popolocan family of the Otomanguean stock located in the southern part of the State of Puebla near Oaxaca.

Popoloca (of Veracruz), a tribe assigned to the Mixe division of the Mizocuavean stock of Mason and Johnson and located on the southern coast of the Bay of Campeche extending south to the mountains in the Peninsula of Tehuantepec, México.

Posalme, a Concho band.

Potlapiqua, a tribe said to have branched off from the Pima though in Opata territory.

Potosino, a body of Indians speaking a dialect of Huastec, Mayan linguistic family.

Prinzo, a body of Indians of the Uluan division of the Chibchan stock, located in the Republic of Nicaragua north of the Río Grande.

Quata, a tribe doubtfully classed in the Matlatzinca division of the Otomian linguistic family.

Quepo, a division or tribe of Boruca Indians belonging to the Talamanca division of the Chibchan linguistic family and located on the Pacific coast of Costa Rica centering about Quepos Point.

Quiche, an important Mayan tribe belonging to the Highland division of the family which is given the name Quichoid by Mason and Johnson. They occupied considerable territory in central Guatemala about the headwaters of Río Motagua, extending thence around the western side of Lake Atitlán and southward to the Pacific Ocean.

Quinicuanes, according to Orozco y Berra (1864), a Tamaulipec tribe.

Rama, a tribe belonging to the Rama-Corobici division of the Chibchan linguistic family. They occupied the southeasternmost part of the present Republic of Nicaragua between the Río San Juan and the Atlantic but the greater part of them are now on Rama Key in Bluefields Lagoon.

Sabaibo, a division of the Acaxee.

Sainoscos, a Tamaulipec tribe about Padilla.

Salineros, a division of the Seri on the mainland of the State of Sonora opposite Tiburón Island.

San Blas, a Cuna tribe of the Chibchan stock at San Blas on the north coast of the Republic of Panamá.

San Salvador, name given to a detached body of Pokomam of the Quichoid division of the Mayan family located about the capital of the Republic of El Salvador.

Santa Cruz, a division of Maya Indians in northeastern Yucatán.

Sayula, a division of the Popoloca of Veracruz.

Sayultec, a tribe of the Aztecoidan division of the Uto-Azecan stock occupying two areas, one on the Pacific coast in the southern part of Jalisco, and the other inland, south and southwest of the Lago de Chapala.

Seco, a division of the Paya Indians (Payan stock).

Seri, a tribe formerly placed in an independent stock but now classed with the Yuman family and Hokan stock. They lived on Tiburón Island in the Gulf of California and on the eastern coast of the latter from the Río San José nearly to the Altar, State of

Sonora.   The following subdivisions are mentioned: Guayma (in the southern part of the Seri territory), Salineros (on the mainland opposite Tiburón Island), Tepocas (in the northernmost part of the Seri territory), Tiburón (on Tiburón Island), Upanguayma (near the Guayma).

Serrano, a Seri division. (See **Seri.**)

Serrano, a northern division of Otomi near the Río Moctezuma.

Sibayones (1), a Tamaulipec tribe about Aguayo.

Sibayones (2), a Tamaulipec tribe on the Río de los Infantes.

Sigua, a Nahuatlan (Uto-Aztecan) tribe classed in the same group as the Pipil and located on the Río Telorio in the Bahia de Almirante, on the Atlantic coast of Panamá.

Silam, a Sumo division belonging to the Misumalpan linguistic stock living on the lower course of Wanks River, in the territory of Nicaragua and Honduras.

Similaton, a dialectic division of the Lenca Indians (Lencan stock) located in the territory of the present Republic of Honduras.

Sinacantan, a division of the Xinca Indians in southeastern Guatemala.

Sobaibo, a division of the Acaxee Indians in the southern part of their territory on the Río San Lorenzo, State of Sonora.

Soltec, a division of the Chatino of the Zapotecan linguistic stock.

Subinha, a tribe of the Mayan linguistic stock believed to have been related to the Jacaltec.   All that is known of their language is contained in a vocabulary in the Lenguas Indígenas de Centro-America en el Siglo XVIII (Fernández, 1892.).

Subtiaba, a tribe forming with the Tlapanec and Maribichicoa of Guerrero the Supanecan linguistic family which has been connected with the Hokan stock,   They lived in the region of Léon, Republic of Nicaragua, on the Pacific slope.

Sucayi, a Concho band.

Suerre, a tribe of the Talamanca division of the Chibchan linguistic stock located on the Atlantic slope of Costa Rica south of the mouth of the Río San Juan Bajo.

Suma, a tribe or group of tribes which extended along the Río Grande south of the present El Paso and westward to the Río Casas Grandes.   If, as is probable, Jumano is only another form of the name, their boundary would be carried down the Río Grande beyond the mouth of the Concho.   (See **Shuman** under Texas.) Probably related to the Uto-Aztecan stock.

Sumo, a tribe or group of tribes of the Suman family and Misumalpan linguistic stock in the northwestern interior of the Republic of Nicaragua and a fringe of territory adjoining in Honduras. Subdivisions: Bawihka (east of Wanks River towards its mouth),

Boa (near the head of the Río Grande), Coco, Panamaka (on the Río Bokay and Río Hamaca), and the Lakus and Pispis Indians (on the Río Uani, in Uasabane, on the upper course of the Río Pispis, and on the Río Bambana), and Wasabane. The Ku and Silam (on the middle course of Wanks River) should probably be added.

Sumo-Sirpe, a mixed Mosquito-Sumo tribe.

Tagualilos, given by Orozco y Berra (1864) as the name of a Tamaulipec tribe.

Tahue, a tribe of the Taracahitian family of the Uto-Aztecan linguistic stock on the Pacific coast northward of Mazatlán, extending to the mouth of the Río San Lorenzo and from that point inland and northward to about latitude 25°30' N. The following villages are mentioned: Atamura, Ategualato, Culiacán, Diareacato, Guachimeto, Hiluruto, Naboloto, Teboloto, Teculimeto, Yebalito—all but the third situated below Culiacán.

Talamanca, a tribe associated with the Bribri and located in central Costa Rica. It gave its name to a division of the Chibchan linguistic stock.

Tamaulipec, a group of small tribes named from the State of Tamaulipas in the central and southeastern parts of which they lived. It is probable that they were related to the Coahuilteco and Karankawa (see Texas), but the merest fragment of any of their languages survives. Through the Coahuilteco they are conjecturally connected with the Hokan stock. The Mexican Publicaciones del Archivo General de la Nación XV (Reyes, 1944) gives the following Tamaulipec tribes: Anachiguaies (about Escandón), Apostatas (about Burgos), Aracanaes (about Altamira), Borrados (about Dolores), Cacalotes (about Mier), Cadimas (about Guemes), Camaleones (about Santillán), Carrizos (about Camargo), Comecamotes (about Soto la Marina), Comecrudo (about San Fernando), Cuercos quemados (about Revilla), Inocoples (about Hoyos), Mariguanes (about Horcasitas), Pitas (about Santander), Sainoscos (about Padilla), Serranos (about Santa Barbara), Sibayones (1) (about Aguayo), Sibayones (2) (about Río de los Infantes), Tepemacas (about Laredo). Orozco y Berra (1864) repeats some of these names, sometimes in an altered form, and adds: Aretines, Canaynes, Caramariguanes, Caramiguais, Caribayes, Guisolotes, Malinchenos, Panguayes, Pasitas, Pintos (=Pitas?), Quinicuanes, Tagualilos, Tamaulipecos.

Tamazulteca, a tribe of unknown connections living in western Michoacán.

Tapachultec (1), (or Tapachula) a detached branch of the Zoque and so, according to Mason and Johnson, in the Mizocuavean stock. They lived on the border between México and Guatemala.

Tapachultec (2), a tribe of unknown affiliations, but distinct from the preceding, located on the México-Guatemalan border.

Tapixulapan, a division of the Zoque tribe of the Mizocuavean stock.

Tarahumare, a hispanized form, according to Lumholtz (*in* Hodge, 1910, p. 692) of the native name Ralámari which probably signifies "foot-runners," a large tribe belonging to the Taracahitian branch of the Uto-Aztecan linguistic stock, living in the Sierra Madre Mountains and on the headwaters of the San Pedro, Conchos, Urique, Otero, and Papigochic Rivers, southern Sonora and Chihuahua. The Pachera (at the extreme headwaters of the northern branch of the Río Nonoava, under the municipality of Guerrero) are given as a subdivision.

Tarasco, a tribe forming the Tarascan linguistic stock and occupying almost the whole of the State of Michoacán, except for the coastal section, and some small areas outside.

Tariaca, a division of Cabecar Indians of the Talamanca branch of the Chibchan linguistic stock living on the north coast of Costa Rica southeast of Point Limón.

Tatamaste, a Concho band.

Tatimolo, a division of Totonac Indians (Totonacan stock).

Tatiquilhati, a Totonac division of the Totonacan linguistic stock.

Tawahka, a tribe of the Sumo group and Misumalpan linguistic stock, living on the upper course of Wanks River, Honduras and Nicaragua. (See **Tanaxka** on map.)

Tawira, a tribe of Mosquito Indians (Misumalpan stock) in northeastern Nicaragua on the coast.

Tayopan, given by Peralta (1895) as a Guetare "province."

Tebaca, a division of the Acaxee of the Taracahitian family and Uto-Aztecan stock, living in the southwestern part of the Acaxee territory on the Río Culiacán.

Tecaya, given as a division of the Acaxee.

Teco-Tecoxquin, a tribe belonging to the Aztecoidan branch of the Uto-Aztecan linguistic stock located inland in southern Nayarit and in two detached areas in western Michoacán.

Tecual, a tribe placed by Sauer (1934) in one group with the Huichol and by Mason and Johnson in the Aztecoidan branch of the Uto-Aztecan stock. There were two sections of this tribe, one on the Río Grande de Santiago and the other on the Río San Pedro in Nayarit.

Tecuexe, a division of the Cazcan Indians, Aztecoidan branch of the

Uto-Aztecan stock, living north of Lago de Chapala, State of Jalisco.

Tedexenos, given by Orozco y Berra (1864) as the name of a Tamaulipec tribe.

Tehueco, a tribe of the Cahita Indians on the Río Oteros, State of Chihuahua.

Teluski, a tribe whose exact affiliations are unknown but they probably belonged to the Chibchan stock.

Temori, a tribe assigned by Mason and Johnson to the Varohío group in the Taracahitian family and Uto-Aztecan stock. They lived between the Río Chinipa or Oteros and the Río Urique, State of Chihuahua.

Tepahue, a tribe belonging to the Taracahitian family and Uto-Aztecan stock closely connected with the Cahita. They lived on the Río Cedros, a northern branch of the Río Mayo, Sonora.

Tepanec, a Nahuatl tribe.

Tepecano, derived by Hrdlička (1903; *in* Hodge, 1910) from Nahuatl tepetl, "mountain," and aco, "on top of," a southern Tepehuane division of the Piman family and Uto-Aztecan stock, living in the sierras of northern Jalisco.

Tepehua, a tribe belonging to the Totonacan linguistic stock occupying a small territory where the Mexican States of Veracruz, Hidalgo, and Puebla come together.

Tepehuan, according to Buelna (1891) from Nahuatl tepetl, "mountain," and huan, "at the junction of," a tribe belonging to the Piman division of the Uto-Aztecan linguistic stock, located mainly in Durango, on the eastern slope of the sierra between latitude 21° and 27° N., extending also into the States of Chihuahua, and Zacatecas and from the headwaters of the Río Fuerte to the Río Grande de Santiago in Jalisco.

Tepemacas, a Tamaulipec tribe about Laredo.

Tepocas, a division of the Seri in the northernmost part of their territory on the coast of the Gulf of California about latitude 30° N.

Tequistlatec, often called Chontal, an Aztec word meaning "stranger," a tribe in the districts of Yautepec and Tehuantepec on the Pacific coast of the State of Oaxaca. It was originally made into an independent linguistic stock, the Tequistlatecan from the name Tequistlateca suggested by D. G. Brinton (1891, p. 113). Brinton, however, classed it as a dialect of Yuman and this has recently been confirmed by Kroeber (1915), who allies it through that family with the Hokan stock.

Térraba, a tribe belonging to the Talamanca division of the Chibchan linguistic stock located in the extreme northwestern part of the Republic of Panamá, between Río Tarire and Río Telorio.

Teshbi, a Chibchan tribe related to the Térraba.

Tetiquilhatí, a Totonac division.

Teul, a tribe in southern Zacatacas on the Río Juchipila connected with the Tepecano and Tepehuan and through them with the Piman family of the Uto-Aztecan stock.

Texixtepec, a division of the Popoloca (of Veracruz) connected with the Mixe and through them with the Mizocuavean stock.

Tice, a tribe of the Rama-Corobici branch of the Chibchan linguistic stock.

Tlacopan, one of the three Nahuatl tribes in the Valley of México, which formed the Mexican confederation.

Tlacotepehua-Tepuzteca, an unclassified tribe centering around Chilpancingo, Guerrero.

Tlapanec, or **Tlapaneco-Yopi,** given by Orozco y Berra (1864) as a name applied to the Chocho Indians by the Indians of Guerrero, but made independent by Lehmann (1920), who connects the Tlapanec with the Maribio and Subtiaba which would place it in the Hokan stock.

Tlascala, a Nahuatl tribe in the present State of Tlaxcala, México.

Toboso, the name of a predatory tribe living in the seventeenth century in the Bolson de Mapimi and extending northward at least to the Río Grande, State of Coahuila, México. On circumstantial evidence they have been classed as Athapascan but this is not beyond question. Orozco y Berra's Cocoyome and Cabezas should perhaps be classed with them.

Tocone, a Concho band.

Tojar, a Chibchan tribe related to the Térraba (Chibchan stock) and located on an island of the same name on the north coast of Panamá.

Tolimeca, a tribe of uncertain affiliations in western Guerrero.

Topacolme, a Concho band.

Toquegua, a tribe belonging to the Choloid branch of the Mayan linguistic family and located in northwestern Honduras on the coast of the Gulf of Honduras.

Totonac, the principal tribe of the Totonacan linguistic stock which is now regarded as independent though formerly thought to have affinities with the Mayan people. They lived in the northern part of the State of Puebla and that part of Veracruz between the City of Veracruz and latitude 21° N. Subdivisions: Mason and Johnson give three, the Coast, Papantla, and Sierra, but Zembrano (1752) states that there were four dialects: Chacahuaxtli (in the Pueblos of Xalpan and Pentepec), Ipapana (in the missions of the Augustines), Tatimolo (in the Pueblo of Noalingo), and Tetiquilhati (in the high sierras).

Totorame, a tribe closely connected with the Cora Indians and through them with the Aztecoidan branch of the Uto-Aztecan stock. They occupied the coast of Sinaloa from Mazatlán southward.

Trique, a tribe entered by Mason and Johnson as a substock of their Otomanguean stock. Mechling (1912) connected them with Mazatec and Lehmann (1920) with the Chiapanec and Otomi. They were in the midst of the Mixtec country west of the City of Oaxaca. The dialect of the town of Copala was said to differ considerably from the rest.

Tubar, a tribe placed by Mason and Johnson in the Tahue group of the Taracahitian linguistic family, Uto-Aztecan stock, and located in the hot river gorge between the debouchure of the Chínipas and Urique Rivers.

Tucurrique, a tribe believed to have been Chibchan but otherwise of uncertain affiliations.

Tule, a Cuna tribe in eastern Panamá.

Tungla, a mixed Mosquito-Sumo tribe.

Tunki, a subdivision of the Panamaka.

Turriarba, a Guetare tribe in southwestern Costa Rica.

Turrin, a Rama-Corobici tribe of the Chibchan stock.

Turucaca, a Chibchan tribe related to the Boruca living north of the Golfo Dulce, on the Pacific coast of the Republic of Panamá.

Tzeltal or **Tzental,** a tribe belonging to the Tzeltaloid division of the Mayan stock and located in eastern Chiapas northeast of the Chiapanec and between the Río San Pedro and the Río Grande, México.

Tzotzil (Quelene and **Chamula** probably synonyms), a tribe belonging to the Tzeltaloid division of the Mayan stock and located on the Río Grande in central Chiapas east of the Chiapanec.

Tzutuhil, a tribe belonging to the Quichoid division of the Mayan stock, living around the southern shore of Lake Atitlán, Guatemala.

Uchita, or **Utciti,** a division of the Waicuri on the west coast of the peninsula of Baja California between latitude 24° N. and the Pericu.

Ulua, originally a type tribe of the Uluan linguistic stock, they were connected by Lehmann (1920) with the Tawahka, Yosko, Mosquito, and Matagalpa and all ultimately with Chibchan. Mason and Johnson, however, treat the Suman family as a division of their Misumalpan stock and more remotely connected with the Chibchan tribes. They occupied much of the interior of the present Republic of Nicaragua from the Bay of Fonseca eastward to Lake Nicaragua and from the latter northward to the lower Río Grande and the Mosquito territory. The following subdivisions are given: Guanexico (location not given), Prinzo (north of the Río Grande), Ulua (on the Río Grande and Río Sigua).

Upanguayma, a body of Seri Indians near Guaymas, Sonora.

Uren, a Chibchan tribe not otherwise fixed as to status.

Ures, a body of Pima Bajo on the flood plain of the Río Sonora below the gorge of Ures and beyond, Sonora.

Urinama, a Chibchan tribe connected with the Bribri.

Urraca, a tribe of unknown affiliations living on the south coast of the Republic of Panamá.

Uspanteca, a tribe of the Quiche group, Quichoid division, of the Mayan linguistic family, located at the point of meeting of the Quiche, Ixil, and Pokonchi and in the great bend of the Chixoy (Río Negro), Guatemala.

Vacoregue, a division of the Guasave Indians of the Taracahitian family, Uto-Aztecan stock, on the Pacific coast north of the mouth of the Río Fuerte, Sonora.

Varohío, by Mason and Johnson made the type tribe of a group belonging to the Taracahitian linguistic family and Uto-Aztecan stock. They were on the headwaters of the Río Mayo on the boundary between Chihuahua and Sonora, México.

Vassapalles, a Lagunero band.

Veracruzano, a Huastec dialectic division, Mayan stock.

Viceita, a Chibchan tribe connected with the Bribri.

Vigitega, a detached body of Indians near Tepic in Nayarit believed to have belonged to the Piman family and Uto-Aztecan stock.

Voto, a tribe forming, with the neighboring Rama and Guatuso, one dialectic group of the Chibchan stock located in the northwestern part of the present Republic of Costa Rica just south of the Río San Juan.

Wahmi, a division of the Chinantec, Chorotegan stock.

Waicuri, the largest body of Indians belonging to the Waicurian linguistic stock which Mason and Johnson classify conjecturally under the Hokan. They covered all of Baja California south of latitude 26° N. except a small area in the extreme southwest. Subdivisions: Aripa (located by Orozco y Berra (1864) in the extreme northwestern part of Waicuri territory), Cora (on the east coast from near Dolores to the southeastern point of the peninsula), Monqui (on the east coast between Dolores and Loreto), Uchita or Utciti (on the west coast between latitude 24° N. and the Pericu), Waicuri (on the west coast from latitude 24° to 25° N.). The Edú, Didú, and Ika, given by others as

Cochimi divisions, were probably Waicuri but their locations are uncertain.

Wanki, a Mosquito subdivision.

Xilotlantzinca, an unclassified tribe in western Michoacán.

Xinca, a tribe placed in the Zoquean stock by Lehmann (1920) but given independent status by Thomas (1911) and more recently by Mason and Johnson except that the last mentioned place it in their great Macro-Penutian phylum. They lived in the extreme southeastern part of Guatemala between two areas of Pipil Indians. There were three closely allied dialects spoken in the pueblos of Sinacantan, Xupiltepec, and Xutiapa, to which Conguaco should probably be added, although Juarros (1824) and Thomas (1911) call it Lencan.

Xixime, a tribe of the Taracahitian branch of the Uto-Aztecan stock, their nearest relatives apparently being the Acaxee. They occupied the upper courses of the San Lorenzo, Piaxtla, Presidio, and Baluarte Rivers in the States of Durango and Sinaloa. The following subdivisions are reported: Aibine, Hine (on the head-waters of the Río Piaxtla), Hume (on the Presidio and Baluarte Rivers).

Xiximole, a Concho band.

Xorrhue, an otherwise unidentified Chibchan tribe.

Xupiltepec, a town whose inhabitants spoke a Xinca dialect. It is located in Guatemala.

Xurru, a tribe belonging to the Rama-Corobici branch of the Chibchan stock.

Xutiapa, a town of Guatemala in which a dialect of the Xinca language was spoken.

Yacchicaua, a Concho band.

Yaculsari, a Concho band.

Yanabopos, a Lagunero band.

Yaochane (Ahuchan or Ochan), a Concho band.

Yaqui, a tribe or tribal division of the Cahita living on the Río Yaquí in the State of Sonora, México.

Yasika, a Suman tribe belonging to the Misumalpan stock.

Yecora, a division of Pima Bajo along the boundary line between the states of Chihuahua and Sonora, México.

Yeguacat, a Concho band.

Yolox, a division of the Chinantec, Chorotegan stock.

Yosco, a tribe of the Misumalpan stock most closely connected with the Sumo and Ulua people, in central Nicaragua on the Río Lisauei and the Río Hamaka.

Zacateco, a tribe related to the Cazcan of the Aztecoidan family and Uto-Aztecan stock, occupying a large part of the State of Zacatecas and also part of Durango, México.

Zapotec, the type tribe of the Zapotecan family, occupying the greater part of central Oaxaca and extending from the Chinantec country to the Pacific coast. Mason and Johnson give the following major divisions: Zapotec of the Northern Mountains, Zapotec of the Southern Mountains, and Zapotec of the Valleys, and the following dialects: the Zapotec Cajono, Zapotec Etla, Zapotec Ixtepexi, Zapotec Nexitza, Zapotec Ocotlan, Zapotec Zaachilla, and the Tehuantepec.

Zayahueco, a division of the Cora Indians, Taracahitian family, Uto-Aztecan stock, living in the southern and southwestern margins of the Cora country.

Zegua, a Chibchan tribe, otherwise unclassified.

Zhorquin, a Chibchan tribe, otherwise unclassified.

Zoe, according to Buelna (1891), from tzoi, "wax," "pitch tree," regarded by Sauer (1934) as belonging to the same group as the Comanito Indians which were members of the Taracahitian family and Uto-Aztecan stock. They lived in the rough hill country of the Río Fuerte above the Cahita and along the Sinaloa-Chihuahua boundary. Two related tribes are mentioned, the Zoe proper and the Baimena.

Zoque, the type tribe of the Zoquean linguistic family placed by Mason and Johnson in their Mizocuavean stock. They lived in the extreme eastern part of Oaxaca, in northwestern Chiapas, and in the adjoining parts of Tabasco. Tapixulapan is given as a dialect.

Zuaque, a division of the Cahita Indians of the Uto-Aztecan stock living on the lower course of the Río del Fuerte, State of Sinaloa.

Authorities.—Brinton, D. G., 1891; Buelna, 1891; Conzemius, 1932; Hrdlička, 1903; Johnson, 1940; Juarros, 1824; Kroeber, 1925; Lehmann, 1920; Lumholtz, 1894; Mason, 1940; Mechling, 1912; México, Archivo General de la Nación, Publicaciones, vol. XV (on Tamaulipas, 1944); Orozco y Berra, 1864; Peralta, 1895; Peter Martyr, 1912; Sauer, 1934; Thomas, 1911; Zembrano, 1752;

BIBLIOGRAPHY

ADAIR, JAMES.
   1775. The history of the American Indians. London. (Reprint ed. by
      Samuel Cole Williams under auspices of Nat. Soc. Colonial Dames,
      in Tenn. The Watauga Press, Johnson City, Tenn., 1930.)
ALARCON, FERNANDO.
   1810. Relation. 1540. *In* Hakluyt, Voyages, vol. 3, 1600, reprinted 1810.
   1838. Relation de la navigation et de la découverte . . . 1540. *In* Ternaux-
      Compans, Voyages, vol. 9, Paris.
ALLEN, HENRY T.
   1887. Report on an expedition to the Copper, Tanana, and Koyukuk Rivers,
      in the Territory of Alaska, in the year 1885. Washington.
ALLIS, SAMUEL. *See* DUNBAR, JOHN B.
ALVORD, CLARENCE WALWORTH, and BIDGOOD, LEE.
   1912. The first explorations of the Trans-Allegheny Regions by the Vir-
      ginians, 1650–1674. Cleveland.
AMDRUP, L. BOBÉ. *See* VAHL, G. C., ET AL.
AMERICAN STATE PAPERS.
   1832, 1834. Documents, legislative and executive, of the Congress of the
      United States. Class II, Indian Affairs, vols. 1–2.
   1832–1861. Documents of the Congress of the United States in relation to
      the Public Lands. Class VIII, Public Lands, vols. 1–8.
ANGHIERA, PIETRO MARTIRE D' (PETER MARTYR).
   1912. De orbe novo decades: The Eight Decades of Peter Martyr d'Anghiera.
      Trans. from the Latin with notes and introd. by Francis Augustus
      MacNutt. 2 vols. New York. (First decade originally published
      in 1511.)
ANZA, LIEUT. COL. JUAN BAUTISTA DE.
   1774, 1775. *See* Garcés Diary *in* Coues, 1900.
ARBER, EDWARD, EDITOR. *See* SMITH, JOHN, 1884.
ARMSTRONG, MAJ. FRANCIS W.
   1835. Correspondence on the subject of the emigration of Indians, &c., Sen-
      ate Document No. 512, 1833. Washington.
BABCOCK, WILLIAM H.
   1899. The Nanticoke Indians of Indian River, Delaware. Amer. Anthrop.,
      n. s., vol. 1, pp. 277–282.
BACK, GEORGE.
   1836. Narrative of the Arctic land expedition in the years 1833, 1834, and
      1835. Philadelphia and London.
   1838. Narrative of an expedition in H. M. S. *Terror*, on the Arctic shores,
      in the years 1836–37. London.
BALLARD, EDWARD.
   1871. Geographical names on the coast of Maine. U. S. Coast Survey Rep.
      for 1868.
BANCROFT, HUBERT HOWE.
   1886–90. The works of. 39 vols. San Francisco. (Vols. 1–5, Native
      races.)

BANDELIER, ADOLF F.

1881. Historical introduction to studies among the sedentary Indians of New Mexico. Pap. Archaeol. Inst. Amer., Amer. Ser., vol. 1. Boston.

1884. Reports on his investigations in New Mexico during the years 1883–84. Fifth Ann. Rep. Archaeol. Inst. Amer. Cambridge.

1890–92. Final report of investigations among the Indians of the southwestern United States, carried on mainly in the years from 1880 to 1885. Pap. Archaeol. Inst. Amer., Amer. Ser., vol. 3, 1890; vol. 4, 1892. Cambridge.

1890. Contributions to the history of the southwestern portion of the United States. Pap. Archaeol. Inst. Amer., Amer. Ser. vol. 5. Cambridge.

1892. Documentary history of the Zuñi tribe. Journ. Amer. Ethnol. and Archaeol., vol. 3. Boston, New York.

See also Nuñez Cabeza de Vaca, Alvar.

BANDELIER, FANNY. See NUÑEZ CABEZA DE VACA, ALVAR.

BANKS, CHARLES E.

1911. History of Martha's Vineyard. 3 vols. Boston.

BARBEAU, C. MARIUS.

1915. Huron and Wyandot mythology. With an appendix containing earlier published records. Canada Dept. Mines, Geol. Surv., Anthrop. Ser., Mem. 80, No. 11. Ottawa.

1929. Totem poles of the Gitksan, Upper Skeena River, British Columbia. Nat. Mus. Canada, Anthrop. Ser. No. 12, Bull. 61. Ottawa.

BARCIA CARBALLIDO Y ZUÑIGA, ANDRES G.

1723. Ensayo cronologico para la historia general de la Florida, 1512–1722, por Gabriel de Cardenas Z. Cano (pseud.) Madrid.

BARNWELL, COL. JOHN.

1908. The Tuscarora expedition. Letters of Colonel John Barnwell. South Carolina Hist. and Geneal. Mag., vol. 9, No. 1, pp. 28–58.

BARRETT, S. A.

1908 a. The ethno-geography of the Pomo and neighboring Indians. Univ. Calif. Publ. Amer. Arch. and Ethnol., vol. 6, No. 1, pp. 1–332.

1908 b. The geography and dialects of the Miwok Indians. Univ. Calif. Publ. Amer. Arch. and Ethnol., vol. 6, Nos. 2 and 3, pp. 333–380.

1910. The material culture of the Klamath Lake and Modoc Indians. Univ. Calif. Publ. Amer. Arch. and Ethnol., vol. 5, No. 4, pp. 239–292.

1917 a. Ceremonies of the Pomo Indians. Univ. Calif. Publ. Amer. Arch. and Ethnol., vol. 12, No. 10, pp. 397–441.

1917 b. The Washo Indians. Bull. Public Mus. Milwaukee, vol. 2, No. 1.

1919. The Wintun Hesi Ceremony. Univ. Calif. Publ. Amer. Arch. and Ethnol., vol. 14, pp. 437–488.

BARROWS, DAVID PRESCOTT.

1900. Ethno-botany of the Coahuilla Indians of southern California. Univ. Chicago, Dept. Anthrop. Chicago.

BARTLETT, J. R.

1854. Personal narrative of explorations and incidents . . . connected with the United States and Mexican Boundary Commission, 1850–53. Vols. 1–2. New York.

BARTRAM, WILLIAM.
    1792. Travels through North and South Carolina, Georgia, East and West
        Florida, the Cherokee country, the extensive territories of the
        Muscogulges or Creek Confederacy, and the country of the Choc-
        taws. London.
    1909. Observations on the Creek and Cherokee Indians. 1879. With
        prefatory and supplementary notes by E. G. Squier. Report.
        Complete. Trans. Amer. Ethnol. Soc., vol. 3, pt. 1, pp. 1–81.
        (Facsimile reprint of 1853 ed.)
    1943. Travels in Georgia and Florida, 1773–74. A report to Dr. John Fother-
        gill. Annotated by Francis Harper. Trans. Amer. Phil. Soc., n. s.,
        vol. 33, pt. 2.

BATTS, THOMAS. See ALVORD, CLARENCE W., and BIDGOOD, LEE; and BUSHNELL,
    DAVID I., JR., 1907.

BEALS, RALPH L.
    1932. The comparative ethnology of Northern Mexico before 1750. Ibero-
        Americana: 2. Univ. Calif. Press.
    1933. Ethnology of the Nisenan. Univ. Calif. Publ. Amer. Arch. and
        Ethnol., vol. 31, No. 6, pp. 335–414. Univ. Calif. Press.

BEAUCHAMP, WILLIAM M.
    1892. The Iroquois trail; or, footprints of the Six Nations. Fayetteville,
        N. Y.
    1897 a. Aboriginal chipped stone implements of New York. Bull. N. Y.
        State Mus., No. 16. Albany.
    1897 b. Polished stone articles used by the New York aborigines. Bull.
        N. Y. State Mus., No. 18. Albany.
    1900. Aboriginal occupation of New York. Bull. N. Y. State Mus., No.
        32. Albany.
    1901. Wampum and shell articles used by the New York Indians. Bull.
        N. Y. State Mus., No. 41. Albany.
    1902. Horn and bone implements of the New York Indians. Bull. N. Y.
        State Mus., No. 50. Albany.
    1903. Metallic ornaments of the New York Indians. Bull. N. Y. State
        Mus., No. 73. Albany.
    1905. A history of the New York Iroquois. Bull. N. Y. State Mus., No. 78.
        Albany.
    1907. Aboriginal place names of New York. Bull. N. Y. State Mus., No. 108.
        Albany.

BEAURAIN, LE SIEUR. See LA HARPE, BERNARD DE, 1831.

BECKWITH, HIRAM M.
    1883. Indian names of water courses in the State of Indiana. Ind. Dept.
        Geol. and Nat. Hist., 12th Ann. Rept., 1882.

BENAVIDES, ALONSO DE.
    1630. Memorial. Madrid. (Also translation in Land of Sunshine, vol. 13.
        Los Angeles, Calif., 1900.)

BERREMAN, JOEL V.
    1937. Tribal distribution in Oregon. Mem. Amer. Anthrop. Assoc. No. 47.

BERRY, BREWTON; CHAPMAN, CARL; and MACK, JOHN.
    1944. Archaeological remains of the Osage. Amer. Antiquity, vol. 10,
        pp. 1–11.

BERRY, BREWTON; CHAPMAN, CARL; WRENCH, J. E.; and SEITZ, WILBUR.
    1938. Archaeological investigations in Boone County. Missouri Archae-
        ologist, Columbia, Mo., vol. 4, pp. 1–36.
BEVERLEY, ROBERT.
    1722. History of Virginia, by a native and inhabitant of the place. 2d ed.
        London.
BIEDMA, LUIS HERNANDEZ DE. See BOURNE, EDWARD GAYLORD, EDITOR.
BIENVILLE, JEAN BAPTISTE LE MOYNE, SIEUR DE.
    1932. Journal du voyage de M. de Bienville des Taensas au village des
        Yataches, par les terres. 22 mars-18 mai, 1700. Printed in Miss.
        Provincial Archives, French Dominions, ed. Rowland, Dunbar, and
        Sanders, Albert Godfrey, vol. 3. (Also in Margry, Pierre, 1875–86,
        vol. 4, pp. 432–444; MS. memoir in Newberry Library, Chicago.)
BLOSSOM, L. See LAPHAM, I. A.
BLYTH, BEATRICE. See RAY, VERNE F.
BOAS, FRANZ.
    1888. The Central Eskimo. 6th Rep. Bur. Amer. Ethnol, pp. 399–669.
    1897. The social organization and secret societies of the Kwakiutl Indians,
        based on personal observations and on notes made by Mr. George
        Hunt. Rep. U. S. Nat. Mus. for 1895.
    1898. The mythology of the Bella Coola Indians. Mem. Amer. Mus. Nat.
        Hist., vol. 2, Anthropology 1. New York.
    1901, 1907. The Eskimo of Baffin Land and Hudson Bay. Bull. Amer.
        Mus. Nat. Hist., vol. 15. New York. (Pt. 1, 1901; pt. 2,
        1907.)
    1916. Tsimshian mythology. 31st Ann. Rep. Bur. Amer. Ethnol., 1909–
        1910, pp. 29–1037.
    1921. The ethnology of the Kwakiutl, based on data collected by George
        Hunt. 35th Ann. Rep. Bur. Amer. Ethnol., 1913–14, pp. 43–794.
    1927. Map showing the distribution of Salish tribes and their neighbors about
        the end of the 18th century. (Accompanying a paper on "Sound
        Shifts in Salishan Dialects," by Franz Boaz and Herman Haeberlin.
        Int. Journ. Amer. Ling., vol. 4, Nos. 2–4.) New York.
    See also Reports of the Committee appointed by the British Association
        for the Advancement of Science to report on the northwest tribes
        of Canada, in Reports Brit. Assoc. Adv. Sci., 1885–1898. London.
        Report of 1895 referred to particularly. And Haeberlin, H. K.;
        Teit, James A; and Roberts, Helen H.
BOGORAS, WALDEMAR.
    1904. The Chuckchee. 1. Material culture. Mem. Amer. Mus. Nat. Hist.,
        Publ. Jesup N. Pacific Exped., vol. 7. Leiden and New York.
BOLLAERT, WILLIAM.
    1850. Observations on the Indian tribes in Texas. Journ. Ethnol. Soc.
        London, vol. 2.
BOLTON, HERBERT EUGENE.
    1914. Athanase de Mézières and the Louisiana-Texas Frontier, 1768–1780.
        2 vols. Cleveland.
    1916. Spanish explorations in the Southwest, 1542–1706. Ed. by Herbert
        Eugene Bolton. In Original narratives of early American history.
        New York.

BOLTON, HERBERT EUGENE—Continued
1919. Kino's historical memoirs of Pimería Alta, 1681–1711. 2 vols. Ed. by Herbert Eugene Bolton. Cleveland.

1925. Arredondo's historical proof of Spain's title to Georgia. A contribution to the history of one of the Spanish borderlands. Univ. Calif. Press.

BOSCANA, GERONIMO.
1846. Chinigchinich: A historical account of the origin, customs, and traditions of the Indians at the missionary establishment of St. Juan Capistrano, Alta California; called the Acagchemem Nation. (English trans. in Robinson, Alfred, "Life in California." New York. The Spanish original is probably lost. Alexander Taylor reprinted the English version in the California Farmer, vol. 13, 1860. The Robinson book has also been reprinted, but without the Chinigchinich.)

BOSSU, N.
1771. Travels through that part of North America formerly called Louisiana. Trans. by J. R. Forster. 2 vols. London.

BOURKE, JOHN G.
1892. The medicine-men of the Apache. 9th Ann. Rep. Bur. Ethnol., 1887–88, pp. 443–603.

BOURNE, EDWARD GAYLORD, EDITOR.
1904. Narratives of the career of Hernando de Soto. 2 vols. New York. (Note: Reprints of op. cit. are in "Great American explorers," by David Nutt, London, 1905; and "American explorers," Allerton Book Co., New York, 1922.)

BOYD, MARK F.
1934. A topographical memoir on east and west Florida with itineraries of General Jackson's army, 1818. By Capt. Hugh Young, Corps of Topographical Engineers, U. S. A. With an introduction and annotations by Mark F. Boyd and Gerald M. Ponton. Florida Hist. Soc. Quart., vol. 13, No. 1, pp. 16–50, and No. 2, pp. 82–104.

BRACKETT, COL. ALBERT G.
1880. The Shoshonis, or Snake Indians, their religion, superstitions, and manners. Ann. Rep. Smithsonian Inst. for 1879, pp. 328–333.

BRANNON, PETER A.
1909. Aboriginal remains in the middle Chattahoochee Valley of Alabama and Georgia. Amer. Anthrop., n. s., vol. 11, pp. 186–198.

BRINTON, DANIEL G.
1859. Notes on the Floridian Peninsula, its literary history, Indian tribes and antiquities. Philadelphia.

1882–85. Library of aboriginal American literature, 6 vols. Philadelphia. (1. Chronicles of the Mayas. 2. The Iroquois book of rites. 3. The Comedy-ballad of Güegüence. 4. A migration legend of the Creek Indians, vol. 1. 5. The Lenâpé and their legends. 6. The annals of the Cakchiquels.) Ed. by Daniel G. Brinton.

1891. The American Race. New York.

1893. Vocabulary of the Nanticoke dialect. Proc. Amer. Philos. Soc., vol. 31, pp. 325–333. Philadelphia.

BUELNA, EUSTAQUIO.
   1891. Arte de la Lengua Cahita. Vol. 1. México.
BUREAU OF AMERICAN ETHNOLOGY, SMITHSONIAN INSTITUTION. Annual Reports
   1-48, 1881-1933. Bulletins, 1-143, 1887-1949. Introductions, 1-4, 1877-1880.
   Miscellaneous Publications, 1-12, 1880-1944. Contributions to North American Ethnology, vols. 1-9, 1877-1893.
BURK, JOHN D.
   1804-5. History of Virginia. 3 vols. Petersburg.
BUSCHMANN, JOHANN C. E.
   1859. Spuren der Aztek. Sprache.
BUSHNELL, DAVID I., Jr.
   1907. Discoveries beyond the Appalachian Mountains in September 1671.
      Amer. Anthrop., n. s., vol. 9, pp. 45-56.
   1908. The account of Lamhatty. Amer. Anthrop., n. s., vol. 10, No. 4,
      Oct.-Dec.
   1909. The Choctaw of Bayou Lacomb, St. Tammany Parish, Louisiana.
      Bur. Amer. Ethnol. Bull. 48.
   1930. The five Monacan towns in Virginia, 1607. Smithsonian Misc. Coll.,
      vol. 82, No. 12.
BUSTAMANTE AND GALLEGOS.
   1582. Reprinted in Colección de documentos inéditos . . . Vol. 15. Madrid,
      1864-84.
BYRD, WILLIAM.
   1866. History of the dividing line and other tracts. 2 vols. Richmond.
CABEZA DE VACA, ALVAR NUÑEZ. See NUÑEZ CABEZA DE VACA, ALVAR, 1851.
CABRILLO, JUAN RODRIGUEZ. See FERREL, BARTOLOMÉ.
CADZOW, DONALD A.
   1925. Habitat of Loucheux Bands. Mus. Amer. Indian, Indian Notes, vol.
      2, No. 3.
CANADA. DEPARTMENT OF CITIZENSHIP AND IMMIGRATION, INDIAN AFFAIRS
   BRANCH.
   Report. Ottawa, 1876-19—.
CARDENAS Z. CANO, GABRIEL DE. See BARCIA CARBALLIDO Y ZUNIGA, ANDRES G.
CARMACK ON THE BEOTHUK IN BEOTHUK INSTITUTE.
   1907. In Handbook of American Indians. Bull. 30, vol. 1., art. Beothukan
      Family. (See Hodge, Frederick Webb, 19C7, 1910.)
CARROLL, B. R.
   1836. Historical collections of South Carolina; embracing many rare and
      valuable pamphlets, and other documents, relating to the history
      of that State, from its first discovery to its independence, in the year
      1776. 2 vols. New York.
CARTIER, JACQUES.
   1545. Brief recit, et succincte narration, de la nauigation faicte es ysles de
      Canada. Paris. (Reprinted, Paris, 1863.)
CARVER, JONATHAN.
   1778. Travels through the interior parts of North America, in the years
      1766, 1767, and 1768. London.

CARVER, JONATHAN—Continued
  1796. Three years' travels through the interior parts of North America for
        more than five thousand miles. Philadelphia.
  1838. Carver's travels in Wisconsin. New York.
CASAÑAS, DE JESUS MARIA, FRAY FRANCISCO. See SWANTON, JOHN R. 1942.
CASAS, BARTOLOMÉ DE LAS.
  1875–76. Historia de las Indias. 5 vols. Madrid.
CASTAÑEDA, CARLOS E.
  1936. The Mission Era: Vol. 1, The finding of Texas, 1519–1693.
CASTAÑEDA DE NAGERA, PEDRO DE.
  1838. Relation du voyage de Cibola, entrepris en 1540. [1596. Ternaux-
        Compans, Voyages, vol. 9. Paris.
CATLIN, GEORGE.
  1844. Letters and notes on the manners and customs and condition of the
        North American Indians. 2 vols. New York and London.
CENSUS. UNITED STATES BUREAU OF THE CENSUS. See PORTER.
CHAMBERLAIN, ALEXANDER F.
  1892. In 10th Report on Northwest tribes of Canada for the British Associ-
        ation for the Advancement of Science.
  MS. Manuscript on the Malesit, 1882, in archives of Bureau of American
        Ethnology.
CHAMPLAIN, SAMUEL DE.
  1830. Voyages: ou journals ès decouvertes de la Nouvelle France. 2 t.
        Paris.
  1870. Oeuvres de Champlain publiées sous le patronage de l'Université Laval.
        Par l'Abbé C.-H. Laverdière, M. A. 2e ed. 5 t. Quebec.
  1922–36. The works of Samuel de Champlain. 6 vols. Trans. and ed. by
        H. H. Laughlin and William F. Ganong. The Champlain Soc.
        Toronto.
CHAPMAN, CARL. See BERRY, BREWTON, ET AL.
CHARLEVOIX, PIERRE F. S. DE.
  1744. Histoire et description generale de la Nouvelle France. 3 t. Paris.
  1761. Journal of a voyage to North America. 2 vols. London.
CHAUVIGNERIE, WRITING IN 1736.
  1853. In Schoolcraft, Henry R., 1851–57, vol. 3, pp. 554–555.
CHURCH, THOMAS.
  1825. The history of King Philip's War, and also expeditions against the
        French and Indians in the eastern parts of New England. To which
        is added copious notes and corrections by Samuel G. Drake. Boston.
        (Also in Library of New England History, vols. 2–3. Boston,
        1865–67.)
COLDEN, CADWALLADER.
  1747. The history of the Five Indian Nations of Canada, which are dependent
        on the province of New York in America. London. (Reprint,
        1755.)
COLECCIÓN DE DOCUMENTOS INÉDITOS, RELATIVOS AL DESCUBRIMIENTO, CON-
  QUISTA Y COLONIZACIÓN DE LAS ANTIGUAS POSESIONES ESPAÑOLAS EN AMÉRICA
  Y OCEANÍA. 41 vols. Madrid, 1864–84.

CONGRÉS INTERNATIONAL DES AMÉRICANISTES.
1907. Compte rendu. Quinzieme session, Quebec, 1906. Quebec.

CONNELLEY, WILLIAM ELSEY.
1918. The Prairie Band of Pottawatomie Indians. Coll. Kansas State Hist. Soc., vol. 14, pp. 488–570.

CONZEMIUS, EDUARD.
1932. Ethnographical survey of the Miskito and Sumu Indians of Honduras and Nicaragua. Bur. Amer. Ethnol. Bull. 106.

COOK, S. F.
1940. Population trends among the California Mission Indians. Ibero-Americana, vol. 17. Univ. Calif. Press.

COOKE, ANN M. *See* PARK, WILLARD Z.

COPWAY, GEORGE.
1847. Life, history, and travels of Copway, a young Indian chief of the Ojibwa nation; sketch of the present state of the nation. Albany.

CORBUSIER, WILLIAM HENRY.
1886. *In* American Antiquarian, vol. 8. p. 276.
MS. Manuscript on Yavapai, 1873–75, in archives of Bureau of American Ethnology.

COUES, ELLIOTT, EDITOR.
1893. History of the expedition of Lewis and Clark to the sources of the Missouri River, and to the Pacific in 1804–5–6. A new edition. 4 vols. New York.
1900. On the trail of a Spanish pioneer. The diary and itinerary of Francisco Garcés, 1775–76. 2 vols. New York.

COVILLE, FREDERICK V.
1892. The Panamint Indians of California. Amer. Anthrop., o. s., pp. 351–361.
1897. Notes on the plants used by the Klamath Indians of Oregon. Contr. U. S. Nat. Herb., vol. 5, No. 2.

COX, ISAAC JOSLIN, EDITOR.
1905. The journeys of Réné Robert Cavelier, Sieur de La Salle. 2 vols. Trail Makers (series). New York.

COX, ROSS.
1831. Adventures on the Columbia River. 2 vols. London.

COXE, DANIEL.
1741. A description of the English province of Carolana. By the Spaniards called Florida, and by the French, La Louisiane. London. (*Also in* French, B. F., Historical Collections of Louisiana. 2d ed., pt. 2. Philadelphia, 1750.)

CRANE, VERNER W.
1929. The Southern Frontier, 1670–1732. Duke Univ., Durham, N. C.

CRANTZ, DAVID.
1767. History of Greenland. 2 vols. London. (Other eds., London, 1780, 1820.)

CROZIER, ARCHIBALD.
1938. Indian towns near Wilmington, Delaware. Bull. Archaeol. Soc. Delaware, vol. 2. No. 6. June. Frank Martine Heal, ed.

Curtis, Edward S.
1907–30. The North American Indian. 14 vols. (1, Apache, Jicarillas, Navaho; 2, Pima, Papago, Qahatika, Yuma, Maricopa, Walapai, Hava-
supai, Apache-Mohave; 3, Teton Sioux, Yanktonai, Assiniboin;
4, Apsaroke, Hidatsa; 5, Mandan, Arikara, Atsina: 6, Piegan,
Cheyenne, Arapaho; 7, Yakima, Klickitat, Interior Salish,
Kutenai; 8, Nez Percés, Wallawalla, Umatilla, Cayuse, Chinookan
tribes; 9, Salishan tribes of the Coast, Chimakum, Quilliute,
Willapa; 10, the Kwakiutl; 11, Nootka, Haida; 12, the Hopi; 13,
Hupa, Yurok, Wiyot, Tolowa, Tututni, Shasta, Achomawi,
Klamath; 14, Kato, Wailaki, Yuki, Pomo, Wintun, Maidu,
Yokuts.) New York.

Cushing, Frank Hamilton.
1883. Zuñi fetishes. 2d. Ann. Rep. Bur. Ethnol., pp. 3–45.
1886. A study of Pueblo pottery as illustrative of Zuñi culture-growth. 4th
Ann. Rep. Bur. Ethnol., pp. 490–564.
1896. Outlines of Zuñi creation myths. 13th Ann. Rep. Bur. Ethnol., pp.
321–447.
1901. Zuñi folk-tales. New York.

Cusick, David.
1828. Sketches of ancient history of the Six Nations. 2d ed. Tuscarora,
N. Y.

Dall, William H.
1870 a. On the distribution of the native tribes of Alaska and the adjacent
territory. Proc. Amer. Assoc. Adv. Sci. 1869. Cambridge.
1870 b. Alaska and its resources. Boston.
1877. Tribes of the extreme northwest. Contr. N. Amer. Ethnol., vol. 1,
pp. 1–156.
1886. The native tribes of Alaska. Proc. Amer. Assoc. Adv. Sci. 1885,
vol. 34. Salem.

Dawson, George M.
1880 a. Report on the Queen Charlotte Islands. Rep. Geol. Surv. Canada
for 1878–79. Montreal.
1880 b. Report of progress of the [Canadian] Geological Survey. 30B.
1881. Report on an exploration from Port Simpson on the Pacific coast to
Edmonton on the Saskatchewan, embracing a portion of the northern
part of British Columbia and the Peace River country. 1879.
Rep. Geol. Surv. Canada. Montreal.
1888 a. Notes and observations on the Kwakiool people of the northern part
of Vancouver Island and adjacent coasts made during the summer
of 1885, with vocabulary of about 700 words. Proc. and Trans.
Roy. Soc. Canada. 1887, vol. 5. Montreal.
1888 b. Report on an exploration in the Yukon district, N. W. T. and
adjacent northern portion of British Columbia. Ann. Rep. Geol.
and Nat. Hist. Surv. Canada, n. s. vol. 3, pt. 1, Rep. B, 1887–88.
Montreal.
1922. Notes on the Shuswap people of British Columbia. Proc. and Trans.
Roy. Soc. Canada 1891, vol. 9, sec. 2. Montreal.

DE CRENAY MAP.
    1733. Copy in Bureau of American Ethnology. Sections of this are repro-
        duced in Hamilton, Peter J., Colonial Mobile, revised and enlarged
        ed. Boston and New York, 1910.

DE FOREST, JOHN W.
    1851. History of the Indians of Connecticut from the earliest known period
        to 1850. Hartford. (Reprinted 1852, 1853.)

DE KERLÉREC, CHEVALIER.
    1907. Rapport du Chevalier de Kerlérec, Gouverneur de la Louisiane
        française sur les peuplades des vallées du Mississippi et du Missouri
        (1758). C. R. Congress Int. Amér., 15th sess., vol. 1, pp. 61–
        86. Québec.

DELANGLEZ, JEAN.
    1938. The journal of Jean Cavelier, the account of a survivor of La Salle's
        Texas expedition, 1684–1688. Trans. and annot. by Jean Delanglez.
        Inst. Jesuit Hist. Publ. Chicago.

DENIG, EDWIN THOMPSON.
    1930. Indian tribes of the Upper Missouri. Ed. by J. N. B. Hewitt. 46th
        Ann. Rep. Bur. Amer. Ethnol., 1928–29, pp. 375–628.

DENSMORE, FRANCES.
    1929. Chippewa customs. Bur. Amer. Ethnol. Bull 86.

DENYS, NICOLAS.
    1908. The description and natural history of the coasts of North America.
        Trans. and ed. by William F. Ganong. Champlain Soc., Toronto.

DE SOTO, HERNANDO. See BOURNE, E. G.

DICKENSON, JONATHAN.
    1803. Narrative of a shipwreck in the Gulph of Florida. 6th ed. Stanford, N. Y.

DIRON D'ARTAGUIETTE. See MERENESS, NEWTON D., EDITOR.

DIXON, ROLAND B.
    1905. The Northern Maidu. Bull. Amer. Mus. Nat. Hist., vol. 17, pt. 3.
        New York.
    1907. The Shasta. Bull. Amer. Mus. Nat. Hist., vol. 17, pp. 381–498.
    1910. The Chimariko Indians and language. Univ. Calif. Publ. Amer.
        Archeol. and Ethnol., vol. 5, pp. 293–380.

DIXON, ROLAND B., and KROEBER, A. L.
    1919. Linguistic families in California. Univ. Calif. Publ. Amer. Archaeol.
        and Ethnol., vol. 16, pp. 47–118.

DOMENECH, EMMANUEL.
    1860. Seven years' residence in the great deserts of North America. Vols.
        1–2. London.

DORSEY, GEORGE A.
    1904 a. Mythology of the Wichita. Carnegie Inst. Washington Publ. No. 21.
    1904 b. Folk-lore Soc., vol. 8. Boston and New York.
    1905. The Cheyenne. Pt. 1, Ceremonial organization. Pt. 2, The Sun
        dance. Publ. Field Col. Mus. Anthrop. Ser., vol. 9, Nos. 1 and 2.
        Chicago.
    1906. The Pawnee—Mythology, pt. 1. Carnegie Inst. Washington Publ. No. 59.

DORSEY, GEORGE A., and KROEBER, A. L.
    1903. Traditions of the Arapaho. Publ. Field Col. Mus. Anthrop. Ser.,
        vol. 5. Chicago.

DORSEY, J. OWEN.
    1884. Omaha sociology.   3d Ann. Rep. Bur. Ethnol., pp. 205–370.
    1896. Omaha dwellings, furniture, and implements.   13th Rep. Bur. Ethnol., pp. 263–288.
    1897. Siouan Sociology.   15th Ann. Rep. Bur. Ethnol., 1893–94, pp. 205–244.
    MS. Naltunnetuñne vocabulary.   Oct. 1884.   (*In* Archives Bur. Amer. Ethnol.)

DORSEY, J. OWEN, and SWANTON, JOHN R.
    1912. A dictionary of the Biloxi and Ofo languages.   Bur. Amer. Ethnol. Bull. 47.

DOUAY, FATHER ANASTASIUS.
    1905. Narrative of La Salle's attempt to ascend the Mississippi in 1687 . . . *In* Journeys of La Salle, edited by Isaac Joslin Cox, vol. 1, pp. 222–247.

DOUSMAN, G. D.   *See* LAPHAM, I. A.

DRAKE, SAMUEL G.
    1848. Book of the Indians of North America.   xi.   Boston.
    See also Church, Thomas.

DRIVER, HAROLD EDSON.
    1937. Southern Sierra Nevada.   Anthrop. Rec. Univ. Calif., vol. 1, No. 2. Berkeley.
    1939. Northwest California.   Anthrop. Rec. Univ. Calif., vol. 1, No. 6. Berkeley.

DRUCKER, PHILIP.
    1937. The Tolowa and their Southwest Oregon kin.   Univ. Calif. Publ. Amer. Archaeol. and Ethnol., vol. 36, No. 4, pp. 221–300.

DU BOIS, CORA.
    1935. Wintu ethnography.   Univ. Calif. Publ. Amer. Archaeol. and Ethnol., vol. 36, No. 1, iv + 148 pp.

DUMONT DE MONTIGNY.
    1753. Mémoires historiques sur La Louisiane.   2 vols.   Ed. by Le Mascrier. Paris.

DUNBAR, JOHN B.
    1880–82. The Pawnee Indians.   Mag. Amer. Hist., vols. 4, 5, 8.   Morrisiana, N. Y.

DU ROULLET, RÉGIS.
    1732. Journal of a visit made to the Choctaw nation in 1732.   (In the Archives of the Naval Hydrographic Service, Paris.   Copy in the Library of Congress, MS. Div.)

DYER, J. O.
    1916. The early history of Galveston, pt. 1.   Galveston, Tex.
    1917. The Lake Charles Atakapas (cannibals), period of 1817–1820.

ECKSTORM, FANNIE HARDY.
    1941. Indian place-names of the Penobscot Valley and the Maine coast. Univ. Maine Studies, 2d ser., No. 55.   Univ. Maine Press, Orono, Maine.

EELLS, MYRON.
    1877. The Twana Indians of the Skokomish Reservation in Washington Territory.   Bull. U. S. Geol. and Geogr. Surv., vol. 3, No. 1.
    1889. The Twana, Chemakum, and Klallam Indians of Washington Territory.   Ann. Rep. Smithsonian Inst. for 1887, pp. 605–681.

EGEDE, HANS.
1745. Description of Greenland. Trans. from the Danish. London.

EISELEY, LOREN C. See SPECK, FRANK G., and EISELEY, LOREN C.

EIXARCH, TOMÁS. See COUES, 1900.

ELVAS, NARRATIVE OF A GENTLEMEN OF. See ROBERTSON, JAMES A., TRANSLATOR AND EDITOR; also BOURNE, EDWARD GAYLORD.

EMMONS, GEORGE T.
1910. Articles on Niska and Tahltan in Handbook of American Indians, Bur. Amer. Ethnol. Bull. 30. (See Hodge, 1907, 1910.)
1911. The Tahltan Indians. Univ. Pennsylvania Mus. Anthrop. Publ. vol. 4, No. 1.

EMORY, W. H.
1848. Notes of a military reconnaissance from Fort Leavenworth in Missouri to San Diego in California, made in 1846–47. Washington.

ESCALANTE, FRAY SILVESTRE VELEZ DE.
1882. In Duro, Cesareo F., "Don Diego de Peñalosa y su descubrimiento del reino de Quivira." Madrid.

ESPEJO, ANTONIO DE.
1600. Viaje en el año de 1583. In Hakluyt, Voyages. Reprint 1810.
1871. Relación del viage. In Col. Doc. Inédit., t. 15, pp. 163–189.

EWING, HENRY P.
1892. Great Divide. Dec., p. 203.

FAIRBANKS, C. R.
1871. History of Florida, 1512–1842. Philadelphia.

FERNÁNDEZ, LEÓN.
1892. Lenguas indigenas de Centro-America en el Siglo XVIII. segun copia del Archivo de Indias. San José de Costa Rica.

FERREL, BARTOLOMÉ.
1879. Relation, or diary, of the voyage which Rodriguez Cabrillo made with two ships, from the 27th of June, 1542, until the 14th of April of the following year. Wheeler Surv. Rep., vol. 7, pt. 1, app., Washington. (English translation in Bolton, H. E., "Spanish exploration in the Southwest," pp. 13–39, New York, 1916.)

FEWKES, JESSE WALTER.
1897 a. Tusayan katcinas. 15th Ann. Rep. Bur. Ethnol., 1893–94, pp. 245–313.
1897 b. Tusayan Snake ceremonies. 16th Ann. Rep. Bur. Amer. Ethnol., 1894–95, pp. 267–312.
1900 a. Tusayan migration traditions. 19th Ann. Rep. Bur. Amer. Ethnol., 1897–98, pt. 1, pp. 573–633.
1900 b. Tusayan Flute and Snake ceremonies. 19th Ann. Rep. Bur. Amer. Ethnol., 1897–98, pt. 2, pp. 957–1011.
1903. Hopi katcinas, drawn by native artists. 21st Ann. Rep. Bur. Amer. Ethnol., 1899–1900, pp. 3–126.

FLETCHER, ALICE C.
1904. The Hako, a Pawnee ceremony. 22d Rep. Bur. Amer. Ethnol., 1900–1, pt. 2, pp. 5–368.

FLETCHER, ALICE C., and LA FLESCHE, FRANCIS.
1911. The Omaha tribe. 27th Ann. Rep. Bur. Amer. Ethnol., 1905–6, pp. 17–654.

FONTANEDA, HERNANDO DE ESCALANTE.
    1866. Memoria de las cosas y costa Indios de la Florida. Doc. Inéd., t. 5,
        pp. 532–548. Madrid. (*Also in* Smith, B., Letter of Hernando de
        Soto, and Memoir of Hernando de Escalante Fontaneda, Washing-
        ton, 1854; and *French trans. in* Ternaux-Compans, Voyages, t. 20,
        pp. 9–42, Paris.)

FOOTE, HENRY S.
    1841. Texas and the Texans. 2 vols. Philadelphia.

FORDE, C. DARYLL.
    1931. Ethnography of the Yuma Indians. Univ. Calif. Publ. Amer. Archaeol.
        and Ethnol., vol. 28, No. 4, pp. 83–278.

FOREMAN, GRANT.
    1930. A traveler in Indian Territory. The Journal of Ethan Allen Hitchcock,
        late Major-General in the United States Army. Cedar Rapids,
        Iowa.
    1946. The last trek of the Indians. Univ. Chicago Press.

FORNEY, JACOB.
    1858. United States Office of Indian Affairs, Report, p. 213.

FORSTER, J. R. *See* BOSSU, N.

FRACHTENBERG, LEO J.
    1911. Siuslawan (Lower Umpqua). Bur. Amer. Ethnol. Bull. 40, pt. 2, pp.
        431–629.
    1918. Comparative studies in Takelman, Kalapuyan, and Chinookan. Int.
        Journ. Amer. Ling., vol. 1, pp. 175–182.

FRANCISCAN FATHERS, THE.
    1910. An ethnologic dictionary of the Navaho language. 2 vols. St.
        Michaels, Arizona.

FRANKLIN, JOHN.
    1823. Narrative of a journey to the shores of the Polar Sea, in the years 1819,
        20, 21, and 22. London. (Other eds., London, 1824; Philadelphia,
        1824.)
    1828. Narrative of a second expedition to the Polar Sea, 1825–27. London.

FRANQUELIN, JOHANNES LUDOVICUS.
    1688. Map in Library of Congress.

FRENCH, B. F.
    1846–53. Historical collections of Louisiana, embracing many rare and valu-
        able documents relating to the natural, civil, and political history
        of that state. Pts. 1–5. New York. (Other eds: New ser.,
        New York, 1869; second ser., New York, 1875.)

GAIRDNER, DR.
    1841. Notes on the geography of Columbia River. Journ. Roy. Geogr. Soc.
        London, vol. 11.

GALLATIN, ALBERT.
    1836. A synopsis of the Indian tribes within the United States east of the
        Rocky Mountains, and in the British and Russian possessions in
        North America. Trans. and Coll. Amer. Antiq. Soc., Archaeologia
        Americana, vol. 2. Cambridge.

GANONG, WILLIAM F. *See* CHAMPLAIN, SAMUEL DE, 1922–36; Dennys, Nicolas;
    Leclerq, Chrétian, 1910.

GARCÉS, FRANCISCO. *See* COUES, ELLIOTT, EDITOR.

GARCILASO DE LA VEGA.
    1723. La Florida del Inca. Historia del adalantado, Hernando de Soto.
        Madrid.
GATSCHET, ALBERT S.
    1877-80. The Timucua language. Proc. Amer. Philos. Soc., vols. 16-18.
        Philadelphia.
    1877-92. Der Yuma-Sprachstamm nach den neuesten handschriftlichen
        Quellen. Zeitschr. Ethnol., B. 9-24. Berlin.
    1883. The Shetimasha Indians of St. Mary's Parish, Southern Louisiana.
        Trans. Anthrop. Soc. Washington, vol. 2.
    1884, 1888. A migration legend of the Creek Indians. Vol. 1. Brinton's
        Lib. Aborig. Amer. Lit., No. 4. Philadelphia. Vol. 2.
        Trans. Acad. Sci. St. Louis, vol. 5, Nos. 1 and 2. St. Louis.
    1891 a. The Karankawa Indians, the coast people of Texas. Archaeol. and
        Ethnol. Pap. Peabody Mus., vol. 1, No. 2, Cambridge.
    1891 b. The Klamath Indians of southwestern Oregon. Contr. N. Amer.
        Ethnol., vol. 2, pts. 1 and 2. Cambridge.
    MS. Wyandot MS., 1877, in archives of Bureau of American Ethnology.
GERARD, WM. R. See HODGE, F. W., 1907, 1910.
GIBBS, GEORGE.
    1867. Notes on the Tinneh or Chepewyan Indians of British and Russian
        America. 1. The eastern Tinneh, by Bernard Ross. 2. The
        Loucheux Indians, by William Hardisty. 3. The Kutchin tribes,
        by Strachan Jones. Ann. Rep. Smithsonian Inst. for 1866.
    1877. Tribes of western Washington and northwestern Oregon. Contr. N.
        Amer. Ethnol., vol. 1.
GIFFORD, E. W.
    1931. The Kamia of Imperial Valley. Bur. Amer. Ethnol. Bull. 97.
    1933. The Cocopa. Univ. Calif. Publ. Amer. Archaeol. and Ethnol., vol.
        31, No. 5, pp. 257-334.
    1936. Northeastern and Western Yavapai. Univ. Calif. Publ. Amer.
        Archaeol. and Ethnol. vol. 34, No. 4, pp. 247-354.
    1932. The Southeastern Yavapai. Univ. Calif. Publ. Amer. Archaeol. and
        Ethnol., vol. 29, pp. 177-252.
    1932. The Northfork Mono. Univ. Calif. Publ. Amer. Archaeol. and
        Ethnol., vol. 31, pp. 15-65.
GILES, JOHN.
    1869. Memoirs of Odd Adventures, Strange Deliverences, etc., in the Cap-
        tivity of John Giles, Esq., Commander of the Garrison on Saint
        George River, in the District of Maine. Written by Himself.
        Originally published at Boston, 1736. Cincinnati.
GILMORE, MELVIN R.
    1927. Notes on Arikara tribal organization. Mus. Amer. Ind., Heye Foun-
        dation, Indian Notes, vol. 4, No. 4, Oct., pp. 333-350.
GODDARD, PLINY EARLE.
    1903. Life and culture of the Hupa. Univ. Calif. Publ., Amer. Archaeol.
        and Ethnol., vol. 1, No. 1.
    1914 a. Dancing societies of the Sarsi Indians. Anthrop. Pap. Amer. Mus.
        Nat. Hist., vol. 11, pt. 5.
    1914 b. Notes on the Chilula Indians of northwestern California. Univ.
        Calif. Publ. Amer. Archaeol. and Ethnol., vol. 10, pp. 265-288.

GODDARD, PLINY EARLE—Continued
    1916. The Beaver Indians. Anthrop. Pap. Amer. Mus. Nat. Hist., vol. 10, pt. 4.

GOODWIN, GRENVILLE.
    1935. The social divisions and economic life of the western Apache. Amer. Anthrop., n. s., vol. 37, pp. 55–64.

GOOKIN, DANIEL.
    1806. Historical collections of the Indians in New England, 1792. Coll. Mass. Hist. Soc., 1st ser., vol. 1. Boston.

GRAVIER, J. See SHEA, JOHN GILMARY, 1852, pp. 115–163; and THWAITES, REUBEN GOLD, Jesuit relations, 1896–1901, vol. 65, pp. 100–179.

GREENLAND. 3 vols. Edited by M. Vahl, G. C. Amdrup, L. Bobé, and A. S. Jensen. Published by the Commission for the Direction of the Geological and Geographical Investigations in Greenland. C. A. Reitzel, Copenhagen; Oxford University Press, London, 1928 and 1929.

GRINNELL, GEORGE BIRD.
    1889. Pawnee hero stories and folk tales. New York.
    1892. Blackfoot lodge tales. New York.
    1905. Social organization of the Cheyenne. Rep. Int. Congr. Amer., 13th sess., 1902. New York.
    1923. The Cheyenne Indians: Their history and ways of life. 2 vols. Yale Univ. Press. New Haven.
    1926. Cheyenne camp fires. London.

GÜNTHER, ERNA.
    1927. Klallam Ethnology. Univ. Washington Publ. Anthrop., vol. 1, No. 5, pp. 171–314. Seattle.
    See also Haeberlin, Hermann, and Günther, Erna.

HAEBERLIN, HERMANN, and GÜNTHER, ERNA.
    1924. Ethnographische Notizen über bie Indianerstämme des Puget Sundes. Zeitschr. f. Ethnol., pp. 1–74. Berlin.
    1930. The Indians of Puget Sound. Univ. Washington Publ. Anthrop., vol. 4, No. 1, pp. 1–84. Seattle.

HAEBERLIN, H. K.; TEIT, JAMES A.; and ROBERTS, HELEN H.
    1928. Coiled basketry in British Columbia and surrounding region, under direction of Franz Boas. 41st Ann. Rep. Bur. Amer. Ethnol., 1919–24, pp. 119–484.

HALBERT, HENRY SALE.
    1901. District divisions of the Choctaw nation. Publ. Ala. Hist. Soc., Misc. Coll., vol. 1, pp. 375–385. Montgomery, Ala.

HALE, HORATIO.
    1846. Ethnology and philology. U. S. Exploring Exped. 1836–1842, under command of Charles Wilkes, U. S. N., vol. 6. Philadelphia.
    1883 a. Iroquois book of rites. Philadelphia.
    1883 b. The Tutelo tribe and language. Proc. Amer. Philos. Soc., vol. 21, No. 114. Philadelphia.

HALL, C. F.
    1865. Arctic researches and life among the Esquimaux. New York.

HARBY, MRS. LEE C.
    1895. The Tejas: Their habits, government, and superstitions. Ann. Rep. Amer. Hist. Assoc. for 1894. Washington.

HARE, LLOYD C. M.
   1932. Thomas Mayhew, Patriarch to the Indians. New York and London.
HARIOT, THOMAS.
   1893. Narrative of the first English plantation of Virginia. 1588 and 1590.
      Reprint. London.
HARPER, FRANCIS. See BARTRAM, WILLIAM, 1943.
HARRINGTON, JOHN PEABODY.
   1908. A Yuma account of origins. Journ. Amer. Folk-lore, vol. 21, pp. 324–348.
   1910. On phonetic and lexic resemblances between Kiowan and Tanoan.
      Archaeol. Inst. Amer., School Amer. Archaeol., No. 12.
HARRINGTON, M. R.
   1913. A preliminary sketch of Lenápe culture. Amer. Anthrop., n. s., vol.
      15, pp. 208–235.
HARRIS, JACK. See RAY, VERNE F.
HARRIS, JOHN.
   1705. Naviganteum atque itinerantium bibliotheca, or a complete collection
      of voyages and travels. 2 vols. London. (2d ed. London, 1764.)
HARVEY, HENRY.
   1855. History of the Shawnee Indians, from the year 1681 to 1854, inclusive.
      Cincinnati.
HAWKES, E. W.
   1916. The Labrador Eskimo. Canada Geol. Surv., Anthrop. Ser., Mem.
      91, No. 14.
HAWKINS, BENJAMIN.
   1848. A sketch of the Creek country, in 1798 and 99. Georgia Hist. Soc.
      Coll., vol. 3. Savannah.
   1916. Letters of Benjamin Hawkins 1796–1806. Georgia Hist. Soc. Coll.,
      vol. 9. Savannah.
HAYDEN, FERDINAND V.
   1862. Contributions to the ethnography and philology of the Indian tribes
      of the Missouri Valley. Trans. Amer. Philos. Soc., n. s., vol. 12.
      Philadelphia.
HAYWOOD, JOHN.
   1823. The natural and aboriginal history of Tennessee, up to the first settle-
      ments therein by the white people, in the year 1768. Nashville.
HEARNE, SAMUEL.
   1795. Journey from Prince of Wales' Fort in Hudson's Bay to the northern
      ocean. London. (Reprint, Dublin, 1796.)
HECKEWELDER, JOHN G. E.
   1819. An account of the history, manners, and customs of the Indian nations
      who once inhabited Pennsylvania and the neighboring states.
      Philadelphia. (Reprinted Mem. Hist. Soc. Pa., vol. 12. Phila-
      delphia, 1876.)
   1907. Narrative of the mission of the United Brethren among the Delaware
      and Mohegan Indians from its commencement in the year 1740 to
      the close of the year 1808. W. E. Connelley, ed. Cleveland.
HEINZELMAN, MAJ. S. P.
   1857. In Indian affairs on the Pacific. Message from the President of the
      United States transmitting report in regard to Indian affairs. (Pp.
      34–53.) H. R. Ex. Doc. 76, 34th Congr., 3d sess., p. 44.

HEINZELMAN, MAJ. S. P.—Continued
    1858. *In* Annual Report of the Commissioner of Indian Affairs for the year
        1857, p. 392.

HENLEY, THOMAS A.
    1857. California Indians. *In* Schoolcraft, H. S., 1851–57, vol. 6, table 35,
        pp. 715–718. Philadelphia.

HENRY, ALEXANDER.
    1809. Travels and adventures in Canada, and the Indian territories, between
        1760 and 1776. New York.
    MS. Comparative vocabularies of the Ojeebois, Kinistineau, and Assiniboine.
        Copied from the Journal of Alexander Henry, 1799–1811, by Charles
        N. Bell, F. R. G. S., 1887. (In archives Bur. Amer. Ethnol.)

HEWETT, EDGAR L.
    1906. Antiquities of the Jemez Plateau, New Mexico. Bur. Amer. Ethnol.
        Bull. 32.

HEWITT, J. N. B.
    1892. Legend of the founding of the Iroquois league. Amer. Anthrop., o. s.,
        vol. 5, pp. 131–148.
    1903. Iroquoian cosmology. 21st Ann. Rep. Bur. Amer. Ethnol., 1899–1900,
        pp. 127–339.
    1928. Iroquoian cosmology. Second Part. 43d Ann. Rep. Bur. Amer.
        Ethnol., 1925–26, pp. 449–819.
    See also Denig, Edwin Thompson; *and* Hodge, F. W., 1907, 1910.

HILL-TOUT, CHARLES.
    1900. Notes on the Sk'qo'mic of British Columbia, a branch of the great
        Salishan stock. *In* Rep. Comm. on Ethnol. Surv. Canada for Brit.
        Assoc. for Advancement of Science, pp. 472–559. London.
    1902. Report on the ethnology of the Siciatl of British Columbia, a coastal
        division of the Salishan stock. *In* Rep. Comm. on Ethnol. Surv.
        Canada for Brit. Assoc. for Advancement of Science, pp. 472–549.
        London.

HIND, HENRY Y.
    1863. Explorations in the interior of the Labrador Peninsula, the country of
        the Montagnais and Nasquapee Indians. 2 vols. London.

HODGE, FREDERICK WEBB.
    1907, 1910. Handbook of American Indians north of Mexico. Bur. Amer.
        Ethnol. Bull. 30, pts. 1 and 2. Ed. Frederick Webb Hodge.
    1910. The Jumano Indians. Proc. Amer. Antiquarian Soc., vol. 20, pp.
        249–268.

HODGSON, WILLIAM B.
    1848. The Creek Confederacy. Georgia Hist. Soc. Coll., vol. 3, pt. 1.
        Savannah.

HOEBEL, E. ADAMSON. *See* RAY, VERNE F.

HOFFMAN, WALTER JAMES.
    1886. Remarks on Indian tribal names. Proc. Amer. Phil. Soc., vol. 23,
        pp. 294–303.
    1891. The Midē'wiwin, or "grand Medicine Society" of the Ojibwa. 7th
        Ann. Rep. Bur. Ethnol., 1885–86, pp. 143–300.

HOFFMAN, WALTER JAMES—Continued
    1896. The Menomini Indians. 14th Ann. Rep. Bur. Ethnology, pt. 1, pp.
        3–328.
    MS. In archives of Bureau of American Ethnology.
HOIJER, HARRY.
    1938. The Southern Athapaskan languages. Amer. Anthrop., n. s., vol. 40,
        No. 1, pp. 75–87.
HOLMES, WILLIAM H.
    1905. Notes on the antiquities of Jemez Valley, New Mexico. Amer.
        Anthrop., n. s., vol. 7, No. 2.
HOOPER, LUCILE.
    1920. The Cahuilla Indians. Univ. Calif. Publ. Amer. Archaeol. and
        Ethnol., vol. 16, pp. 315–380.
HOOPER, WILLIAM H.
    1853. Ten months among the tents of the Tuski. London.
HOPKINS, SARAH WINNEMUCCA.
    1883. Life among the Piutes. Ed. by Mrs. Horace Mann. Boston.
HOUGH, WALTER.
    1915. The Hopi Indians. Cedar Rapids, Iowa.
HOWLEY, JAMES P.
    1915. The Beothucks or Red Indians: The aboriginal inhabitants of New-
        foundland. Cambridge [Eng.].
HRDLIČKA, ALEŠ.
    1906. Notes on the Pima of Arizona. Amer. Anthrop., n. s., vol. 8, No. 1,
        pp. 39–46.
    1903. The region of the ancient "Chichimecs," with notes on the Tepecanos
        and the ruin of La Quemada, Mexico. Amer. Anthrop., n. s., vol. 5,
        pp. 385–440.
HUNT, GEORGE. See BOAS, FRANZ, 1897, 1921.
HUNTER, JOHN D.
    1823. Memoirs of a captivity among the Indians of North America. London.
IAPI OAYE.
    1871–87. The Word Carrier. Vols. 1–16. Greenwood, Dakota; Santee
        Agency, Nebraska.
IBERVILLE, PIERRE LE MOYNE d'. See MARGRY, PIERRE, 1875–86, vol. 4, p. 514.
INDIAN AFFAIRS (UNITED STATES).
    Office of Indian Affairs, War Department. Reports. 1825–1848. Report
        of the Commissioner, Department of the Interior, 1849–1932. In Report
        of the Department of the Interior, 1933—.
JACOBS, MELVILLE.
    1937. Historic perspectives in Indian languages of Oregon and Washington.
        Pacific Northwest Quarterly, Jan., pp. 55–74.
JAMES, EDWIN.
    1823. Account of an expedition from Pittsburgh to the Rocky Mountains,
        performed in the years 1819 and '20, by order of the Hon. J. C.
        Calhoun, Sec'y of War: under the command of Major Stephen H.
        Long. 2 vols. and atlas. Philadelphia. (Same, London, 1823.)
JEFFERSON, THOMAS.
    1801. Notes on the State of Virginia; with a map of Virginia, Maryland,
        Delaware, and Pennsylvania. Philadelphia. (2d ed., Philadelphia, 182.5)

JEFFERYS, THOS.
   1761. The natural and civil history of the French dominions in North and
      South America. Parts 1–2. London.
JENKS, ALBERT ERNEST.
   1900. The wild-rice gatherers of the upper lakes: A study in American prim-
      itive economics. 19th Ann. Rep. Bur. Amer. Ethnol., 1897–98,
      pt. 2, pp. 1013–1137.
JENNESS, DIAMOND.
   1922 a. The life of the Copper Eskimos. Rep. Canadian Arctic Exped.,
      1913–18, vol. 12, pt. A. Ottawa.
   1922 b. The Copper Eskimos; physical characteristics of the Copper Eski-
      mos. Rep. Canadian Arctic Exped., 1913–18, vol. 2. pt. B.
   1923 a. Eskimo folk-lore. Myths and traditions from Northern Alaska, the
      Mackenzie Delta, and Coronation Gulf. Rep. Canadian Arctic
      Exped., 1913–18, vol. 13, pt. A.
   1923 b. Eskimo folk-lore. Eskimo string figures. Rep. Canadian Arctic
      Exped., 1913–18, vol. 13, pt. B.
   1932. The Indians of Canada. Nat. Mus. Canada, Bull. 65, Anthrop. Ser.
      No. 15. Ottawa.
   1937. The Sekani Indians of British Columbia. Nat. Mus. Canada, Bull.
      No. 84, Anthrop. Ser., No. 20. Ottawa.
   1938. The Sarcee Indians of Alberta. Nat. Mus. Canada, Bull. 90, Anthrop.
      Ser. No. 23. Ottawa.
JENSEN, A. S. *See* VAHL, G. C., ET AL.
JESUIT RELATIONS AND ALLIED DOCUMENTS.
   1858. Relations des Jesuites contenant ce qui s'est passé de plus remarquable
      dans les missions des pères de la Compagnie de Jesus dans la Nou-
      velle-France. Embrassant les années 1611–1672. T. 1–3. Quebec.
   1896–1901. Travels and explorations of the Jesuit missionaries in New France,
      1610–1791. Reuben Gold Thwaites, ed. 73 vols. Cleve-
      land.
JEWITT, JOHN R.
   1815. A narrative of the adventures and sufferings of John R. Jewitt; only
      survivor of the crew of the ship *Boston*, during a captivity of nearly
      three years among the savages of Nootka Sound. Middletown,
      Conn. (2d ed., Ithaca, N. Y., 1849.)
JOCHELSON, WALDEMAR.
   1933. History, ethnology, and anthropology of the Aleut. Carnegie Inst.
      Washington, Publ. No. 4320.
JOHNSON, ELIAS.
   1881. Legends, traditions, and laws of the Iroquois, or Six Nations. Lock-
      port, N. Y.
JOHNSON, FREDERICK.
   1940. The linguistic map of Mexico and Central America. *In* The Maya
      and their neighbors: (Tozzer volume), pp. 88–114. New York and
      London.
JONES, PETER.
   1861. History of the Ojebway Indians; with especial reference to their con-
      version to Christianity. London.

JOUTEL, HENRI.
    1713. Journal historique du dernier voyage que M. de la Sale fit dans le golfe
        de Mexique pour trouver l' embouchure de la riviere de Mississippi.
        Paris. (Also in Margry, Pierre, 1875–86, vol. 3, pp. 89–534.)

JUARROS, DOMINGO.
    1808–1818. Compendio de la Historia de la Ciudad de Guatemala, 1808–1818.
    1824. English edition of above entitled "A statistical and commercial history
        of the Kingdom of Guatemala."

KEATING, WILLIAM H.
    1824. Narrative of an expedition to the source of St. Peter's River, Lake
        Winnepeek, Lakes of the Woods, etc. Compiled from the notes of
        Major Long, Messrs. Say, Keating, and Calhoun. 2 vols. Phila-
        delphia. (Same, London, 1825.)

KELLY, ISABEL T.
    1932. Ethnography of the Surprise Valley Paiute. Univ. Calif. Publ. Amer.
        Archaeol. and Ethnol., vol. 31, No. 3, pp. 67–210.
    1934. Southern Paiute bands. Amer. Anthrop., n. s., vol. 36, No. 4, pp.
        548–560.
        Also see Park, Willard Z.

KENDALL, EDWARD AUGUSTUS.
    1809. Travels through the northern parts of the United States in the years
        1807 and 1808. 3 vols. New York.

KER, HENRY.
    1816. Travels through the western interior of the United States, from the
        year 1808 up to the year 1816. Elizabethtown.

KINIETZ, W. VERNON.
    1940. The Indians of the Western Great Lakes 1615–1760. Occasional
        Contr. Mus. Anthrop. Univ. Michigan, No. 10. Univ. Michigan
        Press, Ann Arbor.

KINO, EUSEBIUS.
    1726. Tabula Californiae, Anno 1702. In Stöcklein, Der Neue Welt-Bott,
        pt. 2, facing p. 74. Augspurg und Grätz.

KRAUSE, AUREL.
    1885. Die Tlinkit Indianer. Ergebnisse einer Reise nach der Nordwestkuste
        von America und der Beringstrasse. Auftrage der Bremer geograph-
        ichen Gesellschaft, 1880–81. Jena.

KROEBER, ALFRED L.
    1900. The Eskimo of Smith Sound. Bull. Amer. Mus. Nat. Hist., vol. 12,
        Art. 21, pp. 265–327.
    1902 a. Preliminary sketch of the Mohave Indians. Amer. Anthrop., n. s.,
        vol. 4, pp. 276–285.
    1902 b. The Arapaho. Bull. Amer. Mus. Nat. Hist., vol. 18.
    1903. The coast Yuki of California. Amer. Anthrop., n. s., vol. 5, pp. 729–
        730.
    1904. Types of Indian culture in California. Univ. Calif. Publ. Amer.
        Archaeol. and Ethnol., vol. 2, pp. 81–103.
    1907 a. Shoshonean dialects of California. Univ. Calif. Publ. Amer.
        Archaeol. and Ethnol., vol. 4, No. 3.
    1907 b. The religion of the Indians of California. Univ. Calif. Publ. Amer.
        Archaeol. and Ethnol., vol. 4, pp. 319–356.

Kroeber, Alfred L.—Continued

1908 a. Ethnography of the Cahuilla Indians. Univ. Calif. Publ. Amer. Archaeol. and Ethnol., vol. 8, pp. 29–68.

1908 b. Ethnology of the Gros Ventre. Anthrop. Pap. Amer. Mus. Nat. Hist., vol. 1, pt. 4.

1909. Notes on Shoshonean dialects of Southern California. Univ. Calif. Publ. Amer. Archaeol. and Ethnol., vol. 8, No. 5.

1915. Serian, Tequistlatecan and Hokan. Univ. Calif. Publ. Archaeol. and Ethnol., vol. 11, No. 4.

1920 a. Yuman tribes of the Lower Colorado. Univ. Calif. Publ. Amer. Archaeol. and Ethnol., vol. 16, No. 8.

1920 b. Californian culture provinces. Univ. Calif. Publ. Amer. Archaeol. and Ethnol., vol. 17, pp. 151–169.

1922. Elements of culture in native California. Univ. Calif. Publ. Amer. Archaeol. and Ethnol., vol. 13, pp. 259–328.

1925. Handbook of the Indians of California. Bur. Amer. Ethnol. Bull. 78.

1931. The Seri. Southwest Mus. Pap., No. 6, April.

1932. The Patwin and their neighbors. Univ. Calif. Publ. Archaeol. and Ethnol., vol. 29, No. 4, pp. 253–323.

1934. Uto-Aztecan languages of Mexico. Ibero-Americana, No. 8, Univ. Calif. Press.

1935. Material collected by Fred Kniffen, Gordon MacGregor, Robert McKennan, Scudder Mekeel, and Maurice Mook. Edited by A. L. Kroeber. Mem. Amer. Anthrop. Assoc., No. 42, Contr. Lab. Anthrop. No. 1.

1939. Cultural and natural areas of native North America. Univ. Calif. Publ. Amer. Archaeol. and Ethnol., vol. 38.

Krogman, Wilton Marion.

1935. The physical anthropology of the Seminole Indians of Oklahoma. With an introduction by Corrado Gini. Comitato Italiano per lo Studio dei Problemi della Popolazione. Seri 3, vol. 2. Rome, Italy.

Krzywicki, Ludwik.

1934. Primitive society and its vital statistics. App. 2, North American Indian Tribes, pp. 318–509. App. 3, North American confederacies and their equivalents, pp. 510–543.

La Flesche, Francis.

1921. The Osage tribe. Rite of the chiefs; sayings of the ancient men. 36th Ann. Rep. Bur. Amer. Ethnol., 1914–15, pp. 37–597.

1925. The Osage tribe. The rite of vigil. 39th Ann. Rep. Bur. Amer. Ethnol., 1917–18, pp. 31–630.

1928. The Osage tribe. Two versions of the child-naming rite. 43d Ann. Rep. Bur. Amer. Ethnol., 1925–26, pp. 23–164.

La Harpe, Bernard de.

1831. Journal historique de l'établissement des Français a la Louisiane. Nouvelle Orleans. (*Eng. trans. in* French, B. F., Hist. Coll. La., vol. 3. New York, 1851.)

Lamhatty, Account of. *See* Bushnell, David I., Jr., 1908.

Lane, Joseph.

1850. *In* Report of United States Office of Indian Affairs for 1850, p. 161.

LAPHAM, I. A., BLOSSOM, L., and DOUSMAN, G. D.
1870. Number, locality, and times of removal of the Indians of Wisconsin. Milwaukee.

LA SALLE, NICOLAS DE. *See* MARGRY, PIERRE, vol. 1, pp. 547–570.

LA SALLE, RÉNÉ ROBERT CAVELIER, SIEUR DE.
For account of La Salle's voyage, *see* Shea, John Gilmary, 1861, pp. 15–42.
See also Cox, Isaac Joslin, Editor; and Delanglez, Jean.

LAS CASAS. *See* CASAS, BARTOLOMÉ LAS.

LAUDONNIÈRE, RENÉ.
1586. Histoire notable de la Florida située ès Indes Occidentales, contenant, les trois voyages faits en icelle par certains capitaines et pilotes François a laquelle a esté adjousté un quatriesme voyage fait par le Captaine Gourgues, mise en lumière par M. Basnier. Paris. (New ed., Paris, 1853.)

LAUGHLIN, H. H., and GANONG, WILLIAM F., TRANSLATORS AND EDITORS. *See* CHAMPLAIN, SAMUEL DE, 1922–36.

LAVERDIÈRE, C. H. *See* CHAMPLAIN, SAMUEL DE, 1870.

LAWSON, JOHN.
1709. A new voyage to Carolina; containing the exact description and natural history of that country; together with the present state thereof, and a journal of a thousand miles travel thro' several nations of Indians. London.
1714. History of Carolina, containing the exact description and natural history of that country. London. (Reprint, Raleigh, 1860; Richmond, 1937.)

LECLERQ, CHRÉTIEN.
1691. Nouvelle relation de la Gaspésie. Paris.
1881. First establishment of the faith in New France; now first translated with notes by J. G. Shea. 2 vols. New York.
1910. New relation of Gaspesia, with the customs and religion of the Gaspesian Indians. Trans. by William F. Ganong. The Champlain Society. Toronto.

LEDERER, JOHN.
1912. The discoveries of John Lederer in three several marches from Virginia to the west of Carolina and other parts of this continent; begun in March 1669, and ended September 1670. Together with a general map of the whole territory which he traversed. Collected and translated by Sir William Talbot, Baronet. *In* Alvord, Clarence W., and Bidgood, Lee. (Note: Other eds. of op. cit. are London, 1672; *in* Harris, vol. 2, London, 1705; and Rochester, 1902.)

LEHMANN, WALTER.
1920. Die Sprachen Zentral-Amerikas. Zentral-Amerikas, pt. 1, 2 vols. Berlin.

LE MOYNE, JACQUES.
1875. Narrative of Le Moyne, an artist who accompanied the French expedition to Florida under Laudonnière, 1564. Trans. from Latin of De Bry. Boston.

LENGUAS INDÍGENAS DE CENTRO-AMERICA EN EL SIGLO XVIII segun copia del Archivo de Indias hecha por León Fernández y publicada por Ricardo Fernández Guardia y Juan Fernández Ferraz para el 9° Congreso de Americanistas. San José de Costa Rica. Tip. nacional, 1892.

Le Page du Pratz, Antoine S.
    1758. Histoire de la Louisiane. 3 t. Paris. (Eng. trans., London, 1763, 1764.)
Leroux, Joseph.
    1888. Le medaillier du Canada. Montréal.
Lescarbot, Marc.
    1612. Histoire de la novvelle France. Paris.
    1907–14. History of New France. Trans. by W. L. Grant. The Champlain
        Society. 3 vols. Toronto. (Vol. 1, 1907; vol. 2, 1911; vol. 3, 1914.)
Lesser, Alexander, and Weltfish, Gene.
    1932. Composition of the Caddoan linguistic stock. Smithsonian Misc.
        Coll., vol. 87, No. 6.
Le Sueur, Narrative of. See Margry, Beaurain, and Pénicaut.
Lewis, Albert Buell.
    1906. Tribes of the Columbia Valley and the coast of Washington and
        Oregon. Mem. Amer. Anthrop. Assoc., vol. 1, pt. 2.
Lewis, Meriwether, and Clark, Wm.
    1840. The journal of Lewis and Clark, to the mouth of the Columbia River
        beyond the Rocky Mountains. Dayton, Ohio.
Lieber, Oscar M.
    1858. Vocabulary of the Catawba language with some remarks on its gram-
        mar, construction, and pronunciation. Coll. S. C. Hist. Soc., vol. 2,
        pp. 327–342. Charleston.
Long, John.
    1791. Voyages and travels of an Indian interpreter and trader, describing
        the manners and customs of the North American Indians. London.
Long, Stephen H. See James, Edwin; Keating, William H.
Loud, Llewellyn L.
    1918. Ethnogeography and archaeology of the Wiyot territory. Univ. Calif.
        Publ. Amer. Archaeol. and Ethnol., vol. 14, pp. 221–436.
Lowery, Woodbury.
    1901. The Spanish settlements within the present limits of the United States.
        1513–1561 and 1564–1574, 2 vols. New York and London.
Lowie, Robert H.
    1917. Notes on the social organization and customs of the Mandan, Hidatsa,
        and Crow. Anthrop. Pap., Amer. Mus. Nat. Hist., vol. 21, pt. 1.
    1939. Ethnographic notes on the Washo. Univ. Calif. Publ. Amer. Archaeol.
        and Ethnol., vol. 36, No. 5, pp. 301–352.
        (Also numerous writings on the Crow Indians.)
Lumholtz, Carl.
    1894. Proceedings International Congress of Anthropology.
    1898. Huichol Indians of Mexico. Bull. Amer. Mus. Nat. Hist., vol. 10.
        New York.
Lyon, G. F.
    1824. Private journal during voyage of discovery under Captain Parry.
        Boston. (Reprint, London, 1825.)
MacCauley, Clay.
    1887. The Seminole Indians of Florida. 5th Rep. Bur. Ethnol., 1883–84,
        pp. 469–531.
McClintock, Walter.
    1910. The Old North Trail. London.

McILWRAITH, THOMAS F.
    1948. The Bella Coola Indians. Univ. Toronto Press, 2 vols.

MACK, JOHN. *See* BERRY, BREWTON, ET AL.

McKENNAN, ROBERT.
    1935. Note "Anent the Kutchin Tribes." Amer. Anthrop., n. s., vol. 37, No. 2, p. 369.

McKENNEY, THOMAS L.
    1846. Vol. 1: Memoirs, official and personal; with sketches of travels among the northern and southern Indians; embracing a war excursion, and descriptions of scenes along the western borders. Vol. 2: On the origin, history, character, and the wrongs and rights of the Indians, with a plan for the preservation and happiness of the remnants of that persecuted race. (Two volumes in one.) New York.

McKENNY, THOMAS L., and HALL, JAMES.
    1933–34. The Indian tribes of North America. 3 vols. Edinburgh.

MACKENZIE, ALEXANDER.
    1801. Voyages from Montreal, on the river St. Lawrence, through the continent of North America, to the Frozen and Pacific Oceans; in the years 1789 and 1793. London. (Reprint, Philadelphia, 1802.)

MacNUTT, FRANCIS AUGUSTUS. *See* ANGHIERA, PIETRO MARTIRE D'.

MAINE HISTORICAL SOCIETY. Collections, vols. 1–6, Portland, 1831–59. Vol. 7, Bath, 1876. Vols. 8–10, Portland, 1881–91. 2d ser., vols. 1–10. Portland, 1890–99.

MARBURY.
    1792. MS. A census taken by the State of Georgia.

MARGRY, PIERRE.
    1875–86. Découvertes et établissements des Français dans l'ouest et dans le sud de l'Amérique Septentrionale (1614–1754). Mémoires et documents originaux. Pts. 1–6. Paris.

MARQUETTE'S MAP, 1673. *See* JESUIT RELATIONS.

MASON, J. ALDEN.
    1912. The ethnology of the Salinan Indians. Univ. Calif. Publ. Amer. Archaeol. and Ethnol., vol. 10, pp. 97–240.
    1940. The native languages of Middle America. *In* The Maya and their neighbors (Tozzer Volume), pp. 52–87. D. Appleton-Century Co., New York and London.

MASSACHUSETTS HISTORICAL SOCIETY. Collections, vols. 1–10, Boston, 1792–1809 (vol. 1 reprinted in 1806 and 1859; vol. 5 in 1816 and 1835). 2d ser., vols. 1–10, Boston, 1814–23 (reprinted 1838–43). 3d ser., vols. 1–10, Boston, 1825–49 (vol. 1 reprinted 1846). 4th ser., 1–10, Boston, 1852–71.

MAURAULT, J. A.
    1866. Histoire des Abenakis depuis 1605 jusqu'a nos jours. Quebec.

MAXIMILIAN, ALEXANDER P.
    1843. Travels in the interior of North America. Trans. from German by H. Evans Lloyd. London.

MAYHEW, THOMAS, JR.
    1928. *In* Territorial subdivisions and boundaries of the Wampanoag, Massachusetts, and Nauset, by Frank G. Speck. Ind. Notes and Monogr., Misc. Ser., No. 44, p. 110. Mus. Amer. Ind., Heye Found. New York.

MECHLING, WILLIAM H.
   1912. The Indian linguistic stocks of Oaxaca, Mexico. Amer. Anthrop.
        n. s., vol. 14, pp. 643–682.

MEIGS, PEVERIL, 3D.
   1939. The Kiliwa Indians of Lower California. Ibero-Americana, No. 15.
        Univ. Calif. Press, Berkeley, Calif.

MENGARINI, GREGORY.
   1871–72. Indians of Oregon. Journ. Anthrop. Inst., N. Y., vol. 1. New
        York.

MERENESS, NEWTON D., EDITOR.
   1916. Travels in the American Colonies. New York.

MERRIAM, C. HART.
   1905. The Indian population of California. Amer. Anthrop., n. s., vol. 7,
        pp. 594–606.
   1907. Distribution and classification of the Mewan stock of California.
        Amer. Anthrop., n. s., vol. 9, pp. 338–357.
   1914. Distribution of Indian tribes in the southern Sierra and adjacent parts
        of the San Joaquin Valley, California. Science, n. s., vol. 19, pp.
        912–917.
   1926. The classification and distribution of the Pit River Indian tribes of
        California. Smithsonian Misc. Coll., vol. 78, No. 3.
   1929. The Cop-éh of Gibbs. Amer. Anthrop., n. s., vol. 31, pp. 136–137.
   1930 a. The New River Indians Tló-hōm-taĥ-hoi. Amer. Anthrop., n. s.,
        vol. 32, No. 2, pp. 280–293.
   1930 b. The Em'-tim'-bitch, a Shoshonean tribe. Amer. Anthrop., vol. 32,
        No. 3, pt. 1, pp. 496–499.

MÉXICO. ARCHIVO GENERAL DE LA NACIÓN, vol. 15. On Tamaulipas.

MÉZIÈRES, ATHANASE DE. See BOLTON, HERBERT EUGENE, 1914.

MICHEL, FRANCIS LOUIS.
   1916. Report of the journey of Francis Louis Michel from Berne, Switzerland,
        to Virginia, October 2, 1701–December 1, 1702. Va. Mag. Hist. and
        Biog., Va. Hist. Soc., vol. 24, pp. 1–43, 113–141, 275–303. Trans-
        lated and edited by Prof. William J. Hinke.

MICHELSON, TRUMAN.
   1912. Preliminary report on the linguistic classification of Algonquian tribes.
        28th Ann. Rep. Bur. Amer. Ethnol., 1906–7, pp. 221–290b.
   1916. Ritualistic origin myths of the Fox Indians. Journ. Washington Acad.
        Sci., vol. 6, No. 8, pp. 209–211.
   1919. Some general notes on the Fox Indians. Journ. Washington Acad.
        Sci., vol. 9, No. 16, pp. 482–494; No. 17, pp. 521–528.
   1921. The Owl Sacred Pack of the Fox Indians. Bur. Amer. Ethnol. Bull. 72.
   1925. The mythical origin of the White Buffalo Dance of the Fox Indians.
        The autobiography of a Fox Indian woman. Notes on Fox mortuary
        customs and beliefs. Notes on the Fox society known as "Those
        Who Worship the Little Spotted Buffalo." 40th Ann. Rep. Bur.
        Amer. Ethnol., 1918–19, pp. 23–658.
   1927. Contributions to Fox Ethnology. Bur. Amer. Ethnol. Bull. 85.
   1928. Notes on the Buffalo-head Dance of the Thunder Gens of the Fox
        Indians. Bur. Amer. Ethnol. Bull. 87.

MILFORT, LE CLERC.
    1802. Memoire ou coup-d'oeil rapide sur mes differens voyages et mon sejour dans la nation Crëck. Paris.
MILLING, CHAPMAN J.
    1940. Red Carolinians. Univ. N. C. Press, Chapel Hill, N. C.
MINDELEFF, COSMOS.
    1900. Localization of Tusayan clans. 19th Ann. Rep. Bur. Amer. Ethnol., 1897–98, pt. 2, pp. 635–653.
MINNESOTA HISTORICAL SOCIETY. Collections. Vols. 1–11. St. Paul, 1872–1905.
MISSISSIPPI PROVINCIAL ARCHIVES, FRENCH DOMINIONS.
    Particularly vol. 3, ed. Rowland, Dunbar, and Sanders, Albert Godfrey, Jackson, Miss., 1932. See Bienville, Jean Baptiste le Moyne, Sieur de.
MOONEY, JAMES.
    1895. The Siouan tribes of the east. Bur. Amer. Ethnol. Bull. 22.
    1896. The Ghost-dance religion and the Sioux outbreak of 1890. 14th Ann. Rep. Bur. Amer. Ethnol., 1892–93, pt. 2, pp. 641–1110.
    1898. Calendar history of the Kiowa Indians. 17th Ann. Rep. Bur. Amer. Ethnol., 1895–96, pt. 1, pp. 129–445.
    1900. Myths of the Cherokee. 19th Ann. Rep. Bur. Amer. Ethnol., 1897–98, pt. 1, pp. 3–548.
    1907. The Cheyenne Indians. Mem. Amer. Anthrop. Assoc., vol. 1, pt. 6.
    1928. The aboriginal population of America north of Mexico. Smithsonian Misc. Coll., vol. 80, No. 7.
MORGAN, LEWIS H.
    1851. League of the Ho-de-no-sau-nee, or Iroquois. Rochester, New York, and Boston. (2d ed., New York, 1904.)
MORICE, A. G.
    1889. The Western Dénés. Their manners and customs. Proc. Can. Inst., 3d ser., vol. 6, No. 2. Toronto.
    1895. Notes, archaeological, industrial and sociological, on the Western Dénés. Trans. Can. Inst., vol. 4, 1892–93. Toronto.
    1904 a. History of the northern interior of British Columbia, formerly New Caledonia. Toronto.
    1904 b. In Transactions of the Royal Canadian Institute, vol. 7, p. 518.
    1906. The Great Déné Race. Anthropos, vol. 1 and succeeding vols.
MORSE, JEDEDIAH.
    1822. A report to the Secretary of War of the United States, on Indian affairs, comprising a narrative of a tour performed in the summer of 1820. New Haven, Conn.
MOTT, MILDRED.
    1938. The relation of historic Indian tribes to archaeological manifestations in Iowa. Iowa Journ. Hist. and Politics, vol. 36, No. 3, pp. 227–327. (Published quarterly by the State Hist. Soc. of Iowa, Iowa City, Iowa.)
MULLAN, JOHN.
    1855. Report on the Indian tribes in the eastern portion of Washington territory, 1853. Pac. R.R. Rep., vol. 1, pp. 437–441. Washington.
MULLOY, WILLIAM T. See PARK, WILLARD Z.

MURDOCH, JOHN.
　　1892. Ethnological results of the Point Barrow Expedition.   9th Ann. Rep.
　　　　Bur. Ethnol., 1887–88, pp. 3–441.

MURDOCK, GEORGE PETER.
　　1941. Ethnographic bibliography of North America.   Published for the
　　　　Department of Anthropology.   Yale Univ. Press.
　　　　See also Ray, Verne F., 1938.

MURIE, JAMES R.
　　1914. Pawnee Indian Societies.   Anthrop. Pap., Amer. Mus. Nat. Hist.,
　　　　vol. 11, pp. 543–644.

MYERS, ALBERT COOK.
　　1912. Narratives of early Delaware, New Jersey, and Pennsylvania.   In
　　　　Original narratives of early American history.   New York.

NANSEN, F.
　　1893. Eskimo life.   Trans. by William Archer.   London.   (2d ed., London,
　　　　1894.)

NEIGHBORS, MAJOR ROBERT S.
　　1857. Report of United States Office of Indian Affairs.   (See also Swanton,
　　　　1942, p. 20.)

NELSON, E. W.
　　1899. The Eskimo about Bering Strait.   18th Ann. Rep. Bur. Amer. Ethnol.,
　　　　1896–97, pt. 1, pp. 3–518.

NELSON, WILLIAM.
　　1894. Indians of New Jersey.   Paterson, N. J.

NEW YORK.   DOCUMENTS RELATING TO THE COLONIAL HISTORY OF THE STATE
　　Vols. 1–15, 1853–87.   Albany.

NIZA, MARCOS DE.
　　1810. Relation, 1539.   In Hakluyt, Voy., vol. 3, pp. 438–446, 1600.   (Re-
　　　　print, 1810.   There are several other editions of this work.)

NOMLAND, GLADYS AYER.
　　1935. Sinkyone Notes.   Univ. Calif. Publ. Amer. Archaeol. and Ethnol.,
　　　　vol. 36, No. 2, pp. 149–178.
　　1938. Bear River ethnography.   Anthrop. Rec., vol. 2, No. 2, pp. 91–124.
　　　　Univ. Calif. Press.

NORTH CAROLINA, THE COLONIAL RECORDS OF.   Vols. 1–9.   Raleigh, 1886–90.

NORTH DAKOTA, STATE HISTORICAL SOCIETY.   Collections.   Vols. 1–2.   Bismarck,
　　N. D., 1906–08.

NORTHWESTERN TRIBES OF CANADA.   Reports on the physical characters, lan-
　　guages, industrial and social condition of the northwestern tribes of the Dominion
　　of Canada.   In Reports of the British Association for the Advancement of
　　Science, 1885 to 1898, London, 1886–99.

NUÑEZ CABEZA DE VACA, ALVAR.
　　1851. Relation.   Trans. by Buckingham Smith.   New York.   (2d ed., New
　　　　York, 1871.)
　　1905. The journey of Alvar Nuñez Cabeza de Vaca . . . translated from his
　　　　own narrative by Fanny Bandelier.   Trail Makers (series).   New
　　　　York.

OLDMIXON, JOHN.
　　1708. British Empire in America.   2 vols.   London.

OLSON, RONALD L.
    1936. The Quinault Indians. Univ. Washington Publ. Anthrop., vol. 6, No. 1, pp. 1–190. Seattle, Washington.

OÑATE, JUAN DE.
    1871. Memorial sobre el descubrimiento del Nuevo México y sus acontecimientos. Años desde 1595 á 1602. Col. Doc. Inédit., t. 16, pp. 188–227. Madrid.

OPLER, MARVIN K. See PARK, WILLARD Z.

ORCUTT, S.
    1882. Indians of the Housatonic and Naugatuck Valleys.

OROZCO Y BERRA, MANUEL.
    1864. Geografía de las lenguas y carta etnográfica de México. México.

OSGOOD, CORNELIUS.
    1934. Kutchin tribal distribution and synonymy. Amer. Anthrop., n. s., vol. 36, No. 2, pp. 168–179.
    1936. Contributions to the ethnography of the Kutchin. Yale Univ. Publ. Anthrop., No. 14.

OWEN, MARY ALICIA.
    1904. Folk-lore of the Musquakie Indians of North America. Publ. Folk-lore Soc., vol. 51. London.

PACIFIC RAILROAD REPORTS. Reports of explorations and surveys to ascertain the most practicable route for a railroad from the Mississippi River to the Pacific Ocean. Made under the direction of the Secretary of War. 1853–54. Vols. 1–12, in 13 vols. Washington, 1855–60.

PAIGE, G. A.
    1858. In Annual Report of the Commissioner of Indian Affairs for the year 1857, p. 329. Washington.

PALMER, WILLIAM R.
    1928. Utah Indians past and present: An etymological and historical study of tribes and tribal names from original sources. Utah Hist. Quart., vol. 1, No. 2, pp. 35–52.

PAREJA, FRANCISCO DE.
    1612. Cathecismo, en lengua Castellana y Timuquana. México.
    1613. Confessionario, en lengua Castellana y Timuquana. México.
    1886. Arte de la lengua Timuquana compuesta en 1614. Bibl. Ling. Amér., vol. 11. Paris.

PARK, WILLARD Z., AND OTHERS.
    1938. Tribal distribution of the Great Basin. Amer. Anthrop., n. s., vol. 40, No. 4, pt. 1, pp. 622–638. (Containing: The organization and habitat of Paviotso Bands, by Willard Z. Parks, pp. 622–626; Washo Territory, by Edgar E. Siskin, pp. 626–627; The Northern Ute, by Anne M. Cooke, pp. 627–630; Groups of central and southern Nevada, by William T. Mulloy, pp. 630–632; The Southern Ute, by Marvin K. Opler, pp. 632–633; Band organization of the Southern Ute, by Isabel T. Kelly, pp. 633–634; Kawaiisu Territory, by Maurice L. Zigmond, pp. 634–638.)

PARKER, SAMUEL.
    1840. Journal of an exploring tour beyond the Rocky Mountains. Ithaca, 1838, 1840, 1842, 1846. (See 1840 vol., p. 257.)

PARSONS, ELSIE CLEWS.
    1929. The social organization of the Tewa of New Mexico. Mem. Amer.
        Anthrop. Assoc. No. 36.

PENHALLOW, SAMUEL.
    1726. The history of the wars of New England with the eastern Indians.
        Boston. (Other eds: In Coll. N. H. Hist. Soc., vol. 1, Concord.
        1824; reprint, 1871.)

PÉNICAUT, M.
    1869. Annals of Louisiana from the establishment of the first colony under
        d'Iberville, to 1722. In French, B. F., Hist. Coll. La. and Fla.,
        n. s., New York; also in Margry, Pierre, pt. 5 (q. v.).

PERALTA, MANUEL M. DE.
    1895. In the Ethnology of Costa Rica. In Brinton's "Report upon the col-
        lection exhibited at the Columbian Historical Exposition at Madrid."
        Washington.

PEREA, ESTEVAN DE.
    1632–33. Verdadera [y Segvnda] relación, de la grandiosa conversión que ha
        avido en el Nuevo Mexico. Sevilla.

PERRIN DU LAC, F. M.
    1805. Voyages dans les deux Louisianes, et chez les nations sauvages du
        Missouri, par les Etats-Unis, en 1801–1803. Paris, 1805. (Same,
        Lyon, 1805.)

PERROT, NICOLAS.
    1864. Mémoire sur les mœurs, coustumes et relligion des sauvages de l'Améri-
        que Septentrionale, publié pour la premiére fois par le R. P. J.
        Tailhan. Leipzig et Paris.

PETER MARTYR OF ANGHIERA. See ANGHIERA, PIETRO MARTIRE d'.

PETITOT, EMILE.
    1875. Géographie de l'Athabaskaw-Mackenzie et des grands lacs du bassin
        arctique. Bull. Soc. Géogr. Paris, 6e ser., t. 10. Paris.
    1876 a. Monographie des Dènè-Dinjié. In Dictionnaire de la langue Dènè-
        Dindjié dialectes Montagnais ou Chippéwayan, Peaux de Lièvre
        et Loucheux, etc. Bibl. Ling. et Ethnogr. Amér., t. 2. Paris.
    1876 b. Vocabulaire Francais-Esquimau. Bibl. Ling. et Ethnogr. Amér.,
        t. 3. Paris.
    1883. On the Athabascan district of the Canadian North West Territory.
        Proc. Roy. Geogr. Soc. and Monthly Rec. of Geogr., vol. 5. London.
    1884. On the Athapasca district of the Canadian North-west Territory.
        Montreal Nat. Hist. Soc., Rec. Nat. Hist. and Geol. Montreal.
        (Reprinted in Canadian Rec. Sci., vol. 1, Montreal, 1884.)
    1887 a. Traditions indiennes du Canada nordouest. Alençon.
    1887 b. En route pour la mer glaciale. Paris.
    1891. Autour du grand lac des Esclaves. Paris.
    1893. Exploration de la region de grand lac des Ours. Paris.
    MS. Comparative vocabulary of the Montagnais-Tinne. Includes Chippe-
        wyananock des Crees, Esclaves-Tribu des Peaux de Lièvre (Hares).
        1865. (In archives of Bur. Amer. Ethnol.)

PETROFF, IVAN.
    1884. Report on the population, industries, and resources of Alaska. U. S.
        Dept. Int., Census Office, 10th Census, vol. 8.

POLLARD, J. G.
    1894. The Pamunkey Indians of Virginia. Bur. Amer. Ethnol. Bull. 17.

POPPLE MAP.
   1733. *In* Swanton, John R., 1922, pl. 4.
PORTER, ROBERT T.
   1893. *In* Report on population and resources of Alaska at the eleventh
         census, 1890.   United States Bureau of the Census.   Washington.
PORTER, GEN. PETER B.   *See* SCHOOLCRAFT, HENRY B., 1851–57, vol. 3, p. 497.
POWELL, JOHN WESLEY.
   1881. Wyandot government: A short study of tribal society.   1st Ann. Rep.
         Amer. Ethol., 1879–80, pp. 57–69.
   1891. Indian linguistic families of America north of Mexico.   7th Ann. Rep.
         Bur. Ethnol., 1885–1886, pp. 1–142.
POWELL, JOHN WESLEY, and INGALLS, G. W.
   1874. Report of the special commissioners J. W. Powell and G. W. Ingalls
         on the condition of the Ute Indians of Utah; the Pai-Utes of Utah,
         northern Arizona, southern Nevada, and southeastern California;
         the Go-si Utes of Utah and Nevada; the northwestern Shoshones of
         Idaho and Utah; and the western Shoshones of Nevada.   Wash-
         ington.
POWERS, STEPHEN.
   1877. Tribes of California.   Contr. N. A. Ethnol., vol. 3.   Washington.
PRINCE, J. DYNELEY.
   1897. The Passamaquoddy wampum records.   Proc. Amer. Philos. Soc.,
         vol. 36, pp. 479–495.   Philadelphia.
PURCELL MAP.   *See* SWANTON, 1922, pl. 7.
RADIN, PAUL.
   1923. The Winnebago tribe.   37th Ann. Rep. Bur. Amer. Ethnol., 1915–1916,
         pp. 35–550.
RAND, SILAS T.
   1894. Legends of the Micmacs.   New York and London.
RASMUSSEN, KNUD.
   1908. People of the Polar north; a record compiled from the Danish originals
         and edited by G. Herring.   Philadelphia.
   1919. Scientific results of the second Thule expedition to northern Greenland,
         1916–1918.
RAY, VERNE F.
   1932. The Sanpoil and Nespelem: Salishan peoples of northeastern Washing-
         ton.   Univ. Washington Publ. Anthrop., vol. 5, Dec. 1932.   Seattle.
   1938. Lower Chinook ethnographic notes.   Univ. Washington Publ. Anthrop.
         vol. 7, No. 2, pp. 29–165.   Seattle.
RAY, VERNE F., AND OTHERS.
   1938. Tribal distribution in eastern Oregon and adjacent regions.   Amer.
         Anthrop., n. s., vol. 40, No. 3, pp. 384–415.   (Containing: Tribal
         distribution in northeastern Oregon, by Verne F. Ray, pp. 384–395;
         Notes on the Tenino, Molala, and Paiute of Oregon, by George Peter
         Murdock, pp. 395–402; Northern Paiute bands in Oregon, by
         Beatrice Blyth, pp. 402–405; Northern Paiute, by Omer C. Stewart,
         pp. 405–407; Western Shoshoni, by Jack Harris, pp. 407–410; Bands
         and distribution of the Eastern Shoshone, by E. Adamson Hoebel,
         pp. 410–413; Wind River Shoshone geography, by D. B. Shimkin,
         pp. 413–415.

REICHARD, GLADYS A.
   1928. Social life of the Navajo Indians. New York.
REID, HUGO.
   1852. The Indians of Los Angeles County. Los Angeles Star. (Republished by Alexander S. Taylor in the California Farmer, vol. 14, Jan. 11–Feb. 8, 1861.)
REPORTS OF THE COMMITTEE APPOINTED BY THE BRITISH ASSOCIATION FOR THE ADVANCEMENT OF SCIENCE TO REPORT ON THE NORTHWEST TRIBES OF CANADA. 1889–98. Rep. Brit. Assoc. Adv. Sci. London.
REYES, CANDELARIO.
   1944. Apuntes para la historia de Tamaulipas en los siglos XVI y XVII. México (Talleres graficos Laguna).
RICHARDSON, JOHN.
   1851. Arctic searching expedition: A journal of a boat-voyage through Rupert's land and the Arctic sea. 2 vols. London.
RIDER, SIDNEY S.
   1904. The lands of Rhode Island as they were known to Caunounicus and Miantunnomu. Providence.
RIGGS, A. L. See IAPI OAYE.
RIGGS, STEPHEN RETURN.
   1894. Dakota grammar, texts, and ethnography. Contr. N. A. Ethnol., vol. 9.
RIGHTS, DOUGLAS L.
   1947. The American Indian in North Carolina. Duke University Press, Durham, N. C.
RINK, HENRY.
   1875. Tales and traditions of the Eskimo. London.
   1887. The Eskimo tribes. Medelelser om Grønland, vol. 11. Copenhagen and London.
RIVERS, WILLIAM J.
   1856. Sketch of the history of South Carolina. Charleston.
ROBERTS, HELEN H.; HAEBERLIN, H. K.; and TEIT, JAMES A.
   1928. Coiled basketry in British Columbia and surrounding region, under direction of Franz Boas. 41st Ann. Rep. Bur. Amer. Ethnol., 1919–24, pp. 119–484.
ROBERTSON, JAMES ALEXANDER, EDITOR AND TRANSLATOR.
   1933. True relation of the hardships suffered by Governor Fernando de Soto and certain Portuguese gentlemen during the discovery of the Province of Florida, now newly set forth by a Gentleman of Elvas. 2 vols. Fla. State Hist. Soc. De Land.
ROMANS, BERNARD.
   1775. A concise natural history of East and West Florida. Vol. 1. (Vol. 2 unpublished.) New York.
ROSS, ALEXANDER.
   1849. Adventures of the first settlers on the Oregon or Columbia River. London.
   1855. The fur hunters of the far west; a narrative of adventures in the Oregon and Rocky Mountains. 2 vols. London.

Ross, Bernard.
   1867. The eastern Tinneh. Smithsonian Rep. 1866.
   MS. Manuscript 1858 in archives of Bureau American Ethnology.
Rowland, Dunbar, and Sanders, Albert Godfrey. See Bienville, Jean
   Baptiste le Moyne, Sieur de.
Royal Canadian Institute. Proceedings: Ser. 1: The Canadian Journal: A
   Repertory of Industry, Science and Art; and a Record of the Proceedings
   of the Canadian Institute. Vols. 1–3, Toronto, 1852–55. Ser. 2: The
   Canadian Journal of Science, Literature, and History. Vols. 1–15, Toronto,
   1856–78. Ser. 3: Proceedings of the Canadian Institute. Vols. 1–7,
   Toronto, 1879–90. Annual Reports: 1886–94. (App. Rep. Min. Education
   Ont., Toronto, 1888–94). Transactions: Vols. 1—. Toronto, 1889–19—.
Royal Society of Canada.
   Proceedings and Transactions. 1st ser., vols. 1–12. Montreal, 1883–95.
   2d ser., vols. 1–12, Montreal, 1895–1905. 3d ser., 1913—.
Royce, C. C.
   1887. The Cherokee nation of Indians: A narrative of their official relations
      with the Colonial and Federal governments. 5th Rep. Bur. Ethnol.,
      1883–84, pp. 121–378.
   1899. Indian land cessions in the United States. 18th Ann. Rep. Bur.
      Amer. Ethnol., 1896–97, pt. 2, pp. 521–964.
Russell, Frank.
   1908. The Pima Indians. 26th Ann. Rep. Bur. Amer. Ethnol., 1904–5,
      pp. 3–389.
Ruttenber, Edward M.
   1872. History of the Indian tribes of Hudson's River; their origin, manners,
      and customs; tribal and sub-tribal organizations; wars, treaties, etc.
      Albany.
Sagard Theodat, Gabriel.
   1865. Le grand voyage du pays des Hurons situé en l'Amérique vers la mer
      douce avec un dictionnaire de la langue Huronne. 2 t. Paris.
Salley, Alexander S., Jr., Editor.
   1911. Narratives of early Carolina. In Original Narratives of Early Ameri-
      can History. New York.
Sapir, Edward.
   1909. Wishram texts, together with Wasco tales and myths. Collected by
      Jeremiah Curtin and ed. by Edward Sapir. Leyden. Publ. Amer.
      Ethnol. Soc., vol. 2.
   1913. Wiyot and Yurok, Algonkin Languages of California. Amer. Anthrop.,
      vol. 15, No. 4, pp. 617–646.
   1915 a. The Na-déné Languages, a preliminary report. Amer. Anthrop.,
      n. s., vol. 17, No. 3, pp. 534–558.
   1915 b. A sketch of the social organization of the Nass River Indians.
      Canada Geol. Surv., Mus. Bull. No. 19. Ottawa.
      See also Spier, Leslie, and Sapir, Edward.
Sauer, Carl O.
   1934. The distribution of aboriginal tribes and languages in Northwestern
      Mexico. Ibero-Americana: No. 5. Univ. Calif. Press, Berkeley,
      Calif.
   1935. Aboriginal population of Northwestern Mexico. Ibero-Americana:
      No. 10. Univ. Calif. Press, Berkeley, Calif.

SCAIFE, H. LEWIS.
1896. History and condition of the Catawba Indians of South Carolina. Publ. Ind. Rights Assoc. Philadelphia.

SCHOOLCRAFT, HENRY R.
1851-57. Historical and statistical information, respecting the history, condition, and prospects of the Indian tribes of the United States. 6 vols. Philadelphia.

SCHRADER, F. C.
1900. Reconnaissances in Prince William Sound. 20th Ann. Rep. U. S. Geol. Surv., pt. 7, pp. 341-423.

SCHULTZ, J. W.
1907. My life as an Indian. New York.

SCOTT, HUGH LENOX.
1907. The early history and the names of the Arapaho. Amer. Anthrop., n. s., vol. 9, pp. 545-560.

SEITZ, WILBUR. See BERRY, BREWTON, ET AL.

SEMMES, RAPHAEL.
1929. Aboriginal Maryland, 1608-1689. Maryland Hist. Mag., vol. 24, pt. 1, pp. 157-171; pt. 2, pp. 195-209.

SERRANO Y SANZ, EDITOR.
1913. Documentos historicos de la Florida y la Luisiana siglos 16 al 18. Madrid.

SHAWNEE, W. H.
1903. Absentee Shawnee Indians. Gulf States Hist. Mag., vol. 1, p. 415. Montgomery.

SHEA, JOHN GILMARY.
1852. Discovery and exploration of the Mississippi Valley. New York. (2d ed. Albany, 1903.)
1861. Early voyages up and down the Mississippi. Albany.
See also Charlevoix, Pierre F. X. de, 1774; and Leclerq, Chrétien, 1881.

SHIMKIN, D. B. See RAY, VERNE F., 1938.

SIBLEY, JOHN.
1832. Historical sketches of the several Indian tribes in Louisiana, south of the Arkansas River, and between the Mississippi and River Grande. (Message from the President communicating discoveries made by Captains Lewis and Clark, Washington, 1806.) In Amer. State Pap., Class II, Ind. Affairs, vol. 1. (Also in Ann. Congr., 9th Congr., 2d sess., cols. 1076-1088.)

SIMPSON, JOHN.
1855. Observations on the western Esquimaux. In Further papers relative to the recent Arctic Expeditions. London.

SISKIN, EDGAR E. See PARK, WILLARD Z.

SKINNER, ALANSON.
1914. Political organization, cults, and ceremonies of the Plains-Ojibway and Plains-Cree Indians. Anthrop. Pap. Amer. Mus. Nat. Hist., vol. 11, pt. 6. New York.
1921. Material culture of the Menomini. Indian Notes and Monographs. Misc. No. 20, Mus. Amer. Ind., Heye Foundation. New York.
1923, 1925. Observations on the ethnology of the Sauk Indians. Bull. Public Mus. City of Milwaukee, vol. 5, Nos. 1-3. Milwaukee.

SKINNER, ALANSON—Continued
    1924–27. The Mascoutens or Prairie Potawatomi. Bull. Public Mus. City
        of Milwaukee, vol. 6, pt. 1: Social life and ceremonies.
    1925. Notes on Mahican ethnology. Bull. Public Mus. City of Milwaukee,
        vol. 2, No. 3.
    1926. Ethnology of the Ioway Indians. Bull. Public Mus. City of Milwaukee,
        vol. 5, No. 4, pp. 181–354. Milwaukee.
SMET, PIERRE J. DE.
    1847. Oregon missions and travels over the Rocky Mountains, in 1845–46.
        New York.
SMITH, BUCKINGHAM. See NUÑEZ CABEZA DE VACA, ALVAR. 1851.
SMITH, ERMINNIE A.
    1883. Myths of the Iroquois. 2d Ann. Rep. Bur. Ethnol., 1880–81, pp.
        47–116.
SMITH, HURON H.
    1923 a. Ethnobotany of the Menomini Indians. Bull. Public Mus. City of
        Milwaukee, vol. 4, No. 1, pp. 1–174.
    1923 b. Ethnobotany of the Meskwaki Indians. Bull. Public Mus. City of
        Milwaukee, vol. 4, No. 2, pp. 177–326.
    1923 c. Ethnobotany of the Ojibwe Indians. Bull. Public Mus. City of
        Milwaukee, vol. 4, No. 3, pp. 327–525.
SMITH, JOHN.
    1819. The true travels, adventures, and observations of Captaine John
        Smith, in Europe, Asia, Africke, and America; beginning about the
        yeere 1593, and continued to this present 1620. 2 vols. Vol. 2.
        The generall historie of Virginia, New England, and the Summer
        iles. Richmond. (Reprint of London ed. of 1620.)
    1884. Works, 1608–1631. Ed. by Edward Arber. English Scholar's Library,
        No. 16. Birmingham.
SMITH, MARIAN W.
    1940. The Puyallup-Nisqually. Columbia Univ. Contr. Anthrop., vol. 32.
        New York.
    1941. The Coast Salish of Puget Sound. Amer. Anthrop., n. s., vol. 43,
        No. 2, pt. 1, pp. 197–211.
SOUTH CAROLINA HISTORICAL AND GENEALOGICAL MAGAZINE, VOL. 9.
SOUTH CAROLINA HISTORICAL SOCIETY.
    1857–97. Collections. Vols. 1–5. Charleston and Richmond.
SPARKMAN, PHILIP STEDMAN.
    1908. The culture of the Luiseño Indians. Univ. Calif. Publ. Amer. Archaeol.
        and Ethnol., vol. 8, pp. 187–234.
SPECK, FRANK G.
    1907. The Creek Indians of Taskigi town. Mem. Amer. Anthrop. Asso.,
        vol. 2, pt. 2.
    1909 a. Ethnology of the Yuchi Indians. Anthrop. Publ. Univ. Mus.,
        Univ. Pa., vol. 1, No. 1. Philadelphia.
    1909 b. Notes on the Mohegan and Niantic Indians. Anthrop. Pap. Amer.
        Mus. Nat. Hist., vol. 3, pp. 181–210.
    1915 a. The Nanticoke Community of Delaware. Contr. Mus. Amer. Ind.,
        Heye Foundation, vol. 2, No. 4. New York.
    1915 b. The Eastern Algonkian Wabanaki Confederacy. Amer. Anthrop.,
        n. s., vol. 17, pp. 492–508.

SPECK, FRANK G.—Continued

1915 c. Family hunting territories and social life of various Algonkian Bands of the Ottawa Valley. Canada Geol. Surv., Mem. 70. Ottawa.

1915 d. Myths and folk-lore of the Timiskaming Algonquin and Timagami Ojibwa. Canada Geol. Surv., Mem. 71, Anthrop. Ser. No. 9. Ottawa.

1917. Game totems among the Northwestern Algonkians. Amer. Anthrop., n. s., vol. 19, pp. 9–18.

1922. Beothuk and Micmac. Indian Notes and Monographs. Mus. Amer. Ind., Heye Foundation. New York.

1925. The Rappahannock Indians of Virginia. Indian Notes and Monographs, vol. 5, No. 3. Mus. Amer. Ind., Heye Foundation. New York.

1928 a. Chapters on the ethnology of the Powhatan tribes of Virginia. Indian Notes and Monographs, vol. 1, No. 5. Mus. Amer. Ind., Heye Foundation. New York.

1928 b. Territorial subdivisions and boundaries of the Wampanoag, Massachusett, and Nauset Indians. Indian Notes and Monographs, No. 44, Mus. Amer. Ind., Heye Foundation. New York.

1928 c. Native tribes and dialects of Connecticut. 43d Ann. Rep. Bur. Amer. Ethnol., 1925–26, pp. 199–267.

1928 d. Wawenock myth texts from Maine. 43d Ann. Rep. Bur. Amer. Ethnol., 1925–26, pp. 165–197.

1929. Boundaries and hunting groups of the River Desert Algonquin. Indian Notes, vol. 6, No. 2, pp. 77–120, Mus. Amer. Ind., Heye Foundation.

1931. Montagnais-Naskapi Bands and early Eskimo distribution in the Labrador Peninsula. Amer. Anthrop., n. s., vol. 33, No. 4, pp. 557–600.

1935. Siouan tribes of the Carolinas as known from Catawba, Tutelo, and documentary sources. Amer. Anthrop., n. s., vol. 37, pt. 2, pp. 201–225.

SPECK, FRANK G., and EISELEY, LOREN C.

1942. Montagnais-Naskapi Bands and family hunting districts of the Central and Southeastern Labrador Peninsula. Proc. Amer. Philos. Soc., vol. 85, No. 2, pp. 215–242.

SPIER, LESLIE.

1927. Tribal distribution in southwestern Oregon. Oregon Hist. Quart., vol. 28, No. 4.

1928. Havasupai ethnography. Anthrop. Pap. Amer. Mus. Nat. Hist., vol. 29, pt. 3. New York.

1930 a. Klamath ethnography. Univ. Calif. Publ. Amer. Archaeol. and Ethnol., vol. 30, pp. x+1–338. Univ. Calif. Press.

1936. Tribal distribution in Washington. Amer. Anthrop. Assoc., Gen. Ser. Anthrop., No. 3.

SPIER, LESLIE, and SAPIR, EDWARD.

1930 b. Wishram ethnography. Univ. Washington Publ. Anthrop., vol. 3, No. 3, pp. 151–300. Seattle.

SPIESS, MATHIAS, COMPILER.

1934. Connecticut circa 1625, its Indian trails, villages, and sachemdoms. Publ. by Connecticut Soc. Colonial Dames of America, Inc., from data collected by Mathias Spiess. Ed. by Elinor H. Bulkeley, Chairman Publ. Comm.

SPINDEN, H. J.
1908. The Nez Percé Indians. Mem. Amer. Anthrop. Assoc., vol. 2, pt. 3.
SQUIER, E. G. See BARTRAM, WILLIAM, 1909.
STATISTIK AARBOG 1922, COPENHAGEN.
STEFÁNSSON, VILHJÁLMUR.
1914 a. Prehistoric and present commerce among the Arctic Coast Eskimo. Canada Geol. Surv., Bull. No. 6. Ottawa.
1914 b. The Stefánsson-Anderson Arctic Expedition of the American Museum: Preliminary ethnological report. Anthrop. Pap. Amer. Mus. Nat. Hist., vol. 14, pp. 1–395. New York.
STEM, JESSE.
1851. In Report of United States Office of Indian Affairs, pp. 260–261.
STERN, BERNHARD J.
1934. The Lummi Indians of northwest Washington. Columbia Univ. Publ. Anthrop., vol. 17. Columbia Univ. Press, New York.
STEVENSON, MATILDA COXE.
1894. The Sia. 11th Ann. Rep. Bur. Ethnol., 1889–90, pp. 3–157.
1904. The Zuñi Indians: Their mythology, esoteric fraternities, and ceremonies. 23d Ann. Rep. Bur. Amer. Ethnol., 1901–2, pp. 3–608.
STEWARD, JULIAN H.
1933. Ethnography of the Owens Valley Paiute. Univ. Calif. Publ. Amer. Archaeol. and Ethnol., vol. 33, No. 3, pp. 233–250.
1937. Linguistic distributions and political groups of the Great Basin Shoshoneans. Amer. Anthrop., n. s., vol. 39, No. 4 (pt. 1), pp. 625–634.
1938. Basin-plateau aboriginal sociopolitical groups. Bur. Amer. Ethnol. Bull. 120.
1941. Culture element distributions: 13, Nevada Shoshone. Anthrop. Rec., vol. 4, No. 2. Univ. California Press.
STEWART, OMER C.
1941. Culture element distributions: 14, Northern Paiute. Anthrop. Rec., vol. 4, No. 3. Univ. Calif. Press.
See also RAY, VERNE F.
STONE, DORIS.
1941. Archaeology of the north coast of Honduras. Mem. Peabody Mus. Archaeol. and Ethnol., Harvard Univ., vol. 9, No. 1. Cambridge.
STRACHEY, WILLIAM.
1849. The historie of travaile into Virginia Britannia, expressing the cosmographie and comodities of the country, together with the manners and customs of the people. Hakluyt Soc. Publ., vol. 6. London.
STRONG, WILLIAM DUNCAN.
1935. Archaeological investigations in the Bay Islands, Spanish Honduras. Smithsonian Misc. Coll., vol. 92, No. 14, Feb. 12.
SWAN, JAMES G.
1857. The northwest coast, or three years residence in Washington Territory. New York.
1870. Indians of Cape Flattery. Smithsonian Contr. to Knowledge, vol. 16.
SWANTON, JOHN R.
1904–5. Social conditions, beliefs, and linguistic relationship of the Tlingit Indians. 26th Ann. Rep. Bur. Amer. Ethnol., 1904–5, pp. 391–485.
1905. Contributions to the ethnology of the Haida. Mem. Amer. Mus. Nat. Hist., Jesup N. Pac. Exped., vol. 5, pt. 1. Leiden and New York.

SWANTON, JOHN R.—Continued

1911. Indian tribes of the Lower Mississippi Valley and adjacent coast of the Gulf of Mexico. Bur. Amer. Ethnol. Bull. 43.

1918. An early account of the Choctaw Indians. Mem. Amer. Anthrop. Assoc., vol. 5, pt. 2.

1922. Early history of the Creek Indians and their neighbors   Bur. Amer. Ethnol. Bull. 73.

1928 a. Social organization and social usages of the Indians of the Creek Confederacy. 42d Ann. Rep. Bur. Amer. Ethnol., 1924–25, pp. 23–472. 1928.

1928 b. Religious beliefs and medical practices of the Creek Indians. 42d Ann. Rep. Bur. Amer. Ethnol., 1924–25, pp. 473–672.

1931. Source material for the social and ceremonial life of the Choctaw Indians. Bur. Amer. Ethnol. Bull. 103.

1942. Source material on the history and ethnology of the Caddo Indians. Bur. Amer. Ethnol. Bull. 132.

1946. The Indians of the Southeastern United States. Bur. Amer. Ethnol Bull. 137.

See also Thomas, Cyrus, and Swanton, John R.

TANNER, JOHN.

1830. Narrative of captivity and adventures during thirty years' residence among the Indians in North America. Prepared for the press by Edwin James. New York.

TAYLOR, ALEXANDER S.

1860–63. Indianology of California. Calif. Farmer and Journ. Useful Sci., vols. 13–20, Feb. 22, 1860, to Oct. 30, 1863. San Francisco.

TEIT, JAMES.

1900. The Thompson Indians of British Columbia. Mem. Amer. Mus. Nat. Hist., vol. 2, Publ. Jesup N. Pac. Exped., vol. 1, No. 4, Anthrop. vol. 1, pt. 4. New York.

1906 a. Notes on the Tahltan Indians of British Columbia. *In* Boas anniversary volume. Anthropological papers written in honor of Franz Boas, Professor of Anthropology in Columbia University, on the twenty-fifth anniversary of his doctorate. New York.

1906 b. The Lillooet Indians. Mem. Amer. Mus. Nat. Hist., vol. 4, pt. 6, Publ. Jesup. N. Pac. Exped., vol. 2, No. 5.

1909. The Shuswap. Mem. Amer. Mus. Nat. Hist., vol. 4, pt. 7. Publ. Jesup N. Pac. Exped., vol. 2, No. 7.

1928. The Middle Columbia Salish. Univ. Washington Publ. Anthrop., vol. 2, No. 4, pp. 83–128. Seattle.

TEIT, JAMES, and BOAS, FRANZ.

1930. The Salishan tribes of the Western Plateaus. 45th Ann. Rep. Bur. Amer. Ethnol., 1927–38, pp. 23–396.

TEIT, JAMES A.; HAEBERLIN, H. K.; and ROBERTS, HELEN H.

1928. Coiled basketry in British Columbia and surrounding region, under direction of Franz Boas. 41st Ann. Rep. Bur. Amer. Ethnol., 1919–24, pp. 119–484.

TEN KATE, H.

1884. Materiaux pour servir à l'anthropologie de la presqu'ile californienne. Bull. Soc. d'Anthrop., pp. 551–569.

1885. Reizen en Onderzoekingen in Noord-Amerika. Leiden.

THALBITZER, WILLIAM.
> 1950. A note on the derivation of the word "Eskimo" (Inuit). Amer.
> Anthrop., n. s., vol. 52, No. 4, pt. 1, p. 564.

THOMAS, CYRUS, and SWANTON, JOHN R.
> 1911. Indian languages of Mexico and Central America and their geographical
> distribution. Bur. Amer. Ethnol. Bull. 44.

THOMPSON, DAVID.
> 1916. Narrative of his explorations in western America, 1784–1812. Ed. by
> J. B. Tyrrell. Publ. Champlain Soc., No. 12. Toronto.

THWAITES, REUBEN GOLD, EDITOR.
> 1896–1901. Travels and explorations of the Jesuit missionaries in New
> France, 1610–1791. 73 vols. Cleveland.
> 1904–7. Early western travels, 1748–1846. 32 vols. Cleveland.

TIMBERLAKE, HENRY.
> 1765. Memoirs of Lieut. Henry Timberlake (who accompanied the three
> Cherokee Indians to England in the year 1762) . . . containing an
> accurate map of their Over-hill settlement. London.

TOLMIE, W. F., and DAWSON, GEORGE M.
> 1884. Comparative vocabularies of the Indian tribes of British Columbia.
> With a map illustrating distribution. Geol. and Nat. Hist. Surv.
> of Canada. Montreal.

TONTI, HENRI DE. See MARGRY, PIERRE, 1875–86, vol. 1, pp. 572–616; and COX,
ISAAC JOSLIN, EDITOR, 1905, vol. 1, pp. 1–65.

TOOKER, W. W.
> 1895. Algonquian appellatives of the Siouan tribes of Virginia. Amer.
> Anthrop., o. s., vol. 8, pp. 376–392.

TOWNSHEND, CHARLES H.
> 1900. The Quinnipiack Indians and their reservation. New Haven.

TRUMBULL, BENJAMIN.
> 1818. Complete history of Connecticut from 1630 to 1764. 2 vols. New
> Haven.

TURNER, LUCIEN M.
> 1894. Ethnology of the Ungava district. 11th Ann. Rep. Bur. Ethnol.,
> 1889–90, pp. 159–350.

TURNEY-HIGH, HARRY HOLBERT.
> 1937. The Flathead Indians of Montana. Mem. Amer. Anthrop. Assoc.,
> No. 48 (suppl. Amer. Anthrop., vol. 39, No. 4, pt. 2: Contr. Montana
> State Univ.).
> 1941. Ethnography of the Kutenai. Mem. Amer. Anthrop. Assoc., No. 56
> (suppl. Amer. Anthrop., vol. 43, No. 2, pt. 2 E).

UHDE, ADOLPH.
> 1861. Die Länder am untern Rio Bravo del Norte. Heidelberg.

UMFREVILLE, EDWARD.
> 1790. The present state of Hudson's Bay, containing a full description of
> that settlement and the adjacent country; and likewise of the fur
> trade. London.
> 1859. Idem. Maine Hist. Soc. Coll., vol. 6, p. 270.

VAHL, G. C.; AMDRUP, L. BOBÉ; and JENSEN, A. S., EDITORS.
> 1928–29. Greenland. 3 vols. Published by the Commission for the Direc-
> tion of the Geological and Geographic Investigations in Green-
> land. C. A. Reitzel, Copenhaven; Oxford Univ. Press, London.

VANCOUVER, GEORGE.
    1801. Voyage of discovery to the North Pacific Ocean, and round the world.
        1790–95. 6 vols. London.
VENEGAS, MIGUEL.
    1757. Noticia de la California, y de su conquista temporal y espiritual hasta
        el tiempo presente. T. 3. Madrid.
    1758. A natural and civil history of California. Translated from the original
        Spanish. Madrid. Vols. 1–2. London, 1759.
    1767. Histoire naturelle et civile de la California. T. 3. Paris.
VENIAMÍNOFF, IVAN.
    1840. Zapíski ob ostraváx Unaláshkinskago otdailo. 2 vols. St. Petersburg.
        [In Russian.]
VÉRENDRYE, PIERRE GAULTIER DE VARENNES (AND HIS SONS).
    1927. Journals and letters of. Ed. by Lawrence J. Burpee. Champlain
        Soc., Toronto.
VETANCURT, AGUSTIN DE.
    1870–71. Teatro Mexicano. T. 4. México (Reprint). (Tomo 3 contains
        the Crónica de la provincia del Santo Evangello de México, and
        tomo 4 the Menologio Franciscano de los varones, etc.)
VETROMILE, EUGENE.
    1866. The Abnakis and their history, or historical notices on the aborigines
        of Acadia. New York.
VICTOR, FRANCIS F.
    1871. The Oregon Indians. Overland Monthly, vol. 7, October. San
        Francisco.
VOEGELIN, ERMINIE W.
    1938. Tübatulabal ethnography. Anthrop. Rec., vol. 2, No. 1. Univ.
        Calif. Press.
WARREN, WILLIAM W.
    1885. History of the Ojibways based upon traditions and oral statements.
        Coll. Minn. Hist. Soc., vol. 5. St. Paul.
WATERMAN, T. T.
    1918. The Yana Indians. Univ. Calif. Publ. Amer. Archaeol. and Ethnol.,
        vol. 13, pp. 35–102.
    1920. Yurok Geography. Univ. Calif. Publ. Amer. Archaeol. and Ethnol.,
        vol. 16, pp. 177–314.
WEEDEN, WILLIAM B.
    1884. Indian money as a factor in New England civilization. Johns Hopkins
        Univ. Studies in Hist. and Polit. Sci., 2d. ser., vols. 8–9. Baltimore.
WELLCOME, HENRY B.
    1887. The story of Metlakahtla. New York.
WHEELER SURVEY REPORT.
    1875–78. Report upon United States Geographical Survey west of the one
        hundredth meridian. In charge of First Lieut. Geo. M. Wheeler.
        Ann. Rep.
    1879. Idem., vol. 7. Archaeology.
WHIPPLE, A. W.
    1656. Pacific Railroad Report, vol. 3, pt. 3, p. 103.
WHITE, FRANCES J.
    1903. Old-time haunts of the Norwottock and Pocumtuck Indians. Spring-
        field, Mass.
WHITMAN, WILLIAM.
    1937. The Oto. Columbia Contr. Anthrop., vol. 28. Columbia Univ. Press,
        New York.

WHORF, BENJAMIN L.
1935. The comparative linguistics of Uto-Aztecan. Amer. Anthrop., n. s., vol. 37, pp. 600–608.
WHYMPER, FREDERICK.
1868. A journey from Norton Sound, Bering Sea, to Fort Youkon (junction of Porcupine and Youkon Rivers.) Journ. Roy. Geogr. Soc., vol. 38. London.
WILKES, CHARLES.
1849. Western America, including California and Oregon, with maps of those regions and of the Sacramento valley. Philadelphia.
WILL, G. F., and SPINDEN, HERBERT J.
1906. The Mandans. A study of their culture, archaeology, and language. Pap. Peabody Mus. Amer. Archaeol. and Ethnol., Harvard Univ., vol. 3, No. 4. Cambridge, Mass.
WILLIAMS, ROGER.
1643. A key into the language of America. London. (Repr. in Rhode Island Hist. Soc. Coll., vol. 1, Providence, 1827; also in Mass. Hist. Soc. Coll., 1st ser., vol. 3, Boston, 1794; also in Narragansett Club Publ., 1st ser., vol. 1, Providence, 1866.)
WILLOUGHBY, C. C.
1905. Dress and ornament of the New England Indians. Amer. Anthrop., vol. 7, pp. 499–508.
1905. Textile fabrics of the New England Indians. Amer. Anthrop., vol. 7, pp. 85–93.
1906. Houses and gardens of the New England Indians. Amer. Anthrop., vol. 8, pp. 115–132.
1907. The adze and ungrooved axe of the New England Indians. Amer. Anthrop., vol. 9, pp. 296–306.
1908. Wooden bowls of the Algonkian Indians. Amer. Anthrop., vol. 10, pp. 423–434.
WILSON, EDWARD F.
1890. Indian tribes. Paper No. 11. The Kootenay Indians. In Our Forest Children, vol. 3, No. 13. Owen Sound, Ontario.
WISSLER, CLARK.
1910. Material culture of the Blackfoot Indians. Amer. Mus. Nat. Hist., Anthrop. Pap., vol. 5, pt. 1. New York.
1938. The American Indian. 3d ed.
WRENCH, J. E. See BERRY, BREWTON, ET AL.
WRIGHT, JULIA McNAIR.
1883. Among the Alaskans. Philadelphia.
YARROW, H. C.
1879. Report of the operations of a special party for making ethnological researches in the vicinity of Santa Barbara. Rep. U. S. Geogr. Surv. west of the 100th Meridian [Wheeler Surv. Rep.], vol. 7, Archaeology, pp. 32–46. Washington.
YOAKUM, H.
1855–56. History of Texas from its first settlement to its annexation to the United States in 1846. 2 vols. New York.
YOUNG, CAPT. HUGH. See BOYD, MARK F., 1934.
ZEMBRANO BONILLA, JOSÉ.
1752. Arte de la lengua totonaca. Ortega, printer.
ZIGMOND, MAURICE L. See PARK, WILLARD Z.

INDEX[1]

Aä'ninĕna, see Atsina.
Ạ-ar-ke, see Hopi.
Ậ'-ậ'tam, see Pima.
Ậ'a'tam ậ'kimûlt, see Pima.
Aays, see Eyeish.
Abasopalme, 613, 619
Ab-boin-ug, see Dakota.
Abercrombie, Lt. [W. R.], explorer, 530
Abihka, 153, 157, 222, 228
Abnaki, 13–15*, 16, 17, 18, 28, 44, 579,
    580
    joined by Pennacook, 18
    removal to Canada, 14, 18
    See also Delaware.
Abra, 613, 622
Absaroka, see Crow.
Absároke, see Crow.
Absentee Shawnee, see Shawnee.
Acapatos, see Atsina.
Acarred Arms, see Cheyenne.
Acasaquastlan, 613, 628
Acaxee, 613–614, 631, 634, 636, 641
Accerri, 614, 622
Accohanoc, see Powhatan.
Accominta, see Pennacook.
Achire, 614, 621
Achomawi, 479–480*, 481
Achuachapan, 614
Acolapissa, 168, 174, 175, 192, 195–196*,
    200, 207, 208, 210, 211
    joined by Natchitoches, 206
    massacre of Natchitoches by, 206
    merged with Houma, 196, 200
Acolhua, 614, 628
Acoste, see Koasati.
Acuera, 120*, 130, 131
Acuyé, see Pecos.
Adai, 196–197*, 201, 206, 212, 309, 314,
    315, 316, 318, 320
    probably joined Caddo, 197
Ạ da ka' da ho, see Arikara.
Ậ'dal-k'ato'igo, see Nez Percé.
Addle-Heads, see Menominee.
Adshusheer, town of, 79, 84
Adwanuqdji, see Atsugewi.
Afúlakin, see Wasco.
Aguacadiba, 611
Aguacaleyquen, see Utina.
Aguacatec I, 614
Aguacatec II, 614
Agueynaba, 611
A-gutch-a-ninne-wug, see Hidatsa.
Ah'alakát, see Chemehuevi.
Ahálpam, see Santiam.
Ahantchuyuk, 452*
Ah-hi'-tä-pe, see Siksika.
Ahihinin, see Pawnee.

Ah-mo-kái, see Hopi.
Ahomama, 614, 625
Ahome, 614, 621, 622
Ah-pen-ope-say, see Arikara.
Aht, see Nootka.*
Ahtena, 529–530*
Ahuádjĕ, see Apache.
Ahuchan, see Yaochane.
Ähyä'to, see Arapaho.
Ai-a'-ta, see Apache.
Aibine, 614, 641
Aígspalo, see Klamath.
Aígspaluma, see Klamath, Modoc.
Ais, 121–122*, 131, 133
Aíspalu, see Klamath.
Aix, see Eyeish.
Ai-yah-kín-nee, see Hopi.
Ajoica mission, 135
Ạkansa, see Quapaw.
Ạk'-ba-sū'-pai, see Havasupai.
Akênuq'lā'lâm, see Okanagon.
Akhrakouaehronon, see Susquehanna.
A'kimmash, see Clackamas.
Ak-min'-e-shu'-me, see Kalispel.
Akochakaneñ, see Mahican.
Akokisa, 198, 199, 307, 308, 324
    fate unknown, 199
    See also Atakapa.
Ạ-ko-t'ăs'-kă-ro'reⁿ', see Tuscarora.
Ạ-ko-tcă-kă'nĕⁿ, see Delaware.
Akwa'ala, 614
Alabama, 122, 130, 134, 135, 139, 144,
    145, 153–156*, 157, 159, 167,
    168, 180, 197, 210, 224, 299, 304,
    307, 324
    joined by Muskogee, 204
    joined by Pawokti, 136, 154, 170
    joined by Tawasa, 154, 211
    member of Creek Confederacy, 299
    migrations, 155, 197, 299, 307
    relations with French, 154
    uniting of some with Seminole, 155
Alabama language, 154, 160
Alabama [State of] 153–174
    Abihka, 153
    Alabama, 153–156*
    Apalachee, 156
    Apalachicola, 156
    Atasi, 156
    Chatot, 156
    Cherokee, 156
    Chickasaw, 156
    Choctaw, 156
    Creek Confederacy, 156–157
    Eufaula, 157
    Fus-hatchee, 157
    Hilibi, 157
    Hitchiti, 157

[1] Asterisk indicates main account of tribe.

683

Alabama [State of]—Continued
Kan-hatki, 157
Kealedji, 157
Koasati, 157–159*
Kolomi, 159
Mobile, 159–160*
Muklasa, 160*
Muskogee, 160–168*
Napochi, 168–169*
Natchez, 169
Okchai, 169
Okmulgee, 169
Osochi, 169
Pakana, 170
Pawokti, 170
Pilthlako, 170
Sawokli, 170–171*
Shawnee, 171
Taensa, 171
Tohome, 171–172*
Tukabahchee, 172*
Tuskegee, 172–173*
Wakokai, 173
Wiwohka, 174
Yamasee, 174
Yuchi, 174
Alachua, 140
Ala'dshūsh, see Chinook.
Alaguilac, 614
Alähó, see Kansa.
Alakĕma'yuk, see Luckiamute.
Alamama, 614, 625
Alámmimakt ísh, see Klamath.
Alarcón, Hernando de, 349, 350, 354,
    357, 366, 369
Alaska [Territory of], 529–544
Ahtena, 529–530*
Aleut, 530–533*
Dihai-kutchin, 533*
Eskimo, 533
Haida, 533
Han, 533*
Ingalik, 533–534*
Koyukon, 534–536*
Kutcha-kutchin, 536–537*
Nabesna, 537*
Niska, 538
Natsit-kutchin, 538*
Tanaina, 538–539*
Tanana, 539–540*
Tennuth-kutchin, 540*
Tlingit, 540–543*
Tranjik-kutchin, 543*
Tsimshian, 543
Vunta-kutchin, 543–544*
A'látskné-i, see Clatskanie.
Alcoholic liquors, effect on Indians, 99
Aleut, 530–533*, 539, 557, 568
Algonkin, 544–545*
Algonquian tribes, 65, 66, 74, 77, 78, 80,
    82, 83, 246, 392, 545, 548
Aliatan, see Shoshoni, Northern.
Aliche, see Eyeish.
Allebome, see Comanche.
Alleghanys, see Cherokee.
Allen, Lt. Henry T., explorer, 530, 540

Alligewi, see Cherokee.
Alliklik, 480, 497
Allouez, French priest, 242, 253
Alnânbaĭ, see Abnaki.
Älsé, see Alsea.
Alsea, 452–453*, 469
Altamaha Yamasee, 113
Al-ta-tin, see Sekani.
A'lvayê'lĭlĭt, see Eskimo.
Amacano, 122, 128, 129
Amacapiras, see Macapiras.
Amadas and Barlowe, explorers, 82
Amahami, 276
Amayes, see Jemez.
Ameias, see Jemez.
Amejes, see Jemez.
A-me-she', see Hidatsa.
Ameyao, 611
Amgútsuish, see Umpqua.
Amishgo, see Amusgo.
Amojave, see Mohave.
Amolélish, see Molala.
Ampχänkni, see Wasco.
A'-mu-kwi-kwe, see Hopi.
Amusgo, 614
Ana, see Cree.
Anacana, see Aracanaes.
Anacasiguais, see Anachiquaies.
Anachiquaies, 614, 635
Anadarko, member of Hasinai Confed-
    eracy, 307, 316
Anagonges, see Abnaki.
Anahou, see Osage.
Anakwanckĭ, see Delaware.
Ananis, see Biloxi.
Anaxis, see Biloxi.
Anaya, 611
Anda-kρoen, see Eskimo.
Andaste, see Susquehanna.
Andatahouats, see Ottawa.
Ani'-Gu'sa, see Muskogee.
Ani'-Kĭtu'hwagĭ, see Cherokee.
Ani'-Na'tsĭ, see Natchez.
Anípörspi, see Nez Percé.
Ani'-Sawănu'gĭ, see Shawnee.
An-ish-in-aub-ag, see Chippewa.
Ani'-Skâla'lĭ, see Tuscarora.
Ani'-Suwa'lĭ, see Cheraw.
Ani'ta'guă, see Catawba.
Ani'-Tsa'ta, see Choctaw.
Ani'-Tsĭ'ksû, see Chickasaw.
Ani'-Yûn'-wigâ', see Cherokee.
Ani'-Yu'tsĭ, see Yuchi.
Annah, see Cree.
Annocchy, see Biloxi.
Ano's-anyotskano, see Arapaho.
Anza, Lt. Col. Juan Bautista de, 370
Apache, 292, 293, 296, 299, 307, 313,
    314, 319, 325, 326, 327–330*,
    335, 337, 339, 343, 348, 349, 363,
    365, 370, 593, 614, 624
group of tribes, 299, 300, 301, 322,
    371
Shuman destroyed by, 325
See also Chiricahua Apache, Kiowa
    Apache, Mimbreño Apache.

Chetco, 456–457*, 483
    removed to reservation, 457
Che-wae-rae, see Oto.
Cheyenne, 260, 275, 278–280*, 284, 285,
    292, 295, 296, 299, 370, 372, 385,
    386, 390
    Custer massacre, participated in by,
    280
    migrations of, 279, 285
    placed on reservation, 390
    Northern, 279, 280, 386, 390
    Southern, 279, 280, 299, 385
Chiaha, 92, 93, 104, 105–107*, 113, 129,
    130, 133, 157, 169, 224
Chiapanec, 617, 618, 639
Chibchan tribes, 614, 615, 616, 617, 618,
    619, 620, 621, 622, 625, 626, 627,
    628, 631, 632, 633, 637, 638, 639,
    640, 641, 642
Chickahominy, 71
Chickanee, see Wateree.
Chickasaw, 93, 107, 154, 156, 168, 176,
    177–180*, 187, 188, 190, 192, 195,
    196, 201, 209, 212, 222, 224, 227,
    229, 233, 299, 319
    allies of English, 178, 180, 196
    relations with French, 178
    relations with Spaniards, 178
Chickasaw Government, merged with
    State of Oklahoma, 179, 299
Chickasaw language, 159, 195
Chickasaw Nation, 306, 307
Chicktaghiks, see Illinois.
Chicomuceltec, 617
Chicora, 84, 100
Chief Joseph, Nez Percé chief, 301, 402
Chiguas, see Tiwa Pueblos.
Chilanga, 617, 625
Chilcotin, 550–551*
Chilkat, 584
Chilluckittequaw, 414, 416–417*
Chilowhist, see Methow.
Chilucan, possibly Timucuan, 129
Chilula, 483*, 492
Chimakum, 414, 417*, 419, 435
    at war with Clallam, 417
Chimariko, 483*, 495, 497, 507
Chinantec, 617, 623, 627, 629, 640, 641
Chinarra, 617, 619
Chine, 122, 123, 128, 129
    See also Chatot.
Chine, possibly Chatot chief, 129
Chinipa, 617
Chinook, 417–419*, 467
    joined Chehalis, 418
Chinook, Upper, 475
    See also Wishram.
Chinook jargon, trade language, 418, 419
Chipewyan, 551–552*, 603
    expelled Cree from country, 551
Chippewa, 40, 230, 236, 240, 241, 243,
    244, 246, 247, 248, 250, 251, 256,
    260–264*, 265, 275, 279, 283, 292,
    298, 390, 544, 551
    migrations of, 263, 292, 298
    myths about, 264

Chiricahua Apache, 624
Chirikoff, explorer, 532, 542
Chiripo, see Cabecar.
Chiru, 617
Chirumas, see Yuma.
Chïshyë, see Apache.
Chiska, see Yuchi.
Chita, 618
Chitimacha, 193, 197, 201, 202–204*,
    206, 210
    noted as basket makers, 204
    war with French, 203
Chiwere group, 258, 266, 270, 287
Chizo, 617, 619
Choch-Katit, see Siksika.
Chocho, 617, 638
Choco, 618
    See also Popoloca.
Choctaw, 127, 128, 129, 136, 156, 159,
    176, 177, 180–185*, 187, 188, 191,
    194, 195, 204, 208, 212, 224, 299,
    309
    allied with French, 176, 183, 185,
    189
    became citizens of United States,
    299
    migrations of, 204, 309
    probably absorbed Mobile, 159, 172
    relations with English, 183, 184
    relations with United States Gov-
    ernment, 184, 185
    Tohome, absorbed by, 172
Choctaw, Yowani, 309
Choctaw language, 136, 144, 154, 159,
    160, 195, 200
Choctaw Nation, 92, 175, 184, 194, 204
Chol, 618
Cholera, suffered by Indians, 280
Cholo, 618
Cholutec, 618
Chonque, see Mosopelea.
Chontal, 618
    See also Tequistlatec.
Choptank, a subdivision of the Nanti-
    coke, 60
Chopunnish, see Nez Percé.
Chorti, 618
Choula, 185, 187
Chouman, see Shuman.
"Chousa," see Sutaio.
Chowan, 88
Chowanoc, 77–78*
    disappearance of, 77
    treaty with English, 77
"Christian Indians," see Munsee.
Chuchures, 618
Chucunaque, 618
Chuj, 617, 618
Chuje, see Chuj.
Chu-mai-a, see Yuki.
Chumash, 383, 484–487*, 490
Chumulu, 618
Church of England Missions, 573, 607
Cibao, see Cahibo.
Cibola, see Zuñi.
Ci-cta'-qwŭt-me'tŭnnĕ, see Umpqua.

Cicujé, *see* Pecos.
Ciguayo, *see* Hubabo.
Cinaloa, 618
Cintu-aluka, *see* Comanche.
Circee, *see* Sarcee.
Ciriés, *see* Sarcee.
Ci-sta'-qwût, *see* Umpqua.
Ci-sta'-qwût-mĕ'tunnĕ', *see* Kuitsh.
Civil War, 321
Clackamas, 419, 457*, 459
Clackstar, *see* Clatskanie.
Clallam, 417, 419–420*
    at war with Chimakum, 417
Clamcoets, *see* Karankawan Tribes.
Classet, *see* Makah.
Clatskanie, 458
Clatsop, 425, 458*
Clowwewalla, 458–459*
    apparently extinct, 459
Club Indians, *see* Yuma.
Coahuiltecan Tribes, 308, 309–312*, 321,
    618
Coahuiltecan Tribes, list of, 309–311*
Coahuilteco, 635
Coamo, 611
Coano, 618, 620
    See also Kohuana.
Coaque, Karankawan tribe, 320
Coast Yuki, *See* Yuki, Coast.
Coça, 106, 616, 618
Cochimi, 618, 625, 641
Cocking, Matthew, 592
Coco, *see* Coaque.
Cocomacaque, 619, 631
Cocomaricopa, *see* Maricopa.
Coconino, *see* Havasupai.
Cocopa, 349*, 350, 351, 354, 619
Cocora, 619
Cocoyome, 638
Cocto, *see* Coto.
Coeur d'Alêne, *see* Skitswish.
Cofitachequi, possibly Kasihta, 111, 165
Cohpáp, *see* Maricopa.
Coiba, 619
Colapissas, *see* Acolapissa.
Coligua, possibly a synonym of Koroa,
    187
Colima, possibly a synonym of Koroa,
    187
Colorado [State of], 370–372
    Apache, 370
    Arapaho, 370
    Bannock, 370
    Cheyenne, 370
    Comanche, 370
    Jicarilla, 370–372*
    Kiowa, 372
    Kiowa Apache, 372
    Navaho, 372
    Pueblos, 372
    Shoshoni, 372
    Ute, 372
Colotlan, 619
Columbia Indians, 420–421*, 429
Colville, 400, 421–422*, 431, 440

Comanche, 285, 292, 295, 296, 299–300,
    312–314*, 319, 323, 330, 337, 370,
    372, 385, 386
    attacked Pecos, 337
    became citizens of United States, 300
    horses introduced to Indians by, 314
    placed on reservation, 314
    relations with Whites, 313–314
Comanito, 619, 642
Comecamotes, 619, 635
Comecrudo, 619, 635
Comeya, *see* Kamia.
Comopori, 619, 621
Comox, 552–553*
Comstock Lode, effect on Indians, 410
Concho, 614, 615, 617, 619, 620, 621,
    622, 624, 625, 627, 629, 632, 634,
    636, 638, 641
Conejo, 619
Conestoga, 40, 57, 58, 66, 70
    Meherrin adopted by, 62
    See also Susquehanna.
Confederate Indians, *see* Iroquois.
Congaree, 93
    joined Catawba, 93
Conguaco, 619, 625, 641
Conicari, 615, 619, 625
Connecticut [State of], 29–33
    Mahican, 29
    Mohegan, 29–30*
    Niantic, Western, 30–31*
    Nipmuc, 31
    Pequot, 31–33*
    Wappinger, 33
Conoy, 48, 57–59*, 61, 66, 74
    found by Captain John Smith and
        Maryland Colonists, 58
    migration of, 58
Consumption, suffered by Indians, 573
Cooc, 619, 622
Cook, Captain [James], 539, 588
Coosa, 93, 95, 96
Coosawda, *see* Koasati.
Copalis, 422*
Copper Indians, *see* Tatsanottine.
Copper River Indians, *see* Ahtena.
Coquille, *see* Mishikhwutmetunne.
    Lower, *see* Miluk.
    Upper, *see* Mishikhwutmetunne.
Cora, 618, 631, 639, 640, 642
Cora (1), 620, 622
Cora (2), 620
Coranine, *see* Coree.
Cordova [Francis Hernandez de], ex-
    plorer, 126
Coree, 78*, 81, 82, 86
    disappearance of, 78
Corn eaters, *see* Arikara.
Corobici, 620, 622
Coronado, Francisco Vasquez de, 110,
    290, 294, 306, 329, 331, 333, 336,
    339, 343, 345, 347, 348, 352, 362,
    371
Cosapuya, *see* Cusabo.
Cosnino, *see* Havasupai.

Georgia [State of]—Continued
    Kasihta, 111
    Oconee, 112*
    Okmulgee, 112–113*
    Osochi, 113
    Sawokli, 113
    Shawnee, 113
    Tamathli, 113–114*
    Timucua, 114
    Yamasee, 114–116*
    Yuchi, 116–120*
Ghecham, see Luiseño.
Ghost Dance religion, cause of Dakota uprising, 283, 284, 319
Gi-aucth-in-in-e-wug, see Hidatsa.
Gibbs, George, 402, 419, 422, 426, 442, 458
Gikidanum, see Serrano.
Gilā′q!ulawas, see Kwalhioqua.
Gilā′wēwalamt, see Clowwewalla.
Gila′xicatck, see Watlala.
Gillamooks, see Tillamook.
Gīnä′s, see Kiowa Apache.
Ginebigōnini, see Shoshoni, Northern.
Gitanemuk, see Serrano.
Gitā′q!ēmas, see Clackamas.
Gīts′ajĭ, see Kichai.
Gocoyome, 621
Goddard, Pliny Earle, 605
Gohún, see Yavapai.
Gold, discovery of, 478, 536, 537, 585, 602
Gōnana, see Nahane.
Gorretas, see Manso.
Gosiute, 372–373, 375
Gosnold, [Bartholomew], explorer, 26
Gotane, 621
Gourgues, [Dominique] de, French commander, 139, 144
Grand River, Ute band, 374
Grant, Col. James, 222
Grashoffer, Father Juan Bautista, 363
Grasshopper Indians, see Ute.
Gravier, J., 186, 195, 200
Great Osage, see Osage.
Greek Church, effect on natives, 532
Green Wood Indians, see Nez Percé.
Greenville, treaty with Delaware, 54
    treaty with English, 54
Greenwood, Old, 380
Gregorief, explorer, 530
Grigra, adopted by Natchez, 185*, 189
Gros Ventres, see Atsina, Hidatsa.
Gros Ventres de la Rivière, see Hidatsa.
Gros Ventres des Plaines, see Atsina.
Gros Ventres of the Plains, see Atsina.
Guacata, 121, 131*
    disappearance of, 131
Guacaya, see Waccamaw.
Guaccaiarima, 609*
Guachichile, 621, 623
Guaes, see Kansa.
Guaimaro, 610
Gualaca, 621

Guale, 94, 108–111*, 116, 123, 131, 144, 150, 165
    joined Yamasee, 110, 115
    relations with Spaniards, 165
Gualiba, see Walapai.
Guamahaya, 610
Guamichicorama, 619, 621
Guanacahibes, 609, 610
Guanexico, 621, 640
Guanica, 611
Guaniguanico, 610
Guapo, see Wappo.
Guarco, 621, 622
Guarionex, 611
Guasámas, see Cathlamet.
Guasapar, 621
Guasave, 614, 619, 621, 640
Guasco, 315
Guatari, see Wateree.
Guatijigua, 622, 625
Guatinicamame, 622
Guatuso, 620, 622, 640
Guaxiquero, 622, 625
Guaygata, 611
Guayma, 622 634
Guaymi, 621, 622, 628, 631
Guelasiguicme, 619, 622
Guerriers de pierre, see Assiniboin.
Guetare, 619, 621, 622, 630, 639
Gueza, 102
Guiaquita, 619, 622
Guichita, see Wichita.
Guichyana, see Yuma.
Guisoletes, 635
Guithla′kimas, see Clackamas.
Guithlamethl, see Cathlamet.
Guixolotes, 622
Gū′ta′k, see Kiowa Apache.
Guyandot, see Wyandot.
Gyai′-ko, see Comanche.
Gyitkshan, see Kitksan.

Haāninin, see Atsina.
Haħatonwan, see Chippewa.
Ḣaħatonway, see Chippewa.
Hahderuka, see Crow.
Hai-ai′-nĭma, see Sanpoil.
Haida, 533, 540, 570–573*
    noted for their arts, 573, 607
Haideroka, see Crow.
Haiʻluntchi, see Cayuse.
Hainai, 315
Ḣáish, see Eyeish.
Haiti, 608–610
    Bainoa, 608
    Cahibo or Cibao, 608–609
    Caizcimu, 609
    Guaccaiarima, 609
    Hubabo (or Ciguayo), 609–610
    Maguana, 610
    Marien, 610
Halchidhoma, 349–350*, 354, 369, 492
    absorbed by Maricopa, 350
Hale, Horatio, 426
Halkōme′lēm, see Stalo.

Kalispel, 391, 399–400*, 411, 424
   Lower, 400
Ka-lŏX-la'-tce, see Kadohadacho.
Kalu-χnádshu, see Kadohadacho.
Kamaiakan, Yakima chief, 451
Kamia, 488, 490, 494–495*, 624
Kamiyahi, see Kamia.
Kamiyai, see Diegueño, Kamia.
Kamŭ'inu, see Nez Percé.
Ka'-nan-in, see Arikara.
Kanawha, see Conoy.
Ka'neaheăwastsĭk, see Cheyenne.
Kangitoka, see Crow.
Kan-hatki, division of the Muskogee, 157
Kā'nína, see Havasupai.
Kaninahoish, see Arapaho.
Kanit', see Mandan.
Kan'kaⁿ, see Ponca.
Kănk.'utlā'atlam, see Okanagon.
Kansa, 213, 270, 271, 286, 291, 293–294*, 300
   removed to reservation, 300.
Kansas, 286, 288
Kansas [State of], 292–298
   Apache, 292
   Arapaho, 292
   Cherokee, 292
   Cheyenne, 292
   Chippewa, 292
   Comanche, 292
   Delaware, 292
   Foxes, 292
   Illinois, 292
   Iowa, 292–293
   Iroquois, 293
   Jicarilla, 293
   Kansa, 293–294*
   Kickapoo, 294
   Kiowa, 294–296*
   Kiowa Apache, 296–297*
   Miami, 297
   Missouri, 297
   Munsee, 297
   Osage, 297
   Oto, 297
   Ottawa, 297
   Pawnee, 297
   Potawatomi, 297–298
   Quapaw, 298
   Sauk, 298
   Seneca, 298
   Shawnee, 298
   Wyandot, 298
Kantcati, 155
Kantsi, see Kiowa Apache.
K'á-pätop, see Kiowa Apache.
Karankawa, 308, 635
Karankawan Tribes, 308, 309, 320–321*
Karawala, 630
Kariko, see Tonkawan Tribes.
Karok, 495–496*
Kasahá únûⁿ, see Chickasaw.
Kasihta, division of Muskogee, 111, 118
Kaska, 606
Kaskaias, see Kiowa Apache.

Kaskaskia, 242, 300
   joined by Michigamea, 212
Kaskinampo, 158, 212, 224–225*
   disappearance of, 225
Kasseye'i, see Kadohadacho.
Katce, see Siksika.
Kathlamet, see Cathlamet.
Katlagakya, see Watlala.
Kato, 496*
Kattera, see Tutelo.
Katuku, see Chastacosta.
Kaw, see Kansa.
Kawaiisu, 496*, 517
Kawchottine, 569, 574*
Kawia, 357
   See also Cahuilla.
Ka-wi-'na-han, see Siksika.
Ka'-xi, see Crow.
K°op-tagúi, see Jicarilla.
K'çu-qwic'tŭnnĕ, see Siuslaw.
Kealedji, division of the Muskogee, 157
Ke-at, see Koso.
Kebiks, see Montagnais-Naskapi.
Keew-ahomomy, see Tuscarora.
Kekchi, 624
Keller, Padre Ignacio Javier, 363
Kenāke'n, see Okanagon.
Kenistenoag, see Cree.
Kentucky [State of], 229–230
   Cherokee, 229
   Chickasaw, 229
   Mosopelea, 230
   Shawnee, 230
   Yuchi, 230
K'eres, see Keresan Pueblos.
Keresan Pueblos, 332–334*, 340
   origin myth, 333
Kerlérec, Chevalier de, 160, 172
Kern River Indians, see Tübatulabal.
Ketschetnäer, see Ahtena.
Kettle Falls Indians, see Colville.
Keyauwee, 66, 76, 77, 79, 80–81*, 96
   discovered by Lawson, 80
   probably joined Catawba, 81, 96
Khecham, see Luiseño.
Khoso, see Hopi.
Kiawa, 96, 107
Kichai, 300, 306, 321–322*
   joined Wichita, 322
Ki'-çi-ku'-çuc, see Wichita.
Ki-çi'-tcac, see Kichai.
Kickapoo, 225, 231, 237, 238, 242, 243, 250, 252–254*, 256, 269, 294, 301
   Mexican, 253, 301
Kidder, Dr. A. V., archeologist, 337
Kighetawkigh Roanu, see Illinois.
Kihnatsa, see Crow.
Kij, see Gabrielino.
Kikima, see Halyikwamai.
Kikitamkar, see Kitanemuk.
Kikitanum, see Kitanemuk.
Kiliwa, 488, 624
Kiliwi, see Kiliwa, 624
Kilat, see Tsimshian.
Kilgat, see Tsimshian.
Killamook, see Tillamook.

La Flesche, Dr. Francis, 272, 287
La Harpe, Bernard de, 185, 186, 193, 196, 198, 199, 202, 206, 207, 304, 306, 318, 319
La Pérouse, explorer, 542, 573
La Plais, see Comanche.
La Purificacion Mission de la Tama, 113
La Purísima de Zuñi, see Zuñi.
La Salle [Sieur de], murder of, 316, 317, 318
La Salle, Nicholas, 118, 186, 188, 189, 192, 195, 207, 208, 209, 210, 214, 242, 279, 288, 296, 315, 316, 320, 321
Lacandon, 625, 626
Lagoons, see Tolowa.
Lagunero, 614, 616, 620, 622, 623, 625, 627, 629, 630, 640, 641
Lake Indians, see Senijextee.
Lakmiut, see Luckiamute.
Lakota, see Dakota.
Lakus, 625, 635
Lakweip, 606
La-la-cas, see Modoc.
Laleshiknom, see Kato.
Lameco, see Chiaha.
Lamhatty, Tawasa Indian informer, 145
Lane, Joseph, 442, 472
Lanos, see Manso.
Lapiene's House Indians, see Takkuth-kutchin.
Lari, 625
La'-ri'hta, see Comanche.
Lar-ti-e-lo, see Spokan.
Lassik, 498*, 507, 515
Lastóchkin, explorer, 530
Latgawa, 462*, 469
Láti-u, see Molala.
Laudonnière, René, French writer, 120, 135
Lawson, John, explorer, 66, 72, 73, 74, 78, 79, 80, 83, 84, 86, 88, 89, 90, 93, 98, 99, 100, 101, 102
execution of, 86
Laymon, 618, 625
Leapers, see Chippewa.
LêcLē'cuks, see Spokan.
Lederer, John, explorer, 64, 65, 72, 76, 79, 84, 91, 101, 102, 118
Lemhi Reservation, 399, 404
Le Moyne, Jacques, 135, 143
Lenca, 617, 619, 622, 624, 625, 630, 634
Lenni Lenape, see Delaware.
Leon, Ponce de, explorer, 126, 127, 131, 150, 312, 320
Le Page du Pratz, Antoine S., 187, 188, 191, 192, 195, 199, 207, 210, 214
Leroux, Joseph, 351, 357, 370
Le Sueur [Pierre Charles], 264, 288
Lewis, Meriwether, and Clark, Wm., 394, 400, 402, 404, 405, 412, 413, 414, 418, 422, 425, 428, 433, 434, 436, 442, 444, 447, 449, 450, 451, 455, 457, 458, 459, 467, 471, 472, 476
Lewis, Prof. T. M. N., 117
Lhtaten, see Sekani.

Lihit', see Ponca.
Lillooet, 577-578*, 593
Lower, 577, 578
Upper, 578
Lintcanre, see Thlingchadinne.
Lipan, 296, 301, 307, 322-323*, 330, 334
See also Apache.
Liquor, effects on Indians, 573
Little Crow, Dakota chief, 283
Little Osage, see Osage.
Little Taensa, see Avoyel.
Little Turtle, Miami chief, 240
Lku'ngen, see Songish.
Loaiza, 611
Lohim, 462*
disappearance of, 462
Long Tom Creek Indians, see Chelamela.
Longfellow, H. W., poem by, 264
Long-haired Indians, see Crow.
Lopas, see Tolowa.
Loreto, 625
Los Angeles, see Pecos.
Los Mecos, see Comanche.
Loucheux, see Nakotcho-kutchin.
Louchieux Proper, see Takkuth-kutchin.
Louisiana [State of], 195-212
Acolapissa, 195-196*
Adai, 196-197*
Alabama, 197
Apalachee, 197
Atakapa, 197-199*
Avoyel, 199-200*
Bayogoula, 200-201*
Biloxi, 201
Caddo, 201
Chatot, 201
Chawasha, 201-202*
Chitimacha, 202-204*
Choctaw, 204
Doustioni, 204
Houma, 204
Koasati, 204
Koroa, 204
Mugulasha, 204
Muskogee, 204
Natchez, 204-205
Natchitoches Confederacy, 205-207*
Ofo, 207
Okelousa, 207*
Opelousa, 207-208*
Ouachita, 208
Pascagoula, 208
Quapaw, 208
Quinipissa, 208-209*
Souchitioni, see Natchez Confederacy.
Taensa, 209-210*
Tangipahoa, 210-211*
Tawasa, 211
Washa, 211-212*
Yatasi, 212
Loup, see Delaware.
Loups, see Mahican.
Lower Rogue River Indians, see Tututni.
Lowland People, see Kutcha-kutchin.
Ltsxe'als, see Nisqually.

Mashukhara, see Shasta.
Maskegon, 556
Massachuset, 19–20*, 23, 24, 27
    contact with Captain John Smith, 20
Massachusetts [State of], 19–27
    Mahican, 19
    Massachuset, 19–20*
    Nauset, 21–22*
    Nipmuc, 22–23*
    Pennacook, 23
    Pocomtuc, 23–24*
    Wampanoag, 24–27*
Massasoit, Wampanoag chief, 26, 27
Massasoits, see Wampanoag.
Mastutc'-kwe, see Hopi.
Matagalpa, 615, 617, 626, 627, 639
Matávĕkĕ-Paya, see Walapai.
Mat-che-naw-to-waig, see Iroquois.
Mat-hat-e-vátch, see Chemehuevi.
Matlame, 626
Matlatzinca, 614, 626, 629, 632
Matokatági, see Oto.
Mattapony, 71
Mattapony, Upper, 71
Mattole, 481, 501–502*
Matu-ĕs'-wi skitchi-nú-ûk, see Micmac.
Mauilla, see Mobile.
Mauvais Monde des Pieds-Noirs, see Sarcee.
Mauvila, see Mobile.
Mauwehu, Pequot Indian, 47
Mavila, see Mobile.
Mawatani, see Mandan.
Maximilian, Alexander P., 278
Maya, 623, 626
Mayaguex, 611
Mayajuaca, 131
Maynoa, 611
Mayo, 615, 616, 625, 626
Mazahua, 627, 630
Mazatec, 622, 627, 639
McDougall, James, explorer, 594
McGillivray, Alexander, Scotch trader, 166
McLeod, John M., chief trader, 584
Mednofski, see Ahtena.
Meguenodon, see Tututni.
Meherrin, 62–63*, 65, 73, 82
    Conestoga adopted by, 62
Melchora, 627
Mĕli'-lĕma, see Tenino.
Menendez [Pedro], 131, 151
Mengwe, see Nottaway.
Menominee, 243, 244, 254*, 256
Mepontsky, 62
Merriam, C. Hart, 492
Merrimac, see Pennacook.
Meshingomesia's band, see Miami.
    citizens of Indiana, 239
Mĕshkwa kihŭgⁱ, see Foxes.
Mesquite, 619, 627
Metacom, see Metacomet.
Metacomet, Wampanoag chief, 26
Methodist Missions, 573
Methow, 428*

Metitlanec, 627
Métutahanke, see Mandan.
Meviras, 625, 627
Mexicano, see Nahautl.
Mexico and Central America, classification of the languages, 611–613
    tribes listed, 613–642
Meyemma, see Chimariko.
Mézières, Athanase de, 197, 306
Meztitlanec, 628
Miami, 54, 230, 231, 237–240*, 241, 242, 243, 249, 255, 297, 300, 301
    citizens of Oklahoma, 239, 297
Mical, 428*
Michigamea, division of Illinois, 212
    united with Kaskaskia, 212
    See also Illinois.
Michigan, [State of], 243–250
    Chippewa, 243
    Foxes, 243
    Kickapoo, 243
    Menominee, 243
    Miami, 243
    Neutrals, 243
    Noquet, 243–244*
    Ottawa, 244–246*
    Potawatomi, 247–250*
    Sauk, 250
    Wyandot, 250
Michilimackinac, 235
Mĭ-Çlauq'-tcu-wûn'-ti, see Klickitat.
Micmac, 13, 548, 579–581*
    Beothuk driven north by, 548
Miká-atí, see Shoshoni, Northern.
Mikadeshitchísi, see Nez Percé.
Mikasuki, 104, 107, 119, 129, 130, 133–134*, 301
Miko Lusa (Black Chief), Chakchiuma chief, 176
Mikonopi, Oconee chief, 135
Mi'kyashĕ, see Shoshoni, Northern.
Millbank Sound Indians, see Bellabella.
Miluk, 459, 463*
Mimbreño Apache, 624
Mingwe, see Iroquois.
Minitari, see Hidatsa.
Minnesota [State of], 260–265
    Arapaho, 260
    Cheyenne, 260
    Chippewa, or Ojibwa, 260–264*
    Dakota, 264
    Foxes, 264
    Iowa, 264
    Missouri, 264
    Omaha, 264
    Oto, 264
    Ottawa, 265
    Ponca, 265
    Sauk, 265
    Winnebago, 265
    Wyandot, 265
Minnetarees of the Plains, see Atsina.
Minnetarees of the Prairies, see Atsina.
Minnishúpsko, see Dakota.
Minqua, see Susquehanna.
Miopacoas, 625, 627

Mooachaht, *see* Nootka.
Moore, Col. James, 87, 114, 123, 124, 151, 221
Moosehead Lake Indians, *see* Penobscot.
Mopan, 626, 627
Moratok, 82*
Moravian Indians, 47, 54
Moravians, missionaries, 54, 568
Morgan, Lewis H., 40
Morice, Rev. A. G., 550, 594, 604
Mormon missionaries, 92
Morris, Robert, 87
Morse, Jedediah, 191, 194, 308, 475
Moscoso, successor to De Soto, 205, 211, 315
Moses-Columbia band, *see* Sinkiuse-Columbia.
Moshome, *see* Navaho.
Mosnala, 619, 627
Mosopelea, 190, 213, 225, 230, 231–232*, 240
    See also Ofo.
Mosquito Indians, 615, 624, 625, 626, 627–628, 636, 639
Mosquito-Sumo, 615, 624, 625, 635, 639
Motozintlec, 628
Motútatak, *see* Oto.
Mouilla, missionary, 151
Mountain Comanche, *see* Apache.
Mountain Indians, *see* Tsethaottine, Tutchone.
Mountaineers, *see* Chipewyan.
Move, 622, 628
Muckleshoot, 428–429*
Mucoço, *see* Mocoço.
Mugulasha, 192, 200, 204, 208
    destroyed by Bayogoula, 200, 208
    possibly identical with Quinipissa, 208
Muite, 622, 628
Mukkudda Ozitunnug, *see* Siksika.
Muklasa, 134, 157, 160*, 301
    disappearance of, 160
    migration of, 160
Muklasa language, 154
Multnomah, 466–467*
Mûn-an'-nĕ-qu' tûnnĕ, *see* Klickitat.
Munceys, 54
Munsee, 42, 49, 54, 55, 255, 257, 292, 293, 297, 301
Muoi, 622, 628
Murire, 622, 628
Muruam, 326
Muskogee, 104, 105, 108, 111, 130, 133, 134, 139, 142, 155, 157, 159, 160–168*, 169, 170, 204, 225, 301, 314, 323
    disappearance of, 204
    immigration of, 134, 142, 204
    joined Alabama, 204
Muskogee language, 106, 111, 114, 132, 134, 145, 160, 168, 169
Muskrats, *see* Malecite.
Muspa, *see* Calusa.
Musutepes, 628
Mûtsíănă-täníu, *see* Kiowa Apache.
Mutsun, *see* Costanoan.

Muχtsuhintan, *see* Apache.
Nabedache, member of Hasinai Confederacy, 316, 323
Nabesna, 537*, 608
Nabiltse, *see* Hupa.
Nabuggindebaig, *see* Choctaw.
Nacachau, member of Hasinai Confederacy, 323
Nacanish, member of Hasinai Confederacy, 316, 323
Nachittoos, *see* Natchitoches.
Nachtichoukas, *see* Natchitoches.
Nacitos, *see* Natchitoches.
Naco, *see* Chamelcon.
Nacogdoche, member of Hasinai Confederacy, 323
Nactythos, *see* Natchitoches.
Nadaco, member of Hasinai Confederacy, 323
Nadchito, *see* Natchitoches.
Nadíisha-déna, *see* Kiowa Apache.
Nadouessioux, *see* Dakota, Iowa.
Nadowa, *see* Iroquois, Wyandot.
Nagaieff, explorer, 530
Nagrandan, 626, 628
Nahane, 583–585*, 601, 602
Nahankhotane, 459
Nahaunee, *see* Tutchone.
Nahuatl, 614, 616, 617, 628, 631, 638
Nahuatlato, 628, 629
Nahyssan, 64*
    joined Saponi and Tutelo, 64
Nai-tĕ'-zi, *see* Zuñi.
Na-izhă'ñ, *see* Lipan.
Naked Indians, *see* Miami.
Naketosh, *see* Natchitoches.
Nakota, *see* Dakota.
Nakotcho-kutchin, 585*, 603
Na-Kotchρô-tschig-Kouttchin, *see* Kutcha-kutchin.
Näks'-ăt, *see* Mohave.
Na''lani, *see* Comanche.
Na'la'ni, *see* Kiowa.
Namidish, member of Hasinai Confederacy, 323
Nanaimo, 585*
Nanatsoho, member of Kadohadacho Confederacy, 323
Naniaba, 160, 172
Na'nita, *see* Comanche.
Nanoníks-karĕ'níki, *see* Cheyenne.
Nansemond, 71
Nanticoke, 42, 47, 48, 57, 58, 59–61*, 74
    found by Maryland Colonists, 60
    migration of, 60
Napgitache, *see* Natchitoches.
Napissa, 195, 208
Napochi, 165, 168–169*, 195, 208
Naquitoches, *see* Natchitoches.
Nar-a-tah, *see* Comanche.
Narraganset, 19, 23, 24, 27*, 29, 31, 32, 43
    joined in King Philip's War, 28
Narsh-tiz-a, *see* Zuñi.

Notchitoches, *see* Natchitoches.
Nottaway, 62, 65*
   discovered by Virginia Colonists, 65
   See also Eskimo, 556.
Nottoway, *see* Nottaway.
Nouga, *see* Kawchottine.
Nó-zi, *see* Yana.
N'poch-le, *see* Sanpoil.
Nsekau's, *see* Clackamas.
.n.selixtcī'n, *see* Sanpoil.
Nsietshawas, *see* Tillamook.
Ns tiwat, *see* Clackamas.
Ntlakyapamuk, 430, 432, 577, 588–
   591*, 601
   absorbed Stuwihamuk, 601
Nuestra Señora de Guadalupe de los
   Mansos, mission, 334
Nuestra Señora de Guadalupe de Zuñi,
   see Zuñi.
Nuestra Señora de la Candelaria de
   la Tama, mission, 113
Nuestra Señora de la Luz, mission, 199
Nuestra Señora de los Angeles de
   Porciúncula, *see* Pecos.
Nuestra Señora de los Dolores, mis-
   sion, 315
Nuestra Señora del Pilar de los Adaes,
   military post, 197
Nuh-lum-mi, *see* Lummi.
Nuktusem, *see* Dakota.
Nüma, *see* Paiute, Southern.
Numakaki, *see* Mandan.
Num-ee-muss, *see* Hupa.
Nuñez Cabeza de Vaca, Alvar, 198,
   312, 320, 321, 325, 326
Nu-sklaim, *see* Clallam.
Nū-sō-lupsh, *see* Cowlitz, Kwaiailk.
Nutaa, *see* Paiute, Northern.
Nwǎ'-kǎ, *see* Chippewa, 260.
Nyavapai, *see* Yavapai, 367.

Obome, 619, 629
Obwahnug, *see* Dakota.
Ocale, 134–135*
   disappearance of, 135
Occaneechi, 65–66*, 73, 74, 79, 80, 81, 83
   discovered by Lederer, 65
   united with Saponi and Tutelo, 66
Ochan, *see* Yaochane.
Ocheese, 117
Ochesee, *see* Muskogee.
Ocheti shakowin, *see* Dakota.
Ochie'tari-ronnon, *see* Cherokee.
Ochoes, 625, 629
Oçita, *see* Pohoy.
Ocklawaha, *see* Seminole.
Oconee, 104, 112*, 123, 130, 135, 142
   migrations of, 112, 135
Oconi, *see* Oconee.
Ocoroni, 623, 629
Octoctatas, *see* Oto.
Ocuiltec, 626, 629
Ocute, *see* Hitchiti.
O-dug-am-eeg, *see* Foxes.
O-e'-tun'-i-o, *see* Crow.

Ofo, 74, 188, 190, 194, 195, 207, 213,
   225, 231, 232
   united with Tunica.
   See also Mosopelea.
Ofogoula, *see* Ofo.
Ogden, Peter Skene, 380
Oglethorpe, Governor [James Edward],
   118
Ogoize, *see* Bannock.
Ohio [State of], 230–236
   Chippewa, 230
   Delaware, 230
   Erie, 230–231*
   Honniasont, 231
   Illinois, 231
   Iroquois, 231
   Kickapoo, 231
   Miami, 231
   Mosopelea, 231–232*
   Neutrals, 232
   Ofo, 232
   Ottawa, 233
   Potawatomi, 233
   Seneca, 233
   Shawnee, 233
   Wyandot, 233–236*
Ojibwa, *see* Chippewa.
Ojitlan, 617, 629
Okanagon, 400, 430–433*, 440, 441, 591
Okchai, division of the Muskogee,
   169, 170
Oke-choy-atte, *see* Alabama.
Okelousa, 190, 202, 207*
   disappearance of, 207
OkEnā.qai'n, *see* Okanagon.
Oklahoma [State of], 299–307
   Alabama, 299
   Apache, 299
   Apalachee, 299
   Arapaho, 299
   Biloxi, 299
   Caddo, 299
   Cherokee, 299
   Cheyenne, 299
   Chickasaw, 299
   Choctaw, 299
   Comanche, 299–300
   Creeks, 300
   Delaware, 300
   Foxes, 300
   Hitchiti, 300
   Illinois, 300
   Iowa, 300
   Iroquois, 300
   Jicarilla, 300
   Kansa, 300
   Kichai, 300
   Kickapoo, 301
   Kiowa, and Kiowa Apache, 301
   Koasati, 301
   Lipan, 301
   Miami, 301
   Mikasuki, 301
   Missouri, 301
   Modoc, 301

Oklahoma [State of]—Continued
  Muklasa, 301
  Munsee, 301
  Muskogee, 301
  Natchez, 301
  Nez Percé, 301
  Okmulgee, 301
  Osage, 302
  Oto, 302
  Ottawa, 302
  Pawnee, 302
  Peoria, 302
  Piankashaw, 302
  Ponca, 302
  Potawatomi, 302
  Quapaw, 302
  Sauk, 302
  Seminole, 302
  Seneca, 302
  Shawnee, 302–303
  Tawakoni, 303*
  Tawehash, 303–304*
  Tonkawa, 304
  Tuskegee, 304
  Waco, 304–305*
  Wea, 305
  Wichita, 305–306*
  Wyandot, 307
  Yscani, 307*
  Yuchi, 307
Okmulgee, 104, 107, 112–113*, 157, 169, 301
  Creek tribe, 169, 301
Okwanuchu, 497, 507*
Olancho, 629
Olive, 629
Olmec, 629
Olobayaguame, 619, 629
Olojasme, 619, 629
Olomega, see Nahuatlato.
Oluta, 629
Omaha, 213, 259, 264, 265, 268, 271, 284, 285, 286–287, 291, 293
  citizens of United States, 286
Omanominee, see Menominee.
Onagungees, see Abnaki.
Oñate, Juan de, Governor, 325, 329, 333, 336, 339, 348, 349, 350, 351, 352, 354, 356, 357, 368, 369
Onatheaqua, 135
Ondatawawat, see Ottawa.
Oneida, 40, 57, 252, 256, 257
  Tuscarora adopted by, 87
  See Iroquois.
Ongniaahra, 44
Oñgwanᵃsioñni', see Iroquois.
Oní'häᵒ, see Omaha.
Onnogonges, see Abnaki.
Onondaga, 40
O-no'-ni-o, see Arikara.
Ontponea, 62
Ontwagana, see Shawnee.
O-o'-ho-mo-i'-o, see Dakota.
Oohp, see Navaho, Walapai.
Oop, see Apache, Navaho.
Op, see Apache.

Opata, 325, 621, 624, 629–630*, 633
Opatoro, 625, 630
Opechancanough, Powhatan chief, 70, 71
  massacre of English by, 70, 71
Opelousa, 197, 202, 207–208*
  disappearance of, 208
O'pimmitish Ininiwuc, see Cree.
Opos(i)me, see Obome, 619, 629
Oregon [State of], 451–478
  Ahantchuyuk, 452*
  Alsea, 452–453*
  Atfalati, 453–454*
  Bannock, 454
  Calapooya, 454*
  Cayuse, 454–455*
  Chastacosta, 455–456*
  Chelamela, 456*
  Chepenafa, 456*
  Chetco, 456–457*
  Clackamas, 457*
  Clatskanie, 458*
  Clatsop, 458*
  Clowwewalla, 458–459*
  Dakubetede, 459*
  Hanis, 459*
  Klamath, 459–461*
  Kuitsh, 461–462*
  Latgawa, 462*
  Lohim, 462*
  Luckiamute, Lakmiut, 463*
  Miluk, 463*
  Mishikhwutmetunne, 463–464*
  Modoc, 464–466*
  Molala, 466*
  Multnomah, 466–467*
  Nez Percé, 467*
  Paiute, Northern, 467
  Santiam, 467–468*
  Shasta, 468
  Siletz, 468*
  Siuslaw, 468–469*
  Skilloot, 469
  Snake, 469
  Takelma, 469–470*
  Taltushtuntude, 470*
  Tenino, 469–471*
  Tillamook, 471–472*
  Tututni, 472–473*
  Tyigh, 473–474*
  Umatilla, 474*
  Umpqua, 474–475*
  Wallawalla, 475
  Walpapi, 475
  Wasco, 475*
  Watlala, 476*
  Yahuskin, 476
  Yamel, 476–477*
  Yaquina, 477–478*
  Yoncalla, 478*
Oristan, 611
Orleans Indians, see Karok.
Ornofay, 611
Orontony, Wyandot chief, 235
Orosi, 630
Orotiña, 618, 630

Spring Creeks, see Bidai.
Squakson, see Squaxon.
Squawmish, 587, 597–599*
Squaxon, 445*, 447
S'qŭles'tshi, see Arikara.
Squint-Eyes, see Takkuth-kutchin.
Stak-ta-mish, see Kwaiailk.
Stalo, 600–601*
Staq-tûbc, see Chehalis.
Stâr-râh-he', see Arikara.
Stefánsson, Vilhjalmur, explorer, 568
Stegaraki, 62
Stem, Jesse, 319
Stémchi, see Crow.
Stémtchi, see Crow.
Stevenson, Matilda Coxe, 348
Steward, Julian H., on Shoshoni.
Stewart, Rev. Alex., missionary, 80, 81
Stimk, see Crow.
Stinkards, see Winnebago.
Stla'thiumн, see Lillooet.
Stobshaddat, see Yakima.
Stockbridges, 254, 255, 257–258
    removed to Wisconsin, 42
    See also Mahican.
Stone Indians, see Assiniboin.
Stonies, see Assiniboin.
Stono, 95, 96, 119
Stuart, John, British Indian Agent, 214
Stuwihamuk, 601*
    absorbed by Ntlakyapamuk, 601
Stχuaíχn, see Siksika.
Suali, see Cheraw.
Subinha, 634
Subtiaba, 634
Sucayi, 619, 634
Suck-a-mier, see Luckiamute.
Su'-dȼĕ, see Kadohadacho.
Suerre, 634
Sugeree, 85, 100*, 102, 103
    probably united with Catawba, 100
Suketī'kenuk, see Nisqually.
Sukotī'kenuk, see Nisqually.
Sulatelik, see Wiyot.
Sullivan, Indian towns destroyed by,
    40, 73
Suma, 618, 624, 626, 634
    See also Shuman.
Sumo, 615, 621, 624,▼625, 627, 632,
    634–635, 636, 641
Sumo-Sirpe, 635
Sun caste, Natchez institution, 190
Sunset Indians, see Natchez.
Sŭ'nyitsa, see Zuñi.
Sünyítsi, see Zuñi.
Supai, see Havasupai.
Suquamish, 445*
Surruque, 143*
    probably joined Timucua, 143
Susquamish, see Suquamish.
Susquehanna, 33, 55, 56–57*, 58, 61, 62,
    64, 65, 74
    conquest by Iroquois, 57
    encounter with Dutch, 57
    encounter with English, 57
    encounter with French, 57

Susquehanna—Continued
    Honniasont destroyed by, 55
    massacred by Whites, 57
Susquehannock, see Susquehanna.
Sussee, see Sarcee.
Sussekoon, see Sarcee.
Sutaio, 278, 279, 280, 284, 285*
    migrations of, 285
Suturees, see Sugeree.
Suwa'dabc, see Sinkiuse-Columbia.
Suχwa'pmuχ, see Shuswap.
.swā'dab.c, see Sinkiuse-Columbia.
Swalash, see Swallah.
Swallah, 445–446*
Swan, James G., 418
.swa'namc, see Sinkiuse-Columbia.
Swedes, contact with Delaware, 54
    contact with Unalachtigo, 54
Swinomish, 442, 446*

Tá-ashi, see Apache.
Tâa Ashiwani, see Zuñi.
Tabby, Ute Chief, 374
Tabeguache, Ute band, 374
Täbkĕpáya, see Walapai.
Ta-cáb-cí-nyu-mûh, see Navaho.
Tacatacuru, 144*
    joined Timucua, 144
    relations with French, 144
    relations with Spanish, 144
Tadirighrones, see Catawba.
Taensa, 124, 171, 188, 197, 203, 205, 206,
    209–210*, 232
    destroyed Bayogoula, 200, 209
    disappearance of, 210
    human sacrifices made by, 209, 210
    migrations of, 171, 209, 210
    relations with French, 209
Tagualilos, 635
Tâ'gugala, see Kiowa Apache.
Tagúi, see Apache, Kiowa Apache.
Tágukerésh, see Apache.
Tágukerish, see Kiowa Apache.
Tâ'hana, see Ute.
Tá'hba, see Maricopa.
Táh'ba, see Papago.
Ta'hlï'mnïn, see Navaho.
Tahltan, 601–602*, 606
Tahogaléwi, see Yuchi.
Tahue, 635
Taidnapam, 446*
    extinct as tribe, 446
Ta-ih, see Tyigh, 473
Taitinapam, 425
Taíwi, see Tabby.
Takadhé, see Takkuth-kutchin.
Takelma, 469–470*
Takelma, Lowland, see Takelma.
Takhayuna, see Aleut.
Takhtam, see Serrano.
Takulli, see Carriers.
Takkuth-kutchin, 602–603*
Ta-kutchi, see Eskimo.
Tä-Kuth-Kutchin, see Takkuth-kutchin.
Talamanca, 615, 633, 634, 635, 636
Tálĕmaya, see Tututni.

Washa, 137, 200, 201, 202, 207, 211-212*, 519
  disappearance of, 211
Washakie, Shoshoni chief, 404, 405
Washington [State of], 412-451
  Cathlamet, 414*
  Cathlapotle, 414-415*
  Cayuse, 415
  Chehalis, 415-416*
  Chelan, 416*
  Chilluckittequaw, 416-417*
  Chimakum, 417*
  Chinook, 417-419*
  Clackamas, 419
  Clallum, 419-420*
  Columbia, 420-421*
  Colville, 421-422*
  Copalis, 422*
  Cowlitz, 422-423*
  Duwamish, 423*
  Hoh, 424*
  Humptulips, 424*
  Kalispel, 424
  Klickitat, 424-425*
  Kwaiailk, 426*
  Kwalhioqua, 426*
  Lummi, 427*
  Makah, 427-428*
  Methow, 428*
  Mical, 428*
  Muckleshoot, 428-429*
  Neketemeuk, 429
  Nespelem, 429
  Nez Percé, 429
  Nisqually, 429-430*
  Nooksack, 430*
  Ntlayapamuk, 430
  Okanagon, 430-433*
  Ozette, 433*
  Palouse, 433-434*
  Pshwanwapam, 434*
  Puyallup, 434*
  Queets or Quaitso, 434-435*
  Quileute, 435*
  Quinault, 435-436*
  Sahehwamish, 436-437*
  Samish, 437*
  Sanpoil, 437-439*
  Satsop, 439-440*
  Semiahmoo, 440*
  Senijextee, 440*
  Sinkaietk, 440-441*
  Sinkakaius, 441*
  Skagit, 441-442*
  Sinkiuse-Columbia, 420-421*
  Skilloot, 442*
  Skin, 442-443*
  Snohomish, 443*
  Snoqualmie, 443-444*
  Spokan, 444-445*
  Squaxon or Squakson, 445*
  Suquamish, 445*
  Swallah, 445-446*
  Swinomish, 446*
  Taidnapam, 446*
  Twana, 447*

Washington [State of]—Continued
  Wallawalla, 447-448*
  Wanapam, 448*
  Watlala, 448
  Wauyukma, 448*
  Wenatchee (Wīna't;ca), 448-449
  Wishram, 449-450*
  Wynoochee, 450*
  Yakima, 450-451*
Washo, 383-384*, 519
  conquered by Paiute, Northern, 384
Watawawininiwok, see Ottawa.
Wateknasi, see Tübatulabal.
Wateni'hte, see Siksika.
Wateree, 88, 101-102*
  joined Catawba, 101
Watlala, 448, 476*
Watohtata, see Oto.
Wat'ota, see Oto.
Watútata, see Oto.
Wauyukma, 448*
Wawáh, see Maidu, Wintun.
Waxhaw, 88, 102*
  destruction of, 102
Wa-yä-tä-no'-ke, see Miami.
Waymouth, [Capt. George], 14
Wazhazhe, see Osage.
Wazikute, band of Yanktonai, 388
Wa-zi'-ya-ta Pa-da'-nin, see Arikara.
Wdǫwǫ, see Ottawa.
Wea, 239, 242, 297, 300, 305
  subdivision of Miami, 297, 305
Weapemeoc, 88-89*
Weepers, see Assiniboin.
Weesock, see Waxhaw.
Wehrman, Lt., Russian explorer, 543
Weitchpec, see Yurok.
Wenatchee, 448-449*
Wenrohronon, 48*, 57
  allied with Neutral Nation, 48
  destruction of, 48
Werowocomoco, 71
Wĕs'ǎnikaciⁿga, see Shoshoni, Northern.
Weskarini, see Algonkin.
West Indies, 608-611
  Cuban Tribes, 610-611
  Haitian Tribes, 608-610
  Jamaican Tribes, 611
  Porto Rican Tribes, 611
West Virginia [State of], 74
  Cherokee, 74
  Conoy, 74
  Delaware, 74
  Honniasont, 74
  Moneton, 74*
  Shawnee, 74
  Susquehanna, 74
Western Dakota, see Dakota.
Western Niantic, see Niantic.
Westo, see Yuchi.
Wɛtc.nāqei'n, see Okanagon.
Wetitsaán, see Hidatsa.
Whe-el-po, see Colville.
Whilkut, 483, 492, 519*
White Indians, see Menominee.
White Minqua, see Susquehanna.

○